Lecture Notes in Computer Science 4260

Commenced Publication in 1973
Founding and Former Series Editors:
Gerhard Goos, Juris Hartmanis, and Jan van Leeuwen

Zhiming Liu Jifeng He (Eds.)

Formal Methods and Software Engineering

8th International Conference
on Formal Engineering Methods, ICFEM 2006
Macao, China, November 1-3, 2006
Proceedings

Springer

Volume Editors

Zhiming Liu
The United Nations University
International Institute for Software Technology
UNU-IIS, Casa Silva Mendes Ext. do Engenheiro Trigo No. 4
P.O. Box 3058, Macao SAR, China
E-mail: z.liu@iist.unu.edu

Jifeng He
East China Normal University
Software Engineering Institute
3663 Zhongshan Road (North), Shanghai 200062, China
E-mail: jifeng@sei.ecnu.edu.cn

Library of Congress Control Number: 2006934465

CR Subject Classification (1998): D.2.4, D.2, D.3, F.3

LNCS Sublibrary: SL 2 – Programming and Software Engineering

ISSN 0302-9743
ISBN-10 3-540-47460-9 Springer Berlin Heidelberg New York
ISBN-13 978-3-540-47460-9 Springer Berlin Heidelberg New York

Springer is a part of Springer Science+Business Media

springer.com

Printed in Germany

Typesetting: Camera-ready by author, data conversion by Scientific Publishing Services, Chennai, India
Printed on acid-free paper SPIN: 11901433 06/3142 5 4 3 2 1 0

Preface

Formal methods for the development of computer systems have been extensively researched and studied. A range of semantic theories, specification languages, design techniques, and verification methods and tools have been developed and applied to the construction of programs of moderate size that are used in critical applications. The challenge now is to scale up formal methods and integrate them into engineering development processes for the correct construction and maintenance of computer systems. This requires us to improve the state of the art by researching the integration of methods and their theories, and merging them into industrial engineering practice, including new and emerging practice.

ICFEM, the *International Conference on Formal Engineering Methods*, aims to bring together those interested in the application of formal engineering methods to computer systems. Researchers and practitioners, from industry, academia, and government, are encouraged to attend, and to help advance the state of the art. The conference particularly encourages research that aims at a combination of conceptual and methodological aspects with their formal foundation and tool support, and work that has been incorporated into the production of real systems.

This volume contains the proceedings of ICFEM 2006, which was the 8th ICFEM and held in Macao SAR, China on 1-3 November 2006. The Program Committee received 108 submissions from over 30 countries and regions. Each paper was reviewed, mostly by at least three referees working in relevant fields, but by two in a few cases. Borderline papers were further discussed during an online meeting of the Program Committee. A total of 38 papers were accepted based on originality, technical soundness, presentation and relevance to formal engineering and verification methods. We sincerely thank all the authors who submitted their work for consideration. We thank the Program Committee members and the other referees for their effort and professional work in the reviewing and selecting process. In addition to the regular papers, the proceedings also include contributions from the keynote speakers: Zhou Chaochen, Gary T. Leavens and John McDermid.

Three associated events were held: an Asian Working Conference on Verified Software (AWCVS06, 29-31 October), a Refinement Workshop (REFINE06, 31 October) and a Workshop on Formal Methods for Interactive Systems (FMIS06, 31 October). We thank the organizers for bringing their events to ICFEM 2006.

ICFEM 2006 was jointly organized and sponsored by the International Institute for Software Technology of the United Nations University (UNU-IIST), the University of Macau, and Macao Polytechnic Institute. We would like to thank all the members of staff and students who helped in the organization, in particular Pun Chong Iu, Pun Ka, Sandy Lee, Ho Sut Meng, Chan Iok Sam, Hoi Iok Wa, and Lu Yang. Acknowledgement also goes to Formal Method Europe for its support to the FME Keynote Speaker.

August 2006 Zhiming Liu and He Jifeng

Organization

Conference Chairs

Honorary Chair:	Vai Pan Iu (Rector, University of Macau, Macao)
Conference Chairs:	Yiping Li (University of Macau, Macao)
	George Michael Reed (UNU-IIST, Macao)
Program Chairs:	He Jifeng (East China Normal University, China)
	Zhiming Liu (UNU-IIST, Macao)
Organization Chairs:	Iontong Iu (UNU-IIST, Macao)
	Xiaoshan Li (University of Macau, Macao)
Publicity Chair:	Chris George (UNU-IIST, Macao)
Workshop Chair:	Bernhard K. Aichernig (Graz Univ. of Tech., Austria)

Program Committee

Farhad Arbab
Ralph Back
Luis Soares Barbosa
Tommaso Bolognesi
Jonathan P. Bowen
Manfred Broy
Michael Butler
Ana Cavalcanti
Yoonsik Cheon
Philippe Darondeau
Jim Davies
Colin Fidge
John Fitzgerald
Marc Frappier
Marcelo Frias
Atsushi Igarashi
Mathai Joseph
Kung-Kiu Lau
Xuandong Li
Tiziana Margaria
Hong Mei H
Huaikou Miao
Ernst-Ruediger Olderog
Shengchao Qin
Zongyan Qiu
Anders P. Ravn
Ken Robinson
Abhik Roychoudhury
Motoshi Saeki
Hassen Saidi
Augusto Sampaio
Davide Sangiorgi
Peter H. Schmitt
Klaus-Dieter Schewe
Wolfram Schulte
Joseph Sifakis
Joao Pedro Sousa
Sofiene Tahar
T.H. Tse
Farn Wang
Mark Utting
Martin Wirsing
Qiwen Xu
Hongseok Yang
Wang Yi
Jian Zhang

External Referees

Poonam Agarwal
Frank Atanassow
Richard Banach
Pontus Boström
Judy Bowen
Leonid Kof
Pavel Krcal
Marco Kuhrmann
Vinay Kulkarni
Shrawan Kumar
Katharina Spies
David Streader
Kim Solin
Jun Sun
Bernhard Thalheim

Steering Committee

Table of Contents

Keynote Talks

Specification and Verification

Internetware and Web-Based Systems

Concurrent, Communicating, Timing and Probabilistic Systems

Object and Component Orientation

Testing and Model Checking

Tools

Fault-Tolerance and Security

Specification and Refinement

Program Verification Through Computer Algebra

Zhou Chaochen

Laboratory of Computer Science
Institute of Software
Chinese Academy of Sciences
Beijing, China
zcc@ios.ac.cn

Abstract. This is to advocate the approach to reducing program verification to the algebraic symbolic computation. Recent advances indicate that various verification problems can be reduced to semi-algebraic systems (SAS for short), and resolved through computer algebra tools. In this talk, we report our encouraging attempts at applying DISCOVERER to program termination analysis and state reachability computation. DISCOVERER is a Maple program implementing an algorithm of real solution classification and isolation for SAS, which is based on the discovery of complete discrimination systems of parametric polynomials. The talk also concludes that this approach deserves further attention from the program verification community.

For theoretical and technical details of the work, we refer the reader to [1,2,3,4,5].

References

1. B. Xia and L. Yang. An algorithm for isolating the real solutions of semi-algebraic systems. *J. Symbolic Computation,* 34:461–477, 2002.
2. L. Yang. Recent advances on determining the number of real roots of parametric polynomials. *J. Symbolic Computation*, 28:225–242, 1999.
3. L. Yang, X. Hou and Z. Zeng. A complete discrimination system for polynomials. *Science in China (Ser. E)*, 39:628–646, 1996.
4. L. Yang and B. Xia. Real solution classifications of a class of parametric semi-algebraic systems. In *Proc. of Int'l Conf. on Algorithmic Algebra and Logic*, pp. 281–289, 2005.
5. L. Yang, N. Zhan, B. Xia and C. Zhou. Program verification by using DISCOVERER. To appear in the Proc. VSTTE'05 held in Zürich, Oct. 10-Oct. 13, 2005.

Z. Liu and J. He (Eds.): ICFEM 2006, LNCS 4260, p. 1, 2006.

JML's Rich, Inherited Specifications for Behavioral Subtypes*

Gary T. Leavens

Department of Computer Science, Iowa State University
229 Atanasoff Hall, Ames, IA 50011-1041, USA
leavens@cs.iastate.edu

Abstract. The Java Modeling Language (JML) is used to specify detailed designs for Java classes and interfaces. It has a particularly rich set of features for specifying methods. This paper describes those features, with particular emphasis on the features related to specification inheritance. It shows how specification inheritance in JML forces behavioral subtyping, through a discussion of semantics and examples. It also describes a notion of modular reasoning based on static type information, supertype abstraction, which is made valid in JML by methodological restrictions on invariants, history constraints, and initially clauses and by behavioral subtyping.

1 Introduction

Work on formal methods is interesting for at least two reasons: it can lead to practical tools (such as runtime assertion checkers or model checkers) and it can be used to give insight into informal programming practice. Both of these reasons drive the work on the Java Modeling Language, JML [10, 12, 44, 45, 47]. While JML is technically limited to precisely describing the syntactic interfaces and functional behavior of sequential Java classes and interfaces at the detailed design level, its rich set of specification constructs can be used to explain concepts that can be informally applied in other settings. This paper attempts to give such an explanation for ideas related to behavioral subtyping.

1.1 Context

JML builds on the ideas of Eiffel [58, 59] and the Larch family of behavioral interface specification languages [17, 30, 39, 81]. While JML also uses ideas from other sources [8, 35, 48, 49, 61, 62, 67, 71, 79], at its core it blends these two language traditions.

From Eiffel JML takes the idea of writing assertions (e.g., pre-and postconditions) in program notation; hence JML assertions are written as Java expressions. This helps make JML easy to read by Java programmers.

From Larch JML takes the idea of using mathematical values to specify complete functional behavior. These mathematical values are specified in JML as the values of "model fields" [18, 48]. (Examples of model fields are given below.) Because model fields are only used in assertions, their time and space efficiency is not important. (One

* This work was supported by NSF grant CCF-0429567.

Z. Liu and J. He (Eds.): ICFEM 2006, LNCS 4260, pp. 2–34, 2006.

can always turn off assertion checking to gain efficiency.) Thus the type of a model field can be something closer to mathematics, such as a set, sequence, or relation, instead of a binary search tree, an array, or a hash table. This allows users to focus on clarity.

JML has been successful in attracting researchers working with formal methods at the level of detailed design for Java. To date there are at least 19 groups doing research with JML. (See `http://www.jmlspecs.org/` for a list.)

1.2 JML's Tools

Part of JML's attraction for researchers is that they can build on a rich language and use several different tools [10]. This set of tools helps researchers be more productive. For example, since program verification with a theorem prover is time-consuming, it helps to use other tools to find bugs first.

While JML's tools could use more polish, they have been used in several college classes and in work on Java smart cards [9, 10, 11, 33, 57].

The JML research community is dedicated to finding ways to help make the cost of writing specifications worthwhile for its users by providing added value through tools. This includes basic tools such as a documentation generator (jmldoc), and a runtime assertion checker (jmlc) [14, 16]. There are also several tools designed to do formal verification with interactive theorem provers, including LOOP [33, 34], JACK [9], KRAKATOA [57], Jive [73], and KeY [1]. One of JML's principal design goals is to support the use of both runtime assertion checking and formal verification with theorem provers. But JML is also supported by several other novel tools, including:

- ESC/Java2 [36], a descendant of the extended static checker ESC/Java [29], which statically detects bugs and uses specifications to improve the accuracy of bug reports,
- Daikon [27], a tool that mines execution traces to find likely program invariants, which can synthesize specifications,
- The jmlunit tool [15], which uses JML specifications to decide the success or failure of unit tests, and
- SpEx-JML [77], which uses the model checker Bogor [76] to check properties of JML specifications.

Most of these tools are open source products. The JML community itself is also open and encourages more participation from the formal methods community.

1.3 Overview

JML has evolved from its roots in Larch and Eiffel into a language with a rich set of features. The goal of this paper is to use a subset of these features to help explain the ideas connected with behavioral subtyping in a way that will help readers apply them in programming practice, e.g., in documenting and informally reasoning about object-oriented programs. A secondary goal is to aid readers who would like to use some of the JML tools or would like to reuse or build on the ideas of JML's language design. This paper assumes the reader is familiar with basic concepts in formal methods, such as first-order logic and pre- and postconditions [25, 30, 31, 59, 60].

This paper focuses on behavioral subtyping [2, 3, 4, 23, 28, 38, 41, 42, 43, 55, 59, 74] for several reasons. The first is because of its utility in organizing and reasoning about object-oriented software [19, 37, 43, 53, 59]. The second is that JML embodies a set of features that make working with behavioral subtyping particularly convenient, but these features and their combination in JML have not previously had a focused explanation. While the key language design ideas of specification cases [80] and their use in specification inheritance [79] to force behavioral subtyping have been explained in the context of Larch/C++ [23, 40], they are found in a simpler and thus more understandable form in JML. And while these ideas have been previously explained from a theoretical perspective [42], their embodiment in JML makes the explanation more concrete and accessible to the practice of programming and specification language design.

2 Background: JML Specifications for Methods and Types

This section gives background on JML and several examples. This background is necessary to explain the concept of supertype abstraction in the context of JML, since supertype abstraction involves reasoning about specifications. The examples in this section will also be used in the remainder of the paper.

2.1 JML Basics

For example, take the Java interface `Gendered` given in Fig. 1. `Gendered`'s behavior is specified in its JML annotations.[1]

```
public interface Gendered {
  //@ model instance String gender;

  //@ ensures \result <==> gender.equals("female");
  /*@ pure @*/ boolean isFemale();
}
```

Fig. 1. A JML specification of the interface `Gendered`. The JML annotations are written in comments that start with an at-sign (`@`). The rest of the JML notation is explained in the text.

The second line of the figure is an annotation that declares a field `gender`. In that declaration, the modifier **`model`** says that the field is a specification-only field that is an abstraction of some concrete state [18, 48]. The modifier **`instance`** means that this abstraction is based on instance fields, and thus this modeling feature can be thought of as a field in each object that implements the `Gendered` interface.

In JML, specifications for methods precede the header of the method being specified. In Fig. 1, the **`ensures`** clause, specifies the postcondition of the method `isFemale`. This postcondition says that the value returned by the method, **`\result`**, is equivalent (written `<==>`) to whether the model field `gender` equals the string `"female"`. The `isFemale` method is also specified using the modifier **`pure`**, which says that the method cannot have side effects and may thus be used in assertions.

[1] JML annotations should not be confused with Java 5's annotations, which are quite different.

2.2 Specification for Fields

The class `Animal` in Fig. 2 will be used to explain JML's features related to fields. Since `Animal` is a subtype of `Gendered`, it inherits the model instance field `gender` (declared in Fig. 1). Inheritance of instance fields means that specifications for instance methods written in supertypes make sense when interpreted in their subtypes. For example, the ensures clause of the method `isFemale` specified in the interface `Gendered` makes sense in its subtype `Animal`.[2]

```
public class Animal implements Gendered {
  protected boolean gen; //@ in gender;
  //@ protected represents gender <- (gen ? "female" : "male");

  protected /*@ spec_public @*/ int age = 0;

  //@ requires g.equals("female") || g.equals("male");
  //@ assignable gender;
  //@ ensures gender.equals(g);
  public Animal(final String g) { gen = g.equals("female"); }

  public /*@ pure @*/ boolean isFemale() { return gen; }

  /*@   requires 0 <= a && a <= 150;
    @   assignable age;
    @   ensures age == a;
    @ also
    @   requires a < 0;
    @   assignable age;
    @   ensures age == \old(age);   @*/
  public void setAge(final int a) { if (0 <= a) { age = a; } }
}
```

Fig. 2. Class `Animal` from the file `Animal.java`. In a multi-line annotation at-signs at the beginnings of lines are ignored. The other new JML features are explained in the text.

The **in** clause, which occurs immediately after the declaration of the protected boolean field gen, is used to declare datagroup membership. It says that gen is in `gender`'s data group [49]. The data group of a field f can be thought of as a set of fields that are allowed to be assigned to when f is mentioned in an assignable clause. The data group of a model field f includes all the fields needed to determine f's value, but may also include other fields. Thus the **in** clause in the declaration of gen tells JML that: (a) the value of gender may depend on the value of gen and (b) gen may be assigned whenever `gender` is allowed to be assigned by a method. For example the constructor's **`assignable`** clause lists `gender`, which means that it may assign to all locations in gender's data group, which includes gen. (See below for more about assignable clauses.)

[2] Inherited specifications make sense even if there are shadowing field declarations in subtypes. However, in this paper I will assume that there is no such field shadowing, as this simplification does not lose any generality.

The **represents** clause gives an expression for the value of the model field gender. Thus, whenever gender occurs in a specification, such as in the constructor's postcondition, its value is the value of the expression (gen ? "female": "male"). However, not only is gender more concise, it is public, whereas gen and the design decision about how gender is represented are hidden from clients. This illustrates how model fields in JML can be used to hide design details [18, 48]. The represents clause specifies an abstraction function [32] from part of the concrete state of an Animal object to a model field. Since the model field gender is inherited from Gendered, this abstraction function can be thought of as mapping part of the state of an Animal object to the state of a Gendered object [55].

The **spec_public** modifier in the declaration of age can be thought of as shorthand for the declaration of a public model field (named age), and clauses saying that the protected field (renamed to, say, _age) is in the model field's data group, and that the model field's value is the value of the concrete field. Use of **spec_public** is often convenient when documenting existing code. It allows the protected field that is used in the representation to be changed (e.g., renamed) at a later date without affecting the specification's clients. If such a change is made in the future, at that time one has to unpack these shorthands and rename all uses of the protected field.

The **requires** clauses in the constructor and method specifications of Fig. 2 specify preconditions. For example, the precondition of the constructor says that the argument g must be either "female" or "male".

An **assignable** clause gives a frame axiom [6, 62]. It lists the fields whose data groups may be assigned during the execution of the method. All locations that are not in the data group of a listed field are not allowed to be even temporarily changed. (In this sense JML's assignable clauses are more strict than the modifies clauses found in Larch.) Such frame axioms are important for formal verification [6, 12]. An assignable clause can be thought of as syntactic sugar for part of the method's postcondition. For example the assignable clause of the constructor can be thought of as shorthand for adding **only_assigned**(gender) to the constructor's postcondition. The method modifier **pure** is, in part, a shorthand for the clause **assignable \nothing** and hence can also be thought of as shorthand for part of a postcondition.

2.3 Joining Specification Cases with also

The setAge method in Fig. 2 on the preceding page has a specification with two specification cases connected by **also**. A JML *specification case* consists of several clauses, including requires, assignable, and ensures clauses [47]. Each specification case has a precondition (which might default to true), that tells when that specification case applies to a call. JML's **also** joins together specification cases in a way that makes sure that, whenever a specification case's precondition holds for a call, its postcondition must also hold. That is, in general a JML method specification may consist of several specification cases, and all these specification cases must be satisfied by a correct implementation.

One reason for using **also** and separate specification cases is to make distinct execution scenarios clear to the specification's reader. In the setAge example, a call that satisfies the first specification case's precondition must set age to the value of the argument a. The second specification case describes the method's behavior for negative arguments. In this case the value of the age field must be unchanged. This is specified with the postcondition `age == \old(age)`, which says that the post-state value of `age` must equal its pre-state value, `\old(age)`. The `\old()` operator is often used in the postconditions for methods that change the state of an object [59].

I will refer to the combination of two method specifications with **also** as their "join," since it is technically the join with respect to the refinement ordering on method specifications [42, 50, 64]. (It is also easier to talk about "joining" specification cases.)

To define the join operation precisely I will use a bit of notation. As we have seen, specification cases are essentially pairs of pre- and postconditions (the assignable clause being shorthand for part of a postcondition, as explained above). So, in what follows, I will write $T \triangleright (pre, post)$ for a specification case of an instance method that type checks when its receiver (**this**) has static type T. Thus you can think of $T \triangleright spec$ as being written in type T. In JML, $T \triangleright spec$ will also type check in a context where **this** has some subtype of T. I omit the receiver's type when it is clear from context. Also, since there is little difference between a simple method specification and a specification case, I will often just call them method specifications. With this notation, the definition of the join operation for specification cases is as follows [23, 40, 42, 50, 64, 80].

Definition 1 (Join of JML method specifications, $\sqcup^U$). *Let $T' \triangleright (pre', post')$ and $T \triangleright (pre, post)$ be specifications of an instance method m. Let U be a subtype of both T' and T. Then the* join of $(pre', post')$ and $(pre, post)$ for U, *written $(pre', post') \sqcup^U (pre, post)$, is the specification $U \triangleright (p, q)$ with precondition p:*

$$pre' \;\; || \;\; pre \tag{1}$$

and postcondition q:

$$(\backslash\mathbf{old}(pre') \;\; ==> \;\; post') \;\; \&\& \;\; (\backslash\mathbf{old}(pre) \;\; ==> \;\; post). \tag{2}$$

In the above definition, the precondition of the join of two method specifications is their disjunction (with `||` as in Java). The postcondition of the join is a conjunction of implications (written `==>` in JML's notation), which says that when one of the preconditions holds (in the pre-state), then the corresponding postcondition must hold.

The ability to join method specification cases is useful in specification inheritance, which joins specification cases from subtypes with those inherited from supertypes. However, when the join's receiver type is clear from context, I omit the superscript U.

For example, the join of the two specification cases for `setAge` in Fig. 2 on page 5 is equivalent to the specification case shown in Fig. 3. Of course, one could write this specification directly, but when one compares it to the specification of `setAge` in Fig. 2, one can see that the postcondition of Fig. 3 contains within it a repetition of the

```
//@   requires (0 <= a && a <= 150) || a < 0;
//@   assignable age;
/*@   ensures (\old(0<=a && a<=150) ==> age==a)
  @           && (\old(a<0) ==> age==\old(age));    @*/
public void setAge(final int a);
```

Fig. 3. The join of the specification cases for the `setAge` method from Fig. 2 on page 5

preconditions from Fig. 2. This repetition is a maintenance problem and distracts from the clarity of the specification. JML's **also** avoids these problems.

2.3.1 Using \same to Make Refinements

Often in writing a method specification in a subtype, one wants the precondition of the overriding method to be the same as that of the specification of the method being overridden. This often occurs for a method m in a subclass that calls super.m and then does something extra. JML's predicate **\same** can be used in the precondition of such a specification to say that the method's precondition is the same as that of the method being overridden [47]. For example, in Fig. 4, the precondition of the given specification case for setAge is equal to that in the specification of setAge in Animal. In this example, that precondition is equivalent to the disjunction of setAge's preconditions from the two specification cases in Figure 2 (as shown in Fig. 3), and is thus is equivalent to a <= 150.

```
public class Person extends Animal {
  protected /*@ spec_public @*/ boolean ageDiscount = false; //@ in age;

  /*@ also
    @   requires \same;
    @   assignable age, ageDiscount;
    @   ensures 65 <= age ==> ageDiscount;    @*/
  public void setAge(final int a) {
    super.setAge(a);
    if (65 <= age) { ageDiscount = true; }
  }

  //@ requires g.equals("female") || g.equals("male");
  //@ assignable gender;
  //@ ensures gender.equals(g);
  public Person(final String g) { super(g); }
}
```

Fig. 4. A JML specification of the class Person. The notation **\same** is explained in the text. In JML, **also** must be used in a method specification whenever one overrides a method, to remind the specification's reader about specification inheritance, as will be explained later.

2.4 Invariants, History Constraints, and Initially Clauses

In addition to field declarations and method specifications, a type specification in JML may also contain invariants, history constraints, and **initially** clauses.[3] An invariant [32] is a predicate that should hold in all *visible states*, i.e., in the pre-state and post-state of each (non-helper[4]) method execution [47, 63], and in the post-state of each constructor execution. Invariants are one-state predicates; i.e., they cannot use **\old()**. By contrast a history constraint [55, 56] is a two-state predicate that uses **\old()** to state a monotonic relationship between pre-states and post-states. A history constraint

[3] This list is a simplification, but it covers the most important features.

[4] In JML a private method or constructor can be declared with the modifier **helper**. This exempts it from having to preserve invariants, or establish history constraints and initially clauses.

must hold in the post-state of every (non-helper) method execution [47]. An initially clause [26] is a predicate that should hold in all post-states of (non-helper) constructors. Initially clauses are one-state predicates.

In JML all of these clauses may be omitted (as in the examples given previously), in which case a default predicate, **true**, is used. These defaults allow us to speak of "the invariant" etc. declared by a type, even if none is explicitly declared.

2.4.1 Invariants

To explain invariants in JML, consider Fig. 5. This figure has two **invariant** clauses, both of which declare public (client-visible) instance invariants. Declaring two invariants is equivalent to declaring a single invariant whose predicate conjoins the predicates declared in the two clauses. The first invariant clause says that the value of the age field is always between 0 and 150 (inclusive). Although this invariant is true for objects whose dynamic type is exactly `Animal`, it is not necessarily true for subtypes of `Animal`; a subtype could declare a method that would allow values outside this range to be assigned to age. Thus it is necessary to explicitly declare this invariant [55]. In effect, this invariant prohibits methods that set age outside the range specified in the invariant.

```
import java.util.*;
public class Patient extends Person {
  //@ public invariant 0 <= age && age <= 150;

  protected /*@ spec_public rep @*/ List history;
  /*@ public initially history.size() == 0;
    @ public invariant (\forall int i; 0 <= i && i < history.size();
    @                            history.get(i) instanceof rep String);
    @ public constraint \old(history.size()) <= history.size();
    @ public constraint (\forall int i; 0 <= i && i < \old(history.size());
    @                            history.get(i).equals(\old(history.get(i))));
    @*/

  /*@ requires !obs.equals("");
    @ assignable history.theCollection;
    @ ensures history.size() == \old(history.size()+1)
    @       && history.get(\old(history.size()+1)).equals(obs);    @*/
  public void recordVisit(String obs) {
    history.add(new /*@ rep @*/ String(obs));
  }

  //@ requires g.equals("female") || g.equals("male");
  //@ assignable gender, history;
  //@ ensures gender.equals(g);
  public Patient(String g) { super(g); history = new /*@ rep @*/ ArrayList(); }
}
```

Fig. 5. A JML specification of the class `Patient`. The **invariant** clause in a class declares an invariant, and **constraint** declares a history constraint. The **rep** annotations declare ownership properties. JML's specification of `List` includes a data group named `theCollection`.

The second invariant clause in part documents a design decision, since it says that all elements of the List `history` are instances of type `String`. So it is closely related to what some authors call a "representation invariant" [32, 54]. However, since `history` is public for specification purposes, the invariant is public and visible to clients.

JML distinguishes instance invariants from static invariants. Instance invariants can refer to the state of an instance of the enclosing type using the keyword **`this`** and the names of instance (non-static) fields. Static invariants cannot refer to the state of an instance. Both of the invariants in Fig. 5 are instance invariants.

2.4.2 History Constraints

History constraints are taken from Liskov and Wing's work [55, 56], and specify a very simple kind of temporal property. They are used to declare monotonic relationships that are preserved by methods of a type.

The two **`constraint`** clauses in Fig. 5 declare two history constraints for the type `Patient`. (Again, having two history constraints is equivalent to having one constraint which conjoins the two predicates.) The first constraint says that the size of the `history` list never shrinks; that is, the size of `history` is monotonically non-decreasing. The second says that elements in the `history` list are never deleted.

In JML history constraints can be used to collect common postconditions, in much the same way that invariants can be used to collect common pre- and postconditions. For example, the ensures clause of the `recordVisit` method does not need to specify that the elements of `history` are preserved, as this is implicit in the second history constraint. This helps make specifications more understandable.

2.4.3 Initially Clauses

The **`initially`** clause in Fig. 5 on the preceding page gives a predicate that is to be true in the post state of each (non-helper) constructor. It can thus be thought of as conjoined to the postcondition for `Patient`'s constructor. In JML initially clauses can be used to collect postconditions from constructors. While initially clauses are not involved in reasoning about dynamic dispatch, they are useful for reasoning with invariants and history constraints. When used with the invariants declared in a type, they provide a basis for datatype induction. When used with history constraints the provide a basis for computing the set of reachable object states. When an object is created its state must satisfy each declared initially clause. When its state is mutated, the method doing the mutation must satisfy each history constraint. Thus using an initially clause and a history constraint one may restrict the set of reachable states for a type and its subtypes in a way that would otherwise not be expressible.

In JML a type may have several initially clauses. As with invariants and history constraints, writing multiple initially clauses in a type specification is equivalent to writing one initially clause with the conjunction of their predicates. In the following the phrase "*the initially predicate*" for a type refers to this conjunction.

2.5 Specification Inheritance

In JML specifications of subtypes inherit not only fields and methods from their supertypes, but also specifications. Thus, to fully understand the examples given so far, you need to understand how JML's specification inheritance works.

To explain specification inheritance it helps to fix a bit of notation for type specifications. For a type T, let $added\_inv^T$ be the invariant predicate declared in T's specification (i.e., without inheritance), let $added\_hc^T$ be the history constraint declared in T's specification, and let $added\_init^T$ be the initially predicate declared in T's specification. Let $supers(T)$ be the set of all supertypes of T (including T) and let $methods(\mathcal{T})$ be the set of all instance method names declared in the specifications of the types in a set $\mathcal{T}$. (For simplicity, I assume that statically overloaded methods have been distinguished by adding to each method name a list of the method's argument types; thus each method name is associated unambiguously with a list of argument types. I also assume that there is no shadowing of fields and that all overriding methods use the same formal parameter names as the methods they override; these assumptions can also be made with no loss of generality by use of renamings.)

For methods, I use the notation $added\_spec^T_m = (added\_pre^T_m, added\_post^T_m)$ for the pre/post specification declared in type T for method m. Such a specification is the join of the specification cases specified in type T for m. If there are no specification cases in type T for method m, this notation should still be defined, but one has to distinguish two cases. If m is declared in T with no specification and is not overriding any methods in T, then $added\_spec^T_m = (true, true)$. This corresponds to the JML default specification, which places no limits on callers or on the implementation. However, if m is not declared in T (and hence has no specification in T), then we want a method specification that will not affect the join of other method specifications. Hence in this case we define $added\_spec^T_m = (false, true)$, which is the identity with respect to the join of method specifications. Appropriately, this least useful specification is also the join of the empty set of method specifications, $\bigsqcup \emptyset$.

As in Java, a JML specification for a type inherits instance field declarations from its proper supertypes, including the modifiers (such as **spec_public**) and data group declarations that are part of such field declarations. This inheritance applies to model (and ghost) fields, as well as Java fields. As noted earlier, inheritance of such declarations is important for making sense of predicates inherited from supertypes. Represents clauses, which specify how to retrieve the values of model fields are also inherited in JML. Overriding of (functional) represents clauses in subtypes presents semantic problems [52], and thus I will assume that the type checker prohibits it. Since represents clauses and fields are merely collected and not combined like method specifications or invariants, I omit them from the definition below.

With these conventions, the mechanism JML uses to inherit specifications can be explained by constructing an extended specification [23, 42].

Definition 2 (Extended specification). *Suppose T has supertypes $supers(T)$, which includes T itself. Then* the extended specification of T *is a specification such that:*

methods: *for all methods $m \in methods(supers(T))$, the extended specification of m is the join of all added specifications for m in T and all its proper supertypes:*

$$ext\_spec^T_m = \bigsqcup\nolimits^T \{added\_spec^U_m \mid U \in supers(T)\},$$

invariant: *the extended invariant of T is the conjunction of all added invariants in T and its proper supertypes:*

$$ext\_inv^T = \bigwedge\{added\_inv^U \mid U \in supers(T)\},$$

history constraint: *the extended history constraint of T is the conjunction of all added history constraints in T and its proper supertypes:*

$$ext\_hc^T = \bigwedge\{added\_hc^U \mid U \in supers(T)\},$$

initially predicate: *the extended initially predicate of T is the conjunction of all added initially predicates in T and its proper supertypes:*

$$ext\_init^T = \bigwedge\{added\_init^U \mid U \in supers(T)\}.$$

2.6 Examples of Specification Inheritance

Specification inheritance for invariants, history constraints, and initially clauses is simple. It simply conjoins the appropriate predicates from a type and its supertypes. For example, the type `FemalePatient` specified in Fig. 6 would inherit these clauses from `Patient` (see Fig. 5 on page 9). The history constraints and initially predicates are inherited without change. However, the invariant of `FemalePatient` is the conjunction of the invariant added in Fig. 6 and the invariant of `Patient` (which is the conjunction of the two invariants in Fig. 5).

```
public class FemalePatient extends Patient {
  //@ public invariant gender.equals("female");

  //@ assignable gender;
  public FemalePatient() { super("female"); }
}
```

Fig. 6. A JML specification of the class `FemalePatient`

Specification inheritance for methods simply joins together all the method specifications from a type and its supertypes. For example, the extended specification of the `isFemale` method of `Gendered` from Fig. 1 on page 4 is just the specification $(true, Q)$, where Q is the postcondition from that figure. This is the extended specification because `isFemale` is not specified in any supertypes of `Gendered`. This same specification for `isFemale`, $(true, Q)$, is inherited unchanged by `Animal`, because Fig. 2 does not have any added specification cases for `isFemale`, so $added\_spec^{\texttt{Animal}}_{\texttt{isFemale}}$ is the identity specification $(false, true)$. Thus the extended specification for `isFemale` is $\bigsqcup\{(true, Q), (false, true)\}$, which equals $(true, Q)$. Similarly, `isFemale` has the same extended specification in the classes `Person` and `Patient`.

A more interesting example is the `setAge` method. This method is specified for the type `Animal` in Fig. 2 on page 5, and in its subtype `Person` in Fig. 4 on page 8. The extended specification of `setAge` in type `Person` is thus the join of these two specifications. (This join is also inherited by the type `Patient` specified in Fig. 5 on page 9.)

Using the definitions given above, one can compute a single specification case that is equivalent to this join. However, when reading a JML specification with multiple specification cases, it is not necessary to calculate the specification of their join. Instead, the reader of such a specification just has to remember that each specification case must be obeyed by a correct implementation. For this reason, the jmldoc tool shows the join using **also** instead of the more complex, calculated specification. For example, compare the specification in Fig. 7 to that in Fig. 3 on page 7.

```
/*@  requires 0 <= a && a <= 150;              // from Animal
  @  assignable age;
  @  ensures age == a;
  @ also
  @  requires a < 0;
  @  assignable age;
  @  ensures age == \old(age);
  @ also
  @  requires \same;                            // from Person
  @  assignable age, ageDiscount;
  @  ensures 65 <= age ==> ageDiscount;    @*/
public void setAge(int a);
```

Fig. 7. The join of the 3 specification cases for `setAge` for the type `Person`, presented as a join of specification cases. In such contexts the precondition `\same` means the disjunction of the other (non-`\same`) preconditions.

With specification inheritance it is impossible to make a method's precondition strictly stronger than what is inherited. Consider the class `Senior` specified in Fig. 8 on the next page. At first glance, the `setAge` method in Fig. 8 seems to specify a method with a stronger precondition than `setAge`'s extended precondition in `Person`, which is `a <= 150`. However, taking specification inheritance into account, the extended precondition of `setAge` in `Senior` is the disjunction of `a <= 150` and the precondition in the added specification case, and hence is equivalent to `a <= 150`. Thus the argument to `setAge` can legally be 18, for example, and in this case the `Senior`'s age will be set to 18.

Findler and Felleisen [28] note that it might be better for the specification language to point out this situation as a problem. Since it is not possible with specification inheritance to strengthen an inherited precondition, it would be reasonable to disallow what seem like attempts to strengthen a method's precondition if there is no good use for writing such a precondition. One reason for stating a stronger precondition would be to say that some extra effects happen in a subset of the cases in which the method may be called, as shown in Fig. 9 on the following page. However, such examples can be specified without changing the precondition, as shown in Fig. 4 on page 8. Another reason for writing a stronger precondition would be to redundantly specify some effect of the method, to bring it to the reader's attention. However, JML has a way to mark redundant specification cases explicitly, by putting them in the **implies_that** section or **for_example** sections of a method specification [40, 47]. So it may be sensible for JML to at least give a warning if such a non-redundant method specification strengthens the inherited precondition.

```
public class Senior extends Person {
  /*@ also
    @   requires 65 < a && a <= 150;
    @   assignable age;
    @   ensures age == a;
    @*/
  public void setAge(final int a) { super.setAge(a); }

  //@ requires g.equals("female") || g.equals("male");
  //@ assignable gender, age;
  //@ ensures gender.equals(g) && age == 66;
  public Senior(final String g) { super(g); age = 66; ageDiscount = true; }
}
```

Fig. 8. A JML specification of the class `Senior`

```
  /*@ also
    @   requires 65 <= age;
    @   assignable age, ageDiscount;
    @   ensures ageDiscount;   @*/
  public void setAge(final int a);
```

Fig. 9. Specifying an extra effect in `Person`'s `setAge` method when `65 <= age`

3 Supertype Abstraction

Subtyping causes a fundamental problem for reasoning about object-oriented programs. The problem is that since one generally does not know the dynamic (runtime) type of an object, the specification the object obeys is also unknown. Early discussions of this problem focused on reasoning about dynamically-dispatched method calls [3, 4, 38, 43, 53], but the problem also applies to invariants, history constraints, and initially clauses.

To explain the reasoning problems caused by dynamic dispatch, consider Fig. 10 on the next page. In that example, the `isFemale` method of the `Gendered` interface is called on each element of the List argument `s`. This works even if the List contains objects of different dynamic (runtime) types, thanks to dynamic dispatch.

The pre- and postconditions in this specification use universal quantifiers. In JML a universal quantifier has the form (**\forall** $T\ x$; $R(x)$; $B(x)$), which is true when for all x of type T, if the range predicate $R(x)$ holds, then $B(x)$ holds. The modifier **nullable** in the precondition is used to allow `e` to range over null as well as other objects. By default declarations in JML do not allow null as a value, but null is a possible element of a List in Java. Thus the precondition says that all the elements of the argument `s` must be instances of the type `Gendered` (and in particular not null). The postcondition says that all elements of the result were in the argument `s` and are female.

To reason about the functional correctness of the `females` method in Fig. 10 one has to know how to reason about calls to methods with possibly unknown specifications. For example, `e.isFemale()` calls a method with a possibly unknown specification because the exact dynamic type of `e` is unknown; all that is known is that it implements the interface `Gendered`. The receiver `e` could represent a person, animal, or German noun.

```
/*@ requires (\forall nullable Object e; s.contains(e);
  @                                          e instanceof Gendered);
  @ ensures (\forall Gendered e; \result.contains(e);
  @                         s.contains(e) && e.gender.equals("female")); @*/
public List females(List s) {
  List r = new ArrayList();
  Iterator elems = s.iterator();
  while (elems.hasNext()) {
    Gendered e = (Gendered)elems.next();
    if (e.isFemale()) { r.add(e); }
  }
  return r;
}
```

Fig. 10. A method that extracts a list of females

The technique of *supertype abstraction* [42, 43] uses the specification of the static type of the receiver to reason about such calls. Thus, since e's static type is `Gendered`, supertype abstraction tells us to reason about the call `e.isFemale()` using the specification given in Fig. 1 on page 4. This specification has no precondition, so we can conclude that the call returns true just when the gender of e is `"female"`. This allows us to conclude that e is only added to `r` if it is female, which helps establish the postcondition of the method `females`.

However, supertype abstraction and the problems it solves are not limited to reasoning about method calls. The same technique of using static type information solves problems in reasoning that uses invariants and history constraints [55] and also in reasoning that uses initially predicates. For example, if p is a variable that has static type `Patient` (see Fig. 5 on page 9), then using supertype abstraction, one could look at the invariant declared in type `Patient`, and conclude that `p.age <= 150`. Without supertype abstraction this conclusion could only be made if one knew the invariant of the dynamic type of p. Similarly, supertype abstraction works with history constraints. For example, it would allow one to conclude, after invoking a method with receiver p of static type `Patient`, that the size of `p.history` has not become smaller. Finally, supertype abstraction works with initially predicates. For example, it would allow one to prove the assertion in the following code fragment.

```
Patient p;
if (B) { p = new Patient("male"); } else { p = new FemalePatient(); }
//@ assert p.history.size() == 0;
```

Supertype abstraction was essentially invented by the first object-oriented programmers. It embodies the idea that objects of all subtypes of a type (including that type itself) can be treated uniformly.[5] These programmers reasoned (informally) that whenever they added a new proper subtype of an existing type to their program, unchanged code would continue to work correctly even when it operated on these new objects. For

[5] Conversely, reasoning using supertype abstraction embodies this treatment of each method name and type as standing for a common behavior.

example, if they added a proper subtype of Gendered to the program, they would expect that the method females would still work correctly on objects of this new type.

Supertype abstraction is so ingrained in object-oriented thinking that it is hard to imagine alternative ways of reasoning about dynamic dispatch. Yet doing so helps illustrate the benefits (and limitations) of supertype abstraction.

An alternative to using supertype abstraction is to use the specification of each possible dynamic type of an expression's value. For example, suppose we know that in a call to the method females, the argument s only contains objects of type Person (which must be a subtype of Gendered). Then we could use the specification of Person's method isFemale to reason about the call e.isFemale(). If e might have dynamic types Person and GermanNoun, then we would have to consider two cases in the proof, one for each of these specifications. In general, if e can have n different types, we would have to consider n cases. The advantage of using supertype abstraction is that we avoid this case analysis, since we only use a single specification, namely the one associated with Gendered. The disadvantage of supertype abstraction is that, since it does no case analysis, it cannot exploit special properties of these subtypes, such as Person or GermanNoun. Supertype abstraction thus trades specificity and reasoning power for uniformity and simplicity of reasoning.

However, there is a way to sidestep this disadvantage of supertype abstraction by moving the case analysis into the program's code, using downcasts and type tests. An example of this idea is given in Fig. 11, which takes an object of static type Gendered that must dynamically have type GermanNoun (see Fig. 12 on the next page) or GreekNoun (which is similar, but not shown). In Fig. 11 **instanceof** tests are used to do a case analysis, and within the different cases the code does downcasts. Due to these downcasts, one can again use supertype abstraction to reason about the variables gern and grkn. In particular one can reason about the call gern.isMale() using the specification of isMale() in the type GermanNoun. And one can use the invariant of GermanNoun to conclude that if gern is neither female nor male, then it must be neuter. This shows how case analysis (in code) and supertype abstraction (in reasoning) can be used together. Thus insisting on supertype abstraction is not as limiting as it might at first appear.

Another advantage of supertype abstraction is that it permits reasoning with fewer assumptions. In particular, reasoning that uses supertype abstraction can be valid

```
/*@ requires n instanceof GermanNoun || n instanceof GreekNoun;
  @ ensures \result <==> n.gender.equals("neuter");    @*/
public boolean isNeuter(final Gendered n) {
  if (n instanceof GermanNoun) {
    GermanNoun gern = (GermanNoun) n;
    return !(gern.isFemale() || gern.isMale());
  } else {
    GreekNoun grkn = (GreekNoun) n;
    return !(grkn.isFemale() || grkn.isMale());
  }
}
```

Fig. 11. A method that uses downcasts so that reasoning about calls can use both the special properties of the dynamic types GermanNoun, GreekNoun, and supertype abstraction

```
public interface GermanNoun extends Gendered {
  /*@ public instance invariant gender.equals("female")
    @             || gender.equals("male") || gender.equals("neuter");  @*/

  //@ ensures \result <==> gender.equals("male");
  /*@ pure @*/ boolean isMale();
}
```

Fig. 12. A JML specification of a type `GermanNoun`. The type `GreekNoun` is similar

without assuming knowledge of all possible dynamic subtypes. In other words, supertype abstraction does not need knowledge of a whole program, and permits reasoning about programs that are open to the addition of new subtypes. For example, supertype abstraction allows reasoning about the correctness of the method `females` using the specifications of `Gendered`, without the need to know what dynamic subtypes are possible. Supertype abstraction allows reasoning about calls such as `e.isFemale()` even before subtypes of `Gendered`, such as `Person`, have been written. In this sense supertype abstraction is a modular reasoning technique.

4 Behavioral Subtyping

JML is designed to make supertype abstraction valid by making each type a behavioral subtype of each of its supertypes. To do this, it uses specification inheritance [23, 42, 45, 47, 75, 79] and methodological restrictions on invariants, etc. [24, 62, 63].

Much of the material below is adapted from my work with Dhara [23] and Naumann [42]. Interested readers should consult the latter [42] for details and proofs. I follow it in defining behavioral subtyping using the concept of refinement of method specifications, and in discussing the property needed from a methodology for invariants, etc.

4.1 Refinement of Method Specifications

Refinement is a binary relation on method specifications [42, 61]. Recall that $T \triangleright spec$ is a specification of a method that type checks with a receiver of static type T.

Definition 3 (refinement w.r.t. T', $\sqsupseteq^{T'}$). *Let $T' \triangleright spec'$ and $T \triangleright spec$ be specifications of an instance method m, such that T' is a subtype of T. Then spec'* refines *spec* with respect to *T', written spec' $\sqsupseteq^{T'}$ spec, if and only if for all calls of m where the receiver's dynamic type is a subtype of T', every correct implementation of spec' satisfies spec.*

The refining specification, *spec'* is stronger than *spec* in the sense that it restricts implementations more than does *spec*. Thus it may be that fewer implementations satisfy *spec'* compared to those that satisfy *spec*. >From a client's point of view, *spec'* may be more useful, while from the implementor's point of view *spec'* may be more difficult.

In the above definition, the condition on the receiver's dynamic type allows a specification for method m in a subtype to refine m's specification in one of its supertypes.

(This condition would be dropped if one were considering refinement of Java static methods or constructors, which have no receiver.)

For an example of refinement, I will show that the first specification case of `setAge` in Fig. 2 on page 5 is refined by the specification given in Fig. 3 on page 7.[6] Showing this refinement means showing that if an implementation satisfies the specification in Fig. 3, then it satisfies the specification for `setAge` given in Fig. 2. This is true, for example, of the implementation given in Fig. 2, which satisfies both specifications, due to the conditional. However, if this conditional were omitted and the method's body always assigned to `age`, then the body would still be a correct implementation of the specification in Fig. 2. However, it would not correctly implement the specification in Fig. 3. For example, with the omitted conditional, a call such as `setAge(-1)` would assign to `age`, possibly violating the first conjunct of the ensures clause in Fig. 3. It follows that the specification in Fig. 2 is not a refinement of the specification in Fig. 3.

4.1.1 Proving Refinements

To show that the specification in Fig. 3 really is a refinement of the first specification case in Fig. 2, one must show that every implementation that satisfies this specification satisfies the specification given in Fig. 2.

A general way to do such a proof is to prove a relationship between the specifications in question. Java and JML's type checking implies that if $T' \triangleright (pre', post')$ is to refine $T \triangleright (pre, post)$, then T' must be a subtype of T. Furthermore, in Java, both must have the same argument types. For simplicity, I will assume that the formal parameter names are the same. I will also use the notation $\mathrm{Spec}(T') \vdash P$ to mean that P is provable using the semantics of Java and the specification of T'. (Also, the notation && means logical conjunction as in JML.) With these conventions we have the following theorem [13, 42, 50, 64, 68].

Theorem 1. *Let* $T' \triangleright (pre', post')$ *and* $T \triangleright (pre, post)$ *be specifications of an instance method* m*, where* T' *is a subtype of* T*. Then* $(pre', post') \sqsupseteq^{T'} (pre, post)$ *if and only if the following two conditions hold:*

$$Spec(T') \;\vdash\; pre \;\&\&\; (\textbf{this instanceof}\; T') \implies pre' \tag{3}$$

$$Spec(T') \vdash \backslash\textbf{old}(pre \&\& (\textbf{this instanceof}\; T')) \implies (post' \implies post). \tag{4}$$

∎

Condition (3) says that the refinement's precondition *pre′* cannot make more assumptions than *pre*, except perhaps about the receiver's type. Since subtypes inherit the fields of their supertypes, *pre* makes sense for all objects of type T'. Note that if both specifications are for the same type, T', then Java guarantees the receiver is an instance of T' (or a subtype), and so in this case (3) just says that *pre* implies *pre′*. Condition (4) says that whenever a call whose receiver has type T' satisfies *pre*, and the refinement's postcondition *post′* is true, then *post* must hold. It can also be simplified if the receiver types are the same (T'), since in that case we can again ignore the conjunct (**this instanceof** T').

[6] This comparison ignores the second specification case in Fig. 2.

In the `setAge` example, we can prove (3), because `0 <= a && a <= 150` implies the disjunction of that condition and `a <= 150`. And we can prove (4) because whenever `0 <= a && a <= 150` holds in the pre-state, and the postcondition of Fig. 3 holds, it follows that `age == a`. We can ignore the assignable clauses in this proof, since they are identical and in such a case JML's semantics implies that the translation of the assignable clauses will be the same.

An important point is that simplifying (4) by omitting its dependence on *pre* makes the notion of refinement too restrictive (i.e., unable to prove some refinements that meet the definition). For example, note that the postcondition of `setAge` in Fig. 3 does not imply the postcondition in the first specification case of Fig. 2. To see this, consider what happens if `a` is `-1`, in which case in the postcondition in Fig. 3 simplifies to `age == \old(age)`, which does not imply the postcondition in the first specification case of Fig. 2, `age == a`. However, as we have just shown, (4) does hold for this example. Thus a refining specification is unconstrained for states that do not satisfy the precondition of the specification it refines.

4.1.2 Refinement and Assignable Clauses

Although assignable clauses can be considered as shorthand for part of a postcondition, it is useful to be able to treat them separately in a proof of refinement. To do this, suppose that the assignable clause of *spec*′ has the list L' and that the assignable clause of *spec* is L. Then one has to prove:

$$\begin{aligned}\mathrm{Spec}(T') \;\vdash\; & \texttt{\textbackslash old}(\mathit{pre}\ \texttt{\&\&}\ (\texttt{this instanceof}\ T')) \\ & \Longrightarrow (\texttt{\textbackslash only\_assigned}(L') \Longrightarrow \texttt{\textbackslash only\_assigned}(L)).\end{aligned} \tag{5}$$

Doing this allows one to omit the translation of the assignable clauses in the proof of (4). Informally, (5) means that the frame of *spec*′ can be more restrictive than that of *spec*, but data group membership has to be decided based on the specification of the refinement's receiver type, T'. That data group membership matters can be seen by considering Fig. 13, where the subtype `Animal`'s specification is needed to show that gen is a member of `gender`'s data group, and hence when at most the locations in the data groups of `gender` and gen are assigned, then at most the locations in `gender`'s data group are assigned [49].

```
//@ refines "Animal.refines-jml";
public class Animal implements Gendered {
  /*@ also
    @   protected behavior
    @     assignable gender, gen;
    @     ensures gen == g.equals("female");  @*/
  public Animal(String g);
}
```

Fig. 13. A JML refinement file that refines the specification of the constructor in Fig. 2 on page 5. The **`refines`** directive says that this file is to be used to refine the file `Animal.java`. The annotation **`protected behavior`** says that this is a specification of protected visibility.

4.1.3 Refinement of Binary Methods Such as equals

"Binary" methods, which operate on one or more arguments of the same type as the receiver [7], pose special pitfalls for refinement (and hence for behavioral subtyping [55]).

These pitfalls can be demonstrated by considering Java's `equals(Object)` method. For example, consider a specification for `Gendered`'s `equals` method as in Fig. 14. This is almost certainly an overly strong specification, since it allows no variation in refinements (and hence in subtypes). The specification says that when two objects that are subtypes of `Gendered` are compared, the method must return true just when their genders are equal, and it must return false otherwise. Thus, this specification says that the only attribute of an object of any subtype of `Gendered` that matters for `equals` is the object's gender. However, as in real life, other attributes do matter. For example, we might wish to distinguish two objects of type `Animal` if they have different ages or if they have different identities (i.e., if they are not ==). But, as the reader can check, such specifications are not refinements of the one in Fig. 14.

A better way to specify the `equals(Object)` method is shown in Fig. 15. This is a looser specification, since it allows the method to always return false. This freedom allows refinements (and hence subtypes) to specialize the method by considering other attributes of `Gendered` objects, such as their age or object identity. The specification in Fig. 15 says (in the first ensures clause) that for the case where the argument `obj` is an instance of `Gendered`, when the method returns true, then the argument must have the same gender as the receiver. The reader should check that this allows the method to return false even if the argument is an instance of `Gendered` and the genders are equal.

Two equivalent ways of writing this specification are given in the **`implies_that`** section of Fig. 15 [40, 47]. The first ensures clauses following **`implies_that`** says that when the argument is a `Gendered` object with a different gender, then the method returns

```
/*@ also
  @   ensures obj instanceof Gendered
  @       ==> \result == gender.equals(((Gendered)obj).gender);   @*/
public /*@ pure @*/ boolean equals(/*@ nullable @*/ Object obj);
```

Fig. 14. A bad (unrefinable) specification of the `equals` method of type `Gendered`

```
/*@ also
  @   ensures obj instanceof Gendered
  @       ==> (\result ==> gender.equals(((Gendered)obj).gender));
  @ implies_that
  @   ensures obj instanceof Gendered
  @       ==> (!gender.equals(((Gendered)obj).gender) ==> !\result);
  @   ensures obj instanceof Gendered && \result
  @       ==> gender.equals(((Gendered)obj).gender);      @*/
public /*@ pure @*/ boolean equals(/*@ nullable @*/ Object obj);
```

Fig. 15. A good (refinable) specification of the `equals` method for the type `Gendered`. The section following **`implies_that`** states redundant consequences of the specification. This **`implies_that`** section can be omitted without changing the meaning of the specification.

false. The last redundant ensures clause is a logically equivalent way of writing the non-redundant ensures clause that follows **also**.

This problem of overspecifying the `equals` method mainly affects types with immutable objects, because for a type with mutable objects, the `equals` method should usually be specified to compare object identities. However, this problem does occur in real examples. For instance when we first specified the type `java.util.Date` we used a specification of its `equals` method that only allowed comparison of the millisecond times (written in a way similar to Fig. 14 on the previous page). However, this was too strong because there could be subtypes, that need to distinguish objects based on other attributes, such as a number of nanoseconds.

4.1.4 Using `also` to Make Refinements

JML makes sure that an implementation refines all specification cases given for it by joining them together. This is the reason for the using **also** in the syntax to connect specification cases. The connection between the join of specification cases using **also** and refinement is shown in the following nice little theorem [13, 23, 40, 42, 50, 64, 80]. The proof assumes that **\old**() is *monotonic* in the sense that: $(Q \implies P) \implies$ $(\texttt{\textbackslash old}(Q) \implies \texttt{\textbackslash old}(P))$.

Theorem 2. *Suppose* **\old**() *is monotonic. Let* $T' \rhd (pre', post')$ *and* $T \rhd (pre, post)$ *be specifications of an instance method* m*, where* T' *is a subtype of* T*. Then*

$$((pre', post') \sqcup^{T'} (pre, post)) \sqsupseteq^{T'} (pre, post).$$

Proof: Let m, $T' \rhd (pre', post')$, and $T \rhd (pre, post)$, be as stated. Theorem 1 gives two conditions to prove using Spec(T'). To show (3) we can calculate as follows.

$$
\begin{array}{ll}
 & pre \;\&\&\; (\textbf{this instanceof } T') \\
\implies & \langle \text{by } (P \;\&\&\; I) \implies P \rangle \\
 & pre \\
\implies & \langle \text{by } P \implies (P' \;||\; P) \rangle \\
 & (pre' \;||\; pre)
\end{array}
$$

To show (4) assume that $\texttt{\textbackslash old}(pre \;\&\&\; \textbf{this instanceof } T')$ holds. Since **\old**() is monotonic by assumption, $\texttt{\textbackslash old}(pre)$ holds. Now we can calculate as follows.

$$
\begin{array}{ll}
 & (\texttt{\textbackslash old}(pre') \texttt{==>} post') \;\&\&\; (\texttt{\textbackslash old}(pre) \texttt{==>} post) \\
\implies & \langle \text{by } (X' \;\&\&\; X) \implies X \rangle \\
 & \texttt{\textbackslash old}(pre) \texttt{==>} post \\
\implies & \langle \text{by assumption that } \texttt{\textbackslash old}(pre) \text{ holds} \rangle \\
 & post
\end{array}
$$

∎

A more involved proof is needed to show that there is no better definition of the join of method specifications; i.e., that the join of method specifications is their least upper bound in the refinement ordering [13, 42, 50, 64]. This justifies the notation "⊔".

4.1.5 Methodologies for Invariants

Besides refinement of method specifications, behavioral subtyping involves the other elements of a type specification. Initially clauses and history constraints have not been studied in much detail in academic papers, but they are similar enough to invariants that most research on invariants should apply to them. By contrast, invariants have been the subject of much recent research in object-oriented programming methodology [5, 51, 62, 63, 65, 66]. The reason that invariants are such a focus of research is that they have interesting interactions with aliasing, reentrance, and subtyping.

Aliasing can cause problems if objects contained in an object *o* are exposed to clients, who may break *o*'s invariant without calling one of *o*'s methods.

Reentrance causes problems for invariants when a method being run on some receiver object *o* breaks an invariant temporarily, and then while still running, makes a call that (eventually) runs a method whose receiver is *o*. In such a situation, the invariant may not hold in the pre-state of the call back to *o*.

Subtyping causes problems because, in a subtype, invariants can be strengthened [55]. However, since they can also be thought of as conjoined to the preconditions (and postconditions) of instance methods, this means that a stronger invariant in a subtype will strengthen the subtype's precondition. But, as described in condition (3) of Theorem 1 on page 18, strengthening the precondition of a refining specification is not allowed. To see the problem, consider the dynamic dispatch code in Fig. 10 on page 15. When the call is made to `e.isFemale()` and `e` has dynamic type `Patient`, how do we know that the invariant of `Patient` holds in the pre-state of the execution of `isFemale`?

To resolve these problems, the essential insight is that some set of restrictions on programs, i.e., a programming methodology, is needed. A programming methodology must validate the implicit assumption that each invariant holds in each (non-helper) method's pre-state [42, §2.3]. A programming methodology that allows one to safely assume invariants in pre-states is needed to validate reasoning with supertype abstraction, even if invariants cannot be weakened in behavioral subtypes [42, Lemma 23].

There are, broadly speaking two general approaches that are being investigated for such programming methodologies in the context of JML-like specification languages.

The first is the relevant invariant semantics [62, 63], which is based on an ownership type system [24]. Ownership is used both to prevent problems of representation exposure [54, 62, 66] and to deal with layered abstractions. Reentrance is dealt with by mandating that invariants are established at the point of calling a (non-helper) method.

This approach is being investigated in the context of JML. Dietl and Müller have integrated the Universe type system [24] into the JML checker, which can use ownership annotations to check that specifications follow the methodology. In particular the checker uses the **`rep`** annotations to indicate when contained objects are owned by an enclosing object. For example, in Fig. 5 the **`rep`** annotation in the declaration of `history` says that `history` is owned by the enclosing `Patient` object; i.e., that `history` is part of the representation of `Patient`. The construction of a rep `String` object in the body of `recordVisit` places the newly created string in the `Patient` object's universe (ownership domain). Similarly, the **`rep`** annotation in the constructor's **`new`** expression says that the new object is in its owner's universe. Type checking ensures that invariants only depend on the state of owned objects and are never violated outside of the classes in which they are declared. For example, the type system checks that the object referred to by `history` is never exposed directly to clients, which would allow them to mutate it in ways that would violate the invariant or history constraint of `Patient`.

The second approach is the "Boogie" methodology [5, 51, 65], which is used in the specification language Spec#. To explain the Boogie methodology briefly, I will translate it into JML terms. Suppose each object has a ghost field, which I will call `validFor`. This ghost field could be declared in JML's specification of `Object` as follows.

```
//@ public ghost Class validFor = null;
```

In JML a ghost field is a specification-only field, like a model field, but which is not an abstraction of concrete fields. Instead, a ghost field is manipulated by using **set** statements, which are written in annotations and thus considered part of the program's specification. However, the `validFor` field is special in that the Boogie methodology only allows it to be assigned by two special statements **pack**(T) and **unpack**(T).

This field is used to weaken each declared invariant as follows. Suppose a type T declares an instance invariant inv^T. The Boogie methodology transforms this invariant into an implication: `this.validFor <: \type(`T`) ==>` inv^T. (In JML the operator `<:` means "is a subtype of" and `\type()` is used to enclose type names in expressions.) Thus this transformed invariant says that the declared invariant, inv^T, only has to hold when `this.validFor` is a subtype of T. In the Boogie methodology, this transformed invariant holds in every state, including the pre-state of each method. This is fundamental to solving the invariant problems.

In the Boogie methodology, one can only assign to the fields of an object o that are declared in a type T when an object is "unpacked for T," meaning that o`.validFor` is not a subtype of T. Unpacking an object is the job of the **unpack**(T) statement. When done changing an object's fields, one uses the **pack**(T) statement to check inv^T and to set `validFor` to T. Thus, whenever the program is able to assign to the fields of an object, that object must be unpacked, and hence the declared invariant does not have to hold. This may seem complicated, but the special statements are often implicitly wrapped around the body of a method using default annotations in Spec#.

Because it is based on dynamic manipulations of the `validFor` field, the Boogie methodology is more flexible than the relevant invariant approach. For example, the declared invariants do not have to be re-established on each call to a (non-helper) method, since the object's `validFor` field can be used to dynamically test whether the declared invariant holds. However, as one can see from this translation, some of these ideas (like the dependency of an invariant of part of a program's state) can be used in JML to gain some of the flexibility of the Boogie methodology. Whether these approaches can be usefully blended together is an interesting problem for future research.

Fortunately, the validity of supertype abstraction does not depend on the details of these methodologies. All that is needed is that they allow one to safely assume invariants in the pre-states of non-helper methods [42].

4.1.6 Semantic Implication for Objects of a Type

Predicates used in invariants, history constraints, and initially clauses written in the specification of a type T are written to use the fields (including model fields) and instance methods of that type. Because these are inherited by all subtypes of T, they make sense for all subtypes of T. In the following we will say that a predicate P is for T to describe this association between a predicate and this type context; technically P *is for* T if P type checks in the context of T, assuming that **this** has static type T. Note that if P is for T and T is a supertype of T', then P is also for T'. This notion is used in comparing the relative strength of invariants and history constraints.

Definition 4 (Implies for objects of type T'). *Let P' and P be predicates that are for a type T'. Then P'* implies P for objects of type T' *if and only if whenever* **`this`** *has a dynamic type that is a subtype of T' and P' holds, then P holds.*

It is a corollary that P' implies P for objects of type T' if and only if:

$$\text{Spec}(T') \;\vdash\; \texttt{this instanceof}\; T' \implies (P' \implies P). \tag{6}$$

4.2 A Definition of Behavioral Subtyping for JML

The following definition of behavioral subtyping strays a bit beyond the technical results in Leavens and Naumann's recent work [42] because the definition also treats history constraints and initially clauses. They only prove define behavioral subtyping for types with pre/post method specifications and invariants. However, in adapting their definition to JML I have followed the ideas in their work, which should again be consulted for details.

JML supports two notions of behavioral subtyping. There is an experimental notion of "weak behavioral subtyping" [20, 22, 23]. However, that notion relies on an untested programming methodology [21] which JML does not currently enforce. Thus the most important notion of behavioral subtyping for JML, which corresponds to Liskov and Wing's constraint-based definition [55, p. 1823], is the following.

Definition 5 (strong behavioral subtype). *Let T' be a type specification and let T be a specification for a supertype of T'. Then T'* is a strong behavioral subtype of T *if and only if:*

methods: *for all instance methods m in T, the method specification for m in T' refines that of m in T with respect to T',*
invariant: *the instance invariant of T' implies the instance invariant of T for objects of type T',*
history constraint: *the instance history constraint of T' implies the instance history constraint of T for objects of type T', and*
initially predicate: *the initially predicate of T' implies the initially predicate of T for objects of type T'.*

Notice that the definition above says nothing directly about constructors and thus applies equally well to Java interfaces. However, as Liskov and Wing emphasized [55, 56], constructors are constrained by the invariant of each type. Furthermore, the **`initially`** predicate in a type specification also constrains constructors.

Normally the concept defined above will be referred to as "behavioral subtyping." However, it is useful to keep in mind that the above definition is designed for JML and how one reasons about JML programs using supertype abstraction. As discussed in the next subsection, when working with a specification language X, one needs a definition of behavioral subtyping that validates X's notion of supertype abstraction [2, 38]. Thus there really is no single, normative definition of behavioral subtyping.

4.3 Connection to Supertype Abstraction

The fundamental property of a definition of behavioral subtyping is that it makes supertype abstraction valid [38, 42, 43]. Ideally, a definition would also be no stronger than needed to make supertype abstraction valid. For example, since calls to constructors and static methods are not directly involved in reasoning using supertype abstraction, there is no need for a syntactic (or type) relationship between the constructors and static methods of a behavioral subtype and its supertypes. However, the definition must indirectly limit constructors and static methods (e.g., by enforcing invariants) so that supertype abstraction is valid.

Thus, ideally, behavioral subtyping would be both necessary and sufficient for supertype abstraction to be valid. To prove a theorem about this requires a precise formulation of supertype abstraction. Leavens and Naumann [42] have given such a precise formulation for reasoning with pre/post specifications about dynamically dispatched calls (i.e., in the absence of invariants, history constraints, and initially predicates). Their formulation uses two semantics for such calls, the normal (dynamic) one and a static one. With this notion of supertype abstraction, they shown that it is both necessary and sufficient that each (non-abstract) class be a behavioral subtype of all its supertypes [42, Corollary 13]. Somewhat surprisingly, it turns out that it is not necessary to have an interface (or an abstract class) be a behavioral subtype of its supertypes. They conjecture that with a suitable definition of supertype abstraction (i.e., one that allows reasoning about invariants based on static type information) there is again such an equivalence for specifications with invariants. However, their formal treatment only gives soundness in this case, using some invariant methodology that validates the assumption of invariants in method pre-states (see Section 4.1.5 on page 21).

The notion of supertype abstraction for JML described in this paper involves reasoning using pre/post specifications, invariants, history constraints, and initially predicates. The definition of behavioral subtyping is designed to make the following true.

Conjecture 1 (Supertype abstraction valid). Suppose JML enforces sensible methodological restrictions on invariants, history constraints, and initially predicates.

Then supertype abstraction for JML is valid if and only if each non-abstract class C is a behavioral subtype of all of its supertypes.

Proving a technically precise version of this conjecture would be an important check on the definitions of the programming methodology, supertype abstraction, and strong behavioral subtyping.

Although it is not necessary for the soundness of supertype abstraction, most treatments of behavioral subtyping make interfaces and abstract classes also be behavioral subtypes of their supertypes. JML does this also, through specification inheritance.

4.4 Connection to Specification Inheritance

With specification inheritance each subtype is forced to be a behavioral subtype of each of its supertypes [23, 42]. The following uses the notation from Section 2.5 on page 10.

Theorem 3 (Specification inheritance forces behavioral subtyping). *Let T and V be types where T is a subtype of V. Then the extended specification of T is a strong behavioral subtype of the extended specification of V.*

Proof: Let T and $V \in \mathit{supers}(T)$ be given. We must show that the extended specifications of T and V satisfy Definition 5 on page 24.

methods: Let m be an instance method in $\mathit{methods}(V)$. We show that $\mathit{ext\_spec}_m^T$ refines $\mathit{ext\_spec}_m^V$ with respect to T by the following calculation.

$$\begin{array}{ll}
 & \mathit{ext_spec}_m^T \\
= & \quad \langle \text{by Definition 2} \rangle \\
 & \bigsqcup^T \{\mathit{added_spec}_m^U \mid U \in \mathit{supers}(T)\} \\
= & \quad \langle \text{by set theory, to separate out } V \text{ and its supertypes} \rangle \\
 & \bigsqcup^T \{\mathit{added_spec}_m^U \mid U \in ((\mathit{supers}(T) \setminus \mathit{supers}(V)) \cup \mathit{supers}(V))\} \\
= & \quad \langle \text{by definition of join with respect to } T \rangle \\
 & \quad \left(\bigsqcup^T \{\mathit{added_spec}_m^U \mid U \in (\mathit{supers}(T) \setminus \mathit{supers}(V))\}\right) \\
 & \sqcup^T \left(\bigsqcup^V \{\mathit{added_spec}_m^W \mid W \in \mathit{supers}(V)\}\right) \\
\sqsupseteq^T & \quad \langle \text{by Theorem 2 on page 21, since } T \text{ is a subtype of } V \rangle \\
 & \bigsqcup^V \{\mathit{added_spec}_m^W \mid W \in \mathit{supers}(V)\} \\
= & \quad \langle \text{by Definition 2} \rangle \\
 & \mathit{ext_spec}_m^V
\end{array}$$

invariant: We calculate as follows.

$$\begin{array}{ll}
 & \mathit{ext_inv}^T \\
= & \quad \langle \text{by Definition 2} \rangle \\
 & \bigwedge \{\mathit{added_inv}^U \mid U \in \mathit{supers}(T)\} \\
= & \quad \langle \text{by set theory, to separate out } V \text{ and its supertypes} \rangle \\
 & \bigwedge \{\mathit{added_inv}^U \mid U \in ((\mathit{supers}(T) \setminus \mathit{supers}(V)) \cup \mathit{supers}(V))\} \\
= & \quad \langle \text{by definition of conjunction} \rangle \\
 & \quad (\bigwedge \{\mathit{added_inv}^U \mid U \in (\mathit{supers}(T) \setminus \mathit{supers}(V))\}) \\
 & \wedge (\bigwedge \{\mathit{added_inv}^W \mid W \in \mathit{supers}(V)\}) \\
\Rightarrow & \quad \langle \text{by } A \wedge B \implies B \rangle \\
 & \bigwedge \{\mathit{added_inv}^W \mid W \in \mathit{supers}(V)\} \\
= & \quad \langle \text{by Definition 2} \rangle \\
 & \mathit{ext_inv}^V
\end{array}$$

history constraint and initially predicate: these implications follow by the same reasoning as the implication for the invariant above. ∎

4.5 Examples of Behavioral Subtyping

The above theorem shows that, with specification inheritance, subtypes may only refine and strengthen specifications they inherit from their supertypes. However, specification inheritance can easily cause subtypes to not be satisfiable. For example, the invariant of class `OldAnimal` specified in Fig. 16 on the next page can be violated by the inherited `setAge` method, which is unsatisfiable, since no implementation of `setAge` will be able to both satisfy the inherited specification case and the added invariant.

However, it is possible to strengthen an invariant without making the specification unsatisfiable, as shown in the type `FemalePatient` from Fig. 6 on page 12. Liskov

```
public class OldAnimal extends Animal {
  //@ public invariant 65 < age;

  //@ requires g.equals("female") || g.equals("male");
  //@ assignable gender, age;
  //@ ensures gender.equals(g) && age == 66;
  public OldAnimal(String g) { super(g); age = 66; }
}
```

Fig. 16. A JML specification of the class `OldAnimal`

```
public abstract class Dog extends Animal {
  public static final int D2PY = 7;   // conversion factor
  private /*@ spec_public @*/ int dogAge = 0; //@ in age;
  //@ public invariant dogAge == D2PY*age;

  //@ assignable \nothing;
  //@ ensures \result == dogAge;
  public int getDogAge() { return dogAge; }

  public void setAge(final int a) { super.setAge(a); dogAge = D2PY*age; }
  /* ... */
}
```

Fig. 17. A JML specification of the class `Dog`

and Wing would call this type a "constrained" behavioral subtype [55] of `Patient` (see Fig. 5 on page 9). `FemalePatient`'s invariant limits the values of the model field gender to be the string `"female"`. Unlike the situation with the strengthened invariant in the type `OldAnimal`, there are no inherited methods that can change the `gender`, and hence this added invariant does not make the extended specification unsatisfiable.

In addition to constraining choices allowed by supertypes, a behavioral subtype may also add information and methods. Such a type is an "extension subtype" in Liskov and Wing's terminology [55]. The class `Dog`, given in Fig. 17, extends the type `Animal` in this sense. `Dog`'s added invariant allows the specification of the method `setAge` to be inherited without change. This invariant implies that in its supertype, since by specification inheritance it is the conjunction of the added invariant and `Animal`'s invariant, which is just the default (true). This subtype also adds method `getDogAge`.

5 Related Work

The present paper is based on a recent semantical account that has a formal treatment of supertype abstraction and proves results about its connection to behavioral subtyping and specification inheritance [42]. The following draws on that paper's more detailed discussion of related work.

Several program logics for sequential Java incorporate a notion of supertype abstraction [62, 69, 70, 72]. They mostly require each overriding method implementation in a type to satisfy the corresponding specification in each of its supertypes, which is effectively the same as specification inheritance.

Liskov and Wing's paper [55] also discusses the idea of supertype abstraction to some extent. Their "subtype requirement" [55, p. 1812], says that properties of a supertype hold for all subtypes. However, the properties they consider are only those obtainable by inductive reasoning with invariants and history constraints, because they consider concurrent programs and do not require alias control. Due to concurrency their subtype requirement does not encompass the use of supertype abstraction to do pre/post reasoning about the correctness of method implementations, although their definition of behavioral subtyping is adequate for such reasoning if one were to consider a sequential language and impose a methodology to deal with the problems of invariants described in Section 4.1.5 on page 21. Liskov and Wing's formalization of behavioral subtyping uses abstraction functions. Abstraction functions are not needed in the formalization presented here, because all fields (including model fields) are inherited in JML, which makes the predicates used to specify supertypes automatically meaningful in subtypes. They give many interesting examples of their notion of behavioral subtyping.

Dhara and Leavens [23] explained specification inheritance for Larch/C++ and gave the first proof that it forces behavioral subtyping.

Wills introduced the idea of specification inheritance for combining "capsules" in his Fresco system [79]. In Fresco one can write several "capsules" for a method, which must all be obeyed by a correct implementation. Specification cases in JML are based on this idea. The idea of combining separate specification cases first appeared in Wing's dissertation [80]. That work introduced the Larch family of behavioral interface specification languages [30, 81], which were a precursor of JML.

Eiffel [59], another precursor of JML, also has behavioral subtyping and a form of specification inheritance. Mitchell and McKim describe an idea similar to the join of method specifications in their chapter on inheritance [60, Chapter 6].

Early work on behavioral subtyping is surveyed in a paper by Leavens and Dhara [41], including the work of America [3, 4], which has the first proof of the soundness of reasoning in the context of behavioral subtyping.

6 Conclusions

JML is a cooperative effort to enhance the utility of specification languages and associated tools. While the concepts presented in this paper seem well established, many challenges remain [46]. The main future work related to the present paper is limiting the notion of specification inheritance by warning where it appears that the specifier is trying to strengthen the precondition of an overriding method's specification [28]. Static analysis tools for JML could also warn when a subtype's specification was inconsistent, due to conflicts between inherited and added specifications. More work on JML's semantics, including a proof of Conjecture 1 on page 25 would also be interesting.

Specification inheritance in JML forces all subtypes to be behavioral subtypes. This ensures that one can use supertype abstraction to do modular reasoning using static type information. The key feature of JML that supports specification inheritance is JML's **`also`**, which automatically produces a refinement of the specification cases that it joins.

These ideas can also be used informally [54]. For example, when writing informal documentation for a method, one can mimic JML's use of **`also`** by starting with a phrase like "In addition to the inherited behavior, this method ..."

Similarly, when designing a type as a subtype of various classes and interfaces, one can keep in mind the demands of behavioral subtyping [19, 37, 59]. For example one has to be careful not to strengthen the invariant of a class in a way that would contradict the specification of inherited methods. One should be especially careful not to overspecify when specifying binary methods, such as the `equals` method, which would make behavioral subtypes unable to consider additional attributes.

Finally, the notion of behavioral subtyping validates informal reasoning based on static type information. When the specifications associated with static types are not sufficient to draw a desired conclusion, one can use type tests and downcasts to record the need for stronger assumptions about the types of objects. This blends special case reasoning with the uniformity of supertype abstraction.

Acknowledgments

Special thanks to David Naumann, who co-developed the theory behind this paper with me [42], and with whom I have had many interesting conversations about this paper's topics. Thanks also to my other collaborators on topics related to behavioral subtyping: William Weihl, Krishna Kishore Dhara, Cesare Tinelli, and Don Pigozzi. Thanks to Barbara Liskov for starting me on the topic of object-oriented programming, and for her inspirational examples of how to explain ideas for programmers. Thanks to Jeannette Wing for her work on Larch, and for suggesting the Larch/C++ project, which eventually led to JML. Thanks to Yoonsik Cheon for joint work on Larch/C++ and to Al Baker, Clyde Ruby, and Tim Wahls for their collaboration on the initial design of JML, including the core features described in this paper. Thanks to Patrice Chalin, Yoonsik Cheon, Curtis Clifton, David Cok, Joseph Kiniry, Rustan Leino, Peter Müller, Arnd Poetzsch-Heffter, Erik Poll and the rest of the JML community (`jmlspecs.org`) for many discussions about JML, its design, semantics, and tool support. Thanks to Samik Basu, Kristina Boysen, David Cok, Faraz Hussain, David Naumann, Hridesh Rajan, Clyde Ruby, and Tim Wahls for comments on earlier drafts of this paper.

Bibliography

[1] W. Ahrendt, T. Baar, B. Beckert, R. Bubel, M. Giese, R. Hähnle, W. Menzel, W. Mostowski, A. Roth, S. Schlager, and P. H. Schmitt. The KeY tool. *Software and System Modeling*, 4: 32–54, 2005.

[2] S. Alagic and S. Kouznetsova. Behavioral compatibility of self-typed theories. In B. Magnusson, editor, *ECOOP 2002 — Object-Oriented Programming, 16th European Conference, Máalaga, Spain, Proceedings*, volume 2374 of *Lecture Notes in Computer Science*, pages 585–608, Berlin, June 2002. Springer-Verlag.

[3] P. America. Inheritance and subtyping in a parallel object-oriented language. In J. Bezivin et al., editors, *ECOOP '87, European Conference on Object-Oriented Programming, Paris, France*, pages 234–242, New York, NY, June 1987. Springer-Verlag. Lecture Notes in Computer Science, volume 276.

[4] P. America. Designing an object-oriented programming language with behavioural subtyping. In J. W. de Bakker, W. P. de Roever, and G. Rozenberg, editors, *Foundations of Object-Oriented Languages, REX School/Workshop, Noordwijkerhout, The Netherlands, May/June 1990*, volume 489 of *Lecture Notes in Computer Science*, pages 60–90. Springer-Verlag, New York, NY, 1991.

[5] M. Barnett, R. DeLine, M. Fähndrich, K. R. M. Leino, and W. Schulte. Verification of object-oriented programs with invariants. *Journal of Object Technology*, 3(6):27–56, 2004. URL `http://tinyurl.com/m2a8j`.

[6] A. Borgida, J. Mylopoulos, and R. Reiter. On the frame problem in procedure specifications. *IEEE Transactions on Software Engineering*, 21(10):785–798, Oct. 1995.

[7] K. Bruce, L. Cardelli, G. Castagna, T. H. O. Group, G. T. Leavens, and B. Pierce. On binary methods. *Theory and Practice of Object Systems*, 1(3):221–242, 1995.

[8] M. Büchi and W. Weck. The greybox approach: When blackbox specifications hide too much. Technical Report 297, Turku Center for Computer Science, Aug. 1999. http://www.abo.fi/~mbuechi/publications/TR297.html.

[9] L. Burdy, A. Requet, and J.-L. Lanet. Java applet correctness: a developer-oriented approach. In K. Araki, S. Gnesi, and D. Mandrioli, editors, *FME 2003: Formal Methods, International Symposium of Formal Methods Europe*, volume 2805 of *Lecture Notes in Computer Science*, pages 422–439. Springer, Sept. 2003.

[10] L. Burdy, Y. Cheon, D. R. Cok, M. D. Ernst, J. R. Kiniry, G. T. Leavens, K. R. M. Leino, and E. Poll. An overview of JML tools and applications. *International Journal on Software Tools for Technology Transfer (STTT)*, 7(3):212–232, June 2005.

[11] N. Cataño and M. Huisman. Formal specification of Gemplus's electronic purse case study. In L. H. Eriksson and P. A. Lindsay, editors, *FME 2002*, volume LNCS 2391, pages 272–289. Springer-Verlag, 2002.

[12] P. Chalin, J. R. Kiniry, G. T. Leavens, and E. Poll. Beyond assertions: Advanced specification and verification with JML and ESC/Java2. In *Formal Methods for Components and Objects (FMCO) 2005, Revised Lectures*, Lecture Notes in Computer Science. Springer-Verlag, 2006. URL `http://tinyurl.com/o4nxa`.

[13] Y. Chen and B. H. C. Cheng. A semantic foundation for specification matching. In G. T. Leavens and M. Sitaraman, editors, *Foundations of Component-Based Systems*, pages 91–109. Cambridge University Press, New York, NY, 2000.

[14] Y. Cheon. A runtime assertion checker for the Java Modeling Language. Technical Report 03-09, Department of Computer Science, Iowa State University, Ames, IA, Apr. 2003. URL `ftp://ftp.cs.iastate.edu/pub/techreports/TR03-09/TR.pdf`. The author's Ph.D. dissertation.

[15] Y. Cheon and G. T. Leavens. A simple and practical approach to unit testing: The JML and JUnit way. In B. Magnusson, editor, *ECOOP 2002 — Object-Oriented Programming, 16th European Conference, Máalaga, Spain, Proceedings*, volume 2374 of *Lecture Notes in Computer Science*, pages 231–255, Berlin, June 2002. Springer-Verlag.

[16] Y. Cheon and G. T. Leavens. A runtime assertion checker for the Java Modeling Language (JML). In H. R. Arabnia and Y. Mun, editors, *Proceedings of the International Conference on Software Engineering Research and Practice (SERP '02), Las Vegas, Nevada, USA, June 24-27, 2002*, pages 322–328. CSREA Press, June 2002. URL `ftp://ftp.cs.iastate.edu/pub/techreports/TR02-05/TR.pdf`.

[17] Y. Cheon and G. T. Leavens. The Larch/Smalltalk interface specification language. *ACM Transactions on Software Engineering and Methodology*, 3(3):221–253, July 1994.
[18] Y. Cheon, G. T. Leavens, M. Sitaraman, and S. Edwards. Model variables: Cleanly supporting abstraction in design by contract. *Software—Practice and Experience*, 35(6):583–599, May 2005.
[19] W. R. Cook. Interfaces and specifications for the Smalltalk-80 collection classes. *ACM SIGPLAN Notices*, 27(10):1–15, Oct. 1992. *OOPSLA '92 Proceedings*, Andreas Paepcke (editor).
[20] K. K. Dhara. Behavioral subtyping in object-oriented languages. Technical Report TR97-09, Department of Computer Science, Iowa State University, 226 Atanasoff Hall, Ames IA 50011-1040, May 1997. The author's Ph.D. dissertation.
[21] K. K. Dhara and G. T. Leavens. Preventing cross-type aliasing for more practical reasoning. Technical Report 01-02a, Department of Computer Science, Iowa State University, Ames, Iowa, 50011, Nov. 2001. URL `ftp://ftp.cs.iastate.edu/pub/techreports/TR01-02/TR.pdf`. Available from archives.cs.iastate.edu.
[22] K. K. Dhara and G. T. Leavens. Weak behavioral subtyping for types with mutable objects. In S. Brookes, M. Main, A. Melton, and M. Mislove, editors, *Mathematical Foundations of Programming Semantics, Eleventh Annual Conference*, volume 1 of *Electronic Notes in Theoretical Computer Science*. Elsevier, 1995. Available from `http://www.sciencedirect.com/science/journal/15710661`.
[23] K. K. Dhara and G. T. Leavens. Forcing behavioral subtyping through specification inheritance. In *Proceedings of the 18th International Conference on Software Engineering, Berlin, Germany*, pages 258–267. IEEE Computer Society Press, Mar. 1996. A corrected version is ISU CS TR #95-20c, `http://tinyurl.com/s2krg`.
[24] W. Dietl and P. Müller. Universes: Lightweight ownership for JML. *Journal of Object Technology (JOT)*, 4(8):5–32, Oct. 2005. URL `http://www.jot.fm/issues/issue_2005_10/article1.pdf`.
[25] E. W. Dijkstra. *A Discipline of Programming*. Prentice-Hall, Inc., Englewood Cliffs, N.J., 1976.
[26] S. H. Edwards, W. D. Heym, T. J. Long, M. Sitaraman, and B. W. Weide. Part II: Specifying components in RESOLVE. *ACM SIGSOFT Software Engineering Notes*, 19(4):29–39, Oct 1994.
[27] M. Ernst, J. Cockrell, W. G. Griswold, and D. Notkin. Dynamically discovering likely program invariants to support program evolution. *IEEE Transactions on Software Engineering*, 27(2):99–123, Feb. 2001.
[28] R. B. Findler and M. Felleisen. Contract soundness for object-oriented languages. In *OOPSLA '01 Conference Proceedings, Object-Oriented Programming, Systems, Languages, and Applications, October 14-18, 2001, Tampa Bay, Florida, USA*, pages 1–15, Oct. 2001.
[29] C. Flanagan, K. R. M. Leino, M. Lillibridge, G. Nelson, J. B. Saxe, and R. Stata. Extended static checking for Java. In *Proceedings of the ACM SIGPLAN 2002 Conference on Programming Language Design and Implementation (PLDI'02)*, volume 37, 5 of *SIGPLAN*, pages 234–245, New York, June 17–19 2002. ACM Press.
[30] J. V. Guttag, J. J. Horning, S. Garland, K. Jones, A. Modet, and J. Wing. *Larch: Languages and Tools for Formal Specification*. Springer-Verlag, New York, NY, 1993.
[31] C. A. R. Hoare. An axiomatic basis for computer programming. *Commun. ACM*, 12(10): 576–583, Oct. 1969.
[32] C. A. R. Hoare. Proof of correctness of data representations. *Acta Informatica*, 1(4):271–281, 1972.

[33] B. Jacobs and E. Poll. Java program verification at Nijmegen: Developments and perspective. Technical Report NIII-R0318, Computing Science Institute, University of Nijmegen, 2003. URL http://www.cs.kun.nl/research/reports/full/NIII-R0318.ps.gz.

[34] B. Jacobs, J. van den Berg, M. Huisman, M. van Berkum, U. Hensel, and H. Tews. Reasoning about Java classes (preliminary report). In *OOPSLA '98 Conference Proceedings*, volume 33(10) of *ACM SIGPLAN Notices*, pages 329–340. ACM, Oct. 1998.

[35] C. B. Jones. *Systematic Software Development Using VDM*. International Series in Computer Science. Prentice Hall, Englewood Cliffs, N.J., second edition, 1990.

[36] J. R. Kiniry and D. R. Cok. ESC/Java2: Uniting ESC/Java and JML: Progress and issues in building and using ESC/Java2, including a case study involving the use of the tool to verify portions of an Internet voting tally system. In *Construction and Analysis of Safe, Secure, and Interoperable Smart devices (CASSIS)*, volume 3362 of *Lecture Notes in Computer Science*, pages 108–128. Springer-Verlag, 2004.

[37] W. R. LaLonde, D. A. Thomas, and J. R. Pugh. An exemplar based Smalltalk. *ACM SIGPLAN Notices*, 21(11):322–330, Nov. 1986. OOPSLA '86 Conference Proceedings, Norman Meyrowitz (editor), September 1986, Portland, Oregon.

[38] G. T. Leavens. Verifying object-oriented programs that use subtypes. Technical Report 439, Massachusetts Institute of Technology, Laboratory for Computer Science, Feb. 1989. The author's Ph.D. thesis.

[39] G. T. Leavens. An overview of Larch/C++: Behavioral specifications for C++ modules. In H. Kilov and W. Harvey, editors, *Specification of Behavioral Semantics in Object-Oriented Information Modeling*, chapter 8, pages 121–142. Kluwer Academic Publishers, Boston, 1996. An extended version is TR #96-01d, Department of Computer Science, Iowa State University, Ames, Iowa, 50011.

[40] G. T. Leavens and A. L. Baker. Enhancing the pre- and postcondition technique for more expressive specifications. In J. M. Wing, J. Woodcock, and J. Davies, editors, *FM'99 — Formal Methods: World Congress on Formal Methods in the Development of Computing Systems, Toulouse, France, September 1999, Proceedings*, volume 1709 of *Lecture Notes in Computer Science*, pages 1087–1106. Springer-Verlag, 1999. URL http://tinyurl.com/qv84o.

[41] G. T. Leavens and K. K. Dhara. Concepts of behavioral subtyping and a sketch of their extension to component-based systems. In G. T. Leavens and M. Sitaraman, editors, *Foundations of Component-Based Systems*, chapter 6, pages 113–135. Cambridge University Press, 2000. URL http://www.cs.iastate.edu/~leavens/FoCBS-book/06-leavens-dhara.pdf.

[42] G. T. Leavens and D. A. Naumann. Behavioral subtyping, specification inheritance, and modular reasoning. Technical Report 06-20a, Department of Computer Science, Iowa State University, Ames, Iowa, 50011, Aug. 2006. URL ftp://ftp.cs.iastate.edu/pub/techreports/TR06-20/TR.pdf.

[43] G. T. Leavens and W. E. Weihl. Specification and verification of object-oriented programs using supertype abstraction. *Acta Informatica*, 32(8):705–778, Nov. 1995.

[44] G. T. Leavens, Y. Cheon, C. Clifton, C. Ruby, and D. R. Cok. How the design of JML accommodates both runtime assertion checking and formal verification. *Science of Computer Programming*, 55(1-3):185–208, Mar. 2005. URL http://dx.doi.org/10.1016/j.scico.2004.05.015.

[45] G. T. Leavens, A. L. Baker, and C. Ruby. Preliminary design of JML: A behavioral interface specification language for Java. *ACM SIGSOFT Software Engineering Notes*, 31(3):1–38, Mar. 2006. http://doi.acm.org/10.1145/1127878.1127884.

[46] G. T. Leavens, K. R. M. Leino, and P. Müller. Specification and verification challenges for sequential object-oriented programs. Technical Report 06-14, Department of Computer Science, Iowa State University, Ames, Iowa, May 2006. URL ftp://ftp.cs.iastate.edu/pub/techreports/TR06-14/TR.pdf.

[47] G. T. Leavens, E. Poll, C. Clifton, Y. Cheon, C. Ruby, D. R. Cok, P. Müller, J. Kiniry, and P. Chalin. JML reference manual. Department of Computer Science, Iowa State University. Available from http://www.jmlspecs.org, Jan. 2006.

[48] K. R. M. Leino. *Toward Reliable Modular Programs*. PhD thesis, California Institute of Technology, 1995. Available as Technical Report Caltech-CS-TR-95-03.

[49] K. R. M. Leino. Data groups: Specifying the modification of extended state. In *OOPSLA '98 Conference Proceedings*, volume 33(10) of *ACM SIGPLAN Notices*, pages 144–153. ACM, Oct. 1998.

[50] K. R. M. Leino and R. Manohar. Joining specification statements. *Theoretical Comput. Sci.*, 216(1-2):375–394, Mar. 1999.

[51] K. R. M. Leino and P. Müller. Object invariants in dynamic contexts. In M. Odersky, editor, *European Conference on Object-Oriented Programming (ECOOP)*, volume 3086 of *Lecture Notes in Computer Science*, pages 491–516. Springer-Verlag, 2004.

[52] K. R. M. Leino and P. Müller. A verification methodology for model fields. In P. Sestoft, editor, *European Symposium on Programming (ESOP)*, volume 3924 of *Lecture Notes in Computer Science*, pages 115–130. Springer-Verlag, 2006. URL http://tinyurl.com/pzll8.

[53] B. Liskov. Data abstraction and hierarchy. *ACM SIGPLAN Notices*, 23(5):17–34, May 1988. Revised version of the keynote address given at OOPSLA '87.

[54] B. Liskov and J. Guttag. *Program Development in Java*. The MIT Press, Cambridge, Mass., 2001.

[55] B. Liskov and J. Wing. A behavioral notion of subtyping. *ACM Trans. Prog. Lang. Syst.*, 16(6):1811–1841, Nov. 1994.

[56] B. Liskov and J. M. Wing. Specifications and their use in defining subtypes. *ACM SIGPLAN Notices*, 28(10):16–28, Oct. 1993. *OOPSLA '93 Proceedings*, Andreas Paepcke (editor).

[57] C. Marché, C. Paulin-Mohring, and X. Urbain. The KRAKATOA tool for certification of JAVA/JAVACARD programs annotated in JML. *Journal of Logic and Algebraic Programming*, 58(1-2):89–106, Jan.–Mar. 2004.

[58] B. Meyer. *Eiffel: The Language*. Object-Oriented Series. Prentice Hall, New York, NY, 1992.

[59] B. Meyer. *Object-oriented Software Construction*. Prentice Hall, New York, NY, second edition, 1997.

[60] R. Mitchell and J. McKim. *Design by Contract by Example*. Addison-Wesley, Indianapolis, IN, 2002.

[61] C. Morgan. *Programming from Specifications: Second Edition*. Prentice Hall International, Hempstead, UK, 1994.

[62] P. Müller. *Modular Specification and Verification of Object-Oriented Programs*, volume 2262 of *Lecture Notes in Computer Science*. Springer-Verlag, 2002. URL http://tinyurl.com/jtwot.

[63] P. Müller, A. Poetzsch-Heffter, and G. T. Leavens. Modular invariants for layered object structures. *Sci. Comput. Programming*, 62(3):253–286, Oct. 2006. URL http://dx.doi.org/10.1016/j.scico.2006.03.001.

[64] D. A. Naumann. Calculating sharp adaptation rules. *Inf. Process. Lett.*, 77:201–208, 2001.

[65] D. A. Naumann and M. Barnett. Towards imperative modules: Reasoning about invariants and sharing of mutable state. *Theoretical Comput. Sci.*, 2006. To appear.

[66] J. Noble, J. Vitek, and J. Potter. Flexible alias protection. In E. Jul, editor, *ECOOP '98 – Object-Oriented Programming, 12th European Conference, Brussels, Belgium*, volume 1445 of *Lecture Notes in Computer Science*, pages 158–185. Springer-Verlag, July 1998.

[67] W. F. Ogden, M. Sitaraman, B. W. Weide, and S. H. Zweben. Part I: The RESOLVE framework and discipline — a research synopsis. *ACM SIGSOFT Software Engineering Notes*, 19(4):23–28, Oct. 1994.

[68] E. Olderog. On the notion of expressiveness and the rule of adaptation. *Theoretical Comput. Sci.*, 24:337–347, 1983.

[69] M. J. Parkinson. Local reasoning for Java. Technical Report 654, University of Cambridge Computer Laboratory, Nov. 2005. URL `http://www.cl.cam.ac.uk/TechReports/UCAM-CL-TR-654.pdf`. The author's Ph.D. dissertation.

[70] C. Pierik. *Validation Techniques for Object-Oriented Proof Outlines*. PhD thesis, Universiteit Utrecht, 2006. URL `http://igitur-archive.library.uu.nl/dissertations/2006-0502-200341/index.htm`.

[71] A. Poetzsch-Heffter. Specification and verification of object-oriented programs. Habilitation thesis, Technical University of Munich, January 1997. URL `http://tinyurl.com/g7xgm`.

[72] A. Poetzsch-Heffter and P. Müller. A programming logic for sequential Java. In S. D. Swierstra, editor, *European Symosium un Programming (ESOP '99)*, volume 1576 of *Lecture Notes in Computer Science*, pages 162–176. Springer-Verlag, 1999. URL `http://tinyurl.com/krjle`.

[73] A. Poetzsch-Heffter, P. Müller, and J. Schäfer. The Jive tool. `http://softech.informatik.uni-kl.de/twiki/bin/view/Homepage/Jive`, Apr. 2006. Checked August 2, 2006.

[74] E. Poll. A coalgebraic semantics of subtyping. In H. Reichel, editor, *Coalgebraic Methods in Computer Science (CMCS)*, number 33 in Electronic Notes in Theoretical Computer Science. Elsevier, Amsterdam, 2000.

[75] A. D. Raghavan and G. T. Leavens. Desugaring JML method specifications. Technical Report 00-03e, Iowa State University, Department of Computer Science, May 2005. URL `ftp://ftp.cs.iastate.edu/pub/techreports/TR00-03/TR. pdf`.

[76] Robby, M. B. Dwyer, and J. Hatcliff. Bogor: An extensible and highly-modular model checking framework. In *Proceedings of the 9th European Software Engineering Conference held jointly with the 11th ACM SIGSOFT Symposium on the Foundations of Software Engineering*, volume 28 number 5 of *SIGSOFT Softw. Eng. Notes*, pages 267–276. ACM, 2003.

[77] Robby, E. Rodríguez, M. Dwyer, and J. Hatcliff. Checking strong specifications using an extensible software model checking framework. In *Proceedings of the 10th International Conference on Tools and Algorithms for the Construction and Analysis of Systems*, volume 2988 of *Lecture Notes in Computer Science*, pages 404–420. Springer-Verlag, 2004. ISBN 3-540-21299-X.

[78] S. Stepney, R. Barden, and D. Cooper, editors. *Object Orientation in Z.* Workshops in Computing. Springer-Verlag, Cambridge CB2 1LQ, UK, 1992.

[79] Specification in Fresco. In Stepney et al. [78], chapter 11, pages 127–135.

[80] J. M. Wing. A two-tiered approach to specifying programs. Technical Report TR-299, Massachusetts Institute of Technology, Laboratory for Computer Science, 1983.

[81] J. M. Wing. Writing Larch interface language specifications. *ACM Trans. Prog. Lang. Syst.*, 9(1):1–24, Jan. 1987.

Three Perspectives in Formal Engineering

John McDermid and Andy Galloway

Department of Computer Science, University of York
Heslington, York. YO10 5DD, UK
{jam, andyg}@cs.york.ac.uk

Abstract. We present three perspectives of the use of formalism in the construction of High-Integrity Embedded Real-time Systems. In the first, we describe the long-term research aims. The scope is the entire system, the goal is to demonstrate *intentional* correctness, and the emphasis is on *scientific certainty*. In the second, we present medium-term research aims. The scope is more on the software in the system, and the emphasis shifts to the notion of *engineering confidence*. Following on from the medium-term view we propose a set of challenges for formal engineering methods research, based on our perception of the *technical* issues surrounding the provision of viable engineering solutions. In the third perspective we discuss the short term. In particular, we describe how our recent research is attempting to meet some of the proposed challenges, as a first step towards our medium and long-term aspirations.

1 Introduction

The primary motivation for this paper is the question "How do we construct a system and know that the fruit of our efforts behaves as we intended?" Due emphasis is placed on the word *intended*, as opposed to *specified*. We are interested in whether a system "does what we want" not just whether it "does what we say."

The focus on intent is vital. Traditional development is inductive; the requirements specification is the "base-case", and *validation* and *verification* are the means ("inductive steps") by which we demonstrate *correctness*. By thinking immediately in terms of the V&V model, we run the risk of avoiding essential considerations such as whether our choice of base-case was a wise one.

In what follows we present three perspectives, long-term, medium-term and short-term, on the use of formalism in the construction of High Integrity Embedded Real-time Systems (HIRTS). In doing so, we aim to amalgamate our recent efforts on three fronts. The long-term view is based on on-going work supporting the *Grand Challenges* initiative. In it we begin to set out a view based on the aspiration of *scientific certainty*. The medium-term perspective represents our endeavours to provide a coherent technical framework, and "bigger picture", for the aims of our current research. The aspiration here is *engineering confidence*, rather than certainty. Following the medium-term view, we present a set of challenges for research in Formal Engineering Methods. We view the challenges in two ways: firstly as a

Z. Liu and J. He (Eds.): ICFEM 2006, LNCS 4260, pp. 35 – 54, 2006.

positive agenda for future work, given in terms of what we perceive as the outstanding problems; and secondly, considering the items on that agenda as a synergistic whole, as a set of potential pitfalls for proposed solutions to avoid – i.e. it is both a "wish" list and a "watch out for" list. Finally, the short-term perspective briefly describes our own research in attempting to meet some of these challenges. The paper builds on ideas originally presented at ICFEM 98 [1].

2 The Long-Term

The systems we build are complex. They can contain digital software and hardware, analogue electronics, and pneumatic, hydraulic and mechanical sub-systems. They affect the real-world (temperatures, pressures, motions) in ways we have to understand in order to predict what the systems we fabricate will actually do. Systems also contain human beings – we sometimes make assumptions about human responses, such as their expected physiological, psychological, rational or procedural behaviour in particular situations. We may need to take into account *all* of these factors in order to assure ourselves that what we have produced is what we *intended* to produce.

In providing the long-term view of Formal Engineering, our aim is to present a vision of *intentional correctness* based on the notion of *scientific certainty*. This may seem at odds with the title of the paper, which explicitly mentions "Engineering" – a term which one might define as the process by which we creatively apply different *sciences* in order to produce something of value. However, our assertion here is that having something to aim at helps. By considering the long-term, we hope to be able to set better intermediate objectives for our work.

There are many *computational models* in Formal Methods, one of the most general is Parnas' 4-variable model [2]. Our long-term view is presented in terms of a modification of Parnas' model, which, along with an appropriate interpretation, serves as a mathematical metaphor for our aspirations. The Parnas model distinguishes *monitored*, *input*, *output* and *controlled* variables. Systems and their software components are characterised in terms of various relations NAT, REQ, INPUT, OUTPUT, SOFTREQ, which collectively describe the real-world (nature, the input/output devices) and our requirements over it (how we want the real-world to be, what the software does to achieve it). See section 3 for more detail. Variables (e.g. monitored) are modeled as trajectories – functions from a dense time domain to the vector of their prospective values. Relationships between variables are captured as relations between their trajectories, e.g. between the monitored and controlled variables. The relationships described between variables form the basis of rigorous engineering documentation.

Since our metaphor is not intended as a basis for engineering practices we can be more general; we do not insist on the variable classification and prescribed set of relations (further justification for this is provided below). A system is characterised as a single set of trajectories – a function from a dense time domain to the significant variables of the system (their valuation function). Variables might represent any quantity of significance: a temperature, the position of a stepper motor in an actuator, the pressure on a human-operated inceptor, a digital electronic signal, a variable in a program. Variable values are generally *real*, and may exhibit both continuous and discontinuous mathematical properties. Note that selecting which variables are significant is itself a problem and one which we will leave open.

Another interesting issue is what the domains of the trajectories represent. One interpretation is that each trajectory represents one possible use of the software from power-up to power-down. However, this interpretation is probably over-restrictive. Hardware can be reset during a mission, and environmental faults will persist during the power cycle – intentional correctness is an ideal which spans more than single uses of the software. For this reason, and for the metaphor to apply to persistent components as well as software, we assume the domains represent entire *missions*, although we leave the specific definition of *mission* open.

Before completing the metaphor, it is interesting to note that many other formalisms can be interpreted as abstractions of the trajectory model. A Machine in B might be said to abstract away time to leave behavioural ordering, and then characterise the ordering by focusing on specific variables and relationships of interest. The main variables of interest represent software state, and the relationship is that of a *step* in state, along with how the input and output variables are allowed to vary with that *step*[1]. It might be viewed as a set of first-order difference equations. Likewise, basic CSP might be said to abstract time, but now the variables of interest represent the willingness or refusal of processes to engage in shared actions.

The final step in the construction of our metaphor is to augment the trajectory model with the notion of probability. Probability is key to our ideal of intentional correctness. We cannot model everything; we cannot have an infinite set of variables representing the world at sub-atomic level. Even if we could, we know uncertainty and probability pervade all our models of reality, whatever lens we view the universe through. Probability is vital when abstracting reality to a manageable set of variables. For example, a shaft breaking in the gas turbine engine powering an aircraft is far less likely to happen in a given time frame – thankfully – than a small change in ambient temperature. Accordingly, the sets of trajectories associated with each phenomenon have very different probabilistic weightings. Moreover, considering our *intentional* view of correctness, there is no absolute notion of a system being *correct*. For example, flying is an inherently risky business. The requirements on the system cannot be stated as simply as "we are not going to kill anyone", because, at least for the present, we ARE. It is merely a question of whether the likelihood of that happening is "tolerable". If everything went wrong on an aircraft that could do (including the pilot!) no piece of software, or wider notion of computation, is going to avert a disaster – we might consider this the alternative "law of the excluded miracle." Instead, the fundamental requirement of our fabricated computations (software or otherwise) is to mitigate the risk of something bad happening rather than stopping it completely.

In order to capture essential considerations about probability we associate a probability distribution with the set of trajectories. Once again we leave open questions. In particular, we avoid the question of how the distribution is produced, and indeed, how to integrate over its intervals. The metaphor is illustrated in Figure 1.

---

[1] Note that we are not suggesting this is a correct, or the only, interpretation, just that interpretation is possible.

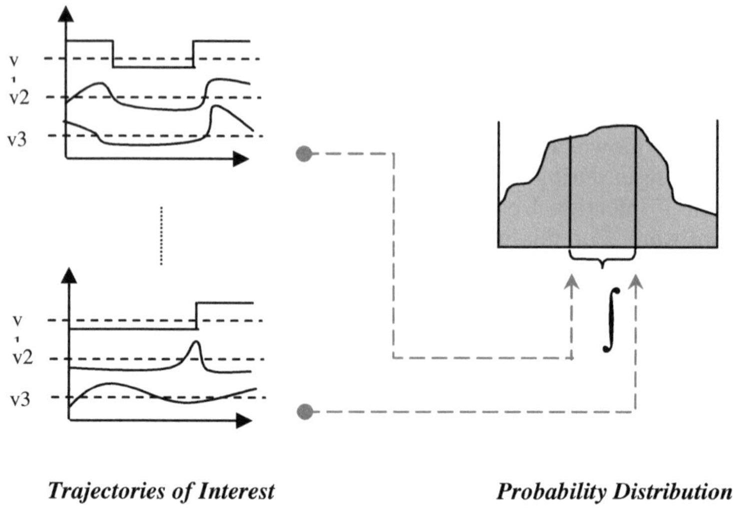

Fig. 1. The Metaphor

It is now possible to state our intent – the basis against which correctness needs to be demonstrated. The intent of the system can be given as limits on the probabilities associated with particular sets of trajectories. We require the probability of bad things happening (i.e. those associated with loss of life) to be below some limit, and the probability of (only) good things happening (i.e. a useful outcome) to be above some limit. To use mathematical rhetoric, if we had a logic expressive enough to identify the trajectories of interest, and a property P expressed in this logic, then a requirement is that:

$$\int_{trj \models P} \text{Prob (trj)}$$

is in some stipulated bisect of *0..1*.

Clearly, we are avoiding answering many important questions, such as: how the trajectories and their associated probabilities are calculated, how important classes of trajectory and their limits are identified for requirements purposes, and how systems are *composed* and *refined*. These questions *are* difficult to answer – and avoiding some of them allows the metaphor to be more abstract. For example, any practical theory is likely to be underpinned by a causal model, which characterises the dependencies between phenomena of interest (e.g. faults, failures, hazards). The variable classification *monitored*, *input*, *output*, *controlled*, might be seen as a first step towards such a model – viewed this way the decision abstract away from the classification is a natural consequence of the issues left open. In addition, although the emphasis has been on probability, the distribution might, for practical purposes, represent alternative *weightings*. In particular, the notions of *risk* and *value* are central in resolving conflicting interests. Trajectory probabilities may be modified according to *severity* and *benefit*, and certain limits (requirements) may be better expressed in these terms than by probability alone.

Note that we are not proposing the metaphor as a mathematical framework for developing systems – that is one of the reasons it is presented as a *metaphor*. However, if the goal is scientific certainty, and given the complexity of the systems we build, we are arguing that something of at least the expressive power implied by the metaphor is necessary. Accepting this, the first thing to acknowledge is that intentional correctness is a muti-discipline affair. The information repesented by the metaphor has to be instantiated, and this can include, for example, techniques in, material science, mechanical engineering, aerodynamics, psychology, control theory, electrical engineering, statistical modelling, Markov modelling, causal modelling and risk analysis. We must remain humble regarding our role in the *big picture* and to the contribution of skilled others – we software engineers cannot demonstrate intentional correctness by ourselves.

To reach the aspiration of scientific certainty, each of the techniques used to insert information into the model must do so with scientific certainty. Considering the magnitude of the questions left open in the description of the metaphor, the multi-discipline nature of the problem, and the ambition of the scientific agenda, we do not believe that long-term vision is going be a working reality any time soon!

3 The Medium Term

For the medium term view our aspiration is *engineering confidence* rather than scientific certainty, and we now consider the targeted use of formalism within a wider engineering process. The wider process, for example, can be assumed to help manage the probabilistic and risk/value-based aspects of the metaphor presented in the previous section. This occurs through the application of engineering judgement, along with analysis techniques for structuring, gaining great confidence in, and articulating the decision making process based on appropriate models (e.g. design representations, fault trees, HAZOP, goal structuring notation etc.). In particular, not only is risk/value assessed, but design changes (derived requirements) emerge out of this process, which minimise risk (and maximise value). Thus, engineering discipline provides the link from *specification* to *intent*, rather than some formal model (as implied by the metaphor).

Formal development is widely seen as a way to achieve the extremely low failure rates (cf the risk/value model) demanded for safety-critical software. Indeed, this principle is embodied by a number of standards [3, 4]. However, whilst there are good examples of the application of static program analysis techniques to safety-critical software, e.g. [5], there are very few examples of the use of “classical” formal approaches such as those based on the notion of refinement ([6] is a rare example). Indeed, there are many practical and theoretical difficulties in applying such models.

The ideas presented in this section were borne out of endeavours to provide a sound technical basis for the use of formal development within the wider engineering context. This led to the identification of a set of practical challenges associated with the development of safety-critical systems, based on our experience with a range of avionics applications. The results were originally published in [7]. This section reprises the technical proposals from [7], and in the next section we present a revised and extended version of the challenges.

3.1 Development Models

In a safety-critical engineering setting we need to model the environment (air, passengers, roads, etc.), the top-level system, e.g. an aero-engine, which we term the "platform", the control, or embedding, system, e.g. a Full Authority Digital Engine Controller (FADEC) and the embedded system (computing system and software). Moreover, we need to distinguish the variables (real-world quantities, logical values) on either side of each interface – the metaphor presented in the previous section was not practical in this respect. The distinction supports other engineering activities such as causal and risk-based analysis, and resolves how different values of interest are treated in the development (e.g. refinement) process. Few software development models relate the software to the embedding system/environment. We have already seen from the previous section that the Parnas' four variable model does make such distinctions; another example is Jackson's Problem Frames [8].

Recall that Parnas' model distinguishes *monitored*, *controlled*, *input* and *output* variables. The first two represent the environment and/or platform; the control system senses the monitored variables and attempts to control the environment by influencing the controlled variables (both the sensing and influencing processes may be indirect i.e. via other real-world variables). For example a FADEC senses cockpit thrust demands, various air temperatures and pressures along with engine shaft speeds (the monitored variables), and modifies fuel flow (amongst other things) in order to influence the level of thrust (the controlled variable) in the required way.

The input and output variables are the values seen or produced by the computer – perhaps the output of an analogue to digital (A/D) converter at the input, and the contents of a register which goes through digital to analogue (D/A) conversion to produce a current to drive a motor or valve.

Abstractly, *requirements* for the control system are stated in terms of relationships over the monitored and controlled variables, whilst *specifications* for the computer system are stated in terms of input and output variables. To give a complete specification also requires a definition of the relationship between the monitored variables and the inputs, as well as between the output variables and controlled variables.

Jackson's approach is not constrained to embedded systems, and so does not identify specific classes of variables. It does however introduce the notion of domain models, which encapsulate properties of the wider system; these can be used to represent the nature of the environment, platform and embedding system. Thus, for example, a domain model could be used to explain the relationship between the monitored and input variables in Parnas' approach.

In Parnas' approach the behaviour of the physical environment (Nature) is described by a relation, NAT. The basic model is illustrated in Fig. 2, which shows the system decomposition on the left and the relationship of elements of the specification set on the right:

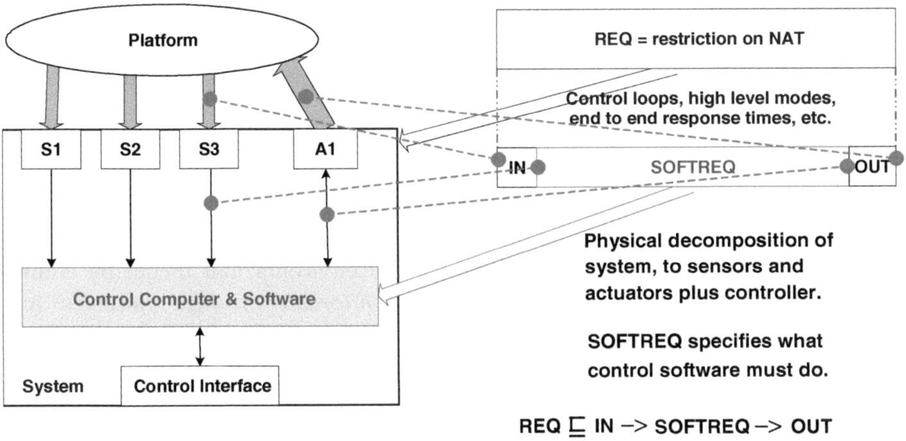

Fig. 2. Representation of Parnas' Four Variable Model

The arrows from the platform are the monitored variables; the reverse arrow is the controlled variable. The input and output variables relate to the control computer and software. The sensors (e.g. S1) map the monitored variables to inputs, represented by relation IN, and the actuators (e.g. A1) map the outputs to the controlled variables, represented by relation OUT. (Here we have made the decision to align IN and OUT with elements of the embedding system.) REQ gives the required behaviour in "real world" terms (environment and platform); SOFTREQ is the analogous specification at the level of computing system and software. A control interface is also shown; this would be a cockpit interface if the platform were an engine. The interface can be thought of as a further set of monitored, controlled, input and output variables, albeit with a very different inter-relationships determined by the design of other systems on the aircraft.

In problem frames, the domain models would encompass necessary properties of the environment, platform, the embedding system, the sensors and actuators – NAT, IN and OUT in Parnas' terms.

Both Parnas' and Jackson's approaches are relevant to the development of embedded systems; but experience with embedded systems such as FADECs suggests the need for an elaboration of these models. As a technical basis for our medium-term perspective, we propose two orthogonal, but complimentary, enhancements of Parnas' four variable model. The first enhancement identifies additional structure outside the control computer, whilst the second focuses on the structure inside the computer.

3.2 Adding External Structure

An important practical consideration regarding domain modelling and the elucidation of NAT, REQ, IN and OUT is how to manage the considerable complexity that may be inherent. From our experience with aerospace applications we are aware of many subtleties to be addressed. A key concern is to reflect better the role of the embedding system, and to distinguish it from the environment and platform. Our view is that such distinctions provide a useful basis for abstraction, and that they need to be acknowledged and clarified within the development model. By achieving a greater separation of concerns, we believe it will be easier to develop and validate specifications and to handle change.

A further problem that we need to contend with is the difficulty of sensing key properties of the environment/platform. For example it is not practical to manage engine thrust directly – although it is a key controlled variable – instead it is necessary to use surrogates such as shaft speed or engine pressure ratio.

Our first proposal is, therefore, to enhance the environmental model by adding additional variables. Thus, in addition to *monitored/controlled* variables and *inputs/outputs*, we might further distinguish:

- *sensed* and *actuated* variables: those real-world variables which directly affect (and are directly affected by) the system under development, and which are influenced by (and influence) the monitored (and controlled) variables;
- *embeddingInput* and *embeddingOutput* variables: those variables which represent the inputs and outputs of the embedding system.

Thus, for instance, whilst REQ might still define the high-level requirements (thrust in terms of demand), we could also distinguish EFFECTREQ over *sensed* and *actuated* variables and EMBEDDINGREQ over *EmbeddingInput* and *EmbeddingOutput* variables. We would also need to provide the equivalent of the IN/OUT relations to define how the new variables are related. For example, IN_{Emb} could describe the relationship between the real-world "sensed" variables and the inputs to the embedding system. See Fig. 3.

We can illustrate the above principle by revisiting the earlier engine example. The monitored variables are demands, temperatures, pressures and shaft speeds; the controlled variable is thrust. The sensed variables are the same as the monitored variables, whereas the actuated variable is fuel flow. The inputs to the embedding system might be analogue electronic signals from several sensing devices (with multiplex redundancy for some of the sensed variables). The output might be control signals to a stepper motor which changes the "throat" on a control valve. Finally, the inputs to the computer are digital representations of the analogue sensor inputs, and the output is a digital representation of the stepper motor signal. The relation IN_{Emb} in this context would relate the sensed input signals to the real-world variables they are sensing – this might reflect assumptions, for instance, about "noise".

It is now possible to state the relationships between the various abstractions:

$$\text{EMBEDDINGREQ} \sqsubseteq \text{IN} \rightarrow \text{SOFTREQ} \rightarrow \text{OUT}$$
$$\text{EFFECTREQ} \sqsubseteq \text{IN}_{Emb} \rightarrow \text{EMBEDDINGREQ} \rightarrow \text{OUT}_{Emb}$$

Where $\sqsubseteq$ is the appropriate refinement relation, and $\rightarrow$ represents composition of Parnas' relations. The above is a generalisation of the usual relationship between REQ and IN, SOFTREQ and OUT. However, once in the "real world" this generalisation, whilst valid, may be impractical to define as the relationships between *sensed/actuated* variables and *monitored/controlled* variables are likely to be too

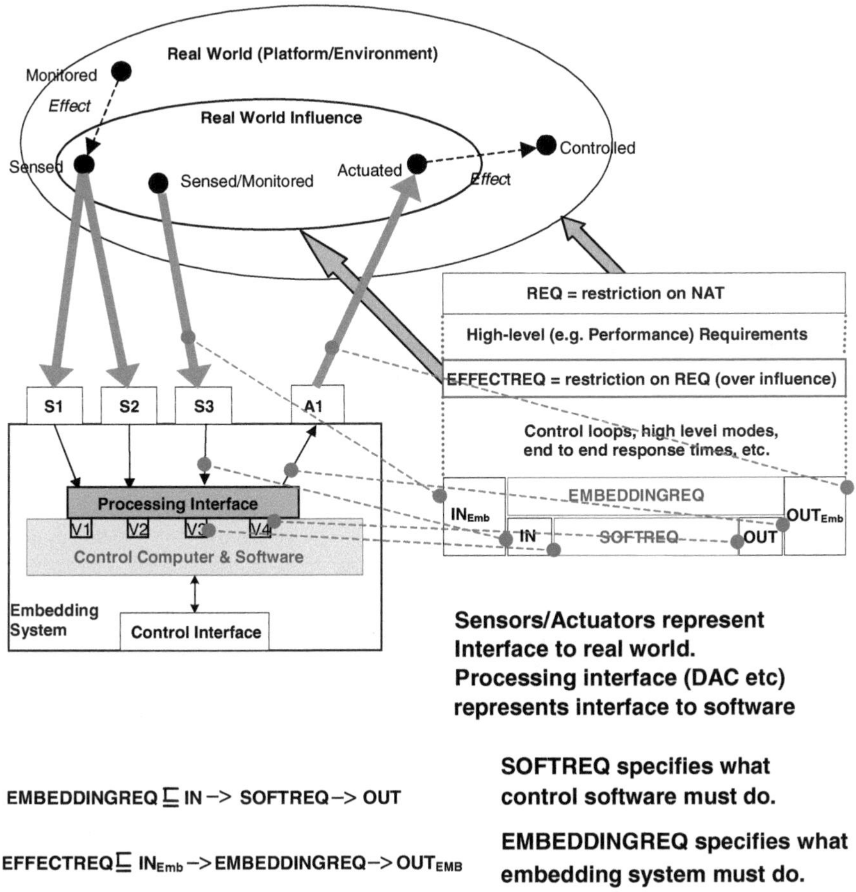

Fig. 3. Elaboration of Environmental Model

complex to represent as IN/OUT style relations between interface[2] variables (c.f. closed-loop control). Instead we would propose the following:

NAT is defined as a relation over all monitored/controlled and sensed/actuated variables, representing a model of the *real world*.

REQ is defined as a relation over *monitored*, *controlled*, *sensed* and *actuated* variables, with the condition that:

$$\mathrm{NAT} \sqsubseteq \mathrm{REQ}$$

i.e. that REQ is consistent with (i.e. a refinement of) NAT. EFFECTREQ is defined as a relation over *sensed* and *actuated* variables, with the condition that:

[2] i.e. between monitored and sensed, and between actuated and controlled.

$$REQ \setminus ((monitored \cup controlled) \setminus (sensed \cup actuated)) \sqsubseteq EFFECTREQ$$

i.e. that EFFECTREQ is consistent with REQ (where all monitored/controlled variables that are not also sensed/actuated variables have been hidden).

Finally, although we have distinguished *an* embedding system, for certain applications there may be a *hierarchy* of embedding systems. Thus, it may be desirable to distinguish more than one set of embedding system variables and requirements etc. We presented the "simple" case as an example of the general case.

3.3 Adding Internal Structure

SOFTREQ is expressed rather monolithically. In fact there will be computing hardware, application software and also other software elements, e.g. an operating system, functions for managing faults, etc. Our second proposal is to elaborate the four variable model as shown in Fig 4.

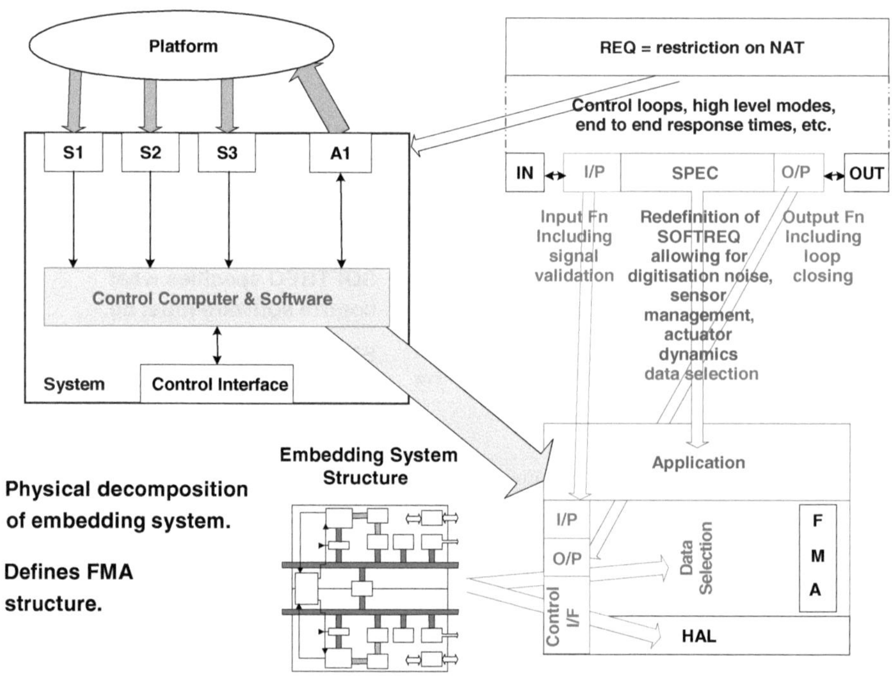

Fig. 4. Representation of Software Structure

This expanded model shows further decomposition of the software specification, reflecting the hardware structure of the embedding system. The control system software will include device drivers (represented as I/P and O/P) which will map the output of the sensors to meaningful values in software, e.g. the output of a 6 bit A/D converter to a temperature in degrees C, represented as an Ada variable; similarly O/P represents drivers for actuators (note these may be complex and read back values from actuators, running them "closed loop"). A hardware abstraction layer (HAL), or primitive operating system, provides basic services such as scheduling, timers, etc.

The controller computer hardware is usually multiplex redundant, and there are often multiple sources of sensed data. Thus there is fault management and accommodation (FMA), or data selection, logic deriving "healthy" values from the various inputs to provide validated data to the application. A "disconnect" is shown between IN and I/P, and O/P and OUT to reflect that input/output variables may correspond to different embedding system inputs and outputs depending on which input values are selected. In highly critical applications, e.g. aircraft flight control, the validation and data selection logic (dealing with redundant processing hardware, sensors and actuators) might account for 80% or more of the embedded code.

In problem frame terms, the controller structure is another (part of the) domain model. There is another important factor in such a development, the introduction of a software architecture to structure the code. Jackson has been developing problem frames in this direction [9]; this is important, but for brevity we focus here on more "black box" specifications. Finally the definition of HAL seems to be a "free choice"; in practice the application-programming interface (API) is likely to be defined by a standard, e.g. ARINC653 [10].

4 Medium-Term Challenges for Formal Engineering

Following the medium-term perspective, the principal aim of a Formal Engineering process is to maximise engineering confidence by:

- acknowledging the structure of the environment shown in Fig 3. (cf. sensed/actuated, embeddingInput/embeddingOutput variables);
- respecting and supporting the physical and logical decomposition of the design, such as that outlined in Fig 4[3].

To achieve this aim we believe there are several challenges to address. These are presented in the remainder of the section, *roughly* split into *essential* challenges (those that apply especially to high-integrity embedded systems and *others* (those which are also important, but more general in their nature). Note that we have omitted critical sociological issues, such as those associated with changes in engineering culture and human communication, but we acknowledge their importance in deploying such solutions.

4.1 Essential Challenges for High-Integrity Embedded Systems

The key challenges are as follows:

- *Computational Models*: Most formal methods represent computations using the idioms familiar to us as Computer Scientists. For example, in Z, VDM or B we think of an operation as an input, a change of state and an output – a set of constraints distinguishes valid instances of the variables during this *step*. A

[3] Further elaboration of the structure may be required to allow for more complex designs e.g. distributed solutions.

control engineer, on the other hand, thinks of a processing system as implementing a *transfer function*, that is a function from a set of inputs and their differentials to a set of outputs and their differentials. There may be more appropriate computational models than those we are presently using, e.g. for expressing properties of interest and managing the shift from engineering (i.e. *intent*) to computing (i.e. software *specification*) viewpoints.

- *Abstraction and Refinement*: In classical "IT" we are familiar with the process of studying the environment in which the software will be used (systems analysis and requirements analysis), providing an *abstract* specification for the *intended* behaviour of the software, and *refining* that specification into an implementation. We would argue strongly that this kind of approach is inappropriate for the development of safety-critical embedded systems. The reason for this is that, as we have seen, *intent* is a system-wide notion – shoehorning intent into the software variable space has serious ramifications for abstraction and the process of refinement.

  Abstraction is crucial to formal development. Without supreme confidence in the initial specification the use of formal verification can become irrelevant – one might as well use traditional verification techniques as the main source of defects will continue to be the specification. Abstraction is hard to employ at the software interface. The data being manipulated is a reflection of real-world properties, e.g. temperatures and pressures, making classical data abstraction of little value. Other approaches, e.g. loose or algebraic specifications, are also of limited relevance – it is necessary to specify precisely what happens under all physically permissible circumstances to ensure safety, and so on.

  The usual rules of refinement, e.g. weakening pre-conditions and strengthening post-conditions, are also difficult to apply. For example, requirements will be met under normal conditions and under certain classes of input failure, but will be violated when inadequate input data is available. The important thing to note is that the pre-condition representing "adequate input data" cannot usually be expressed over the program variables; it is a "real world" property. Thus, without adequate treatment of the problem structure external to the software, one might have no recourse but to weaken the post-condition in this situation. From a development process perspective, one abstract data value (monitored), e.g. air pressure, may have multiple representations at different points in the environment and software – "real-world", "raw" values from sensors, value after fault accommodation for that sensor, value after voting between alternative data sources or derivation from other sensors etc. It is difficult to see how these "design steps" accord with the classical rules of refinement, especially if we are restricted to discussing only the variables within scope of the software.

- *The Environment*: Clearly, one solution to the problems with abstraction and refinement is to model the environment. However, this is not necessarily straightforward. As we have seen from the long and medium-term perspectives, once we step outside the software the mathematical relationships are continuous (e.g. differential equations of motion) and discrete events (such as component failures) are probabilistic in nature. The challenge is how to represent this information in a way that supports verification, rather than rendering its analysis techniques (model-checking etc.) intractable.

In many ways this is the single most important technical factor in the applicability of formal techniques to this domain – and if not the applicability of formal techniques per se, then certainly of the literature that champions them.

- *Link to Continuous Mathematics*: Many embedded control systems employ some form of continuous (e.g. closed-loop) control. The *intent* here is to manage the transition between "stable" states (e.g. a demand), compensate for variance in the environment, and avoid engineering "limits" (such as undue stress on materials). The software achieves this by implementing discrete approximations to transfer functions. Once again, the issue is how to relate the *specification* (SOFTREQ) to the *intent* (REQ) – especially when control engineers are interested in continuous properties such as the *stability* of the control strategies they adopt, yet ultimately these must be implemented in the discrete world of software.

  There are several issues. Firstly, the mathematics of *discretisation* produces both functional and non-functional requirements. Functional requirements involve not just the control algorithm (e.g. in proportional/integral terms), but also constraints on mathematical precision and saturation etc., which make the discrete algorithm valid with respect to its continuous counterpart. This "ideal to real" transformation does not sit easily with the usual notion of refinement. The non-functional requirements include for instance end-to-end timing constraints (possibly across a distributed architecture), which are also essential to the validity of the control algorithm. Reconciling functional and non-functional properties within formal development can be difficult. Secondly, continuous analyses may be partial and usually assume ideal conditions. When requirements are added to *knit* together partial models, validate inputs and manage failure conditions, it is important that these additional requirements do not adversely affect the continuous dynamics of the system (e.g. inadvertently introduce discontinuities.) These additional requirements often have an intimate relationship with the timing properties of the system – e.g. the difference between what is judged to be a *good* signal and a *noisy* signal depends upon how often the signal is processed.

  Finally, when devising methods to bridge the continuous/discrete divide it is essential we avoid "reinventing the wheel". Certain aspects of development have established solutions that work. For example, control theory is a **Formal** method; it has been subjected to the same sociological validation as our "reductionist" mathematical systems of set theory and logic. It would be hopelessly inefficient, if not impossible, to try to reduce control theory to set theory and logic. Instead, we need to find a way to co-exist peacefully with other techniques but do so within a robust framework. Real-time techniques such as scheduling theory, and numerical analysis, are also very important bodies of work that we need to reuse rather than reinvent.

- *Safety as a goal*: In order for our techniques to be applied in situations that could lead to loss of life, we have to be able to argue that they are safe enough. Every system needs to carry a safety case (e.g. see [3]), and if we use technology across the development of systems, then their associated safety cases will need to be constructed on top of a generic soundness argument for that technology. It is important to avoid safety-related pitfalls. For instance, providing a complex transformation between two mathematical systems, when there is no suitable way to validate the transformation or its implementation, may severely limit how the technology can be used on real projects.

4.2 Other Important Challenges

We briefly outline three further challenges. These are less specific to safety-critical embedded systems, but just as important as the above:

- *Partiality of (and consistency between) models*: Systems are complex. The models presented in the medium-term perspective involve time, continuous and discrete relationships; they can represent various phenomena, such as the real world, a sequential computation or the patterns of communication across a distributed architecture. The long-term perspective also involves uncertainty and probability. No one formal development technique incorporates all of these facets, and if it did, arguably, it would not be practical to use. On the other hand, using separate techniques is also troublesome. Consistency across notations is crucial; one needs to be able to validate mathematically unrelated models and ultimately one has to be able to reconcile different viewpoints via an implementation. One solution might be to use multi-perspective mathematical models as a *rendez-vous* for the different views, with generic transformations defined in advance for use by the developer – rather than using the multi-perspective model itself. This is a broad research area, which encompasses work on Hybrid Systems, Integrated Formal Methods, Unifying Theories of Programming, and probabilistic extensions to existing notations (e.g. **wp**, process algebra.)

- *Cost of reasoning*: Even before economic arguments are considered, our analysis techniques need to be tractable – and this is especially the case for complex (hybrid, probabilistic, multi-faceted) models. Automated techniques need to consume reasonable levels of resources (time and space); manual techniques need to be "man-sized". For example, we do not want to see developers sifting through thousands of supplied and derived hypotheses trying to find the formula needed to unlock a proof.

  Economic considerations are key to the practical value of formal techniques, and are more subtle than "time in front of screen" measurements. Techniques need to be predictable and provide rapid feedback (in the same way that, say, testing does). Even if formal verification is a one-off activity this is difficult enough: How much effort is involved in discharging a *verification condition* (VC)? But this is an over simplification. What happens when VCs cannot be discharged? What is the impact in terms of rework of correcting a defect? What is the risk associated with leaving a VC undischarged, both to the product and to the process? All these considerations, and more, make up the complex "cost/value" function that determines the usefulness of the techniques.

The effectiveness of reasoning techniques is improving thanks to the sterling efforts of the theoreticians on model-checking (e.g. SAT) and automated theorem proving. Formal Methodists should hold firm to their tenets of compositionality and monotonicity. Perhaps more research is needed from traditional software engineering schools on the measurement, management and risk analysis of formal approaches.

- *Requirements changes*: Removing defects is one source of rework; another is changes in requirements. Requirements changes are not (just) a product of bad requirements engineering, they are a fact of life – i.e one cannot avoid the problem by inventing technical solutions to add rigour to the specification phase. Embedded systems are developed in a concurrent engineering environment, and the engineering processes (e.g. at airframe level, at engine level, and control system level) are processes of discovery. Hardware changes, mathematical models need to be honed, derived requirements are produced to mitigate the risks associated with loss of life, and so on. As a consequence the software requirements change. Change is a complication that adds to the importance of the "cost of reasoning" challenge. However, its impact on the development process is more widespread than that, say, of defect correction. Processes need to be iterative, and respecification and revalidation become important factors in cost. Formal techniques need to be *adaptive* to change, and the perception is certainly that they are not. Research into the application of Patterns (to proof, to specification) (e.g. see [11]), and into Agile Methods for HIRTS (e.g. see [12]), have the potential to improve practice in this area.

5 The Short Term

This section briefly describes the direction of the work we are currently engaged in, especially how it aims, in the short term, to address some of the challenges outlined in the previous section. The discussion is based on ideas developed through the "Practical Formal Specification" (PFS) project e.g. [13,14,15], which ran[4] for approximately 10 years from 1996. PFS was principally funded by the UK Ministry of Defence, with contributions from Rolls-Royce plc and BAE SYSTEMS. Initially conceived as an investigation into how developers of safety-critical embedded software could meet the spirit of the UK Defence Standards e.g. [3], later phases of the project concentrated on concurrency and then tool-support. Results from the early parts of the project are now supported by the "Simulink/Stateflow Analyser" (SSA) [14,15], which extends The Mathworks' Matlab/Simulink/Stateflow environment (MSS). MSS includes graphical interfaces for specifying and analysing "control law" block diagrams and hierarchical state machines in the State Charts style. SSA adds facilities for annotating diagrams with assumptions, expressed as formal statements, and provides deeper *discrete* reasoning capabilities via the generation and discharge of "healthiness" proof obligations on models.

---

[4] Although, we are optimistic the work will continue.

The emphasis in PFS has been on *validation*, with the assumption that other technologies, such as ClawZ [16], would provide "route to code". We have, and continue to be, especially interested in the link from specification (in this case control laws, state machines etc.) to intent – the primary motivation for this paper.

In essence PFS consists of two strands: a set of techniques for developing "sequential" control software (where concurrency exists only for the purposes of redundancy), and some additional proposals for use on solutions involving distributed architectures. The sequential strand concerns the addition of annotations to state machines and block diagrams, in the latter case as *contracts* over sub-systems. The annotations are used to express the intent of the specifier; proof obligations (in Z) are generated to demonstrate consistency between intent and specification. The emphasis is on managing the complexity of formal statements through the use of tables (as inspired by Parnas, Leveson etc.). This is now implemented in SSA. The distributed strand adds to the sequential techniques, by allowing the specifier to provide "communication interfaces" between subsystems, which describe how they interact with their environment (performing blocking/non-blocking reads and writes, invoking computations etc.). Further proof obligations are generated to demonstrate that the distortion introduced by asynchrony does not violate consistency between the specification and the expressions of intent (assumptions guaranteed by context etc.). The formal underpinning for the distributed strand was originally expressed in terms of an integration of B and CCS, called CGSL [17]. The distributed techniques are not yet supported by SSA.

In the remainder of the section we will contrast what has been achieved so far with PFS and SSA against some of the challenges described in the previous section. In doing so, we aim to give more details of our work, identify some of the remaining weaknesses and describe our aspirations for the short-term.

5.1 Computational Models

The sequential strand of PFS, as implemented in SSA, uses a contract language based on the notion of a discrete transfer function. Behaviour is specified in terms of relations whose input/output alphabet includes an arbitrary number of *prior instances* of the variable of interest. Thus, contracts are able to capture information about variables' differentials as well as their current value. Similarly, abstraction in state machines is achieved by defining a first-order assumption on the input variables: by knowing some property held on the values that took the machine into a particular state, and by knowing how those values change over the course of time, it is possible to *scope* the values relevant to the outgoing transitions. We believe this model is allied closely to that of the control engineers, and provides a natural medium for expressing intent.

Consistency reasoning is supported by an elaboration of **wp**, which takes into account previous instances of variables. The theory extends that presented in [18,19]; we believe the technique provides a greater degree of automation than that of alternative approaches, for example the use of *history variables*.

The main immediate weaknesses in this area are: i) the **wp** theory has not been subjected to rigorous validation; and ii) the distributed strand of PFS was not designed with the *prior instances* model in mind. For i) further work is required to show the validity of the symbolic treatment of prior instances, especially given the challenge associated with arguing that the techniques are "safe". This might be achieved, say, with respect to some more fundamental expression of behaviour – for example regular **wp** over *sequences* of values. Future work associated with ii) has an interesting Integrated Formalism perspective. At present, assumptions in the underlying formalism have to be 0th order. Relaxing this restriction raises several issues concerning the interaction between asynchrony, time and differential (prior instance) assumptions. These issues are complicated by the essential difference between sample time (of a sensor) and time after propagation (through a distributed computation).

5.2 Abstraction and Refinement

Despite our earlier comments, abstraction in PFS is based on looseness in the classical "weaken pre-condition, strengthen post-condition" sense. Refinement (of a contract into a sub-system design, possibly containing further contracts) amounts to logical implication. There are alternatives, such as the retrenchment model [20]. However, we were concerned about the possible misuse of its concession constructs. Instead we would hope that by properly respecting the structure of the environment (see 5.3), we can avoid having to retrench to *fall-back* requirements. However, retrenchment of arithmetic types (e.g. infinite to finite, real to approximate) is a vital issue for linking to the continuous mathematics (see 5.4).

Abstraction features prominently in the distributed strand of PFS. The main reason for this is to minimise the cost of reasoning (and make it a tractable problem in the first place). The computational model for the distributed strand includes time, communications and data manipulation. Various abstractions are advocated, including the removal of time, and use of symbolic techniques, from e.g. [21], to leave properties over the data in the system (e.g. to show assumptions hold). Alternatively, data might be removed to leave a pure (conservative) timing model (e.g. for end-to-end timing etc.).

There are two main weaknesses in this area. Firstly methodological guidance in PFS needs to be more robust, especially in respect of the structures outlined in sections 3.2 and 3.3. The danger here is that weakening sets of assumptions in the environment might lead to prohibitively expensive restructuring of the design (c.f. *cost of reasoning*, *requirements changes*). Secondly, the abstraction techniques in the distributed work have not been validated, and there may be an issue here concerning arguing their soundness (c.f. *safety as a goal*). As a step towards greater maturity, our aim in the future is to continue this work using the Circus notation [22].

5.3 The Environment

The main way environmental properties have to date been represented in PFS is through the use of assumptions. For example, if a control algorithm has been designed specifically for use in a particular situation (say engine above idle), then the assumptions on the algorithm express this *domain of applicability*. This is inadequate in two important ways. Firstly, there is no formal link between such assumptions and the environment to which they pertain. That is, assumptions are produced on an *ad hoc* basis, rather than derived from somewhere. For example, the environmental model used to produce the control algorithm might have been produced by simulation, or other empirical means, using control points selected from a particular domain. There ought to be a symbolic link, transporting the domain assumptions between this model and that of the design. Secondly, even on an *ad hoc* basis, there is only a tenuous link between the variables over which the assumptions are stated and the variables in the environment to which they apply. The assumptions are stated over variables that have undergone input conditioning in various ways (value checks, clamping, noise reduction) and may have been modified further due to fault accommodation logic (input source selection, model value derivation, default value setting). The practice of providing assumptions on an *ad hoc* basis carries with it the precept that the variables in the environment are equivalent – they might not be; the environmental variables *might* be *outside* the applicable domain whilst the "validated/ fault-accommodated" variables are *inside*. The result is that we lose formal control over the weakening of the precondition and the introduction of detail.

In the future we hope to model more of the environment in order to address some of these issues. However, this is by no means easy. The difficulty is in finding the relevant abstractions needed to prove something of value, whilst avoiding "reinventing the wheel" (c.f. *link to continuous mathematics*). In essence, this means capturing enough information to provide rigorous validation of the parts of the specification we have the least confidence in. This is very much an open question. But we believe a good start will be to begin explicitly representing the structure described in section 3.2. In this way we would hope to provide, and subsequently weaken, more realistic assumptions on the system (e.g. sensors equal real world values, sensors approximate real-world values, sensors approximate real-world values subject to a tolerable set of failure circumstances etc.).

5.4 Link to Continuous Mathematics

Hitherto, the link to the continuous mathematical world in PFS has been through abstraction (looseness). The aim has been to characterise enough of the algorithms which derive from continuous models, via contracts, to validate the important discrete features of the specification. I.e. a contract *envelope* is specified over a subsystem which is *tight* enough to discharge important healthiness conditions (such as assumptions guaranteed by context) but *weak* enough to avoid complex reasoning. The characterisation is, we believe, made easier by the computational model, that of a discrete transfer function. A detailed design for the subsystem described by the contract – such as one produced via the discretisation of a continuous model – can subsequently be proven consistent with that contract.

The reasoning is currently based on natural numbers, leading to *scaling* and *dimensionality* issues, and there is no formal link to the continuous model in terms of precision and saturation of arithmetic. At present this is achieved by conventional means, i.e. analysis of continuous model for precision and saturation tolerances, numerical and static analysis of the final code (e.g. see [23]). The retrenchment issue is effectively avoided by deferring the problem to later in the lifecycle. Another important issue is how (discrete) input validation and fault accommodation affect the stability of control laws. I.e. the emergent properties of attempting to mitigate for failure, e.g. on continuity etc. This is an open problem. For brevity we omit a discussion on time, which is largely left to real-time scheduling techniques.

6 Conclusions

We have presented three perspectives of Formal Engineering: our view of the long, medium and short terms. Each has its associated set of goals (c.f. scientific certainty, engineering confidence, steps in the right direction). Our aim has been to provide a coherent landscape for research into the formal engineering of high-integrity embedded control systems, describe a little of our recent work, and indicate its current direction. The problems are complex, and in our opinion there is much work to be done and many open research issues. We are hopeful that reaching the goals implied by the medium-term perspective, at least, is a realistic aspiration.

References

1. John McDermid, Andy Galloway et al. Towards Industrially Applicable Formal Methods: Three Small Steps, and One Giant Leap. In *Proceedings of International Conference on Formal Engineering Methods (ICFEM) 1998*. IEEE Press, 1998.
2. D Parnas, J Madey. Functional Documents for Computer Programs. *Science of Computer Programming*, Vol. 25, No. 1, 1995.
3. UK Ministry of Defence, Defence Standard 00-56 Issue 2: Safety Management Requirements for Defence Systems. 1996.
4. Australian Department of Defence, Australian Defence Standard Def(Aust) 5679: Procurement of Computer-based Safety Critical Systems. 1998.
5. A German. Software Static Code Analysis, Lessons Learned, *Crosstalk*. November 2003.
6. S King, J Hammond, R Chapman, A Pryor. Is Proof more Cost-Effective than Tesing? *IEEE Transactions on Software Engineering*. Vol. 26, No. 8, 2000.
7. Andy Galloway, Frantz Iwu, John McDermid and Ian Toyn. On the Formal Development of Safety-Critical Software, In *Proceedings of Verified Software: Theories, Tools, Experiments*. To appear in LNCS. Springer. 2006.
8. M A Jackson. *Problem Frames*, Addison Wesley, 2001.
9. L Rapanotti, J G Hall, M A Jackson, B Nuseibeh, Architecture-driven Problem Decomposition. In *Proceedings of RE04*. IEEE Computer Society Press, 2004
10. Airline Electronic Engineering Committee, ARINC, Supplement 1 to ARINC Specification 653: Avionics Application Software Standard Interface, Standard 03-116/SWM-89, Annapolis Maryland, 2003.
11. S. Stepney, F. Polack and I. Toyn. Patterns to Guide Practical Refactoring: examples targetting promotion in Z. In *Proceedings of ZB2003: Formal Specification and Development in Z and B*. LNCS 2651, Springer, 2003.
12. R. F Paige, H Chivers, J. A. McDermid, Z. R. Stephenson. High Integrity Extreme Programming. *Symposium on Applied Computing*. ACM. 2005.
13. A. J. Galloway, T. J. Cockram and J. A. McDermid. Experiences with the Application of Discrete Formal Methods to the Development of Engine Control Software. In *Proceedings of Distributed Computer Control Systems (DCCS) 98*. IFAC - International Federation of Automatic Control, 1998.

14. F Iwu, A Galloway, I Toyn and J A McDermid. Practical Formal Specification For Embedded Control Systems. *In Proceedings of the 11th IFAC Symposium on Information Control Problems in Manufacturing, INCOM 2004.* Salvador, Brazil April 5-7, 2004.
15. I Toyn and A Galloway. Proving Properties of Stateflow Models using ISO Standard Z and CADiZ. In *Proceedings of ZB 2005*. LNCS 3455, Springer, 2005.
16. R Arthan, P Caseley, C O'Halloran and A Smith. ClawZ: Control Laws in Z. In *Proceedings of ICFEM 2000*. S Liu, J A McDermid, M G Hinchey (Eds). IEEE Computer Society, 2000.
17. Andy Galloway and James Blow. Multilayered Domain Specific Formal Methods. In *Proceedings of The Joint Workshop on Formal Specification of Computer Based Systems.* Washington DC, April 2001. University of Stirling. 2001.
18. James Blow and Andy Galloway. Generalised Substitution Language and Differentials, In *Proceedings of ZB2002: Formal Specification and Development in Z and B*. Grenoble, France, January 2002. LNCS vol. 2272. Springer. 2002.
19. J. R. Blow. *Use of Formal Methods in the Development of Safety-critical Control Software*. DPhil thesis, Department of Computer Science, University of York. YCST-2003-08. 2003.
20. M Poppleton, R Banach. Retrenchment, Refinement and Simulation. In *Proceedings of ZB 2000*. J P Bowen, S Dunne, A Galloway, S King (Eds). LNCS 1878, Spinger, 2000.
21. M. Hennessy and H. Lin. Symbolic Bisimulations, *Theoretical Computer Science*, no 138, 1995.
22. J. C. P. Woodcock and A. L. C. Cavalcanti. The Semantics of Circus, in *Proceedings of ZB2002: Formal Specification and Development in Z and B*. LNCS 2272, pp 184-203, 2002.
23. D. M. Atiya. On extending the SPARK toolset for reasoning about floating point arithmetic: II. Technical Report, UTC, Department of Computer Science, University of York. YUTC/TR/2005/06. 2005. (See also YUTC/TR/2005/01)

A Method for Formalizing, Analyzing, and Verifying Secure User Interfaces*

Bernhard Beckert and Gerd Beuster

Institute for Computer Science, University of Koblenz-Landau
beckert@uni-koblenz.de, gb@uni-koblenz.de

Abstract. We present a methodology for the formalization of human-computer interaction under security aspects. As part of the methodology, we give formal semantics for the well-known GOMS methodology for user modeling, and we provide a formal definition of an important aspect of human-computer interaction security. We show how formal GOMS models can be augmented with formal models of (1) the application and (2) the user's assumptions about the application. In combination, this allows the pervasive formal modeling of and reasoning about secure human-computer interaction. The method is illustrated by a simple eVoting example.

1 Introduction

1.1 Overview

We present a methodology for the pervasive formal specification and verification of user interfaces under security aspects. We define formal semantics for GOMS [10], a well-established user modeling methodology. We augment formal GOMS models with formal models of (1) the application and (2) formal models of the user's assumptions about the application. We adapt the common definitions of computer security to the field of human-computer interaction (HCI). For Integrity, an important aspect of HCI security, we provide a formal definition. In combination with a formal definition of human-computer interaction (HCI) security, this allows formal reasoning about the security of user interfaces. Our approach is illustrated by a simple eVoting example.

While formal methods are used extensively in many fields of computer security, they are rarely used in HCI—even for security critical systems. The reason is that HCI does not deal with the interaction of two machines but with the interaction of a machine and a human. While the behavior of a machine can be described precisely with formal methods, human behavior is more difficult to describe in a precise way and it can be formalized to a limited extend only. This makes comprehensive modeling of all aspects

* This work was partially funded by the German Federal Ministry of Education, Science, Research and Technology (BMBF) in the framework of the Verisoft project under grant 01 IS C38. The responsibility for this article lies with the authors. See http://www.verisoft.de for more information about Verisoft.

Z. Liu and J. He (Eds.): ICFEM 2006, LNCS 4260, pp. 55–73, 2006.

of user behavior an unreachable goal. However, we argue that, nevertheless it is possible to formally describe human behavior under computer security aspects.

Our approach addresses real world security threats and shows how to counter them. It is directly applicable for the security evaluation of existing systems, as well as to the specification of new systems.

The user modeling methodology presented in this paper is based on the well-established GOMS methodology [10]. GOMS is extensively used for the modeling of user behavior. For our purposes, however, it has two weaknesses: A strict formal semantics is missing, and GOMS models the user behavior independently from the behavior of the system. Both of these short-comings are overcome in this paper.

The structure of this paper is as follows. In Section 2, we develop a formal semantics for GOMS models and illustrate it with an example. In Section 3, that example is completed by adding components representing the application and the user's assumptions about the application. In Section 4, the common definition of computer security is adapted for HCI-security, an a formal definition of Integrity, an important aspect of HCI-security, is developed. In Section 5, our approach is extended to hierarchical models. This allows the *pervasive* description of HCI security and to prove security for all aspects of a user interface—from the pixel level up to high-level functionality of the user interface. Finally, in Section 6, we summarize our work.

1.2 User Modeling Formalisms

User models are routinely used in computer system usability studies. Such user models usually draw on psychological models of the user. They model the user's tasks, goals, motivations, etc. While this is essential under a usability point of view, it makes a comprehensive formal modeling of the effects of user actions infeasible because complex psychological activities can be modeled to a limited extend only. From a usability point of view, this is not necessarily a severe drawback. To guarantee a certain level of usability, it suffices to give plausible evidence that the application's interface is usable, assuming certain goals and behaviors of the user. Security, however, requires a stricter notion of human-computer interaction. While a usability glitch in some dialog window may decrease the general usability of the application a bit, a security glitch can have more severe consequences. Even worse, a security glitch will encourage attackers to seek methods to actually exploit the glitch. The different view on the user and the different goals of usability and security, make it possible and advisable to apply formal methods to security aspects of user interfaces with user models adapted to the particular needs of security.

The computer security problem of proper visual representation of system state is addressed by Duke, Harrison, and others in a number of papers[1,6,7,8]. Their focus is to define the relationship between the functional component and the representational component of applications. In [8], they present a theory of how to describe representations of system state. Our approach is orthogonal to the approach of Duke et al. We present a formal method to reason about correspondence of the application's state and the user's representation of the state *under the assumption* that the visualization is adequate.

Process oriented formalisms like the well known PIE model developed by Dix and Runciman [5] and its more recent variations (e.g. [4]) allow to describe the interaction of the system and a user formally, but they focus on describing the computer system's side of the interaction. In PIE, the behavior of a user interface is described by a sequence of commands (issued by the user) leading to a sequence of effects. While PIE and similar formalisms put an emphasis on describing the I/O behavior of a computer system and are suitable for automated reasoning (e.g., with model checkers), other approaches like Task Knowledge Structures (TKS) [9], (Extended) Task Action Grammar ((E)TAG) [2], and Goals Operators Methods Selection-rules (GOMS) [10] focus on providing cognitive models of the user. TKS provides an explicit representation of the cognitive model of the user. GOMS is more oriented towards psychological analysis of user behavior and timed measurement of user activity. TAGs allow a precise formal description of the user actions, the user's knowledge and the user's internal representation of the system (what the user thinks about the system).

We base our formalization on GOMS, because GOMS is a well established formalism, and—in the incarnation CMN-GOMS [10]—it allows to describe user models hierarchically. This is an important property for modeling a user interface under security aspects because of the large variety of errors in human-computer interaction. Some of these errors are on a very low level (for example, the user may push the mouse button twice instead of once), while others are on a very high level of abstraction (e.g., the user may misinterpret the meaning of an error message). A hierarchical modeling mechanism allows to model all kinds of errors within one formalism. GOMS models are semi-formal. We provide formal semantics for GOMS models. The formal GOMS model is augmented by formal models of the application and formal models of the user's assumptions about the application. With a formal definition of secure human-computer interaction, this allows to determine the security of a user interface by automated reasoning.

2 Formal Semantics for GOMS User Models

In this section we define formal semantics of GOMS models. In Section 2.1 the formal methods used throughout this paper are defined. Based on these formal methods, formal semantics for GOMS are defined in Section 2.2, and the example used throughout this paper is introduced. In Section 2.3, the formal semantics are extended by defining semantics of selection criteria. In combination with the formal model of the application (Section 3), and a formal definition of HCI security (Section 4), automated reasoning about the security of a HCI interaction model becomes possible.

2.1 Components

Our methodology for the formal description of and reasoning about GOMS makes use of Input Output Labeled Transition Systems (IOLTS) and Linear Temporal Logic (LTL). Below, we define these concepts and some related notions used throughout this paper.

Definition 1. *A* Labeled Transition System *(LTS) is a tuple* $L = (S, \Sigma, s_0, \rightarrow)$ *where* S *is a set of* states, $s_0 \in S$ *is an* initial state, Σ *is a set of* labels, *and* $\rightarrow \subseteq S \times \Sigma \times S$ *is a* transition relation. *We use the notation* $p \xrightarrow{\sigma} q$ *for* $(p, \sigma, q) \in \rightarrow$.

Definition 2. *An* Input Output Labeled Transition System *(IOLTS) is an LTS* $L = (S, \Sigma, s_0, \rightarrow)$ *with* $\Sigma = \Sigma? \cup \Sigma! \cup \Sigma I$. *We call* $\Sigma?$ *the* input alphabet, $\Sigma!$ *the* output alphabet, *and* ΣI *the* internal alphabet.

We use state transition diagrams to visualize IOLTS. An example is shown in Figure 1.

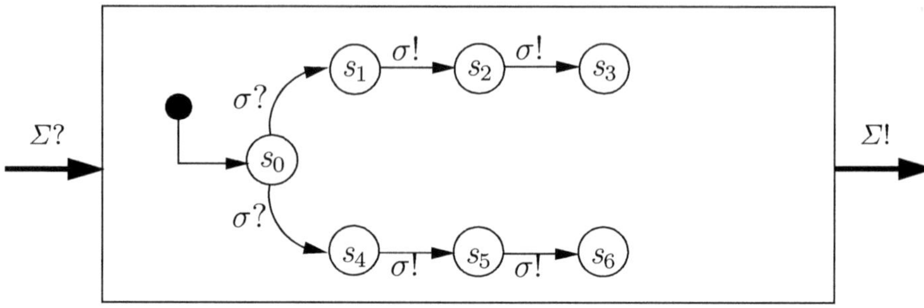

Fig. 1. State Transition Diagram representation of an IOLTS

The combination of two IOLTSs L_a and L_b where the output alphabet of L_a is the input alphabet of L_b is called a *composition*:

Definition 3. *Let* $L_a = (S_a, \Sigma_a, s_{0a}, \rightarrow_a)$, $L_b = (S_b, \Sigma_b, s_{0b}, \rightarrow_b)$ *be two IOLTS with* $\Sigma!_a = \Sigma?_b$. *The* composition $(L_a \,||\, L_b) = (S, \Sigma, s_0, \rightarrow)$ *of* L_a *and* L_b *is defined by:*

$$
\begin{aligned}
S &= S_a \times S_b \\
\Sigma? &= \Sigma?_a \\
\Sigma! &= \Sigma!_b \\
\Sigma I &= \Sigma I_a \cup \Sigma I_b \cup \Sigma!_a \\
s_0 &= (s_{0a}, s_{0b}) \\
\rightarrow &= \{((s_a, s_b), \sigma, (s'_a, s_b)) \mid s_a \xrightarrow{\sigma}_a s'_a \textit{ with } \sigma \in \Sigma?_a \cup \Sigma I_a\} \cup \\
&\quad\; \{((s_a, s_b), \sigma, (s_a, s'_b)) \mid s_b \xrightarrow{\sigma}_b s'_b \textit{ with } \sigma \in \Sigma!_b \cup \Sigma I_b\} \cup \\
&\quad\; \{((s_a, s_b), \sigma, (s'_a, s'_b)) \mid s_a \xrightarrow{\sigma}_a s'_a \textit{ and } s_b \xrightarrow{\sigma}_b s'_b \textit{ with } \sigma \in \Sigma!_a\}
\end{aligned}
$$

Often, components are combined by *mutual* composition. In mutual composition, the output of L_a serves as input for L_b, and the output of L_b serves as input of L_a (this is illustrated in Figure 2).

Definition 4. *Let* $L_a = (S_a, \Sigma_a, s_{0a}, \rightarrow_a)$ *and* $L_b = (S_b, \Sigma_b, s_{0b}, \rightarrow_b)$ *be IOLTS.*

We assume the input and output alphabets of L_a *and* L_b *to consist of internal and external subsets, where the internal input is denoted with* $\Sigma?I$, *the external input with* $\Sigma?I$, *the internal output with* $\Sigma!I$, *and the external output with* $\Sigma!E$. *And we demand that these subsets are chosen such that* $\Sigma!I_a = \Sigma?I_b$ *and* $\Sigma!I_b = \Sigma?I_a$.

Then, the mutual composition $(L_a \,||_m\, L_b) = (S, \Sigma, s_0, \rightarrow)$ *of* L_a *and* L_b *is defined by:*

$$
\begin{aligned}
S &= S_a \times S_b \\
\Sigma? &= \Sigma?E_a \cup \Sigma?E_b \\
\Sigma! &= \Sigma!E_a \cup \Sigma!E_b \\
\Sigma I &= \Sigma I_a \cup \Sigma I_b \cup \Sigma!I_a \cup \Sigma!I_b \\
s_0 &= (s_{0a}, s_{0b}) \\
\rightarrow &= \{((s_a, s_b), \sigma, (s'_a, s_b)) \mid s_a \xrightarrow{\sigma}_a s'_a \textit{ with } \sigma \in \Sigma?E_a \cup \Sigma!E_a \cup \Sigma I_a\} \cup \\
&\quad\ \{((s_a, s_b), \sigma, (s_a, s'_b)) \mid s_b \xrightarrow{\sigma}_b s'_b \textit{ with } \sigma \in \Sigma?E_b \cup \Sigma!E_b \cup \Sigma I_b\} \cup \\
&\quad\ \{((s_a, s_b), \sigma, (s'_a, s'_b)) \mid s_a \xrightarrow{\sigma}_a s'_a \textit{ and } s_b \xrightarrow{\sigma}_b s'_b \textit{ with} \\
&\quad\qquad \sigma \in \Sigma!I_a \cup \Sigma!I_b\}
\end{aligned}
$$

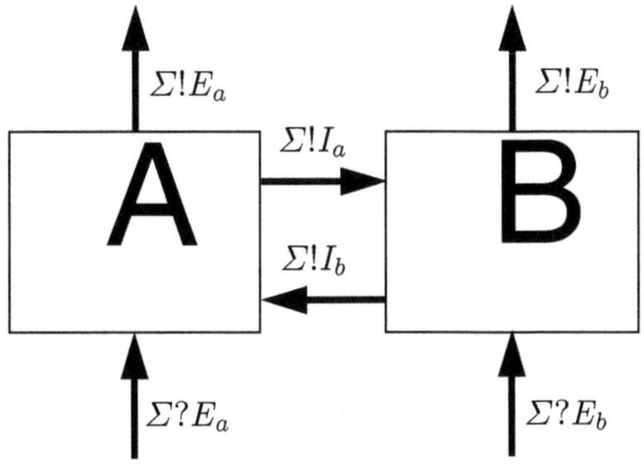

Fig. 2. Mutual composition of IOLTSs

The input/output behavior of a component is described by *traces*, which are (possibly infinite) sequences of elements from the alphabet Σ, and *paths*, which are corresponding sequences of states.

Definition 5. *Let $L = (S, \Sigma, s_0, \rightarrow)$ be an IOLTS. Then, a* path *is a sequence $\langle s_0, s_1, \ldots \rangle$ of states from S with $s_i \rightarrow s_{i+1}$ for all $i \geq 0$. A* trace *(of L) is a sequence $\langle \sigma_0, \sigma_1, \ldots \rangle$ of elements of Σ such that there is a path $\langle s_0, s_1, \ldots \rangle$ with $s_i \xrightarrow{\sigma_i} s_{i+1}$ ($i \geq 0$).*

We use Linear Temporal Logic (LTL) to describe properties of components. The syntax of LTL is defined as usual, i.e., given a set P of atomic propositions, LTL formulae ϕ are constructed inductively by:

$$\phi ::= p \mid \phi \vee \phi \mid \phi \wedge \phi \mid \neg\phi \mid X\phi \mid \phi U \phi \mid G\phi \mid F\phi \qquad (p \in P)$$

Now, we can use IOLTSs to interpret LTL formulas—in combination with valuations λ that map atomic propositions to the states in which they are true. The satisfaction relation is extended to more complex formulae as usual.

Definition 6. *Given an IOLTS $L = (S, \Sigma, s_0, \rightarrow)$ and a set P of atomic propositions, a* valuation *λ is a mapping from P to S. An atom $p \in P$ is said to be true in $s \in S$ iff $s \in \lambda(p)$.*

Given a path $c = \langle s_0, s_1, \ldots \rangle$, *by* c^i *we denote the sub-path of* c *starting at* s_i.

Whether an LTL formula ϕ *is satisfied by a path* c *and a valuation* λ, *denoted by* $L, \lambda, c \models \phi$, *is inductively defined as follows:*

- $L, \lambda, c \models \top$
- $L, \lambda, c \models \phi$ *if* $\phi \in P$ *and* $s_0 \in \lambda(\phi)$
- $L, \lambda, c \models \neg\, \phi$ *if not* $L, \lambda, c \models \phi$
- $L, \lambda, c \models \phi \wedge \psi$ *if* $L, \lambda, c \models \phi$ *and* $L, \lambda, c \models \psi$
- $L, \lambda, c \models \phi \vee \psi$ *if* $L, \lambda, c \models \phi$ *or* $L, \lambda, c \models \psi$
- $L, \lambda, c \models \boldsymbol{X}\phi$ *if* $L, \lambda, c^1 \models \phi$
- $L, \lambda, c \models \phi \boldsymbol{U} \psi$ *if (a)* $L, \lambda, c \models \psi$ *or (b) there is some* $i \geq 1$ *s.t.* $L, \lambda, c^i \models \psi$ *and* $L, \lambda, c^k \models \phi$ *for all* $0 \leq k < i$
- $L, \lambda, c \models \boldsymbol{G}\phi$ *if* $L, c^i \models \phi$ *for all* $i \geq 0$
- $L, \lambda, c \models \boldsymbol{F}\phi$ *if* $L, c^i \models \phi$ *for some* $i \geq 0$

An LTL formula ϕ *is said to be satisfied by a valuation* λ, *denoted by* $L, \lambda \models \phi$, *iff* $L, \lambda, c \models \phi$ *for all paths* c *of* L. *And* ϕ *is said to be satisfied by* L, *denoted by* $L \models \phi$ *iff* $L, \lambda \models \phi$ *for all valuations* λ.

2.2 Using IOLTS Traces to Define the Semantics of GOMS Models

We now provide a formal semantics for the GOMS user modeling methodology. GOMS describes human behavior in categories of

*G*oals	The user's goals
*O*perators	Atomic actions available to the user
*M*ethods	Sequences of operators and sub-goals
*S*election Rules	Rules to decide between alternative methods

We formalize the CMN-GOMS variant of GOMS [10]. In difference to other GOMS variants, CMN-GOMS satisfies the two core requirements for the formal description of human behavior under security aspects: It allows to model user behavior on different levels of abstractions, and CMN-GOMS's informal semantic is suitable for formalization. In CMN-GOMS, methods for achieving a goal consist of sequences of sub-goals and atomic operators (the only difference between sub-goals and atomic operators is that operators cannot be further decomposed). If there is more than one way to reach a goal, a selection rule is used to choose between alternatives.

Figure 3 gives an example. It models the user of an eVoting machine. In order to achieve the goal "VOTE FOR CANDIDATE('Bob')", the user executes the method consisting of the atomic operations "WAIT FOR UNLOCK OF VOTING MACHINE" and "CHOOSE CANDIDATE('Bob')". Then he reviews his vote. The sub-goal "REVIEW VOTE" can be achieved in two ways: (1) If the user has selected the right candidate, he confirms. (2) If he has selected the wrong candidate, he pursues sub-goal "CHANGE VOTE". Changing the vote leads to the sub-goal "REVIEW VOTE(2)". If the user has selected the right candidate this time, he confirms; otherwise, voting fails.

We give a formal semantics for GOMS models using the notion of IOLTS traces. That is, an IOLTS corresponds to a GOMS model if the traces of the IOLTS are identical to the possible sequences of user decisions (selections) and operations. In order to

GOAL: VOTE FOR CANDIDATE("Bob")
  OPERATOR: WAIT FOR UNLOCK OF VOTING MACHINE
  OPERATOR: CHOOSE CANDIDATE("Bob")
  GOAL: REVIEW VOTE
  SELECT:
    OPERATOR: CONFIRM VOTE. . . if candidate "Bob" selected
    GOAL: CHANGE VOTE . . . otherwise
      OPERATOR: CANCEL VOTE
      OPERATOR: CHOOSE CANDIDATE("Bob")
      GOAL: REVIEW VOTE(2)
      SELECT:
        OPERATOR: CONFIRM VOTE. . . if candidate "Bob" selected
        OPERATOR: FAIL . . . otherwise

Fig. 3. GOMS model for eVoting

$T = (G, O, M, R, C, g_0)$ with

$$G = \{\text{VOTE\_FOR\_CANDIDATE("Bob")},\ \text{REVIEW\_VOTE},\ \text{CHANGE\_VOTE},\ \text{REVIEW\_VOTE(2)}\}$$

$$O = \{\text{WAIT\_FOR\_UNLOCK},\ \text{CHOOSE\_CANDIDATE},\ \text{CONFIRM\_VOTE},\ \text{CANCEL\_VOTE},\ \text{FAIL}\}$$

$$C = \{\text{Candidate "Bob" selected}, \neg(\text{Candidate "Bob" selected})\}$$

$$M(g) = \begin{cases} \langle \text{WAIT\_FOR\_UNLOCK, CHOOSE\_CANDIDATE, REVIEW\_VOTE} \rangle \\ \quad \text{if } g = \text{VOTE\_FOR\_CANDIDATE} \\ \langle \text{CANCEL\_UNLOCK, CHOOSE\_CANDIDATE, REVIEW\_VOTE(2)} \rangle \\ \quad \text{if } g = \text{CHANGE\_VOTE} \end{cases}$$

$$R(g, c) = \begin{cases} \text{CONFIRM\_VOTE} & \text{if } g = \text{REVIEW\_VOTE and} \\ & c = \text{Candidate "Bob" selected} \\ \text{CHANGE\_VOTE} & \text{if } g = \text{REVIEW\_VOTE and} \\ & c = \neg\ (\text{Candidate "Bob" selected}) \\ \text{CONFIRM\_VOTE} & \text{if } g = \text{REVIEW\_VOTE(2) and} \\ & c = \text{Candidate "Bob" selected} \\ \text{FAIL} & \text{if } g = \text{REVIEW\_VOTE(2) and} \\ & c = \neg\ (\text{Candidate "Bob" selected}) \end{cases}$$

Fig. 4. Formal GOMS model for the eVoting model from Figure 3

formally define, which IOLTS correspond to a given GOMS model, we use the following formal syntax for GOMS models:

Definition 7. *Given a GOMS model, the corresponding* formal GOMS model *is*

$$T = (G, O, M, R, C, g_0)$$

where

- *G is the set of (sub-)goals;*
- *O is the set of operators;*

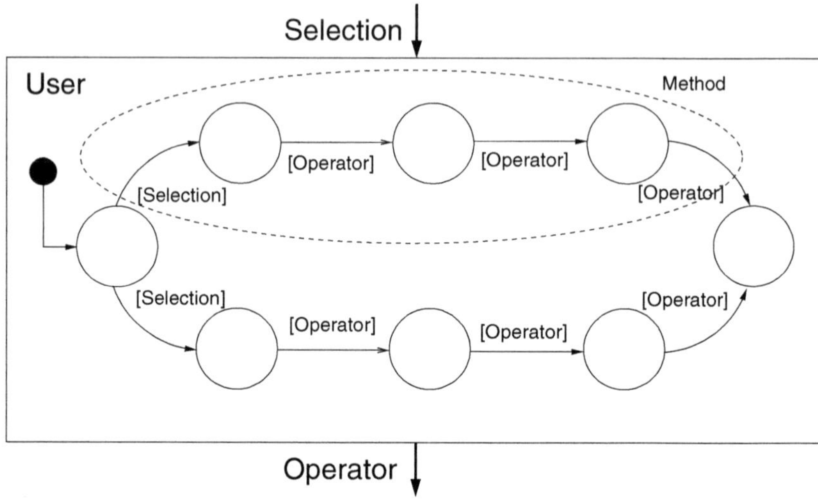

Fig. 5. Translating GOMS categories to state transition diagrams

- *C is the set of selection criteria;*
- *M is a function mapping goals to their sequences of sub-goals/operators.*
- *The function $R\colon G \times C \longrightarrow G$ is defined by: $R(g, c) = g'$ iff the goal g is achieved by sub-goal/operator g' in case criteria c holds;*
- *g_0 is the top-level goal.*

The formal GOMS model corresponding to the eVoting GOMS model from Figure 3 is shown in Figure 4.

We define a formal semantics for GOMS models by translating the formal GOMS model into an IOLTS. The idea is to represent operators as elements of the output alphabet, selections as elements from the input alphabet, and methods as (sub-)paths. Selection rules are branching points in the IOLTS. Figure 5 illustrates this translation.

Definition 8. *Let $T = (G, O, M, R, C, g_0)$ be a formal GOMS model. And let $(S, \Sigma, S_0, \rightarrow)$ be the (generalized) IOLTS constructed for T and $S_0 = \{s_0\}$ by the algorithm shown in Figure 6.*

Then $(S, \Sigma, s_0, \rightarrow)$ is the IOLTS corresponding to T.

Note that the algorithm in Figure 6 constructs an IOLTS that is generalized in the sense that is may have more than one initial state. If the algorithm is started with a singleton set $S_0 = \{s_0\}$ of initial states, a standard IOLTS is constructed (the more general case is only needed for the recursive calls within the algorithm). An implementation of the algorithm in the Perl programming language has been used for constructing the example IOLTSs presented in this paper.

Applying the algorithm to the eVoting example results in the following IOLTS that corresponds to the GOMS model shown in Figure 3 resp. 4. The IOLTS is shown graphically in Figure 7.

Require: GOMS model $T = (G, O, M, R, c, g_0)$, and a set S_0 of initial states
Ensure: (Generalized) IOLTS $L = (S, \Sigma, S_0, \rightarrow)$ and set F of states,
s.t. $\Sigma? = C$, $\Sigma! = O$, and F contains the final states of L

if $g_0 \in O$ **then**
  {initial goal is an atomic operator}
  create new state s_1
  $S := S_0 \cup \{s_1\}$
  $\Sigma? := \varnothing$
  $\Sigma! := \{g_0\}$
  $\rightarrow := \{(s_0, g_0, s_1) \mid s_0 \in S_0\}$
  $F := \{s_1\}$
else if $M(g_0) = \langle m_1, \ldots, m_n \rangle$ **then**
  {initial goal has sub-goals $g_1, \ldots, g_n$}
  $S := \varnothing$
  $\Sigma? := \varnothing$
  $\Sigma! := \varnothing$
  $\rightarrow := \varnothing$
  $F := S_0$
  for $i = 1 \ldots n$ **do**
    create an IOLTS $L_i = (S_i, \Sigma_i, S_0^i, \rightarrow_i)$ with final states F_i
      for $T_i = (G, O, M, R, c, g_i)$ and set $S_0^i := F$ of initial states
      by recursion
    $S := S \cup S_i$
    $\Sigma? = \Sigma? \cup \Sigma?_i$
    $\Sigma! = \Sigma! \cup \Sigma!_i$
    $\rightarrow = \rightarrow \cup \rightarrow_i$
    $F = F_i$
  end for
else
  {initial goal is a selection point}
  for all g_i, c_i such that $R(g_0, c_i) = g_i$ **do**
    create a new state s_i
    $S := S \cup \{s_i\}$
    $\rightarrow = \rightarrow \cup \{(s_0, c_i, s_i) \mid s_0 \in S_0\}$
    create an IOLTS $L_i = (S_i, \Sigma_i, S_0^i, \rightarrow_i)$ with final states F_i
      for $T_i = (G, O, M, R, c, g_i)$ and set $S_0^i := \{s_i\}$ of initial state
      by recursion
    $S := S \cup S_i$
    $\Sigma? = \Sigma? \cup \Sigma?_i$
    $\Sigma! = \Sigma! \cup \Sigma!_i \cup \{c_i\}$
    $\rightarrow = \rightarrow \cup \rightarrow_i$
    $F = F \cup F_i$
  end for
end if

Fig. 6. Algorithm for constructing an IOLTS corresponding to a given GOMS model

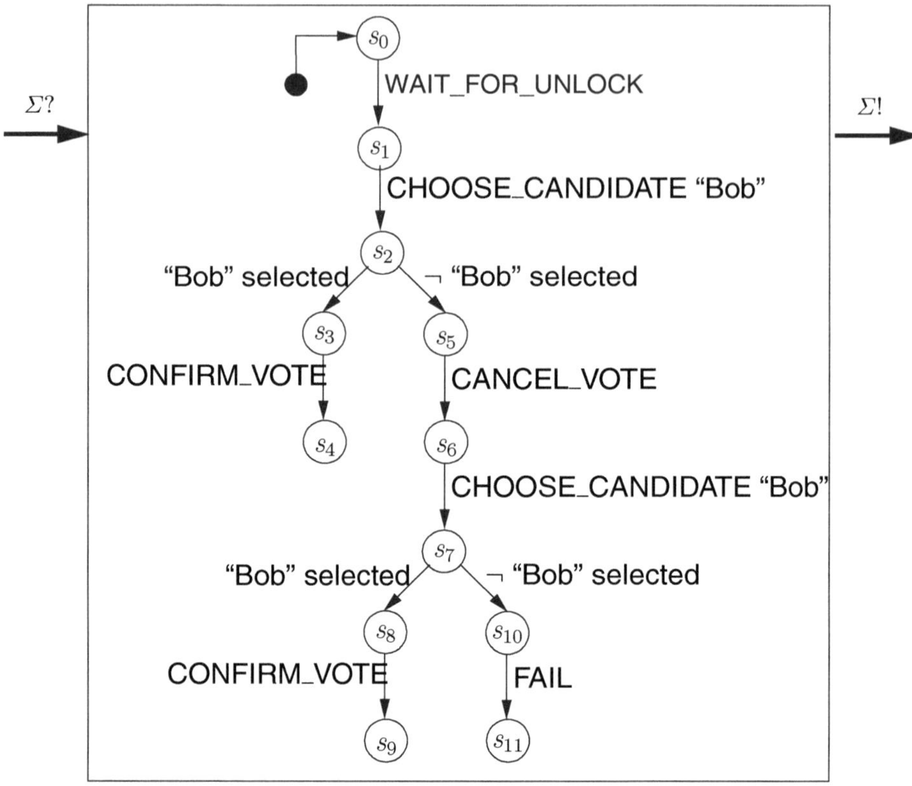

Fig. 7. IOLTS corresponding to the eVoting GOMS model

$$S = \{s_0, \ldots, s_{11}\}$$

$$\Sigma = \Sigma? \cup \Sigma!$$

$$\Sigma? = \{\text{“Bob” selected}, \neg\ (\text{“Bob” selected}\}$$

$$\Sigma! = \{\text{WAIT\_FOR\_UNLOCK, CONFIRM\_VOTE, CANCEL\_VOTE, FAIL, CHOOSE\_CANDIDATE}\}$$

$$\begin{aligned} \rightarrow = \{ & (s_0, \text{WAIT\_FOR\_UNLOCK}, s_1), \\ & (s_1, \text{CHOOSE\_CANDIDATE(“Bob”)}, s_2), \\ & (s_2, \text{“Bob” selected}, s_3), \\ & (s_3, \text{CONFIRM\_VOTE}, s_4), \\ & (s_2, \neg\ (\text{“Bob selected}), s_5), \\ & (s_5, \text{CANCEL\_VOTE}, s_6), \\ & (s_6, \text{CHOOSE\_CANDIDATE(“Bob”)}, s_7), \\ & (s_7, \text{“Bob” selected}, s_8), \\ & (s_8, \text{CONFIRM\_VOTE}, s_9), \\ & (s_7, \neg\ (\text{“Bob” selected}), s_{10}), \\ & (s_{10}, \text{FAIL}, s_{11})\} \end{aligned}$$

2.3 Assumptions as Selection Rules

Selection rules in GOMS models require decision criteria. In GOMS, these criteria are only specified in an informal way. Since our goal is to provide a formal semantics for GOMS models suitable for automated reasoning, a methodology for the formal description of selection criteria is required.

If a user is in the situation to choose between multiple options, his decision will be based on the current system configuration or, more precisely, on his *perception* of the system configuration. In the eVoting example, the decision whether to confirm his vote or to change it, depends on the candidate selection shown by the voting machine and the user's corresponding perception of the machine's internal configuration.

Following our component-based approach, we define the user's assumption about the system configuration as a component. This component is combined with the (IOLTS corresponding to the) formal GOMS model by mututal composition. The rational behind mutual composition is that not only do the user's presumptions about the applicaton state influence his behavior but his assumptions about the state of the application are influenced by his actions as well. For example, when the user pushes the "confirm vote" button, he will asume that the voting process is completed, even if it takes some time before the next message appears on the screen. The other input for the assumption component—besides the users actions, i.e., the operators in the GOMS model—comes from the output of the application (application output is defined in Section 3). Figure 8 illustrates the composition of an interactive formal user model.

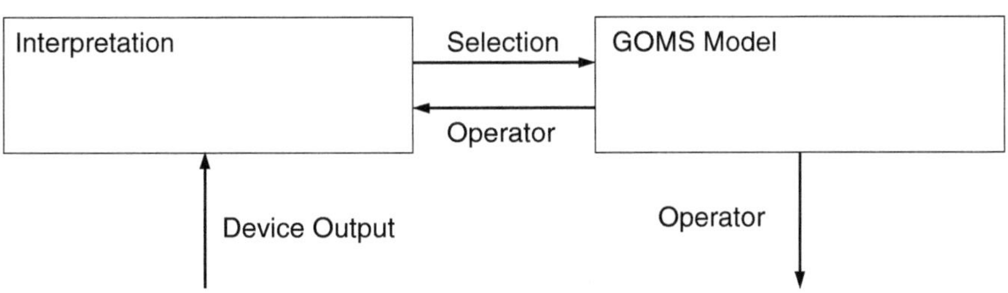

Fig. 8. Combination of GOMS model and user's interpretation of the application's configuration

Definition 9. *An IOLTS* $L = (S, \Sigma, s_0, \rightarrow)$ *is called a* user assumption IOLTS, *if*

- $\Sigma = \Sigma? \cup \Sigma!$,
- $\Sigma? = \Sigma?_D \cup \Sigma?_A$ *where* $\Sigma?_D$ *atomic application (device) output and* $\Sigma?_A$ *are GOMS operators,*
- $\Sigma!$ *consists of GOMS selection criteria.*

An interactive formal user model $L = (L_A \; ||_m \; L_I)$ *is the mutual composition of the IOLTS* L_U *corresponding to a formal GOMS model (user model) and a user assumption IOLTS* L_I.

2.4 Formal HCI Model: Summary

We have defined formal semantics for GOMS models and for selection criteria. Selection criteria are defined by a component modeling the user's assumptions about the application. The combination of a formal GOMS models of the user and a model of the user's assumptions allows the formal description of human behavior.

In order to reason about security of HCI, a formal application model and a formal definition of HCI security is required in addition. In Section 3, we complete the eVoting example. We provide an application model and two alternative user assumption components. In Section 4, definitions of generic formal HCI security requirements are given and applied to the eVoting example.

3 Completing the eVoting Model

In order to apply automated reasoning to human-computer interaction, we need three components: (1) A formal GOMS model and its corresponding IOLTS; (2) a component representing the assumptions of the user about the application; and (3) a component representing the application itself. In this section, we provide the missing two components for the eVoting example, starting with the application.

We assume that the eVoting machine is initially in a locked state. After some time, the machine is unlocked and the user can cast his vote. After he has selected a candidate, the machine shows the user's choice and asks for confirmation. If he confirms, the voting process finishes. If he cancels, he can change the vote. Figure 9 sketches an IOLTS modeling the voting machine. The input alphabet is identical to the output alphabet of the user model IOLTS, i.e., the operators available to the user. The output alphabet is an abstract representation of the application's output (in Section 5 we introduce hierarchical models which allow to model application output down to the pixel level). In order to make the example interesting, we have built a bug into the IOLTS: If a user votes for "Bob", the eVoting machine may mistakenly interpret this as a vote for "Fred":

$$
\begin{aligned}
S &= \{s_0, s_1, s_2\} \cup \bigcup\nolimits_{c \in \text{Candidates}} \{s_c, s'_c, s''_c, s'''_c\} \\
\Sigma &= \Sigma? \cup \Sigma! \\
\Sigma? &= \{\text{WAIT\_FOR\_UNLOCK, CONFIRM\_VOTE, CANCEL\_VOTE, FAIL,} \\
&\qquad \text{CHOOSE\_CANDIDATE}\} \\
\Sigma! &= \{\text{locked, unlocked}\} \cup \bigcup\nolimits_{c \in \text{Candidates}} \{\text{Vote cast}(c), \text{Vote confirmed}(c)\} \\
\rightarrow &= \{(s_0, \text{WAIT\_FOR\_UNLOCK}, s_1), \\
&\qquad (s_1, \text{unlocked}, s_2)\} \cup \\
&\quad \{(s_2, \text{CHOOSE\_CANDIDATE}[c], s_c) \mid c \in \text{Candidates}\} \cup \\
&\quad \{(s_c, \text{Vote cast}(c), s'_c) \mid c \in \text{Candidates}\} \cup \\
&\quad \{(s'_c, \text{CHANGE\_VOTE}, s_2) \mid c \in \text{Candidates}\} \cup \\
&\quad \{(s'_c, \text{CONFIRM\_VOTE}, s''_c) \mid c \in \text{Candidates}\} \cup \\
&\quad \{(s''_c, \text{Vote confirmed}(c), s'''_c) \mid c \in \text{Candidates}\} \cup \\
&\quad \{(s_{\text{“Bob”}}, \text{Vote cast (“Fred”)}, s'_{\text{“Fred”}})
\end{aligned}
$$

For the completion of the example, we still need a model of the user's assumptions. As defined in the last section, a user assumption component has an input alphabet consisting

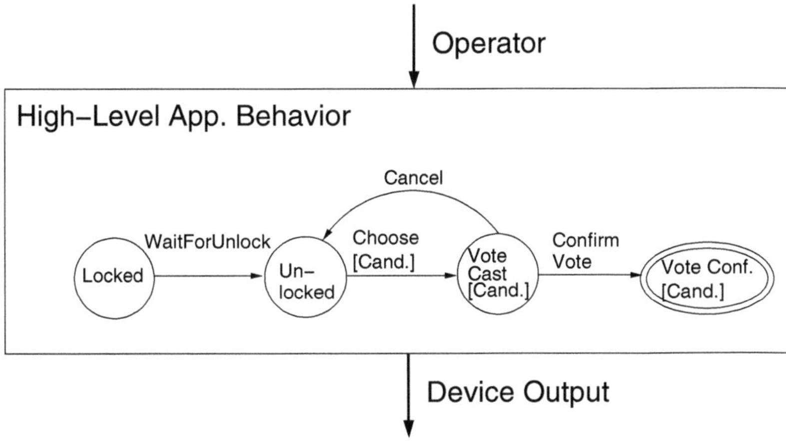

Fig. 9. Application Model for the eVoting example

of the application's output and the user's operators, and an output alphabet consisting of the user's selection criteria. In this example we use user assumption components that only use the application's output as input (in order to keep the example simple). Selection rules are used at two points in the GOMS model: When the user reviews his voting decision for the first time, and when he reviews his voting decision for the second time. The user's assumption is that the eVoting application works correctly. Thus, the assumption component will output "candidate 'Bob' selected" for the input "Vote cast('Bob')", and "¬(Candidate 'Bob' selected)" for the input "Vote cast(c)" with $c \neq$ "Bob". This "error-free" model corresponds to the following user assumption IOLTS:

$$\begin{aligned}
S &= \{s_0, s_{bob}, s_{other}\} \\
\Sigma &= \Sigma? \cup \Sigma! \\
\Sigma? &= \{\text{locked, unlocked}\} \cup \textstyle\bigcup_{c \in \text{Candidates}} \{\text{Vote cast}(c), \text{Vote confirmed}(c)\} \\
\Sigma! &= \{\text{Candidate 'Bob' selected, } \neg\text{(Candidate 'Bob' selected)}\} \\
\rightarrow &= \{(s_0, \sigma, s_0) \mid \sigma \neq \text{Vote cast}(c) \text{ for all candidates } c\} \cup \\
&\quad \{(s_0, \text{Vote cast('Bob')}, s_{bob})\} \cup \\
&\quad \{(s_0, \text{Vote cast}(c), s_{other}) \mid c \neq \text{“Bob”}\} \cup \\
&\quad \{(s_{bob}, \text{Candidate 'Bob' selected}, s_0)\} \cup \\
&\quad \{(s_{other}, \neg \text{ (Candidate 'Bob' selected)}, s_0)
\end{aligned}$$

While standard GOMS does not allow to model user errors, our component-based approach does. As an example, we model a user who may think the system is in a state where he voted for "Bob" while in fact he voted for someone else. The changed relation $\rightarrow$ is shown below:

$$\begin{aligned}
\rightarrow \; = \; & \{(s_0, \sigma, s_0) \mid \sigma \neq \text{Vote cast}(c) \text{ for all candidates } c\} \cup \\
& \{(s_0, \text{Vote cast}(c), s_{bob}) \mid c \in \text{Candidates}\} \cup \\
& \{(s_0, \text{Vote cast}(c), s_{other}) \mid c \neq \text{“Bob”}\} \cup \\
& \{(s_{bob}, \text{Candidate 'Bob' selected}, s_0)\} \cup \\
& \{(s_{other}, \neg \text{ (Candidate 'Bob' selected)}, s_0)
\end{aligned}$$

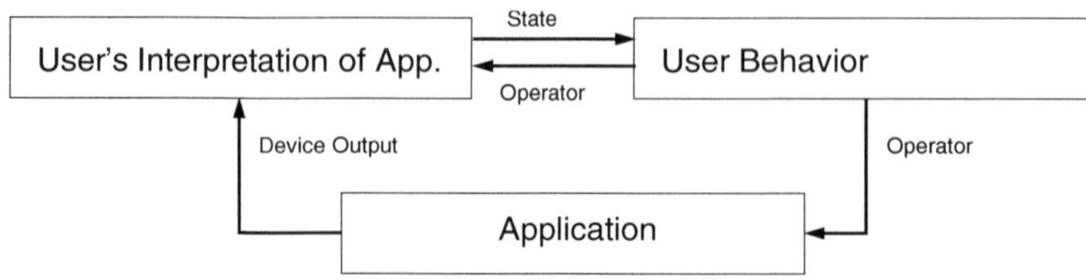

Fig. 10. Basic system model

In this section, we showed how system models are created from formal GOMS models, user assumption components, and application models. The mutual compositions of these three components—as shown in Figure 10—provide a complete model. With this, complete formal modeling of human-computer interaction becomes possible. In difference to traditional methods, our method also allows to model erroneous user behavior.

In the next section, we define HCI security properties as LTL formulae. With the formal definition of HCI security properties and the modeling methodology developed in this section, formal methods can be used for reasoning about security of user interaction.

4 HCI Security Definitions

The aim of computer security is to guarantee access to services and resources to authorized persons, while preventing access and manipulation by unauthorized parties. The basic security threats are *Data Leaking*, *Data Manipulation*, and *Program Manipulation* [3]. These are countered by the core security requirements, usually abbreviated as *CIA*:

Confidentiality: Information is available to authorized parties only.
Integrity: Both the assumptions of the user about the application, and the assumptions of the application about the user are correct.
Availability: Accessibility of services and data is guaranteed.

Adapting these concepts to user interface security is straightforward:

HCI Confidentiality: No secret information is leaked via the user interface.
HCI Integrity: There is a correspondence between the configuration of the application (defined by its internal state and data), and the user's assumption about the data and the state.
HCI Availability: The user interface must guarantee reachability of desirable states, and it must prevent user interactions that lead to transitions into undesirable states.

In the following, we concentrate on formalizing the integrity requirement. Informally, we define HCI Integrity as follows:

Definition 10. *HCI Integrity: Whenever the system is in a critical state, all critical properties are the same in the application and in the user's assumption about the application.*

Let the set P of atomic propositions contains the following atoms:

- $appCritical$ is true whenever the application is in a critial state.
- $a_0, \ldots, a_n$ represent the critical properties of the application.
- $u_0, \ldots, u_n$ represent the user's assumption about critical properties.

Then, we can formalize HCI Integrity using the LTL formula

$$\mathbf{G}(appCritical \rightarrow ((a_0 \leftrightarrow u_0) \wedge (a_1 \leftrightarrow u_1) \wedge \ldots \wedge (a_n \leftrightarrow u_n)))$$

In the eVoting example, the critical property is the user's vote, and the critical state is reached once the user has finished voting. If in that state the user thinks he selected the candidate of his choice, while in fact he voted for some other candidate, human-computer interaction was erroneous. Thus, we choose u_0 to represent "the user has voted for 'Bob"' and a_0 to represent "the user thinks he has voted for 'Bob"'. Critical states are those states of the application model where a vote has been confirmed.

We can now use automated reasoning techniques (e.g., model checking) to confirm that, whenever the valuation λ reflect this interpretation of the atoms, the HCI Integrity formula holds.

In the example, despite the bug in the application model (choosing "Bob" may be credited to "Fred"), the Integrity requirement holds for the model where the user makes correct assumptions about the system state, because the user will recognize the error when he is asked to confirm the vote for "Fred". In the variant of the eVoting model with the erronous user assumptions model, Integrity does not hold, because the user may mistakely confirm the vote for "Fred".

5 Hierarchical Model

In the models introduced so far, the application, the user's actions, and the user's assumptions are modeled as monolithic components. When we start to add more details to our models—for example, when application output and user perception is modeled in more detail—the components become unwieldy.

To counter this problem, we introduce hierarchical components. In a model of hierarchical components, components of different levels of abstraction are layered above each other. This allows to describe user interfaces and human-computer interaction at all levels of detail with model still managable by humans and computers.

Both in the construction of graphical user interfaces and in the perception (and interpretation) of graphical user interfaces, there are generic abstraction levels shared over a large class of interfaces. By identifying these abstraction levels and modeling user interfaces along these lines, it becomes possible to model complex user interfaces (and potential error sources in complex user interfaces) while still preserving maintainability of the models. The proposed model pattern is shown in Figure 11.

The sub-concepts of the user interface follow the well established hierarchical view of interfaces. On the uppermost level, a user interface consists of distinct screens. Each screen represents a specific view on the application. Screens themselves are built from a number of windows, windows are built from widgets, and these are built from elementary symbols.

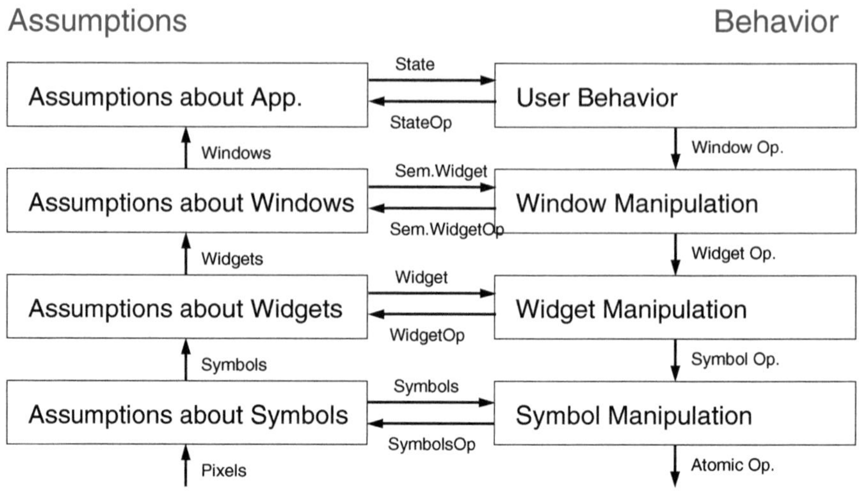

Fig. 11. Generic Hierarchical User Model

Creating a hierarchical user interface where each component represents one level of abstraction makes it possible to model typical errors on their respective levels. For example, the typical error that a user misses a button and pushes a wrong one, is modeled on a low level, while the error that a user misinterprets a screen is modeled on a high level.

In our eVoting example, a user may accidently push the button for "Fred" if it is next to the button for "Bob." This error can be modeled on the symbol manipulation level by the GOMS sub-model for the "CHOOSE_CANDIDATE('Bob')" operator shown in Figure 12 and the following assumption component about widget manipulation:

$$\begin{aligned}
S &= \{s_0, s_1, \ldots, s_n\} \\
\Sigma &= \Sigma? \cup \Sigma! \\
\Sigma? &= \{(\text{“Bob's Button”} = 1), \\
&\quad\; (\text{“Bob's Button”} = 2), \\
&\quad\; \ldots, \\
&\quad\; (\text{“Bob's Button”} = n)\} \\
\Sigma! &= \{(\text{“Bob's Button”} = 1), \\
&\quad\; (\text{“Bob's Button”} = 2), \\
&\quad\; \ldots, \\
&\quad\; (\text{“Bob's Button”} = n) \\
\rightarrow &= \{(s_0, (\text{“Bob's Button”} = i), s_i) \mid 1 \leq i \leq n\} \cup \\
&\quad \{(s_0, (\text{“Bob's Button”} = i - 1), s_i)) \mid 1 < i \leq n\} \cup \\
&\quad \{(s_0, (\text{“Bob's Button”} = i + 1), s_i) \mid 1 \leq i < n\}
\end{aligned}$$

Our approach to the construction of sub-models of GOMS models is depicted in Figure 13. Each method for achieving a sub-goal becomes a GOMS model on its own. The IOLTSs corresponding to these GOMS models can then be combined into one

```
GOAL: CHOOSE_CANDIDATE("Bob")
    SELECT:  OPERATOR: PUSH_BUTTON(0) ... if "Bob's Button" = 0
             OPERATOR: PUSH_BUTTON(1) ... if "Bob's Button" = 1
             OPERATOR: PUSH_BUTTON(2) ... if "Bob's Button" = 2
             ⋮
```

Fig. 12. Sub-Model for CHOOSE_CANDIDATE("Bob")

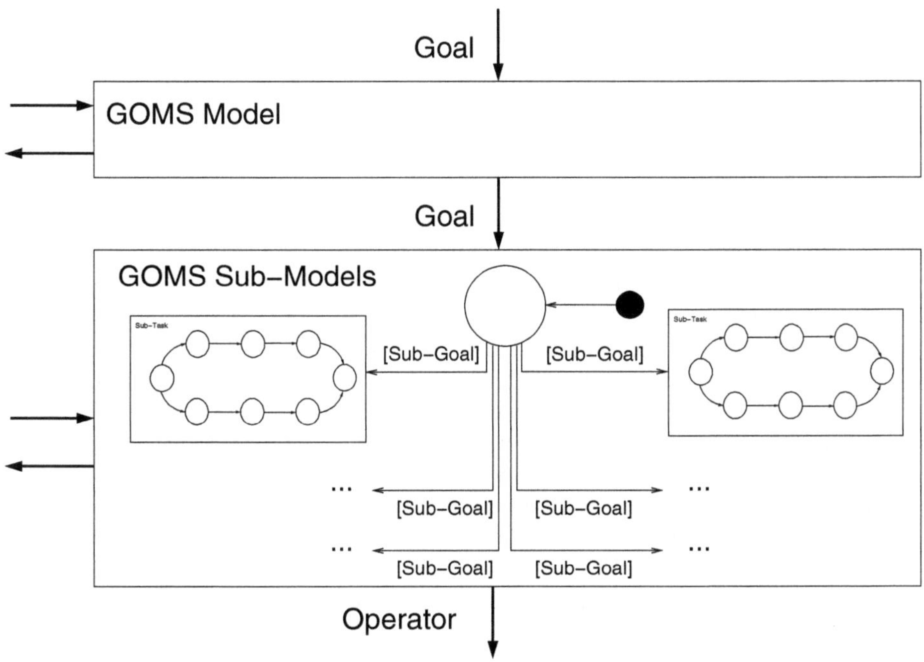

Fig. 13. Hierarchical GOMS model

component such that the operators from the higher GOMS model become selection criteria. Formally, this is defined as follows:

Definition 11. *Let*

- $T = (G, O, M, R, C, g_0)$ *be a GOMS model with the corresponding IOLTS* $L = (S, \Sigma, s_0, \rightarrow)$, *and let*
- $T_i = (G_i, O_i, M_i, R_i, C_i, g_0^i)$ *be GOMS models* ($1 \leq i \leq n$) *with the corresponding IOLTSs* $L_i = (S_i, \Sigma, s_0^i, \rightarrow_i)$

such that $O = \{g_0^1, \ldots, g_0^n\}$, *i.e., the operators of* T *are the top-level goals of* $T_1, \ldots, T_n$.

Then, the IOLTS $L' = (S', \Sigma', s_0', \rightarrow')$ *for the hierarchical model consisting of* T *and* $T_1, \ldots, T_n$ *is defined by*

$$S' = \{s'_0\} \cup \bigcup_{1 \le i \le n} S_i$$
$$\Sigma' = \Sigma!' \cup \Sigma?'$$
$$\Sigma?' = \bigcup_{1 \le i \le n} \Sigma?_i$$
$$\Sigma!' = \bigcup_{1 \le i \le n} \Sigma!_i$$
$$\rightarrow' = \{s'_0 \xrightarrow{g_0^i} s_0^i) \mid 1 \le i \le n\} \cup \bigcup_{1 \le i \le n} \rightarrow_i$$

6 Summary

In this paper, we have introduced a methodolgy for formalizing, analyzing, and verifying user interfaces and human-computer interaction under computer security aspects. The main point of this work is to provide a formal semantics for an extended version of GOMS that is suitable for automatic reasoning. In this paper:

- We have introduced a formal semantics for GOMS models describing user behavior, which is based on input/output latbelled transition systems (IOLTS).
- We showed how the component-based formalization of GOMS can be augmented with components modeling the user's assumptions about the application. That allows to model both successful HCI and erroneous HCI.
- The method used to formalize GOMS models and the user's assumption can be applied to model the application as well. Combining all three components leads to a complete model of human-computer interaction suited for automated reasoning.
- We have introduced a methodology to formally describe hierarchical user interfaces. That allows to pervasively model all aspects of user interface security.
- We have formalized generic concepts of user interface security in linear temporal logic. In combination with a formal model of HCI, that allows to use automated reasoning to determine if a user interface is secure.

References

1. C. Bramwell. Formal development methods for interactive systems: Combining interactors and design rationale, 1996.
2. Geert de Haan. *ETAG: A Formal Model of Competence Knowledge for User-Interface Design.* PhD thesis, Vrije Universiteit, Amsterdam, 2000.
3. Rüdiger Dierstein. Sicherheit in der Informationstechnik: Der Begriff IT-Sicherheit. *Informatik Spektrum*, 27(4), August 2004.
4. Alan Dix and Gregory Abowd. Modelling status and event behaviour of interactive systems. *Software Engineering Journal*, 11(6):334–346, 1996.
5. Alan Dix and Colin Runciman. Abstract models of interactive systems. In P. Johnson and S. Cook, editors, *HCI'85: People and Computers I: Designing the Interface*, pages 13–22. Cambridge: Cambridge University Press, 1985.
6. Gavin Doherty and Michael D. Harrison. A Representational Approach to the Specification of Presentations. *Eurographics Workshop on Design Specification and Verification of Interactive Systems, DSVIS 97, Granada, Spain*, June 1997.
7. D. Duke, P. Barnard, D. Duce, and J. May. Systematic development of the human interface, 1995.

8. D. J. Duke and M. D. Harrison. A Theory of Presentations. In M. Naftalin, T. Denvir, and M. Bertran, editors, *Proceedings of FME'94: Industrial Benefit of Formal Methods*, pages 271–290. Srpinger-Verlag, 1994.
9. F. Hamilton. Predictive evaluation using task knowledge structures. In *Companion Proceedings of CHI'96, Vancouver, Canada*, 1996.
10. B. E. John and D. E. Kieras. The GOMS family of user interface analysis techniques: Comparison and contrast. *ACM Transactions on Computer-Human Interaction*, 3(4):320–351, 1996.

Applying Timed Interval Calculus to Simulink Diagrams

Chunqing Chen and Jin Song Dong

School of Computing
National University of Singapore
{chenchun, dongjs}@comp.nus.edu.sg

Abstract. Simulink has been used widely as an industry tool to model and simulate embedded systems. With increasing usage of embedded systems in real-time safety-critical situations, Simulink is deficient to cope with the requirements of high-level assurance and timing analysis. In this paper, we present a systematic approach to translate Simulink diagrams to Timed Interval Calculus (TIC), a notation extending Z to support real-time system specification and verification. This work is based on the same angle chosen by Simulink and TIC where they model systems in terms of continuous time. Translated TIC specifications preserve the functional and timing aspects of the diagrams, and cover a wide range of Simulink blocks. After the translation, we can increase the design space by specifying important requirements, especially timing constraints exactly on the system or its components. Moreover, we can take advantage of TIC reasoning rules to formally verify systems with requirements, and hence elevate the design quality of Simulink.

Keywords: Simulink, Real-Time Specification, Z, Verification.

1 Introduction

Simulink [18] is a graphical environment used widely for modelling and simulating embedded systems. A Simulink diagram is formed by connecting blocks with wires to represent a set of mathematical functions that model system behavior over time. Simulink adopts continuous-time semantics [12] to support discrete (multi-rate), continuous and hybrid systems. Its simulation facility assists designers to analyze system behavior visually under specific parameters, initial conditions and simulation period.

With increasing usage of embedded systems in real-time safety-critical situations, high-level assurance is required and timing analysis becomes necessary [21]. Simulink is deficient to cope with the complexity by two factors: one is that each simulation in Simulink reflects system behavior under a particular circumstance, and hence it is infeasible to examine the behavior of infinite values of parameters or an infinite simulation period; the other is that Simulink is difficult in specifying and analyzing timing constraints, since it adopts an idealized timing model for block execution and communication. Recently, formal methods receive more attention to complement Simulink by their rigorous semantics and formal verification capability [25]. We propose to apply a real-time formal notation, i.e. Timed Interval Calculus (TIC) [8] to model Simulink diagrams, and thus to complement Simulink by TIC formal verification capability.

TIC [8] is set-theory based and extends the work of Mahony and Hayes [14]. It makes use of the continuous functions of time to model system, and defines interval brackets to

Z. Liu and J. He (Eds.): ICFEM 2006, LNCS 4260, pp. 74–93, 2006.

concisely express properties in terms of intervals. TIC reuses Z [26] mathematical and schema notations. It has been applied to a number of real-time systems, including a mine-shaft pump system [14, 24], a speedometer [8] and a controller for barometric altimeter [6]. Dawson and Goré [5] have formalized TIC reasoning rules using generic theorem prover Isabelle [20] for machine-assisted proof. The similar formalism that can handle real-time systems is Duration Calculus (DC) [27]. It uses the integration of Boolean-valued states over closed and bounded intervals to specify critical duration constraints. Its extensions, Mean Value Calculus [28] adopts the mean value of states to express properties in point intervals, and Extended Duration Calculus [29] defines two functions to give the values of state at the endpoints of an interval. Because they describe system behavior without the explicit references to absolute time, they are limited to represent the constraints which restrict the values of the interval endpoints for specific intervals.

The approach is based on the same angle adopted by Simulink and TIC when modelling systems in terms of continuous time. It can cover a wide range of Simulink blocks of different categories. The behavior of Simulink library blocks is described informally in [17], so we focuses on capturing their denotational semantics, i.e. the mathematical functions between their inputs and outputs over time. We thus define a set of TIC library functions to model the library blocks. Based on the TIC library, we develop a strategy to translate Simulink diagrams into TIC specifications by modelling the components and connections of the diagrams. The strategy can derive and keep the sample time of elementary blocks during the translation. Furthermore, Simulink conditionally executed subsystems are taken into account as well. Hence, the generated TIC specifications preserve the functional and timing aspects of the diagrams. A tool has been implemented using JAVA to experiment our strategy. After the translation, we can precisely and easily express important requirements such as timing related *safety* and *liveness* on a system or one of its components. Verification is a deduction to show that the system satisfies requirements with the use of TIC reasoning rules. Our approach even allows the analysis of open systems which are not checkable by simulation in Simulink. Therefore, using TIC can increase the design space and elevate the design quality of Simulink.

Recently, there are a number of work on translating Simulink into other formal notations or programming languages. Arthan et al [2], Adams and Clayton [1] translate Simulink diagrams into Z by capturing the functional behavior of one cycle. Cavalcanti et al [4] extend the work by using Circus to capture the functionality and concurrency of Simulink diagrams. Their approaches aim to verify that Simulink diagrams are correctly implemented in programming language Ada, and that is different from ours. Our goal is to validate that Simulink diagrams satisfy different requirements. Moreover, they consider only single-rate discrete systems, and timing information is missing. Similarly, Caspi et al [3] focus on only discrete Simulink blocks though it supports multi-rate systems. Other approaches [22, 23, 9] take Simulink/ Stateflow [1] Models (SSMs) into account. Sims et al [22] verify SSMs with an invariant checker, and the translation from SSMs to the input language of the checker is performed by hand. Tiwari et al [23] reduce certain accuracy grade by discretizing differential equations represented by Simulink diagrams into difference equations denoting discrete transition systems. Gupta et al [9]

[1] Stateflow [16] combines flow diagrams and statecharts for control logic and can be integrated into Simulink.

develop a tool *CheckMate* that can automatically verify customized SSMs, but the type of constraints supported is limited to the linear inequality that allows one variable only. Jersak et al [13] report on translating Simulink diagrams to SPI models for timing analysis. However, the communication in SPI models is represented by FIFO queues, and that is different from wires in Simulink. In short, our approach covers more types of Simulink blocks and supports more complex requirements.

The rest of the paper is organized as follows. Section 2 introduces Simulink and TIC. Section 3 defines the set of TIC library functions for Simulink library blocks. Section 4 presents the translation strategy. Section 5 shows that the TIC verification capability can complement Simulink. Section 6 concludes the paper with possible future work.

2 Background

2.1 Simulink

A Simulink diagrams is formed by connecting blocks with wires to represent a set of mathematical functions which specify system behavior over time. Elementary blocks are units. Each denotes a primitive mathematical relationship over its inputs and outputs, for example, a summation of two inputs. An elementary block is an instance of a Simulink library block using parameterization technique, i.e., generated by assigning specific values to the parameters of the library block. Hence, given different values of parameters, a library block can create the elementary blocks with different functionalities. To support hierarchical modelling, a Simulink block can be a Simulink diagram as well to represent a subsystem. A wire is a directed edge to indicate dependency relationships between connected blocks. Namely, the source block (destination block) can write (read) the value to (from) the wire according to its sample time.

Every Simulink elementary block is assigned a sample time as the rate at which the block executes in simulation. A sample time of a block can be determined by parameter *SampleTime*, by *sample time propagation* rules, or by block type (e.g. blocks from continuous library always have a continuous sample time). Simulink supports various systems such as continuous, discrete and hybrid systems. It adopts continuous-time semantics as a unifying domain. Hence the discrete systems behave piecewise-constant continuously. Simulink also supports conditionally executed subsystems whose executions depend on the value of an input, i.e. control signal. For instances, an *enabled* subsystem is active when the control signal is positive, and a *triggered* subsystem is active when a trigger event in the control signal occurs.

Example 1. We introduce a water tank system as a running example to explain and illustrate our main ideas and results. The system consists of a tank, a drainage outlet, a gate, a detector sensing water volume every 1 second, and a controller for the gate based on the value from the detector. Initially, the tank is full of water as represented by value 4 and the gate is closed. When the gate closes, the water flow rate (denoted by *flow*) is $-1 \leq \mathit{flow} < 0$ where the negative sign indicates that the water volume decreases. When the gate opens, water flows into the tank with the range $0 \leq \mathit{flow} \leq 1$. The objective is to prevent the tank from overflow or being empty. The Simulink diagram for the system with constant water flow rates is shown in Figure 1. In the diagram, each box is a Simulink block. Subsystems are used to provide a hierarchical structure of the system. Each ellipse inside a subsystem block represents an interface. To be specific, subsystem *plant* outputs different water flow rate (denoted by *flow*) according to the value from the input (denoted by *gate*); subsystem *detector* continuously integrates the water flow rate, as well as samples and holds the result every 1 second; subsystem *controller* implements the logic to control the gate. Namely, it opens the gate by outputting value 1 when the water volume (denoted by *water*) is not greater than value 1, and closes the gate by yielding value 0 when the water volume is not less than value 3.

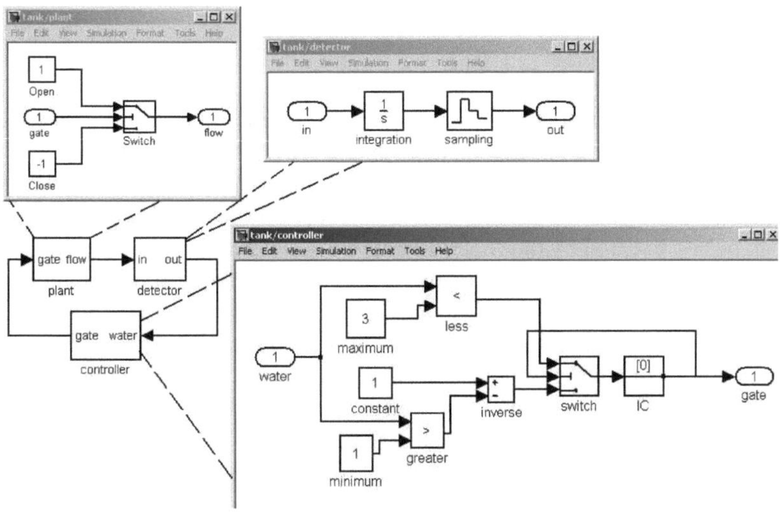

Fig. 1. The *water tank* system with its subsystems in Simulink

A Simulink diagram is stored in a structured ASCII file which is called *model file*. The file describes the Simulink diagram by keywords and parameter-value pairs. The parameter-value pairs capture the contents of the Simulink diagram by assigning values to relevant parameters. The use of keywords followed by a pair of brackets arranges contents in the same hierarchical order of the Simulink diagram. For example, part of the contents of the block *integration* in the subsystem *detector* is given below.

```
System { Name                               "detector"
         Block { BlockType                  Integrator
                 Name                       "integration"
                 InitialCondition           "4" } }
```

In the above example, the parameter-value pair "*BlockType Integrator*" indicates that the block named *integration* executes an integration function. Note that the exact mathematical expression, i.e. the integration is not shown directly. As the contents of the block is within the pair of brackets following the keyword *System*, it shows that the block is a component of the system *detector*. Moreover, the model file contains more information which is not expressed graphically, for example, the initial value 4 is not shown in Figure 1. Thus, the model file is the input of our translation from Simulink to Timed Interval Calculus.

2.2 Timed Interval Calculus

TIC is set-theory based and reuses the Z mathematical and schema notations. It adopts total functions of time to model system behavior, and defines interval brackets to concisely express properties in terms of intervals.

Time domain $\mathbb{T}$ is nonnegative real numbers, i.e., $\mathbb{R}_+ \cup \{0\}$. An interval is a contiguous range of time points. There are four types based on whether the endpoints are included, namely, left-open ($($), left-closed ($[$), right-open ($)$) and right-closed ($]$). For example, a left-closed, right-open interval is defined below.

$$[\_\ldots\_) : \mathbb{T} \times \mathbb{T} \rightarrow \mathbb{P}\mathbb{T}$$
$$\forall x, y : \mathbb{R} \bullet [x \ldots y) = \{z : \mathbb{T} \mid x \leq z < y\}$$

Note that a point interval can be depicted by a left-closed, right-closed interval, and the empty set is not an interval. Symbol $\mathbb{I}$ denotes the set of all nonempty intervals. Operators α, ω and δ return the infimum, supremum and length of an interval respectively.

TIC defines each system variable as a total function of time. For example, a water height can be represented by the function $height : \mathbb{T} \rightarrow \mathbb{R}$.

A TIC expression denotes a set of intervals during which a predicate holds everywhere. A predicate is a function from time to Boolean ($\mathbb{B}$ ::= true | false). Since the operators α, ω and δ which are the functions of intervals can be applied in a predicate, the predicate is evaluated with respect to time points and intervals simultaneously by applying the *lifting* function [15]. The lifting function ($\uparrow$) can generalize operators of simple type to complex type. For example, the predicate, $height(\alpha) \leq height$, would be lifted to a lambda abstraction which assigns a time point and an interval to the appropriate place in the predicate at the same time.

$$(height(\alpha) \leq height) \uparrow^{\mathbb{I},\mathbb{T}} = \lambda \Delta : \mathbb{I};\ t : \mathbb{T} \bullet height(\alpha(\Delta)) \leq height(t)$$

The following specification defines a set of left-closed, right-open intervals of the predicate $TP : \mathbb{T} \rightarrow \mathbb{B}$ with the use of lifting function. Note that there are other three types of sets of intervals and they can be defined in the similar way.

$$[\_) : (\mathbb{T} \rightarrow \mathbb{B}) \twoheadrightarrow \mathbb{I}$$
$$\forall TP : \mathbb{T} \rightarrow \mathbb{B} \bullet$$
$$[TP) = \{x, y : \mathbb{T} \mid \forall t : [x \ldots y) \bullet TP \uparrow^{\mathbb{I},\mathbb{T}} ([x \ldots y), t) \bullet [x \ldots y)\}$$

For example, applying the brackets to previous predicate, $height(\alpha) \leq height$, it returns all the left-closed, right-open intervals during which the water height is not less then the height at the beginning of the interval as expanded below.

$$[\, height(\alpha) \leq height\,) = \{x, y : \mathbb{T} \mid \forall t : [x \ldots y) \bullet (height(\alpha) \leq height) \uparrow^{\mathbb{I},\mathbb{T}} ([x \ldots y), t) \bullet [x \ldots y)\}$$

In general, a set of intervals with unspecified endpoints is defined:

$$[\![\_]\!] : (\mathbb{T} \rightarrow \mathbb{B}) \twoheadrightarrow \mathbb{I}$$
$$\forall TP : \mathbb{T} \rightarrow \mathbb{B} \bullet [\![TP]\!] = (TP) \cup (TP] \cup [TP) \cup [TP]$$

Since TIC is based on the set theory, the set operators such as union ($\cup$) and intersection ($\cap$) can be used to construct new sets of intervals. In addition, to capture the sequences of behaviors, a concatenation operator ($\frown$) is defined to connect consecutive intervals end-to-end.

$$\_ \frown \_ : \mathbb{I} \times \mathbb{I} \nrightarrow \mathbb{I}$$

$$\forall X, Y : \mathbb{I} \bullet X \frown Y = \{x : X;\ y : Y;\ z : \mathbb{I} \mid z = x \cup y \wedge (\forall t1 : x;\ t2 : y \bullet t1 < t2) \bullet z\}$$

A TIC predicate is formed from the TIC expressions with logical operators ($\neg$, $\vee$ and so on). We transform system logical properties into real-time properties. Namely, they can be represented by constraints on different sets of intervals. For example, the timing constraint, "*within any closed interval which starts from a multiple of 5 seconds and lasts for 1 second, the critical property P must hold.*", can be specified by the TIC predicate $[\exists k : \mathbb{N} \bullet \alpha = 5 * k \wedge \delta = 1] \subseteq [P]$.

To manage predicates in a structured way, we utilize the Z schema to group a list of variables in the declaration part and constrain the relationships among the variables in the predicate part. For example, a timing liveness property, that when the water height exceeds the maximum for more than 10 time units an alarm should be on and last till the end, can be modelled below.

AlarmON

$height : \mathbb{T} \rightarrow \mathbb{R};\ maximum : \mathbb{R};\ alarm : \mathbb{T} \rightarrow \mathbb{B}$

$[height > maximum \wedge \delta > 10) \subseteq [true] \frown [\![alarm)$

In the above predicate part, the expression $[height > maximum \wedge \delta > 10)$ represents the intervals in which the variable *height* exceeds the constant *maximum* and whose length exceeds 10 time units; while another expression $[true] \frown [\![alarm)$ denotes the intervals in which the variable *alarm* remains true from some time [2]. The relation between these two sets of intervals is hence constrained by the set comparison operator $\subseteq$. The specification is called a TIC schema which extends the conventional Z schema to support the TIC-defined operators. Hence in TIC, a system is modelled by a collection of TIC schemas.

TIC provides a rich set of reasoning rules [8, 6, 24]. They are derived from the set theory to capture the properties of sets of intervals and the interval concatenations. A typical verification is a deduction to show that system design implies requirements where they are specified in TIC. Due to the page limit, we list below some rules used in our later verification. Symbols *P, Q* and *R* denote predicates; *S, T, S'* and *T'* represent sets of intervals .

Rule 1: If the predicate that *P* implies *Q* holds all the time, then
$(\forall t : \mathbb{T} \bullet P \uparrow^{\mathbb{T}} t \Rightarrow Q \uparrow^{\mathbb{T}} t) \Rightarrow [\![P]\!] \subseteq [\![Q]\!]$. A derivative is: $[\![P \wedge Q]\!] \subseteq [\![P]\!]$

Rule 2: Transitivity on sets of intervals :
$([\![P]\!] \subseteq [\![Q]\!]) \wedge ([\![Q]\!] \subseteq [\![R]\!]) \Rightarrow [\![P]\!] \subseteq [\![R]\!]$

2 $[true]$ denotes any nonempty interval in the form of $[\_]$

Rule 3: Monotonicity on concatenation:
$(S \subseteq S' \wedge T \subseteq T') \Rightarrow (S \frown T \subseteq S' \frown T')$

Rule 4: Concatenate duration: If α, ω and δ do not occur in P, and r, s are positive values of type $\mathbb{T}$, then $[\![P \wedge \delta = r + s]\!] = [\![P \wedge \delta = r]\!] \frown [\![P \wedge \delta = s]\!]$

3 TIC Library Functions for Simulink Library Blocks

Simulink library blocks act as templates to produce elementary blocks by the parameterization technique. Simulink elementary blocks are the units to construct Simulink diagrams. In this section, we firstly describe the general structure of TIC schema for the elementary blocks, and then construct a set of TIC library functions for the library blocks.

3.1 TIC Schemas for Simulink Elementary Blocks

An elementary block denotes a mathematical function between its inputs and outputs at all points in time. In general, it can be characterized by a tuple $\{Ins, Out, Ps, \mathcal{F}\}$ where Ins is a set of inputs, Out is an output, Ps is a set of parameters and $\mathcal{F}$ is the mathematical function. The function computes output based on its inputs and parameters, i.e. $\mathcal{F} : (Ins \times Ps) \rightarrow Out$.

We translate each elementary block to a TIC schema. The schema declares each input and output as a total function from time to real numbers. The assumption of the range type of the function is acceptable since different data types in Simulink only affect simulation efficiency. Furthermore, in a Simulink diagram, each elementary block is assigned a specific sample time value as the rate at which it is executed during simulation. To capture this timing aspect, a schema variable $st : \mathbb{T}$ is declared in the translated schema. The basic schema structure of an elementary block can be modelled as below.

BasicBlk

$Ins : \mathbb{P}(\mathbb{T} \rightarrow \mathbb{R}); \; Out : \mathbb{T} \rightarrow \mathbb{R}; \; Ps : \mathbb{P}\mathbb{R}$
$\mathcal{F} : (\mathbb{P}(\mathbb{T} \rightarrow \mathbb{R}) \times \mathbb{P}\mathbb{R}) \rightarrow (\mathbb{T} \rightarrow \mathbb{R}); \; st : \mathbb{T}$

Blocks having sample time value 0 are said to have continuous sample times. Such a block executes its function at every time point. Its output depends on its inputs either at current time point or through a period, for example, an integration requires calculation over an interval. Hence the block behavior is modelled in terms of intervals instead of time points by a TIC predicate $\mathbb{I} = [\![\mathcal{F}(Ins \; Ps) = Out]\!]$. The schema structure for a continuous block can be represented as below.

$$EleBlk\_C \mathrel{\widehat{=}} [BasicBlk \mid st = 0 \wedge \mathbb{I} = [\![\mathcal{F}(Ins, Ps) = Out]\!]]$$

Blocks having positive sample time values are said to have discrete sample times. As Simulink adopts the continuous-time semantics, a discrete system behaves piecewise constantly continuously. Namely, blocks execute their functions only at sample time points, and remain constant between the sample time points. To capture this timing behavior, we decompose the time domain into a sequence of left-closed, right-open intervals, where the length is the sample time value. This feature is represented by the expression $\lceil\exists k : \mathbb{N} \bullet \alpha = k * st \wedge \omega = (k+1) * st\rceil$ where $\mathbb{N}$ includes the value 0. Moreover, the update of the function is modelled by the expression $\mathcal{F}(Ins, Ps)(\alpha) = Out$. The expression restricts that all values of the output over an interval relies on the values of the inputs at the beginning of the interval. Hence, the schema structure for a discrete block can be defined as below.

$$EleBlk\_D \mathrel{\widehat{=}} [BasicBlk \mid st > 0 \wedge \lceil\exists k : \mathbb{N} \bullet \alpha = k * st \wedge \omega = (k+1) * st\rceil = \lceil\mathcal{F}(Ins, Ps)(\alpha) = Out\rceil]$$

Every elementary block is either discrete or continuous and thus can be modelled by the following schema: $EleBlk \mathrel{\widehat{=}} EleBlk\_C \vee EleBlk\_D$.

3.2 Construction of TIC Library

Parameterization technique is the key for Simulink library blocks to create elementary blocks. As we focus on the mathematical function, the parameters for block visual appearance or simulation efficiency are deliberately ignored. For example, the parameter about a block font size is omitted. According to the effect to the mathematical function, the remaining parameters are classified into three groups: operand parameters, sample times and operator parameters.

A library block is represented by a TIC library function. The function accepts a set of arguments which correspond to the operand parameters or sample time of the library block, and returns the TIC schema which specifies the behavior of generated elementary block. Based on the general structure of the TIC schemas of elementary blocks defined in the previous section, we model the general structure of the TIC library functions as follows.

- A *continuous* library block has the sample time value 0. The structure of its TIC function can be depicted by the function function $Lib\_C : \mathbb{P}\,\mathbb{R} \rightarrow \mathbb{P}\,EleBlk\_C$ that considers only the values of relevant operand parameters.
- A *discrete* library block has positive sample time values. The structure of its TIC library function can be depicted by the function $Lib\_D : (\mathbb{T} \times \mathbb{P}\,\mathbb{R}) \rightarrow \mathbb{P}\,EleBlk\_D$ that takes into account both the sample time and the operand parameters of the block.
- Other library blocks can produce either discrete or continuous elementary blocks. Thus, their structure of the TIC library function can be depicted by the following function which covers both kinds of behavior with corresponding sample time constraint.

$$Lib\_I : (\mathbb{T} \times \mathbb{P}\,\mathbb{R}) \rightarrow \mathbb{P}\,EleBlk$$

$$\forall t : \mathbb{T};\ ps : \mathbb{P}\,\mathbb{R} \bullet (t = 0 \Rightarrow Lib\_I(t, ps) = Lib\_C(ps)) \wedge (t > 0 \Rightarrow Lib\_I(t, ps) = Lib\_D(t, ps))$$

With the expressive power, TIC supports a wide range of library blocks. One advantage is that we can handle continuous library blocks. For example, the continuous library block *Integrator* adds an initial value and the integral of its input from time 0 to current time point. In the TIC library function *Integrator* shown below, the variables In_1 and *Out* relate to the input and the output respectively, as well as the variable *IniVal* for the initial value. The parameter of the function denote the initial value from the Simulink when creating an elementary block. The product of the function is the TIC schema that specifies the behavior of the elementary block in terms of a higher level, i.e. intervals instead of time points. Note that the operator $\int$ is defined in [7].

$$Integrator : \mathbb{R} \rightarrow \mathbb{P}[In_1, Out : \mathbb{T} \rightarrow \mathbb{R};\ IniVal : \mathbb{R};\ st : \mathbb{T}]$$

$$\begin{aligned} \forall\, init : \mathbb{R} \bullet Integrator(init) = [&In_1, Out : \mathbb{T} \rightarrow \mathbb{R};\ IniVal : \mathbb{R};\ st : \mathbb{T} \mid \\ &st = 0 \wedge IniVal = init \wedge Out(0) = IniVal \wedge \\ &\mathbb{I} = ⦃Out(\omega) = Out(\alpha) + \textstyle\int_{\alpha}^{\omega} In_1⦄] \end{aligned}$$

Another advantage is that the timing feature, i.e., the sample times of the elementary blocks can be preserved in the generated TIC schemas. For example, the discrete library block *Zero Order Hold* samples and holds its input for a specified sample time. As the TIC library function *ZOH* shown below, the returned schema which stores the sample time value by the variable *st*, and captures the discrete behavior by the TIC expression $Out = In_1(\alpha)$.

$$ZOH : \mathbb{T} \rightarrow \mathbb{P}[In_1, Out : \mathbb{T} \rightarrow \mathbb{R};\ st : \mathbb{T}]$$

$$\begin{aligned} \forall\, t : \mathbb{T} \bullet ZOH(t) = [&In_1, Out : \mathbb{T} \rightarrow \mathbb{R};\ st : \mathbb{T} \mid st > 0 \wedge st = t \wedge \\ &⦇\exists\, k : \mathbb{N} \bullet \alpha = k * st \wedge \omega = (k+1) * st⦈ = ⦇Out = In_1(\alpha)⦈] \end{aligned}$$

We have demonstrated how TIC library functions deal with the operand parameters and the sample times. Next we consider the analysis of the operator parameters. This kind of parameters is special since it allows a library block to generate elementary blocks with different functionalities. One example is the library block *Sum* which adds two inputs by default. While it can produce elementary blocks that can either execute a subtraction or an addition of three inputs according to the value of its parameter *Inputs*. To cope with the complexity, we adopt the overloading technique. Namely, we define multiple TIC library functions for a single type of library block, and each function models one kind of functionality of the library block. Regarding the previous example, three TIC library functions capture three different functions of the library block *Sum* respectively.

In this section, we showed the general structure of TIC schemas for Simulink elementary blocks and TIC library functions for Simulink library blocks. The arguments of a library function correspond to the operand parameters or the sample time of a library block. Overloading technique is applied to handle the operator parameters. The TIC library serves as a foundation for automatic translation. Currently, we formally defined 50 TIC library functions [3] for 25 often used library blocks from 8 categories including *continuous*, *discrete* and *discontinuities* libraries. We also identified that the library blocks from the *Ports and Subsystems* category are not suitable to be specified in this phase. They are usually used to construct subsystems. Hence, their functionalities are

[3] They can be found at `www.comp.nus.edu.sg/~chenchun/TIC_Lib/` and Appendix A shows part of them used for the water tank system.

unpredictable until they are instantiated in specific Simulink diagrams. We will discuss their solution in the next section.

4 Translating Simulink Diagrams to TIC Specifications

A Simulink diagram represents a set of mathematical functions over time. In this section we will show how the translation from Simulink diagrams to TIC specifications can preserve the functional and timing aspects. As Simulink models systems in a hierarchical way, we illustrate the translation in the bottom-up order, namely, from elementary blocks, wires to diagrams. A discussion for handling conditionally executed subsystems is provided in the end.

4.1 Translating Elementary Blocks

A Simulink elementary block denotes a primitive mathematical function in a diagram. It is produced by a library block using the parameterization technique. Similarly, an elementary block is translated into a TIC schema by applying an appropriate TIC library function to relevant Simulink parameters. Two important factors are taken into account in the translation.

One is the criteria to choose a suitable TIC library function that produces a TIC schema to correctly model the functional behavior of the elementary block. The primary criterion is the parameter *BlockType* which indicates the mathematical function implicitly. Recalling the *integration* example given in Section 2.1, the value *Integrator* of the parameter *BlockType* denotes that the block performs an integration function. Furthermore, some library blocks can generate different functionalities of their instances by different values assigned of their operator parameters. Thus, these relevant operator parameters are additional criteria as well. Taking the library block *Sum* example from 3.2, parameters *BlockType* and *Inputs* compose the criteria to select an appropriate TIC library function.

The other is the sample time which represents the rate at which a block is executed. A block sample time can be assigned explicitly by the parameter *SampleTime* with positive value; or implied by the type of its library block, for example, a continuous block always has sample time value 0; or derived from sample time propagation, which is a process to calculate the sample time of a block from the sample times of the inputs of the block. A method is developed below to derive the sample time of an elementary block based on the instructions in [18]. We assume that the sample time values of the block inputs (each is a function of time and denoted by $Blk\_In == \mathbb{T} \rightarrow \mathbb{R}$) are known and represented by the function $InST : Blk\_In \rightarrow \mathbb{T}$.

1. If all inputs have the same sample time values, then the value is assigned to the sample time of the block. The following function returns the desired sample time value if it exists, value 0 otherwise.

$$AllEq : \mathbb{P}\, Blk\_In \rightarrow \mathbb{T}$$

$$\forall\, ins : \mathbb{P}\, Blk\_In \bullet \exists\, res : \mathbb{T} \bullet$$
$$\quad AllEq(ins) = \textsf{If}\ \forall\, in : ins \bullet InST(in) = res\ \textsf{Then}\ res\ \textsf{Else}\ 0$$

2. Otherwise, if a sample time value of an input is the common integer divisor of other sample time values, then the value is the result. The following function specifies the computation and returns value 0 if no such a sample time exists.

$$
\begin{array}{l}
ExiFast : \mathbb{P}\, Blk\_In \rightarrow \mathbb{T} \\
\hline
\forall\, ins : \mathbb{P}\, Blk\_In \bullet \exists\, res : \mathbb{T} \bullet ExiFast(ins) = \\
\quad \text{If } \exists\, in1 : ins \bullet \forall\, in2 : ins \mid in1 \neq in2 \bullet \\
\quad\quad \exists\, k : \mathbb{N} \mid k > 1 \bullet InST(in2) = InST(in1) * k \wedge InST(in1) = res \\
\quad \text{Then } res \text{ Else } 0
\end{array}
$$

3. Otherwise, if the Simulink *variable-step* solver [4] is used, then the block is assigned the continuous sample time; if the Simulink *fixed-step* solver is used, and the greatest common integer divisor (GCD) of the sample time values of all inputs can be derived, then GCD is the result, otherwise, it is value 0. In the following function *STP*, $Solver == \{Fixed\_Step, Variable\_Step\}$, and the function *CalGCD* returns GCD if it exists, otherwise value 0. The function *STP* checks whether any of the previous two conditions holds before it computes the sample time based on the solver type. Note that the previous two conditions are mutually exclusive.

$$
\begin{array}{l}
STP : \mathbb{P}\, Blk\_In \times Solver \rightarrow \mathbb{T} \\
\hline
\forall\, ins : \mathbb{P}\, Blk\_In;\ s : Solver \bullet STP(ins, s) = \\
\quad \text{If } AllEq(ins) \neq 0 \vee ExiFast(ins) \neq 0 \text{ Then } AllEq(ins) + ExiFast(ins) \\
\quad \text{Else (If } s = Variable\_Step \text{ Then } 0 \text{ Else } CalGCD(ins))
\end{array}
$$

Hence, after the translation, the functional aspect of an elementary block is captured by a TIC schema, and the timing information, i.e. the sample time value, is calculated and kept in the schema.

Taking the elementary block *less* in Figure 1 as an example, the selection criteria consists of the parameters *BlockType* and *Operator*, so their respective values *RelationalOperator* and "<" determine that the proper library function is *Relation_1* shown in Appendix A. In addition, the sample time value is 0, which is derived by the sample time propagation method as the block *maximum* has the continuous sample time. Thus, the block is translated into the TIC schema: $tank\_controller\_less \mathrel{\widehat{=}} Relation\_1(0)$. We adopt a conventional naming manner to capture the hierarchical structure of the Simulink diagram. To be specific, a TIC schema name of a block is formed by appending the names of the block and systems along the structure path of the diagram using the symbol "_". Hence, the schema name *tank_controller_less* indicates that the block *less* is the component of the system *controller* which is the subsystem of the system *tank*.

4.2 Translating Wires

In Simulink, wires represent input and output relations between connected blocks. They have values at all points in time. Source (Destination) block writes (reads) value to

[4] Variable-step solvers vary the simulation step size in simulation, while fixed-step solvers keep the simulation step size constant.

(from) a wire according to its sample time. Hence, it supports the communication between blocks which have different sample time values. We convert a wire into an equation which consists of two variables denoting the output of the source block and the input of the destination block respectively. The equivalence remains the Simulink communication feature, i.e. the destination block receiving the same value that is produced by the source block at the same time. The general structure can thus be modelled in the schema.
$Line \mathrel{\widehat{=}} [src, dst : \mathbb{T} \rightarrow \mathbb{R} \mid src = dst]$

4.3 Translating Diagrams

A Simulink diagram is formed by connecting Simulink blocks with wires. Hence the formal specification of a diagram should capture the components and connection. Our method is similar to the way presented in [2]. A diagram into a TIC schema after translating its components into corresponding TIC schemas. The schema declares each component to be a schema variable which is an instance of the TIC schema of the component. It hence depicts the connection by translating each wire into an equation using the variables in the declaration part. The structure of the schema can be modelled by the following mutually recursive free type definition [11].

$$\begin{array}{l} Diagram ::= System\langle\langle [InS, OutS : \mathbb{P}(\mathbb{T} \rightarrow \mathbb{R});\ Blks : \mathbb{P}_1\, Block;\ Ls : \mathbb{P}_1\, Line] \rangle\rangle \\ \& \\ Block ::= Subsystem\langle\langle [subsys : Diagram] \rangle\rangle \mid LibBlk\langle\langle [blk : EleBlk] \rangle\rangle \end{array}$$

The above definition indicates that a Simulink block can be either an elementary block or a subsystem which is a diagram as well. Moreover, it restricts that a Simulink diagram must have at least one wire to connect two components.

4.4 Additional Translation Issues

As mentioned at the end of Section 3, the library blocks from the *Ports and Subsystems* category would be analyzed during the translation. As they are mainly used to construct subsystems, we demonstrate the solution by considering the *plain* subsystems and *conditionally executed* subsystems below.

A plain subsystem reduces virtually the number of blocks displayed in a Simulink diagram without changing the system behavior. Hence, it is treated in the same way translating diagrams. In particular, the instances generated by the library blocks *Inport* and *Outport* are represented by functions from time to real numbers as they represent the interface of the subsystems.

A conditionally executed subsystem restricts its execution within special periods. Namely, the execution depends on the value of the *control signal*. In our approach, such a subsystem is translated into a TIC schema in the similar way for a plain subsystem, besides two additional TIC predicates constraining the relationship between the execution and the control signal in terms of intervals. To be specific, each predicate contains two TIC expressions. One expression (*TE1*) specifies the intervals when the system is (or is not) executable, the other expression (*TE2*) depicts the corresponding behavior.

Hence, the predicate is generally in the format $TE1 \subseteq TE2$. As the execution of subsystems can be arbitrary, it is hard to predict the contents of the expression *TE2*, and we thus focus on the way to construct the expression *TE1* for two prominent conditionally executed subsystems respectively.

- An *enabled* subsystem is executed when the control signal is positive. The control signal is defined by the function $enabled : \mathbb{T} \rightarrow \mathbb{R}$. The set of intervals when the subsystem is enabled is thus expressed by the expression $[\!(enabled > 0)\!]$, while the expression $[\!(enabled \leq 0)\!]$ represents the set of intervals when the subsystem is disabled.
- A *triggered* subsystem is executed when a trigger event in the control signal occurs. That is to say, it is active at single time points. The control signal is defined by the function $triggered : \mathbb{T} \rightarrow \mathbb{B}$ which returns true when an event occurs, and false otherwise. Thus, the set of intervals when the subsystem is active is specified by the expression $\lceil triggered \rceil$, while the expression $(\neg\ triggered)$ denotes the set of intervals when the system is inactive.

We experiment our strategy by translating the water tank system displayed in Figure 1 into corresponding TIC schemas shown in Appendix B. For simplicity, we choose the subsystem *detector* which is plain as the example.

The subsystem contains four elementary blocks. Two of them, *integration* and *sampling* are translated to two TIC schemas below which capture the initial value and the sample time of the blocks respectively.

$$tank\_detector\_integration \mathrel{\widehat{=}} Integrator(4)$$
$$tank\_detector\_sampling \mathrel{\widehat{=}} ZOH(1)$$

Other blocks, *in* and *out* denote the interface of the subsystem. They are declared as functions over time in the following TIC schema *tank_detector*. The schema models the subsystem by declaring its components as instances of the translated TIC schemas, and confining the connections by three equations.

tank_detector

$in : \mathbb{T} \rightarrow \mathbb{R};\ sampling : tank\_detector\_sampling$
$integration : tank\_detector\_integration;\ out : \mathbb{T} \rightarrow \mathbb{R}$

$sampling.Out = out \wedge in = integration.In_1$
$integration.Out = sampling.In_1$

We remark that in the subsystem *controller*, there is an algebraic loop made up by the blocks *switch* and *IC*. In practical, solving an algebraic loop is difficult, and unnecessary if it is not involved in analysis. Thus, in our approach, the structure of the loop, i.e. the components and the connections, is preserved after the translation, so the loop can be retrieved by relevant TIC schemas and equations when needed.

In this section, we presented a strategy to translate Simulink diagrams into TIC specifications in the bottom-up manner. The translation preserves the functional and timing aspect. We also discussed the solution to handle conditionally executed subsystems.

Currently we have been implementing the strategy using JAVA so the translation can be accomplished automatically, for example, the TIC specifications of the water tank system are generated successfully by the translator.

5 Simulink Diagrams Verification in TIC

In TIC, verification is a deduction to show that a system implies requirements. This section will firstly describe the way to specify requirements based on the translated TIC specifications, and then show the benefits from utilizing the TIC verification capability by analyzing the water tank system.

5.1 Specification of Requirements

TIC models system behavior in terms of intervals. It supports various requirements specifications represented as TIC predicates. For example, a *safety* requirement that a predicate P holds always can be expressed in the TIC predicate $\mathbb{I} = [\![P]\!]$ that restricts the requirement in a higher level, i.e., in any non-empty level. With the TIC-defined operators on interval endpoints and length, timing constraints that are difficult to be supported in Simulink, can be represented precisely and concisely in TIC. For example, a timing *liveness* requirement that for any interval lasting more than K time units and during which a predicate P holds, then a predicate Q should hold within K time units and last till the end of the interval, can be specified by the following TIC predicate $[\![P \wedge \delta > K]\!] \subseteq [\![\delta \leq K]\!] \frown [\![Q]\!]$.

In our approach, requirements are formed based on the TIC schemas translated from Simulink diagrams. We can specify them over the whole system or some of its components. For example, in the water tank system, the requirement of the subsystem *detector* is "*for any period lasting more than 1 second and during which the water volume in a tank is not greater than 1, then the gate must open within 1 second (including 1) till the end.*". From the translated TIC specifications shown in Appendix B, the variable *gate* of the schema *tank_controller* denotes the gate status, and the output of the schema *tank_detector_integration* represents the real-time water volume in the tank. Moreover, the requirement is about timing-related liveness, so it can be specified easily in the similar format of the previous TIC predicate. Namely, the requirement is modelled as below:

$$\forall sys : tank \bullet [\![sys.detector.integration.Out \leq 1 \wedge \delta > 1)\!) \subseteq [\![\delta \leq 1)\!) \frown [\![sys.controller.gate = 1)\!)$$

We remark that Simulink Verification and Validation [19] provides a function to link requirements documents (e.g. a Word or Excel file) with Simulink components. The function aims to assists users to quickly look over requirements in the modelling phase, and it is different from ours in that we can formally verify systems against requirements directly.

5.2 Checking Beyond Simulink

As Simulink diagrams are constructed in a hierarchical manner, we adopt a common approach [10] to analyze system behavior in a bottom-up order. We start with checking requirements of subsystems, so the proved requirements act as lemmas for the analysis of higher-level system. During the verification, the translated TIC specifications serve as assumptions to depict the blocks behavior and the connections in the diagram. Each deductive step is reached by formally applying assumptions, reasoning rules, common mathematical theories, or lemmas. We take the verification of the requirement mentioned above as an example and give manually developed deduction outlines by necessity:

1. Start with the premise $\lceil sys.detector.integration.Out \leq 1 \wedge \delta > 1 \rceil$. Let $r = 1 > 0$ and $s = \delta - 1 > 0$, and based on *rule 4*, we can obtain a concatenation of two sets of intervals. Two sets are named by *E1* and *E2*.

$$
\begin{aligned}
&\lceil sys.detector.integration.Out \leq 1 \wedge \delta > 1 \rceil \\
= &\lceil sys.detector.integration.Out \leq 1 \wedge \delta = 1 \rceil && \text{[E1]} \\
&\frown \lceil sys.detector.integration.Out \leq 1 \rceil && \text{[E2]}
\end{aligned}
$$

2. In *E1*, since $\delta = 1 \Rightarrow \delta \leq 1$, we applied *rule 1* and *rule 2* in turn to obtain $E1 \subseteq \lceil \delta = 1 \rceil \subseteq \lceil \delta \leq 1 \rceil$.
3. As $integration.Out = out$ in the schema *tank_detector*, and in the schema *tank*, $detector.out = controller.water$, after two substitutions of the equations in turn, we have

$$
\begin{aligned}
E2 &= \lceil sys.detector.out \leq 1 \rceil \\
&= \lceil sys.controller.water \leq 1 \rceil
\end{aligned}
$$

4. A proved requirement of the *controller* subsystem is used as a lemma below: **Lemma** : $\forall con : tank\_controller \bullet \llbracket con.water \leq 1 \rrbracket \subseteq \llbracket con.gate = 1 \rrbracket$. It states that whenever the controller detects that the input water volume is not lager then 1, it opens the gate. Thus, after applying *rule 1* and *2* several times, we have:

$$E2 \subseteq \lceil sys.controller.gate = 1 \rceil$$

5. From step 2 and 4, after applying *rule 3*, we can conclude that

$$
\begin{aligned}
&\lceil sys.detector.integration.Out \leq 1 \wedge \delta > 1 \rceil \\
\subseteq &\lceil \delta \leq 1 \rceil \frown \lceil sys.controller.gate = 1 \rceil
\end{aligned}
$$

□

Besides the above proof, we have successfully shown that the water tank system satisfied other important requirements [5] including the safety requirement that the tank would be neither empty nor overflow always. In the verification, mathematical analysis, e.g. integral calculus, is applied freely in the TIC logic, and hence it provides a flexible

[5] Details of other requirements verification are available in the technical report at www.comp.nus.edu.sg/~chenchun/water_tank/

interface to conventional control theory. Furthermore, one advantage is that open systems can be analyzed if certain constraints of their input functions are given. Simulink can only simulate closed systems, and it is often impractical to know the exact input functions. This limitation can be solved in our approach by specifying the constraints in TIC and treating them as assumptions in the verification.

The proof so far is achieved by hand. The calculations however are simple and stereotypic, so there is a reasonable hope for machine-assisted proof. Currently we are exploring the way to reuse the existent work [5] which formalized several reasoning rules in the generic theorem prover Isabelle [20]. Based on the real numbers and set theories available in Isabelle/HOL, intervals can be implemented as connected sets of real numbers, and TIC specifications can be encoded into Isabelle theorems to be checked by the validated reasoning rules.

6 Conclusion

In this paper, we propose to apply Timed Interval Calculus (TIC), a set-theoretic notation, to formally model and verify Simulink diagrams. The work is based on the same angle adopted by Simulink and TIC where they specify systems in terms of continuous time. We defined a set of TIC library functions to model Simulink library blocks and cover a wide range of categories such as *continuous*, *discrete* and *discontinuous* libraries. Moreover, the TIC schemas produced by their library functions can capture the functional behavior over time of the Simulink elementary blocks.

We presented a strategy to translate Simulink diagrams to TIC specifications in the bottom-up order. The timing information can be derived and kept in the generated TIC schemas. Hence, the translation preserves the functional and timing aspects of the diagrams. Moreover, we discussed the way to handle conditionally executed subsystems, such as *enabled* and *triggered* subsystems. A translator has been implemented in JAVA to experiment our strategy.

With the expressive power of TIC, we can precisely and concisely specify requirements, especially the timing constraints, over a system or its components after the translation. This way yields a larger design space. Using TIC reasoning rules, we can formally verify systems against requirements beyond Simulink, for example, a safety requirement needs a possible infinite simulation period. During the verification, mathematical analysis, e.g., control theory, can be applied freely in TIC logic. Furthermore, open systems which are not checkable by simulation in Simulink can be analyzed in our approach. Thus, using TIC can elevate the design quality in Simulink.

We are enhancing the capability of the translator with more complex Simulink diagrams. In the future, we plan to extend the TIC library functions to support Stateflow. Embedding TIC into Isabelle/HOL for machine-assisted proof is one of our goals as well.

Acknowledgements

We thank Brendan Mahony for providing materials about TIC notation. We also thank Anders P. Ravn and Zhou Chaochen and Mark Adams for their insightful discussion on the related work. This work is supported by the A*Star research Grants "Formal Design Techniques for Reactive Embedded Systems".

References

1. M. M. Adams and Peter B. Clayton. Clawz: Cost-effective formal verification for control systems. In *ICFEM 2005*, pages 465–479, 2005.
2. R. D. Arthan, P. Caseley, C. O'Halloran, and A. Smith. ClawZ: Control laws in Z. In *ICFEM 2000*, pages 169–176. IEEE Press, 2000.
3. P. Caspi, A. Curic, A. Maignan, C. Sofronis, and S. Tripakis. Translating discrete-time Simulink to Lustre. In *EMSOFT 2003*, Philadelphia, PA, USA, 2003.
4. A. Cavalcanti, P. Clayton, and C. O'Halloran. Control law diagrams in Circus. In *FM 2005*, University of Newcastle upon Tyne, UK, July 2005.
5. J. E. Dawson and R. Goré. Machine-checking the timed interval calculus. In *Australian Joint Conference on Artificial Intelligence*, pages 95–106, 2002.
6. C. J. Fidge. Modelling discrete behaviour in a continuous-time formalism. In *IFM 1999*, pages 170–188. Springer-Verlag, June 1999.
7. C. J. Fidge, I. J. Hayes, and B. P. Mahony. Defining differentiation and integration in Z. In *ICFEM 1998*. IEEE Computer Society, 1998.
8. C. J. Fidge, I. J. Hayes, A. P. Martin, and A. Wabenhorst. A set-theoretic model for real-time specification and reasoning. In *MPC 1998*, pages 188–206, 1998.
9. S. Gupta, B. H. Krogh, and R. A. Rutenbar. Towards formal verification of analog designs. In *ICCAD 2004*, pages 210 – 217, 2004.
10. J. Hooman. *Specification and Compositional Verification of Real-Time Systems*. Springer-Verlag New York, Inc., Secaucus, NJ, USA, 1991.
11. ISO/IEC. *Information Technology — Z Formal Specification Notation — Syntax, Type System and Semantics*, 1st edition, July 2002. 13568.
12. A. Jantsch and I. Sander. Models of computation and languages for embedded system design. *IEE Pro. on Comp. and Dig. Tech.*, 152(2):114–129, March 2005.
13. M. Jersak, Y. Cai, D. Ziegenbein, and R. Ernst. A transformational approach to constraint relaxation of a time-driven simulation model. In *ISSS 2000*, 2000.
14. B. P. Mahony and I. J. Hayes. A case-study in timed refinement: A mine pump. *IEEE Transactions on Software Engineering*, 18(9):817–826, 1992.
15. A. Martin and C. J. Fidge. Lifting in Z. *Electronic Notes in Theoretical Computer Science*, 42, 2001.
16. The MathWorks. *Stateflow and Stateflow coder - For Complex Logic and State Diagram Modeling*, 2003.
17. The MathWorks. *Simulink - Simulation and Model-based Design - Simulink Reference Version 6*, 2004.
18. The MathWorks. *Simulink - Simulation and Model-based Design - Using Simulink Version 6*, 2004.
19. The MathWorks. *Simulink Verification and Validation User's Guide*, March 2006.
20. T. Nipkow, L. C. Paulson, and M. Wenzel. *Isabelle/HOL — A Proof Assistant for Higher-Order Logic*. Springer, 2002.
21. A. Pnueli. Embedded systems: Challenges in specification and verification. In *EMSOFT 2002*, pages 1–14, London, UK, 2002. Springer-Verlag.
22. S. Sims, R. Cleaveland, K. Butts, and S. Ranville. Automated validation of software models. In *ASE 2001*, pages 91–96. IEEE Computer Society, 2001.

23. A. Tiwari, N. Shankar, and J. Rushby. Invisible formal methods for embedded control systems. *Proceedings of the IEEE*, 91(1):29–39, January 2003.
24. A. Wabenhorst. Induction in the timed interval calculus. *Theoretical Computer Science*, 300(1-3):181–207, 2003.
25. F. Wang. Formal verification of timed systems: A survey and perspective. *Proceedings of the IEEE*, 92(8):1283–1307, August 2004.
26. J. Woodcock and J. Davies. *Using Z: Specification, Refinement and Proof.* Prentice Hall International, 1996.
27. C. C. Zhou and M. R. Hansen. *Duration Calculus: A Formal Approach to Real-Time Systems.* Springer Verlag, 2004.
28. C. C. Zhou and X. S. Li. A mean value calculus of durations. In *A classical mind: essays in honour of C. A. R. Hoare.* Prentice-Hall International, 1994.
29. C. C. Zhou, A. P. Ravn, and M. R. Hansen. An extended duration calculus for hybrid real-time systems. In *Hybrid Systems*, pages 36–59. Springer-Verlag, 1993.

A TIC Library Functions of the Water Tank System

$$ZOH : \mathbb{T} \rightarrow \mathbb{P}[In_1, Out : \mathbb{T} \rightarrow \mathbb{R};\ st : \mathbb{T}]$$

$$\forall t : \mathbb{T} \bullet ZOH(t) = [In_1, Out : \mathbb{T} \rightarrow \mathbb{R};\ st : \mathbb{T} \mid st > 0 \wedge st = t \wedge \lfloor Out = In_1(\alpha) \rfloor = \lfloor \exists k : \mathbb{N} \bullet \alpha = k * st \wedge \omega = (k+1) * st \rfloor]$$

$$Integrator : \mathbb{R} \rightarrow \mathbb{P}[In_1, Out : \mathbb{T} \rightarrow \mathbb{R};\ IniVal : \mathbb{R};\ st : \mathbb{T}]$$

$$\forall init : \mathbb{R} \bullet Integrator(init) = [In_1, Out : \mathbb{T} \rightarrow \mathbb{R};\ IniVal : \mathbb{R};\ st : \mathbb{T} \mid st = 0 \wedge init = IniVal \wedge Out(0) = IniVal \wedge \mathbb{I} = \llbracket Out(\omega) = Out(\alpha) + \int_\alpha^\omega In_1 \rrbracket]$$

$$Switch : (\mathbb{T} \times \mathbb{R}) \rightarrow \mathbb{P}[TH : \mathbb{R};\ st : \mathbb{T};\ In_1, In_2, In_3, Out : \mathbb{T} \rightarrow \mathbb{R}]$$

$$\begin{aligned}
&\forall t : \mathbb{T};\ th : \mathbb{R} \bullet \\
&(t = 0 \Rightarrow Switch(t, th) = [TH : \mathbb{R};\ st : \mathbb{T}; \\
&\quad In_1, In_2, In_3, Out : \mathbb{T} \rightarrow \mathbb{R} \mid \\
&\quad st = 0 \wedge th = TH \wedge \\
&\quad \llbracket In_2 > TH \rrbracket = \llbracket Out = In_1 \rrbracket \wedge \\
&\quad \llbracket In_2 \leq TH \rrbracket = \llbracket Out = In_3 \rrbracket]) \wedge \\
&(t > 0 \Rightarrow Switch(t, th) = [TH : \mathbb{R};\ st : \mathbb{T}; \\
&\quad In_1, In_2, In_3, Out : \mathbb{T} \rightarrow \mathbb{R} \mid \\
&\quad t = st \wedge st > 0 \wedge th = TH \wedge \\
&\quad \lfloor \exists k : \mathbb{N} \bullet \alpha = k * st \wedge \omega = (k+1) * st \rfloor = \\
&\quad \lfloor (In_2(\alpha) > TH \Rightarrow Out = In_1(\alpha)) \wedge \\
&\qquad (In_2(\alpha) \leq TH \Rightarrow Out = In_3(\alpha)) \rfloor])
\end{aligned}$$

$$Sum\_PM : \mathbb{T} \rightarrow \mathbb{P}[In_1, In_2, Out : \mathbb{T} \rightarrow \mathbb{R};\ st : \mathbb{T}]$$

$$\begin{aligned}
&\forall t : \mathbb{T} \bullet (t = 0 \Rightarrow Sum_PM(t) = \\
&\quad [In_1, In_2, Out : \mathbb{T} \rightarrow \mathbb{R};\ st : \mathbb{T} \mid \\
&\quad st = 0 \wedge \mathbb{I} = \llbracket Out = In_1 - In_2 \rrbracket]) \wedge \\
&(t > 0 \Rightarrow Sum_PM(t) = \\
&\quad [In_1, In_2, Out : \mathbb{T} \rightarrow \mathbb{R};\ st : \mathbb{T} \mid \\
&\quad t = st \wedge st > 0 \wedge \\
&\quad \lfloor Out = In_1(\alpha) - In_2(\alpha) \rfloor = \\
&\quad \lfloor \exists k : \mathbb{N} \bullet \alpha = k * st \wedge \omega = (k+1) * st \rfloor])
\end{aligned}$$

$$Relation\_l : \mathbb{T} \rightarrow \mathbb{P}[In_1, In_2 : \mathbb{T} \rightarrow \mathbb{R};\ Out : \mathbb{T} \rightarrow \{0,1\};\ st : \mathbb{T}]$$

$$\begin{aligned}
&\forall t : \mathbb{T} \bullet \\
&(t = 0 \Rightarrow Relation_l(t) = [In_1, In_2 : \mathbb{T} \rightarrow \mathbb{R}; \\
&\quad Out : \mathbb{T} \rightarrow \{0,1\};\ st : \mathbb{T} \mid st = 0 \wedge \\
&\quad (\llbracket In_1 < In_2 \rrbracket = \llbracket Out = 1 \rrbracket) \wedge \\
&\quad (\llbracket In_1 \geq In_2 \rrbracket = \llbracket Out = 0 \rrbracket)]) \wedge \\
&(t > 0 \Rightarrow Relation_l(t) = [In_1, In_2 : \mathbb{T} \rightarrow \mathbb{R}; \\
&\quad Out : \mathbb{T} \rightarrow \{0,1\};\ st : \mathbb{T} \mid \\
&\quad t = st \wedge st > 0 \wedge \\
&\quad \lfloor \exists k : \mathbb{N} \bullet \alpha = k * st \wedge \omega = (k+1) * st \rfloor = \\
&\quad \lfloor (In_1(\alpha) < In_2(\alpha) \Rightarrow Out = 1) \wedge \\
&\qquad (In_1(\alpha) \geq In_2(\alpha) \Rightarrow Out = 0) \rfloor])
\end{aligned}$$

$$Relation\_g : \mathbb{T} \rightarrow \mathbb{P}[In_1, In_2 : \mathbb{T} \rightarrow \mathbb{R};\ Out : \mathbb{T} \rightarrow \{0,1\};\ st : \mathbb{T}]$$

$$\begin{aligned}
&\forall t : \mathbb{T} \bullet \\
&(t = 0 \Rightarrow Relation_g(t) = [In_1, In_2 : \mathbb{T} \rightarrow \mathbb{R}; \\
&\quad Out : \mathbb{T} \rightarrow \{0,1\};\ st : \mathbb{T} \mid st = 0 \wedge \\
&\quad (\llbracket In_1 > In_2 \rrbracket = \llbracket Out = 1 \rrbracket) \wedge \\
&\quad (\llbracket In_1 \leq In_2 \rrbracket = \llbracket Out = 0 \rrbracket)]) \wedge \\
&(t > 0 \Rightarrow Relation_g(t) = [In_1, In_2 : \mathbb{T} \rightarrow \mathbb{R}; \\
&\quad Out : \mathbb{T} \rightarrow \{0,1\};\ st : \mathbb{T} \mid \\
&\quad t = st \wedge st > 0 \wedge \\
&\quad \lfloor \exists k : \mathbb{N} \bullet \alpha = k * st \wedge \omega = (k+1) * st \rfloor = \\
&\quad \lfloor (In_1(\alpha) > In_2(\alpha) \Rightarrow Out = 1) \wedge \\
&\qquad (In_1(\alpha) \leq In_2(\alpha) \Rightarrow Out = 0) \rfloor])
\end{aligned}$$

$$InitCond : (\mathbb{T} \times \mathbb{R}) \rightarrow \mathbb{P}[In_1, Out : \mathbb{T} \rightarrow \mathbb{R};\ IniVal : \mathbb{R};\ st : \mathbb{T}]$$

$$\begin{aligned}
&\forall t : \mathbb{T};\ init : \mathbb{R} \bullet \\
&(t = 0 \Rightarrow InitCond(t, init) = \\
&\quad [In_1, Out : \mathbb{T} \rightarrow \mathbb{R};\ IniVal : \mathbb{R};\ st : \mathbb{T} \mid \\
&\quad init = IniVal \wedge Out(0) = IniVal \wedge \\
&\quad st = 0 \wedge \llbracket 0 < \alpha \rrbracket = \llbracket Out = In_1 \rrbracket]) \wedge \\
&(t > 0 \Rightarrow InitCond(t, init) = \\
&\quad [In_1, Out : \mathbb{T} \rightarrow \mathbb{R};\ IniVal : \mathbb{R};\ st : \mathbb{T} \mid \\
&\quad t = st \wedge Out(0) = IniVal \wedge \\
&\quad st > 0 \wedge init = IniVal \wedge \\
&\quad \lfloor \alpha = 0 \wedge \omega = st \rfloor = \lfloor Out = IniVal \rfloor \wedge \\
&\quad \lfloor Out = In_1(\alpha) \rfloor = \\
&\quad \lfloor \exists k : \mathbb{N}_1 \bullet \alpha = k * st \wedge \omega = (k+1) * st \rfloor])
\end{aligned}$$

$$\begin{array}{|l}
Constant : \mathbb{R} \rightarrow \mathbb{P}[Out : \mathbb{T} \rightarrow \mathbb{R};\ IniVal : \mathbb{R}] \\
\hline
\forall cv : \mathbb{R} \bullet Constant(cv) = \\
\quad [Out : \mathbb{T} \rightarrow \mathbb{R};\ IniVal : \mathbb{R} \mid \\
\quad\ cv = IniVal \wedge \mathbb{I} = \llbracket Out = IniVal \rrbracket]
\end{array}$$

B TIC Specifications of the Water Tank Simulink Diagram

Controller Subsystem

$tank\_controller\_maximum \mathrel{\widehat=} Constant(3)$
$tank\_controller\_less \mathrel{\widehat=} Relation\_l(0)$
$tank\_controller\_minimum \mathrel{\widehat=} Constant(1)$
$tank\_controller\_greater \mathrel{\widehat=} Relation\_g(0)$
$tank\_controller\_inverse \mathrel{\widehat=} Sum\_PM(0)$
$tank\_controller\_switch \mathrel{\widehat=} Switch(0, 0)$
$tank\_controller\_IC \mathrel{\widehat=} InitCond(0, 0)$
$tank\_controller\_constant \mathrel{\widehat=} Constant(1)$

$$\begin{array}{|l}
\multicolumn{1}{l}{__ tank_controller __} \\
water : \mathbb{T} \rightarrow \mathbb{R} \\
maximum : tank_controller_maximum \\
minimum : tank_controller_minimum \\
less : tank_controller_less \\
greater : tank_controller_greater \\
constant : tank_controller_constant \\
inverse : tank_controller_inverse \\
switch : tank_controller_switch \\
IC : tank_controller_IC \\
gate : \mathbb{T} \rightarrow \mathbb{R} \\
\hline
water = less.In_1 \wedge inverse.Out = switch.In_3 \\
constant.Out = inverse.In_1 \wedge IC.Out = gate \\
less.Out = switch.In_1 \wedge water = greater.In_1 \\
switch.Out = IC.In_1 \wedge IC.Out = switch.In_2 \\
greater.Out = inverse.In_2 \\
maximum.Out = less.In_2 \\
minimum.Out = greater.In_2 \\
\hline
\end{array}$$

Detector Subsystem

$tank\_detector\_integration \mathrel{\widehat=} Integrator(4)$
$tank\_detector\_sampling \mathrel{\widehat=} ZOH(1)$

$$\begin{array}{|l}
\multicolumn{1}{l}{__ tank_detector __} \\
in : \mathbb{T} \rightarrow \mathbb{R} \\
integration : tank_detector_integration \\
sampling : tank_detector_sampling \\
out : \mathbb{T} \rightarrow \mathbb{R} \\
\hline
sampling.Out = out \wedge in = integration.In_1 \\
integration.Out = sampling.In_1 \\
\hline
\end{array}$$

Plant Subsystem

$tank\_plant\_switch \mathrel{\widehat=} Switch(0, 0)$
$tank\_plant\_Open \mathrel{\widehat=} Constant(1)$
$tank\_plant\_Close \mathrel{\widehat=} Constant(-1)$

$$\begin{array}{|l}
\multicolumn{1}{l}{__ tank_plant __} \\
gate : \mathbb{T} \rightarrow \mathbb{R} \\
switch : tank_plant_switch \\
Open : tank_plant_Open \\
Close : tank_plant_Close \\
flow : \mathbb{T} \rightarrow \mathbb{R} \\
\hline
Open.Out = switch.In_1 \wedge gate = switch.In_2 \\
Close.Out = switch.In_3 \wedge switch.Out = flow \\
\hline
\end{array}$$

Water Tank System

$$\begin{array}{|l}
\multicolumn{1}{l}{__ tank __} \\
plant : tank_plant \\
detector : tank_detector \\
controller : tank_controller \\
\hline
plant.flow = detector.in \\
detector.out = controller.water \\
controller.gate = plant.gate \\
\hline
\end{array}$$

Reducing Model Checking of the Few to the One

E. Allen Emerson[1,⋆], Richard J. Trefler[2,⋆⋆], and Thomas Wahl[1,⋆]

[1] Department of Computer Sciences and Computer Engineering Research Center,
The University of Texas, Austin/TX 78712, USA
[2] David R. Cheriton School of Computer Science,
University of Waterloo, Waterloo/Ontario N2L 3G1, Canada
{emerson, wahl}@cs.utexas.edu, trefler@uwaterloo.ca

Abstract. Verification of parameterized systems for an arbitrary number of instances is generally undecidable. Existing approaches resort to non-trivial restrictions on the system or lack automation. In practice, applications can often provide a suitable bound on the parameter size. We propose a new technique toward the bounded formulation of parameterized reasoning: how to efficiently verify properties of a family of systems over a *large finite* parameter range. We show how to accomplish this with a single verification run on a model that aggregates the individual instances. Such a run takes significantly less time than if the systems were considered one by one. Our method is applicable to a completely inhomogeneous family of systems, where properties may not even be preserved across instances. In this case the method exposes the parameter values for which the verification fails. If symmetry is present in the systems, it is inherited by the aggregate representation, allowing for verification over a reduced model. Our technique is fully automatic and requires no approximation.

1 Introduction

Model checking is an algorithmic technique for the verification of programs with respect to temporal logic specifications [QS82, CE81]. It is suitable for systems representable by a finite model, which includes many safety-critical applications such as flight-controllers. The method is successfully applied in industry to technical protocols, to computer hardware, and also, more recently, to software.

In practice, many systems are composed of replicated components. Examples include communication and cache coherence protocols, where the components are concurrent processes, and hardware designs, where the components are black-box pieces of logic, such as memory units. To allow for re-usability, descriptions of such systems are usually parameterized by the number of components. The *parameterized verification problem* is to decide whether a given property holds for all (i.e. infinitely many) instances of the size parameter. Due to its broad nature, this problem is generally undecidable [AK86].

⋆ Authors supported in part by NSF grants CCR-009-8141 and CCR-020-5483.
⋆⋆ Author supported in part by grants from NSERC of Canada and Nortel Networks.

Z. Liu and J. He (Eds.): ICFEM 2006, LNCS 4260, pp. 94–113, 2006.

There are two principle ways of approaching parameterized verification algorithmically. One is to identify decidable subclasses of parameterized systems. To this end, many authors quite heavily restrict both the systems and the properties [CGB86, CG87, EK00, see also sections 8 and 9], and give more or less efficiently verifiable conditions under which these properties hold for all instances. The other way is to realize that it is often possible and sufficient to consider a bound on the parameter size. Some applications suggest such a bound themselves, for example the number of components that fit on a particular circuit board. In other cases, verification engineers may find a correctness result that holds for a large number of components acceptable if all-inclusive parameterized techniques cannot handle their design.

In this paper, we propose a new approach to *bounded* parameterized verification. The goal is to verify—automatically and efficiently—temporal logic properties of an arbitrary parameterized system for a large finite range of values of the parameter. Of course, this can be accomplished (in an unsophisticated way) by analyzing the individual systems one by one, ignoring their common origin. This approach quickly becomes inefficient if the range for the parameter is non-trivial: in each run, both the modeling step and the verification are repeated, perhaps with only minor changes.

To address these shortcomings, we present a simple but effective technique to merge all instances in the given finite range into a single *aggregate* structure capable of simulating all systems from the range in one fell swoop. States of small systems (with few components) can be embedded in states of larger systems. The key in our approach is that we annotate each such embedding in a space-efficient way with the number of components in the embedded state, thereby making the merging lossless. Symbolic data structures such as BDDs (see section 2.2) can then be used to explore the aggregate structure in only little more time than (sometimes the same time as) it takes to traverse the largest of the original structures. This compares well to the cumulative time to analyze *all* structures one by one.

It is not obvious that the aggregate method outperforms the naive one. In fact, our findings seem to contradict the principle of decomposing large systems into small, verifiable units, and then re-composing the results into a final report. The reason why in our case aggregation outperforms decomposition is that the components—here: instances of a parameterized system—are of similar form, suitable for a monolithic model. Moreover, we exert the power of *symbolic data structures* to compactly represent a large number of similar structures, at a cost much less than the sum of the costs to describe the individual entities.

The suggested method is applicable to an arbitrary, *inhomogeneous*, finite system family, irrespective of any restrictions on the syntax of the system description or property. Given this much flexibility, it is well possible that the property under investigation is true for some but not for all instances, i.e. formulas may not be preserved across system sizes. In such cases, most traditional parameterized techniques are unlikely to be useful (see comments in [CGB86]; an exception is [KM89]). In contrast, our technique is capable of reporting the exact set of parameter values for which the property is incorrect, still with a single verification run. This provides an invaluable hint for debugging.

In the second part of the paper, we consider the special case of *symmetric*, i.e. more homogeneous, families. We show that the aggregate representation of all instances M_n by a single one, M, preserves the symmetry. Permutations, commonly used to formalize symmetry, are restricted to those that respect the special format of the states in the aggregate structure. We then demonstrate that with a careful encoding of M, this restriction can be ignored in an implementation: existing symmetry reduction algorithms can be applied without any changes. We emphasize that even though for homogeneous systems full parameterized verification *may* apply, a front-end is still required that checks whether the given system conforms to the imposed restrictions. Furthermore, this check may very well turn out negative, since symmetry alone is not enough. None of this is of any concern with our method.

In summary, we view our approach as a complement to parameterized verification, which is generally intractable. The proposed method trades the benefit of solving the verification problem for infinitely many instances of a system, in exchange for greatly enhanced practicability. Indeed, the technique does not require any manual reasoning, imposes no restrictions on the input syntax, and is easy to implement. We document its efficacy by experimental results in section 8.

2 Background

The following paragraphs contain some basic material about symbolic model checking and temporal logics; the reader familiar with these topics is invited to skip ahead to section 3.

2.1 Model Checking and Temporal Logic

Model checking requires that the system under investigation be expressed as a finite-state model, and that the desired properties be written in a temporal logic that is understood by the model checker at hand. Formally, a model M consists, at a minimum, of a finite set of states, S, and a transition relation, R. The set of states is usually obtained as the set of all possible valuations of system variables. R is a relation in order to allow modeling non-determinism. Finally, sometimes we also explicitly define a labeling function, L, which provides the "glue" between the model and the properties to be verified: it assigns to each state atomic properties that are true at that state, such as "error state" or "initial state". These *atomic propositions*, forming a set AP, are used as atoms in temporal logic formulas. Summarizing, given a finite set S, we have $R \subset S \times S$ and L: $S \to 2^{AP}$.

Popular temporal logics used for the specification of program properties are (enhanced versions of) LTL [Pnu77] and CTL [EC82]. Both logics can be thought of as propositional logic extended by operators related to the evolving nature of programs through states. More precisely, LTL features temporal operators such as X, F, and G, which express that their argument is true in the next state, in some future state, and in all future states, respectively. CTL, on the other hand, has operators characterizing both temporal and branching behavior of programs, such as AX, EF, AG, which express that their argument is true in all successors of the current state, in some future state along some execution path, and in all future states along all execution paths, respectively. For example, the LTL formula GF *executed* states that with respect to the current state, the atomic predicate *executed* is always (G)eventually (F) true, i.e. infinitely often. The CTL formula EF *sorted* states that along some execution path of the program, at some point the predicate *sorted* will be true (we say the predicate is *reachable*). Neither of the two logics subsumes the other; the quite powerful logic CTL* is a superset of LTL ∪ CTL. A formal treatment of these logics is beyond the scope of this paper; plenty of literature is available on these topics [Eme90].

Both the system model and the temporal logic properties are presented to a model checker. Given sufficient resources, the result is either a confirmation of the satisfaction of the property with respect to the model, or a failure, in which case often a counter example can be presented. Assuming the property is a desirable one, the counter example is used in debugging the system.

2.2 Symbolic Model Checking

A phenomenon impacting the usability of model checking in practice is the *state explosion problem*, referring to the fact that the state space of a system is often exponentially larger than its description. One successful approach to combat this problem is *symbolic model checking* [McM93]. The idea is that instead of representing the system model $M = (S, R)$ using sets that enumerate the states and transitions, S and R can also be expressed as boolean formulas. For example, the formula $x = 4 \wedge y = 3$ succinctly represents the set of states where x has the value 4 and y the value 3 (with other variables' values unspecified). A formula over current-state and next-state variables can be used to express the effect of a transition. For instance, $next(x) = x + 1$ represents the assignment $x := x + 1$.

Once states and transitions are modeled as boolean formulas, a data structure is needed to encode these formulas. In its original form [McM93], symbolic model checking was implemented using *binary decision diagrams* (BDDs) [Bry86]; today alternative structures are used as well. BDDs can represent many practically occurring systems succinctly, although for some they are provably unsuitable, for instance those involving non-linear arithmetic. One disadvantage of BDDs is that the degree of conciseness depends on quite a few parameters, many of which can only be determined experimentally. An advantage that makes them blend nicely with model checking is canonicity: for a fixed set of parameters, every propositional formula has a unique BDD representation. This facilitates termination detection in model checking routines.

3 Preliminaries

The parameterized systems we consider consist of replicated components, i.e. collections of processes whose behavior is described by a single program. The program can have shared variables; each process is characterized at any time by its local state. We present such programs using the graph-like notation of *synchronization skeletons* [CE81]. Local states are shown as nodes in the graph, transitions as edges. As an example, consider a token-ring solution to the n-process Mutual Exclusion problem with a shared variable $tok \in [1..n]$, and the skeleton in figure 1.

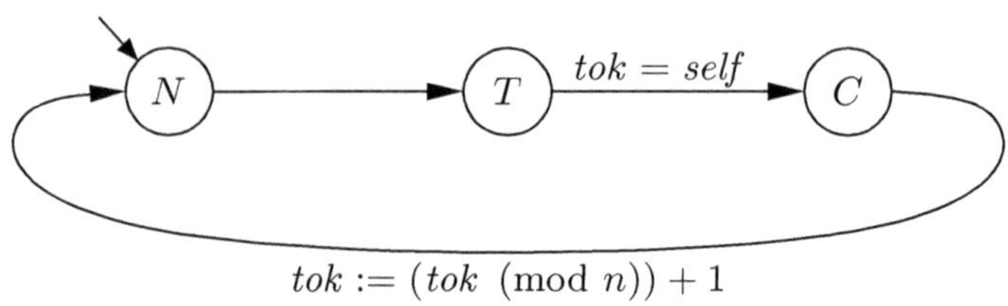

Fig. 1. Synchronization skeleton for a token version of the Mutual Exclusion problem

A skeleton's arcs can be labeled with guards (shown in the figure above the arc) and actions (shown below the arc). Guards are boolean-valued expressions on local states of processes and shared variables. Actions are assignments to shared variables. The actions are executed after the local state change. The skeleton in figure 1 allows a process to enter its critical section C if it currently possesses the token ($tok = self$). Upon leaving C, it passes the token on to the next process.

A synchronization skeleton gives rise to a system of n concurrent processes in the obvious way. To keep the notation simple, we omit shared variables from our state description for now. (Their presence is mostly immaterial to the techniques developed in this paper, as we will discuss in section 9.) A global state s is thus a tuple $(s^1, \ldots, s^n)$ of local states of processes; transitions do not have actions associated with them. Given two states s and t, let the notation $s^i \xrightarrow{g} t^i \in \mathit{SKEL}$ express that there is an edge in the skeleton from a node labeled s^i to a node labeled t^i such that s satisfies guard g. The transition relation R_n of the n-process concurrent system is defined as

$$R_n = \Big\{(s,t) : \exists i : i \leq n : \Big(s^i \xrightarrow{g} t^i \in \mathit{SKEL} \;\wedge\; \forall j : j \neq i : s^j = t^j\Big)\Big\}. \quad (1)$$

In practice, the behavior of the processes will rarely be given as a synchronization skeleton, but perhaps in a programming language. Deriving a skeleton from a program is fairly straightforward: each valuation of all local process variables defines a local state; local atomic computation of a process (such as assignments to local variables) is abstracted into a single transition.

4 The Aggregate System

The goal of this paper is to develop an approach to parameterized verification that works for any bounded family of systems derived from a synchronization skeleton parameterized by the number n of processes, and arbitrary CTL* properties. Let l be the number of local states occurring in the skeleton and AP be a set of atomic propositions to be used in temporal logic formulas. The skeleton gives rise to a family $(M_n)_{n\in\mathbb{N}}$ of Kripke structures with $M_n = (S_n, R_n, L_n)$. With R_n as in (1), we have

$$S_n = [0..(l-1)]^n, \quad R_n \subset S_n \times S_n, \quad L_n\colon S_n \to 2^{AP}.$$

Let now N be an integer specifying the maximum number of processes we are interested in, i.e. we consider $n \leq N$. We will represent all systems $M_1..M_N$ in a single *aggregate* structure by forming their disjoint union, in the following sense. A state of a particular instance M_n is given by the local states of n processes, which can be embedded in a local state vector of length N. In order to be able to recognize the state as a member of M_n, we fill the remaining $N-n$ vector positions with a fresh local state symbol, say \$. Every state vector is thus a sequence of non-\$ symbols followed by a sequence of \$ symbols. Intuitively, a process resides in local state \$ if its index is outside the range of the system to which the global state belongs.

Formally, we define a new Kripke structure $M = (S, R, L)$ over the state space $S = [0..l]^N$. Every state in S is a vector of length N over $l+1$ local states. The embedding of the systems M_n in M is achieved as follows.

Definition 1. *For $n \leq N$, the* completion *of a state $s_n = (s^1, \ldots, s^n) \in S_n$ and of an edge $(s_n, t_n) \in R_n$, respectively, are defined as*

$$c(s^1, \ldots, s^n) = (s^1, \ldots, s^n, \underbrace{\$, \ldots, \$}_{N-n}) \in S, \quad c(s_n, t_n) = (c(s_n), c(t_n)) \in R. \tag{2}$$

The completion of sets of states and sets of transitions is defined pointwise.

The completion upgrades states and transitions to members of the aggregate structure. We call a state $s \in S$ *proper* if there exists a number n such that s is of the form $(s^1, \ldots, s^n, \$, \ldots, \$)$, $s^j \neq \$$ for all $j \in [1..n]$. If s is proper, this number n is unique, called the *width* of proper state s. A state is proper of width n exactly if it is the completion of some state in S_n.

We are now ready to define the transition relation of the aggregate system:

$$R = \bigcup_{n\leq N} c(R_n). \tag{3}$$

R can be viewed as the disjoint union of the R_n, the disjointness being guaranteed by the fresh local state symbol \$. This definition ensures that the aggregate structure allows only proper paths, in the following sense.

Property 2. *For $(s,t) \in R$, both s and t are proper and have the same width.*

Corollary 3. *All states along non-empty paths in the aggregate structure M are proper and have the same width.*

Finally, the labeling function L of M is defined as follows.

$$L(s^1, \ldots, s^N) = \begin{cases} L_n(s^1, \ldots, s^n) & \text{if } (s^1, \ldots, s^N) \text{ is proper of some width } n \\ \emptyset & \text{otherwise.} \end{cases} \tag{4}$$

We remark that L is well-defined since the width of a proper state is unique.

5 Efficiently Constructing the Aggregate System

In this section we illustrate how to efficiently implement the system representation outlined before with symbolic data structures such as BDDs. The main result will be that building a BDD for the aggregate R differs only slightly from building a BDD for any R_n.

The first step is to make sure there is enough space to accommodate the additional $(l + 1)$st local state, for each process. Representing state space S requires $\lceil \log(l + 1) \rceil$ bits per process, which is equal to $\lceil \log l \rceil$ bits unless l happens to be a power of 2. Hence, S can often be represented with no more bits than the largest of the original state spaces, S_N. When l is a power of 2, the number of bits increases by 1 per process, compared with S_N.

Second, how do we implement the transition relation R? Equation (3) is suitable for proving theorems about the aggregate system, but not for implementing R, because it refers to the individual relations R_n, which we want to circumvent. Fortunately, there exists a different characterization of R, paving the way for a better solution.

Theorem 4. *Let the family of systems $(S_n, R_n)_{n \leq N}$ be given as a synchronization skeleton. Then*

$$\bigcup_{n \leq N} c(R_n) = \{(s, t) : s \textit{ is proper of some width } n, \textit{ and} \\ \exists i : i \leq n : \left(s^i \xrightarrow{g} t^i \in \mathit{SKEL} \;\wedge\; \forall j : j \neq i : s^j = t^j\right)\} \tag{5}$$

(In the expression $s^i \xrightarrow{g} t^i \in \mathit{SKEL}$, guard g is evaluated over $(s^1, \ldots, s^n)$.)

Proof.

"⇒": Let $(s, t) \in c(R_n)$. Then by the definition of *completion*, s is proper of width n, and $((s^1, \ldots, s^n), (t^1, \ldots, t^n)) \in R_n$. By equation (1), there exists an index i with the property required in (5).

"⇐": Consider (s, t). From (1) and the second line in (5), we conclude $((s^1, \ldots, s^n), (t^1, \ldots, t^n)) \in R_n$. From the properness of s, we conclude $s^k = \$$ and hence $t^k = \$$ for $k > n$. Thus, $c(s^1, \ldots, s^n) = s$, similarly for t, and therefore $(s, t) \in c(R_n)$. □

Discussion. This theorem provides the ingredients for an efficient implementation of R. The left side of equation (5) is identical to the expression defining R in (3). The right side of (5) is almost identical to the right side of (1), which defines the transition relation R_n of a single system. The only difference is the requirement that s be proper. The reason for this requirement is that the width of a proper source state tells us the number n of processes in the system instance that contains the state. This number is needed when a guard or an action of a skeleton edge refer to it. An example is a guard like $\forall i : s^i = T$, where n determines the range for i. Another example is the action $tok := (tok \pmod{n}) + 1$, where n determines the value at which the token is reset to 1.

To implement R, we divide the skeleton edges in two classes: those that are independent of the system size n, such as the edge $N \to T$ in figure 1, and those that depend on n. For the former class, we simply translate every edge as if it was an edge of the largest system, M_N. For the latter class, we need an additional loop that iterates through the possible system sizes; see figure 2. In the figure, $e(p)$ stands for the propositional formula representing the system size independent skeleton edge e executed by process p. Similarly, $e(p, n)$ stands for the formula representing edge e executed by p in system M_n. The term $\mathit{proper}(n)$ in line 8 symbolizes the set of proper states of width n (expressed in current-state variables). It ensures that transition $e(p, n)$ can only be executed from a state that belongs to M_n. (The computation of $\mathit{proper}(n)$ can of course be pulled out of the loop beginning in line 6.)

1. $R := \emptyset$;
2. **for** $p := 1$ **to** N **do**:
3.   **for** every edge e independent of the system size:
4. $R := R \vee e(p)$
5. **for** $n := 1$ **to** N **do**:
6.   **for** $p := 1$ **to** n **do**:
7.   **for** every edge e dependent on the system size:
8. $R := R \vee (\mathit{proper}(n) \wedge e(p, n))$

Fig. 2. Implementation of the aggregate transition relation R

We can see that for the second class of edges, the number of systems N we consider enters the complexity directly. We remark, however, that the majority of the edges in a skeleton defining a parameterized system usually belong to the first class, since dependence of transitions on the system size tends to destroy the regular system structure. Moreover, quite frequently edges that seem to depend on n can be rewritten such that the dependence goes away. Consider a conjunctive guard of the general form $\forall i : h(i)$. In the context of the aggregate structure, we can think of this guard as expressing the condition that every index i satisfy $h(i)$ *unless* i is greater than the width of the current state (i.e. i is "out-of-scope"). In this case the guard is to be ignored. Thus, the formula can be rewritten as $\forall i : (h(i) \vee s^i = \$)$ over the entire range $[1..N]$, independent of the actual system size. Similarly, disjunctive guards $\exists i : h(i)$ can be rewritten as $\exists i : h(i) \wedge i \neq \$$.

Finally, consider a system in which no edge depends on the system size. In this case, equation (5) can essentially be replaced by (1). In particular, the properness requirement need not be enforced in source or target states in R, since properness is propagated from the initial states during model checking (see next paragraph how proper initial states are constructed). In other words, it is then $R = R_N$, making the solution space-optimal. Although this exact situation may be rare in practice, it shows the asymptotic complexity of our technique as the number of dependencies on the system size decreases. We emphasize that our method does not require *checking* for these dependencies a priori—their existence is a matter of efficiency, not effectiveness.

Implementing the labeling function L amounts to computing sets of states labeled with a particular atomic proposition. As an example, suppose I is a distinguished initial local state. For any n, this entails an initial global state of M_n with components $s^1 = \ldots = s^n = I$. According to (4), we can aggregate the initial states of all systems M_n into the following set of initial states of M:

$$\begin{array}{rl} 1. & (I, \$, \$, \ldots, \$) \\ 2. & (I, I, \$, \ldots, \$) \\ & \vdots \\ N. & (I, I, I, \ldots, I) \end{array}$$

A BDD for this set can efficiently be derived from the set P of proper states using the formula $P \wedge \forall i : i \leq N : (s^i = I \vee s^i = \$)$. The BDD representing the set of proper states of a certain width n has no more nodes than there are bits used to represent a state. It is computed with a loop over all conceivable indices $1, \ldots, N$. Indices greater than n are constrained to be equal to \$, all others are constrained to be different from \$. The set of *all* proper states (of any width) can be obtained as the union over sets of proper states of a specific width. These BDDs are all small in practice and have to be computed only once.

6 Verifying the Aggregate System

We are now ready to realize the main goal of this paper: to reduce the verification of all systems up to size N to the verification of the aggregate system M. We accomplish this by establishing N bisimulations, one between each M_n and M, which contain pairs of a state and its completion:

Lemma 5. *For any $n \leq N$, the relation $s_n \in S_n \sim c(s_n) \in S$ is a bisimulation relation between structures M_n and M.*

Proof. Let $s_n = (s^1, \ldots, s^n) \in S_n$, hence $c(s_n) = (s^1, \ldots, s^n, \$, \ldots, \$) \in S$. (i) By the definition of the labeling function L, we have $L(c(s_n)) = L_n(s_n)$, since $c(s_n)$ is proper of width n. (ii) For t_n such that $(s_n, t_n) \in R_n$, we have $t_n \sim c(t_n)$. Since $(s_n, t_n) \in R_n$, we get $(c(s_n), c(t_n)) = c(s_n, t_n) \in c(R_n) \subset R$ by (3). (iii) Conversely, consider some $t \in S$ such that $(c(s_n), t) \in R$. By (3), there exists $m \leq N$ such that $(c(s_n), t) \in c(R_m)$. From $c(s_n) \in c(S_m)$, we derive $m = n$, hence $t \in c(S_n)$. This allows us to conclude the existence of t_n with $c(t_n) = t$, thus $(c(s_n), c(t_n)) \in c(R_n)$ and $(s_n, t_n) \in R_n$. □

We point out that structures M_n and M are not bisimilar, since there is in general no way to define an initial state of M such that for every n, the initial states of M_n and M are bisimilar (if there was, the M_n would all be bisimilar to each other by transitivity). All we can say is that M *simulates* each of the M_n. For our purposes, however, lemma 5 is strong enough (relation $\sim$ is rich enough) to prove that a property true of all individual systems M_n is also true of the aggregate system M, and vice versa. For $n \leq N$, let $s_n \in S_n$ be the state of M_n with respect to which the property is to hold, and define

$$\Sigma = \{c(s_n) \in S : n \leq N\}.$$

All states $c(s_n)$ are proper and thus suitable as a start state of a path in M. We can now formulate the main result of this section:

Theorem 6. *Let f be a CTL* formula, and s_n, Σ as above. Then*

$$\forall n : n \leq N : M_n, s_n \models f \quad \textit{iff} \quad \forall s : s \in \Sigma : M, s \models f. \tag{6}$$

Proof. We exploit that structures with a bisimulation relation between them satisfy the same CTL* formulas with respect to bisimilar states.

$\Rightarrow$: Given $s \in \Sigma$, let s_n such that $s = c(s_n)$. Then $s_n \sim s$. Further $M_n, s_n \models f$ as given, and hence $M, s \models f$ follows with lemma 5.

$\Leftarrow$: Given $n \leq N$, we have $M, s \models f$ for $s = c(s_n) \in \Sigma$. Since $s_n \sim c(s_n)$, the claim $M_n, s_n \models f$ follows with lemma 5. □

Discussion. Theorem 6 can be viewed as identifying a claim of the form "for all numbers n: ..." and a claim of the form "for all states s: ...". The latter is suitable to be approached with symbolic data structures that reason over sets of states, such as BDDs. Indeed, if BDD_f denotes the set of states of M that satisfy formula f, then the condition on the right of equation (6) is equivalent to $\Sigma \subset BDD_f$.

We remark that the meaning of formula f implicitly depends on n, namely through the labeling functions L_n. These may assign a given atomic proposition to "different" (even after completion) states in different systems; thus $\mathsf{EF}\, q$ may mean different things depending on the system.

How do negative verification results over M relate to the family of structures $(M_n)_{n \leq N}$? Assume the proof of $\forall s : s \in \Sigma : M, s \models f$ (right side of (6)) fails. Then there exists a non-empty set $F \subset \Sigma$ of states s such that $M, s \not\models f$. By the definition of Σ, all states in F are proper; the set $width(F) = \{width(s) : s \in F\}$ contains precisely the parameter values pointing to the delinquent systems. This set can give valuable information for debugging; section 8 presents an example of this phenomenon. Moreover, consider a particular $n \in width(F)$. If the failed verification of f over M admits a counterexample path, say p, then p can be mapped to a path in M_n by projecting every state along p to the first n components. The result is a valid counterexample path in M_n, due to the bisimulation between the structures: the two paths *correspond*.

Another consequence of the path correspondence is that the diameter and the girth of Kripke structure M, i.e. the distance between its most distant nodes and the length of its longest simple path, respectively, are equal to the maximum diameter, resp. girth, of any of the M_n. These numbers are important complexity measures in symbolic model checking. For example, the diameter is an upper bound on the number of image computations it takes for reachability analysis to converge. As a result, the time complexity of model checking the CTL formula $\mathsf{EF}\, \mathit{bad}$ over M, measured in number of image steps, is equal to the maximum time complexity, over all structures M_n, of model checking this formula over M_n.

7 Families of Symmetric Systems

In this section we briefly review *symmetry reduction* in model checking and then demonstrate that the aggregate system inherits contingent symmetry from the individual systems. We conclude by showing how to efficiently exploit the (slightly non-standard) symmetry in the aggregate with literally no change to existing symmetry reduction algorithms.

7.1 Symmetries in Kripke Structures

A Kripke structure $M = (S, R)$ modeling a system of n concurrently executing processes is said to be *(fully) symmetric* if the transition relation R is immune to permutations. More precisely, let Sym_n be the group of permutations on $[1..n]$ and let $\pi \in \mathit{Sym}_n$ act on a state $s \in S$ in the form $\pi(s^1, \ldots, s^n) = (s^{\pi(1)}, \ldots, s^{\pi(n)})$, i.e. by permuting the process indices. Then, M is symmetric if for every $\pi \in \mathit{Sym}_n$ the condition $R = \pi(R)$ holds, i.e. [CEFJ96]

$$(s,t) \in R \quad \text{iff} \quad (\pi(s), \pi(t)) \in R. \tag{7}$$

Intuitively, a system is symmetric if its set of transitions remains invariant when the participating processes are renamed. A structure induced by a synchronization skeleton is a promising candidate for symmetry, since all processes execute the same parameterized program. This fact alone, however, is insufficient: guards and actions on local state transitions can depend on the identity of the executing process in a way that limits or destroys the otherwise apparent symmetry. For instance, the action $\mathit{tok} := (\mathit{tok} \pmod n) + 1$ of the skeleton in figure 1 permits only the n rotation permutations and thus inhibits full symmetry. Some conditions can be placed on the skeleton to guarantee that the derived structure is indeed symmetric; see [EW03] for a possible strategy. In this section, we assume such conditions are satisfied.

The *orbit relation* $s \equiv t$ iff $\exists \pi : \pi(s) = t$ is an equivalence relation on the state space; based on it a quotient $\bar{M} = (\bar{S}, \bar{R})$ of M can be constructed in the usual style of existential abstraction: $\bar{S}$ is a set of unique representatives of the equivalence classes (*orbits*), and

$$\bar{R} = \{(\bar{s}, \bar{t}) : \exists s \equiv \bar{s}, t \equiv \bar{t} : (s,t) \in R\}. \tag{8}$$

Given an appropriate set of atomic propositions that respect the equivalence classes, the quotient turns out to be bisimulation equivalent to the original M. Any CTL* formula over such atomic propositions can thus be verified over the smaller $\bar{M}$ instead of over M. Technical details of symmetry reduction are available in the literature [ES96, CEFJ96].

7.2 Uniformly Symmetric Systems

Intuitively, due to the strong correspondence between the given system family $(M_n)_{n \le N}$ and the aggregate M, one might expect that symmetry *uniformly* present in all of the M_n carries over to M. In proving this conjecture, one encounters the difficulty that the M_n have different numbers of replicated components. Thus permutations act on different sets of indices and cannot be compared across the M_n or related to M. A unifying solution is to let permutations from Sym_N act on all states, even with less than N components, after upgrading the states to dimension N using the completion operator. This step introduces the \$ symbol into the state, which, due to its special meaning, requires special treatment: we have to make sure permutations preserve the properness of a state. Otherwise, a transition between proper states could be permuted into a pair of improper states (by definition not a transition). We therefore first define a restricted permutation action, as follows.

Definition 7. *For any $\pi \in Sym_N$ and $s \in S$, define*

$$\pi[s] = \begin{cases} \pi(s) & \text{if } s \text{ is proper of some width } n \\ & \text{and } \forall i : i > n : \pi(i) = i \\ s & \text{otherwise,} \end{cases} \tag{9}$$

where as usual $\pi(s) = \pi(s^1, \ldots, s^N) = (s^{\pi(1)}, \ldots, s^{\pi(N)})$. This definition extends in the pointwise fashion to transitions and to sets of states and transitions. It can be shown that the relation $s \equiv t$ iff $\exists \pi : \pi[s] = t$ is an equivalence. The condition $\forall i : i > n : \pi(i) = i$ guarantees that no value i is permuted across the boundary between n and $n+1$. Since $s^i = \$$ for all $i > n$ in a proper state s, it is irrelevant how permutations act on such i, as long as they respect this boundary. The weaker condition $\forall i : i > n : \pi(i) > n$ has the same effect. Regarding the "otherwise" case of (9), note that it applies not only to improper states, but also to proper states for which π violates the boundary.

Property 8. *For any $\pi \in Sym_N$ and $s \in S$, s is proper if and only if $\pi[s]$ is proper. If both proper, they have the same width.*

Proof. If s is improper, then $\pi[s] = s$, so $\pi[s]$ is also improper. If s is proper, but π violates the properness boundary, then again $\pi[s] = s$, so $\pi[s]$ is proper. Otherwise, with n as in (9), $\pi(i) = i > n$ for all $i > n$, hence $s^{\pi(i)} = \$$. Due to bijectivity of π, we have $\pi(i) \le n$ for all $i \le n$, hence $s^{\pi(i)} \ne \$$, so $\pi[s]$ is proper; the claim of property 8 about the same width is immediate. □

We now define the notion of uniform symmetry for a parameterized system. In order to overcome the technical barrier that permutations acting on different systems have different domains, we use once again completions.

Definition 9. *The family* $(M_n)_{n \leq N}$ *of systems is called* uniformly symmetric *if*

$$\forall n : n \leq N : \forall \pi : \pi \in Sym_N : \ \pi[c(R_n)] = c(R_n). \tag{10}$$

It is easy to see that $(M_n)_{n \leq N}$ is uniformly symmetric exactly if each system M_n satisfies $\pi(R_n) = R_n$ for all permutations on $[1..n]$. Definition 9 provides a closed formulation of this fact and refers to only a single permutation group, Sym_N. This makes reasoning about uniformly symmetric systems convenient. We point out that in equation (10), permutations $\pi[\cdot]$ act according to equation (9), whereas in the expression $\pi(R_n) = R_n$, they act in the standard fashion; there is no notion of proper states in individual systems.

The main result in this section relates symmetry in the M_n and in M:

Theorem 10. *If* $(M_n)_{n \leq N}$ *is uniformly symmetric, then* M *is fully symmetric.*

Proof. Let an arbitrary $\pi \in Sym_N$ be given; we show $\pi[R] = R$:

$$\pi[R] \overset{(3)}{=} \pi\left[\bigcup_{n \leq N} c(R_n)\right] \overset{(*)}{=} \bigcup_{n \leq N} \pi[c(R_n)] \overset{(10)}{=} \bigcup_{n \leq N} c(R_n) \overset{(3)}{=} R,$$

where $(*)$ follows from function application distributing over finite set union. □

Using this result, it remains to show that the quotient of M with respect to the orbit equivalence relation $\equiv$ and the special permutation action from equation (9) is bisimulation equivalent to M, so that we can verify CTL* properties over the quotient without losing information. This proof is similar to the argument used in standard symmetry reduction, provides no new insights and is thus omitted here.

7.3 Symmetry-Reducing the Aggregate System

Looking at the somewhat ungainly equation (9) defining permutation action, one might suspect that exploiting the symmetry in the aggregate system is more difficult or less efficient since only certain permutations can be effectively applied to a state. In the rest of this section, we will show that such is not the case: restricting permutations in this way preserves the quotient size.

Symmetry reduction algorithms proceed by mapping an encountered state s to a unique representative of its equivalence class $orbit(s)$ with respect to the orbit relation [CEFJ96, ID99]. A common choice for the representative is the orbit's lexicographically least element, $\min_{\text{lex}}(orbit(s))$, given some total order $\leq_L$ on the local states. For example, in a 3-process system with local states A and B, the global states (A, A, B), (A, B, A) and (B, A, A) form an orbit, which can be represented by the lexicographically least of the three states, (A, A, B). We demonstrate in the following that such representatives can be computed without worrying about the special permutation action introduced in (9); instead permutations can be applied in the traditional way, with the same result:

Theorem 11. *Let s be a proper state. Then*

$$\min_{\text{lex}}\{\pi[s] : \pi \in Sym_N\} \;=\; \min_{\text{lex}}\{\pi(s) : \pi \in Sym_N\}. \tag{11}$$

Proof. Let n be the width of s, and let $P_{[s]}$ and $P_{(s)}$ be the two sets in the scope of the $\min_{\text{lex}}$ operator in (11). Then $\min_{\text{lex}} P_{[s]} \geq \min_{\text{lex}} P_{(s)}$ follows from $P_{[s]} \subset P_{(s)}$. To see the subset property, consider an element $\pi[s]$. If $\forall i : i > n : \pi(i) = i$, then $\pi[s] = \pi(s) \in P_{(s)}$. If not, then $\pi[s] = s = id(s) \in P_{(s)}$, for the identity permutation $id \in Sym_N$.

For the converse, let $s = (s^1, \ldots, s^n, \$, \ldots, \$)$. Since, by the choice of the numerical value of the special local state \$, $s^i \leq_L \$$ for all i, the state $\min_{\text{lex}} P_{(s)}$ has the form $m = (m^1, \ldots, m^n, \$, \ldots, \$)$. We have to show that $m \in P_{[s]}$, from which then $\min_{\text{lex}} P_{[s]} \leq m = \min_{\text{lex}} P_{(s)}$ follows. To map the **proper** state s to m, we can choose a permutation π that leaves all i with $i > n$ invariant ($\forall i : i > n : \pi(i) = i$) and only permutes the first n components of s into their lexicographically least arrangement. For this permutation, it is $m = \pi(s) = \pi[s] \in P_{[s]}$. □

Theorem 11 shows that in order to map a proper state s to its orbit representative, there is no need to worry about the special permutation action. The key is, of course, that the local state of out-of-bounds processes, represented by \$, was chosen greater, with respect to the local state order $\leq_L$, than any other local state. Thus, representative mappings never move this symbol to the left in the local state vector and therefore preserve properness of states. As a result, the quotient of M with respect to the restricted permutation action defined in (9) is of the same size (in fact, is the same) as the standard symmetry quotient.

8 Applications

In this section we compare our technique with two alternative methods for verifying parameterized systems: the naive method that simply considers all systems individually ("one-by-one"), and general parameterized model checking approaches. Experimental results are obtained using BDD-based symbolic model checking. In tables, "N" refers to the parameter bound. "Peak Number of BDD Nodes" is the maximum number of BDD nodes live at any point during execution and thus is a measure of the memory requirements of the method. Running times are given in seconds (s), minutes (m), or hours (h), as appropriate. We used the *CUDD* BDD package [Som], with a BDD variable order statically chosen to best-fit each problem. All experiments were performed on a 1.6GHz PC with 512MB of RAM running a variant of the Linux operating system.

8.1 Comparison to the One-by-One Method

The one-by-one method and our aggregate technique have the same theoretical power: they can be used to verify arbitrary parameterized systems up to some finite bound. We show experimental results demonstrating the superiority of our method in terms of efficiency.

The first example, "McsLock", is a model of a queuing lock algorithm [MS91]. It has a shared variable that counts processes in the queue (such counters are disallowed by many fully parameterized techniques). It also has a transition that causes several processes to change their local state simultaneously; this transition depends on the number of components in the system. We show in table 1 how our method scales for an increasing number of components. As can be seen, the BDD size for the transition relation R is only slightly bigger than that for R_N. The benefit of our technique is to reduce the verification time, which it does by more than an order of magnitude for the larger instances, and this factor increases with N.

The second example is a parallel program. Written for a particular cluster of machines, such programs have a natural upper bound on the parameter: the physical number of CPUs in the cluster. Due to the possibility of failures and down-times, such programs are parameterized by the number of available processors. These characteristics make them a suitable application domain for bounded parameterized verification.

We present here a variant of parallel *odd-even sort* [KGGK94]. This algorithm proceeds in rounds; during even rounds processors compare each even-indexed element they own with its right neighbor (which may be owned by the next processor), analogously for odd rounds. The odd-even split ensures mutual exclusion when changing the position of elements. The initial state is unconstrained; the number of elements to be sorted grows with N. The CTL property we verified is of the form AF *sorted*.

The results in table 1 show again clearly the time savings obtained through our method. In contrast to the McsLock example, the BDD for the aggregate happens to be of a form that allows it to be traversed with fewer live BDD nodes compared with the one-by-one technique. Note that the number of live BDD nodes depends strongly on implementation details in the BDD package. On the other hand, the number of nodes of a particular BDD does not, and indeed the sizes of R_N vs. R are as expected. The differences between R_N and R are bigger than with McsLock since the sorting problem is much less homogeneous—individual transition relations depend a lot on the instance size.

8.2 Comparison to PMC Approaches

If applicable, successful approaches to parameterized model checking (PMC) (see e.g. [Lub84, GS92, many others]) have the clear advantage that they show correctness for all sizes. Interestingly, the bounded and unbounded formulations of PMC synergize when unbounded techniques reduce the correctness for infinitely many instances to correctness up to some finite *cutoff*. This cutoff depends on

Table 1. Comparison one-by-one and aggregate verification method

N	One-by-one method for $n \in [1..N]$ BDD Size of R_N	Peak Number of BDD Nodes	Time	Aggregation method for N BDD Size of R	Peak Number of BDD Nodes	Time
McsLock (N = number of processes):						
5	924	19,165	2.4s	958	19,176	0s
10	2,012	384,449	1:30m	2,057	384,796	53s
15	3,082	1,797,874	39:08m	3,147	1,797,711	15:17m
20	4,173	5,142,717	6:23h	4,346	5,142,890	1:50h
Parallel Sorting (N = number of parallel processors):						
5	962	37,699	3s	2,021	26,106	3s
7	1,614	144,111	52s	3,643	90,249	30s
10	2,881	673,727	21m	6,911	371,529	7m
13	4,450	2,190,163	3:30h	11,129	1,099,196	54m

the communication complexity of the parameterized system and is not guaranteed to be small [EK00, BHV03, CMP04]. Our method can therefore be used as a follow-up to cutoff-based approaches, picking up the task of verifying the remaining finite-size family.

The disadvantage of unbounded methods is that, targeting a generally undecidable problem, a fully automated solution that works for any input system does not exist. Many authors forfeit completeness by imposing restrictions on the input syntax in order to allow an algorithmic solution. In an early work, Clarke, Grumberg and Browne assume the absence of shared variables [CGB86], which could be used to distinguish the number of components. The McsLock example discussed above contains such a shared counter variable. Counters may also occur in dynamic systems that monitor the number of active components, for instance for performance reasons. Interestingly, if an "energy-saving" mode of operation has a bug, the dynamic system may be correct for a large number of processes, but not for a small one.

The logic used in [CGB86] also bans the next-time operator X and arbitrarily nested $\exists$ and $\forall$ quantifiers over processes indices. This makes some natural properties cumbersome to express, such as deadlock reachability [EK02] or even mutual exclusion [CGB86]. In contrast, our method—being less ambitious—requires no restrictions on the input syntax, and is valid for full CTL* (and even the μ-calculus).

Other approaches sacrifice full automation. In [CG87], the notion of a *closure process* is introduced, whose definition depends on the parameterized system at hand to a degree that seems to undermine mechanization. In [KM89], the authors present a fairly broad induction method to reduce a family of systems to a single system, using an *invariant process*, which enforces a partial order among the processes. Finding such an invariant requires help from the designer and can be non-trivial. The Murφ tool supports replicated components for fully symmetric systems [ID99]. The tool automatically checks whether the given program allows generalizing the verification result to larger systems. The designer, however, is still left with checking the authenticity of returned error traces. Since our method is exact, there is no need to solicit human interaction for path-lifting, or other forms of manual assistance.

Looking back at the parallel sorting example, the Kripke structure derived from this algorithm is asymmetric, since the processors have a translational (non-cyclic) communication pattern. Because of this irregularity and the liveness-type property, we believe that most existing parameterized techniques are not immediately applicable to automatically verify this algorithm correct for all size instances.

Finally, we present the response of our method to situations in which a property is true for some but not all size instances. The sorting procedure requires comparing each processor's final element to the first of the next processor; the last processor must be treated specially. The parity (even/odd) of the final element owned by each processor alternates if the number of elements per processor is odd. It is easy to get the communication of the boundary cases wrong. Below is the output of our method for a version of the algorithm that fails to compare the last two elements of the last processor if the number of processors is odd:

```
Initial states violating "AF sorted" for N=10:
  -   $   $   $   $   $   $   $   $
  -   -   -   $   $   $   $   $   $
  -   -   -   -   -   $   $   $   $
  -   -   -   -   -   -   -   $   $
  -   -   -   -   -   -   -   -   -
```

Here, '$' represents as before the local state of out-of-bounds processors. The values carried by active processors have been abstracted away and replaced by '-' to more conspicuously expose the delinquent systems: The number of '-' in a global state (i.e. in one row) equals the state's width and thus indicates the parameter size of the system. In our case, these sizes are all odd (1, 3, 5, 7, 9), giving a potentially substantial hint as to where the problem lies.

9 Conclusion

In this paper we have shown how to collapse a range of instances derived from an arbitrary parameterized system into a single aggregate, which is detailed enough to be able to simulate each instance. Further, initial states of the original systems can be converted appropriately to states of the aggregate, enabling us to verify arbitrary CTL* properties for all instances up to some finite size in one fell swoop. The large time savings obtained in this manner come at little or no additional space cost, the difference sometimes being masked by the fluctuating performance of BDD-based symbolic model checking procedures. As a special case, if the systems are individually symmetric, then so is the aggregate system, which can thus be symmetry-reduced. Our method can be viewed as, instead of symmetry reducing and verifying all systems individually and then combining the result ("does any of them have an error?"), combining the systems first and then applying the reduction and verification once.

We have presented experimental results using a BDD-based implementation of our technique. We believe the method can likewise be used with SAT-based symbolic verification such as *Bounded Model Checking* (BMC) [BCCZ99]; crucial is the capability to operate on sets of states in one step. We remark on the side that despite the common "bounded", the goals of BMC (investigating bounded time lines over a fixed structure) and of our technique (investigating unbounded time lines over a bounded family of structures) are quite different.

Treatment of shared variables. Shared variables are used for communication and synchronization among processes, and they may appear in atomic propositions of CTL* formulas. Their presence is mostly orthogonal to our techniques. To form the aggregate system M, we distinguish two types of shared variables. Those with range independent of the system size n (such as a boolean semaphore) are introduced into M with the same range. *Id-sensitive* shared variables, i.e. those ranging over process indices and thus with range $[1..n]$ in M_n, are assigned a range of $[1..N]$ in the aggregate structure, equal to their range in structure M_N. An example is the variable *tok* in figure 1 earlier. Regarding the definition of *proper*, a variable like *tok* must be restricted to $[1..n]$ in a proper state of width n, despite the variable's range $[1..N]$ in the aggregate. The *completion* operator leaves the values of all shared variables unchanged.

Other related work. In addition to the results on parameterized verification mentioned in section 8, there are some that make use of the apparent symmetry in systems defined using a single process template. Full symmetry of Kripke structures can be exploited using some form of counters [EN96, ID99], or by appealing to *state symmetry* [ES96] of the property [EN96, EK00]. In contrast, we show how to take advantage of *internal symmetry* of the property and the Kripke structure through a quotient construction.

Future Work. A topic for further investigation is which reductions other than symmetry are preserved during the aggregation. This seems promising since the aggregate *faithfully* simulates the individuals. The success will depend on how much existing reduction algorithms have to be adjusted to work on the aggregate, and how much efficiency and compression is lost as a result of such adjustments.

References

[AK86] Krzysztof R. Apt and Dexter Kozen. Limits for automatic verification of finite-state concurrent systems. *Information Processing Letters (IPL)*, 1986.

[BCCZ99] Armin Biere, Alessandro Cimatti, Edmund M. Clarke, and Yunshan Zhu. Symbolic model checking without bdds. In *Tools and Algorithms for the Construction and Analysis of Systems (TACAS)*, 1999.

[BHV03] Ahmed Bouajjani, Peter Habermehl, and Tomás Vojnar. Verification of parametric concurrent systems with prioritized fifo resource management. In *Concurrency Theory (CONCUR)*, 2003.

[Bry86] Randy E. Bryant. Graph-based algorithms for boolean function manipulation. *IEEE Transactions on Computers*, 1986.

[CE81] Edmund M. Clarke and E. Allen Emerson. The design and synthesis of synchronization skeletons using temporal logic. In *Logic of Programs (LOP)*, 1981.

[CEFJ96] Edmund M. Clarke, Reinhard Enders, Thomas Filkorn, and Somesh Jha. Exploiting symmetry in temporal logic model checking. *Formal Methods in System Design (FMSD)*, 1996.

[CG87] Edmund M. Clarke and Orna Grumberg. Avoiding the state explosion problem in temporal logic model checking. In *Principles of Distributed Computing (PODC)*, 1987.

[CGB86] Edmund M. Clarke, Orna Grumberg, and Michael C. Browne. Reasoning about networks with many identical finite-state processes. In *Principles of Distributed Computing (PODC)*, 1986.

[CMP04] Ching-Tsun Chou, Phanindra K. Mannava, and Seungjoon Park. A simple method for parameterized verification of cache coherence protocols. In *FMCAD*, 2004.

[EC82] E. Allen Emerson and Edmund M. Clarke. Using branching time temporal logic to synthesize synchronization skeletons. *Science of Computer Programming (SOCP)*, 1982.

[EK00] E. Allen Emerson and Vineet Kahlon. Reducing model checking of the many to the few. In *Computer-Aided Design (CAD)*, 2000.

[EK02] E. Allen Emerson and Vineet Kahlon. Model checking large-scale and parameterized resource allocation systems. In *TACAS*, 2002.

[Eme90] Allen E. Emerson. Temporal and model logic. In *Handbook of Theoretical Computer Science*. North-Holland Pub. Co./MIT Press, 1990.

[EN96] E. Allen Emerson and Kedar S. Namjoshi. Automatic verification of parameterized synchronous systems. In *Computer-Aided Verification (CAV)*, 1996.

[ES96] E. Allen Emerson and A. Prasad Sistla. Symmetry and model checking. *Formal Methods in System Design (FMSD)*, 1996.

[EW03] E. Allen Emerson and Thomas Wahl. On combining symmetry reduction and symbolic representation for efficient model checking. In *Conference on Correct Hardware Design and Verification Methods (CHARME)*, 2003.

[GS92] Steven M. German and A. Prasad Sistla. Reasoning about systems with many processes. *Journal of the ACM*, 1992.

[ID99] C. Norris Ip and David L. Dill. Verifying systems with replicated components in Murφ. *Formal Methods in System Design (FMSD)*, 1999.

[KGGK94] Vipin Kumar, Ananth Grama, Anshul Gupta, and George Karypis. *Introduction to Parallel Computing*. Benjamin/Cummings Publishing, 1994.

[KM89] R. P. Kurshan and K. McMillan. A structural induction theorem for processes. In *Principles of distributed computing (PODC)*, 1989.

[Lub84] Boris D. Lubachevsky. An approach to automating the verification of compact parallel coordination programs. *Acta Informatica*, 1984.

[McM93] Kenneth L. McMillan. *Symbolic Model Checking: An Approach to the State Explosion Problem*. Kluwer Academic, 1993.

[MS91] John M. Mellor-Crummey and Michael L. Scott. Algorithms for scalable synchronization on shared-memory multiprocessors. *Transactions on Computer Systems (TOCS)*, 1991.

[Pnu77] Amir Pnueli. The temporal logic of programs. In *FOCS*, 1977.

[QS82] Jean-Pierre Quielle and Joseph Sifakis. Specification and verification of concurrent systems in cesar. In *5th International Symposium on Programming*, 1982.

[Som] Fabio Somenzi. *The CU Decision Diagram Package, release 2.3.1*. University of Colorado at Boulder, `http://vlsi.colorado.edu/~fabio/CUDD/`.

Induction-Guided Falsification

Kazuhiro Ogata, Masahiro Nakano,
Weiqiang Kong, and Kokichi Futatsugi

School of Information Science
Japan Advanced Institute of Science and Technology (JAIST)
{ogata, m-nakano, weiqiang, kokichi}@jaist.ac.jp

Abstract. The induction-guided falsification searches a bounded reachable state space of a transition system for a counterexample that the system satisfies an invariant property. If no counterexamples are found, it tries to verify that the system satisfies the property by mathematical induction on the structure of the reachable state space of the system, from which some other invariant properties may be obtained as lemmas. The verification and falsification process is repeated for each of the properties until a counterexample is found or the verification is completed. The NSPK authentication protocol is used as an example to demonstrate the induction-guided falsification.

Keywords: CafeOBJ, counterexample, induction, invariant, Maude, observational transition system (OTS).

1 Introduction

The OTS/CafeOBJ method [1] is a modeling, specification and verification method. In the method, a system is modeled as an *observational transition system*, or an *OTS*, the OTS is specified in *CafeOBJ* [2], an algebraic specification language, and it is verified that the OTS satisfies a property using the CafeOBJ system as an interactive theorem prover. OTSs are transition systems. Unlike the conventional definition of transition systems, however, the structure of states are not specified explicitly. Instead of use of variables, functions from states to data types are used to obtain the values that characterize states. Such functions are called observers. We have conducted some case studies [3,4,5,6,7,8,9,10] so as to demonstrate the effectiveness of the method and refine the method.

Although CafeOBJ does not have any model checking facilities, *Maude* [11], which is a sibling language of CafeOBJ, is equipped with such facilities. Although the state space of a system to be model checked by Maude does not have to be finite, its reachable state space should be finite. The reachable state space of an OTS is generally infinite, even if the number of some entities such as principals is made finite. Therefore, a way to search a bounded reachable state space of an OTS for a counterexample that the OTS satisfies an invariant property has been proposed [12], which is inspired by *Bounded Model Checking*, or *BMC* [13].

What if no counterexamples that an OTS satisfies an invariant property are found in the bounded reachable state space whose depth is n and the bounded reachable state

Z. Liu and J. He (Eds.): ICFEM 2006, LNCS 4260, pp. 114–131, 2006.

space whose depth is $n + 1$ or more is too large to be exhaustively traversed within a reasonable time? If that is the case, we start verifying that the OTS satisfies the invariant property by mathematical induction on the structure of the reachable state space of the OTS. Some other invariant properties may be obtained as lemmas from the induction. If such invariant properties are obtained, we search the bounded reachable state space whose depth is n for a counterexample that the OTS satisfies each of the invariant properties. If at least one such counterexample is found, the OTS does not satisfy the original invariant property. Otherwise, the verification and falsification process called *the induction-guided falsification* is repeated for each of the invariant properties until a counterexample is found or the verification is completed.

The rest of the paper is organized as follows. Section 2 describes OTSs. Section 3 mentions how to write OTSs in CafeOBJ and Maude. Section 4 outlines how to search a bounded reachable state space of an OTS for a counterexample that the OTS satisfies an invariant property. Sections 5 and 6 describe the induction-guided falsification. Section 7 reports on a case study. The NSPK authentication protocol [14] is used as an example in Sections 3, 4 and 7. Section 8 mentions some related work. Section 9 concludes the paper.

2 Observational Transition Systems (OTSs)

We suppose that there exists a universal state space denoted Υ and that each data type used in OTSs is provided. The data types include Bool for truth values. A data type is denoted D_*.

Definition 1 (OTSs). *An OTS $\mathcal{S}$ [1] is $\langle \mathcal{O}, \mathcal{I}, \mathcal{T} \rangle$ such that*

- $\mathcal{O}$*: A finite set of observers. Each* observer $o_{x_1:D_{o1},\ldots,x_m:D_{om}} : \Upsilon \to D_o$ *is an indexed function that has m indexes $x_1, \ldots, x_m$ whose types are $D_{o1}, \ldots, D_{om}$. The equivalence relation $(v_1 =_\mathcal{S} v_2)$ between two states $v_1, v_2 \in \Upsilon$ is defined as $\forall o_{x_1,\ldots,x_m} : \mathcal{O}. (o_{x_1,\ldots,x_m}(v_1) = o_{x_1,\ldots,x_m}(v_2))$, where $\forall o_{x_1,\ldots,x_m} : \mathcal{O}$ is the abbreviation of $\forall o_{x_1,\ldots,x_m} : \mathcal{O}.\forall x_1 : D_{o1} \ldots \forall x_m : D_{om}$.*
- $\mathcal{I}$*: The set of initial states such that $\mathcal{I} \subseteq \Upsilon$.*
- $\mathcal{T}$*: A finite set of transitions. Each* transition $t_{y_1:D_{t1},\ldots,y_n:D_{tn}} : \Upsilon \to \Upsilon$ *is an indexed function that has n indexes $y_1, \ldots, y_n$ whose types are $D_{t1}, \ldots, D_{tn}$ provided that $t_{y_1,\ldots,y_n}(v_1) =_\mathcal{S} t_{y_1,\ldots,y_n}(v_2)$ for each $[v] \in \Upsilon/{=_\mathcal{S}}$, each $v_1, v_2 \in [v]$ and each $y_k : D_{tk}$ for $k = 1, \ldots, n$. $t_{y_1,\ldots,y_n}(v)$ is called* the successor state *of v with respect to (wrt) $\mathcal{S}$. Each transition $t_{y_1,\ldots,y_n}$ has the condition* $c\text{-}t_{y_1:D_{t1},\ldots,y_n:D_{tn}} : \Upsilon \to$ Bool, *which is called* the effective condition *of the transition. If $c\text{-}t_{y_1,\ldots,y_n}(v)$ does not hold, then $t_{y_1,\ldots,y_n}(v) =_\mathcal{S} v$.* □

Note that although the number of indexed functions is finite, the instances of the indexed functions may be infinite. For example, the number of instances of transition $\text{send1}_{p:\text{Prin},q:\text{Prin}} : \Upsilon \to \Upsilon$ is infinite if Prin is infinite, namely that the number of principals is infinite.

Definition 2 (Reachable states). *Given an OTS $\mathcal{S}$,* reachable states *wrt $\mathcal{S}$ are inductively defined:*

- *Each $\upsilon_{\text{init}} \in \mathcal{I}$ is reachable wrt $\mathcal{S}$.*
- *For each $t_{y_1,\ldots,y_n} \in \mathcal{T}$ and each $y_k : D_{tk}$ for $k = 1\ldots,n$, $t_{x_1,\ldots,x_n}(\upsilon)$ is reachable wrt $\mathcal{S}$ if $\upsilon \in \Upsilon$ is reachable wrt $\mathcal{S}$.*

Let $\mathcal{R}_{\mathcal{S}}$ be the set of all reachable states wrt $\mathcal{S}$. $\mathcal{R}_{\mathcal{S}}$ may be called the reachable state space wrt $\mathcal{S}$. □

Predicates whose types are $\Upsilon \rightarrow$ Bool are called *state predicates*. We suppose that each state predicate includes a finite number of logical connectives. We also suppose that each state predicate p considered in this paper has the form $\forall z_1 : D_{p1} \ldots \forall z_M : D_{pM}.\, P(\upsilon, z_1, \ldots, z_M)$, where $\upsilon, z_1, \ldots, z_M$ are all variables in p and $P(\upsilon, z_1, \ldots, z_M)$ does not contain any quantifiers.

Definition 3 (Invariants). *Any state predicate $p : \Upsilon \rightarrow$ Bool is called* invariant *wrt $\mathcal{S}$ if p holds in all reachable states wrt $\mathcal{S}$, i.e. $\forall \upsilon : \mathcal{R}_{\mathcal{S}}.\, p(\upsilon)$.* □

Definition 4 (Execution fragments). *Given an OTS $\mathcal{S}$, execution fragments wrt $\mathcal{S}$ are inductively defined:*

- *Each $\upsilon_{\text{init}} \in \mathcal{I}$ is an execution fragment (to υ_{init}) wrt $\mathcal{S}$.*
- *For each $t_{y_1,\ldots,y_n} \in \mathcal{T}$ and each $y_k : D_{tk}$ for $k = 1\ldots,n$, $\upsilon_0,\ldots,\upsilon_m, t_{y_1,\ldots,y_n}(\upsilon_m)$ is also an execution fragment (to $t_{y_1,\ldots,y_n}(\upsilon_m)$) wrt $\mathcal{S}$ if $\upsilon_0,\ldots,\upsilon_m$ is an execution fragment wrt $\mathcal{S}$.*

Let $\mathcal{EF}_{\mathcal{S}}$ be the set of all execution fragments wrt $\mathcal{S}$. □

Proposition 1 (Reachable states and Execution fragments). *(1) For each reachable state $\upsilon \in \mathcal{R}_{\mathcal{S}}$, there exists an execution fragment to υ wrt $\mathcal{S}$, and (2) for each execution fragment $\upsilon_0,\ldots,\upsilon_m \in \mathcal{EF}_{\mathcal{S}}$, each υ_k is reachable wrt $\mathcal{S}$ for $k = 0,\ldots,m$.*

Proof. (1) By mathematical induction on υ. (2) By mathematical induction on m. □

Given an execution fragment $e \in \mathcal{EF}_{\mathcal{S}}$, let $\text{depth}(e)$ denote the length of the execution fragment, e.g. $\text{depth}(\upsilon_0,\ldots,\upsilon_n) = n$, and let ef2set$(e)$ denote the set of the states that appear in e, e.g. ef2set$(\upsilon_0,\ldots,\upsilon_n) = \{\upsilon_0,\ldots,\upsilon_n\}$. Let $\mathcal{EF}_{\mathcal{S},\leq n}$ be $\{e \in \mathcal{EF}_{\mathcal{S}} \mid \text{depth}(e) \leq n\}$, the set of all execution fragments wrt $\mathcal{S}$ whose lengths are less than or equal to n.

Definition 5 (Bounded reachable state space). $(\bigcup_{e \in \mathcal{EF}_{\mathcal{S},\leq n}} \text{ef2set}(e))$ *is called* the (n-)bounded reachable state space *wrt $\mathcal{S}$. Let $\mathcal{R}_{\mathcal{S},\leq n}$ denote the set of states.*

From Prop. 1, it is clear that every $\upsilon \in \mathcal{R}_{\mathcal{S},\leq n}$ is reachable wrt $\mathcal{S}$. For a set $\mathcal{A} \subseteq \Upsilon$ of states to be (in)finite wrt $\mathcal{S}$ means that $\mathcal{A}/=_{\mathcal{S}}$ consists of (in)finite elements.

Theorem 1 (Sufficient condition that $\mathcal{R}_{\mathcal{S},\leq n}$ is finite). *If $\mathcal{I}$ is finite wrt $\mathcal{S}$ and the number of the instances of transitions whose effective conditions hold in each state of $\mathcal{R}_{\mathcal{S},\leq(n-1)}$ is finite, then $\mathcal{R}_{\mathcal{S},\leq n}$ is finite wrt $\mathcal{S}$.*

Proof. By mathematical induction on n. □

If $\forall \upsilon : \mathcal{R}_{\mathcal{S}}.\, p(\upsilon)$ does not hold, then there must exist a reachable state $\upsilon \in \mathcal{R}_{\mathcal{S}}$ such that $\neg p(\upsilon)$, and there must exit an execution fragment to υ wrt $\mathcal{S}$ from Prop. 1.

Definition 6 (Counterexamples). *Any execution fragment to* $\upsilon \in \mathcal{R}_{\mathcal{S}}$ *such that* $\neg p(\upsilon)$ *is called* a counterexample *for an invariant* $\forall \upsilon : \mathcal{R}_{\mathcal{S}}.\, p(\upsilon)$. *Let* $\mathcal{CX}_{\mathcal{S},p}$ *be all counterexamples for* $\forall \upsilon : \mathcal{R}_{\mathcal{S}}.\, p(\upsilon)$. □

Any counterexample $cx \in \mathcal{CX}_{\mathcal{S},p}$ such that $\neg(\exists cx' : \mathcal{CX}_{\mathcal{S},p}.\, (\mathrm{depth}(cx') < \mathrm{depth}(cx)))$ is called a *shortest counterexample* for $\forall \upsilon : \mathcal{R}_{\mathcal{S}}.\, p(\upsilon)$. When $\mathcal{CX}_{\mathcal{S},p}$ is not empty, let $cx^{\min}_{\mathcal{S},p} \in \mathcal{CX}_{\mathcal{S},p}$ be a shortest counterexample for $\forall \upsilon : \mathcal{R}_{\mathcal{S}}.\, p(\upsilon)$.

3 Specifying OTSs

OTSs are defined so that they can be straightforwardly specified as behavioral specifications in CafeOBJ. But, OTSs can be specified in Maude as well [15,12]. In this paper, the NSPK authentication protocol [14] is used as an example to describe how to specify OTSs in Maude as well as CafeOBJ.

The protocol can be described as the three message exchanges:

$$\begin{array}{l} \text{Msg 1 } p \longrightarrow q : \mathcal{E}_q(n_p, p) \\ \text{Msg 2 } q \longrightarrow p : \mathcal{E}_p(n_p, n_q) \\ \text{Msg 3 } p \longrightarrow q : \mathcal{E}_q(n_q) \end{array}$$

Each principal is given a pair of keys: public and private keys. $\mathcal{E}_p(m)$ is the message m encrypted with the principal p's public key. n_p is a nonce (a random number) generated by principal p.

3.1 OTS $\mathcal{S}_{\mathrm{NSPK}}$ Modeling NSPK

One of the desired invariant properties that the protocol should have is (*Nonce*) *Secrecy Property* that any nonces cannot be leaked. The protocol is modeled as an OTS $\mathcal{S}_{\mathrm{NSPK}}$ by taking into account the intruder so as to verify that the protocol has Secrecy Property. The data types used in $\mathcal{S}_{\mathrm{NSPK}}$ are: (1) Bool for truth values, (2) Prin for principals; intr denoting the intruder, (3) Rand for random numbers; seed denoting a random number available initially; $\mathrm{next}(r)$ denoting a random number that has never been generated so far, (4) Nonce for nonces; $\mathrm{n}(p, q, r)$ denoting the nonce (generated by principal p for principal q) whose uniqueness is guaranteed by random number r, (5) Cipher for ciphertexts; $\mathrm{enc1}(p, n, q)$ denoting $\mathcal{E}_p(n, q)$; $\mathrm{enc2}(p, n1, n2)$ denoting $\mathcal{E}_p(n1, n2)$; $\mathrm{enc3}(p, n)$ denoting $\mathcal{E}_p(n)$, (6) SetNonce for sets of nonces; empty denoting the empty set; n , s denoting $\{n\} \cup s$; $s1$, $s2$ denoting $s1 \cup s2$, and (7) Network for multisets of ciphertexts; empty denoting the empty multiset; e , m denoting $\{\!|\, e \,|\!\} \uplus m$; $m1$, $m2$ denoting $m1 \uplus m2$.

$\mathcal{S}_{\mathrm{NSPK}}$ is $\langle \mathcal{O}_{\mathrm{NSPK}}, \mathcal{I}_{\mathrm{NSPK}}, \mathcal{T}_{\mathrm{NSPK}} \rangle$ such that

$$\begin{array}{l} \mathcal{O}_{\mathrm{NSLPK}} \triangleq \{\mathrm{rand} : \Upsilon \rightarrow \mathrm{Rand}, \mathrm{nw} : \Upsilon \rightarrow \mathrm{Network}, \mathrm{nonces} : \Upsilon \rightarrow \mathrm{SetNonce}\} \\ \mathcal{I}_{\mathrm{NSLPK}} \triangleq \{\upsilon_{\mathrm{init}} \in \Upsilon \mid \mathrm{rand}(\upsilon_{\mathrm{init}}) = \mathrm{seed} \wedge \mathrm{nw}(\upsilon_{\mathrm{init}}) = \mathrm{empty} \wedge \\ \qquad\qquad\qquad \mathrm{nonces}(\upsilon_{\mathrm{init}}) = \mathrm{empty}\} \end{array}$$

$$\mathcal{T}_{\mathrm{NSLPK}} \triangleq \{\mathrm{send1}_{p:\mathrm{Prin},q:\mathrm{Prin}} : \Upsilon \to \Upsilon,$$
$$\mathrm{send2}_{p:\mathrm{Prin},q:\mathrm{Prin},n:\mathrm{Nonce},nw:\mathrm{Network}} : \Upsilon \to \Upsilon,$$
$$\mathrm{send3}_{p:\mathrm{Prin},q:\mathrm{Prin},n1,n2:\mathrm{Nonce},nw:\mathrm{Network}} : \Upsilon \to \Upsilon,$$
$$\mathrm{fake1}_{p:\mathrm{Prin},q:\mathrm{Prin},n:\mathrm{Nonce},ns:\mathrm{SetNonce}} : \Upsilon \to \Upsilon,$$
$$\mathrm{fake2}_{p:\mathrm{Prin},n1,n2:\mathrm{Nonce},ns:\mathrm{SetNonce}} : \Upsilon \to \Upsilon,$$
$$\mathrm{fake3}_{p:\mathrm{Prin},n:\mathrm{Nonce},ns:\mathrm{SetNonce}} : \Upsilon \to \Upsilon\}$$

Given a state $\upsilon \in \Upsilon$, rand returns a random number available in υ, nw returns a multiset of ciphertexts (denoting the network) that have been sent up to υ, and nonces returns a set of nonces that have been gleaned by the intruder up to υ. The first three transitions model sending messages exactly following the protocol, while the last three transitions model the intruder's faking messages based on the gleaned nonces. The transitions are defined as follows:

- $\mathrm{send1}_{p,q}$: $\mathrm{send1}_{p,q}(\upsilon) \triangleq \upsilon'$ such that

  $\mathrm{rand}(\upsilon') \triangleq \mathrm{next}(\mathrm{rand}(\upsilon))$, $\mathrm{nw}(\upsilon') \triangleq \mathrm{enc1}(q, n(p,q,\mathrm{rand}(\upsilon)), p)$, $\mathrm{nw}(\upsilon)$, and $\mathrm{nonces}(\upsilon') \triangleq \mathbf{if}\ q = \mathrm{intr}\ \mathbf{then}\ n(p,q,\mathrm{rand}(\upsilon))$, $\mathrm{nonces}(\upsilon)\ \mathbf{else}\ \mathrm{nonces}(\upsilon)$.

- $\mathrm{send2}_{p,q,n,nw}$: $c_{\mathrm{send2}_{p,q,n,nw}}(\upsilon) \triangleq (\mathrm{nw}(\upsilon) = \mathrm{enc1}(p,n,q)\ ,\ nw)$.
  If $c_{\mathrm{send2}_{p,q,n,nw}}(\upsilon)$, then $\mathrm{send2}_{p,q,n,nw}(\upsilon) \triangleq \upsilon'$ such that

  $\mathrm{rand}(\upsilon') \triangleq \mathrm{next}(\mathrm{rand}(\upsilon))$, $\mathrm{nw}(\upsilon') \triangleq \mathrm{enc2}(q, n, n(p,q,\mathrm{rand}(\upsilon)))$, $\mathrm{nw}(\upsilon)$, and $\mathrm{nonces}(\upsilon') \triangleq \mathbf{if}\ q = \mathrm{intr}\ \mathbf{then}\ n\ ,\ n(p,q,\mathrm{rand}(\upsilon))$, $\mathrm{nonces}(\upsilon)\ \mathbf{else}\ \mathrm{nonces}(\upsilon)$.

- $\mathrm{send3}_{p,q,n1,n2,nw}$:
  $c_{\mathrm{send2}_{p,q,n1,n2,nw}}(\upsilon) \triangleq (\mathrm{nw}(\upsilon) = \mathrm{enc2}(p,n1,n2)\ ,\ \mathrm{enc1}(q,n1,p)\ ,\ nw)$.
  If $c_{\mathrm{send3}_{p,q,n1,n2,nw}}(\upsilon)$, then $\mathrm{send3}_{p,q,n1,n2,nw}(\upsilon) \triangleq \upsilon'$ such that

  $\mathrm{rand}(\upsilon') \triangleq \mathrm{rand}(\upsilon)$, $\mathrm{nw}(\upsilon') \triangleq \mathrm{enc3}(q,n2)$, $\mathrm{nw}(\upsilon)$, and $\mathrm{nonces}(\upsilon') \triangleq \mathbf{if}\ q = \mathrm{intr}\ \mathbf{then}\ n2$, $\mathrm{nonces}(\upsilon)\ \mathbf{else}\ \mathrm{nonces}(\upsilon)$.

- $\mathrm{fake1}_{p,q,n,ns}$: $c_{\mathrm{fake1}_{p,q,n,ns}}(\upsilon) \triangleq (\mathrm{nonces}(\upsilon) = n\ ,\ ns)$.
  If $c_{\mathrm{fake1}_{p,q,n,ns}}(\upsilon)$, then $\mathrm{fake1}_{p,q,n,ns}(\upsilon) \triangleq \upsilon'$ such that

  $\mathrm{rand}(\upsilon') \triangleq \mathrm{rand}(\upsilon)$, $\mathrm{nw}(\upsilon') \triangleq \mathrm{enc1}(q,n,p)$, $\mathrm{nw}(\upsilon)$, and $\mathrm{nonces}(\upsilon)' \triangleq \mathrm{nonces}(\upsilon)$

- $\mathrm{fake2}_{p,n1,n2,ns}$: $c_{\mathrm{fake2}_{p,n1,n2,ns}}(\upsilon) \triangleq (\mathrm{nonces}(\upsilon) = n1\ ,\ n2\ ,\ ns)$.
  If $c_{\mathrm{fake2}_{p,n1,n2,ns}}(\upsilon)$, then $\mathrm{fake2}_{p,n1,n2,ns}(\upsilon) \triangleq \upsilon'$ such that

  $\mathrm{rand}(\upsilon') \triangleq \mathrm{rand}(\upsilon)$, $\mathrm{nw}(\upsilon') \triangleq \mathrm{enc2}(p,n1,n2)$, $\mathrm{nw}(\upsilon)$, and $\mathrm{nonces}(\upsilon)' \triangleq \mathrm{nonces}(\upsilon)$.

- $\mathrm{fake3}_{p,n,ns}$: $c_{\mathrm{fake3}_{p,n,ns}}(\upsilon) \triangleq (\mathrm{nonces}(\upsilon) = n\ ,\ ns)$.
  If $c_{\mathrm{fake3}_{p,n,ns}}(\upsilon)$, then $\mathrm{fake3}_{p,n,ns}(\upsilon) \triangleq \upsilon'$ such that

  $\mathrm{rand}(\upsilon') \triangleq \mathrm{rand}(\upsilon)$, $\mathrm{nw}(\upsilon') \triangleq \mathrm{enc3}(p,n)$, $\mathrm{nw}(\upsilon)$, and $\mathrm{nonces}(\upsilon)' \triangleq \mathrm{nonces}(\upsilon)$.

Secrecy Property can be expressed as $\forall \upsilon : \mathcal{R}_{\mathcal{S}_{\mathrm{NSPK}}} . \mathrm{SP}(\upsilon)$, where $\mathrm{SP}(\upsilon) \triangleq \forall n :$ Nonce $(n \in \mathrm{nonces}(\upsilon) \Rightarrow (\mathrm{p1}(n) = \mathrm{intr} \vee \mathrm{p2}(n) = \mathrm{intr}))$, $\mathrm{p1}(\mathrm{n}(p,q,r)) \triangleq p$ and $\mathrm{p2}(\mathrm{n}(p,q,r)) \triangleq q$.

3.2 Specifying $\mathcal{S}_{\text{NSPK}}$ in CafeOBJ

We suppose that there exist visible sorts `Bool`, `Prin`, `Rand`, `Nonce`, `Cipher`, `SetNonce` and `Network` corresponding to the data types used in $\mathcal{S}_{\text{NSPK}}$. $\mathcal{S}_{\text{NSPK}}$ is specified as a module `NSPK`. The signature of the module is as follows:

```
op  init   : -> Sys
bop rand   : Sys -> Rand
bop nw     : Sys -> Network
bop nonces : Sys -> SetNonce
bop send1  : Sys Prin Prin -> Sys
bop send2  : Sys Prin Prin Nonce Network -> Sys
bop send3  : Sys Prin Prin Nonce Nonce Network -> Sys
bop fake1  : Sys Prin Prin Nonce SetNonce -> Sys
bop fake2  : Sys Prin Nonce Nonce SetNonce -> Sys
bop fake3  : Sys Prin Nonce SetNonce -> Sys
```

`Sys` is the hidden sort denoting the state space. `bop` is the keyword to declare observation and action operators, while `op` is the keyword to declare other operators. Constant `init` denotes an arbitrary initial state of $\mathcal{S}_{\text{NSPK}}$. The three observation operators correspond to the three observers, and the six action operators correspond to the six transitions. In this paper, the definition of action operator `send3` is shown, which is as follows:

```
op c-send3 : Sys Prin Prin Nonce Nonce Network -> Bool
eq c-send3(S,P1,P2,N1,N2,NW)
   = (nw(S) = enc2(P1,N1,N2), enc1(P2,N1,P1) , NW) .
eq  rand(send3(S,P1,P2,N1,N2,NW)) = rand(S) .
ceq nw(send3(S,P1,P2,N1,N2,NW))
    = (enc3(P2,N2) , nw(S)) if c-send3(S,P1,P2,N1,N2,NW) .
ceq nonces(send3(S,P1,P2,N1,N2,NW))
    = (if P2 = intr then (N2 , nonces(S)) else nonces(S) fi)
    if c-send3(S,P1,P2,N1,N2,NW) .
ceq send3(S,P1,P2,N1,N2,NW) = S if not c-send3(S,P1,P2,N1,N2,NW) .
```

`eq` is the keyword to declare equations, while `ceq` is the keyword to declare conditional equations.

Constant `init` is defined as follows:

```
eq rand(init)   = seed .
eq nw(init)     = empty .
eq nonces(init) = empty .
```

3.3 Specifying $\mathcal{S}_{\text{NSPK}}$ in Maude

We suppose that there exist sorts `Bool`, `Prin`, `Rand`, `Nonce`, `Cipher`, `SetNonce` and `Network` corresponding to the data types used in $\mathcal{S}_{\text{NSPK}}$. $\mathcal{S}_{\text{NSPK}}$ is specified as a module `NSPK`. The signature of the module is as follows:

```
subsorts TRule OValue < Sys .
op none       : -> Sys .
op __         : Sys Sys -> Sys [assoc comm id: none] .
op rand :_    : Rand -> OValue .
op nw :_      : Network -> OValue .
op nonces :_  : SetNonce -> OValue .
op send1      : Prin Prin -> TRule .
op send2      : -> TRule .
op send3      : -> TRule .
op fake1      : Prin Prin -> TRule .
op fake2      : Prin -> TRule .
op fake3      : Prin -> TRule .
```

Sys is the sort denoting the state space. A state is represented by a multiset of variables (which correspond to observers) and transitions. OValue is the sort denoting variables and TRule is the sort denoting transitions. TRule and OValue are declared as subsorts of Sys. Constant none denotes the empty state, and the juxtaposition operator __, which is given associativity, commutativity and none as its identity, is the data constructor of non-empty states. The next three operators denote the three variables, which correspond to the three observers, and the last six operators denote the six transitions. In this paper, the definition of operator send3 is shown, which is as follows:

```
rl [send3] : send3 (rand : R)
  (nw : (enc2(P1,N1,N2), enc1(P2,N1,P1) , NW)) (nonces : Ns)
  => send3 (rand : R)
     (nw : (enc3(P2,N2) , enc2(P1,N1,N2), enc1(P2,N1,P1) , NW))
     (nonces : (if P2 == intr then N2 , Ns else Ns fi)) .
```

rl is the keyword to declare rewriting rules, while crl is the keyword to declare conditional rewriting rules. send3 is the label given to this rewriting rule.

When three principals including the intruder participate in the protocol, the initial state is represented as follows:

```
op init : -> Sys . eq init = send1(p1,p2) send1(p1,intr)
send1(p2,p1) send1(p2,intr) send1(intr,p1) send1(intr,p2) send2
send3 fake1(p1,p2) fake1(p1,intr) fake1(p2,p1) fake1(p2,intr)
fake1(intr,p1) fake1(intr,p2) fake2(p1) fake2(p2) fake2(intr)
fake3(p1) fake3(p2) fake3(intr) (rand : seed) (nw : empty)
(nonces: empty) .
```

4 Falsification of OTSs

Maude is used to falsify $\forall v : \mathcal{R}_{\mathcal{S}}.\, p(v)$, i.e. to find a counterexample for $\forall v : \mathcal{R}_{\mathcal{S}}.\, p(v)$. The way [12] used in this paper is to search $\mathcal{R}_{\mathcal{S},\leq n}$ for a counterexample for $\forall v : \mathcal{R}_{\mathcal{S}}.\, p(v)$. If $\mathcal{R}_{\mathcal{S},\leq n}$ is finite wrt $\mathcal{S}$, this search can be completed within a finite time. A sufficient condition that $\mathcal{R}_{\mathcal{S},\leq n}$ is finite wrt $\mathcal{S}$ is given in Theorem 1. Since Maude is not equipped with any facilities that can be used to search only $\mathcal{R}_{\mathcal{S},\leq n}$ for a counterexample for $\forall v : \mathcal{R}_{\mathcal{S}}.\, p(v)$, however, we need to make a little modification to $\mathcal{S}$.

Definition 7 (Bounded OTSs). *One observer* steps : $\Upsilon \rightarrow$ Nat *is added to* $\mathcal{S}$*, where* Nat *is the type for natural numbers. The initial value returned by* steps *is* 0*, and the inequality* $\text{steps}(v) < n$ *is added to the effective condition of each transition. The value returned by* steps *is incremented whenever each transition is applied in a state where the effective condition holds. The OTS obtained by modifying* $\mathcal{S}$ *in this way is called* the $(n$-)bounded OTS $\mathcal{S}$ *and denoted* $\mathcal{S}^{\leq n}$. □

We have the theorem that guarantees that the search of $\mathcal{R}_{\mathcal{S}^{\leq n}}$ for a counterexample for $\forall v : \mathcal{R}_{\mathcal{S}^{\leq n}} . p(v)$ coincides with the search of $\mathcal{R}_{\mathcal{S},\leq n}$ for a counterexample for $\forall v : \mathcal{R}_{\mathcal{S}} . p(v)$ if the observer steps is not used in p.

Theorem 2 (Coincidence of counterexamples [12]). *If the observer* steps *is not used in a state predicate* $p : \Upsilon \rightarrow$ Bool*, then (1) any counterexample for* $\forall v : \mathcal{R}_{\mathcal{S}^{\leq n}} . p(v)$ *is also a counterexample for* $\forall v : \mathcal{R}_{\mathcal{S}} . p(v)$*, and (2) for any counterexample* $v_0, \ldots, v_m$ *for* $\forall v : \mathcal{R}_{\mathcal{S}} . p(v)$ *such that* $m \leq n$*, there exists a counterexample* $v'_0, \ldots, v'_m$ *for* $\forall v : \mathcal{R}_{\mathcal{S}^{\leq n}} . p(v)$ *such that* $v'_k =_{\mathcal{S}} v_k$ *for* $k = 0, \ldots, m$. □

In the Maude specification of $\mathcal{S}_{\text{NSPK}}$, the following operator declaration is added:

```
op steps :_ : Nat -> OValue .
```

The term `(steps : 0)` is added to constant `init` in Subsect. 3.3. Then, the rewriting rules defining each transition is modified such that the value returned by steps is incremented whenever each transition is applied and the inequality $\text{steps}(v) < n$ is added to the condition of each of the rewriting rules. The rewriting rule labeled `send3` is modified as follows:

```
crl [send3] : send3 (rand : R) (nw :
(enc2(P1,N1,N2),enc1(P2,N1,P1) , NW)) (nonces : Ns) (steps : X)
  => send3 (rand : R)
     (nw : (enc3(P2,N2) , enc2(P1,N1,N2), enc1(P2,N1,P1) , NW))
     (nonces : (if P2 == intr then N2 , Ns else Ns fi))
     (steps : (X + 1)) if X < bound .
```

where constant bound corresponds to n.

The Maude model checker can be used to search $\mathcal{R}^{\leq n}_{\mathcal{S}_{\text{NSPK}}}$ for a counterexample for $\forall v : \mathcal{R}_{\mathcal{S}_{\text{NSPK}}} . \text{SP}(v)$, and so can command `search`. In this paper, we use command `search`. One way to use command `search` is as follows:

search [1] *start* =>* *pattern* **such that** *condition* .

Command `search` performs a breadth-first search to find one state that matches *pattern* and that can be reached from *start* by applying zero or more rewriting rules.

To search $\mathcal{R}^{\leq n}_{\mathcal{S}_{\text{NSPK}}}$ for a counterexample for $\forall v : \mathcal{R}_{\mathcal{S}_{\text{NSPK}}} . \text{SP}(v)$, all we have to do is to feed the following line to the Maude system:

```
search [1] init =>* (nonces : (N , Ns)) S
          such that not(p1(N) == intr or p2(N) == intr).
```

When bound is 4, command `search` finds a state v in which $\text{SP}(v)$ does not hold. Command `show path` can be used to show the path to the state, which is a shortest counterexample for $\forall v : \mathcal{R}_{\mathcal{S}_{\text{NSPK}}} . \text{SP}(v)$.

5 Interaction Between Verification and Falsification

When bound is less than 4, command search does not find any states υ in which $\mathrm{SP}(\upsilon)$ does not hold. What if $\mathcal{R}_{\mathcal{S}_{\mathrm{NSPK}},\leq 4}$ is too large for the Maude system to search it within a reasonable time? If so, we start verifying $\forall \upsilon : \mathcal{R}_{\mathcal{S}_{\mathrm{NSPK}}}. \mathrm{SP}(\upsilon)$. One standard way to prove $\forall \upsilon : \mathcal{R}_{\mathcal{S}}. p(\upsilon)$ is to use mathematical induction on υ. In the rest of the paper, let $p(\upsilon)$ be $\forall z_1 : D_{p1} \ldots \forall z_M : D_{pM}. P(\upsilon, z_1, \ldots, z_M)$.

Theorem 3 (Mathematical induction on $\mathcal{R}_{\mathcal{S}}$). *Let (I) be $\forall \upsilon_{\mathrm{init}} : \mathcal{I}. p(\upsilon_{\mathrm{init}})$, (II) be $\forall \upsilon : \mathcal{R}_{\mathcal{S}}. (p(\upsilon) \Rightarrow A. p(t_{y_1,\ldots,y_n}(\upsilon)))$, let (III) be $\forall \upsilon : \mathcal{R}_{\mathcal{S}}.B. (P(\upsilon, z_{\iota_1}, \ldots, z_M) \Rightarrow A. P(t_{y_1,\ldots,y_n}(\upsilon), z_1, \ldots, z_M))$, where A is $\forall t_{y_1,\ldots,y_n} : \mathcal{T}. \forall y_1 : D_{t1} \ldots \forall y_n : D_{tn}$ and B is $\forall z_1 : D_{p1} \ldots \forall z_M : D_{pM}$. Then, (1) $\forall \upsilon : \mathcal{R}_{\mathcal{S}}. p(\upsilon) \Leftrightarrow ((I) \wedge (II))$ and (2) $((I) \wedge (II)) \Leftrightarrow ((I) \wedge (III))$.*

Proof. (1) From the mathematical induction principle. (2) $\Leftarrow$: Straightforward. $\Rightarrow$: It is clear that $((I) \wedge (II)) \Rightarrow (I)$. We assume $(I) \wedge (II)$. From (1), we have $\forall \upsilon : \mathcal{R}_{\mathcal{S}}. p(\upsilon)$, which implies (III). □

We use $\forall \upsilon : \mathcal{R}_{\mathcal{S}}. p(\upsilon) \Leftrightarrow ((I) \wedge (III))$ from Theorem 3 in order to prove (and disprove) $\forall \upsilon : \mathcal{R}_{\mathcal{S}}. p(\upsilon)$. We often need lemmas to prove $\forall \upsilon : \mathcal{R}_{\mathcal{S}}. p(\upsilon)$.

Definition 8 (Effective case splits and Necessary lemmas). *Let us consider proving $\forall \upsilon : \mathcal{R}_{\mathcal{S}}. p(\upsilon)$ by mathematical induction on υ. In an induction case where $t_{y_1,\ldots,y_n} \in \mathcal{T}$ is taken into account, all we have to do is to prove $P(\upsilon^{\mathrm{c}}, z_1^{\mathrm{c}}, \ldots, z_M^{\mathrm{c}}) \Rightarrow P(t_{y_1^{\mathrm{c}},\ldots,y_n^{\mathrm{c}}}(\upsilon^{\mathrm{c}}), z_1^{\mathrm{c}}, \ldots, z_M^{\mathrm{c}})$, where υ^{c} is a constant denoting an arbitrary state and each y_k^{c} (z_k^{c}) is a constant denoting an arbitrary value of D_{tk} (D_{pk}). We suppose that a proposition $q_1 \vee \ldots \vee q_L$ is a tautology, where each q_l is in the form $Q_l(\upsilon^{\mathrm{c}}, y_1^{\mathrm{c}}, \ldots, y_n^{\mathrm{c}}, z_1^{\mathrm{c}}, \ldots, z_M^{\mathrm{c}})$. If the truth value of $P(\upsilon^{\mathrm{c}}, z_1^{\mathrm{c}}, \ldots, z_M^{\mathrm{c}}) \Rightarrow P(t_{y_1^{\mathrm{c}},\ldots,y_n^{\mathrm{c}}}(\upsilon^{\mathrm{c}}), z_1^{\mathrm{c}}, \ldots, z_M^{\mathrm{c}})$ can be determined assuming each q_l, then $q_1 \vee \ldots \vee q_L$ is called* an effective case split *for this induction case. Moreover, if the truth value is* false, *then $\forall \upsilon : \mathcal{R}_{\mathcal{S}}. \forall y_1 : D_{t1}, \ldots, \forall y_n : D_{tn}, \forall z_1 : D_{p1}, \ldots, \forall z_M : D_{pM}. \neg Q_l(\upsilon, y_1, \ldots, y_n, z_1, \ldots, z_M)$ is called* a necessary lemma *of $\forall \upsilon : \mathcal{R}_{\mathcal{S}}. p(\upsilon)$. Given an effective case split for each induction case, let $\mathcal{NL}_{\mathcal{S},p}$ be the set of all necessary lemmas of $\forall \upsilon : \mathcal{R}_{\mathcal{S}}. p(\upsilon)$ obtained by the effective case splits. Generally, there are multiple such sets, which depend on effective case splits.* □

In the rest of this section, let $q(\upsilon)$ be $\forall \upsilon : \mathcal{R}_{\mathcal{S}}. \forall y_1 : D_{t1}, \ldots, \forall y_n : D_{tn}, \forall z_1 : D_{p1}, \ldots, \forall z_M : D_{pM}. \neg Q_l(\upsilon, y_1, \ldots, y_n, z_1, \ldots, z_M)$, and let q_l be $Q_l(\upsilon^{\mathrm{c}}, y_1^{\mathrm{c}}, \ldots, y_n^{\mathrm{c}}, z_1^{\mathrm{c}}, \ldots, z_M^{\mathrm{c}})$.

Lemma 1 (Counterexamples induced by necessary lemmas). *Let $\forall \upsilon : \mathcal{R}_{\mathcal{S}}. q(\upsilon)$ be a necessary lemma of $\forall \upsilon : \mathcal{R}_{\mathcal{S}}. p(\upsilon)$. If there exists a counterexample $ce_q \in \mathcal{CX}_{\mathcal{S},q}$ such that* $\mathrm{depth}(ce_q) = N$, *then $ce_q \in \mathcal{CX}_{\mathcal{S},p}$ or there exists a counterexample $ce_p \in \mathcal{CX}_{\mathcal{S},p}$ such that* $\mathrm{depth}(ce_p) = N + 1$.

Proof. We suppose that $\forall \upsilon : \mathcal{R}_{\mathcal{S}}. q(\upsilon)$ is found in an induction case where a transition $t_{y_1,\ldots,y_n} \in \mathcal{T}$ is taken into account. Let ce_q be $\upsilon_0, \ldots, \upsilon_N$. From the assumption, there exist $y_1^{\mathrm{d}}, \ldots, y_n^{\mathrm{d}}, z_1^{\mathrm{d}}, \ldots, z_M^{\mathrm{d}}$ such that $Q(\upsilon_N, y_1^{\mathrm{d}}, \ldots, y_n^{\mathrm{d}}, z_1^{\mathrm{d}}, \ldots, z_M^{\mathrm{d}})$

holds. (1) $\neg p(\upsilon_N)$: Clearly $ce_q \in \mathcal{CX}_{\mathcal{S},p}$. (2) $p(\upsilon_N)$: Since both $p(\upsilon_N)$ and $Q(\upsilon_N, d_{j_1}, \ldots, d_{j_n}, d_{\iota_1}, \ldots, d_{\iota_\alpha})$ holds, $P(t_{d_{j_1},\ldots,d_{j_n}}(\upsilon_N), d_{\iota_1}, \ldots, d_{\iota_\alpha})$ must not hold because $\forall \upsilon : \mathcal{R}_\mathcal{S}.\, q(\upsilon)$ is a necessary lemma of $\forall \upsilon : \mathcal{R}_\mathcal{S}.\, p(\upsilon)$ and is found in the induction case concerned. Therefore, $\upsilon_0, \ldots, \upsilon_N, t_{y_1^{\mathrm{d}},\ldots,y_n^{\mathrm{d}}}(\upsilon_N)$ is a counterexample of $\forall \upsilon : \mathcal{R}_\mathcal{S}.\, p(\upsilon)$. □

Lemma 2 (Existence of necessary lemmas that induce counterexamples). *If $\mathcal{CX}_{\mathcal{S},p}$ is not empty and* $\mathrm{depth}(cx^{\min}_{\mathcal{S},p}) = N + 1$, *then there exists a necessary lemma $\forall \upsilon : \mathcal{R}_\mathcal{S}.\, q(\upsilon)$ of $\forall \upsilon : \mathcal{R}_\mathcal{S}.\, p(\upsilon)$ such that $\mathcal{CX}_{\mathcal{S},q}$ is not empty and* $\mathrm{depth}(cx^{\min}_{\mathcal{S},q}) = N$, *and such a necessary lemma can be found in any $\mathcal{NL}_{\mathcal{S},p}$.*

Proof. Let $cx^{\min}_{\mathcal{S},p}$ be $\upsilon_0, \ldots, \upsilon_N, \upsilon_{N+1}$. From the assumption, $p(\upsilon_N)$ holds and there exist $t_{y_1,\ldots,y_n} \in \mathcal{T}$ and $y_1^{\mathrm{d}}, \ldots, y_n^{\mathrm{d}}, z_1^{\mathrm{d}}, \ldots, z_M^{\mathrm{d}}$ such that $\upsilon_{N+1} =_\mathcal{S} t_{y_1^{\mathrm{d}},\ldots,y_n^{\mathrm{d}}}(\upsilon_N)$ and $\neg P(t_{y_1^{\mathrm{d}},\ldots,y_n^{\mathrm{d}}}(\upsilon_N), z_1^{\mathrm{d}}, \ldots, z_M^{\mathrm{d}})$. Let $q_1 \vee \ldots \vee q_L$ be an arbitrary effective case split for the induction case where $t_{y_1,\ldots,y_n}$ is taken into account. There must exist $l \in \{1, \ldots, L\}$ such that the truth value of $P(\upsilon^{\mathrm{c}}, z_1^{\mathrm{c}}, \ldots, z_M^{\mathrm{c}}) \Rightarrow P(t_{y_1^{\mathrm{c}},\ldots,y_n^{\mathrm{c}}}(\upsilon^{\mathrm{c}}), z_1^{\mathrm{c}}, \ldots, z_M^{\mathrm{c}})$ is false assuming q_l because otherwise there does not exist the supposed counterexample. Therefore, $Q_l(\upsilon^{\mathrm{c}}, y_1^{\mathrm{c}}, \ldots, y_n^{\mathrm{c}}, z_1^{\mathrm{c}}, \ldots, z_M^{\mathrm{c}})$ holds and then $\upsilon_1, \ldots, \upsilon_N$ is a counterexample for $\forall \upsilon : \mathcal{R}_\mathcal{S}.\, q(\upsilon)$. We suppose that $\mathrm{depth}(cx^{\min}_{\mathcal{S},q}) < N$. If so, $\mathrm{depth}(cx^{\min}_{\mathcal{S},p}) < N + 1$ from Lemma 1, which contradicts the assumption. □

We give a procedure with which we alternately falsify and verify $\forall \upsilon : \mathcal{R}_\mathcal{S}.\, p(\upsilon)$.

Definition 9 (Procedure IGF). *Given an OTS $\mathcal{S}$, a state predicate p and a natural number n, the procedure is defined as follows:*

1. $\mathcal{P} := \{p\}$ *and* $\mathcal{Q} := \emptyset$.
2. *Repeat the following until* $\mathcal{P} = \emptyset$.
   (a) *Choose a state predicate q from $\mathcal{P}$ and* $\mathcal{P} := (\mathcal{P} - \{q\})$.
   (b) *Search $\mathcal{R}_{\mathcal{S}\leq n}$ for a counterexample for $\forall \upsilon : \mathcal{R}_\mathcal{S}.\, q(\upsilon)$.*
   If a counterexample is found, terminate and return Falsified.
   (c) *Try to prove $\forall \upsilon : \mathcal{R}_\mathcal{S}.\, q(\upsilon)$ by mathematical induction on υ and compute $\mathcal{NL}_{\mathcal{S},q}$.*
   (d) $\mathcal{Q} := \mathcal{Q} \cup \{q\}$ *and* $\mathcal{P} := \mathcal{P} \cup (\mathcal{NL}_{\mathcal{S},q} - \mathcal{Q})$.
3. *Terminate and return* Verified. □

We have the the soundness and completeness theorem on procedure IGF.

Theorem 4 (Soundness and Completeness of IGF wrt Falsification). *Given an arbitrary OTS $\mathcal{S}$, an arbitrary state predicate p and an arbitrary natural number n, (1) if* IGF *terminates and returns* Falsified, *then $\neg(\forall \upsilon : \mathcal{R}_\mathcal{S}.\, p(\upsilon))$, and (2) if $\mathcal{CX}_{\mathcal{S},p}$ is not empty,* $\mathrm{depth}(cx^{\min}_{\mathcal{S},p})$ *is finite, $\mathcal{R}_{\mathcal{S}\leq n}$ is finite wrt $\mathcal{S}$ and $\mathcal{NL}_{\mathcal{S},q}$ can be computed for an arbitrary state predicate q, then* IGF *terminates and returns* Falsified.

Proof. From Lemmas 1 and 2. □

Note that when n is large, the search of $\mathcal{R}_{\mathcal{S}\leq n}$ may not be completed within a reasonable time, which implies that IGF may not terminate within a reasonable time, and when $\mathrm{depth}(cx^{\min}_{\mathcal{S},p})$ is large, IGF may not terminate within a reasonable time.

The following should be noted. The number of some entities such as principals may have to be made finite so as to make the n-bounded reachable state space wrt an OTS finite. Even when there exists a counterexample for an invariant in the n-bounded reachable state space wrt an OTS $\mathcal{S}$ in which there are an infinite number of some entities, no such counterexamples may be found in the n-bounded reachable state space wrt $\mathcal{S}$ in which there are a finite number of the entities, which depends on the number of the entities. Let us consider $\mathcal{S}_{\rm NSPK}$ for example. When the number of principals is infinite, $\mathcal{R}_{\mathcal{S}_{\rm NSPK},\leq n}$ is also infinite if $n \geq 2$. The number of principals should be made finite to make $\mathcal{R}_{\mathcal{S}_{\rm NSPK},\leq n}$ finite. When there are three or more principals, one of which is the intruder, a counterexample that $\mathcal{S}_{\rm NSPK}$ satisfies Secrecy Property is found in $\mathcal{R}_{\mathcal{S}_{\rm NSPK},\leq n}$ if $n \geq 4$. Otherwise, however, no such counterexamples are found in $\mathcal{R}_{\mathcal{S}_{\rm NSPK},\leq n}$ for any n.

6 A Way to Compute Necessary Lemmas

Since Theorem 4 relies on whether $\mathcal{NL}_{\mathcal{S},p}$ can be computed for an arbitrary state predicate p, we need to argue the feasibility. Given an arbitrary OTS $\mathcal{S}$ and an arbitrary state predicate p, we show a way to compute an effective case split for each induction case when we prove $\forall v : \mathcal{R}_{\mathcal{S}}.\, p(v)$ by mathematical induction on v and to obtain $\mathcal{NL}_{\mathcal{S},p}$ based on the effective case splits. The solution employs the CafeOBJ system that uses the Hsiang TRS [16] as a decision procedure of propositional logic. The CafeOBJ system reduces a proposition that is always true (false) to `true` (`false`). Generally, the CafeOBJ system reduces a proposition to an exclusive-or normal form.

We suppose that $\mathcal{S}$ is written as a module $\mathtt{M}_{\mathcal{S}}$ in CafeOBJ. We also suppose that when all equations available in $\mathtt{M}_{\mathcal{S}}$ are regarded as a set of left-to-right rewrite rules, the set, i.e. the TRS, is confluent and terminating. The TRS will be referred as $\mathrm{TRS}_{\mathcal{S}}$. In a module `INV`, which imports $\mathtt{M}_{\mathcal{S}}$, we declare the following operator and equation:

$$\mathtt{op}\ \mathtt{inv}_p : \mathtt{H}\ \mathtt{V}_{p1}\ \ldots\ \mathtt{V}_{pM}\ \texttt{->}\ \mathtt{Bool}$$
$$\mathtt{eq}\ \mathtt{inv}_p(\mathtt{S}, \mathtt{Z}_1, \ldots, \mathtt{Z}_M) = \mathtt{P}(\mathtt{S}, \mathtt{Z}_1, \ldots, \mathtt{Z}_M)\ .$$

where `H` is a hidden sort denoting Υ, `S` is a CafeOBJ variable of sort `H`, each $\mathtt{Z}_k$ is a CafeOBJ variable of sort $\mathtt{V}_{pk}$, and $\mathtt{P}(\mathtt{S}, \mathtt{Z}_1, \ldots, \mathtt{Z}_M)$ is a term denoting $P(v, z_1, \ldots, z_M)$. In `INV`, for each $\mathtt{V}_{pk}$, we also declare a constant $\mathtt{y}_k^{\mathtt{c}}$ of the sort, which denotes an arbitrary value of the sort. In a module `ISTEP`, which imports `INV`, we declare the following operator and equation:

$$\mathtt{op}\ \mathtt{istep}_p : \mathtt{V}_{p1}\ \ldots\ \mathtt{V}_{pM}\ \texttt{->}\ \mathtt{Bool}$$
$$\mathtt{eq}\ \mathtt{istep}_p(\mathtt{Z}_1, \ldots, \mathtt{Z}_M) = \mathtt{inv}_p(\mathtt{s}, \mathtt{Z}_1, \ldots, \mathtt{Z}_M)\ \mathtt{implies}\ \mathtt{inv}_p(\mathtt{s}', \mathtt{Z}_1, \ldots, \mathtt{Z}_M)\ .$$

where `s` and `s'` are constants of sort `H` declared in the module, and the operator `_implies_` corresponds to the logical implication. Constant `s` denotes an arbitrary state, and constant `s'` denotes a successor state of the state.

Let us consider an induction case in which a transition $t_{y_1,\ldots,y_n} \in \mathcal{T}$ is taken into account. We suppose that the transition and its effective condition are represented by the action operator `t` and the operator `c-t`, respectively, declared in $\mathtt{M}_{\mathcal{S}}$ as follows:

bop t : H V_{t1} ... V_{tn} -> H
op c-t : H V_{t1} ... V_{tn} -> Bool

We also have the following equation:

eq $s' = t(s, y^c_{j_1}, \ldots, y^c_{j_n})$.

where each y^c_k is a constant of V_{tk} denoting an arbitrary value of V_{tk}.

We give a procedure that computes an effective case split for the induction case.

Definition 10 (Procedure CaseSplit). *The procedure is defined as follows:*

1. $\mathcal{C} := \{\texttt{c-t}(s, y^c_{j_1}, \ldots, y^c_{j_n}), \neg\texttt{c-t}(s, y^c_{j_1}, \ldots, y^c_{j_n})\}$ *and* $\mathcal{C}' := \emptyset$.
2. *Repeat the following until* $\mathcal{C} = \emptyset$.
   (a) *Choose a proposition* q *from* $\mathcal{C}$ *and* $\mathcal{C} := \mathcal{C} - \{q\}$.
   (b) *Reduce* $\texttt{istep}_p(z^c_1, \ldots, y^c_M)$ *assuming* q *in module* ISTEP.
   Let r *be the result.*
   - *If* r *is* true, *do nothing.*
   - *If* r *is* false, $\mathcal{C}' := \mathcal{C}' \cup \{q\}$.
   - *Otherwise, choose a primitive proposition* ρ *from* r *and* $\mathcal{C} := \mathcal{C} \cup \{q \wedge \rho, q \wedge \neg\rho\}$.
3. *Terminate and return* $\mathcal{C}'$. □

When $\texttt{istep}_p(z^c_1, \ldots, y^c_M)$ is reduced assuming q in module ISTEP, q should be written as one or more equations. A way to write q in equations is described in [17]. Since $\text{TRS}_\mathcal{S}$ is terminating and p includes a finite number of logical connectives, procedure CaseSplit terminates. CaseSplit clearly computes an effective case split for the induction case, and when CaseSplit terminates, $\mathcal{C}'$ consists of all the propositions in the effective case split such that $\texttt{istep}_p(z^c_1, \ldots, y^c_M)$ reduces to false assuming each of the propositions. From $\mathcal{C}'$, it is straightforward to construct all necessary lemmas (of $\forall v : \mathcal{R}_\mathcal{S}.\, p(v)$) that are found in the induction case.

7 A Case Study

We try to prove $\forall v \in \mathcal{R}_{\mathcal{S}_\text{NSPK}}.\, \text{SP}(v)$ by mathematical induction on v based on the CafeOBJ specification of $\mathcal{S}_\text{NSPK}$. We first declare a module INV, which imports module NSPK. In module INV, the following operator and equation are declared:

```
op inv1 : Sys Nonce -> Bool
eq inv1(S,N)
   = ((N \in nonces(S)) implies (p1(N) = intr or p2(N) = intr)) .
```

where the operator _or_ corresponds to the logical disjunction. We also declare a constant n of sort Nonce in module INV. We next declare a module ISTEP, which imports module INV. In module ISTEP, the following operator and equation are declared:

```
op istep1 : Nonce -> Bool
eq istep1(N) = inv1(s,N) implies inv1(s',N) .
```

where s and s' are constants of sort Sys declared in module ISTEP.

We have the two cases in which `istep1(n)` reduces to `false`. The corresponding proof passages (basic fragments of a proof, or a proof score) are as follows:

```
open ISTEP
-- arbitrary values
  ops p1 p2 : -> Prin .  op m : -> Nonce .  op nw : -> Network .
-- assumptions
  -- eq c-send2(s,p1,p2,m,nw) = true .
  eq nw(s) = enc1(p1,m,p2) , nw .
  --
  eq p2 = intr .  eq (p1(n) = intr) = false .
  eq (p2(n) = intr)=false.eq m = n. eq n \in nonces(s)=false.
-- successor state
  eq s' = send2(s,p1,p2,m,nw) .
-- check
  red istep1(n) .
close
open ISTEP
-- arbitrary values
  ops p1 p2:-> Prin . ops m1 m2 : -> Nonce. op nw :->Network.
-- assumptions
  -- eq c-send3(s,p1,p2,m1,m2,nw) = true  .
  eq nw(s) = enc2(p1,m1,m2), enc1(p2,m1,p1) , nw .
  --
  eq p2 = intr .  eq m2 = n .  eq (p1(n) = intr) = false .
  eq (p2(n) = intr) = false .  eq n \in nonces(s) = false .
-- successor state
  eq s' = send3(s,p1,p2,m1,m2,nw) .
-- check
  red istep1(n) .
close
```

The CafeOBJ command `open` constructs a temporary module that imports a given module and the CafeOBJ command `close` destroys such a temporary module. A comment starts with `--` and terminates at the end of the line.

From the two proof passages, we obtain the two necessary lemmas of $\forall v \in \mathcal{R}_{\mathcal{S}_{\mathrm{NSPK}}}.\,\mathrm{SP}(v)$. The two necessary lemmas are $\forall v \in \mathcal{R}_{\mathcal{S}_{\mathrm{NSPK}}}.\,\mathrm{NL}_1(v)$ and $\forall v \in \mathcal{R}_{\mathcal{S}_{\mathrm{NSPK}}}.\,\mathrm{NL}_2(v)$, where $\mathrm{NL}_1(v) \triangleq \forall n : \mathrm{Nonce}.\forall q : \mathrm{Prin}.\,(\mathrm{enc1}(q, n, \mathrm{intr}) \in \mathrm{nw}(v) \Rightarrow (n \in \mathrm{nonces}(v) \vee \mathrm{p1}(n) = \mathrm{intr} \vee \mathrm{p2}(n) = \mathrm{intr}))$ and $\mathrm{NL}_2(v) \triangleq \forall n1, n2 : \mathrm{Nonce}.\forall q : \mathrm{Prin}.\,((\mathrm{enc2}(q, n1, n2) \in nw(v) \wedge \mathrm{enc1}(\mathrm{intr}, n1, q) \in \mathrm{nw}(v)) \Rightarrow (n2 \in \mathrm{nonces}(v) \vee \mathrm{p1}(n2) = \mathrm{intr} \vee \mathrm{p2}(n2) = \mathrm{intr}))$.

To search $\mathcal{R}_{\mathcal{S}_{\mathrm{NSPK}},\leq n}$ for a counterexample for $\forall v : \mathcal{R}_{\mathcal{S}_{\mathrm{NSPK}}}.\,\mathrm{NL}_1(v)$, all we have to do is to feed the following line to the Maude system:

```
search [1] init =>* (nw : (enc1(Q,N,intr) , Ms)) (nonces : Ns) S
      such that not(N \in Ns or p1(N) == intr or p2(N) == intr).
```

Command `search` does not find any states v such that $\mathrm{NL}_1(v)$ does not hold when `bound` is up to 5. Actually, we have proved $\forall v \in \mathcal{R}_{\mathcal{S}_{\mathrm{NSPK}}}.\,\mathrm{NL}_1(v)$ by mathematical induction on $\mathcal{R}_{\mathcal{S}_{\mathrm{NSPK}}}$ without any lemmas.

```
state 0, Sys: send2 send3 rand : seed nw : empty nonces : empty fake2(intr)
    fake2(p1) fake2(p2) fake3(intr) fake3(p1) fake3(p2) steps : 0 send1(intr,
    p1) send1(intr, p2) send1(p1, intr) send1(p1, p2) send1(p2, intr) send1(p2,
    p1) fake1(intr, p1) fake1(intr, p2) fake1(p1, intr) fake1(p1, p2) fake1(p2,
    intr) fake1(p2, p1)
===[ ... [label send1] ... ]===>
state 3, Sys: send2 send3 rand : next(seed) nw : enc1(intr, n(p1, intr, seed),
    p1) nonces : n(p1, intr, seed) fake2(intr) fake2(p1) fake2(p2) fake3(intr)
    fake3(p1) fake3(p2) steps : 1 send1(intr, p1) send1(intr, p2) send1(p1,
    intr) send1(p1, p2) send1(p2, intr) send1(p2, p1) fake1(intr, p1) fake1(
    intr, p2) fake1(p1, intr) fake1(p1, p2) fake1(p2, intr) fake1(p2, p1)
===[ ... [label fake1] ... ]===>
state 31, Sys: send2 send3 rand : next(seed) nw : (enc1(intr, n(p1, intr,
    seed), p1),enc1(p2, n(p1, intr, seed), p1)) nonces : n(p1, intr, seed)
    fake2(intr) fake2(p1) fake2(p2) fake3(intr) fake3(p1) fake3(p2) steps : 2
    send1(intr, p1) send1(intr, p2) send1(p1, intr) send1(p1, p2) send1(p2,
    intr) send1(p2, p1) fake1(intr, p1) fake1(intr, p2) fake1(p1, intr) fake1(
    p1, p2) fake1(p2, intr) fake1(p2, p1)
===[ ... [label send2] ... ]===>
state 436, Sys: send2 send3 rand : next(next(seed)) nw : (enc1(intr, n(p1,
    intr, seed), p1),enc1(p2, n(p1, intr, seed), p1),enc2(p1, n(p1, intr,
    seed), n(p2, p1, next(seed)))) nonces : n(p1, intr, seed) fake2(intr)
    fake2(p1) fake2(p2) fake3(intr) fake3(p1) fake3(p2) steps : 3 send1(intr,
    p1) send1(intr, p2) send1(p1, intr) send1(p1, p2) send1(p2, intr) send1(p2,
    p1) fake1(intr, p1) fake1(intr, p2) fake1(p1, intr) fake1(p1, p2) fake1(p2,
    intr) fake1(p2, p1)
```

Fig. 1. An excerpt from the counterexample for $\forall v : \mathcal{R}_{\mathcal{S}_{\mathrm{NSPK}}} . \mathrm{NL}_2(v)$.

```
state 0, Sys: send2 send3 rand : next(next(seed)) nw : (enc1(intr, n(p1, intr,
    seed), p1),enc1(p2, n(p1, intr, seed), p1),enc2(p1, n(p1, intr, seed), n(
    p2, p1, next(seed)))) nonces : n(p1, intr, seed) fake2(intr) fake2(p1)
    fake2(p2) fake3(intr) fake3(p1) fake3(p2) steps : 3 send1(intr, p1) send1(
    intr, p2) send1(p1, intr) send1(p1, p2) send1(p2, intr) send1(p2, p1)
    fake1(intr, p1) fake1(intr, p2) fake1(p1, intr) fake1(p1, p2) fake1(p2,
    intr) fake1(p2, p1)
===[ ... [label send3] ... ]===>
state 9, Sys: send2 send3 rand : next(next(seed)) nw : (enc3(intr, n(p2, p1,
    next(seed))),enc1(intr, n(p1, intr, seed), p1),enc1(p2, n(p1, intr, seed),
    p1),enc2(p1, n(p1, intr, seed), n(p2, p1, next(seed)))) nonces : (n(p1,
    intr, seed),n(p2, p1, next(seed))) fake2(intr) fake2(p1) fake2(p2) fake3(
    intr) fake3(p1) fake3(p2) steps : 4 send1(intr, p1) send1(intr, p2) send1(
    p1, intr) send1(p1, p2) send1(p2, intr) send1(p2, p1) fake1(intr, p1)
    fake1(intr, p2) fake1(p1, intr) fake1(p1, p2) fake1(p2, intr) fake1(p2, p1)
```

Fig. 2. An excerpt from the path to a state v such that $\neg\mathrm{SP}(v)$ from s436

To search $\mathcal{R}_{\mathcal{S}_{\mathrm{NSPK}},\leq n}$ for a counterexample for $\forall v : \mathcal{R}_{\mathcal{S}_{\mathrm{NSPK}}} . \mathrm{NL}_2(v)$, all we have to do is to feed the following line to the Maude system:

```
search [1] init =>*
    (nw : (enc2(Q1,N1,N2) , enc1(intr,N1,Q1),Ms)) (nonces:Ns)S
    such that not(N2 \in Ns or p1(N2)==intr or p2(N2)==intr).
```

When bound is 3, command search finds a state v in which $\mathrm{NL}_2(v)$ does not hold. Command show path can be used to show the path to the state, which is a shortest counterexample for $\forall v : \mathcal{R}_{\mathcal{S}_{\mathrm{NSPK}}} . \mathrm{NL}_2(v)$. An excerpt from the counterexample generated is shown in Fig. 1.

The counterexample and $\text{send3}_{p,q,n1,n2,nw}$ make a counterexample for $\forall v : \mathcal{R}_{\mathcal{S}_{\text{NSPK}}}.\, \text{SP}(v)$. Command `search` can also be used to make such a counterexample. Let a constant `s436` equal the term of state 436 appearing in Fig. 1. Instead of `init`, `s436` is used to find a state such v that $\text{SP}(v)$ does not hold by feeding the following line into the Maude system:

```
search [1] s436 =>* (nonces : (N , Ns)) S
      such that not(p1(N) == intr or p2(N) == intr) .
```

When `bound` is 1, such a state is found. An excerpt from the path to the state from `s436` is shown in Fig. 2. The two paths shown in Fig. 1 and Fig. 2 are combined to make a counterexample for $\forall v : \mathcal{R}_{\mathcal{S}_{\text{NSPK}}}.\, \text{SP}(v)$.

8 Related Work

There are two main methods of falsifying (software and/or hardware) systems: testing and model checking [18]. Model checking is superior to testing in terms of coverage provided that systems should be basically modeled as finite-state transition systems. Even when a system can be modeled as a finite-state transition system, the system may not be model checked because the state space is too large for a computer on which model checking is performed. Bounded model checking, or BMC [13] can alleviate the problem. BMC uses a propositional SAT solver to search $\mathcal{R}_{\mathcal{S},\leq n}$ for a counterexample for a property written in propositional LTL for a fixed n, although a Kripke structure is used instead of an OTS. If no counterexample is found, BMC repeatedly increments n and performs the search until a counterexample is found, the search becomes intractable, or some pre-computed completeness threshold is reached.

In addition to modeling systems as finite-state transition systems, abstract data types such as lists and queues should be encoded in basic data types such as arrays and bounded integers because most existing model checkers do not allow to use abstract data types freely in a system to be model checked. The Maude model checker [19] allows to use abstract data types including inductively defined data types in a system to be model checked and does not require the state space of a system to be finite, although the reachable state space of a system should be finite. That is why we have decided to use Maude to falsify OTSs. Since Maude is not equipped with any BMC facilities, however, a way to search $\mathcal{R}_{\mathcal{S}\leq n}$ for a counterexample for $\forall v : \mathcal{R}_{\mathcal{S}}.\, p(v)$ has been devised [12]. Note that the `search` command can be used to search an infinite state space of an OTS for a counterexample that the OTS satisfies an invariant property, but the termination is not guaranteed, which is required by procedure IGF.

A way to implement a local (or bounded) μ-calculus model checker in Maude using the Maude reflective facilities has been proposed [20]. The primary purpose of implementing or specifying the model checker in Maude is toward verification of the model checker. The bounded μ-calculus model checker could be used to search the bounded reachable state space $\mathcal{R}_{\mathcal{S},\leq n}$ for a counterexample for $\forall v : \mathcal{R}_{\mathcal{S}}.\, p(v)$. In terms of speed, however, the Maude `search` command and the Maude model checker are superior to the bounded μ-calculus model checker.

The induction-guided falsification can be considered a possible solution to the state explosion problem, which we often encounter when we try to model check if a system satisfies a property. Several possible solutions to the problem have been proposed. Their primary purpose is verification. One of the most popular methods is abstraction [21], which requires an original transition system and property to be modified. Instead of abstraction, our solution uses mathematical induction on the structure of the reachable state space of a transition system, which does not require an original transition system to be modified.

The induction-guided falsification can also be regarded as one possible combination of BMC and mathematical induction. There exists another possible combination of them: k-induction [22]. k-induction has been implemented in SAL (Symbolic Analysis Laboratory) [23], which is a toolkit for analyzing transition systems. The primary purpose of k-induction is verification.

9 Conclusion

The induction-guided falsification has been described. The NSPK authentication protocol has been used as an example to demonstrate the induction-guided falsification. We have been developing a translator [24], which takes a CafeOBJ specification of an OTS and generates a Maude specifications of the OTS, and an automatic invariant verifier [25,26] for OTSs, which uses an automatic case splitter that computes necessary lemmas. One piece of our future work is to use the translator and the automatic case splitter to automate the induction-guided falsification.

The basic idea in the proposed solution to find a counterexample that an OTS $\mathcal{S}$ satisfies an invariant property is as follows. When no counterexamples are found in the bounded reachable state space $\mathcal{R}_{\mathcal{S}}^{\leq n}$ and it is impossible to search $\mathcal{R}_{\mathcal{S}}^{\leq(n+1)}$ entirely, first discover all necessary lemmas of the invariant property and then search $\mathcal{R}_{\mathcal{S}}^{\leq n}$ for each of the necessary lemmas. The proposed solution guarantees if there exists a counterexample for the invariant property in $\mathcal{R}_{\mathcal{S}}^{\leq(n+1)}$, there exists a counterexample for at least one of the necessary lemmas in $\mathcal{R}_{\mathcal{S}}^{\leq n}$, and vice versa. Some may wonder how efficient it is to search $\mathcal{R}_{\mathcal{S}}^{\leq n}$ when compared to the search of $\mathcal{R}_{\mathcal{S}}^{\leq(n+1)}$. We suppose that $\mathcal{S}$ has one initial state and there are x (≥ 2) (instances of) transitions whose effective conditions hold in each state. Then, the number of states in $\mathcal{R}_{\mathcal{S}}^{\leq n}$ is $\sum_{i=0}^{n} x^i$, which equals $(x^{n+1} - 1)/(x - 1)$. The difference between the number of states in $\mathcal{R}_{\mathcal{S}}^{\leq(n+1)}$ and that in $\mathcal{R}_{\mathcal{S}}^{\leq n}$ is x^{n+1}, which is greater than the number of states in $\mathcal{R}_{\mathcal{S}}^{\leq n}$ because $x^{n+1} - \sum_{i=0}^{n} x^i$ is $(x^{n+1}(x-2)+1)/(x-1)$. The greater x is, the greater the difference is. There are more than two (instances of) transitions whose effective conditions hold in each state in most applications. Therefore, the search of $\mathcal{R}_{\mathcal{S}}^{\leq n}$ is more efficient than that of $\mathcal{R}_{\mathcal{S}}^{\leq(n+1)}$. When three principles including the intruder participate the NSPK protocol, the number of states in $\mathcal{R}_{\mathcal{S}_{\mathrm{NSPK}}}^{\leq 3}$ is 807, while that in $\mathcal{R}_{\mathcal{S}_{\mathrm{NSPK}}}^{\leq 4}$ is 11323 and that in $\mathcal{R}_{\mathcal{S}_{\mathrm{NSPK}}}^{\leq 5}$ is 180475.

Although procedure IGF can be used to verify that a state predicate p is invariant wrt an OTS $\mathcal{S}$, it is not efficient for the verification. This is because necessary lemmas are useful for finding counterexamples, i.e. falsification but they may not for verification. It is often the case that necessary lemmas should be strengthened to make the corresponding proofs more tractable. It is another piece of our future work to make the procedure useful for both verification and falsification.

As described at the end of Section 5, it depends on the number of some entities in an OTS whether procedure IGF works effectively if the number of the entities should be made finite. Therefore, we need to come up with something that can decide how many entities in an OTS $\mathcal{S}$ are enough to make sure that there exists a counterexample for an invariant in the n-bounded reachable state space wrt $\mathcal{S}$ in which there are a finite number of the entities if there does so in the n-bounded reachable state space wrt $\mathcal{S}$ in which there are an infinite number of the entities.

References

1. Ogata, K., Futatsugi, K.: Proof scores in the OTS/CafeOBJ method. In: FMOODS 2003. LNCS 2884, Springer (2003) 170–184
2. Diaconescu, R., Futatsugi, K.: CafeOBJ Report. Volume 6 of AMAST Series in Computing. World Scientific (1998)
3. Ogata, K., Futatsugi, K.: Formally modeling and verifying Ricart&Agrawala distributed mutual exclusion algorithm. In: 2nd APAQS, IEEE CS Press (2001) 357–366
4. Ogata, K., Futatsugi, K.: Formal analysis of Suzuki&Kasami distributed mutual exclusion algorithm. In: 5th FMOODS, Kluwer (2002) 181–195
5. Ogata, K., Futatsugi, K.: Rewriting-based verification of authentication protocols. In: 4th WRLA 2002. ENTCS 71, Elsevier (2002)
6. Ogata, K., Futatsugi, K.: Formal analysis of the iKP electronic payment protocols. In: 1st ISSS. LNCS 2609, Springer (2003) 441–460
7. Ogata, K., Futatsugi, K.: Formal verification of the Horn-Preneel micropayment protocol. In: 4th VMCAI. LNCS 2575, Springer (2003) 238–252
8. Ogata, K., Futatsugi, K.: Equational approach to formal verification of SET. In: 4th QSIC, IEEE CS Press (2004) 50–59
9. Ogata, K., Futatsugi, K.: Formal analysis of the NetBill electronic commerce protocol. In: 2nd ISSS. LNCS 3233, Springer (2004) 45–64
10. Ogata, K., Futatsugi, K.: Equational approach to formal analysis of TLS. In: 25th ICDCS, IEEE CS Press (2005) 795–804
11. Clavel, M., Durán, F., Eker, S., Lincoln, P., Martí-Oliet, N., Meseguer, J., Quesada, J.: Maude: Spesification and programming language in rewriting logic. TCS **285** (2002) 187–243
12. Ogata, K., Kong, W., Futatsugi, K.: Falsification of OTSs by searches of bounded reachable state spaces. In: 18th SEKE. (2006) 440–445
13. Biere, A., Cimatti, A., Clarke, E.M., Strichman, O., Zhu, Y.: Bounded model checking. In: Advances in Computers. 58. Academic Press (2003)
14. Needham, R.M., Schroeder, M.D.: Using encryption for authentication in large networks of computers. CACM **21** (1978) 993–999
15. Kong, W., Ogata, K., Futatsugi, K.: Model-checking observational transition system with Maude. In: 20th ITC-CSCC. (2005) 5–6
16. Hsiang, J., Dershowitz, N.: Rewrite methods for clausal and nonclausal theorem proving. In: 10th ICALP. LNCS 154, Springer (1983) 331–346
17. Ogata, K., Futatsugi, K.: Some tips on writing proof scores in the OTS/CafeOBJ method. In: Algebra, Meaning, and Computation: A Festschrift Symposium in Honor of Joseph Goguen. LNCS 4060, Springer (2006) 596–615

18. Edmund M. Clarke, J., Grumberg, O., Peled, D.A.: Model Checking. The MIT Press (2001)
19. Eker, S., Meseguer, J., Sridharanarayanan, A.: The Maude LTL model checker. In: WRLA 2002. ENTCS 71, Elsevier (2002) 143–168
20. Wang, B.Y.: Specification of an infinite-state local model checker in rewriting logic. In: 17th SEKE. (2005) 442–447
21. Clarke, E.M., Grumberg, O., Long, D.E.: Model checking and abstraction. ACM TOPLAS **16** (1994) 1512–1542
22. de Moura, L., Rueß, H., Sorea, M.: Bounded model checking and induction: From refutation to verification. In: 15th CAV. LNCS 2392, Springer (2003) 14–26
23. de Moura, L., Owre, S., Rueß, H., Rushby, J., Shankar, N., Sorea, M., Tiwari, A.: SAL 2. In: 16th CAV. LNCS 3114, Springer (2004) 496–500
24. Kong, W., Ogata, K., Seino, T., Futatsugi, K.: Lightweight integration of theorem proving and model checking for system verification. In: 12th APSEC, IEEE CS Press (2005) 59–66
25. Nakano, M., Ogata, K., Nakamura, M., Futatsugi, K.: Automatic verification of the STS authentication protocol with Crème. In: 20th ITC-CSCC. (2005) 15–16
26. Nakano, M., Ogata, K., Nakamura, M., Futatsugi, K.: Automating invariant verification of behavioral specifications. In: 6th QSIC, IEEE CS Press (2006)

Verifying χ Models of Industrial Systems with SPIN

Nikola Trčka*

Department of Mathematics and Computer Science, Eindhoven University of Technology, P.O. Box 513, NL-5600 MB Eindhoven, The Netherlands

Abstract. The language χ has been developed for modeling of industrial systems. Its simulator has been successfully used in many industrial areas for obtaining performance measures. For functional analysis simulation is less applicable and such analysis can be done in other environments. The purpose of this paper is to describe an automatic translator from χ to PROMELA, the input language of the well known model-checker SPIN. We highlight the differences between the two languages and show, in a step by step manner, how some of them can be resolved. We conclude by giving a translation scheme and apply the translator in a small industrial case study.

1 Introduction

The language χ [19] is a modeling language developed for detecting design flaws and for optimizing performance of industrial systems (machines, manufacturing lines, warehouses, factories, etc.) It allows for the specifying of discrete-event, continuous and probabilistic aspects of systems. Its simulator has been successfully applied to a large number of industrial cases, such as a car assembly line (NedCar [10]), a multi-product, multi-process wafer fab (Philips [6]), a brewery (Heineken), a fruit juice blending and packaging plant (Riedel [8]) and process industry plants ([1]). Simulation is a powerful technique for performance analysis, like calculating throughput and cycle time, but it is less suitable for functional analysis (sometimes called verification). It can for instance reveal that a system has a deadlock (it is unable to proceed) or that it sometimes has a certain behavior, but it cannot show that the system is deadlock-free nor that it always has a certain behavior.

A most widely used verification technique today is model checking. This technique performs an exhaustive search of the state space checking if a certain property of the system holds. The property is represented as a formula of some temporal logic, a logic that allows us to say things like: if a machine is given input then it will eventually produce a correct output. There are many variants of these logics (consult e.g. [20]). They can be linear (reasoning is about a single sequence of states) or branching (reasoning involves several different branches starting from a state), action based (reasoning is about what action can be performed in a state) or state based (reasoning about the value of variables in a state), etc. Once the property is stated, model checking becomes a completely automated process.

* Research supported by the Netherlands Organization for Scientific Research (NWO) under project number 612.064.205.

Z. Liu and J. He (Eds.): ICFEM 2006, LNCS 4260, pp. 132–148, 2006.

To facilitate model checking, either verification tools have to be developed especially for χ, or existing verification tools and techniques have to be made available for use with χ. Currently, the latter approach is pursued [4,3,19]. The idea is to extend χ with facilities for doing formal verification by establishing a connection with other state-of-the-art verification tools and techniques on the level of the specification language. That is, formal verification of a χ model is done by first translating it into the input language of some model checker and then performing the actual verification there. Preferably, the translation closely resembles the original, so that counterexamples produced by the model checker can be related to the original specification. However, it should also look, as much as possible, as it were written in the target language and not translated from some other language. This is to ensure that the full power of the verification tool is used.

The aim of this paper is to present techniques that were used to build a translator from χ specifications to PROMELA, the input language of a popular (state-based, linear-temporal) model checker SPIN. Aspects in which χ and PROMELA differ from each other are given in a step by step manner and treated in detail. For each aspect, difficulties of translation are discussed, pitfalls and solutions presented and explained. We cover many important features of χ such as time, nested parallelism, urgency etc. that are usually present in models of industrial systems. We (syntactically) define a subset of χ models that can be translated to PROMELA, present a translation scheme and explain the translation process.

Note that here we take a wide but a less formal approach to the problem. In [17] we support a part of our translation with a formal correctness proof. There we define a notion of equivalence for (a slightly different version of) χ, prove that it is a congruence and that it preserves validity of temporal logic formulas. Then, we identify a subset of χ that resembles PROMELA's syntax closely and thus can map to PROMELA straightforwardly. We also show how a bigger subset of χ can be reduced, modulo the equivalence, to that form.

Our work can be seen as an extension of that presented in [4] and [3]. In [4], the authors present a translation of a χ model of a turntable machine to PROMELA and verify properties, like the absence of deadlock and no product loss, with SPIN. The focus is on the verification and not on the translation; general guidelines for translating arbitrary χ models to PROMELA are not provided. In [3], a more detailed model of the same machine is translated to PROMELA, μCRL [2] and UPPAAL timed automata [16]. Even though this paper shows some techniques and difficulties of the translation to PROMELA, its aim is to compare the different approaches for the functional analysis of χ models, like comparing state based and action based model checking, and to a lesser extent on the aspect of translation.

The structure of the paper is as follows. In Section 2 we give an introduction to χ; its syntax and (informal) semantics. As an illustration we present (a part of) a χ model of a small manufacturing line. In Section 3 we briefly introduce PROMELA, pointing out features that we need. Section 4 is the main section of this paper. There we explain how we deal with the aspects of χ that are uncommon to PROMELA: parallelism, scoping and complex data types, guarded processes, time etc. For each feature we show what the problems of translating it to PROMELA are and how we can circumvent them. Then, we present a translatable subset of χ and a translation scheme. We explain the translation process that serves as a base of the translator and apply the translator on the manufacturing line χ model introduced in Section 2. In the last section we give some conclusions. We also provide an appendix in which the complete χ specification of the manufacturing line and its PROMELA translation are given.

2 The χ Language

For the translation to PROMELA we take the discrete-event subset of χ as our starting point. We give a short and informal introduction to the language and refer to [19] for a complete syntax definition and a formal semantics.

Data Types. The basic data types of χ are booleans, natural, integer, rational and real numbers and typed channels. Most of the usual constants, operators and relations are defined for every data type and can be used together with variables to build expressions. Furthermore, χ provides a mechanism to build compound types such as, among others, tuples (notation $<\mathsf{type}, \mathsf{type}>$) and lists (notation $[\mathsf{type}]$) from the basic types (but not channels).

Time domain. The time domain in χ is dense, i.e. timing is measured on a continuous time scale. Delaying is enforced by the delay operator but some processes can also implicitly delay (see the next paragraph). The weak time determinism principle, sometimes called the time factorization property (time does not make a choice), is implicitly adopted. Maximal progress (a process can delay only if it cannot do anything else) is sometimes implicit and for delayable processes can be enforced by an operator.

2.1 Syntax and Semantics

Atomic processes. The atomic processes of χ are process constructors and cannot be split into smaller processes. We explain each one of them.

The *skip* process performs the internal action τ and cannot delay. The *delay* process Δe delays any number of time units less or equal to the value of the expression e. The *(multi)assignment* process $x_1, \ldots, x_n := e_1, \ldots, e_n$ assigns the value of the expression e_i to the variable x_i, $1 \leq i \leq n$. It does not have the possibility to delay. The *send* process $m!!e$ sends the value of the expression e along the channel m and cannot delay. The *delayable send* $m!e$ behaves as $m!!e$ but it can delay arbitrarily long. The *receive* process $m??x$ inputs a value over the channel m and cannot delay. The *delayable receive* $m?x$ is the same as $m??x$ but can delay.

Compound processes. Here we give an informal explanation for each of the eleven operators in χ. The *guarded* process $b \rightarrow p$ behaves as p when the value of the guard b is true and blocks otherwise. The *sequential composition* $p\,;q$ behaves as p followed by the process q. The *alternative composition* $p \,[]\, q$ stands for a non-deterministic choice between p and q. It delays only if both p and q delay. The *repetition* operator $*p$ behaves as p infinitely many times. The *guarded repetition* process $b \overset{*}{\rightarrow} p$ is interpreted as 'while b do $(skip\,; p)$'. The *parallel composition* operator $\|$ executes p and q concurrently in an interleaved fashion. In addition, if one of the processes can execute a send action and the other one can execute a receive action on the same channel, then they can also communicate, i.e. $p \parallel q$ can also execute the communication action on this channel. Parallel composition delays if both components delay. The *scope* operator is used for declarations of local variables. The process $[\![s \mid p]\!]$ behaves as p in a local state s. The *encapsulation* operator $\partial_A(p)$ disables all actions of p that occur in the parameter set A. The *abstraction* operator $\tau_I(p)$ 'hides' (renames to τ) all actions of p that occur in the parameter set I. The *urgent communication* operator $\mathcal{U}_\mathcal{H}$ gives communication actions via channels from $\mathcal{H}$ a higher priority over the passage of time.

The language χ also allows for process definitions. They are given once but can be instantiated many times (possibly with different parameters) by the *process instantiation* operator.

2.2 A Manufacturing Line in χ

To give an impression of the language we give an example, a slight modification of the one given in [19]. Consider a manufacturing line that consists of a generator, a distributor, a rejector, two manufacturing cells, an assembly machine and exit. The system is pictured in Fig. 1. The generator generates products every 7 time units and delivers them to the distributor. The distributor waits 6 time units for one of the cells to be ready and then sends it a product. If in 5 time units none of the cells are ready the distributor sends a product to the rejector. Each manufacturing cell consists of two machines and a 5-place buffer in between. Every product is processed by the cell twice. After processing, products are sent to the assembly machine where they are processed

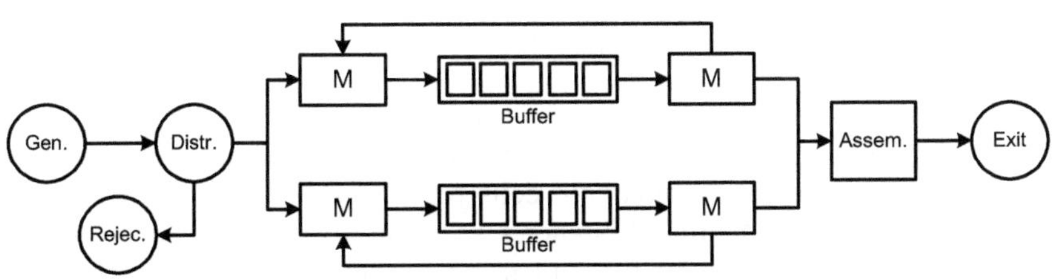

Fig. 1. Manufacturing Line

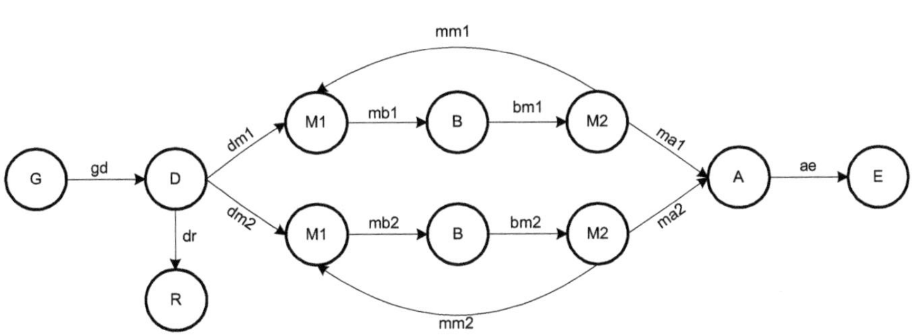

Fig. 2. Manufacturing Line - Process Diagram

further, combined and sent to the exit. All machines take 4 time units to perform their operation.

We now give a complete χ specification of the manufacturing line. The process diagram is depicted in Figure 2.

$$
\begin{array}{l}
\mathbf{G}(\textsf{chan}\ out : \textsf{bool}, \textsf{disc}\ d : \textsf{int}) = |[\ \textsf{disc}\ x : \textsf{bool} = \mathit{false} \mid *\,(\Delta d\ ;\ out!x))\ ]| \\
\mathbf{D}(\textsf{chan}\ in, out_1, out_2 : \textsf{bool}, \textsf{disc}\ d : \textsf{int}) = |[\ \textsf{disc}\ x : \textsf{bool} \mid \\
\quad *(\ in?x\ ;\ (out_1!x\ [\!]\ out_2!x\ [\!]\ \Delta d\ ;\ out_r!x)\ )\ ]| \\
\mathbf{R}(\textsf{chan}\ in : \textsf{bool}) = |[\ \textsf{disc}\ x : \textsf{bool} = \mathit{false} \mid *\,(in?x)\ ]| \\
\mathbf{M_1}(\textsf{chan}\ in_1, in_2, out : \textsf{bool}, \textsf{disc}\ d : \textsf{int}) = |[\ \textsf{disc}\ x : \textsf{bool} \mid \\
\quad *(\ (in_1?x\ [\!]\ (in_2?x\ ;\ x := \mathit{true}))\Delta d\ ;\ out!x\ )\ ]| \\
\mathbf{B}(\textsf{chan}\ in, out : \textsf{bool}, \textsf{disc}\ n : \textsf{int}) = |[\ \textsf{disc}\ x : \textsf{bool}, buf : [\textsf{bool}] = [\,]\ \mid \\
\quad *(\ len(buf) < n \rightarrow (in?x\ ;\ buf := buf +\!\!+ [x]) \\
\quad\ \ [\!]\ len(buf) > 0 \rightarrow (out!hd(buf)\ ;\ buf := tl(buf))\ )\ ]| \\
\mathbf{M_2}(\textsf{chan}\ in, out_m, out_a : \textsf{bool}, \textsf{disc}\ d : \textsf{int}) = |[\ \textsf{disc}\ x : \textsf{bool} \mid \\
\quad *(\ in?x\ ;\ \Delta d\ ;\ (x \rightarrow out_a!x [\!] \neq x \rightarrow out_m!x)\ )\ ]| \\
\mathbf{A}(\textsf{chan}\ in_1, in_2, out : \textsf{bool}, \textsf{disc}\ d : \textsf{int}) = |[\ \textsf{disc}\ x, y : \textsf{bool}\ \mid \\
\quad *(\ (in_1?x \parallel in_2?y)\ ;\ \Delta d\ ;\ out!(x \wedge y)\ )\ ]| \\
\mathbf{E}(\textsf{chan}\ in : \textsf{bool}) = |[\ \textsf{disc}\ x : \textsf{bool} \mid *\,(in?x)\ ]| \\
\textsf{sys}() = \mathcal{U}_{\mathcal{H}}\partial_{\mathcal{A}}(|[\ \textsf{chan}\ gd, dm_1, dm_2, dr, mb_1, mb_2, bm_1, bm_2, \\
\qquad\qquad\qquad\qquad\qquad ma_1, ma_2, mm_1, mm_2, ae : \textsf{bool}\ \mid \\
\qquad\quad \mathbf{G}(gd, 7) \parallel \mathbf{D}(gd, dm_1, dm_2, dr, 6) \parallel \mathbf{R}(dr) \parallel \\
\qquad\quad \parallel \mathbf{M_1}(dm_1, mm_1, mb_1, 4) \parallel \mathbf{M_1}(dm_2, mm_2, mb_2, 4) \parallel \\
\qquad\quad \parallel \mathbf{B}(mb_1, bm_1, 5) \parallel \mathbf{B}(mb_2, bm_2, 5) \parallel \\
\qquad\quad \parallel \mathbf{M_2}(bm_1, mm_1, ma_1, 4) \parallel \mathbf{M_2}(mm_2, mm_2, ma_2, 4) \parallel \\
\qquad\quad \parallel \mathbf{A}(ma_1, ma_2, me, 4) \parallel \mathbf{E}(ae)\ ]|\ )
\end{array}
$$

Variable x models products. It is a boolean variable (the prefix disc stands for discrete; in discrete-event models all variables are discrete) so that we can distinguish cases when the product was not processed by the cells yet (x is *false*) from when it is already processed once (x is *true*). Symbol $[\,]$ denotes an empty list, and the operator $+\!\!+$ concatenates two lists. $\mathcal{H}$ contains all channel names; $\mathcal{A}$ contains all send/receive actions. This is to ensure that sending and receiving cannot happen individually but only as an instant communication.

3 PROMELA/SPIN

PROMELA's syntax is derived from C [15], with communication primitives from CSP [12] and control flow statements based on the guarded command language [7]. It has many language constructs similar to χ constructs. The full presentation of the language, is beyond the scope of this paper so we only give a brief overview mentioning only those parts of the language that we are interested in. For more information, see [13,9,14] or consult SPIN's web page `http://spinroot.com`.

PROMELA has a rather limited set of data types, only `bool`, `byte`, `short`, `int` (all with the `unsigned` possibility) and channels. It also provides a way to build records and arrays and to define C-like macros. Message channels are declared, for instance, as `chan m = [2] of {int}` meaning that the channel is buffered and that it can store (at most) two values of (its field's) type integer. Channels can be of length 0, i.e. unbuffered, to model synchronous communication. They can also have more than one field, not necessarily of the same type.

Any expression is also a statement, executable precisely if it evaluates to a non-zero value. Assignments are also statements and have the usual semantics. The `skip` statement executes the action `(1)` and has no effect on variables. The send statement (`m!e_1,...,e_n`) sends a tuple of values of the expressions `e_i` to the channel `m`. The receive statement (`m?E_1,...,E_n`) retrieves a message from the non-empty channel `m`, for every `E_i` that is a variable assigns a value of `e_i` to it and for every other `E_j` makes sure that its value matches the value of the `e_j`. If the channel is buffered, a send is enabled if the buffer is not full; a receive is enabled if the buffer is non-empty. On an unbuffered channel, a send (receive) is enabled only if there is a corresponding receive (send) that can be executed simultaneously. There are also many variants of these statements.

There are several ways to combine statements. The alternative composition `if ::stmt_1 ... ::stmt_n fi` nondeterministically selects among its options an executable statement and executes it. It blocks until there is at least one selectable option. The repetition `do ::stmt_1 ... ::stmt_n od` is similar to the alternative composition except that the choices are executed repeatedly, until control is explicitly transferred to outside the statement by the `break` or `goto` statement. The `break` statement terminates the innermost repetition statement in which it is executed and cannot be used outside a repetition. The sequential composition is denoted `p;q` or `b -> p`. The latter form is usually used to emphasize that `p` is guarded by the conditional expression/statement `b`.

The original version of PROMELA/SPIN is untimed but there is a discrete time extension, called DTPROMELA/DTSPIN [5]. The idea is to divide time into slices and then frame actions into these slices. The time between actions is measured in ticks of a global digital clock. By having a variable `t` declared as `timer`, setting its value to some expression that evaluates to a natural number (by doing `set(t,e)`) and waiting for `t` to expire (by stating `expire(t)`) a process can be enforced to postpone its execution for `n` time slices (where `n` is the value of `e`). When DTSPIN executes the `timeout` action, all timers synchronize and time progresses to a next slice. This action is executed only if no other actions can be executed, meaning that maximal progress is implicit. Deadlock is recognized when `timeout` is enabled and all timers are off (not set or already expired).

PROMELA provides two constructs, `atomic{stmt_1;...;stmt_n}` and `d_step{stmt_1;...;stmt_n}` that can be used to model indivisible events and to reduce a state space. Their purpose is to forbid the statements from inside to interleave with other statements in the specifications. The difference is that additionally `d_step` executes all statements as one (one state in the state space). These constructs are very useful but have limitations: statements other than the first may not block.

A common specification consists of global channel declarations, variable declarations and process declarations. Process declarations (`proctype`)contain local variables and channels declarations not visible to other processes. Once declared, every process can be started (with different parameters) by the process creation mechanism, the `run` statement. With the prefix `active`, a process is considered initially active and need not be started explicitly. Once started processes execute in parallel with the interleaving semantics. This is the only way to achieve parallelism because there is no explicit parallel operator. Processes communicate with each other through global variables and channels.

4 Translating χ to PROMELA

First we introduce some mild assumptions about the χ processes we consider for translation. SPIN is a state based model checker and hiding of actions does not play a role so we assume that our models do not contain the τ_I operator. In addition, because the main form of communication in χ is synchronous, we assume that the encapsulation operator ∂_A, with A the set of all send and receive actions, is applied to our process. Since there is no explicit encapsulation in PROMELA, we do not allow ∂_A to occur anywhere else. The last assumption concerns timing. Because time progresses in SPIN only if nothing else is possible, our process is prefixed by the $\mathcal{U}_\mathcal{H}$ operator. This is the only place where $\mathcal{U}_\mathcal{H}$ is allowed. To summarize, we consider only processes of the form $\mathcal{U}_\mathcal{H}\partial_A(p)$ where p does not contain abstraction, encapsulation nor the urgent communication (experience shows that most χ specifications of discrete-event systems are of this shape). From now on when we refer to the process we translate, we mean p.

4.1 Translation Techniques

We now explain the translation of every feature in which χ and PROMELA differ from each other. The PROMELA translation of some χ construct x is denoted `x`.

4.2 Translation of Data Types

From the set of basic data types a χ specification to be translated can contain channels, booleans, natural numbers and integers. Translation of bool, nat and int variable declarations is straightforward. For the translation of channel declarations note that, in PROMELA, forcing the communication on some channel to be handshake communication is automatically done if the channel is declared of zero length. So, the translation of chan m : int is `chan m = [0] of {int}`.

Complex data types can be implemented using PROMELA's support for records, arrays and macro definitions. For example, a tuple of an integer and a boolean value is represented as

```
 typedef TUPLE_INT_BOOL {
    int elem_1;
    bool elem_2;
} .
```

To model *bounded* lists we can use buffered channels (a similar approach was taken in [11]). A list of maximal length n is defined as a tuple of a channel `l` of capacity `n` (the actual list) and a variable `head` that holds the first element of the list. Adding an item to a list is represented as sending it to a channel that represents the list. Transformation of a list into its tail is done by receiving an element from this channel. To keep the `head` variable up-to-date, we use a predefined PROMELA function `len`, that returns the length of a channel, and a variant of the send statement (`m?<x>`), that behaves as `m?x` only that the message from the channel `m` is not erased upon executing. All lists are required to be initially empty. A list of (max. n) integers is represented as:

```
typedef LIST_INT {
   chan l = [n] of {int};
   int head = 0;
} .
```

To make the usage of lists simpler and closer to χ syntax we define four macros. They represent some usual functions on lists (note that χ has more): `add(x,lst)` adds `x` to the list `lst`, `hd(lst)` returns a first element of `lst`, `tail(lst)` transforms the list `lst` into its tail and `length(lst)` gives the length of `lst`.

```
#define add(x,lst) d_step{ lst.l!x;\
                           if\
                            :: len(lst.l) == 1 -> lst.head = x\
                            :: else\
                           fi;\
                         }
#define hd(lst) (lst.head)
#define tail(lst) d_step{ lst.l?_;\
                          if\
                           :: len(lst.l) > 0 -> lst.l?<lst.head>\
                           :: else\
                          fi;\
                        }

#define length(lst) (len(lst.l)) .
```

4.3 Translation of Processes Terms

Translation of the *skip* statement, sequential and alternative composition is straightforward since they have direct equivalents in PROMELA. The multi-assignment $x_1, \ldots, x_n$:= $e_1, \ldots, e_n$ is also easily translated as

```
d_step {x_1 = e_1; ... x_n = e_n}.
```

Due to the nature of timing in PROMELA, every process is delayable. Therefore, the delayable send $m!e$ and the delayable receive $m?x$ are translated to `m!e` and `m?x`. The undelayable send $m!!e$ (the undelayable receive is similar) is translated as

```
if
 :: m!e
 :: atomic { timeout; false }
fi .
```

This statement says that the send is available but the passage of time leads to an immediate deadlock.

Parallelism. As said before, process definitions in PROMELA are implicitly executed in parallel and there is no (explicit) parallel operator. The `run` statement cannot be used to translate nested parallelism. Suppose that $(p \parallel q) \; [\!] \; r$ is translated as:

```
if
 :: atomic { run(p); run(q) }
 :: r
fi ,
```

where p and q are separate process definitions in PROMELA. In this PROMELA specification the choice does not depend on the executability of $p \parallel q$; the `run` statement is always executable. Similar problems arise with nested process instantiation.

Nested parallelism, therefore, must be eliminated. Note that not all parallelism should be eliminated (e.g. by linearizing) because this would take time, it would drastically move us away from the original specification, and we would not be able to use SPIN's powerful verification features.

We now discuss some cases in which there are techniques to deal with nested parallelism.

Note that a sequential composition can be simulated by a parallel composition at the expense of introducing an extra synchronization variable. Thus process $(p \parallel q) \; ; r$ is equal to

$$[\![\mathsf{disc}\ w : \mathsf{nat} = 0 \mid p \, ; w := w + 1 \parallel q \, ; w := w + 1 \parallel w = 2 \rightarrow r]\!]$$

and similarly $p \, ; (q \parallel r)$ is equal to

$$[\![\mathsf{disc}\ w : \mathsf{bool} = \mathit{false} \mid p \, ; w := \mathit{true} \parallel w \rightarrow q \parallel w \rightarrow r]\!] \, .$$

This technique can easily be extended from two to an arbitrary number of parallel components.

If parts of a process that run in parallel do not communicate with each other, the parallel operator is just an interleaving operator. In both χ and PROMELA interleaving of atomic processes can sometimes be achieved with one loop and a few additional guards (boolean variables). The idea is to associate one guard to each atomic process. If there is a choice between two atomic processes then they share the same guard. Only atomic processes available from the start have their guards initially set to *true*. When an atomic process is executed, its guard is put to *false* and the guard of the atomic process that comes next is assigned *true*. This is done in a loop that is exited when all the guards are *false*. Note that this does not work when there is repetition operator involved.

We illustrate the technique with an example. Suppose a,b,c,d and e are atomic processes. Then, process $a \, ; b \parallel c \, ; (d \; [\!] \; e)$ is transformed to:

$$\begin{array}{l}
[\![\ \mathsf{disc}\ b_1 : \mathsf{bool} = \mathit{true}, b_2 : \mathsf{bool} = \mathit{false}, b_3 : \mathsf{bool} = \mathit{true}, b_4 : \mathsf{bool} = \mathit{false} \mid \\
b_1 \vee b_2 \vee b_3 \vee b_4 \overset{*}{\rightarrow} \\
\quad (\ b_1 \rightarrow a \, ; b_1 := \mathit{false} \, ; b_2 := \mathit{true} \\
\quad [\!]\ b_2 \rightarrow b \, ; b_2 := \mathit{false} \\
\quad [\!]\ b_3 \rightarrow c \, ; b_3 := \mathit{false} \, ; b_4 := \mathit{true} \\
\quad [\!]\ b_4 \rightarrow d \, ; b_4 := \mathit{false} \\
\quad [\!]\ b_4 \rightarrow e \, ; b_4 := \mathit{false} \\
\quad)\ ]\!] .
\end{array}$$

Note that this solution introduces many additional assignments and therefore enlarges the state space of a process. When translating the example to PROMELA one can put a guarded command and the assignments following in a `d_step` statement.

Scoping. In PROMELA there are only two scope levels. Process local, in process declarations, and global, outside of them. It is not possible to introduce blocks with block-local variables inside the process declarations. This is not a serious limitation because for almost every process we can always find an equivalent one of the form $[\![s \mid [\![s_1 \mid p_1]\!] \parallel \ldots \parallel [\![s_n \mid p_n]\!]]\!]$ where the p_i's do not contain the scope operator. First note that $[\![- \mid p]\!]$ is equivalent to p and that $[\![s_1 \mid [\![s_2 \mid p]\!]]\!]$ is equivalent to $[\![\gamma(s_1, s_2) \mid p]\!]$ (where γ is a function that adds variables from s_2 to s_1, overwriting those already present in s_1). This allows us to eliminate scope when its declaration section is empty or when it is immediately nested. Further, it is not hard to prove that, when q does not contain free variables (a variable is free in q if it is not used within a scope that declares it) that are declared in s, then $[\![s \mid p]\!] \circ q$ is equivalent to $[\![s \mid p \circ q]\!]$ for all $\circ \in \{;, [\,], \parallel\}$. Similarly, $b \longrightarrow [\![s \mid p]\!]$ is the same as $[\![s \mid b \longrightarrow p]\!]$ when b does not contain variables also declared in s, and $p\,; [\![s \mid q]\!]$ is the same as $[\![s \mid p\,; q]\!]$ when the free variables of p are not declared in s.

Elimination of a scope in the context of a repetition is more complicated. Note that the process $*\,[\![s \mid p]\!]$ has different behavior than $[\![s \mid *p]\!]$. This is because p in $*\,[\![s \mid p]\!]$, when it has finished executing, starts again in the 'fresh' state s while p in $[\![s \mid *p]\!]$ starts from a possibly modified state. A solution is to make p restore the old state when it is done. In other words, if s is of the form $\textsf{disc}\ x_1 : \textsf{type}_1 = c_1, \ldots, x_n : \textsf{type}_n = c_n, \textsf{chan}\ m_1 : \textsf{type}_1, \ldots, \textsf{chan}\ m_k : \textsf{type}_k$, we transform $*\,[\![s \mid p]\!]$ to $[\![s \mid *(p\,; x_1 := c_1\,; \ldots; x_n := c_n)]\!]$. If some of the x_i's are not initialized (i.e. the part $= c_i$ is missing) we simply omit $x_i := c_i$. The guarded repetition $b \overset{*}{\longrightarrow} [\![s \mid p]\!]$ similarly translates to $[\![s \mid b \overset{*}{\longrightarrow} (p\,; x_1 := c_1\,; \ldots; x_n := c_n)]\!]$.

The summary of all the transformations that (after adequately renaming variables) can be used for nested scopes elimination is given in Table 1.

Table 1. Elimination of nested scopes

$[\![- \mid p]\!]$	p
$b \longrightarrow [\![s \mid p]\!]$	$[\![s \mid b \longrightarrow p]\!]$
$[\![s \mid p]\!]\,;q$	$[\![s \mid p\,; q]\!]$
$p\,; [\![s \mid q]\!]$	$[\![s \mid p\,; q]\!]$
$[\![s \mid p]\!]\,[\,]q$	$[\![s \mid p\,[\,]\,q]\!]$
$[\![s \mid p]\!] \parallel q$	$[\![s \mid p \parallel q]\!]$
$[\![s_1 \mid [\![s_2 \mid p]\!]]\!]$	$[\![\gamma(s_1, s_2) \mid p]\!]$
$*\,[\![s \mid p]\!]$	$[\![s \mid *(p\,; x_1 := c_1\,; \ldots; x_n := c_n)]\!]$
$b \overset{*}{\longrightarrow} [\![s \mid p]\!]$	$[\![s \mid b \overset{*}{\longrightarrow} (p\,; x_1 := c_1\,; \ldots; x_n := c_n)]\!]$

Timing. DTPROMELA is a discrete time extension so we require delays to be natural numbers. This is not a real limitation because for rational delays there is always a number we can multiply all of them by, and obtain natural delays of the same ratio. The Δe

statement is translated to the DTPROMELA statement `expire(t)`, where `t` is of type `timer` and is previously set to the value of e. For each Δ statement a new timer should be introduced. In cases where Δe is not involved in a choice, `set(t,e)` can be present immediately before the `expire(t)` (there is a PROMELA macro `delay(t,e)` defined as `set(t,e); expire(t)` that can be used instead). However, when there is a choice of Δe and another process we have to be more careful. If, for example, we translate $\Delta e \;[\!]\; p$ as

```
if
  :: set(t,e); expire(t)
  :: p
fi ,
```

then because `set(t,e)` is always executable, SPIN can choose to execute it. This means that, if `p` can do a send or receive action, then we lose an option to communicate which contradicts the fact that send and receive processes are delayable and that alternatives delay together. Also, if `p` is an assignment, SPIN should not execute `set(t,e)` because the assignment should have priority.

To prevent time from making a choice `set(t,e)` must be moved before the alternative composition. This is enough to assure the right behavior since `expire(t)` is a boolean expression/statement that is blocked until n (the value of `e`) time slices later. Therefore, the right translation of $\Delta e \;[\!]\; p$ is:

```
set(t,e);
if
  :: expire(t)
  :: p
fi.
```

Guards. Statements of type $b \rightarrow p$, in general cannot be just translated as `b -> p`. This is because in PROMELA operator `->` is equivalent to the sequential operator and the boolean expression `b` is also a statement. This means, if the value of `b` is `true`, SPIN will execute the action `(1)` (e.g. it will pass the guard) even though process `p` cannot execute anything. This is different from χ which looks for both b to be $true$ and for p to be executable before taking the step. For example, in χ, the process $true \rightarrow p \;[\!]\; true \rightarrow skip$ will execute $skip$ if p is not executable. In PROMELA however, process

```
if
  :: true -> p
  :: true -> skip
fi ,
```

since it does not look 'behind' guards, can pick the first `true`, execute it and deadlock afterwards. Thus, the PROMELA statement `b -> p` actually corresponds to the process $(b \rightarrow skip) \, ; p$ in χ.

In the special case when p is an atomic process it is always possible to translate process $b \rightarrow p$. A guarded $skip$ is translated to a PROMELA expression/statement `b`. Guarded delays $b \rightarrow \Delta e$ are simply translated as `set(t,e); (b && expire(t))`.

A guarded assignment $b \rightarrow x := e$ we translate as `d_step{b; x = e}`. With the `d_step` operator we force the statement to be executed as one action, like in χ. If the value of `b` is `false` the statement is blocked, and if it is `true`, since an assignment is always executable, both statements execute at once.

In order to translate guarded send/receive processes we must apply a different trick because these processes can block. We change the channel declaration by adding another field argument to it, one of type integer (for another possibility to translate guarded send and receive statements on unbuffered channels, see [13, page 398]). We use this extra argument to synchronize on guards and we translate $b \rightarrow m!e$ to `m!e,b` and $B \rightarrow m?x$ to `m?x,eval(2-B)`. We take `2-B` instead of just `B` to avoid the communication between a guarded send and a guarded receive when both guards evaluate to false (`2-B = b` is equivalent to `B=1` and `b=1`). The `eval` function is used to force the evaluation of the expression `2-B`. SPIN does not do this automatically in receive statements because the expression can be a variable in which case it should not serve as a match but instead it would be assigned the incoming value. Correspondingly, the guarded undelayable send $b \rightarrow m!!e$ is translated as

```
if
 :: m!e,b
 :: atomic {timeout; false}
fi.
```

Like in the case of the scope operator, the restriction that only atomic processes are guarded is not so serious since most processes have equivalents in that form. Transformations that simplify guards in the context of other guards, alternative and sequential composition, and repetition are shown in Table 2 (how guarded scopes are simplified we have shown in the paragraph on scoping). Translation is simpler if *all* atomic processes are guarded, so we also have a rule that transforms p to the obvious equivalent $true \rightarrow p$.

Table 2. Simplification of guards

p	$true \rightarrow p$
$b_1 \rightarrow b_2 \rightarrow p$	$b_1 \wedge b_2 \rightarrow p$
$b \rightarrow (p \mathbin{[]} q)$	$(b \rightarrow p) \mathbin{[]} (b \rightarrow q)$
$b \rightarrow (p; q)$	$(b \rightarrow p)\ ;\ q$
$b \rightarrow *p$	$(b \rightarrow p)\ ;\ *p$
$b_1 \rightarrow b_2 \overset{*}{\rightarrow} p$	$b_1 \wedge b_2 \rightarrow skip\ ;\ b \overset{*}{\rightarrow} p \mathbin{[]} b_1 \wedge \neg b_2 \rightarrow skip$

Note that, in general, $b \rightarrow (p \parallel q)$ is not equivalent to $(b \rightarrow p) \parallel (b \rightarrow q)$. This is because when the value of b is $true$, after executing an action (for example from p) process $b \rightarrow (p \parallel q)$ proceeds as $p' \parallel q$ and process $(b \rightarrow p) \parallel (b \rightarrow q)$ as $p' \parallel (b \rightarrow q)$ and the action might have changed the value of b to $false$. Only when p and q do not change the value of b, e.g. when they do not contain atomic processes that influence variables present in b, we can distribute the guard over the parallel operator.

Repetition. The guarded repetition $b \xrightarrow{*} p$ is translated to

```
do
  :: b; p
  :: !b
od.
```

Note that the repetition operator $*p$ is not equivalent to $true \xrightarrow{*} p$. The difference between the two becomes apparent in the context of alternative composition. The process $(true \xrightarrow{*} p) \,[\!]\, q$ chooses between the $skip$, which is always executable, and the process q. The process $(*p) \,[\!]\, q$ chooses between p and q. The correct translation of $*p$ is, of course,

```
do
  :: p
od.
```

4.4 Translation Process

In accordance to the previous discussion, χ specifications that can be translated to PROMELA belong to the set P generated by the following:

$$S ::= - \mid \mathsf{disc}\ x : \mathsf{type} = c, S' \mid \mathsf{chan}\ x : \mathsf{type}, S' \mid p : <\mathsf{type}, \mathsf{type}>, S' \mid l : [\mathsf{type}] = [\,], S'$$

$$A ::= skip \mid x := e \mid m!e \mid m?x \mid m!!e \mid m??x \mid \Delta e$$

$$BP ::= A \mid b \rightarrow BP \mid BP \,;\, BP \mid BP \,[\!]\, BP \mid *BP \mid b \xrightarrow{*} BP \mid [\![S \mid BP]\!]$$

$$P ::= \mathcal{U}_{\mathcal{H}} \partial_{\mathcal{A}}([\![S \mid BP(\ldots) \parallel \ \ldots \ \parallel BP(\ldots)]\!])$$

where $\mathcal{H}$ contains all channel names, $\mathcal{A}$ contains all send/receive actions, the symbol e represents any expression, the symbol b represents a boolean expression. The statement $BP(\ldots)$ denotes a process instantiation of a process definition that belongs to BP. We assume the restriction on allowed data types and the restriction for the allowed operators on lists. Note that we completely disallow nested parallelism and nested process instantiations. Although in the previous section we explained how in some cases they can be eliminated, it is hard to syntactically identify those cases. The translatable subset is restrictive but usually corresponds to the current practice.

The first step of the translator is to check if the χ specification belongs to the required subset, and if not, to issue an error message. Note that the grammar above allows nested scopes and arbitrary guarded processes. These statements cannot be directly translated to PROMELA, so the second step of the translator, called the preprocessing step, is to perform the transformations from Tables 2 and 1. This step changes the definition of BP into

$$BP ::= [\![S \mid BP']\!]$$

$$BP' ::= b \rightarrow A \mid BP' \,;\, BP' \mid BP' \,[\!]\, BP' \mid *BP' \mid b \xrightarrow{*} BP'.$$

The third step is the application of the following scheme:

$$S \longmapsto \begin{cases} \texttt{-} & S \equiv - \\ \texttt{type x = c; S} & S \equiv \mathsf{disc}\,x : \mathsf{type} = c, S \\ \texttt{chan c[0] of \{type,int\}; S} & S \equiv \mathsf{chan}\,c : \mathsf{type}, S \\ \texttt{TUPLE\_TYPE\_TYPE p; S} & S \equiv p : <\mathsf{type}, \mathsf{type}>, S \\ \texttt{LIST\_TYPE l; S} & S \equiv l : [\mathsf{type}] = [], S \end{cases}$$

$$b \rightarrow A \longmapsto \begin{cases} \texttt{d\_step}\{\texttt{b}; \texttt{x} := \texttt{e}\} & A \equiv x := e \\ \texttt{b} & A \equiv skip \\ \texttt{c!Expr, b} & A \equiv c!e \\ \texttt{c?x, eval(2 - b)} & A \equiv c?x \\ \begin{array}{l}\texttt{if} \\ \;\texttt{:: c!Expr,b} \\ \;\texttt{:: atomic \{timeout; false\}} \\ \texttt{fi}\end{array} & A \equiv c!!e \\ \begin{array}{l}\texttt{if} \\ \;\texttt{:: c?x,eval(2 - b)} \\ \;\texttt{:: atomic \{timeout; false\}} \\ \texttt{fi}\end{array} & A \equiv c??x \\ \texttt{set(t,e); (b \&\& expire(t))} & A \equiv \Delta e \end{cases}$$

$$BP' \,;\, BP' \longmapsto \texttt{BP'; BP'} \qquad BP' \mid BP' \longmapsto \begin{array}{l}\texttt{if} \\ \;\texttt{:: BP'} \\ \;\texttt{:: BP'} \\ \texttt{fi}\end{array}$$

$$*BP' \longmapsto \begin{array}{l}\texttt{do} \\ \;\texttt{:: BP'} \\ \texttt{od}\end{array} \qquad b \overset{*}{\rightarrow} BP' \longmapsto \begin{array}{l}\texttt{do} \\ \;\texttt{:: b; BP'} \\ \;\texttt{:: !b} \\ \texttt{od}\end{array}$$

$P \longmapsto$
```
S;
proctype BP(...) {
   S
   BP'
}
 ...
active proctype BP(...) {
   S
   BP'
}
```

Note that only the last process is given the prefix `active`.

To correctly translate delays, a postprocessing step that declares and renames timers and that moves `set` functions to outside of `if :: fi` and `do :: od` statements, is performed.

The translator is developed by Ralph Meijer and can be obtained from [18]. It is still a prototype, the preprocessing and postprocessing steps are not implemented but only a warning is issued.

4.5 The Manufacturing Line in PROMELA

We now give the PROMELA translation of the χ model of the manufacturing line presented in Section 3. Note that, before applying the translator, we manually removed the simple (interleaving) nested parallelism in the process A. We also, after applying the translator, moved the `set` statement of the process D to the outside of the `if :: fi` statement.

```
#include "dtime.h"
#include "list.h"

proctype G(chan out; int d) {
    timer t;
    bool x = 0;

    do :: delay(t,d); out!x,1 od;
}

proctype D(chan in,out1,out2,outr; int d) {
    timer t;
    bool x;

    do
     :: in?x,eval(2-1); set(t,d);
        if
         :: out1!x,1
         :: out2!x,1
         :: expire(t); outr!x,1
        fi
    od
}

proctype R(chan in) {
    bool x;

    do :: in?x,eval(2-1) od
}

proctype M1(chan in1,in2, out; int d) {
    bool x;
    timer t;

    do
     :: if
         :: in1?x,eval(2-1)
         :: in2?x,eval(2-1); x = 1
        fi;
        delay(t,d);
        out!x,1
    od
}

 proctype B(chan in,out; int n) {
    bool x;
    LISTBOOL buf;

    do
     :: in?x,eval(length(buf) < n);
        add(x,buf)
     :: out!hd(buf),(length(buf) > 0);
        tail(buf)
    od
}

proctype M2(chan in,outm,outa;int d){
    bool x;
    timer t;

    do
     :: in?x,eval(2-1);
        delay(t,d);
        if
         :: outa!x,x
         :: outm!x,(!x)
        fi
    od
}

proctype A(chan in1,in2,out; int d) {
  bool x,y;
  timer t;

  do
   :: if
     ::in1?x,eval(2-1);in2?y,eval(2-1)
     ::in2?y,eval(2-1);in1?x,eval(2-1)
      fi;
      delay(t,d);
      out!(x && y),1
    od
}

proctype E(chan in) {
    bool x;

    do :: in?x,eval(2-1) od
}

active proctype sys() {
    chan gd = [0] of {bool,int};
    chan dm1 = [0] of {bool,int};
    chan dm2 = [0] of {bool,int};
    chan dr = [0] of {bool,int};
    chan mb1 = [0] of {bool,int};
    chan mb2 = [0] of {bool,int};
    chan bm1 = [0] of {bool,int};
    chan bm2 = [0] of {bool,int};
    chan ma1 = [0] of {bool,int};
    chan ma2 = [0] of {bool,int};
    chan mm1 = [0] of {bool,int};
```

```
   chan mm2 = [0] of {bool,int};
   chan ae = [0] of {bool,int};

   atomic{
      run G(gd,7);
      run D(gd,dm1,dm2,dr,6);
      run R(dr);
      run M1(dm1,mm1,mb1,4);
      run M1(dm2,mm2,mb2,4);
      run B(mb1,bm1,5);
      run B(mb2,bm2,5);
      run M2(bm1,mm1,ma1,4);
      run M2(bm2,mm2,ma2,4);
      run A(ma1,ma2,ae,4);
      run E(ae);
   }
}
```

To illustrate the usefulness of our approach we verify the property that products that are only assembled once do not leave the system. First note that this is equivalent to saying that, in all states of the system, the variable `x` from the process `E` has the value `1` (if also it was initially `1`). In the linear temporal logic built in SPIN this is expressed as `[] (x == 1)`. Since this logic allows reasoning only about global variables, we have to move `x` to the global scope (and initialize it to `1`). SPIN verified this property almost instantly.

5 Conclusion

In this paper we discussed the automatic translator of χ models to PROMELA. Comparing the two languages in detail, we showed that most χ specifications have equivalents in PROMELA, but also that sometimes, what seems to be an obvious translation, can have very different behavior.

We were able to syntactically define a translatable subset and we presented a translation scheme. We also defined the phases of the translation process on which the translator is based.

Most χ specifications encountered in practice either belong to the translatable subset or can be easily modified to fit the form of the subset. For example, nested parallelism almost never appears guarded or in an alternative composition. However, it still is a problem that we cannot (yet) deal with in a satisfactory way. This is a subject for further investigations.

Together, the simulator of χ and a tool that translates χ models into PROMELA constitute an effective environment in which performance analysis and functional analysis of industrial systems are combined.

At last, we think that our results can also be used in building a translator from χ to some other process-like formalisms like e.g. μCRL, and in building a translator from any process algebra like language to PROMELA.

Acknowledgements. I would like to thank Bas Luttik for commenting on a draft of this paper, and to other members of the TIPSy project for discussions.

References

1. D. A. van Beek, A. van der Ham, and J.E. Rooda. Modelling and control of process industry batch production systems. In *15th Triennial World Congress of the International Federation of Automatic Control*, Barcelona, Spain, 2002.
2. S. Blom, W. Fokkink, J.F. Groote, I. van Langevelde, B. Lisser, and J.C. van de Pol. μCRL: A toolset for analysing algebraic specifications. In *Proceedings of CAV2001*, LNCS 2102, pages 250–254, 2001.

3. E. Bortnik, N. Trčka, A.J. Wijs, S.P. Luttik, J.M. van de Mortel-Fronczak, J.C.M. Baeten, W.J. Fokkink, and J.E. Rooda. Analyzing a χ model of a turntable system using SPIN, CADP and UPPAAL. *Journal Of Logic and Algebraic Programming*, 65:51–104, 2005.
4. V. Bos and J.J.T. Kleijn. Automatic verification of a manufacturing system. *Robotics and Computer Integrated Manufacturing*, 17:185–198, 2001.
5. D. Bošnački. *Enhancing State Space Reduction Techniques for Model Checking*. PhD thesis, Eindhoven University of Technology, 2001.
6. E. J. J. van Campen. *Design of a Multi-Process Multi-Product Wafer Fab*. PhD thesis, Eindhoven University of Technology, 2000.
7. E. W. Dijkstra. *A Discipline of Programming*. Prentice-Hall, 1976.
8. J.J.H. Fey. *Design of a Fruit Juice Blending and Packaging Plant*. PhD thesis, Eindhoven University of Technology, 2000.
9. R. Gerth. Concise Promela reference. Obtainable from: `http://spinroot.com/spin/Man/Quick.html`.
10. J. A. Govaarts. Efficiency in a lean assembly line: a case study at NedCar born. Master Thesis, October, 1997.
11. Klaus Havelund, Mike Lowry, and John Penix. Formal analysis of a space-craft controller using SPIN. *IEEE Trans. on Software Engineering*, 27(8):749–765, 2001.
12. C. A. R. Hoare. *Communicating Sequential Processes*. Prentice Hall, 1985.
13. G. J. Holzmann. *The SPIN model checker*. Addison-Wesley, 2003.
14. G.J. Holzmann. The model checker SPIN. *IEEE Trans. on Software Engineering*, 23(5):279–295, May 1997. Special issue on Formal Methods in Software Practice.
15. B. W. Kernighan and D. M. Ritchie. *The C Programming Language, Second Edition*. Prentice-Hall, 1988.
16. K.G. Larsen, P. Pettersson, and W. Yi. UPPAAL in a nutshell. *Int. Journal on Software Tools for Technology Transfer*, 1(1-2):134–152, 1997.
17. B. Luttik and N. Trčka. Stuttering congruence for χ. In *SPIN'05*, San Francisco, California, USA, 2005.
18. Ralph Meijer. χ to Promela translator. Obtainable from the TIPSy project web site: `http://www.cwi.nl/~wijs/TIPSy/main.htm`.
19. R.R.H. Schiffelers and K.L. Man. *Formal Specification and Analysis of Hybrid Systems*. PhD thesis, Eindhoven University of Technology, 2006.
20. C. Stirling. *Modal and Temporal Properties of Processes*. Springer, 2001.

Stateful Dynamic Partial-Order Reduction*

Xiaodong Yi, Ji Wang, and Xuejun Yang

National Laboratory for Parallel and Distributed Processing,
Changsha, P.R. China
{xdyi, jiwang}@mail.edu.cn

Abstract. State space explosion is the main obstacle for model checking concurrent programs. Among the solutions, partial-order reduction (POR), especially dynamic partial-order reduction (DPOR) [1], is one of the promising approaches. However, DPOR only supports stateless explorations for acyclic state spaces. In this paper, we present the stateful DPOR approach for may-cyclic state spaces, which naturally combines DPOR with stateful model checking to achieve more efficient reduction. Its basic idea is to summarize the interleaving information for all transition sequences starting from each visited state, and infer the necessary partial-order information based on the summarization when a visited state is encountered again. Experiment results on two programs coming from [1] show that both of the costs of space and time could be remarkably reduced by stateful DPOR with rather reasonable extra memory overhead.

1 Introduction

Model checking has been acknowledged as not only an effective but also a practical technology for the verification of concurrent programs. However, the state space explosion problem is still the main obstacle preventing model checking from scaling to large practical programs. Among the various state space reduction solutions, both the partial-order reduction (POR) and the stateful exploration of the program/model are proven to be simply but effective.

The research of POR mainly focuses on two main core partial-order reduction techniques [1-4]: persistent/stubborn sets and sleep sets. This paper (as well as [1]) focuses on the former one, and the sleep set techniques may be well complemented with ours (see the experiments). The partial-order among transitions, which is used by existing persistent/stubborn set techniques to perform reduction, is collected by static analysis techniques (see [2-6]). It therefore may be very imprecise in practice and consequently cause the efficiency loss of partial-order reduction (as indicated in [1]). To this problem, Cormac and Godefroid present the dynamic partial-order reduction (DPOR) to perform a precise state space reduction. Its basic idea is to dynamically collect the information on how processes have communicated with each other on a specific execution trace, such as which memory locations were read or written by which processes and in what orders. The information is then analyzed to add backtracking points along the trace that

* Partially supported by the National NSF of China under grant No. 60233020, National Hi-Tech Programme of China under the grant 2005AA113130 and Program for New Century Excellent Talents in University under grant No. NCET-04-0996.

Z. Liu and J. He (Eds.): ICFEM 2006, LNCS 4260, pp. 149–167, 2006.

identify the alternative transitions that need to be explored because they might lead to other execution traces that are not equivalent to the current one (i.e., are not linearizations of the same partial-order execution) [1].

For temporal safety properties, stateful exploration of the program/model may dramatically reduce the generated state space by preventing each state from being explored more than once. In comparison, stateless exploration usually needs to repeatedly explore a state for even exponential times because software programs always have many fork-join structures caused by branches. The algorithm presented in [1] fits in with stateless model checking, i.e., no states are stored during the state space exploration. Therefore, it is suitable for stateless model checkers, such as Verisoft [7] and Java PathExplorer [8, 9]. However, because stateless model checking is of low efficiency for the verification of temporal safety properties, many projects acknowledge stateful model checking techniques, such as SLAM [10, 11], MAGIC [12, 13], ComFoRT [14, 15], Zing [16, 17] for C programs and Java PathFinder [18, 19] for Java programs.

DPOR and stateful exploration are two well complementary state space reduction techniques. The combination of them may achieve a considerable efficiency improvement on state space reduction comparing with using each alone. However, at first glance, it seems that there is no way to perform stateful exploration while still applying DPOR [1]. As illustrated above, DPOR selects at each state only one arbitrary process to explore, and the other necessary ones that leads to different partial-order linearizations are identified and backtracked to explore when traversing all necessary transition sequences starting from that state. Therefore, if a future transition sequence reaches a visited state s, it could not simply ignore s and backtrack because both the backtracking points and the alternative processes of that sequence could not be identified until all necessary transition sequences starting from s have been explored.

As the contribution of this paper, we extend the dynamic partial-order reduction to support stateful model checking. The extended variant is called stateful DPOR (SDPOR). Its basic idea is to summarize at each state s the interleaving information on how processes have communicated with each other in all the transition sequences starting from s, and then all necessary backtracking points and alternative processes of each future transition sequence that reaches s may be identified by checking that summary. We use the *happens-before transition mapping* to represent the *summary of the interleaving information* for a transition sequence that leads from s, and consequently the summary of state s is represented by a set of such mappings. Under the depth-first state space exploration strategy, the summarization may be achieved by performing an extra action at the backtracking step to relay the interleaving information of current state to its predecessors. Therefore, although equipped with DPOR, the stateful model checking may also perform as before.

It is nontrivial to implement the above idea since there exist many (even infinite) transition sequences starting from each state s, and the interleaving information of all transition sequences should be summarized at s to identify all necessary backtracking points and processes for the future transition sequences that reach s. Also, it is critical to store and manipulate such summary with lower time and space cost. Moreover, exploration of cyclic state spaces will reach a state that only part of its successive transition sequences have been explored, i.e., the summary of the interleaving information at that state is incomplete. To deal with the problems, a variant of depth-first state space exploration strategy is also presented.

We also give the experimentation based on the two concurrent programs coming from [1]. The experiment results show that the state space reductions achieved by stateful exploration and by DPOR are well complementary, and a considerable reduction may be achieved through the SDPOR method presented in the paper. For example, the reduced state space by SDPOR may be up to 66 times smaller than that by the stateless one. Along with the reduction of state spaces, the time for model checking the programs is also remarkable reduced. It is also illustrated that, the extra memory overhead introduced by SDPOR is rather low comparing with the memory for state storage.

The rest of the paper is organized as follows. After some introductions of the preliminaries in Section 2, we present in Section 3 the happen-before transition mapping, the summarization of interleaving information and the stateful exploration strategy with SDPOR. In Section 4, we present the implementations of the presented definition and algorithm. The experimentation is performed in Section 6, and we conclude in Section 7.

Related work. The most related work is dynamic partial-order reduction presented in [1]. The significant improvement of our method lies in the stateful exploration, which surpasses the stateless one in usual model checking cases. The presented method combines the two complementary state space reduction methods (i.e., stateful exploration and DPOR) together with rather little time and space overhead. The idea of summarization has been used in the interprocedural analysis such as [16, 20] to summarize procedures. The procedure summaries are then reused at all call sites such as the verification by Zing [16, 17]. Sharing a similar idea, our method summarizes the interleaving information for the transition sequences starting from a state, and the summaries are reused for dynamic partial-order reduction.

Traditional partial-order state space reduction methods are also relevant to ours. There are two main core partial-order reduction techniques: persistent/stubborn sets and sleep sets. Basically, persistent/stubborn set [2-4] (moreover, ample set [5, 6]) techniques select out a subset of transitions enabled in each state such that the unselected transitions are proven not to interfere with the execution of those selected. In contrast, sleep set techniques (see [2]) compute the unnecessary enabled transitions in each state by considering the information of past explorations. These two techniques are also complementary with our method and may be used simultaneously. A latest research on partial-order reduction is cluster-based partial-order reduction [21, 22], which introduces the concept of cluster hierarchy to capture the system hierarchy and the induced dependencies among the processes in the hierarchical structured programs.

2 Preliminaries

2.1 Concurrent Program Models

We consider a concurrent program composed of a finite set of processes, which may have their private local variables and execute a sequence of statements in a deterministic order. The processes communicate by performing atomic operations on communication objects, such as shared variables, semaphores, locks, and so on. In this paper, it is assumed that the communications among processes are implemented as some operations on several global variables with the aid of two synchronous primitives *P* and *V* defined in C-like codes as follows:

$$P(x) \;::\; block \text{ if } x \leq 0 \mid x{-}{-} \text{ otherwise}$$
$$V(x) \;::\; x{+}{+}$$

where $block$ means that the execution of $P(x)$ cannot be completed currently. We assume that all statements never block except $P(x)$.

For simple representation as in [1], the paper only considers the reachability safety properties, such as detecting deadlocks and assertion failures. Under this assumption, the partial-order-equivalence of two transition sequences is of no relevance to the verifying property.

The interleaving execution of a concurrent program can be treated as a LTS. Let a concurrent program have m sequential processes (we use the integer $p \in \{1, \ldots, m\}$ to identify each process), and let $CFG_p = \langle N_p, E_p \rangle$ be the control flow graph (CFG) of pth sequential process. Then the execution graph of the concurrent program is written $CP = \langle S, s_0, T, \Delta \rangle$ where S is the state space defined as follows:

$$S \subseteq N_1 \times \ldots \times N_m \times LS_1 \times \ldots \times LS_m \times SS$$

where N_p is the node set in CFG of the pth process, LS_p is local state space of the pth process and SS is the shared state space of all communication objects. Each state $ls \in LS_p$ and $ss \in SS$ may be represented by an explicit evaluation or implicit symbolic expression of the local and shared objects, respectively. One may infer that, if a state $s \in S$ is verified to be safe, i.e., all interleaving transition sequences starting from s do not violate the reachability properties, then s need not to be re-explored when reached again from other directions.

As for other elements of $CP = \langle S, s_0, T, \Delta \rangle$, $s_0 \in S$ is the initial state, and T is the set of all transitions of the concurrent program. We call an operation to be visible if it operates at least one shared object, and invisible otherwise. Following [1], a transition $t \in T$ is defined to be a visible operation followed by a finite sequence of invisible operations of the same process. And last, $\Delta \subseteq S \times T \times S$ is the set of state transitions.

A transition sequence π of $CP = \langle S, s_0, T, \Delta \rangle$ is a sequence of transitions $t_1 t_2 \ldots t_n$ where $t_1, \ldots, t_n \in T$ and there exist states $s_1, \ldots, s_{n+1} \in S$ such that s_1 is the initial state s_0 and $\langle s_i, t_i, s_{i+1} \rangle \in \Delta$ for each $1 \leq i \leq n$. For the transition sequence $\pi = t_1 t_2 \ldots t_n$ and a set of states $s_1, \ldots, s_{n+1} \in S$ where each state s_i is the unique state reached by the transition sequence $t_1 t_2 \ldots t_{i-1}$, the following notations [1] are used:

- π_i refers to the transition t_i;
- $proc(t)$ is the integer process identifier of transition t;
- $\pi.t$, $t.\pi$ and $\pi.\pi'$ denote extending π with an additional transition t, inserting the transition t before π and jointing two transition sequences π and π' together, respectively;
- $pre(\pi, i)$ for $i \in \{1, \ldots, n\}$ refers to the state s_i; and
- $last(\pi)$ refers to the state s_{n+1}. And $last(\pi) = s_0$ if $\pi = \emptyset$.

If several transition sequences are involved, we use πi (such as $\pi 1, \pi 2, \ldots$) to denote the ith one. We use Π to denote a set of transition sequences, and $[\![\Pi]\!]$ to denote the set of all transition sequences.

Following [1], to simplify the presentation, three assumptions are preset:

- It is assumed that there exists only one transition for each process at any state. For branch statements, we therefore assume that only one branch is feasible[1]. The unique transition of process p at state s is denoted by $next(s, p)$.
- Each transition $t \in T$ of $CP = \langle S, s_0, T, \Delta \rangle$ is assumed to operate on at most one shared object. The shared object of a visible transition t is denoted by $\alpha(t) \in [\![Object]\!]$ where $[\![Object]\!]$ denotes all shared objects.
- Two visible transitions t_1 and t_2 are assumed to be dependent iff they access the same shared object, i.e., $\alpha(t_1) = \alpha(t_2)$.

Let $enabled(s)$ be the set of *non-blocked* processes at state $s = \langle s_1, \ldots, s_m \rangle$. For a process p, $p \in enabled(s)$ (we call process p is enabled) iff there exists at least one *non-blocked* transition $\langle s, t, s' \rangle \in \Delta$ such that $proc(t) = p$. If s is the last state of the system, we have $p \notin enabled(s)$ as there is no outgoing transition leaving s. Otherwise, as only the primitive $P(x)$ may be blocked provided $x \leq 0$, one may infer that the process p may be possibly *blocked* only if a P primitive is encountered.

2.2 Dynamic Partial-Order Reduction (DPOR)

The "happens-before" ordering relation $\rightarrow_\pi$ [1] for a transition sequence $\pi = t_1 t_2 \ldots t_n$ is defined to be the smallest relation on $\{t_1, \ldots, t_n\}$ such that[2]:

- if $i \leq j$ and t_i is dependent with t_j then $t_i \rightarrow_\pi t_j$; and
- $\rightarrow_\pi$ is transitively closed.

By construction, the happens-before relation $\rightarrow_\pi$ is a partial-order relation, and the sequence of transitions in π is one of the linearizations of this partial order. As in [1], a variant of the happens-before relation, $\pi_i \rightarrow_\pi p$, is used to identify backtracking points. The relation $\pi_i \rightarrow_\pi p$ holds for $i \in \{1, \ldots, n\}$ and process p if either $proc(\pi_i) = p$ or there exists $k \in \{i+1, \ldots, n\}$ such that $\pi_i \rightarrow_\pi \pi_k$ and $proc(\pi_k) = p$. Intuitively, if $\pi_i \rightarrow_\pi p$, then the next transition of process p from the state $last(\pi)$ cannot be the next transition of process p in the state right before transition π_i in either this transition sequence or in any equivalent sequence obtained by swapping adjacent independent transitions[3].

The DPOR algorithm in [1] is implemented by recursive calls of the function Explore. To be compatible with the presented SDPOR algorithm, we equivalently rewrite the algorithm based on a stack. In Figure 1, *Stack* is a stack storing a list of transition sequences as usual, and has three standard operations: *push*, *pop* and *top*. The global

[1] The nondeterministic branch operations, i.e., the both branches could be feasible, may be easily supported by extending the algorithm.

[2] We define $\rightarrow_\pi$ over $\{t_1, \ldots, t_n\}$, instead of over $\{1, \ldots, n\}$ as in [1], to avoid the confusion of indices among partial-order-equivalent transition sequences of π.

[3] We call such transition sequences partial-order-equivalent.

variables $backtrack$ and $done$ map a state to its backtracking and done processes, respectively, and they are initially empty for all states. The algorithm of Figure 1 performs a standard depth-first exploration for acyclic state spaces. Acyclic state space means that the state space contains no circle or loop. The function RefineBackTrackDpor is called to identify the backtracking points for the transition sequence π', and the details of its implementation are described in [1]. By implementation, we may use the clock vector to

$Stack$: A list of transition sequence π;
$backtrack, done$: $S \mapsto 2^{\mathbb{N}}$;
Explore()
{
1 for all $s \in S$ let $backtrack(s) = done(s) = \emptyset$;
2 $Stack$.push($\emptyset$);
3 if ($\exists p \in enabled(s_0)$) $backtrack(s_0) := \{p\}$;
4 while (!$Stack$.empty()){
5 let $\pi = Stack$.top() and let $s = last(\pi)$;
6 $Stack$.pop();
7 if ($\exists p \in backtrack(s) \setminus done(s)$) {
8 $done(s) := done(s) \cup \{p\}$;
9 let $\pi' = \pi.next(s,p)$ and $s' = last(\pi')$;
10 RefineBackTrackDpor(π');
11 if ($\exists p \in enabled(s')$) $backtrack(s') := \{p\}$;
12 $Stack$.push(π');
13 } else if($\exists \pi', t : \pi'.t = \pi$) $Stack$.push(π');
14 }
}

RefineBackTrackDpor(π)
{
1 let $s = last(\pi)$;
2 for all processes p {
3 if $\exists i = max(\{i \in dom(\pi) \mid \pi_i$ is dependent and may be co-enabled with $next(s,p)$ and $i \not\to_\pi p\})$
{
4 let $E = \{q \in enabled(pre(\pi,i)) \mid q = p$ or $\exists j \in dom(\pi) : j > i$ and $q = proc(\pi_j)$ and $j \to_\pi p\}$;
5 if($E \neq \emptyset$) add any $q \in E$ to $backtrack(pre(\pi,i))$;
6 else add all $q \in enabled(pre(\pi, i))$ to $backtrack(pre(\pi,i))$;
}
}
}

Fig. 1. Dynamic partial-order reduction algorithm for acyclic state spaces

represent the happens-before relation of each transition sequence. Thus both the backtracking points and the conditions of line 3 of the function RefineBackTrackDpor could be determined directly. For simplicity, however, the paper does not involve any clock vector, but clock vectors could be naturally integrated with the presented techniques. In fact, it is implemented in the tool for us to carry out experiments.

3 Stateful Dynamic Partial-Order Reduction (SDPOR)

3.1 Summary of Interleaving Information (SII)

We first introduce the happens-before transition mapping to represent the summary of the interleaving information for a transition sequence. To do so, we lift the function α over transition sequences, i.e., $\alpha(\pi) = \{\alpha(\pi_i)\}$ is the set of shared objects involved in π. For a transition sequence π, the function $MinIndex(\pi, o)$ is defined to return the minimum index of the transitions in π which operate the shared object $o \in \alpha(\pi)$, i.e.,

$MinIndex(\pi, o) = min\{i|\alpha(\pi_i) = o\}$. Another function *MinObjTrans*, which returns the set of minimum-indexed transitions operating each object $o \in \alpha(\pi)$, is defined as:

$$MinObjTrans(\pi) \triangleq \{\pi_i \mid \exists o \in \alpha(\pi) : i = MinIndex(\pi, o)\}$$

The happens-before transition mapping of a transition sequence π, written Υ_π, is defined as:

$$\Upsilon_\pi : MinObjTrans(\pi) \mapsto 2^T$$

We define the function $dom(\Upsilon_\pi)$ to return the domain of the mapping Υ_π, i.e., $dom(\Upsilon_\pi) = MinObjTrans(\pi)$. Over the happens-before relation $\rightarrow_\pi$, for each transition $t \in dom(\Upsilon_\pi)$, $\Upsilon_\pi(t)$ is defined as:

$$\Upsilon_\pi(t) \triangleq \{\pi_i \mid \pi_i \rightarrow_\pi t\}$$

In other words, Υ_π maps the first transition π_i, which operates each $o \in \alpha(\pi)$, to the set of transitions that must happen-before π_i in either π or its partial-order-equivalent sequences obtained by swapping adjacent independent transitions.

Example 1. In the following transition sequence:

$$\pi = p_1 : x{+}{+};\, p_2 : x{+}{+};\, p_1 : y{+}{+};\, p_2 : y{+}{+};$$

We have $\alpha(\pi) = \{x, y\}$, $MinIndex(\pi, x) = 1$ and $MinIndex(\pi, y) = 3$, where π_1 and π_3 are $p_1 : x{+}{+}$ and $p_1 : y{+}{+}$, respectively. So $dom(\Upsilon_\pi) = MinObjTrans(\pi) = \{p_1 : x{+}{+}, p_1 : y{+}{+}\}$, and $\Upsilon_\pi(p_1 : x{+}{+}) = \emptyset$, $\Upsilon_\pi(p_1 : y{+}{+}) = \{p_1 : x{+}{+}\}$ because $p_1 : x{+}{+} \rightarrow_\pi p_1 : y{+}{+}$.

The happens-before transition mapping $\Upsilon_{t.\pi}$ for the new transition sequence $t.\pi$ (i.e., obtained by inserting the transition t at the head of π) may be derived from Υ_π. First of all, the domain of $\Upsilon_{t.\pi}$ changes to $dom(\Upsilon_{t.\pi}) = dom(\Upsilon_\pi) \cup \{t\} \setminus \{t^*\}$, where $t^* \in dom(\Upsilon_\pi)$ such that $\alpha(t) = \alpha(t^*)$. That is to say, we add t to and remove t^* from $dom(\Upsilon_\pi)$, where t^* is the transition that operates the same shared object as t. Then, we define:

$$\Upsilon_{t.\pi}(t') \triangleq \begin{cases} \emptyset & \text{if } t = t' \\ \Upsilon_\pi(t') \cup \{t\} \setminus \{t^*\} & \text{if } t \rightarrow_{t.\pi} t' \vee \exists t'' \in \Upsilon_\pi(t') : t \rightarrow_{t.\pi} t'' \\ \Upsilon_\pi(t') \setminus \{t^*\} & \text{otherwise} \end{cases}$$

The summary of interleaving information for a state s is represented by a set of happens-before transition mappings, and each mapping corresponds to one transition sequence that starts form s.

Let $\Pi = \{\pi 1, \ldots, \pi n\}$ be a set of transition sequences starting from the unique state s. The *summary of interleaving information* (SII) of the state s with respect to Π, written $SII_\Pi(s)$, is defined as:

$$SII_\Pi \triangleq \{\Upsilon_{\pi 1}, \ldots, \Upsilon_{\pi n}\}$$

We also use the symbol $[\![SII]\!]$ to denote the set of all kinds of summaries of interleaving information.

If the state space is finite and acyclic, the number of the transition sequences that start from any state is finite. For any state s, let Π be the finite set of all transition sequences starting form s, and let SII_{Π} be the summary of interleaving information of s. If the state s is reached again after executing the transition sequence π, the backtracking points of π may be refined based on SII_{Π} by the procedure RefineBackTrackSII shown in Figure 2. Intuitively in line 3, the first condition says that $\pi_i \not\rightarrow_{\pi.t} t$, and the second one says that $\pi_i \not\rightarrow_{\pi.t'} t'$ for all t' such that $t' \rightarrow_{\pi k} t$. One may therefore infer that $\pi_i \not\rightarrow_{\pi.\pi k} t$. As t is the first transition of πk that operates the same shared object as π_i, we need to introduce a backtracking point in the state $pre(\pi, i)$. The correctness is promised by Theorem 1.

RefineBackTrackSII(π, SII_{Π})
{
1 for all $\Upsilon_{\pi k} \in SII_{\Pi}$ do
2 for all $t \in dom(\Upsilon_{\pi k})$ do
3 if the following two conditions hold:
- $\exists i = max(\{i \in dom(\pi) \mid \pi_i$ is dependent and may be co-enabled with t and $\pi_i \not\rightarrow_{\pi.t} t\})$; and
- $\forall t' \in \Upsilon_{\pi k}(t) : \pi_i \not\rightarrow_{\pi.t'} t'$
{
4 let $E = \{q \in enabled(pre(\pi, i)) \mid q = proc(t)$ or $\exists t' \in \Upsilon_{\pi k}(t) : q = proc(t')$ or $\exists j \in dom(\pi) : j > i$ and $q = proc(\pi_j)$ and $j \rightarrow_{\pi} proc(t)\}$;
5 if ($E \neq \emptyset$) then add any $q \in E$ to $backtrack(pre(\pi, i))$;
6 else add all $q \in enabled(pre(\pi, i))$ to $backtrack(pre(\pi, i))$;
}
}

Fig. 2. Backtracking points Refinement based on SII for acyclic state spaces

Theorem 1. *If the state space is finite and acyclic, then for all states $pre(\pi, i)$ of a transition sequence π, each backtracking point set $backtrack(pre(\pi, i))$ obtained by the procedure RefineBackTrackSII of Figure 2 is equal to the one obtained by exploring the set of transition sequences Π with standard DPOR algorithm shown in Figure 1.*

Proof. See Appendix.

3.2 Stateful Exploration with SDPOR

The stateful exploration with SDPOR for may-cyclic state spaces is shown in Figure 3. Both explicit and implicit state representations are supported. The global variables $backtracking$, $done$ and $Stack$ are defined in Figure 1. The global mapping SII records the SII for each state to avoid repeated explorations. If the state space contains circles, the SII of a state may be incomplete in the case that its some necessary processes have not been explored. Therefore, the depends-on relation between a transition sequence and a state, denoted $\longrightarrow$, is introduced. If a transition sequence $\pi = t_1 \ldots t_n$ reaches a visited state s_{n+1}, we set $\pi \longrightarrow s_{n+1}$ and then backtrack. Thereafter, if the SII of s_{n+1} is updated, the backtracking points for π need to be recomputed.

```
backtrack, done: S ↦ 2^ℕ;
Stack: A list of transition sequece π;
SII: S ↦ ⟦SII⟧;
⟶: ⟶⊆ ⟦Π⟧ × S;
Explore()
{
1  for all s ∈ S let backtrack(s) =
          done(s) = SII(s) = ∅;
2  Stack.push(∅);
3  if(∃p ∈ enabled(s0))
4     backtrack(s0) := {p};
5  while(!Stack.empty()) {
6     let π = Stack.top();
7     Stack.pop();
8     let s = last(π);
9     if(∃p ∈ backtrack(s) \ done(s)){
10       done(s) := done(s) ∪ {p};
11       let π' = π.next(s,p)
12       let s' = last(π');
13       if(s' has not been visited){
14          RefineBackTrackDpor(π');
15          if(∃p ∈ enabled(s'))
16             backtrack(s') := {p};
17       }else RefineBackTrackSII(π',SII(s'));
                and set π' ⟶ s';
18       Stack.push(π');
19    } else if (∃π', t : π'.t = π) {
20       Stack.push(π');
21       let s' = last(π');
22       let oldSII = SII(s');
23       for all Υπi ∈ SII(s);
               add Υt.πi to SII(s');
24       if(oldSII ≠ SII(s'))
25          for all π'' such that π'' ⟶ s' do {
26             RefineBackTrackSII(π'',SII(s'));
27             Stack.push(π'');
28          }
29    }
30 }
}
```

Fig. 3. Stateful exploration with SDPOR for may-cyclic state spaces

We will go to line 17 when a visited state s' is reached again in line 13. The transition sequences starting from the visited state s' do not need to be explored again, and the backtracking points of π' could be identified by the procedure RefineBackTrack-SII based on the SII of s'. We also should set the depends-on relation $\pi' \longrightarrow s'$ in case of the later changes of $SII(s')$. When backtracking from s to s' (lines 19-29), each happens-before transition mapping $\Upsilon_{\pi i} \in SII(s)$ is updated to $\Upsilon_{t.\pi i}$ and added to $SII(s')$ in line 23. If the merged $SII(s')$ is not equal to the one before merging in line 24, the backtracking sets of any transition sequence π'' which depends-on s' should be recomputed (line 26) and π'' should be re-traversed (line 27) because there may be extra backtracking points introduced. It is worth to notice that when exploring acyclic state spaces, there is no transition sequence that depends-on any visited state (otherwise a circle exists). That is to say, there exists no transition sequence π'' such that $\pi'' \longrightarrow s'$ in line 25 of Figure 3.

Theorem 2. *When the procedure in Figure 3 terminates, the set of transitions that have been explored from every state is a persistent set in that state.*

In [1], it is shown that, for acyclic state spaces, the set of the transitions that have been explored by stateless DPOR algorithm is a persistent set (see Theorem 1 of [1]). Theorem 1 (in subsection 3.1) says that although the visited states are not explored again, the backtracking points identified are equal to those by stateless DPOR. That is to say, for acyclic state spaces, the set of transitions that have been explored from every state is equal to that of stateless DPOR.

For may-cyclic state spaces, if we can prove that the SII of each state is complete when the procedure terminates, we may infer that the theorem also holds. In lines 24-28 of Figure 3, if $SII(s')$ is updated, any transition sequence π'' which depends-on s' would be re-traversed until $SII(s')$ does not change anymore. So, no matter how many times the circle path is unrolled, exploring the corresponding transition sequence will never cause $SII(s')$ to change. That is to say, $SII(s')$ is the complete SII of s' although there may be infinite transition sequences starting from s'.

One may doubt whether the procedure of Figure 3 could terminate because the circled transition sequences would keep re-traversed until the SII does not change. However, when SII is implemented as in the following section, we can promise the termination of that procedure if the state space is finite.

4 Implementation

We discuss in this section how to implement SII and the general algorithm in Figure 3. To discuss the complexity of the algorithm, we assume that there are m processes and total n shared objects in the concurrent program.

4.1 Implementation of SII

The happens-before transition mapping Υ_π only records the first transition t that operates each shared object as well as the transitions happen-before t in the transition sequence π. Also, we only consider $proc(t)$ and $\alpha(t)$ for each transition t of Υ_π. Therefore, we may use the pair $\langle proc(t), \alpha(t)\rangle$ to represent the transition t, and we therefore also call such pair a transition. Based on this representation, a simplified variant of happens-before transition mapping Υ_π, written $\hat{\Upsilon}_\pi$, is defined as:

$$\hat{\Upsilon}_\pi : \mathbb{N} \times [\![Object]\!] \mapsto 2^{\mathbb{N} \times [\![Object]\!]}$$

Based on Υ_π, $\hat{\Upsilon}_\pi$ is constructed by translating each transition t to the pair $\langle proc(t), \alpha(t)\rangle$. If $\hat{\Upsilon}_{\pi 1}$ is exactly equal to $\hat{\Upsilon}_{\pi 2}$ for two transition sequences $\pi 1$ and $\pi 2$, we define that $\pi 1$ and $\pi 2$ are $\hat{\Upsilon} - equivalent$. There are total $(m \times n)!$ different transition sequences that are not $\hat{\Upsilon} - equivalent$ to each other. That is to say, there could exist at most $(m \times n)!$ different happens-before transition mappings.

Let $\Pi = \{\pi 1, \ldots, \pi n\}$ be a set of transition sequences starting from a unique state s. The SII of the state s with respect to Π, i.e., $SII_\Pi(s)$, is alternatively defined as $SII_\Pi(s) = \{\hat{\Upsilon}_{\pi 1}, \ldots, \hat{\Upsilon}_{\pi n}\}$ and implemented by two mappings:

$$OI : \mathbb{N} \times [\![Object]\!] \mapsto 2^{\mathbb{N}}$$
$$DI : \mathbb{N} \times [\![Object]\!] \mapsto 2^{\mathbb{N}}$$

where OI stands for the mapping for object indices and DI stands for the mapping for depend indices. They are constructed as follows: for each $\hat{\Upsilon}_{\pi i} \in SII_\Pi(s)$, each transition $\langle p, o\rangle \in dom(\hat{\Upsilon}_{\pi i})$ is assigned an integer index k in OI. And k is inserted into the set $DI(\langle p', o'\rangle)$ for each transition $\langle p', o'\rangle \in \hat{\Upsilon}_{\pi i}(\langle p, o\rangle)$. Intuitively, for each transition sequence $\pi i \in \Pi$, OI maps the first transition t of each object to an integer k. And for all transitions t' such that $t' \rightarrow_{\pi i} t$, $DI(\langle proc(t'), \alpha(t')\rangle)$ contains k. In other words, if there exists some integer k such that $k \in OI(\langle proc(t), \alpha(t)\rangle)$ and $k \in DI(\langle proc(t'), \alpha(t')\rangle)$, then there exists a transition sequence πi such that $t' \rightarrow_{\pi i} t$.

Since the above indices $k \in \mathbb{N}$ can be arbitrarily selected, two summaries may have the same meaning but with different forms. So we define that $SII_{\Pi}(s) = \langle OI, DI\rangle$ is equivalent to $SII_{\Pi'}(s) = \langle OI', DI'\rangle$, written $SII_{\Pi}(s) \equiv SII_{\Pi'}(s)$, iff there exists a one-one mapping $KT : \mathbb{N} \mapsto \mathbb{N}$ such that:

- $\forall\langle p, o\rangle \in dom(OI)$ and $\forall k \in OI(\langle p, o\rangle)$, $\exists k' \in OI'(\langle p, o\rangle) : k' = KT(k)$;
- $\forall\langle p, o\rangle \in dom(OI')$ and $\forall k' \in OI'(\langle p, o\rangle)$, $\exists k \in OI(\langle p, o\rangle) : k' = KT(k)$;
- $\forall\langle p, o\rangle \in dom(DI)$ and $\forall k \in DI(\langle p, o\rangle)$, $\exists k' \in DI'(\langle p, o\rangle) : k' = KT(k)$; and
- $\forall\langle p, o\rangle \in dom(DI')$ and $\forall k' \in DI'(\langle p, o\rangle)$, $\exists k \in DI(\langle p, o\rangle) : k' = KT(k)$.

Example 2. Let us consider the following two transition sequences starting from a unique state s:

$$\pi 1 = \langle 1, x\rangle\langle 2, x\rangle\langle 1, y\rangle\langle 2, y\rangle$$
$$\pi 2 = \langle 1, y\rangle\langle 2, y\rangle\langle 2, x\rangle\langle 1, x\rangle$$

We have $dom(\hat{\Upsilon}_{\pi 1}) = \{\langle 1, x\rangle, \langle 1, y\rangle\}$, $dom(\hat{\Upsilon}_{\pi 2}) = \{\langle 1, y\rangle, \langle 2, x\rangle\}$. And we also have $\hat{\Upsilon}_{\pi 1}(\langle 1, x\rangle) = \emptyset$, $\hat{\Upsilon}_{\pi 1}(\langle 1, y\rangle) = \{\langle 1, x\rangle\}$, $\hat{\Upsilon}_{\pi 2}(\langle 1, y\rangle) = \emptyset$ and $\hat{\Upsilon}_{\pi 2}(\langle 2, x\rangle) = \{\langle 1, y\rangle, \langle 2, y\rangle\}$. We then construct the mapping OI as follows. For $dom(\hat{\Upsilon}_{\pi 1})$, we use the integers 1 and 2 to denote the transitions $\langle 1, x\rangle$ and $\langle 1, y\rangle$, respectively. For $dom(\hat{\Upsilon}_{\pi 2})$, we use 3 and 4 to denote $\langle 1, y\rangle$ and $\langle 2, x\rangle$, respectively. Therefore, we have for example $OI(\langle 1, y\rangle) = \{2, 3\}$ (see Table 1). The mapping DI is then constructed as follows. As $\hat{\Upsilon}_{\pi 1}(\langle 1, y\rangle) = \{\langle 1, x\rangle\}$, the integer that denotes the transition $\langle 1, y\rangle$ of $\pi 1$ (i.e., the integer 2) should be added to $DI(\langle 1, x\rangle)$. Note that we do not add the integer 3 to $DI(\langle 1, x\rangle)$, because 3 denotes $\langle 1, y\rangle$ of $\pi 2$.

The two mappings OI and DI constructed above are shown in Table 1. Notice that we may obtain another equivalent summary by assigning another integer (for example, 5) to denote each transition (for example, $\langle 1, x\rangle$).

Table 1. Example mappings

Transition t	$OI(t)$	Transition t	$DI(t)$
$\langle 1, x\rangle$	$\{1\}$	$\langle 1, x\rangle$	$\{2\}$
$\langle 1, y\rangle$	$\{2, 3\}$	$\langle 1, y\rangle$	$\{4\}$
$\langle 2, x\rangle$	$\{4\}$	$\langle 2, y\rangle$	$\{4\}$

Besides the assumption that the concurrent program has m processes and total n shared objects, we assume that Π has at most l transition sequences that are not $\hat{\Upsilon} - equivalent$ to each other (we have $l \leq (m \times n)!$). We may do a conservative estimation for the time and space requirements. OI could have at most $m \times n$ transitions and each transition could have at most l indices. As a result, OI could have $m \times n \times l$ indices and occupy $O(m \times n \times l)$ space at most. DI could have at most $m \times n$ transitions and each transition could have at most $m \times n \times l$ indices (all indices in OI). So DI may require at most $O(m^2 \times n^2 \times l)$ space, and so does $DI_{\Pi}(s)$. In practice, however, the space required is far less than that, because the amounts of indices of each transition in OI and in DI are far less than l and $m \times n \times l$, respectively.

One may infer from above construction that, there exists no explicit transition sequence in both mappings, which remarkably reduces the time and space costs. Furthermore, as there are total $(m \times n)!$ different happens-before transition mappings, the total amount of different $SII_{\Pi}(s) \triangleq \langle OI, DI \rangle$ is $2^{(m \times n)!}$ no matter how many (even infinite) transition sequences in Π. Note that $2^{(m \times n)!}$ is only a very conservative estimation, and the amount of different $SII_{\Pi}(s)$ used in practice is far less than that.

As no transition sequence is explicitly involved, the *summary of interleaving information* is denoted by $SII(s)$ instead of $SII_{\Pi}(s)$ in the following context. As the total amount of different SIIs is finite, the algorithm of Figure 3 that explores finite and may-cyclic state spaces should always terminate.

4.2 Implementation of the Exploration with SDPOR

To implement the exploration with SDPOR for may-cyclic state spaces shown in Figure 3, we need to replace the condition $oldSII \neq SII(s')$ with $oldSII \not\equiv SII(s')$ in line 24 to decide whether two SIIs are equivalent. We also should implement the function RefineBackTrackSII used in lines 17 and 26. Moreover, there are two extra functions involved in line 23 of Figure 3 when computing $\Upsilon_{t.\pi i}$ from $\Upsilon_{\pi i}$ and adding it to $SII(s')$. One function, UpdateSII, is to update $SII(s)$ when inserting a transition t at the head of the corresponding transition sequences. The other function, MergeSII, is to merge the updated SII and the original SII into one. And the codes of line 23 should be implemented by three statements: $SII' = SII(s)$, UpdateSII(SII') and MergeSII($SII(s')$, SII').

The function RefineBackTrackSII for the transition sequence π based on the new representation $SII(s) = \langle OI, DI \rangle$ is shown in Figure 4 where $s = last(\pi)$ (i.e., π reaches the visited state s). After executing the first for-loop of lines 1-2, a may-backtrack map BT is constructed where each transition $\langle p, o \rangle \in dom(BT)$ may happen-before π_i, the last dependent and co-enabled transition of π. Thereafter in the following codes of lines 3-5, we check whether there exists an integer k such that $k \in BT(\langle p, o \rangle)$ and $k \in DI(\langle p', o' \rangle)$ (see line 4). If it is the case, we know that there exists a happens-before transition mapping $\hat{\Upsilon}_{\pi'}$ for some transition sequence π' such that $\langle p', o' \rangle \in \hat{\Upsilon}_{\pi'}(\langle p, o \rangle)$. If the condition $\pi_i \rightarrow_{\pi} \langle p', o' \rangle$ holds (see line 5), we know that $\pi_i \rightarrow_{\pi.\pi'} \langle p, o \rangle$ because $\langle p', o' \rangle \in \hat{\Upsilon}_{\pi'}(\langle p, o \rangle)$. So k is removed out from $BT(\langle p, o \rangle)$ to indicate that the transition $\langle p, o \rangle$ in π' cannot happen-before π_i. If $BT(\langle p, o \rangle) \neq \emptyset$ in line 7, then let $k \in BT(\langle p, o \rangle)$, and we know that there exists some transition sequence such that the transition $\langle p, o \rangle$ (denoted by k) may happen-before the transition π_i. So the backtracking set refinement is performed in lines 9-10 as standard DPOR algorithm does [1]. Theoretically, the RefineBackTrack algorithm requires $O(m^2 \times n^2 \times l)$ time and space in the worst case, but actually in practice, the cost is far less than that.

$BT : \mathbb{N} \times [\![Obj]\!] \mapsto 2^{\mathbb{N}}$;
$BL : \mathbb{N} \times [\![Obj]\!] \mapsto \mathbb{N}$;
RefineBackTrackSII(π, $\langle OI, DI \rangle$)
{
for all $\langle p, o\rangle \in dom(OI)$ do
  if $\exists i = max(\{i \in dom(\pi) \mid \pi_i$ is dependent and may be co-enabled with $\langle p, o\rangle$
    and $\pi_i \not\rightarrow_\pi \langle p, o\rangle\})$ then $BT(\langle p, o\rangle) := OI(\langle p, o\rangle)$, $BL(\langle p, o\rangle) := i$;
for all $\langle p', o'\rangle \in dom(DI)$ do
  for all k such that $k \in BT(\langle p, o\rangle)$ and $k \in DI(\langle p', o'\rangle)$ do
    if $\pi_i \rightarrow_\pi \langle p', o'\rangle$ where $i = BL(\langle p, o\rangle)$, then remove k from $BT(\langle p, o\rangle)$;
for all $\langle p, o\rangle \in dom(BT)$ do
  if ($BT(\langle p, o\rangle) \neq \emptyset$) {
    let $i = BL(\langle p, o\rangle)$;
    if $p \in enabled(pre(\pi, i))$ then add p to $backtrack(pre(\pi, i))$;
    else add $enabled(pre(\pi, i))$ to $backtrack(pre(\pi, i))$;
  }
}

Fig. 4. Implementation of the function RefineBackTrackSII

Example 3. Let us refine the backtracking points of the transition sequence

$$\pi = \langle 1, x\rangle\langle 2, y\rangle\langle 1, y\rangle\langle 2, x\rangle$$

based on the $SII(s)$ shown in Table 1 of Example 2 in subsection 4.1. In Example 2, we have $dom(OI) = \{\langle 1, x\rangle, \langle 1, y\rangle, \langle 2, x\rangle\}$ (refer to the first column of Table 1). For the transition $\langle 1, x\rangle$, the last dependent and co-enabled transition of π is $\pi_4 = \langle 2, x\rangle$. Because $\pi_4 \rightarrow_\pi \langle 1, x\rangle$, we should add $\langle 1, x\rangle$ to $dom(BT)$ and set $BT(\langle 1, x\rangle) = OI(\langle 1, x\rangle) = \{1\}$. As the integer 1 does not appear in the DI mapping, we cannot remove 1 from $BT(\langle 1, x\rangle)$. So $\langle 1, x\rangle$ can happen-before π_4 and the corresponding backtracking points refinement should be performed.

Figure 5 presents the algorithms for updating and merging SIIs. We first consider the procedure UpdateSII, which is used by the depth-first exploration to relay the SII of a state to its predecessors. If $o = o'$ in line 3, then $\langle p', o'\rangle$ should be removed from $dom(OI)$ in line 5, because $\langle p', o'\rangle$ is no longer the first transition operating object o after inserting $\langle p, o\rangle$ at the head of any transition sequence. Also, all indices in $OI(\langle p', o'\rangle)$ should be removed from DI(line 12). In line 6, $p = p'$ implies that $\langle p, o\rangle$ happens-before $\langle p', o'\rangle$, which is set in line 7. Then, a new index is assigned for the transition $\langle p, o\rangle$ in line 10. In lines 11-15, we remove the useless indices as well as construct the depend-on relations. If the condition in line 13 holds, we know that $\langle p', o'\rangle$ depends on $\langle p, o\rangle$ (i.e., $\langle p, o\rangle$ happens-before $\langle p', o'\rangle$), thus all the transitions depending on $\langle p', o'\rangle$ also depend on $\langle p, o\rangle$ (as what we do in line 14). Again, the algorithm requires $O(m^2 \times n^2 \times l)$ time and space in the worst case.

We then consider the procedure MergeSII of Figure 5, which is used by the depth-first exploration to merge the SIIs at the states which have two or more successors. The codes of lines 1-8 replace each index in OI' and DI' with a new index, and then put the new index into OI and DI, respectively. The codes of lines 9-14 check whether there

```
RS : RS ⊂ ℕ;
UpdateSII(⟨OI, DI⟩, t)
{
let p = proc(t) and o = α(t);
for all ⟨p', o'⟩ ∈ dom(OI) do {
  if(o = o') {
    add OI(⟨p', o'⟩) to RS;
    remove ⟨p', o'⟩ from dom(OI);
  } else if(p = p') {
    add OI(⟨p', o'⟩) to DI(⟨p, o⟩);
  }
}
add a new index k ∈ ℕ to OI(⟨p, o⟩);
For all ⟨p', o'⟩ ∈ dom(DI) do {
  DI(⟨p', o'⟩) := DI(⟨p', o'⟩) \ RS;
  if(p = p' or o = o')
    add DI(⟨p', o'⟩) to DI(⟨p, o⟩);
}
}
```

```
CHG : ℕ ↦ ℕ;
IT : ℕ ↦ 2^(ℕ×⟦Obj⟧);
MergeSII(⟨OI, DI⟩, ⟨OI', DI'⟩)
{
for all ⟨p, o⟩ ∈ dom(OI') do
  for all k ∈ OI'(⟨p, o⟩) do {
    add a new index k' ∈ ℕ to OI(⟨p, o⟩);
    set CHG(k) = k';
  }
for all ⟨p, o⟩ ∈ dom(DI') do
  for all k ∈ DI'(⟨p, o⟩) do
    add index k' = CHG(k) to DI(⟨p, o⟩);
for all ⟨p, o⟩ ∈ dom(DI) do
  for all k ∈ DI(⟨p, o⟩) do
    add ⟨p, o⟩ to IT(k);
for all ⟨p, o⟩ ∈ dom(OI) do
  if there exist k, k' ∈ OI(⟨p, o⟩) such
      that IT(k) ⊆ IT(k') then
    remove k' from OI and DI;
}
```

Fig. 5. Implementation of UpdateSII (left) and MergeSII (right)

exist two indices $k, k' \in OI(\langle p, o \rangle)$ such that the set of transitions depended by k (i.e., $IT(k)$) is a subset of the one depended by k' (i.e., $IT(k')$). If $IT(k) \subseteq IT(k')$, one may infer that k' is redundant and can be safely removed from both OI and DI.

Example 4. Let us refer to Table 1 of Example 2 in subsection 4.1. The transition $\langle 1, y \rangle$ is mapped to two indices 2 and 3, and the transition sets depended by indices 2 and 3 are $\{\langle 1, x \rangle\}$ and $\emptyset$, respectively. That is to say, if $\langle 1, y \rangle$ may happen-before π_i for some transition sequence π, then $\langle 1, x \rangle$ should be checked when considering index 2, but nothing need to be checked for index 3. Therefore, the index 2 is redundant and can be further removed from both mappings.

The algorithm requires also $O(m^2 \times n^2 \times l)$ time and space at most, where $IT(k) \subseteq IT(k')$ is assumed to be able to judge during construction of IT. In practice, however, all the three algorithms require only a little space and time, because many transition sequences may be merged due to the redundant indices.

5 Experimentation

We use the same two benchmarks presented in [1], namely *Indexer* and *File System*, to demonstrate the stateful dynamic partial-order reduction. The Indexer benchmark consists of several processes/threads manipulating a shared hash table. Each process receives a massage w and inserts it into the hash table with the index $h = hash(w)$. If a hash table collision occurs, the next free entry is used. An array $mutex$ is used to protect each table entry from being accessed by more than one process at the same time.

The File System Benchmark has two kernel data structures *inode* and *busy*, which are protected by two arrays of locks *locki* and *lockb*, respectively. Each process picks an inode i and searches a free block to allocate to it if i has no associated block.

We implement all algorithms presented in the paper and thus do not need an extra model checker. The state is explicitly represented in the implementation, i.e., a state is composed of the evaluations of all program variables. We compare four strategies: Stateless DPOR, Stateless DPOR with sleep sets, Stateful DPOR and Stateful DPOR with sleep sets. The sleep set reduction technique exploits information on dependencies exclusively among the transitions enabled in the current state, as well as information recorded about the past of the search. As shown in [1], there exists a nice complementarity between DPOR and sleep sets.

The experiment results are shown in Table 2 and Table 3. These data are generated by a machine of 1.6 GHz Athlon CPU with 1 GB memory. "DPOR" denotes stateless DPOR, and "SDPOR" denotes stateful DPOR. "Procs" is the number of concurrent processes. "All Trans." is the number of all transitions explored, including the invisible transitions followed by the visible ones. "Time" is the exploring time in seconds. And "Mem" is the number of memory in kilo-bytes used to store the summary of interleaving information of each state. Note that we only count the memory occupied by SIIs. The memory which is used to store states and clock vectors are not counted in.

Table 2. Experiment results of Indexer

Procs	DPOR		DPOR+sleep set		SDPOR			SDPOR + sleep set		
	All Trans.	Time (s)	All Trans.	Time (s)	All Trans.	Time (s)	Mem (KB)	All Trans.	Time (s)	Mem (KB)
11	604	0.2	604	0.2	604	0.4	4.3	604	0.4	4.3
12	14479	4.6	4546	1.4	2399	1.9	511	2355	1.7	499
13	169661	59.3	23529	7.7	5196	5.3	1403	4124	3.7	1064
14	3837429	1814.4	182841	70.2	20901	30.7	5436	14406	16.1	3659
15			1508101	695.9	94506	248.0	25573	47623	77.7	12995
16			12507473	7072.8	450340	1718.4	143208	188452	594.6	48084

If the number of processes is less than or equal to 11 and 13 in Table 2 and Table 3, respectively, there exists no conflict among visible objects, and the state space is reduced to contain only one transition sequence by all four strategies. When the number of processes continues increasing, one may infer that stateful DPOR may achieve much better state space reduction effect than stateless DPOR, and stateful DPOR with sleep sets also performs better than stateless DPOR with sleep sets. For example in Table 2, the state space reduced by stateful DPOR with sleep sets is 66 times smaller than that by stateless DPOR with sleep sets, when the number of processes is 16. As the number of transitions directly determines the exploring time, the DPOR strategy spends 1814.4 seconds to explore the Indexer example with 14 processes, but the SDPOR with sleep sets strategy only spends 16.1 seconds for 14 processes and 594.6 seconds for 16 processes. In Table 3, however, the time for SDPOR with sleep sets is more than that for DPOR with sleep sets although both transitions are the same. The additional time is

Table 3. Experiment results of File System

Procs	DPOR		DPOR+sleep set		SDPOR			SDPOR + sleep set		
	All Trans.	Time (s)	All Trans.	Time (s)	All Trans.	Time (s)	Mem (KB)	All Trans.	Time (s)	Mem (KB)
13	142	0.1	142	0.1	142	0.1	30	142	0.1	30
14	434	0.2	298	0.1	303	0.2	68	298	0.2	68
15	1102	0.4	505	0.2	691	0.4	162	505	0.3	120
16	3226	1.3	960	0.4	1776	1.2	432	960	0.6	228
17	9922	4.0	1943	0.8	4945	3.5	1276	1943	1.2	463
18	30946	13.2	4046	1.6	14173	10.6	3951	4046	2.5	981
19	96790	41.8	8517	3.5	40924	33.0	12407	8517	5.4	2134
20	302602	140.0	17980	7.7	118261	103.5	39014	17980	12.1	4701
21	944842	474.7	37939	16.7	341493	317.9	122682	37939	26.5	10403
22			79914	36.2				79914	59.0	23012
23			167969	79.4				167969	137.2	51086
24			352280	175.4				352280	321.4	113923
25			737295	394.8				737295	769.9	255187
26			1540102	895.3						

used to manipulate states, such as storing and comparing, and we will discuss it later in this subsection.

We may see in Table 2 that, stateful DPOR without sleep sets is even better than stateless DPOR with sleep sets. This is because stateful DPOR may avoid the re-explorations of a same state reached by different transition sequences that are not partial-order-equivalent. In Table 3, however, stateless DPOR with sleep sets achieves better effect than stateful DPOR without sleep sets. Table 3 also shows that, by applying sleep sets technique, the state spaces after stateful DPOR and stateless DPOR are exactly the same. It is because all the transition sequences reaching same states are partial-order-equivalent and thus can be reduced by stateless DPOR in the File System program. However, as acknowledged in practical programs that stateful model checking usually achieves much better state space reduction performance than stateless one, the stateful DPOR is therefore expected to have much better state space reduction performance than stateless one.

The drawback of SDPOR is that extra memory is needed to store the summaries of interleaving information. However, as shown in above two tables, the additional memory needed for SDPOR is relatively low comparing with the memory for states. In the experiments, Indexer and File System have 256 and 116 visible objects, respectively, and they also have tens of concurrent processes, but the average amount of memory used for one SII is 200 to 300 bytes per state. For the File System example with 24 processes, the memory needed by SIIs is 114MB. In comparison, about 800 MB memory is needed to store states. Currently we directly store the visible object names in the SII of each state, which could be optimized by assigning an index for each object and storing the indices instead. Moreover, traditional methods such as compression may be used to remarkably reduce the memory consumption.

Stateful model checking also needs additional time to search and compare to infer whether current state has been visited before. For example in Table 3, two strategies "DPOR + sleep set" and "SDPOR + sleep set" have same amount of transitions, but for the File System example with 24 concurrent processes, the latter strategy costs 321.4 seconds and the former only costs 175.4 seconds. However, as there always exist large number of execution paths leading to the same states in practical programs and especially in the abstracted models (such as those abstracted by slicing execution [23, 24]), stateful DPOR usually achieves much better performance.

6 Conclusions

In the paper, we present a novel strategy, i.e., stateful DPOR, to combine stateful model checking with dynamic partial-order reduction. The approach summarizes at each state the information on how communication objects have been manipulated by the transition sequences starting form that state. Therefore, all backtracking points may be identified by checking the summary of a visited state, and each state does not need to be explored more than once. The paper also presents a modified depth-first exploration strategy for applying stateful DPOR in model checking of the programs with may-cyclic state spaces. As a result, the presented method may perform a more effective state space reduction with reasonable overhead.

As this paper only focuses on the reachability safety properties, part of our future work is to extend the presented method to model check full temporal safety properties. Another part of future work is to combine stateful DPOR with slicing execution [23, 24] to model check practical programs.

References

[1] Cormac Flanagan and Patrice Godefroid. Dynamic partial-order reduction for model checking software. In proceedings of POPL 2005. Long Beach, California, USA.

[2] P.Godefroid. Partial-Order Methods for the Verification of Concurrent Systems - An Approach to the State-Explosion Problem. 1996. Vol. 1032 of Lecture Notes in Computer Science.

[3] A.Valmari. Stubborn sets for reduced state space generation. pp. 491-515. 1991. In Advances in Petri Nets 1990.

[4] Kimmo Varpaaniemi, Minimizing the Number of Successor States in the Stubborn Set Method. Journal of Fundamental Informatics, 51(1-2), pp.215-234 (2001).

[5] D.Peled, Combining partial order reductions with on-the-fly model checking. Computer Aided Verification, CAV '94, LNCS 818, Springer (1994).

[6] G.J.Holzmann and D.Peled, An improvement in formal verification. In Formal Descriptions Techniques VII, FORTE'94, Chapman & Hall (1995).

[7] Juergen Dingel, Computer-Assisted Assume/Guarantee Reasoning with VeriSoft. In proceedings of the 25th International Conference on Software Engineering (ICSE'03) pp. 138-148 (2003).

[8] Klaus Havelund and Grigore Rosu. Java PathExplorer - A Runtime Verification Tool. Proc.ISAIRAS '01: 6th International symposium on AI, Robotics and Automation in Space. 2001. Nordwijk, The Netherlands.

[9] Klaus Havelund and Grigore Rosu. Monitoring Java Programs with Java PathExplorer. In proceedings of RV '01: 1st Workshop on Runtime Verification, Springer LNCS, vol.55, issue 2. 2001. Paris, France.
[10] T.Ball, R.Majumdar, T.Millstein and S.K.Rajamani, Automatic predicate abstraction of C programs. PLDI2001: Programming Language Design and Implementation (2001).
[11] T.Ball and S.K.Rajamani, Generating abstract explanations of spurious counterexamples in C programs. Technical Report MSR-TR-2002-09, Microsoft Research, Microsoft Corporation (2002).
[12] Sagar Chaki, Edmund Clarke and Alex Groce, Modular Verification of Software Components in C. ACM-SIGSOFT Distinguished Paper in the 25th International Conference on Software Engineering (ICSE) 2003 385-395 (2003).
[13] Sagar Chaki, Joel Ouaknine, Karen Yorav and Edmund Clarke. Automated Compositional Abstraction Refinement for Concurrent C Programs: A Two-Level Approach. 2nd Workshop on Software Model Checking (SoftMC) . 2003.
[14] Sagar Chaki, Edmund Clarke, Nishant Sinha and Prasanna Thati. Automated Assume-Guarantee Reasoning for Simulation Conformance. LNCS 3576, pp. 534-547. 2005. Proceedings of Computer Aided Verification (CAV), 2005.
[15] Sagar Chaki, James Ivers, Natasha Sharygina and Kurt Wallnau. The ComFoRT Reasoning Framework. pp. 164-169. 2005. Proceedings of Computer Aided Verification (CAV), 2005, LNCS 3576.
[16] T.Andrews, S.Qadeer, S.K.Rajamani, J.Rehof and Y.Xie, Zing: Exploiting Program Structure for Model Checking Concurrent Software. In Proceedings of CONCUR 2004 (2004).
[17] T.Andrews, S.Qadeer, S.K.Rajamani, J.Rehof and Y.Xie, Zing: A Model Checker for Concurrent Software. MSR Technical Report: MSR-TR-2004-10 (2004).
[18] S.Khurshid, C.S.Pasareanu and W.Visser, Generalized symbolic execution for model checking and testing. TACAS, 2003 (2003).
[19] Corina S.Pasareanu and Willem Visser, Verification of Java Programs using Symbolic Execution and Invariant Generation. SPIN 2004 (2004).
[20] Shaz Qadeer, Sriram K.Rajarnani and Jakob Rehof, Summarizing Procedures in Concurrent Programs. In proceedings of POPL '04 (2004).
[21] Twan Basten, Dragan Bosnacki and Marc Geilen, Cluster-based Partial-Order Reduction. Automatic Software Engineering 11(4) 365-402 (2004).
[22] T.Basten and D.Bosnacki, Enhancing Partial-Order Reduction via Process Clustering. In proceedings of Automated Software Engineering, ASE '01, IEEE Computer Society Press (2001).
[23] Xiaodong Yi, Ji Wang and Xuejun Yang. Verification of C Programs using Slicing Execution. In proceeding of Fifth International Conference on Quality Software (QSIC'05), Melbourne, Australia. 2005. IEEE Computer Society press.
[24] Xiaodong Yi, Ji Wang and Xuejun Yang, Slicing Execution for Model Checking C Programs. Special Issue on Quality Software of International Journal of Software Engineering and Knowledge Engineering, Accepted (2006).

Appendix. Proof of Theorem 1

Lemma 1. *Given two transition sequences π and π', for any two transitions π_i and $t \in dom(\Upsilon_{\pi'})$, if $\pi_i \not\rightarrow_{\pi.t} t$ and $\pi_i \not\rightarrow_{\pi.t'} t'$ for all $t' \in \Upsilon_{\pi'}(t)$, then $\pi_i \not\rightarrow_{\pi.\pi'} t$ holds.*

Proof. Let $t = \pi'_k$ and we consider the transition π'_j such that $j = max\{j \mid j < k \wedge \pi'_j \not\rightarrow_{\pi'} \pi'_k\}$, i.e., π'_j is the last transition before t which does not happen-before

t. One may infer that $\pi'_j \not\rightarrow_{\pi'} \pi'_l$ for all $l : j < l < k$ (otherwise, $\pi'_j \rightarrow_{\pi'} t$ should hold), i.e., π'_j also does not happen-before any transition between π'_j and t. Hence, one may get an equivalent transition sequence by moving down π_j to the position just after t. Repeatedly doing this will generate a partial-order-equivalent transition sequence $\bar{\pi}'$ of π' where all the transitions before t belong to $\Upsilon_{\pi'}(t)$. Therefore, all the transitions before t in $\bar{\pi}'$ may happen-before π_i in $\pi.\bar{\pi}'$. Consequently, $\pi_i \not\rightarrow_{\pi.\bar{\pi}'} t$ holds and hence $\pi_i \not\rightarrow_{\pi.\pi'} t$ holds. □

Theorem 1. *If the state space is finite and acyclic, then for all states $pre(\pi, i)$ of a transition sequence π, each backtracking point set $backtrack(pre(\pi, i))$ obtained by the procedure RefineBackTrackSII of Figure 2 is equal to the one obtained by exploring the set of transition sequences Π with standard DPOR algorithm shown in Figure 1.*

Proof. We only need to prove that for each transition sequence $\pi' \in \Pi$, each backtracking point set $backtrack(pre(\pi, i))$ identified by considering $\Upsilon_{\pi'}$ in procedure RefineBackTrackSII is equal to the one by exploring the transition sequence $\pi.\pi'$ with standard DPOR algorithm.

If the procedure RefineBackTrackSII identifies that the set $backtrack(pre(\pi, i))$ needs to be refined, one knows that there exists a transition $t \in dom(\Upsilon_{\pi'})$ such that $\pi_i \not\rightarrow_{\pi.t} t$ and $\pi_i \not\rightarrow_{\pi.t'} t'$ for all $t' \in \Upsilon_{\pi'}(t)$. Following Lemma 1, one knows $\pi_i \not\rightarrow_{\pi.\pi'} t$. Let $t = \pi'_l$, then we know $t = next(pre(\pi', l), proc(t))$. So we have $\pi_i \not\rightarrow_{\pi.\pi'|l} proc(t)$ at state $pre(\pi', l)$ where $\pi.\pi'|l \triangleq \pi.(\pi'_1\pi'_2 \ldots \pi'_{l-1})$ is the first part transition sequence of $\pi.\pi'$ just before π'_l. When the standard DPOR algorithm reaches the state $pre(\pi', l)$ of $\pi.\pi'$, it will also identify $backtrack(pre(\pi, i))$ as the backtracking point, because $\pi_i \not\rightarrow_{\pi.\pi'|l} proc(t)$ and t is the first transition that operates the visible object $\alpha(\pi_i)$ in π'. In what follows, we prove that the sets of processes added to $backtrack(pre(\pi, i))$ by RefineBackTrackSII and standard DPOR algorithm are the same. We only need to prove the set E of RefineBackTrackSII is equal to that of standard DPOR algorithm. Actually, the condition "$\exists t' \in \Upsilon(t) : q = proc(t')$ or $\exists j \in dom(\pi) : j > i$ and $q = proc(\pi_j)$ and $j \rightarrow_\pi proc(t)$" is equivalent to the condition "$\exists j \in dom(\pi.\pi'|l) : j > i$ and $q = proc((\pi.\pi'|l)_j)$ and $j \rightarrow_{\pi.\pi'|l} proc(t)$".

On the other side, let the backtracking set $backtrack(pre(\pi, i))$ be identified by the standard DPOR algorithm when reaching the state $pre(\pi', l)$ of $\pi.\pi'$, then $\pi_i \not\rightarrow_{\pi.\pi'} \pi'_l$ holds. Also, we know that π_i is the last transition that operates the same visible object as π'_l in the transition sequence $\pi.\pi'|l$, so π'_l is the first transition of π' that operates $\alpha(\pi'_l)$ and thus $\pi'_l \in dom(\Upsilon_{\pi'})$. $\pi_i \not\rightarrow_{\pi.\pi'} \pi'_l$ implies $\pi_i \not\rightarrow_{\pi.\pi'_l} \pi'_l$ and $\pi_i \not\rightarrow_{\pi.t'} t'$ for all $t' \in \Upsilon_{\pi'}(\pi'_l)$ (otherwise, $\pi_i \rightarrow_{\pi.\pi'} \pi'_l$ holds since $t' \rightarrow_{\pi'} \pi'_l$). As the set E of RefineBackTrackSII is the same as that of the standard DPOR algorithm, the same backtracking set $backtrack(pre(\pi, i))$ will be identified. □

User-Defined Atomicity Constraint: A More Flexible Transaction Model for Reliable Service Composition

Xiaoning Ding[1,2], Jun Wei[1], and Tao Huang[1]

[1] Institute of Software, Chinese Academy of Sciences, Beijing, China
[2] Graduate School of Chinese Academy of Sciences, Beijing, China
{dxn, wj, tao}@otcaix.iscas.ac.cn

Abstract. Transaction is the key mechanism to make service composition reliable. To ensure the relaxed atomicity of transactional composite service (TCS), existing research depends on the analysis to composition structure and exception handling mechanism. However, this approach can not handle various application-specific requirements, and causes lots of unnecessary failure recoveries or even aborts. In this paper, we propose a relaxed transaction model, including system mode, relaxed atomicity criterion, static checking algorithm and dynamic enforcement algorithm. Users can define different relaxed atomicity constraint for different TCS according to the specific application requirements, including accepted configurations and the preference order. The checking algorithm determines whether the constraint can be satisfied. The enforcement algorithm monitors the execution and performs transaction management works according to the constraint. Compared to existing work, our approach is flexible enough to handle complex application requirements and performs the transaction management works automatically. We apply the approach into web service composition language WS-BPEL and illustrate the above advantages through a concrete example.

1 Introduction

Internetware [1,2] is a new software form designed for the open and dynamic nature of internet computing environment. An internetware application is built upon the composition of existing individual services, referred to as primitive services. Transaction is a key mechanism to make the composition reliable. A service composed of transactional primitive services is called a transactional composite service (TCS).

The transactional capability of primitive services is usually described by two properties: retriable and compensable [3]. A service is said to be retriable if it can ultimately succeed after finite times of retrying. A service is said to be compensable if it provides an operation to semantically undo the execution effect. Due to the heterogeneous nature of internetware, different primitive services may have different transactional capabilities, while the composition may also be long-running and complex in structure. The traditional "all or nothing" atomic transaction semantics [4] is too strict and not suitable.

Various relaxed transaction models [5] are employed to provide a relaxed atomicity: either the TCS terminates normally or all completed services are compensated [6]. To

Z. Liu and J. He (Eds.): ICFEM 2006, LNCS 4260, pp. 168–184, 2006.

enforce relaxed atomicity, existing research analyzes the composition structure of TCS and guarantee there exists at least one must-success path after the non-compensable service [7]. During runtime stage, any possible failures are trapped by the exception handling mechanism [8]. Then a backward recovery or a forward recovery is applied. The entire TCS would not abort if all services inside dependency sphere are recovered.

However, above approach can not deal with some application-specific requirements and cause some unnecessary failure recoveries. For example, since the service-oriented environment has a native built-in capability of parallelism, it is common to invoke several candidate services in parallel. Suppose two candidate services (*Flight* and *Train*) are invoked in parallel and only one of them need to succeed. It is not necessary to do any failure recoveries if only one of them fails. On the other hand, system should compensate one service if both of them succeed. However, there is no exception occurring in this situation and current mechanism can not handle the requirement.

Furthermore, users may have some preferences, such as preferring *Flight* to *Train*. If both services succeed, the one should be compensated is service *Train* instead of *Flight*. However, current exception handling mechanism can not handle it and users have to process all these works manually.

In essence, the above shortcomings are brought by the fact that the existing approach is not aware of application-specific semantics. In this paper, we propose a relaxed transaction model based on a user-defined relaxed atomicity constraint, which implicitly expresses the application semantics. The checking and enforcement are unified and driven by the constraint.

The rest of the paper is organized as follows. In the next section, we introduce a motivating example. Section 3 presents our relaxed transaction model ASRTM (Application Semantics-based Relaxed Transaction Model), including system model and relaxed atomicity criterion. Section 4 gives the static checking algorithm ASRTM-RAC (Relaxed Atomicity Checking). Section 5 gives the dynamic enforcement algorithm ASRTM-EAE (Relaxed Atomicity Enforcement). We apply our approach into the motivating example in section 6 and demonstrate the advantages. Section 7 reviews the related work. And we conclude the paper in the last section.

2 Motivation

A travel agency provides an online service to arrange a travel for its clients. It includes reserving hotel, booking transportation tickets, payment, and etc. The service is named *TravelPlan*, which is composed of eight existing primitive services. Figure 1 shows the composition structure.

The primitive services are provided by the travel agency itself and its business partners, such as airport, hotel and bank. Each primitive service performs a single business logic unit: *CheckUser* checks whether the service requester is a registered client. *Hotel* reserves a hotel room. *Flight* books a flight ticket to the destination, while *Train* books a train ticket. *Calfees* calculates the total fees, and *Payment* performs the online payment job. Finally, *FedEx* or *EMS* arranges a ticket delivery on line.

To complete *TravelPlan* as soon as possible, we invoke the ready services in parallel, including (*Hotel, Flight, Train*) and (*FedEx, EMS*). According to the application

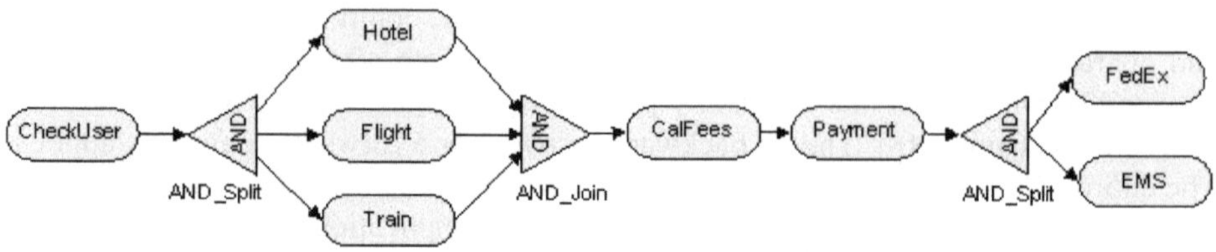

Fig. 1. A Transactional Composite Service

semantics, there are following requirements: (1) Service *Hotel* should succeed (2) One and only one service between *Flight* and *Train* should succeed, and *Flight* is more preferred. (3) One and only one service between *FedEx* and *EMS* should succeed, without any peference.

After we have designed the composite service *TravelPlan*, there are some issues we want to ensure.

First, we want to ensure the composition is correct, i.e., it wouldn't generate an unacceptable result during execution. For example, Suppose *Calfees* is non-compensable and *Payment* is non-retriable. When *Calfees* executes successfully and *Payment* fails, the *TravelPlan* can not be forward recovered (*Payment* is non-retriable). It also can not be backward recovered (*Calfees* is non-compensable). Obviously we can not accept this result.

Second, when there are multiple choices, we want a more favorite one. For example, if both services *Flight* and *Train* succeed, we want to reserve *Flight* service and compensate *Train* service.

Finally, all these works related to transaction management, such as retrying service or compensating service, should be performed automatically by system instead of by users manually.

In summary, system should provide following abilities:

- Users can define the relaxed atomicity constraint for a TCS according to the specific application requirements.
- In design stage, it should be able to decide whether the specific constraint can be satisfied.
- In runtime stage, system should perform transactional works according to the constraint automatically.

Our work in the rest of paper is divided into three parts according to the above requirements.

3 Transaction Model

3.1 System Model

We construct the system model from service types. Retriablity and compensability are two independent properties, therefore there are four service types on different combinations.

Definition 3.1 (Service Type). The type of a primitive service *s* is denoted as type(*s*), type(*s*)∈ {*trivial, retriable, compensable, pivot*}.

A *trivial* service is both retriable and compensable, while a *pivot* service is neither retriable nor compensable.

Definition 3.2 (Service State). According to the service type, a service may be in different states during its life cycle. Figure 2 shows the possible states and transitions:

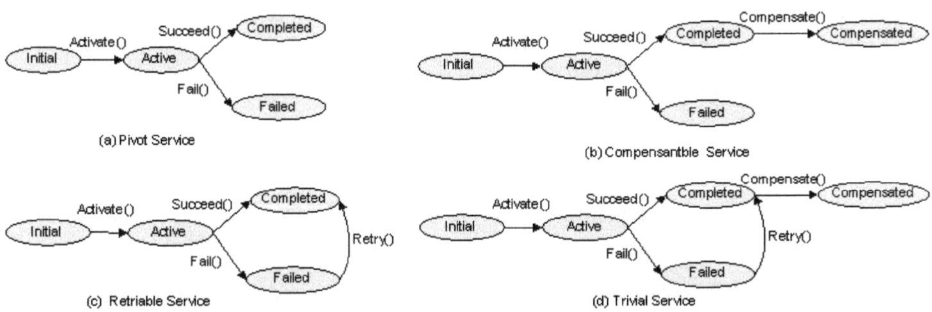

Fig. 2. States and Transitions of Primitive Services

The initial state of a service is *initial*. A state is transited to another state through a *transition*. When a service enters *completed* state, the desired effect has been made. If the service is compensable, the effect can be undone through compensate() transition. If the service enters *failed* state, the desired effect has not been made and compensation is not needed.

In our model, we can determine whether need to activate a service in advance according to the atomicity constraint, and do not need canceling a service when it is under execution. Therefore there is no cancel() or abort() transitions in our model.

Among all these transitions, activate(), retry() and compensate() is called "*external transition*". External transitions are invoked by system on demand and we can predict the resulting state. Succeed() and fail() is called "*internal transition*". Internal transitions occur automatically when the service is under *active* state and system can not predict which transitions will occur.

The state of service *s* is denoted as state(*s*), and its all possible states are denoted as set PS(*s*). When a specific type of service is at state *p*, we denote the states set that one-step transition can reach is PostState(*type, p*), and the states set that multiple steps can reach is AllPostState(*type, p*).

Only one time of retry() transition may not work and the service is still in the original state. But it can ultimately enter state *completed* after finite times of retrying. To simplify the system model, we simplify the possible multiple times of retry() to only one time. The simplification does not affect any conclusion in our model.

Definition 3.3 (Control Dependency). Control dependency describes the different control structures of primitive services. A service *s* can not be activate() until some other services ends. The set of these services is denoted as Pre(*s*).

Definition 3.4 (Transactional Composite Service). A service composed of primitive services is called a Transactional Composite Service (TCS). TCS = (id, T, $<_T$). Among the definition:

- id is the identifier of TCS
- T is the set containing all primitive services
- $<_T$ is the set of control dependencies in T

Definition 3.5 (TCS Configuration). A TCS configuration describes the states of all its primitive services at a given time. TCS configuration is defined as a n-slots tuple of service states, with a state space of Cartesian set

$$\prod_{s \in TCS.T} PS(s).$$

Since the initial state of each primitive service is *initial*, the initial configuration of TCS is (*initial, initial, . . . , initial*).

Definition 3.6 (TCS Execution). An execution of TCS is a sequence of configurations: $P_0, P_1, P_2, \ldots, P_n$. P_0 is the initial configuration. There is one and only one service *s* has difference states in P_{i-1} and P_i. Suppose the different states are k_{i-1} and k_i, then $k_i \in$ PostState(type(*s*), k_{i-1}).

The activation and termination of services would not occur at the exactly same time in reality, and any transition changes the configuration immediately. Therefore there is still only one service has different states between P_{i-1} and P_i even there is a parallel structure in TCS.

3.2 Relaxed Atomicity Criterion

In our model, the relaxed atomicity criterion is defined by users according to the application-specific semantic requirements.

Users express their specific requirements through the set and order of TCS configurations. All accepted TCS configurations are organized into an ordered set ε, with the preference order. If an execution ends in a configuration in ε, the execution is thought to be acceptable. The bigger set ε is, the more relax atomicity is. In the extreme situation,ε is an empty set and it is not satisfiable.

Definition 3.7 (Relaxed Atomicity Criterion). ε is an ordered set of TCS configurations. If an execution of TCS ends in configuration *p* and $p \in \varepsilon$, then the execution is said to satisfy the relaxed atomicity ε. Each configuration in ε is called a legal configuration. The order inside ε represents user's preference, and a legal configuration in front is more favorite than the one in latter.

The traditional "all or nothing" atomicity semantics can also be described by this criterion. Its ε is < (*completed, completed, . . . , completed*), (*failed, failed, . . . , failed*) >.

We adopt a compact recording method to reduce the size of set ε. In the method, a slot of TCS configuration can also be an ordered set containing all possible state values. For example, an ε can be recorded as $\varepsilon =< (< K_1, K_2 >, < K_3, K_4 >) >$, it means $\varepsilon =< (K_1, K_3), (K_1, K_4), (K_2, K_3), (K_2, K_4) >$.

4 Relaxed Atomicity Checking

A TCS may be a critical business process among organizations. It is important to find out any possible errors during its design time. After a specific atomicity constraint is assigned to a TCS, it should be guaranteed that the constraint can be satisfied. i.e., no matter which service succeeds or fails, the execution can end in a legal configuration.

Our checking algorithm is based on the concept of Configuration Transition Diagram.

4.1 Configuration Transition Diagram

If a TCS configuration is denoted as a node and a transition is denoted as a directed edge, we get a graph named Configuration Transition Diagram (CTD). Any possible execution of a TCS is a path in CTD, with an initial node (*initial, initial, ..., initial*). Since there is no cycle in the state transition graph of primitive services, CTD is a Directed Acyclic Graph (DAG).

Generating the full-size CTD in advance is unaffordable in time complexity and also unnecessary. We adopt a dynamic method to generate CTD by steps on demand. In each step, we only generate all child nodes of current node.

Table 1 shows the algorithm, which generates all child nodes for a specific node: *CurrentNode*. In the algorithm, ES is a set including all ended services, while RS is a set including all ready services.

Table 1. CTD Generating Algorithm

```
Initialize ES and RS to empty set;
for each service s in CurrentNode do
   if state(s) is completed, failed or compensated then
      add s to ES;
for each service s in CurrentNode do
   if Pre(s) ⊆ ES then put s into RS;
for each service s in RS do
   for each state k in PostState(type(s),state(s)) do
   {
      Create a new node named NewNode;
      Copy CurrentNode to NewNode, and change state of s to k;
      Insert NewNode to graph as a child node of CurrentNode;
   }
```

Suppose the number of primitive services in TCS.T is n, then we need O(n) time to construct set ES and RS. There are at most two possible transitions under any given state for any service type, so there are at most 2*n child nodes need to be generated. The overall time complexity of the algorithm is O(n).

Since the complete CTD of *TravelPlan* is too large, we only illustrate the CTD of a composition fragment. We still choose the composition fragment (*Calfees, Payment*) which we have discussed in section 2. Figure 3 shows the CTD generated by the above algorithm.

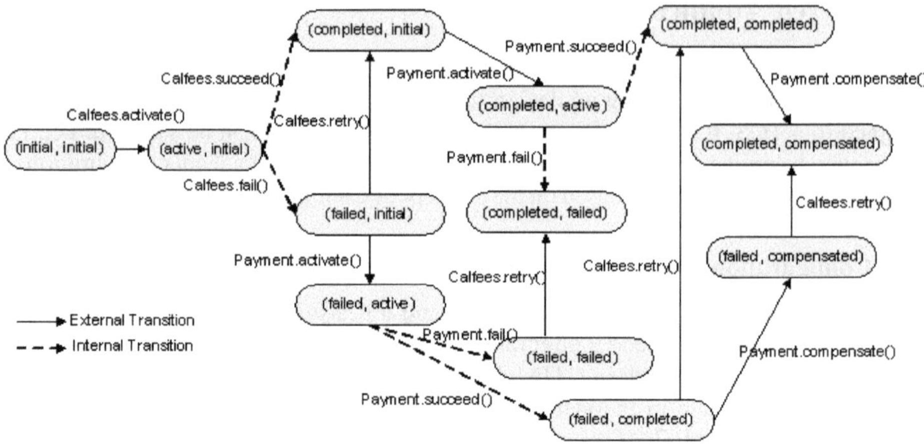

Fig. 3. Configuration Transition Diagram

4.2 Well-Behaved Criterion

To discuss the checking rules, we first define some special nodes in CTD.

Definition 4.1 (Reachability). Suppose p and p' are two different nodes in CTD. If there is at least one path from p to p' in CTD, then p' is reachable from p, otherwise p' is unreachable from p.

Definition 4.2 (Reachable Configuration & Unreachable Configuration). Suppose p is a node in CTD, if it is reachable from the initial node, then it is a reachable configuration, otherwise it is an unreachable configuration.

We illustrate the above concepts still by the example of (*Calfees, Payment*). Suppose ε is specified as <(*completed, completed*), (*compensated, completed*)> , as is shown in figure 4. We can see that configuration (*completed, completed*) is reachable, while (*compensated, completed*) is unreachable.

Definition 4.3 (Dead Configuration & Live Configuration). Suppose p is a node in CTD. If all nodes in ε are unreachable from node p, then p is called a dead configuration, otherwise it is called an live configuration.

As we can see from figure 4, (*completed, failed*), (*failed, failed*), (*failed,compensated*) and (*completed, compensated*) are all dead configurations.

When the execution of TCS enters a dead configuration, it can not reach any legal configurations. Obviously we should avoid dead configurations during execution. Some dead configurations are avoidable, but some are not.

For example, the dead configuration (*failed, compensated*) is generated by an external transition: *Payment*.compensated(). The transition is fired by system, and system can predict the result configuration. So we can avoid this dead configuration in its parent node (*failed, completed*),.

On the other hand, dead configuration (*completed, failed*) is unavoidable. An execution may enter one of its parent node (*completed, active*), which is a live configuration. The available transitions under this configuration are all internal configurations.

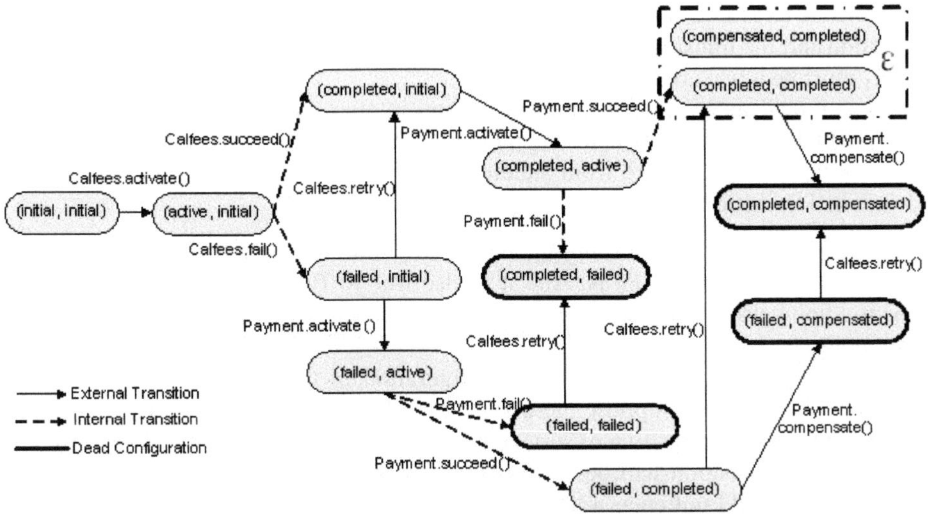

Fig. 4. Unreachable configurations and dead configurations

However, we can not predict which transition will occur, succeed() or fail(). If the fail() transition occurs, the execution will enter the dead configuration (*completed, failed*) immediately.

As we can see, an unavoidable dead configuration is dangerous and deadly. We call such configuration a trap configuration.

Definition4.4 (Trap Configuration). Suppose p is a node in CTD, p is a trap configuration if and only if: (1) p is a dead configuration by itself (2) At least one parent node p' of p is a live configuration, and the transition from p' to p is an internal transition.

Now we can give the relaxed atomicity checking rules:

Well-behaved Criterion: Given a TCS and a relaxed atomicity constraint ε, the constraint is guaranteed to be satisfied if and only if: (1) The initial configuration is a live configuration (2) There is no trap configuration.

Proof
(→) Any possible execution is a sequence of configurations P_0, P_1, P_2, ..., P_n. The sequence can be represented as a path in CTD and each node is the child node of the previous node.

From the assumption we know that P_0 is a live configuration, which implies that at least one of its child nodes is also a live configuration. Suppose all possible transitions under node P_0 is set M. M can be categorized into the following three classes:

- All transitions in M are external transitions: Since external transition is fired by system and system can predict the result configuration. And, at least one child node of P_0 is a live configuration. So we can choose a live configuration as P_1.
- All transitions in M are internal transitions: In this situation, all child nodes must be live configurations, otherwise there is a trap configuration and the supposition is

violated. (It is a dead configuration by itself. One of its parent nodes is live configuration and the transition is an internal transition). Therefore, the next configuration P_1 must be a live configuration.
- M is mixed up by external transitions and internal transitions: In this situation, system does not fire any external transitions, but just wait for an internal transition to occur. As we can see from situation 2, the configuration P_1 generated by the internal transition must be a live configuration.

As a conclusion, we can ensure the next configuration P_1 is a live configuration no matter what configuration P_0 is. And it is also true to P_2, P_3 until P_n. Furthermore, CTD is a finite graph without cycles. Thus the execution is guaranteed to end in a legal configuration.

(←) The execution can reach a legal configuration, so the initial configuration must be a live configuration. Suppose there exist a trap configuration P_1 with a live parent node P_0 and internal transition of service s. Under configuration P_0, we can not predict which internal transition will occur, succeed() or fail(). So we can not guarantee that the execution would not enter a dead configuration. But this is in contradiction to the assumption. So there is no trap configuration in CTD.

4.3 Checking Algorithm

In this section, we discuss the relaxed atomicity checking algorithm.

First, check whether the initial configuration is a live configuration. To preserve this property, at least one legal configuration in ε should be reachable from the initial configuration.

Second, check whether there exists a trap configuration. A straightforward approach is to travel the whole CTD and check each node. However, it is unaffordable on time complexity.

We check any possible trap configurations according to its characteristics. A trap configuration is generated by an internal transition from a live configuration. Suppose the live configuration P_0=(K_1, K_2,..., *active*, ..., K_n), and the internal transition occurs on service s. The internal transition can only produce two configurations: P_1=(K_1, K_2, ..., *completed*, ..., K_n) and P_2=(K_1, K_2, ..., *failed*, ..., K_n). One of them could be trap configuration.

P_0 is a live configuration, suppose all legal configurations it can transit to form set M, and all possible states of service s in M form set K. If P_1 is a dead configuration, the only possible state in set K must be *failed*. If P_2 is a dead configuration, service s must be non-retriable and the possible states in set K are *completed* and *compensated*.

We check the above two situations for each service s. Take the first situation as an example. The constraint ε is divided into two subsets. All configurations with state of s is *failed* are put into M, and all the other configurations are put into set N. If there exists a configuration p which can transit to set M but can not transit to set N, it is a trap configuration when the state of s in p is replaced by *completed*. The checking to the second situation is similar to the first one.

The algorithm is described in table 2.

We analyze the time complexity of ASRTM-RAC algorithm briefly. Suppose the number of primitive services in TCS.T is n, the number of legal configurations is m.

Table 2. Algorithm ASRTM_RAC

```
Input: TCS, ε
Output: boolean
{
  //Check whether the initial configuration is live
  flag := false;
  for each legal configuration p in ε do
  {
    p.reachability := true;
    for each service s in TCS.T do
      if (the required state of s in p) ∉ PS(s) then
        p.reachability := false;
    if p.reachability == true then
      flag := true;
  }
  if flag==false then return false;
  //Check trap configurations: succeed()
  for each service s in TCS.T do
  {
    Initialize M and N to empty set;
    Put all legal configurations with state(s) is failed into M;
    Put all the other configurations into N;
    J := all possible configurations which can not
    transit to any configurations in N;
    for each configuration p in M do
    {
      Q := all possible configurations which can transit to p;
      if the intersection between Q and J is not empty then
        return false;
    }
  }
  //Check trap configurations: succeed()
  for each service s in TCS.T do
  {
    if type(s) is retriable or trivial then continue;
    Initialize M and N to empty set;
    Put all legal configurations with state(s)
      is completed or compensated into M;
    Put all the other configurations into N;
    J := all possible configurations which can not
    transit to any configurations in N;
    for each configuration p in M do
    {
      Q := all possible configurations which can transit to p;
      if the intersection between Q and J is not empty then
        return false;
    }
  }
  //All checking passed
  return true;
```

Checking initial configuration only needs to do a loop on TCS.T and ε. The required time complexity is O(m*n). Checking trap configurations needs to do a loop on TCS.T. In the loop body, the most complex operation is determining the configuration set J and Q. To reduce the time complexity, we represent the set as a Cartesian set of each service states set, like < {},{},...,{}>. The searching and intersection works are performed on this data structure. It requires a time complexity of $O(n^2)$. Therefore the whole loop needs $O(n^3)$ and the overall time complexity of the algorithm is $O(n^3)$. Since the number of primitive services and the legal configurations would not be a large number, $O(n^3)$ complexity is acceptable.

5 Relaxed Atomicity Enforcement

5.1 Goal

The goal of relaxed atomicity enforcement is to monitor the execution of TCS and ensure the execution ends in a legal configuration. When there are several available choices, choose the most favorite one.

Since the static checking algorithm has guaranteed that the constraint is satisfiable and there is no trap configuration. The enforcement algorithm only needs to monitor the execution and adjust the state of services according to constraint. It changes the state of services through invoking retry() and compensate() transition of services. While the activate() transition is invoked by the service composition engine.

Relaxed atomicity enforcement is not just the failure recovery. Sometimes it also needs to adjust the state of services even if there are no failures.

5.2 Enforcement Algorithm

Our relaxed atomicity enforcement algorithm is named ASRTM-RAE. It is invoked after the end of each primitive service. The algorithm is described in table 3.

In the algorithm, ES is the set of all ended services. *s* is the ended primitive service which fires the current execution of algorithm.

ASRTM-RAE first adds service *s* to the ended service set ES and constructs a configuration prefix from the set. Then, scan and find out the first legal configuration *p* which current prefix can transit to. There must exist a legal configuration which prefix can transit to. It is guaranteed by the previous execution of the algorithm.

If the according part of *p* is same to the prefix, it means that current configuration is already the most favorite one we can reach, so algorithm does nothing but exit. Otherwise, adjust the state of each ended service to the required state in *p*. If the required state is *completed*, we keep doing retry() until it succeed. If the required state is *compensated*, we invoke the compensate() transition of the service. Since *p* is the configuration that current configuration can transit to, above transitions are under the transactional capability of the service.

When the state of a service is not *initial* or *failed*, no external transitions can change it to *initial* or *failed*. But *p* is reachable from current configuration, which implies that current state of service must already be *initial* or *failed*. So, if the required state is *initial* or *failed*, the algorithm does nothing.

Table 3. Algorithm ASRTM_RAE

```
Input: TCS, ε, s
Output: void
{
  Add s to ES;
  prefix := sequence of states of all services in ES;
  For each configuration p in do
  {
    for each service s in TCS.T do
    {
      k := required state of s in p;
      if k ∉ (state(s) + AllPostState(type(s), state(s))) then
        break; //current configuration can not transit to p
    }
    //p is the configuration that current configuration can transit to
    prefix' = NULL;
    for each service s in ES do
      prefix' := prefix' + required state of s in p;
    if prefix' == prefix then
      exit algorithm; //Nothing need to do
    else
      exit loop; //adjust service states according to p
  }
  for each service s in ES do
  {
    k := required state of s in p;
    if state(s) == k then continue;
    If k == completed then
      while state(s)≠ completed do
        invoke s.retry()
    else If k == compensated then
      invoke s.compensate();
    //if k is failed or initial, do nothing
  }
}
```

The above processing also avoids dead configurations. Since the adjusted configuration at least can transit to the legal configuration *p*, it must be a live configuration.

We analyze the time complexity of the algorithm briefly. Suppose the number of primitive services in TCS.T is n, the number of legal configurations is m. Constructing configuration prefix needs O(n), finding out p needs O(m*n), comparing prefixes needs O(n), and adjusting states according to configuration *p* needs O(n). Therefore the overall time complexity of the algorithm is $O(n^2)$.

6 Demonstration

In this section, we apply our approach into the motivating example *TravelPlan* and show the advantages of our approach. Since web service is the most popular implementation technology of internetware, we discuss *TravelPlan* in web service environment.

6.1 Relaxed Atomicity in WS-BPEL

WS-BPEL [9] is the most promising web service composition language nowadays. To integrate our approach into WS-BPEL, the first job is to express the relaxed atomicity constraint ε in the language.

Each composite service in WS-BPEL is called a *process*, and each process is associated with a deployment descriptor. We extend the deployment descriptor and record ε in it as a XML-structure.

At the same time, a default ε is generated for each WS-BPEL process. It includes two legal configurations. The first one is (*completed, completed, ..., completed*), which expresses the atomicity constraint for the success of TCS. The second one is (*<initial, failed, compensated>*, *<initial, failed, compensated>*, ..., *<initial, failed, compensated>*), which expresses the atomicity constraint for the failure of TCS. If the primitive service is non-compensable, the according slot is only *<initial, failed>* and not includes *compensated*.

6.2 Specification of TravelPlan

After process *TravelPlan* is deployed, system generates a default atomicity constraint for it, as shown in table 4. Since system does not know the specific requirements of *TravelPlan*, the default atomicity constraint is not very suitable.

Table 4. Default Relaxed Atomicity Constraint ε

CheckUser	Hotel	Flight	Train	Calfees	Payment	FedEx	EMS
completed	completed	completed	completed	completed	completed	completed	completed
<initial, failed, compensated>	<initial, failed, compensated>	<initial, failed, compensated>	<initial, failed, compensated>	<initial, failed, compensated>	<initial, failed>	<initial, failed>	<initial, failed, compensated>

User modifies the default constraint to the following one according to the specific requirements, as shown in table 5. Note the order inside ε also implies the application requirements (such as preferring *Flight* to *Train*).

The type of each service is showed in table 6.

Through the relaxed atomicity checking algorithm, we can ensure that the initial configuration is a live configuration and there is no trap configuration in the CTD of *TravelPlan*.

Table 5. User-defined Relaxed Atomicity Constraint ε

CheckUser	Hotel	Flight	Train	Calfees	Payment	FedEx	EMS
completed	completed	completed	<failed, compensated>	completed	completed	completed	<initial, failed, compensated>
completed	completed	<failed, compensated>	completed	completed	completed	completed	<initial, failed, compensated>
completed	completed	completed	<failed, compensated>	completed	completed	<initial, failed>	completed
completed	completed	<failed, compensated>	completed	completed	completed	<initial, failed>	completed
<initial, failed, compensated>	<initial, failed, compensated>	<initial, failed, compensated>	<initial, failed, compensated>	<initial, failed, compensated>	<initial, failed>	<initial, failed>	<initial, failed, compensated>

Table 6. Service Type

CheckUser	Hotel	Flight	Train	Calfees	Payment	FedEx	EMS
compensable	compensable	compensable	trivial	compensable	pivot	pivot	trivial

6.3 Typical Scenarios

In this section, we show the processing of our approach on several typical scenarios during the execution of TravelPlan.

■ All candidate services succeed

Suppose the first four services succeed and we get the configuration prefix = (*CheckUser.completed, Hotel.completed, Flight.completed, Train.completed*).

Scan ε according to the order, since *failed* ∉ AllPostState(*trivial, completed*), we can not change the state of *Train* from *completed* to *failed*. So any legal configurations with prefix=(*CheckUser.completed, Hotel.completed, Flight.completed, Train.failed*) are unreachable from current configuration. The next legal configuration (*CheckUser.completed, Hotel.completed, Flight.completed, Train.compensated*) is reachable, which requires the state of *Train* to be *compensated*. So ASRTM-RAE invoke the compensate() transition of service *Train*.

In this scenario, utilizing the implicit application semantics in ε, ASRTM-RAE chooses a more favorite configuration: *Flight* first.

■ Some candidate services fail

Now suppose service *Flight* failed, and we get the configuration prefix = (*CheckUser.completed, Hotel.completed, Flight.failed, Train.completed*). Scan ε according to the order, since *completed* ∉ AllPostState(*compensable, failed*), current configuration can not transit to the legal configurations with prefix = (*CheckUser.completed, Hotel.completed, Flight.completed, Train.failed*) or (*CheckUser.completed, Hotel.completed, Flight.completed, Train.compensated*). While the next legal configuration has a same prefix, so ASRTM-RAE does nothing.

This scenario shows that utilizing the implicit application semantics in ε, we can avoid unnecessary failure recoveries and decrease the transactional capability requirements to services.

■ Service fails before the non-compensable service
Suppose service *Payment* failed, we get a configuration prefix = (*CheckUser.completed, Hotel.completed, Flight.completed, Train.compensated, Calfees.completed, Payment.failed*). The first four legal configurations require state of *Payment* to be *completed*, but type (*Payment*)=*pivot* and *completed* $\notin$ AllPostState(*pivot, failed*). So these configurations are unreachable from current configuration. The only legal configuration we can transit to is the final one, which requires the state of services *CheckUser, Hotel, Flight*, and *Calfees* to be *compensated*.

We can understand this scenario more clearly from the angle of failure recovery. A non-retriable service failed, and the service is vital to the process. So we have to roll-back the whole process. Fortunately the failed service is before any non-compensable services, so we just need to compensate all completed services.

■ Service fails after the non-compensable service
Suppose both service *FedEx* and *EMS* failed, we get a configuration prefix = (*CheckUser.completed, Hotel.completed, Flight.completed, Train.compensated, Calfees.completed, Payment.completed, fedEx.failed, EMS.failed*). Scan ε and we can learn that since type(*Payment*)=*pivot*, we can not transit the prefix to any legal configurations except (*CheckUser.completed, Hotel.completed, Flight.completed, Train.compensated, Calfees.completed, Payment.completed, Fedex.failed, EMS.completed*). The legal configuration requires the state of service *EMS* to be *completed*. The checking algorithm ASRTM-RAC has ensured service *EMS* is *retriable*, so ASRTM-RAE retries service *EMS* until it succeeds.

From the angle of failure recovery, there should exit a must-success executing path after the non-compensable service. In the approaches based on syntax analysis, it requires both *FedEx* and *EMS* to be retriable. But in our approach, we only require one of them to be retriable utilizing the implicit application semantics of ε. i.e., the unnecessary transactional capability requirements to services are avoided.

7 Related Work

The research on relaxed atomicity traditionally comes from database systems, and also be studied in workflow and cooperative systems. While the more recent research is usually performed in web service environment.

Current web service transaction specification usually defines its own relaxed transaction model, including Business Activity in WS-Transaction [10], Cohesion in BTP [11], and TX-LRA, TX-BP in WS-TXM [12]. However, these relaxed transaction models only define the message exchange protocol among participants. They did not state how to manage transactions in the service composition. Users have to do all the works related to the transaction management by themselves, such as retrying service or compensating service.

WebTransact [7] is a transactional composition model for web services. It guarantees the relaxed atomicity through the analysis to the composition structure. For example, there should exist a must-success path after the non-compensable service. Our approach also needs to ensure this property. However, our judgment is based on the application semantics provided by instead of composition structure. It is more precise and can reduce the transactional capability requirements to services.

Accepted Termination States (ATS) [13] is a mechanism to express the relaxed atomicity which comes from transactional workflow systems. However, ATS does not preserve the order of each item inside constraint, which is an important part of application semantics. There are lots of work based on ATS [13,14,15]. But it is still thought difficult to ensure every execution preserve these properties [13]. Paper [16] applies ATS to transactional service composition to ensure the required failure atomicity. The approach used is analyzing composition structures, based on a series of transactional rules according to different syntax structures. It did not discuss the enforcement issues such as failure recoveries.

WSTx [17] is a framework for transactional web service composition, which also supports user-defined relaxed atomicity constraint. The concept in WSTx expresses the constraint is called *outcome condition*. An outcome condition is a plain text string, which includes the names of all services. Each service can be success or failed, with a value of true and false. WSTx parse the string as a boolean expression and calculate the result during runtime. The transaction can only be committed when the result is true. This approach is very flexible. However, the outcome condition is hard-coded in the program as a string, it is difficult to analyze and check it.

8 Conclusion

Ensuring the relaxed atomicity of TCS is a key problem to support reliable service composition in internetware. Existing approaches are based on the analysis to composition syntax and exception handling mechanism. Without knowledge of the specific application semantics, it can not handle complex requirements and causes some unnecessary failure recoveries.

In this paper, we propose a relaxed transaction model to handle above problems. In the model, the relaxed atomicity criterion of a TCS is defined by users according to specific application semantics. The static checking and dynamic enforcement works are driven by the atomicity constraint. Compared to the existing work, our approach has several advantages.

First, the relaxed atomicity constraint describes specific application semantics implicitly. Utilizing the implicit application semantics, the checking and enforcement works are performed more precisely. Unnecessary failure recoveries or transactional capability requirements are avoided. And system can choose a more favorite result for users.

Second, the transaction management is integrated into service composition. The routine transactional works, such as retrying service or compensating service, are performed by system automatically instead of by users manually. Thus the non-functional concern is separated from business logic.

Finally, our model is based on a simple and clear correctness criterion, which can be applied into various service composition languages easily.

Acknowledgments. This paper was supported by the Major State Basic Research Development Program of China (973 Program) under Grant No.2002CB312005, and the National Science Foundation of China under Grant No.60573126.

References

1. Yang FQ. Thinking on the development of software engineering technology. Journal of Software, 16(1): 1-7, 2005
2. Lu Jian, Tao Xianping, Ma Xiaoxing, et al., Research on Agent-Based Software Model for Internetware. Science in China, Series F-Information Sciences, 35(12): 1233-1253, 2005 9.
3. A. Zhang, M. Nodine, and B. Bhargava, Global Scheduling for Flexible Transactions in Heterogeneous Distributed Database Systems, IEEE Transactions on Knowledge and Data Engineering, 13(3):pp.439-450, 2001
4. J. Gray and A. Reuter, Transaction Processing: Concepts and Techniques, Morgan Kaufmann Publishers, San Mateo, California, 1993
5. Mohan C. Tutorial: Advanced Transaction Models Survey and Critique. In ACM SIGMOD International Conference on Management of Data, Minneapolis, 1994
6. P. Grefen, J. Vonk, E. Boertjes, and P. Apers, Semantics and Architecture of Global Transaction Support in Workflow Environments, In Proceedings of the Fourth IFCIS International Conference on Cooperative Information Systems, pp.348-359, Edinburgh, Scotland, September 2-4, 1999
7. P. F. Pires. WebTransact: A Framework For Specifying And Coordinating Reliable Web Services Compositions. Technical report ES-578/02, Coppe Federal University of Rio De Janeiro, Brazil, April 2002
8. Yi Ren, Quanyuan Wu, Yan Jia, et al., Transactional Business Coordination and Failure Recovery for Web Services Composition. GCC 2004, pp.26-33, 2004
9. IBM, BEA Systems, Microsoft, SAP AG, Siebel Systems. Business Process Execution Language for Web Services, version 1.1. http://www-128.ibm.com/developerworks/library/specification/ws-bpel/, 2005
10. Microsoft, BEA and IBM. Web Services Transaction (WS-Transaction), http://www.ibm.com/developerworks/library/ws-transpec/., 2002
11. Oasis Committee. Business Transaction Protocol (BTP), Version1.0. http://www.oasis-open.org/committees/business-transactions/., 2002
12. D. Bunting et al. Web Services Transaction Management (WS-TXM) Version 1.0. Arjuna, Fujitsu, IONA, Oracle, and Sun, July 28, 2003
13. Marek Rusinkiewicz , Amit Sheth, Specification and execution of transactional workflows, Modern database systems: the object model, interoperability, and beyond, ACM Press/Addison-Wesley Publishing Co., New York, NY, 1995
14. Mansoor Ansari , Linda Ness , Marek Rusinkiewicz , Amit P. Sheth, Using Flexible Transactions to Support Multi-System Telecommunication Applications, Proceedings of the 18th International Conference on Very Large Data Bases, pp.65-76, 1992
15. A. Elmagarmid , Y. Leu , W. Litwin , Marek Rusinkiewicz, A multidatabase transaction model for InterBase, Proceedings of the sixteenth international conference on Very large databases, pp.507-518, 1990
16. Sami Bhiri, Olivier Perrin, Claude Godart, Ensuring required failure atomicity of composite Web services, In Proceedings of the 14th international conference on World Wide Web(WWW '05), pp. 138-147, 2005
17. Thomas Mikalsen, Stefan Tai, and Isabelle Rouvello. Transactional Attitudes: Reliable Composition of Autonomous Web Services. International Conference on Dependable Systems and Networks (DSN 2002). 2002

Environment Ontology-Based Capability Specification for Web Service Discovery

Puwei Wang[1,3], Zhi Jin[1,2], and Lin Liu[4]

[1] Institute of Computing Technology, Chinese Academy of Sciences
[2] Academy of Mathematics and System Sciences, Chinese Academy of Sciences
[3] Graduate University of Chinese Academy of Sciences
[4] School of Software, Tsinghua University
Beijing 100080, China
wangpw@ict.ac.cn

Abstract. During Web service discovery, capabilities of Web services are of major concern. This paper proposes an environment ontology based approach for specifying Web service capability semantically. First, a meta-level environment ontology is adopted in the proposed approach to provide formal and sharable specifications of environment resources in a particular domain. For each environment resource, we build a corresponding hierarchical state machine specifying its dynamic characteristics. Second, we propose to use the effect of a Web service on its environment resources for specifying the Web service capability and to designate the effect as the traces of the state transitions the Web service can impose on its environment resources. Finally, we give the mechanism to match service query with service capability description.

Keywords: Environment Ontology, Capability Specification, Service Discovery.

1 Introduction

Service discovery is one of the major challenges in the emerging area of Web services. For discovering a Web service, what humans or other Web services care about are the capabilities of Web services. Therefore, capability specification is a fundamental for service discovery. Conventional approaches usually consider Web service capability specification as a one-step process. In OWL-S [1] and WSMO [2], the one-step process is modelled as inputs, outputs, preconditions and results (i.e., IOPR schema). Then, a published service is matched with a required service when the inputs and outputs of the required service match with those of the published service, as well as the preconditions and results. Consider a common scenario in our daily life. Assume that the subject is a regular traveller, who wants to have a pleasurable budget trip, might request that "*I need a travel agency service who provides flight ticket selling and hotel room ordering service, whose service fees are charged by credit card.*" Obviously, the Web service, which satisfies the user's request, can be easily described by the following IOPR schema:

Z. Liu and J. He (Eds.): ICFEM 2006, LNCS 4260, pp. 185–205, 2006.

```
Capability
   :cap-id BudgetTravelAgency
   :input (?creditCardNo ?start ?destination ?time ?hotelLocation)
   :output (!ticketReceipt !hotelReceipt)
   :precondition (creditcard-isvalid ticket-available hotelroom-vacancy)
   :result (creditcard-ischarged ticket-sold hotelroom-ordered)
```

However, more particular requests from users arise. For instance, the traveller may want to put the flight seats and the hotel room on hold without charge. Therefore, he may have a particular request that "*I want the travel agency service to provide flight ticket ordering, i.e., I can order flight ticket, and if there is an emergency, I can cancel the ticket on hold.*" Obviously, we cannot describe a service that exactly matches the traveller's request, because when the service is considered as a one-step process, the internal state in which ticket is pending is not expressible. Then, these queries cannot be done by current discovery mechanisms. Therefore, more elaborate model than the conventional one-step process based model is needed to achieve precise service discovery. A tempting idea is to use behavior description to specify service capability for service discovery.

In [3][4], A.Wombacher presents an approach for more precise service matching by using behavior description rather than the one-step process based description. In [5], behavior as operational level description using automata is used to be as an advertisement for Web service discovery. Moreover, [6] also argues that the Web service discovery process is based on the specification of behavior, that is the process model. These efforts have a common ground that **service's behaviors** are for advertising Web service capabilities. However, they also have their limitations. For example, service's behavior may be tied too closely with implementation which reflects personal preferences of each developer.

Based on some earlier exploratory works [7] in our group, this paper proposes an environment ontology-based capability specification for Web service discovery. Different from above efforts, our behavior description isn't about Web services themselves. Its distinct feature is to introduce environment as the objective reference of Web service capability. Because that, in a particular domain, there are some sharable environment resources focused by diversified services, environment resources can gap the diversified services. In our approach, we view environment of a Web service to be composed of those controllable resources (or called "environment resources") that the Web service can impose effects on. And then, capability of a Web service is specified as the effects that the Web service imposes on its environment resources during execution, i.e., a Web service's behavior is observable to its environment.

For example, capability of a simple ticket-selling service can be specified as its effect on the environment resource `ticket` that changes the state of `ticket` from `available` to `sold`. Hence, our approach relates behavior descriptions of environment resources to the capability specification of Web services. The environment resources can constitute knowledge of sharable environment for different Web services, i.e., environment ontology. This ontology enables the behavior descriptions of environment resources, which form capability specification of Web services, to be encoded in an unambiguous and machine-understandable form.

The rest of this paper is structured as follows: Section 2 presents definition of the environment ontology and a sample environment ontology is given. Section 3 describes the approach for specifying semantically the capabilities of Web service. a mechanism to match service query with service capability specification is given. Section 4 analyzes current related works. Finally, section 5 draws a conclusion and discusses our future works.

2 Environment Ontology

Environment in dictionary is generally defined as, "the totality of circumstances surrounding an organism or group of organisms". By analogy with the organism, it is harmless to say that the circumstances of a Web service are those resources that the Web service can impose effects on. In this sense, environment of a Web service is viewed as a finite set of various environment resources (or called "controllable resources") surrounding the Web service. An environment resource is a stateful entity, and its state transitions are triggered by input messages. For example, `ticket` is an environment resource. It has two states: `available` and `sold`. And we can change its state from `available`, i.e., `ticket` is available, to `sold`, i.e., `ticket` is sold. Moreover, environment resources are domain-relevant and independent to any Web services. Therefore, the conceptualization of environment resources, i.e., the environment ontology, constitutes the sharable domain knowledge for different Web services.

Current general ontology structures, such as the one defined in [8], only contain the declarations of the concepts and the relations between them. They don't characterize the states of the concepts and the relations between the states. We extend the current general ontology representation in the following aspects.

First, we extend the general ontology structure with state machines for specifying the states and the state transitions. And a rich theory of state machine had been developed regarding to their expressive power, their operations and the analysis of their properties. On the basis of the state machine, dynamic characteristics of an environment resource can be presented, and an effect that a Web service imposes on these resources can be described with the triplet of the initial state, the target state, and a set of middle states (these middle states are included in the traces from the initial state to the target state).

Second, we propose to use the hierarchical state machine for supporting different granularity of the conceptualization. The states in a hierarchical state machine may be ordinary states or super-states which can be further subdivided (refined). Hierarchical skeleton assures that hierarchical state machine has different granularity. [9] has proposed hierarchical state machine to specify software requirement and has shown its efficiency. For example, the environment resource *ticket* may have a state *sold*, which means the *ticket* is sold. Moreover, *sold* can be further subdivided into two states: *non-delievered* and *delivered*. They mean that whether the *ticket* is delivered to purchaser or not. Moreover, hierarchical state machine is implemented as a tree-like structure. That is to reduce the computational complexity.

2.1 Definitions of the Environment Ontology

The definition of the environment ontology is presented as follows:

Definition 1. *Environment Ontology is depicted as a 6-tuple,* $\mathcal{E}nv\mathcal{O} \stackrel{\text{def}}{=} \{Rsc, \mathcal{X}^c, \mathcal{H}^c, \mathcal{HSM}, inter, res\}$, *in which:*

- *Rsc is a finite set of environment resources,*
- $\mathcal{X}^c \subseteq Rsc \times Rsc$ *is a component relation between the environment resources,* $\forall c_{r1}, c_{r2} \in Rsc$, $\langle c_{r1}, c_{r2}\rangle \in \mathcal{X}^c$ *means that* c_{r1} *is a component of* c_{r2},
- $\mathcal{H}^c \subseteq Rsc \times Rsc$ *is a taxonomic relation between the environment resources.* $\forall c_{r1}, c_{r2} \in Rsc$, $\langle c_{r1}, c_{r2}\rangle \in \mathcal{H}^c$ *means that* c_{r1} *is a subconcept of* c_{r2},
- $\mathcal{HSM}$ *is a finite set of tree-like hierarchical state machines (called "THSM"),*
- $inter \subseteq \mathcal{HSM} \times \mathcal{HSM}$ *is a message exchange relation between THSMs.* $hsm_1, hsm_2 \in \mathcal{HSM}$, $\langle hsm_1, hsm_2\rangle \in inter$ *means that* hsm_1 *and* hsm_2 *interact with each other by message exchange,*
- $res : Rsc \leftrightarrow \mathcal{HSM}$ *is a bijective relation.* $\forall c_r \in Rsc$, *there is one and only one* $hsm \in \mathcal{HSM}$, $hsm{=}res(c_r)$. *It says that hsm is the THSM of* c_r.

A THSM structure is proposed to model the possible state transitions of an environment resource. A THSM of environment resource c_r is described as $hsm(c_r) = \{\mathcal{S}, \Sigma, \mathcal{T}, f, \lambda_0, \preccurlyeq\}$, in which,

- $\mathcal{S}$ is a finite set of states of environment resource c_r;
- Σ is a finite set that is composed of two subsets: Σ^{in} and Σ^{out} for inputs and outputs respectively;
- $\delta : \mathcal{S} \times \Sigma^{in} \rightarrow \mathcal{S}$ is a deterministic transition function ($\langle s, \alpha, s'\rangle \in \mathcal{T}$ is a state transition, if $\exists \alpha \in \Sigma^{in}$, such that $s' = \delta(s, \alpha)$);
- f is an output function $f : \mathcal{S} \rightarrow \Sigma^{out}$;
- $\lambda_0 \in \mathcal{S}$ is the start state;
- $\preccurlyeq$ is a tree-like partial ordering with a topmost point. This relation defines the hierarchy relation on the states in $\mathcal{S}$ ($x \preccurlyeq y$ meaning that x is a descendant of y, or x is equal to y). Tree-like means that $\preccurlyeq$ has the property: $\neg(a \preccurlyeq b \vee b \preccurlyeq a) \Rightarrow \neg\exists x : (x \preccurlyeq a \wedge x \preccurlyeq b)$. If the state x is a descendant of y ($x \prec y$), and there is no z such that $x \prec z \prec y$, we say that the state x is a child of y, i.e., x *child* y (or the state y is the parent of x, $y = parent(x)$, i.e., y *parent* x). we define $\gamma(y) \in \mathcal{S}$ as the set of all children of the state y, that is $\gamma(y) = \{x | x \ child\ y\}$. There exists one and only one default child $x_d \in \gamma(y)$. It denotes that there is only one destination state $x_d \in \gamma(y)$ of the transition from parent-state y.

Given $\mathcal{T}_{\gamma(y)} \in \mathcal{T}$ denotes state transitions between states in $\gamma(y)$, $\Sigma_{\gamma(y)} \in \Sigma$ denotes inputs of $\mathcal{T}_{\gamma(y)}$ and outputs from $\gamma(y)$ and $f_{\gamma(y)}$ is the output function whose domain is $\gamma(y)$, an ordinary finite state machine (FSM) then can be obtained as $\mathcal{N}_{\gamma(y)} = \{\gamma(y), \Sigma_{\gamma(y)}, \mathcal{T}_{\gamma(y)}, f_{\gamma(y)}, x_d \in \gamma(y)\}$. The relation between y (called "super-state") and $\mathcal{N}_{\gamma(y)}$ (called "sub-FSM") is called subdivision (or refining) relation. Therefore, the THSM of c_r can be described in another form: $hsm(c_r) = \{\{\mathcal{N}_1, ..., \mathcal{N}_n\}, \mathcal{D}\}$, in which $\mathcal{N}_i (i \in [1, n])$ is an ordinary finite state machine, and $\mathcal{D}$ is the subdivision relation. For example, a THSM of environment resource *ticket* is given as Fig.1.

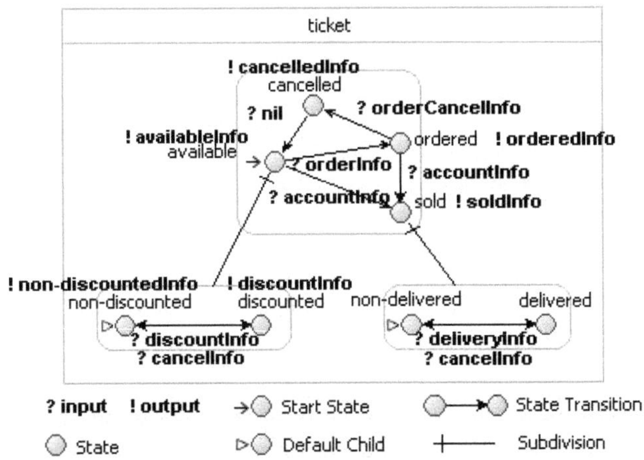

Fig. 1. THSM of Environment Resource *ticket*

We then define the message exchange relation $inter \in \mathcal{E}nv\mathcal{O}$ between THSMs. Let hsm_1 and hsm_2 be two THSMs, $\mathcal{S}(hsm_i)$ be the set of states in hsm_i, and $\mathcal{T}(hsm_i)$ be the set of transitions in hsm_i $(1 \leqslant i \leqslant 2)$.

Definition 2. *The message exchange relation on THSMs is defined as:*

$$inter \stackrel{\text{def}}{=} \{\langle hsm_1, hsm_2\rangle | \exists s \in \mathcal{S}(hsm_i), t \in \mathcal{T}(hsm_j), 1 \leqslant i \neq j \leqslant 2, s \uparrow t\}$$

where $s \uparrow t$ means that output message of state s can trigger state transition t and $s \uparrow t$ is called a message exchange. For example, in terms of Table.1, there exists a message exchange relation between THSM *hsm*(*creditcard*) of environment resource *creditcard* and THSM *hsm*(*ticket*) of environment resource *ticket*.

Table 1. Message Exchanges

State↑Transition
$valid \uparrow \langle ordered$, accountInfo, $sold\rangle$
The output from *creditcard*'s state *valid* can trigger the state transition of *ticket* from *ordered* to *sold*.
$valid \uparrow \langle available$, accountInfo, $sold\rangle$
The output from *creditcard*'s state *valid* can trigger the state transition of *ticket* from *available* to *sold*.
$sold \uparrow \langle non\text{-}charged$, feeInfo, $charged\rangle$
The output from *ticket*'s state *sold* can trigger state transition of *creditcard* from *non-charged* to *charged*.

2.2 A Sample Environment Ontology

The budget travelling environment ontology (called "*BTO*") is given to illustrate our ideas. It captures the domain knowledge about budget travelling environment. In *BTO*, five environment resources are focused. Table 2 summarizes these environment resources and their THSMs.

Table 2. Environment Resources and their THSMs in *BTO*

Environment Resources	THSMs
hotelroom	*hsm(hotelroom)*
ticket	*hsm(ticket)*
itinerary	*hsm(itinerary)*
creditcard	*hsm(creditcard)*
merchandise	*hsm(merchandise)*

Environment resource *ticket* is for taking travellers to their destinations, environment resource *hotelroom* is for accommodating travellers, and environment resource *creditcard* is a method of payment. Both *ticket* and *hotelroom* are subconcepts of environment resource *merchandise*. Moreover, environment resource *itinerary* that describes a trip from start to destination is a component of *ticket*. Table 3 summarizes the relations between them and their THSMs.

Table 3. Relations in *BTO*

Relations
$\mathcal{H}^c$
$ticket \rightarrow merchandise$
$hotelroom \rightarrow merchandise$
$\mathcal{G}^c$
$itinerary \rightarrow ticket$
res
$ticket \leftrightarrow hsm(ticket)$
$hotelroom \leftrightarrow hsm(hotelroom)$
$itinerary \leftrightarrow hsm(itinerary)$
$creditcard \leftrightarrow hsm(creditcard)$
$merchandise \leftrightarrow hsm(merchandise)$
$inter$
$hsm(ticket) \parallel hsm(creditcard)$
$hsm(hotelroom) \parallel hsm(creditcard)$

The THSM *hsm(ticket)* is formalized in the XML representation as follows (segments). Other THSMs can be formalized in the same way.

```
<?xml version="1.0" encoding="UTF-8"?>
<thsm Id="ticket">
 ...
 <fsm Id="salecond">
```

```
  <state Id="available" output="availableInfo"/>
  <state Id="ordered" output="orderedInfo"/>
  <state Id="cancelled" output="cancelledInfo"/>
  <state Id="sold" output="soldInfo"/>
  <transition src="available" dest="ordered">
    <input>orderInfo</input>
  </transition>
  <transition src="available" dest="sold">
    <input>accountInfo</input>
  </transition>
  <transition src="ordered" dest="sold">
    <input>accountInfo</input>
  </transition>
  <transition src="ordered" dest="cancelled">
    <input>orderCancelInfo</input>
  </transition>
  <transition src="cancelled" dest="available">
    <input></input>
  </transition>
 </fsm>

 <fsm Id="deliverycond">
  <state Id="non-delivered" output="non-deliveredInfo">
  <state Id="delivered" output="deliveredInfo">
  <transition src="non-delivered" dest="delivered">
   <input>deliveryInfo</input>
  </transition>
  <transition src="delivered" dest="non-delivered">
   <input>cancelInfo</input>
  </transition>
 </fsm>

 <subdivision super-state="salecond.sold" sub-FSM="deliverycond">
 ...
</thsm>
```

A message exchange relation has been introduced between $hsm(creditcard)$ and $hsm(ticket)$ (Table.1). In the same way, $hsm(creditcard)$ also has a message exchange relation with $hsm(hotelroom)$, in terms of Table.4.

Table 4. Message Exchanges

State↑Transition
creditcard-valid ↑ ⟨*hotelroom-ordered*, accountInfo, *hotelroom-paid*⟩
creditcard-valid ↑ ⟨*hotelroom-vancay*, accountInfo, *hotelroom-paid*⟩
hotelroom-paid ↑ ⟨*creditcard-non-charged*, feeInfo, *creditcard-charged*⟩

The message exchanges in Table.4 are formalized in the XML representation as follows.

```
<mesexchanges>
 <mesexchange>
    <state Id="creditcard-valid">
    <transition src="hotelroom-ordered" dest="hotelroom-paid">
      <input>accountInfo</input>
    </transition>
 </mesexchange>
 <mesexchange>
    <state Id="creditcard-valid">
    <transition src="hotelroom-vancancy" dest="hotelroom-paid">
      <input>accountInfo</input>
    </transition>
 </mesexchange>
 <mesexchange>
    <state Id="hotelroom-paid">
    <transition src="creditcard-non-charged" dest="creditcard-charged">
      <input>feeInfo</input>
    </transition>
 </mesexchange>
<mesexchanges>
```

The THSMs of environment resources *ticket* and *creditcard* are depicted in Fig.2. They are obtained from their XML representations. The message exchange relation is denoted by the thick light-gray line with double arrowheads.

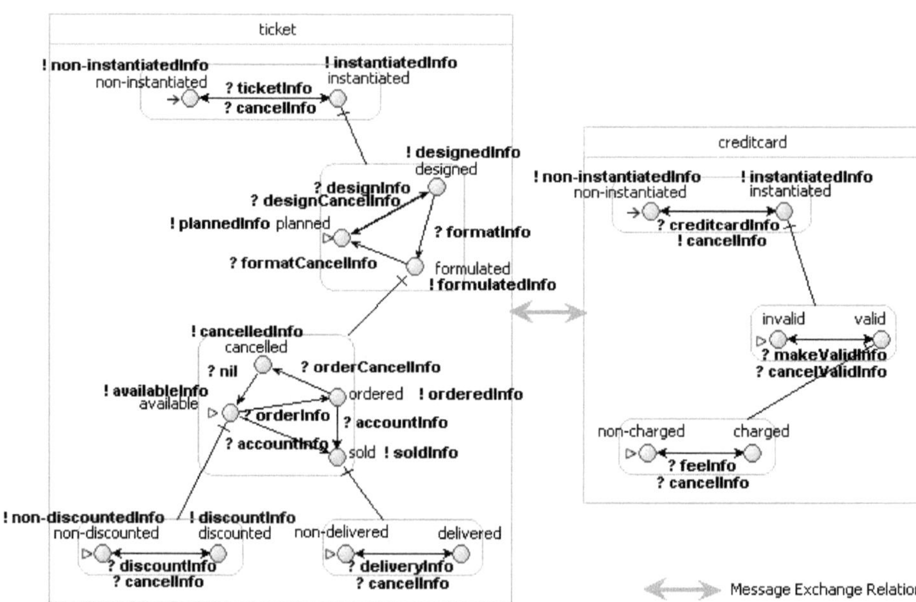

Fig. 2. Screenshot of *hsm*(*ticket*) and *hsm*(*creditcard*)

3 Capability Specification for Web Service Discovery

With the explicit representation of the environment ontology, we specify the capability of a Web service as the state transitions of the environment resources which are the environment entities of this Web service. For example, the capability of a simple ticket-selling service that customers should order tickets before they purchase them can be specified as the state change of resource *ticket* that is from the initial state, i.e., *available* to the target state, i.e., *sold* via the middle state, i.e., *ordered* as: $ticket.available \rightarrow ticket.ordered \rightarrow ticket.sold$

Actually, these state transitions can be acquired from the hierarchical state machine of *ticket* in *BTO* (shown in Fig.2). Therefore, what providers of Web services need to publish is the effects on environment resources, i.e., the initial state, the target state and the middle states of the environment resources. And then, we provide a novel way to discover published Web services. That makes the Web service matchmaking more flexible. The following two subsections introduce the rules for service capability specification and service discovery.

3.1 Capability Specification of Web Services

To introduce capability specification of a Web service, we first define effect that the Web service imposes on its environment resources. The effect on an environment resource is described as a triplet which contains an initial state, a target state and a set of middle states (these middle states are included in the traces from the initial state to the target state) of this environment resource. Let c_r be an environment resource.

Definition 3. $effect(c_r) \stackrel{\text{def}}{=} \langle s_i, \mathcal{S}_m, s_t \rangle, s_i, s_t \in c_r.State, \mathcal{S}_m \subseteq c_r.State$, *in which* s_i *is an initial state,* s_t *is a target state and* $\mathcal{S}_m$ *is a set of middle states.*

The traces from s_i to s_t via $\mathcal{S}_m$ consist of: (1) state transition in a basic state machine, or (2) transition from a state to its default child, or (3) transition from a state to its parent-state. For example, an effect that a simple ticket-selling service imposes on environment resource *ticket* can be described as $\langle available, \phi, sold \rangle$.

The environment ontology is a knowledge base for both the registry and the providers of Web services. The capability profile to advertise capability of the Web service can be described based on the effects that the Web service imposes on its environment resources. The capability profile of Web service is defined as follows:

Definition 4. $CapProfile \stackrel{\text{def}}{=} \{Rsc_{sub}, \mathcal{M}s, effs\}$, *in which,*

- $Rsc_{sub} = \{c_{r1}, ..., c_{rn}\}$ *is a set of environment resources that Web service can impose effects on,*
- $\mathcal{M}s = \{\mathcal{M}(c_{r1}), ..., \mathcal{M}(c_{rn})\}$. $\mathcal{M}(c_{ri})$ *is composed of two subsets:* $\mathcal{M}^{in}(c_{ri})$ *and* $\mathcal{M}^{out}(c_{ri})$ *for denoting inputs and outputs that Web service needs and produces about the environment resource* $c_{ri} (i \in [1, n])$,
- $effs = \{effect(c_{r1}), ..., effect(c_{rn})\}$ *is a set of effects (called "effect set") that Web service imposes on* $c_{r1}, .., c_{rn}$.

The environment ontology is a sharable knowledge base for Web services. The THSM of an environment resource in the ontology (called "domain THSM") describes all possible state transitions of the environment resource as sharable knowledge. By traversing the domain THSM of an environment resource, traces from initial state to target state via a set of middle states (i.e., going through an effect $\langle s_i, \mathcal{S}_m, s_t \rangle$ on the environment resource) triggered by a series of inputs can be generated. These traces constitute a THSM (called "specific THSM"). Hence, each specific THSM is corresponding to an effect on an environment resource.

And then, a model $\mathcal{I} = \{\mathcal{K}, inter_k\}$ is described, in which,

- $\mathcal{K} = \{k_{cr1}, ..., k_{crn}\}$ is a set of specific THSMs corresponding to a set of effects $effs = \{effect(c_{r1}), ..., effec(c_{rn})\}$,
- $inter_k$ is a message relation on $\mathcal{K}$.

The model $\mathcal{I}$ is called the *semantic schema* of the effect set $effs$. It can be viewed to a capability specification of Web service. Let c_r be an environment resource, and $hsm(c_r)$ be the domain THSM of c_r in an environment ontology. The algorithm for generating model $\mathcal{I}$ is given as *Algorithm*.1.

Algorithm 1. Model Generation

Require: *Environment Ontology* $\mathcal{E}nv\mathcal{O}$, *Capability Profile* $\{Rsc_{sub}, \mathcal{M}s, effs\}$
Ensure: *Semantic Schema of* $effs$: $\mathcal{I} = \{\mathcal{K}, inter_k\}$
  $Rsc_{sub} = \{c_{r1}, ..., c_{rn}\}$,
  $\mathcal{M}s = \{\mathcal{M}(c_{r1}), ..., \mathcal{M}(c_{rn})\}$,
  $effs = \{effect(c_{r1}), ..., effect(c_{rn})\}$,
  Instantiating $\mathcal{I}$: $\mathcal{K} = \phi, inter_k = \phi$.
  for all $c_r \in Rsc_{sub}$ ***do***
    /* k_{cr} is the specific THSM reduced from the domain THSM $hsm(c_r)$ in $\mathcal{E}nv\mathcal{O}$ corresponding to $effect(c_r)$ */
    if (k_{cr} *isn't instantiated*)
      then *Instantiating* $k_{cr} = \{\phi, \phi\}$.
    $effect(c_r) = \langle s_i(c_r), \mathcal{S}_m(c_r), s_t(c_r) \rangle$,
    /* Invoking a procedure for constructing k_{cr} */
    GeneratingTHSM($s_i(c_r)$, $\mathcal{S}_m(c_r)$, $s_t(c_r)$, $\mathcal{M}(c_r)$, k_{cr}).
  end for

The recursive procedure *GeneratingTHSM* is designed for constructing the specific THSMs. Let c_r be an environment resource, $effect(c_r) = \langle s_i, \mathcal{S}_m, s_t \rangle$ be an effect on c_r, $\mathcal{M}(c_r) = \{\mathcal{M}^{in}, \mathcal{M}^{out}\}$ be inputs and outputs of Web service about c_r, and k be the specific THSM reduced from domain THSM $hsm(c_r)$ as a result. Then, the procedure is described summarily as follows.

GeneratingTHSM(InitialState s_i, MiddleSet $\mathcal{S}_m$, TargetState s_t, InputsOutputs $\mathcal{M}$, SpecificHSM k)
Ensure: *specific THSM k which is reduced from* $hsm(c_r)$
  /* $\mathcal{N}_i (i \in [1, n])$ is a FSM, and $\mathcal{D}_k$ is the subdivision relation. */
  $k = \{\{\mathcal{N}_1, ..., \mathcal{N}_n\}, \mathcal{D}_k\}$,

Creating $\mathcal{N}_x, 1 \leqslant x \leqslant n$, $\mathcal{S}(\mathcal{N}_x) = \mathcal{S}(\mathcal{N}_x) \cup \{s_i\}$,
/* Target state s_t is reached, the specific THSM k is generated */
if $(s_i == s_t)$ ***then***
$\mathcal{K} = \mathcal{K} \cup \{k\}$, **exit**.
end if
for all *subdivision* $ud(s_i)$ *from state* s_i *to its sub-HSM* $subhsm(s_i)$ *in* $hsm(c_r)$, *where target state* s_t *or middle states* $s_m \in \mathcal{S}_m$ *are in* $subhsm(s_i)$ ***do***
$isVisited(ud(s_i)) = true$,
/* λ_0 is default start state in $subhsm(s_i)$*/
if $(\lambda_0 \in \mathcal{S}_m)$ ***then*** $\mathcal{S}_m = \mathcal{S}_m - \{\lambda_0\}$,
Creating $\mathcal{N}_y, 1 \leqslant y \leqslant n, y \neq x$,
$\mathcal{S}(\mathcal{N}_y) = \mathcal{S}(\mathcal{N}_y) \cup \{\lambda_0\}$, $\mathcal{D}_k = \mathcal{D}_k \cup \{\langle s_i, \mathcal{N}_y \rangle\}$,
GeneratingTHSM(λ_0, S_m, s_t, $\mathcal{M}$, k).
end for
for all *transition* t *in* $hsm(c_r)$ *where source state is* s_i ***do***
$isVisited(t) = true$,
/* Let $in(t)$ be the input of state transition t,
The transition t can't be triggered by Web service.*/
if $(in(t) \notin \mathcal{M}^{in})$ ***then***
/* Acquiring state $s_{iner}(c_r')$ of another environment resource c_r' through the message exchange $s_{iner}(c_r') \uparrow t$. Output of this state can trigger state transition t*/
$s_{iner}(c_r') = MessgeExchange(t)$,
if $(s_{iner}(c_r')$==*null*$)$ ***then exit***.
Acquiring $s_{cur}(c_r')$ *that is current state of* c_r'.
if ($k_{cr'}$ *isn't instantiated*)
then *Instantiating* $k_{cr'} = \{\phi, \phi\}$,
GeneratingTHSM($s_{cur}(c_r')$,ϕ,$s_{inter}(c_r')$,$\mathcal{M}(c_r')$,$k_{cr'}$),
/* Creating a message exchange relation between k and $k_{cr'}$ */
$inter_k = inter_k \cup \{\langle k, k_{cr'} \rangle\}$.
end if
/* $dest(t)$ is the destination state of transition t */
$\mathcal{S}(\mathcal{N}_x) = \mathcal{S}(\mathcal{N}_x) \cup \{dest(t)\}$,
$\mathcal{T}(\mathcal{N}_x) = \mathcal{T}(\mathcal{N}_x) \cup \{\langle s_i, in(t), dest(t) \rangle\}$,
if $(dest(t) \in \mathcal{S}_m)$ ***then*** $\mathcal{S}_m = \mathcal{S}_m - \{dest(t)\}$,
GeneratingTHSM($dest(t)$, $\mathcal{S}_m$, s_t, $\mathcal{M}$, k).
end for

For example, there is a Web service *Budget Travelling Agency* (called "*BTA*"). It provides the travelling arrangement service for travellers. *BTA* is supposed to have the basic capabilities: flight ticket selling and hotel room ordering. The environment which *BTA* is situated in has been depicted as *BTO* (shown in Table.3). There are three environment resources in *BTO* which *BTA* can impose effects on. They are *ticket*, *hotelroom* and *creditcard* respectively, and their THSMs have been depicted in Fig.2. The XML-style capability profile of *BTA* is presented as follows.

```
<capability Id="BudgetTravellingAgency">
  xmlns:resource="http://www.ecf4ws.org/EnvO"
  <resources>BTO:ticket,BTO:hotelroom,BTO:creditcard</resources>
  <inputs>
    <input res="ticket">orderInfo,orderCancelInfo,deliveryInfo</input>
    <input res="hotelroom">orderInfo,orderCancelInfo</input>
  </inputs>
  <outputs>
    <output res="ticket">deliveredInfo</output>
    <output res="hotelroom">orderedInfo</output>
    <output res="creditcard">chargedInfo</output>
  </outputs>
  <effects>
    <effect res="ticket">
      <initialState>available</initialState>
      <middleSet>ordered,cancelled<middleSet>
      <targetState>delivered</targetState>
    </effect>
    <effect res="hotelroom">
      <initialState>vacancy</initialState>
      <middleSet>cancelled<middleSet>
      <targetState>ordered</targetState>
    </effect>
    <effect res="creditcard">
      <initialState>valid</initialState>
      <targetState>charged</targetState>
    </effect>
  </effects>
</capability>
```

This capability profile can be translated to a statement in natural language: BTA provides a ticket-selling service and tickets can be delivered to customers. Before purchasing tickets, ordering service is provided. If ordered tickets aren't satisfying, customers have opportunities to cancel the orders. Moreover, BTA provides a hotel room ordering service. And if ordered rooms aren't satisfying, customers also have opportunities to cancel the orders. These service fees are charged by credit card.

Fig.3 is the screenshot showing the model $\mathcal{I}_{bta}$, which is the capability specification of BTA. The *ws_ticket* depicts a specific THSM (denoted by $k(ticket)$), which is generated corresponding to the effect that BTA imposes on *ticket*. In the same way, $k(hotelroom)$ and $k(creditcard)$ are generated (i.e., *ws_hotelroom*, *ws_creditcard* in Fig.3). Moreover, there is a message exchange relation between $k(ticket)$ and $k(creditcard)$. Therefore, $\mathcal{I}_{bta}$ is formalized as follows: $\{\{k(ticket), k(creditcard), k(hotelroom)\}, \{\langle k(ticket), k(creditcard)\rangle\}\}$.

Asterisk ($*$) in Fig.3 denotes a special input provided by other THSMs through message exchange. They are neither provided by customers nor described in the capability profile. For example, the input `*creditcard-validInfo` in $k(ticket)$ is provided by $k(creditcard)$, instead of the inputs described in the capability profile of BTA.

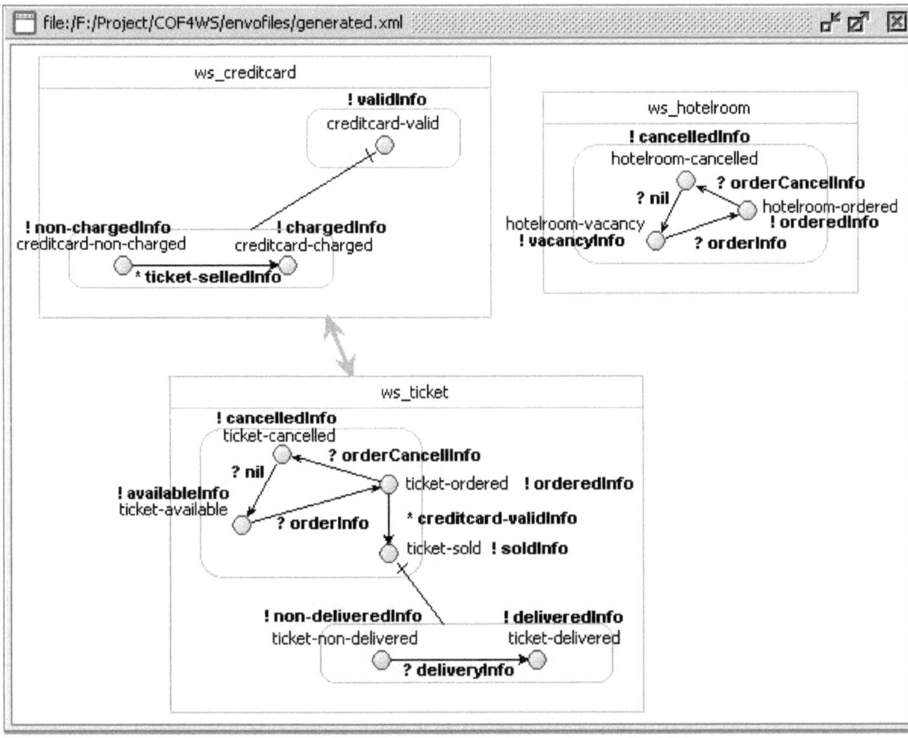

Fig. 3. Screenshot of the model $\mathcal{I}_{bta}$ generated from the capability profile of BTA

3.2 Flexible Web Service Discovery

Now, we already have declared the environment ontology BTO which has been described in section 2.2, and a Web service BTA in section 3.1. On the basis of BTO, capability profile of BTA is also presented. Here, we present an approach for flexible Web service discovery.

For example, a scenario that a user wants to have a pleasant budget travelling can be focused. Now, we have a well-defined environment ontology BTO and the capability profile of BTA. Then the request, which has been described in our introduction section, is that "*I find the service that provides flight ticket-selling and hotel room ordering, and I can order ticket and hotel room, and if there is an emergency, I have opportunities to cancel the ticket or hotel room on hold.*" And then, It can be formalized as an effect-based capability profile as a query profile in XML respresentation:

```
<query Id="RequestBudgetTravelling">
  xmlns:resource="http://www.cof4ws.org/EnvO"
  <resources>BTO:ticket,BTO:hotelroom</resources>
  <inputs>
    <input res="ticket">orderInfo,orderCancelInfo,accountInfo</input>
    <input res="hotelroom">orderInfo,orderCancelInfo</input>
```

```
  </inputs>
  <outputs>
    <output res="ticket">soldInfo</output>
    <output res="hotelroom">orderedInfo</output>
  </outputs>
  <effects>
    <effect res="ticket">
      <initialState>available</initialState>
      <middleSet>ordered,cancelled<middleSet>
      <targetState>sold</targetState>
    </effect>
    <effect res="hotelroom">
      <initialState>vacancy</initialState>
      <middleSet>cancelled<middleSet>
      <targetState>ordered</targetState>
    </effect>
  </effects>
</query>
```

To identify existing services that can be used to implement a required service, we need a way to match the requirements and capabilities of services i.e, identify semantic distance between services. A matchmaking between the capability profile of BTA **BudgetTravellingAgency** and the query profile **RequestBudgetTravelling** (called "**Ava**"and "**Req**"for short) can be performed with help of the environment ontology. Let $Cap_{ava} = \{Rsc_{sub}^{ava}, \mathcal{M}s^{ava}, effs^{ava}\}$ and $Cap_{req} = \{Rsc_{sub}^{req}, \mathcal{M}s^{req}, effs^{req}\}$ be capability profile of a Web service and a query profile respectively. The main matchmaking process is described as following:

Step 1. For **environment resources**, two different types of relationships, namely, subConceptOf(a, b), ComponentOf(a, b) are modelled where $a, b \in Rsc$ are two given environment resources. We first introduce the matching degree between **Req**:Rsc_{sub} and **Ava**:Rsc_{sub}, which describe which environment resources will be imposed effects on. Then, we call them **effect spaces**.

- If $Rsc_{sub}^{req} \cap Rsc_{sub}^{ava} == \phi$,
  - $\nexists a \in Rsc_{sub}^{req}, b \in Rsc_{sub}^{ava}$, such that subConceptOf$(a, b)$ or ComponentOf(a, b), we say **Irrelevant**
    It means that requested effect space is completely irrelevant with provided effect space. In the condition, *the matchmaking process terminates.*
  - $\exists a \in Rsc_{sub}^{req}, b \in Rsc_{sub}^{ava}$, such that subConceptOf$(a, b)$ or ComponentOf(a, b), we say **weak-Intersection**
    It means that requested effect space has a weak relation with provided effect space.
- If $Rsc_{sub}^{req} == Rsc_{sub}^{ava}$, we say **Exact Match**.
  It means that they have identical effect space.
- If $Rsc_{sub}^{req} \subset Rsc_{sub}^{ava}$, we say **Plug-In Match**.
  It means that requested effect space is covered by provided effect space. In the

condition, the requestor has opportunities to achieve its requirements completely.

- If $Rsc_{sub}^{req} \supset Rsc_{sub}^{ava}$, we say **Subsume Match**.
  It means that requested effect space covers provided effect space. In the condition, the provider might satisfy requestor's requirements partly.
- If $Rsc_{sub}^{req} \cap Rsc_{sub}^{ava} \neq \phi$ and $\nexists Rsc_{sub}^{req} \supseteq Rsc_{sub}^{ava} \vee Rsc_{sub}^{req} \subset Rsc_{sub}^{ava}$, we say **strong-Intersection**.
  It means that requested effect space intersects with provided effect space.

For above instance, because that **Req**:{`BTO:ticket,BTO:hotelroom`} $\subseteq$ **Ava**: {`BTO:ticket,BTO:hotelroom,BTO:creditcard`}, there is a **Plug-In Match** between their effect spaces. And then, on the basis of the environment ontology *BTO*, a matchmaking between **Req**:$effs$ and **Ava**:$effs$ can be performed in the next step.

Step 2. If there is **Relevancy** (no **Irrelevant**) between Rsc_{sub}^{req} and Rsc_{sub}^{ava}, the requestor and the provider have common or related effect space. The step is to perform a flexible matchmaking between their effects on the common or related effect space with the aid of environment ontology. We generate a model $\mathcal{I}$ according to effects on environment resources grounded on the environment ontology. Then, matchmaking between two effects is regarded as the matchmaking between the two models generated from the two effects respectively. For example, Fig.3 depicts the model $\mathcal{I}_{bta}$ which is generated according to **Ava** grounded on *BTO*. Similarly, the model $\mathcal{I}_{req}$ according to **Req** can be generated as Fig.4.

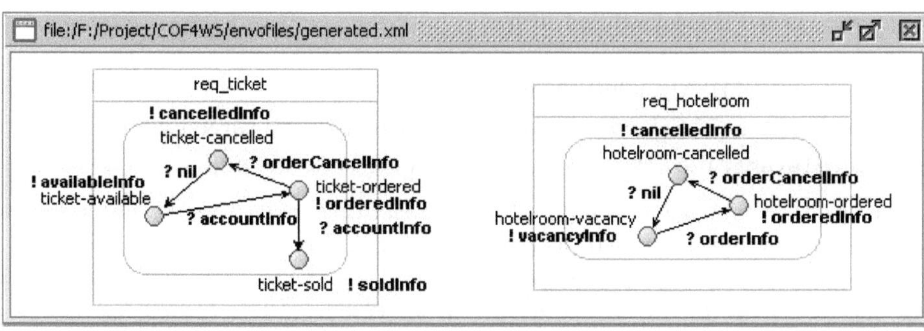

Fig. 4. Screenshot of a model $\mathcal{I}_{req}$ generated from **Req**

Now, the problem we encounter is how to match THSM models. [3] proposes an approach for automata matchmaking when they have a non-empty intersection. Here, we define the intersection of two given THSMs.

Definition 5. *Intersection of two THSMs*
$hsm_1 = \{\mathcal{S}_1, \Sigma_1, \mathcal{T}_1, f_1, \lambda_{01}, \preccurlyeq_1\}$ *and* $hsm_2 = \{\mathcal{S}_2, \Sigma_2, \mathcal{T}_2, f_2, \lambda_{02}, \preccurlyeq_2\}$ *be two THSMs. Their intersection is* $hsm = \{\mathcal{S}, \Sigma, \mathcal{T}, f, \lambda_0, \preccurlyeq\} = hsm_1 \sqcap hsm_2$, *in which*

there is an injective function $g : \mathcal{S} \rightarrow \mathcal{S}_1$, $\forall m^{in} \in \Sigma^{in}$ *and* $s \in \mathcal{S}$, $t \in \mathcal{T}$, $t_1 \in \mathcal{T}_1$, *satisfying:*
$g(t(s, m^{in})) = t_1(g(s), m^{in})$, $g(parent(s)) = parent_1(s)$, $f(s) = f_1(g(s))$ *and there is an injective function* $l : \mathcal{S} \rightarrow \mathcal{S}_2$, $\forall m^{in} \in \Sigma^{in}$ *and* $s \in \mathcal{S}$, $t \in \mathcal{T}$, $t_2 \in \mathcal{T}_2$, *satisfying:*
$g(t(s, m^{in})) = t_2(l(s), m^{in})$, $g(parent(s)) = parent_2(s)$, $f = f_2(l(s))$.

For example, the intersection of *ws_ticket* in Fig.3 and *req_ticket* in Fig.4 is depicted in Fig.5. As shown in this figure, the intersection is *req_ticket*.

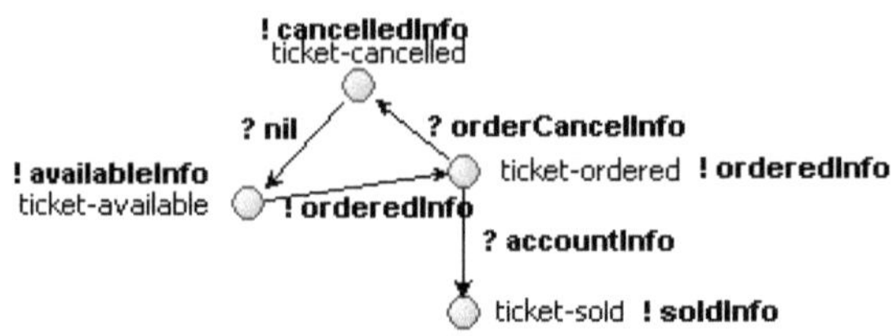

Fig. 5. Intersection of *ws_ticket* and *req_ticket*

And then, we can define the matching degree between THSMs. Let hsm_{req} and hsm_{ava} be two THSMs, which are generated from capability profile and query description respectively, and their intersection is hsm.

- **`Exact Match`**, if $|\mathcal{S}(hsm_{req})| == |\mathcal{S}(hsm)| == |\mathcal{S}(hsm_{ava})|$. In other words, hsm_{req}, hsm_{ava} and hsm are identical.
- **`Plug-In Match`**, if $|\mathcal{S}(hsm_{req})| == |\mathcal{S}(hsm)| < |\mathcal{S}(hsm_{ava})|$. In other words, hsm_{req} is a THSM included in hsm_{ava},
- **`Subsume Match`** if $|\mathcal{S}(hsm_{ava})| == |\mathcal{S}(hsm)| < |\mathcal{S}(hsm_{req})|$. In other words, hsm_{ava} is a THSM included in hsm_{req},
- **`Intersection`**, if $\mathcal{S}(hsm) \neq \phi$ and there aren't above three matches.
- **`Not Relevant`**, if $\mathcal{S}(hsm) == \phi$, i.e., the intersection is null.

Because that model $\mathcal{I}$ is composed of THSMs, we can get the matching degree between the models grounded on matching degree between THSMs. We generate two models $\mathcal{I}_{req} = \{\mathcal{K}_{req}, inter_{\mathcal{K}_{req}}\}$ and $\mathcal{I}_{ava} = \{\mathcal{K}_{ava}, inter_{\mathcal{K}_{ava}}\}$ based on **`Req`**:$effs$ and **`Ava`**:$effs$, in which $\mathcal{K}_{req} = \{k_r(ticket), k_r(hotelroom), k_r(credit-card)\}$ and $\mathcal{K}_{ava} = \{k_a(ticket), k_a(hotelroom)\}$. Then, the matching degree between $\mathcal{I}_{req}$ and $\mathcal{I}_{ava}$ can be obtained by integrating the matching degrees of $Degree : \langle k_r(ticket), k_a(ticket)\rangle$ and $Degree : \langle k_r(hotelroom), k_a(hotelroom)\rangle$. Table.5 depicts how to integrate matching degree between THSMs/$\mathcal{I}$s.

For example, there is a **`Plug-In Match`** between $k_r(ticket)$ and $k_a(ticket)$. And there is **`Exact Match`** between $k_r(hotelroom)$ and $k_a(hotelroom)$. Therefore, the integration matching degree between **`Req`**:$effs$ and **`Ava`**:$effs$ is **`Plug-In Match`** according to Table.5.

Finally, on the basis of the degrees of match between environment resources and effects on these environment resources. The degree of match between capability profile and query description can be presented in Table.6.

Table 5. Integrated Degree of Match between two $\mathcal{I}$s

Degree between two THSMs/$\mathcal{I}$s	Degree between two THSMs/$\mathcal{I}$s	Degree between two $\mathcal{I}$s
Irrelevant	Irrelevant	Irrelevant
Relevancy	Irrelevant	Intersection
Exact Match	Exact Match	Exact Match
	Plug-In Match	Plug-In Match
	Subsume Match	Subsume Match
	Intersection	Intersection
Plug-In Match	Plug-In Match	Plug-In Match
Plug-In Match	Subsume Match	Intersection
	Intersection	Intersection
Subsume Match	Subsume Match	Subsume Match
	Intersection	Intersection

Table 6. Matching Degree between Capability Profile and Query Profile

Degree:EffectSpaces	Degree:$\mathcal{I}$s	Final Degree
All	Irrelevant	Irrelevant
Irrelevant	All	Irrelevant
Weak-intersection	Relevant	Weak-intersection
Strong-Intersection	Relevant	Strong-Intersection
Relevancy	Intersection	Intersection
Exact Match	Exact Match	Exact Match
	Plug-In Match	Plug-In Match
	Subsume Match	Subsume Match
Plug-In Match	Subsume Match	Intersection
	Exact Match	Plug-In Match
	Plug-In Match	Plug-In Match
Subsume Match	Plug-In Match	Intersection
	Subsume Match	Subsume Match
	Exact Match	Subsume Match

For the matchmaking between **req** and **ava**, there is **Plug-In Match** between **req**:Rsc_{sub} and **ava**:Rsc_{sub}. And there is **Plug-In Match** between their effects. Therefore, we say that there is **Plug-In Match** between **req** and **ava**.

4 Related Work

Web service discovery is a fast growing research area. Capability specification constitutes a necessary step for service publication and service request. In this field, earlier efforts include the XML-based standards, such as Web Service Description Language (WSDL)[10]. It's designed to provide descriptions of message exchange mechanisms, and for describing the service interface. However, keyword-based approach taken by WSDL is for the automatic service discovery. Universal Description Discovery Integration (UDDI)[11] provides a registry of Web services. It describes Web services by their physical attributes such as name, address and the services that they provide. As UDDI dose not touch service capabilities.

OWL-S [4] takes up the challenge of representing the functionalities of Web services. It attempts to bridge the gap between the semantic Web and Web services. The main contribution of the OWL-S approach is its service ontology, which builds on the series of semantic Web standards. OWL-S capability model is based on functional procedure which includes the information transformation performed by service and the state transition as consequence of the execution of the service, i.e., IOPR schema. WSMO [2] and METEOR-S [12] are two other efforts to bridge the semantic Web and Web services. Their capability models still assume a Web service a one step process. [13][14] argues that a limitation of OWL-S is the lack of logical relationships underlying the inputs and outputs of its capability model. They propose the OWL-S Process model, which is primarily designed for specifying how a Web service works, to be the capability specification of Web services.

By describing the constraints between inputs and outputs and allowing creating gradually concepts directly with the advertisements and requests, LARKS [15] makes improvement to OWL-S. LARKS is a matching engine that allows matching of advertisements and requests on the basis of the capabilities that they describe to some extent.

Currently, the behavior description for service discovery is also hotspot. Wombacher proposes an extended finite state automata as description of Web services [3][4]. However, it requires that the process description should be globally predefined to ensure consistency during service matchmaking. The loosely coupled Web services are often developed by different teams, and are described in different conceptual framework without agreement. Hence, key problem of such setting is that process description of a Web service should be understood by other Web services without prior knowledge. Recently, [5] proposes a behavior model for Web services using automata and logic formalisms. It adopts the IOPR schema in OWL-S to describe activities of Web services. [6] proposes a solution for service retrieval based on behavioral description using a graph representation formalism for services. It assumes that the semantic information including name of operation, inputs and outputs of activities has been attached to each service. Moreover, [16] argues that essential facets of Web services can be described using process algebraic notations, i.e., capability description and message exchange could be specified by process algebra.

In fact, context was a key concern in the requirements modelling and is getting more and more attentions [17]. It has been recognized as the semantic basis of the meaning of the requirements [18]. Currently, [19] proposes an OWL encoded context ontology (CONON) for modeling context in pervasive computing environments, and for supporting logic-based context reasoning. [20] proposes an agent-based and context-oriented approach that supports the composition of Web services. In these efforts, the context is perceived as the static relevant information that characterizes a situation, such as identifier, location and preferences etc [21]. Different from these efforts, we view environment (a kind of context) of a Web service to be composed of those controllable resources (i.e., environment resources) that this Web service can impose effects on. Our approach pays a special attention to the effects that Web services impose on their environment resources for specifying capability of Web service semantically. For each environment resource, there is a corresponding hierarchical state machine specifying its dynamic characteristics. The environment resources are domain-relevant and independent to any Web services.

5 Conclusion and Future Work

This paper proposes a solution for specifying Web Service capabilities based on the environment ontology. Behavior description could be automatically derived from the effects that Web service imposes on its environment resources. The hierarchical state machines representing behavior of environment resource are designed to reflect Web service capabilities. Consequently, the model, which is semantic schema of effect set, can be semantics of the capability specification of Web Services. Then, we propose a flexible matchmaking method for Web service discovery. The approach has the following characteristics:

- The state transitions of the environment resources are formalized as sharable knowledge in environment ontology.
- Designing a lightweight and explicit effects-based capability profile of Web services. Lightweight means that capability specification can be generated by adding rich semantics (i.e., state transitions) automatically to the capability profile from environment ontology.
- Researches on model checking of general HSM have made many successful steps, such as intersection, inclusion and equivalence problems, etc. Hence, our capability specification has better expressive power than conventional one-step process based specification.
- This capability specification supports more intelligent Web Service discovery because of its good expressive power.
- Finally, for derived from sharable environment ontology, the capability specification wouldn't be tied too closely with implementation.

In our future work, a logic formalism will be given to express the constraints on Web services. Furthermore, the algorithm for intelligent service discovery and matchmaking based on our capability specification also will be specified.

Acknowledgment

Partly supported by the National Natural Science Key Foundation of China under Grant No.60233010 and Grant No.60496324, the National Key Research and Development Program of China under Grant No.2002CB312004, the Knowledge Innovation Program of the Chinese Academy of Sciences, and MADIS of the Chinese Academy of Sciences

References

1. The OWL Services Coalition, OWL-S: Semantic Markup for Web Services, 2004 http://www.daml.org/services/owl-s/1.1/overview/
2. WSMO project site (Web Service Modeling Ontology), http://www.wsmo.org
3. Andreas Wombacher, Peter Fankhuaser, Bendick Mahleko et al, "Matchmakeing for Business Processes based on Choreographies," Proceedings of the 2004 IEEE Conference on and Enterprise Computing, E-Commerce and E-Services
4. B. Mahleko, and A.Wombacher, "A grammar-based index for matching business processes," Proceedings of the 2005 IEEE International Conference on Web Services
5. Zhongnan Shen, Jianwen Su, "Web Service Discovery Based on Behavior Signatures," Proceedings of the 2005 IEEE International Conference on Services Computing
6. Daniela Grigori, Mokrane Bouzeghoub, "Service retrieval based on behavioral specification," Proceedings of the 2005 IEEE International Conference on Services Computing
7. Puwei Wang, Zhi Jin and Lin Liu, "On Constructing Environment Ontology for Semantic Web Services", Proceedings of the First International Conference on Knowledge Science, Engineering and Management, 2006 (to appear)
8. Alexander Maedche and Steffen Staab, "Ontology Learning for the Semantic Web," IEEE intelligent systems, Mar./Apr. 2001, pp.72-79
9. Mats P.E. Heimdahl and Nancy G. Leveson, Completeness and Consistency in Hierarchical State-Based Requirments, IEEE Transaction on software engineering, VOL.22, No.6, June 1996
10. E.Christensen, F.Curbera, GMeredith et al, "Web Services Description Language (WSDL) 1.1 Technical Report", W3C, 2001, http://www.w3.org/TR/2001/NOTE-wsdl-20010315
11. L.Clement, A.Hately, C.von Riegen et al, "UDDI version 3.0", http://uddi.org/pubs/uddi_v3.htm, 2004
12. METOR-S project site (METEOR for Semantic Web Service), http://lsdis.cs.uga.edu/projects/meteor-s/
13. Sharad Bansal and Jose M.Vidal. "Matchmaking of Web Services Based on the DAML-S Service Model," AAMAS 2003, July 14-18, 2003, ACM.
14. Antonio Brogi et al. "Flexible Matchmaking of Web Services Using DAML-S Ontologies," ICSOC 2004 November 15-18.
15. K.Sycara, S.Widoff, M.Klusch et al, "LARKS: Dynamic Matchmaking Among Heterogeneous Software Agents in Cyberspace," Autonomous Agents and Multi-Agent Systems, volume 5, pages 173-203, Kluwer Academic Publishers, 2002
16. Gwen Salaun, Lucas Bordeaux, Marco Schaerf, "Describing and Reasoning on Web Services using Process Algebra," Proceeding of the 2004 IEEE international Conference on Web Service
17. P.Zave and M.Jackson, "Four dark corners of requirements engineering," ACM Transactions on Software Engineering and Methodolgy, 6(1):1-30, January 1997
18. C.A.Gunter, E.L.Gunter,M.Jackson et al, "A reference model for requirements and specification" IEEE Software, 17(3):37-43, May/June 2000
19. Xiao Hang Wang, Da Qing Zhang and Tao Gu, "Ontology Based Context Modeling and Reasoning using OWL", Proceedings of the Second IEEE Annual Conference on Pervasive Computing and Communications Workshops

20. Zakaria Maamar, Soraya Kouadri Mostefaoui, and Hamdi Yahyaoui, "Toward an Agent-Based and Context-Oriented Approach for Web Services Composition", IEEE transaction on knowledge and data engineering, vol.17, no.5, May 2005
21. A.K. Dey, G.D. Abowd, and D. Salber, A Conceptual Framework and a Toolkit for Supporting the Rapid Prototyping of Context-Aware Applications, Human-Computer Interaction J., special issue on context-aware computing, vol.16, no.1, 2001.

Scenario-Based Component Behavior Derivation*

Yan Zhang, Jun Hu, Xiaofeng Yu, Tian Zhang,
Xuandong Li, and Guoliang Zheng

State Key Laboratory of Novel Software Technology
Department of Computer Science and Technology
Nanjing University, Nanjing, P.R. China 210093
zhangyan@seg.nju.edu.cn, lxd@nju.edu.cn

Abstract. The reusability of components affects how much benefit we can get from the component based software development (CBSD). For enhancing the reuse of components, we propose an approach to derive the desired behavior from a component in terms of the user's requirement given by a scenario specification. In our proposal, a special environment, i.e., sup-inclusive environment (SIE), is automatically constructed to adjust the component's behavior based on the scenario specification. All behavior of a component that is specified by the scenario specification can be preserved in the composition of the component and its SIE, and other behavior of the component is discarded to the most extent. We use interface automata to model the behavior of components and a set of action sequences to abstract the scenario specification in Message Sequence Charts (MSCs). The composition of components is modelled by the product of interface automata. We give the algorithm for constructing SIE and illustrate our approach by an example.

1 Introduction

Component based software development (CBSD) provides a pragmatic approach for efficiently building complex systems by the reuse of existing software components and the plug-and-play mechanisms. In CBSD, users find desired components in repositories and compose them to creat a new system. However, the reusability of components affects how much benefit we can get from CBSD. Frequently, existing components could not exactly meet the requirement of users. Users have to face with the trouble that resists the reuse of components. This problem generally takes on two types: one is that the functionalities of components are less than users' needs; the other is that there are some redundant functionalities in components besides users' needs. The former can be solved by the composition of components. In academia, many researches had been undertaken on this aspect [1,2]. For the latter, we can release it by extracting the

* This paper is supported by the National Grand Fundamental Research 973 Program of China (No. 2002CB312001), the National Natural Science Foundation of China (No. 60425204, No. 60233020), and by Jiangsu Province Research Foundation (No. BK2004080).

Z. Liu and J. He (Eds.): ICFEM 2006, LNCS 4260, pp. 206–225, 2006.

desired functionality (behavior) or removing the undesired functionality from the components based on the user's requirements.

Usually, users give their requirements by the descriptions of scenarios, which is called the *scenario specifications.* A scenario specification can describe the user's desired behavior of a component (i.e., good scenario) or the user's undesired behavior (i.e., bad scenario). The *scenario-based behavior derivation* of a component requires to preserve all behavior specified by the good scenario in the component and discard other behavior as much as possible. The *scenario-based behavior filtration* of a component requires to discard all behavior specified by the bad scenario in the component and preserve other behavior as much as possible. The scenario-based behavior derivation and filtration are complementary, and theoretically either can be used for a given user's requirement. However, since the way to adjust the behavior of a component is limited, that is, only by means of the inputs provided for the component (see Sect. 5.2), these two approaches will result in the different outputs. Thus, it is necessary to study the scenario-based behavior derivation and filtration respectively. In [3], we had studied the scenario-based behavior filtration for a component.

In this paper, we focus on the scenario-based behavior derivation and propose an solution for it. Based on the scenario, an environment (an environment can be seen as a component too) for a component is automatically constructed to make only the desired behavior of the component to be extracted when the component works in the environment. In other words, only the behavior of the component that is specified by the scenario can be preserved in the composition of the component and the environment. Interface automata [4] are used to model the behavior of components. Scenarios are specified by Message Sequence Charts (MSCs) [5] and the MSC is abstracted as a set of action sequences further. The composition of components is modelled by the product of interface automata. We extend the concept of environment in the interface automata theory and introduce *sup-inclusive environment* (SIE). By constructing the SIE $E_{\mathcal{L}}$ for a given interface automaton R under a known set $\mathcal{L}$ of action sequences, the behavior of R that contains any element of $\mathcal{L}$ is preserved in the composition $R \otimes E_{\mathcal{L}}$, and other behavior of R is not preserved to the most extent.

A primary reason for selecting interface automata as the modelling language is that interface automata are appropriate to specify the components in an open system. The environment assumptions [4] and the behavior of components are integrated into the same model, i.e., interface automata.

The remainder of this paper is organized as follows. Section 2 considers related research work. Section 3 introduces interface automata and Message Sequence Charts briefly. Section 4 gives some relevant concepts about our proposal. Section 5 discusses the approach to scenario-based behavior derivation of components in detail and shows the constructive algorithm of SIE. Finally, in Section 6 we conclude this paper and discuss the future work. Additionally, we use an example to illustrate our approach throughout the paper.

2 Related Works

There are many researches related to our work. The most pertinent research, presented by Inverardi and her colleagues [6,7] , is the software architecture based approach to components coordination for desired behavior of the system. Their approach is based on a specific architecture style — Connector Based Architecture (CBA). With the system specification in bMSCs (basic Message Sequence Charts) and HMSC (High level MSC) and the coordination properties (i.e., the desired behavior) in Linear-time Temporal Logic (LTL), they can automatically synthesize a connector (both model and code) for composed components. The connector synthesized by their algorithm can restrict the behavior of the components composition to the desired behavior. However, there are many differences between our approach and theirs. Firstly, the connector in [6] restricts the behavior of components composition by not accepting the outputs of composed components. On the contrary, the environment in our approach must accept all outputs of components. An environment can affect components behavior only by the inputs provided for the components. It is reasonable to assume that the environment must accept all outputs of components. Secondly, our approach is not based on CBA. The connector in [6] is like a "delegator" and intervenes the communication between components. The environment in our approach is like a "wrapper" that is not able to influence the messages interchange among the composed components. The environment can change the components (or compositions) behavior only by their inputs. This characteristic of environment is useful, particularly, in the component-based self-organizing systems. Thirdly, our modelling language, i.e., interface automata, integrates the behavior model of components and the environment assumption (i.e., components' requirements on environment) into one model, but in [6] the behavior model of environment (AS-Graph) need to derive from the behavior model of components (AC-Graph). Finally, the complexity of synthesis algorithm in [7] is exponential in time, but our algorithm is polynomial. Nevertheless, only the model of SIE can be constructed by our approach. By comparison, not only the model but also the code of a connector can be derived by the approach of Inverardi et al.

Other pertinent researches can be found in the area of discrete event systems (DES) [8]. In the control of DES, the synthesis problem is to construct a supervisor (also called controller) that can restrict the behavior of the controlled object (called plant) to the desired behavior. A generalization of the synthesis problem and its solution are studied by Bochmann in the context of relational databases [9]. Unlike the synthesis problem, in which at every state of the plant must be receptive towards every possible input from the controller, in the component-based system, the environment must provide for the component the input that can be accepted at the current state of the component. Therefore, in the control of DES, the plant and the synthesized controller are usually modelled by automata [10] that are input-enabled [4], but the component and the constructed environment in our research are modelled by interface automata that are environment-constraining [4].

Our research is also related to works in adapter synthesis [1,2]. These works mainly solve the behavioral compatibility of components composition. Similarly, in [11], we compose two behaviorally incompatible components by constructing an environment for them. These works do not concern whether the behavior of the composition is the needs of users. By using environment, our approach in this paper can extract desired behavior from components or their compositions in terms of requirements given by scenario specification. Our approach overcomes the limitation in those works mentioned above.

In our previous work [12], we only present the algorithm to check whether there exists desired behavior in a software component. In this paper, we further give the approach to derive the desired behavior from software components by constructing environments.

3 Background

In the section, we briefly introduce some basic concepts about interface automata and MSCs, most of which refer to [4] and [5] respectively.

3.1 Interface Automata

Definition 1 (interface automaton, IA). *An* interface automaton $P = \langle V_P, V_P^{init}, \mathcal{A}_P^I, \mathcal{A}_P^O, \mathcal{A}_P^H, \mathcal{T}_P \rangle$ *consists of the following elements:*

- V_P *is a finite set of* states.
- $V_P^{init} \subseteq V_P$ *is a set of* initial states. *If* $V_P^{init} = \emptyset$ *then* P *is called* empty.
- $\mathcal{A}_P^I$, $\mathcal{A}_P^O$ *and* $\mathcal{A}_P^H$ *are mutually disjoint sets of* input, output *and* internal *actions.* $\mathcal{A}_P = \mathcal{A}_P^I \cup \mathcal{A}_P^O \cup \mathcal{A}_P^H$ *denotes the set of all* actions.
- $\mathcal{T}_P \subseteq V_P \times \mathcal{A}_P \times V_P$ *is a set of* steps. *If* $\tau = (v, a, u) \in \mathcal{T}_P$, *then we say that action* a *is* enabled *at state* v, *and write* $label(\tau) = a$, $head(\tau) = v$, $tail(\tau) = u$.

If $a \in \mathcal{A}_P^I$ (resp. $a \in \mathcal{A}_P^O$, $a \in \mathcal{A}_P^H$), then (v, a, v') is called an input (resp. output, internal) step. Let $\mathcal{T}_P^I = \{(v, a, v') \mid v, v' \in V_P \wedge a \in \mathcal{A}_P^I \wedge (v, a, v') \in \mathcal{T}_P\}$, $\mathcal{T}_P^O = \{(v, a, v') \mid v, v' \in V_P \wedge a \in \mathcal{A}_P^O \wedge (v, a, v') \in \mathcal{T}_P\}$ and $\mathcal{T}_P^H = \{(v, a, v') \mid v, v' \in V_P \wedge a \in \mathcal{A}_P^H \wedge (v, a, v') \in \mathcal{T}_P\}$ be respectively the set of input, output and internal steps. For $v \in V_P$, let $\mathcal{A}_P^I(v) = \{a \in \mathcal{A}_P^I \mid \exists v' \in V_P . (v, a, v') \in \mathcal{T}_P\}$, $\mathcal{A}_P^O(v) = \{a \in \mathcal{A}_P^O \mid \exists v' \in V_P . (v, a, v') \in \mathcal{T}_P\}$ and $\mathcal{A}_P^H(v) = \{a \in \mathcal{A}_P^H \mid \exists v' \in V_P . (v, a, v') \in \mathcal{T}_P\}$ be respectively the subset of input, output and internal actions that are enabled at the state v. Let $\mathcal{A}_P(v) = \mathcal{A}_P^I(v) \cup \mathcal{A}_P^O(v) \cup \mathcal{A}_P^H(v)$.

For simplicity, we require that all interface automata referred in this paper are deterministic, i.e., for any IA P, it satisfies $\left|V_P^{init}\right| = 1$ and $\forall (v, a, u), (v, a, u') \in \mathcal{T}_P . u = u'$. An example of IA is shown in Fig. 1.

Example 1. The IA *Seller* (see Fig. 1) specifies the behavior of a component, the seller in a business to business system, when it interacts with other. The

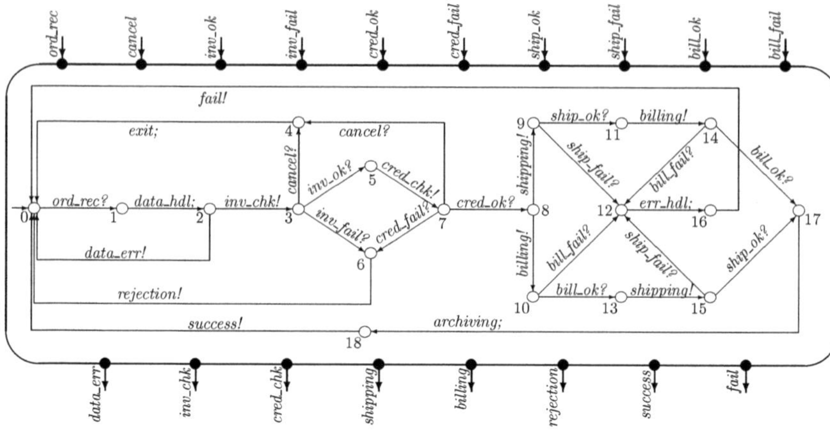

Fig. 1. Interface automaton *Seller*. The action whose name is followed by the symbol "?" (resp. "!", ";") is an input (resp. output, internal) action. An arrow without source denotes the initial state of the interface automaton.

seller receives an order (*ord_rec*) from a customer and handles data in the order (*data_hdl*), e.g., transform of data format. If some error is found in the order, the seller will report it (*data_err*) to the customer, otherwise the seller will check the inventory (*inv_chk*) from the supplier and the customer credit (*cred_chk*) from the bank. Contingent on availability of inventory (*inv_ok*) and valid credit (*cred_ok*), the seller will inform the shipper to ship product (*shipping*) and the bank to bill the customer for the order (*billing*). Either unavailability of inventory (*inv_fail*) or invalid credit (*cred_fail*) will lead to reject the order (*rejection*). The seller can receive some information (*cancel*) from the customer to terminate (*exit*) the order. If shipping and billing finish successfully (*ship_ok* and *bill_ok*), the seller will make archive (*archiving*) and give the notification (*success*) to the customer. Otherwise, the negative notification (*fail*) will be given after processing the exception (*err_hdl*).

In IA P, an *execution fragment* $v_0 a_0 v_1 a_1 \cdots a_{n-1} v_n$ is a sequence consisted of states and actions alternately, where $(v_i, a_i, v_{i+1}) \in \mathcal{T}_P$, for all $0 \leq i < n$. For any two states $v, u \in V_P$, we say that u is *reachable from* v if there is an execution fragment with v as the first state and u as the last state. The state u is *reachable in* P if u is reachable from an initial state $v \in V_P^{init}$.

Definition 2 (interface automata product). *Two IAs P and Q are* composable *if* $\mathcal{A}_P^H \cap \mathcal{A}_Q = \emptyset$, $\mathcal{A}_Q^H \cap \mathcal{A}_P = \emptyset$, $\mathcal{A}_P^I \cap \mathcal{A}_Q^I = \emptyset$ *and* $\mathcal{A}_P^O \cap \mathcal{A}_Q^O = \emptyset$. *Let* $shared(P,Q) = \mathcal{A}_P \cap \mathcal{A}_Q = (\mathcal{A}_P^I \cap \mathcal{A}_Q^O) \cup (\mathcal{A}_P^O \cap \mathcal{A}_Q^I)$ *be the set of shared actions of P and Q. The* product *of composable IAs P and Q, denoted by $P \otimes Q$, is the IA defined by*

$$
\begin{aligned}
V_{P\otimes Q} &= V_P \times V_Q \\
V_{P\otimes Q}^{init} &= V_P^{init} \times V_Q^{init} \\
\mathcal{A}_{P\otimes Q}^{I} &= (\mathcal{A}_P^I \cup \mathcal{A}_Q^I) \setminus \mathit{shared}(P,Q) \\
\mathcal{A}_{P\otimes Q}^{O} &= (\mathcal{A}_P^O \cup \mathcal{A}_Q^O) \setminus \mathit{shared}(P,Q) \\
\mathcal{A}_{P\otimes Q}^{H} &= \mathcal{A}_P^H \cup \mathcal{A}_Q^H \cup \mathit{shared}(P,Q) \\
\mathcal{T}_{P\otimes Q} &= \{((v,u),a,(v',u)) \mid (v,a,v') \in \mathcal{T}_P \wedge a \notin \mathit{shared}(P,Q) \wedge u \in V_Q\} \\
&\quad \cup \{((v,u),a,(v,u')) \mid (u,a,u') \in \mathcal{T}_Q \wedge a \notin \mathit{shared}(P,Q) \wedge v \in V_P\} \\
&\quad \cup \{((v,u),a,(v',u')) \mid (v,a,v') \in \mathcal{T}_P \wedge (u,a,u') \in \mathcal{T}_Q \wedge a \in \mathit{shared}(P,Q)\}\,.
\end{aligned}
$$

At some state of $P \otimes Q$, one IA, say P, may produces an output action that is an input action of Q, but is not enabled at the current state in Q. Such state is an *illegal states* of $P \otimes Q$. For two composable IAs P and Q, the set of illegal states of $P \otimes Q$ is denoted by $\mathit{Illegal}(P,Q) \subseteq V_P \times V_Q$,

$$
\mathit{Illegal}(P,Q) = \left\{ (v,u) \in V_P \times V_Q \,\middle|\, \exists\, a \in \mathit{shared}(P,Q)\,.\, \begin{pmatrix} a \in \mathcal{A}_P^O(v) \wedge a \notin \mathcal{A}_Q^I(u) \\ \vee \\ a \in \mathcal{A}_Q^O(u) \wedge a \notin \mathcal{A}_P^I(v) \end{pmatrix} \right\}.
$$

Definition 3 (environment). *An IA E is an* environment *for an IA R if: (1) E and R are composable, (2) E is not empty, (3) $\mathcal{A}_E^I = \mathcal{A}_R^O$, and (4) if $\mathit{Illegal}(R,E) \neq \emptyset$, then no state in $\mathit{Illegal}(R,E)$ is reachable in $R \otimes E$.*

The third condition ensures that the environment must accept all output of R. In other words, the environment does not constrain R by not accepting some of its outputs. The fourth condition ensures that IA R can work in its environment without running into any illegal state.

3.2 Message Sequence Charts

MSC [5] is a trace description language for visualization of selected system runs. It concentrates on message interchange by communicating entities and their environment. Every MSC specification has an equivalent graphical and textual representation. Especially the graphical representation of MSCs gives an intuitive understanding of the described system behavior. Therefore, MSC is a widely used scenario specification language.

The fundamental language constructs of MSCs are component and message flow. Vertical time lines with a heading represent components. The heading contains the component name. Along these time lines, MSC events are arranged that gives an order to the events connected to this component. Such events can be message send and receive events, timer and local events. A message is depicted by an arrow, horizontal or downward slope, from the send to the receive event. The fact that a message must be sent before it can be received imposes a total order on the send and receive event of a message and, furthermore, a partial order on all events in a MSC.

Definition 4 (message sequence chart, MSC). *A* message sequence chart $Ch = \langle \mathcal{C}, \mathcal{E}, \mathcal{M}, \mathcal{F}, \mathcal{O} \rangle$ *is a 5-tuple, where*

- $\mathcal{C}$ *is a finite set of* components.
- $\mathcal{E}$ *is a finite set of* events *corresponding to sending or receiving a message.*
- $\mathcal{M}$ *is a finite set of* messages. *For any* $m \in \mathcal{M}$, *let* $s(m)$ *and* $r(m)$ *to denote the events that correspond to sending and receiving message* m *respectively.*
- $\mathcal{F} : \mathcal{E} \to \mathcal{C}$ *is a* labelling function *which maps each event* $e \in \mathcal{E}$ *to a component* $\mathcal{F}(e) \in \mathcal{C}$ *.*
- $\mathcal{O} \subseteq \mathcal{E} \times \mathcal{E}$ *is a* partial order relation *over the set of events. For every* $(e, e') \in \mathcal{O}$ *, it is the case that* $e \neq e'$ *.* (e, e') *represents a visual order displayed in* Ch *.*

Figure 2 shows an example of MSC. Each MSC describes a set of message sequences.

Definition 5 (message sequence of MSC). *Let* $Ch = \langle \mathcal{C}, \mathcal{E}, \mathcal{M}, \mathcal{F}, \mathcal{O} \rangle$ *is a MSC. A sequence* $m_0 m_1 \cdots m_n$ *is a* message sequence *of* Ch *if and only if it satisfies the following conditions:*

- $\{m_0, m_1, \ldots m_n\} = \mathcal{M}$ *;*
- $m_i \neq m_j$ $(0 \leq i \leq n,\ 0 \leq j \leq n,\ i \neq j)$ *; and*
- *for any* m_i, m_j $(0 \leq i < j \leq n)$ *, it is the case that* $(s(m_j), s(m_i)) \notin \mathcal{O}$ *and* $(r(m_j), r(m_i)) \notin \mathcal{O}$ *.*

A message sequence of one MSC must be composed of all messages of the MSC and any message occurs only once in the sequence. For any two messages in the sequence, if one precedes the other then their send events and receive events should not violate the partial order relation over the set of events.

Observe that messages in MSCs correspond to actions in IA. Hence, we call a message sequence of MSC as an *action sequence* derived from the MSC and write it as $\varrho = \varrho(0)\varrho(1) \cdots \varrho(n)$, where $\varrho(i)$ is a message in the message sequence for all $0 \leq i \leq n$.

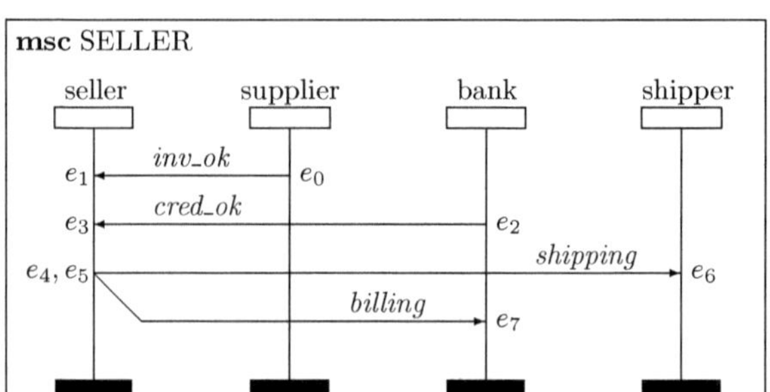

Fig. 2. MSC 'SELLER' specifying a scenario of the interaction between the seller component and other components

Example 2. The MSC 'SELLER' (see Fig. 2) shows a specification of the seller component (in Example 1) interacting with other components, which contains all desired behavior of a user about the seller component. It describes a scenario: if the seller receives *inv_ok* and *cred_ok* , it should produce *shipping* to the shipper and *billing* to the bank simultaneously. We can derive a set of action sequences $\mathcal{L}_S = \{inv\_ok\hat{\ }cred\_ok\hat{\ }shipping\hat{\ }billing, cred\_ok\hat{\ }inv\_ok\hat{\ }shipping\hat{\ }billing,$ $inv\_ok\hat{\ }cred\_ok\hat{\ }billing\hat{\ }shipping, cred\_ok\hat{\ }inv\_ok\hat{\ }billing\hat{\ }shipping\}$ from the MSC 'SELLER'. For legibility, we use the symbol "^" to separate two adjacent actions in an action sequence.

4 Sup-inclusive Environment

For any execution fragment $\eta = v_i a_i v_{i+1} a_{i+1} \cdots a_{j-1} v_j$ $(i < j)$ of IA P, where $v_i \in V_P^{init}$, if $v_i = v_j$ or $\mathcal{A}_P(v_j) = \emptyset$ then η is a run in P. Informally, a run is a special execution fragment which begins with an initial state and end with the same initial state (i.e., non-blocking case), or end with a state without any enabled action at it (i.e., blocking case). Let Γ_P and Σ_P denote the set of all execution fragments and the set of all runs of IA P respectively. Obviously, there is $\Sigma_P \subseteq \Gamma_P$. For any execution fragment $\eta = v_i a_i v_{i+1} a_{i+1} \cdots a_{j-1} v_j \in \Gamma_P$ $(i < j)$, we say that execution fragment $\eta' = v_s a_s v_{s+1} a_{s+1} \cdots a_{t-1} v_t$ $(i \le s < t \le j)$ *is on* η, denoted by $\eta' \sqsubseteq \eta$. Specifically, if $\eta' = v_s a_s v_{s+1}$ $(i \le s < j)$, then we say that the step $\tau = (v_s, a_s, v_{s+1}) \in \mathcal{T}_P$ *is on* the execution fragment η, denoted by $\tau \sqsubseteq \eta$. For every $\eta \in \Gamma_P$, write the first state of η as *first*(η) , the last state of η as *last*(η) and the set of all states in η as $V(\eta)$.

The *trace* of an execution fragment $\eta = v_0 a_0 v_1 a_1 \cdots a_{n-1} v_n$ is a subsequence of η , which consists of all actions in η . We write $trace(\eta) = a_0 a_1 \cdots a_{n-1}$. Given an execution fragment $\eta \in \Gamma_{P \otimes Q}$ and $trace(\eta) = a_0 a_1 \cdots a_{n-1}$, the *projection* of the trace of η on IA P, denoted by $\pi_P(trace(\eta))$, is a subsequence of $trace(\eta)$, which is obtained by deleting all actions $a_i \in \mathcal{A}_Q \setminus shared(P,Q)$, $0 \le i \le n-1$ from $trace(\eta)$. Informally, $\pi_P(trace(\eta))$ only contains those elements in $trace(\eta))$ that are actions of IA P.

Definition 6 (cover, corresponding step and state). *For two composable IAs P and Q , let $\eta = v_0 a_0 v_1 a_1 \cdots a_{n-1} v_n \in \Gamma_P$ and $\alpha \in \Sigma_{P \otimes Q}$. If there exists an execution fragment $\zeta \sqsubseteq \alpha$ satisfying $\pi_P(trace(\zeta)) = trace(\eta)$ and for any $v_i a_i v_{i+1} \sqsubseteq \eta$ it is the case that $(v_i, u_i) a_i (v_{i+1}, u_{i+1}) \sqsubseteq \zeta$, where $u_i, u_{i+1} \in V_Q$ and $0 \le i < n$, then we say that η is* covered *by α . At the same time, (u_i, a_i, u_{i+1}) is called the* corresponding step *of (v_i, a_i, v_{i+1}) if $a_i \in shared(P,Q)$, and u_i, u_{i+1} is called the* corresponding state *of v_i, v_{i+1} respectively.*

If an execution fragment of IA P can be covered by a run of IA $P \otimes Q$, then it means that the behavior represented by the execution fragment of P can be preserved in $P \otimes Q$. Note that for any $(v, a, v') \in \mathcal{T}_P$ and $a \notin shared(P,Q)$, there are only corresponding states of v and v' in Q if vav' can be covered by runs of $P \otimes Q$.

Definition 7 (occurrence). *Given a run α of IA P and an action sequence ϱ, if ϱ is a subsequence of $trace(\alpha)$, then we say action sequence ϱ* occurs *on run α, denoted by $\varrho \propto \alpha$.*

We can consider an action sequence and the trace of a run as behavior. The occurrence of an action sequence on a run of one IA means that in the IA there is a behavior containing the behavior represented by the action sequence.

Suppose that action sequence $\varrho = \varrho(0)\varrho(1)\cdots\varrho(m)$ occurs on run $\alpha \in \Sigma_R$. If there exists an execution fragment $\eta \sqsubseteq \alpha$ satisfying that ϱ is a subsequence of $trace(\eta) = a_0 a_1 \cdots a_n$ $(n \geq m)$ and $\varrho(0) = a_0$, $\varrho(m) = a_n$, then η is a *proper occurrence* of ϱ on α. Suppose that $\eta_0, \eta_1, \ldots, \eta_n \sqsubseteq \alpha$ are the proper occurrences of action sequences $\varrho_0, \varrho_1, \ldots, \varrho_n$ on α respectively. For any $\eta \sqsubseteq \alpha$, if $(V(\eta) \setminus \{first(\eta), last(\eta)\}) \cap V(\eta_i) = \emptyset$, $i = 0, 1, \ldots, n$, then η is a *proper inoccurrence* of $\varrho_0, \varrho_1, \ldots, \varrho_n$ on α. Intuitively, the proper occurrence of ϱ on α is an execution fragment on α, whose trace "contains" ϱ properly. Other execution fragments on α without any overlap with the proper occurrence are the proper inoccurrences of ϱ on α.

Given an IA P and a set $\mathcal{L}$ of action sequences, the function $\phi_{\mathcal{L}} : 2^{\Sigma_P} \to 2^{\Sigma_P}$ partitions any set $\Sigma \subseteq \Sigma_P$ as two sets: $\phi_{\mathcal{L}}(\Sigma) = \{\alpha \in \Sigma \mid \exists\, \varrho \in \mathcal{L} \,.\, \varrho \propto \alpha\}$ and $\overline{\phi_{\mathcal{L}}(\Sigma)} = \Sigma \setminus \phi_{\mathcal{L}}(\Sigma)$. Thus, Σ_P is partitioned as $\phi_{\mathcal{L}}(\Sigma_P)$ and $\overline{\phi_{\mathcal{L}}(\Sigma_P)}$. For every run in set $\phi_{\mathcal{L}}(\Sigma_P)$, there exists at least one action sequence in $\mathcal{L}$ that occurs on it. For any run in set $\overline{\phi_{\mathcal{L}}(\Sigma_P)}$, no action sequence in $\mathcal{L}$ occurs on it.

Example 3. IAs P and Q (see Fig. 3(a) and 3(b)) are composable and their product is shown in Fig. 3(c). The run $\alpha = 0a1b2c3d0$ of P is covered by run $\gamma = (0,v)a(1,u)b(2,u)c(3,u)d(0,v)$ of $P \otimes Q$ since $\pi_P(trace(\gamma)) = trace(\alpha) = abcd$. (v,a,u) and (u,d,v) are the corresponding steps in Q of $(0,a,1)$ and $(3,d,0)$ in P respectively. Suppose action sequence $\varrho = a\hat{\ }c$. ϱ occurs on α. The proper occurrence of ϱ on α is $0a1b2c3$ and the proper inoccurrence of ϱ on α is $3d0$. We can find the behavior represented by ϱ is preserved in $P \otimes Q$, since the run of P with occurrence of ϱ can be covered by a run of $P \otimes Q$.

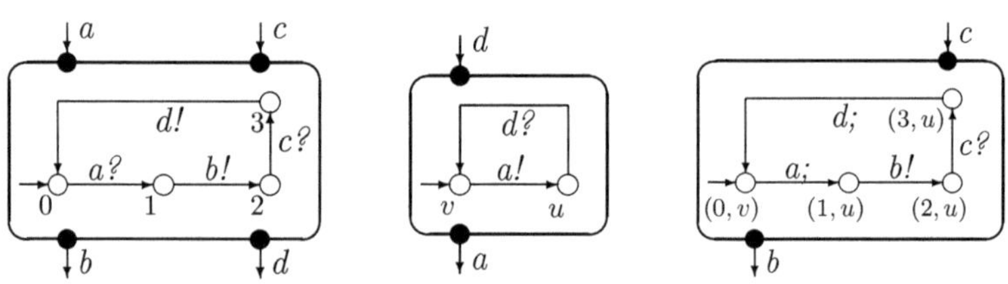

(a) IA P (b) IA Q (c) IA $P \otimes Q$

Fig. 3. Explanation for cover, corresponding step and occurrence

Definition 8 (sup-inclusive environment, SIE). *Let R be an IA and $\mathcal{L}$ a set of action sequences satisfying $\exists\, \varrho \in \mathcal{L} \,.\, \exists\, \alpha \in \Sigma_R \,.\, \varrho \propto \alpha$. The* inclusive environment *of R under $\mathcal{L}$ is an environment E of R such that for any $\varrho \in \mathcal{L}$,* *if ϱ occurs on a run α of R, then α must be covered by a run of $R \otimes E$. An inclusive environment E of R under $\mathcal{L}$ is the* sup-inclusive environment *if and only if for any inclusive environment E' of R under $\mathcal{L}$, any execution fragment of R that can be covered by some run of $R \otimes E$ must be covered by some run of $R \otimes E'$.*

Given an IA R and a set $\mathcal{L}$ of action sequences, if we consider $\mathcal{L}$ as the representation of a set of behavior, then two types of behavior in R are preserved in $R \otimes E$, where E is an inclusive environment of R under $\mathcal{L}$: (I) all behavior containing the behavior in $\mathcal{L}$, and (II) some behavior not containing the behavior in $\mathcal{L}$. However, the least of (II) is preserved in $R \otimes E_{\mathcal{L}}$, besides all of (I), than in the products of R and its any other inclusive environments, where $E_{\mathcal{L}}$ is the SIE of R under $\mathcal{L}$.

Theorem 1 (existence of SIE). *For any IA R and set $\mathcal{L}$ of action sequences, there exists a SIE $E_{\mathcal{L}}$ of R under $\mathcal{L}$ if and only if there exist an inclusive environment of R under $\mathcal{L}$.*

Theorem 2 (properties of SIE). *An environment E of IA R is the SIE of R under the set $\mathcal{L}$ of action sequences if and only if E holds all of the following properties at the same time:*

1. *for any step $\tau \sqsubseteq \alpha \in \phi_{\mathcal{L}}(\Sigma_R)$, there exists the corresponding step of τ in E if $label(\tau) \in shared(R, E)$ and there exist the corresponding states of $head(\tau)$ and $tail(\tau)$ in E if $label(\tau) \notin shared(R, E)$;*
2. *for any step $\tau \sqsubseteq \eta \in \Gamma_R$, $\eta \sqsubseteq \alpha \in \phi_{\mathcal{L}}(\Sigma_R)$, where η satisfies that $first(\eta) \in V_R^{init}$ and for any $\tau' \sqsubseteq \eta$, if $\tau' \in \mathcal{T}_R^I$ then there is $\beta \in \phi_{\mathcal{L}}(\Sigma_R)$ such that $\tau' \sqsubseteq \beta$, there exists the corresponding step of τ in E if $label(\tau) \in shared(R, E)$ and there exist the corresponding states of $head(\tau)$ and $tail(\tau)$ in E if $label(\tau) \notin shared(R, E)$;*
3. *for any other step $\tau \in \mathcal{T}_R$ except in 1 and 2, there does not exist the corresponding step of τ in E if $label(\tau) \in shared(R, E)$ and there do not exist the corresponding states of $head(\tau)$ and $tail(\tau)$ in E if $label(\tau) \notin shared(R, E)$.*

Theorem 2 describes properties of the SIE of arbitrary IA under a known set of action sequence. On the other hand, Theorem 2 indicates what runs and execution fragments in R are covered by the runs of $R \otimes E_{\mathcal{L}}$ and what runs and execution fragments in R are not covered by the runs of $R \otimes E_{\mathcal{L}}$.

5 Construction of Sup-inclusive Environment

The behavior of a component, say COMP, can be specified by an IA R. A scenario specification describes the user's desired behavior of COMP in MSC. Deriving behavior from COMP based on the scenario specification amounts to constructing the SIE $E_{\mathcal{L}}$ of R under $\mathcal{L}$, where $\mathcal{L}$ is the set of action sequences derived from the MSC. When $E_{\mathcal{L}}$ has been constructed, all of desired behavior in R, which is specified by the MSC, is extracted to the composition $R \otimes E_{\mathcal{L}}$. At the same time, other behavior in R that is out of $\mathcal{L}$ is not preserved in $R \otimes E_{\mathcal{L}}$ as much as possible.

In this section, we will discuss the basic idea for constructing SIE, how to decide the inclusive environment of R under $\mathcal{L}$ existing and how to construct $E_{\mathcal{L}}$ for R in detail and give the algorithm of constructing SIE.

5.1 Basic Approach to Constructing SIE

An environment of one IA, say R, can affect the runs of R only by the input actions of R. For arbitrary input step τ on arbitrary run of R, when the label of τ is a shared action of R and its environment, if the environment does not provide the input action for R when R needs it, then R cannot go on along the run. For example, if the environment does not provide input action *cancel* for IA *Seller* (see Fig. 1) when *Seller* stays at state 3, then *Seller* cannot run along execution fragment 3 *cancel* 4 *exit* 0 back to initial state. That the environment does not provide input action $label(\tau)$ for R, when R needs it, amounts to no corresponding step of τ in the environment.

Based on the above analysis, we can obtain the SIE $E_{\mathcal{L}}$ of IA R by the following procedure. Firstly, for every run $\alpha \in \overline{\phi_{\mathcal{L}}(\Sigma_R)}$, traverse steps on α from the state $first(\alpha)$. On run α find the first input step τ that is not on any run in $\phi_{\mathcal{L}}(\Sigma_R)$, delete τ from IA R and all unreachable states produced by this deletion. Secondly, construct corresponding steps in an empty IA E for all residual steps in R. When the second step finishes, E is the SIE $E_{\mathcal{L}}$ of R.

Note that if there exists $\eta \in \Gamma_R$, $first(\eta) = last(\eta)$ and $first(\eta), last(\eta) \notin V_R^{init}$, called η as a *loop*, then Σ_R is an infinite set and the *lengths* of some runs in Σ_R, i.e., the number of steps on a run, may be also infinite. Accordingly, $\phi_{\mathcal{L}}(\Sigma_R)$, $\overline{\phi_{\mathcal{L}}(\Sigma_R)}$ and the lengths of some runs in them may be infinite. Thus, it is unfeasible to traverse all runs in $\overline{\phi_{\mathcal{L}}(\Sigma_R)}$ directly. For getting a feasible approach, we introduce the concepts of the simple run and simple loop.

Given an IA R and a set $\mathcal{L}$ of action sequences, a run $\alpha = v_0 a_0 v_1 a_1 \cdots a_{n-1} v_n \in \Sigma_R$ is a *simple run* when it satisfies the following conditions:

1. if $\alpha \in \overline{\phi_{\mathcal{L}}(\Sigma_R)}$, then there is $v_i \neq v_j$ $(0 < i < n,\ 0 < j < n,\ i \neq j)$;
2. if $\alpha \in \phi_{\mathcal{L}}(\Sigma_R)$, then
   (a) for any proper inoccurrence $\eta = v_i a_i v_{i+1} a_{i+1} \cdots a_{j-1} v_j$ $(0 \le i < j \le n)$ on α, there is $v_s \neq v_t$ $(i \le s \le j,\ i \le t \le j,\ s \neq t)$; and
   (b) for any proper occurrence ζ of $\varrho = \varrho(0)\varrho(1)\cdots\varrho(m) \in \mathcal{L}$ on α, if there is $\zeta' = v_i a_i v_{i+1} a_{i+1} \cdots a_{j-1} v_j \sqsubseteq \zeta$ $(0 \le i < j \le n)$, and $a_i = \varrho(k)$, $a_{j-1} = \varrho(k+1)$, $0 \le k < m$, then there is $v_s \neq v_t$ $(i < s < j,\ i < t < j,\ s \neq t)$.

We put some constrains for loops on runs and get the simple runs. The meaning of condition 1 is that there is not any loop on a simple run without occurrence of action sequences in $\mathcal{L}$. The meaning of condition 2a is that there is not any loop on a proper inoccurrence of action sequences on a simple run. The meaning of condition 2b is that on a proper occurrence of an action sequence on a simple run, there is not any loop between the occurrence of two neighbor actions in the action sequence.

The set of all simple runs of IA R under $\mathcal{L}$ is denoted by $\Omega_R^{\mathcal{L}}$. Similarly, $\Omega_R^{\mathcal{L}}$ can be partitioned as $\phi_{\mathcal{L}}(\Omega_R^{\mathcal{L}})$ and $\overline{\phi_{\mathcal{L}}(\Omega_R^{\mathcal{L}})}$. Obviously, there are $\Omega_R^{\mathcal{L}} \subseteq \Sigma_R$, $\phi_{\mathcal{L}}(\Omega_R^{\mathcal{L}}) \subseteq \phi_{\mathcal{L}}(\Sigma_R)$ and $\overline{\phi_{\mathcal{L}}(\Omega_R^{\mathcal{L}})} \subseteq \overline{\phi_{\mathcal{L}}(\Sigma_R)}$.

Given an IA R and a set $\mathcal{L}$ of action sequences, an execution fragment $\eta = v_i a_i v_{i+1} a_{i+1} \cdots a_{j-1} v_j \in \Gamma_R$ $(i < j)$ is a *simple loop* if: (1) $v_i = v_j$, $v_i, v_j \notin V_R^{init}$, (2) $v_s \neq v_t$ $(i \leq s < j$, $i \leq t < j$, $s \neq t)$ and (3) $\forall \alpha \in \phi_{\mathcal{L}}(\Omega_R^{\mathcal{L}}) . \eta \not\sqsubseteq \alpha$.

The first and second conditions ensure that except the first and the last states, there are not duplicate states in a simple loop. The third condition ensures that a simple loop is not the loop on a proper occurrence of some action sequence in $\mathcal{L}$. For given IA R and set $\mathcal{L}$ of action sequences, $\Lambda_R^{\mathcal{L}}$ denotes the set of all simple loops of R. We say that simple loop $\eta \in \Lambda_R^{\mathcal{L}}$ *associates* with simple run $\alpha \in \Omega_R^{\mathcal{L}}$ if $V(\eta) \cap V(\alpha) \neq \emptyset$ or $V(\eta) \cap V(\eta') \neq \emptyset$, where $\eta' \in \Lambda_R^{\mathcal{L}}$ associates with α. Informally, if a simple loop has a common state with a simple run, then the simple loop associates with the simple run. Additionally, if a simple loop has a common state with a simple loop that associates with a simple run, then the simple loop also associates with the simple run. Let $\psi_{\mathcal{L}}(\Lambda_R^{\mathcal{L}}) = \{\eta \in \Lambda_R^{\mathcal{L}} \mid \exists \alpha \in \phi_{\mathcal{L}}(\Omega_R^{\mathcal{L}}) . \eta \text{ associates with } \alpha\}$ and $\overline{\psi}_{\mathcal{L}}(\Lambda_R^{\mathcal{L}}) = \left\{\eta \in \Lambda_R^{\mathcal{L}} \mid \exists \alpha \in \overline{\phi_{\mathcal{L}}(\Omega_R^{\mathcal{L}})} . \eta \text{ associates with } \alpha\right\}$.

Example 4. In Fig. 4, we give a succinct representation of one IA for explaining the concept of simple run and simple loop. It is reasonable not to distinguish the input, output and internal action for this purpose. Suppose action sequence $\varrho = a\hat{\ }d\hat{\ }d$ and $\varrho' = g$. The runs with occurrence of ϱ are $0a(1b(2c)^*2d)^*1e3f0$, where $(\cdot)^*$ represents that the content in parentheses can repeat arbitrary times. The number of these runs is infinite, but the simple run with occurrence of ϱ is only one, i.e., $\alpha = 0a1b2d1b2d1e3f0$. The simple loop associated with α is $2c2$. There is not any simple run with occurrence of ϱ'. The simple run without occurrence of ϱ' is $\alpha' = 0a1e3f0$ and the simple loops associated with α' are $1b2d1$ and $2c2$. The numbers of simple runs and simple loops are finite.

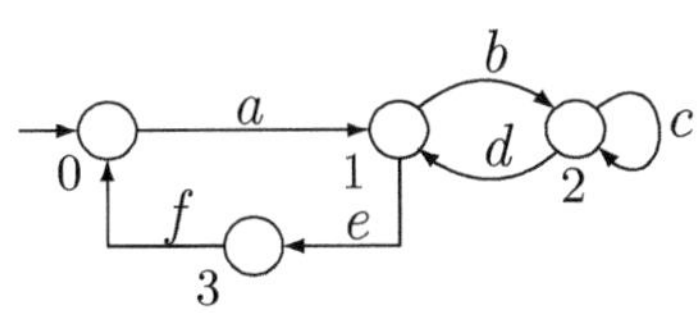

Fig. 4. Explanation for simple run and simple loop

Notice that every step on any run in Σ_R corresponds to a step on some simple run in $\Omega_R^{\mathcal{L}}$ or on some simple loop in $\Lambda_R^{\mathcal{L}}$. However, $\Omega_R^{\mathcal{L}}$ and $\Lambda_R^{\mathcal{L}}$ are finite sets and the lengths of all simple runs and simple loops are finite. Thus, we can apply the approach for getting SIE of R mentioned previously to $\Omega_R^{\mathcal{L}}$ and $\Lambda_R^{\mathcal{L}}$. Since these sets are finite, the approach becomes feasible.

5.2 Decision of Existence of Inclusive Environment

According to Definition 8, if all action sequences in $\mathcal{L}$ do not occur on any runs of R, then there does not exist any inclusive environment of R under $\mathcal{L}$. Furthermore, we had proven that there maybe exist some kind of execution fragments in one IA, say P, for any environment E of P, which cannot be covered by any run of $P \otimes E$ [11]. Suppose that some action sequences in $\mathcal{L}$ occur on runs with such kind of execution fragments on it. Because these runs cannot be covered by any run in the product of R and R's any environment, there does not exist any inclusive environment of R under $\mathcal{L}$ according to Definition 8.

We give the decision of the existence of inclusive environment in the following theorem.

Theorem 3. *For any IA R and set $\mathcal{L}$ of action sequences, there does not exist an inclusive environment E of R under $\mathcal{L}$ if any one of the followings holds:*

1. $\phi_{\mathcal{L}}(\Omega_R^{\mathcal{L}}) = \emptyset$.
2. *For some $\alpha \in \phi_{\mathcal{L}}(\Omega_R^{\mathcal{L}})$, there are $\eta_1, \eta_2 \in \Gamma_R$, $\eta_2 \sqsubseteq \alpha$ and η_1, η_2 satisfy any of the following conditions:*
   (a) $\eta_1 = v_i a v_j$ and $\eta_2 = v_j b v_k$, where $i \neq j \neq k$, $a \notin shared(R, E)$, $b \in \mathcal{A}_R^I \cap shared(R, E)$ and $b \notin \mathcal{A}_R(v_i)$.
   (b) $\eta_1 = v_i a v_j$ and $\eta_2 = v_i b v_k$, where $i \neq j \neq k$, $a \notin shared(R, E)$, $b \in \mathcal{A}_R^I \cap shared(R, E)$ and $b \notin \mathcal{A}_R(v_j)$.
   (c) $\eta_1 = v_i a_i v_{i+1} a_{i+1} \cdots a_{j-1} v_j$ and $\eta_2 = v_i b v_i'$, where $i < j$, $v_i' \notin V(\eta_1)$, $a_k \notin shared(R, E)$, $k = i, i+1, \ldots, j-1$, $b \in \mathcal{A}_R^I \cap shared(R, E)$ and $\exists v \in V(\eta_1) \,.\, b \notin \mathcal{A}_R(v)$.

According to Theorem 1, if the inclusive environment of R under $\mathcal{L}$ does not exist, the SIE of R under $\mathcal{L}$ does not exist either.

5.3 Algorithm of Constructing SIE

The skeleton of the constructive algorithm for SIE is described as follows. Firstly, decide whether inclusive environments of R under $\mathcal{L}$ exist by Theorem 3. If no inclusive environment exists then there is no SIE of R. Secondly, if inclusive environments of R exist, then we can obtain the SIE of R by three steps. Step one, for every simple run without occurrence of action sequences in $\mathcal{L}$ and every simple loop associated with it, traverse it from the first state and find the first input steps on it, which is not on any simple run with occurrence of action sequences in $\mathcal{L}$ or any simple loop associated with it. Step two, remove the input steps from R and all unreachable states after the removal. Step three, construct corresponding steps in one IA for all residual steps in R.

Algorithm. Make the convention of $\mathcal{A}_{E_{\mathcal{L}}}^H = \emptyset$ and $\mathcal{A}_{E_{\mathcal{L}}}^O = \mathcal{A}_R^I$ [11]. Let $R \downharpoonright \mathcal{T}$ denote the IA obtained by removing all steps in $\mathcal{T} \subset \mathcal{T}_R$ from R and all unreachable states in R after the removal. The algorithm of constructing SIE $E_{\mathcal{L}}$ of R is shown in Algorithm 1.

Algorithm 1. Constructing SIE $E_{\mathcal{L}}$ of IA R

Input: Interface automaton R and set $\mathcal{L}$ of action sequences.
Output: The SIE $E_{\mathcal{L}}$ of R under $\mathcal{L}$.
Variables: $\mathcal{T} \subset \mathcal{T}_R$, step τ, IA R' and boolean found

1: Traverse R to get $\phi_{\mathcal{L}}(\Omega_R^{\mathcal{L}})$, $\overline{\phi_{\mathcal{L}}(\Omega_R^{\mathcal{L}})}$, $\psi_{\mathcal{L}}(\Lambda_R^{\mathcal{L}})$ and $\overline{\psi}_{\mathcal{L}}(\Lambda_R^{\mathcal{L}})$.
2: **if** no inclusive environment exists **then** // by Theorem 3
3:     **return** $E_{\mathcal{L}}$ does not exist
4: **else**
5:     $\mathcal{T} \longleftarrow \emptyset$
6:     **for all** $\eta \in \overline{\phi_{\mathcal{L}}(\Omega_R^{\mathcal{L}})} \cup \overline{\psi}_{\mathcal{L}}(\Lambda_R^{\mathcal{L}})$ **do**
7:         found $\longleftarrow$ **true**
8:         $\tau \longleftarrow$ the first step on η // $head(\tau) = first(\eta) \wedge \tau \sqsubseteq \eta$
9:         **while** $(\tau \notin \mathcal{T}_R^I \vee \exists \zeta \in (\phi_{\mathcal{L}}(\Omega_R^{\mathcal{L}}) \cup \psi_{\mathcal{L}}(\Lambda_R^{\mathcal{L}})).\tau \sqsubseteq \zeta) \wedge$ found **do**
10:             **if** τ is not the last step on η **then** // $tail(\tau) \neq last(\eta) \wedge \tau \sqsubseteq \eta$
11:                 $\tau \longleftarrow$ the next step on η
12:             **else** found $\longleftarrow$ **false**
13:             **end if**
14:         **end while**
15:         **if** found **then** $\mathcal{T} \longleftarrow \mathcal{T} \cup \{\tau\}$
16:         **end if**
17:     **end for**
18:     $R' \longleftarrow R \downharpoonright \mathcal{T}$
19:     Initialize $E_{\mathcal{L}}$: $V_{E_{\mathcal{L}}} \longleftarrow \{u_0\}$, $V_{E_{\mathcal{L}}}^{init} \longleftarrow \{u_0\}$
20:     **for all** $\tau \in \mathcal{T}_{R'}$ **do**
21:         Construct the corresponding step of τ in $E_{\mathcal{L}}$
22:     **end for**
23:     **return** $E_{\mathcal{L}}$
24: **end if**

Analysis. We can prove that the return (i.e., line 23) of Algorithm 1 is an inclusive environment of R under $\mathcal{L}$ and holds all properties in Theorem 2. It means that the IA constructed by Algorithm 1 is the SIE of R under $\mathcal{L}$. Thus, Algorithm 1 is correct.

About line 1 in Algorithm 1, we had given an algorithm to find which simple run of an IA has the occurrence of a given action sequence [12]. About line 21 in Algorithm 1, we had given a method of constructing corresponding steps [11].

Suppose that $n = \max\{length(\eta) \mid \eta \in \Omega_R^{\mathcal{L}} \cup \Lambda_R^{\mathcal{L}}\}$ is the maximal length of all simple runs and simple loops of R, where $length(\eta)$ is the number of steps on η. Suppose that $m_1 = |\phi_{\mathcal{L}}(\Omega_R^{\mathcal{L}})|$, $m_2 = |\overline{\phi_{\mathcal{L}}(\Omega_R^{\mathcal{L}})}|$ are the number of simple runs in $\phi_{\mathcal{L}}(\Omega_R^{\mathcal{L}})$, $\overline{\phi_{\mathcal{L}}(\Omega_R^{\mathcal{L}})}$ respectively, and $k_1 = |\psi_{\mathcal{L}}(\Lambda_R^{\mathcal{L}})|$, $k_2 = |\overline{\psi}_{\mathcal{L}}(\Lambda_R^{\mathcal{L}})|$ are the number of simple loops in $\psi_{\mathcal{L}}(\Lambda_R^{\mathcal{L}})$, $\overline{\psi}_{\mathcal{L}}(\Lambda_R^{\mathcal{L}})$ respectively. In the worst case, line 6 to 15 in Algorithm 1 can be done in $O\left((m_1 + k_1)(m_2 + k_2)n^2\right)$ time. According to [12] and [11], line 1 and line 21 in Algorithm 1 need $O((m_1 + m_2)n)$ and $O(|V_{R'}|)$ time respectively, where $|V_{R'}|$ is the number of states of IA R'. In general, there are $length(\eta) \ll length(\alpha)$ for $\eta \in \Lambda_R^{\mathcal{L}}$ and $\alpha \in \Omega_R^{\mathcal{L}}$ and $|V_{R'}| \ll (m_1 + m_2)n$. Hence, the complexity of Algorithm 1 is $O(m_1 m_2 n^2)$.

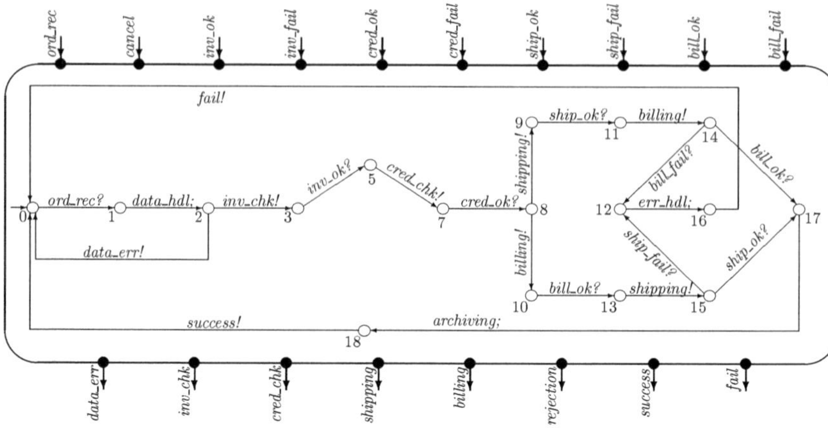

Fig. 5. IA R'. The intermediate result of Algorithm 1 with inputs of *Seller* and $\mathcal{L}_S$

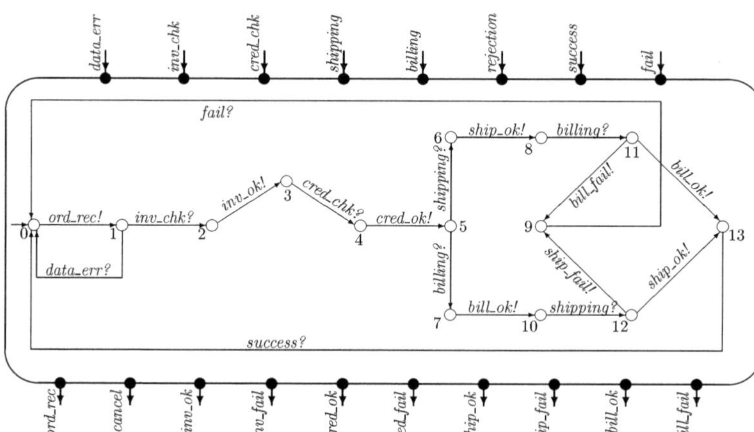

Fig. 6. The SIE $E_{\mathcal{L}_s}$ of *Seller* under $\mathcal{L}_S$

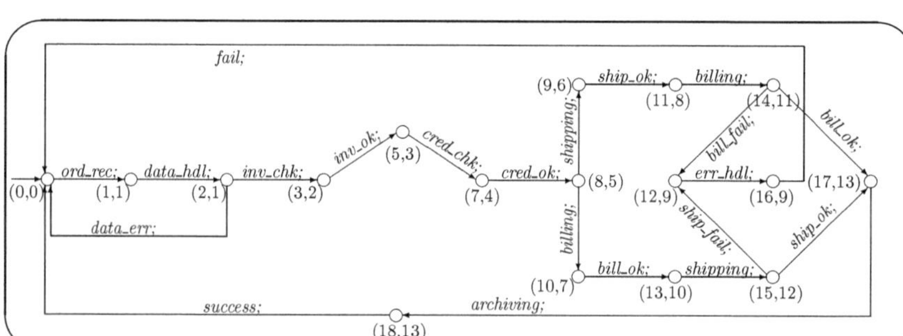

Fig. 7. *Seller* $\otimes E_{\mathcal{L}_s}$. The composition of *Seller* and $E_{\mathcal{L}_S}$.

Example 5. By Algorithm 1, we can obtain the SIE $E_{\mathcal{L}_S}$ (see Fig. 6) of the IA *Seller* (see Fig. 1) under $\mathcal{L}_S$ derived from the MSC 'SELLER' (see Fig. 2). For instance, since $\alpha = 0\,ord\_rec1\,data\_hdl2inv\_chk3cancel4exist0$ of *Seller* is a simple run without occurrence of any action sequence in $\mathcal{L}_S$, there is $\alpha \in \phi_{\mathcal{L}_S}\left(\Omega_{Seller}^{\mathcal{L}_S}\right)$. According to line 8 to 14 in Algorithm 1, we traverse α from state 0 and find the first input step $(3, cancel, 4)$ that is not on any simple run with occurrence of any action sequence in $\mathcal{L}_S$. Note that we find the input step $(0, ord\_hdl, 1)$ before $(3, cancel, 4)$, but $(0, ord\_hdl, 1)$ is on a simple run with occurrence of an action sequence in $\mathcal{L}_S$. Similarly, we can get all input steps like $(3, cancel, 4)$, that is, $(3, inv\_fail, 6)$, $(7, cancel, 4)$, $(7, cred\_fail, 6)$, $(9, ship\_fail, 12)$ and $(10, bill\_fail, 12)$, on other simple runs in $\phi_{\mathcal{L}_S}\left(\Omega_{Seller}^{\mathcal{L}_S}\right)$. After delete these steps from *Seller* and unreachable states 4 and 6 produced by the deletion, we get the intermediate result R' (see line 18 in Algorithm 1) shown in Fig. 5. Constructing the corresponding step for every step in R' by the method given in [11], we obtain the SIE $E_{\mathcal{L}_S}$ finally. For instance, we construct the corresponding step $(1, inv\_chk, 2)$ in $E_{\mathcal{L}_S}$ for output step $(2, inv\_chk, 3)$ in R'.

It can be found that the user's desired behavior specified by MSC 'SELLER' is extracted from *Seller* to the composition of *Seller* and $E_{\mathcal{L}_S}$, i.e., $Seller \otimes E_{\mathcal{L}_S}$ (see Fig. 7). Except the user's desired behavior, other behavior of *Seller* is discarded as much as possible in $Seller \otimes E_{\mathcal{L}_S}$.

6 Conclusion

We study the behavior derivation of components based on scenarios. By constructing a special environment, i.e., SIE, for a component, the user's desired behavior specified by a scenario specification can be derived from the component to the composition of the component and its SIE, and other behavior of the component is discarded to the most extent. We use interface automata to model the behavior of components and a set of action sequences to abstract the scenario specified by MSC. The composition of components is modelled by the product of interface automata. We give the algorithm of constructing SIE for a given interface automaton under a known set of action sequences, and illustrate our approach by an example.

In service-based systems, e.g., web services, services are the basic building blocks and interact each other to perform some tasks. Services have some common characteristics with components, such as modularity, composablity and reusability. Because services can be implemented by components, our proposal is also appropriate to services. We are trying to apply our approach given in this paper to web services. Additionally, we have designed a prototype of the tool supporting our approach for scenario-based behavior derivation. For the space limitations, we will discuss the prototype in other paper. The tool is being implemented until this paper has been published.

There are some limitations about our approach given in this paper. Firstly, in comparison with [6], only the model of SIE can be constructed by our approach.

Secondly, our approach assume that SIE and component share all inputs of the component (i.e., $\mathcal{A}^O_{E_\mathcal{L}} = \mathcal{A}^I_R$). In some circumstances, the assumption can be relaxed. We will study how to release these limitations in the future.

References

1. Bracciali, A., Brogi, A., Canal, C.: A formal approach to component adaptation. Journal of Systems and Software **74** (2004) 45–54
2. Yellin, D.M., Strom, R.E.: Protocol specifications and component adaptors. ACM Transactions on Programming Languages and Systems **19** (1997) 292–333
3. Zhang, Y., Yu, X., Zhang, T., Li, X., Zheng, G.: Scenario-based component behavior filtration. In: Proceedings of IFIP Working Conference on Software Engineering Techniques (SET 2006). Lecture Notes in Computer Science, Springer-Verlag (2006) (Accepted).
4. de Alfaro, L., Henzinger, T.A.: Interface automata. In: Proceedings of the 9th Annual ACM Symposium on Foundations of Software Engineering (FSE 2001), New York, ACM Press (2001) 109–120
5. ITU-TS: ITU-TS recommendation Z.120: Message Sequence Chart (MSC). ITU-TS, Geneva (1999)
6. Inverardi, P., Tivoli, M.: Software architecture for correct components assembly. In Bernardo, M., Inverardi, P., eds.: Formal Methods for Software Architectures, Third International School on Formal Methods for the Design of Computer, Communication and Software Systems: Software Architectures (SFM 2003). Volume 2804 of Lecture Notes in Computer Science. Springer-Verlag (2003) 92–121
7. Tivoli, M., Autili, M.: SYNTHESIS: a tool for synthesizing "correct" and protocol-enhanced adaptors. L'Object Journal **12** (2005)
8. Ramadge, P.J., Wonham, W.M.: The control of discrete event systems. Proceedings of the IEEE **77** (1989) 81–98
9. v. Bochmann, G.: Submodule construction for specifications with input assumptions and output guarantees. In: Proceedings of the 22nd IFIP WG 6.1 International Conference on Formal Techniques for Networked and Distributed Systems (FORTE 2002). Volume 2804 of Lecture Notes in Computer Science., Berlin Heidelberg New York, Springer-Verlag (2002) 17–33
10. Phoha, V.V., Nadgar, A.U., Ray, A., Phoha, S.: Supervisory control of software systems. IEEE Transactions on Computers **53** (2004) 1187–1199
11. Zhang, Y., Hu, J., Yu, X., Zhang, T., Li, X., Zheng, G.: Available behavior all out from incompatible component compositions. In: Proceedings of the 2nd International Workshop on Formal Aspects of Component Software (FACS'05). Electronic Notes in Theoretical Computer Science, Elsevier (2006) (To appear).
12. Hu, J., Yu, X., Zhang, Y., Zhang, T., Wang, L., Li, X., Zheng, G.: Scenario-based verification for component-based embedded software designs. In: Proceedings of the 34th International Conference on Parallel Processing Workshops (ICPP 2005 Workshop), Los Alamitos, California, IEEE Computer Society (2005) 240–247

Appendix. Proof of Theorems and the Correctness of Algorithm

For concision, we introduce some notation. If an execution fragment $\eta \in \Gamma_P$ can be covered by a run $\alpha \in \Sigma_{P \otimes Q}$ then we denote it by $\alpha C \eta$. For any two execution fragments $\eta_1, \eta_2 \sqsubseteq \zeta$, $\zeta \in \Gamma_P$, if $last(\eta_1) = first(\eta_2)$ or $\exists\, \eta' \sqsubseteq \zeta \,.\, last(\eta_1) = first(\eta') \wedge last(\eta') = first(\eta_2)$, then we say that η_1 *precedes* η_2 on ζ, denoted by $\eta_1 \prec_\zeta \eta_2$. Specifically, if $\eta_1 = vav'$ and $\eta_2 = ubu'$ we can say that step $\tau_1 = (v, a, v')$ precedes $\tau_2 = (u, b, u')$ on ζ, denoted by $\tau_1 \prec_\zeta \tau_2$. For given IA R and set $\mathcal{L}$ of action sequences, let $\mathrm{IE}_{\mathcal{L}}(R)$ denote the set of all inclusive environments of R under $\mathcal{L}$.

Proof of Theorem 1. Sufficiency is obvious according to Definition 8. It is enough to prove necessity.

Suppose that $E \in \mathrm{IE}_{\mathcal{L}}(R)$ satisfies that for any $E' \in \mathrm{IE}_{\mathcal{L}}(R)$, any execution fragment of R that can be covered by some run of $R \otimes E'$ must be covered by some run of $R \otimes E$ [1]. For any run $\alpha \in \overline{\phi_{\mathcal{L}}(\Sigma_R)}$, find the non-laps of α with all runs in $\phi_{\mathcal{L}}(\Sigma_R)$, denoted the set of all these non-laps by $\mathrm{NL}_R(\alpha)$. A so-called non-lap η of run α with run β is an execution fragment $\eta \sqsubseteq \alpha$ satisfying $\forall\, \eta' \sqsubseteq \eta \,.\, \eta' \not\sqsubseteq \beta$. For any step τ_R on any execution fragment in $\mathrm{NL}_R(\alpha)$, after deleting its corresponding step τ_E from E, E is still an inclusive environment of R under $\mathcal{L}$. In other words, after deleting τ_E from E, all of runs in $\phi_{\mathcal{L}}(\Sigma_R)$ can still be covered by runs of $R \otimes E$. $\zeta \in \mathrm{NL}_R(\alpha)$ is called a relative maximal non-lap in $\mathrm{NL}_R(\alpha)$ if and only if $\forall\, \zeta' \in \mathrm{NL}_R(\alpha) \,.\, \zeta \sqsubseteq \zeta' \longrightarrow \zeta = \zeta'$. Denote the set of all relative maximal non-laps in $\mathrm{NL}_R(\alpha)$ as $\mathrm{LMNL}_R(\alpha)$. Observe that there are $\mathcal{A}_E^I = \mathcal{A}_R^O$ and Definition 2, so only for steps in $\mathcal{T}_R^I$ their corresponding steps can be not constructed in E. For any $\tau_R \sqsubseteq \eta, \tau_R \in \mathcal{T}_R^I, \eta \in \Gamma_R$, if there does not exist τ_R's corresponding step in E, then for any $\tau_R' \sqsubseteq \eta, \tau_R \prec_\eta \tau_R'$ there does not exist τ_R''s corresponding step in E. Thus, for any $\eta \in \mathrm{LMNL}_R(\alpha), \alpha \in \overline{\phi_{\mathcal{L}}(\Sigma_R)}$, make back traversal of η from $last(\eta)$ to $first(\eta)$. For every traversed τ_R, if there is some $\tau_R' \in \mathcal{T}_R^I, \tau_R' \sqsubseteq \eta$ and $\tau_R' \prec_\eta \tau_R$, then delete the corresponding step of τ_R from E. Repeat this operation until the traversal of η finishes. For every run α in $\overline{\phi_{\mathcal{L}}(\Sigma_R)}$, repeat above process, i.e., compute $\mathrm{LMNL}_R(\alpha)$, for every execution fragment in $\mathrm{LMNL}_R(\alpha)$ traverse it backward and delete the corresponding steps from E for traversed steps that satisfy the mentioned conditions above. Finally, residual steps in E form an IA that is the SIE $E_{\mathcal{L}}$ of R under $\mathcal{L}$. Since runs of $R \otimes E$ cover all runs of R, for any other $E' \in \mathrm{IE}_{\mathcal{L}}(R)$, runs of $R \otimes E'$ cover no more execution fragments of R than runs of $R \otimes E$ do. Thus, the above process is appropriate to E' too. So the necessity holds. □

Proof of Theorem 2. (Sufficiency) By property 1 in the theorem, it is possible to conclude that for any run of R with occurrence of action sequences in $\mathcal{L}$, it can be covered by a run of $R \otimes E$. Thus E is an inclusive environment of R under $\mathcal{L}$, i.e., $E \in \mathrm{IE}_{\mathcal{L}}(R)$.

As follows, we prove that E is the SIE of R under $\mathcal{L}$ by contradiction.

Assume that there is $E' \in \mathrm{IE}_{\mathcal{L}}(R)$, $shared(R, E') = shared(R, E)$ and $E' \neq E$ such that an execution fragment $\eta \in \Gamma_R$ satisfies $\exists\, \gamma \in \Sigma_{R \otimes E} \,.\, \gamma C \eta$ and $\forall\, \gamma \in \Sigma_{R \otimes E'} \,.\, \neg(\gamma C \eta)$. Without loss of generality, it is possible to suppose $\eta = vav'$.

[1] In fact, E amounts to the comprehensive legal environment (CLE) of R when $V = \emptyset$, where V is the set of desired unreachable states. The definition of CLE refers to [11].

According to the theorem, step (v,a,v') must satisfy the precondition of property 2. If $a \in shared(R,E)$, then there are two cases. Case 1, if $(v,a,v') \in \mathcal{T}_R^I$ then there is $\exists\,\alpha \in \phi_{\mathcal{L}}(\Sigma_R)\,.\,vav' \sqsubseteq \alpha$. Since $\forall\,\gamma \in \Sigma_{R\otimes E'}\,.\,\neg(\gamma C \eta)$, E' is not an inclusive environment of R under $\mathcal{L}$. This contradicts the assumption. Case 2, if $(v,a,v') \in \mathcal{T}_R^O$ then there must exist the corresponding step of (v,a,v') in any environment of R by Definition 3. Similarly, if $a \notin shared(R,E)$, then there must exist the corresponding states of v and v' in any environment of R. Thus, vav' must be covered by runs of $R \otimes E'$. This also contradicts the assumption. In a word, the assumption is wrong. Hence, E is a SIE of R under $\mathcal{L}$ by Definition 8.

(Necessity) By Definition 8, there is $\forall\,\alpha \in \phi_{\mathcal{L}}(R)\,.\,\exists\,\gamma \in \Sigma_{R\otimes E}\,.\,\gamma C \alpha$. Thus, property 1 in the theorem holds obviously by Definition 6.

Suppose that $\eta = v_0 a_0 v_1 a_1 \cdots a_i v_{i+1} \cdots a_{n-1} v_n \in \Gamma_R$, $0 \le i < n$ satisfies that $v_0 \in V_R^{init}$, $\exists\,\alpha \in \overline{\phi_{\mathcal{L}}(R)}\,.\,\eta \sqsubseteq \alpha$ and $\forall\,\tau \sqsubseteq \eta\,.\,\exists\,\beta \in \phi_{\mathcal{L}}(R)\,.\,\tau \in \mathcal{T}_R^I \longrightarrow \tau \sqsubseteq \beta$. If $a_0 \in shared(R,E)$, then there are two cases. Case 1, if $(v_0,a_0,v_1) \in \mathcal{T}_R^I$ then there must exist the corresponding step of (v_0,a_0,v_1) in E by property 1 in the theorem. Case 2, if $(v_0,a_0,v_1) \in \mathcal{T}_R^O$ there must exist the corresponding step of (v_0,a_0,v_1) in E by Definition 3 and 6. If $a_0 \notin shared(R,E)$ then there must exist the corresponding state of v_0 and v_1 in E by Definition 6. Assume that in E there exists the corresponding step of (v_k,a_k,v_{k+1}), $0 < k < i-1$ if $a_k \in shared(R,E)$ and there exist the corresponding states of v_k and v_{k+1} if $a_k \notin shared(R,E)$. Observe the situation when $k = i$. If $a_i \in shared(R,E)$ then there are two cases. Case 1, if $a_i \in \mathcal{A}_R^I$ then there must be $(v_i,a_i,v_{i+1}) \in \mathcal{T}_R^I$. Since $\exists\,\beta \in \phi_{\mathcal{L}}(R)\,.\,v_i a_i v_{i+1} \sqsubseteq \beta$, there must exist the corresponding step of (v_i,a_i,v_{i+1}) in E by property 1 in the theorem. Case 2, if $a_i \in \mathcal{A}_R^O$ then there must exist the corresponding step of (v_i,a_i,v_{i+1}) in E because of $\mathcal{A}_R^O = \mathcal{A}_E^I$ by Definition 3. If $a_i \notin shared(R,E)$ then there must exist the corresponding state of v_{i+1} that is the corresponding state of v_i in E by Definition of 6. Thus, property 2 holds by induction.

As follows, we prove that property 3 holds by contradiction.

Assume that there are the corresponding step of $\tau \in \mathcal{T}_R$ when $label(\tau) \in shared(R,E)$ or the corresponding states of $head(\tau)$ and $tail(\tau)$ when $label(\tau) \notin shared(R,E)$, where step τ does not satisfy the preconditions of property 1 and 2. Without loss of generality, suppose that $\tau = (v,a,v')$ and there is $\forall\,\alpha \in \Sigma\,.\,\forall\,\beta \in \overline{\phi_{\mathcal{L}}(\Sigma_R)} \setminus \Sigma\,.\,\tau \sqsubseteq \alpha \wedge \tau \not\sqsubseteq \beta$, where $\Sigma \subseteq \overline{\phi_{\mathcal{L}}(\Sigma_R)}$. This meaning is that τ is only on runs in $\Sigma \subseteq \overline{\phi_{\mathcal{L}}(\Sigma_R)}$. If $\tau \in \mathcal{T}_R^I \wedge label(\tau) \in shared(R,E)$ then a new IA E' can be obtained by deleting the corresponding step of τ from E. It is possible to conclude that $E' \in \mathrm{IE}_{\mathcal{L}}(R)$ and vav' is not covered by runs of $R \otimes E'$. Thus, E is not the SIE of R under $\mathcal{L}$. This contradicts the known condition. If $\tau \notin \mathcal{T}_R^I \vee label(\tau) \notin shared(R,E)$ then there must be $\forall\,\alpha \in \Sigma\,.\,\exists\,\tau' \prec_\alpha \tau\,.\,\forall\,\beta \in \phi_{\mathcal{L}}(\Sigma_R)\,.\,\tau' \in \mathcal{T}_R^I \wedge \tau' \not\sqsubseteq \beta$. Otherwise, τ must satisfy the precondition of property 2. Let $T(\tau) = \{\tau' \in \mathcal{T}_R^I \mid \forall\,\alpha \in \Sigma\,.\,\exists\,\tau' \prec_\alpha \tau\,.\,\forall\,\beta \in \phi_{\mathcal{L}}(\Sigma_R)\,.\,\tau' \not\sqsubseteq \beta\}$. A new IA E' can be obtained by deleting the corresponding steps of all step in $T(\tau)$ from E. Note that the corresponding state of v is unreachable in E after the deletion. It is possible to conclude that $E' \in \mathrm{IE}_{\mathcal{L}}(R)$ and vav' is not covered by runs of $R \otimes E'$. Thus, E is not the SEI of R under $\mathcal{L}$. This contradicts the known condition. To sum up, the assumption is wrong. Hence, property 3 holds.

In conclusion, if E is the SIE of R under $\mathcal{L}$ then it holds property 1, 2 and 3. Therefore, necessity holds. □

Proof of Theorem 3

1. According to Definition 8, the conclusion holds obviously.
2. According to Theorem 3.10 in [11], it is possible to conclude that for any environment E of R, η_2 cannot be covered by any runs of $R \otimes E$ if any one of (a) to (c) holds. Since $\eta_2 \sqsubseteq \alpha$, α cannot be covered by any runs of $R \otimes E$ either. Also, since $\exists \varrho \in \mathcal{L} . \varrho \propto \alpha$, inclusive environment of R under $\mathcal{L}$ does not exist according to Definition 8.

By 1 and 2, the theorem holds. □

Proof of the Correctness of Algorithm 1. According to the algorithm, there is $\phi_{\mathcal{L}}(\Sigma_R) = \phi_{\mathcal{L}}(\Sigma_{R'})$. Thus, the return of Algorithm 1 holds property 1 in Theorem 2. By line 5 to 18 in Algorithm 1, it is possible to conclude that all steps of R that satisfy the precondition of property 2 in Theorem 2 are steps of R'. Thus, the return of Algorithm 1 holds property 2 in Theorem 2. By line 5 to 18, it is possible to conclude that any step of R, say τ, which satisfies the property 3 in Theorem 2 is not the step of R', because there is $\tau \in \mathcal{T}$ or $head(\tau)$ is unreachable in R after deleting all steps in $\mathcal{T}$ from R. Thus, the return of Algorithm 1 holds property 3 in Theorem 2.

Accordingly, the return of Algorithm 1 is the SIE of R under $\mathcal{L}$ by Theorem 2. In conclusion, the correctness of Algorithm 1 holds. □

Verification of Computation Orchestration Via Timed Automata

Jin Song Dong, Yang Liu*, Jun Sun, and Xian Zhang

School of Computing,
National University of Singapore
Tel.: +65 68742834; Fax: +65 6779 4580
{dongjs, liuyang, sunj, zhangxi5}@comp.nus.edu.sg

Abstract. Recently, a promising programming model called *Orc* has been proposed to support a structured way of orchestrating distributed web services. *Orc* is intuitive because it offers concise constructors to manage concurrent communication, time-outs, priorities, failure of sites or communication and so forth. The semantics of *Orc* is also precisely defined. However, there is no verification tool available to verify critical properties against *Orc* models. Instead of building one from scratch, we believe the existing mature model-checkers can be reused. In this work, we first define a Timed Automata semantics for the *Orc* language, which we prove is semantically equivalent to the original operational semantics of *Orc*. Consequently, Timed Automata models are systematically constructed from *Orc* models. The practical implication of the construction is that tool supports for Timed Automata, e.g., UPPAAL, can be used to model check *Orc* models. An experimental tool is implemented to automate our approach.

1 Introduction

The prevalence of the Internet and web services raises the request of service-oriented computing [22], which can invoke remote services, process the results and communicate results with other terminals. However, it is very difficult and complex to design an orchestrating system with concurrency and synchronization using practical programming languages because these traditional languages use threads for concurrency and semaphores for synchronization. Even the higher-level libraries, like channel and working pool, have to be built up based on these primary elements.

Recently, a promising programming language Orc [17, 6] has been proposed for orchestrating distributed services in a structured manner. It abstracts all computations, web services and time control mechanisms as site calls, which are implemented by primitive remote procedures. With this abstraction, it provides a concise syntax for concurrent site call executions, threads synchronization and message passing. In addition, slow response and service failure can be easily handled using timing site calls. Using Orc, complicated orchestrating problems can be easily understood and constructed without worrying about the programming details.

Orc is as well precise and elegant. Both operational semantics [17] and denotational semantics (a tree semantics [18]) are defined. However, as a new emerging language,

* Corresponding author.

Z. Liu and J. He (Eds.): ICFEM 2006, LNCS 4260, pp. 226–245, 2006.

there are no formal verification mechanisms to systematically verify critical properties over systems modelled in Orc. In this work[1], we address the verification problem of the Orc language. Our aim is to detect possible violations of critical properties, especially timing properties, of Orc programs using an existing mature model checker. Our approach starts with defining an executable model in Timed Automata [1] for Orc expressions, which conforms with the semantics of the Orc language as defined in [6]. As a natural consequence, existing tool support for Timed Automata, e.g., UPPAAL [4], can be used for verification of Orc models. We use two examples, namely Auction Site and Purchase Order Handling System, to demonstrate our approach. Moreover, we implement a tool to construct UPPAAL models automatically from Orc models. Constrained by the Timed Automata theories, our approach focuses a subset of Orc language that is regular, type-safe and with a finite number of threads.

Orc has a strong theoretical foundation in process algebras, particularly CCS [15], CSP [12] and π-calculus [16]. These process algebras provide fundamental models of concurrency in which processes communicate over channels. However, Orc is different from the above process algebras as Orc permits integration of arbitrary components (sites) in a computation. More importantly, Orc has timing control to handle the site failures. Traditional process algebras have well established model checking theories and tool supports, e.g., FDR2 [20] for CSP, and FO$\lambda^{\Delta\nabla}$ [24] for π-calculus. Because of the absence of quantitative timing support, none of these tools can model and verify timing aspects of complex systems. There are some process algebras with time extensions, e.g., Timed CSP [21]. Unfortunately, there is no good model checker available[2]. Timed Automaton [1] is a notation developed for modelling and verification of real-time systems. It is a specialized finite state machine with clocks. Well developed automatic verification tools are available for Timed Automata [4, 7, 23]. This gives the inspiration of this work. Our Timed Automata semantics for Orc would allow Timed Automata verification techniques, theories and tools, to be applied to Orc.

Our work is related to works on BPEL4WS verification [10, 19] as BPEL4WS shares many common elements with Orc. BPEL4WS [13] (Business process orchestration languages for web services) is an XML based business process orchestration language. Both BPEL4WS and Orc orchestrate the web services by using process composition (sequential and parallel) and communication (synchronous and asynchronous). However they are different in several ways. BPEL4WS has a rich set of the language structures to ease the process design. Orc's concise syntax allows the reuse of the process definitions. BPEL4WS has variables to store the state of the communications and is able to receive calls from client web services. Orc is more abstract and as it focuses on process and communication. Orc has a well-defined semantics. Our work therefore focuses on defining an equivalent semantics for Orc in Timed Automata so as to use existing tools.

The rest of the paper is organized as follows: Section 2 briefly introduces the Orc language and the notation of Timed Automata. Section 3 presents an executable modelling

[1] Besides this work, our research team recently starts to work on a reasoning tool for Timed CSP.

[2] To our knowledge, the only tool support for TCSP is the preliminary PVS encoding of TCSP in Brooke's PhD thesis [5].

in Timed Automata for each and every constructor in Orc. Section 4 demonstrates how UPPAAL is used to verify the Orc language using two case studies. Section 5 concludes the paper with possible future works.

2 Background

This section is devoted to a brief introduction to the relevant languages and notations, namely the Orc computation model and Timed Automata.

2.1 Orchestration Language Orc

The syntax and informal semantics of Orc are described in this section. Formal definition of Orc semantics can be found elsewhere at [6].

In the following syntax, E is an expression name, M a site name, x a variable, c a constant, P a list of actual parameters and Q a list of formal parameters.

$$\begin{array}{lll} D \in Decl & ::= & E(Q) \widehat{=} f \\ f, g \in Expression & ::= & \mathbf{0} \parallel M(P) \parallel E(P) \parallel f >x> g \parallel f \mid g \parallel f \textbf{ where } x :\in g \\ p \in Actual & ::= & x \parallel c \parallel M \\ q \in Formal & ::= & x \parallel M \end{array}$$

Declaration $E(Q) \widehat{=} f$ defines expression E whose formal parameter list is Q and body is expression f. An expression is either elementary or a composition of two expressions. An elementary expression is either: (1) $\mathbf{0}$, a site which never responds, (2) a site call $M(P)$, or (3) an expression call $E(P)$. Orc has three composition operators: (1) $>x>$ for sequential composition, (2) $\mid$ for symmetric parallel composition, and (3) **where** for asymmetric parallel composition.

Site. The basic element of Orc expression is a site call. A site is a separately defined procedure, e.g., a web service implemented on a remote machine. A site call can give at most one response; it is possible that a site never responds to a call, which is treated as non-terminating computation. A site call has the same form as a function call: the name of a site followed by an optional list of parameters. For example, calling site $Google(w)$ where $Google$ is an internet search engine and w is a keyword, may return the web sites links related to the keyword. Calling $Email(a,m)$ sends message m to address a, causing a permanent change in the recipient's mailbox, and returns a signal to denote completion of the operation. Site calls are strict, i.e., a site is called only if all its parameters have values. Table 1 lists the fundamental sites used in Orc for effective programming.

Sequential Composition Operator. Sequential operator $>x>$ allows strict sequencing of site calls. For example, $Google(w) >m> Email(a,m)$ will first call site $Google$, and name the returned value as m. After that $Email(a,m)$ is called. If either site fails to respond, then the evaluation returns no value. The simpler notation $M \gg N$ is used when the value returned by site M is of no significance. To send two emails in sequence and then call Notify, we write

$$Email(addr1, m) \gg Email(addr2, m) \gg Notify$$

Table 1. Fundamental Sites

0	never responds. It can be used to terminate a computation.
$let(x, y, ...)$	returns a tuple consisting of the values of its arguments.
Clock	returns the current time at the server of this site as an integer.
$Atimer(t)$	where t is integer and $t \geq Clock$, returns a signal at time t.
$Rtimer(t)$	where t is integer and $t \geq 0$, returns a signal after exactly t time units.
$if(b)$	where b is boolean, returns a signal if b is true, and remains silent (no response) if false.
Signal	returns a signal immediately. It is the same as $Rtimer(0)$.

Symmetric Parallel Operator. Symmetric parallel operator $|$ gives the power of multi-threaded computation. Evaluation of $f \mid g$, creates two threads to compute f and g respectively. The result from $f \mid g$ is the interleaving of these two streams in time order. If both threads produce values simultaneously, they are merged arbitrarily. Operator $|$ is commutative and associative. An interesting expression is $(Google(w) \mid Yahoo(w)) > m > Email(a, m)$. Here, the first part $(Google(w) \mid Yahoo(w))$ may publish multiple values, and for each value v, we call $Email(a, m)$ where m is set to v. Therefore, the evaluation can cause up to two emails to be sent, one with the value from *Google* and the other from *Yahoo*.

Asymmetric Parallel Operator. The asymmetric parallel operator **where** is used to prune portions of a computation selectively: $Email(a, m)$ **where** $m :\in (Google(w) \mid Yahoo(w))$ sends at most one email, with the first value received from either *Google* or *Yahoo*. In this expression, $Email(a, m)$ and $(Google(w) \mid Yahoo(w))$ are evaluated simultaneously. $Email(a, m)$ is blocked because m does not have a value. Evaluation of $(Google(w) \mid Yahoo(w))$ may return up to two values; the first value is assigned to m and further evaluation of this expression is then terminated. After that, $Email(a, m)$ is unblocked and executed.

Expression Definition. An expression is defined like a procedure, with a name and possible parameters, though it may return a stream of values. As an example, consider the following restaurant reservation process, where $R1$ and $R2$ are two restaurants, and t is the meal time. The user is notified for the first acknowledgement received from the two restaurants, if any.

$$Reservation(t) \mathrel{\widehat{=}} Notify(x) \textbf{ where } x :\in R1(t) \mid R2(t)$$

Recursive definition is also supported in Orc. The following expression defines a *Clock* using $Rtimer(t)$, which emits a signal every time unit, starting immediately.

$$Clock \mathrel{\widehat{=}} Signal \mid Rtimer(1) \gg Clock$$

Dining Philosophers. An example of using Orc is the classical dining philosophers problem, originally presented in [17]. There are N Philosophers, sitting around a table. Every pair of neighbors shares a fork. The fork to the left of Philosopher i is $Fork_i$ and to his right is $Fork_{i'}$ ($i' = (i+1)$ *mod* N). Philosopher i can eat only if it holds both left and right forks. A philosopher's life cycle consists of the following activities: acquire the two adjacent forks, eat, and release the forks. Because of the seating arrangement, neighboring philosophers can not eat simultaneously.

Each $Fork_i$ is modelled as a FIFO buffered channel which is either empty (if some philosopher holds the corresponding fork) or has one signal (if no philosopher holds the fork). We write $Fork_i.put$ to send a signal along the channel and $Fork_i.get$ to get a signal from the channel. Initially, each channel holds a signal. In this example, P_i $(0 \leq i < N)$ depicts philosopher i, where the right neighbor of P_i is $P_{i'}$ ($i' = (i+1)$ *mod* N), and *Eat* returns a signal on completion of eating.

$$\begin{aligned} P_i \mathrel{\widehat{=}} (&let(x,y) \gg Eat \gg Fork_i.put \gg Fork_{i'}.put \\ &\textbf{where } x :\in Fork_i.get, y :\in Fork_{i'}.get) \gg P_i \end{aligned}$$

The dining philosophers problem can be represented as:

$$DP \mathrel{\widehat{=}} P_0 \mid P_1 \mid \cdots \mid P_{N-1}$$

This definition of dining philosophers can lead to deadlock. To avoid deadlock, philosophers should pick up their forks in a specific order. For instance, all except P_0 pick up their left and then their right forks, and P_0 picks up its right and then its left fork.

$$\begin{aligned} &P'_0 \mathrel{\widehat{=}} Fork_1.get \gg Fork_0.get \gg Eat \gg Fork_1.put \gg Fork_0.put \gg P'_0 \\ &P'_i(1 \leq i < N) \mathrel{\widehat{=}} Fork_i.get \gg Fork_{i'}.get \gg Eat \gg Fork_i.put \gg Fork_{i'}.put \gg P'_i \\ &DP' \mathrel{\widehat{=}} P'_0 \mid P'_1 \mid \cdots \mid P'_{N-1} \end{aligned}$$

2.2 Timed Automata and UPPAAL

Timed Automata are finite state machines equipped with clocks. It is a formal notation to model behaviors of real-time systems. Its definition provides a general way to annotate state transition graphs with timing constraints using finitely many real-valued clock variables. Given a set of clock C, the set of clock constraints $\Phi(C)$ is defined as:

$$\phi := x \leq c \mid c \leq x \mid x < c \mid c < x \mid \phi_1 \wedge \phi_2$$

where x is a clock variable and c is a real number.

Definition 1 (Timed Automata). *A timed automaton $\mathcal{A}$ is a 6-tuple $\langle S, s_0, \Sigma, C, I, T\rangle$, where S is a finite set of states, s_0 is the initial state, Σ is the alphabet, C is a finite set of clocks, $I : S \to \Phi(C)$ is a mapping from a state to a state invariant, and $T \subseteq S \times \Sigma \times 2^C \times \Phi(C) \times S$ is the transition relation.* □

In Timed Automata, a state is associated with an invariant, while a transition is labelled with a synchronization action, a guard (a constraint on clocks) and a clock reset (a set of clocks to be reset). Intuitively, a timed automaton starts execution with all clocks initialized to zero. The automaton can stay at a node, as long as the invariant of the node is satisfied, with all clocks increasing at the same rate. A transition can be taken if the values of the clocks fulfill the guard. By taking the transition, all clocks in the clock reset are set to zero, while the clocks not in the clock reset keep their values. For example, Figure 1 illustrates some simple timed automata. Graphically, a double-lined circle indicates an initial state. Typically, a Timed Automata modelling of complex systems would consist of a network of timed automata[3].

Definition 2 (Timed Automata Network). *A network of timed automata is the parallel composition of a collection of $\mathcal{A}_1, \ldots, \mathcal{A}_n$, denoted as $\mathcal{A}_1 \parallel \cdots \parallel \mathcal{A}_n$. A transition of the network of timed automata is either a local step of one of the automata where $(s_1, e, c, i, s_2) \in \mathcal{A}_i \wedge e \notin (\bigcup_{k:1..n \wedge k \neq i} \Sigma_k)$ or a pairwise synchronization between two automata where $(s_1, e!, c, i, s_2) \in \mathcal{A}_i$ and $(s_1', e?, c', i', s_2') \in \mathcal{A}_j$.* □

UPPAAL [4] is our choice of model-checker for verifying a network of timed automata because of its efficiency (both for model-checking and simulation) as well as its wide recognition. UPPAAL is a tool for modelling, simulation and verification of real-time systems modelled as timed automata. It consists of three main parts, a system editor which provides a graphical interface to design timed automata, a simulator and a model checker. The simulator is a validation tool which enables examination of possible dynamic executions of a system and thus provides an inexpensive mean of fault detection prior to verification by the model checker which covers the exhaustive dynamic behavior of the system. The model checker checks invariant and bounded liveness properties by exploring the symbolic state space of a system. The properties are expressed as a rich subset of TCTL [11]. In a nutshell, UPPAAL is a model checker for systems that can be modelled as a collection of non-deterministic processes with finite control structure and real valued clocks, communicating through channels or shared variables. Typical applications include real-time controllers and communication protocols, e.g., those where timing aspects are critical. In this work, we extend its application to orchestration of web services.

3 Timed Automata Semantics for Orc

This section is devoted to a definition of Timed Automata semantics for Orc models, which allows us to systematically construct the Timed Automata model from an Orc model. The practical implication is that we may then reuse existing tools and theories for Timed Automata to achieve various purposes, for instance, synthesis of implementation [3], simulation [2], theorem proving [14] or more importantly formal verification [4]. In the following, the Timed Automata semantics for Orc expressions is formally defined. The dining philosophers example is used as a running example.

Definition 3 (Zero Site). *A zero site* **0** *is modelled as an automaton $\mathcal{A}_\mathbf{0}$ where $S = \{s_i, s_1\}$ and $\Sigma = \{call_\mathbf{0}\}$ and $C = \varnothing$ and $I = \varnothing$ and $T = \{s_i, call_\mathbf{0}, \varnothing, true, s_1\}$.* □

A zero site is a site that never responds. Thus there is no *publish* event, as illustrated in Figure 1(a). The formal definition of the automaton for the fundamental site *Rtimer*(t) is presented below, which plays the central role in the timing aspect of the orchestration.

[3] We may treat an automata network as one automata by constructing the product. However, leaving it as a network saves us from the state space explosion problem as well as allowing us to benefit from optimization built in the timed automata tools.

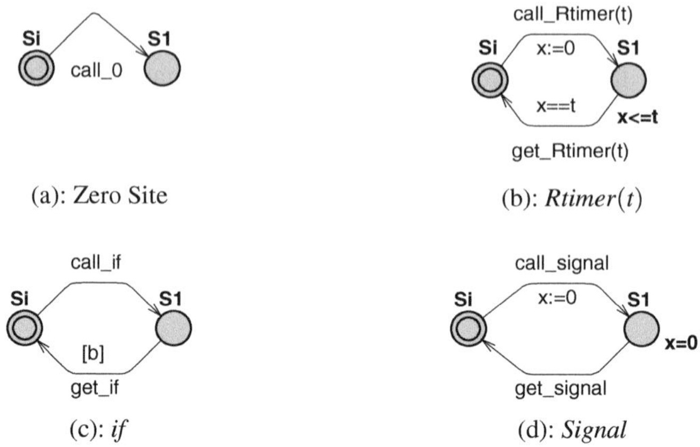

Fig. 1. Fundamental Sites

Definition 4 **($Rtimer(t)$).** *A $Rtimer(t)$ site is modelled as an automaton $\mathcal{A}_{Rtimer(t)}$ where $S = \{s_i, s_1\}$ and $\Sigma = \{call_{Rtimer(t)}, get_{Rtimer(t)}\}$ and $C = \{x\}$ and $I = \varnothing$ and $T = \{(s_i, call_{Rtimer(t)}, \{x\}, true, s_1), (s_1, get_{Rtimer(t)}, \varnothing, x = t, s_i)\}$.* □

The Timed Automaton for $Rtimer(t)$ is illustrated in Figure 1(b). Once the site is called via the synchronization on the $call_{Rtimer(t)}$ event, the local clock x is reset to 0. After exactly t time units, the calling site is notified via the $get_{Rtimer(t)}$ event. Notice that we adopt the synchronous semantics of Orc in this definition. In the asynchronous semantics, arbitrary delays in processing events are allowed, including the $call_{Rtimer(t)}$ event. Consequently, all we can assert about the call to $Rtimer(t)$ is that client will receive the signal *sometime* after t unit delay, which is too weak for program time-outs or timed-interrupts. We believe that the synchronous semantics is intuitive and powerful. However, the asynchronous semantics can be easily captured by changing the $\Phi(C)$ on the transition from s_1 to s_i as $x \geq t$ and removing the state invariant on state s_1.

Similarly, fundamental sites $call_{if}$ and $call_{Signal}$ are defined as timed automata as well, which are illustrated in Figure 1 (c) and (d) respectively. $call_{Atimer(t)}$ is ignored since $Atimer(t)$ can represented as $Rtimer(t - c)$, where c is the current clock value. $call_{let}$ is a simple Timed Automaton similar to $call_{if}$, but the second transition is the *publish* event without condition b.

The fundamental sites presented so far are defined as the complete expression calls (see definition 9). If we only consider timed automata for the Orc contracts of the fundamental sites, then the *call* events should be removed, e.g., the zero site **0** contains just a single state without any transitions.

Definition 5 **(Site Call).** *A site call $M(P)$ is modelled as an automaton $\mathcal{A}_{M(P)}$ where $S = \{s_i, s_1, s_2, s_3\}$, $\Sigma = \{call_{M(P)}, get_{M(P)}, publish_{M(P)}\}$, $C = \varnothing$, $I = \varnothing$, and $T = \{(s_i, call_{M(P)}, \varnothing, true, s_1), (s_1, get_{M(P)}, \varnothing, true, s_2), (s_2, publish_{M(P)}, \varnothing, true, s_3)\}$.* □

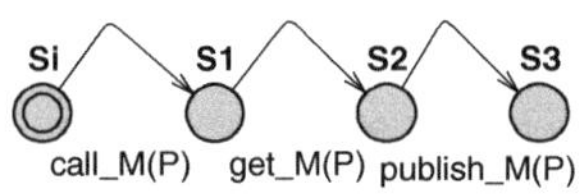

Fig. 2. TA for Site Call

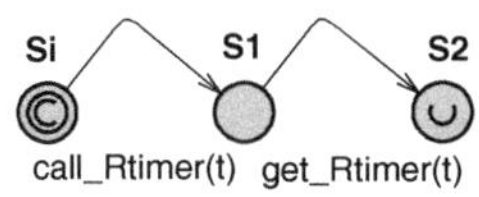

Fig. 3. TA for *Rtimer*(t) Call

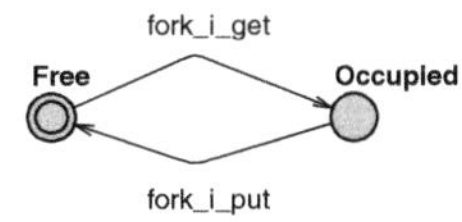

Fig. 4. TA for $Fork_i$

A site call is modelled as a timed automaton allowing a *call* event which invokes the service and a *get* event which gets the response from the called site and a *publish* event which publishes the response, illustrated in Figure 2. This conforms the operational semantics of site call, i.e., the three steps of invocation, response, publication as in [6].

A special kind of site calls is the calls to *Rtimer*(t) and *Signal* because of the timing constraints. The invocation of *Rtimer*(t) site is shown in Figure 3 (*Signal* calls are ignored for the similarity). The initial state is set as committed state[4], which will fire the outgoing event $call_{Rtimer(t)}$ immediately with the top priority among all transitions. The finishing state is set as an urgent state[5], which stops the timer in the finishing state. By using the committed and urgent states, we can get exactly t time units between the initial state and finishing state.

The behavior of the external called site must be specified as a separate timed automaton for the sake of verification. For example, the behaviors of the forks in the dining philosophers example are modelled as in Figure 4, where the user may repeatedly get the fork and then put it back. Consequently, a site call $Fork_i.put$ is interpreted as a synchronization on the $call_{Fork_i.out}$ (simplified as $Fork_i.put$ in this example). For an abstract site call like *Eat*, instead of building a trivial automaton which synchronizes on the *call* event and then returns a signal, it is treated as an abstract local event for the sake of efficient verification[6].

Definition 6 (Sequential Composition). *Let the automata network of g be* $\mathcal{A}_g \mathrel{\widehat{=}} \mathcal{A}_1 \parallel \ldots \parallel \mathcal{A}_n$. *A sequential composition* $f >x> g$ *is modelled as a timed automata network* $\mathcal{A}_{f>\!x\!>g} \mathrel{\widehat{=}} \mathcal{A}_f \parallel \mathcal{A}'_g$ *where,* $\mathcal{A}'_g \mathrel{\widehat{=}} (\mathcal{A}'_1 \parallel \ldots \parallel \mathcal{A}'_n)^k$ *and for all* $i : 1 \,..\, n$, $\mathcal{A}'_i \mathrel{\widehat{=}} \langle S, s_i, \Sigma, C, I, T\rangle$ *where* $S = \mathcal{A}_i.S \cup \{s_i\}$ *and* $\Sigma = \mathcal{A}_i.\Sigma \cup \{publish_x\}$ *and* $C = \mathcal{A}_i.C$ *and* $I = \mathcal{A}_i.I$ *and* $T = \mathcal{A}_i.T \cup \{(s_i, publish_x, \varnothing, true, \mathcal{A}_i.s_i)\}$. □

Notice that a channel[7] named $publish_x$ is defined to synchronize the publishing of a value of x and the receiving of the value.

A sequential composition is modelled as, in general, a network of timed automata. The network of f is untouched, whereas the automata in the network of g have to synchronize on the event $publish_x$ before making a step. If there is no value passing between

[4] In UPPAAL, committed states freeze time. If any process is in a committed location, the next transition must involve an edge from one of the committed locations.

[5] In UPPAAL, urgent states are semantically equivalent to adding an extra clock x, that is reset on all incoming edges, and having an invariant $x \leq 0$ on the location. Hence, time is not allowed to pass when the system is in an urgent location.

[6] In UPPAAL, it corresponds to a transition labelled with no channel event.

[7] In UPPAAL, a broadcast channel is used here in order to do the synchronization for all paralleled automata in the g.

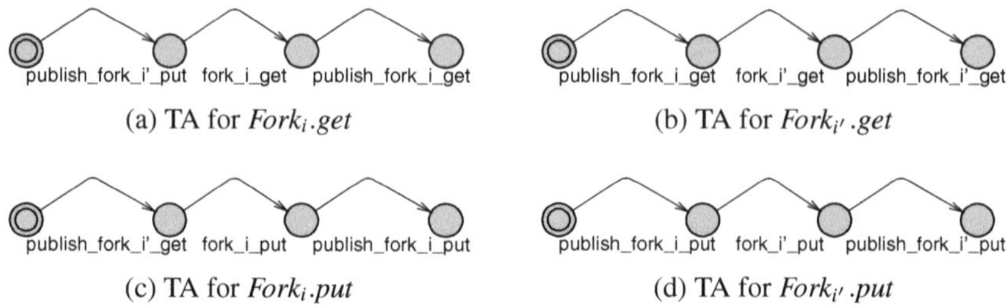

(a) TA for $Fork_i.get$ (b) TA for $Fork_{i'}.get$

(c) TA for $Fork_i.put$ (d) TA for $Fork_{i'}.put$

Fig. 5. Network of Automata for $P'_i(1 \leq i \leq N)$

the Orc expressions, the first publishing signal, i.e., event $publish_x$, is used to precede the automata for expression g.

To abuse the notations, we use $\mathcal{A}^k$ to denote a network containing k copies of the same automaton $\mathcal{A}$. The network of f is parallel-composed with multiple copies of network of g. Every time a new value of x is published, a new instance of the g component is created and starts execution. In general, there would be infinite number of overlapping activations of the g component. However, if we assume the g part executes reasonably fast (and terminating), we need only a finite number of copies of g to fork and reuse them once they are terminated. For the sake of verification of real world applications, we always assume that there is an upper bound on the number of overlapping activation of the g part. For example, Figure 5 presents the automata interpretation of the $P'_i(1 \leq i \leq N)$ in the dining philosophers example, where each site call is model as a TA and local event *eat* has been removed for simplicity. In general, multiple copies of each of the automata is required. However, only one copy for each automaton is shown as that is all that is needed in this case.

Definition 7 (Symmetric Parallel Composition). *A symmetric parallel composition* $f \mid g$ *is modelled as a network of two timed automata (networks)* $\mathcal{A}_f \parallel \mathcal{A}_g$. □

A symmetric parallel composition is modelled as two automata (networks) running in parallel. There is no communication between the f and g. f and g are probably remote site call to services which run independently on remote machines. Thus, two automata (networks) sharing no common event are used to capture the interleaving behaviors. For example, the automata network for DP' in the dining philosophers example is the network containing the networks in Figure 5 (one for each i).

The last compositional constructor of Orc is the asymmetric parallel composition, denoted f **where** $x :\in g$. According to the semantics in [6], the g expression terminates as soon as one value of x is published. This kind of dynamic termination of timed automata is achieved through the use of a shared global flag.

Definition 8 (Asymmetric Parallel Composition). *Let flag be a global boolean variable. It is initially true. Let the network of the expression g be* $\mathcal{A}_g \mathrel{\widehat=} \mathcal{A}_1 \parallel \cdots \parallel \mathcal{A}_n$. *An asymmetric parallel composition* f **where** $x :\in g$ *is modelled as a network of timed automata* $\mathcal{A}_{f\ \mathbf{where}\ x:\in g} \mathrel{\widehat=} \mathcal{A}_f \parallel \mathcal{A}'_g$ *where,* $\mathcal{A}'_g = \mathcal{A}'_1 \parallel \cdots \parallel \mathcal{A}'_n$ *and for all* $i : 1 \mathrel{..} n$, $\mathcal{A}'_i \mathrel{\widehat=} \langle \mathcal{A}_i.S, \mathcal{A}_i.s_i, \mathcal{A}_i.\Sigma, \mathcal{A}_i.C, \mathcal{A}_i.I, T \rangle$ *where*

$T = \{(s_1, publish_x, cl', gc, s_2) \mid (s_1, publish_x, cl, gc, s_2) \in \mathcal{A}_i.T\}$
$\cup\{(s_1, e, cl, gc \wedge flag, s_2) \mid e \neq publish_x \wedge (s_1, e, cl, gc, s_2) \in \mathcal{A}_i.T\}$
wherecl'setsflagtofalseandresetstheclocksinclusingassignmentin UPPAAL. □

As soon as a publishing of x is achieved, the global flag is set to be *false* (this is atomic since they are on the same transition). Consequently all transitions in the network of the expression g are blocked. Therefore, the network of g terminates. Notice that the flag is carefully implemented so that it is local to the automata in $\mathcal{A}'_g$ (by defining a unique global variable for each activation of the network). The execution of $\mathcal{A}_f$ is not blocked until a synchronization on event $publish_x$ is required. Therefore, it may make steps in parallel or even before g does. We remark that while our definitions of timed automata interpretation for Orc expression are generic, there are plenty of simplifications and optimizations to be performed on the constructed timed automata. For example, the P_i expression is modelled (and simplified) as the automaton in Figure 6.

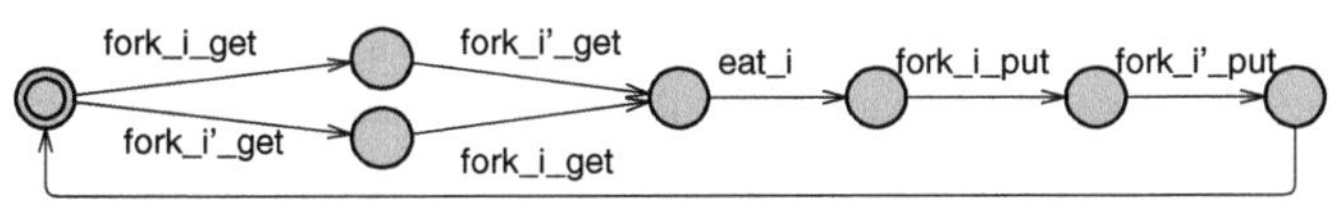

Fig. 6. Timed Automata for P_i

Definition 9 (Expression Call). *An expression call is $E(P)$ with $E(P) \mathrel{\widehat{=}} f$ is modelled as the network of timed automata for f prefixed by the $call_E(P)$ event, i.e., $\mathcal{A}_{E(P)} \mathrel{\widehat{=}} \langle S, s_i, \Sigma, C, I, T\rangle$, where $S = \{s_i \cup \mathcal{A}_f.S\}$ and $\Sigma = \{call_{E(P)} \cup \mathcal{A}_f.\Sigma\}$ and $C = \mathcal{A}_f.C$ and $I = \mathcal{A}_f.I$ and $T = \{(s_i, call_{E(P)}, \varnothing, true, \mathcal{A}_f.s_i) \cup \mathcal{A}_f.T\}$..* □

For each parameter x of the expression call, a channel $publish_x$ is defined to synchronize with the publishing of a value of the parameter x. In case there are multiple parameters, the expression call is executed only after all the parameters get their values (via synchronization on the corresponding channels). Publishing of the parameters may occur in any order.

For simple recursion where there is only one automaton instead of an automata network when the recursion call is reached (with our simplification and optimization done), we connect the last state to the initial state to make a loop, e.g., the automaton in Figure 6. In general, recursion is resolved by replacing it with the least fixed point. However, Orc does allow expressions like $N = f \mid N$ where there could be infinite number of copies of f. These kinds of expressions are disallowed for the sake of model checking.

The soundness of the Timed Automata modelling is proved by showing that there is a weak bi-simulation relation between the timed automata and the operational semantics of Orc. The following theorem is proved by a structural induction over our definitions and the operational semantics of Orc defined in [17] (see Appendix for the proof details).

Theorem 1. *For any Orc expression[8] f, $\mathcal{A}_f \approx \mathcal{O}_f$, where $\mathcal{O}_f$ is the state transition system constructed from the operational semantics of Orc in [17].* □

[8] We focus on a subset of Orc langauge that is regular, type-safe and with a finite number of threads (see Section 4 for details).

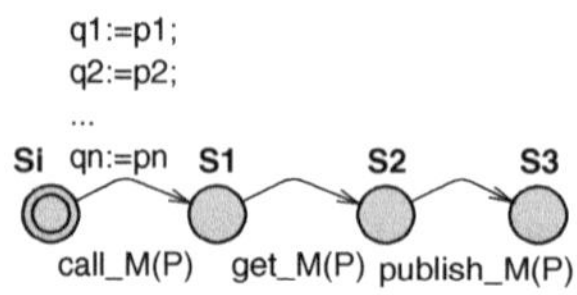

Fig. 7. TA for Site Call with Value Passing

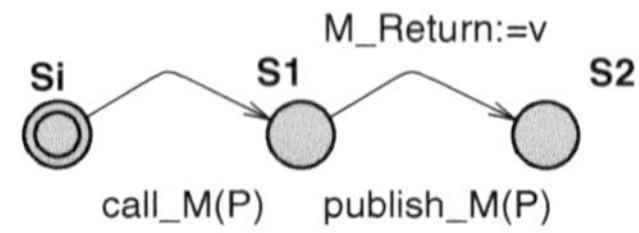

Fig. 8. TA for Site with Value Passing

Value Passing Handling

Timed Automata do not have notions for variables and assignments. Fortunately UPPAAL as an extension of Timed Automata introduces variables (both local and global) and variable assignments (in events). Hence parameter passing can be realized through some globally shared variables since no data can be attached along a channel communication. It is obvious that these shared variables must have unique names. Because the names of site calls are unique, we prefix all the formal parameters' names with their site call names. The return values of each site call are named as site call name + "Return".

To invoke a site call, the formal parameters are assigned to the value of actual parameters in the *call* event in the Site Call model. The complete model of $call_{M(P)}$ is shown in Figure 7. The return value of a site is assigned in the *publish* event in the Site model (Figure 8). The sequential composition $f >x> g$ has an additional assignment $x := f_{Return}$ for variable x in the *publish* event of f. Similarly for asymmetric parallel composition f **where** $x :\in g$, we add the assignment $x := g_{Return}$ in the *publish* event of g. The expression call $E(P) \mathrel{\widehat{=}} f$ has also an assignment in the *publish* event for its return value.

4 Verification Using UPPAAL

This section is devoted to a discuss on how to use tool support for Timed Automata, in particular UPPAAL, to formally analyze the constructed Timed Automata. In general, our modelling of Orc may end up with a network containing an infinite number of automata (see Definitions 6 and 9). One piece of evidence of an possibly infinite number of automata is that Orc in general allows an irregular language (as in automata theory). Our target is therefore a subset of Orc langauge that is regular, type-safe and only allows a finite number of threads. Some Orc examples that we regard as problematic are as the following:

$P \mathrel{\widehat{=}} b \mid a \gg P \gg c$, where a, b, c are sites or even expressions
$M \mathrel{\widehat{=}} f(x)\ where\ let(0) \mid Signal$
$N \mathrel{\widehat{=}} x$ **where** $x :\in N$

P in general allows the language of the form $a^n bc^n$ which is a typical example of an irregular language. It is a known fact that such languages can not be expressed using finite automata. Therefore, they are beyond automata-based model checking. M is not type safe because the type of x can be either integer 0 or a signal. In general, x could be any type. This as well presents a problem to current model-checking techniques. Lastly,

N allows an infinitely number of threads of f running independently, which would result in an infinite internal loop without returning a value, i.e., a divergence in CSP's terms.

4.1 Automated Construction

We developed an experimental tool to automatically construct UPPAAL models from Orc models using XML and Java technology. We start with parsing the Orc program and building an Abstract Syntax Tree. Afterwards, each Orc language construct is converted to a timed automaton or a network of time automata according to our definitions in Section 3. The output of the program is an XML representation of the UPPAAL model, which is ready to be employed and verified. The experimental tool and Orc examples appeared in this paper can be found on the web [9].

We briefly mention some of the implementation issues here. Because UPPAAL does not allow data to pass through channels, global variables are carefully defined to pass along the values, i.e., a *publish* event is always attached with an assignment to the respective global variable. An aggressive simplification procedure is applied whenever possible to simplify and optimize the constructed Timed Automata. For instance, when we apply Definition 6, if we are certain there is only one copy of g required, we may do the product of the two automata and remove the *publish* event given that it does not affect the rest of the model. We also try to minimize the number of clock variables by reusing the same ones as so to speed up the verification. However, the simplification and optimization remains as a challenging task and we may improve it by considering Orc laws.

Once the UPPAAL model is built, we may import it using UPPAAL and do verification. For example, it can be easily verified that the first Orc model of the dining philosophers can lead to deadlock. In our experiment, we created 5 philosophers and 5 fork instances. Afterwards we checked if the model is deadlock free using the following property: $A[]$ *not deadlock*. UPPAAL reports that the property does not hold for the system. A counterexample where all philosophers pick up their left fork can be found via random simulation. In the case that the first philosopher always picks up the right fork, we verify that the Orc model is deadlock-free and it satisfies properties like that no more than half of the philosophers can be eating at the same time etc.

4.2 Case Study: Orchestrating an Auction

In this subsection, we demonstrate the construction of the UPPAAL model from Orc as well as property checking through a typical web-based application, i.e., running an auction for an item. This example was originally presented in [17].

First, the item is advertised by calling site $Adv(v_0)$, which posts its description and a minimum bid price at a web site. Bidders put their bids on specific channels. In UPPAAL, a template called *Bidder* is built, which outputs a bid on channel *bid*. In general, there are multiple *Bidders*. A *Multiplexor* is used to merge all the bids into a single channel, i.e., *bid*. The Timed Automata for the sites (like, $Adv(v_0)$, $PostNext(m)$ and $PostFinal(n)$) used in this example are not shown, because they have the same structure as the TA in Figure 8.

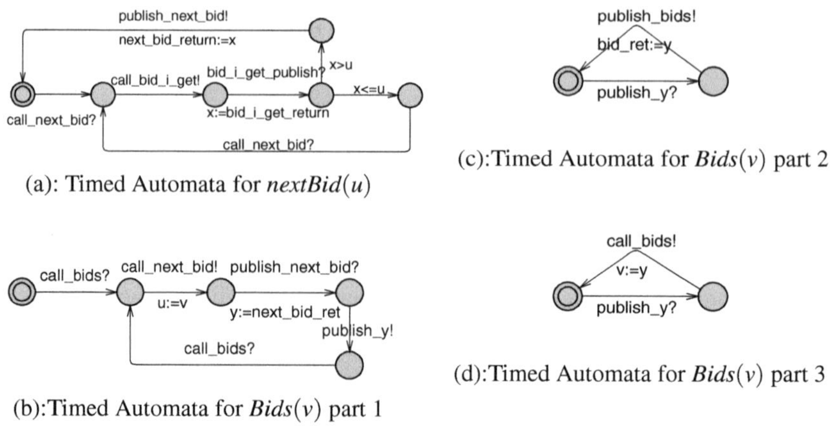

(a): Timed Automata for $nextBid(u)$

(c):Timed Automata for $Bids(v)$ part 2

(b):Timed Automata for $Bids(v)$ part 1

(d):Timed Automata for $Bids(v)$ part 3

Fig. 9. Basic Sites in Auction Example

$$Multiplexor_i \mathrel{\widehat{=}} bid_i.get >y> bid.put(y) \gg Multiplexor_i$$
$$Multiplexor \mathrel{\widehat{=}} Multiplexor_1 \mid Multiplexor_2 \mid \ldots \mid Multiplexor_i$$

Three variations on the auction strategy, $Auction_i(v)$ $(1 \leq i \leq 3)$ are considered. We start the auction by executing $z :\in Auction_i(V)$ where V is the minimum acceptable bid.

Non-terminating Auction . The first solution continually takes the next bid from channel *bid* which exceeds the current (highest) bid and posts it at a web site by calling *PostNext*.

$$nextBid(u) \mathrel{\widehat{=}} bid.get >x> \{(if(x > u) \gg let(x)) \mid (if(x \leq u) \gg nextBid(u))\}$$
$$Bids(v) \mathrel{\widehat{=}} nextBid(v) >y> (let(y) \mid Bids(y))$$

Orc expression $nextBid(v)$ returns the next bid from c exceeding v. The site call $if(x > v)$ returns a signal if $x > v$ and remains silent otherwise. $Bids(v)$ returns a stream of bids from *bid* where the first bid exceeds v and successive bids are strictly increasing. The following strategy starts the auction by advertising the item, and posts successively higher bids at a web site. But the expression evaluation never terminates. The Timed Automata of $nextBid(u)$ and $Bids(v)$ are shown in Figure 9. The Timed Automata of $nextBid(u)$ is simplified by combining the two if-condition automata with the main $nextBid(u)$ TA, because the two conditions $(x > u)$ and $(x \leq u)$ are exclusive.

$$Auction_1(p) \mathrel{\widehat{=}} Adv(p) \gg Bids(p) >z> PostNext(z) \gg \mathbf{0}$$

Following the Timed Automata semantics defined in Section 3, $Auction_1(v)$ is interpreted as the automata in Figures 10 and 11.

By checking with UPPAAL, we can see that this version of the auction system is deadlock free, which means it never terminates. In this example, we assume that expression $let(y)$ in $Bids(v)$ is carried out fast enough so that there will not be an infinite number of threads of $let(y)$. In addition to deadlock-freeness, we may verify properties like a bid is never lower than the minimum (see examples in Table 2).

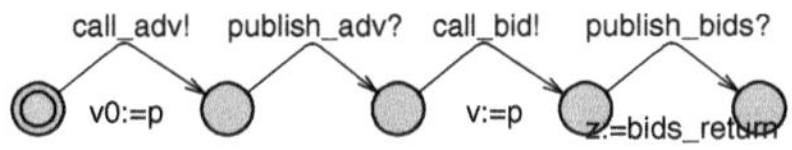

Fig. 10. TA for $Auction_1$ part 1

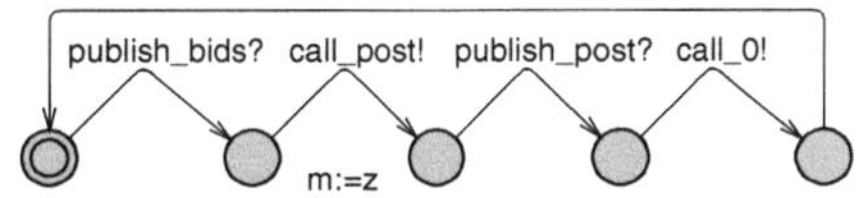

Fig. 11. TA for $Auction_1$ part 2

Table 2. Experiment Results

Orc	Property	Result	Time(s)	Remark
$Auction_1$	*A[] not deadlock*	true	20	Non-terminating.
$Auction_1$	*A[] not (PostNext.posted<250)*	true	3	No bid price lower 250.
$Auction_1$	*A[] not(old==0) imply new>old*	true	90	Price posted on the *PostNext* site keeps increasing.
$Auction_1$	*E<> PostNext.posted == 500*	true	1	Possible to post 500.
$Auction_2$	*A[] not deadlock*	false	1	Terminating.
$Auction_2$	*A[] PostFinal.postFinal imply Auc.c>=h*	true	150	Auction terminates after *h* time units.
$Auction_2$	*A[] PostFinal.final == 1000 imply Bidder10.bid == true*	true	10	The final bid comes from the respective bidder.
$Auction_3$	*A[] not deadlock*	false	1	Terminating.
$Auction_3$	*E[] not(PostNext.p1<h and PostNext.p1>0)*	true	60	It is not possible to post a highest bid before *h* time units.

In order to save space, the automata in the next two examples have been simplified whenever possible. Committed states are used to prevent undesired interleaving behaviors. For example, it is used to publish multiple signals at once for expressions like $let(x,y,z)$.

Terminating Auction. The previous program is modified so that the auction terminates if no higher bid arrives for *h* time units (say, *h* is an hour). The winning bid is then posted by calling *PostFinal*, and the goal variable is assigned the value of the winning bid. The expression $Tbids(v)$, where v is a bid, returns a stream of pairs $(x, flag)$, where x is a bid value, $x \geq v$, and *flag* is boolean. If *flag* is *true*, then x exceeds its previous bid, and if *false* then x equals its previous bid, i.e., no higher bid has been received in an hour.

$$\begin{aligned} &Tbids(v) \mathrel{\widehat{=}} let(x, flag) \mid if(flag) \gg Tbids(x) \\ &\qquad \textbf{where } (x, flag) :\in nextBid(v) >y> let(y, true) \mid Rtimer(h) \gg let(v, false) \\ &Auction_2(v) \mathrel{\widehat{=}} Adv(v) \gg Tbids(v) >(x, flag)> \\ &\qquad \{if(flag) \gg PostNext(x) \gg \mathbf{0} \mid if(flag) \gg PostFinal(x) \gg let(x)\} \end{aligned}$$

In this auction, a new site call named *PostFinal* is added which is quite similar to *PostNext*. The difference between a non-terminating auction and a terminating auction is that a *time-out* (*h* time unit) process is added. As *time-out* (or *timed-interrupt*) is a typical timing behavior, we do define some templates to treat them specially and effectively. A list of typical composable timing patterns formally defined in terms of Timed Automata is available elsewhere in [8]. For example in Figure 12, we can use the

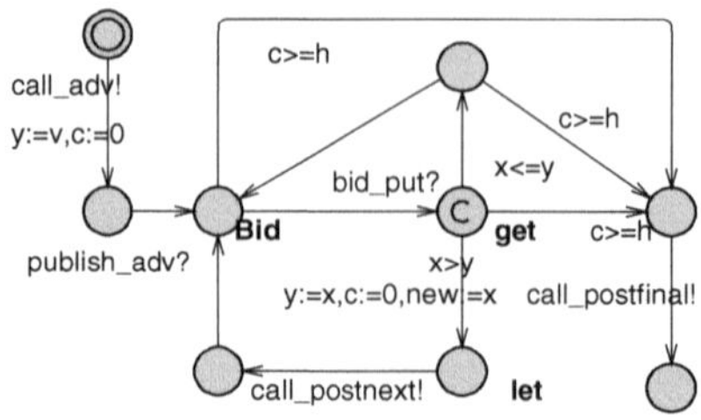

Fig. 12. Auction$_2$: Terminating Auction

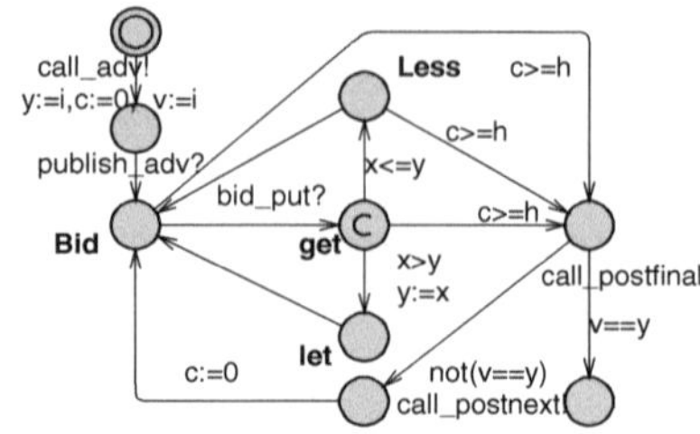

Fig. 13. Auction$_3$: Batch Processing

typical way of dealing with *time-out* in Timed Automata by adding a clock to record the time, as well as some clock constraints to guard the transitions. The constructed Timed Automata for $Auction_2$ is shown in Figure 12, in which c denotes the clock and h is a constant.

Batch Processing. The previous solution posts every higher bid as it appears in channel *bid*. It is reasonable to post higher bids only once each hour. Thus, the last solution collects the best bid over an hour and posts it. If this bid does not exceed the previous posting, i.e., no better bid has arrived in an hour, the auction is closed, the winning bid is posted and its value is returned as the result. In the interest of space, we skip the Orc model and the construction. The detail of the auction is available elsewhere in [17]. The constructed Timed Automaton is presented in Figure 13.

In the verification experiment of auction example using UPPAAL, we created 10 Bidders whose bid prices are from 200 to 1100, while the minimum bid price is 250. UPPAAL version 3.4 is installed on a machine running Windows XP with 3GHz Pentium 4 processor and 512MB memory. Some properties concerning all three auction strategies together the verification time are illustrated in Table 2.

4.3 Case Study: Purchase Order Handling

In this subsection, we present an example for handling purchase order, which was originally presented by Mistra and Cook [13].

$$
\begin{array}{l}
GetInv(custInfo, PO) \mathrel{\widehat=} ProduceInv(price, prodSchd) > inv > let(inv)\\
\quad \textbf{where}\ (price, prodSchd) :\in\\
\quad\quad (let(x,y)\\
\quad\quad\quad \textbf{where}\ x :\in InitPriceCal(PO) \gg GetPrice(shpInfo) > x > let(x)\\
\quad\quad\quad\quad y :\in (InitProdSchd(PO) \gg GetProdSchd(shpSchd) > y > let(y)\\
\quad\quad\quad\quad\quad \textbf{where}\ shpSchd :\in GetShpSchd(shpInfo)))\\
\quad\quad \textbf{where}\ shpInfo :\in GetShpInfo(custInfo))\\
POHandling(custInfo, PO) \mathrel{\widehat=} MailInv(inv, custInfo)\\
\quad \textbf{where}\ inv :\in GetInv(custInfo, PO) \mid Rtimer(t) \gg let(error)
\end{array}
$$

On receiving the purchase order from a customer, the process initiates three tasks concurrently: calculating the final price for the order, selecting a shipper, and scheduling the production and shipment for the order. While some of the processing can proceed concurrently, there are control and data dependencies between the three tasks. In particular, the shipping price is required to finalize the price calculation, and the shipping date is required for the complete fulfillment schedule. When the three tasks are completed, invoice processing can proceed and the invoice is mailed to the customer. If the invoice can not be generated within t time units, an error message is sent to the customer.

The purpose of this example is to show that the complex Orc expression can be represented by a clear UPPAAL model and the verification of time and data dependency. The UPPAAL model and property checking of this example are skipped (refer to [9]).

5 Conclusion and Future Works

The contribution of our work is threefold. Firstly, we defined an automata-based semantics for the Orc language, which allows a systematic construction of Timed Automata models from Orc models. Secondly, we explored ways of use UPPAAL to verify critical properties over Orc models. Lastly, we developed a tool to automate our approach.

There are some possible future works. One is better tool support of our approach, e.g., a graphical user interface for editing Orc models, hiding UPPAAL programs and visualizing counter examples if there are any, a better simplification and optimization strategy, etc. Another possible future work concerns the inadequate data passing capability of Orc, i.e., no complex data structure is supported. Therefore, we might provide a mechanism for introducing and manipulating data structures like arrays and tuples in our tool. The long term objective of this work is to investigate the relationship between process algebras and automata theories, e.g., provide theories and tools for applying automata-based model-checking to languages and notations based on process algebra.

Acknowledgements

The authors would like to thank Prof. Jayadev Misra for insightful discussion on the Orc language and pointing out relevant papers.

References

1. R. Alur and D. L. Dill. A Theory of Timed Automata. *Theor. Comput. Sci.*, 126(2):183–235, 1994.
2. T. Amnell, A. David, and Y. Wang. A Real-Time Animator for Hybrid Systems. In J. W. Davidson and S. L. Min, editors, *LCTES*, volume 1985 of *Lecture Notes in Computer Science*, pages 134–145. Springer, 2000.
3. T. Amnell, E. Fersman, P. Pettersson, H. Sun, and Y. Wang. Code Synthesis for Timed Automata. *Nord. J. Comput.*, 9(4):269–300, 2002.
4. J. Bengtsson, K. G. Larsen, F. Larsson, P. Pettersson, and Y. Wang. UPPAAL - a Tool Suite for Automatic Verification of Real-Time Systems. In R. Alur, T. A. Henzinger, and E. D. Sontag, editors, *Hybrid Systems*, volume 1066 of *Lecture Notes in Computer Science*. Springer, 1995.
5. P. Brooke. *A Timed Semantics for a Hierarchical Desgn Notation.* PhD thesis, University of York, 1999.

6. W. R. Cook and J. Misra. A Structured Orchestration Language. 2005. Available for download at http://www.cs.utexas.edu/users/wcook/projects/orc.
7. C. Daws, A. Olivero, S. Tripakis, and S. Yovine. The tool KRONOS. *In Hybrid System III: Verification and Control*, pages 208–219, 1996.
8. J. S. Dong, P. Hao, S. Qin, J. Sun, and Y. Wang. Timed Patterns: TCOZ to Timed Automata. In J. Davies, W. Schulte, and M. Barnett, editors, *ICFEM'04*, volume 3308 of *Lecture Notes in Computer Science*, pages 483–498. Springer, 2004.
9. J. S. Dong, Y. Liu, J. Sun, and X. Zhang. http://nt-appn.comp.nus.edu.sg/fm/orc, 2006.
10. H. Foster, S. Uchitel, J. Magee, and J. Kramer. Model-based Verification of Web Service Compositions. In *Automated Software Engineering 2003*, 2003.
11. T. A. Henzinger, X. Nicollin, J. Sifakis, and S. Yovine. Symbolic Model Checking for Real-Time Systems. In *7th. Symposium of Logics in Computer Science*, pages 394–406, 1992.
12. C. A. R. Hoare. *Communicating Sequential Processes.* International Series in Computer Science. Prentice-Hall, 1985.
13. IBM, BEA Systems, Microsoft, SAP AG, and Siebel Systems. BPEL4WS, Business Process Execution Language for Web Service version 1.1, 2003. http://www.siebel.com/bpel.
14. H. M. Lin and Y. Wang. A Proof System for Timed Automata. In J. Tiuryn, editor, *FoSSaCS*, volume 1784 of *Lecture Notes in Computer Science*, pages 208–222, 2000.
15. R. Milner. *Communication and Concurrency.* Prentice-Hall International, 1989.
16. R. Milner. *Communicating and Mobile Systems: the π Calculus.* Cambridge University Press, 1999.
17. J. Misra and W. Cook. *Computation Orchestration: A Basis for Wide-Area Computing.* To appear in the Journal of Software & Systems Modeling, 2006.
18. J. Misra, T. Hoare, and G. Menzel. A Tree Semantics of an Orchestration Language. In *M. Broy (ed.) Proc. of the NATO Advanced Study Institute, Engineering Theories of Software Intensive Systems, NATO ASI Series*, Marktoberdorf, Germany, August 2004.
19. G. G. Pu, X. P. Zhao, S. L. Wang, and Z. Y. Qiu. Towards the semantics and verification of BPEL4WS. In *International Workshop on Web Languages and Formal Methods*, UK, 2005.
20. A.W. Roscoe. *The Theory and Practice of Concurrency.* Prentice-Hall, 1997.
21. S. Schneider and J. Davies. A Brief History of Timed CSP. *Theoretical Computer Science*, 138, 1995.
22. M. P. Singh and M. N. Huhns. *Service-Oriented Computing.* John Wiley & Sons, Ltd, 2005.
23. M. Sorea. TEMPO: A Model-checker for Event-recording Automata. In *Proceedings of Workshop on Real-time Tools*, August 2001.
24. A. Tiu. Model Checking for Pi-calculus Using Proof Search. In *CONCUR'05*, San Francisco, August 2005.

Appendix. Correctness Proof

This section presents the proof of the weak bi-simulation relation between the timed automata and the operational semantics of Orc. In this proof, the Orc expressions refer to a subset of Orc langauge that is regular, type-safe and with a finite number of threads (see Section 4 for details).

Definition 10. *Given an Orc expression, the transition system associated with the expression is* $(\mathcal{O}, o_0, \Sigma, \longrightarrow_1)$ *where* $\mathcal{O}$ *is the set of possible Orc configurations,* o_0 *is the initial given Orc expression,* Σ *is the alphabet which includes all events in the Orc semantics [17], and* $\longrightarrow_2$ *is the transition relation by the transition rules [17].*

Definition 11. *Given a Timed Automaton, the transition system associated with the automaton is* $(\mathcal{S}, s_0, \Sigma \cup \mathbb{T}, \longrightarrow_2)$ *where* $\mathcal{S} \mathrel{\widehat{=}} S \times V$ *is the set of all possible states. Each state is composed of a control state and a valuation of the clocks. The initial state* $s_0 = \langle i, v_0 \rangle$ *comprises the initial state i and a zero valuation* v_0. $\longrightarrow_2 \subseteq \mathcal{S} \times (\Sigma^\tau \cup \mathbb{T}) \times \mathcal{S}$ *comprises all possible transitions of the following two kinds:*

- *a time passing move* $\langle s, v \rangle \xrightarrow{\delta}_2 \langle s, v + \delta \rangle$.
- *an action execution* $\langle s, v \rangle \xrightarrow{a}_2 \langle s', v' \rangle$ *iff* $s \xrightarrow{a;\, X;\, \varphi} s'$. *That is, the clock interpretation meets the guard* ($v \models \varphi$)*, and the new clock valuation satisfies:* $v'(x) = 0$ *for all* $x \in X$ *and* $v'(x) = v(x)$*, for all* $x \notin X$.

Definition 12. *For any* $o \in \mathcal{O}$ *and* $s \in \mathcal{S}$, $c \approx s$ *if and only if,*

- $\forall \alpha \in \Sigma, o \xrightarrow{\alpha}_1 o'$ *implies there exists* s' *such that* $s \xrightarrow{\alpha}_2 s'$, *and* $o' \approx s'$.
- $\forall \alpha \in \Sigma, s \xrightarrow{\alpha}_2 s'$ *implies there exists* o' *such that* $o \xrightarrow{\alpha}_1 o'$, *and* $o' \approx s'$.

Theorem 2. *Given an Orc expression Orc, let* $LTS_{Orc} \mathrel{\widehat{=}} (\mathcal{O}, o_0, \Sigma, \longrightarrow_2)$ *be the transition system associated with the expression. Let* $\mathcal{A}_{Orc}$ *be the corresponding Timed Automaton defined using definition 3 to 9 in the paper. Let* $LTS_{\mathcal{A}_{Orc}} \mathrel{\widehat{=}} (\mathcal{S}, s_0, \Sigma \cup \mathbb{T}, \longrightarrow_1)$ *be the transition system associated with the Timed Automaton.* $o_0 \approx s_0$.

Proof: The theorem can be proved by a structural induction on the Orc expressions. To abuse notations, we write $Orc \approx \mathcal{A}_{Orc}$ to mean $LTS_{Orc}.o_0 \approx LTS_{\mathcal{A}_{Orc}}.s_0$.

- $\mathbf{0}$: In Orc semantics, there is no transition rule for $\mathbf{0}$, so $LTS_{\mathbf{0}}$ is a single state transition system without any transitions. The same is $LTS_{\mathcal{A}_{\mathbf{0}}}$. Thus, $\mathbf{0} \approx \mathcal{A}_{\mathbf{0}}$.
- $let(z)$: In Orc semantics, the only transition for $LTS_{let(z)}$ is $let(z) \xrightarrow{publish_z}_1 \mathbf{0}$. It is also the only transition in the responding Timed Automaton. Thus, $let(z) \approx \mathcal{A}_{let(z)}$.
- $Rtimer(t)$: In Orc semantics [17], there is no transition rules for this basic site. However, it plays an important role in our work. After being called, the only transition allowed is time passing,

$$Rtimer(t) \xrightarrow{\delta_{t_1}}_1 Rtimer(t - t_1);\;\; Rtimer(t) \xrightarrow{\delta_t}_1 \mathbf{0}$$

  The calling site is blocked until the t time units has elapsed. By definition 4 and 11, the Timed Automaton bi-simulates the site $Rtimer(t)$.
- The proof for fundamental sites *if* and *Signal* are skipped. There are no formal semantics defined for them. We can treat them as the normal site calls.
- Site call $M(P)$: According to Orc's operational semantics [17], the transitions in $LTS_{M(P)}$ are $M(P) \xrightarrow{call_{M(P)}}_1 ?k$ and $?k \xrightarrow{get_{M(P)}}_1 let(v)$. According to our definition 5, the two transitions have one-to-one correspondence to the transitions in the Timed Automaton shown in figure 2. In particular, $s_2 \approx let(v)$ and, therefore, $s_1 \approx ?k$ and, lastly, $s_i \approx M(P)$. Thus, $M(P) \approx \mathcal{A}_{M(P)}$.
- Sequential composition $f >x> g$: According to the operational semantics of Orc, the two transitions available for the sequential composition are:

$$f >x> g \xrightarrow{a}_1 f' >x> g \;\; if \;\; f \xrightarrow{a}_1 f'$$
$$f >x> g \xrightarrow{publish_v}_1 (f' >x> g) \mid [v/x].g \;\; if \;\; f \xrightarrow{publish_v}_1 f'$$

Assume $f \approx \mathcal{A}_f$ and $g \approx \mathcal{A}_g$. For every a such that if $f \xrightarrow{a}_1 f'$, there is a transition in $LTS_{f \gg\!\triangleright g}$. Because $\mathcal{A}_{f \gg\!\triangleright g}$ is $\mathcal{A}_f \parallel \mathcal{A}'_g$ (by definition 6), there is a corresponding transition in $\mathcal{A}_{f \gg\!\triangleright g}$ because a is local to automaton $\mathcal{A}_f$ and by definition 2 the local actions are free to occur. Moreover, $f' \approx \mathcal{A}_{f'}$ by assumption. If $f \xrightarrow{publish_v}_1 f'$, then $f >x> g \xrightarrow{publish_v}_1 (f' >x> g) \mid [v/x].g$. By definition 6, there is a corresponding transition in $\mathcal{A}'_g$. As long as the number of *publish* events are finite, there is always a corresponding transition in one of the A'_g.

In the other direction, for every transition a from the initial state of $\mathcal{A}_{f \gg\!\triangleright g}$, if a is a *publish* event, it must be a synchronization between $\mathcal{A}_f$ and one of the $\mathcal{A}'_g$. By assumption, there must be a transition $f \xrightarrow{a}_1 f'$. Therefore, there is a corresponding transition in $f >x> g \xrightarrow{publish_v}_1 (f' >x> g) \mid [v/x].g$. If a is a local event, then it must belong to $\mathcal{A}_f$ because the only transition in $\mathcal{A}'_g$ at its initial state is a synchronized *publish* event. There must be a corresponding transition in LTS_f and $LTS_{f \gg\!\triangleright g}$. By induction, we conclude $f >x> g \approx \mathcal{A}_{f \gg\!\triangleright g}$.

– Symmetric composition $f \mid g$: According to the operational semantics of Orc, the two transitions available for the sequential composition are:

$$f \mid g \xrightarrow{a}_1 f' \mid g \;\; if \;\; f \xrightarrow{a}_1 f'$$
$$f \mid g \xrightarrow{a}_1 f \mid g' \;\; iff \;\; g \xrightarrow{a}_1 g'$$

Therefore, f and g are interleaving. By definition 7, the corresponding Timed Automaton is defined as $\mathcal{A}_{f|g} \mathrel{\widehat{=}} \mathcal{A}_f \parallel \mathcal{A}_g$. The events in both f and g are renamed so that there is no synchronization between f and g. Assume $f \approx \mathcal{A}_f$ and $g \approx \mathcal{A}_g$. By definition 2 and the above, transitions rules, we conclude $f \mid g \approx \mathcal{A}_{f|g}$.

– Asymmetric composition f **where** $x :\in g$: According to the operational semantics of Orc, the two transitions available for the sequential composition are:

$$f \textbf{ where } x :\in g \xrightarrow{a}_1 f' \textbf{ where } x :\in g \;\; if \;\; f \xrightarrow{a}_1 f'$$
$$f \textbf{ where } x :\in g \xrightarrow{a}_1 [v/x].f \;\; if \;\; g \xrightarrow{a}_1 g'$$
$$f \textbf{ where } x :\in g \xrightarrow{a}_1 f \textbf{ where } x :\in g' \;\; if \;\; g \xrightarrow{a}_1 g' \; and \; a \neq !v$$

Form the transaction rules we can conclude the following three properties: 1) f and g run in parallel; 2) the first returned value of g is passed to f and g stops; 3) f is blocked if x is not available. From the three properties, the transition system $LTS_{f \textbf{ where } x:\in g}$ is the production of LTS_f and LTS_g, where they synchronized on the transition $publish_x$ and g is stopped after the synchronization. $LTS_{\mathcal{A}_{f \textbf{ where } x:\in g}}$ is exactly the same transition according to the definition 7, which uses the shared flag to stop the execution of g.

– Expression call $E(P) \mathrel{\widehat{=}} f$: According to the operational semantics of Orc, the transition available for expression call composition is: $E(P) \xrightarrow{\tau}_1 [P/x].f$ *iff* $[\![E(x) \mathrel{\widehat{=}} f]\!] \in D$. The internal event τ acts as the initial event of the expression. It passes the input value to formal parameters. The equivalent event in the TA model is $call_E(P)$

event in the definition 9. The one-to-one mapping is shown in the following two transition systems.

$$\begin{aligned} LTS_{E(P)} &\mathrel{\widehat{=}} (\{LTS_f.S \cup o_0\}, \{LTS_f.\Sigma \cup \tau\}, o_0, \\ &\qquad \{LTS_f. \longrightarrow_1 \cup (o_0, \tau, LTS_f.o_0)\}) \\ LTS_{\mathcal{A}_{E(P)}} &\mathrel{\widehat{=}} (\{LTS_{\mathcal{A}_f}.S \cup (i, v_0)\}, \{LTS_{\mathcal{A}_f}.\Sigma \cup \tau\}, (i, v_0), \\ &\qquad \{LTS_f. \longrightarrow_1 \cup ((i, v_0), \tau, (LTS_f.s_0.i, v_0)))\}) \end{aligned}$$

Therefore, we conclude that our Timed Automata semantics is sound.

Towards the Semantics for Web Service Choreography Description Language*

Jing Li, Jifeng He, Geguang Pu, and Huibiao Zhu

Software Engineering Institute, East China Normal University
Shanghai, China, 200062
{jli, jifeng, ggpu, hbzhu}@sei.ecnu.edu.cn

Abstract. A choreography is a multi-part contract which describes peer to peer collaboration of services regardless of any specific programming language or supporting platform. WS-CDL, issued from W3C, is the first language for describing choreography. In this paper, we propose a language CDL_0 to capture the important features of WS-CDL, including choreography composition, compensation and exception handling. An adjunctive concept *role reference* is introduced with the aim of distinguishing multiple participants which provide the same kind of service within a choreography model. The semantics is given by an operational approach to provide a formal base for the choreography language. We believe this formalism work helps to clear ambiguous points in the WS-CDL specification and promote the usage of choreography languages.

Keywords: WS-CDL, choreography, operational semantics, compensation, exception handling.

1 Introduction

The goal of Web Services is to collaborate within or across the trusted domains of an organization resulting in accomplishing a common business goal. Interoperability between services is achieved by standard protocols that provide uniform ways to define the interface a web service exhibits (namely WSDL), to exchange messages (i.e., SOAP), and to look for particular services (i.e., UDDI). However, there still remain open challenges when it comes to the management of complex systems composed by a large number of services, where interactions go far beyond simple sequences of requests and responses. For this purpose, two different although overlapping viewpoints are currently investigated. The first one, referred to as web services orchestration, deals with the description of the interactions in which a given service engages with other services, as well as its internal actions. The second one, referred to as web services choreography, describes the external observable behavior across multiple web services from a global perspective, in which each participant is responsible for adhering to a specific protocol. R.Dijkman and M.Dumas [2] introduces a foundational model, in terms of Petri nets, for describing the viewpoints and their interrelationships.

* Supported by National Basic Research Program of China (No. 2002CB312001).

Z. Liu and J. He (Eds.): ICFEM 2006, LNCS 4260, pp. 246–263, 2006.

A number of standardization proposals that describe web services orchestration have been put forward over the past years (e.g. BPML, XLANG, WSFL), and BPEL4WS [11] is the more recent proposal for this viewpoint. On the other hand, the Web Services Choreography Description Language (WS-CDL) [12] is the first proposal for describing web services choreography which is recommended by W3C in November 2005. WS-CDL is an XML-based language which is aimed at being able to precisely describe collaborations between any type of service regardless of the supporting platform or programming model used by the implementation of the hosting environment. One feature of WS-CDL is that it supports choreography composition which allows scalable modeling. That is, smaller choreographies are built first and then combined together to form a larger choreography. Another important feature is the ability to deal with long-running transactions. When a failure occurs during the execution, mechanisms are provided to capture such an exception and fire the corresponding compensation activity to recover from errors. The mechanisms are referred to as exception handling and compensation.

At present, WS-CDL is not fully developed and a number of issues remain open [1]. One problem is that this language cannot differentiate multiple participants providing the same kind of service in a collaboration so as not able to identify which interaction is related to each participant. In this paper, we propose a language called CDL_0, the "untagged" version of WS-CDL, the syntax of which is written in the BNF format instead of XML. CDL_0 captures many features of WS-CDL, including choreography composition, compensation and exception handling. Moreover, CDL_0 introduces a new concept *role reference* to distinguish different participants providing the same kind of service within a choreography model. The operational semantics of CDL_0 is carefully studied, through which we clearly illustrate how to deal with scalable modeling and long-running transactions.

This paper is organized as follows. Section 2 provides an introduction of the CDL_0 language. Section 3 presents the operational semantics especially for composition, compensation and exception handling. Some related work is discussed in Sect.4. The last section gives the conclusion and future work.

2 The Language CDL_0

This section presents an overview of CDL_0. Firstly, the syntax of choreography and activity is presented accompanying with the formal definition of choreography. Secondly, we give a description for the kinds of activities: basic activities, ordering structured activities and workunits. Finally, we talk about choreography life-line which is a key character of choreography.

2.1 The Syntax of CDL_0

Formally, a system is described by a set of choreographies. A choreography defines re-usable common rules that govern the ordering of exchanged messages, and the provisioning patterns of collaborative behavior, as agreed upon between two or more interacting participants. It is composed of five parts: name, role reference declarations, body activity, exception handlers and finalizer blocks. The syntax is described below:

$$\begin{array}{ll} choreography & ::= c(A, RDec, EHandler, FBlock) \\ RDec & ::= \{\rho : r\}^+ \\ EHandler & ::= \{et : A\}^* \\ FBlock & ::= \{f : A\}^* \end{array}$$

In the syntax above, c denotes a choreography name; et stands for any exception type; f represents the name of a finalizer block; A represents an activity which may be defined within a choreography body, an exception handler or a finalizer Block. The activity defined within a choreography body is called *body activity.* Exception handlers are used to deal with exceptions, whereas finalizer blocks are used to define the compensations for the body activity. It is not necessary for a choreography to include exception handlers or finalizer blocks.

Currently, the interaction described in WS-CDL specification only specifies the requesting and the accepting role types. There is no corresponding concept to denote a specific role instance or a concrete web service. Therefore, if two or more service providers of the same role type participate in one collaboration, there is no way to tell which one is involved in a specific interaction. In order to solve this problem, we introduce the concept *role reference* to denote a distinct service. Consequently, all the role references declared in the same choreography represent different web services. Two role references defined in different choreographies may bind together to refer to the same service participating in the activities of both choreographies. Every role reference has a *role type* enumerating potential observable behaviors. A role type is described by a name, a set of variables and the set of operations it exhibits. Let $RTName$ be the set of role type names ranged over by ρ, Var be the set of variables ranged over by x, y, u, v, and $Oper$ be the set of operations ranged over by op. The set $RType$ containing all the possible role types is defined as follows ($\mathbb{P}(S)$ denotes the powerset of S):

$$RType = \{(\rho, \ell, o) | \rho \in RTName, \ell \in \mathbb{P}(Var), o \in \mathbb{P}(Oper)\}$$

There exists a *root* choreography which is enabled by the system by default. We use a distinct name *root* to mark this choreography, which has no finalizer blocks. The root choreography declares all participating services denoted by role references. For example, if the whole collaboration includes one customer and two sellers, then there are two role types needed and three role references declared to denote such three participants. The non-root choreography only needs to declare these role references which just participate in this sub-collaboration. We regard the role references defined in the root choreography as the *global participants.* Any role reference of a non-root choreography is bound directly or indirectly to the global participant defined in the root choreography. Thus we can deduce which action is performed by each participant, meanwhile, we can also trace how the state changes for each participant.

Let e range over XPath expressions; r, s range over the set of role references denoted by $RRef$; b, g range over XPath boolean expressions; and $\overline{x}$ stands for a sequence $\langle x_1, x_2, ..., x_n \rangle$ (similarly for $\overline{e}$, $\overline{r}$, etc). The syntax of activity is defined below:

$$
\begin{array}{lll}
A, B ::= & skip & (skip) \\
& \mid silent(r.\overline{x}) & (silent) \\
& \mid r.\overline{x} := \overline{e} & (assignment) \\
& \mid OW(r_1.x \rightarrow r_2.y, op) & (one-way) \\
& \mid RR(r_1.x \rightarrow r_2.y, r_1.u \leftarrow r_2.v, op) & (request-response) \\
& \mid perform(c, id, \overline{r_1} \Leftrightarrow \overline{r_2}) & (perform) \\
& \mid finalize(c, f, id) & (finalize) \\
& \mid A; B & (sequence) \\
& \mid A \parallel B & (parallel) \\
& \mid A \sqcap B & (choice) \\
& \mid \talloblong_{i \in I}.(g_i \rightarrow A_i) & (guard) \\
& \mid A * b & (repetition) \\
& \mid throw(et) & (throw)
\end{array}
$$

Now we define the choreography in a formal way. The set *chor* contains all the choreographies, which is defined as follows:

$$
\begin{aligned}
chor = \{(c, R, A, E, F) \mid\ & c \in CName, R \in \mathbb{P}(RDec), A \in Activity, \\
& E \in \mathbb{P}(EHandler), F \in \mathbb{P}(FBlock)\}
\end{aligned}
$$

$$RDec = \{(\rho, r) | \rho \in RTName, r \in RRef\}$$

$$EHandler = \{(et, A) | et \in EType \cup \{all\}, A \in Activity\}$$

$$FBlock = \{(f, A) | f \in FName, A \in Activity\}$$

where $CName$ is the set of choreography names, $EType$ is the set of exception types, and $FName$ is the set of finalizer block names.

2.2 CDL_0 Activities

According to WS-CDL specification, the activities are classified into three types: basic activities, ordering structures, and workunits. Basic activities describe the lowest level actions performed within a choreography, such as skip, assignment, interaction, etc. Ordering structures express the ordering rules of actions, including sequence, choice, and parallel. Workunits provide a way of adding conditionality and provide repetition based on some predicate. The introduction of all these activities is given below.

Skip and Silent: The activity *skip* denotes that no action is specified to be performed. From a deep semantic view, it means an activity terminates successfully.

silent is an explicit designator used for marking the point where unobservable operations within a specific role must be performed. This activity just announces some variables residing in a specific role may change during the non-observable operations without showing how the change occurs. Such kind of activity will influence the following collaborations. Consider the example that a customer asks for quotes from two sellers. After obtaining the quotes, the customer compares the two quotes in a way that the sellers cannot observe and then decides from which seller he should order goods based on this comparison.

Assignment: This activity is used to create or change the value of one or more variables using the value of another variable or expression. All the variables belong to a specific role reference, that is, this action is performed by one participant.

Interaction: Interaction results in information exchange between two collaborating participants. According to the specification [12], interaction is classified into three types: request, respond, and request-respond. Here, we treat *request* and *respond* in the same way in which the information is transferred through one way. Therefore, we call this kind of interaction as one-way interaction. When the information is received, the operation *op* performed by recipient specifies what to do with the exchanged information.

Perform: The perform activity realizes the composition of choreographies by combining existing choreographies to create new ones. In terms of composition, this activity is similar to *procedure call* in other languages. When choreography c_1 performs another choreography c_2 through perform activity, c_1 is called the immediately enclosing choreography of c_2, and c_2 is called the immediately enclosed choreography of c_1. If there exists a sequence $c_1, c_2, ..., c_n$, in which c_i is the immediately enclosing choreography of c_{i+1} (where $1 \leq i < n$), then c_j is called an enclosed choreography of c_i and c_i is called an enclosing choreography of c_j for each i, j satisfying $j > i$.

The root choreography is performed once by system, so it has only one choreography instance. However, a non-root choreography may be performed more than once. This kind of choreography may have more than one choreography instances, thus unique identifiers for choreography instances are required. In most cases, the identifier is determined statically and the guarantee of uniqueness is provided by designers. However, if the perform activity appears within a repetition, then each performing must be dynamically assigned a different identifier. In this case, the designer consigns this assignment to the system, leaving the identifier assigned during runtime.

In perform activity $perform(c, id, \overline{r_1} \Leftrightarrow \overline{r_2})$, c is the name of the enclosed choreography, id is an unique identifier for this new choreography instance, and $\overline{r_1}$ are these role references defined in the enclosing choreography which should be bound to the role references $\overline{r_2}$ defined in the enclosed choreography thus leading to refer to the same participants respectively. According to the specification, this activity has two kinds of working modes: blocking mode and non-blocking mode. The former one means the enclosing choreography must wait for the enclosed choreography to complete, whereas the latter one allows the enclosing choreography to be active concurrently with the enclosed choreography. However, the semantics is quite bewildering when the working mode is combined with the sequential or parallel operators. Consider the following simple sequential activity:

$$perform(c, id, \overline{r_1} \Leftrightarrow \overline{r_2}); B$$

If the perform activity is in non-blocking mode, it means the body activity of c is executed concurrently with B. This semantics conflicts with the original meaning of sequential operators. The case is similar to a parallel activity $perform(c, id, \overline{r_1} \Leftrightarrow \overline{r_2}) \parallel B$ in which the perform activity is executed in blocking mode. To clear up the ambiguity, we choose to abandon the working mode in our CDL_0 language, just using the suitable operators to describe the desired working patterns between different choreographies.

Finalize: After a choreography instance has successfully completed, it needs to provide compensating activities, from a semantic point of view, which undo the actions performed by its completed body activity in case the corresponding transaction fails in later stage. CDL_0 suggests a way to provide several alternative compensations, and each of them is defined in a finalizer block. A compensation becomes valid only after the body activity of its choreography has completed successfully, and becomes active only when it is invoked by a finalize activity specifying its finalizer block name. Thus, a set of finalizer blocks can be selected as desired, invoked in any order. This compensation mechanism is quite similar to the concept *multiple compensation* introduced in [18], an extension to StAC [17].

In a finalize activity $finalize(c, f, id)$, the identifier id is bound to an existing choreography instance with name c to explicitly specify which instance is to be finalized. If the desired identifier is assigned at runtime, we can resort to a *name directory* for the sake of dynamic binding. f is a finalizer block name, used to denote which compensation is expected to undo the completed activities.

Sequential and Parallel: The sequential construct $A; B$ indicates that A is executed first, and only when A terminates successfully can B be executed.

In parallel activity $A \parallel B$, the execution of A and B is interleaved, but must support synchronization on terminal events. The whole parallel activity fails when either A or B throws an exception.

Guard and Choice: The guard activity $[]_{i \in I}.(g_i \rightarrow A_i)$ includes one or more activities, each of which is guarded by a boolean function g_i. This boolean function may just evaluate data, may only wait for some event to happen or mix the two together. The guard activity is put into two categories, guarded choice and conditional activity.

When the set I has more than one member, the guard activity can be expanded to such a form: $g_1 \rightarrow A_1 \, [] \, g_2 \rightarrow A_2 \, [] \, ... \, [] \, g_n \rightarrow A_n$ $(n \geq 2)$, which shows itself as a guarded choice. The guarded choice selects one activity to be performed, depending on whose guard is matched. If none of the guards is matched, this activity will block, waiting for the guards to be triggered.

When the set I has only one member, $g \rightarrow A$ (the index is omitted) denotes a conditional activity which behaves as A whenever g evaluates to true. Conversely, if g is false, the conditional activity will block. The conditional activity is also called blocking condition. Workunits also supports non-blocking condition: if the guard evaluates to false, then A is not considered to be executed. The non-blocking condition is a special form of guarded choice: $(g \rightarrow A) \, [] \, (\neg g \rightarrow skip)$.

The choice $A \sqcap B$, different from guarded choice, nondeterministically selects one activity A or B to be performed.

Repetition: In the repetition activity $A * b$, activity A is performed first and b is evaluated after A terminates successfully. If b is true, this repetition activity is performed again, otherwise, this activity is skipped.

Throw: There is no such corresponding activity in the specification of WS-CDL, but such an activity is necessary to explicitly notice an application exception. Exceptions related to communication or security issues are thrown by the underlying protocols. Concerning application failures (e.g., the credit check fails while processing the order fulfillment), a mechanism is needed to throw such exceptions explicitly. On the other hand, the exception handler needs to propagate exceptions to its enclosing choreography explicitly in the case that it cannot solve the exceptions completely, which requires further compensations for its previous sibling choreographies.

2.3 Choreography Life-Line

A choreography life-line expresses the progression of a collaboration. It has four distinct states: enabled, successful, failed, and closed.

enabled. When a choreography is performed by the system or another choreography, it enters the enabled state. The exception handlers are enabled when the choreography they belong to is enabled. All these exception handlers behave as monitors, trying to catch the exceptions occurring in this and its enclosed choreographies. The life cycle of any role reference starts at this time when its choreography is enabled.

successful. A choreography in the enabled state enters the successful state when there are no more activities within its body. In other words, the body activity of this choreography has completed successfully. The finalizer blocks are installed at this time, and one of them may be activated by a $finalize$ activity whenever an exception takes place afterwards during its immediately enclosing choreography.

failed. Any occurrence or propagation of an exception causes a choreography to enter the failed state. The exception handlers may capture the occurred exception or not, if not, the exception is propagated. In this case, the compensating activities defined in finalizer blocks does not work.

closed. When the choreography enters the closed state, the life cycle of any role reference defined in this choreography expired. There are six cases in which a choreography enters the closed state.

1. When a choreography is in the successful state and there are no finalizer blocks specified in this choreography, it implicitly enters the closed state.
2. A choreography in the successful state with finalizer blocks specified enters the closed state when one of its finalizer blocks is enabled by a finalize activity and completes successfully.
3. A choreography in the successful state with finalizer blocks implicitly enters the closed state when its immediate enclosing choreography enters the closed state without enabling any of its finalizer blocks.

4. A choreography in the failed state enters the closed state when an exception is captured in its exception handlers and the corresponding handler is performed successfully.
5. A choreography in the failed state without any exception handlers implicitly enters the closed state. The exception occurred is recursively propagated to the immediately enclosing choreography until the exception is handled.
6. A choreography in the failed state with exception handlers specified implicitly enters the closed state when the exception occurred is not captured by its own handlers. In this case, the exception occurred is also recursively propagated to the immediately enclosing choreography.

The choreography life-line decides whether a compensation can be activated or not, e.g., finalizing a choreography in the closed state has no effect. It also works on the mechanism of exception handling, shown in Sect.3.2. As we will see, all transitions among the four states are clearly reflected in the following operational semantics.

3 Operational Semantics for CDL_0

This section presents the operational semantics for CDL_0. The operational semantics [9] is a way of defining the behavior of activities in terms of transition rules between configurations. For the semantics of CDL_0, a configuration is defined as a tuple:

$$\langle A, C, id, \sigma \rangle \in Activity \times Context \times CIns \times State$$

where

$$Context = CIns \nrightarrow CName \times CIns \times CState \times (RRef \nrightarrow RRef)$$
$$State = RRef \times Var \nrightarrow Val$$
$$CState = \{enabled, successful, failed, closed\}$$

In the above tuple, A is not just a CDL_0 activity. For the semantics necessity, we introduce another five activities: $\Omega, \Xi, [A]_{id}, fail_{et}, early_{et}$, which will be explained in the later sections. $CIns$ represents the set of all possible choreography instances. We introduce an important element *choreography context* C, a function which provides the context for each choreography instance, including its choreography name, its state, its immediately enclosing choreography instance, and the global participants bound by role references declared in this choreography. For simplicity, we use $C(id).name$, $C(id).state$, $C(id).parent$ to denote the choreography name, choreography state and immediately enclosing choreography instance respectively, and $C(id.r)$ to represent the global participant defined in the root choreography, bound by $id.r$ (id is the legal scope of r, an instance of the choreography in which r is declared). We do not need to offer the scope of $C(id.r)$ explicitly, since it has a default scope *root*. If the choreography instance is related to *root* choreography, then its enclosing choreography instance denoted by ϵ, and $C(id.r)$ is r itself for every role reference r defined in the root choreography. id represents the performing choreography instance in which an activity A (the first element of a configuration) is executed. We call id the scope identifier of A. σ represents data state which is a partial function from the variables of participants to values. It records the global state of all participants defined within the root choreography. Val is the set of all possible values, ranged over by ν. We use $\sigma[s.x \mapsto \nu]$ to denote variable x of participant s is set to the value ν, and there is an implicit scope $root$ for this participant s.

The set Λ of all possible transition labels is defined as:

$$\Lambda = EType \cup \{\alpha, \tau, \checkmark\}$$

where an exception type denotes that an exception occurs. α is a visible event representing a communication between two services. It has two specific forms, one represents one-way interaction, while the other represents request-response interaction. τ and $\checkmark$ are two special labels, the former one represents an event invisible to the external environment and the latter one represents successful termination. In the transition rules, we consider $a \in \{\alpha, \tau\}$.

Skip: The skip activity leads to *termination* activity Ω through one step, and the semantics of Ω is shown later:

$$\langle skip, C, id, \sigma\rangle \xrightarrow{\checkmark} \langle \Omega, C, id, \sigma\rangle$$

Silent: This activity changes the data state in an unobservable way. The values of variable $\overline{x}$ within r may change and such change is reflected in σ':

$$\langle silent(r.\overline{x}), C, id, \sigma\rangle \xrightarrow{\tau} \langle skip, C, id, \sigma'\rangle$$

Assignment: $r.\overline{x} := \overline{e}$ causes the associated participant bound by r to change its data state:

$$\frac{s = C(id.r) \wedge \overline{\nu} = \overline{e}(\sigma)}{\langle r.\overline{x} := \overline{e}, C, id, \sigma\rangle \xrightarrow{\tau} \langle skip, C, id, \sigma[s.\overline{x} \mapsto \overline{\nu}]\rangle}$$

Interaction: Two services interact with each other to exchange information, thus the corresponding state change is recorded:

$$\frac{s_1 = C(id.r_1) \wedge s_2 = C(id.r_2)}{\langle OW(r_1.x \rightarrow r_2.y, op), C, id, \sigma\rangle \xrightarrow{r_1?r_2.op\uparrow} \langle skip, C, id, \sigma[s_2.y \mapsto \sigma(s_1.x)]\rangle}$$

$$\frac{s_1 = C(id.r_1) \wedge s_2 = C(id.r_2)}{\begin{array}{l}\langle RR(r_1.x \rightarrow r_2.y,\ r_1.u \leftarrow r_2.v, op), C, id, \sigma\rangle \xrightarrow{r_1?r_2.op\updownarrow} \\ \qquad\qquad \langle skip, C, id, \sigma[s_2.y \mapsto \sigma(s_1.x), s_1.u \mapsto \sigma(s_2.v)]\rangle\end{array}}$$

Repetition: This repetition activity is a kind of composition of sequence, guarded choice and repetition itself:

$$\langle A * b, C, id, \sigma\rangle \xrightarrow{\tau} \langle A; (b \rightarrow A * b \mathbin{[]} \neg b \rightarrow skip), C, id, \sigma\rangle$$

Choice: This activity decides nondeterministically which activity A or B will take place:

$$\langle A \sqcap B, C, id, \sigma\rangle \xrightarrow{\tau} \langle A, C, id, \sigma\rangle \qquad \langle A \sqcap B, C, id, \sigma\rangle \xrightarrow{\tau} \langle B, C, id, \sigma\rangle$$

Guard: The rule states that if more than one guards are matched, then the first matched one is selected.

$$\frac{\bigwedge_{j<k.}\, g_j(\sigma) = false \wedge g_k(\sigma) = true}{\langle [\!]_{i\in I.}(g_i \rightarrow A_i), C, id, \sigma\rangle \xrightarrow{\tau} \langle A_k, C, id, \sigma\rangle}$$

Sequence: In the sequential activity $A; B$, A performs first while B is preserved:

$$\frac{\langle A, C, id, \sigma\rangle \xrightarrow{a} \langle A', C', id', \sigma'\rangle}{\langle A; B, C, id, \sigma\rangle \xrightarrow{a} \langle A'; B, C', id', \sigma'\rangle}$$

If the first activity A terminates successfully, then B starts and the $\checkmark$action is hidden from outside:

$$\frac{\langle A, C, id, \sigma\rangle \xrightarrow{\checkmark} \langle \Omega, C', id', \sigma'\rangle}{\langle A; B, C, id, \sigma\rangle \xrightarrow{\tau} \langle B, C', id', \sigma'\rangle}$$

Parallel: In parallel activity, either activity may progress independently by performing a non-terminal event:

$$\frac{\langle A, C, id, \sigma\rangle \xrightarrow{a} \langle A', C', id', \sigma'\rangle}{\langle A \parallel B, C, id, \sigma\rangle \xrightarrow{a} \langle A' \parallel B, C', id', \sigma'\rangle} \qquad \frac{\langle B, C, id, \sigma\rangle \xrightarrow{a} \langle B', C', id', \sigma'\rangle}{\langle A \parallel B, C, id, \sigma\rangle \xrightarrow{a} \langle A \parallel B', C', id', \sigma'\rangle}$$

The rule below states that the parallel activity $A \parallel B$ terminates successfully when both A and B terminate successfully:

$$\frac{\langle A, C, id, \sigma\rangle \xrightarrow{\checkmark} \langle \Omega, C', id', \sigma'\rangle \wedge \langle B, C, id, \sigma\rangle \xrightarrow{\checkmark} \langle \Omega, C', id', \sigma'\rangle}{\langle A \parallel B, C, id, \sigma\rangle \xrightarrow{\checkmark} \langle \Omega, C', id', \sigma'\rangle}$$

3.1 Operational Semantics for Composition and Compensation

There are two special activities: $perform$ and $finalize$, the former one deals with choreography composition while the latter one is related to compensation. Two other activities are introduced for the sake of semantics: termination activity Ω and scope activity $[A]_{id}$. The meaning of the two activities is explained later in this section.

Perform: When a choreography is performed, its body activity is enabled in a new scope. An unique identifier is allocated to denote this new produced choreography instance, the state of which becomes *enabled*:

$$\begin{aligned}&\langle perform(c, id', \overline{r_1} \Leftrightarrow \overline{r_2}), C, id, \sigma\rangle \xrightarrow{\tau} \\ &\qquad \langle [c.body]_{id'}, C[id' \mapsto (c, id, enabled, binding(C, id, \overline{r_1}, \overline{r_2}))], id, \sigma\rangle\end{aligned}$$

If the assignment for id' is a dynamic requirement, thus the system is responsible for allocating a fresh instance identifier at runtime. $c.body$ represents the body activity of choreography c, which satisfies:

$$(c, R, c.body, E, F) \in chor$$

$C[id' \mapsto (c, id, enabled, binding(C, id, \overline{r_1}, \overline{r_2}))]$ records the context for this enclosed choreography instance. The immediately enclosing choreography instance of the newly produced instance id' is the current performing instance id.

$binding(C, id, \overline{r_1}, \overline{r_2})$ is such a function which makes the role references $id'.\overline{r_2}$ point to the same participants as those to which $id.\overline{r_1}$ refer. As mentioned earlier, $\overline{r_1} = \langle r_{11}, r_{12}, ..., r_{1n}\rangle, \overline{r_2} = \langle r_{21}, r_{22}, ..., r_{2n}\rangle$, so its definition is as follows:

$$binding(C, id, \overline{r_1}, \overline{r_2}) = \{(r_{2i}, C(id.r_{1i}))|1 \leq i \leq n\}$$

Finalize: Every finalizer block is defined as a compensation activity which is specified by its name. The finalize activity is used to enable a specific finalizer block in a successfully completed choreography instance to recover from a failure. A finalizer block can only be enabled by its immediately enclosing choreography instance. When a finalizer block is enabled, the compensating activity begins to execute in a new scope:

$$\frac{C(id') = (c, id, successful, ?)}{\langle finalize(c, f, id'), C, id, \sigma\rangle \xrightarrow{\tau} \langle [compensation(c, f)]_{id'}, C, id, \sigma\rangle}$$

If id' is a dynamic binding, a *name directory* is provided, allowing for the retrieval of a specific choreography instance based on the choreography name and the involved participants. The *choreography context C* contains all the needed information for dynamic binding, which can also act as a name directory.

$C(id') = (c, id, successful, ?)$ means the performed choreography instance must be situated in the successful state and its immediately enclosing choreography instance is the current performing instance. The symbol ? represents the value we do not care. In the above rule, we do not care about which participants are involved in this collaboration.

$compensation(c, f)$ represents the compensating activity in the finalizer block named f within the choreography c, which satisfies:

$$(c, R, A, E, F) \in chor \wedge (f, compensation(c, f)) \in F$$

The following rule states that the finalize activity does nothing if the context does not satisfy $C(id') = (c, id, successful, ?)$:

$$\frac{C(id') \neq (c, id, successful, ?)}{\langle finalize(c, f, id'), C, id, \sigma\rangle \xrightarrow{\tau} \langle skip, C, id, \sigma\rangle}$$

Termination: When the body activity, a finalizer block or an exception handler completes successfully, the states of the choreography instances must be updated. The final derived activity is defined as Ξ which has no further transition rules:

$$\langle \Omega, C, id, \sigma\rangle \xrightarrow{\tau} \langle \Xi, C', id, \sigma\rangle$$

where:

$$C' = SetClosed(UpdCState(C, id))$$

Here, we introduce two functions: *UpdCState* and *SetClosed*. The *UpdCState* function updates the state of the choreography instance specified by *id* according to the state transition rules in Sect.2.3. It is defined as follows:
$UpdCState(C, id) =$

$$\begin{cases} C[id \mapsto (!, !, successful, !)] & if\ C(id).state = enabled \wedge \\ & (C(id).name, R, A, E, F) \in chor \wedge F \neq \emptyset \\ C[id \mapsto (!, !, closed, !)] & \text{otherwise} \end{cases}$$

The symbol ! represents no change, so $C[id \mapsto (!, !, successful, !)]$ denotes that only the state of *id* is changed to the successful state, while other properties remain the same as before.

When a choreography instance enters the closed state, all its enclosed choreographies are closed implicitly. Thus we must set all the enclosed choreography instances to the closed state. The *SetClosed* function is recursively defined as follows ($\oplus$ represents the 'relation coverage' operator):
$SetClosed(C) =$

$$\begin{cases} C & \text{if } \forall id \cdot C(id).state \neq closed \Rightarrow C(C(id).parent).state \neq closed \\ SetClosed(C \oplus \{(id, (!, !, closed, !)) | C(C(id).parent).state = closed\}) & \text{otherwise} \end{cases}$$

Moreover, all closed choreography instances become useless which should be deleted:

$$C' = \{id | C(id).state = closed\} \trianglelefteq C'$$

Where $\trianglelefteq$ represents the 'domain elimination' operator.

Scope: We have introduced a new activity $[A]_{id}$ named *scope* during the semantics for *perform* and *finalize* activities. This new activity confines an activity A to a scope in which A is executed. The scope identifier *id* is derived from a choreography instance identifier. Scope activities can be nested, consider the following activity:

$$[[A_1]_b \parallel ([A_2]_c; A_3)]_a$$

A_1, A_2 and A_3 lie in different scopes.
The scope activity follows the inner activity to execute step by step:

$$\frac{\langle A, C, id, \sigma\rangle \xrightarrow{a} \langle A', C', id'', \sigma'\rangle}{\langle [A]_{id}, C, id', \sigma\rangle \xrightarrow{a} \langle [A']_{id}, C', id', \sigma'\rangle}$$

Recall that, in a configuration $\langle A, C, id, \sigma\rangle$, *id* is the scope identifier of A. In the above rule, the scope identifier of the inner activity A is *id* rather than id' and the scope for the scope activity $[A]_{id}$ itself stays stable during the transition.

The following rule states that the scope activity hides the terminal event to the environment. If we do not do so, the choreography instance denoted by the scope identifier id has no chance to update its choreography state:

$$\frac{\langle A, C, id, \sigma\rangle \xrightarrow{\checkmark} \langle A', C', id'', \sigma'\rangle}{\langle [A]_{id}, C, id', \sigma\rangle \xrightarrow{\tau} \langle [A']_{id}, C', id', \sigma'\rangle}$$

The Ξ activity means that the normal flow or the compensating flow of an choreography instance has completed successfully and the corresponding choreography state is updated. Thus, the scope activity $[\Xi]_{id}$ leads to $skip$:

$$\langle [\Xi]_{id}, C, id', \sigma\rangle \xrightarrow{\tau} \langle skip, C, id', \sigma\rangle$$

To behave consistently, the body activity of the root choreography must be transformed into scope activity at the beginning.

3.2 Operational Semantics for Exception Handling

A choreography may sometimes fail as a result of an exceptional circumstance or an "error" that occurs during its performance. There are different types of exceptions, including interaction failures, security failures, timeout errors, application failures and so on. A choreography may define several exception handlers to capture these exceptions. An exception handler is such a tuple:

$$(et, A) \in EType \cup \{all\} \times Activity$$

If $et = all$, this exception handler is called the *default* exception handler which captures any exception.

In order to deal with exceptions, we introduce two kinds of activities: $early_{et}$, $fail_{et}$. $early_{et}$ denotes that an exception of the exception type et takes place, which may be caught by exception handlers depending upon its type. $fail_{et}$ represents that a choreography cannot resolve the exception of type et. In this case, it is suggested that the unresolved exception should be propagated to the immediately enclosing choreography.

Exception handlers for a choreography are meant to handle exceptions during the body activity within that choreography. In other words, the exception handlers are uninstalled once their associated choreography enters the successful state. Therefore, the disposal of exceptions occurring within the exception handlers or finalizer blocks is the responsibility of the enclosing choreography.

When an exception occurs, its type is matched first with the type specified by non-default exception handlers. If such a match fails, the default exception handler deals with this exception:

$$\frac{C(id).state = enabled \wedge (C(id).name, R, A, E, F) \in chor \wedge (et, A') \in E}{\langle early_{et}, C, id, \sigma\rangle \xrightarrow{\tau} \langle A', C[id \mapsto (!, !, failed, !)], id, \sigma\rangle}$$

$$\frac{C(id).state = enabled \wedge (C(id).name, R, A, E, F) \in chor \wedge et \notin dom(E) \wedge (all, A') \in E}{\langle early_{et}, C, id, \sigma\rangle \xrightarrow{\tau} \langle A', C[id \mapsto (!, !, failed, !)], id, \sigma\rangle}$$

When a choreography has no exception handlers or all its handlers cannot capture the occurred exception, it leads to $fail_{et}$:

$$\frac{C(id).state = enabled \wedge (C(id).name, R, A, \emptyset, F) \in chor}{\langle early_{et}, C, id, \sigma\rangle \xrightarrow{\tau} \langle fail_{et}, C', id, \sigma\rangle}$$

$$\frac{C(id).state = enabled \wedge (C(id).name, R, A, E, F) \in chor \wedge \{et, all\} \cap dom(E) = \emptyset}{\langle early_{et}, C, id, \sigma\rangle \xrightarrow{\tau} \langle fail_{et}, C', id, \sigma\rangle}$$

When the choreography instance is not in the enabled state, we propagate the exception instead of dealing with it:

$$\frac{C(id).state \neq enabled}{\langle early_{et}, C, id, \sigma\rangle \xrightarrow{\tau} \langle fail_{et}, C', id, \sigma\rangle}$$

In the above three rules which lead to the activity $fail_{et}$, the current choreography instance and all its enclosed choreography instances must enter the closed state. The computation for C' is as follows:

$$C' = \{id | C(id).state = closed\} \trianglelefteq SetClosed(C[id \mapsto (!, !, closed, !)])$$

The function *SetClosed* is defined in the part of termination activity Ω.

Then we should add some rules to deal with the occurrence of exception in kinds of basic activities, and the composition of exception with other structural activities.

The exceptions which take place during such activities as *silent*, *assignment* and *interaction* are thrown from the low level implementations or protocols.

Silent

$$\langle silent(r.\overline{x}), C, id, \sigma\rangle \xrightarrow{et} \langle early_{et}, C, id, \sigma\rangle$$

Assignment

$$\langle r.\overline{x} := \overline{e}, C, id, \sigma\rangle \xrightarrow{et} \langle early_{et}, C, id, \sigma\rangle$$

Interaction

$$\langle OW(r_1.x \rightarrow r_2.y, op), C, id, \sigma\rangle \xrightarrow{et} \langle early_{et}, C, id, \sigma\rangle$$

$$\langle RR(r_1.x \rightarrow r_2.y, r_1.u \leftarrow r_2.v, op), C, id, \sigma\rangle \xrightarrow{et} \langle early_{et}, C, id, \sigma\rangle$$

Throw: This activity throws an exception of a specific type explicitly.

$$\langle throw(et), C, id, \sigma\rangle \xrightarrow{et} \langle early_{et}, C, id, \sigma\rangle$$

Scope: $fail_{et}$ makes the scope activity abandon the scope symbol '[ ]' and propagate the non-handled exception to the immediately enclosing choreography:

$$\langle [fail_{et}]_{id}, C, id', \sigma\rangle \xrightarrow{et} \langle early_{et}, C, id', \sigma\rangle$$

Scope activity hides the exceptions occurred within the scope:

$$\frac{\langle A, C, id, \sigma\rangle \xrightarrow{et} \langle A', C', id'', \sigma'\rangle}{\langle [A]_{id}, C, id', \sigma\rangle \xrightarrow{\tau} \langle [A']_{id}, C', id', \sigma'\rangle}$$

Sequence: When an exception occurs during the first activity A, the whole sequential composition is abnormally terminated:

$$\frac{\langle A, C, id, \sigma\rangle \xrightarrow{et} \langle early_{et}, C', id', \sigma'\rangle}{\langle A; B, C, id, \sigma\rangle \xrightarrow{et} \langle early_{et}, C', id', \sigma'\rangle}$$

Considering the activity $[A]_{id}; B$, it means A and B are situated in different choreographies. Thus if an exception occurring within A is captured by the corresponding exception handler, we cannot terminate the whole sequential activity immediately. Only if the exception is not captured within A's scope, then the sequential activity terminates abnormally. Profitted by the *scope* activity, the captured exception within A's scope is hidden from environment, so the above rule also applies to $[A]_{id}; B$.

Parallel: The whole parallel composition terminates abnormally when at least one branch has terminated prematurely with an exception occurred. The occurred exception within one branch can not prevent another branch from continuing until another branch terminates successfully or also terminates prematurely:

$$\frac{\langle A, C, id, \sigma\rangle \xrightarrow{et} \langle early_{et}, C', id', \sigma'\rangle \wedge \langle B, C, id, \sigma\rangle \xrightarrow{\checkmark} \langle \Omega, C', id', \sigma'\rangle}{\langle A \parallel B, C, id, \sigma\rangle \xrightarrow{et} \langle early_{et}, C', id', \sigma'\rangle}$$

$$\frac{\langle A, C, id, \sigma\rangle \xrightarrow{\checkmark} \langle \Omega, C', id', \sigma'\rangle \wedge \langle B, C, id, \sigma\rangle \xrightarrow{et} \langle early_{et}, C', id', \sigma'\rangle}{\langle A \parallel B, C, id, \sigma\rangle \xrightarrow{et} \langle early_{et}, C', id', \sigma'\rangle}$$

$$\frac{\langle A, C, id, \sigma\rangle \xrightarrow{et_1} \langle early_{et_1}, C', id', \sigma'\rangle \wedge \langle B, C, id, \sigma\rangle \xrightarrow{et_2} \langle early_{et_2}, C', id', \sigma'\rangle}{\langle A \parallel B, C, id, \sigma\rangle \xrightarrow{et} \langle early_{et}, C', id', \sigma'\rangle}$$

The last rule states that when both branches terminate prematurely, the type of the exception derived from the whole parallel activity is a new type which represents the combination of the two original types.

4 Related Work

Up to now, there are only a few works focusing on formalizing choreography languages compared with orchestration languages. Busi et al [4] designs a simple choreography language CL whose main concepts are based on WS-CDL. A choreography in CL is defined by two parts. A declarative part describes the involved entities and a conversational part models the ordering of interactions among services. Paralleled with our language, CL just covers a few concepts without mentioning workunits, guarded choice and even the important features with regard to reusability and long running transactions. Brogi et al [6] formalizes web service choreography interface (WSCI) using a process algebra approach CCS [13]. Based on such formalization, compatibility, replaceability and the automatic generation of adaptors are discussed. WSCI [19] permits to specify a global model of service composition from a different point of view with respect to WS-CDL. More precisely, WSCI just provides a set of connections between pairs of individual operations in each service on the basis of respective behaviors of each participant. Instead, WS-CDL directly describes the interdependencies among different interactions between services.

One of the important features in CDL_0 is to deal with compensation to reverse the effects of a partial work. The concept compensation has its root to the seminal work of Sagas [5]. In the recent years, some works have been done towards the formal definition of this concept. StAC [7] proposes a formal framework for automatic invocation of compensations in the reverse order with respect to the order of their installation. The semantics of StAC was defined on its semantic language $StAC_i$ which has a operational semantics based on the indexed compensation tasks. Butler and Ripon [3] develops an operational semantics for the compensating CSP (cCSP) language in the framework of CSP [8] process algebra. The invocation of compensations is automatic depending on the success or failure of transactions, whereas a compensation in CDL_0 is explicitly activated by the finalize activity lying on the choreography life-line. Bocchi et al [15] designs a language πt-calculus, an extension of the asynchronous π-calculus with long running transactions. A transaction defined in this language contains a body activity, a compensation handler and a failure manager, similar to the structure of a choreography in CDL_0. However, none of them gives the choice for enabled compensation to be selected as desired, invoked in any order as CDL_0 does.

We have done the research on BPEL which is a de facto standard of execution workflow specification for web service orchestration. In [10], the operational semantics for a simplified version μ-BPEL is presented and time-related properties can be verified in model checker UPPAAL based on a formal mapping form μ-BPEL to timed automata. [14,16] studies the semantics of the fault and compensation handling in the BPEL vein. The concepts *compensation closure* and *compensation context* are proposed in the semantic to capture the execution structure and the process of programmable compensation.

5 Conclusion

Choreography is concerned with peer to peer observable collaborations of multiple services that need to interact in order to achieve some business goal. WS-CDL is a language in which a choreography model is specified, and behavior is described from a global or neutral perspective rather than from the perspective of any single service. A choreography is such a scope that provides exception handling and compensation. This language also provides choreography composition to enable scalable modeling and reusability.

This paper has proposed a language CDL_0 enlightened by WS-CDL, where the complicated XML syntactical style is abandoned, but almost all the important features are included. A new concept called *role reference* is introduced into this language in order to distinguish different participants providing the same kind of service. We place a constraint that every role reference in a non-root choreography must be bound directly or indirectly to the participant defined in the root choreography. This constraint enables us to clarify the exact actions performed by a specific service, which facilitates the generation of code skeleton for every participating service. Moreover, CDL_0 adds a *throw* activity to explicitly throw exceptions in the case of application failures or incomplete solutions to exceptions within exception handlers. The operational semantics for CDL_0 is carefully studied. In the semantics, we propose the concept *choreography context*, which captures choreography relations and choreography life-line to enable the process of choreography composition, compensation and exception handling.

Currently, we are also working on the verification of business behavior within a choreography model using process algebra approach. Furthermore, based on the work of the semantics of BPEL [10,14,16], we plan to investigate the relationship between WS-CDL and BPEL. This work can be done from two aspects: how to derive web service skeletons written in BPEL from a given choreography model; check whether a specific BPEL model is consistent against the global choreography model.

References

1. A. Barros, M. Dumas and P. Oaks. A critical overview of web service choreography description language(WS-CDL). *BPTrends*, March 2005.
2. R. Dijkman and M. Dumas. Service-oriented design: a multi-viewpoint approach. *International Journal of Cooperative Information Systems*, vol.13(4), pp. 337-368, 2004.
3. M. Butler and S. Ripon. Executable semantics for compensating CSP. In *Proceedings of 2nd International Workshop on Web Services and Formal Methods*, LNCS 3670, pp. 243-256, 2005.
4. N. Busi, R. Gorrieri, C. Guidi, R. Lucchi and G. Zavattaro. Towards a formal framework for choreography. In *Proceedings of the 14th IEEE International Workshops on Enabling Technologies: Infrastructure for Collaborative Enterprise*, pp. 107-112, 2005.
5. H. Garcia-Molina and K. Salem. Sagas. In *Proc. of ACM SIGMOD'87*, pp. 249-259. ACM Press, 1987.
6. A. Brogi, C. Canal, E. Pimentel, and A. Vallecillo. Formalizing web services choreographies. In *Proc. of WS-FM'04*, ENTCS 105, 2004.
7. M. Butler and C. Ferreira. An operational semantics for StAC, a language for modelling long-running business transactions. In *Proc. of Coordination'04*, LNCS 2949, pp.87-104. Springer, 2004.
8. A.W. Roscoe. The Theory and Practice of Concurrency. Prentice Hall, pearson edition, 1998.
9. G. D. Plotkin. A structural approach to operational semantics. Technical report, Aarhus University, 1981.

10. Pu Geguang, Zhao Xiangpeng, Wang Shuling, and Qiu Zongyan. Towards the semantics and verification of BPEL4WS. In *International Workshop on Web Languages and Formal Methods, WLFM2005*, to appear in Electronic Notes in Theoretical Computer Science, Elsevier 2006.
11. F. Curbera, Y. Goland, J. Klein, F. Leymann, D. Roller, S. Thatte, and S. Weerawarana. Business Process Execution Language for Web Services (BPEL4WS 1.1). http://www-106.ibm.com/developerworks/webservices/library/ws-bpel/, 2003.
12. World Wide Web Consortium. Web Services Choreography Description Language Version 1.0. Candidate Recommendation 9 November 2005. http://www.w3.org/TR/2005/CR-ws-cdl-10-20051109.
13. Robin Milner. Communication and Concurrency. Prentice-Hall, 1989.
14. Pu Geguang, Zhu Huibiao, Qiu Zongyan, Wang Shuling, Zhang Xiangpeng, and He Jifeng. Theoretical foundations of scope-based compensable flow languange for Web Service. In *IFTP FMOODS'06*, LNCS 4307, pp. 251-266. Springer, 2006.
15. L. Bocchi, C. Laneve, and G. Zavattaro. A calculus for long-running transactions. In *FMOODS*, LNCS 2884, pp. 124-138. Springer-Verlag, 2003.
16. Qiu Zongyan, Wang Shuling, Pu Geguang, and Zhao Xiangpeng. Semantics of BPEL4WS-like fault and compensation handling. In *FM2005*, LNCS 3582, pp. 350-365. Springer, 2005.
17. M. Butler and C. Ferreira. A process compensation language. In *Integrated Formal Methods(IFM2000)*, LNCS 1945, pp. 61-76. Springer-Verlag, 2000.
18. M. Chessell, D. Vines, C. Griffin, M. Butler, C. Ferreira, and P. Henderson. Extending the concept of transaction compensation. *IBM Systems Journal*, vol.41(4), pp. 743-758, 2002.
19. World Wide Web Consortium. Web Service Choreography Interface (WSCI) 1.0. http://www.w3.org/TR/wsci, 2002.

Type Checking Choreography Description Language*

Hongli Yang[1], Xiangpeng Zhao[1], Zongyan Qiu[1], Chao Cai[1], and Geguang Pu[2]

[1] LMAM and Department of Informatics, School of Math.,
Peking University, Beijing 100871, China
{yhl, zxp, qzy, toppi}@math.pku.edu.cn
[2] Software Engineering Institute
East China Normal University, Shanghai, 200062, China
ggpu@sei.ecnu.edu.cn

Abstract. The Web Services Choreography Description Language (WS-CDL) is a W3C specification developed for the description of peer-to-peer collaborations of participants from a global viewpoint. Currently WS-CDL has no rigorous static type checking. We believe that introducing a type system will exclude many design and description errors, and ensure desirable properties of the choreography specifications. In this paper, we took a core language CDL, which covers most of the important features of the WS-CDL, and is more convenient for the study. We developed the abstract syntax and operational semantics of CDL, and defined a collection of rules which can be used to check if choreography is well-typed. Moreover, we also proved some type safety theorems for CDL in the sense that well-typed choreography cannot get stuck. We show how the use of type information can allow us to gain confidence in the correctness of choreography.

Keywords: Choreography, WS-CDL, Formal model, Type checking.

1 Introduction

Web services have been becoming more and more important in recent years, and promising the interoperability of various applications running on heterogeneous platforms over Internet. Web service composition refers to the process of combining various web services to provide a value-added service, which has received much interest in supporting enterprise application integration. The recently released web service choreography description language (WS-CDL)[10] is a W3C candidate recommendation for web service composition. WS-CDL is an XML-based language designed for describing the common and collaborative observable behavior of multiple services that interact with each other to achieve a goal. WS-CDL focuses on specifying the business protocol among participant roles. All the behaviors are performed by the participants, and the WS-CDL specification gives a global observation.

One of requirements for WS-CDL success factors is to provide static type checking for ensuring desirable properties of choreography [2]. There are various types that need to be defined before describing a choreography. For instance, the information types that describe variables and general messages in interaction; the tokens that are aliases to information types; the role types that define a set of behaviors; the relationship types that

* Supported by National Natural Science Foundation of China (No. 60573081).

Z. Liu and J. He (Eds.): ICFEM 2006, LNCS 4260, pp. 264–283, 2006.

describe how role types are connected; and the channel types that describe communication links between role types [12]. Mistaken references among number of types can easily cause inconsistency. Although the detection of such inconsistency is essential to a choreography, this detection is beyond the scope of the XML Schema based validation.

We have previously provided a small language CDL with its operational semantics [8], which is a formal model of the simplified WS-CDL. Based on the formal model, we can project a given choreography to orchestration views, which provide a basis for the implementation of the choreography by a number of web services. Moreover, we have translated WS-CDL to the input language of the model-checker SPIN [7], thus allowing us to automatically verify the properties of a given choreography [13]. Since type systems are widely used in programming languages to detect program inconsistency, we moved our attention here toward type system. Our aim is to detect type errors statically. In this paper, we extend CDL language of [8], and define a collection of typing rules to determine if a choreography is well-typed. Moreover, we proved that the type safety for choreography in the sense that well-typed choreography cannot get stuck. "Stuckness" gives us a simple notion of run-time error situations where the operational semantics does not know what to do because the program has reached a "meaningless state"[11]. Finally, we showed how the use of type information allows us to gain confidence in the correctness of a choreography, with an example.

The rest of the paper is organized as follows. We first briefly introduce the syntax of CDL in Section 2. Then we introduce a type system for it (Section 3). Section 4 presents an operational semantics of CDL and the proof the theorems about the type safety. Section 5 gives an example choreography and its type checking process, to illustrate the type system and operational semantics defined. Some related work is discussed in Section 6. Finally, in Section 7, we conclude the paper and discuss some future research directions.

2 CDL Language Definition

The language used in this paper, CDL, can be seen as a core language of WS-CDL of W3C. It includes a large part of the important features related to web service choreography. We present the syntax of CDL in this section, and its type system in Section 3. For the study to be more practical, we include in this language a lot of details from WS-CDL, rather than take the approach towards a minimal core.

In the definitions below, the meta-variable p ranges over package names; I ranges over information type names; k ranges over token names; R, R_1 and R_2 range over role type names; b, b_1 and b_2 range over role behavior names; S ranges over relationship type names; CH ranges over channel type names; C ranges over choreography names; A, B and BA range over activities; e ranges over expressions; x, y, m and n range over variable names; g, g_1, g_2 and q range over XPath boolean expressions; op ranges over the operations offered by the roles; ch ranges over channel variable names. We will use $\overline{Idecl}$ to express a sequence of zero or more $Idecl$(s) (Similarly, for $\overline{Kdecl}$, $\overline{Rdecl}$, $\overline{Sdecl}$, etc.). The notation $\underline{b}$ expresses one or more b (Similarly, for $\underline{b_1}$, $\underline{b_2}$, $\underline{S}$, etc.). We use $R.x$ to refer to the variable x located in role type R.

At the top level of CDL, there is a package declaration $Pdecl$ with name p and a set of type declarations: $Idecl$ for an information type declaration, $Kdecl$ for token, $Rdecl$ for role type, $Sdecl$ for relationship type, $Hdecl$ for channel type, $Cdecl$ for choreography declaration. An information type has a name I and an external type XT which is defined within an XML Schema document or a WSDL document; A token has a name k and an information type I; A role type has a name R and one or more behaviors $\underline{b}$; A relationship type has a name S and two referenced role types: R_1 with behaviors b_1 and R_2 with behaviors b_2; A channel type has a name CH, a receipt role type R with a behavior b, and a token k referencing receipt physical address; A choreography has a name C, one or more relationship types $\underline{S}$, zero or more variable declarations $\overline{Vdecl}$ and an activity A. Finally, a variable is either a message variable x with type I in role types $\underline{R}$, or a channel variable x with type CH in role types $\underline{R}$.

$$
\begin{array}{lll}
Pdecl ::= & \mathsf{pkg}\ \{p\ \overline{Idecl}\ \overline{Kdecl}\ \overline{Rdecl}\ \overline{Sdecl}\ \overline{Hdecl}\ Cdecl\} & \text{(package)} \\
Idecl ::= & \mathsf{info}\ I\ \{XT\} & \text{(infoType)} \\
Kdecl ::= & \mathsf{token}\ \{k\ I\} & \text{(token)} \\
Rdecl ::= & \mathsf{role}\ R\ \{\underline{b}\} & \text{(roleType)} \\
Sdecl ::= & \mathsf{rela}\ S\ \{R_1(\underline{b_1})\ R_2(\underline{b_2})\} & \text{(relationType)} \\
Hdecl ::= & \mathsf{chan}\ CH\ \{\overline{R(b)\ k}\} & \text{(channelType)} \\
Cdecl ::= & \mathsf{chor}\ C\ \{\underline{S}\ \overline{Vdecl}\ A\} & \text{(choreography)} \\
Vdecl ::= & \mathsf{var}\ \{x\ I\ \underline{R}\} \mid \mathsf{var}\ \{x\ CH\ \underline{R}\} & \text{(var definition)}
\end{array}
$$

$$
\begin{array}{lll}
A ::= & BA & \text{(basic)} \\
 & \mid q?A & \text{(condition)} \\
 & \mid q * A & \text{(repeat)} \\
 & \mid g\!:\!A\!:\!q & \text{(workunit)} \\
 & \mid A; B & \text{(sequence)} \\
 & \mid A \sqcap B & \text{(non-determ.)} \\
 & \mid g_1 \Rightarrow A \,[]\, g_2 \Rightarrow B & \text{(general-choice)} \\
 & \mid A \parallel B & \text{(parallel)} \\
BA ::= & \mathsf{skip} & \text{(skip)} \\
 & \mid R.x := e & \text{(assign)} \\
 & \mid \mathsf{comm}\ (S, R_1.x \rightarrow R_2.y, rec, ch, op) & \text{(request)} \\
 & \mid \mathsf{comm}\ (S, R_1.x \leftarrow R_2.y, rec, ch, op) & \text{(response)} \\
 & \mid \mathsf{comm}\ (S, R_1.x \rightarrow R_2.y, R_1.m \leftarrow R_2.n, rec, ch, op) & \text{(req-resp)} \\
e ::= & R.x \mid xp & \text{(expression)}
\end{array}
$$

An activity A is either a basic activity BA or a control-flow activity. Basic activities include $skip$, assignment and interaction. The assignment activity $R.x := e$ assigns, within the role type R, the value of expression e to the variable x. Here the expression e is either an XPath expression xp or a variable $R.x$, which represents a variable x belonging to role type R.

The most complex forms of basic activities are the interaction, which is represented here by three different comm $(\ldots)$. In an interaction, S denotes a relationship type; R_1 and R_2 are two participant role types; ch is a channel variable; and rec is the shorthand for the assignments $R_1.\overline{x_1} := \overline{e_1}, R_2.\overline{y_2} := \overline{e_2}$, where $\overline{x_1}$ and $\overline{y_2}$ are two lists of state variables on the role types R_1 and R_2, respectively. Note that here we use overline rather than underline.

The Well-formedness of *Pdecl*. A package declaration

$$Pdecl ::= \mathsf{pkg}\ \{\, p\ \overline{Idecl}\ \ \overline{Kdecl}\ \ \overline{Rdecl}\ \ \overline{Sdecl}\ \ \overline{Hdecl}\ \ Cdecl\}$$

is well-formed, if all the following conditions hold:

- All type names, i.e. $I_1, \ldots, I_i, R_1, \ldots, R_j, S_1, \ldots, S_m, CH_1, \ldots, CH_n, C$, are distinct from each other.
- The token names $k_1, \ldots, k_k$ in the package are different from each other.
- The variable names $x_1, \ldots, x_k$ in the package are different from each other.

In the following, we only consider well-formed package declaration.

In the definition of this language, we omitted some features of WS-CDL for the simplicity. The important features omitted here include some details of the channels, exceptions, and finalize blocks. We will consider them in our future work.

3 Type System of CDL

Now we define a type system for CDL.

3.1 Typing Context

A type T in the type system is either an imported external type XT, an information type $\mathsf{info}(XT)$, a token $\mathsf{token}(I)$, a role type $\mathsf{role}(\underline{b})$, a relationship type $\mathsf{rela}(R_1(\underline{b_1})\ R_2(\underline{b_2}))$, an information variable type $\mathsf{var}(I\ \ \underline{R})$, a channel variable type $\mathsf{var}(CH\ \ \underline{R})$, or a channel type $\mathsf{chan}(R)$. Here we omit other information from the channel type, only care about the receiving role type R for the information exchange.

Following is the formal definition of the forms of type T:

$$\begin{array}{rll} T ::= & XT & \text{(imported types)} \\ & |\,\mathsf{info}(XT) & \text{(infoType)} \\ & |\,\mathsf{token}(I) & \text{(token)} \\ & |\,\mathsf{role}(\underline{b}) & \text{(roleType)} \\ & |\,\mathsf{rela}(R_1(\underline{b_1})\ \ R_2(\underline{b_2})) & \text{(relationshipType)} \\ & |\,\mathsf{chan}(R) & \text{(channelType)} \\ & |\,\mathsf{var}(I\ \ \underline{R}) & \text{(infoVariable)} \\ & |\,\mathsf{var}(CH\ \ \underline{R}) & \text{(channelVariable)} \end{array}$$

The typing context Γ is a sequence of the pair $n : T$, where n is a name and T is a type defined above. It is constructed and used during the static analysis of CDL specifications. We define a function build to extract type information from CDL descriptions. The results of the extractions will be used in the construction of typing context Γ. Here is the definition of the function build:

$$\text{build (info } I\ \{XT\}) = I : \text{info}(XT)$$
$$\text{build (token}\{k\ \ I\}) = k : \text{token}(I)$$
$$\text{build (role } R\ \{\underline{b}\}) = R : \text{role}(\underline{b})$$
$$\text{build (rela } S\ \{R_1(\underline{b_1})\ \ R_2(\underline{b_2})\}) = S : \text{rela}(R_1(\underline{b_1})\ \ R_2(\underline{b_2}))$$
$$\text{build (chan } CH\ \{R(b)\ \ k\}) = CH : \text{chan}(R)$$
$$\text{build (var}\{v\ \ I\ \ \underline{R}\}) = x : \text{var}(I\ \ \underline{R})$$
$$\text{build (var}\{v\ \ CH\ \ \underline{R}\}) = x : \text{var}(CH\ \ \underline{R})$$

Now we are ready to present the typing rules for CDL. Firstly, we have a basic rule as follows: if the pair $x : T$ exists in Γ, then we have the result that under the context Γ, we know that the type of x is T.

$$\frac{x : T \in \Gamma}{\Gamma \vdash x : T}$$

Type checking a choreography is, in some sense, quite different from type checking a program. A choreography is not an independent entity. Its features and behaviors depend closely on its environment, in fact, the boundless Internet. Thus, for the successfully type checking the choreography described in CDL, we are going to isolate (introduce in) a set of basic functions which dependent on the information outside the choreography under checking, and indispensable in the checking process. We can reasonably assume that the implementation of the checking system offers these functions.

3.2 Typed Rules for Expressions

We present initially rules for the expressions. Our language have two kinds of expressions corresponding to the variables and XPath expressions in WS-CDL. Because each variable is located in some role types, we define here only the type rule for the variable form $R.x$. We omit the type rule for general variable form x.

The type of a variable $R.x$ comes from the type context Γ directly.

$$\frac{\Gamma \vdash I : \text{info}(XT), \quad \Gamma \vdash x : \text{var}(I, \underline{R}), \quad R \in \underline{R}}{\Gamma \vdash R.x : \text{info}(XT)} \qquad \text{(VarType1)}$$

$$\frac{\Gamma \vdash CH : \text{chan}(R), \quad \Gamma \vdash x : \text{var}(CH, \underline{R}), \quad R \in \underline{R}}{\Gamma \vdash R.x : \text{chan}(R)} \qquad \text{(VarType2)}$$

We suppose, in the first, that there is a function *xptype* which returns the type of an XPath expression xp, and infers the type of xp in Γ as following rule. Here XT expresses an external data type.

$$\frac{xptype(xp) = \text{info}(XT)}{\Gamma \vdash xp : \text{info}(XT)} \qquad \text{(XpathType1)}$$

$$\frac{xptype(xp) = \text{chan}(R)}{\Gamma \vdash xp : \text{chan}(R)} \qquad \text{(XpathType2)}$$

3.3 Well-Typed Type Declarations

We will use "$\Gamma \vdash \ldots$ ok" to express that a type declaration "..." is well-typed in context Γ. For simplicity and cleanness, in the presentation of the rules below, we may omit some internal construct of some type descriptions, and just write down the type label in the case that the detailed construct is not used in the rule. For instance, in some cases, we will use the shorten form I : info instead the full form I : $\mathsf{info}(XT)$, to express that I is an information type when we don't care about its full type details.

If XT refers to the data type defined within an XML Schema document or a WSDL document, then the information type $\mathsf{info}\ I\ \{XT\}$ is well-typed. Here we assume a function $check$ which checks if XT is a valid external data type.

$$\frac{check(XT)\ \text{ok}}{\mathsf{info}\ I\ \{XT\}\ \text{ok}} \qquad \text{(Info)}$$

If type definition I : $\mathsf{info}(XT)$ exists in Γ, then $\mathsf{token}\ \{k\ \ I\}$ is well-typed. Here k is the token name.

$$\frac{\Gamma \vdash I : \mathsf{info}}{\Gamma \vdash \mathsf{token}\ \{k\ \ I\}\ \text{ok}} \qquad \text{(Token)}$$

Role type $\mathsf{role}\ R\ \{\underline{b}\}$ is always ok.

$$\vdash \mathsf{role}\ R\ \{\underline{b}\}\ \text{ok} \qquad \text{(Role)}$$

If role types R_1 with behaviors $\underline{a_1}$ and R_2 with behaviors $\underline{a_2}$ have been defined in Γ, the behaviors $\underline{b_1}$ are a subset of $\underline{a_1}$, and the behaviors $\underline{b_2}$ are a subset of $\underline{a_2}$, then relationship type $\mathsf{rela}\ S\ \{R_1(\underline{b_1})\ \ R_2(\underline{b_2})\}$ is well-typed. A behavior specifies the observable operations which participant exhibits.

$$\frac{\Gamma \vdash R_1 : \mathsf{role}(\underline{a_1}),\quad \Gamma \vdash R_2 : \mathsf{role}(\underline{a_2}),\quad \underline{b_1} \subseteq \underline{a_1},\quad \underline{b_2} \subseteq \underline{a_2}}{\Gamma \vdash \mathsf{rela}\ S\ \ \{R_1(\underline{b_1})\ \ R_2(\underline{b_2})\}\ \text{ok}} \qquad \text{(Rela)}$$

If role type R with behaviors $\underline{a}$ and token k are defined in Γ, and behavior b belongs to the set of behaviors $\underline{a}$, then channel type $\mathsf{chan}\ CH\{R(b)\ \ k\}$ is well-typed.

$$\frac{\Gamma \vdash R : \mathsf{role}(\underline{a}),\quad \Gamma \vdash k : \mathsf{token},\quad b \in \underline{a}}{\Gamma \vdash \mathsf{chan}\ \ CH\ \ \{R(b)\ \ k\}\ \text{ok}} \qquad \text{(Chan)}$$

3.4 Well-Typed Activities and Choreography

Variable Declarations. An information variable $\mathsf{var}\ \ \{x\ \ I\ \ \underline{R}\}$ is ok if information type I is defined in Γ, and role types $\underline{R}$ are defined in Γ too.

$$\frac{\Gamma \vdash I : \mathsf{info},\quad \Gamma \vdash \underline{R} : \underline{\mathsf{role}}}{\Gamma \vdash \mathsf{var}\ \ \{x\ \ I\ \ \underline{R}\}\ \text{ok}} \qquad \text{(Var1)}$$

The rule for a well-typed channel variable is similar:

$$\frac{\Gamma \vdash CH : \mathsf{chan},\quad \Gamma \vdash \underline{R} : \underline{\mathsf{role}}}{\Gamma \vdash \mathsf{var}\ \ \{x\ \ CH\ \ \underline{R}\}\ \text{ok}} \qquad \text{(Var2)}$$

In order to make sure that the assignment activity is well-typed, we assume a relation $compatible(T_1, T_2)$ which can determine if the value of type T_2 can be assigned to the variable of type T_1. This function should be reflective and transitive, that is:

$$compatible(T, T) \qquad \text{(Reflexivity)}$$

$$\frac{compatible(T_1, T_2), \quad compatible(T_2, T_3)}{compatible(T_1, T_3)} \qquad \text{(transitivity)}$$

Basic Activities. A skip activity is always ok.

$$\Gamma \vdash \mathsf{skip\ ok} \qquad \text{(Skip)}$$

An information variable assignment $R.x := e$ is ok, if $R.x$ has type $\mathsf{info}(XT_1)$, expression e has type $\mathsf{info}(XT_2)$, and types $\mathsf{info}(XT_1)$ and $\mathsf{info}(XT_2)$ are assignment compatible.

$$\frac{\Gamma \vdash R.x : \mathsf{info}(XT_1), \quad \Gamma \vdash e : \mathsf{info}(XT_2) \quad compatible(\mathsf{info}(XT_1), \mathsf{info}(XT_2))}{\Gamma \vdash R.x := e \ \text{ ok}} \qquad \text{(Assign1)}$$

Similarly we have rule for well-typed channel variable assignment.

$$\frac{\Gamma \vdash R.x : \mathsf{chan}(R_1), \quad \Gamma \vdash e : \mathsf{chan}(R_2), \quad R_1 = R_2}{\Gamma \vdash R.x := e \ \text{ ok}} \qquad \text{(Assign2)}$$

Before defining the well-typedness of an interaction activity, we need to define the condition that a message exchange $R_1.x \to R_2.y$ is ok.

$$\frac{\Gamma \vdash R_1.x : T_1, \quad \Gamma \vdash R_2.y : T_2, \quad T_1 = T_2}{\Gamma \vdash R_1.x \to R_2.y \ \text{ ok}}$$

A request interaction $\mathsf{comm}\,(S, R_1.x \to R_2.y, rec, ch, op)$ is well-typed, if relationship type S is defined in Γ, message exchange and the state variables records are all ok in Γ, both channel type CH and channel variable ch exist in Γ. In the rule below, condition $R_1 \in \underline{R}$ means that the role type R_1 must own the channel variable ch for its communication; condition $op \in \underline{b_2}$ means that operation op is one of the behaviors of role type R_2. Please note rec is the shorthand for the assignments $R_1.\overline{x_1} := \overline{e_1}, R_2.\overline{y_2} := \overline{e_2}$.

$$\frac{\begin{array}{c}\Gamma \vdash S : \mathsf{rela}(\ R_1(\underline{b_1})\ \ R_2(\underline{b_2})) \\ \Gamma \vdash R_1.x \to R_2.y \ \text{ ok} \\ \Gamma \vdash R_1.\overline{x_1} := \overline{e_1} \ \text{ ok}, \quad \Gamma \vdash R_2.\overline{y_2} := \overline{e_2} \ \text{ ok} \\ \Gamma \vdash CH : \mathsf{chan}(R_2), \quad \Gamma \vdash ch : \mathsf{var}(CH\ \underline{R}) \\ R_1 \in \underline{R}, \quad op \in \underline{b_2}\end{array}}{\Gamma \vdash \mathsf{comm}\,(S, R_1.x \to R_2.y, rec, ch, op) \ \text{ ok}} \qquad \text{(Request)}$$

Similarly we have rule to check whether a response interaction is well-typed. Here $R_2 \in \underline{R}$ means that role type R_2 must own channel variable ch through which it can communicate with role type R_1. It is necessary that operation op is one of the behaviors of role type R_1.

$$\frac{\begin{array}{c} \Gamma \vdash S : \mathsf{rela}(\ R_1(\underline{b_1})\ \ R_2(\underline{b_2})) \\ \Gamma \vdash R_1.x \leftarrow R_2.y \ \text{ ok} \\ \Gamma \vdash R_1.\overline{x_1} := \overline{e_1} \ \text{ ok}, \quad \Gamma \vdash R_2.\overline{y_2} := \overline{e_2} \ \text{ ok} \\ \Gamma \vdash CH : \mathsf{chan}(R_1), \quad \Gamma \vdash ch : \mathsf{var}(CH\ \underline{R}) \\ R_2 \in \underline{R}, \quad op \in \underline{b_1} \end{array}}{\Gamma \vdash \mathsf{comm}\,(S, R_1.x \leftarrow R_2.y, rec, ch, op) \ \text{ ok}} \quad \text{(Response)}$$

For a request-response interaction, we need both request message exchange and response message exchange are ok in Γ. Here we also assume that operation op is one of the behaviors of role type R_2.

$$\frac{\begin{array}{c} \Gamma \vdash S : \mathsf{rela}(\ R_1(\underline{b_1})\ \ R_2(\underline{b_2})) \\ \Gamma \vdash R_1.x \rightarrow R_2.y \ \text{ ok}, \quad \Gamma \vdash R_1.m \leftarrow R_2.n \ \text{ ok} \\ \Gamma \vdash R_1.\overline{x_1} := \overline{e_1} \ \text{ ok}, \quad \Gamma \vdash R_2.\overline{y_2} := \overline{e_2} \ \text{ ok} \\ \Gamma \vdash CH : \mathsf{chan}(R_2), \quad \Gamma \vdash ch : \mathsf{var}(CH\ \underline{R}) \\ R_1 \in \underline{R}, \quad op \in \underline{b_2} \end{array}}{\Gamma \vdash \mathsf{comm}\,(S, R_1.x \rightarrow R_2.y, R_1.m \leftarrow R_2.n, rec, ch, op) \ \text{ ok}} \quad \text{(RR)}$$

Control Flow Activities. Following are the rules of well-typed control flow activities. As an example, a condition activity $q?A$ is well-typed, if both activity A is ok and XPath expression q has type $Bool$ in Γ. The type $Bool$ is an XML schema data type. Here we use $Bool$ as a shorthand for $\mathsf{info}(Bool)$.

$$\frac{\Gamma \vdash A \ \text{ ok}, \quad \Gamma \vdash q : Bool}{\Gamma \vdash q?A \ \text{ ok}} \quad \text{(Condition)}$$

Other rules are listed here. The meaning of these rules are quite regular. We omit the explanations about them.

$$\frac{\Gamma \vdash A \ \text{ ok}, \quad \Gamma \vdash q : Bool}{\Gamma \vdash q * A \ \text{ ok}} \quad \text{(Repeat)}$$

$$\frac{\Gamma \vdash A \ \text{ ok}, \quad \Gamma \vdash g : Bool, \quad \Gamma \vdash q : Bool}{\Gamma \vdash g{:}A{:}q \ \text{ ok}} \quad \text{(WorkUnit)}$$

$$\frac{\Gamma \vdash A \ \text{ ok}, \quad \Gamma \vdash B \ \text{ ok}}{\Gamma \vdash A; B \ \text{ ok}} \quad \text{(Sequence)}$$

$$\frac{\Gamma \vdash A \ \text{ ok}, \quad \Gamma \vdash B \ \text{ ok}}{\Gamma \vdash A \sqcap B \ \text{ ok}} \quad \text{(Non-Det)}$$

$$\frac{\Gamma \vdash A \ \text{ ok}, \quad \Gamma \vdash B \ \text{ ok}, \quad \Gamma \vdash g_1 : Bool, \quad \Gamma \vdash g_2 : Bool}{\Gamma \vdash g_1 \Rightarrow A \,[\!]\, g_2 \Rightarrow B \ \text{ ok}} \quad \text{(Gen-Choice)}$$

$$\frac{\Gamma \vdash A \ \text{ ok}, \quad \Gamma \vdash B \ \text{ ok}}{\Gamma \vdash A \parallel B \ \text{ ok}} \quad \text{(Parallel)}$$

Choreography. A choreography is well-typed if relationship types $\underline{S}$ are defined in Γ, variable declarations $\overline{Vdecl}$ are ok in Γ, and activity A is ok in type environment $\Gamma; \mathsf{build}(\overline{Vdecl})$. Please note that we use ; to express the order of type context which is constructed step by step during static analysis.

$$\frac{\Gamma \vdash \underline{S} : \underline{\mathsf{rela}}, \quad \Gamma \vdash \overline{Vdecl} \text{ ok}, \quad \Gamma; \mathsf{build}(\overline{Vdecl}) \vdash A \text{ ok}}{\Gamma \vdash \mathsf{chor}\ C\ \{\underline{S}\ \overline{Vdecl}\ A\} \text{ ok}}$$

Here a set of variable declarations $\overline{Vdecl}$ are ok if each variable declaration $Vdecl_i$ ($i \in 1 \ldots n$) is ok. We extend build to variable declarations $\overline{Vdecl}$ which build a sequence of type pairs for variables. In the following, we adopt the similar extension for other declaration sequences, such as $\mathsf{build}(\overline{Idecl})$.

3.5 Well-Typed Package

Here is the rule for the well-typed package:

$$\frac{\begin{array}{c} \overline{Idecl} \text{ ok}, \quad \mathsf{build}(\overline{Idecl}) \vdash \overline{Kdecl} \text{ ok} \\ \overline{Rdecl} \text{ ok}, \quad \mathsf{build}(\overline{Rdecl}) \vdash \overline{Sdecl} \text{ ok} \\ \mathsf{build}(\overline{Kdecl}); \mathsf{build}(\overline{Rdecl}) \vdash \overline{Hdecl} \text{ ok} \\ \mathsf{build}(\overline{Idecl}); \mathsf{build}(\overline{Hdecl}); \mathsf{build}(\overline{Rdecl}) \vdash \overline{Vdecl} \text{ ok} \\ \mathsf{build}(\overline{Idecl}); \ldots; \mathsf{build}(\overline{Vdecl}) \vdash Cdecl \text{ ok} \end{array}}{\vdash \mathsf{pkg}\,\{\, p\ \overline{Idecl}\ \overline{Kdecl}\ \overline{Rdecl}\ \overline{Sdecl}\ \overline{Hdecl}\ Cdecl\} \text{ ok}}$$

4 Operational Semantics and Type Safety

In this section, we will always assume that a choreography declaration $Cdecl$ under consideration is well-typed, unless explicitly specified. The type context Γ constructed has forms $I_1 : \mathsf{info}_1, \ldots, I_h : \mathsf{info}_h, k_1 : \mathsf{token}_1, \ldots, k_i : \mathsf{token}_i, R_1 : \mathsf{role}_1, \ldots, R_j : \mathsf{role}_j, S_1 : \mathsf{rela}_1, \ldots, S_m : \mathsf{rela}_m, CH_1 : \mathsf{chan}_1, \ldots, CH_n : \mathsf{chan}_n, x_1 : \mathsf{var}_1, \ldots, x_p : \mathsf{var}_p$. Please note that here we use the shortening forms of types.

4.1 Auxiliary Definition

For convenience to discuss types of variables, we define Σ_Γ as a mapping from variables of the roles to their types. Note that here the role types R and R' may be identical.

$$\Sigma_\Gamma(R.x) \stackrel{\text{def}}{=} \begin{cases} \mathsf{info}(XT) & \text{if } \Gamma \vdash R.x : \mathsf{info}(XT) \\ \mathsf{chan}(R'(b)\ k) & \text{if } \Gamma \vdash R.x : \mathsf{chan}(R'(b)\ k) \end{cases}$$

4.2 State and Configuration

A state Δ of a choreography is a composition of each participant role's state.

$$\Delta \stackrel{\text{def}}{=} \langle \Delta_{R_1}, \Delta_{R_2}, \cdots, \Delta_{R_n} \rangle$$

where $R_1, R_2, \ldots, R_n$ are the all roles in the choreography.

A role state Δ_{R_i} $(i = 1, \cdots, n)$ is a function from the variable names of the role R_i to their values, with the form $R_i.x_1 : v_1, R_i.x_2 : v_2, \cdots, R_i.x_k : v_k$ $(k \geq 0)$. We will always suppose that each variable name is decorated with a role name on which it resides. For convenience, we use the form $\Delta[\overline{v}/R.\overline{x}]$ to denote a global state obtained from global state Δ with some variable assignments $R.\overline{x} := \overline{v}$ on the given role R.

A value here is a value v_{inf} of any information type, or a channel instance v_{ch} of any channel type.

$$\begin{array}{lll} v ::= & v_{inf} & \text{(information value)} \\ & \mid v_{ch} & \text{(channel value)} \end{array}$$

A configuration is of the form $\langle s, \Delta \rangle$, where s is a piece of CDL specification, and Δ is a state. We use $\langle \epsilon, \Delta \rangle$ to denote a terminated configuration with empty specification.

4.3 Evaluation of Expression

We use $\Delta \models e \rightarrow v$ to express that expression e is evaluated to a value v under state Δ. When dealing with XPath expressions, we will not care about the inner structure of them and simply assume that these expressions can be evaluated. We assume a function *xpeval* such that $xpeval(xp, \Delta)$ returns the value of XPath expression xp under state Δ.

The evaluations of expressions are formally defined by the following rules.

$$\frac{\Delta(R.x) = v}{\Delta \models R.x \rightarrow v} \qquad \text{(VAR)}$$

$$\frac{xpeval(xp, \Delta) = v_{inf}}{\Delta \models xp \rightarrow v_{inf}} \qquad \text{(XPATH1)}$$

$$\frac{xpeval(xp, \Delta) = v_{ch}}{\Delta \models xp \rightarrow v_{ch}} \qquad \text{(XPATH2)}$$

We say that the state Δ is consistent with the type context Γ if:

- $dom(\Delta) = dom(\Sigma_\Gamma)$;
- For any $R.x \in dom(\Delta)$, $compatible(\Sigma_\Gamma(R.x), valType(\Delta(R.x)))$.

Here the function *valType* returns the type of a value, $valType(\Delta(R.x))$ returns the type of the value of variable $R.x$ in state Δ. In the following, we always use notation $valType(v)$ to denote the type of the value v, and $valType(\overline{v})$ to denote a sequence of the types of the values $\overline{v}$.

Theorem 1 (Type safety of expression). For any type context Γ, an expression e, if there exists a type T such that $\Gamma \vdash e : T$, then for any state Δ that is consistent with Γ, there exists a value v such that $\Delta \models e \rightarrow v$ and $compatible(T, valType(v))$.

Proof. By the induction on the structure of e.

- Case $R.x$. We discuss each possible type of $R.x$:
  - Case $\mathsf{info}(XT)$
    Since $\Gamma \vdash R.x : \mathsf{info}(XT)$ can only be resulted from rule (VarType1), we have $T = \mathsf{info}(XT)$ and $\Sigma_\Gamma(R.x) = T$, i.e., $R.x \in dom(\Sigma_\Gamma)$. Since Δ is consistent with type context Γ, we have immediately $R.x \in dom(\Delta)$ and $compatible(\Sigma_\Gamma(R.x), valType(\Delta(R.x)))$, i.e., there is a value v such that $(R.x : v) \in \Delta$ and $compatible(T, valType(v))$. From rule (VAR), we have that $\Delta \models R.x \rightarrow v$.
  - Case $\mathsf{chan}(R)$
    The proof is same as above.
- Case xp. We discuss each possible type of xp:
  - Case $\mathsf{info}(XT)$
    Since $\Gamma \vdash xp : \mathsf{info}(XT)$ can only be resulted from rule (XpathType1), we have $T = \mathsf{info}(XT)$. From rule (XPATH1), we know that $\Delta \models xp \rightarrow v_{inf}$. This implies that $compatible(\mathsf{info}(XT), valType(v_{inf}))$.
  - Case $\mathsf{chan}(R)$
    The proof is same as above. □

4.4 Execution of Activity

In this subsection, we define an operational semantics for our language. We use the big-step style to define the semantics in order to prove features of our type system. We write $(A, \Delta) \rightarrow (\varepsilon, \Delta')$ to denote that the execution of activity A under state Δ will terminate and reach a new state Δ'.

Basic Activities. The semantics of the basic activities are defined as follows:

The execution of skip activity always terminates successfully, and leaves everything unchanged.

$$\langle \mathsf{skip}, \Delta \rangle \longrightarrow \langle \epsilon, \Delta \rangle \qquad \text{(SKIP)}$$

The assignment activity updates variable $R.x$ with the value v of expression e.

$$\frac{R.x \in dom(\Delta), \Delta \models e \rightarrow v}{\langle R.x := e,\ \Delta \rangle \longrightarrow \langle \epsilon, \Delta[v/R.x] \rangle} \qquad \text{(ASS)}$$

In the execution of an interaction activity, some information may exchange between two participant roles. After the interaction, there may be some variable updates on both roles. Here we suppose that rec is a shorthand for the assignments $R_1.\overline{x_1} := \overline{e_1}$ and $R_2.\overline{y_2} := \overline{e_2}$.

$$\frac{\begin{array}{c}\Delta \models R_1.x \rightarrow v,\ \ R_2.y \in dom(\Delta), \\ R_1.\overline{x_1} \in dom(\Delta),\ \ R_2.\overline{y_2} \in dom(\Delta),\ \ \Delta \models \overline{e_1} \rightarrow \overline{v_1},\ \ \Delta \models \overline{e_2} \rightarrow \overline{v_2},\end{array}}{\begin{array}{c}\langle \mathsf{comm}\,(S, R_1.x \rightarrow R_2.y, rec, ch, op),\ \Delta \rangle \longrightarrow \\ \langle \epsilon, \Delta[v/(R_2.y)][\overline{v_1}/(R_1.\overline{x_1}), \overline{v_2}/(R_2.\overline{y_2})] \rangle\end{array}} \qquad \text{(REQ)}$$

$$\frac{\begin{array}{c}\Delta \models R_2.y \rightarrow v,\ \ R_1.x \in dom(\Delta), \\ R_1.\overline{x_1} \in dom(\Delta),\ \ R_2.\overline{y_2} \in dom(\Delta),\ \ \Delta \models \overline{e_1} \rightarrow \overline{v_1},\ \ \Delta \models \overline{e_2} \rightarrow \overline{v_2},\end{array}}{\begin{array}{c}\langle \mathsf{comm}\,(S, R_1.x \leftarrow R_2.y, rec, ch, op),\ \Delta \rangle \longrightarrow \\ \langle \epsilon, \Delta[v/(R_1.x)][\overline{v_1}/(R_1.\overline{x_1}), \overline{v_2}/(R_2.\overline{y_2})] \rangle\end{array}} \qquad \text{(RESP)}$$

$$\frac{\begin{array}{c}\Delta \models R_1.x \to v,\;\; R_2.y \in dom(\Delta),\;\; \Delta \models R_2.n \to v',\;\; R_1.m \in dom(\Delta),\\ R_1.\overline{x_1} \in dom(\Delta),\;\; R_2.\overline{y_2} \in dom(\Delta),\;\; \Delta \models \overline{e_1} \to \overline{v_1},\;\; \Delta \models \overline{e_2} \to \overline{v_2},\end{array}}{\begin{array}{c}\langle \mathsf{comm}\,(S, R_1.x \to R_2.y, R_1.m \leftarrow R_2.n, rec, ch, op),\; \Delta\rangle \longrightarrow \\ \langle \epsilon, \Delta[v/(R_2.y)][v'/(R_1.m)][\overline{v_1}/(R_1.\overline{x_1}), \overline{v_2}/(R_2.\overline{y_2})]\rangle\end{array}} \quad \text{(REQ-RESP)}$$

In the WS-CDL specification, there are more detailed control mechanisms for the execution time of assignments on the state variables. We omit them for the focus of this paper on type-related issues.

Control Flow Activities. The semantics of many control flow activities are rather standard. We need not to explain them in details.

In the first place, the conditionals and the iterations:

$$\frac{\Delta \models q \to \textbf{false}}{\langle q?A, \Delta\rangle \longrightarrow \langle \epsilon, \Delta\rangle} \quad \text{(IF-FALSE)}$$

$$\frac{\Delta \models q \to \textbf{true},\;\; \langle A, \Delta\rangle \longrightarrow \langle \epsilon, \Delta'\rangle}{\langle q?A, \Delta\rangle \longrightarrow \langle \epsilon, \Delta'\rangle} \quad \text{(IF-TRUE)}$$

$$\frac{\Delta(q) = \textbf{false}}{\langle q * A, \Delta\rangle \longrightarrow \langle \epsilon, \Delta\rangle} \quad \text{(REP-FALSE)}$$

$$\frac{\Delta(q) = \textbf{true},\;\; \langle A, \Delta\rangle \longrightarrow \langle \epsilon, \Delta''\rangle,\;\; \langle q * A, \Delta''\rangle \longrightarrow \langle \epsilon, \Delta'\rangle}{\langle q * A, \Delta\rangle \longrightarrow \langle \epsilon, \Delta'\rangle} \quad \text{(REP-TRUE)}$$

The workunit $(g : A : q)$ will blocked until the guard g evaluates to true. When the guard is trigged, the activity A is executed. If A terminates successfully, and if the repetition condition q evaluates to true, the workunit will be considered again; otherwise, it finishes. The formal rules are defined as follows.

$$\frac{\Delta(g) = \textbf{true},\;\; \langle A, \Delta\rangle \longrightarrow \langle \epsilon, \Delta'\rangle,\;\; \Delta'(q) = \textbf{false}}{\langle g{:}A{:}q, \Delta\rangle \longrightarrow \langle \epsilon, \Delta'\rangle} \quad \text{(BLOCK1)}$$

$$\frac{\Delta(g) = \textbf{true},\;\; \langle A, \Delta\rangle \longrightarrow \langle \epsilon, \Delta'\rangle,\;\; \Delta'(q) = \textbf{true},\;\; \langle g{:}A{:}q, \Delta'\rangle \longrightarrow \langle \epsilon, \Delta''\rangle}{\langle g{:}A{:}q, \Delta\rangle \longrightarrow \langle \epsilon, \Delta''\rangle} \quad \text{(BLOCK2)}$$

The sequential compositions and non-deterministic structures are regular:

$$\frac{\langle A, \Delta\rangle \longrightarrow \langle \epsilon, \Delta''\rangle,\;\; \langle B, \Delta''\rangle \longrightarrow \langle \epsilon, \Delta'\rangle}{\langle A; B, \Delta\rangle \longrightarrow \langle \epsilon, \Delta'\rangle} \quad \text{(SEQ)}$$

$$\frac{\langle A, \Delta\rangle \longrightarrow \langle \epsilon, \Delta'\rangle}{\langle A \sqcap B, \Delta\rangle \longrightarrow \langle \epsilon, \Delta'\rangle} \quad \text{(NON-DET1)}$$

$$\frac{\langle B, \Delta\rangle \longrightarrow \langle \epsilon, \Delta'\rangle}{\langle A \sqcap B, \Delta\rangle \longrightarrow \langle \epsilon, \Delta'\rangle} \quad \text{(NON-DET2)}$$

In the definition of WS-CDL, branches in a choice activity is not symmetric, but ordered. The branch comes first has a higher priority. That is, if the guards of two branches evaluate to true simultaneously, the first branch will take the control. Following this spirit, the rules for the choice activities in CDL are as follows.

$$\frac{\Delta(g_1) = \textbf{true}, \langle A, \Delta\rangle \longrightarrow \langle \epsilon, \Delta'\rangle}{\langle g_1 \Rightarrow A \,[]\, g_2 \Rightarrow B, \Delta\rangle \longrightarrow \langle \epsilon, \Delta'\rangle} \qquad \text{(CHOICE1)}$$

$$\frac{\Delta(g_1) = \textbf{false},\ \Delta(g_2) = \textbf{true}, \langle B, \Delta\rangle \longrightarrow \langle \epsilon, \Delta'\rangle}{\langle g_1 \Rightarrow A \,[]\, g_2 \Rightarrow B, \Delta\rangle \longrightarrow \langle \epsilon, \Delta'\rangle} \qquad \text{(CHOICE2)}$$

Now comes the parallel structures. In the development of this operational semantics, our intention is to make it a medium for the proof of the properties of our type system, especially, the Type Safety Theorem in Section 4.5. We all know that the parallel activities will introduce many subtle problems into the execution. However, these subtleties are dynamic problems, and can not be detected and prevented, in general, by the type checking. In defining type systems, we can ignore these dynamic problems. Following this recognition, in the semantical rule of parallel structures, we will not care about the interactions between the parallel execution of activities, and only consider whether they terminate. We simply define that if both the execution of A and B terminate, then $A \parallel B$ will terminate. Thus, the rule for the parallel composition is rather simple:

$$\frac{\langle A, \Delta\rangle \longrightarrow \langle \epsilon, \Delta'\rangle, \langle B, \Delta\rangle \longrightarrow \langle \epsilon, \Delta''\rangle}{\langle A \parallel B, \Delta\rangle \longrightarrow \langle \epsilon, \Delta' \oplus \Delta''\rangle} \qquad \text{(PARA)}$$

Operator $\oplus$ denotes a state combination. If Δ' and Δ'' update one variable to two same values, then $\Delta' \oplus \Delta''$ update this variable to any one of the values. Here we don't care which value will be taken by one variable in $\Delta' \oplus \Delta''$ when Δ' and Δ'' update this variable to two different values.

Please note that the execution of activity $q * A$ and $g : A : q$ might not come to a terminated configuration due to infinite loops. The general choice activity will blocked if the guards of two branches evaluate to false simultaneously.

Lemma 1. *If* $\langle A, \Delta\rangle \longrightarrow \langle \epsilon, \Delta'\rangle$, *then* $dom(\Delta) = dom(\Delta')$.

Proof. By induction on the structure of the derivative rules. Note that none of these rules changes $dom(\Delta)$. Therefore, the correctness of the lemma is obvious. □

4.5 Type Safety of Activity

We list in the first some abnormal cases which cannot be statically checked.

Abnormal Case 1: The execution of an activity may not terminate due to an infinite loop.

Abnormal Case 2: The execution of a workunit activity $g : A : q$ will block when g evaluates to false for ever.

Abnormal Case 3: The execution of a general choice activity $g_1 \Rightarrow A \,[]\, g_2 \Rightarrow B$ will block when the guards g_1 and g_2 evaluate to false for ever.

Theorem 2 (Type safety of activity). For any type context Γ and activity A, if $\Gamma \vdash A$ ok, then for any state Δ which is consistent with Γ, there exists a state Δ' such that $\langle A, \Delta\rangle \longrightarrow \langle \epsilon, \Delta'\rangle$ and Δ' is consistent with Γ, unless the abnormal cases listed above happen in the execution.

Proof. By the induction on the structure of A.

- Case skip
  >From rule (SKIP), we know that $\langle \mathsf{skip}, \Delta\rangle \longrightarrow \langle \epsilon, \Delta\rangle$. Obviously, Δ is consistent with Γ.
- Case $R.x := e$
  We discuss each possible type of $R.x$:
  - Case $\mathsf{info}(XT)$
    Since $\Gamma \vdash R.x := e$ ok can only be resulted from rule (Assign1), we have $\Sigma_\Gamma(R.x) = \mathsf{info}(XT)$, $\Gamma \vdash e : T$, and $compatible(\mathsf{info}(XT), T)$. From Theorem 1, there is a value v such that $\Delta \models e \to v$ and $compatible(T, valType(v))$. Noticing that $R.x \in dom(\Sigma_\Gamma)$, since Γ is consistent with Δ, we have $R.x \in dom(\Delta)$. Thus, from rule (ASS), we know that $\langle R.x := e,\ \Delta\rangle \longrightarrow \langle \epsilon, \Delta'\rangle$, where $\Delta' = \Delta[v/R.x]$. Noticing that $valType(\Delta'(R.x)) = valType(v)$, from rule (Transmission), we have $compatible(\mathsf{info}(XT), valType(v))$. From these facts and Lemma 1, we have $dom(\Delta') = dom(\Delta) = dom(\Sigma_\Gamma)$. Therefore, Δ' is consistent with Γ.
  - Case $\mathsf{chan}(R)$
    The proof is same as above.
- Case comm $(S, R_1.x \to R_2.y, rec, ch, op)$
  Since $\Gamma \vdash \mathsf{comm}\,(S, R_1.x \to R_2.y, rec, ch, op)$ ok can only be resulted from rule (Request), we have $\Gamma \vdash R_1.x \to R_2.y$ ok, $\Gamma \vdash R_1.\overline{x_1} := \overline{e_1}$ ok, and $\Gamma \vdash R_2.\overline{y_2} := \overline{e_2}$ ok, i.e. $\Sigma_\Gamma(R_1.x) = \Sigma_\Gamma(R_2.y) = T$, $\Sigma_\Gamma(R_1.\overline{x_1}) = \overline{T_{x_1}}$, $\Gamma \vdash \overline{e_1} : \overline{T_{e_1}}$, $compatible(\overline{T_{x_1}}, \overline{T_{e_1}})$, $\Sigma_\Gamma(R_2.\overline{y_2}) = \overline{T_{y_2}}$, $\Gamma \vdash \overline{e_2} : \overline{T_{e_2}}$, $compatible(\overline{T_{y_2}}, \overline{T_{e_2}})$. Since Δ is consistent with Γ, we have $R_2.y \in dom(\Delta)$, $R_1.\overline{x_1} \subset dom(\Delta)$, and $R_2.\overline{y_2} \subset dom(\Delta)$. From Theorem 1, there exists value v such that $\Delta \models R_1.x \to v$ and $compatible(T, valType(v))$; there exists values $\overline{v_1}$ such that $\Delta \models \overline{e_1} \to \overline{v_1}$ and $compatible(\overline{T_{e_1}}, valType(\overline{v_1}))$; there exists values $\overline{v_2}$ such that $\Delta \models \overline{e_2} \to \overline{v_2}$ and $compatible(\overline{T_{e_2}}, valType(\overline{v_2}))$. Thus, from rule (REQ), we know that $\langle \mathsf{comm}\,(S, R_1.x \to R_2.y, rec, ch, op),\ \Delta\rangle \longrightarrow \langle \epsilon, \Delta'\rangle$, where $\Delta' = \Delta[v/(R_2.y)]$ $[\overline{v_1}/(R_1.\overline{x_1}), \overline{v_2}/(R_2.\overline{y_2})]$. Besides, noticing that $valType(\Delta'(R_2.y)) = valType(v)$, $valType(\Delta'(R_1.\overline{x_1})) = valType(\overline{v_1})$, and $valType(\Delta'(R_2.\overline{y_2})) = valType(\overline{v_2})$, from rule (Transmission), we will have $compatible(\Sigma_\Gamma(R_2.y), valType(v))$, $compatible(\Sigma_\Gamma(R_1.\overline{x_1}), valType(\overline{v_1}))$, and $compatible(\Sigma_\Gamma(R_2.\overline{y_2}), valType(\overline{v_2}))$. >From these facts and Lemma 1, we have $dom(\Delta') = dom(\Delta) = dom(\Sigma_\Gamma)$. Therefore, Δ' is consistent with Γ.

  Similarly, we can prove other two cases: comm $(S, R_1.x \leftarrow R_2.y, rec, ch, op)$ and comm $(S, R_1.x \to R_2.y, R_1.m \leftarrow R_2.n, rec, ch, op)$.
- Case $q?A$
  Since $\Gamma \vdash q?A$ ok can only be resulted from rule (Condition), we have $\Gamma \vdash A$ ok and $\Gamma \vdash q : Bool$. If $\Delta \models q \to false$, from rule (IF-FALSE), we have $\langle q?A, \Delta\rangle \longrightarrow \langle \epsilon, \Delta\rangle$. Obviously, Δ is consistent with Γ. If $\Delta \models q \to true$, from

the deduction hypothesis, there exists state Δ' such that $\langle A, \Delta\rangle \longrightarrow \langle \epsilon, \Delta'\rangle$ and Δ' is consistent with Γ. From rule (IF-TRUE), we have $\langle q?A, \Delta\rangle \longrightarrow \langle \epsilon, \Delta'\rangle$.

- Case $q * A$
  Since $\Gamma \vdash q * A$ ok can only be resulted from rule (Repeat), we have $\Gamma \vdash A$ ok, and $\Gamma \vdash q : Bool$. If $\Delta \models q \rightarrow false$, then from rule (REP-FALSE) we have $\langle q * A, \Delta\rangle \longrightarrow \langle \epsilon, \Delta\rangle$. If $\Delta \models q \rightarrow true$, then from the deduction hypothesis, there exists state Δ'' such that $\langle A, \Delta\rangle \longrightarrow \langle \epsilon, \Delta''\rangle$ and Δ'' is consistent with Γ. Since abnormal case 1 will not happen, there exists state Δ' such that $\langle q * A, \Delta''\rangle \longrightarrow \langle \epsilon, \Delta'\rangle$ and Δ' is consistent with Γ. From rule (REP-TRUE), we have $\langle q * A, \Delta\rangle \longrightarrow \langle \epsilon, \Delta'\rangle$.
- Case $g : A : q$
  Since $\Gamma \vdash g : A : q$ ok can only be resulted from rule (WorkUnit), we have $\Gamma \vdash A$ ok, $\Gamma \vdash g : Bool$ and $\Gamma \vdash q : Bool$. Since abnormal case 2 will not happen, we have $\Delta \models g \rightarrow true$, from the deduction hypothesis, there exists state Δ' such that $\langle A, \Delta\rangle \longrightarrow \langle \epsilon, \Delta'\rangle$ and Δ' is consistent with Γ. If $\Delta' \models q \rightarrow false$, then from rule (BLOCK1) we have $\langle g : A : q, \Delta\rangle \longrightarrow \langle \epsilon, \Delta'\rangle$. If $\Delta' \models q \rightarrow true$, Since abnormal case 1 will not happen, from the deduction hypothesis, there exists state Δ'' such that $\langle g : A : q, \Delta'\rangle \longrightarrow \langle \epsilon, \Delta''\rangle$ and Δ'' is consistent with Γ. From rule (BLOCK2), we have $\langle g : A : q, \Delta\rangle \longrightarrow \langle \epsilon, \Delta''\rangle$.
- Case $A; B$
  Since $\Gamma \vdash A; B$ ok can only be resulted from rule (Sequence), we have $\Gamma \vdash A$ ok and $\Gamma \vdash B$ ok. From the deduction hypothesis, there exists state Δ'' such that $\langle A, \Delta\rangle \longrightarrow \langle \epsilon, \Delta''\rangle$ and Δ'' is consistent with Γ. From the deduction hypothesis, there exists state Δ' such that $\langle B, \Delta''\rangle \longrightarrow \langle \epsilon, \Delta'\rangle$ and Δ' is consistent with Γ. From rule (SEQ) we have $\langle A; B, \Delta\rangle \longrightarrow \langle \epsilon, \Delta'\rangle$.
- Case $A \sqcap B$
  Since $\Gamma \vdash A \sqcap B$ ok can only be resulted from rule (Non-Det), we have $\Gamma \vdash A$ ok and $\Gamma \vdash B$ ok. From the deduction hypothesis, there exists state Δ' such that $\langle A, \Delta\rangle \longrightarrow \langle \epsilon, \Delta'\rangle$ and Δ' is consistent with Γ. From rule (NON-DET1) we have $\langle A \sqcap B, \Delta\rangle \longrightarrow \langle \epsilon, \Delta'\rangle$.
- Case $g_1 \Rightarrow A \,[]\, g_2 \Rightarrow B$
  Since $\Gamma \vdash g_1 \Rightarrow A \,[]\, g_2 \Rightarrow B$ ok can only be resulted from rule (Gen-Choice), we have $\Gamma \vdash A$ ok and $\Gamma \vdash B$ ok. Since abnormal case 3 will not happen, we only consider following two subcases: If $\Delta \models g_1 \rightarrow true$,from the deduction hypothesis, there exists state Δ' such that $\langle A, \Delta\rangle \longrightarrow \langle \epsilon, \Delta'\rangle$ and Δ' is consistent with Γ. From rule (CHOICE1) we have $\langle g_1 \Rightarrow A \,[]\, g_2 \Rightarrow B, \Delta\rangle \longrightarrow \langle \epsilon, \Delta'\rangle$. If $\Delta \models g_1 \rightarrow false, \Delta \models g_2 \rightarrow true$, from the deduction hypothesis, there exists state Δ' such that $\langle B, \Delta\rangle \longrightarrow \langle \epsilon, \Delta'\rangle$ and Δ' is consistent with Γ. From rule (CHOICE2) we have $\langle g_1 \Rightarrow A \,[]\, g_2 \Rightarrow B, \Delta\rangle \longrightarrow \langle \epsilon, \Delta'\rangle$.
- Case $A \parallel B$
  Since $\Gamma \vdash A \parallel B$ ok can only be resulted from rule (Parallel), we have $\Gamma \vdash A$ ok and $\Gamma \vdash B$ ok. From the deduction hypothesis, there exists state Δ' such that $\langle A, \Delta\rangle \longrightarrow \langle \epsilon, \Delta'\rangle$ and Δ' is consistent with Γ, there exists state Δ'' such that $\langle B, \Delta\rangle \longrightarrow \langle \epsilon, \Delta''\rangle$ and Δ'' is consistent with Γ. From rule (PARA) we have $\langle A \parallel B, \Delta\rangle \longrightarrow \langle \epsilon, \Delta' \oplus \Delta''\rangle$, where $\Delta' \oplus \Delta''$ is consistent with Γ. □

Theorem 3 (Type safety of choreography). If a choreography chor $C\ \{\underline{S}\ \overline{Vdecl}\ A\}$ is well-typed in Γ, then there exists a state Δ' such that $\langle A, \{\underline{R.x} : \underline{v_{ini}}\}\rangle \longrightarrow \langle \epsilon, \Delta' \rangle$, unless the abnormal cases above happen.

Proof. Since choreography chor $C\ \{\underline{S}\ \overline{Vdecl}\ A\}$ is well-typed in Γ, we have $\Gamma \vdash A$ ok. Besides, Γ is consistent with initial state $\{\underline{R.x} : \underline{v_{ini}}\}$. According to Theorem 2, we know that there exists a state Δ' such that $\langle A, \{\underline{R.x} : \underline{v_{ini}}\}\rangle \longrightarrow \langle \epsilon, \Delta' \rangle$. □

From this theorem, we know that if no the abnormal case happens in the execution, then a well-typed choreography must terminate as expected.

5 An Example

In this section we give a simple example choreography to illustrate how our type system and operational semantics work together.

5.1 Package

A *ConsRetPkg* package is defined as follows:

$$
\begin{array}{l}
\textsf{pkg}\ \{\ ConsRetPkg \\
\quad \textsf{info}\ poType\ \{poMsg\}, \\
\quad \textsf{info}\ poAckType\ \{poAckMsg\}, \\
\quad \textsf{info}\ uriType\ \{string\}, \\
\quad \textsf{token}\ \{retRef\ \ uriType\}, \\
\quad \textsf{token}\ \{consRef\ \ uriType\}, \\
\quad \textsf{role}\ Cons\ \{consForRet, consForWare\}, \\
\quad \textsf{role}\ Ret\ \{retForCons\}, \\
\quad \textsf{rela}\ consRetRela\ \{Cons(consForRet)\ \ Ret(retForCons)\}, \\
\quad \textsf{chan}\ consChan\ \{Cons(consForRet)\ \ consRef\}, \\
\quad \textsf{chan}\ retChan\ \{Ret(retForCons)\ \ retRef\}, \\
\quad \textsf{chor}\ ConsRetChor\ \{\ consRetRela \\
\qquad\qquad \textsf{var}\ \{po\ \ poType\ \ \{Cons, Ret\}\}, \\
\qquad\qquad \textsf{var}\ \{poAck\ \ poAckType\ \ \{Cons, Ret\}\}, \\
\qquad\qquad \textsf{var}\ \{consC\ \ consChan\ \ \{Cons, Ret\}\}, \\
\qquad\qquad \textsf{var}\ \{retC\ \ retChan\ \ \{Cons, Ret\}\}, \\
\qquad\qquad \textsf{comm}\ (consRetRela, Cons.po \rightarrow Ret.po, \\
\qquad\qquad Cons.poAck \leftarrow Ret.poAck, , retC, poHandle)\} \\
\}
\end{array}
$$

This choreography involves a consumer role type *Cons* sending a request for a purchase order to a retailer role types *Ret* to which the *Ret* role type responds with a purchase order acknowledgement. The execution of the choreography involves one interaction performed from *Cons* to *Ret* on the retailer-channel *retC* as a request/response exchange. The purchase order message *po* is sent from the *Cons* to the *Ret* as a request message; and the purchase Order acknowledge message *poAck* is sent from the *Ret* to the *Cons* as a response message.

5.2 Type Checking

We perform type checking to the package. Initially, the type context Γ is empty. We suppose the external data types *poMsg*, *poAckMsg* and *string* are predefined.The type contexts used in the type checking process are abbreviations with their complete forms as follows:

$$\Gamma_1 = \{poType : \mathsf{info}(poMsg), poAckType : \mathsf{info}(poAckMsg), uriType : \mathsf{info}(string)$$

$$\Gamma_2 = \Gamma_1 \cup \{Cons : \mathsf{role}(consForRet, consForWare), Ret : \mathsf{role}(retForCons)\}$$

$$\Gamma_3 = \Gamma_2 \cup \{consRef : \mathsf{token}(uriType), retRef : \mathsf{token}(uriType)\}$$

$$\Gamma_4 = \Gamma_3 \cup \{consRetRela : \mathsf{rela}(Cons(consForRet)\ Ret(retForCons)), consChan : \mathsf{chan}(Cons(consForRet)\ \ consRef), retChan{:}\mathsf{chan}(Ret(retForCons)\ \ retRef)\}$$

$$\Gamma_5 = \Gamma_4 \cup \{po : \mathsf{var}(poType\ \ \{Cons, Ret\}), poAck : \mathsf{var}(poAckType\ \ \{Cons, Ret\}), consC : \mathsf{var}(consChan\ \ \{Cons, Ret\}), retC : \mathsf{var}(retChan\ \ \{Cons, Ret\})\}$$

The list below show the process of the type checking:

1) $check(poMsg)$ ok	
2) $check(poAckMsg)$ ok	
3) $check(string)$ ok	
4) $\mathsf{info}\ poType\ \{poMsg\}$ ok	(Info),1
5) $\mathsf{info}\ poAckType\ \{poAckMsg\}$ ok	(Info),2
6) $\mathsf{info}\ uriType\ \{string\}$ ok	(Info),3
7) $\Gamma_1 \vdash \mathsf{token}\ \{consRef\ \ uriType\}$ ok	(Token),6
8) $\Gamma_1 \vdash \mathsf{token}\ \{retRef\ \ uriType\}$ ok	(Token),6
9) $\mathsf{role}\ Cons\ \{consForRet, consForWare\}$ ok	(Role)
10) $\mathsf{role}\ Ret\ \{retForCons\}$ ok	(Role)
11) $\Gamma_2 \vdash \mathsf{rela}\ consRetRela\ \{Cons(consForRet)\ Ret(retForCons)\}$ ok	(Rela),9,10
12) $\Gamma_3 \vdash \mathsf{chan}\ consChan\ \{Cons(consForRet)\ \ consRef\}$ ok	(Chan), 7,9
13) $\Gamma_3 \vdash \mathsf{chan}\ retChan\ \{Ret(retForCons)\ \ retRef\}$ ok	(Chan),8,10
14) $\Gamma_4 \vdash \mathsf{var}\ \{po\ poType\ \{Cons, Ret\}\}$ ok	(Var1),4,9,10
15) $\Gamma_4 \vdash \mathsf{var}\ \{poAck\ \ poAckType\ \ \{Cons, Ret\}\}$ ok	(Var1),5,9,10
16) $\Gamma_4 \vdash \mathsf{var}\ \{consC\ \ consChan\ \ \{Cons, Ret\}\}$ ok	(Var2),9,10,12
17) $\Gamma_4 \vdash \mathsf{var}\ \{retC\ \ retChan\ \ \{Cons, Ret\}\}$ ok	(Var2),9,10,13
18) $\Gamma_5 \vdash \mathsf{comm}\ (consRetRela, Cons.po \rightarrow Ret.po, Cons.poAck \leftarrow Ret.poAck, , retC, poHandle)$ ok	(RR),11,14,15,17
19) $\Gamma_5 \vdash \mathsf{chor}\ \ ConsRetChor\ \ \{\cdots\}$ ok	def

Since *ConsRetChor* is ok, we have proved that *ConsRetChor* is a well-typed choreography.

If any step of typing checking fails, *ConsRetChor* will not be a well-typed choreography, and will get stuck during execution because there is no applicable rule. For example, suppose that type checking $check(poMsg)$ fails in step 1, in this case, step 4, 14, 18, and 19 will fail too. Thus *ConsRetChor* is not a well-typed choreography, and will get stuck when executing the communication activity.

5.3 Performing Choreography

We perform choreography $ConsRetChor$ according to our operational semantics.

The state Δ is a composition of local states of role types $Cons$ and Ret, both of which have four variables: $\Delta = \{Cons.po : v_{po},\ Cons.poAck : 0,\ Cons.consC : v_{ch},\ Cons.retC : v_{ch'},\ Ret.po{:}0,\ Ret.poAck : v_{ack},\ Ret.consC : v_{ch},\ Ret.retC : v_{ch'}\}$. Here we use 0 to express the empty value.

Based on the rule (REQ-RESP), after execution of the interaction activity, the choreography terminates properly, and finally enters a state Δ', where $\Delta' = \Delta[v_{po}/(Ret.po)][v_{ack}/(Cons.poAck)]$.

6 Related Work

It is widely recognized that the most popular and best established lightweight formal methods are type systems. Type systems and type checking techniques are widely used and have been proved to be very useful in detecting subtle inconsistency, or unconscious and accidental errors, and checking various properties of programs. Recently, people pay much attention to define type systems for various new languages and features, for example, to establish type system for the Object-Oriented languages. A good example here is the work of Igarashi et al. [1], in which a small OO language called Featherweight Java (FJ) is studied, which covers some fundamental features of Java. The authors created a typing environment for FJ, studied the cast problems, and proved the type soundness theorem.

There is also existing work on type systems in the field of XML. Hosoya and Pierse [9] describe a statically typed XML processing language called XDuce, which provides a simple, clean, and powerful type system for XML processing. Draper et al. [6] describe the XPath/XQuery type system based on XML Schema. The type system can check various properties, such as whether a data instance matches a type and whether a type is a subtype of another.

In a recent paper [5], N.Busi et al. proposed a simple choreography language, equipped with a formal semantics, which was intended as the starting point for the development of a framework for the design and analysis of choreographies in Service Oriented Computing. Different from our language, the author want to minimize the language features, there were no state record variables. Particularly, it didn't consider the type system of web service choreography language. Moreover, Barros et al. discussed some important issues of WS-CDL in [3]. Brogi et al. presented the formalization of Web Service Choreography Interface (WSCI) using a process algebra approach, and discussed the benefits of such formalization [4]. The developing team of WS-CDL in W3C suggested that type checking WS-CDL will be very useful. From our knowledge, there is no real work on definition of the type system for WS-CDL style languages.

7 Conclusion and Future Work

In this paper, we describe a choreography description language CDL as a formal model of the simplified WS-CDL, then develop a type system for CDL, and prove some type safety theorems.

Type safety is the most important property of type systems [11]. It is commonly proved as the progress and preservation theorems. Progress means either a well-typed item is a value or it can take a step according to the evaluation rules. Preservation means if a well-typed item can take a step in the evaluation, then the resulting item is also well-typed. The preservation theorem shows the evaluation of an expression preserves well-typedness. It particularly adapts to functional languages that focus on the concepts such as functions, values and types. But our language CDL is not a functional language. In type checking CDL, we focus on checking for context consistencies. That is the reason why we don't mention the preservation theorem in our type system, and just present the progress theorem, which is actually composed of our type safety theorems 1, 2 and 3.

Our type system has two contributions:(1) preventing mistaken references among various entities in the choreography. For example, let us consider a relationship type S which refers to role types R_1 and R_2. It is inconsistent if either R_1 or R_2 is not defined, or the behaviors of R_1 or R_2 required by S are not the subset of the pre-defined behaviors of R_1 or R_2. (2) making sure a well-typed choreography can terminate as expected. Additionally, in this work, we also determined a clear set of primitive functions which are required for any type checking systems of CDL (and also WS-CDL). They are:

- $xptype(xp)$: It returns the type of XPath expression xp.
- $check(XT)$: It checks if XT is a valid external data type.
- $compatible(T_1, T_2)$: It determines if the value of type T_2 can be assigned to the variable of type T_1.

We regard CDL as a core calculus for modeling WS-CDL's type system. The goal in the design of CDL is to make the proof of type safety as concise as possible. CDL includes most of the important features of WS-CDL. The features of WS-CDL that CDL does model include kinds of types, variables, activities (control-flow, workunit, skip, assignment, interaction) and choreography. CDL also omits some advanced features such as some details of the channel, exception and finalize blocks. Extending CDL to include more features of WS-CDL will be one direction of our further work. As another future work, we are working on the development of a type checker for WS-CDL based on our model. Currently, XML Schema based validation cannot detect inconsistency of type references.

Acknowledgements. We would like to thank Liang Zhao, Shengchao Qin and Xiwu Dai for many helpful comments.

References

1. A. Igarashi and B. Pierce and P. Wadler. Featherweight Java: A minimal core calculus for Java and GJ. In *ACM SIGPLAN Conference on Object-Oriented Programming, Systems, Languages and Applications*, 1999.
2. Daniel Austin, Abbie Barbir, Ed Peters, and Steve Ross-Talbot. Web Services Choreography Requirements. W3C Working Draft, March 2004. http://www.w3.org/TR/2004/WD-ws-chor-reqs-20040311/.

3. Alistair Barros, Marion Dumas, and Phillipa Oaks. A Critical Overview of the Web Services Choreography Description Language. 2005. http://www.bptrends.com.
4. A. Brogi, C. Canal, E. Pimentel, and A. Vallecillo. Formalizing web service choreography. In *WS-FM 2004*. Electronic Notes in Theoretical Computer Science, 2004.
5. N. Busi, R. Gorrieri, C. Guidi, R. Lucchi, and G. Zavattaro. Towards a formal framework for Choreography. In *Proceedings of the 14th IEEE International Workshops on Enabling Technologies: Infrastructure for Collaborative Enterprise*. IEEE Computer Society, 2005.
6. D. Draper et al. XQuery 1.0 and XPath 2.0 Formal Semantics. W3C Working Draft, September 2005. http://www.w3.org/TR/2005/WD-xquery-semantics-20050915/.
7. Gerard J. Holzmann. *The SPIN Model Checker:Primer and Reference Manual*. Addison-Wesley, 2003.
8. Hongli Yang and Xiangpeng Zhao and Zongyan Qiu and Geguang Pu and Shuling Wang. A Formal Model for Web Service Choreography Description Language (WS-CDL). to appear in the proceedings of International Conference on Web Services(ICWS)2006.
9. H. Hosoya and B. C. Pierce. XDuce: A Statically Typed XML Processing Language. May 2003. http://wam.inrialpes.fr/people/roisin/mw2004/Hosoya2003.pdf.
10. N. Kavantzas, D. Burdett, G. Ritzinger, T. Fletcher, Y. Lafon, and C. Barreto. Web Services Choreography Description Language Version 1.0. November 2005. http://www.w3.org/TR/2005/CR-ws-cdl-10-20051109/.
11. Benjamin C. Pierce. *Types and Programming Languages*. MIT Press, 2002.
12. Steve Ross-Talbot and Tony Fletcher. Web Services Choreography Description Language: Primer Version 1.0. May 2006. http://www.w3.org/TR/Year/WD-ws-cdl-10-primer-YearMMDD/.
13. Xiangpeng Zhao, Hongli Yang, and Zongyan Qiu. Towards the Formal Model and Verification of Web Service Choreography Description Language. to appear in the proceedings of 3rd International Workshop on Web Services and Formal Methods(WS-FM)2006.

Formalising Progress Properties of Non-blocking Programs

Brijesh Dongol

ARC Centre for Complex Systems,
School of Information Technology and Electrical Engineering,
University of Queensland

Abstract. A non-blocking program is one that uses non-blocking primitives, such as load-linked/store-conditional and compare-and-swap, for synchronisation instead of locks so that no process is ever blocked. According to their progress properties, non-blocking programs may be classified as wait-free, lock-free or obstruction-free. However, a precise description of these properties does not exist and it is not unusual to find a definition that is ambiguous or even incorrect. We present a formal definition of the progress properties so that any confusion is removed. The formalisation also allows one to prove the widely believed presumption that wait-freedom is a special case of lock-freedom, which in turn is a special case of obstruction-freedom.

1 Introduction

It has become clear that non-blocking programs provide a practical alternative to synchronisation via lock-based techniques [GC96]. By removing locks, programs are able to scale more easily, tend to be more efficient, and problems such as deadlock are averted by the nature of the program. However, as a result of their inherent complexity, non-blocking implementations are hard to trust without formal justification. In fact, there is more than one example of errors being discovered in published programs through formal verification [CG05, Doh03].

Much work has been devoted to verifying safety properties [Doh03, HLM03] [DGLM04, CG05], but formal proofs of progress properties have largely been ignored. Yet, progress properties are important enough to warrant classification of non-blocking programs as *wait-free*, *lock-free*, and *obstruction-free*. Existing definitions of these properties are given in natural language making them imprecise and subject to interpretation. In fact, side-by-side examination of the definitions provided in the literature reveals that interpretations vary among different authors. Informality of the definitions also makes it difficult to decide exactly when a non-blocking program satisfies a given property. Formalisation allows one to *prove* that a property holds, thus removing any ambiguity. Furthermore, a failed proof might reveal errors, and point to the changes necessary to correct them.

Our definitions are based on the notion of *leads-to* (denoted $\rightsquigarrow$) which allows proofs of temporal 'eventuality' properties. The logic we use, [DG06], combines

Z. Liu and J. He (Eds.): ICFEM 2006, LNCS 4260, pp. 284–303, 2006.

the safety logic of Owicki and Gries [OG76], and the progress logic of Chandy and Misra [CM88].

The formalisation of progress has allowed us to prove the postulation that wait-free programs are lock-free and that lock-free programs are obstruction-free. The relationship between progress properties of non-blocking programs and properties such as starvation and deadlock freedom has also been established.

This paper is organised as follows. Section 2 presents the programming model, while Section 3 describes the safety and progress logic. The informal and formal definitions of the different progress properties are presented in Section 4. Then, in Section 5, a description of the hierarchy of known progress properties is given. The proofs of the counter-examples in this section provide examples of applications of our definitions to real programs. Some other benefits of formalisation is given in Section 6.

2 Programming Model

The sequential part of the programming language we use is based on Dijkstra's language of guarded commands [Dij76]. However, to accommodate representation of a program's control state and thus allow reasoning about progress, our statements are labelled [DG06]. Each label in the program is distinct from the other labels. Below, when we write "$i\colon S\ j\colon$", the label i corresponds to S and j corresponds to the statement that follows S sequentially. Immediately after execution of S, we expect control to be updated to j. The existence of a special label τ is assumed, which is used to denote termination. Statements in our model take the following form.

$$\begin{aligned} S \ \widehat{=}\ & i\colon skip\ j\colon \mid i\colon\ \textbf{exit}\ \tau\colon \mid i\colon \overline{x} := \overline{E}\ j\colon \mid i\colon \langle S\rangle\ j\colon \mid i\colon S_1;\ j\colon S_2\ k\colon \mid \\ & i\colon \textbf{if}\ B_1 \longrightarrow j_1\colon S_1\ [\!]\ \ B_2 \longrightarrow j_2\colon S_2\ \textbf{fi}\ k\colon \mid i\colon \textbf{do}\ B \longrightarrow j\colon S\ \textbf{od}\ k\colon \end{aligned}$$

Statements *skip*, **exit**, $\overline{x} := \overline{E}$ and $\langle S\rangle$ are atomic. We use the term *control point* to refer to the point between two atomic statements.

The intended operational meaning of statements is as follows. A *skip* does nothing, $\overline{x} := \overline{E}$ is the multiple assignment statement, and $\langle S\rangle$ executes S atomically. We describe the operational behaviour of **exit** later. Guard evaluation of an **if**, written as $(B_1 \longrightarrow j_1\colon\ [\!]\ \ B_2 \longrightarrow j_2\colon)$, atomically evaluates B_1 and B_2 then updates control to j_1 if B_1 holds and j_2 if B_2 holds. When $B_1 \vee B_2 \ \equiv\ \mathit{false}$, the guard evaluation statement blocks (unlike Dijkstra [Dij76]), and when multiple guards hold, one of them is chosen non-deterministically and control updated correspondingly. We may also have guard evaluations of the form $(\langle B_1 \longrightarrow S_1\rangle\ j_1\colon\ [\!]\ \ \langle B_2 \longrightarrow S_2\rangle\ j_2\colon)$, in which case evaluation of B_1 and B_2, execution of S_1 or S_2 (depending on which guard holds), and update of control takes place atomically.

Non-atomic statements may be decomposed as follows. Statement $i\colon \textbf{if}\ B_1 \longrightarrow j_1\colon S_1\ [\!]\ \ B_2 \longrightarrow j_2\colon S_2\ \textbf{fi}\ k\colon$ consists of:

1. an atomic guard evaluation statement $(B_1 \longrightarrow j_1\colon \,[\!]\, B_2 \longrightarrow j_2\colon)$, and
2. statements $j_1\colon S_1\ k\colon$ and $j_2\colon S_2\ k\colon$.

Statement $i\colon \mathbf{do}\ B \longrightarrow j\colon S\ \mathbf{od}\ k\colon$ consists of:

1. an atomic guard evaluation statement $(B \longrightarrow j\colon \,[\!]\, \neg B \longrightarrow k\colon)$ and
2. statement $j\colon S\ i\colon$.

Finally, the sequential composition $i\colon S_1;\ j\colon S_2\ k\colon$ consists of statements $i\colon S_1\ j\colon$ and $j\colon S_2\ k\colon$.

As the programs we consider are non-blocking, we do not expect blocking **if** statements to occur in the final program. Furthermore, as we frequently perform a *skip* when all guards are *false*, a non-blocking conditional **ife** is defined as:

$$\begin{array}{l} i\colon\ \mathbf{ife}\ B_1 \longrightarrow j_1\colon S_1 \\ \quad\ [\!]\quad B_2 \longrightarrow j_2\colon S_2 \\ \quad\ \mathbf{efi} \\ k\colon \end{array} \quad \widehat{=} \quad \begin{array}{l} i\colon\ \mathbf{if}\ B_1 \longrightarrow j_1\colon S_1 \\ \quad\ [\!]\ B_2 \longrightarrow j_2\colon S_2 \\ \quad\ [\!]\ \langle \neg(B_1 \vee B_2) \longrightarrow skip\rangle \\ \quad\ \mathbf{fi} \\ k\colon \end{array}$$

Loops with a guard of *true* are also a common feature. Here, we follow [FvG99] and define:

$$*[\ S\ ] \ \widehat{=}\ \ \mathbf{do}\ true \longrightarrow S\ \mathbf{od}$$

A *program*[1] is a 3-tuple $(OP, PROC, Init)$ where OP is a finite set of operations, $PROC$ is a finite set of process ids, and $Init$ is a predicate describing the initial state of the program. An *operation* is a sequential statement parameterised by the calling process and is *non-blocking* if for each guard evaluation statement $(B_1 \longrightarrow j_1\colon [\!]\ B_2 \longrightarrow j_2\colon)$ in the operation, $B_1 \vee B_2 \equiv true$. A program is *non-blocking* if each operation in OP is non-blocking. A *process* is the active entity of the program and sequentially executes the atomic statements of operations it invokes. So, we may consider each process $p \in PROC$ as the statement:

$$*[\ \ \mathbf{if}\quad ([\!]_{O \in OP}\ true \longrightarrow O_p)\quad \mathbf{fi}\ \ ].$$

Hence, a process repeatedly chooses an operation in OP non-deterministically and invokes it by executing its statements. Invocation of an operation may be followed by a response (which means the operation terminates) [HW90], but we do not force this as a requirement, so non-terminating operations are allowed.

A program's execution consists of an interleaving of the atomic statements of the operations each process has invoked. As demanded by our progress logic (Section 3), we assume weak fairness so that each process is eventually able to execute if it is continuously enabled.

Program variables are either *shared* (may be accessed and modified by any process) or *local* (may only be accessed by the process it belongs to). It is also

[1] In the literature, programs are also referred to as algorithms, data structures, or objects.

possible to introduce *auxiliary* variables [OG76] in order to aid proofs. For each process p, we assume the existence of a local auxiliary variable pc_p, which models the *program counter* of p. Following [DG06], pc_p is updated implicitly after execution of each atomic statement and hence, must not explicitly appear in any statement. We expect $pc_p = i$ to be an implicit precondition to each statement $i{:}\, S$ executed by process p to reflect the fact that control of p must be at i before execution of S. Statement **exit** terminates the current operation by setting the pc value of the executing process to τ. To rule out the case of an atomic statement terminating partway through its execution, we require that **exit** may not appear within $\langle\ \rangle$.

We use PC_X to represent the set of labels of operation X, and PC to represent the set of all labels of the program. Hence, $PC = \bigcup_{X \in OP} PC_X$. Label τ is the only label shared among all operations, i.e., $\bigcap_{X \in OP} PC_X = \{\tau\}$. For this reason, we may refer to a statement in an operation by its corresponding label. Also, note that process p is only able to invoke a new operation when $pc_p = \tau$. Finally, we use PC_{start} to be the set containing the label at the start of each operation.

We also require that snapshots of the current state of the program counters be taken. Thus, we define the type SS as follows.

$$SS \;\widehat{=}\; PROC \to PC$$

The type SS can be thought of as the set of all functions that return a label for a given process. Notice that pc has type SS.

A common proviso to many of the informal definitions is that progress be made in the face of delay or failure of other processes. Given that our programs are non-blocking and that we are assuming weak fairness, one might conclude that each process always executes a statement. However, this is not necessarily true. Underlying mechanisms such as scheduler implementations or process failure can prevent processes from doing so. In fact, some definitions of progress are dependant on these underlying mechanisms, for instance from [HLM03], "... we need to provide some mechanism to reduce the contention so that progress is achieved."

We introduce a condition ξ_p for process p, whose value is changed externally such that p is able to execute iff ξ_p holds. No statement in the program is allowed to modify ξ_p. We will say that p is *enabled* when ξ_p holds, and *disabled* when $\neg\xi_p$ holds. Now, we may think of each *skip*, assignment, or a coarse-grained atomic statement $i{:}\, S\ j{:}$ as the statement $i{:}\, \langle \textbf{if}\ \xi_p \to S\ \textbf{fi}\rangle\ j{:}$ and each guard evaluation statement $i{:}\, (B_1 \to j_1{:} \,[\!]\ B_2 \to j_2{:})\ k{:}$ as the statement $i{:}\, (B_1 \wedge \xi_p \to j_1{:} \,[\!]\ B_2 \wedge \xi_p \to j_2{:})\ k{:}$. Although this means process executions can be blocked, the crucial difference is that the blocking takes place via underlying mechanisms not controlled by the program. As an example, in a system that uses round-robin scheduling where $PROC \;\widehat{=}\; 0..n-1$, one might implement the scheduler as in Fig. 1.

The exact details of specifying when processes are enabled and disabled lies outside the scope of this paper, as they reflect factors external to the program. However, failure can be modelled with little added cost, therefore, we assume

$$Init \mathrel{\widehat{=}} (\forall_{p \in PROC}\ \neg\xi_p) \wedge e = 0$$

```
ξe = true ;
*[
   ξe := false ;
   e := (e + 1) mod n ;
   ξe := true
]
```

Fig. 1. Round-robin scheduling

that processes only become disabled due to failure, i.e., once a process is disabled, it is never re-enabled.[2] As the condition ξ_p for process p is modified externally, we will assume that it appears in our programs implicitly, i.e., our programs will not mention ξ_p.

3 A Logic of Safety and Progress

We now present a logic for our programming model. Here, notation $[\ F\ ]$ is used to denote "in all states F holds", and $(x := E).F$ to denote the textual replacement of all free occurrences of the variable x in F by expression E.

3.1 Safety

Formal semantics for the programming language is provided using the weakest liberal precondition (*wlp*) predicate transformer [Dij76]. We define the *wlp* for labelled atomic statements, and assume knowledge of *wlp* for unlabelled statements (see [FvG99]). Due to the importance of the calling process, we parameterise the *wlp* by process p.

Definition 1 (Weakest Liberal Precondition). *Assuming the statements are executed by process p, the wlp of a labelled atomic statement $i{:}\,S\ j{:}$ with respect to a postcondition P computes the weakest condition required for a terminating execution of $i{:}\,S\ j{:}$ to establish P. It is defined as follows.*

1. $[\ wlp_p.(i{:}\,skip\ j{:}).P \equiv \xi_p \Rightarrow (pc_p := j).P\ ]$
2. $[\ wlp_p.(i{:}\,\overline{x} := \overline{E}\ j{:}).P \equiv \xi_p \Rightarrow (\overline{x}, pc_p := \overline{E}, j).P)\ ]$
3. $[\ wlp_p.(i{:}\,\mathbf{exit}\ \tau{:}).P \equiv \xi_p \Rightarrow (pc_p := \tau).P\ ]$
4. $[\ wlp_p.(i{:}\,\langle S\rangle\ j{:}).P \equiv \xi_p \Rightarrow wlp_p.S.((pc_p := j).P)\ ]$
5. $[\ wlp_p.(B_1 \longrightarrow j_1{:}\ [\!]\ B_2 \longrightarrow j_2{:}).P \equiv (B_1 \wedge \xi_p \Rightarrow (pc_p := j_1).P) \wedge (B_2 \wedge \xi_p \Rightarrow (pc_p := j_2).P)\ ]$

We now define the criteria necessary to judge correctness of assertions in a concurrent environment. Assertions must accommodate for interference from

[2] This assumption does not prevent one from implementing other scheduling algorithms, but the algorithm should make sure that a disabled process is not re-enabled until at least some some process has made progress.

other processes. Our presentation follows the (calculational) reformulation of [OG76] as presented in [FvG99]. We note that as guard evaluation can have the side-effect that the program counter is updated, we have an extra clause in the definition of local correctness wrt [FvG99].

Definition 2 (Correctness). *An assertion P occuring in operation X executed by process p is* correct *if it is both locally and globally correct where:*

1. *P is* locally correct *whenever*
   (a) *if P occurs at the start of the operation, then $[\ Init \Rightarrow P\ ]$.*
   (b) *if P is textually preceded by $\{Q\}\ X_i$, where Q is correct, then* $[\ Q \Rightarrow wlp_p.X_i.P\ ]$.
   (c) *if P is textually preceded by $\{Q\}\ B \longrightarrow j$: where Q is correct, then* $[\ Q \wedge B \Rightarrow (pc_p := j).P)\ ]$.
2. *P is* globally correct *if for each atomic $\{Q\}\ Y_j$ executed by a process q where $q \neq p$ and Q is correct, $[\ P \wedge Q \Rightarrow wlp_q.Y_j.P\ ]$.*

So, an assertion in an operation executed by a process is correct if it is established by execution of the operation (locally correct), and maintained by execution of operations performed by other processes (globally correct). The safety logic also allows one to use invariants.

Definition 3 (Invariant). *Assertion P is* invariant *if $[\ Init \Rightarrow P\ ]$ and for all atomic X_i with correct pre-assertion U, executed by any process p, $[\ P \wedge U \Rightarrow wlp_p.X_i.P\ ]$.*

Hence, an invariant is a predicate that holds initially, and is preserved by execution of any atomic statement by any process, i.e., it is a property that holds in every state of the program.

3.2 Progress

The progress logic [DG06] is a reformulation of Chandy and Misra's UNITY formalism [CM88], which allows axiomatic proofs of temporal [MP92] eventuality properties. Here, we will assume knowledge of weakest preconditions (wp) for unlabelled statements (see [Dij76]). Our presentation follows [DM06]. The basis for the logic is the unless (**un**) relation.

Definition 4 (Unless). *For any predicates P and Q, P **un** Q holds if for all atomic X_i with correct pre-assertion U, executed by any process p, $[\ P \wedge \neg Q \wedge U \Rightarrow wlp_p.X_i.(P \vee Q)\ ]$.*

If P **un** Q holds, then P continues to hold until Q holds. Hence, execution of each statement either preserves P or establishes Q. Note that even when P **un** Q holds, there is no guarantee that Q will ever become *true*, for example, if P is invariant, then P **un** *false* holds. Thus, to make sure that Q is established by execution of the program from a state that satisfies P, we must prove that $P \leadsto Q$ (which is equivalent to proving the temporal formula $\Box(P \Rightarrow \Diamond Q)$ [MP92]). We first define the weakest precondition for labelled atomic statements. The wp of an unlabelled statement is interpretated according to [Dij76].

Definition 5 (Weakest precondition). *Assuming the statements are executed by process p, the wp of a labelled atomic statement $i\colon S\ j\colon$ with respect to a postcondition P computes the weakest condition required to guarantee termination of $i\colon S\ j\colon$, such that P is established upon termination of $i\colon S\ j\colon$.*

1. If S is one of *skip*, $\overline{x} := \overline{E}$, or **exit**, or a guard evaluation statement then,
$$[\ wp_p.(i\colon S\ j\colon).P \ \equiv\ wlp_p.(i\colon S\ j\colon).P\ ]$$
2a. If S is of the form **if** $B_1 \longrightarrow T_1 [\!] \ B_2 \longrightarrow T_2$ **fi**
$$[\ wp_p.(i\colon \langle S\rangle\ j\colon).P \ \equiv\ (\xi_p \wedge B_1 \Rightarrow wp_p.T_1.((pc_p := j).P)) \wedge (\xi_p \wedge B_2 \Rightarrow wp_p.T_2.((pc_p := j).P))\ ]$$
2b. If S is not of the form **if** $B_1 \longrightarrow T_1 [\!] \ B_2 \longrightarrow T_2$ **fi**
$$[\ wp_p.(i\colon \langle S\rangle\ j\colon).P \ \equiv\ \xi_p \Rightarrow wp_p.S.((pc_p := j).P)\ ]$$

Definition 6 (Leads-to). *Under weak fairness, for any predicates P and Q, $P \leadsto Q$ if it can be proved via a finite number of applications of the following rules.*

1. (Immediate progress) *$P \leadsto Q$ holds by immediate progress if P **un** Q holds, and there is an atomic statement X_i, executed by any process p such that $[\ P \wedge \neg Q \ \Rightarrow\ pc_p = i \wedge wp.X_i.Q \wedge \neg wp.X_i.\mathit{false}\ ]$ holds.*
2. (Transitivity) *$P \leadsto Q$ if there is a predicate R such that $P \leadsto R$ and $R \leadsto Q$.*
3. (Disjunction) *If $P \mathrel{\widehat{=}} (\exists_{i:W} P_i)$ for some set W, then $P \leadsto Q$ if $(\forall_{i:W} P_i \leadsto Q)$.*

By the immediate progress rule, some process p is guaranteed to execute a statement from a state that satisfies P so that the next state satisfies Q. Notice that as P **un** Q holds, every other process either preserves P or establishes Q. The transitivity rule allows intermediate states in the proof of $P \leadsto Q$. Finally, disjunction allows us to establish, for example, that if $P \equiv P_1 \vee P_2$, to show that $P \leadsto Q$, we may prove $P_1 \leadsto Q$ and $P_2 \leadsto Q$ individually.

The operator $\leadsto$ binds weaker than any logical operator, i.e., $\neg P \leadsto Q \equiv (\neg P) \leadsto Q$ and $P \oplus Q \leadsto R \equiv (P \oplus Q) \leadsto R$ where $\oplus \in \{\vee, \wedge, \Rightarrow, \Leftrightarrow\}$. In addition, we find the following lemmata for $\leadsto$ to be of use.

Lemma 1. *For any predicates P, Q and R:*

1. *$\leadsto$ is monotonic (or isotonic) in its second argument* [DM06], *i.e.,*
$$(P \leadsto Q) \wedge [\ Q \Rightarrow R\ ] \ \Rightarrow\ (P \leadsto R)$$
2. *$\leadsto$ is anti-monotonic (or antitonic) in its first argument* [DM06], *i.e.,*
$$[\ P \Rightarrow Q\ ] \wedge (Q \leadsto R) \ \Rightarrow\ (P \leadsto R)$$
3. *Implication* [CM88]*:*
$$[\ P \Rightarrow Q\ ] \ \Rightarrow\ (P \leadsto Q)$$
4. *Induction* [CM88]*:*
For any well-founded order $(W, \prec)$ and M which is an expression on program variables evaluating to an element of W,
$$(\forall_{m:W}\ P \wedge M = m \ \leadsto\ (P \wedge M \prec m) \vee Q) \ \Rightarrow\ (P \leadsto Q).$$

4 Progress Properties of Non-blocking Programs

We now present a sample of the definitions of wait, lock and obstruction-free provided by various authors, which allows us to highlight the differences and ambiguities introduced through the use of natural language. These are formalised in the subsequent sections.

Wait-free

[Her88]	"A *wait-free* implementation of a concurrent object is one that guarantees that any process can complete any operation in a finite number of steps"
[HLM03]	"An algorithm is *wait-free* if it ensures that all processes make progress even when faced with arbitrary delay or failure of other processes."
[Mic04]	"A lock-free shared object is also *wait-free* if progress is guaranteed per operation."
[Sun04]	"*Wait-free* algorithms guarantee progress of all operations, independent of the actions performed by the concurrent operations."

Lock-free

[MP91]	"An object is *lock-free* if it guarantees that some operation will complete in a finite number of steps."
[HLM03]	"An algorithm is *lock-free* if it guarantees that some thread always makes progress."
[Mic04]	"A shared object is *lock-free* if whenever a thread executes some finite number of steps towards an operation on the object, some thread must have completed an operation on the object during execution of these steps."
[Sun04]	"*Lock-free* algorithms guarantee progress of always at least one operation, independent of the actions performed by the concurrent operations."

Obstruction-free

[HLM03]	"A non-blocking algorithm is *obstruction-free* if it guarantees progress for any thread that eventually executes in isolation. Even though other threads may be in the midst of executing operations, a thread is considered to execute in isolation as long as the other threads do not take any steps."
[SS05]	"The core of an *obstruction free* algorithm only needs to guarantee progress when one single thread is running (although other threads may be in arbitrary states)"
[Sun04]	"Recently, some researchers also proposed *obstruction-free* algorithms to be non-blocking, although this kind of algorithms do not give any progress guarantees."

We do not follow any one of these definitions in particular, and to avoid further confusion, we do not present our interpretation using natural language.

Instead, we jump straight into formalisation, then relate the definitions presented above to our formal definitions. However, at this stage we point out that [Mic04] presumes that a wait-free program is lock-free.

4.1 Formalising Progress Properties

To describe the desired progress properties of a program, we define a progress function

$$\Pi : PC \longrightarrow \mathbb{P}(PC)$$

which for any control point returns the set of control points such that a control point in the set must be reached to make progress. Hence, for any label i and for any $j \in \Pi.i$, if $pc_p = j$ ever holds, then process p has made progress from i. Notice that in defining Π, we formalise the progress requirement of the program.

The progress function Π of a program specifies the progress requirements of each operation in the program. Hence, any progress property must be defined with respect to a particular definition of Π. It is possible for different definitions of Π to allow the same program to be classified differently.

Assuming that Π is given allows us to express progress properties in a very general manner. By relating the definitions of the progress properties to a progress function, we are able to provide definitions that do not refer to any particular program. However, to rule out trivial cases, we place a few restrictions on the definition of Π. Clearly, progress cannot occur if a process does not take a step. We also do not allow Π to be defined from a control point of one operation to the control point of another. Furthermore, a process that invokes a new operation is considered to have made progress. Thus, the following healthiness conditions on Π are imposed:

$$(\forall_{i:PC}\ i \notin \Pi.i) \tag{1}$$

$$(\forall_{X:OP}\ (\forall_{i:PC_X} \Pi.i \subset PC_X)) \tag{2}$$

$$\Pi.\tau \ = \ PC_{start} \tag{3}$$

As $P \rightsquigarrow Q$ is a two state predicate, one or more statements may need to be executed[3] to reach a state that satisfies Q from one that satisfies P. Hence, values of variables in states that satisfy P may be different to their values in states that satisfy Q. This is definitely the case with our proofs which are usually of the form $pc_p = i \rightsquigarrow pc_p \in \Pi.i$. By (1), this means that $pc_p \neq i$ on the right side of the $\rightsquigarrow$, i.e., the value of pc_p has changed. Thus, to show that a state that satisfies $pc_p = i$ reaches a state that satisfies $pc_p \in \Pi.i$, we need to record the value of pc_p at the start. As properties such as lock-freedom require the system as a whole to make progress, we must record the value of the program counters of *all* processes. To do this we use a snapshot ss of type SS with which we are able to record the state of all the program counters. By considering all ss in SS,

[3] Execution of statements is not always necessary. For instance when $[\ P \Rightarrow Q\ ]$, by Lemma 1 (implication), $P \rightsquigarrow Q$.

every possible configuration of the program counters can be considered. We note that in real life, some of these ss might not be reachable, but for the purposes of this paper, we will assume that they are.

From the informal definitions, we can see that it is common for Π to be defined so that progress for each operation occurs when the operation terminates. For this reason, we define the constraint:

$$(\forall_{i:PC-\{\tau\}}\ \Pi.i = \{\tau\}) \tag{4}$$

If the progress function Π satisfies (4), progress occurs whenever a currently executing operation terminates.

4.2 Wait-Freedom

A program exhibits the wait-free property if each process makes progress independently of the other processes.

Definition 7 (Wait-free). *A non-blocking program is* wait-free *with respect to a progress function Π iff it satisfies WF_Π, where*

$$WF_\Pi \ \widehat{=}\ (\forall_{i:PC}\ (\forall_{p:PROC}\ pc_p = i \ \leadsto\ pc_p \in \Pi.i \vee \neg\xi_p)).$$

If a program satisfies WF_Π, then for every value, i, of the program counter, and for every process p in the program, given that the recorded value of pc_p is i, either we eventually reach a state for which the value of pc_p is in $\Pi.i$, i.e., p has made progress, or p is disabled (possibly forever).

Let us now compare WF_Π to the informal definitions compiled in Section 4.1. WF_Π implies the definitions in [HLM03, Mic04, Sun04] as when WF_Π holds, each process that is not disabled (eg., through failure) makes progress. For [Her88], we constrain Π so that it satisfies (4). Now, if the program is wait-free, then $pc_p = i \leadsto pc_p = \tau$ holds for each $p \in PROC$. By the definition of $\leadsto$, any proof of the form $pc_p = i \leadsto pc_p = \tau$ is proved using a finite number of applications of immediate progress. As each application of immediate progress corresponds to a step in the operation, it follows that each operation terminates after a finite number of steps.

4.3 Lock-Freedom

Lock-freedom is a weaker property than wait-freedom that only requires the system as a whole to make progress. Being a system-wide property, we need to take a snapshot the program counters of *all* processes, then show that *one* of these processes has made progress.

Definition 8 (Lock-free). *A non-blocking program is* lock-free *with respect to a progress function Π iff it satisfies LF_Π, where*

$$LF_\Pi \ \widehat{=}\ (\forall_{ss:SS}\ pc = ss \ \leadsto\ (\exists_{p:PROC}\ pc_p \in \Pi.ss_p) \vee (\forall_{p:PROC}\ \neg\xi_p)).$$

If a program satisfies LF_Π, given that we record the value of the program counters of all processes in ss, eventually either some process makes progress or all processes are disabled. As we check all ss, we consider every configuration of the program counters.

Let us compare LF_Π with the informal definitions of lock-freedom. The definition in [HLM03] states that some process always makes progress which implies LF_Π. We can relate [Mic04] to LF_Π by constraining Π so that it satisfies (4). The fact that each $\rightsquigarrow$ proof consists of a finite number of applications of immediate progress means that some operation has taken a finite number of steps, and furthermore, some operation has completed. However, notice that the definitions in [Mic04] can be misinterpreted. The phrase "...some finite number of steps..." could mean that there is a finite number n, and "...some thread must have completed an operation during execution of these steps..." could mean that if any process takes n steps, then some operation must have completed. Against [MP91], we may once again constrain Π to satisfy (4). As the proof involves a finite number of applications of immediate progress, some operation completes in a finite number of steps. The definition in [Sun04] is a rewording of [MP91] where progress can occur without a process terminating, and the requirement that a finite number of steps be taken is removed.

Examining these definitions also provides us with an opportunity to show how natural language definitions can be ambiguous. Consider the following definition.

$$LFA_\Pi \;\widehat{=}\; (\exists_{p:PROC}\ (\forall_{ss:SS}\ pc = ss \;\rightsquigarrow\; pc_p \in \Pi.ss_p \vee (\forall_{q:PROC}\ \neg\xi_q)))$$

Assuming that processes are not disabled, if a program satisifies LFA_Π, then we are required to show that there is a distinguished process that always makes progress. Notice that LFA_Π is a possible interpretation of the definition in [HLM03] as there exists a process that always makes progress. We can prove that $LFA_\Pi \Rightarrow LF_\Pi$, however, a lock-free program does not need to guarantee that a particular process that always makes progress exists.

To see this for a two process case, consider a program for which $PROC = \{q, r\}$. Against any progress function Π, if the program satisfies LFA_Π then the following holds.

$$\begin{aligned} &(\forall_{ss:SS}\ pc = ss \;\rightsquigarrow\; pc_q \in \Pi.ss_q \vee (\forall_{p:PROC}\ \neg\xi_p))) \\ \vee\ &(\forall_{ss:SS}\ pc = ss \;\rightsquigarrow\; pc_r \in \Pi.ss_r \vee (\forall_{p:PROC}\ \neg\xi_p))) \end{aligned} \tag{5}$$

However, if the program satisfies LF_Π it satisfies:

$$(\forall_{ss:SS}\ pc = ss \;\rightsquigarrow\; pc_q \in \Pi.ss_q \vee pc_r \in \Pi.ss_r \vee (\forall_{p:PROC}\ \neg\xi_p))) \tag{6}$$

which is equivalent to

$$\begin{aligned} (\forall_{ss:SS}\ &(pc = ss \rightsquigarrow pc_q \in \Pi.ss_q) \;\vee\; (pc = ss \rightsquigarrow pc_r \in \Pi.ss_r) \\ &\vee\; (pc = ss \rightsquigarrow (\forall_{p:PROC}\ \neg\xi_p)))) \end{aligned}$$

and now it is clear that (6) is a weaker property than (5). Thus LF_Π does not imply LFA_Π.

4.4 Obstruction-Freedom

Our definition of obstruction-freedom follows from the original source [HLM03]. The first part of their definition seems to require that there are no other contending (concurrently executing) processes. However, by the second part of [HLM03] and by the definition in [SS05], we realise that contending processes are allowed as long as they do not take any steps.

A process p executes in isolation, i.e., without any contending processes, if all other processes are disabled. That is, for every process q other than p, condition $\neg\xi_q$ holds. Recall that we assume a process is that is disabled is never re-enabled.

Definition 9 (Obstruction-free). *A non-blocking program is* obstruction-free *with respect to a progress function Π iff it satisfies OF_Π, where*

$$OF_\Pi \ \widehat{=}\ (\forall_{i:PC}\ (\forall_{p:PROC}\ pc_p = i \wedge (\forall_{q:PROC}\ p = q \vee \neg\xi_q) \ \rightsquigarrow \\ pc_p \in \Pi.i \vee \neg\xi_p)).$$

If a program satisfies OF_Π, then for all processes p, given that we record the value of pc_p in i, if p is ever executing in isolation, the program eventually reaches a state where p has made progress from i, or p is itself disabled.

Notice that obstruction-freedom allows processes to prevent each other from making progress, and as long as a process is not executing in isolation, no progress guarantees are provided. An objective of Herlihy et al [HLM03] is the separation of safety and progress concerns during program development. In their words, "We believe a clean separation between the two [safety and progress] concerns promises simpler, more efficient, and more effective algorithms." The definition we have provided allows one to observe this intended separation more easily as it is now clear that the other half of ensuring progress is concerned with developing an effective underlying mechanism that ensures each process eventually executes in isolation. We leave exploration of the sorts of mechanisms necessary as a topic for further work as it lies outside the scope of this paper.

Comparing our definition to those in natural language, we have developed our definition of OF_Π using [HLM03, SS05]. We believe the definition given in [Sun04] is incorrect, as OF_Π does provide progress guarantees, although they are quite weak.

5 Progress Hierarchy

In this section we prove the widely believed presumption that wait-free programs are a special case of lock-free programs and lock-free programs a special case of obstruction-free programs. We will use notation $x = y = z$ as shorthand for $x = z \wedge y = z$. For our proof, we will be using a well-founded lexicographical (or dictionary) ordering which we define below.

Definition 10 (Lexicographical ordering). *Given a collection of sets A_1, $A_2, \ldots, A_n$ and respective total-orderings $\prec_1, \prec_2, \ldots, \prec_n$, the* lexicographical ordering $\prec\!\!\!\prec$ *of $A_1 \times A_2 \times \ldots \times A_n$ is defined as*

$$[a_1, a_2, \ldots, a_n] \lll [a'_1, a'_2, \ldots, a'_n] \;\equiv\; (\exists_{t:1..n}(\forall_{u:1..t-1}\; a_u = a'_u \wedge a_t \prec_t a'_t)).$$

Definition 11 (Well-founded). *An ordering is* well-founded *if it does not contain any infinite descending chains, and a lexicographical ordering is* well-founded *if each* $(A_i, \prec_i)$ *is well-founded.*

Hence, for example, for $W \mathrel{\widehat{=}} (\mathbb{N} \times \mathbb{N} \times \mathbb{N}, \lll)$ where $\prec$ is just $<$ on the natural numbers, the relation $[33, 1, 100] \lll [33, 100, 1]$ holds.

Theorem 1. *Any wait-free program is also lock-free, but a lock-free program is not necessarily wait-free.*

Proof $(\Rightarrow)$. For some arbitrary progress function, Π, we prove that $WF_\Pi \Rightarrow LF_\Pi$ as follows:

$$
\begin{array}{ll}
 & (\forall_{i:PC}\; (\forall_{p:PROC}\; pc_p = i \;\leadsto\; pc_p \in \Pi.i \vee \neg\xi_p)) \\
\equiv & \quad \{\text{as } SS\colon PROC \to PC\ \} \\
 & (\forall_{ss:SS}\; (\forall_{p:PROC}\; pc_p = ss_p \;\leadsto\; pc_p \in \Pi.ss_p \vee \neg\xi_p)) \\
\Rightarrow & \quad \{\text{LHS of } \leadsto \text{ is anti-monotonic}\} \\
 & \quad \{\text{RHS of } \leadsto \text{ is monotonic}\} \\
 & (\forall_{ss:SS}\; (\forall_{p:PROC}\; pc = ss \;\leadsto\; (\exists_{q:PROC}\; pc_q \in \Pi.ss_q) \vee \neg\xi_p)) \\
\Rightarrow & \quad \{\text{as processes do not become re-enabled}\} \\
 & (\forall_{ss:SS}\; pc = ss \leadsto (\exists_{q:PROC}\; pc_q \in \Pi.ss_q) \vee (\forall_{p:PROC}\; \neg\xi_p))
\end{array}
$$

□

Proof $(\Leftarrow)$.

```
PROC ≙ {q, r}
Init ≙ pc_q = pc_r = τ
------------------------------
X(k: PROC)
      *[
X2:   t_k := T;
X1:   ife ⟨T = t_k → T := t_k + 1⟩
X0:         exit
      efi
      ]
τ:
```

Fig. 2. A lock-free program

To prove that lock-freedom does not imply wait-freedom, we consider the program in Fig. 2. To simplify our reasoning, we will assume that ξ_p for each process p is never set to *false* which means no process is ever disabled. We define the progress function for the program in Fig. 2 as:

$$(\lambda_{c:PC}\; \mathsf{if}\; c = \tau\; \mathsf{then}\; \{X_2\}\; \mathsf{else}\; \{\tau\})$$

Hence, progress occurs either if a process invokes a new X operation, or if a currently executing operation terminates. Due to weak fairness, we can guarantee that the following holds:

$$(\forall_{p:PROC}\ pc_p = X_0 \ \rightsquigarrow\ pc_p = \tau)$$

and hence, the progress function becomes:

$$\Pi_1 \ \widehat{=}\ (\lambda_{c:PC} \text{ if } c = \tau \text{ then } \{X_2\} \text{ else } \{X_0\}).$$

The program in Fig. 2 is lock-free wrt Π_1. We let $\tau \prec X_0 \prec X_1 \prec X_2$ be the ordering on PC and prove LF_{Π_1} using lexicographical orderings and induction.

$$\begin{array}{ll} & (\forall_{ss:SS}\ pc = ss \ \rightsquigarrow\ (\exists_{p:PROC}\ pc_p \in \Pi_1.ss_p)) \\ \Leftarrow & \quad \{\text{anti-monotonicity of} \rightsquigarrow\} \\ & (\forall_{ss:SS}\ true \ \rightsquigarrow\ (\exists_{p:PROC}\ pc_p \in \Pi_1.ss_p)) \\ \Leftarrow & \quad \{\text{Lemma 1 (induction)}\} \\ & \quad \{(P := true),\ (Q := pc_p \in \Pi_1.ss_p),\ (M := pc),\ (m := ss),\ (W := SS)\} \\ & (\forall_{ss:SS}\ pc = ss \ \rightsquigarrow\ pc \lll ss \vee (\exists_{p:PROC}\ pc_p \in \Pi_1.ss_p)) \end{array}$$

Hence, LF_{Π_1} is satisfied if the value of one of the program counters is decreased, or one of the processes makes progress. For the rest of the proof, we will consider process q in detail realising that a symmetric argument can be applied to r. Due to weak fairness, all but two actions of q trivially satisfies $pc = ss \rightsquigarrow pc \lll ss$. The steps that q may perform which increase the value of pc_q are:

(*a*) When a (currently idle) q invokes a new operation, where the value of pc_q changes from τ to X_2.
(*b*) When the test at X_1 fails, i.e., $pc_q = X_1 \wedge t_q \neq T$ holds and q is executed. Here, the value of pc_q changes from X_1 to X_2.

Of these, (*a*) may be disregarded by (3), as Π_1 is satisfied if pc_q changes from τ to X_2. Hence, our proof obligation becomes:

$$(\forall_{z:PC}\ pc = [X_1, z] \wedge t_q \neq T \ \rightsquigarrow\ pc \lll [X_1, z] \vee pc_q \in \{\tau\} \vee pc_r \in \Pi_1.z).$$

To prove this, we perform case analysis on the value of pc_r, and show that the left side of $\rightsquigarrow$ does indeed reach the right side. To save space we introduce notation $[\![i, j]\!]$ to mean $pc = [i, j]$. Notice that most of our steps below are of the form $[\![i, j]\!] \rightsquigarrow [\![i', j]\!] \vee [\![i, j']\!]$. This is because the immediate progress rule forces us to consider both a step taken by q and a step taken by r. From a state that satisfies $[\![i, j]\!]$, if q takes a step, then we reach $[\![i', j]\!]$ and if r takes a step, then we reach $[\![i, j']\!]$. Our program is non-blocking and hence no deadlock exists. This means one of the two things is guaranteed to happen. Thus, we are guaranteed to reach a state that satisfies $[\![i', j]\!] \vee [\![i, j']\!]$.

For our proof we use the property: $K \ \widehat{=}\ pc_p = pc_r = X_1 \wedge t_q \neq T \Rightarrow t_r = T$. K is a safety property; its proof is omitted.

case $pc_r = X_2$:

$$\begin{array}{ll} & [\![X_1, X_2]\!] \wedge t_q \neq T \\ \rightsquigarrow & \quad \{\text{imm. progress on } X_1 \text{ (or } X_2)\} \\ & [\![X_2, X_2]\!] \vee [\![X_1, X_1]\!] \\ \rightsquigarrow & \quad \{\text{imm. progress on } X_2\} \\ & ([\![X_1, X_2]\!] \wedge t_q = T) \\ & \vee ([\![X_2, X_1]\!] \wedge t_r = T) \vee [\![X_1, X_1]\!] \\ \rightsquigarrow & \quad \{\text{imm. progress on } X_1 \text{ (or } X_2)\} \\ & [\![X_0, X_2]\!] \vee [\![X_2, X_0]\!] \vee [\![X_1, X_1]\!] \end{array}$$

case $pc_r = X_1$:

$$\begin{array}{ll} & [\![X_1, X_1]\!] \wedge t_q \neq T \\ \rightsquigarrow & \quad \{\text{by } K\}\{\text{Lemma 1 (implication)}\} \\ & [\![X_1, X_1]\!] \wedge t_q \neq T \wedge t_r = T \\ \rightsquigarrow & \quad \{\text{imm. progress on } X_1\} \\ & ([\![X_2, X_1]\!] \wedge t_r = T) \vee [\![X_1, X_0]\!] \\ \rightsquigarrow & \quad \{\text{imm. progress on } X_2\} \\ & ([\![X_1, X_1]\!] \wedge t_q = t_r = T) \\ & \vee [\![X_2, X_0]\!] \vee [\![X_1, X_0]\!] \end{array}$$

case $pc_r = X_0$:

$$\begin{array}{ll} & [\![X_1, X_0]\!] \wedge t_q \neq T \\ \rightsquigarrow & \quad \{\text{imm. progress on } X_1\} \\ & [\![X_2, X_0]\!] \vee [\![X_1, \tau]\!] \\ \rightsquigarrow & \quad \{\text{imm. progress on } X_2\} \\ & ([\![X_1, X_0]\!] \wedge t_q = T) \vee [\![X_2, \tau]\!] \\ & \vee [\![X_1, \tau]\!] \end{array}$$

case $pc_r = \tau$:

$$\begin{array}{ll} & [\![X_1, \tau]\!] \wedge t_q \neq T \\ \rightsquigarrow & \quad \{\text{imm. progress on } X_1 \text{ (or } \tau)\} \\ & [\![X_2, \tau]\!] \vee [\![X_1, X_2]\!] \\ \rightsquigarrow & \quad \{\text{imm. progress on } X_2 \text{ (or } \tau)\} \\ & ([\![X_1, \tau]\!] \wedge t_q = T) \vee [\![X_2, X_2]\!] \\ & \vee [\![X_1, X_2]\!] \\ \rightsquigarrow & \quad \{\text{imm. progress on } X_1 \text{ (or } \tau)\} \\ & [\![X_0, \tau]\!] \vee [\![X_2, X_2]\!] \vee [\![X_1, X_2]\!] \end{array}$$

Thus, with all four cases, either the value of $[pc_q, pc_r]$ is reduced with respect to $\lessdot$, or progress is made with respect to Π_1. This completes the proof that X satisfies LF_{Π_1}.

The program in Fig. 2 is not wait-free wrt Π_1. To show that the program satisfies WF_{Π_1}, we must prove $(\forall_{ss:SS}\ (\forall_{p:PROC}\ pc_p = ss_p \ \rightsquigarrow\ pc_p \in \Pi_1.ss_p))$. We choose to prove this for process q realising that a symmetric argument applies to r. Below, we present the attempted proof of progress for q from a state that satisfies $pc_q = X_2$.

$$\begin{array}{ll} & pc_q = X_2 \ \rightsquigarrow\ pc_q \in \Pi_1.X_2 \\ \equiv & \quad \{\text{transitivity, as } pc_q \text{ is local to } q\}\{\text{definition of } \Pi_1\} \\ & (pc_q = X_2 \rightsquigarrow pc_q = X_1) \ \wedge\ (pc_q = X_1 \rightsquigarrow pc_q = X_0) \ \wedge\ (pc_p = X_0 \rightsquigarrow pc_p = \tau) \\ \equiv & \quad \{\text{immediate progress on } X_2 \text{ and } X_0\} \\ & pc_q = X_1 \ \rightsquigarrow\ pc_q = X_0 \end{array}$$

However,

$$\begin{array}{ll} & pc_q = X_1 \\ \rightsquigarrow & \quad \{\text{Lemma 1 (implication), case analysis on guard of } X_1\} \\ & (pc_q = X_1 \wedge t_q = T) \vee (pc_q = X_1 \wedge t_q \neq T) \\ \rightsquigarrow & \quad \{\text{by immediate progress}\} \\ & pc_q = X_0 \vee (pc_q = X_1 \wedge t_q \neq T) \vee pc_q = X_2 \\ \rightsquigarrow & \quad \{\text{by immediate progress}\} \\ & pc_q \in \{X_0, X_2\} \end{array}$$

Thus, when $pc_q = X_1$, either pc_q is set to X_0 as we hoped, or it fails and pc_q is set to X_2. That is, the trace $[X_1, pc_r], [X_2, pc_r]$ may be infinitely repeated, whereby q never makes progress. This shows that the program in Fig. 2 is not wait-free and concludes the proof that a lock-freedom does not imply wait-freedom. □

Theorem 2. *Any lock-free program is also obstruction-free, but an obstruction free program is not necessarily lock-free.*

Proof (⇒). For any progress function Π, we prove that $LF_\Pi \Rightarrow OF_\Pi$ as follows:

$$
\begin{array}{ll}
& (\forall_{ss:SS}\ pc = ss \ \leadsto\ (\exists_{p:PROC}\ pc_p \in \Pi.ss_p) \vee (\forall_{p:PROC}\ \neg\xi_p)) \\
\equiv & \quad \{\text{logic, } q \text{ is free}\} \\
& (\forall_{ss:SS}\ (\forall_{q:PROC}\ pc = ss \ \leadsto\ (\exists_{p:PROC}\ pc_p \in \Pi.ss_p) \vee (\forall_{p:PROC}\ \neg\xi_p))) \\
\Rightarrow & \quad \{\text{LHS of} \leadsto \text{is anti-monotonic}\} \\
& (\forall_{ss:SS}\ (\forall_{q:PROC}\ pc = ss \wedge (\forall_{p:PROC}\ p = q \vee \neg\xi_p) \ \leadsto \\
& \qquad\qquad (\exists_{p:PROC}\ pc_p \in \Pi.ss_p) \vee (\forall_{p:PROC}\ \neg\xi_p))) \\
\Rightarrow & \quad \{\text{RHS of} \leadsto \text{is monotonic}\} \\
& (\forall_{ss:SS}\ (\forall_{q:PROC}\ pc = ss \wedge (\forall_{p:PROC}\ p = q \vee \neg\xi_p) \ \leadsto \\
& \qquad\qquad (\exists_{p:PROC}\ pc_p \in \Pi.ss_p) \vee \neg\xi_q)) \\
\Rightarrow & \quad \{\text{all } p \text{ for which } p \neq q \text{ are disabled}\} \\
& (\forall_{ss:SS}\ (\forall_{q:PROC}\ pc_q = ss_q \wedge (\forall_{p:PROC}\ p = q \vee \neg\xi_p) \ \leadsto\ pc_q \in \Pi.ss_q \vee \neg\xi_q)) \\
\equiv & \quad \{\text{as } SS: PROC \to PC\ \} \\
& (\forall_{i:PC}\ (\forall_{q:PROC}\ pc_q = i \wedge (\forall_{p:PROC}\ p = q \vee \neg\xi_p) \ \leadsto\ pc_q \in \Pi.i \vee \neg\xi_q))
\end{array}
$$

□

Proof (⇐).

<table>
<tr><td colspan="2">PROC ≙ {q,r}
Init ≙ $pc_q = pc_r = \tau$</td></tr>
<tr><td>X(k: PROC)
    *[
X_2: B := true ;
X_1: ife B →
X_0:   exit
      efi
    ]
τ:</td><td>Y(k: PROC)
    *[
Y_2: B := false ;
Y_1: ife ¬B →
Y_0:   exit
      efi
    ]
τ:</td></tr>
</table>

Fig. 3. An obstruction-free program

To see that the implication does not hold in the other direction, we consider the program in Fig. 3. The progress requirement, as before will be that each operation terminates. However, due to the fact that $(\forall_{p \in PROC}\ pc_p \in \{X_0, Y_0\} \leadsto pc_p = \tau \vee \neg\xi_p)$ holds, we may define our progress function to be

$$\Pi_2 \ \widehat{=}\ (\lambda_{c:PC}\ \mathsf{if}\ c = \tau\ \mathsf{then}\ \{X_2, Y_2\}\ \mathsf{else}\ \{X_0, Y_0\})$$

The program in Fig. 3 is obstruction-free wrt Π_2. We assume that r is disabled, i.e., $\neg\xi_r$ holds which means q is executing in isolation. If q has invoked X, then $pc_q = X_2$. Recalling that we assume r does not get re-enabled, it is not hard to see that by repeated applications of immediate progress, $pc_q = X_2 \leadsto pc_q = X_0 \vee \neg\xi_q$ holds. Similarly, if q has invoked Y, we can easily prove that $pc_q = Y_2 \leadsto pc_q = Y_0 \vee \neg\xi_q$. Which shows that our program is obstruction-free.

The program in Fig. 3 is not lock-free wrt Π_2. Suppose processes q and r have invoked X and Y respectively, so $pc_q = X_2 \wedge pc_r = Y_2$. We get:

$$\begin{array}{ll} & [\![X_2, Y_2]\!] \\ \leadsto & \quad \{\text{immediate progress on } X_2 \text{ (or } Y_2)\} \\ & ([\![X_1, Y_2]\!] \wedge B) \vee ([\![X_2, Y_1]\!] \wedge \neg B) \vee \xi_q \vee \xi_r \\ \leadsto & \quad \{\text{immediate progress on } X_1 \text{ (or } Y_2)\} \\ & [\![X_0, Y_2]\!] \vee ([\![X_1, Y_1]\!] \wedge \neg B) \vee ([\![X_2, Y_1]\!] \wedge \neg B) \vee \xi_q \vee \xi_r \end{array}$$

Considering just the second disjunct we have:

$$\begin{array}{ll} & [\![X_1, Y_1]\!] \wedge \neg B \\ \leadsto & \quad \{\text{immediate progress on } X_1 \text{ (or } Y_1)\} \\ & ([\![X_2, Y_1]\!] \wedge \neg B) \vee [\![X_1, Y_0]\!] \vee \neg\xi_q \vee \neg\xi_r \\ \leadsto & \quad \{\text{immediate progress on } X_2 \text{ (or } Y_1)\} \\ & ([\![X_1, Y_1]\!] \wedge B) \vee [\![X_2, Y_0]\!] \vee [\![X_1, Y_0]\!] \vee \neg\xi_q \vee \neg\xi_r \end{array}$$

Again, considering the first disjunct separately gives us:

$$\begin{array}{ll} & [\![X_1, Y_1]\!] \wedge B \\ \leadsto & \quad \{\text{immediate progress on } X_1 \text{ (or } Y_1)\} \\ & [\![X_0, Y_1]\!] \vee ([\![X_1, Y_2]\!] \wedge B) \vee \neg\xi_q \vee \neg\xi_r \end{array}$$

Thus, our program may infinitely repeat the trace $[X_1, Y_2], [X_1, Y_1], [X_2, Y_1], [X_2, Y_1], [X_1, Y_1]$ during which no process makes progress wrt Π_2, showing that the program is not lock-free. Thus, we are able to conclude that obstruction-freedom does not imply lock-freedom. □

6 Benefits of Formalisation

In this section we present some other theoretical results obtained through formalisation of the progress properties. The relationship between progress properties of blocking and non-blocking algorithms is presented in Section 6.1 and in Section 6.2 we briefly describe how other progress properties may be formalised.

6.1 Progress Properties of Blocking Programs

As we have a formal description of progress, we are able to investigate whether other progress properties can be discovered. By placing restrictions on the definition of Π, we can define starvation and deadlock freedom in terms of WF_Π, LF_Π and OF_Π. These definitions apply to any concurrent program, not necessarily those that are non-blocking.

Definition 12 (Starvation-free, deadlock-free). *For a program, suppose we define Π so that the following holds:*

$$(\forall_{X:OP}\ (\forall_{i:PC_X}\ \Pi.i = PC_X - \{i\}))$$

i.e., progress occurs from any label i whenever any process takes a step. Then,

1. *a concurrent program is* starvation-free *iff it satisfies* WF_Π.
2. *a concurrent program is* deadlock-free *iff it satisfies* LF_Π *or it satisfies* OF_Π.

6.2 Other Progress Properties

Another benefit of having a formal description of progress is that we are able to define progress properties other than wait, lock, and obstruction freedom. We have already seen an example of this in LFA_Π (see Section 4.3) which defines a property stronger than LF_Π. For some progress function Π, we may also define a property such as

$$AF_\Pi \;\widehat{=}\; (\exists_{is \subseteq PC, i:PC}\ (\forall_{p:PROC}\ pc_p = i \wedge i \in is \;\rightsquigarrow\; pc_p \in \Pi.i \vee \neg\xi_p))$$

that is, there is a set of control points (in the program) from which all processes that do not get disabled make progress. For a program that satisfies AF_Π, to show that a process makes progress, we only need to prove that the process reaches a control point from which progress is guaranteed.

By placing different restrictions on Π, it might be possible to discover other relationships among progress properties. Also, by careful manipulation of the formulae, we might be able to discover some other progress properties and build a more complete hierarchy. We leave exploration of both these ideas as a subject for further work.

7 Conclusion

Formally describing progress properties of concurrent programs is not an easy task, and subtle variations in assumptions on the programming model can result in widely varying proof obligations. We have presented definitions for the three well known progress properties of non-blocking programs using the logic of [DG06]. The relationship between wait-free, lock-free, and obstruction-free programs have also firmly been established and we have been able to express properties of blocking programs such as starvation and deadlock-freedom using our definitions.

By defining the progress properties of a program in a precise and provable manner, confusion on what is required for a program to have a given progress property is avoided. A program has a given property precisely when it satisfies the definition. The proofs of the programs in Fig. 2 and 3 provide examples of applications of our definitions to real programs, although a large case study has not been presented. We leave this as further work. As we have already seen, the formalisation allows one to describe new progress properties, and in the future, we hope that a more complete hierarchy of progress properties can be constructed.

In a blocking program, proving progress usually amounts to proving progress past the blocking statements, which provide useful reference points in stating the required progress property. The fact that no blocking occurs in a non-blocking program makes stating and proving their progress property much more difficult. Furthermore, proofs of properties such as lock-freedom are complicated by the fact that they are system-wide properties, as opposed to one that is per-process. The complicated nature of the relatively simple programs Fig. 2 and 3 are indicative of the possible underlying complexity. Future work should thus address this and aim to make proofs of progress of non-blocking programs easier.

We note that our model is complicated by the fact that we take underlying mechanisms into consideration. However, one of the aims of this paper has been that the definitions of wait, lock and obstruction freedom be kept similar, a decision that has paid off as can be seen by the relative ease with which one has been able to prove Theorems 1 and 2. It might certainly be possible to simplify the definitions and abstract away from mention of underlying mechanisms, however, we leave exploration of this idea as another avenue of further research.

While this paper has concentrated on verifying programs, the definitions given in this paper assist formal derivations [FvG99] of non-blocking programs. Derivations of non-blocking programs are presented in [Moo02], but like Feijen and van Gasteren [FvG99], the logic of Owicki and Gries [OG76] is used, thus only safety properties are formally considered. Derivations that consider both safety and progress using the logic in [DG06] is described in [DG06, GD05, DM06], however, as they consider lock-based synchronisation, the lessons learnt may not be directly applicable to a non-blocking context.

Acknowlegements. The author wishes to thank Ian Hayes, Robert Colvin, and anonymous referees for their valuable comments on earlier drafts. Many thanks also goes out to Arjan Mooij for pointing out the necessity of modelling failure, and to Lindsay Groves and Ray Nickson for pointing out possible relationships between progress properties of non-blocking and blocking programs.

References

[CG05] R. Colvin and L. Groves. Formal verification of an array-based nonblocking queue. In *10th IEEE International Conference on Engineering of Complex Computer Systems (ICECCS)*, pages 507–516. IEEE Computer Society, 2005.

[CM88] K. M. Chandy and J. Misra. *Parallel Program Design: A Foundation.* Addison-Wesley Longman Publishing Co., Inc., 1988.

[DG06] B. Dongol and D. Goldson. Extending the theory of Owicki and Gries with a logic of progress. *Logical Methods in Computer Science*, 2(6):1–25, March 2006.

[DGLM04] S. Doherty, L. Groves, V. Luchangco, and M. Moir. Formal verification of a practical lock-free queue algorithm. In *FORTE*, volume 3235 of *Lecture Notes in Computer Science*, pages 97–114. Springer, 2004.

[Dij76] E. W. Dijkstra. *A Discipline of Programming.* Prentice Hall, 1976.

[DM06] B. Dongol and A. J. Mooij. Progress in deriving concurrent programs: Emphasizing the role of stable guards. In Tarmo Uustalu, editor, *Proceedings of the 8th International Conference on Mathematics of Program Construction*, volume 4014, pages 140–161. Lecture Notes in Computer Science, Jun 2006.

[Doh03] S. Doherty. Modelling and verifying non-blocking algorithms that use dynamically allocated memory. Master's thesis, Victoria University of Wellington, 2003.

[FvG99] W. H. J. Feijen and A. J. M. van Gasteren. *On a Method of Multiprogramming*. Springer Verlag, 1999.

[GC96] Michael Greenwald and David R. Cheriton. The synergy between non-blocking synchronization and operating system structure. In *Operating Systems Design and Implementation*, pages 123–136. ACM Press, 1996.

[GD05] D. Goldson and B. Dongol. Concurrent program design in the extended theory of Owicki and Gries. In M. Atkinson and F. Dehne, editors, *CATS*, volume 41, pages 41–50, Newcastle, Australia, 2005. Conferences in Research and Practice in Information Technology.

[Her88] M. Herlihy. Impossibility and universality results for wait-free synchronization. In *PODC '88: Proceedings of the 7th annual ACM Symposium on Principles of Distributed Computing*, pages 276–290, New York, NY, USA, 1988. ACM Press.

[HLM03] M. Herlihy, V. Luchangco, and M. Moir. Obstruction-free synchronization: Double-ended queues as an example. In *23rd IEEE International Conference on Distributed Computing Systems*, page 522, 2003.

[HW90] M. P. Herlihy and J. M. Wing. Linearizability: A correctness condition for concurrent objects. *ACM Trans. Program. Lang. Syst.*, 12(3):463–492, 1990.

[Mic04] M. M. Michael. Practical lock-free and wait-free LL/SC/VL implementations using 64-bit CAS. In Rachid Guerraoui, editor, *DISC*, volume 3274 of *Lecture Notes in Computer Science*, pages 144–158, Amsterdam, The Netherlands, October 2004. Springer.

[Moo02] A. J. Mooij. Formal derivations of non-blocking multiprograms. Master's thesis, Technische Universiteit Eindhoven, 2002.

[MP91] H. Massalin and C. Pu. A lock-free multiprocessor OS kernel. Technical Report CUCS-005-91, Columbia University, New York, 1991.

[MP92] Z. Manna and P. Pnueli. *Temporal Verification of Reactive and Concurrent Systems: Specification*. Springer-Verlag New York, Inc., 1992.

[OG76] S. Owicki and D. Gries. Verifying properties of parallel programs: An axiomatic approach. *Commun. ACM*, 19(5):279–285, 1976.

[SS05] W. N. Scherer and M. L. Scott. Advanced contention management for dynamic software transactional memory. In *PODC*, pages 240–248. ACM Press, 2005.

[Sun04] H. Sundell. *Efficient and practical non-blocking data structures*. PhD thesis, Department of Computer Science, Chalmers University of Technology and Göteborg University, 2004.

Towards a Fully Generic Theory of Data

Douglas A. Creager and Andrew C. Simpson

Oxford University Computing Laboratory
Wolfson Building, Parks Road, Oxford, OX1 3QD
United Kingdom

Abstract. Modern software systems place a large emphasis on heterogeneous communication. For disparate applications to communicate effectively, a generic theory of data is required that works at the *inter-application* level. The key feature of such a theory is *full generality*, where the data model of an application is not restricted to any particular modeling formalism. Existing solutions do not have this property: while any data can be encoded in terms of XML or using the Semantic Web, such representations provide only *basic generality*, whereby to reason about an arbitrary application's data model it must be re-expressed using the formalism in question. In this paper we present a theory of data which is fully generic and utilizes an extensible design to allow the underlying formalisms to be incorporated into a specification only when necessary. We then show how this theory can be used to investigate two common data equivalence problems — canonicalization and transformation — independently of the datatypes involved.

1 Introduction

Modern software systems must contend with many issues of communication and data exchange that did not exist previously. This raises an interesting class of new problems involving *data equivalence* — the question of whether two data somehow "mean" the same thing, taking into account the data's format, structure, semantics, and application. Two examples are canonicalization and transformation.

Canonicalization involves two equivalences that disagree. For example, in the world of XML [6], digital signatures are problematic, as cryptographic signature algorithms are defined in terms of byte streams. Since a single XML document has many possible binary encodings, a mismatched signature does not necessarily mean that an XML document was modified in transit — it may be a different sequence of bytes that represents the same document.

Transformation, on the other hand, involves maintaining an equivalence between two datatypes. This problem occurs frequently when two applications are linked with a communications channel: the data models of the two applications will likely not be the same, even though they refer to semantically equivalent concepts. Assuming that one cannot easily rewrite the applications, some form of transformation is needed to bridge the mismatch between the two datatypes.

Z. Liu and J. He (Eds.): ICFEM 2006, LNCS 4260, pp. 304–323, 2006.

The transformation, however, must ensure that it maintains the semantic equivalence between the two datatypes.

These problems are particularly troublesome, especially when applied to real-world applications, since they must take into account the low-level encoding details of the datatypes. This constrasts with most existing approaches to data modeling and data typing, which abstract away encoding details to simplify the formalism. This abstraction is beneficial to the application designer, since one can exploit *data independence* to separate the high-level application logic from the low-level data storage issues. However, when integrating multiple applications, these low-level issues must be considered.

Further complicating matters, these problems must handle multiple underlying data formalisms. Many data formalisms are *complete*, meaning that any feasible application data model can be represented in the formalism. Complete formalisms, at varying levels of abstraction, include XML, the relational model of data [8], algebraic and co-algebraic datatypes [10], and Shannon's information theory [16]. One can investigate canonicalization and transformation within one of these formalisms. The W3C, for instance, has developed solutions to both within the context of XML [9,7]. However, these data equivalence issues are problems with data in general, and cross formalism boundaries. No XML transformation method can solve the transformation problem in general.

Fundamentally, existing solutions are not general because multiple data formalisms exist not just in theory, but in practice. There are applications that do not use XML, or do not use the relational model, for perfectly valid reasons. Though these formalisms are complete, they only maintain *basic generality* — to reason about an arbitrary application's data model, it must first be re-expressed in terms of the formalism in question. Instead, we strive for a theory of data with *full generality*, which would allow us to reason formally about an application's data model *as it exists in the application*. Requiring the application to present a separate, theory-compatible, view of its data is not a desirable solution.

This paper presents a fully generic theory of data. It has two key features. The first is that, in addition to the data itself, datatypes and data equivalences are both treated as first-class objects. This lets us reason about generic problems like canonicalization and transformation independently of the particular datatypes and underlying data formalisms used. The second is that the theory is designed in an extensible way; for instance, one can represent an XML datatype in this theory without requiring a complete description of the XML formalism. Of course, including an XML formalism increases the number of properties one can deduce about an XML datatype; however, as we will show, many interesting problems do not require this level of detail.

The remainder of this paper is organized as follows. Section 2 provides a basic description of datatypes and data equivalence. Section 3 provides a formal description of the data theory. We will present this formalism using the Z notation, introductions to which can be found in [19,20,21]. We will digress slightly from the standard notation, however, by allowing certain operators to be overloaded — to be defined, for instance, for both datatypes and sequences of datatypes.

Section 4 shows how we can use this formalism to investigate canonicalization and transformation. Finally, Section 5 presents our conclusions and suggests an area for future work.

2 Overview

In this section we provide an overview of our data theory. First, we highlight some of the complications that arise when considering the supposedly simple notion of "equivalence". Next, we mention an existing classification that can help illuminate some of the issues involved. Finally, we use this classification to present informal descriptions of several datatypes that we want our theory to support.

2.1 Data Equivalences

A key feature to take into account when designing a data theory is *data equivalence*. What do we mean when we say that two data are "equivalent"? A naïve answer would be to define this based on binary equality — two program variables that both contain the 32-bit integer "73" are obviously equivalent. However, this does not capture the entire picture. We present a few obvious counterexamples.

First, we can consider low-level encoding details that can affect data equivalence. For instance, computer processors have a property called *endianness* that affects how multi-byte numbers are stored in memory. "Big-endian" processors store these numbers with their most-significant byte first, whereas "little-endian" processors store the number's least-significant byte first. As an example, consider the number 1,000, which can be encoded in hexadecimal as the 16-bit quantity 03E8. As shown in Figure 1, when encoded on a big-endian machine, the number is represented by the byte string ⟨⟨03 E8⟩⟩. When encoded on a little-endian machine, however, the byte string becomes ⟨⟨E8 03⟩⟩. In one sense, that of binary equality, the data are not equivalent; in another, equally valid sense, that of integer equality, they are. This inconsistency holds in reverse, as well. Consider the byte string ⟨⟨03 E8⟩⟩. As before, on a big-endian machine, this evaluates to the integer 1,000. On the little-endian machine, however, this is interpreted as the hexadecimal number E803, or 59,395. In this case, the data are equivalent according to binary equality, but not according to integer equality.

To further complicate matters, both of the previous examples assumed that the integers were unsigned. Modern computers encode signed integers using *two's complement notation*, which has the beneficial property that the same binary addition operator can be used for signed and unsigned numbers. This is

⟨⟨03 E8⟩⟩			⟨⟨E8 03⟩⟩	
Signed	Unsigned		Signed	Unsigned
1,000	1,000	Big-endian	-6,141	59,395
-6,141	59,395	Little-endian	1,000	1,000

Fig. 1. Differing semantic interpretations of binary integers

a further inconsistency in how a particular byte string can be interpreted as an integer. For example, on a big-endian machine, the byte string ⟪`E8 03`⟫ is interpreted differently as an signed integer (-6,141) and unsigned integer (59,395). This is another case of the data being equivalent according to binary equality, but not according to integer equality.

Similar inconsistencies can appear at higher abstraction levels. For instance, in the HTML markup language [15], it is possible to specify the background color of a Web page with the `bgcolor` attribute of the opening `body` tag. To give a Web page a white background, for instance, one could use the following:

```
<body bgcolor="white">
```

This example represents the color using one of the values in the list of named color strings specified by the HTML standards. It is also possible to specify the color by giving an explicit color value in the RGB color space, such as:

```
<body bgcolor="#ffffff">
```

This example specifies a background color that has the maximum value of 255 ("`ff`" in hexadecimal) for its red, green, and blue components; this color happens to be the color white. These two examples are not equivalent according to binary equality, or even according to character string equality. However, the semantics of the `bgcolor` attribute, as defined by the HTML standard, are such that the character strings "`white`" and "`#ffffff`" represent equivalent colors.

Thus, it is easy to see that a true notion of data equivalence is very application-dependent. It is also a notion that is very dependent on the level of abstraction being used — two data that have different binary encodings might be semantically equivalent, and vice versa. Sometimes semantic equivalence will be more important; sometimes syntactic equivalence will.

2.2 S Classification

As seen in the previous section, many different kinds of data equivalence exist, depending on the application and the desired level of abstraction. It will be useful to classify these different equivalences. Ouksel and Sheth identify one possible classification in their study of heterogeneity in information systems [14,17]: *system*, *syntax*, *structure*, and *semantics*. System heterogeneity refers to the particular combination of hardware and software used to implement an application or datastore. Syntactic heterogeneity refers to the low-level representation of the data — usually in terms of a specific binary encoding. Structural heterogeneity refers to the underlying data primitives used to model an application domain. Semantic heterogeneity refers to the inherent meaning and interpretation of data — the terms *information* and *knowledge* are often used instead of *data* to refer to semantic content.

Ouksel and Sheth introduce this classification, which we will refer to as the *S classification*, to study heterogeneity of information systems — the applications that process data. It is equally effective at describing the data itself. Data equivalence is ambiguous because of its dependence on the desired level of abstraction. The S classification allows us to describe which level of abstraction we are using when analyzing a particular data equivalence, and to highlight differences between data equivalences.

2.3 Datatypes

Any study of data needs to think about datatypes. Broadly speaking, we define a *datatype* to be some set of data. Notionally, a datatype is different than an arbitrary set of data, because the data that constitute a type are supposed to be "similar" in some way. Exactly what form this similarity takes will be application-dependent, just like our notion of data equivalence. To illustrate this, we present several example datatypes, and show how the S classification helps classify them.

Integers. As our first example we can consider the integer types. This is a very low-level set of types; its syntax is a binary string, or sequence of bytes. As we have seen in previous sections, our interpretation of these bytes depends on several factors. At the system level, we must know the integer's endianness, as this affects the order of the bytes in the sequence. At the structural level, we must know the length (and therefore range) of the integer; this is necessary, for instance, to know how much space to reserve in memory for the integer value. At the semantic level, we must know whether the application intends to use this integer as a signed or unsigned value.

Each of these levels can be seen as imposing constraints on which particular data can appear in the datatype's set: an integer datatype contains all of the data that are encoded as a byte string of a particular length, and are interpreted as integers with a particular endianness and signedness. Taken together, this constraint-based definition of the datatype's set brings our original vague notion of "similarity" into focus — but only for this particular datatype.

Postal address (XML). Next we look at a higher-level type — a postal address encoded in XML. This data type might, for example, be used to send "electronic business cards" between address book applications. An instance of this datatype is shown in Figure 2.

At the semantic level, this datatype represents a postal address. As people who have grown up with a postal system, we are able to encapsulate quite a bit of semantic meaning into this concept. This datatype does not provide us with a means of directly encoding this semantic meaning in the data, but it will inform how we write applications that use this data.

At the syntax level, we are using the Extensible Markup Language (XML). Therefore, by extension, our datatype implicitly includes all of the syntactic

```
<address>
  <name>Douglas Creager</name>
  <company>Oxford University Computing Lab</company>
  <line1>Wolfson Building</line1>
  <line2>Parks Road</line2>
  <city>Oxford</city>
  <postcode>OX1 3QD</postcode>
  <country>UK</country>
</address>
```

Fig. 2. Example instance of the postal address XML type

assumptions and requirements of the XML standard [6]: for instance, a binary string that is not well-formed XML cannot be a valid instance of our datatype.

At the structural level, we have an XML schema (not shown) that specifies which XML tags must be used, the content of those tags, and the order in which the tags must appear. Like at the syntax level, this implicitly includes into the datatype definition all of the structural assumptions and requirements of our XML schema: a well-formed XML document that does not match our schema is not a valid instance of our datatype.

At the system level, things are more vague, and will depend in part on the details of the application that is accessing the data. Further, the different aspects of the system interpretation of the datatype are interrelated with the interpretations of the other three levels. Our application will need to have some sort of XML parser, which will handle the syntax level. It will also need application-level logic for parsing the abstract document tree, taking care of the structural level. The application itself will be written with some intuitive notion of what an address actually *is*, taking care of the semantic level. In addition, there will be the low-level details of the application itself, such as the hardware and operating system that it is running on, and any shared libraries that it uses.

Again, we can look at these levels as imposing constraints on the members of the datatype's set: the set contains all of those data that are encoded in XML, using this particular address schema, and that are used as "postal addresses" within the context of some application.

Postal address (database). As another example, we might decide to store these postal addresses in a relational database. This could correspond to an address book application's internal state of the various business cards that someone has collected. An instance of this datatype is shown in Figure 3.

Semantically, this datatype represents a postal address, just as in the previous example. Specifically, this means that the semantic-level constraints imposed on the corresponding sets are the same for both of these datatypes.

Structurally, however, they are obviously quite different. The tables used in this example are based on the relational model, which is quite different than the hierarchical model of XML. Instead of using an XML schema to define which

ADDRESSES table

ADDRESS_ID	13
NAME	"Douglas Creager"
COMPANY	"Oxford University Computing Lab"
LINE_1	"Wolfson Building"
LINE_2	"Parks Road"
CITY	"Oxford"
POST_CODE	"OX1 3QD"
COUNTRY_ID	30

COUNTRIES table

COUNTRY_ID	30
NAME	"United Kingdom"
ABBREV	"UK"

Fig. 3. Example instance of the postal address database type

tags must appear in the tree of XML data, we have a database schema that defines which relational tables we use, and how the tables relate to each other.

The system and syntax levels of this example are rather blurred. Relational databases do provide an application-visible syntax in the SQL query language, but this is not the syntactic representation of the data itself. In fact, we have several similar datatypes that are equivalent semantically and structurally, but different syntactically. We could be referring to the internal representation used by a particular database server, such as PostgreSQL or Oracle. We could be referring to the wire format used by the database server to send the results of a query back to the application. We could be referring to the equivalent SQL `INSERT` statement that could be used to reconstruct the data. We could be referring to the abstract notion of a relational tuple, in which case there is no actual low-level syntax that can be represented in a computer. Often, these syntactic differences will not matter, and we can exploit data independence by ignoring them. Other times, they will be important, and must be included in the datatype definition.

Postal address (Semantic Web). As one final example, we can describe a third postal address datatype, which uses the formalisms and notations of the Semantic Web [3]. The Semantic Web provides a data representation that is better able to express the semantics of the data involved. It does this by representing data using *subject-predicate-object* triples as defined by the Resource Description Framework (RDF) [11,1]. One can envision these triples as edges in a graph, with the subject being a source node, the object being a destination node, and the predicate being a labeled edge connecting the two. This graph notation is used in Figure 4 to show how a postal address could be expressed in the Semantic Web. (Technically, we should give full URIs [2] for the labels of the edges and the address1 and uk nodes; we provide shorter labels for brevity.)

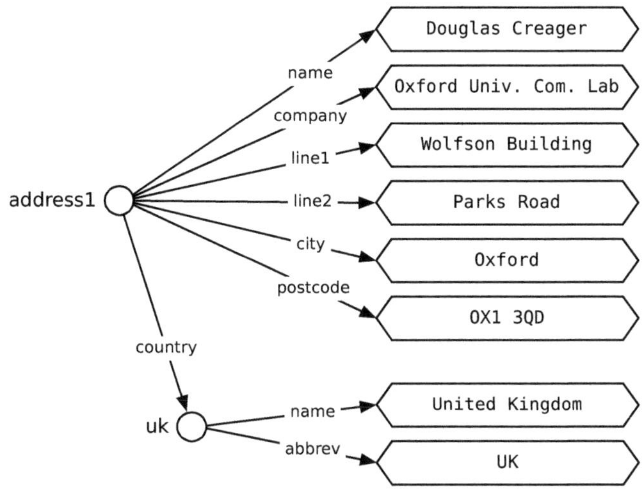

Fig. 4. Example instance of the postal address Semantic Web type

Semantically, this datatype once again represents a postal address; however, by using subject-predicate-object triples, we have encoded a version of these semantics into the data more directly.

Syntactically, the Semantic Web uses XML to encode these graphs of RDF triples, so in one very specific, low-level sense, this datatype is similar to the XML postal datatype described previously. Structurally, however, not just any XML data is allowed — Semantic Web data must exist in a well-formed RDF graph, encoded in XML in a specific way. So while the XML syntax is used for both datatypes, they differ greatly in structure. As with the previous examples, the Semantic Web provides a schema language, the Web Ontology Language (OWL) [13,18], for stating which particular semantic structures are used. Our datatype would include an OWL ontology describing the overall structure of the graph in Figure 4. RDF graphs that do not match this ontology would not be instances of this datatype.

3 Formalization

The example datatypes described in the previous section were not particularly complex. Even so, they were able to incorporate several formalisms that represent data in completely different ways. A fully generic theory of data must be able to incorporate all of this data, regardless of the differences in the underlying formalisms. In this section we describe such a theory, using a simple running example to provide clarity.

In order to talk about data, we must first define it. Since we are aiming for full generality in this type theory, we cannot assume any kind of structure when referring to data — it must be considered completely opaque. We also define *equivalences*, which are relations between data that are reflexive, symmetric, and transitive:

$$[Datum]$$

$$
\begin{array}{|l}
Equivalence : \mathbb{P}(Datum \leftrightarrow Datum) \\
\hline
\forall \triangleq : Datum \leftrightarrow Datum \bullet \\
\quad \triangleq \in Equivalence \Leftrightarrow \\
\quad\quad \forall d : \mathrm{dom} \triangleq \bullet d \triangleq d \land \\
\quad\quad \forall d_1, d_2 : Datum \bullet (d_1 \triangleq d_2) \Rightarrow (d_2 \triangleq d_1) \land \\
\quad\quad \forall d_1, d_2, d_3 : Datum \bullet (d_1 \triangleq d_2 \land d_2 \triangleq d_3) \Rightarrow (d_1 \triangleq d_3)
\end{array}
$$

As mentioned above, datatypes are represented as sets of data. We can define a simple is-a relation between data and datatypes. Note that this definition says nothing about polymorphism; it is neither mandated nor prohibited.

$$Datatype == \mathbb{P}\, Datum$$

$$
\begin{array}{|l}
\_ \;\mathsf{is\text{-}a}\; \_ : Datum \leftrightarrow Datatype \\
\hline
\forall d : Datum;\ t : Datatype \bullet d \;\mathsf{is\text{-}a}\; t \Leftrightarrow d \in t
\end{array}
$$

However, we have also said that a datatype is not just any set of data; the data in question must be similar in some way. We will express this similarity by defining *interpretations* and *constraints* for each datatype. The interpretations and constraints can both be classified using the S classification.

We can apply this to one of the integer types mentioned in Section 2.3. There are multiple integer datatypes, since bit length, endianness, and signedness all affect the integer interpretation. For simplicity, we will look at one integer datatype in particular: 16-bit, little-endian, and unsigned.

$$
\begin{array}{|l}
Integer_{\mathsf{16,L,U}} : Datatype
\end{array}
$$

Our first task is to specify the datatype's interpretations. In the case of the integer datatypes, there are two interpretations: its binary encoding, and its integer value. We use the $_{\mathsf{Syn}}$ subscript to denote that the binary interpretation is syntactic, and the $_{\mathsf{Sem}}$ subscript to denote that the integer interpretation is semantic. Both interpretations are defined as partial functions:

$$
\begin{array}{|l}
\mathrm{binary}_{\mathsf{Syn}} : Datum \rightarrow\!\!\!\!\!+ ByteString \\
\mathrm{integer}_{\mathsf{Sem}} : Datum \rightarrow\!\!\!\!\!+ \mathbb{Z}
\end{array}
$$

In the first case, we define the binary interpretation using the byte string type specified in Appendix A. Similarly, we define an integer interpretation in terms of Z's integer type ($\mathbb{Z}$). It is important to point out that this integer interpretation is not the same as any concrete representation of an integer — rather, it is an abstract mathematical concept that fully captures the semantics of an "integer".

With these interpretations in place, we can formalize our notion of binary equivalence and integer equivalence. Two data are binary-equivalent if their binary interpretations are equal; a similar definition applies to integer equivalence.

$$
\begin{array}{|l}
\_ \stackrel{\circ}{=}_{\text{bin}} \_ : \textit{Equivalence} \\
\_ \stackrel{\circ}{=}_{\text{int}} \_ : \textit{Equivalence} \\
\hline
\forall\, d_1, d_2 : \textit{Datum} \bullet \\
\quad (d_1 \stackrel{\circ}{=}_{\text{bin}} d_2) \Leftrightarrow (\text{binary}_{\mathsf{Syn}}\ d_1 = \text{binary}_{\mathsf{Syn}}\ d_2) \land \\
\quad (d_1 \stackrel{\circ}{=}_{\text{int}} d_2) \Leftrightarrow (\text{integer}_{\mathsf{Sem}}\ d_1 = \text{integer}_{\mathsf{Sem}}\ d_2)
\end{array}
$$

In both cases, we have defined the interpretation as a generic property that can be applied to any *Datum*, since there are many other datatypes that might be encoded in binary or interpreted as an integer. They are both partial functions, though, because not every *Datum* has a binary or integer interpretation. We must then apply these generic properties to our specific datatype:

$$
\begin{array}{l}
\textit{Integer}_{16,\mathsf{L},\mathsf{U}} \subseteq \operatorname{dom} \text{binary}_{\mathsf{Syn}} \\
\textit{Integer}_{16,\mathsf{L},\mathsf{U}} \subseteq \operatorname{dom} \text{integer}_{\mathsf{Sem}}
\end{array}
$$

After defining the interpretations, we must also specify the datatype's constraints. Each of these constraints will depend in some way on at least one of the interpretations. First we have the structural constraint that our integer type is 16 bits long. This is defined in terms of the datatype's binary interpretation. Note that this is a two-way constraint; we must not only say that each of our integers is 16 bits long, but also that every 16-bit binary string can be interpreted as an integer of this type.

$$\forall\, i : \textit{Integer}_{16,\mathsf{L},\mathsf{U}} \bullet \text{binary}_{\mathsf{Syn}}\ i \in \mathsf{Bytes}\, 2$$

$$\forall\, b : \mathsf{Bytes}\ 2 \bullet \exists_1\, i : \textit{Integer}_{16,\mathsf{L},\mathsf{U}} \bullet \text{binary}_{\mathsf{Syn}}\ i = b$$

Our other constraint states how the binary and integer interpretations relate to each other, which we can calculate using the functions in Appendix A. This constraint is informed by both the system-level endianness property and the semantic-level signedness property. As before, the constraint is two-way: we must explicitly state that every integer interpretation in the correct numeric range has a corresponding $\textit{Integer}_{16,\mathsf{L},\mathsf{U}}$.

$$\forall\, i : \textit{Integer}_{16,\mathsf{L},\mathsf{U}} \bullet \text{integer}_{\mathsf{Sem}}\ i = \mathsf{unsignedInt}\ \text{binary}_{\mathsf{Syn}}\ i$$

$$\forall\, z : 0..(2^{16} - 1) \bullet \exists_1\, i : \textit{Integer}_{16,\mathsf{L},\mathsf{U}} \bullet \text{integer}_{\mathsf{Sem}}\ i = z$$

This completes a formal specification of this particular integer type. The other integer types can be defined analagously.

The amount of detail that went into the description of this integer datatype highlights an important distinction in our formalism. The $\textit{Integer}_{16,\mathsf{L},\mathsf{U}}$ datatype had a *full specification* — we provided a complete, formal description of both of the datatype's interpretations, and of the constraints that relate them. In this particular case, this full specification was not overly verbose. We were able to use Z's existing mathematical integer type ($\mathbb{Z}$) to model the semantics of an integer, and it was relatively straightforward to provide a formal definition of binary data (*ByteString*) in Appendix A.

Often a complete formal description is not readily available, and the effort involved in developing a precise definition might not be worth the benefit gained from doing so. In these cases, it is possible to provide a datatype with a *partial specification*, where we define some of the interpretations and constraints as abstract entities. This becomes especially useful when considering how multiple partially-specified datatypes relate to each other.

For instance, we can revisit the postal address types, which have new interpretations that were not used by the integer datatype. However, whereas we provided (or were given) full definitions of the $\mathbb{Z}$ and *ByteString* types, we will leave these new interpretations abstract:

$$[XMLDocument, XMLSchema]$$
$$[RelationalTuple, RelationalSchema]$$
$$[PostalAddress]$$

XMLDocument represents the logical document tree of an XML document, while *RelationalTuple* represents a row from some relational table. In both cases, we have also mentioned a type that represents the schema that describes the data's structure. *PostalAddress* represents the semantic meaning of a postal address. We can now define interpretations and equivalences for these three Z types, similarly to the integer example:

$$\begin{array}{l}
\mathrm{xml}_{\mathsf{Struct}} : Datum \nrightarrow XMLDocument \\
\mathrm{relational}_{\mathsf{Struct}} : Datum \nrightarrow RelationalTuple \\
\mathrm{address}_{\mathsf{Sem}} : Datum \nrightarrow PostalAddress
\end{array}$$

$$\begin{array}{l}
_ \mathrel{\stackrel{\circ}{=}_{\mathrm{xml}}} _ : Equivalence \\
_ \mathrel{\stackrel{\circ}{=}_{\mathrm{rel}}} _ : Equivalence \\
_ \mathrel{\stackrel{\circ}{=}_{\mathrm{addr}}} _ : Equivalence \\
\hline
\forall d_1, d_2 : Datum \bullet \\
\quad (d_1 \mathrel{\stackrel{\circ}{=}_{\mathrm{xml}}} d_2) \Leftrightarrow (\mathrm{xml}_{\mathsf{Struct}}\ d_1 = \mathrm{xml}_{\mathsf{Struct}}\ d_2) \land \\
\quad (d_1 \mathrel{\stackrel{\circ}{=}_{\mathrm{rel}}} d_2) \Leftrightarrow (\mathrm{relational}_{\mathsf{Struct}}\ d_1 = \mathrm{relational}_{\mathsf{Struct}}\ d_2) \land \\
\quad (d_1 \mathrel{\stackrel{\circ}{=}_{\mathrm{addr}}} d_2) \Leftrightarrow (\mathrm{address}_{\mathsf{Sem}}\ d_1 = \mathrm{address}_{\mathsf{Sem}}\ d_2)
\end{array}$$

With these interpretations defined, we can define the types themselves. The XML address datatype will have binary, XML, and address interpretations; the relational address datatype will have relational and address interpretations. (We ignore the syntax of the relational datatype to maintain data independence.)

$$\begin{array}{l}
Address_{\mathsf{XML}} : Datatype \\
\hline
Address_{\mathsf{XML}} \subseteq \mathrm{dom}\,\mathrm{binary}_{\mathsf{Syn}} \\
Address_{\mathsf{XML}} \subseteq \mathrm{dom}\,\mathrm{xml}_{\mathsf{Struct}} \\
Address_{\mathsf{XML}} \subseteq \mathrm{dom}\,\mathrm{address}_{\mathsf{Sem}}
\end{array}$$

$$\begin{array}{|l} Address_{\mathsf{Rel}} : Datatype \\ \hline Address_{\mathsf{Rel}} \subseteq \mathrm{dom}\,\mathrm{relational}_{\mathsf{Struct}} \\ Address_{\mathsf{Rel}} \subseteq \mathrm{dom}\,\mathrm{address}_{\mathsf{Sem}} \end{array}$$

Next we specify the constraints, for which we will need several helper functions and relations, which, again, we do not provide full definitions for:

$$\mathsf{encodes}: ByteString \twoheadrightarrow XMLDocument$$

$$\begin{array}{l} \mathsf{instanceof}: XMLDocument \leftrightarrow XMLSchema \\ \mathsf{instanceof}: RelationalTuple \leftrightarrow RelationalSchema \\ AddressSchema_{\mathsf{XML}} : XMLSchema \\ AddressSchema_{\mathsf{Rel}} : RelationalSchema \end{array}$$

$$\begin{array}{l} \mathsf{interpret}: XMLDocument \twoheadrightarrow PostalAddress \\ \mathsf{interpret}: RelationalTuple \twoheadrightarrow PostalAddress \end{array}$$

The encodes function maps a byte string to the XML document that it represents. (The function is partial since not all byte strings represent valid XML documents.) The two flavors of the instanceof relation allow us to verify that an XML document or relational tuple matches its corresponding schema. We also mention the particular schemas used by our XML and relational datatypes. The two flavors of interpret allow us to determine the semantic meaning of an XML document or relational tuple. These are then applied to the datatypes as constraints:

$$\begin{array}{l} \forall\, d : Address_{\mathsf{XML}} \bullet \\ \quad (\mathrm{binary}_{\mathsf{Syn}}\ d)\ \mathsf{encodes}\ (\mathrm{xml}_{\mathsf{Struct}}\ d) \wedge \\ \quad (\mathrm{xml}_{\mathsf{Struct}}\ d)\ \mathsf{instanceof}\ AddressSchema_{\mathsf{XML}} \wedge \\ \quad (\mathrm{xml}_{\mathsf{Struct}}\ d)\ \mathsf{interpret}\ (\mathrm{address}_{\mathsf{Sem}}\ d) \end{array}$$

$$\begin{array}{l} \forall\, d : Address_{\mathsf{Rel}} \bullet \\ \quad (\mathrm{relational}_{\mathsf{Struct}}\ d)\ \mathsf{instanceof}\ AddressSchema_{\mathsf{Rel}} \wedge \\ \quad (\mathrm{relational}_{\mathsf{Struct}}\ d)\ \mathsf{interpret}\ (\mathrm{address}_{\mathsf{Sem}}\ d) \end{array}$$

This provides a formal rendering of the datatype definitions in Section 2.3. For an XML postal address, its binary encoding must match its logical XML document; this XML document must match the postal address schema; and the document must have some valid real-world interpretation as a postal address. Similar constraints apply to relational postal addresses.

4 Canonicalization and Transformation

The formalism presented in the previous section allowed us to give formal definitions for the datatypes from Section 2.3. However, we only provided a partial specification for the postal address types. If we were so inclined, it would certainly have been possible to give them full specifications. This would have required a formal specification of each of the datatypes' interpretations. For XML, it would be relatively straightforward to define in terms of trees of data nodes; for relational data, we have the underlying relational model to work with. The real-world semantics could have been modeled using a knowledge-representation framework such as the Semantic Web. All of these specifications are possible; however, they would also be much more verbose than what we have presented, and time-consuming to produce and verify. As will be shown in this section, we can still describe and reason about useful properties of these datatypes with partial specifications, rendering this cost unnecessary much of the time. We look specifically at canonicalization and transformation.

4.1 Canonicalization

One example that highlights the importance of differing notions of equivalence is *data canonicalization*. A well-known current example of canonicalization involves XML documents and digital signatures [9,4,5].

The problem stems from the fact that every XML document has many different encodings as a concrete sequence of bytes. Three aspects of the XML syntax, in particular, affect the encoding of a document: attributes, namespaces, and whitespace. In most XML applications, these differences are not a problem, since the application works with a high-level view of the XML content, often in the form of the Document Object Model API [12], which represents an XML document by its abstract tree structure. However, one application area where these differences are important is *digital signatures*. Briefly, digital signatures are a more cryptographically-secure version of checksums and error-correcting codes. They provide a means of attesting that the content of a document has not been modified in transit between two parties. This is an important security feature in modern applications that helps prevent, among other things, man-in-the-middle attacks.

The algorithms used to implement digital signatures are not constrained to XML documents; they work on any binary payload. Alice can send an XML document to Bob, signing it before sending it along the communications channel. However, there might be communications gateways in between Alice and Bob that modify the binary representation of an XML document without modifying the document structure. When Bob receives the document, its binary representation will have changed, and Alice's signature will no longer match the document.

Looking at this in terms of our datatype formalism, we can define a function that can sign a byte string:

$$[\mathit{Signature}]$$

$$\mathsf{sign} : \mathit{ByteString} \rightarrow \mathit{Signature}$$

$$\forall\, b_1, b_2 : \mathit{ByteString} \bullet (\mathsf{sign}\, b_1 = \mathsf{sign}\, b_2) \Leftrightarrow (b_1 = b_2)$$

This captures the essence of a digital signature: if the signatures match, the byte strings most likely match as well; conversely, if the signatures do not match, the byte strings are different. (It should be noted that is not technically a true equivalence. The number of signatures is much smaller than the number of binary strings, so some overlap is inevitable. Rather than a full guarantee, matching signatures *strongly imply* that the binary strings are the same. However, for the purposes of this example, this distinction is not important, and we will treat it as an equivalence.)

We can define a similar function for signing data that simply signs a datum's binary interpretation; signatures then work for arbitrary data, too, *but only under binary equivalence*:

$$\mathsf{sign} : Datum \twoheadrightarrow Signature$$

$$\forall\, d : Datum \bullet \mathsf{sign}\; d = \mathsf{sign}\, \mathrm{binary}_{\mathsf{Syn}}\; d$$
$$\forall\, d_1, d_2 : Datum \bullet (\mathsf{sign}\; d_1 = \mathsf{sign}\; d_2) \Leftrightarrow (d_1 \mathrel{\stackrel{\circ}{=}_{\mathrm{bin}}} d_2)$$

We run into a problem in the case of XML. Alice's and Bob's applications do not care about binary equivalence; they care about XML equivalence. The hope, then, is that the signature predicate holds for XML equivalence, too:

$$\forall\, d_1, d_2 : Datum \bullet (\mathsf{sign}\; d_1 = \mathsf{sign}\; d_2) \stackrel{?}{\Leftrightarrow} (d_1 \mathrel{\stackrel{\circ}{=}_{\mathrm{xml}}} d_2)$$

For this to be the case, we would need the following implication to hold:

$$\forall\, d_1, d_2 : Datum \bullet (d_1 \mathrel{\stackrel{\circ}{\neq}_{\mathrm{bin}}} d_2) \stackrel{?}{\Rightarrow} (d_1 \mathrel{\stackrel{\circ}{\neq}_{\mathrm{xml}}} d_2)$$

However, we know this is not true; two different byte strings *can* represent the same XML document.

What is needed is a *canonicalization function*. In the case of XML documents, we need to choose one particular binary encoding for each logical XML document. We would then define a function $\mathsf{canon}_{\mathrm{xml}}$ that maps an XML datum to its canonical binary encoding. The required property would then hold:

$$\forall\, d_1, d_2 : Datum \bullet (\mathsf{canon}_{\mathrm{xml}}\; d_1 \mathrel{\stackrel{\circ}{=}_{\mathrm{bin}}} \mathsf{canon}_{\mathrm{xml}}\; d_2) \Leftrightarrow (d_1 \mathrel{\stackrel{\circ}{=}_{\mathrm{xml}}} d_2)$$

Two XML documents that have the same logical structure, when canonicalized, would also have the same binary encoding. Expressed another way, two data that are XML-equivalent, when canonicalized, would also be binary-equivalent. In fact, we can define canonicalization as a generic property that a function might provide between any two equivalences:

$$DataFunction == Datum \twoheadrightarrow Datum$$

$$\_\ \mathsf{canonicalizes}\ [\_/\_] : DataFunction \leftrightarrow (Equivalence \times Equivalence)$$

$$\forall\, f : DataFunction;\ \stackrel{\circ}{=}_1, \stackrel{\circ}{=}_2 : Equivalence \bullet$$
$$f\ \mathsf{canonicalizes}\ [\stackrel{\circ}{=}_1 / \stackrel{\circ}{=}_2] \Leftrightarrow$$
$$\forall\, d_1, d_2 : Datum \bullet (d_1 \mathrel{\stackrel{\circ}{=}_1} d_2) \Leftrightarrow (f\; d_1 \mathrel{\stackrel{\circ}{=}_2} f\; d_2)$$

With this generic property defined, we can easily state that the canon_{xml} function canonicalizes XML equivalence in terms of binary equivalence:

$$\begin{array}{|l} \mathsf{canon}_{xml} : DataFunction \\ \hline \mathsf{canon}_{xml}\ \mathsf{canonicalizes}\ [\,\stackrel{\circ}{=}_{xml} / \stackrel{\circ}{=}_{bin}\,] \end{array}$$

It should be noted that this formalism does not help us find a detailed definition of the canon_{xml} function. In general, the definition of a canonicalization function will be highly dependent on the details of the underlying data formalism and how this relates to its binary encodings.

4.2 Transformations

The canonicalizations described in the previous section provide one category of special data function. *Transformations* provide another. They differ in how they relate to the data equivalences that hold on particular types. In the case of canonicalization, the function is used to ensure that two equivalences agree with each other. A transformation, on other hand, only deals with a single equivalence; the function provides a bridge between two datatypes that maintains this equivalence.

One situation where transformations are useful arises often in application integration: linking two heterogeneous applications with a communications channel. These applications will often have completely different datatypes for their inputs and outputs; however, as implied by the fact that we want them to communicate, there is at least some semantic equivalence between the datatypes. (If there were not, what communication would be possible?) We can return once again to the postal address example, and consider two address book applications: one which uses the relational datatype, and one which uses the XML datatype. Since the datatypes both refer to postal addresses, they are semantically equivalent; therefore, in theory, the two applications can communicate. However, before we can even begin to consider the details of the communications channel itself, we must reconcile the difference in datatypes. Assuming that rewriting the applications is impossible or too expensive, some transformation is needed to link the applications. This transformation would translate data from one datatype to another, while maintaining the semantic equivalence.

We can model this situation similarly to the canonicalization example and reuse the *DataFunction* type from that section. We need to introduce the notion of *typing* the data functions, however:

$$\begin{array}{|l} \_\ \mathsf{source}\ \_ : Datatype \leftrightarrow DataFunction \\ \_\ \mathsf{dest}\ \_ : Datatype \leftrightarrow DataFunction \\ \hline \forall\, t : Datatype;\ f : DataFunction \bullet \\ \qquad t\ \mathsf{source}\ f \Leftrightarrow \mathrm{dom}\, f \subseteq t \land \\ \qquad t\ \mathsf{dest}\ f \Leftrightarrow \mathrm{ran}\, f \subseteq t \end{array}$$

We can define the *source* and *destination* datatypes for a data function; this simply states that all of the function's input or output values come from the respective datatype. Since we have not prohibited polymorphism, we must define this as a relation — i.e., there might be many datatypes that encompass the input values for a particular function; all of them can be said to be sources of the function. A data function *links* each of its sources to each of its destinations:

$$
\begin{array}{|l}
\_\ \mathsf{links}\ [\_ \rightharpoonup \_] : \\
\quad DataFunction \leftrightarrow (Datatype \times Datatype) \\
\hline
\forall f : DataFunction;\ t_S, t_D : Datatype \bullet \\
\quad f\ \mathsf{links}\ [\, t_S \rightharpoonup t_D \,] \Leftrightarrow (t_S\ \mathsf{source}\ f) \land (t_D\ \mathsf{dest}\ f)
\end{array}
$$

Lastly, a data function *maintains* an equivalence if that equivalence holds between each of the function's inputs and the corresponding output:

$$
\begin{array}{|l}
\_\ \mathsf{maintains}\ \_ : DataFunction \leftrightarrow Equivalence \\
\hline
\forall f : DataFunction;\ \mathrel{\hat{=}} : Equivalence \bullet \\
\quad f\ \mathsf{maintains} \mathrel{\hat{=}} \Leftrightarrow \\
\qquad \forall d : \mathrm{dom} f \bullet d \mathrel{\hat{=}} (f\ d)
\end{array}
$$

With these definitions in place, we can state the existence of the required transformation: it links the XML and relational postal address datatypes, and maintains the postal address semantic equivalence.

$$
\begin{array}{|l}
\mathsf{xform}_{\mathrm{Address}} : DataFunction \\
\hline
\mathsf{xform}_{\mathrm{Address}}\ \mathsf{links}\ [\, Address_{\mathsf{XML}} \rightharpoonup Address_{\mathsf{Rel}} \,] \\
\mathsf{xform}_{\mathrm{Address}}\ \mathsf{maintains} \mathrel{\hat{=}}_{\mathrm{addr}}
\end{array}
$$

The $\mathsf{xform}_{\mathrm{Address}}$ function is a transformation since it links the $Address_{\mathsf{XML}}$ and $Address_{\mathsf{Rel}}$ datatypes while maintaining the $\mathrel{\hat{=}}_{\mathrm{addr}}$ equivalence. Note that once again, we have abstracted away a lot of unnecessary detail — we have said nothing about how $\mathsf{xform}_{\mathrm{Address}}$ performs this transformation.

Since transformations are modeled as functions between data, they are also composable. This allows us to consider sequences of datatypes, and sequences of data functions:

$$
\begin{array}{l}
TypeSequence == \mathrm{seq}_1\ Datatype \\
FunctionSequence == \mathrm{seq}_1\ DataFunction
\end{array}
$$

$$
\begin{array}{|l}
\_\ \mathsf{types}\ \_ : TypeSequence \leftrightarrow FunctionSequence \\
\_\ \mathsf{source}\ \_ : Datatype \leftrightarrow FunctionSequence \\
\_\ \mathsf{dest}\ \_ : Datatype \leftrightarrow FunctionSequence \\
\hline
\forall ts : TypeSequence;\ fs : FunctionSequence \bullet \\
\quad ts\ \mathsf{types}\ fs \Leftrightarrow \\
\qquad \#ts = \#fs + 1 \land \\
\qquad \forall i : 1 \mathinner{..} \#fs \bullet ts(i)\ \mathsf{source}\ fs(i) \land ts(i+1)\ \mathsf{dest}\ fs(i) \land \\
\qquad (head\ ts)\ \mathsf{source}\ fs \land \\
\qquad (last\ ts)\ \mathsf{dest}\ fs
\end{array}
$$

A sequence of functions is *well-typed* if the destination type of each data function matches the source type of its successor. We can then define the source and dest operators for sequences, much as they are defined for individual functions: the source (destination) of a function sequence is the source (destination) of the first (last) function in the sequence.

With these definitions, we can define a compose operator on function sequences:

$$\mathsf{compose}\ \_ : \mathit{FunctionSequence} \rightarrow \mathit{DataFunction}$$

$$\begin{array}{l}
\forall f : \mathit{DataFunction} \bullet \mathsf{compose}\,\langle f \rangle = f \\
\forall \mathit{fs}_1, \mathit{fs}_2 : \mathit{FunctionSequence} \bullet \\
\quad \mathsf{compose}\ \mathit{fs}_1 \frown \mathit{fs}_2 = (\mathsf{compose}\ \mathit{fs}_2) \circ (\mathsf{compose}\ \mathit{fs}_1) \\
\forall t : \mathit{Datatype};\ \mathit{fs} : \mathit{FunctionSequence} \bullet \\
\quad t\ \mathsf{source}\ \mathit{fs} \Leftrightarrow t\ \mathsf{source}\ (\mathsf{compose}\ \mathit{fs}) \wedge \\
\quad t\ \mathsf{dest}\ \mathit{fs} \Leftrightarrow t\ \mathsf{dest}\ (\mathsf{compose}\ \mathit{fs})
\end{array}$$

The operator is defined in the obvious way using structural induction, exploiting the fact that functional composition is associative. Note the order reversal; for the $\circ$ operator, the function to apply first is on the right, whereas in a function sequence, it is on the left.

5 Discussion

In this paper we have provided a formalism for an inter-application theory of data. This formalism features *full generality*, in that any application data model can be represented as is, without requiring conversion to another data formalism. This theory represents data as abstract entities with several *interpretations* and *constraints*, with the constraints defining how the interpretations of a datatype relate to each other. Underlying formalisms such as the XML or relational models can be incorporated into a specification to give a precise meaning to an interpretation; however, this is optional. It is also valid for an interpretation to remain abstract.

Our formalism is able to represent the low-level encoding details of a datatype in addition to the usual high-level semantic descriptions. At first glance, this seems to violate the data independence principle. However, this is not the case. Data independence can be maintained, when necessary, simply by leaving the datatype's low-level syntactic and structural interpretations abstract, as in the case of the $\mathit{Address}_{\mathsf{Rel}}$ datatype.

However, data independence is not useful when studying problems like canonicalization and transformation in a fully generic way. First, we must be able to handle different data formalisms, and cannot rely on a single abstraction to provide data independence. Second, we must be able to handle the data's binary encoding, which are exactly the details that are hidden by data independence. By allowing (but not requiring) our formalism to include descriptions of these low-level details, we are able to reason about this class of problems.

The similar notion of data refinement [21, Chapter 16] tackles many of these issues from a slightly different viewpoint. Looking at the example of integer endianness, one would consider the mathematical set of integers ($\mathbb{Z}$) to be a datatype that happens to be defined at a high, abstract level. One could then define a lower-level type, such as $\mathit{Integer}_{\mathsf{16,L,U}}$, that represents a binary string interpreted in a particular way. One would then prove that $\mathit{Integer}_{\mathsf{16,L,U}}$ *refines* $\mathbb{Z}$ — that a specification written in terms of $\mathbb{Z}$ could use $\mathit{Integer}_{\mathsf{16,L,U}}$ as a drop-in replacement without affecting the specification.

Data refinement is also possible with our framework. Instead of writing an application specification in terms of the $\mathbb{Z}$ "datatype", it is written in terms of any *Datum* that has an $\text{integer}_{\mathsf{Sem}}$ interpretation. The refinement proof then consists of showing how a datatype's $\text{integer}_{\mathsf{Sem}}$ interpretation correctly relates to one of its other interpretations. Our approach is different in two ways. First, $\mathbb{Z}$ is defined as an interpretation rather than as a first-class datatype, which allows multiple datatypes to have an integer interpretation. This difference does not mean much in terms of expressiveness; with data refinement, it is just as easy to define multiple types that all refine $\mathbb{Z}$. It does, however, make possible the second difference: that data equivalences are first class objects that might be defined abstractly. This allows problems like canonicalization and transformation to be investigated generically in terms of abstract equivalences, without having to rely on the details of the datatypes involved.

It is important to note that this data theory is not meant to be a replacement for any of the other data formalisms that have been mentioned. For instance, our description of canonicalization is not meant to replace the work of the XML Digital Signature initiative [9]; rather, it is meant to provide a higher-level framework in which to ground the XML-specific canonicalization. We envision this framework serving two purposes: as a bridge between data formalisms, and an abstraction away from them. Again, this allows us to reason about generic data without being forced to consider the particular formalism that it is defined in.

Further work in this area will focus on the transformation formalism mentioned in Section 4.2. The current type theory allows one to state the existence of transformations, and to provide specifications of these transformations at whatever detail is necessary. However, the theory provides no mechanism for *discovering* transformations. We hope to exploit the composability of transformation to develop a transformation framework that supports efficient discovery, while retaining the full generality of the type theory.

Acknowledgments

Doug Creager's work is funded by the Software Engineering Programme of the Oxford University Computing Laboratory. The authors would like to thank David Faitelson for providing valuable feedback on the manuscript of this paper. The comments of the anonymous reviewers were also very helpful in improving the readability and content of the paper.

References

1. D. Beckett, editor. *RDF/XML Syntax Specification.* W3C, February 2004. http://www.w3.org/TR/rdf-syntax-grammar/.
2. T. Berners-Lee, R. T. Fielding, and L. Masinter. Uniform Resource Identifier (URI): Generic syntax. *IETF Requests for Comments*, 3986, January 2005. http://www.ietf.org/rfc/rfc3986.txt.
3. T. Berners-Lee, J. Hendler, and O. Lassila. The Semantic Web. *Scientific American*, pages 29–37, May 2001.
4. J. Boyer. *Canonical XML.* W3C, March 2001. http://www.w3.org/TR/xml-c14n/.
5. J. Boyer, D. E. Eastlake, and J. Reagle. *Exclusive XML Canonicalization.* W3C, July 2002. http://www.w3.org/TR/xml-exc-c14n/.
6. T. Bray, J. Paoli, C. M. Sperberg-McQueen, E. Maler, and F. Yergeau, editors. *Extensible Markup Language.* W3C, February 2004. http://www.w3.org/TR/REC-xml/.
7. J. Clark, editor. *XSL Transformations (XSLT).* W3C, November 1999. http://www.w3.org/TR/xslt/.
8. E. F. Codd. A relational model of data for large shared data bases. *Communications of the ACM*, 13(6):377–387, 1970.
9. D. Eastlake, J. Reagle, and D. Solo, editors. *XML-Signature Syntax and Processing.* W3C, February 2002. http://www.w3.org/TR/xml-dsigcore/.
10. B. Jacobs and J. Rutten. A tutorial on (co) algebras and (co) induction. *EATCS Bulletin*, 62(222):222–259, 1997.
11. G. Klyne and J. J. Carroll, editors. *Resource Description Framework (RDF): Concepts and Abstract Syntax.* W3C, February 2004. http://www.w3.org/TR/rdf-concepts/.
12. A. Le Hors, P. Le Hégaret, L. Wood, G. Nicol, J. Robie, M. Champion, and S. Byrne. *Document Object Model (DOM) Level 3 Core Specification.* W3C, April 2004. http://www.w3.org/TR/DOM-Level-3-Core/.
13. D. L. McGuinness and F. van Harmelen, editors. *OWL Web Ontology Language Overview.* W3C, February 2004. http://www.w3.org/TR/owl-features/.
14. A. M. Ouksel and A. Sheth. Semantic interoperability in global information systems. *SIGMOD Record*, 28(1):5–12, 1999.
15. D. Raggett, A. Le Hors, and I. Jacobs. *HTML 4.01 Specification.* W3C, December 1999. http://www.w3.org/TR/html.
16. C. Shannon and W. Weaver. *The Mathematical Theory of Communication.* University of Illinois, 1963.
17. A. Sheth. Changing focus on interoperability in information systems: From system, syntax, structure to semantics. In M. F. Goodchild, M. J. Egenhofer, R. Fegeas, and C. A. Kottman, editors, *Interoperating Geographic Information Systems.* Kluwer Publishers, 1998.
18. M. K. Smith, C. Welty, and D. L. McGuinness, editors. *OWL Web Ontology Language Guide.* W3C, February 2004. http://www.w3.org/TR/owl-guide/.
19. J. M. Spivey. An introduction to Z and formal specification. *Software Engineering Journal*, 4(1):40–50, January 1989.
20. J. M. Spivey. *The Z Notation: A Reference Manual.* Prentice Hall International, 1989.
21. J. C. P. Woodcock and J. W. M. Davies. *Using Z: Specification, refinement, and proof.* Prentice Hall, 1996.

A Z Specification for Binary Integers

Any description of binary data must first define *bits*. Bits are simple — there are exactly two of them: $\mathtt{0}$ and $\mathtt{1}$. We can also define a *bit string*, which is an ordered sequence of bits.

$$Bit ::= \mathtt{0} \mid \mathtt{1}$$

$$BitString == \operatorname{seq} Bit$$

We will often need to translate a binary string into its integer equivalent. (This is not to be confused with interpreting integer datatypes; this is a low-level helper function to get the decimal interpretation of a base-2 integer.)

$$\mathsf{int_{Bit}} : Bit \rightarrowtail \mathbb{N}$$
$$\mathsf{int_{Bits}} : BitString \rightarrow \mathbb{N}$$

$$\mathsf{int_{Bit}}\ \mathtt{0} = 0$$
$$\mathsf{int_{Bit}}\ \mathtt{1} = 1$$

$$\mathsf{int_{Bits}}\ \langle\rangle = 0$$
$$\forall\, b : Bit;\ bin : BitString \bullet \mathsf{int_{Bits}}\ \langle b \rangle \frown bin = (\mathsf{int_{Bits}}\ bin) * 2 + (\mathsf{int_{Bit}}\ b)$$

This allows us to define a *byte*, which is an 8-bit value, and a *byte string*, which is an ordered sequence of bytes. We also define a Bytes function which returns the set of all byte strings of a given length.

$$Byte == \{\, b : BitString \bullet \#b = 8 \,\}$$

$$ByteString == \operatorname{seq} Byte$$

$$\mathsf{Bytes}\ \_ : \mathbb{N} \rightarrowtail \mathbb{P}\, ByteString$$

$$\forall\, n : \mathbb{N} \bullet \mathsf{Bytes}\ n = \{\, b : ByteString \bullet \#b = n \,\}$$

When referring to literal byte strings, we will denote the bytes by their numeric (specifically hexadecimal) values, as in $\langle\!\langle \mathsf{48\ 6F} \rangle\!\rangle$.

The integer representation of a byte string is more complicated, because we must contend with signedness and endianness issues. In this paper we are only considering unsigned, little-endian numbers; this is the simplest case, since we can use distributed concatenation to turn the little-endian byte string into an equivalent little-endian bit string. This bit string can be evaluated using the $\mathsf{int_{Bits}}$ function.

$$\mathsf{unsignedInt} : ByteString \rightarrow \mathbb{N}$$

$$\forall\, b : ByteString \bullet \mathsf{unsignedInt}\ b = \mathsf{int_{Bits}}\ ({\frown}/\ b)$$

Verifying Statemate Statecharts Using CSP and FDR

A.W. Roscoe and Z. Wu*

Oxford University Computing Laboratory
{bill.roscoe, zhenzhong.wu}@comlab.ox.ac.uk

Abstract. We propose a framework for the verification of statecharts. We use the CSP/FDR framework to model complex systems designed in statecharts, and check for system consistency or verify special properties within the specification. We have developed an automated translation from statecharts into CSP and exploited it in both theoretical and practical senses.

1 Introduction

Statecharts are a popular means for designing the hierarchical state machines which are used in embedded systems, telecommunications etc. Clarke and his colleagues have developed the SMV tool for checking finite state systems against specifications in the temporal logic CTL [4,5,6]. Work by Bienmuller, Damm and their colleagues has built up the STVE to model and verify some industrial applications [2,3,7,11].

The CSP/FDR framework is well established as a methodology for analyzing interacting systems and state machines [25]. A number of people have done prototyping work in the translation of statechart problems in a form the FDR can analyze. Work by Fuhrmann and his colleagues [14] shows how a subset of the statechart is expressed and verified by CSP/FDR. In this paper we report on our development of an automated translation from Harel's *Statemate* Statecharts into CSP, and exploit it in both theoretical and practical senses, mainly in defining language semantics and in system verification.

The statecharts formalism derives from conventional finite state machines. It is a structured analysis approach for modelling reactive systems. The Statemate semantics of statecharts was introduced by David Harel [18], and has been proved to be very useful for specifying concurrent systems. It supports both models of timing: *synchronous* and *asynchronous*. Verification techniques for statecharts have often been based on extensive checking or simulation. However, the informality of such approaches can easily lead to important requirements being overlooked and, since testing is rarely exhaustive, failures can be missed.

Our approach to Statemate Statecharts uses the CSP process algebra to specify concurrent systems. A statechart can be represented as a CSP process;

* Supported by QinetiQ.

Z. Liu and J. He (Eds.): ICFEM 2006, LNCS 4260, pp. 324–341, 2006.

statechart constructs such as hierarchy, AND and OR states, and communications all having CSP analogues. CSP-based tools such as FDR can then be used to verify properties of statecharts by performing refinement checks on the translation.

We initially adopted our approach as a way of understanding the semantics of statecharts, but it proved unexpectedly successful at verifying practical systems. We have therefore sought to include as wide a range of statechart constructs as possible in our compiler. In this paper we document which constructs are covered, but only give technical details of the more important ones. The paper is concluded by a case study.

2 Modelling Statecharts in CSP

Before we can describe the simulation we need to understand the basic concept of Statemate Statecharts.

2.1 Statemate Semantics

The statechart concept is based fundamentally on three ideas:

- Hierarchy: a statechart can exist within a single state of a higher level state machine.
- State machines: the basic component of a statechart is a sequential state machine, with guarded actions between states that have the potential to set signals and assign to shared variables.
- Parallelism (AND states): having several sequential machines running side by side.

There are many semantics of statecharts. One of the most important is the Statemate Statecharts of Harel [18], as refined by various developers. The various semantics of statecharts take different views on, for example:

- Concurrency. Statemate has an eager and concurrent model of AND states — if several states can proceed on one step then they all do.
- Timing model. Statemate has a two-level timing model and expects a system to settle through a number of "small" time steps before allowing further external signals to be processed.
- Nondeterminism. Statemate expects (under priority) at most one action of each OR-state to be available at one time, and forbids race conditions on variables.
- Priority. Statemate gives the highest priority to actions that are enabled further up the hierarchy, together with various other rules.

The statechart diagram in Fig. 1 illustrates the uses of these features in Statemate semantics. This statechart module has two input events: *event1* and *event2*. There are two variables: *v1* and *v2*. There is one constant *Limit*. Suppose, for

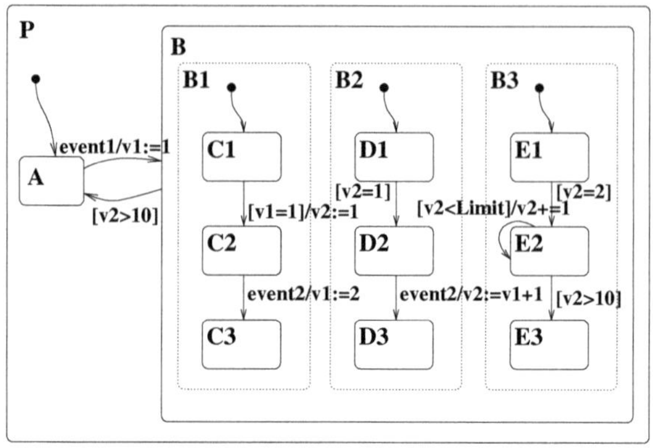

Fig. 1. Example Statemate Statechart

example, that state A is active, *Limit* is set to 11, and two variables are set to 0. If *event1* occurs under these conditions, the transition from state A to state B is enabled, and variable *v1* is set to 1.

State B is an AND-state: states *B1*, *B2* and *B3* are its sub-states. Once an AND-state is entered, all its components become active in parallel. In Fig. 1, states *B1*, *B2*, *B3* are entered simultaneously when entering B so that all three sub-states become active. Once they are entered transitions emerge from *Default Connectors* automatically. States *C1*, *D1* and *E1* are activated.

Under the asynchronous time model, time is not advanced at every single step but at super-steps. Each super-step consists of a collection of steps. Execution of a series of steps within one super-step does not advance the timer, these steps take place at the same point of time without introducing any external changes from the environment. Once the system is in a stable state, i.e., when no enabled transitions exist in the system, a super-step is completed. The environment can generate signals to enable new transitions and subsequently execute another super-step. In Fig. 1, the transition from *C1* to *C2* is taken, setting *v2* to 1. The transition from *D1* to *D2* is enabled and taken afterwards. There are no more enabled transitions at this point and the system becomes stable. So this super-step is completed, then the environment generates *event2* to trigger new transitions.

When multiple actions make changes on one element in the same step, we cannot predict the outcome and this is considered an error. There is a potential danger from reading and writing the same element in different parallel threads; however Statemate semantics are that an assignment to an element does not take effect till next step. In Fig. 1, occurrence of *event2* enables both transitions from *C2* to *C3* and from *D2* to *D3*. There are two actions available at the same time: *v1* will attain the value of 2 and *v2* will be assigned to "*v1+1*". Without the delay described above this would lead to ambiguity. The signals generated and data-items changed cannot take effect until the completion of the step. This suggests that *v1* still and always holds the value 1 in this step so that *v2* will become 2 but not 3 after the assignment "*v2: =v1+1*".

There is a conflict if multiple transitions are enabled from one common state. Those transitions cannot be performed in the same step. Nondeterminism occurs when there are some conflicts and those transitions within each conflict have the same priority. The choice of transitions results in different statuses. Even if two enabled transitions lead to the same state, non-determinism still occurs due to the changes of some other items during the transition, for instance, different signals being generated. In this case the overall result states will be different. In Fig. 1, transition from state *E1* to state *E2* is enabled since the condition is fulfilled, leading to the activation of state *E2*. The self-loop transition is enabled until *v2* reaches 11. There is a potential conflict at this point, three transitions enabled at the same time: the transition pointed to *E2* itself, the transition from state *E2* to state *E3*, and the transition from state *B* to state *A*.

A transition from a lower level state to a higher-level state takes priority over other types of transitions from the same state. This phenomenon, also called "Preemptive Interrupt" [18], happens when a high level transition prevents transitions on lower levels. Transition priority provides a way to pre-determine one transition among a group of enabled transitions and also to avoid the potential nondeterminism. In Fig. 1, the transition from state *B* to state *A* has the highest priority among all three, and so is preferred. There will be no non-determinism in this case. If none of conflicting multiple transitions has higher priority than the others, different semantics treat it in different ways. Some semantics introduce a specific priority of execution. For example, in *Matlab Stateflow*, transitions are taken according to their relative locations in the statechart diagram in clockwise order starting at the "twelve o'clock" position.[1] Our compiler treats nondeterminism as an error which would be returned by the system. This could be altered straightforwardly, but in some cases it would lead to our tool being less efficient as it presently exploits the determinism of statecharts.[2]

2.2 Compiler

The compiler is written as a program in CSP_M [25] making heavy use of functional programming. It consists of three main parts, plus some other functions:

- The mechanism to construct a single sequential chart: each individual chart is described as a transition system and a set of state labels indicate its substates.
- The mechanism to construct a hierarchy of individual sequential statecharts with capability of promotion: the overall hierarchical structure of the system is expressed as a special *tree* data type; all charts are built based on the *root*. Charts with no subcharts are expressed as single-leaf trees.

---

1 See [Mathworks97] for a precise description of the evaluation order [22].

2 The full description of the syntax of Statemate Statecharts is beyond the scope of this paper. I refer the interested readers to a full description in Harel and Naamad [18].

– Constructing variables and timers as processes running in parallel with the main system.

2.3 Timing Model and Step Semantics

Two levels of timing model are supported in the compiler. A small step is indicated by event *step*, and event *tock* represents a super-step. The entire system created has a synchronous timing model represented by *tock* and *step*, which all processes synchronise on. When the possible actions are complete, processes will agree to "step". Once there is no progress that can be made within the system, a "tock" is produced to introduce possible external changes. Another global synchronous event *calculate* is introduced after each *tock* and *step*. It occurs after all external inputs or effects of the previous step have propagated themselves. The sequence of these three actions is shown in Fig. 2.

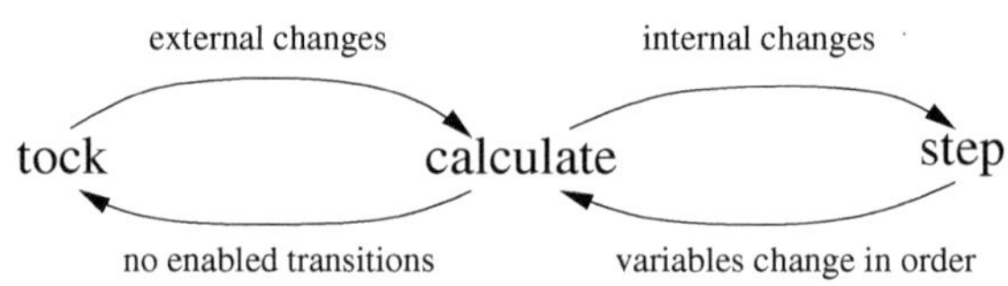

Fig. 2. Sequence of tock, step and calculate

After a super-step, changes can be made to the inputs, and timers are advanced by one time unit. Inputs and changes to timers only happen on super-steps. After this we get as many small steps as are required until no further progress is possible, i.e., there are no possible transitions without external changes made by the environment. Inputs and timers do not change during the execution of a small step. Within a small step, internal changes can be made to variables, which is done by communicating with the variable processes.

2.4 Hierarchical Structuring

Statecharts are structured, and one chart can sit inside a single state of another. The inner one is active only when the enclosing state is, and is turned off if the enclosing one is left.

At the highest level the model of a chart combines three synchronous processes: `Sys` represents the hierarchy of charts, `VARSandTIMERS` holds the values of variables and timers, and the combination of `NOACT` and `TOX` to enforce the timing model and outputs. At the highest level a chart is defined as following:

```
System(Hierarchy) =
        (VARSandTIMERS [|{|tock,calculate,step,ich,xch,iwrite,
            read,readch,timer_read,timer_on,timer_cancel|}|]
         Sys(Hierarchy,true,false))\{|ich,iwrite,read,readch,
```

```
            timer_read,timer_on,timer_cancel|})
            [|{|action,tock,step,turn_me_on,outp,xch|}|]
        (NOACT[|{|tock,step|}|]TOX)
```

The parameter Hierarchy must be defined in the user script or as output from a higher-level tool. The second parameter of Sys is set to "true" meaning that the highest level machine in the hierarchy is initially on.

```
NOACT = action?_ -> ACTS
     [] turn_me_on -> ACTS
     [] STEPTOCK
STEPTOCK = tock ->  NOACT
```

The step semantics is achieved through synchronization with the NOACT process which obliges a *step* to happen as opposed to a *tock* just when there has been an action since the last *step* or *tock*. The highest level chart has no enclosing state which can turn it on and off, so we forbid the actions "turn_me_on" and "turn_me_off".

```
ncSYSTEM(Hierarchy)= System(Hierarchy)
                     [|{|turn_me_on,turn_me_off|}|] STOP
```

Hierarchy. The definition of the main type of chart structures is:

```
datatype Statechart =
     SCTree.SGlabel.Set(ActLabel).Set((Statelabel,Statechart))
```

This recursive definition means that a chart is root behaviour identified by one of these labels, a set of actions labels that are not to be promoted beyond this point, and a set of pairs, each a state label of the present chart with a chart which sits within it. We defined a function Sys()[3] recursively that produces the CSP representation of statechart. A chart with no lower level charts is compiled using the function Machine()[3], which creates a process from the description of a sequential chart. Each sequential machine has an event proceed which is used to enable subcharts to do things (implementing the priority rule). For the case with no sub-machines this action is not required, and therefore we prevent it by synchronisation with STOP. The actions are renamed to progress to discard information unnecessary outside this level and to square the outer alphabet of the process with what will be required outside.

Sys() is applied to all subcharts, which are then appropriately synchronised with each other and also with the top level machine which has itself been created with Machine(). We use many renamings and synchronisations to coordinate the behaviour of these parts.

---

[3] See full definitions of these functions in http://web.comlab.ox.ac.uk/oucl/work/bill.roscoe/publications/115.pdf.

```
Sys(SCTree.label.acts.STs,initon,par_prom) =
 let TopMach = Machine(sm(label),initstate(label),initon,par_prom,sc0)
     ...
 within
  (TopMach[[...]]
  ([|...|]v:{v' | (v',_) <- STs} @
    (let  ...
     par_of_subs_of_V =
       ([|...|]sc:SCsInV @
         ((Sys(sc,v==startstate(label) and initon,par_prom')
         [[action.progress <- proceed.v]][[...]])))
     within
      (if par_prom' then (par_of_subs_of_V
       else par_of_subs_of_V)[[dummy <- peer_turn_off]]))) [[...]]
```

par_of_subs_of_V represents the construction for particular node's subcharts. Processes representing subcharts in different substates are synchronised, together with the TopMach()[3]. Actions progress by inner machines are controlled by events proceed, and all actions within this chart and not controlled outside is renamed to progress.

Implementing Priority and Promotion. Standard CSP, as implemented in FDR has no priority. Any one of a set of the currently available actions can occur next, and this is never made impossible by another action being enabled. This is not the case in statecharts at several levels. It impacts upon the two-level model, and on the relative priorities of transitions at low-level, high-level and inter-level (promoted actions). Actions have names, but there is no synchronisation on them between charts. Our model handles this by giving sequential components an additional action progress which it perform precisely when there is nothing else it can do on a given step. It is then possible to synchronise high-level progress actions with low-level actions so that the latter only happen when no higher-priority action is possible [26].

Consider a high-level sequential machine whose states contain sub-statecharts that run while the given state is enabled. Our model treats these subcharts as separate parallel processes and so we need to link the behaviour of the high-level state machine with the processes representing the subcharts. The model we adopt is to give each chart (other than, perhaps, the highest-level one) events "turn_me_on" and "turn_me_off" with the obvious effects. They are then (after suitable renaming) synchronised with the transitions of the high-level machine.

An inner chart may perform an action which is promoted to be an action of an outer one. Such an action must be named (not "progress") and any higher level chart that promotes it must use the same name. The actions of any state are divided into *primary ones* that the state instigates itself and *secondary ones* which are promoted by or through this state. To ensure charts running in parallel to one with an action that is promoted higher get turned off, the process Prom_Mon is introduced:

```
Prom_Mon = tock -> calculate ->  Prom_Mon'
Prom_Mon' = let
             P = one_prom -> Prom_Mon''
              [] step -> calculate ->  Prom_Mon'
              [] tock -> calculate ->  Prom_Mon'
             within
              P [] local_over -> P

Prom_Mon'' = one_prom -> action.error -> STOP
           [] two_prom -> action.error -> STOP
           [] peer_turn_off -> step -> calculate -> Prom_Mon'
```

2.5 Variables and Timers

Variables are defined as processes running parallel with the system. The variable process implements many features of the semantics including the variable update model. The CSP process shown below codes a variable:

```
VAR(id,range,v,ch)=
    let
VARXI(v,v0) = member(id,InputIds)&xch?(_,v'):wrange(id)->VARXI(v',v0)
            [] calculate -> VARNC(v,member(id,changes) and (v!=v0))
            [] member(id,Outputs) & outp.(id,v) -> VARXI(v,v0)

VARIW(v) =  iwrite.(id,v) ->  VARII(v)

VARNC(v,ch) = step -> VARII(v)
            [] tock -> VARXI(v,if member(id,changes) then v else 0)
            [] ich?(_,v'):wrange(id) -> VARIC(v',ch)
            [] member(id,changes) & readch.(id,ch) -> VARNC(v,ch)

VARII(v) =  calculate -> VARNC(v,false)

VARIC(v,ch) = step -> VARIW(v)
            [] ich?(_,_):wrange(id) -> varerror -> STOP
            [] member(id,changes) & readch.(id,ch) -> VARIC(v,ch)

RdVAR(v) = read.(id,v) -> RdVAR(v)
        [] xch?(_,v'):irange(id) -> RdVAR(v')
        [] iwrite?(_,v'):wrange(id) -> RdVAR(v')

within (tock -> VARXI(v,if member(id,changes) then v else 0))
        [|union({|iwrite.p | p <- wrange(id)|},
        {|xch.p | p <- irange(id)|})|] RdVAR(v)
```

Comments:

– Channels:

`xch`: the channel for external changes, changes the value of variable immediately, only possible on tock
`ich`: the channel for internal changes, informs processes of real internal changes of values after the calculation action
`iwrite`: the channel for internal writes, writes value variables, two of which on the same variable in one step are an error
`outp`: the channel for outputs, helps analyzing
`read`: reads values from variables
`readch`: checks for changes

– The purpose of the parallel composition with process `RdVAR(v)` is to allow a process to read the value of this variable from the previous step even after it has been changed via `ich` on this one. The new value is assigned to take effect after the variable has been changed via `iwrite`.

Note that our definition also has the properties that external inputs and outputs only occur immediately after `tock` and two internal changes on one step are an error. All variables are running in parallel, which produce a process for the entire set of variables:

```
VARS = [|{step,calculate,tock}|] (id,v,r):union(Inputs,Variables)
       @ VAR(id,r,v,false)
```

Timers are also defined as processes running parallel with the system. There are three kinds of timers: one is set up on the entry to a state; one is addressed by its own identifier name; another one is set up as a condition for transitions. A timer is initialized to zero and incremented by one each *tock* until the corresponding limit is reached. The CSP process shown below codes a straightforward timer:

```
Timer(l) = timer_on.l -> Timer_Running(l,0)
        [] timer_read.l.0 -> Timer(l)
        [] timer_cancel.l -> Timer(l)
        [] tock -> Timer(l)
        [] step -> Timer(l)

Timer_Running(l,n) = tock -> (if n==tlimit(l) then Timer_Running(l,n)
                               else Timer_Running(l,n+1))
                  [] step -> Timer_Running(l,n)
                  [] timer_read.l.n -> Timer_Running(l,n)
                  [] timer_cancel.l -> Timer(l)
                  [] timer_on.l -> Timer_Running(l,0)
```

Comments on channels:

`timer_on`: turns the timer on, followed by initializing the timer to 0
`timer_cancel`: cancels the timer, remove the timer from the list of active timers
`timer_read`: reads the current value of the timer

2.6 Translating Statecharts into CSP

We analyse statecharts automatically by simulating them in CSP. In other words we have a CSP process which accepts the description of a statechart S as a parameter and then behaves like S. We can prove things about S by analyzing this simulation on FDR.

The way the simulation is written is therefore as a CSP program which closely resembles a translation from statechart syntax to behaviourally equivalent CSP. The combination of the simulation operation and FDR's own CSP compiler produces a compiler from statecharts to FDR internal state machine code. For simplicity we therefore refer to the code that creates the simulation as a compiler. The current definitions of the CSP language mean that it does not have good string processing. For that reason we supply the input statechart to it as a member of a specially designed CSP type plus various ancillary definitions of sets. In other words, by the time CSP sees the statechart, it has been parsed and symbolized, see Section 4 for more details of this CSP syntax.

3 Specification Checking

Many checks can be implemented after the entire system is built. Typically there are three types of checking: checks for general errors in the system, tests for reachability of states, and checks for consistency with application–specific requirements.

3.1 Checks for Errors

The simulation is written so that finitely detectable run-time errors are all flagged by an error event:

```
error_events = {|action.error, varerror, outofrange, timer_overflow,
                type_error|}
```

Event `action.error` indicates nondeterminism caused by ambiguous branching; event `varerror` indicates multiple writes on a small step; event `outofrange` occurs when assigning a value which is out of range; event `timer_overflow` indicates the attempt to read a timer that has reached the bound limit; event `type_error` occurs when a boolean expression produces result not 0,1.

The following standard check should be used for all charts:

```
delayable = {|xch,turn_me_on,turn_me_off,isat,outp|}
Time_Error_Spec = tock -> Time_Error_Spec
                []（STOP |~| ([] x:delayable @ x -> Time_Error_Spec))

Time_Error_Imp(Hierarchy) = SYSTEM(Hierarchy)\
                diff(Events,Union({{tock},delayable,error_events}))
Time_Error_Spec [FD= Time_Error_Imp(Hierarchy)
```

This refinement tests for all types of run-time errors, plus race conditions.[4] It also ensures that there can never be an infinity of *step* events without an infinity of *tocks*. It is this timing aspect of the check that explains the name. This check uses the full power of failures/divergences refinement. However once it is satisfied all subsequent checks will normally be done. A large proportion of the errors we have discovered in industrial case studies have been via this check.

Race Condition. Multiple writes to a variable on one small step lead to race condition and are considered as an error. As showed in the definition of variables in Section 2.5, an error message "`varerror`" would be returned by checking through FDR.

Nondeterminism. Ambiguous enabled actions by any single process cause nondeterminism. Each sequential machine should have at most one action available at a time. Nondeterminism are considered as an error. If Nondeterminism exists in the system, an event "`action.error`" will be returned by checking it through FDR.

3.2 Reachability

To test whether a certain state in any chart can be reached at some point, the following refinement is used:

```
indstates = {(chartlabel,statelabel)}
assert STOP [T= SYSTEM(Hierarchy)\diff(Events,{|isat|})
```

The set `indstates` [5] is used to indicate the state we want to test for reachability. The refinement fails if and when the intended state is reached and a trace to describe how that state is reached can be provided by FDR. Note that this check does not behave ideally with attempts to prove things about a chart under nondeterministic parameters, since it will simply demonstrate that it is sometimes possible to reach the state, not that it is for all values of the parameter.

3.3 Analysis of Properties

Special requirements can be tested to ensure that they are satisfied by the system. Mostly one wants to check safety or security properties, which hold for the whole lifetime of the system. As already mentioned, we model the formal semantics of statecharts and requirements in the input script. Assume the chart representing the requirement is labeled by `spec_label`, the check can be made as follows:

---

[4] The check would fail if the simulation deadlocked. However deadlock is impossible because of the way the simulation is constructed. This feature was useful in designing the compiler.

[5] See full definitions of `isat` and `indstates` in `http://web.comlab.ox.ac.uk/oucl/work/bill.roscoe/publications /115statechartcompiler.csp`.

```
SysAndSpec_sc = SCTree.Box.{}.{(0,Hierarchy),(0,lift(Spec_label))}
assert STOP [T= SYSTEM(SysAndSpec_sc)\diff(Events,{action.spec_error})
```

The event `action.spec_error` indicates that the requirement is not satisfied.

4 Case Study: Burglar Alarm System

A practical case study is the burglar alarm control system. The system provides a very typical example with the features like multiple parallel subcharts, inter-level transitions etc. (see Fig. 3)

The alarm is constructed of two nearly independent parallel processes: one is the number pad that determines (subject to things like timeout and too many attempts as limitations) when the last D digits input are the code number for arming and disarming the alarm.

The *Main Controller* chart moves the alarm between its principal states: correctly typing in the code number (generating the *go* signal) will move it from *disarmed* to *leaving* (which times out to armed) and back to *disarmed.* If the alarm goes off we can type in the number once to turn off the siren and once to get rid of the signal light that tells us where the alarm came from. The state *Returning* gives some time to disarm the alarm if someone returns and is detected in the area of the controller box (Alarm zone 1). The state *Leaving* gives the user time to leave after arming the alarm.

The *Key_Pad* chart indicates that the pad becomes active when a key is pressed. It goes back to inactive if either the code is correctly entered or if too

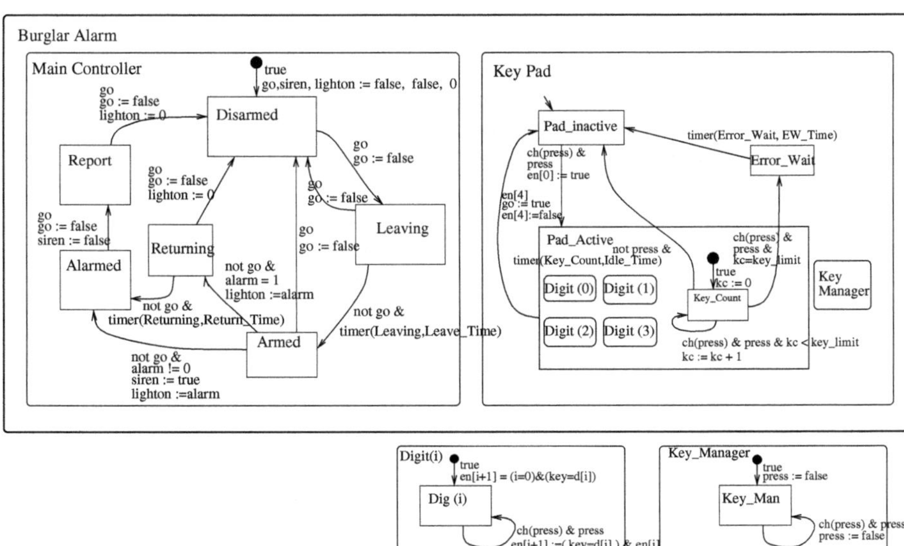

Fig. 3. Burglar Alarm System

long has passed since the previous press. If more than *kc* digits are used in an attempt to key the code, a wait is imposed. The five constituents of *Pad_Active* all run in parallel while that state is running, and similarly the main graph and *Key_Manager*. The chart *Digit* indicates that if the digit just pressed is $d[i]$ and the most recent digits pressed are $d[0]..d[i-1]$ then enable the next process in the chain. The *Key_Manager* chart shows that press will become true each time the user enters a digit, and key takes the value pressed. The function of this process is to ensure that press is only true immediately after the users input so a user-change is always from *false* to *true*.

4.1 Describing the System

The following is part of a CSP file describing the statechart in Fig. 3. In practice the creation of these files is automated by a GUI that inputs details of the statechart from the user.

```
Pad_Digits = 4
digits = {0..Pad_Digits-1}
digit_range = {0..1}
datatype Identifiers = en.{0..Pad_Digits} | d.digit_range | key |
                       press | alarm | lighton | siren | go | kc |
                       key_limit | EW_Time | Idle_Time | Leave_Time |
                       Return_Time | lastdigs
datatype ActLabel = error | progress | spec_error | kc_ew | kc_pa
datatype SGlabel = Digit.digits | Mainpad | Key_Man | KC |
                   Controller | Whole_Alarm | Box | Spec_label
alarm_zones = {0..3}
Inputs = union({(key,0,digit_range),(press,0,nbool)},
               {(alarm,0,alarm_zones)})
Variables = {(lighton,0,alarm_zones),(en.j,0,nbool),(go,0,nbool),
             (kc,0,{0..CV(key_limit)+1}),(siren,0,nbool),
             (lastdigs,<>,prefixes) | j <- {0..Pad_Digits}}
prefixes = {<CV(d.i) | i <- <0..j-1>> | j <- {0..Pad_Digits}}
Outputs = {siren,lighton}
Constants = union({(d.i,i%2)| i <- {0..Pad_Digits-1}},{(EW_Time,1),
                  (Idle_Time,1),(Leave_Time,1),(key_limit,12),
                  (Return_Time,Pad_Digits+1)})
```

We formulate the corresponding process for chart *Main Controller*:

```
Controller_sg =
 let
  State_0 = (0,<(TRUE,progress,<(go,FALSE),(siren,FALSE),
               (lighton,ZERO)>,1)>,<>)
  Disarmed_1 = (1,<(Ival(go),progress,<(go,FALSE)>,2)>,<>)
  Leaving_2 = (2,<(Ival(go),progress,<(go,FALSE)>,1),
                  (andf(notf(Ival(go)),timer(En.(Controller,2),
                  Ival(Leave_Time))),progress, <>,3)>,<>)
  Armed_3 = (3,<(Ival(go),progress,<(go,FALSE)>,1),
```

```
                  (andf(notf(Ival(go)),notf(gt(Ival(alarm),ONE))),
                  progress,<(siren,TRUE),(lighton,Ival(alarm))>,4),
                  (andf(notf(Ival(go)),notf(eqf(Ival(alarm),ONE))),
                  progress,<(lighton,Ival(alarm))>,6)>,<>)
    Alarmed_4 = (4,<(Ival(go),progress,<(go,FALSE),(siren,FALSE)>,5)>,<>)
    Report_5 = (5,<(Ival(go),progress,<(go,FALSE),(lighton,ZERO)>,1)>,<>)
    Returning_6 = (6,<(Ival(go),progress,<(go,FALSE)>,1),
                     (andf(notf(Ival(go)),timer(En.(Controller,6),
                      Ival(Return_Time))),progress,
                      <(siren,TRUE)>,4)>,<>)
   within {State_0,Disarmed_1,Leaving_2,Armed_3,Alarmed_4,Report_5,
          Returning_6}
  Controller_g = (Controller_sg,Controller,0,{go})
```

The processes for charts *Key Pad*, *Digit*, and *Key Manager* are defined similarly to this. We collect information together for whole system:

```
Timed_Nodes_Lim = {((Controller,2),CV(Leave_Time)),
                   ((Controller,6),CV(Return_Time)),
                   ((KC,1),CV(Idle_Time)), ((Mainpad,2),CV(EW_Time))}

AllCharts = {Spec_g,Box_g(Box),kc_g,KeyMan,Digit_g(i),Mainpad_g,
             Controller_g | i <- digits}

Burglar_Alarm_sc = SCTree.Box.{}.{(0,Pad_sc),(0,lift(Controller))}
```

4.2 Property Checking

A property can be verified against the system by trace refinement of the corresponding CSP processes. There are two possible ways of verification depending on the representation of properties: representation as statecharts or implementation as CSP directly.

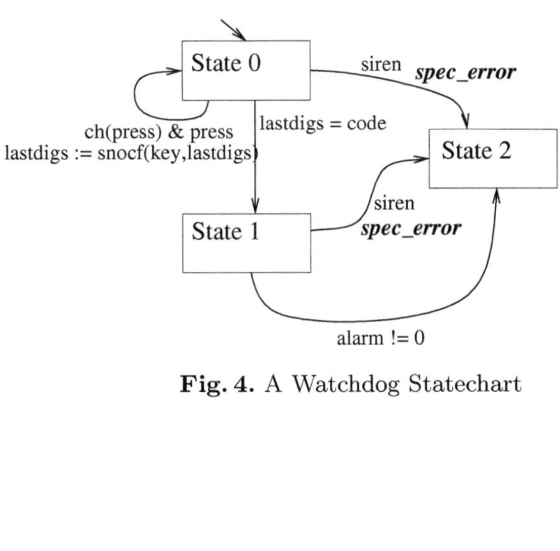

Fig. 4. A Watchdog Statechart

Statechart specification. The first case means trivially using the existing translation. For showing an example of an analysis driven by the presented approach we use the statechart specification of a watch dog (Fig. 4). The requirement is: the siren never goes off until firstly the code number has been typed in and secondly an alarm signal has appeared. Now we translate this statechart into the input script for our compiler:

```
Spec_sg =
   let
     State0 = (0,<(Ival(siren),spec_error,<>,2),
                  (andf(ch(press),Ival(press)),progress,
                     <(lastdigs,snocf(Ival(key),Ival(lastdigs)))>,0),
                  (eqf(Ival(lastdigs),K(<CV(d.i) | i <- <0..3>>)),
                     progress,<>, 1)>,<>)
     State1 = (1,<(Ival(siren),error,<>,2),
                  (notf(eqf(Ival(alarm),K(0))),progress,<>,2)>,<>)
     State2 = (2,<>,<>)
   within {State0,State1,State2}
Spec_g = (Spec_sg,Spec_label,0,{})
```

The specification shows that it moves from *State0* to *State1* when the digits have been correctly entered, and prior to that does the calculations to know when this has been done. It moves from *State1* to *State2* when alarm is not 0, and only then does it not raise an alarm when the siren does off. This is a statechart which is run in parallel with an implementation and can read its variables. It may not, however, write to any variable used by the implementation. Its function is to keep track (as it wishes) of what goes on and to raise a flag (*spec_error*) which can be caught by the Time and Error check if the implementation does something wrong. These conditions mean that it never interferes with the implementation.

```
SysAndSpec_sc =
           SCTree.Box.{}.{(0,Burglar_Alarm_sc),(0,lift(Spec_label))}
```

Now the task is to check the trace refinement relation between the property *Spec_label* and the system *Burglar_Alarm*. For that reason it is necessary to hide all the communication of *SysAndSpec* which is not *spec_error*.

```
assert STOP [T= SYSTEM(SysAndSpec_sc)\diff(Events,{action.spec_error})
```

The used model checker FDR executes the refinement check and returns the CSP model *Burglar_Alarm* meets the Property *Spec_label*:

```
Refine checked 199,245 states.
With 1025751 transitions.
True
```

CSP-style specification. We can specify our burglar alarm directly in terms of the events communicated by the CSP implementation. This particular model is not that good for this type of specification since the event of typing in a code number is rather diffuse (and almost certainly better handled using the watchdog style above). The following specification asserts that the siren cannot sound for at least k time units from the start:

```
SirenWait(0) = outp.(siren,1) -> SirenWait(0)
             [] tock -> SirenWait(0)
SirenWait(k) = tock -> SirenWait(k-1)
```

We can check this for various values via the trace check and the following are the (parameterised) limit.

```
assert SirenWait(CV(Leave_Time)+Pad_Digits+1) [T=
       SYSTEM(Burglar_Alarm_sc)\diff(Events,{tock,outp.(siren,1)})

assert SirenWait(CV(Leave_Time)+Pad_Digits+2) [T=
       SYSTEM(Burglar_Alarm_sc)\diff(Events,{tock,outp.(siren,1)})
```

This is done by the used model checker FDR.

```
Refine checked 185,362 states.
With 955557 transitions.
True.

Refine checked 13,028 states.
With 67109 transitions.
Found 1 example.
```

5 Conclusion

We have used the process algebra CSP and its model checker FDR to model and analyse Statemate Statecharts. Following this approach, the scope of some existing modeling techniques has been widened to address the problems that have arisen in various case studies. We have discovered many errors in practical industrial systems by this approach. For example, our compiler has been successfully used on an automotive system design project, the single lane architecture (QinetiQ), etc. Our compiler provides an efficient way to translate Statemate Statecharts to CSP and has proven to be sufficiently malleable to allow us to capture various properties of the semantics.

As a result of extensive research and studies in Statemate modelling, it is concluded that the idea of modelling statecharts in CSP has opened up, and will continue opening up, many opportunities for researches to model various graphic specifications which are widely used for complex systems. There is enormous scope for future development. The next target is MATLAB Stateflow (which is similar to statecharts). It is hoped that the demonstration of how to apply CSP theory to statecharts will inspire new approaches to standard graphic notations.

References

1. R. Anderson, P. Beame, S. Burns, W. Chan, F. Modugno, D. Notkin, and J. Reese, *Model checking large software specifications*, IEEE Transactions on Software Engineering, Vol. 24, No. 7, pp. 498-520, 1998.
2. T. Bienmuller, J. Bohn, H. Brinkmann, U. Brockmeyer, W. Damm, H. Hungar, and P. Jansen, *Verification of automotive control units*, in E.-R. Olderog and B. Steffen (Eds.), Correct System Design, Springer Verlag, Berlin, 1999,number 1710 in LNCS, pp. 319-341.
3. T. Bienmuller, U. Brockmeyer, W. Damm, G. Dohmen, H.-J. Holberg, H. Hungar, B. Josko, R. Schlor, G. Wittich, H. Wittke, G. Clements, J. Rowlands, and E. Sefton, *Formal verification of an avionics application using abstraction and symbolic model checking*, in F. Redmill and T. Anderson (Eds.), Towards System Safety - Proceedings of the Seventh Safety-critical Systems Symposium, Huntingdon, UK, Safety-critical Systems Club, Springer Verlag, Berlin, 1999, pp. 150-173.
4. J.R. Burch, E.M. Clarke, and D.E. Long, *Symbolic model checking with partitioned transition relations*, In VLSI 91, Edinburgn, Scotland, 1990.
5. J.R. Burch, E.M. Clarke, K.L.McMillan, and D.L.Dill, *Sequential circuit verification using symbolic model checking*, In 27th ACM/IEEE Design Automation Conference, 1990.
6. J.R. Burch, E.M. Clarke, K.L.McMillan, D.L.Dill, and J. Hwang, *Symbolic model checking: 10E20 states and beyond*, In LICS, 1990.
7. T. Bienmuller, W. Damm and H. Wittke, *The Statemeat Verification Environment – Making it real*, In: Proc. CAV, LNCS 1855, pp. 561-561, Springer, 2000.
8. E.M. Clarke, O. Grumberg and D.E. Long, *Model Checking and Abstraction*, In proceedings of the Nineteenth Annual ACM Symposium on Principles of Programming Languages,1992.
9. W. Damm and D. Harel, *LSCs: breathing life into message sequence charts*, in FMOODS'99 IFIP TC6/WG6.1 Third International Conference on Formal Methods for Open Object-Based Distributed Systems, Kluwer Academic Publishers, NY, 1999.
10. W. Damm, B. Josko, H. Hungar, and A. Pnueli, *A compositiona real-time semantics of STATEMATE designs*, in W.-P. de Roever (Ed.), Proceedings, International Symposium on Compositionality-The Significant Diference, Springer-Verlag, 1998, Lecture Notes in Computer Science.
11. W. Damm and J. Klose, *Verification of a radio-based signalling system using the Statemate verification environment*, Formal Methods in System Design 19:121-141, 2001.
12. H. Eshuis and R. Wieringa, *A Formal Semantics for UML Activity Diagrams C Formalising Workflow Models*, Technical Report, 2001.
13. Formal Systems (Europe) Ltd., *Failures-Divergence Refinement*, User Manual, obtainable from `http://www.fsel.com/fdr2_manual.html`
14. K. Fuhrmann and J. Hiemer, *Formal Verification of STATEMATE-Statecharts*, Citeseer.nj.nec.com/255163.html, 2001.
15. W.J. Fokkink and P. Hollingshead, *Verification of interlockings: from control tables to ladder logic diagrams*, in Proceedings of the 3rd Workshop on Formal Methods for Industrial Critical Systems-FMICS'98, Amsterdam. Stichting Mathematisch Centrum, 1998.

16. K. Feyerabend and B. Josko, *VIS: A visual formalism for real time requirement specifications*, in Proceedings of the 4th International AMAST Workshop on Real-Time Systems and Concurrent and Distributed Software, ARTS'97, Lecture Notes in Computer Science 1231, 1997, pp. 156-168.
17. T.V. Group, *VIS: A system for verification and synthesis*, in 8th international Conference on Computer Aided Verification, number 1102 in LNCS, 1996.
18. D. Harel and A. Naamad, *The Statemate Semantics of Statecharts*, Technical Report, i-Logix, 1995.
19. D. Harel, H. Lachover, A. Naamad, A. Pnueli, M. Politi, R. Sherman, and A.S. Trauring, *Statemate: A Working Environment for the Development of Complex Reactive Systems*, IEEE Transactions on Software Engineering, **16**, 4, 1990.
20. J. Hudak, S.C. Dorda, D.P. Gluch, G. Lewis and C. Weinstock, *Model-Based Verification: Abstraction Guidelines*, Technical Note CMU/SEI-2002-TN-001, 2002.
21. D. Harel and M. Politi, *Modeling Reactive Systems with Statecharts: The STATEMATE Approach*, Part No.D-1100-43, i-Logix Inc., Three Riverside Drive, Andover, MA 01810, June 1996.
22. The MathWorks, *Stateflow*, User Manual, obtainable from `http://www.mathworks.com/access/helpdesk/help/toolbox/stateflow/ug/`
23. E. Mikk, Y. Lakhnech, C. Petersohn and M. Siegel, *On Formal Semantics of Statecharts as Supported by STATEMATE*, Technical Report, BCS-FACS Northern Formal Methods Workshop, **2**, Ilkley, 1997.
24. L.E. Moser, Y. Ramakrishna, G. Kutty, P. Melliar-Smith, and L. Dillon, *A graphical environment for design of concurrent real-time systems*, ACM Transactions on Software Engineering and Methodology, Vol.6, No. 1, pp.31-79, 1997.
25. A.W. Roscoe *The theory and practice of concurrency*, Prentice-Hall International, 1998.
26. A.W. Roscoe, *Compiling Statemate Statecharts into CSP and verifying them using FDR – abstract*, Technical Report, 2003.

A Reasoning Method for Timed CSP Based on Constraint Solving

Jin Song Dong, Ping Hao, Jun Sun, and Xian Zhang

School of Computing,
National University of Singapore
{dongjs, haoping, sunj, zhangxi5}@comp.nus.edu.sg

Abstract. Timed CSP extends CSP by introducing a capability to quantify temporal aspects of sequencing and synchronization. It is a powerful language to model real time reactive systems. However, there is no verification tool support for proving critical properties over systems modelled using Timed CSP. In this work, we construct a reasoning method using Constraint Logic Programming (CLP) as an underlying reasoning mechanism for Timed CSP. We start with encoding the semantics of Timed CSP in CLP, which allows a systematic translation of Timed CSP to CLP. Powerful constraint solver like CLP($\mathcal{R}$) is then used to prove traditional safety properties and beyond, e.g., reachability, deadlock-freeness, timewise refinement relationship, lower or upper bound of a time interval, etc. Counter-examples are generated when properties are not satisfied. Moreover, our method also handles useful extensions to Timed CSP. Finally, we demonstrate the effectiveness of our approach through case study of standard real time systems.

1 Introduction

Event-based specification languages like the classic Communicating Sequential Process (CSP) of Hoare's [7] and its timed extension Timed CSP [14], have been proposed for decades. Such specification languages are elegant and intuitive as well as precise. They have been widely accepted and applied to a wide range of systems, including communication protocols, embedded systems, etc [15]. It is important that system specified using CSP or Timed CSP can be proved formally and even better if the proving is fully automated. For CSP, the *de facto* mechanized verification support is its model checker FDR (Failure Divergence Refinement [5, 15]), which verifies various properties by showing that there is a refinement relation from the constructed CSP model to the CSP process capturing the properties. However, there is not yet a mechanized proving method for Timed CSP due to the complexity of time, e.g., the timed trace and failure semantics of Timed CSP is far more complex than the failure semantics of CSP. As far as the authors know, the only attempt is Brooke's work on partial encoding Timed CSP in PVS [2], which relies on heavy user interaction.

Constraint Logic Programming (CLP [9]) is designed for mechanized proving based on constraint solving. CLP has been successfully applied to model

Z. Liu and J. He (Eds.): ICFEM 2006, LNCS 4260, pp. 342–359, 2006.

programs and transition systems for the purpose of verification [6, 11], showing that their approach outperforms the well-know state-of-art systems with higher efficiency. [1] employs a logic program transformation based approach for inductive verification of real-life parameterized protocols. In this work, we propose a constraint-based approach for solving the verification problem of Timed CSP, which readily implies we handle untimed CSP as well. It is the first reasoning mechanism for Timed CSP. The challenge is to cope with the great expressiveness of Timed CSP and allow efficient automatic proving of various assertions.

Our approach starts with a systematic translation of the semantics of Timed CSP into CLP. Both operational and denotational semantics are encoded, which are used for verifying different kinds of properties. We then go beyond by allowing useful extensions to Timed CSP, for example, the concept of *signal* as in [4] for specifying broadcast communication and some liveness conditions, and integration of Timed CSP and state-based specification languages, so that we may specify and verify systems with non-trivial data structures. The practical implication of our translation of Timed CSP to CLP is that powerful constraint solvers like CLP($\mathcal{R}$) [10] can be used to prove properties over systems modelled using Timed CSP. We investigate ways of proving traditional safety properties and beyond, for example reachability, deadlock-freeness, refinement relationship,lower or upper bound of a time interval and etc. Moreover, we are also able to generate counter examples if the properties are not satisfied. We implemented a prototype as a CLP($\mathcal{R}$) program and experimented our encoding with standard real-time systems.

The remainder of the paper is organized as follows. Section 2 briefly introduces Timed CSP and the Constraint Logic Programming. Section 3 illustrates the encoding of both operational and denotational semantics of Timed CSP in CLP. A number of useful extensions to Timed CSP are also considered. Section 4 presents various proving we may perform over systems modelled using Timed CSP and translated to CLP. Section 5 illustrates the effectiveness of our approach with case studies. Section 6 concludes the paper.

2 Background

2.1 Timed CSP

Hoare's CSP [7] is an event based notation primarily aimed at describing the sequencing of behavior within a process and the synchronization of behavior (or *communication*) between processes. Timed CSP extends CSP by introducing a capability to quantify temporal aspects of sequencing and synchronization. Inherited from CSP, Timed CSP adopts a symmetric view of process and environment. Events represent a cooperative synchronization between process and environment. Both process and environment may control the behavior of the other by *enabling* or *refusing* certain events and sequences of events.

The syntactic class of Timed CSP expressions is defined as the following:

$$\begin{array}{rl} P ::= & \textsc{Stop} \mid \textsc{Skip} \mid \textsc{Run} \mid e \xrightarrow{t} P \mid e : E \rightarrow P(e) \mid e \bullet t \rightarrow P(t) \\ \mid & P_1 \Box P_2 \mid P_1 \sqcap P_2 \mid P_1 \ {}_X\|_Y \ P_2 \mid P_1 \,|[\, X \,]|\, P_2 \mid P_1 \,|||\, P_2 \\ \mid & P_1;\ P_2 \mid P_1 \triangledown P_2 \mid P1 \rhd\{d\}\ P2 \mid \textsc{Wait}[d] \mid P_1 \triangledown\{d\}\ P_2 \mid \mu X \bullet P(X) \end{array}$$

$\textsc{Run}_\Sigma$ is a process always willing to engage any event in Σ. $\textsc{Stop}$ denotes a process that deadlocks and does nothing. A process that terminates is written as $\textsc{Skip}$. A process which may participate in event e then act according to process description P is written as $e \bullet t \rightarrow P(t)$. The (optional) timing parameter t records the time, relative to the start of the process, at which the event e occurs and allows the subsequent behavior P to depend on its value. The process $e \xrightarrow{t} P$ delays process P by t time units after engaging event e. The external choice operator ($\Box$) allows a process of choice of behavior according to what events are requested by its environment. Internal choice represents variation in behavior determined by the internal state of the process. The parallel composition of processes P_1 and P_2, synchronized on common events of their alphabets X, Y (or a common set of events A) is written as $P_1 \ {}_X\|_Y \ P_2$ (or $P_1 \,|[\, A \,]|\, P_2$). The sequential composition of P_1 and P_2, written as $P_1;\ P_2$, acts as P_1 until P_1 terminates by communicating a distinguished event $\checkmark$ and then proceeds to act as P_2. The interrupt process $P_1 \triangledown P_2$ behaves as P_1 until the first occurrence of event in P_2, then the control passes to P_2. The timed interrupt process $P_1 \triangledown\{d\}\ P_2$ behaves similarly except P_1 is interrupted as soon as d time units have elapsed. A process which allows no communications for period d time units then terminates is written as $\textsc{Wait}[d]$. The timeout construct written as $P_1 \rhd\{d\}\ P_2$ passes control to an exception handler P_2 if no event has occurred in the primary process P_1 by some deadline d. Recursion is used to give finite representation of non-terminating processes. The process expression $\mu X \bullet P(X)$ describes processes which repeatedly act as $P(X)$.

Example 1 (Timed vending machine). A user may insert some coins and then make a choice between coffee or tea. Once the choice is made, the vending machine dispatches the corresponding drink. Or the user may ask the machine to release the coins and walk away. If the user idles more than 10 seconds after the coin is inserted, the machine will release the coins.

$$\begin{array}{l} \mathit{TVM} \mathrel{\widehat=} \mu X \bullet \mathit{coin} \rightarrow ((\mathit{reqrelease} \rightarrow \mathit{release} \xrightarrow{2} X) \\ \qquad \Box\ (\mathit{coffee} \xrightarrow{3} \mathit{dispatchcoffee} \rightarrow X) \ \Box\ (\mathit{tea} \xrightarrow{2} \mathit{dispatchtea} \rightarrow X)) \\ \qquad \rhd\{10\}\ (\mathit{release} \rightarrow X) \end{array}$$

2.2 CLP Preliminaries

Constraint Logic Programming (CLP) began as a natural merger of two declarative paradigms: constraint solving and logic programming. This combination helps make CLP programs both expressive and flexible, and in some cases, more efficient than other kinds of programs. The CLP scheme defines a class of languages based upon the paradigm of rule-based constraint programming, where CLP($\mathcal{R}$) is an instance of this class. We present some preliminary definitions about CLP [9].

Example 2 (Factorial). The following is typical CLP program:

$$fac(0,1).$$
$$fac(N, X_1 * N) : -N > 0, fac(N-1, X_1).$$

A relation *fac(N, X)* is defined, where X is the factorial of N, denoted as $X = N!$. There are two atoms for the relation *fac(N, X)*, where the first atom is a *fact* and the second one is a *rule*.

The *universe of discourse* $\mathcal{D}$ of our CLP program is a set of terms, integers, and lists of integers. A *Constraint* is written using a language of functions and relations. They are used in two ways, in the basic programming language to describe expressions and conditions, and in user assertions, defined below. In this paper, we will not define the constraint language explicitly, but invent them on demand in accordance with our examples. Thus the terms of our CLP programs include the function symbols of the constraint language.

An *atom*, is as usual, of the form $p(\tilde{t})$, where p is a user defined predicate symbol and $\tilde{t}$ is a sequence of terms. A *rule* is of the form $A : -\tilde{B}, \Psi$ where the atom A is the *head* of the rule, and the sequence of atoms $\tilde{B}$ and the constraint Ψ constitute the *body* of the rule. A *goal* has exactly the same format as the body of the rule of the form $? - \tilde{B}, \Psi$. If $\tilde{B}$ is an empty sequence of atoms, we call this a (constrained) *fact*. All goals, rules and facts are terms. A *ground instance* of a constraint, atom and rule is defined in obvious way. A *ground instance* of a constraint is obtained by instantiating variables therein from $\mathcal{D}$. The *ground instances* of a goal G, written $[\![G]\!]$ is the set of ground atoms obtained by taking all the true ground instances of G and then assembling the ground atoms therein into a set. We write $G_1 \models G_2$ to mean that for all groundings θ of G_1 and G_2, each ground atom in $G_1\theta$ appears in $G_2\theta$.

Let $G = (B_1, ..., B_n, \Psi)$ and P denote a goal and program respectively. Let $R = A : -C_1, ..., C_m, \Psi_1$ denote a rule in P, written so as none of its variables appear in G. Let $A = B$, where A and B are atoms, be shorthand for equations between their corresponding arguments. A *reduct* of G using R is of the form

$$(B_1, ..., B_{i-1}, C_1, ..., C_m, B_{i+1}, ..., B_n, B_i = A \wedge \Psi \wedge \Psi_1)$$

provided $B_i = A \wedge \Psi \wedge \Psi_1$ is satisfiable. A *derivation sequence* is a possibly infinite sequence of goals $G_0, G_1, ...$ where $G_i, i > 0$ is a reduct of G_{i-1}. If there is a last goal G_n with no atoms, notationally $(\square, \Psi)$ and called a *terminal goal*, we say that the derivation is a *successful* and that the *answer constraint* is Ψ. A derivation is ground if every reduction therein is ground.

Example 3 (Derivation). We calculate the 3! through the goal $? - \ fac(3, \ X)$. The following demonstrates a derivation sequence of the goal with three steps. The constraints in the last step which are the termination goal answer $X = 6$.

$$N = 3,\ fac(N,\ X).$$
$$\Downarrow$$
$$N = 3, N > 0, N - 1 = N_1, X = N * X_1, fac(N_1, X_1).$$
$$\Downarrow$$
$$N = 3, N > 0, N - 1 = N_1, X = N * X_1,$$
$$N_1 > 0, N_1 - 1 = N_2, X1 = N_1 * X_2, fac(N_2, X_2).$$
$$\Downarrow$$
$$N = 3, N > 0, N - 1 = N_1, X = N * X_1, N_1 > 0, N_1 - 1 = N_2,$$
$$X1 = N_1 * X_2, N_2 > 0, N_2 - 1 = 0, X_2 = 1.$$

3 Timed CSP Semantics in CLP

This section is devoted to an encoding of the semantics of Timed CSP in CLP. The practical implication is that we may then use powerful constraint solver like CLP(R) [10] to do various proving over systems modelled using Timed CSP. Both the operational semantics and denotational semantics are encoded. The encoding of operational semantics serves most of our purposes. Nevertheless the encoding of the denotational semantics offers an alternative way of proving systems modelled in Timed CSP as well as the correctness of the encoding itself.

The very initial step of our work is the syntax encoding of Timed CSP process in CLP syntax, which can be automated easily by syntax rewriting. A relation of the form $proc(N, P)$ is used to present a process P with name N. For instance, Figure 1 is the syntax encoding of process TVM in CLP, which is a recursive process with name tvm.

$$proc(c1, delay(coffee, eventprefix(dispatchcoffee, tvm), 3)).$$
$$proc(c2, delay(tea, eventprefix(dispatchtea, tvm), 2)).$$
$$proc(c3, eventprefixc(reqrelease, delay(release, tvm, 2))).$$
$$proc(choices, extchoice(extchoice(C, T), R))$$
$$:-proc(c1, C), proc(c2, T), proc(c3, R).$$
$$proc(to, timeout(C, eventprefix(release, tvm), 10))$$
$$:-proc(choices, C).$$
$$proc(tvm, recursion([tvm, eventprefix(coin, P)], eventprefix(coin, P)))$$
$$:-proc(to, P).$$

Fig. 1. Timed Vending Machine in CLP

3.1 Operational Semantics

The operational semantics of Timed CSP is precisely defined by Schneider [17] using two relations: an evolution relation and a timed event transition relation. It is straightforward to verify that our encoding conforms the two relations in [17].

A relation of the form *tos(P1,T1,E,P2,T2)* is used to denote the *t*imed *o*perational *s*emantics, by capturing both evolution relations and timed event transition relations. Informally speaking, *tos(P1,T1,E,P2,T2)* is true if the process *P1* may evolve to *P2* through either a timed transition, i.e., let *T2*-*T1* time units pass, or an event transition by engaging an abstract event instantly[1]. The relation *tos* defines a transition system interpretation of a Timed CSP process, where the state is identified by the combination of the process expression and the time variable. Using tabling mechanism offered in some of the constraint solvers like CLP($\mathcal{R}$) [10] or XSB [19], the termination of the derivation sequence based on relation *tos* depends on the finiteness of the reachable process expressions from the initial one. Therefore, if a process is irregular (i.e. its trace is irregular as in automata theory), proving of goals which need to explore all reachable process expressions is not feasible. However, even for irregular processes, interesting proving like existence of a trace is still possible.

We define the *tos* relation in terms of each and every operator of Timed CSP. For the moment, we assume the process is not parameterized and we shall handle parameterized processes uniformly in Section 3.3. For instance, the primitive process expressions in Timed CSP are defined through the following clauses:

$$tos(stop, T1, [], stop, T2) : -D >= 0, T2 = T1 + D.$$
$$tos(skip, T, [termination], stop, T).$$
$$tos(skip, T1, [], skip, T2) : -D >= 0, T2 = T1 + D.$$
$$tos(run, T, [\_], run, T).$$
$$tos(run, T1, [], run, T2) : -D >= 0, T2 = T1 + D.$$

The only transition for process STOP is time elapsing. Process SKIP may choose to wait some time before engaging event *termination* which is our choice of representation for event ✓ in CLP. Process RUN may either let time pass or engage any event. In the following, we show how hierarchical operators are encoded in CLP using the alphabetized parallel composition operator as an example.

In the operational semantics, the event transition and evolution transition associated with the alphabetized parallel composition operator the alphabetized parallel composition operator $P_1 \;{}_X\|_Y\; P_2$ are illustrated as the following [17]:

$$\frac{P_1 \xrightarrow{e} P_1'}{P_1 \;{}_X\|_Y\; P_2 \xrightarrow{e} P_1' \;{}_X\|_Y\; P_2} [\, e \in X \cup \{\tau\} \setminus Y \,]$$

$$\frac{P_2 \xrightarrow{e} P_2'}{P_1 \;{}_X\|_Y\; P_2 \xrightarrow{e} P_1 \;{}_X\|_Y\; P_2'} [\, e \in Y \cup \{\tau\} \setminus X \,]$$

[1] Or both at the same time by engaging an nontrivial action which takes time (necessary for only extensions to Timed CSP like TCOZ [12] where *E* could be a complicated computation).

```
tos(eventprefix(E, P), T1, [], eventprefix(E, P), T1 + D) : −D > 0.
tos(eventprefix(E, P), T, [E], P, T).
tos(prefixchoice(X, P), T, [Y], P, T) : −member(Y, X).
tos(prefixchoice(_, P), T1, [], P, T1 + D) : −D > 0.
tos(timeout(Q1, _, ), T, [E], P, T) : −tos(Q1, T, [E], P, T).
tos(timeout(, Q2, D), T, [tau], Q2, T) : −D = 0.
tos(timeout(Q1, Q2, D), T, [tau], timeout(P, Q2, D), T)
    : −tos(Q1, T, [tau], P, T).
tos(timeout(Q1, Q2, D), T1, [], timeout(P, Q2, D − T), T1 + T)
    : −T > 0, T <= D, tos(Q1, T1, [], P, T1 + T).
tos(wait(D), T1, E, P, T2) : −tos(timeout(stop, skip, D), T1, E, P, T2).
tos(extchoice(P1,) , T, [E], P3, T) : −tos(P1, T, [E], P3, T).
tos(extchoice(, P2), T, [E], P4, T) : −tos(P2, T, [E], P4, T).
tos(extchoice(P1, P2), T, [tau], extchoice(P3, P2), T) : −tos(P1, T, [tau], P3, T).
tos(extchoice(P1, P2), T, [tau], extchoice(P1, P4), T) : −tos(P2, T, [tau], P4, T).
tos(extchoice(P1, P2), T1, [], extchoice(P3, P4), T2)
    : −T2 > T1, tos(P1, T1, [], P3, T2), tos(P2, T1, [], P4, T2).
tos(interleave(P1, P2), T, E, interleave(P3, P2), T)
    : −tos(P1, T, E, P3, T), (E == []; E == [tau]).
tos(interleave(P1, P2), T, E, interleave(P1, P4), T)
    : −tos(P2, T, E, P4, T), (E == []; E == [tau]).
tos(interleave(P1, P2), T, [E], interleave(P3, P2), T) : −tos(P1, T, [E], P3, T).
tos(interleave(P1, P2), T, [E], interleave(P1, P3), T) : −tos(P2, T, [E], P3, T).
tos(interleave(P1, P2), T1, [], interleave(P3, P4), T1 + D)
    : −D > 0, tos(P1, T1, [], P3, T1 + D), tos(P2, T1, [], P4, T1 + D).
tos(interleave(P1, P2), T, [termination], interleave(P3, P4), T)
    : −tos(P1, T, [termination], P3, T), tos(P2, T, [termination], P4, T).
tos(hiding(P1, X), T, [tau], hiding(P2, X), T)
    : −tos(P1, T, [E], T, P2), member(E, X).
tos(hiding(P1, X), T, [E], hiding(P2, X), T)
    : −tos(P1, T, [E], P2, T), not(member(E, X)).
tos(hiding(P1, X), T1, [], hiding(P2, X), T1 + D)
    : −D > 0, tos(P1, T1, [], P2, T1 + D),
        not(member(A, X), tos(P1, _, [A], _, _)).
tos(sequential(P1, P2), T, [E], sequential(P3, P2), T)
    : −tos(P1, T, [E], P3, T), not(E = termination).
tos(sequential(P1, P2), T, [termination], P2, T) : −tos(P1, T, [termination],, T).
tos(sequential(P1, P2), T1, [], sequential(P3, P2), T1 + D)
    : −D > 0, tos(P1, T1, [], P3, T1 + D), not(tos(P1, _, [termination], _, _)).
tos(interrupt(P1, P2), T, [E], interrupt(P3, P2), T) : −tos(P1, T, [E], P3, T).
tos(interrupt(_, P2), T, [E], P3, T) : −tos(P2, T, [E], P3, T).
tos(interrupt(P1, P2), T1, [], interrupt(P3, P4), T1 + D)
    : −D > 0, tos(P1, T1, [], P3, T1 + D), tos(P2, T1, [], P4, T1 + D).
```

Fig. 2. Operational Semantics of Timed CSP in CLP

$$\frac{P_1 \xrightarrow{e} P_1', P_2 \xrightarrow{e} P_2'}{P_1 \ {}_X\|_Y \ P_2 \xrightarrow{e} P_1' \ {}_X\|_Y \ P_2'} [\, e \in X \cap Y \,]$$

$$\frac{P_1 \overset{d}{\rightsquigarrow} P_1', P_2 \overset{d}{\rightsquigarrow} P_2'}{P_1 \ {}_X\|_Y \ P_2 \overset{d}{\rightsquigarrow} P_1' \ {}_X\|_Y \ P_2'}$$

The $\rightarrow$ represents an event transition, whereas $\rightsquigarrow$ represents an evolution transition. The rules associated with the alphabetized parallel composition operator are as the following:

$$\begin{array}{l} tos(para(P1, P2, X, Y), T, [E], para(P3, P2, X, Y), T) \\ \quad :-tos(P1, T, [E], P3, T), member(E, X), not(member(E, Y)). \\ tos(para(P1, P2, X, Y), T, [E], para(P1, P4, X, Y), T) \\ \quad :-os(P2, T, [E], P4, T), member(E, Y), not(member(E, X)). \\ tos(para(P1, P2, X, Y), T, [E], para(P3, P4, X, Y), T) \\ \quad :-tos(P1, T, E, P3, T), tos(P2, T, E, P4, T), \\ \qquad member(E, X), member(E, Y). \\ tos(para(P1, P2, X, Y), T1, [], para(P3, P4, X, Y), T1 + D) \\ \quad :-tos(P1, T1, [], P3, T1 + D), tos(P2, T1, [], P4, T1 + D). \end{array}$$

The first two rules state that either of the components may engage an event as long as the event is not shared. The third rule states that a shared event can only be engaged simultaneously by both components. The last expresses that the composition may allow time elapsing as long as both the components do. Other parallel composition operation, like $\|[X]\|$ and $|||$, can be defined as special cases of the alphabetized parallel composition operator straightforwardly. There is a clear one-to-one correspondence between our rules and the operators which are partly illustrated in Figure 2 and fully at our website[2]. Therefore, the soundness of the encoding can be proved by showing there is a bi-simulation relationship [13] between the transition system interpretation defined in [17] and ours, and the bi-simulation relationship can be proved easily via a structural induction.

For simplicity, we do restrict the form of recursion to $\mu X \bullet P(X)$, which means mutual recursion through process referencing has to be transformed before hand. The following clauses illustrate how recursion is handled, where N is the recursion point, i.e., X in $\mu X \bullet P(X)$) and P is the process expression, i.e., $P(X)$.

$$\begin{array}{l} tos(recursion([N, P], P1), T, [E], recursion([N, P], P2), T) \\ \quad :-not(P1 == N), tos(P1, T, [E], P2, T). \\ tos(recursion([N, P], P1), T1, [], recursion([N, P], P2), T1 + D) \\ \quad :-D > 0, tos(P1, T1, [], P2, T1 + D). \\ tos(recursion([N, P], N), T, [], recursion([N, P], P), T). \end{array}$$

[2] `http://nt-appn.comp.nus.edu.sg/fm/clp`

3.2 Denotational Semantics

We also encode both the timed traces and the timed failures model of Timed CSP, where the semantics of a Timed CSP process is represented by a set of timed traces or a set of timed failures [16]. A timed failure is a record of an execution, consisting of a timed trace which contains information about event performed, and a timed refusal which contains information about when events could be refused. In contrast to the operational semantics, which focuses on a single step at once, the denotational semantics captures all possible observations of systems modelled using Timed CSP. Therefore, it is easier to prove over all possible behaviors in the denotational semantics model.

In the following, we illustrate our encoding using only a few fundamental constructors for the sake of space saving. A relation *timedfailure(P, f(Tr, R))* is defined to capture the timed failure semantics, where P is a process expression and *Tr* is a sequence of timed events and R is a set of timed refusals. For instance,

$$\begin{array}{l} timedfailure(stop, failure([], \_)).\\ timedfailure(skip, failure([], R))\\ \quad :-sigma(R, S), not(member(termination, S)).\\ timedfailure(skip, failure([tevent(T, termination)], R))\\ \quad :-T >= 0, before(R, T, Z), sigma(Z, N), not\ member(termination, N). \end{array}$$

The relation *sigma(P, S)* is used to retrieve all events S in a process expression P, i.e., $S = \sigma(P)$. Similarly, the relation *before(R, T, Z)* is defined accordingly as $Z = R \upharpoonright T$, i.e., the refusals before time T. Basically, the first rule states that the failures of process STOP are an empty trace with all possible refusals. Process SKIP refuses everything until the occurrence of event *termination*, and all events are refused afterwards. As for compositional operators, we take the interface parallel composition operator as an example.

$$\begin{array}{l} timedfailure(parallel(Q1, Q2, A), failure(S, N))\\ \quad :-timedfailure(Q1, failure(S1, N1)),\\ \qquad timedfailure(Q2, failure(S2, N2)), union(N1, N2, N),\\ \qquad union(A, [termination], AT), remove(N1, AT, N11),\\ \qquad remove(N2, AT, N22), setequal(N11, N22), tsynch(S1, S2, A, S). \end{array}$$

The relation *union(X, Y, Z)* is the set union, i.e., $Z = X \cup Y$. The relation *remove(X, Y, Z)* is the set subtraction, i.e., $Z = X \setminus Y$. The relation *tsynch* defines the ways in which a trace tr_1 from component $Q1$ and a trace tr_2 from component $Q2$ can be combined to form a trace of the parallel (formal definition in [16]). The interface parallel operator requires synchronization on events from the interface event set A, and interleaving on events not in A.

Notice that the denotational semantics focuses on observations of the system, which allows us to query the system behaviors as a whole. For instance, it is more straightforward to check timewise refinement using the denotational semantics, and irregular processes can be handled if we replace the recursion using its fixed point. However, because there is no guarantee that the derivation sequence is terminating, we have to limit the height of the proving tree.

3.3 Handling Extensions to Timed CSP

Timed CSP is introduced in [14]. Since then, various extensions of Timed CSP have been proposed. In this work, we identify some of the effective extensions and show that they can be encoded in the CLP framework. For instance, the idea of *signal* by Davies [4] is a simple yet useful extension to capture liveness as well as model broadcasting effectively. The motivation of the concept *signal* is that when describing the behavior of a real-time process, we may wish to include instantaneous observable events that are not synchronization. For example, an audible bell might form part of the user interface to a telephone network, even though the bell may ring (a *signal*) without the cooperation of the user. Informally, *signal* events are distinguished events that will occur as soon as they become available, and will propagate through parallel composition. A process may ignore any signal performed by another process, unless it is waiting to perform the corresponding synchronization. For any observation that can be extended into the future, the only events that must be observed are signals. Therefore, signals are useful both for modelling broadcast communication and specifying liveness conditions, i.e., some events must be engaged.

$$
\begin{array}{l}
sigTF(eventprefix(E,\_,\_), sigfailure([], X, T)) \\
\quad :-not(E == sig(\_)), sigma(X, Z), \\
\qquad not(member(E, Z)), end(X, T1), T >= T1. \\
sigTF(eventprefix(E, P, D), sigfailure([tevent(T, E) \mid XS], Y, T1 + D + T)) \\
\quad :-T >= 0, not(E == sig(\_)), sigTF(P, sigfailure(S, Y1), T1), \\
\qquad backthrough(Y, T + D, Y1), begin(S, T2), T2 >= T + D, \\
\qquad end(S, Y, T3), max(T, T3, T4), T1 + D + T >= T4, \\
\qquad before(Y, T, Z), sigma(Z, N), \\
\qquad not(member(E, N)), delay(S, T + D, XS). \\
sigTF(eventprefix(sig(E), P, D), sigfailure([], [], 0)). \\
sigTF(eventprefix(sig(E), P, D), sigfailure([tevent(0, E) \mid XS], Y, T)) \\
\quad :-sigTF(P, failure(S, Y1), T1), backthrough(Y, T + D, Y1), \\
\qquad T = T1 + D, before(Y, T, Z), sigma(Z, N), \\
\qquad not(member(E, N)), delay(S, T + D, XS).
\end{array}
$$

The relation $sigTF(P, sigfailure(Tt, Tr, T))$ is used to capture this time failure semantics for signals, where P denotes the process, Tt is the timed trace, Tr denotes the timed refusal set and T denotes a time value. The CLP clauses illustrate the possible evolution of signal event prefixing. The first two clauses denote the semantics for event prefix process $a \rightarrow P$ where a is not a signal, while the last two denote the one with signal event $\hat{a}$, presented as $sig(a)$. In the above rules, *end(X,T)* computes the least upper bound of the time refusal X. *backthrough(Y,T,Y1)* represents the relation: Y - T = Y1, i.e., timed refusal $Y1$ is generated from Y by translating it backwards through time T. *begin(S, T)* retrieves the time of occurrence of the first event in timed trace S.

Another extension of special interest is Timed CSP integrated with state-based languages like Z [20] to model systems with not only complicated control flow but also complex data structures [12, 18]. Instead of adopting a heavy language like TCOZ (Timed Communicating Object-Z [12]), we allow a finite number of variables to be associated with a process[3], called state variables. In addition, we allow a state update transition, i.e., instead of engaging an abstract event, the system may perform a state update which changes the valuation of the state variables. A state update is specified as a predicate involving state variables before and after the update, as in Z style where the after-variables are primed [20].

For instance, there is a fragment of the specification of this vending machine, in which we allow different coins to be inserted via a channel communication $coin?x$ where x is 10, 20 or 50, a data variable *Quota* is requested to accumulate the amount of all coins inserted by the user.

$$Insert(Quota) \mathrel{\widehat{=}} coin?x \rightarrow AddQuota$$

where *AddQuota* is an operation defined in Z, which is:

$$AddQuota \mathrel{\widehat{=}} [x?, quota, quota' : \mathbb{N} \mid quota' = quota + x?]$$

This Timed CSP specification corresponds to the following CLP clauses where both the pre and post values of the process parameter are presented as the parameters, namely *Quota*1 and *Quota*2, of the relation *proc*. The user is responsible to specify exactly how an action updates the data variables, e.g., adding the amount of the coin to *Quota*.

$$\begin{array}{l} proc(coin, eventpreifx(coin(X1), addquota), Quota1, Quota2) \\ \qquad :- action(addquota, X1, Quota1, Quota2). \\ action(addquota, X1, Quota1, Quota2) :- Quota2 = Quota1 + X1. \end{array}$$

4 Proving Properties of Timed CSP

This section is devoted to various proving we may perform over systems modelled using Timed CSP and then encoded in CLP. We implemented a prototype in one of the CLP solver, namely CLP($\mathcal{R}$). Any CLP assertion can be proved against a given real-time system. We also developed a number of shortcuts for easy querying and proving.

4.1 Safety and Liveness

Using CLP, we may make explicit assertion which is neither just a safety assertion, nor just a liveness assertion. Yet it can be used for both purposes using a unique interpretation. In the following, we show how safety properties and liveness properties, like reachability, can be queried. We employ the concept of *coinductive tabling* with the purpose of obtain termination when dealing with recursions, which facilitates verifying safety and liveness properties based on traces. The detailed introduction of *coinductive tabling* can be found in [8].

[3] Which are of types supported by current tools for CLP.

Because Timed CSP is an event-based specification language, it is clearly useful to prove safety and liveness properties in terms of predicate concerning not only state variables but also events. A discussion on how to allow such temporal properties is presented in [3]. In order to explore the full state space, we define the following[4]:

$$\begin{aligned}&treachable(P, P, [], T1, T1).\\&treachable(P, Q, [E \mid N], T1, T2)\\&\quad :-tos(P, T1, E, P1, T3), treachable(P1, Q, N, T3, T2).\end{aligned}$$

The relation *treachable(P, Q, N, T1, T2)* states that it is possible to reach the process expression Q at time *T2* from P at time T1, with trace N. By using the tabling method, we dynamically record the process expressions that have been explored so as to avoid re-exploring them. In this regard, one kind of liveness property namely reachability is easily asserted using *treachable*.

An invariant property (a predicate over time variable and state variables and possible local clocks) is in general expressed as the assertion:

$$inv(P, T, Property) :-not(treachable(P, Q, \_, T, T1), not\ sat(Property)).$$

where *not sat(Property)* is a constraint indicating that the output from the previous atom not satisfying the user defined *Property*.

One safety property of special interest is deadlock-freeness. The following clauses are used to prove it.

$$\begin{aligned}&tdeadlock(P, T1) :-treachable(P, P1, N, T1, T2),\\&\quad (not(tos(P1, T2, [], Q, T), tos(Q, T, [\_], \_, \_)); (tos(P1, T2, [], Q, \_);\\&\quad not(tos, P1, T2, [\_], \_, \_))), printf(\text{"}deadlock\ at: \%\text{"}, [N]).\end{aligned}$$

Basically, it states that a process P at time *T1* may result in deadlock if it can reach the process expression Q at time *T2* where no event transition is available neither at *T2* nor at any later moment. The last line outputs the deadlocked trace as a counterexample. Alternatively, we may present it as a result of the deadlock proving.

We allow trace-based properties (safety or liveness) that can be checked by exploring trace set partially. The retrieve of a trace is done by the predicate $superstep(P, N, Q)$, which finds a sequence of events through which process expression P evolves to Q:

$$\begin{aligned}&superstep(P, [\_], \_) :-not(tos(P, \_, \_, Q, \_), not\ table(Q)).\\&superstep(P, [A \mid N], Q) :-tos(P, \_, M, P1, \_), not(M == []; M == [tau]),\\&\quad M = [A], not\ table(P1), assert(table(P1)), superstep(P1, N, Q).\\&superstep(P, N, Q) :-tos(P, \_, M, P1, \_), (M == []; M == [tau]),\\&\quad not\ table(P1), assert(table(P1)), superstep(P1, N, Q).\end{aligned}$$

We may prove that some event will always eventually be ready to be engaged using the following rule: where rule $member(N, E)$ returns true if event E appears at least once in the event sequence N.

[4] The possible state variables and local clocks are skipped for simplicity.

$$finally(P, E) : -not(superstep(P, N, \_)), not\ member(N, E).$$

Predicate *finally*(P, E) captures the idea that there is no such trace without event E in this process P. In other words, this process will eventually go to event E. Another property based on traces would be identifying the relationship among events, e.g., event A can never happen before (after) event B in a trace or trace fragment. Take the timed vending for example, we would like to ensure that in a round of using the machine, the event *tea* will never be followed by an event *dispatchcoffee*.

Example 4 (Verification). For the timed vending machine, we would like to check that it is deadlock-free by running the following goal and expecting failure:

$$? - proc(vending, P), tdeadlock(P, 0)$$

Moreover, we would expect that whenever we choose *tea*, it would never dispatch *coffee* instead of *tea*, which can be checked by the following goal:

$$\begin{aligned} ? - & proc(vending, P), super(P, N), (not\ in(tea, N); \\ & after(N, dispatchcoffee, tea)). \end{aligned}$$

4.2 Timewise Refinement Checking

The notion of refinement is a particularly useful concept in many forms of engineering activity. If we can establish a relation between components of a system which captures the fact that one satisfies at least the same conditions as another, then we may replace a worse component by a better one without degrading the properties of the system.

Compared to untimed CSP refinements which can be checked by FDR [15], timedwise refinements for Timed CSP contain more information about timing behavior. With the denotational model - timed failure model build in CLP, the refinement relations can be defined for systems described in Timed CSP in several ways, depending on the semantic model of the language which is used. In the timed versions of CSP, we mainly concentrate on two forms of refinement, corresponding to the semantic models which are trace timewise refinement and failure timewise refinement.

Trace timewise refinement. A process Q is a trace timewise refinement of P if all of its timed traces are allowed by P. The trace timewise relation is written $P\ _T\sqsubseteq_{TF}\ Q$ where P is an untimed CSP process, and Q is a timed CSP process. It is defined as:

$$P\ _T\sqsubseteq_{TF}\ Q = \forall (s, \aleph) \in \mathcal{TF}[\![Q]\!] \bullet \#s < \infty \Rightarrow strip(s) \in traces(P)$$

Detailed explanation can be found in [16]. In our timed failure model in CLP, we are able to find any finite timed trace of a process. Instead of testing every timed trace of a process Q by proving that this timed trace s with times removed is also a legal trace for the untimed process P, we test the negation of this predicate.

We introduce the predicate *traceTR* to find a violative timed trace of Q that is not a legal trace of P with its time information removed. The definition of *timedTR* is given by the following CLP clause: where Q is the timed process, P is the untimed process, S is a timed trace of Q and $TimeRmTr$ represents the times removed version of S.

$$traceTR(P, Q, S) :- timedfailure(Q, failure(S, Refusal)),$$
$$strip(S, TimeRmTr), not(trace(P, TimeRmTr)).$$

Failures timewise refinement. The timed process Q is a failure timewise refinement of the untimed process P if all of its timed traces are allowed by P, as well as all its timed failures are allowed by the stable failures of P. It is formally defined as in [16]:

$$P \;_{SF}\sqsubseteq_{TF}\; Q = \forall (s, \aleph) \in \mathcal{TF}[\![\mathcal{Q}]\!] \bullet \#s < \infty \Rightarrow strip(s) \in trace(P) \wedge$$
$$(\exists\, t : R^{+};\; X \subseteq \Sigma \bullet ([t, \infty) \times X) \subseteq \aleph \Rightarrow (strip(s), X) \in \mathcal{SF}[\![\mathcal{P}]\!])$$

We take the similar approach as the trace timewise refinement which tests the negation of the universal predicate. The predicate *failureTR* is introduced to capture this idea, which can be represented by the following CLP clauses:

$$failureTR(P, Q, S, Refusal) :- timedfailure(Q, failure(S, Refusal)),$$
$$((strip(S, TimeRmTr), not(trace(P, TimeRmTr)));$$
$$not(inStableFailure(Q, S, Refusal, P))).$$
$$inStableFailure(Q, S, Refusal, P) :- T > 0, sigma(Q, Sigma),$$
$$subset(Sigma, X), (not(subset(prod(int(T, inf), X), Refusal));$$
$$(strip(S, TimeRmTr), stablefailure(P, failure(TimeRmTr, X)))).$$

4.3 Additional Checking

In reality, most processes are non-terminating, so it would not be possible to retrieve all possible traces of a process. However, by given a specific trace of a trace fragment, we are able to identify whether it is an event sequencing of a given process. For instance, the following clause is used to query if a sequence of event is a trace of the system, where P is a process expression and X is a sequence of events.

$$trace(P, X) :- superstep(P, X,_{)}.$$

In addition to proving pre-specified assertions, one distinguished feature of our approach is that implicit assertions may be proved. For example, we may identify the lower or upper bound of a (time or data) variable, which is very useful for applications like worst or best case analysis of execution time.

$$dur(P, Q, T1, T2) :- tos(P, T1, \_, Q, T2).$$
$$dur(P, Q, T1, T2) :- tos(P, T1, \_, P1, T3), dur(P1, Q, T3, T2).$$

We are able to compute the duration of the execution of one process P to its subsequent process Q by the above two rules, where T_1 is the starting time and

T_2 is the ending time. By using the predicate *dur*, we are able to get identify the lower bound of some processes involving time. The process WAIT(2); $a \xrightarrow{3}$ SKIP should terminate in more than 5 time units, which can be identified by the following goal and expecting T≥5.

$$? - dur(sequ(wait(2), delay(a, skip, 3)), stop, 0, T).$$

5 Experiments and Results

In this section, we compare our method to the mature model checker for CSP, namely FDR (version 2.78), in terms of flexibility as well as efficiency. We implement a prototype as a normal CLP($\mathcal{R}$) program. In the following, we demonstrate our experiments with three examples on a Unix system located at a Sunfire sever with IGB user memory. Because FDR is designed for CSP, the quantitative timing aspects of the examples have been abstracted before FDR verification.

Timed Vending Machine. The specification of the timed vending machine is presented in Example 1. Figure 1 shows the timed vending machine model in CLP. This example is customized into a FDR program (say P), in which the time-out operator is replaced with an external choice. The following are the properties verified:

- *tvm-1* Deadlock-freeness
- *tvm-2* Trace timewise refinement:
  - in CLP, whether the process TVM is a trace timewise refinement of P.
  - in FDR, whether the process P is a trace refinement of TVM.
- *tvm-3* Whether there is such a case that coffee is selected while tea is dispatched.

Dining Philosopher. The classic dining philosopher example is also experimented. The specification is available in [7]. We implemented this example with N philosophers and N forks. The following properties are experimented:

- *philosopherN-1* It is not deadlock-free
- *philosopherN-2* No more than N+1/2 philosophers can eat at the same time.
- *philosopherN-3* It is possible that one philosopher eat all the time with the others starving. This property is checked with trace refinement.

The Railway Crossing. The railway crossing system is modelled and checked, which is complex enough to demonstrate a number of aspects of the modelling and verification of timed systems. The system consists of three components: a train, a gate and a controller. The gate should be up to allow traffic to pass when no train approaching and lowered to obstruct traffic when a train is coming. The controller monitors the approach of a train, and instructs the gate to

Table 1. Properties Verification

Property	Goal in CLP
deadlock-freeness	proc(system, P), tdeadlock(P, 0) $\models$ *false*
if train enters crossing, the gate must be down	proc(system, P), supersetp(P, X), last(X, entercrossing),filter(X, [up,down], X2), last(X2, up) $\models$ *false*
lower bound for a train passes the crossing is 320s	proc(system, P), dur(delay(nearind, _, _), eventprefix(outind, _), T1, T2),T2-T1<320 $\models$ *false*
if the gate is up, the train must have left the crossing	proc(system,P), superstep(P, X), not(not in([up, entercrossing, leavecrossing], X); after(X, leavecrossing, entercrossing))) $\models$ *false*
legal trace checking	proc(system, P),superstep(P, [trainnear, nearind, downcomm,down, confirm, entercrossing, leavecrossing, outind])$\models$*true*

be lowered within the appropriate time. The train is modelled abstractly with behaviors: nearing, entering and leaving the crossing. The Timed CSP modelling is as follows (originally presented in [16]):

$$
\begin{aligned}
&TRAIN \mathrel{\widehat{=}} \mu\, T \bullet trainnear \rightarrow nearind \stackrel{300}{\rightarrow} entercrossing \\
&\qquad \stackrel{20}{\rightarrow} leavecrossing \rightarrow outind \rightarrow T \\
&GATE \mathrel{\widehat{=}} \mu\, G \bullet downcom \stackrel{100}{\rightarrow} down \rightarrow confirm \rightarrow G \\
&\qquad \Box\ upcom \stackrel{100}{\rightarrow} up \rightarrow confirm \rightarrow G \\
&CONTROLLER \mathrel{\widehat{=}} \mu\, C \bullet outind \stackrel{1}{\rightarrow} upcom \rightarrow confirm \rightarrow C \\
&\qquad \Box\ nearind \stackrel{1}{\rightarrow} downcom \rightarrow confirm \rightarrow C \\
&CROSSING \mathrel{\widehat{=}} CONTROLLER\ {}_{C}\|_{G}\ GATE \\
&SYSTEM \mathrel{\widehat{=}} TRAIN\ {}_{T}\|_{C \cup G}\ CROSSING
\end{aligned}
$$

The time information of the system is that: the train takes at least 5 minutes from triggering the near.ind sensor to reach the crossing; and at least 20 seconds to get across the crossing. The controller takes a negligible amount of time, say 1 second, from receiving a signal from a sensor to relaying the corresponding instruction to the gate. The gate process takes 100 seconds to get itself into position following an instruction. A number of interesting properties can be formulated, evidenced in Table 1. The three properties selected for comparing our approach with FDR verification are:

- *railway-1* Deadlock-freeness
- *railway-2* Whether trace $\langle trainnear, nearind, downcomm, down, confirm, entercrossing, leavecrossing, outind\rangle$ is a legal trace or not.
- *railway-3* Whether the lower bound for a train passes the crossing is $320s$.

We summarize our results in Table 2. We ran the examples in both CLP($\mathcal{R}$) and FDR systems and we calculated the execution time of each property if the property is able to be checked in that system. From the table, we can see that

Table 2. Experiment Results

Assertion	CLP($\mathcal{R}$) *(sec)*	FDR *(sec)*
tvm-1	0.00	0.23
tvm-2	0.03	0.27
tvm-3	0.01	–
railway-1	0.25	0.25
railway-2	0.02	0.26
railway-3	0.32	–

Assertion	CLP($\mathcal{R}$) *(sec)*	FDR *(sec)*
phi3-1	0.12	0.25
phi3-2	0.22	–
phi3-3	0.04	0.17
phi4-1	0.84	0.28
phi4-2	2.5	–
phi4-3	0.1	0.3

most of our timing analysis performance are competitive with the well-known system, while in some cases, we are not so competitive. The important metric of our experiments is the flexibility. The results show that our reasoning method based on constraint solver can handle a wider range of properties, including the timed-related properties, bounds of variables, event specified properties, and etc.

6 Conclusions

In this paper, we proposed a reasoning method for Timed CSP based on constraint logic, which to our knowledge, is the first mechanized reasoning support for Timed CSP. The contribution of this work is fourfold. Firstly we showed that event-based process algebra Timed CSP can be encoded in CLP by encoding both the operational and denotational semantics. Our work therefore broadened real-time systems which can be specified and verified by CLP. Secondly, we handled some useful extensions to Timed CSP, most significant one is the concept of *singal* for specifying broadcast communication. Thirdly, we investigated a wide range of properties that may be proved based on constraint solving, for instance we showed that using a unique interpretation, traditional safety and liveness can be proved effectively as well as properties such as lower or upper bound of a variable and refinement. Lastly, we implemented a prototype program and applied our approach to various systems. In our future work, we plan to build a graphical user interface for automatically translating Timed CSP models, inserting properties, visualizing counterexamples if any and etc, which has been partially done recently. Besides, we would also extend our method to verify other integrated formalisms which are based on CSP/Timed CSP.

Acknowledgement

The authors thank Andrew Santosa for insightful discussion on CLP and pointing out relevant documentations.

References

1. R. Abhik and I.V. Ramakrishnan. Automated Inductive Verification of Parameterized Protocols. In *International Conf. on Computer Aided Verification (CAV)*. Springer, 2001.

2. P. J. Brooke. *A Timed Semantics for a Hierarchical Design Notation.* PhD thesis, University of York, April 1999.
3. S. Chaki, E. M. Clarke, J. Ouaknine, N. Sharygina, and N. Sinha. State/Event-based Software Model Checking. In *Proceeding of Integrate Formal Methods 2004*, pages 128–147, 2004.
4. J. Davies. *Specification and Proof in Real-Time CSP.* Cambridge University Press, 1993.
5. Formal Systems (Europe) Ltd. Failure Divergence Refinement: FDR2 User Manual. 1997.
6. G.l Gupta and E. Pontelli. A Constraint-based Approach for Specification and Verification of Real-time Systems. In *IEEE Real-Time Systems Symposium*, pages 230–239, 1997.
7. C. A. R. Hoare. *Communicating Sequential Processes.* International Series in Computer Science. Prentice-Hall, 1985.
8. A. Santosa J. Jaffar and R. Voicu. Modeling Systems in CLP with Coinductive Tabling. In *International Conference on Logic Programming*, 2005.
9. J. Jaffar and M. J. Maher. Constraint Logic Programming: A Survey. *Journal of Logic Programming*, 19/20:503–581, 1994.
10. J. Jaffar, S. Michaylov, P. J. Stuckey, and R. H. C. Yap. The CLP(R) Language and System. *ACM Trans. Program. Lang. Syst.*, 14(3):339–395, 1992.
11. J. Jaffar, A. E. Santosa, and R. Voicu. A CLP Proof Method for Timed Automata. In *Real-Time Systems Symposium*, pages 175–186, 2004.
12. B. P. Mahony and J. S. Dong. Timed Communicating Object Z. *IEEE Trans. Software Eng.*, 26(2):150–177, 2000.
13. R. Milner. *A Calculus of Communicating Systems*, volume 92. Springer-Verlag, 1980.
14. G. M. Reed and A. W. Roscoe. A Timed Model for Communicating Sequential Processes. In L. Kott, editor, *ICALP*, volume 226 of *Lecture Notes in Computer Science*, pages 314–323. Springer, 1986.
15. A. W. Roscoe. *The Theory and Practice of Concurrency.* Prentice-Hall, 1997.
16. S. Schneider. *Concurrent and Real-time System: The CSP Approach.* JOHN WILEY & SONS, LTD, 2000.
17. S. A. Schneider. An Operational Semantics for Timed CSP. In *Proceedings Chalmers Workshop on Concurrency, 1991*, pages 428–456. Report PMG-R63, Chalmers University of Technology and University of Göteborg, 1992.
18. G. Smith and J. Derrick. Specification, Refinement and Verification of Concurrent Systems-An Integration of Object-Z and CSP. *Formal Methods in System Design*, 18(3):249–284, 2001.
19. D. S. Warren. Programming with Tabling in XSB. In *PROCOMET '98: Proceedings of the IFIP TC2/WG2.2,2.3 International Conference on Programming Concepts and Methods*, pages 5–6, London, UK, 1998.
20. J. Woodcock and J. Davies. *Using Z: Specification, Refinement, and Proof.* Prentice-Hall International, 1996.

Mapping RT-LOTOS Specifications into Time Petri Nets

Tarek Sadani[1,2], Marc Boyer[3], Pierre de Saqui-Sannes[1,2], and Jean-Pierre Courtiat[1]

[1] LAAS-CNRS, 7 av. du colonel Roche, 31077 Toulouse Cedex 04, France
[2] ENSICA, 1 place Emile Blouin, 31056 Toulouse Cedex 05, France
[3] IRIT-CNRS/ENSEEIHT, 2 rue Camichel, 31000 Toulouse, France
tsadani@ensica.fr, mboyer@enseeiht.fr, desaqui@ensica.fr, courtiat@laas.fr

Abstract. RT-LOTOS is a timed process algebra which enables compact and abstract specification of real-time systems. This paper proposes and illustrates a structural translation of RT-LOTOS terms into behaviorally equivalent (timed bisimilar) finite Time Petri nets. It is therefore possible to apply Time Petri nets verification techniques to the profit of RT-LOTOS. Our approach has been implemented in RTL2TPN, a prototype tool which takes as input an RT-LOTOS specification and outputs a TPN. The latter is verified using TINA, a TPN analyzer developed by LAAS-CNRS. The toolkit made of RTL2TPN and TINA has been positively benchmarked against previously developed RT-LOTOS verification tool.

1 Introduction

The acknowledged benefits of using Formal Description Techniques (FDTs) include the possibility to verify a model of the system under design against user requirements. These benefits are even higher for systems which are both concurrent and submitted to stringent temporal constraints.

In this paper, formal verification is addressed in the context of RT-LOTOS, a timed extension of the ISO-based LOTOS [1] FDT. RT-LOTOS [2] shares with LOTOS and other process algebras its capability to specify systems as a collection of communicating processes. The paper proposes a transformational approach from RT-LOTOS to Time Petri Nets (TPNs) which, by contrast, are typical example of non compositional FDT. Therefore, it is proposed to embed TPNs into so-called *components* that can be composed relying on different patterns. The latters are carefully defined so as they ensure a very tight relation between the obtained composite TPN and its corresponding RT-LOTOS behavior. This work can be seen as giving a TPN semantics to RT-LOTOS denotationally. A prototype tool implements the translation patterns. It has been interfaced with TINA [3], the Time Petri Net Analyzer developed by LAAS-CNRS. We show that an automatically generated reachability graph of a TPN can be used to reason about and check the correctness of RT-LOTOS specifications.

Z. Liu and J. He (Eds.): ICFEM 2006, LNCS 4260, pp. 360–379, 2006.

The paper is organized as follows. Section 2 introduces the RT-LOTOS language. Section 3 introduces the Time Petri net (TPN) model. Section 4 discusses the theoretical foundations of RT-LOTOS to TPNs mapping. Section 5 addresses practical issues, including tool development and verification results obtained for well-established benchmarks. Section 6 surveys related work. Section 7 concludes the paper.

2 RT-LOTOS

The Language of Temporal Ordering Specifications (LOTOS, [1]), is a formal description technique, based on CCS [4] and extended by a multi-way synchronization mechanism inherited from CSP [5]. In LOTOS, process definitions are expressed by the specification of behavior expressions which are constructed by means of a restricted set of powerful operators making it possible to express behaviors as complex as desired. Among these operators, action prefixing, choice, parallel composition and hiding play a fundamental role.

RT-LOTOS [2] extends LOTOS with three temporal operators: a *deterministic delay* ($\triangle^t$), a *latency*(Ω^t) which enables description of temporal indeterminism and a *time limited offer* $g\{t\}$. The main difference between RT-LOTOS and other timed extensions of LOTOS lies in the way a non-deterministic delay may be expressed. The solution developed for RT-LOTOS is the latency operator. Its usefulness and efficiency have been proved in control command applications and hypermedia authoring [6].

RT-LOTOS formal syntax: Let PV be the set of process variables and X range over PV. Let GV be the set of the user-definable gates. Let g,$g'_1 \dots g'_n \in GV$, let also L be any (possibly empty) subset of GV noted $L = g'_1 \dots g'_n$ and i the internal action.

The formal syntax of RT-LOTOS is recursively given by:

$\mathtt{P} ::= \mathtt{stop} \mid \mathtt{exit} \mid \mathtt{X[L]} \mid g\mathtt{;P} \mid g\{t\}\mathtt{;P} \mid i\{t\}\mathtt{;P} \mid \triangle^t\mathtt{P} \mid \Omega^t\mathtt{P} \mid \mathtt{P\ []\ P} \mid \mathtt{P|[L]|P} \mid$
$\quad \mathtt{hide\ L\ in\ P} \mid \mathtt{P} \gg \mathtt{P} \mid \mathtt{P[>P}$

The syntax of a process definition being "process X[$g'_1 \dots g'_n$]:=P_X endproc". Two alternative syntaxes have been defined for expressing time delays: *delay(t)* which is identical to $\triangle^t$, and latencies, namely *latency(t)* meaning Ω^t.

RT-LOTOS operational semantics in the classical Plotkin's SOS style can be found in [7].

3 Time Petri Nets

Petri nets were, to our knowledge, the first theoretical model augmented with time constraints [8,9], and the support of the first reachability algorithm for timed system [10,11].

The basic idea of time Petri nets (TPN [8,9]) is to associate an interval $I_s(t) = [a, b]$ (static interval) with each transition t. The transition *can* be fired if it

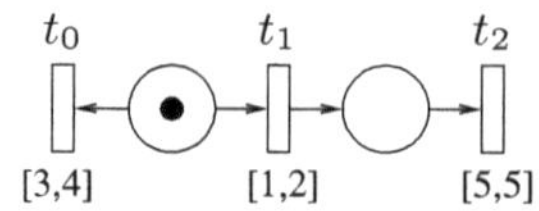

Fig. 1. Priority from urgency

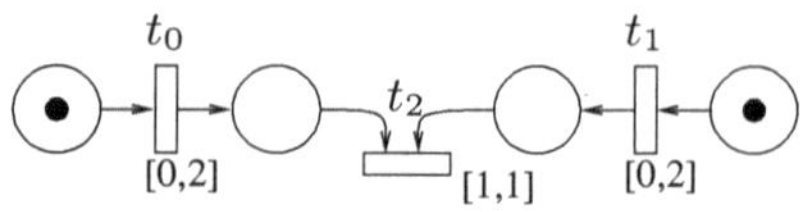

Fig. 2. Synchronization

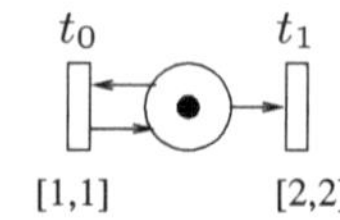

Fig. 3. Continuous enabling

has continuously been enabled during at least a time units, and it *must* fire if continuous enabling time reaches b time units[1].

Figure 1 is a first example: in the initial marking, only t_0 and t_1 are enabled. After one time unit delay, t_1 is firable. Because t_1 reaches its upper interval always before t_0 becomes enable ($3 > 2$), then t_0 can never be fired. t_2 is fired five time units after the firing of t_1. Figure 2 illustrates the synchronization rule: t_0 (resp. t_1) is fired at an absolute date $\theta_0 \leq 2$ (resp. $\theta_1 \leq 2$), and t_2 is fired at $max(\theta_0, \theta_1) + 1$. Figure 3 illustrates another important point: continuous enabling. In that TPN, transition t_1 will *never* be fired, because, at each time unit, t_0 is fired, removing the token and putting it back immediately. Then, t_1 is at most 1 time unit continuously enabled, never 2 time units.

4 Translation Definition

This section gives the translation from RT-LOTOS terms into TPNs. This mapping can also be understood as the definition of an alternative TPNs semantics of RT-LOTOS. It is well known that process algebras (e.g. RT-LOTOS) heavily rely on the concept of compositionality, whereas Petri nets (and their timed versions) lack of compositionality at all. To make the translation possible, a core idea behind our approach is to view a TPN as a composition of number of TPN components. The following section introduces the concept of *TPN Component* as basic building block.

4.1 Time Petri Net Component

A *Component* encapsulates a labeled TPN which describes its behavior. It is handled through its interfaces and interactions points. A component performs an action by firing the corresponding transition. A component has two sets of labels: *Act* which is the alphabet of the component and $Time = \{\text{tv}, \text{delay}, \text{latency}\}$. These three labels are introduced to represent the intended temporal behavior of a component. The tv (for "temporal violation") label represents the expiration of time limited-offering. A delay or latency label represents the expiration of a deterministic delay or a non deterministic delay, respectively.

A component is graphically represented by a box containing a TPN. The black-filled boxes at the component boundary represent interaction points. For instance, the component $C_\mathfrak{P}$ in the Figure 4 is built from a RT-LOTOS term

[1] This urgency when the deadline is reached is called "strong semantics".

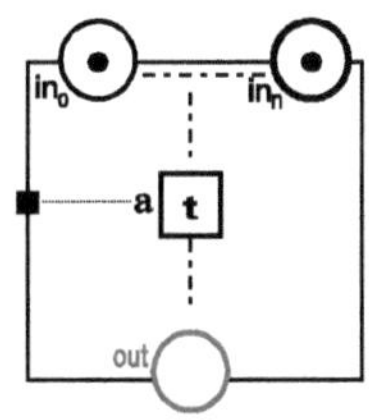

Fig. 4. Component example

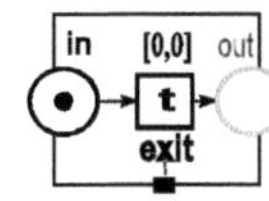

Fig. 5. The `exit` pattern

P. During its execution, it may perform the observable action a. The in_i (initially marked places) represent the component input interface, and the *out* place denotes its output interface. A token in the *out* place of a component means that the component has successfully completed its execution. A component is *activated* by filling its input places. A component is *active* if at least one of its transitions is enabled. Otherwise, the component is *inactive.*

Definition 1 (Component)
Let $Act = A_o \cup A_h \cup \{exit\}$ *be an alphabet of actions, where* A_o *is a set of* observable actions *(with* $i \notin A_o$, $exit \notin A_o$*),* $A_h = \{i\} \times A_o$ *is the set of hidden actions (If* a *is an observable action,* i_a *denotes a hidden action).*
Formally a component is a tuple $C = \langle \Sigma, Lab, I, O \rangle$ *where*

- $\Sigma = \langle P, T, Pre, Post, M_0, IS \rangle$ *is a TPN.*
- $Lab : T \rightarrow (Act \cup Time)$ *is a labeling function which labels each transition in* Σ *with either an action name (Act) or a time-event* ($Time = \{tv, delay, latency\}$*). Let* T^{Act} *(resp.* T^{Time}*) be the set of transitions with labels in Act (resp. Time).*
- $I \subset P$ *is a non empty set of places defining the input interface.*
- $O \subset P$ *is the output interface of the component. A component has an output interface if it has at least one transition labeled by* ***exit****. If so,* O *is the outgoing place of those transitions. Otherwise,* $O = \emptyset$*.*

The following invariants apply to all components:

H1 There is no source transition in a component.
H2 The encapsulated TPN is 1-bounded (cf. *safe* nets in [12]). H2 is called the "safe marking" property. It is essential for the decidability of reachability analysis procedure applied to TPNs.
H3 If all the input places are marked, all other places are empty ($I \subset M \Rightarrow M = I$).
H4 If the *out* place is marked, all other places are empty ($O \neq \emptyset \wedge O \subset M \Rightarrow M = O$).
H5 For each transition t such that $Lab(t) \in Act$, if the label is an observable action ($Lab(t) \in A_0$), its time interval is $[0, \infty)$, otherwise[2], it is $[0, 0]$.

[2] $Lab(t) \in A_h \cup \{exit\}$.

4.2 Translation Patterns

RT-LOTOS behaviour expressions are inductively defined by means of algebraic operators acting on behaviour expressions. Since the translation is meant to be syntax driven we need to endow TPNs with operators corresponding to RT-LOTOS ones, so as to allow one to construct a composite TPN. In the following, we first define components corresponding to nullary algebraic operators (`stop` and `exit`) and, given each RT-LOTOS operator and its operands (i.e. behaviour expressions), we inductively describe how to obtain a new component starting from the one corresponding to the given RT-LOTOS behaviour expressions. The resulting component corresponds to the RT-LOTOS behaviour expression computed by applying the operator to the given operands.

Due to lack of space, the formalization of some patterns is skipped. A complete formal definition can be found in the extended version of this paper [13].

Notation and definition. $f' = f \cup (a, b)$ defines the function $f' : A \cup \{a\} \mapsto B \cup \{b\}$ such that $f'(x) = f(x)$ if $x \in A$ and $f'(a) = b$ otherwise.

Definition 2 (First actions set). *Let C be a component. The set of first actions $\mathcal{FA}(C_P)$ can be recursively built using the following rules*[3]*:*

$$\begin{aligned}
\mathcal{FA}(C_{stop}) &= \emptyset & \mathcal{FA}(C_{exit}) &= \{t_{exit}\} \\
\mathcal{FA}(C_{a;P}) &= \{t_a\} & \mathcal{FA}(C_{\mu X.(P;X)}) &= \mathcal{FA}(C_P) \\
\mathcal{FA}(C_{a\{d\}P}) &= \{t_a\} & \mathcal{FA}(C_{\mathtt{delay}(d)P}) &= \mathcal{FA}(C_P) \\
\mathcal{FA}(C_{\mathtt{latency}(d)P}) &= \mathcal{FA}(C_P) & \mathcal{FA}(C_{P;Q}) &= \mathcal{FA}(C_P) \\
\mathcal{FA}(C_{P|[A]|Q}) &= \mathcal{FA}(C_P) \cup \mathcal{FA}(C_Q) & \mathcal{FA}(C_{P>>Q}) &= \mathcal{FA}(C_P) \\
\mathcal{FA}(C_{P[]Q}) &= \mathcal{FA}(C_P) \cup \mathcal{FA}(C_Q) & \mathcal{FA}(C_{P[>Q}) &= \mathcal{FA}(C_P) \cup \mathcal{FA}(C_Q) \\
\mathcal{FA}(C_{\mathtt{hide}\ a\ \mathtt{in}\ P}) &= h_a(\mathcal{FA}(C_P))
\end{aligned}$$

Low level Petri net operations. The formal definition of the translation patterns uses the following low level Petri nets operators: $\cup, \setminus, \uplus$.

Let $N = \langle P, T, Pre, Post, M_0, IS \rangle$ be a TPN.

Adding a place: Let p be a new place ($p \notin P$), Pre_p and $Post_p$ two sets of transitions of T. Then $N' = N \cup \langle Pre_p, p, Post_p \rangle$ is the TPN augmented with place p such that ${}^\bullet p = Pre_p$ and $p^\bullet = Post_p$.

Adding a transition: Let t be a new transition ($t \notin T$), I its time interval, Pre_t and $Post_t$ two sets of places of P. Then $N' = N \cup \langle Pre_t, (t, I), Post_t \rangle$ is the TPN augmented with transitions t such that ${}^\bullet t = Pre_t$ and $t^\bullet = Post_t$.

Similarly, $\setminus$ is used to remove places or transitions from a net (and all related arcs), and $\uplus$ denotes the free merging of two nets.

[3] where $t_{\mathtt{a}}$ is transition labelled by a. $h_a(\alpha) = \alpha$ if $\alpha \neq a$ and $h_a(a) = i_a$.

Basic components. The $C_{\mathtt{stop}}$ component is simply the empty net (no place, no transition). $C_{\mathtt{exit}}$ is a component which performs a successful termination. It has one input place, one output place, and a single transition labeled with `exit` and a static interval $[0, 0]$ (Fig.5).

Patterns applying to one component. Let us consider the component $C_{\mathtt{P}}$ of Fig. 4. Fig. 6 depicts different patterns applied to $C_{\mathtt{P}}$.

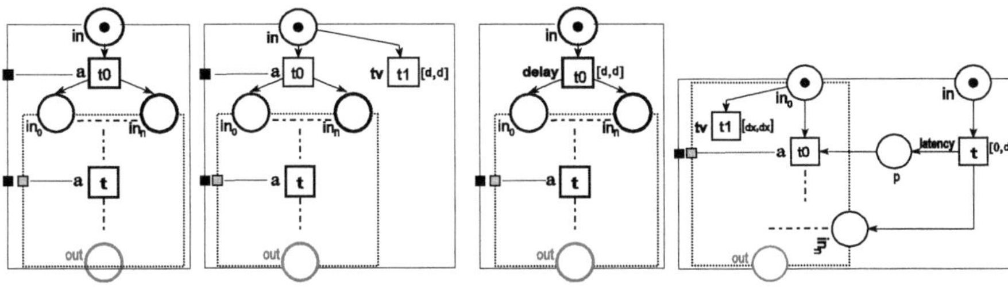

(a) `a;P` (b) `a{d}P` (c) `delay(d)P` (d) `latency(d)P`

Fig. 6. Patterns applying to one component

- $C_{\mathtt{a;P}}$ (Fig. 6(a)) is the component resulting from prefixing $C_{\mathtt{P}}$ with action a. $C_{\mathtt{a;P}}$ executes a then activates $C_{\mathtt{P}}$.
  $C_{\mathtt{a;P}} = \langle \Sigma_{\mathtt{a;P}}, Lab_{\mathtt{a;P}}, \{in\}, O_{\mathtt{P}} \rangle$ where the TPN $\Sigma_{\mathtt{a;P}}$ is obtained by adding a place in and a transition t_0 to $\Sigma_{\mathtt{P}}$, $Lab_{\mathtt{a;P}}$ associates a to transition t_0.

$$\Sigma_{\mathtt{a;P}} = (\Sigma_{\mathtt{P}} \cup \langle \emptyset, (t_0, [0, \infty)), I_{\mathtt{P}} \rangle) \cup \langle \emptyset, in, t_0 \rangle$$
$$Lab_{\mathtt{a;P}} = Lab_{\mathtt{P}} \cup (t_0, \mathtt{a})$$

- $C_{\mathtt{a\{d\};P}}$ (Fig. 6(b)) is the component resulting from prefixing $C_{\mathtt{P}}$ with a limited offer of d units of time on action a. If for any reason, a cannot occur during this time interval, the `tv` transition will be fired (temporal violation situation) and $C_{\mathtt{a\{d\};P}}$ will transform into an inactive component.

$$C_{\mathtt{a\{d\};P}} = \langle \Sigma_{\mathtt{a\{d\};P}}, Lab_{\mathtt{a;P}} \cup \{(t_1, \mathrm{tv})\}, \{in\}, O_{\mathtt{P}} \rangle$$
$$\Sigma_{\mathtt{a\{d\};P}} = \Sigma_{\mathtt{a;P}} \cup \langle \{in\}, (t_1, [d, d]), \emptyset \rangle$$

- $C_{\mathtt{delay(d)P}}$ (Fig 6(c)) is the component resulting from delaying the first action of `P` with a deterministic delay of `d` units of time. This is exactly the same pattern as $C_{\mathtt{a;P}}$ except that the added transition has a delay label and a static interval equal to $[d, d]$.

$$C_{\mathtt{delay(d)P}} = \langle \Sigma_{\mathtt{delay(d)P}}, Lab_{\mathtt{P}} \cup \{(t_0, \mathrm{delay})\}, \{in\}, O_{\mathtt{P}} \rangle$$
$$\Sigma_{\mathtt{delay(d)P}} = (\Sigma_{\mathtt{P}} \cup \langle \emptyset, (t_0, [d, d])), I_{\mathtt{P}} \rangle) \cup \langle \emptyset, in, t_0 \rangle$$

– $C_{\texttt{latency(d)P}}$ (Fig 6(d)) is the component resulting from delaying the first actions of $C_{\texttt{P}}$ with a non deterministic delay of d units of time.

  Like the delay operator, latency is defined by connecting a new transition to the input interface of $C_{\texttt{P}}$. But this time, we add a static interval equal to $[0, d]$. The definition of the latency translation pattern must handle the "subtle" case where one (or several) action(s) among $C_{\texttt{P}}$'s first actions is (are) constrained with a limited offer (this set is denoted by $\mathcal{FA}_{lo}$). For instance, in Fig 6(d), action a is offered to the environment during d_x units of time. The RT-LOTOS semantics states that the latency and the offering of a start simultaneously, which means that if the latency duration goes beyond d_x units of time, the offer on a will expire. To obtain the same behavior, we add the input place in_0 of a to the input interface of the resulting component $C_{\texttt{latency(d)P}}$. In the definition of the pattern, we denote I_{lo} the set of these input places ($I_{lo} \subset I_{\texttt{P}}$). Thus t_1 and t are enabled as soon as the component is activated (all its input places being marked). $C_{\texttt{latency(d)P}}$ is able to execute a (fire t_0) if t_0 is enabled (i.e if in_0 and p are marked) before t_1 is fired (at d_x). Therefore, action a is possibly offered to the environment for no more than d_x units of time, hence conforming to the RT-LOTOS semantics.
  Let $\mathcal{FA}(C_{\texttt{P}})$ be the set of transitions associated to the first actions of P[4], and $\mathcal{FA}_{lo}(C_{\texttt{P}})$ be the set of first actions constrained by a time limited offer:

$$\mathcal{FA}_{lo}(C_{\texttt{P}}) = \{t_a \in \mathcal{FA}(C_{\texttt{P}}) \mid \text{tv} \in ({}^\bullet t_a)^\bullet\}$$

$$I_{lo} = {}^\bullet\mathcal{FA}_{lo}(C_{\texttt{P}})$$

$$C_{\texttt{latency(d)P}} = \langle \Sigma_{\texttt{latency(d)P}}, Lab_{\texttt{P}} \cup \{(t, \text{latency})\}, I_{lo} \cup \{in\}, O_{\texttt{P}} \rangle$$

$$\Sigma_{\texttt{latency(d)P}} = \Sigma_{\texttt{P}} \cup \bigcup_{t_a \in \mathcal{FA}_{lo}(C_{\texttt{P}})} \langle t, p_{t_a}, t_a \rangle \cup \langle \emptyset, in, \emptyset \rangle$$

$$\cup \left\langle \{in\}, (t, [0, d]), (I_{\texttt{P}} \backslash I_{lo}) \cup \bigcup_{t_a \in \mathcal{FA}_{lo}(C_{\texttt{P}})} \{p_{t_a}\} \right\rangle$$

– $C_{\mu\texttt{X.(P;X)}}$ The recursion operator translation is mainly an untimed problem (relying on fixpoint theory). It is not presented in this paper, focused on timed aspects.
– $C_{\texttt{hide a in P}}$ is the component resulting from hiding action a in $C_{\texttt{P}}$. Hiding allows one to transform observable (external) actions into unobservable (internal) actions, then making the latter unavailable for synchronization with other components. In RT-LOTOS, hiding one or several actions induces a notion of urgency on action occurrence. Consequently, a TPN transition corresponding to a hidden action will be constrained by a time interval equal to $[0, 0]$. This implies that as soon as a transition is enabled, it is candidate for being fired.

Patterns applying to a set of components. Each of the following patterns transforms a set of components into one component.

[4] Its formal definition can be found in Def. 2, Sect. 4.2.

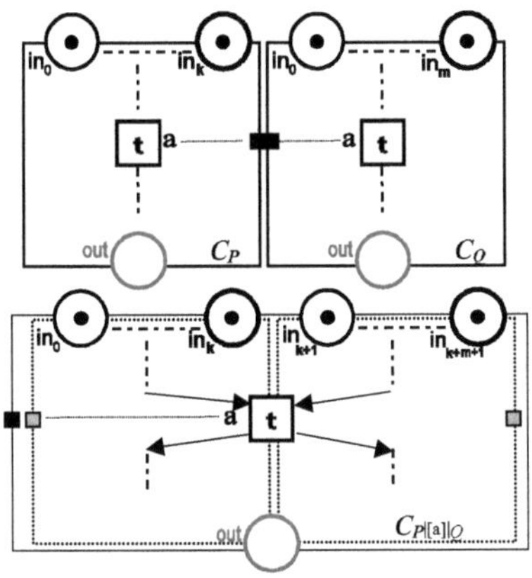

Fig. 7. Parallel synchronization pattern

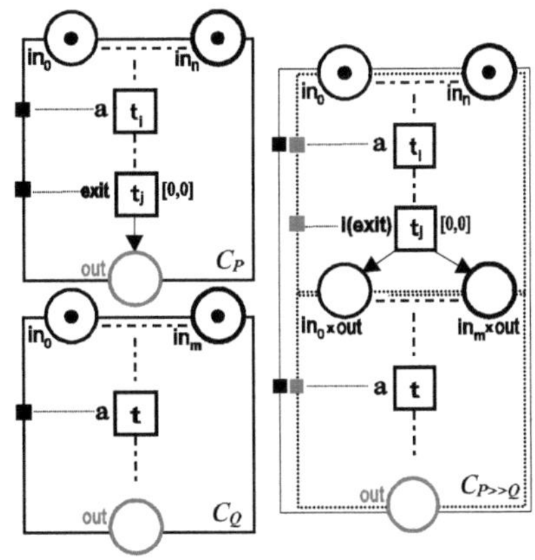

Fig. 8. Sequential composition pattern

– $C_{\mathtt{P|[a]|Q}}$ (Fig.7)
In Petri nets, a multi-way synchronization is represented by a transition with n input places. This transition can fire only if all its input places contain a token (cf. Fig. 2). At the PN level, the synchronization operation is achieved through transition merging. While in untimed Petri nets, the operation of transitions merging is straightforward, it turns to be a rather tricky issue in Time Petri nets. Indeed, it requires explicit handling of the time intervals assigned to the transitions to be merged. Possible incompatibility of these time intervals leads to express global timing constraints as a conjunction of intervals whose consistency is not guaranteed. This problem is not solved in [14] where each transition is assigned a time interval.

To solve this problem and make transitions merging operation always possible, we avoid assigning time intervals to actions transitions. Instead, the timing constraints are assigned to conflicting transitions (cf. time limited offer pattern). The advantage of this solution is twofold:

1) To allow an incremental combination of timing constraints. Figure 7 depicts synchronization between two components $C_{\mathtt{P}}$ and $C_{\mathtt{Q}}$ on action a. Our goal is to define a compositional framework, where each component involved in this synchronization may add timing constraints with respect to the occurrence of action a, such that the global timing constraint on a in $C_{\mathtt{P|[a]|Q}}$ will be the conjunction of several simpler constraints. This implies that when component $C_{\mathtt{P}}$ is ready to execute a, it is forced in the absence of alternative actions, to wait for $C_{\mathtt{Q}}$ to offer a. This may lead for example to the expiration of a limited temporal offer on a in $C_{\mathtt{P}}$. This goal is achieved without explicitly handling time intervals, and the synchronization is modeled as a straightforward transition merging as in untimed Petri nets.
2) Relaxing the TPN's strong semantics. In TPNs the firing of transitions is driven by necessity. Thus an action has to be fired as soon as its

upper bound is reached (except for a transition in conflict with another one). Like process algebras in general, RT-LOTOS favors an interaction point of view, where the actual behavior of a system is influenced by its environment. Thus, an enabled transition may fire within its enabling time window but it cannot be forced to fire. A wide range of real-time systems work on that principle. In particular, soft real-time systems are typical examples of systems that cannot be forced to synchronize with their environment. This behavior would not be possible if the actions transitions were assigned time intervals, because their firing would be driven by necessity. To model necessity in RT-LOTOS we use the `hide` operator. Its combination with the 'temporal limited offering' and the 'latency' operators gives an interesting flexibility in terms of expressiveness.

The synchronization on $\mathtt{a}$ of $C_{\mathtt{P}}$ and $C_{\mathtt{Q}}$ is achieved by merging each $\mathtt{a}$ transition in $C_{\mathtt{P}}$ with each $\mathtt{a}$ transition in $C_{\mathtt{Q}}$, thus creating $n*m$ $\mathtt{a}$ transitions in $C_{\mathtt{P|[a]|Q}}$ (n and m being respectively the number of $\mathtt{a}$ transitions in $C_{\mathtt{P}}$ and $C_{\mathtt{Q}}$).

Let $T_{\mathtt{X}}^{\mathtt{a}}$ be the set of transitions labelled with $\mathtt{a}$ in $C_{\mathtt{X}}$.

$$T_{\mathtt{X}}^{\mathtt{a}} = \{t \in T_{\mathtt{X}} \mid Lab_{\mathtt{X}}(t) = \mathtt{a}\} \qquad\qquad T_{\mathtt{X}}^{\mathtt{A}} = \bigcup_{\mathtt{a}\in\mathtt{A}} T_{\mathtt{X}}^{\mathtt{a}}$$

The net $\Sigma_{\mathtt{P|[A]|Q}}$ is obtained by replacing each transition t_p in $C_{\mathtt{P}}$ with label $\mathtt{a} \in \mathtt{A}$ by a set of transitions (t_p, t_q) such that t_q is also labelled by $\mathtt{a}$, with ${}^\bullet(t_p,t_q) = {}^\bullet t_p \cup {}^\bullet t_q$ and $(t_p,t_q)^\bullet = t_p{}^\bullet \cup t_q{}^\bullet$.
A $[0,\infty)$ temporal interval is associated with the newly created transition (cf. H5).

Note that the two components have to synchronize on `exit` transition to conform to RT-LOTOS semantics. The two output interfaces are merged: $Out = \{out\}$ if $O_{\mathtt{P}} \neq \emptyset \wedge O_{\mathtt{Q}} \neq \emptyset$, $Out = \emptyset$ otherwise.
Let us denote $merge(t_p,t_q) = \langle {}^\bullet t_p \cup {}^\bullet t_q, ((t_p,t_q), IS(t_p)), t_p{}^\bullet \cup t_q{}^\bullet \rangle$; $A' = A \cup \{\mathtt{exit}\}$; $PreOut = T_{\mathtt{P}}^{\mathtt{exit}} \times T_{\mathtt{Q}}^{\mathtt{exit}}$ if $O_{\mathtt{P}} \neq \emptyset \wedge O_{\mathtt{Q}} \neq \emptyset$, $PreOut = \emptyset$ otherwise.

$$\begin{aligned}
C_{\mathtt{P|[A]|Q}} &= \langle \Sigma_{\mathtt{P|[A]|Q}}, Lab_{\mathtt{P|[A]|Q}}, I_{\mathtt{P}} \cup I_{\mathtt{Q}}, Out \rangle \\
\Sigma_{\mathtt{P|[A]|Q}} &= (\Sigma_{\mathtt{P}} \backslash T_{\mathtt{P}}^{\mathtt{A'}} \backslash O_{\mathtt{P}}) \uplus (\Sigma_{\mathtt{Q}} \backslash T_{\mathtt{Q}}^{\mathtt{A'}} \backslash O_{\mathtt{Q}}) \cup \\
\bigcup_{t_p \in T_{\mathtt{P}}^{\mathtt{A'}}, t_q \in T_{\mathtt{Q}}^{\mathtt{A'}}} & merge(t_p,t_q) \cup \langle PreOut, Out, \emptyset \rangle
\end{aligned}$$

$$Lab_{\mathtt{P|[A]|Q}}(t) = \begin{cases} Lab_{\mathtt{X}}(t) & \mathtt{if}\ \ t \in T_{\mathtt{X}}, \mathtt{X} \in \{\mathtt{P},\mathtt{Q}\} \\ \mathtt{a} & \mathtt{if}\ \ t = (t_p,t_q) \wedge t_p \in T_{\mathtt{P}}^{\mathtt{a}} \end{cases}$$

– $C_{\mathtt{P>>Q}}$ (Fig. 8) depicts a sequential composition of $C_{\mathtt{P}}$ and $C_{\mathtt{Q}}$ which means that if $C_{\mathtt{P}}$ successfully completes its execution then it activates $C_{\mathtt{Q}}$. This kind of composition is possible only if $C_{\mathtt{P}}$ has an output interface. The resulting component $C_{\texttt{P>>Q}}$ is obtained by merging the output interface of $C_{\texttt{P}}$ and the input interface of $C_{\texttt{Q}}$, and by hiding the `exit` interaction point of $C_{\texttt{P}}$.

$$C_{\texttt{P>>Q}} = \langle \Sigma_{\texttt{P>>Q}}, Lab_{\texttt{hide exit in P}} \cup Lab_{\texttt{Q}}, I_{\texttt{P}}, 0_{\texttt{Q}} \rangle$$
$$\Sigma_{\texttt{P>>Q}} = \langle P_{\texttt{P}} \backslash O_{\texttt{P}} \cup P_{\texttt{Q}}, T_{\texttt{hide exit in P}} \cup T_{\texttt{Q}}, Pre_{\texttt{P}} \cup Pre_{\texttt{Q}}, Post_{\texttt{P>>Q}}, IS_{\texttt{P}} \cup IS_{\texttt{Q}} \rangle$$
$$Post_{\texttt{P>>Q}} = (Post_{\texttt{P}} \backslash \{(t, O_{\texttt{P}}) \mid t \in {}^{\bullet}O_{\texttt{P}}\}) \cup \{(t, in_{\texttt{Q}}) \mid in_{\texttt{Q}} \in I_{\texttt{Q}} \wedge t \in {}^{\bullet}O_{\texttt{P}}\} \cup Post_{\texttt{Q}}$$

– $C_{\texttt{P[]Q}}$ (Fig. 9) is the component which behaves either as $C_{\texttt{P}}$ or $C_{\texttt{Q}}$.
We do not specify whether the choice between the alternatives is made by the component $C_{\texttt{P[]Q}}$ itself, or by the environment. Anyway, it should be made at the level of the first actions in the component. In other words, the occurrence of one of the first actions in either component determines which component will continue its execution and which one must be deactivated. The problem can be viewed as a competition between $C_{\texttt{P}}$ and $C_{\texttt{Q}}$. These two components compete to execute their first action. As long as the that action has not yet occurred, $C_{\texttt{P}}$ and $C_{\texttt{Q}}$ age similarly, which means that *Time* transitions (labeled by tv, delay or latency) may occur in both components without any consequence on the choice of the wining component. Once one first action has occurred, the control is irreversibly transferred to the winning component, the other one being deactivated, in the sense that it no longer contains enabled transitions. The choice operator is known to cause trouble in presence of initial parallelism. [15] defines a choice operator where each alternative has just one initial place. Therefore, none of the alternative allows any initial parallelism. We think that it is a strong restriction. We do not impose any constraint on the choice alternatives.
The solution we propose to define a choice between two components is as follows: to obtain the intended behavior, we introduce a set of special places, called *lock* places. Those places belong to the input interface of component $C_{\texttt{P[]Q}}$. Their function is to undertake control transfer between the two components. For each first action of $C_{\texttt{P}}$ we introduce one lock place per concurrent first action in $C_{\texttt{Q}}$ (for instance `a` has one concurrent action in $C_{\texttt{Q}}$: `c`, while `c` has two concurrent actions in $C_{\texttt{P}}$: `a` and `b`) and vice versa. A lock place interacts only with those transitions representing the set of initial actions and the time labeled transitions they are related with (delay for `a` and tv for `b`). *Time* transitions restore the token in the lock place, since they do not represent an action occurrence, but a time progression which has not to interfere with the execution of the other component (as long as the first action has not occurred, the two components age similarly). The occurrence of an initial action of $C_{\texttt{P}}$ (respectively $C_{\texttt{Q}}$) locks the execution of $C_{\texttt{Q}}$ (respectively $C_{\texttt{P}}$) by stealing the token from the lock places related to all $C_{\texttt{Q}}$'s (respectively $C_{\texttt{P}}$'s) first actions.
A unique *out* place is created by merging the *out* places of $C_{\texttt{P}}$ and $C_{\texttt{Q}}$.

– $C_{\texttt{P[>Q}}$ (Fig. 10) is the component representing the behavior where component $C_{\texttt{P}}$ can be interrupted by $C_{\texttt{Q}}$ at any time during its execution. It means that at any point during the execution of $C_{\texttt{P}}$, there is a choice between executing one of the next actions from $C_{\texttt{P}}$ or one of the first actions from $C_{\texttt{Q}}$. For

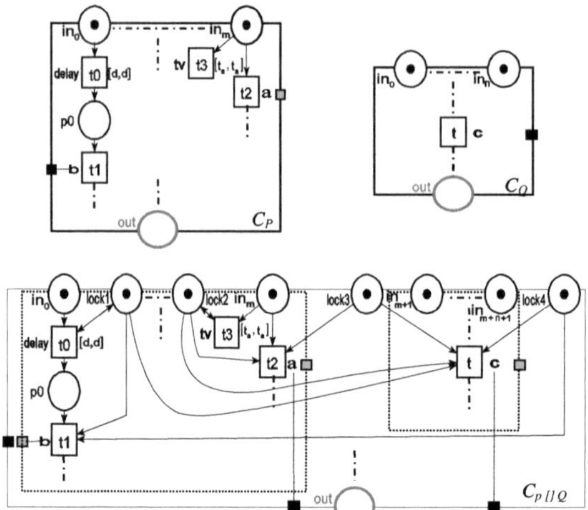

Fig. 9. Choice between $C_{\mathtt{P}}$ and $C_{\mathtt{Q}}$

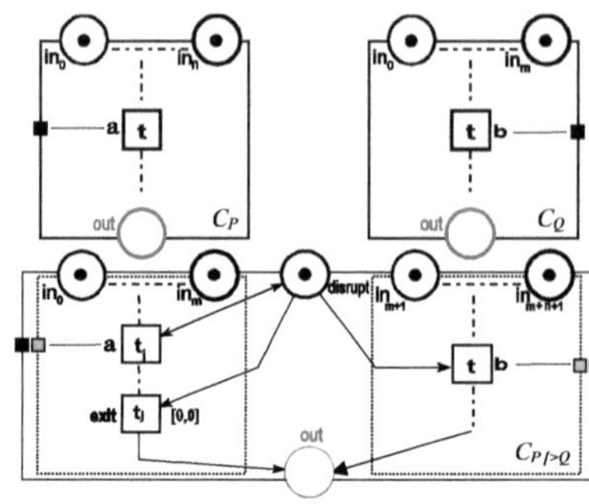

Fig. 10. The disrupt pattern

this purpose, $C_{\mathtt{Q}}$ *steals* the token from the shared place named `disrupt` (which belongs to the input interface of $C_{\mathtt{P\,[>Q}}$), thus the control is irreversibly transferred from $C_{\mathtt{P}}$ to $C_{\mathtt{Q}}$ (`disrupt` is an *input* place for $C_{\mathtt{Q}}$ first action and `exit` transition of $C_{\mathtt{P}}$, it is also an *input/output* place for all the others transitions of $C_{\mathtt{P}}$). Once an action from $C_{\mathtt{Q}}$ is chosen, $C_{\mathtt{Q}}$ continues executing, and transitions of $C_{\mathtt{P}}$ are no longer enabled.

4.3 Formal Proof of the Translation Consistency

We prove that the translation preserves the RT-LOTOS semantics and that the defined compositional framework preserves the good properties (H1–H5) of the components. This is done by induction: assuming that some components $C_1, ..., C_n$ are respectively *equivalent* to some RT-LOTOS terms $T_1, ..., T_n$, and given a RT-LOTOS operator Op, we prove that the pattern applied to $C_1, ..., C_n$ gives a component which is equivalent to the term $Op(T_1, ..., T_n)$ (the behavior over time must be accounted for).

The proof is carried out in two steps:

- we first define a more informative RT-LOTOS semantics, which does not introduce any new operation, but explicitly acquaints the occurrence of *time-events*. A *time-event* represents the expiration of an RT-LOTOS temporal operator. As an illustration, let us consider the rule of the limited offering as it appears in the original semantics of RT-LOTOS. In the following rule, any delay $d' > d$ will *silently* transform a process `a{d};P` into `stop`.

$$\mathtt{a\{d\};P} \xrightarrow{d'} \mathtt{stop} \tag{1}$$

In the augmented RT-LOTOS semantics, a "tv" transition is introduced to denote the limited offer expiration (cf 2).

$$\texttt{a\{d\};P} \xrightarrow{d} \texttt{a\{0\};P} \xrightarrow{tv} \texttt{stop} \xrightarrow{d'-d} \texttt{stop} \qquad (2)$$

A delay $d' > d$ is of course still allowed from `a{d};P`, but it is splited into three steps: a delay d, a "temporal violation" (tv), and a delay $d' - d$.

It is easy to define a branching bisimulation[5] which abstracts from the occurence of the newly added *time-event* transitions and show that the new semantics of RT-LOTOS is branching bisimilar to the original semantics of RT-LOTOS.

- We then prove that the semantic model of the components is strongly timed bisimilar to this more informative RT-LOTOS semantics. Intuitively an RT-LOTOS term and a component are timed bisimilar [16] iff they perform the same action at the same time and reach bisimilar states. For each operator, we prove that, from each reachable state, if the occurrence of a time progression (respectively an action) is possible in an RT-LOTOS term, it is also possible in its associated component, and conversely. Therefore, we ensure that the translation preserves the sequences of possible actions but also the occurrence dates of these actions. It is worth to mention that during the execution of a component the structure of the encapsulated TPN remains the same; only the markings are different, while the structure of an RT-LOTOS term may change through its execution. As a result, the TPN encapsulated in a component may not directly correspond to an RT-LOTOS behavior translation but is strongly bisimilar with a TPN which does correspond to an RT-LOTOS expression translation (The same TPN and current state without the unrechable structure).

Let us illustrate the template of the proof on the parallel synchronization.

Notation. A paragraph starting with $\xrightarrow{\mathbb{R}}$ proves that each time progression which applies to the RT-LOTOS term is acceptable in its associated component. Conversely, $\xleftarrow{\mathbb{R}}$ denotes the opposite proof. Similarly $\xrightarrow{a}$ and $\xleftarrow{a}$ are used for the proof on actions occurrences.

Proof of the synchronization Pattern (Fig. 7)

$\xrightarrow{\mathbb{R}}$: A time progression is acceptable in $C_{\texttt{P|[A]|Q}}$ iff it is acceptable for each enabled transition.

By construction, $T_{\texttt{P|[A]|Q}} = (T_{\texttt{P}} \backslash T_{\texttt{P}}^{\texttt{A'}}) \cup (T_{\texttt{Q}} \backslash T_{\texttt{Q}}^{\texttt{A'}}) \cup E$, with E the set of newly created transitions: $E = \bigcup_{t_p \in T_{\texttt{P}}^{\texttt{A'}}, t_q \in T_{\texttt{Q}}^{\texttt{A'}}} merge(t_p, t_q)$.

Let t be an enabled transition of $C_{\texttt{P|[A]|Q}}$.

If t is in $(T_{\texttt{P}} \backslash T_{\texttt{P}}^{\texttt{A'}})$, by construction this time progression is acceptable for t since its initial timing constraint in $C_{\texttt{P}}$ has not been changed, and it is not involved in the synchronization. The same applies if t is in $(T_{\texttt{Q}} \backslash T_{\texttt{Q}}^{\texttt{A'}})$.

[5] Our temporal branching bisimulation looks like the weak bisimulation of CCS which abstracts the internal actions. The difference with ours is that the *time-event* transitions do not resolve the choice and the disabling contrary to the internal actions of CCS.

If t is in E, we show that $Lab(t) \neq \texttt{exit}$. Let us assume that $Lab(t) = \texttt{exit}$. By construction, it exists t_p and t_q such that $t = (t_p, t_q)$ and $Lab(t_p) = Lab(t_q) = \texttt{exit}$. `exit` is a special urgent action (cf. H5), its execution is enforced as soon as it is enabled. By construction ${}^\bullet t = {}^\bullet t_p \cup {}^\bullet t_q$: if t is enabled, then t_p is enabled in $C_{\texttt{P}}$ and t_q is enabled in $C_{\texttt{Q}}$. The enabling of t_p and t_q precludes any time progression. By induction, it precludes time progression in `P` and `Q` and then in `P|[A]|Q` ($\overset{\mathbb{R}}{\not\rightarrow}$).

From H5, we have that all non `exit` transitions in E are associated with a time interval equal to $[0, \infty)$. Therefore, time progression is also acceptable in $C_{\texttt{P|[A]|Q}}$.

$\overset{\mathbb{R}}{\longleftarrow}$**:** The proof is similar to $\overset{\mathbb{R}}{\longrightarrow}$.

$\overset{a}{\longrightarrow}$**:** Assuming `P|[A]|Q` $\overset{a}{\longrightarrow}$, is this action acceptable for $C_{\texttt{P|[A]|Q}}$?

Two cases must be discussed: either action `a` is a synchronization action between `P` and `Q` (`a` $\in$ `A'`), or it is not.

Case a$\in$A': A synchronization action `a` is possible in `P|[A]|Q` iff it is possible in `P` and in `Q`. By induction, it exists transitions t_p and t_q labelled by a firable in $C_{\texttt{P}}$ and in $C_{\texttt{Q}}$.

That is to say, marking ${}^\bullet p_t \subseteq M_{\texttt{P}}$, and the same for `Q`. By construction, we have ${}^\bullet(t_p, t_q) = {}^\bullet t_p \cup {}^\bullet t_q$, then the marking $M_{\texttt{P|[A]|Q}}$ enables (t_p, t_q). After the firing, the marking of $C_{\texttt{P|[A]|Q}}$ can be seen as the union of the one of $C_{\texttt{P'}}$ and $C_{\texttt{Q'}}$ because $(t_p, t_q)^\bullet = t_p{}^\bullet \cup t_q{}^\bullet$.

Case a$\notin$A': If action `a` occurs in `P|[A]|Q` it either is an action of `P` or an action of `Q`. By induction hypothesis, it is either a firable transition in $C_{\texttt{P}}$ or in $C_{\texttt{Q}}$. Since this transition is not modified in $C_{\texttt{P|[A]|Q}}$, it is firable in $C_{\texttt{P|[A]|Q}}$.

$\overset{a}{\longleftarrow}$**:** Similarly to $\overset{a}{\longrightarrow}$.

5 Tools and Experiments

5.1 Tools

RTL. The Real-Time LOTOS Laboratory developed by LAAS-CNRS [17], takes as input an RT-LOTOS specification and generates either a simulation trace or a reachability graph. RTL generates a minimal reachability graph preserving the CTL[6] properties.

TINA. (TIme petri Net Analyzer [3]) is a software environment to edit and analyze Petri nets and Time Petri nets.

TINA offers various abstract state space constructions that preserve specific classes of properties of the concrete state space of the nets. Those classes of properties include general properties (reachability properties, deadlock freeness, liveness), and specific properties.

[6] Computational Tree Logic.

```
specification scenario: exit
behavior hide sA, sBC, eAB, eC in
( (
       (sA; delay(3,6)eAB{3}; exit)
   ||| (sBC; delay(3,8)eC{5}; exit)
  )
  |[sBC, eAB]|
  (sBC; delay(3,5)eAB{2}; exit)
)
|[sA,sBC]|
(sA; latency(inf)sBC; exit)
endspec
```

Fig. 11. RT-LOTOS specification of the Multimedia scenario

RTL2TPN. is a translator prototype, which implements the translation pattern of Sect. 4. It takes as an input an RT-LOTOS specification and outputs a TPN in the format accepted by TINA. RTL2TPN reuses RTL's parser and type-checker.

5.2 Case Studies

Multimedia scenario. The author of this multimedia scenario wants to present 3 medias named A, B and C, respectively. The duration of these medias are respectively defined by the following time intervals [3,6], [3,5] and [3,8]. This means that the presentation of the media A will last at least 3 sec and at most 6 sec. From the author's point of view, any duration of the media presentation is acceptable, as long as it belongs to the specified time interval. Besides, the author expresses the following global synchronization constraints:

1) The presentation of medias A and B must end simultaneously.
2) The presentation of medias B and C must start simultaneously .
3) The beginning of the multimedia scenario is determined by the beginning of A and its termination is determined by the end of A and B, or by the end of C (cf Fig. 12(a)).

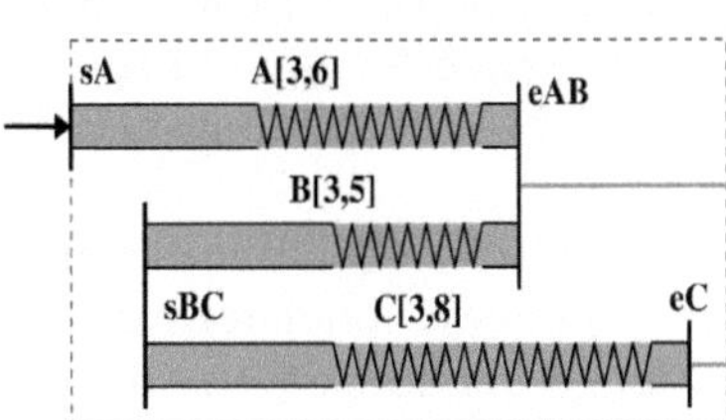

(a) The MM constraints .44

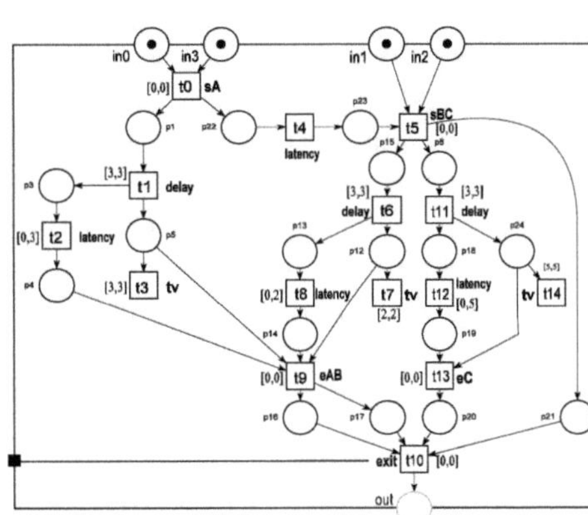

(b) The component

Fig. 12(b) depicts the associated TPN generated by RTL2TPN. For this example TINA builds a graph of 230 classes and 598 transitions.

The scenario is potentially consistent because it exists a path starting by action sA (sA characterizes the beginning of the scenario) and leading to the end of scenario presentation (occurrence of either eAB or eC).

Dinning philosophers. We use one well known multi-process synchronization problem: the Dinning philosophers to check the robustness of the solutions proposed in the paper while facing a state explosion situation. We propose a timed extension of the problem which goes like this: A certain number of philosophers, sitting around a round table spend their lives thinking and eating. Each of them has in front of him a bowl of rice. Between each philosopher and his neighbor is a chopstick. Each philosopher thinks for a while, then gets hungry and wants to eat. In order to eat, he has to get two chopsticks. Once a philosopher picks his left chopstick, it will take him between 0 and 10 seconds to take the right one. Once he possesses two chopsticks, he can begin eating and it will take him 10 to 1000 seconds[7] to finish eating, then he puts back down his left chopstick and the right one in a delay between 0 to 10 seconds.

```
process Philosopher[think,hungry,b_eat,e_eat,
                    pick_left,put_left,pick_right,put_right]:noexit :=
think; hungry; pick_left;latency(10)pick_right; b_eat;
delay(10,1000)e_eat;put_left;latency(10)put_right;
Philosopher[think,hungry,b_eat,e_eat,pick_left,put_left,pick_right,put_right]
endproc

process Chopstick[pick,put] :noexit :=
pick ; put ; Chopstick[pick,put]
endproc
```

Fig. 12. RT-LOTOS specification of the dinning philosophers

The RT-LOTOS specification of the problem consists in the parallel synchronization of different instances of processes Philosopher and Chopstick[8] (cf Fig 12).

Timed Milner scheduler. This is a temporal extension of Milner's scheduler problem [18]. The interesting point about this example is that the timing constraints as introduced in the system, do not increase the state space (compared to the untimed version of the problem). However they complicate the computation of the system's state space.

Let us consider a ring of n process called Cyclers. A Cycler should cycle endlessly as follows: (i) Be enabled by predecessor at g_i, (ii) after a non deterministic delay between 0 and 10 units of time, receive initiation request at a_i, (iii) after a certain amount of time between 10 and 100 units of time, it receives a termination signal at b_i and enables its successor at g_{i+1}(in either order).

[7] delay and latency may be expressed together by a single syntactic construct delay(dmin, dmax)meaning delay(dmin)latency(dmax-dmin).

[8] All the experiments described in this paper have been performed on a PC with 512 Mo memory and a processor at 3.2 GHz.

```
process cycler[g_i,a_i,b_i,g_i+1] : noexit:=

 g_i; latency(10)a_i; delay(10,100)
 (
 (b_i;latency(10)g_i+1;cycler[g_i,a_i,b_i,g_i+1])
  []
 (g_i+1;latency(10)b_i;cycler[g_i,a_i,b_i,g_i+1])
 )

endproc
```

```
Specification SCHEDULER: noexit
Behaviour
Hide g_1..g_n,a_1..a_n,b_1..b_n in
(cycler[g_1,a_1,b_1,g_2]
  |[g_1,g_2]|
  (...
   cycler[g_i,a_i,b_i,g_i+1]
   |[g_i+1]|
   ...
(cycler[g_n,a_n,b_n,g_1] ||| g_1;stop)...)
```

Fig. 13. RT-LOTOS specification of the timed Milner scheduler

Table 1. Performance comparison of RTL2TPN+TINA vs RTL

	RTL2TPN+TINA		RTL	
	Classes/Transitions	CPU(sec)	Classes/Transitions	CPU(sec)
2 **Philosophers**	89/ 150	<1	64/ 120	<1
3	653/ 1536	<1	530/ 1395	3
4	66 251/ 220 488	4	?	>24h
5	876 090/ 3 668 235	103	-	-
2 **Cyclers**	35/ 50	<1	31/ 57	<1
3	81/ 141	<1	58/ 115	<1
4	127/ 232	<1	77/ 153	<1
5	161/ 316	<1	96/ 191	3
6	219/ 414	<1	115/ 229	18
7	232/ 432	<1	134/ 267	97
8	311/ 596	<1	153/ 305	490
9	357/ 687	<1	172/ 343	2363
10	461/ 911	<1	?	>24

The reachability algorithm implemented in RTL is exponential in number of clocks. As the number of philosophers (respectively Cyclers) grows RTL does not challenge TINA's runtime performances. However the size of state space generated by RTL for the RT-LOTOS specifications is more compact than the one generated by TINA for the associated TPNs issued by RTL2TPN. This is due to a useful but however expensive minimization procedure carried out in RTL. This minimization adapted from [19] permits to consider regions larger than the ones required from a strict reachability point of view, thereby minimizing the number of regions.

6 Related Work

Much work has been done on translating process algebras into Petri Nets, by giving a Petri net semantics to process terms [20,15,21]. [21] suggests that a good net semantics should satisfy the retrievability principle, meaning that no new "auxiliary" transitions should be introduced in the reachability graph of the Petri net. [20,15] do not satisfy this criterion. In this paper, we define a one-to-one mapping which is compliant with this strong recommendation.

Untimed models. A survey of the literature indicates that proposals for LOTOS to Petri net translations essentially deal with the untimed version of LOTOS [22,23,24,25,26,27]. The opposite translation has been discussed by [26] where only a subset of LOTOS is considered, and by [28] where the authors addressed the translation of Petri nets with inhibitor arcs into basic LOTOS by mapping places and transitions into LOTOS expressions. [25] demonstrated the possibility to verify LOTOS specifications using verification techniques developed for Petri nets by implementing a Karp and Miller procedure in the LOTOS world.

Among all these approaches, [22,27] is the only one operating a complete translation of LOTOS (it handles both the control and data parts of LOTOS). Moreover, it just considers regular LOTOS terms, and so do we. The LOTOS to PN translation algorithms of [22,27] were implemented in the CAESAR tool. Besides the temporal aspects addressed in this paper, a technical difference with [22,27] lies in the way we structure TPNs. Our solution is based on TPNs components. In our approach, a component may contain several tokens. Conversely, [22,27] structures Petri nets into units, each of them containing one token at most. This invariant limits the size of markings, and permits optimizations on memory consumption. The counterpart is that [22,27] use ϵ-transitions. The latter introduces non determinism. They are eliminated when the underlying automaton is generated (by transitive closure). The use of ϵ-transitions may be inefficient in some particular cases, such as the example provided in [29].

The major theoretical study on taking advantage of both Petri nets and process algebras is presented in [12]. The proposed solution is Petri Box Calculus (PBC), a generic model that embodies both process algebra and Petri nets. The authors start from Petri nets to come up with a CCS-like process algebra whose operators may straightforwardly be expressed by means of Petri nets.

Timed models. [30] pioneered work on timed enhancements of the control part of LOTOS inspired by timed Petri nets models. [31] defined a mapping from TPNs to TE-LOTOS which makes it possible to incorporate basic blocks specified as 1-bounded TPNs into TE-LOTOS specifications. However, because of the strong time semantics of TPNs (a transition is fired as soon as the upper bound of its time interval is reached unless it conflicts with another one) a direct mapping was not always possible.

A Timed extension of PBC has been proposed in [14]. Although the component model proposed in this paper is not a specification model but an intermediate model used as gateway between RT-LOTOS and TPNs, we find it important to compare our work with [14].

Of prime interest to us is the way [14] introduces temporal constraints in his framework by providing each action with two time bounds representing the earliest firing time and latest firing time. This approach is directly inspired by TPNs, where the firing of actions is driven by necessity. However, a well known issue with this strategy is that it is badly compatible with a compositional and incremental building of specifications. The main difficulty is to compose time intervals when dealing with actions synchronization. The operational semantics of

[14] relies on intervals intersection to calculate a unique time interval for a synchronized transition. However, this approach is not always satisfactory(see [13]).

7 Conclusion

Search for efficiency in RT-LOTOS specification verification is the main motivation behind the work presented in this paper. We propose a transformational approach between RT-LOTOS, which is a compositional FDT, and Time Petri Nets, which are not. The semantics of the two FDTS are compared. In order to bridge the gap between RT-LOTOS and TPNs, the latter are embedded into components that may be composed. RT-LOTOS-to-TPN translation patterns are defined in order to match the RT-LOTOS composition operators. The translation has been formally proved to be semantics preserving. The patterns have been implemented in a prototype tool which takes as input an RT-LOTOS specification and outputs a TPN in a format that may be processed by TINA [3]. The benchmarks provided in Section 6 demonstrate the interest of the proposed approach.

One major contribution of the paper is to give RT-LOTOS an underlying semantics expressed in terms of TPNS and to clarify the use of RT-LOTOS operators, in particular the *latency* operator. Discussion in this paper is nevertheless limited to the control part of the RT-LOTOS FDT defined in [2]. We have recently extended our work to the data part of RT-LOTOS. RT-LOTOS specifications will be translated into the new format supported by TINA: Predicates/Actions Time Petri nets. The latter enhance the modelling capabilities of TPNs with global variables associated with the nets together with predicates and actions associated with transitions.

The verification approach developed for RT-LOTOS is being adapted to TURTLE, a real-time UML profile based on RT-LOTOS. We thus expect to develop an interface between the TURTLE toolkit [32] and TINA.

References

1. ISO - Information processing systems - Open Systems Interconnection: LOTOS - a formal description technique based on the temporal ordering of observational behaviour. ISO International Standard 8807:1989, ISO (1989)
2. Courtiat, J.P., Santos, C., Lohr, C., Outtaj, B.: Experience with RT-LOTOS, a temporal extension of the LOTOS formal description technique. Computer Communications **23**(12) (2000)
3. Berthomieu, B., Ribet, P., Vernadat, F.: The TINA tool: Construction of abstract state space for Petri nets and time Petri nets. Int. Journal of Production Research **42**(14) (2004)
4. Milner, R.: Communications and Concurrency. Prentice Hall (1989)
5. Hoare, C.: Communicating Sequential Processes. Prentice-Hall (1985)
6. Courtiat, J.P.: Formal design of interactive multimedia documents. In H.Konig, M.Heiner, A., ed.: Proc. of 23rd IFIP WG 6.1 Int Conf on Formal Techniques for Networked and distributed systems (FORTE'2003). Volume 2767 of LNCS. (2003)

7. Courtiat, J.P., de Oliveira, R.: On RT-LOTOS and its application to the formal design of multimedia protocols. Annals of Telecommunications **50**(11–12) (1995) 888–906
8. Merlin, P.: A study of the recoverability of computer system. PhD thesis, Dep. Comput. Sci., Univ. California, Irvine (1974)
9. Merlin, P., Faber, D.J.: Recoverability of communication protocols. IEEE Transactions on Communications **COM-24**(9) (1976)
10. Berthomieu, B., Menasche, M.: Une approche par énumération pour l'analyse des réseaux de Petri temporels. In: Actes de la conférence IFIP'83. (1983) 71–77
11. Berthomieu, B., Diaz, M.: Modeling and verification of time dependant systems using Time Petri Nets. IEEE Transactions on Software Engineering **17**(3) (1991)
12. Best, E., Devillers, R., Koutny, M.: Petri Net Algebra. Monographs in Theoretical Computer Science: An EATCS Series. Springer-Verlag (2001) ISBN: 3-540-67398-9.
13. Sadani, T., Boyer, M., de Saqui-Sannes, P., Courtiat, J.P.: Effective representation of regular RT-LOTOS terms by finite time petri nets. Technical Report 05605, LAAS/CNRS (2006)
14. Koutny, M.: A compositional model of time Petri nets. In: Proc. of the 21st Int. Conf. on Application and Theory of Petri Nets (ICATPN 2000). Number 1825 in LNCS, Aarhus, Denmark, Springer-Verlag (2000) 303–322
15. Taubner, D.: Finite Representations of CCS and TCSP Programs by Automata and Petri Nets. Number 369 in LNCS. Springer-Verlag (1989)
16. Yi, W.: Real-time behaviour of asynchronous agents. In: Proc. of Int. Conf on Theories of Concurrency: Unification and Extension (CONCUR). Volume 458 of LNCS. (1990)
17. RT-LOTOS: Real-time LOTOS home page. (http://www.laas.fr/RT-LOTOS/)
18. Milner, R.: A calculus of communication systems. Volume 92 of LNCS. (1980)
19. Yannakakis, M., Lee, D.: An efficient algorithm for minimizing real-time transition system. In: Proc. of f the Conf. on Computer-Aided Verification (CAV). Volume 697 of LNCS., Berlin (1993)
20. Goltz, U.: On representing CCS programs by finite Petri nets. In: Proc. of Int. Conf. on Math. Foundations of Computer Science. Volume 324 of LNCS. (1988)
21. Olderog, E.R.: Nets, Terms, and formulas. Cambridge University Press (1991)
22. Garavel, H., Sifakis, J.: Compilation and verification of LOTOS specifications. In Logrippo, L., et al., eds.: Protocol Specification, Testing and Verification, X. Proceedings of the IFIP WG 6.1 Tenth International Symposium, 1990, Ottawa, Ont., Canada, Amsterdam, Netherlands, North-Holland (1990) 379–394
23. Barbeau, M., von Bochmann, G.: Verification of LOTOS specifications: A Petri net based approach. In: Proc. of Canadian Conf. on Electrical and Computer Engineering. (1990)
24. Larrabeiti, D., Quelmada, J., Pavón, S.: From LOTOS to Petri nets through expansion. In Gotzhein, R., Bredereke, J., eds.: Proc. of Int. Conf. on Formal Description Techniques and Theory, application and tools (FORTE/PSV'96). (1996)
25. Barbeau, M., von Bochmann, G.: Extension of the Karp and Miller procedure to LOTOS specifications. Discrete Mathematics and Theoretical Computer Science **3** (1991) 103–119
26. Barbeau, M., von Bochmann, G.: A subset of LOTOS with the computational power of place/transition-nets. In: Proc. of the 14th Int. Conf. on Application and Theory of Petri Nets (ICATPN). Volume 691 of LNCS. (1993)
27. Garavel, H., Lang, F., Mateescu, R.: An overview of cadp 2001. European Association for software science and technology (EASST) Newsletter **4** (2002)

28. Sisto, R., Valenzano, A.: Mapping Petri nets with inhibitor arcs onto basic LOTOS behavior expressions. IEEE Transactions on computers **44**(12) (1995) 1361–1370
29. Sadani, T., Courtiat, J., de Saqui-Sannes, P.: From RT-LOTOS to time Petri nets. new foundations for a verification platform. In: Proc. of 3rd IEEE Int Conf on Software Engineering and Formal Methods (SEFM). (2005)
30. Bolognesi, T., Lucidi, F., Trigila, S.: From timed Petri nets to timed LOTOS. In: Protocol Specification, Testing and Verification X (PSTV), Proceedings of the IFIP WG6.1 Tenth International Symposium on Protocol. (1990) 395–408
31. Durante, L., Sisto, R., Valenzano, A.: Integration of time Petri net and TE-LOTOS in the design and evaluation of factory communication systems. In: Proc. of the 2nd IEEE Workshop on Factory Communications Systems (WFCS'97). (1997)
32. Apvrille, L., Courtiat, J.P., Lohr, C., de Saqui-Sannes, P.: TURTLE : A real-time UML profile supported by a formal validation toolkit. IEEE Transactions on Software Engineering **30**(4) (2004)

Reasoning Algebraically About Probabilistic Loops

Larissa Meinicke and Ian J. Hayes

School of Information Technology and Electrical Engineering,
The University of Queensland, Brisbane, Australia

Abstract. Back and von Wright have developed algebraic laws for reasoning about loops in the refinement calculus. We extend their work to reasoning about probabilistic loops in the probabilistic refinement calculus. We apply our algebraic reasoning to derive transformation rules for probabilistic action systems. In particular we focus on developing data refinement rules for probabilistic action systems. Our extension is interesting since some well known transformation rules that are applicable to standard programs are not applicable to probabilistic ones: we identify some of these important differences and we develop alternative rules where possible. In particular, our probabilistic action system data refinement rules are new.

1 Introduction

Back and von Wright [5] have used algebraic rules from fixpoint theory to derive transformation rules for loop constructs in the refinement calculus [2,15]. Such transformation rules may be used to reason about practical program derivations, such as data refinement and atomicity refinement of action systems. These practical program derivations were traditionally verified using either informal or semantic arguments [5]. The algebraic approach has advantages over these methods because it can be used to construct simpler proofs that are easier to check. Here we extend the work of Back and von Wright to develop transformation rules for loop constructs in the probabilistic refinement calculus [13], and we demonstrate how these rules may be used to generate data refinement rules for probabilistic action systems. Many of the transformation rules that are presented here are the same as those for standard (non-probabilistic) programs, however some of them are not, in particular our data refinement rules for probabilistic action systems are new. Others (for example McIver and Morgan [13] and Hurd [11]) have demonstrated how to reason formally about probabilistic loops, using invariant based techniques, directly in probabilistic program semantics. Our work on reasoning algebraically about loop transformations may be seen as a complement to theirs, and vice versa.

In the standard refinement calculus [2], sequential imperative programs that may include angelic and demonic nondeterminism are represented using *predicate transformers*. The probabilistic refinement calculus [13] is a generalisaton of the refinement calculus, in which programs may also include discrete probabilistic

Z. Liu and J. He (Eds.): ICFEM 2006, LNCS 4260, pp. 380–399, 2006.

choice. Probabilistic programs are modeled using *expectation transformers*. Standard programs that may include demonic, but not angelic nondeterminism, are characterised by the *conjunctive* predicate transformers. Likewise the property that characterises probabilistic programs that may include discrete probabilistic choice and demonic, but not angelic nondeterminism, is *sublinearity*. We find that some well known algebraic laws that apply to conjunctive predicate transformers, do not in general apply to sublinear expectation transformers. We identify some of these important rules and supply alternative ones where possible.

In the following section we briefly describe the *expectation transformer* model of Morgan and McIver [13] for probabilistic programs. We extend this model so that miraculous programs can be expressed, and we verify that sublinear expectation transformers are *cocontinuous*. In Sect. 3 the iteration constructs are introduced, and algebraic properties of these constructs are presented and verified. Probabilistic action systems are introduced in Sect. 4, and algebraic rules are constructed to reason about them: in particular we focus on data refinement rules.

2 Expectation Transformers as Program Statements

Standard (non-probabilistic) imperative programs may be described using a weakest precondition semantics [9], similarly imperative probabilistic programs in which discrete probabilistic choices as well as angelic and demonic nondeterministic choices may be made, may be described using the weakest expectation semantics of McIver and Morgan [13]. We assume that the reader is familiar with such semantics and the basic notions of probabilistic program refinement, as well as the predicate transformer semantics of standard (non-probabilistic programs). We briefly describe the notion of states, expectations and expectation transformers that are used in this paper. Note that we have extended the work of McIver and Morgan to deal with miraculous programs so that we may express guards. This extension is conservative: we explain the minor differences in the model.

2.1 Expectation Transformers

In order to simplify our reasoning we assume that we are only dealing with programs over finite state spaces[1]. An expectation on a state space Σ is a function from Σ to $\mathbb{R}^{\infty}_{\geq 0}$, where $\mathbb{R}^{\infty}_{\geq 0}$ is defined as $\mathbb{R}_{\geq 0} \cup \{\infty\}$. (McIver and Morgan define expectations to be functions from states to the positive real numbers (excluding infinity) [13]. We extend this to include infinity so that we may model miraculous programs.)

Fig. 1 formally defines the set of expectations, and operators that are defined on them. Expectations are ordered with respect to the $\leq$ operator. Predicates,

[1] McIver and Morgan have extended their work on expectation transformer semantics to deal with infinite state spaces [13]. Our finite state space assumption mainly influences our proof of cocontinuity, which we believe will be able to be verified using a more complex proof for infinite state spaces.

Let ϕ and ψ be of type $\mathcal{E}\Sigma$, c be a constant of type $\mathbb{R}_{\geq 0}$. When applied to real numbers, $\sqcap$ is the minimum operator (meet), $\sqcup$ is the maximum operator (join), and $\times$ denotes multiplication.

$\mathcal{E}\Sigma$	$\Sigma \to \mathbb{R}^{\infty}_{\geq 0}$
$\phi \leq \psi$	$\forall \sigma : \Sigma \bullet \phi.\sigma \leq \psi.\sigma$
$\phi \times \psi$	$\lambda \sigma : \Sigma \bullet \phi.\sigma \times \psi.\sigma$
$\phi \sqcup \psi$	$\lambda \sigma : \Sigma \bullet \phi.\sigma \sqcup \psi.\sigma$
$\phi \sqcap \psi$	$\lambda \sigma : \Sigma \bullet \phi.\sigma \sqcap \psi.\sigma$
$\phi * c$	$\lambda \sigma : \Sigma \bullet \phi.\sigma \times c$
$\phi \ominus c$	$\lambda \sigma : \Sigma \bullet (\phi.\sigma - c) \sqcup 0$
$\neg\phi$	$\lambda \sigma : \Sigma \bullet 1 - \phi.\sigma$

Fig. 1. Expectation notation

$\Sigma \to \{0, 1\}$, are a subset of expectations: we equate the boolean value true with 1 and false with 0. Predicate True is defined as $(\lambda\,\sigma \bullet 1)$, and False is defined as $(\lambda\,\sigma \bullet 0)$. For predicates we use the operator $\wedge$ to mean $\sqcap$, and $\vee$ to mean $\sqcup$. The set of all expectations forms a complete lattice, where the top expectation is $(\lambda\,\sigma \bullet \infty)$, and the least expectation is False.

Expectation transformers are used to model probabilistic programs [13]. An expectation transformer is a function from expectations on the output state space, Γ, to expectations on the input state space, Σ. Expectation transformers are the probabilistic equivalent of predicate transformers in the refinement calculus [2]: given an expectation transformer S and an expectation ϕ on the output state space, $S.\phi$ returns the weakest expectation of ϕ in program S. Refinement between two expectation transformers $S, T : \mathcal{E}\Gamma \to \mathcal{E}\Sigma$ is defined as follows.

$$S \sqsubseteq T \triangleq \forall \phi : \mathcal{E}\Gamma \bullet S.\phi \leq T.\phi$$

The set of all expectation transformers forms a complete lattice, where the top element is magic, and the least element is abort (see Fig. 2).

Basic Operators. The four basic composition operators: probabilistic, demonic, and angelic choice, and sequential composition, are shown in Fig. 2. The iteration operators, which are discussed in Sect. 3, have the highest precedence, followed by sequential composition, and then with equal precedence demonic, angelic, and probabilistic choice. From initial state σ, the probabilistic choice statement $S\ {}_p\!\oplus S'$, performs S with probability $p.\sigma$, and S' with probability $1 - p.\sigma$. The demonic choice operator on expectation transformers is defined using the meet (pointwise minimum) operator, while the angelic choice operator is defined using the join (pointwise maximum) operator. Given the definition of refinement between expectation transformers, a demonic choice, $S \sqcap S'$, is able to be refined by any probabilistic choice between S and S'. The unit of sequential composition is skip, the program that does not modify the state, and the unit of demonic choice is magic. For predicate g, the assertion command $\{g\}$ aborts from states in which g does not hold and performs no action from states satisfying g, while the guard $[g]$ is miraculous from states which do not satisfy g, and

Let g be a predicate on state space Σ; θ and ϕ be expectations of type $\mathcal{E}\Sigma$; ψ be an expectation of type $\mathcal{E}\Gamma$; S and S' be expectation transformers of type $\mathcal{E}\Gamma \to \mathcal{E}\Sigma$; $R : \mathcal{E}\Theta \to \mathcal{E}\Sigma$; $R' : \mathcal{E}\Gamma \to \mathcal{E}\Theta$; $T : \mathcal{E}\Sigma \to \mathcal{E}\Sigma$; and p a probability function of type $\Sigma \to [0..1]$, where $[0..1]$ is the closed interval from 0 to 1.

assertion	$\{\theta\}.\phi$	$\lambda\,\sigma : \Sigma \bullet \mathsf{if}\ \theta.\sigma = 0\ \mathsf{then}\ 0\ \mathsf{else}\ \theta.\sigma \times \phi.\sigma$
guard	$[g].\phi$	$\lambda\,\sigma : \Sigma \bullet \mathsf{if}\ g.\sigma\ \mathsf{then}\ \phi.\sigma\ \mathsf{else}\ \infty$
bottom	$\mathsf{abort}.\phi$	False
top	$\mathsf{magic}.\phi$	$(\lambda\,\sigma : \Sigma \bullet \infty)$
unit of composition	$\mathsf{skip}.\phi$	ϕ
sequential composition	$(R;\ R').\psi$	$R.(R'.\psi)$
demonic choice	$(S \sqcap S').\psi$	$S.\psi \sqcap S'.\psi$
angelic choice	$(S \sqcup S').\psi$	$S.\psi \sqcup S'.\psi$
probabilistic choice	$(S\ {}_p\!\oplus S').\psi$	$(\{p\};\ S).\psi + (\{\neg p\};\ S').\psi$
strong iteration	$(T^\omega).\phi$	$(\mu\,X \bullet T;\ X \sqcap \mathsf{skip}).\phi)$
weak iteration	$(T^*).\phi$	$(\nu X \bullet T;\ X \sqcap \mathsf{skip}).\phi$
infinite iteration	$(T^\infty).\phi$	$(\mu\,X \bullet T;\ X).\phi$

Fig. 2. Weakest expectation semantics for probabilistic operators

performs no action from other states. The assertion command is also defined more generally when g is an expectation. Note that in this program model, we have chosen to model miraculous program behaviour in such a way that, for any expectation transformer S, program $S\ {}_p\!\oplus \mathsf{magic}$ is miraculous for states σ from which $p.\sigma$ does not equal one. This may seem to be restrictive, and there are other ways to model miraculous behaviour in probabilistic programs in which we are able to distinguish between programs that are miraculous with certain probabilities. It would be interesting to perform a further investigation into such models, however, for the purpose of reasoning about loops and action systems, we find that we do not need such a richer semantics. We must also take care when using such models, since they are unlikely to share the same properties as our current model.

When predicates are used, guards and assertions satisfy many of the same basic properties as they satisfy in the standard refinement calculus [5]. For predicates p, and q,

$$
\begin{array}{llll}
[p];\ [q] & = [p \wedge q] & \{p\};\ \{q\} & = \{p \wedge q\} \\
[p] \sqcap [q] & = [p \vee q] & \{p\} \sqcap \{q\} & = \{p \wedge q\} \\
[p] & = [p];\ \{p\} & \{p\} & = \{p\};\ [p] \\
\mathsf{skip} & \sqsubseteq [p] & \{p\} & \sqsubseteq \mathsf{skip} \\
\{p\} & = [\neg p];\ \mathsf{abort} \sqcap [p] & [p] & = \{\neg p\};\ \mathsf{magic} \sqcup \{p\}
\end{array}
$$

Healthiness Properties. As for predicate transformers, expectation transformers can be classified by a number of *healthiness* properties [13] (Fig. 3). Primarily we consider *sublinear* expectation transformers. The sublinear set of expectation transformers characterise the set of probabilistic programs that may

Let S be an expectation transformer, c_1, c_2, and c be constants of type $\mathbb{R}_{\geq 0}$, β_1 and β_2 be expectations, $\mathcal{B}$ be a directed set of expectations, and $\mathcal{B}'$ be a co-directed set of expectations.

$$(c_1 * S.(\beta_1) + c_2 * S.(\beta_2)) \ominus c \leq S.((c_1 * \beta_1 + c_2 * \beta_2) \ominus c) \qquad \text{(sublinearity)}$$
$$S.\phi \sqcap S.\psi = S.(\phi \sqcap \psi) \qquad \text{(conjunctivity)}$$
$$\beta_1 \leq \beta_2 \Rightarrow S.\beta_1 \leq S.\beta_2 \qquad \text{(monotonicity)}$$
$$S.(\sqcup\beta : \mathcal{B} \bullet \beta) = (\sqcup\beta : \mathcal{B} \bullet S.\beta) \qquad \text{(continuity)}$$
$$S.(\sqcap\beta : \mathcal{B}' \bullet \beta) = (\sqcap\beta : \mathcal{B}' \bullet S.\beta) \qquad \text{(cocontinuity)}$$

Fig. 3. Healthiness properties for expectation transformers

be expressed using a slight variation[2] of the relational probabilistic model of He et al. [10]: a model that captures probabilistic and demonic nondeterministic behaviour, but not angelic nondeterministic behaviour. The operators given in Fig. 2, apart from angelic choice, preserve sublinearity of their arguments. Standard (non-probabilistic) programs with demonic choice, but no angelic choice, are characterised by the set of conjunctive predicate transformers. We have that not all sublinear expectation transformers are conjunctive.

McIver and Morgan [13] have proved that sublinear expectation transformers are *monotonic*, here we prove that they are also *cocontinuous*. Continuity and cocontinuity are important properties because they simplify the treatment of least and greatest fixpoints over a complete lattice. Their definition involves the use of directed, and codirected sets, which are defined as follows [8]. For any subset $\mathcal{B}$ of a partially ordered set $\mathcal{A}$,

$$\mathit{directed}.\mathcal{B} \triangleq \mathcal{B} \neq \{\} \wedge (\forall \alpha, \beta : \mathcal{B} \bullet (\exists \gamma : \mathcal{B} \bullet \alpha \sqsubseteq \gamma \wedge \beta \sqsubseteq \gamma))$$
$$\mathit{codirected}.\mathcal{B} \triangleq \mathcal{B} \neq \{\} \wedge (\forall \alpha, \beta : \mathcal{B} \bullet (\exists \gamma : \mathcal{B} \bullet \gamma \sqsubseteq \alpha \wedge \gamma \sqsubseteq \beta))$$

A codirected set is the dual of a directed set, and cocontinuity is the dual of continuity. Our proof of cocontinuity is similar to McIver and Morgan's proof of bounded continuity [13].

Theorem 1 (cocontinuity). *Sublinear expectation transformers are cocontinuous.*

[2] The original semantics of He et al. did not facilitate the expression of magical behaviour: programs were expressed as a function from input states to non-empty sets of discrete distributions over the output states that satisfy certain closure properties (see [13] for more details). In order to express magical behaviour, we simply remove the assumption that the sets of distributions must be non-empty. McIver and Morgan expressed and verified the correspondence between non-miraculous sublinear expectation transformers and the original model of He et al. [13]. For our minor extension, the same correspondence and proof used by McIver and Morgan still applies.

Proof. For any sublinear expectation transformer $T : \mathcal{E}\Sigma \to \mathcal{E}\Gamma$, and $\mathcal{B}$ a $\leq$-codirected subset of $\mathcal{E}\Sigma$, we are required to show that

$$T.(\sqcap\beta : \mathcal{B} \bullet \beta) = (\sqcap\beta : \mathcal{B} \bullet T.\beta)$$

By monotonicity of expectation transformers we only need to show that $T.(\sqcap\beta : \mathcal{B} \bullet \beta) \geq (\sqcap\beta : \mathcal{B} \bullet T.\beta)$.

For any constant $c > 0$, for each state $\sigma : \Sigma$, there exists an expectation $\beta_\sigma : \mathcal{B}$ such that $\beta_\sigma.\sigma \ominus c \leq (\sqcap\beta : \mathcal{B} \bullet \beta).\sigma$. Since $\mathcal{B}$ is codirected, and the state space Σ is finite we then have that there exists a $\beta_c : \mathcal{B}$ such that for all $\sigma : \Sigma$, $\beta_c.\sigma \leq \beta_\sigma.\sigma$, and hence $\beta_c \ominus c \leq (\sqcap\beta : \mathcal{B} \bullet \beta)$. We then have that

$$\begin{aligned}
& T.(\sqcap\beta : \mathcal{B} \bullet \beta) \\
\geq\ & \{\text{monotonicity and the above}\} \\
& T.(\beta_c \ominus c) \\
\geq\ & \{\text{sublinearity}\} \\
& T.\beta_c \ominus c \\
\geq\ & \{\beta_c \in \mathcal{B} \text{ and monotonicity}\} \\
& (\sqcap\beta : \mathcal{B} \bullet T.\beta) \ominus c
\end{aligned}$$

Which suffices because c may be arbitrarily close to zero. □

Basic Algebraic Properties. Monotonic expectation transformers share the same set of basic algebraic rules as monotonic predicate transformers [19] (Fig. 4). However, unlike conjunctive predicate transformers, in general sublinear expectation transformers satisfy right sub-distributivity $R;\ (S \sqcap T) \sqsubseteq R;\ S \sqcap R;\ T$, but not right distributivity $R;\ (S \sqcap T) = R;\ S \sqcap R;\ T$. For example, given

$$\begin{aligned}
R &\triangleq (x := 0\ {}_{\frac{1}{2}}\!\oplus x := 1) \\
S &\triangleq [x = 0];\ y := 0 \sqcap [x = 1];\ y := 1 \\
T &\triangleq [x = 0];\ y := 1 \sqcap [x = 1];\ y := 0
\end{aligned}$$

Then,

$$\begin{aligned}
&R;\ (S \sqcap T) = (x := 0\ {}_{\frac{1}{2}}\!\oplus x := 1);\ (y := 0 \sqcap y := 1) \\
&R;\ S \sqcap R;\ T = (x, y := 0, 0\ {}_{\frac{1}{2}}\!\oplus x, y := 1, 1) \sqcap (x, y := 0, 1\ {}_{\frac{1}{2}}\!\oplus x, y := 1, 0)
\end{aligned}$$

In program $R;\ S \sqcap R;\ T$ we have that y is chosen to be 0 with probability $\frac{1}{2}$, and 1 with probability $\frac{1}{2}$, whereas in $R;\ (S \sqcap T)$, y is not guaranteed to be assigned 0 with probability $\frac{1}{2}$, nor is it guaranteed to be assigned 1 with probability $\frac{1}{2}$: the value of y may be chosen nondeterministically.

3 Iteration Constructs

We use the same iteration constructs for probabilistic programs as those that are used for standard programs [5,2]. These constructs are expressed using fixpoints, and may be reasoned about using the usual fixpoint theory [8,5,2].

$R;\ (S;\ T) = (R;\ S);\ T$	(associativity)
$\mathsf{skip};\ S = S$ and $S;\ \mathsf{skip} = S$	(unit)
$R \sqcap (S \sqcap T) = (R \sqcap S) \sqcap T$	(associativity)
$\mathsf{magic} \sqcap S = S$	(unit)
$R \sqcap S = S \sqcap R$	(commutativity)
$R \sqcap R = R$	(idempotence)
$(R \sqcap S);\ T = R;\ T \sqcap S;\ T$	(left distributivity)
$R;\ (S \sqcap T) \sqsubseteq R;\ S \sqcap R;\ T$	(right sub-distributivity)
$\mathsf{magic};\ R = \mathsf{magic}$	(preemption)
$\mathsf{abort};\ R = \mathsf{abort}$	(preemption)

Fig. 4. Basic algebraic properties of monotonic expectation transformers

Lemma 2 (Knaster-Tarski). *Every monotonic function on a complete lattice has a complete lattice of fixpoints.*

Recall from earlier that because we have introduced the ability to express miraculous behaviour in probabilistic programs, we have that the set of probabilistic programs forms a complete lattice. The least, μ, and greatest, ν, fixpoint operators satisfy the following induction and unfolding properties.

$$f.(\mu.f) = \mu.f \text{ and } f.(\nu.f) = \nu.f \qquad \text{(unfolding)}$$
$$f.x \sqsubseteq x \Rightarrow \mu.f \sqsubseteq x \text{ and } x \sqsubseteq f.x \Rightarrow x \sqsubseteq \nu.f \qquad \text{(induction)}$$

We also use the *rolling rules* for fixpoints [5].

Lemma 3 (rolling). *Given monotonic functions f and g on a complete lattice,*

$$f.(\mu.(g \circ f)) = \mu.(f \circ g) \text{ and } f.(\nu.(g \circ f)) = \nu.(f \circ g)$$

The following *fusion* lemma [2] (attributed to Kleene) is used.

Lemma 4 (fusion). *Let f and g be monotonic functions on complete lattices Σ and Γ. If $h : \Sigma \to \Gamma$ is continuous, then*

if $h \circ f \sqsubseteq g \circ h$, then $h.(\mu.f) \sqsubseteq \mu.g$
if $h \circ f = g \circ h$, then $h.(\mu.f) = \mu.g$

And if $h : \Sigma \to \Gamma$ is cocontinuous, then

if $h \circ f \sqsubseteq g \circ h$, then $h.(\nu.f) \sqsubseteq \nu.g$
if $h \circ f = g \circ h$, then $h.(\nu.f) = \nu.g$

The following lemma can be used to simplify reasoning about fixpoints over continuous and cocontinuous functions on a complete lattice [8].

Lemma 5. *The greatest fixed point of a cocontinuous function, f, on a complete lattice is the colimit*

$$\nu.f = (\sqcap i : \mathbb{N} \bullet f^i.\top)$$

where $\top$ is the top element of the complete lattice and $f^0.x \triangleq x$, and $f^{i+1}.x = f.(f^i.x)$. And the least fixed point of the continuous function f on a complete lattice is the limit

$$\mu.f = (\sqcup i : \mathbb{N} \bullet f^i.\bot)$$

where $\bot$ is the bottom element of the complete lattice.

3.1 Iteration Operators

The iteration operators are given in Fig. 2. Informally, T^* executes T any finite number of times, T^∞ executes T an infinite number of times, and T^ω executes T any infinite or finite number of times. From the definition of our iteration operators, and the induction and unfolding properties of fixpoints we immediately get the usual unfolding and induction rules:

$$R^\omega = R;\ R^\omega \sqcap \mathsf{skip} \qquad \text{(unfold strong iteration)}$$
$$R^* = R;\ R^* \sqcap \mathsf{skip} \qquad \text{(unfold weak iteration)}$$
$$R^\infty = R;\ R^\infty \qquad \text{(unfold infinite iteration)}$$
$$R;\ X \sqcap \mathsf{skip} \sqsubseteq X \Rightarrow R^\omega \sqsubseteq X \qquad \text{(strong iteration induction)}$$
$$X \sqsubseteq R;\ X \sqcap \mathsf{skip} \Rightarrow X \sqsubseteq R^* \qquad \text{(weak iteration induction)}$$
$$R;\ X \sqsubseteq X \Rightarrow R^\infty \sqsubseteq X \qquad \text{(infinite iteration induction)}$$

For conjunctive expectation transformer R, R^* satisfies the Kleene axioms of Kozen [12] and Cohen [6], in particular,

$$R^* = (\sqcap i : \mathbb{N} \bullet R^i)$$

But this equivalence does not hold in general for sublinear expectation transformers. Instead the definition of *weak* iteration satisfies the following alternative theorem.

Theorem 6 (Kleene star equivalence). *Let R be a sublinear expectation transformer, and $R^0 \triangleq \mathsf{skip}$ and $R^{i+1} \triangleq R;\ R^i$ for $i \in \mathbb{N}$, then*

$$R^* = \sqcap i : \mathbb{N} \bullet (R \sqcap \mathsf{skip})^i$$

Proof. Before verifying our statement we prove four lemmas. The first lemma is used in the verification of lemmas two and three, and the second and third lemmas are used to verify the fourth.

1. $\forall i : \mathbb{N} \bullet R;\ (R \sqcap \mathsf{skip})^i \sqcap \mathsf{skip} = (R \sqcap \mathsf{skip})^{i+1}$
   (a) Base case: $i = 0$
   $R;\ (R \sqcap \mathsf{skip})^0 \sqcap \mathsf{skip}$
   $= \{\text{definition}\}$
   $R;\ \mathsf{skip} \sqcap \mathsf{skip}$
   $= \{\mathsf{skip}\text{ is unit}\}$
   $(R \sqcap \mathsf{skip})^1$

(b) Inductive case: assume $R;\ (R \sqcap \mathsf{skip})^i \sqcap \mathsf{skip} = (R \sqcap \mathsf{skip})^{i+1}$

$$\begin{aligned}
& (R \sqcap \mathsf{skip})^{i+2} \\
= & \{\text{definition}\} \\
& (R \sqcap \mathsf{skip});\ (R \sqcap \mathsf{skip})^{i+1} \\
= & \{\text{left distributivity}\} \\
& R;\ (R \sqcap \mathsf{skip})^{i+1} \sqcap \mathsf{skip};\ (R \sqcap \mathsf{skip})^{i+1} \\
= & \{\text{inductive assumption}\} \\
& R;\ (R \sqcap \mathsf{skip})^{i+1} \sqcap R;\ (R \sqcap \mathsf{skip})^{i} \sqcap \mathsf{skip} \\
= & \{\text{by monotonicity, } (R \sqcap \mathsf{skip})^{i+1} \sqsubseteq (R \sqcap \mathsf{skip})^{i} \\
& \text{and from basic lattice properties we have that } x \sqsubseteq y \Rightarrow x \sqcap y = x\} \\
& R;\ (R \sqcap \mathsf{skip})^{i+1} \sqcap \mathsf{skip}
\end{aligned}$$

2. $\forall\, i : \mathbb{N} \bullet (\lambda\, X \bullet R;\ X \sqcap \mathsf{skip})^{i+1}.\mathsf{magic} \sqsubseteq (R \sqcap \mathsf{skip})^i$

(a) Base case: $i = 0$

$$\begin{aligned}
& (\lambda\, X \bullet R;\ X \sqcap \mathsf{skip})^{0+1}.\mathsf{magic} \\
= & \{\text{function application}\} \\
& R;\ \mathsf{magic} \sqcap \mathsf{skip} \\
\sqsubseteq & \{\text{general lattice rule } x \sqcap y \sqsubseteq x\} \\
& \mathsf{skip} \\
= & \{\text{definition}\} \\
& (R \sqcap \mathsf{skip})^0
\end{aligned}$$

(b) Inductive case: assume $(\lambda\, X \bullet R;\ X \sqcap \mathsf{skip})^{i+1}.\mathsf{magic} \sqsubseteq (R \sqcap \mathsf{skip})^i$

$$\begin{aligned}
& (\lambda\, X \bullet R;\ X \sqcap \mathsf{skip})^{i+2}.\mathsf{magic} \\
= & \{\text{definition}\} \\
& (\lambda\, X \bullet R;\ X \sqcap \mathsf{skip}).((\lambda\, X \bullet R;\ X \sqcap \mathsf{skip})^{i+1}.\mathsf{magic}) \\
\sqsubseteq & \{\text{inductive assumption and monotonicity}\} \\
& (\lambda\, X \bullet R;\ X \sqcap \mathsf{skip}).(R \sqcap \mathsf{skip})^i \\
= & \{\text{function application}\} \\
& R;\ (R \sqcap \mathsf{skip})^i \sqcap \mathsf{skip} \\
= & \{\text{By 1.}\} \\
& (R \sqcap \mathsf{skip})^{i+1}
\end{aligned}$$

3. $\forall\, i : \mathbb{N} \bullet (R \sqcap \mathsf{skip})^i \sqsubseteq (\lambda\, X \bullet R;\ X \sqcap \mathsf{skip})^i.\mathsf{magic}$

(a) Base case: $i = 0$

$$\begin{aligned}
& (R \sqcap \mathsf{skip})^0 \\
\sqsubseteq & \{\mathsf{magic}\text{ is top element}\} \\
& \mathsf{magic} \\
= & \{\text{definition}\} \\
& (\lambda\, X \bullet R;\ X \sqcap \mathsf{skip})^0.\mathsf{magic}
\end{aligned}$$

(b) Inductive case: assume $(R \sqcap \mathsf{skip})^i \sqsubseteq (\lambda\, X \bullet R;\ X \sqcap \mathsf{skip})^i.\mathsf{magic}$

$$\begin{aligned}
& (\lambda\, X \bullet R;\ X \sqcap \mathsf{skip})^{i+1}.\mathsf{magic} \\
= & \{\text{definition}\} \\
& (\lambda\, X \bullet R;\ X \sqcap \mathsf{skip}).((\lambda\, X \bullet R;\ X \sqcap \mathsf{skip})^{i}.\mathsf{magic}) \\
\sqsupseteq & \{\text{inductive assumption and monotonicity}\} \\
& (\lambda\, X \bullet R;\ X \sqcap \mathsf{skip}).(R \sqcap \mathsf{skip})^i \\
= & \{\text{function application}\} \\
& R;\ (R \sqcap \mathsf{skip})^i \sqcap \mathsf{skip} \\
= & \{\text{By 1.}\} \\
& (R \sqcap \mathsf{skip})^{i+1}
\end{aligned}$$

4. $\sqcap i : \mathbb{N} \bullet (\lambda X \bullet R;\ X \sqcap \mathsf{skip})^i.\mathsf{magic} = \sqcap i : \mathbb{N} \bullet (R \sqcap \mathsf{skip})^i$
For any monotonic function f we have that, $\sqcap i : \mathbb{N} \bullet f^i.\top = \sqcap i : \mathbb{N} \bullet f^{i+1}.\top$, hence from 2 we have that $\sqcap i : \mathbb{N} \bullet (\lambda X \bullet R;\ X \sqcap \mathsf{skip})^i.\mathsf{magic} \sqsubseteq \sqcap i : \mathbb{N} \bullet (R \sqcap \mathsf{skip})^i$. The other direction follows from 3.

We have that function $(\lambda X \bullet R;\ X \sqcap \mathsf{skip})$ is cocontinuous because from Theorem 1 we have that function $(\lambda X \bullet R;\ X)$ is cocontinuous. As a result, the following derivation proves our goal:

$$
\begin{aligned}
& (\nu X \bullet R;\ X \sqcap \mathsf{skip}) \\
= & \{\text{cocontinuity of } (\lambda X \bullet R;\ X \sqcap \mathsf{skip}), \text{ and Lemma 5}\} \\
& \sqcap i : \mathbb{N} \bullet (\lambda X \bullet R;\ X \sqcap \mathsf{skip})^i.\mathsf{magic} \\
= & \{\text{By 4.}\} \\
& \sqcap i : \mathbb{N} \bullet (R \sqcap \mathsf{skip})^i
\end{aligned}
$$

□

Note that for conjunctive R, $(\sqcap i : \mathbb{N} \bullet R^i) = (\sqcap i : \mathbb{N} \bullet (R \sqcap \mathsf{skip})^i)$. For conjunctive predicate transformers we can decompose R^ω into its terminating (R^*) and nonterminating (R^∞) behaviours: that is we have that $R^\omega = R^* \sqcap R^\infty$. For sublinear expectation transformers this is, in general, not the case. The main reason for this difference is that, from a particular initial state, a standard program may either exhibit non-terminating behaviour (that is it may abort) or it may behave miraculously, or it may terminate in a set of states. A probabilistic program may exhibit some probabilistic distribution of these behaviours: for example it may not terminate (abort) with probability a half, and it may produce some distribution of states with the other half. Because of this, we cannot trivially separate out the strong iteration operator into its finite and infinite behaviours. For example, take $R = [x = 1] \sqcap [x = 0];\ (x := 1\ {}_{\frac{1}{2}}\oplus\ x := 2)$, we have that

$$
\begin{aligned}
R^\omega &= [x = 1];\ \mathsf{abort} \sqcap [x = 0];\ (\mathsf{abort}\ {}_{\frac{1}{2}}\oplus\ x := 2) \sqcap \mathsf{skip} \\
R^* &= [x = 1];\ \mathsf{skip} \sqcap ([x = 0];\ (x := 1\ {}_{\frac{1}{2}}\oplus\ x := 2)) \sqcap \mathsf{skip} \\
R^\infty &= [x = 1];\ \mathsf{abort} \sqcap [x = 0];\ \mathsf{magic} \\
R^* \sqcap R^\infty &= [x = 1];\ \mathsf{abort} \sqcap [x = 0];\ (x := 1\ {}_{\frac{1}{2}}\oplus\ x := 2) \sqcap \mathsf{skip}
\end{aligned}
$$

For a conjunctive predicate transformer R, we also have that the strong iteration operator may be expressed in terms of the weak iteration operator as follows [5]: $R^\omega = \{R^\omega.\mathsf{True}\};\ R^*$. Again, this relationship does not hold in general for sublinear expectation transformers. Using our previous example, we can see that

$$
\begin{aligned}
& \{R^\omega.\mathsf{True}\};\ R^* \\
= & \{\lambda \sigma \bullet (\sigma.x \notin \{0,1\}) \times 1 + (\sigma.x = 1) \times 0 + (\sigma.x = 0) \times \tfrac{1}{2}\};\ R^* \\
= & [x = 1];\ \mathsf{abort} \sqcap [x = 0];\ (\mathsf{abort}\ {}_{\frac{1}{2}}\oplus\ ((x := 1\ {}_{\frac{1}{2}}\oplus\ x := 2) \sqcap \mathsf{skip})) \sqcap [x \notin \{0,1\}]
\end{aligned}
$$

Since we equate program non-termination with abortion, the infinite iteration operator is not as interesting as the other two, and so in the remainder of this paper we focus on constructing transformation rules for the weak and strong iteration operators.

3.2 Generalised Induction Properties

The following two lemmas may be used to specify more general induction rules.

Lemma 7. *Given monotonic expectation transformers S and T,*

$$S^{\omega};\ T = (\mu X \bullet S;\ X \sqcap T)$$
$$S^{*};\ T = (\nu X \bullet S;\ X \sqcap T)$$

Proof. The proof presented by Back and von Wright [5] applies to monotonic expectation transformers. □

For conjunctive expectation transformers S and T, we have that

$$T;\ S^{*} = (\nu X \bullet X;\ S \sqcap T)$$

but this equivalence does not hold in general for sublinear expectation transformers, so we present an alternative theorem:

Theorem 8. *Let S and T be sublinear expectation transformers. Then*

$$T;\ S^{*} = (\nu X \bullet X;\ (S \sqcap \mathsf{skip}) \sqcap T)$$

Proof

$$\begin{aligned}
& (\nu X \bullet X;\ (S \sqcap \mathsf{skip}) \sqcap T) \\
= & \ \{\text{Lemma 5 and cocontinuity of } (\lambda X \bullet X;\ (S \sqcap \mathsf{skip}) \sqcap T) \\
& \ \text{follows from left distributivity of monotonic expectation transformers}\} \\
& \sqcap i : \mathbb{N} \bullet (\lambda X \bullet X;\ (S \sqcap \mathsf{skip}) \sqcap T)^{i}.\mathsf{magic} \\
= & \sqcap\{\mathsf{magic},\ T,\ T;\ (S \sqcap \mathsf{skip}),\ T;\ (S \sqcap \mathsf{skip})^{2},\ ...\} \\
= & \sqcap i : \mathbb{N} \bullet T;\ (S \sqcap \mathsf{skip})^{i} \\
= & \ \{\{i : \mathbb{N} \bullet (S \sqcap \mathsf{skip})^{i}\} \text{ is a codirected set, and cocontinuity of} \\
& \ \text{sublinear expectation transformers (Theorem 1)}\} \\
& T;\ (\sqcap i : \mathbb{N} \bullet (S \sqcap \mathsf{skip})^{i}) \\
= & \ \{\text{Theorem 6}\} \\
& T;\ S^{*}
\end{aligned}$$

□

Theorem 9 (general induction). *Let R, S and T be monotonic expectation transformers, then*

$$S;\ X \sqcap R \sqsubseteq X \Rightarrow S^{\omega};\ R \sqsubseteq X \tag{1}$$
$$X \sqsubseteq T;\ X \sqcap R \Rightarrow X \sqsubseteq T^{*};\ R \tag{2}$$
$$X \sqsubseteq X;\ (T \sqcap \mathsf{skip}) \sqcap R \Rightarrow X \sqsubseteq R;\ T^{*} \ \textit{if } T \textit{ and } R \textit{ sublinear} \tag{3}$$

Proof. The first two properties are consequences of Lemma 7 and induction, and the third follows from Theorem 8 and induction. □

3.3 Basic Properties of Iterations

The following properties of iterations hold for both predicate and expectation transformers [5,19]:

Lemma 10. *For monotonic expectation transformer S,*

$$S \sqsubseteq T \Rightarrow S^\omega \sqsubseteq T^\omega \text{ and } S \sqsubseteq T \Rightarrow S^* \sqsubseteq T^* \quad (4)$$
$$S^\omega \sqsubseteq S \text{ and } S^* \sqsubseteq S \quad (5)$$
$$S^\omega \sqsubseteq \mathsf{skip} \text{ and } S^* \sqsubseteq \mathsf{skip} \quad (6)$$
$$S^\omega;\ S^\omega = S^\omega \text{ and } S^*;\ S^* = S^* \quad (7)$$
$$(S^\omega)^\omega = \mathsf{abort} \text{ and } (S^\omega)^* = S^\omega \quad (8)$$
$$(S^*)^\omega = \mathsf{abort} \text{ and } (S^*)^* = S^* \quad (9)$$
$$S^\infty = S^\omega;\ \mathsf{magic} \quad (10)$$

Proof. The proofs provided by Back and von Wright [5,19] for these properties are valid here. They do not require any properties not satisfied by monotonic expectation transformers. □

The *decomposition* property also holds for monotonic expectation transformers (note that we do not require conjunctivity for this proof, we require left, but not right distributivity, which is implied by monotonicity alone (Fig. 4)).

Lemma 11 (decomposition). *For monotonic expectation transformers R and S,*

$$(R \sqcap S)^\omega = R^\omega;\ (S;\ R^\omega)^\omega \text{ and } (R \sqcap S)^* = R^*;\ (S;\ R^*)^*$$

Proof. See Back and von Wright [5]. □

The *leapfrog* property [5] is valid for conjunctive expectation transformers, but not for all sublinear expectation transformers. For monotonic expectation transformers we have a weaker result.

Lemma 12 (leapfrog). *For monotonic expectation transformers R and S. If R is conjunctive then*

$$R;\ (S;\ R)^\omega = (R;\ S)^\omega;\ R \text{ and } R;\ (S;\ R)^* = (R;\ S)^*;\ R$$

otherwise

$$R;\ (S;\ R)^\omega \sqsubseteq (R;\ S)^\omega;\ R \text{ and } R;\ (S;\ R)^* \sqsubseteq (R;\ S)^*;\ R$$

Proof. The proof of the leapfrog property for when R is sublinear, is very similar to the proof for conjunctive R [5]: in the third proof step we have refinement instead of equality. The proof for strong iteration is as follows, the proof for weak iteration is similar.

$R;\ (S;\ R)^\omega$
$= \{\text{definition}\}$
$R;\ (\mu X \bullet S;\ R;\ X \sqcap \mathsf{skip})$

$$
\begin{array}{l}
= \{\text{rolling (Lemma 3) with } f \triangleq (\lambda\, X \bullet R;\ X) \text{ and } g \triangleq (\lambda\, X \bullet S;\ X \sqcap \mathsf{skip})\} \\
\quad (\mu\, X \bullet R;\ (S;\ X \sqcap \mathsf{skip})) \\
\sqsubseteq \{\text{right sub-distributivity and for any functions } f \text{ and } g, \\
\quad f \sqsubseteq g \Rightarrow (\mu\, X \bullet f.X) \sqsubseteq (\mu\, X \bullet g.X)\} \\
\quad (\mu\, X \bullet R;\ S;\ X \sqcap R) \\
= \{\text{Lemma 7}\} \\
\quad (R;\ S)^{\omega};\ R
\end{array}
$$

□

A consequence of the leapfrog rule (with $R = \mathsf{skip}$) is that for sublinear expectation transformer S, we have that $S;\ S^{\omega} \sqsubseteq S^{\omega};\ S$, and $S;\ S^{*} \sqsubseteq S^{*};\ S$, but not necessarily $S;\ S^{\omega} = S^{\omega};\ S$, and $S;\ S^{*} = S^{*};\ S$. For example, take $S \triangleq [x = 0];\ (\mathsf{skip}\ {}_{\frac{1}{2}}\!\oplus x := 1)$, we then have that

$$
\begin{array}{l}
S^{\omega} = [x = 0];\ (\mathsf{skip} \sqcap x := 1) \sqcap [x \neq 0] \\
S;\ S^{\omega} = [x = 0];\ ((x := 1 \sqcap \mathsf{skip})\ {}_{\frac{1}{2}}\!\oplus x := 1) \\
S^{\omega};\ S = [x = 0];\ (\mathsf{skip}\ {}_{\frac{1}{2}}\!\oplus x := 1)
\end{array}
$$

From a start state in which x is 0, S^{ω} may either skip or it may iterate until it assigns x to 1, or it may do some probabilistic combination of these behaviours: it is possible for S^{ω} to assign x to the value 1 because on each iteration of the loop it has a constant, non-zero probability of assigning x to 1.

3.4 Commutativity Properties

In this section we describe how commutativity properties are inherited by iterations. Such properties are useful when reasoning about data refinements of iterations.

Theorem 13. *Let R, S, and T be monotonic expectation transformers,*

$$
\begin{array}{rlr}
R;\ S \sqsubseteq T;\ R \Rightarrow R;\ S^{*} \sqsubseteq T^{*};\ R & & (11) \\
R;\ S \sqsubseteq T;\ R \Rightarrow R;\ S^{\omega} \sqsubseteq T^{\omega};\ R & \textit{if } R \textit{ is continuous} & (12) \\
S;\ R \sqsubseteq R;\ T \Rightarrow S^{*};\ R \sqsubseteq R;\ T^{*} & \textit{if } R \textit{ is conjunctive} & (13) \\
S;\ R \sqsubseteq R;\ T \Rightarrow S^{\omega};\ R \sqsubseteq R;\ T^{\omega} & \textit{if } R \textit{ is conjunctive} & (14) \\
S;\ R \sqsubseteq R;\ (T \sqcap \mathsf{skip}) \Rightarrow S^{*};\ R \sqsubseteq R;\ T^{*} & \textit{if } R \textit{ and } T \textit{ are sublinear} & (15) \\
S;\ R \sqsubseteq R;\ (T \sqcap \mathsf{skip}) \Rightarrow S^{\omega};\ R \sqsubseteq R;\ T^{\omega} & & (16)
\end{array}
$$

Proof. The proofs for the first four commutativity rules have been verified by Back and von Wright [5]: the proofs for these do not require any properties that are not satisfied by monotonic expectation transformers. We focus on proving the last two rules because they differ from the usual rules for conjunctive predicate transformers. Assume R, S, and T are monotonic expectation transformers.

Proof of (15): Assume R and T are sublinear.

$$
\begin{array}{l}
\quad S^*;\ R \sqsubseteq R;\ T^* \\
\Leftarrow \{\text{general induction (Theorem 9(3))}\} \\
\quad S^*;\ R \sqsubseteq S^*;\ R;\ (T \sqcap \mathsf{skip}) \sqcap R \\
\Leftrightarrow \{\text{unfolding and left distributivity}\} \\
\quad S;\ S^*;\ R \sqcap R \sqsubseteq S^*;\ R;\ (T \sqcap \mathsf{skip}) \sqcap R \\
\Leftarrow \{S;\ S^* \sqsubseteq S^*;\ S \text{ is a consequence of Lemma 12}\} \\
\quad S^*;\ S;\ R \sqcap R \sqsubseteq S^*;\ R;\ (T \sqcap \mathsf{skip}) \sqcap R \\
\Leftarrow \{\text{monotonicity}\} \\
\quad S;\ R \sqsubseteq R;\ (T \sqcap \mathsf{skip})
\end{array}
$$

Proof of (16): Assume $S;\ R \sqsubseteq R;\ (T \sqcap \mathsf{skip})$. First we have that

$$
\begin{array}{l}
\quad S^\omega;\ R \sqsubseteq R;\ T^\omega \\
\Leftarrow \{\text{general induction (Theorem 9(1))}\} \\
\quad S;\ R;\ T^\omega \sqcap R \sqsubseteq R;\ T^\omega
\end{array}
$$

We may show that the antecedent follows from the assumption as follows.

$$
\begin{array}{l}
\quad S;\ R;\ T^\omega \sqcap R \\
\sqsubseteq \{\text{general lattice property } x \sqcap y \sqsubseteq x\} \\
\quad S;\ R;\ T^\omega \\
\sqsubseteq \{\text{assumption}\} \\
\quad R;\ (T \sqcap \mathsf{skip});\ T^\omega \\
\sqsubseteq \{\text{general lattice property } x \sqcap y \sqsubseteq x, \text{ and } \mathsf{skip} \text{ is unit}\} \\
\quad R;\ T^\omega
\end{array}
$$

□

For monotonic expectation transformers, Theorem 13 parts (13) and (14) do not hold in general if R is sublinear (and not conjunctive).

Different commutativity rules can be generated for guarded loops: we present two of these. Both rules are used in Sect. 4.1 to verify transformation rules for action systems[3]. Before we introduce these two rules we define some necessary terminology. Given an expectation transformer S, we refer to the set of states from which S may abort with probability one as $\mathsf{fail}.S$:

$$\mathsf{fail}.S \triangleq \lambda\sigma \bullet (S.\mathsf{True}.\sigma = 0)$$

Theorem 14. *Given monotonic expectation transformers R, S and T such that R is continuous, and standard predicates g and p, we have that*

$$R;\ S^\omega;\ [g] \sqsubseteq T^\omega;\ [p];\ R$$

if

$$R;\ S \sqsubseteq T;\ R \qquad (17)$$

$$R;\ [g \vee \mathsf{fail}.S] \sqsubseteq [p];\ R \qquad (18)$$

[3] Note that neither of these rules are present in the work of Back and von Wright [5,19]: the commutativity laws they present for guarded loops are weaker than these.

Proof

$$
\begin{aligned}
& R;\ S^\omega;\ [g] \sqsubseteq T^\omega;\ [p];\ R \\
\Leftrightarrow\ & \{\text{Lemma 7}\} \\
& R;\ (\mu X \bullet S;\ X \sqcap [g]) \sqsubseteq (\mu X \bullet T;\ X \sqcap [p];\ R) \\
\Leftarrow\ & \{\text{fusion (Lemma 4) and continuity of } R\} \\
& (\lambda X \bullet R;\ X) \circ (\lambda X \bullet S;\ X \sqcap [g]) \sqsubseteq (\lambda X \bullet T;\ X \sqcap [p];\ R) \circ (\lambda X \bullet R;\ X) \\
\Leftrightarrow\ & (\lambda X \bullet R;\ (S;\ X \sqcap [g])) \sqsubseteq (\lambda X \bullet T;\ R;\ X \sqcap [p];\ R)
\end{aligned}
$$

$$
\begin{aligned}
& R;\ (S;\ X \sqcap [g]) \\
=\ & \{\text{meet is idempotent}\} \\
& R;\ (S;\ X \sqcap [g]) \sqcap R;\ (S;\ X \sqcap [g]) \\
\sqsubseteq\ & \{\text{right sub-distributivity, general lattice property } x \sqcap y \sqsubseteq x, \\
& \ \text{basic guard rule } \mathsf{skip} \sqsubseteq [g]\ \} \\
& R;\ S;\ X \sqcap R;\ ([\mathsf{fail}.S];\ S;\ X \sqcap [g]) \\
=\ & \{\text{from the definition of } \mathsf{fail},\ [\mathsf{fail}.S];\ S = [\mathsf{fail}.S];\ \mathsf{abort}\} \\
& R;\ S;\ X \sqcap R;\ ([\mathsf{fail}.S];\ \mathsf{abort} \sqcap [g]) \\
\sqsubseteq\ & \{\mathsf{abort} \text{ is the least element and basic guard rules}\} \\
& R;\ S;\ X \sqcap R;\ [\mathsf{fail}.S \vee g] \\
\sqsubseteq\ & \{\text{assumption (17) and (18)}\} \\
& T;\ R;\ X \sqcap [p];\ R
\end{aligned}
$$

□

As suggested by the commutativity rule for iterations, Theorem 13 (16), the conditions required to prove a refinement of the form $([g];\ S)^\omega;\ [\neg g];\ R \sqsubseteq R;\ ([p];\ T)^\omega;\ [\neg p]$, for sublinear expectation transformers S, R, and T, differ from those that one would normally expect for the case when R is conjunctive.

Theorem 15. *Given monotonic expectation transformer R, S and T, and standard predicates g and p, we have that*

$$([g];\ S)^\omega;\ [\neg g];\ R \sqsubseteq R;\ ([p];\ T)^\omega;\ [\neg p]$$

if

$$\{g\};\ S;\ R \sqsubseteq R;\ \{p\};\ T \tag{19}$$

$$R;\ [\neg p] \sqsubseteq [\neg g];\ R \tag{20}$$

Proof

$$
\begin{aligned}
& ([g];\ S)^\omega;\ [\neg g];\ R \sqsubseteq R;\ ([p];\ T)^\omega;\ [\neg p] \\
\Leftarrow\ & \{\text{general induction (Theorem 9 (1))}\} \\
& [g];\ S;\ R;\ ([p];\ T)^\omega;\ [\neg p] \sqcap [\neg g];\ R \sqsubseteq R;\ ([p];\ T)^\omega;\ [\neg p]
\end{aligned}
$$

$$
\begin{aligned}
& [g];\ S;\ R;\ ([p];\ T)^\omega;\ [\neg p] \sqcap [\neg g];\ R \\
=\ & \{\text{basic guard and assertion rules}\} \\
& [g];\ \{g\};\ S;\ R;\ ([p];\ T)^\omega;\ [\neg p] \sqcap [\neg g];\ R \\
\sqsubseteq\ & \{\text{assumption (19)}\} \\
& [g];\ R;\ \{p\};\ T;\ ([p];\ T)^\omega;\ [\neg p] \sqcap [\neg g];\ R \\
=\ & \{\text{basic guard rule } \{p\} = [\neg p];\ \mathsf{abort} \sqcap [p], \text{ left distributivity and preemption}\} \\
& [g];\ R;\ ([p];\ T;\ ([p];\ T)^\omega;\ [\neg p] \sqcap [\neg p];\ \mathsf{abort}) \sqcap [\neg g];\ R
\end{aligned}
$$

$\sqsubseteq$ {abort is the least element}
$[g];\ R;\ ([p];\ T;\ ([p];\ T)^\omega;\ [\neg p] \sqcap [\neg p]) \sqcap [\neg g];\ R$
$=$ {left distributivity and unfolding}
$[g];\ R;\ ([p];\ T)^\omega;\ [\neg p] \sqcap [\neg g];\ R$
$\sqsubseteq$ {basic guard rule $\mathsf{skip} \sqsubseteq [g]$}
$[g];\ R;\ ([p];\ T)^\omega;\ [\neg p] \sqcap [\neg g];\ R;\ [\neg p]$
$=$ {from the basic guard rules $[\neg p];\ [p] = \mathsf{magic}$ and magic is unit}
$[g];\ R;\ ([p];\ T)^\omega;\ [\neg p] \sqcap [\neg g];\ R;\ ([\neg p];\ [p];\ T;\ ([p];\ T)^\omega;\ [\neg p] \sqcap [\neg p])$
$=$ {right and left distributivity of conjunctive programs}
$[g];\ R;\ ([p];\ T)^\omega;\ [\neg p] \sqcap [\neg g];\ R;\ [\neg p];\ ([p];\ T;\ ([p];\ T)^\omega \sqcap \mathsf{skip});\ [\neg p]$
$=$ {unfolding}
$[g];\ R;\ ([p];\ T)^\omega;\ [\neg p] \sqcap [\neg g];\ R;\ [\neg p];\ ([p];\ T)^\omega;\ [\neg p]$
$\sqsubseteq$ {assumption (20) and basic guard rules}
$[g];\ R;\ ([p];\ T)^\omega;\ [\neg p] \sqcap [\neg g];\ R;\ ([p];\ T)^\omega;\ [\neg p]$
$=$ {left distributivity and basic guard rules}
$[g \vee \neg g];\ R;\ ([p];\ T)^\omega;\ [\neg p]$
$=$ {definition of skip}
$R;\ ([p];\ T)^\omega;\ [\neg p]$ □

4 Action Systems

So far we have investigated properties of the general iteration constructs. We now follow the lead of Back and von Wright [5] by applying these results to more well known and useful programming constructs: namely action systems. Action systems can be used to model parallel or distributed systems in which concurrent behaviour is modeled my interleaving atomic actions [3,4]. Probabilistic action systems (originally proposed by Sere and Troubitsyna [16,18]) are an extension of standard action systems in which actions are defined to be sublinear expectation transformers instead of conjunctive predicate transformers. The input/output behaviour of a probabilistic action system is defined in terms of the iteration constructs as follows:

$$\mathsf{do}\ A_1 \sqcap ... \sqcap A_n\ \mathsf{od} \triangleq (A_1 \sqcap ... \sqcap A_n)^\omega;\ [\neg gd.A_1 \wedge ... \wedge \neg gd.A_n]$$

where for all $i : [1, .., n]$, the *action* A_i is a sublinear expectation transformer. $gd.A$ is a standard predicate that specifies the set of states from which A does not behave like magic.

$$gd.A \triangleq \lambda\sigma \bullet (A.\mathit{False}.\sigma = 0)$$

Note that because of how we model magic, for any action A, we have that $[gd.A];\ A = A$, and "$\{gd.A\};\ A$" is strict (an expectation transformer S is strict if $S;\ \mathsf{abort} = \mathsf{abort}$). It is also useful to observe that $gd.(A_1 \sqcap ... \sqcap A_n) = gd.A_1 \vee ... \vee gd.A_n$. In this model infinite behaviours are considered to be aborting: we do not model reactive behaviour. Using our algebraic framework, we construct and verify data refinement rules for probabilistic action systems.

4.1 Data Refinement

An expectation transformer S is said to be data refined by T through R if either

$$R;\ S \sqsubseteq T;\ R \text{ or } S;\ R \sqsubseteq R;\ T$$

In the first instance R can be seen as mapping from the concrete state of T to the abstract state of S, and in the second R can be seen to map the abstract state of S to the concrete state of T. We refer to data refinement in the first instance as *cosimulation*, and *simulation* in the latter.

We present basic cosimulation and simulation rules for probabilistic action systems. These rules are *stuttering insensitive*, that is they require a direct correspondence between actions. The cosimulation rule has a similar form to the cosimulation data refinement rule for standard action systems [1]. The simulation rule has (necessarily) a different form to the corresponding standard action system rule. Our rules are more general than the stuttering insensitive data refinement rules verified by Back and von Wright using algebraic methods for standard action systems [5,19]: they are more general because they take into consideration the failure condition of the actions. We demonstrate our simulation rule using a simple example.

The cosimulation and simulation rules are as follows.

Theorem 16 (cosimulation). *Given sublinear expectation transformers R, S and T, we have that* $R;\ \mathsf{do}\ S\ \mathsf{od} \sqsubseteq \mathsf{do}\ T\ \mathsf{od};\ R$, *if R is continuous and*

$$R;\ S \sqsubseteq T;\ R \tag{21}$$

$$R;\ [\neg gd.S \vee \mathsf{fail}.S] \sqsubseteq [\neg gd.T];\ R \tag{22}$$

Proof. This follows directly from the definition of action systems, assumptions (21) and (22), and Theorem 14. □

Theorem 17 (simulation). *Given sublinear expectation transformers R, S and T, we have that* $\mathsf{do}\ S\ \mathsf{od};\ R \sqsubseteq R;\ \mathsf{do}\ T\ \mathsf{od}$, *if*

$$\{gd.S\};\ S;\ R \sqsubseteq R;\ \{gd.T\};\ T \tag{23}$$

$$R;\ [\neg gd.T] \sqsubseteq [\neg gd.S];\ R \tag{24}$$

Proof. This follows directly from the definition of action systems, assumptions (23) and (24), and Theorem 15. □

We present a simple example to demonstrate how the simulation rule may be used in practice.

Example. Action system $S1$ (see Fig. 5) may be used to represent the behaviour of a unfair scheduler with two processes, $P1$ and $P2$, where both $P1$ and $P2$ are feasible. Predicates $env1$ and $env2$ indicate when processes $P1$ and $P2$ are able to be executed. If both processes are able to be executed at the same time, then the scheduler may demonically chose between executing $P1$ or $P2$, if only one process is ready, then it must execute that process, and if neither process is ready it terminates. We may use representation program R to show that this scheduler is data refined by action system $S2$. $S2$ represents a fair scheduler that has the same processes as $S1$, but, when both processes are able to be executed simultaneously, it chooses between them with equal probability. The fair scheduler, $S2$, uses fresh variable a to determine which process to execute.

$$
\begin{aligned}
&S1 \triangleq \mathsf{do}\ [env1];\ P1 \sqcap [env2];\ P2\ \mathsf{od} \\
&S2 \triangleq \mathsf{do}\ [a = 1];\ P1;\ R \sqcap [a = 2];\ P2;\ R\ \mathsf{od} \\
&R \triangleq [env1 \wedge env2];\ (a := 1\ {}_{\frac{1}{2}}\!\oplus a := 2) \\
&\qquad \sqcap [env1 \wedge \neg env2];\ a := 1 \\
&\qquad \sqcap [\neg env1 \wedge env2];\ a := 2 \\
&\qquad \sqcap [\neg env1 \wedge \neg env2];\ a := 0
\end{aligned}
$$

Fig. 5. Unfair and fair schedulers $S1$ and $S2$

We use Theorem 17 to show that $S1;\ R \sqsubseteq R;\ S2$.

Proof of condition (23): Starting with the right hand side

$$
\begin{aligned}
&\quad R;\ \{a = 1 \vee a = 2\};\ ([a = 1];\ P1;\ R \sqcap [a = 2];\ P2;\ R) \\
&= \{\text{definition of } R\text{, left distributivity of meet and probabilistic choice}\} \\
&\quad [env1 \wedge env2];\ (a := 1;\ \{a = 1 \vee a = 2\};\ ([a = 1];\ P1;\ R \sqcap [a = 2];\ P2;\ R) \\
&\qquad\qquad\qquad {}_{\frac{1}{2}}\!\oplus a := 2;\ \{a = 1 \vee a = 2\};\ ([a = 1];\ P1;\ R \sqcap [a = 2];\ P2;\ R)) \\
&\quad \sqcap [env1 \wedge \neg env2];\ a := 1;\ \{a = 1 \vee a = 2\};\ ([a = 1];\ P1;\ R \sqcap [a = 2];\ P2;\ R) \\
&\quad \sqcap [\neg env1 \wedge env2];\ a := 2;\ \{a = 1 \vee a = 2\};\ ([a = 1];\ P1;\ R \sqcap [a = 2];\ P2;\ R) \\
&\quad \sqcap [\neg env1 \wedge \neg env2];\ a := 0;\ \{a = 1 \vee a = 2\};\ ([a = 1];\ P1;\ R \sqcap [a = 2];\ P2;\ R) \\
&= \{\text{simplify}\} \\
&\quad [env1 \wedge env2];\ (a := 1;\ P1;\ R\ {}_{\frac{1}{2}}\!\oplus a := 2;\ P2;\ R) \\
&\quad \sqcap [env1 \wedge \neg env2];\ a := 1;\ P1;\ R \\
&\quad \sqcap [\neg env1 \wedge env2];\ a := 2;\ P2;\ R \\
&\quad \sqcap [\neg env1 \wedge \neg env2];\ \mathsf{abort} \\
&= \{\text{basic guard rule } \{p\} = [\neg p];\ \mathsf{abort} \sqcap [p] \text{ and left distributivity}\} \\
&\quad \{env1 \vee env2\}; \\
&\quad ([env1 \wedge env2];\ (a := 1;\ P1;\ R\ {}_{\frac{1}{2}}\!\oplus a := 2;\ P2;\ R) \\
&\quad \sqcap [env1 \wedge \neg env2];\ a := 1;\ P1;\ R \\
&\quad \sqcap [\neg env1 \wedge env2];\ a := 2;\ P2;\ R) \\
&\sqsupseteq \{\text{by definition demonic choice is refined by probabilistic choice}\} \\
&\quad \{env1 \vee env2\}; \\
&\quad ([env1 \wedge env2];\ (a := 1;\ P1;\ R \sqcap a := 2;\ P2;\ R) \\
&\quad \sqcap [env1 \wedge \neg env2];\ a := 1;\ P1;\ R \\
&\quad \sqcap [\neg env1 \wedge env2];\ a := 2;\ P2;\ R) \\
&= \{\text{simplify}\} \\
&\quad \{env1 \vee env2\};\ ([env1];\ a := 1;\ P1;\ R \sqcap [env2];\ a := 2;\ P2;\ R) \\
&= \{\text{left distributivity, definition of } R\} \\
&\quad \{env1 \vee env2\};\ ([env1];\ P1 \sqcap [env2];\ P2);\ R
\end{aligned}
$$

Proof of condition (24):

$$
\begin{aligned}
& R;\ [a \neq 1 \wedge a \neq 2] \\
= & \{\text{definition of } R \text{ and left distributivity}\} \\
& [env1 \wedge env2];\ (a := 1\ {}_{\frac{1}{2}}\!\oplus a := 2);\ [a \neq 1 \wedge a \neq 2] \\
& \sqcap [env1 \wedge \neg env2];\ a := 1;\ [a \neq 1 \wedge a \neq 2] \\
& \sqcap [\neg env1 \wedge env2];\ a := 2;\ [a \neq 1 \wedge a \neq 2] \\
& \sqcap [\neg env1 \wedge \neg env2];\ a := 0;\ [a \neq 1 \wedge a \neq 2] \\
= & \{\text{simplify}\} \\
& [\neg env1 \wedge \neg env2];\ a := 0 \\
= & \{\text{definition of } R\} \\
& [\neg env1 \wedge \neg env2];\ R
\end{aligned}
$$

5 Conclusion

Back and von Wright have demonstrated how to reason about standard loops in a concrete algebraic setting [5,2]. We have demonstrated how probabilistic loops may be reasoned about in a similar way. We have identified a number of important transformation rules that are common to both probabilistic and standard loops. In addition, we have identified a number of standard transformation rules that are not applicable to probabilistic programs. For the latter rules, we have developed alternative transformation rules that are suitable in the probabilistic context. In particular, we have constructed new data refinement rules for probabilistic action systems.

There are many benefits to taking an algebraic approach to reasoning about iterations and loops: the main benefit being that it can simplify reasoning about complex theorems. The transformation rules that we have developed may be used as a basis to develop further rules. For instance, they could be used to develop rules for stuttering sensitive data refinement in action systems.

In their earlier work [5,2], Back and von Wright derived their transformation rules within the predicate transformer model. In later work von Wright [19,20], constructed a more abstract refinement algebra that is independent of a particular program model. Solin and von Wright [17] have further extended this abstract refinement algebra with enabledness and termination axioms and used these to reason about action systems on an abstract level. Their algebra is similar to the Kozen's *Kleene algebra with tests* [12], and Cohen's *Omega algebra* [7], however it differs because it deals with total correctness as well as partial correctness. The refinement algebra of von Wright [19] is less general than the *lazy Kleene algebra* of Möller [14]: a relaxation of Kleene algebra in which strictness and right-distributivity are omitted. While Möller's lazy Kleene algebra supports the lack of strictness (R; magic is not in general equal to magic) and right distributivity ($R;\ (S \sqcap T)$ is in general not equal to $R;\ S \sqcap R;\ T$) as required for the probabilistic programs presented here, our probabilistic programs do not satisfy Möller's iteration axioms.

Acknowledgments. This research was supported by Australian Research Council (ARC) Discovery Grant DP0558408, *Analysing and generating fault-tolerant real-time systems.*

References

1. Ralph-Johan Back and Joakim von Wright. Trace refinement of action systems. In *International Conference on Concurrency Theory*, volume 836 of *LNCS*, pages 367–384. Springer Verlag, 1994.
2. Ralph-Johan Back and Joakim von Wright. *Refinement Calculus: A Systematic Introduction.* Springer, 1998.
3. R.J.R. Back and R. Kurki-Suonio. Decentralization of process nets with centralized control. In *Proc. of the 2nd ACM SIGACT-SIGOPS Symp. on Principles of Distributed Computing*, pages 131–142. ACM Press, 1983.
4. R.J.R. Back and R. Kurki-Suonio. Distributed cooperation with action systems. *ACM Trans. Program. Lang. Syst.*, 10(4):513–554, 1988.
5. R.J.R Back and J. von Wright. Reasoning algebraically about loops. *Acta Informatica*, 36:295–334, 1999.
6. Ernie Cohen. Hypotheses in Kleene algebra. Technical Report TM-ARH-023814, Belcore, 1994.
7. Ernie Cohen. Separation and reduction. In *Mathematics of Program Construction*, volume 1837 of *LNCS*, pages 45–59. Springer, 2000.
8. B. A. Davey and H.A Priestley. *Introduction to Lattices.* Cambridge University Press, 1990.
9. Edsger W. Dijkstra. *A Discipline of Programming.* Prentice Hall, 1976.
10. J. He, K. Seidel, and A. McIver. Probabilistic models for the guarded command language. *Science of Computer Programming*, 28(2-3):171–192, 1997.
11. Joe Hurd. A formal approach to probabilistic termination. In *TPHOLs*, volume 2410 of *LNCS*, pages 230–245. Springer-Verlag, 2002.
12. Dexter Kozen. Kleene algebra with tests. *ACM Transactions on Programming Languages and Systems*, 19(3):427–443, 1997.
13. Annabelle McIver and Carroll Morgan. *Abstraction, Refinement and Proof for Probabilistic Systems.* Monographs in Computer Science. Springer, 2005.
14. Bernhard Möller. Lazy Kleene algebra. In *Mathematics of Program Construction*, volume 3125 of *LNCS*, pages 252–273. Springer-Verlag, 2004.
15. C. Morgan. *Programming from Specifications.* Prentice Hall, second edition, 1994.
16. Kaisa Sere and Elena Troubitsyna. Probabilities in action systems. In *Proc. of the 8th Nordic Workshop on Programming Theory*, 1996.
17. Kim Solin and Joakim von Wright. Refinement algebra with operators for enabledness and termination. In *Mathematics of Program Construction*, volume 4014 of *LNCS*, pages 397–415, 2006.
18. Elena A. Troubitsyna. Reliability assessment through probabilistic refinement. *Nordic Journal of Computing*, pages 320–342, 1999.
19. Joakim von Wright. From Kleene algebra to refinement algebra. In *Mathematics of Program Construction*, volume 2386 of *LNCS*, pages 233–262. Springer, 2002.
20. Joakim von Wright. Towards a refinement algebra. *Science of Computer Programming*, 51, 2004.

Formal Verification of the Heap Manager of an Operating System Using Separation Logic

Nicolas Marti[1], Reynald Affeldt[2], and Akinori Yonezawa[1,2]

[1] Department of Computer Science, University of Tokyo
[2] Research Center for Information Security,
National Institute of Advanced Industrial Science and Technology

Abstract. In order to ensure memory properties of an operating system, it is important to verify the implementation of its heap manager. In the case of an existing operating system, this is a difficult task because the heap manager is usually written in a low-level language that makes use of pointers, and it is usually not written with verification in mind. In this paper, our main contribution is the formal verification of the heap manager of an existing embedded operating system, namely Topsy. For this purpose, we develop in the Coq proof assistant a library for separation logic, an extension of Hoare logic to deal with pointers. Using this library, we were able to verify the C source code of the Topsy heap manager, and to find and correct bugs.

1 Introduction

In order to ensure memory properties of an operating system, it is important to verify the implementation of its heap manager. The heap manager is the set of functions that provides the operating system with dynamic memory allocation. Incorrect implementation of these functions can invalidate essential memory properties. For example, task isolation, the property that user processes cannot tamper with the memory of kernel processes, is such a property: the relation with dynamic memory allocation comes from the fact that privilege levels of processes are usually stored in dynamically allocated memory blocks (see [5] for a detailed illustration).

However, the verification of the heap manager of an existing operating system is a difficult task because it is usually written in a low-level language that makes use of pointers, and it is usually not written with verification in mind. For these reasons, the verification of dynamic memory allocation is sometimes considered as a challenge for mechanical verification [15].

In this paper, our main contribution is to formally verify the heap manager of an existing embedded operating system, namely Topsy [2]. For this purpose, we develop in the Coq proof assistant [4] a library for separation logic [1], an extension of Hoare logic to deal with pointers. Using this library, we verify the C source code of the Topsy heap manager. In fact, this heap manager proves harder to deal with than dynamic memory allocation facilities verified in previous studies (see Sect. 8 for a comparison). A direct side-effect of our approach is to

Z. Liu and J. He (Eds.): ICFEM 2006, LNCS 4260, pp. 400–419, 2006.

provide advanced debugging. Indeed, our verification highlights several issues and bugs in the original source code (see Sect. 7.1 for a discussion).

We chose the Topsy operating system as a test-bed for formal verification of memory properties. Topsy was initially created for educational use and has recently evolved into an embedded operating system for network cards [3]. It is well-suited for mechanical verification because it is small and simple, yet it is a realistic use-case because it includes most classical features of operating systems.

The paper is organized as follows. In Sect. 2, we give an overview of the Topsy heap manager, and we explain our verification goal and approach. In Sect. 3, we introduce separation logic and explain how we encode it in Coq. In Sect. 4, we formally specify and prove the properties of the underlying data structure used by the heap manager. In Sect. 5, we formally specify and explain the verification of the functions of the heap manager. In Sect. 6, we discuss practical aspects of the verification such as automation and translation from the original C source code. In Sect. 7, we discuss the outputs of our experiment: in particular, issues and bugs found in the original source code of the heap manager. In Sect. 8, we comment on related work. In Sect. 9, we conclude and comment on future work.

2 Verification Goal and Approach

2.1 Topsy Heap Manager

The heap manager of an operating system is the set of functions that provides dynamic memory allocation. In Topsy, these functions and related variables are defined in the files `Memory/MMHeapMemory.{h,c}`, with some macros in the file `Topsy/Configuration.h`. We are dealing here with the heap manager of Topsy version 2; a browsable source code is available online [2].

The *heap* is the area of memory reserved by Topsy for the heap manager. The latter divides the heap into allocated and free memory blocks: allocated blocks are memory blocks in use by programs, and free blocks form a pool of memory available for new allocations. In order to make an optimal use of the memory, allocated and free memory blocks form a partition of the heap. This is achieved by implementing memory blocks as a simply-linked list of contiguous blocks. In the following, we refer to this data structure as a *heap-list*.

In a heap-list, each block consists of a two-fields header and an array of memory. The first field of the header gives information on the status of the block (allocated or free, corresponding to the `Alloc` and `Free` flags); the second field is a pointer to the next block, which starts just after the current block. For example, here is a heap-list with one allocated block and one free block:

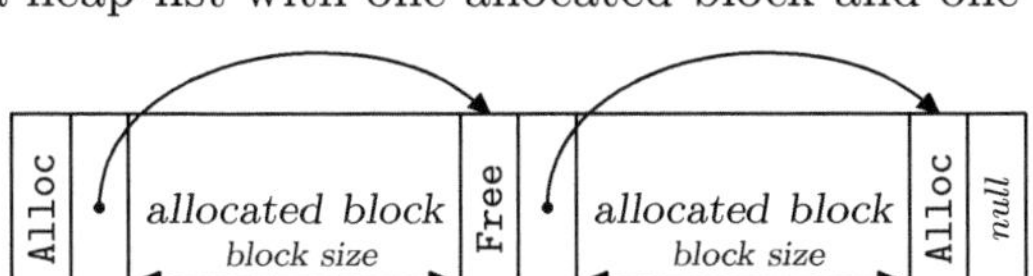

Observe that the size of the arrays of memory associated to blocks can be computed using the values of pointers. (In this paper, when we talk about the size of a block, we talk about its "effective" size, that is the size of the array of memory associated to it, this excludes the header.) The terminal block of the heap-list always consists of a sole header, marked as allocated, and pointing to null.

Initialization of the heap manager is provided by the following function:

```
Error hmInit(Address addr) {...}
```

Concretely, `hmInit` initializes the heap-list by building a heap-list with a single free block that spans the whole heap. The argument is the starting location of the heap. The size of the heap-list is defined by the macro `KERNELHEAPSIZE`. The function always returns `HM_INITOK`.

Allocation is provided by the following function:

```
Error hmAlloc(Address* addressPtr, unsigned long int size) {...}
```

The role of `hmAlloc` is to insert new blocks marked as allocated into the heap-list. The first argument is a pointer provided by the user to get back the address of the allocated block, the second argument is the desired size. In case of successful allocation, the pointer contains the address of the newly allocated block and the value `HM_ALLOCOK` is returned, otherwise the value `HM_ALLOCFAILED` is returned. In order to limit fragmentation, `hmAlloc` performs compaction of contiguous free blocks and splitting of free blocks.

Deallocation is provided by the following function:

```
Error hmFree(Address address) {...}
```

Concretely, `hmFree` turns allocated blocks into free ones. The argument corresponds to the address of the allocated block to free. The function returns `HM_FREEOK` if the block was successfully deallocated, or `HM_FREEFAILED` otherwise.

2.2 Verification Goal and Approach

Our goal is to verify that the implementation of the Topsy heap manager is "correct". By correct, we mean that the heap manager provides the intended service: the allocation function allocates large-enough memory blocks, these memory blocks are "fresh" (they do not overlap with previously allocated memory blocks), the deallocation function turns the status of blocks into free (except for the terminal block), and the allocation and deallocation functions does not behave in unexpected ways (in particular, they do not modify neither previously allocated memory blocks nor the rest of the memory). Guaranteeing the allocation of fresh memory blocks and the non-modification of previously allocated memory blocks is a necessary condition to ensure that the heap manager preserves exclusive usage of allocated blocks. Formal specification goals corresponding to the above informal discussion are explained later in Sect. 5.

Our approach is to use separation logic to formally specify and mechanically verify the goal informally stated above. We choose separation logic for this purpose because it provides a native notion of pointer and memory separation that facilitates the specification of heap-lists. Another advantage of separation logic is that it is close enough to the C language to enable systematic translation from the original source code of Topsy.

In the next sections, we explain how we encode separation logic in the Coq proof assistant and how we use this encoding to specify and verify the Topsy heap manager. All the verification is available online [6].

3 Encoding of Separation Logic

Separation logic is an extension of Hoare logic to reason about low-level programs with shared, mutable data structures [1]. Before entering the details of the formal encoding, we introduce the basic ideas behind separation logic.

Brief Introduction to Separation Logic. Let us consider the program x `*<-` 4 that puts the value 4 into a memory cell pointed to by the variable x. Let us assume that this cell originally contained a pointer to a contiguous cell with the value 2. Informally, the corresponding Hoare triple could be written as follows:

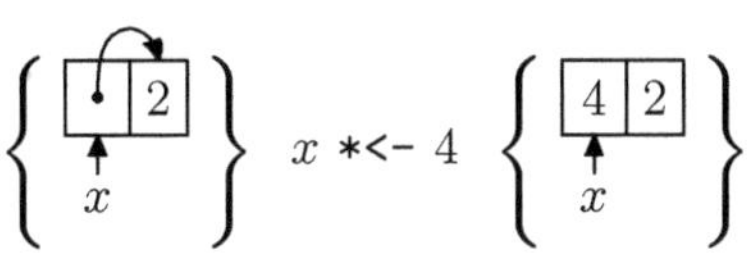

Separation logic provides connectives to conveniently specify and reason about such Hoare triples. In particular, it extends the language of assertions of Hoare logic with a *separating conjunction* $\star$ that asserts that its subformulas hold for disjoint parts of the memory. For illustration, the pre/post-conditions above would be respectively written $(x \mapsto p)\star(p \mapsto 2)$ and $(x \mapsto 4)\star(p \mapsto 2)$, where p is the *location* held by variable x. Separation logic also provides us with "axioms" to verify such triples. For example, by applying the "axiom of backward reasoning for mutation" (to be defined formally later in this section), the verification is reduced to the proof of the (classical) implication $(x \mapsto p) \star (p \mapsto 2) \rightarrow (x \mapsto p) \star ((x \mapsto 4) \mathrel{-\!\!\star} ((x \mapsto 4) \star (p \mapsto 2)))$ where $\mathrel{-\!\!\star}$ is the *separating implication*; this formula is easily provable using the properties of separation logic.

In the rest of this section, we explain the formal definition of separation logic that we implemented in Coq to perform such reasoning as above. The code displayed is directly taken from the implementation; we use traditional mathematical notations instead of ASCII for Coq primitives (e.g., $\forall$, $\exists$, $\rightarrow$, $\wedge$, $\neq$, $\geq$ instead of `forall`, `exists`, `->`, `/\`, `<>`, `>=`).

3.1 The Programming Language

The programming language of separation logic is imperative. The current state of execution is represented by a pair of a store (that maps local variables to values) and a heap (a finite map from locations to values). We have an abstract type `var.v` for variables (ranged over by `x`, `y`), a type `loc` for locations (ranged over by `p`, `adr`), and a type `val` for values (ranged over by `v`, `w`) with the condition that all values can be seen as locations (so as to enable pointer arithmetic).

Our implementation is essentially abstracted over the choice of types, yet, in our experiments, we have taken the native Coq types of naturals `nat` and relative integers `Z` for `loc` and `val` so as to benefit from better automation. Stores and heaps are implemented by two modules `store` and `heap` whose types are (excerpts):

```
Module Type STORE.
 Parameter s : Set. (* the abstract type of stores *)
 Parameter lookup : var.v → s → val.
 Parameter update : var.v → val → s → s.
End STORE.

Module Type HEAP.
 Parameter l : Set. (* locations *)
 Parameter v : Set. (* values *)
 Parameter h : Set. (* the abstract type of heaps *)
 Parameter emp : h. (* the empty heap *)
 Parameter singleton : l → v → h. (* singleton heaps *)
 Parameter lookup : l → h → option v.
 Parameter update : l → v → h → h.
 Parameter union : h → h → h.    Notation "h1 ⊎ h2" := (union h1 h2).
 Parameter disjoint: h→h →Prop. Notation "h1 ⊥ h2" := (disjoint h1 h2).
End HEAP.

Definition state := prod store.s heap.h.
```

To paraphrase the implementation, `(store.lookup x s)` is the value of the variable `x` in store `s`; `(store.update x v s)` is the store `s` in which the variable `x` has been updated with the value `v`; `(heap.lookup p h)` is the contents (if any) of location `p`; `(heap.update p v h)` is the heap `h` in which the location `p` has been mutated with the value `v`; `h ⊎ h'` is the disjoint union of `h` and `h'`; and `h ⊥ h'` holds when `h` and `h'` have disjoint domains.

The programming language of separation logic manipulates arithmetic and boolean expressions that are evaluated w.r.t. the store. They are encoded by the inductive types `expr` and `expr_b` (the parts of the definitions which are not essential to the understanding of this paper are abbreviated with "..."):

```
Inductive expr : Set :=
  var_e : var.v → expr
| int_e : val → expr
| add_e : expr → expr → expr     Notation "e1 '+e' e2" := (add_e e1 e2).
...
Definition null := int_e 0%Z.
Definition nat_e x := int_e (Z_of_nat x).
Definition field x f := var_e x +e int_e f.
                                   Notation "x '-.>' f " := (field x f).
Inductive expr_b : Set :=
  eq_b : expr → expr → expr_b      Notation "e == e'" := (eq_b e e').
| neq_b : expr → expr → expr_b     Notation "e =/= e'" := (neq_b e e').
| and_b : expr_b → expr_b → expr_b Notation "e &&& e'" := (and_b e e').
| gt_b : expr → expr → expr_b      Notation "e >> e'" := (gt_b e e').
...
```

There is an evaluation function `eval` such that `(eval e s)` is the result of evaluating the expression `e` w.r.t. the store `s`.

The commands of the programming language of separation logic are also encoded by an inductive type:

```
Inductive cmd : Set :=
  assign : var.v → expr → cmd           Notation "x <- e" := (assign x e).
| lookup : var.v → expr → cmd           Notation "x '<-*' e" := (lookup x e).
| mutation : expr → expr → cmd          Notation "e '*<-' f" := (mutation e f).
| seq : cmd → cmd → cmd                 Notation "c ; d" := (seq c d).
| while : expr_b → cmd → cmd
| ifte : expr_b → cmd → cmd → cmd       Notation "'ifte' b 'thendo' c 'elsedo' c"
...                                       := (ifte b c d).
```

From this presentation, we omit the memory allocation and deallocation commands of separation logic (they are not useful for our use-case precisely because we verify the implementation of a memory allocation facility).

The operational semantics of the programming language of separation logic is defined by the following inductive type. An object of type (exec s c s') represents the execution of the command c from state s to state s'. Because heaps are finite maps, lookup and mutation may fail; to take this possibility into account, we use an option type.

```
Inductive exec : option state → cmd → option state → Prop :=
    exec_assign : ∀ s h x e,
     exec (Some (s, h)) (x <- e) (Some (store.update x (eval e s) s, h))
  | exec_lookup : ∀ s h x e p v,
     val2loc (eval e s) = p → heap.lookup p h = Some v →
     exec (Some (s, h)) (x <-* e) (Some (store.update x v s, h))
  | exec_lookup_err : ∀ s h x e p,
     val2loc (eval e s) = p → heap.lookup p h = None →
     exec (Some (s, h)) (x <-* e) None
  | exec_mutation : ∀ s h e e' p v,
     val2loc (eval e s) = p → heap.lookup p h = Some v →
     exec (Some (s, h)) (e *<- e') (Some (s, heap.update p (eval e' s) h))
  | exec_mutation_err : ∀ s h e e' p,
     val2loc (eval e s) = p → heap.lookup p h = None →
     exec (Some (s, h)) (e *<- e') None
  ...
```

3.2 Assertions and Reynolds' Axioms

Assertions of Hoare logic are predicate calculus formulas with the same expressions as the programming language. In consequence, the validity of an assertion depends on the current execution state of the program. There are mainly two ways to encode the semantics of such assertions in a proof assistant:

1. *Deep encoding*: define a syntax for assertions and a satisfaction relation between states and assertions.
2. *Shallow encoding*: identify formulas with functions from states to some "boolean type".

The advantage of shallow encoding over deep encoding is that deciding the validity of formulas becomes a function computation, for which the proof assistant provides native facilities (for example, tactics to prove tautologies).

We have developed a shallow encoding of separation logic in Coq. For this purpose, we identify assertions of separation logic with functions from states to `Prop`, the native type for predicate calculus formulas. For example, `True:Prop` represents truth and `∧:Prop → Prop → Prop` represents classical conjunction in Coq. This gives rise to the type `assert` below. By way of example, we also show the encoding of truth and conjunction in separation logic.

```
Definition assert := store.s → heap.h → Prop.
Definition TT : assert := fun s h => True.
Definition And (P Q:assert) : assert := fun s h => P s h ∧ Q s h.
```

Assertions of Separation Logic. The assertion that holds for empty heaps is defined by testing whether the heap is empty:

```
Definition emp : assert := fun s h => h = heap.emp.
```

`e ↦ e'` is the formula that holds for a singleton heap whose only location is the result of evaluating `e` and this location has for contents the result of evaluating `e'`:

```
Definition mapsto e e' s h := ∃ p,
  val2loc (eval e s) = p ∧ h = heap.singleton p (eval e' s).
Notation "e1 ↦ e2" := (mapsto e1 e2).
```

For example, `(var_e x ↦ int_e 4)` asserts that the variable `x` points to a cell that contains the integer 4. The following derived definitions will prove useful later: `e ↦ _` asserts that the cell `e` has some undefined contents, and `e ⇰ l` asserts that there is a list `l` of contiguous cell contents starting from `e`.

The separating conjunction `P ⋆ Q` holds for a heap that can be decomposed into two disjoint heaps for which `P` and `Q` respectively hold:

```
Definition con (P Q:assert) : assert := fun s h =>
  ∃ h1, ∃ h2, h1 ⊥ h2 ∧ h = h1 ⊎ h2 ∧ P s h1 ∧ Q s h2.
Notation "P ⋆ Q" := (con P Q).
```

For example, `(var_e x ↦ nat_e p) ⋆ (nat_e p ↦ int_e 2)` is the formal version of the example given in the beginning of this section.

The separating implication `P -⋆ Q` is less intuitive. It is used to represent logically mutations. In particular, the idiom `(e ↦ _ ⋆ (e ↦ e' -⋆ P))` holds for a heap such that the mutation of location `e` to contents `e'` leads to a heap that satisfies `P`. Section 4.2 gives a concrete example of such a formula together with its utilization. For the time being, we limit ourselves to the formal definition:

```
Definition imp (P Q:assert) : assert := fun s h =>
  ∀ h', h ⊥ h' ∧ P s h' → ∀ h'', h'' = h ⊎ h' → Q s h''.
Notation "P -⋆ Q" := (imp P Q).
```

Reynolds' Axioms. The axioms of separation logic are defined by the following inductive type. An object of type `(semax P c Q)` represents the fact that, going from a state satisfying `P`, the execution of the command `c` leads to a state satisfying `Q`:

```
Inductive semax : assert → cmd → assert → Prop :=
    semax_assign : ∀ P x e,
     semax (update_store2 x e P) (x <- e) P
  | semax_lookup : ∀ P x e,
     semax (lookup2 x e P) (x <-* e) P
  | semax_mutation : ∀ P e e',
     semax (update_heap2 e e' P) (e *<- e') P
  | semax_seq : ∀ P Q R c d,
     semax P c Q → semax Q d R → semax P (c ; d) R
  ...
Notation "{{ P }} c {{ Q }}" := (semax P c Q).
```

where update_store2, etc. are predicate transformers, for example:

```
Definition update_store2 (x:var.v) (e:expr) (P:assert) : assert :=
  fun s h => P (store.update x (eval e s) s) h.
```

Using these definitions, we have implemented much of [1], including the proof of soundness of the axioms of separation logic, the "frame rule", various axioms for backward reasoning, etc. For example, let us just give the axiom for backward reasoning used in the example at the beginning of this section:

```
Lemma semax_mutation_backwards : ∀ P e e',
  {{ fun s h => ∃ e'',(e ↦ e'' ⋆ (e ↦ e' -⋆ P)) s h }} e *<- e' {{ P }}.
```

4 The Heap-List Data Structure

4.1 The Heap-List Assertion

We define an assertion called Heap_List that holds for heaps that contain a well-formed heap-list. Separation logic is very convenient for this purpose. In particular, the property that blocks are disjoint can be expressed using the separating conjunction. The fact the blocks are contiguous relies on pointer arithmetic and this can also be expressed directly in separation logic.

Before defining the Heap_List assertion, we define an assertion to represent arrays of memory, i.e. sets of contiguous locations. Array p sz holds for a heap whose locations p, ..., p+sz-1 have some contents:

```
Fixpoint Array (p:loc) (size:nat) {struct size} : assert :=
  match size with
    O => emp
    | S n => (fun s h => ∃ y, (nat_e p ↦ int_e y) s h) ⋆ Array (p+1) n
  end.
```

We now come to the definition of heap-lists *without* terminal block (let us call them *pre-heap-lists* for convenience). Intuitively, (hl p l) represents the set of headers of a pre-heap-list whose first block starts at location p together with the set of free blocks (the allocated blocks are left outside); information about the blocks is captured by the parameter (l:list (nat*bool)): the list of sizes and flags of the blocks (:: is the list constructor and nil is the empty list):

```
Inductive hl : loc → list (nat*bool) → assert :=
  | hl_last: ∀ s p h,
      emp s h → hl p nil s h
  | hl_Free: ∀ s h p h1 h2 size tl,
      h1 ⊥ h2 → h = h1 ⊎ h2 →
      ((nat_e p ⤇ Free::nat_e (p+2+size)::nil)⋆(Array (p+2) size)) s h1 →
      hl (p+2+size) tl s h2 →
      hl p ((size,free)::tl) s h
  | hl_Allocated: ∀ s h p h1 h2 size tl,
      h1 ⊥ h2 → h = h1 ⊎ h2 →
      (nat_e p ⤇ Allocated::nat_e (p+2+size)::nil) s h1 →
      hl (p+2+size) tl s h2 →
      hl p ((size,alloc)::tl) s h.
```

where `free` and `alloc` are synonymous for booleans. The first constructor specifies empty pre-heap-lists. The second constructor specifies pre-heap-lists that start with a free memory block (that is, a header marked as free and its associated block) followed by a pre-heap-list. The third constructor specifies pre-heap-lists that start with an allocated memory header (in this case, the associated block is left outside). Observe that the definition above uses pointer arithmetic to guarantee that there is no lost space between linked blocks.

Finally, we define heap-lists (*with* terminal block). This is simply the separating conjunction of a pre-heap-list with a terminal block (an allocated block pointing to null):

```
Definition Heap_List (l:list (nat*bool)) (p:nat) : assert :=
  (hl p l) ⋆ (nat_e (get_endl l p) ⤇ Allocated::null::nil).
```

where `(get_endl l p)` returns the location at the end of the list `l` starting from location `p`, i.e., the location of (the header of) the terminal block.

4.2 Properties of Heap-Lists

The heart of our verification of the Topsy heap manager consists of a few basic lemmas capturing the properties of operations such as compaction of blocks, splitting of a block, changing the status of blocks, etc. Since these operations rely on destructive updates, the properties in question are adequately expressed using the separating implication.

For example, the following lemma expresses compaction of two contiguous free blocks (`++` is the list append function of Coq):

```
Lemma hl_compaction: ∀ l1 l2 size size' p s h,
  Heap_List (l1 ++ (size,free)::(size',free)::nil ++ l2) p s h →
  ∃ y, (nat_e (get_endl l1 p + 1) ↦ y ⋆
    (nat_e (get_endl l1 p + 1) ↦ nat_e (get_endl l1 p + size + size' + 4) -⋆
      Heap_List (l1 ++ (size+size'+2,free)::nil ++ l2) p)) s h.
```

The left-hand side of the (classical) implication states the existence of two contiguous free blocks `(size,free)` and `(size',free)`. The right-hand side represents the destructive update of the "next" field of the first block that is made to point to the block following the second block. As a result, the first block sees its size increased by the size of the second block. The function `get_endl` is used to compute the starting location of a block.

We can use this lemma to verify that a destructive update really performs compaction of blocks. Let us consider a concrete example:

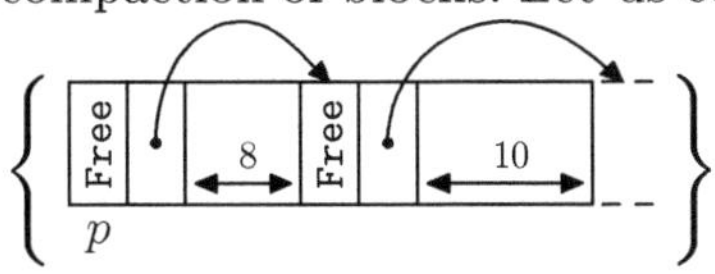

$p + 1$ *<- $p + 22$

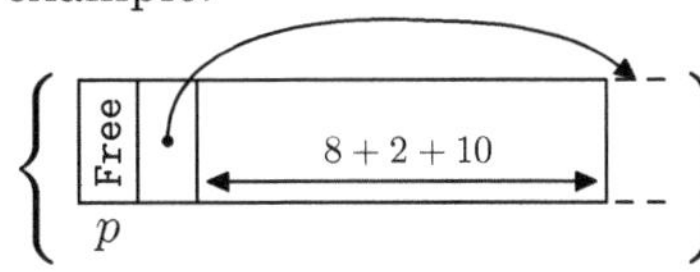

In Coq, we input the following goal, that makes use of `Heap_List` assertions:

```
Goal ∀ p, {{ Heap_List ((8,free)::(10,free)::nil) p }}
           nat_e p +e int_e 1 *<- nat_e p +e int_e 22
          {{ Heap_List ((20,free)::nil) p }}.
```

The application of the axiom for backward reasoning (seen in Sect. 3.2) leads to:

```
  p : nat
  s : store.s
  h : heap.h
  H : Heap_List ((8, free) :: (10, free) :: nil) p s h
  ============================
   ∃ e'' : expr,
     ((nat_e p +e int_e 1) ↦ e'' ⋆
      ((nat_e p +e int_e 1) ↦ (nat_e p +e int_e 22) -⋆
       Heap_List ((20, free) :: nil) p)) s h
```

This new goal is precisely the conclusion of the lemma we gave above. Application of this lemma terminates the proof.

5 Formal Verification

For each function of the heap manager, we give formal specifications using Hoare triples written with the encoding of Sect. 3 and the assertions of Sect. 4. We explain in more details the verification of the allocation function, because it is the most involved.

Prior to verification, the C source code of each function is translated into the programming language of separation logic. As a result of this translation, the signature of each function is augmented with parameters to represent local variables and the return value. This explains the differences between the signatures given in this section and in Sect. 2.1. The translation is explained in Sect. 6.2.

5.1 Formal Verification of Initialization

The initialization function `hmInit` transforms a given area of raw memory into an initial heap-list that consists of a single free block. In the source code, this area starts at location `hmStart` and has a fixed length `KERNELHEAPSIZE`. We formally verify `hmInit` for the general case of any starting location and any size greater than 4: the minimal space needed for two headers (the header of the free block and the header of the terminal block):

```
Definition hmInit_specif := ∀ p size, size ≥ 4 →
 {{ Array p size }} hmInit p size {{ Heap_List ((size-4,free)::nil) p }}.
```

The size of the array of memory corresponding to the free block is the size of the whole area of memory minus the size of the two headers. The verification of this triple is done almost automatically using a tactic provided by our Coq implementation. The non-automatic part is due to the translation of the assertions `Array` and `Heap_List` into the fragment of separation logic handled by this tactic. See Sect. 6.1 for more details.

Despite its apparent simplicity, this function turns out to be buggy, as we explain in Sect. 7.1.

5.2 Formal Verification of Allocation

The allocation function `hmAlloc` searches for a large-enough free block in the heap-list, possibly performing compaction of free blocks if needed. If an adequate block is found, it is split into an allocated block (whose location is returned) and a free block (available for further allocations); otherwise, an error is returned.

We introduce new assertions to simplify specifications. Under the hypothesis that `(Heap_List lst p0)` holds, the assertion `(In_hl lst (p,size,flag) p0)` means that the block starting at location `p` has size `size` and flag `flag`. The assertion `(s |= b)` holds when `b` is true in the store `s`.

As stated informally in Sect. 2.2, the specification of the allocation function consists in checking that (1) newly allocated blocks have at least the requested size, (2) they do not overlap with already allocated memory blocks (they are "fresh"), and (3) neither previously allocated memory blocks nor the rest of the memory is modified.

The formal specification of `hmAlloc` follows. In the pre-condition, we isolate some already allocated block `(x,sizex,alloc)`. In the post-condition, we ensure that (1) the newly allocated block `(y,size'',alloc)` has an appropriate size (i.e., greater than the requested `size`), (2) this newly allocated block does not overlap with previously allocated blocks (more precisely, the newly allocated block is built out of free blocks since `(Heap_List l adr ⋆ Array (y+2) size'')`, and it cannot be the previously allocated block `x` since `x ≠ y`), and (3) previously allocated memory blocks and the rest of the memory are not modified (because these areas are left outside of the area described by the `Heap_List` assertion). The second disjunction in the post-condition applies when allocation fails.

```
Definition hmAlloc_specif := ∀ adr x sizex size, adr > 0 → size > 0 →
  {{ fun s h => ∃ l, Heap_List l adr s h ∧ In_hl l (x,sizex,alloc) adr ∧
     (s |= var_e hmStart == nat_e adr) }}
   hmAlloc result size entry cptr fnd stts nptr sz
  {{ fun s h => (∃ l, ∃ y, y > 0 ∧ (s |= var_e result == nat_e (y+2)) ∧
      ∃ size'', size'' ≥ size ∧ (Heap_List l adr ⋆ Array (y+2) size'') s h ∧
      In_hl l (x,sizex,alloc) adr ∧ In_hl l (y,size'',alloc) adr ∧ x ≠ y)
     ∨
     (∃ l, (s |= var_e result == nat_e 0) ∧
       Heap_List l adr s h ∧ In_hl l (x,sizex,alloc) adr) }}.
```

Other assertions are essentially technical. The equality about the variable hmStart and the location adr is necessary because the variable hmStart is actually global and written explicitly in the original C source code of the allocation function. The inequality about the location adr is necessary because the function implicitly assumes that there is no block starting at the null location. The inequality about the requested size is not necessary, it is just to emphasize that null-allocation is a special case (see Sect. 7.1 for a discussion).

The allocation function relies on three functions to do (heap-)list traversals, compaction of free blocks, and eventually splitting of free blocks. In the rest of this section, we briefly comment on the verification of these three functions.

Traversal. The function findFree traverses the heap-list in order to find a large-enough free block. It takes as parameters the requested size and a return variable entry to be filled with the location of an appropriate block if any:

```
Definition findFree_specif := ∀ adr x sizex size, size > 0 → adr > 0 →
  {{ fun s h => ∃ l, Heap_List l adr s h ∧ In_hl l (x,sizex,alloc) adr ∧
     (s |= (var_e hmStart == nat_e adr) &&& (var_e result == null)) }}
   findFree size entry fnd sz stts
  {{ fun s h => ∃ l, Heap_List l adr s h ∧ In_hl l (x,sizex,alloc) adr ∧
     (s |= (var_e hmStart == nat_e adr) &&& (var_e result == null)) ∧
     ((∃ y, ∃ size'', size'' ≥ size ∧ In_hl l (y,size'',free) adr ∧
      (s |= (var_e entry == nat_e y) &&& (nat_e y >> null)))
      ∨
      s |= var_e entry == null) }}.
```

The post-condition asserts that the search succeeds and the return value corresponds to the starting location of a large-enough free block, or the search fails and the return value is null.

Compaction. The function compact is invoked when traversal fails. Its role is to merge all the contiguous free blocks of the heap-list, so that a new traversal can take place and hopefully succeeds:

```
Definition compact_specif:= ∀ adr size sizex x, size > 0 → adr > 0 →
 {{ fun s h => ∃ l, Heap_List l adr s h ∧ In_hl l (x,sizex,alloc) adr ∧
    (s |= (var_e hmStart == nat_e adr) &&& (var_e result == null) &&&
          (var_e cptr == nat_e adr)) }}
  compact cptr nptr stts
 {{ fun s h => ∃ l, Heap_List l adr s h ∧ In_hl l (x,sizex,alloc) adr ∧
    (s |= (var_e hmStart == nat_e adr) &&& (var_e result == null)) }}.
```

The formal specification of compact asserts that it preserves the heap-list structure. Its verification is technically involved because it features two nested loops and therefore large invariants. The heart of this verification is the application of the compaction lemma already given in Sect. 4.2.

Splitting. The function split splits the candidate free block into an allocated block of appropriate size and a new free block:

```
Definition split_specif := ∀ adr size sizex x, size > 0 → adr > 0 →
  {{ fun s h =>  ∃ l, Heap_List l adr s h ∧ In_hl l (x,sizex,alloc) adr ∧
     (s |= (var_e hmStart == nat_e adr) &&& (var_e result == null)) ∧
     (∃ y, ∃ size'', size'' ≥ size ∧ In_hl l (y,size'',free) adr ∧
       (s |= var_e entry == nat_e y) ∧ y > 0 ∧ y ≠ x) }}
   split entry size cptr sz
  {{ fun s h => ∃ l, In_hl l (x,sizex,alloc) adr ∧
     (∃ y, y > 0 ∧ (s |= var_e entry == int_e y) ∧
       (∃ size'', size'' ≥ size ∧
         (Heap_List l adr ⋆ Array (y+2) size'') s h ∧
         In_hl l (y,size'',alloc) adr ∧ y ≠ x)) }}.
```

The pre-condition asserts that there is a free block of size greater than `size` starting at the location pointed by `entry` (this is the block found by the previous list traversal). The post-condition asserts the existence of an allocated block of size greater than `size` (that is in general smaller than the original free block used to be).

5.3 Formal Verification of Deallocation

The deallocation function `hmFree` does a list traversal; if it runs into the location passed to it, it frees the corresponding block, and fails otherwise. Besides the fact that an allocated block becomes free, we must also ensure that `hmFree` does not modify previously allocated blocks nor the rest of the memory; here again, this is taken into account by the definition of `Heap_List`:

```
Definition hmFree_specif := ∀ p x sizex y sizey statusy, p > 0 →
  {{ fun s h => ∃ l, (Heap_List l p ⋆ Array (x+2) sizex) s h ∧
     In_hl l (x,sizex,alloc) p ∧ In_hl l (y,sizey,statusy) p ∧
     x ≠ y ∧ s |= var_e hmStart == nat_e p }}
   hmFree (x+2) entry cptr nptr result
  {{ fun s h => ∃ l, Heap_List l p s h ∧
     In_hl l (x,sizex,free) p ∧ In_hl l (y,sizey,statusy) p ∧
     s |= var_e result == HM_FREEOK }}.
```

The main difficulty of this verification was to identify a bug that allows for deallocation of the terminal block, as we explain in Sect 7.1.

6 Practical Aspects of the Implementation

6.1 About Automation

Since our specifications take into account many details of the actual implementation, a number of Coq tactics needed to be written to make them tractable.

Tactics to decide disjointness and equality for heaps turned out to be very important. In practice, proofs of disjointness and equality of heaps are ubiquitous, but tedious because one always needs to prove disjointness to make unions of heaps commute; this situation rapidly leads to intricate proofs. For example, the proof of the lemma `hl_compaction` given in Sect. 4.2 leads to the creation of 15 sub-heaps, and 14 hypotheses of equality and disjointness. With these hypotheses, we need to prove several goals of disjointness and equality. Fortunately, the tactic language of Coq provides us with a means to automate such reasoning.

We also developed a certified tactic to verify automatically programs whose specifications belong to a fragment of separation logic without the separating implication (to compare with related work, this is the fragment of [9] without inductively defined datatypes).

We used this tactic to verify the `hmInit` function, leading to a proof script three times smaller than the corresponding interactive proof we made (58 lines/167 lines). Although the code in this case is straight-line, the verification is not fully automatic because our tactic does not deal directly with assertions such as `Array` and `Heap_List`.

Let us briefly comment on the implementation of this tactic. The target fragment is defined by the inductive type `assrt`. The tactic relies on a weakest-precondition generator `wp_frag` whose outputs are captured by another inductive type `L_assrt`. Using this weakest-precondition generator, a Hoare triple whose pre/post-conditions fall into the type `assrt` is amenable to a goal of the form `assrt` → `L_assrt` → `Prop`. Given a proof system `LWP` for such entailments, one can use the following lemma to automatically verify Hoare triples:

```
Lemma LWP_use: ∀ c P Q R,
  wp_frag (Some (L_elt Q)) c = Some R →
  LWP P R →
  {{ assrt_interp P }} c {{ assrt_interp Q }}.
```

—The function `assrt_interp` projects objects of type `assrt` (a deep encoding) into the type `assert` (the shallow encoding introduced in this paper).

Goals of the form `assrt` → `L_assrt` → `Prop` can in general be solved automatically because the weakest-precondition generator returns goals that are inside the range of Presburger arithmetic (pointers are rarely multiplied between each other) for which Coq provides a native tactic (namely, the Omega test).

6.2 Translation from C Source Code

The programming language of separation logic is close enough to the subset of the C language used in the Topsy heap manager to enable a translation that preserves a syntactic correspondence. Thanks to this correspondence, it is immediate to identify a bug found during verification with its origin in the C source code. Below, we explain the main ideas behind the translation in question. Though it is systematic enough to be automated, we defer its certified implementation to future work and do it by hand for the time being.

The main difficulty in translating the original C source code is the lack of function calls and labelled jumps (in particular, the `break` instruction) in separation logic. To deal with function calls, we add global variables to serve as local variables and to carry the return value. To deal with the `break` instruction, we add a global variable and a conditional branching to force exiting where loops can break.

```
static void compact(HmEntry at) {
 HmEntry atNext;

 while (at != NULL) {
  atNext = at->next;


  while ((at->status == HM_FREED) &&
         (atNext != NULL)) {


    if (atNext->status != HM_FREED)
         break;

    at->next = atNext->next;

    atNext = atNext->next;
  }
  at = at->next;}
}
```

```
Definition compact (at
  atNext
  brk tmp cstts nstts:var.v) :=
while (var_e at =/= null) (
  atNext <-* (at -.> next);
  brk <- nat_e 1 ;
  cstts <-* (at -.> status);
  while ((var_e cstts == Free) &&&
         (var_e atNext =/= null) &&&
         (var_e brk == nat_e 1)) (
     nstts <-* (atNext -.> status);
     ifte (var_e nstts =/= Free) thendo (
        brk <- nat_e 0
     ) elsedo (
        tmp <-* atNext -.> next;
        at -.> next *<- var_e tmp;
        atNext <-* atNext -.> next
     ));
  at <-* (at -.> next)
).
```

Fig. 1. Code Translation from C to Coq—Example

Another minor point is that we need to add temporary variables to make up for the restricted set of expressions and commands of separation logic. For example, the evaluation of an expression in separation logic never returns a location, only values, thus we need beforehand to load a location into variable to be able to use it in a boolean expression; also, there is no command to lookup *and* mutate memory at the same time. We overcome these restrictions by decomposing complex expressions and commands, and using temporary variables. These temporary variables correspond to the parameters written without vowels in our specifications.

By way of example, Fig. 1 displays side-by-side the original `compact` function and its Coq counterpart.

The tables below summarize the whole Coq implementation:

Script files	Contents (lines)
`util.v`	Non-standard lemmas about integers, lists, etc. (825)
`heap.v`	Modules for locations, values, and heaps (2388)
`bipl.v`	Separation logic connectives (with tactics) (1579)
`axiomatic.v`	Separation logic triples, frame rule (1080)
`vc.v`	Weakest-precondition generator (196)
`contrib.v`	Various lemmas (arrays, etc.) (1077)
`contrib_tactics.v`	Various tactics (Omega extensions, etc.) (324)
`examples.v`	Small examples (411)
`example_reverse_list.v`	Reverse-list example (383)
`frag.v`	Tactic for a fragment of separation logic (1972)
`frag_examples.v`	Examples for the tactic above (176)

total: 10411 lines

Script files	Contents (lines)
`topsy_hm.v`	Heap-list definition and properties (1015)
`topsy_hmInit.v`	Initialization code, specification, and verification (313)
`topsy_hmAlloc.v`	Allocation code, specifications, and verifications (2762)
`topsy_hmFree.v`	Deallocation code, specification, and verification (536)
`hmAlloc_example.v`	Example of Sect. 7.2 (130)

total: 4756 lines

7 Benefits of Formal Verification

The main output of our experiment is that we have found several issues and bugs in the original source code of the Topsy heap manager. Another output is the Coq implementation of separation logic, that is readily available for other experiments. In particular, the verification of the Topsy heap manager in itself can actually be used for other verifications.

7.1 Issues and Bugs Found in the Original Source Code

Out of Range Initialization. When verifying the initialization function of the heap manager (Sect. 5.1), we found that the header of the terminal block was actually written outside of the memory area reserved for the heap manager. This illegal destructive update made the `Heap_List` assertion unprovable because the latter holds for a fixed area of memory. We corrected this bug by changing a single arithmetic operation, suggesting a programming miss. In all fairness, we must say that this bug was corrected in versions of Topsy posterior to version 2 (that we are using for verification).

Optimizations of Allocation. When verifying the allocation function (Sect. 5.2), we found several useless operations that suggested immediate optimizations.

One such useless operation is the possibility to allocate a non-empty memory block (that is, a header and a non-empty array of memory) when performing a null-size allocation. Since null-size allocations are not filtered out, the alignment calculation is applied anyway, resulting in a non-empty allocation (in addition to the header). This was highlighted when writing assertions. We improved the implementation by forcing failure for null-size allocation.

Among other optimizations, there were useless assignments (to dead variables) and useless tests. For example, there were two identical variables assignments before calling and at the beginning of the `findFree` function; this was highlighted when writing the loop invariant in `findFree`. More interestingly, there was a useless test in the `compact` function. The second conjunct of the test of the inner loop (see Fig. 1) is useless because only the terminal block marked as allocated can point to `null`. Such an optimization cannot be done by an ordinary compilers, contrary to the former one.

Deallocation of the Terminal Block. When verifying the deallocation function (Sect. 5.3), we found that it was possible to suppress allocable space without performing any allocation. This is because it is possible to deallocate the terminal block of the heap-list to trick compaction. The problem is better explained by the following scenario:

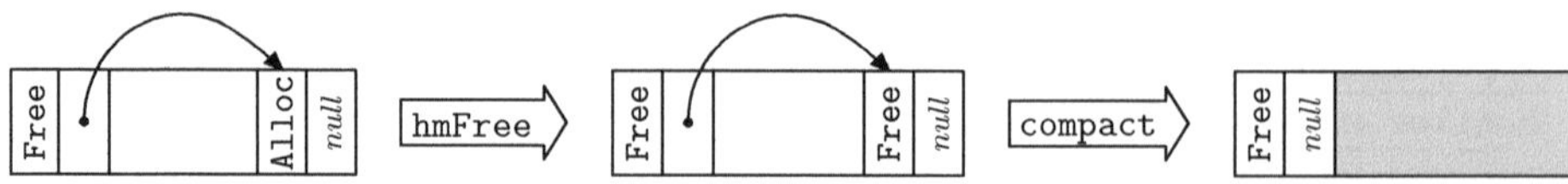

In this scenario, the terminal block is preceded by a free block. If we deallocate the terminal block and try to allocate a too-large block, this will trigger compaction and cause the leading free block to point to null. This problem is easily identified by the `Heap_List` assertion that enforces the terminal block to be marked as allocated. We fixed this problem by adding a test on the "next" field of the block to be deallocated in the deallocation function.

7.2 Using the Verification Result to Verify Other Code

Our verification of the Topsy heap manager provides us with new separation logic axioms that can be used for dynamic memory allocation without resorting to the native malloc/free commands of separation logic. In other words, we can use the specifications of `hmAlloc` and `hmFree` as triples to verify programs. For example, let us consider the following program:

```
Definition hmAlloc_example result entry cptr fnd stts nptr sz v :=
 hmAlloc result 1 entry cptr fnd stts nptr sz;
 ifte (var_e result =/= nat_e 0) thendo (
   (var_e result *<- int_e v)
 ) elsedo ( skip ).
```

This program allocates a new block using `hmAlloc`, stores its location into the variable `result`, and stores some value `v` into this block. Using the specification of `hmAlloc` proved in Sect. 5.2, we can prove the following specification:

```
Definition hmAlloc_example_specif := ∀ v x e p, p > 0 →
 {{ (nat_e x ↦ int_e e) ⋆
    (fun s h => ∃ l, (s |= var_e hmStart == nat_e p) ∧
     Heap_List l p s h ∧ In_hl l (x,1,alloc) p) }}
  hmAlloc_example result entry cptr fnd stts nptr sz v
 {{ fun s h => s |= var_e result =/= nat_e 0 →
    ((nat_e x ↦ int_e e) ⋆ (var_e result ↦ int_e v) ⋆ TT ⋆
     (fun s h => ∃ l, Heap_List l p s h ∧ In_hl l (x,1,alloc) p)) s h }}.
```

The post-condition asserts that, in case of successful allocation, the newly allocated block is separated from any previously allocated block.

8 Related Work

Our use case is reminiscent of work by Yu et al. that propose an assembly language for proof-carrying code and apply it to certification of dynamic storage allocation [7]. The main difference is that we deal with existing C code, whose verification is more involved because it has not been written with verification in mind. In particular, the heap-list data structure has been designed to optimize space usage; this leads to trickier manipulations (e.g., nested loop in `compact`), longer source code, and ultimately bugs, as we saw in Sect. 7.1. Also both allocators differ: the Topsy heap manager is a real allocation facility in the sense that the allocation function is self-contained (the allocator of Yu et al. relies on a pre-existing allocator) and that the deallocation function deallocated only valid blocks (the deallocator of Yu et al. can deallocate partial blocks).

The implementation of separation logic we did in the Coq proof assistant improves the work by Weber in the Isabelle proof assistant [8]. We think that our implementation is richer since it benefits from a substantial use case. In particular, we have developed several practical lemmas and tactics. Both implementations also differ in the way they implement heaps: we use an abstract data type implemented by means of modules for the heap whereas Weber uses partial functions.

Mehta and Nipkow developed modeling and reasoning methods for imperative programs with pointers in Isabelle [12]. The key idea of their approach is to model each heap-based data structure as a mapping from locations to values together with a relation, from which one derives required lemmas such as separation lemmas. The combination of this approach with Isabelle leads to compact proofs, as exemplified by the verification of the Schorr-Waite algorithm. In contrast, separation logic provides native notions of heap and separation, making it easier to model, for example, a heap containing different data structures (as it is the case for the `hmInit` function). The downside of separation logic is its special connectives that call for more implementation work regarding automation.

Tuch and Klein extended the ideas of Mehta and Nipkow to accommodate multiple datatypes in the heap by adding a mapping from locations to types [13]. Thanks to this extension, the authors certified an abstraction of the virtual mapping mechanism in the L4 kernel from which they generate verified C code. Obviously, such a refinement strategy is not directly applicable to the verification of existing code such as the Topsy heap manager. More importantly, the authors point that the verification of the implementation of malloc/free primitives is not possible in their setting because they "break the abstraction barrier" (Sect. 6 of [13]).

Schirmer also developed a framework for Hoare logic-style verification inside Isabelle [11]. The encoded programming language is very rich, including in particular procedure calls, and heap-based data structures can be modeled using the same techniques as Mehta and Nipkow. Thanks to the encoding of procedure calls, it becomes easier to model existing source code (by avoiding, for example, the numerous variables we needed to add to translate the source code of the Topsy heap manager into our encoding of separation logic). However, it is not clear whether this richer encoding scales well for verification of non-trivial examples.

Caduceus [14] is a tool that takes a C program annotated with assertions and generates verification conditions that can be validated with various theorem provers and proof assistants. It has been used to verify several non-trivial C programs including the Schorr-Waite algorithm [15]. The verification of the Topsy heap manager could have been done equally well using a combination of Caduceus and Coq. However, Caduceus does support separation logic. Also, we needed a verification tool for assembly code in Topsy; for this purpose, a large part of our implementation for separation logic is readily reusable (this is actually work in progress). Last, we wanted to certify automation inside Coq instead of relying on a external verification condition generator.

Berdine, Calcagno and O'Hearn have developed Smallfoot, a tool for checking separation logic specifications [10]. It uses symbolic execution to produce verification conditions, and a decision procedure to prove them. Although Smallfoot is automatic (even for recursive and concurrent procedures), the assertions only describe the shape of data structures without pointer arithmetic. Such a limitation excludes its use for data structures such as heap-lists.

9 Conclusion

In this paper, we formally specified and verified the heap manager of the Topsy operating system inside the Coq proof assistant. In order to deal with pointers and ensure the separation of memory blocks, we used separation logic. This verification approach proved very effective since it enabled us to find bugs in the original C source code. In addition, this use-case led us to develop a Coq library of lemmas and tactics that is reusable for other formal verifications of low-level code.

Recent Work. According to the specification described in this paper, an allocation function that always fails is correct. A complementary specification should make clearer the condition under which the allocation function is expected to succeed. In Topsy, allocation always succeeds when there is a list of contiguous free blocks whose compaction has the requested size. We have recently completed the verification of such a specification:

```
Definition hmAlloc_specif2 := ∀ adr size, adr > 0 → size > 0 →
  {{ fun s h => ∃ l1, ∃ l2, ∃ l,
    (Heap_List (l1 ++ (Free_block_list l) ++ l2) adr) s h ∧
    Free_block_compact_size l ≥ size ∧
    (s |= var_e hmStart == nat_e adr) }}
  hmAlloc result size entry cptr fnd stts nptr sz
  {{ fun s h => ∃ l, ∃ y,
      y > 0 ∧ (s |= var_e result == nat_e (y+2)) ∧
      ∃ size'', size'' ≥ size ∧
      (Heap_List l adr ⋆ Array (y+2) size'') s h ∧
      In_hl l (y,size'',alloc) adr }}.
```

This verification turned out to be technically more involved than the one described in this paper because of the numerous clauses required by the verification of `compact`.

Acknowledgments. The authors would like to thank Prof. Andrew W. Appel and his colleagues at INRIA for numerous suggestions that substantially improved the Coq implementation.

References

1. John C. Reynolds. Separation Logic: A Logic for Shared Mutable Data Structures. In *17th IEEE Symposium on Logic in Computer Science (LICS 2002)*, p. 55–74. Invited lecture.
2. Lukas Ruf and various contributors. TOPSY – A Teachable Operating System. `http://www.topsy.net/`.
3. Lukas Ruf, Claudio Jeker, Boris Lutz, and Bernhard Plattner. Topsy v3: A NodeOS For Network Processors. In *2nd International Workshop on Active Network Technologies and Applications (ANTA 2003)*.
4. Various contributors. The Coq Proof assistant. `http://coq.inria.fr`.
5. Nicolas Marti, Reynald Affeldt, and Akinori Yonezawa. Towards Formal Verification of Memory Properties using Separation Logic. In *22nd Workshop of the Japan Society for Software Science and Technology (JSSST 2005)*.
6. Reynald Affeldt and Nicolas Marti. Towards Formal Verification of Memory Properties using Separation Logic. `http://savannah.nongnu.org/projects/seplog`. Online CVS.
7. Dachuan Yu, Nadeem Abdul Hamid, and Zhong Shao. Building Certified Libraries for PCC: Dynamic Storage Allocation. *Science of Computer Programming*, 50(1-3):101–127. Elsevier, Mar. 2004.
8. Tjark Weber. Towards Mechanized Program Verification with Separation Logic. In *13th Conference on Computer Science Logic (CSL 2004)*, volume 3210 of *LNCS*, p. 250–264. Springer.
9. Josh Berdine, Cristiano Calcagno, and Peter W. O'Hearn. A Decidable Fragment of Separation Logic. In *24th International Conference on Foundations of Software Technology and Theoretical Computer Science (FSTTCS 2004)*, volume 3328 of *LNCS*, p. 97–109. Springer.
10. Josh Berdine, Cristiano Calcagno, and Peter W. O'Hearn. Symbolic Execution with Separation Logic. In *3rd Asian Symposium on Programming Languages and Systems (APLAS 2005)*, volume 3780 of *LNCS*, p. 52–68. Springer.
11. Norbert Schirmer. A Verification Environment for Sequential Imperative Programs in Isabelle/HOL. In *11th International Conference on Logic for Programming, Artificial Intelligence, and Reasoning (LPAR 2004)*, volume 3452 of *LNCS*, p. 398–414. Springer.
12. Farhad Mehta and Tobias Nipkow. Proving Pointer Programs in Higher-Order Logic. In *Information and Computation*, 199:200–227. Elsevier, 2005.
13. Harvey Tuch and Gerwin Klein. A Unified Memory Model for Pointers. In *12th International Conference on Logic for Programming, Artificial Intelligence, and Reasoning (LPAR 2005)*, volume 3835 of *LNCS*, p. 474–488. Springer.
14. Jean-Christophe Filliâtre. Multi-Prover Verification of C Programs. In *6th International Conference on Formal Engineering Methods (ICFEM 2004)*. volume 3308 of *LNCS*, p. 15–29. Springer.
15. Thierry Hubert and Claude Marché. A case study of C source code verification: the Schorr-Waite algorithm. In *3rd IEEE International Conference on Software Engineering and Formal Methods (SEFM 2005)*.

A Statically Verifiable Programming Model for Concurrent Object-Oriented Programs

Bart Jacobs[1,⋆], Jan Smans[1,⋆], Frank Piessens[1], and Wolfram Schulte[2]

[1] DistriNet, Dept. Computer Science, K.U. Leuven
Celestijnenlaan 200A, 3001 Leuven, Belgium
{bartj, jans, frank}@cs.kuleuven.be
[2] Microsoft Research
One Microsoft Way, Redmond, WA, USA
schulte@microsoft.com

Abstract. Reasoning about multithreaded object-oriented programs is difficult, due to the non-local nature of object aliasing, data races, and deadlocks. We propose a programming model that prevents data races and deadlocks, and supports local reasoning in the presence of object aliasing and concurrency. Our programming model builds on the multithreading and synchronization primitives as they are present in current mainstream languages. Java or C# programs developed according to our model can be annotated by means of stylized comments to make the use of the model explicit. We show that such annotated programs can be formally verified to comply with the programming model. In other words, if the annotated program verifies, the underlying Java or C# program is guaranteed to be free from data races and deadlocks, and it is sound to reason locally about program behavior. We have implemented a verifier for programs developed according to our model in a custom build of the Spec# programming system, and have validated our approach on a case study.

1 Introduction

Writing correct multithreaded software in mainstream languages such as Java or C# is notoriously difficult. The non-local nature of object aliasing, data races, and deadlocks makes it hard to reason about the correctness of such programs. Moreover, many assumptions made by developers about concurrency are left implicit. For instance, in Java, many objects are not intended to be used by multiple threads, and hence it is not necessary to perform synchronization before accessing their fields. Other objects are intended to be shared with other threads and accesses should be synchronized, typically using locks. However, the program text does not make explicit if an object is intended to be shared, and as a consequence it is practically impossible for the compiler or other static analysis tools to verify if locking is performed correctly.

⋆ Bart Jacobs and Jan Smans are Research Assistants of the Fund for Scientific Research - Flanders (Belgium) (F.W.O.-Vlaanderen).

Z. Liu and J. He (Eds.): ICFEM 2006, LNCS 4260, pp. 420–439, 2006.

We propose a programming model for concurrent programming in Java-like languages, and the design of a set of program annotations that make the use of the programming model explicit. For instance, a developer can annotate his code to make explicit whether an object is intended to be shared with other threads or not. These annotations provide sufficient information to static analysis tools to verify if locking is performed correctly: shared objects must be locked before use, unshared objects can only be accessed by the creating thread. Moreover, the verification can be done modularly, hence verification scales to large programs.

Several other approaches exists to verify race- and deadlock-freedom for multithreaded code. They range from generating verification conditions [1,2,3,4,5,6], to type systems [7,8]. (See Section 7 for an overview of related work.)

Our approach is unique, in that it builds around protecting invariants and that it allows sequential reasoning for multithreaded code. The contributions of this paper are thus as follows:

- We present a programming model and a set of annotations for concurrent programming in Java-like languages.
- Following our programming model ensures absence of data races and deadlocks.
- The generated verification conditions allow sound local reasoning about program behavior. Note that in this paper we ignore null dereference checking to avoid clutter, although our prototype fully supports it.
- We have prototyped a verifier as a custom build of the Spec# programming system [9,10], and in particular its program verifier for sequential programs.
- Through a case study we show the model is usable in practice, and the annotation overhead is acceptable.

The present approach evolved from [11]. It improves upon it by directly supporting platform-standard locking primitives, by preventing deadlocks, by adding support for immutable objects, and by reporting on experience gained using a prototype implementation. As did [11], it builds on and extends the Spec# programming methodology [12] that enables sound reasoning about object invariants in sequential programs.

The rest of the paper is structured as follows. We introduce the methodology in three steps. The model of Section 2 prevents low-level data races on individual fields. Section 3 adds deadlock prevention. The final model, which adds prevention of races on data structures consisting of multiple objects, is presented in Section 4. Each section consists of three subsections, that elaborate the programming model, the program annotations, and the static verification rules, respectively. The remaining sections discuss immutable objects, experience, and related work, and offer a conclusion.

2 Preventing Data Races

A data race occurs when multiple threads simultaneously access the same variable, and at least one of these accesses is a write access. Developers can protect data structures accessed concurrently by multiple threads by associating a mutual exclusion lock with each data structure and ensuring that a thread accesses the data structure only when it holds the associated lock. However, mainstream programming languages such as Java and C# do not force threads to acquire any locks before accessing data structures, and they do not enforce that locks are associated with data structures consistently.

A simple strategy to prevent data races is to lock every object before accessing it. Although this approach is safe, it is rarely used in practice since it incurs a major performance penalty, is verbose, and is prone to deadlocks. Instead, standard practice is to only lock the objects that are effectively shared between multiple threads. However, it is hard to distinguish shared objects (which should be locked) from unshared objects based on the program text. As a consequence, a compiler cannot enforce a locking discipline where shared objects can only be accessed when locked without additional annotations.

An additional complication is the fact that the implementation of a method may assume that an object is already locked by its caller. Hence, the implementation will access fields of a shared object without locking the object first. In such a case, merely indicating which objects are shared does not suffice. The implementor of a method should also make his assumptions about locks that are already held by the calling thread explicit in a method contract.

In this section, we describe a simple version of our programming model that deals with data races on the fields of shared objects. Later sections develop this model further to deal with deadlocks and high-level races on multi-object data structures.

2.1 Programming Model

We describe our programming model in the context of Java, but it applies equally to C# and other similar languages.

In our programming model, accesses to shared objects are synchronized using Java's **synchronized** statement. A thread may enter a **synchronized** (o) block only if no other thread is executing inside a **synchronized** (o) block; otherwise, the thread waits. In the remainder of the paper, we use the following terminology to refer to Java's built-in synchronization mechanism: when a thread enters a **synchronized** (o) block, we say it *acquires o's lock* or, as a shorthand, that it *locks o*; while it is inside the block, we say it *holds o's lock*; and when it exits the block, we say it *releases o's lock*, or, as a shorthand, that it *unlocks o*. Note that, contrary to what the terminology may suggest, when a thread locks an object, the Java language prevents other threads from locking the object but it does not prevent other threads from accessing the object's fields. This is the main problem addressed by the proposed methodology. While a thread holds an object's lock, we also say that the object *is locked* by the thread.

An important terminological point is the following: when a thread t's program counter reaches a **synchronized** (o) block, we say the thread *attempts to lock o*. Some time may pass before the thread *locks o*, specifically if another thread holds o's lock. Indeed, if the other thread never unlocks o, t never locks o. The distinction is important because our programming model imposes restrictions on attempting to lock an object.

Our programming model prevents data races by ensuring that no two threads have access to a given object at any one time. Specifically, it conceptually associates with each thread t an *access set* $t.A$, which is the set of objects whose fields thread t is allowed to read or write at a given point, and the model ensures that no two threads' access sets ever intersect. Access sets can grow and shrink when objects are created, objects are shared, threads are created, or when a thread enters or exits a **synchronized** block. Note that these access sets do not exist at run time: we use them to explain the programming model, and to implement the static verification.

- **Object creation.** When a thread creates a new object, the object is added to the creating thread's access set. This means the constructor can initialize the object's fields without acquiring a lock first. This also means single-threaded programs just work: if there is only a single thread, it creates all objects, and can access them without locking.
- **Object sharing.** In addition to an access set, our model associates with each run-time state a global *shared set* S. We call the objects in S *shared* and objects in the complement of S *unshared*. The shared set, like the access sets, is conceptual: it is not present at run time, but used to explain the model and implement the verification.
  A new object is initially unshared. Threads other than the creating thread are not allowed to access its fields. In addition, no thread is allowed to attempt to lock an unshared object: our programming model does not allow a **synchronized**(o){...} operation unless o is shared. In our programming model, objects that are not intended to be shared are never locked.
  If, at some point in the code, the developer wants to make the object available for concurrent access, he has to indicate this through an annotation (the **share** o annotation). When an object is being shared, the object is removed from the creating thread's access set and added to the shared set. From that point on, the object o is shared, and threads can attempt to acquire the object's lock. If, subsequent to this transition, any thread, including the creating thread, wishes to access the object, it must acquire its lock first. Once shared, an object can never revert to the unshared state.
- **Thread creation.** Starting a new thread transfers the accessibility of the receiver object of the thread's main method (i.e. the *Runnable* object in Java, or the *ThreadStart* delegate instance's target object in the .NET Framework) from the starting thread to the started thread. Otherwise, the thread's main method would not be allowed to access its receiver.
  In addition, the precondition requires this receiver object to be unshared. As a consequence, the invariant that shared objects in a thread's access set are also locked by that thread is maintained.
- **Acquiring and releasing locks.** When an object is being shared, it is removed from the creating thread's access set and added to the shared set. Since the object is now not part of any thread's access set, no thread is

allowed to access it. To gain access to such a shared object, a thread must lock the object first. When a thread acquires an object's lock, the object is added to that thread's access set for the duration of the synchronized block.

As illustrated in Figure 1, an object can be in one of three states: *unshared*, *free* (not locked by any thread and shared) or *locked* (locked by some thread and shared). Initially, an object is unshared. Some objects will eventually transition to the shared state (at a program point indicated by the developer). After this transition, the object is not part of any thread's access set and is said to be *free*. To access a free object, it must be locked first, changing its state to locked and adding the object to the locking thread's access set. Unlocking the object removes it from the access set and makes it free again.

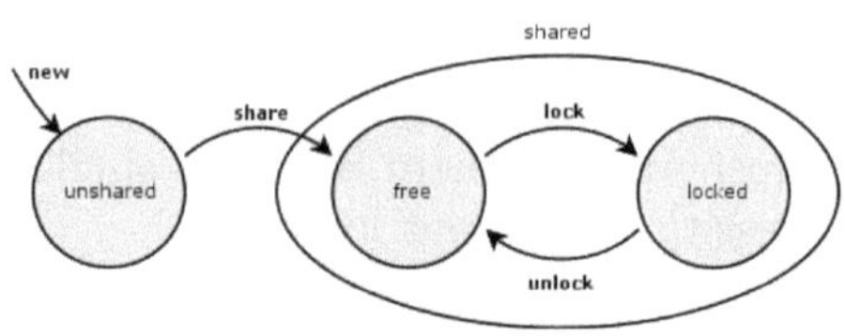

Fig. 1. The three states of an object

Let's summarize. Threads are only allowed to access objects in their corresponding access set. A thread's access set consists of all objects whose lock it holds, the objects it has created but not shared yet, and of the receiver object of the thread's main method, if the thread did not share this object yet. Our programming model prevents data races by ensuring that access sets never intersect.

2.2 Program Annotations

In this section, we elaborate on the annotations needed by our approach by means of the example shown in Figure 2. The example consists of a program that observes events from different sources and keeps a count of the total number of events observed. Since the count is updated by multiple threads, it is subject to data races unless precautionary measures are taken. Our approach ensures that it is impossible to "forget" to take such measures.

In our prototype implementation (see Section 6), annotations are written as stylized comments. But to improve readability, we use a language integrated syntax in this paper. Furthermore, in this paper := denotes assignment and = denotes equality.

The program shown in Figure 2 is a Java program augmented with a number of annotations (indicated by the gray background). More specifically, three sorts of annotations are used: **share** commands, **shared** modifiers and method contracts.

- The **share** command makes an unshared object available for concurrent access by multiple threads. In the example, the *counter* object is shared between all sessions.

```
class Counter {
  int count;
  Counter()
    ensures this ∈ tid.A ∧ this ∉ S;
  {}
}
class Session implements Runnable {
  shared Counter counter;
  int sourceId;
  Session(Counter counter, int sourceId)
    requires counter ∈ S;
    ensures this ∈ tid.A ∧ this ∉ S;
  {
    this.counter := counter;
    this.sourceId := sourceId;
  }
  public void run()
    requires tid.A = {this} ∧ this ∉ S;
  {
    for (;;) {
      // Wait for event from source sourceId (not shown)
      synchronized (counter) {
        counter.count++;
      }
    }
  }
}
class Program {
  static void start()
    requires tid.A = ∅;
  {
    Counter counter := new Counter();
    share counter;
    new Thread(new Session(counter, 1)).start();
    new Thread(new Session(counter, 2)).start();
  }
}
```

Fig. 2. Example program illustrating the approach of Section 2

- Fields and parameters can be annotated with a **shared** modifier, indicating they can only hold shared objects. The field *counter* of *Session* is an example of a field with a **shared** modifier.
- Method contracts are needed to make modular verification possible. They consist of preconditions and postconditions. A precondition states what the method implementation assumes about the current thread's access set

(denoted as $\textbf{tid}.A$) and about the global shared set. For instance, the precondition of *Program*'s *start* method requires the access set to be empty. Postconditions state properties of access sets and the shared set. For example, the postcondition of *Session*'s constructor guarantees that the new object is in the current thread's access set and unshared.

Note that our annotations are entirely erasable, i.e. they have no effect whatsoever on the execution of the program.

The example program is correctly synchronized, and the annotations enable our static verifier to prove this. We discuss in the next subsection how this is done. If the developer forgets to write the **synchronized** block in the *run* method, the program is no longer correctly synchronized. Specifically, the access of *counter.count* in method *run* violates the programming model, since object *counter* is not in the thread's access set.

Thread Creation. To verify the example, we also need the method contracts of all library methods used by the program. These are shown in Figure 3.

The method contracts shown in Figure 3 encode the programming model's rules regarding thread creation.

- The *Thread* constructor requires its argument to be part of the calling thread's access set and unshared. The constructor removes the *Runnable* object from the access set and associates it with the *Thread* object. Indeed, the constructor's postcondition does not state that in the post-state, the *Runnable* object is still in the access set, and therefore the caller cannot assume this and can no longer access the *Runnable* object.
- When method *start* is called, a new thread is started and the *Runnable* object associated with the *Thread* object is inserted into the new thread's access set. Method *run*'s precondition allows the method to assume that its receiver is the only object in the access set and that this object is unshared.

```
public interface Runnable {
  void run();
    requires tid.A = {this} ∧ this ∉ S;
}
public class Thread {
  public Thread(Runnable runnable)
    requires runnable ∈ tid.A ∧ runnable ∉ S;
    ensures this ∈ tid.A ∧ this ∉ S;
  { ... }
  public void start()
    requires this ∈ tid.A;
  { ... }
}
```

Fig. 3. Contracts for the library methods used by the program in Figure 2

2.3 Static Verification

We have explained our programming model informally in the previous sections. In this section we define the model formally, and show how we can statically verify adherence to the model in a modular (i.e. per-method) way.

We proceed as follows: a program P enriched with our annotations is translated to a *verification-time* program P' enriched with assertions and classical method contracts. This translation defines the semantics of our annotations, and is the formal definition of our programming model: the original annotated program P is correct according to our model, if and only if the translated program P' is correct with respect to its assertions and classical method contracts. To check if the translated program P' is correct, we use an existing automatic program verifier for single-threaded programs. Our experiments show (Section 6) that state-of-the-art verifiers are capable of verifying realistic programs in this way.

The contributions of this paper are in the design of the annotation syntax (for the multithreading-specific annotations) and the translation of the annotated program; we use existing technology [10] for sequential program verification. The translation involves two things. In a first step, we insert two verification-only variables into the program (so called ghost variables) to track the state necessary to do the verification. The ghost variable **tid**.A represents the current thread's access set, while S represents the set of shared objects.

Then, in a second step each method of the original program is translated in such a way that the translated method can be verified modularly. The method contracts that the developer writes in annotations are classical method contracts on the ghost state introduced in the first step. The code and other annotations written by the developer are translated into verification-time code and proof obligations (written as assertions) for the verifier. The essence of the translation of code and annotations is shown in Figure 4. It is a formalization of the programming model rules introduced in Section 2.1. We ignore the fact that

```
o := new C; ≡
  o ← new C;
  assume o ∉ S;
  tid.A ← tid.A ∪ {o};

x := o.f; ≡
  assert o ∈ tid.A;
  x ← o.f;

o.f := x; ≡
  assert o ∈ tid.A;
  if (f is declared shared)
    assert x ∈ S;
  o.f ← x;

share o; ≡
  assert o ∈ tid.A;
  assert o ∉ S;
  tid.A ← tid.A \ {o};
  tid.S ← tid.S ∪ {o};

synchronized (o) B ≡
  assert o ∈ S;
  assert o ∉ A;
  havoc o.*;
  tid.A ← tid.A ∪ {o};
  B
  tid.A ← tid.A \ {o};
```

Fig. 4. Translation of source program commands to verification-time commands

object references can be null to reduce clutter. The verification-time code for a **synchronized** block includes a **havoc** operation that assigns an arbitrary value to all fields of the object being locked. This reflects the fact that other threads may have modified these fields. Source program assignment and verification-time assignment are shown as := and $\leftarrow$, respectively.

3 Lock Levels for Deadlock Prevention

The approach of Section 2 prevents data races but it does not prevent deadlocks. In this section, we introduce our approach to deadlock prevention.

For the purpose of this paper, we define a deadlock to be a cycle of threads such that each thread is waiting for the next thread to release some lock. Formally, a deadlock is a sequence of threads $t_0, \ldots, t_{n-1}$ and a sequence of objects $o_0, \ldots, o_{n-1}$ such that t_i holds o_i's lock and is trying to acquire $o_{(i+1) \bmod n}$'s lock. Threads involved in a deadlock are stuck forever.

The prototypical way in which a developer can avoid deadlocks is by defining a partial order over all shared objects, and by allowing a thread to attempt to acquire an object's lock only if the object is less than all objects whose lock the thread already holds.

There are different common strategies for defining such a partial order. A first one is to define the order statically. This approach is common in case the shared objects protect global resources: code will have to acquire these resources in the statically defined order. A second strategy is to define the order based on some field of the objects involved. For instance to define a transfer operation between accounts, the two accounts involved can be locked in order of the account number, thus avoiding deadlocks while locking account objects.

In some cases the developer of a particular module may only wish to impose partial constraints on the locking order or may wish to abstract over a set of objects. For instance the developer of the Subject class in the Subject-Observer pattern may wish to specify that Observers should be locked before locking the Subject and not vice-versa. In other words, all Observers are above the Subject in the deadlock prevention ordering.

3.1 Programming Model

Our programming model is designed to support all three scenarios outlined above. The developer can indicate his intended ordering through the intermediary of *lock levels*. A lock level is a value of the new primitive type (existing only for verification purposes) **locklevel**. A new lock level can be constructed between given existing lock levels using the constructor

$$\mathbf{between}(\{\ell_1^A, \ldots, \ell_m^A\}, \{\ell_1^B, \ldots, \ell_n^B\}),$$

where $0 \le m, n$, provided that each specified lower bound is below each specified upper bound; formally, for each $1 \le i \le m$ and $1 \le j \le n$, $\ell_i^A < \ell_j^B$. The new value is above $\ell_1^A, \ldots, \ell_m^A$ and below $\ell_1^B, \ldots, \ell_n^B$. There is no other way to construct a lock level, which ensures that the less-than ($<$) relation on lock levels is always a partial order.

In the model, a lock level is associated with an object the moment the object is shared. This defines the lock order: for shared objects o_1 and o_2, we have $o_1 < o_2$ iff $o_1.lockLevel < o_2.lockLevel$. A thread is only allowed to lock an object if the object is less than the objects whose lock the thread already holds.

The level of indirection introduced by the lock levels provides an easy way to abstract over sets of objects. In the Subject-Observer example discussed above, all Observer objects can be given the same lock level (that should be above the Subject lock level).

3.2 Program Annotations

In a concurrent Java or C# program, a lock ordering adopted by the developers of a program for the purpose of deadlock prevention is not explicit in the program text, although it can be documented informally in comments. We propose annotations that make it possible for a developer to document the intended ordering formally. As a consequence, static verification of adherence to the ordering is possible (Section 3.3).

Three kinds of annotations are important. We discuss them using the example of the Dining Philosophers program in Figure 5. The program implements a deadlock-free solution to the Dining Philosophers problem with three philosophers. Our annotations explain formally why the program is deadlock-free.

The first kind of annotation is the creation of a lock level using the **between** constructor. The example defines the lock levels and their ordering statically in class *Program*'s *start* method. Three linearly ordered levels are defined: $level1 < level2 < level3$.

The second kind of annotation associates lock levels with shared objects. The **share** annotation is extended to accept a lock level as the second argument. Again, this happens three times in the example: each of the forks is shared with its associated lock level. As a consequence, fork objects are totally ordered, with $fork1 < fork2 < fork3$. Hence, forks can only be locked in descending order.

The third kind of annotations are the method contracts that make modular static verification possible. Method contracts make explicit what assumptions the method makes about the ordering of parameter objects, or about locks already held by the current thread. For instance the constructor of *Philosopher* expects its first argument to have a lower lock level than the second argument, and the *run* method requires that the current thread holds no locks.

These annotations enable a formal static verification of deadlock-freeness.

3.3 Static Verification

Static verification is again done by translating the annotated program P into a program P' enriched with proof obligations for a static verifier (in the form of classical method contracts and assertions). The translation adds ghost fields and variables to track the necessary state. To track the lock level of objects, we add to each object a ghost field called *lockLevel*, whose value is either *null* or a

```
class Fork {
}
class Philosopher implements Runnable {
  shared Fork fork1;
  shared Fork fork2;

  Philosopher( shared Fork fork1, shared Fork fork2)
    requires fork1.lockLevel < fork2.lockLevel;
    ensures this ∈ tid.A ∧ this ∉ S
  {
    this.fork1 := fork1;
    this.fork2 := fork2;
  }
  public void run()
    requires tid.A = {this} ∧ this ∉ S;
    requires tid.lockStack.isEmpty();
  {
    for (;;) {
      synchronized (fork2) {
        synchronized (fork1) {
          // Use the forks to eat...
        }
      }
    }
  }
}
class Program {
  static void start()
    requires tid.lockStack.isEmpty();
  {
    locklevel level1 := between({}, {});
    locklevel level2 := between({level1}, {});
    locklevel level3 := between({level2}, {});
    Fork fork1 := new Fork();
    share (fork1, level1);
    Fork fork2 := new Fork();
    share (fork2, level2);
    Fork fork3 := new Fork();
    share (fork3, level3);
    new Thread(new Philosopher(fork1, fork2)).start();
    new Thread(new Philosopher(fork2, fork3)).start();
    new Thread(new Philosopher(fork1, fork3)).start();
  }
}
```

Fig. 5. Deadlock prevention for the Dining Philosophers

lock level and whose initial value is *null*. The field is written only once: when the object is shared a non-null lock level is assigned to this field. This way, each shared object has an immutable association with a lock level.

To track the locks that the current thread holds, we introduce a ghost variable **tid**.*lockStack*, which is a stack containing the objects whose lock the thread holds. Whenever a thread acquires an object's lock, the object is pushed onto the stack. Note that it follows that the top of the stack is always the least of all objects on the stack. A thread is allowed to acquire an object *o*'s lock only if the lock stack is empty or *o*'s lock level is strictly less than the lock level of the object at the top of the stack.

The essence of the translation of an annotated program is summarized in Figure 6. Note that the rules for object creation and field access have been omitted since they are unchanged from the previous section.

share (o, l); $\equiv$
  assert $o \in$ **tid**.A;
  assert $o \notin S$;
  tid.$A \leftarrow$ **tid**.$A \setminus \{o\}$;
  tid.$S \leftarrow$ **tid**.$S \cup \{o\}$;
  $o.lockLevel \leftarrow l$;

synchronized (o) B $\equiv$
  assert $o \in S$;
  assert **tid**.$lockStack.isEmpty() \vee$
    $o.locklevel <$ **tid**.$lockStack.top().locklevel$;
  tid.$lockStack.push(o)$;
  havoc $o.*$;
  tid.$A \leftarrow$ **tid**.$A \cup \{o\}$;
  B
  tid.$A \leftarrow$ **tid**.$A \setminus \{o\}$;
  tid.$lockStack.pop()$;

Fig. 6. Translation of source program commands to verification-time commands

4 Invariants and Ownership

The approach as described in the preceding sections ensures absence of low-level data races and deadlocks. However, it does not prevent higher-level race conditions, where the programmer protects individual field accesses, but not updates involving accesses of multiple fields or objects that are part of the same data structure. As a result, accesses may be interleaved in such a way that the data structure's consistency is not maintained.

4.1 Programming Model

To prevent race conditions that break the consistency of multi-object data structures, we integrate the Spec# methodology's object invariant and ownership system [12] into our approach, to obtain the final programming model of this paper. This model supports objects that use other objects to represent their state, and object invariants that express consistency constraints on such multi-object structures.

The programming model requires the programmer to designate a subset of each class's fields as the class's *rep fields.* The objects pointed to by an object *o*'s non-null *rep* fields in a given program state are called *o*'s *rep objects.* An object's *rep* objects may have *rep* objects themselves, and so on; we refer to all of these as the object's transitive *rep* objects. The fields of an object, along with those of its transitive *rep* objects, are considered in our approach to constitute the entire representation of the state of the object; hence the name. As will be explained later, a shared object *o*'s lock protects both *o* and its transitive *rep* objects.

In addition to a set of *rep* fields, the programming model requires the programmer to designate, for each class C, an *object invariant*, denoted $Inv_C(o)$ when applied to an object o of C. $Inv_C(o)$ is a predicate that may depend on the state of o, i.e. the fields of o and of its transitive *rep* objects.

The object invariant for an object o need not hold in each program state; rather, the programming model associates with each object a boolean state variable called its *inv bit.*[1] The programming model requires the object invariant to hold only when the *inv* bit is *true.*

The programming model requires an object's *inv* bit to be *true* when a thread shares the object or unlocks it, i.e. when the object becomes free. It follows that each free object's *inv* bit is *true* and its object invariant holds. As a result, when a thread locks an object, it may assume that the object's *inv* bit is true and its object invariant holds.

At the start of an object's constructor, its *inv* bit is *false.* The programming model requires the programmer to designate the regions of code where an object's invariant is supposed to hold by designating the points where **pack** *o*; and **unpack** *o*; operations occur. The former sets *o*'s *inv* bit to *true*, and the latter sets it to *false.*

To ensure that whenever an object's *inv* bit is *true*, its object invariant holds, the programming model imposes the following restrictions:

- A thread may assign to an object's fields only when the object is in the thread's access set *and* the object's *inv* bit is *false.* Furthermore, the remaining restrictions ensure that whenever an object's *inv* bit is *true*, then so are those of its transitive *rep* objects. As a result, an object's state does not change while its *inv* bit is *true.*
- A thread is allowed to perform a **pack** *o*; operation only when *o*'s object invariant holds, its *inv* bit is *false*, and the *inv* bits of *o*'s *rep* objects are *true.* Furthermore, besides setting *o*'s *inv* bit to *true*, the operation removes *o*'s *rep* objects from the thread's access set.
- A thread is allowed to perform an **unpack** *o*; operation only when *o*'s *inv* bit is *true.* The operation sets *o*'s *inv* bit to *false* and adds *o*'s *rep* objects to the thread's access set.

We say that an object *owns* its *rep* objects whenever its *inv* bit is *true.* It follows from the above restrictions that an object has at most one owner.

[1] The *inv* bit is not a field in the actual program; it is a variable introduced only to explain the programming model.

```
class Point {
  int x, y;
  void move(int dx, int dy)
    requires this ∈ tid.A ∧ this.inv; ensures this ∈ tid.A ∧ this.inv;
  { unpack this; x := x + dx; y := y + dy; pack this; }
}
class Rectangle {
  rep Point ul, lr;
  invariant ul.x ≤ lr.x ∧ ul.y ≤ lr.y;
  void move(int dx, int dy)
    requires this ∈ tid.A ∧ this.inv; ensures this ∈ tid.A ∧ this.inv;
  { unpack this; ul.move(dx, dy); lr.move(dx, dy); pack this; }
  int getHeight()
    requires this ∈ tid.A ∧ this.inv; ensures this ∈ tid.A ∧ this.inv;
    ensures 0 ≤ result;
  { unpack this; int h := lr.y − ul.y; pack this; return h; }
}
class Application {
  shared Rectangle windowBounds;
  void paint()
    requires tid.lockStack.isEmpty();
    requires this ∈ tid.A ∧ this.inv; ensures this ∈ tid.A ∧ this.inv;
  {
    int height;
    synchronized (windowBounds) {
      height := windowBounds.getHeight();
    }
    ...
  }
}
class WindowManager {
  shared Rectangle windowBounds;
  void mouseDragged(int dx, int dy)
    requires tid.lockStack.isEmpty();
    requires this ∈ tid.A ∧ this.inv; ensures this ∈ tid.A ∧ this.inv;
  {
    synchronized (windowBounds) {
      windowBounds.move(dx, dy);
    }
  }
}
```

Fig. 7. An example illustrating our data race and deadlock prevention strategy, combined with object invariants and ownership

Note that our approach supports ownership transfer; a *rep* object can be moved from one owner to another by first unpacking both owners and then simply updating the relevant *rep* fields.

4.2 Program Annotations

The example in Figure 7 shows the annotations required by our final methodology. A *Rectangle* object is used to store the bounds of an application's window. The *Rectangle*'s state is represented internally using two *Point* objects, that represent the location of upper-left and lower-right corner, respectively. If the user drags the window's title bar, the window manager moves the window, even if the application is painting the window contents. Our methodology ensures that the application sees only valid states of the *Rectangle* object.

Developers designate a class's *rep* fields using the **rep** modifier, they define a class's object invariant using **invariant** declarations, and they insert **pack** and

```
o := new C; ≡
  o ← new C;
  assume o ∉ S;
  tid.A ← tid.A ∪ {o};
  o.inv ← false;

pack o; ≡
  assert o ∈ tid.A;
  assert ¬o.inv
  assert (∀p ∈ repobjects(o) •
    p ∈ tid.A ∧ p ∉ S ∧ p.inv);
  assert Inv(o);
  o.inv ← true;
  foreach (p ∈ repobjects(o))
    tid.A ← tid.A \ {p};

unpack o; ≡
  assert o ∈ tid.A;
  assert o.inv;
  o.inv ← false;
  foreach (p ∈ repobjects(o)){
    tid.A ← tid.A ∪ {p};
    assume p ∉ S;
  }

x := o.f; ≡
  assert o ∈ tid.A;
  x ← o.f;

o.f := x; ≡
  assert o ∈ tid.A;
  assert ¬o.inv;
  if (f is declared shared)
    assert x ∈ S;
  o.f ← x;

share (o, l); ≡
  assert o ∈ tid.A;
  assert o.inv;
  assert o ∉ S;
  o.lockLevel ← l;
  S ← S ∪ {o};
  tid.A ← tid.A \ {o};

synchronized (o) B ≡
  assert o ∈ S;
  assert tid.lockStack.isEmpty()∨
             o.locklevel < tid.lockStack.top().locklevel;
  tid.lockStack.push(o);
  foreach (p ∉ tid.A) havoc p.*;
  tid.A ← tid.A ∪ {o};
  assume o.inv;
  B
  assert o.inv;
  tid.A ← tid.A \ {o};
  tid.lockStack.pop();
```

Fig. 8. Translation of source program commands to verification-time commands (with invariants and ownership)

unpack commands in method bodies. Additionally, developers may denote an object o's *inv* bit in method contracts, using the $o.inv$ notation.

4.3 Static Verification

Figure 8 shows the translation of source program commands to input for the sequential program verifier.

Note that the verification-time commands for a **synchronized** (o) block havoc all objects that are not in the thread's access set, rather than just object o. This is necessary since other threads may have modified not just o, but o's transitively owned objects as well. Also, the assumption encoded by the **assume** statement is justified by the programming model, as explained above.

The verifier is additionally made aware of the following properties:

$$(\forall o \bullet o.inv \Rightarrow Inv(o))$$
$$(\forall o, p \bullet o.inv \wedge p \in \text{repobjects}(o) \Rightarrow p.inv)$$

These are guaranteed to hold in each program state by the programming model, as explained above.

5 Immutable Objects

In this section we briefly describe how the approach we implemented supports sharing immutable objects without synchronization.

If after an object is shared, it is only ever inspected and never mutated, then there's no need to synchronize accesses. Our approach supports this by splitting a thread's access set into a *read set* and a *write set*, and by splitting the shared sharing mode into a lockprotected mode and an immutable mode. Correspondingly, the **share** command is replaced with a **share_lockprotected** command and a **share_immutable** command. Sharing an object as immutable requires that it is unshared and in the current thread's write set. It removes the object from the write set and adds it to each thread's read set (even if the thread has not yet been started). If the object has *rep* objects, they are recursively shared as immutable and added to all read sets.

Whether an object is shared as lock-protected or as immutable, it must be fully packed in both cases. As a result, an immutable object's invariant holds at all times.

Our approach supports writing classes that allow client code the freedom to use some of the class's objects as thread-local (unshared) objects, to share some and protect them by their lock, and to share some as immutable. Such a class typically provides inspector methods and mutator methods. Only inspector methods can be called on immutable objects.

The **unpack** o; command requires o to be in the thread's write set. To allow an inspector method to access its receiver's *rep* objects, regardless of whether the receiver is writable or only readable, our approach includes a **read** (o) block that adds o's *rep* objects to the thread's read set for the duration of the block. It also temporarily removes o itself from the write set (but not the read set); this is required for soundness.

6 Experience

To verify the applicability of our approach to realistic, useful programs, we implemented it in a custom build of the Spec# program verifier [10] and used it to verify a chat server application written in C# with annotations inserted in the form of specially marked comments. The application verifies successfully; this guarantees the following:

- The program is free from data races and deadlocks
- Object invariants, loop invariants, method preconditions and postconditions, and assert statements declared by the program hold
- The program is free from null dereferences, array index out of bounds errors, and typecasting errors
- The program is free from races on platform resources such as network sockets. This is achieved by enforcing concurrency contracts on the relevant API methods.

Table 1 shows the annotation overhead of four programs which we annotated and verified. Programs chat and phone were derived from the ones used in [7].

Table 1. Annotation overhead

Program	Lines of Code	Lines Changed or Added	Overhead
chat	344	117	34%
phone	222	50	23%
prod-cons	84	24	29%
philosophers	64	21	33%

The prototype verifier and the sample programs are available from the first author's web site at http://www.cs.kuleuven.be/~bartj/.

7 Related Work

The Extended Static Checkers for Modula-3 [1] and for Java [2] attempt to statically find errors in object-oriented programs. These tools include support for the prevention of data races and deadlocks. For each field, a programmer can designate which lock protects it. However, these two tools trade soundness for ease of use; for example, they do not take into consideration the effects of other threads between regions of exclusion. Moreover, various engineering tradeoffs in the tools notwithstanding, the methodology used by the tools was never formalized enough to allow a soundness proof.

Method specifications in our methodology pertain only to the pre-state and post-state of method calls. Some systems [4,3] additionally support specification and verification of the atomic transactions performed during a method call. We focus on verification of object invariants, which does not require such specifications.

A number of type systems have been proposed that prevent data races in object-oriented programs. For example, Boyapati *et al.* [7] parameterize classes by the protection mechanism that will protect their objects against data races. The type system supports thread-local objects, objects protected by a lock (its own lock or its root owner's lock), read-only objects, and unique pointers. However, the ownership relationship that relates objects to their protection mechanism is fixed. Also, the type system does not support object invariants.

Boyapati *et al.* prevent deadlocks by allowing the developer to declare a fixed set of lock levels. Lock levels are assigned to objects as type arguments. Additional expressiveness is gained by supporting locking the nodes of a mutable tree data structure or an immutable DAG data structure, and by ordering the objects of designated classes at run time.

We enable sequential reasoning and ensure consistency of aggregate objects by preventing data races. Some authors propose pursuing a different property, called *atomicity*, either through dynamic checking [13], by way of a type system [8], or using a theorem prover [6]. An atomic method can be reasoned about sequentially. However, we enable sequential reasoning even for non-atomic methods, by assuming only the object invariant for a newly acquired object (see Figure 8). Also, in [8] the authors claim that data-race-freedom is unnecessary for sequential reasoning. It is true that some data races are benign, even in the Java and C# memory models; however, the data races allowed in [8] are generally not benign in these memory models; indeed, the authors prove soundness only for sequentially consistent systems, whereas we prove soundness for the Java memory model, which is considerably weaker.

Ábrahám-Mumm *et al.* [5] propose an assertional proof system for Java's reentrant monitors. It supports object invariants, but these can depend only on the fields of **this**. No claim of modular verification is made.

The rules in our methodology that an object must be consistent when it is released, and that it can be assumed to be consistent when it is acquired, are taken from Hoare's work on monitors and monitor invariants [14].

There are also tools that try dynamically to detect violations of safe concurrency. A notable example is Eraser [15]. It finds data races by looking for locking-discipline violations. The tool has been effective in practice, but does not come with guarantees about the completeness nor the soundness of the method.

In the straightforward implementation proposed in this paper, mutual exclusion is achieved through coarse-grained locking. However, the methodology allows one to use other semantically equivalent techniques that may be more appropriate for particular contention patterns, while preserving the same reasoning framework and safety guarantees. Possible alternatives include fine-grained locking of the objects within an ownership domain, or a form of optimistic concurrency, such as transactional monitors [16].

The present approach evolved from [11]. It improves upon it by supporting standard locking primitives, by preventing deadlocks, by supporting immutable objects, and by reporting on experience gained using a prototype verifier.

8 Conclusion

We propose a programming model for concurrent programming in Java-like languages, and the design of a set of program annotations that make the use of the programming model explicit and that enable automated verification of compliance. Our programming model ensures absence of data races and deadlocks, and provides a sound approach for local reasoning about program behavior. We have prototyped the verifier as a custom build of the Spec# programming system. Through a case study we show the model is usable in practice, and the annotation overhead is acceptable.

Our verification approach is sound; the proof of soundness is largely analogous to the one given in [17] for an earlier version of the approach.

We are currently further extending the programming model to encompass static fields, lock re-entry, and read-write locks.

References

1. Detlefs, D.L., Leino, K.R.M., Nelson, G., Saxe, J.B.: Extended static checking. Research Report 159, Compaq Systems Research Center (1998)
2. Flanagan, C., Leino, K.R.M., Lillibridge, M., Nelson, G., Saxe, J.B., Stata, R.: Extended static checking for Java. In: PLDI 2002. Volume 37 of SIGPLAN Notices., ACM (2002) 234–245
3. Freund, S.N., Qadeer, S.: Checking concise specifications for multithreaded software. Journal of Object Technology **3**(6) (2004) 81–101
4. Qadeer, S., Rajamani, S.K., Rehof, J.: Summarizing procedures in concurrent programs. In: POPL 2004. Volume 39 of SIGPLAN Notices., ACM (2004) 245–255
5. Ábrahám-Mumm, E., de Boer, F.S., de Roever, W.P., Steffen, M.: Verification for Java's reentrant multithreading concept. In: FoSSaCS 2002. Volume 2303 of LNCS., Springer (2002) 5–20
6. Rodríguez, E., Dwyer, M., Flanagan, C., Hatcliff, J., Leavens, G.T., Robby: Extending sequential specification techniques for modular specification and verification of multi-threaded programs. In: ECOOP 2005. Volume 3586 of LNCS., Springer (2005) 551–576
7. Boyapati, C., Lee, R., Rinard, M.: Ownership types for safe programming: Preventing data races and deadlocks. In: OOPSLA 2002. Volume 37 of SIGPLAN Notices., ACM (2002) 211–230
8. Flanagan, C., Qadeer, S.: A type and effect system for atomicity. In: PLDI 2003, ACM (2003) 338–349
9. Barnett, M., Leino, K.R.M., Schulte, W.: The Spec# programming system: An overview. In: CASSIS. Volume 3362 of LNCS., Springer (2004)
10. Barnett, M., Chang, B.Y.E., DeLine, R., Jacobs, B., Leino, K.R.M.: Boogie: A modular reusable verifier for object-oriented programs. In: Proceedings of the Fourth International Symposium on Formal Methods for Components and Objects (FMCO 2005). (2006) To appear.
11. Jacobs, B., Leino, K.R.M., Piessens, F., Schulte, W.: Safe concurrency for aggregate objects with invariants. In: Proc. Int. Conf. Software Engineering and Formal Methods (SEFM 2005), IEEE Computer Society (2005) 137–146

12. Barnett, M., DeLine, R., Fähndrich, M., Leino, K.R.M., Schulte, W.: Verification of object-oriented programs with invariants. Journal of Object Technology **3**(6) (2004) 27–56
13. Flanagan, C., Freund, S.N.: Atomizer: A dynamic atomicity checker for multithreaded programs. In: POPL 2004. Volume 39 of SIGPLAN Notices., ACM (2004) 256–267
14. Hoare, C.A.R.: Monitors: An operating system structuring concept. Communications of the ACM **17**(10) (1974) 549–557
15. Savage, S., Burrows, M., Nelson, G., Sobalvarro, P., Anderson, T.E.: Eraser: A dynamic data race detector for multi-threaded programs. ACM Transactions on Computer Systems **15**(4) (1997) 391–411
16. Welc, A., Jagannathan, S., Hosking, A.L.: Transactional monitors for concurrent objects. In: ECOOP 2004. Volume 3086 of LNCS., Springer (2004)
17. Jacobs, B., Leino, K.R.M., Piessens, F., Schulte, W.: Safe concurrency for aggregate objects with invariants: Soundness proof. Technical Report MSR-TR-2005-85, Microsoft Research (2005)

Model Checking Dynamic UML Consistency*

Xiangpeng Zhao[1], Quan Long[1,2], and Zongyan Qiu[1]

[1] LMAM and Department of Informatics, School of Math., Peking University, Beijing, China
[2] IBM China Research Laboratory
{zxp, qzy}@math.pku.edu.cn, longquan@cn.ibm.com

Abstract. UML is widely accepted and extensively used in software modeling. However, using different diagrams to model different aspects of a system brings the risk of inconsistency among diagrams. In this paper, we investigate an approach to check the consistency between the sequence diagrams and statechart diagrams using the SPIN model checker. To deal with the hierarchy structure of statechart diagrams, we propose a formalism called Split Automata, a variant of automata, which is helpful to bridge the statechart diagrams to SPIN efficiently. Compared with the existing work on model checking UML which do not have formal verification for their translation from UML to the model checker, we formally define the semantics and prove that the automatically translated model (i.e. Split Automata) does simulate the UML model. In this way, we can guarantee that the translated model does represent the original model.

Keywords: UML, Consistency, Semantics, Simulation, Model Checking, Algorithm.

1 Introduction

Model Checking has been proven an effective approach in formally verifying finite-state concurrent systems [3]. Efficient algorithms are used to traverse the model defined by the system and check whether the given specification holds or not. However, in contrast to its good acceptance in hardware industry, there is few large success case studies in software development [2,17]. One of the main reasons is that the state space of software systems, or even components is too large, thus causes the infamous "state exploration" problem in model checking. To reduce the state space, how to model the software system in an abstract way has been recognized as a central task.

Being the de facto standard of software modeling industry, the Unified Modeling Language (UML) [10] is now widely used in the development of software intensive systems. Compared to the other programming languages, UML is an abstract language for specifying software requirements, specifications, and designs in the early stages of development. This offers a natural platform to scale up the use of model checking.

Furthermore, the model checking technique can be helpful in solving new problems aroused in applying UML. In a UML-based development process, several kinds of models are used to represent and analyze the artifacts created in certain phases of the system development. This multi-view modeling has its advantages. Each view focuses on

* Supported by NNSF of China (No. 605730081).

Z. Liu and J. He (Eds.): ICFEM 2006, LNCS 4260, pp. 440–459, 2006.

a different aspect, so that the analysis and understanding of the various features of the modeled system can be done separately [1]. These different views might come from different people relative to the system, and reflect their requirements or expectations. Splitting a system model into several views can also decompose the model into chunks of manageable sizes, which is also important for tool development such as code generation and verification. However, a multi-view model is confronted with the problem of inconsistency among the different models in the whole system, since the aspects of the system described by these models may be overlapped. In this case, the developers hope to recognize these inconsistencies as early as possible.

Researchers, e.g. [5,1], have realized that the difficulties in consistency checking lie in the fact that the syntax and semantics of UML are informal and imprecise compared with formal modeling notations. For example, many features including role names in class diagrams and object names in sequence diagrams are optional and may not appear in the diagrams. This is not harmful if UML is only used in sketchy mode, but not satisfactory in the modes of blueprint and programming language [4], nor for code generation. According to our knowledge, current popular UML tools, such as Rational Rose, MagicDraw and Fujaba support very poor functionality in consistency checking, especially for the consistency between sequence diagrams and statechart diagrams.

We have investigated the consistency issue and the code generation problem in our earlier work [14], where the consistency of class diagrams and sequence diagrams is discussed and rCOS [7][1] code for the method bodies is generated. In this paper, we discuss the consistency issue between sequence diagrams and statechart diagrams. A sequence diagram is described by a modeler who cares about the interaction between some objects, but has less knowledge about the internal behavior of the objects reflected by the statechart diagrams; and vice versa for the modeler of the statechart diagrams. The consistency issue between statechart diagrams and sequence diagrams is dynamic, hence quite complicated. We choose to use the SPIN model checker [8] to solve this problem in this paper. Besides, note that collaboration diagrams can be realized by sequence diagrams, and vice versa. This implies that the solution to the consistency issue between sequence diagrams and statechart diagrams also apply to collaboration diagrams.

The basic idea is that invocation between different objects in a sequence diagram should conform to the transitions of the corresponding statechart diagrams. Firstly, we formalize sequence diagrams and statechart diagrams by giving the syntax of both diagrams in textual form[2], and then the semantics. Then we present algorithms for translating diagrams to SPIN specifications. Sequence diagrams can be formalized as a "never claim" assertion, which is a sequence of events describing unwanted behaviors; while the statechart diagrams are translated into a set of processes. SPIN can automatically verify whether the never claim is a valid trace of the system, thus answers the consistency problems.

An essential difficulty in the above scenario is the translation of statecharts. In general, model checkers can only deal with automata without hierarchical states, which is clearly not the case for statecharts. Motivated by this problem, we propose a formalism

[1] rCOS is an object-oriented design language equipped with a relational semantics.

[2] In our ongoing work, we have developed a tool to support this process.

named *Split Automata* which is an automata network plus a special control mechanism. Any statechart diagram can be mapped to a split automaton. The idea is to encode the data structures of statechart diagram as control structure. The mapping preserves dynamic behaviors of statecharts, and the interactions of the hierarchy are managed by the events passed between different automata. The semantics of split automata is quite similar to the semantics of process in Promela (the input language of SPIN), hence it is straightforward to be implemented.

To prove the fact that the mapping preserves the dynamic behavior of statechart diagrams, we use the notion of *Simulation*. We give formal operational semantics for both statechart diagrams and split automata. Supported by these semantics, we prove that a given statechart diagram can be *simulated* by a split automaton, hence guaranteeing the correctness of the translation.

Related works. There are many research work on model checking UML diagrams. Lilius and Paltor [13] provide a full operational semantics for UML state machines, and allows model checking using a tool called vUML. They perform unfolding of the hierarchical structure only when encoding the states, thus also having a similar benefit compared with our split automata mechanism. However, they do not prove the correctness of the translation from state machines to vUML. Küster et al. [12] present a translation from sequence and statechart diagrams to CSP processes, and use the FDR model checker to verify the consistency issue. Gallardo et al. [6] first translate the sequence diagram to MSC diagram, and the statechart diagram to SDL diagram, and then perform model checking to detect inconsistency in a similar manner. Inverardi et al. [9] use SPIN to check the consistency between diagrams and provides a systematic development methodology starting from software requirement. Hugo/RT [16,11] also use SPIN to verify the consistency between sequence diagrams and statechart diagrams, but they support timed verification by translating the model into the timed model checker UPPAAL instead of SPIN. However, they do not provide semantics and do not have formal treatment on their approaches. Therefore, whether the translated models checked by the tools really represent the original models with respect to the checking motivation remains doubtable. To solve this problem, we have defined and proved the simulation between the UML model and our formalism, which assures the correctness of the translation.

The rest of the paper is organized as follows. Section 2 introduces the formalization of sequence diagrams. Section 3 presents our treatment of statechart diagrams, including the syntax and semantics of both statechart diagrams and split automata, the mapping between them, and the proof of the simulation relation. In Section 4 we give two translation algorithms: an algorithm for translating a statechart diagram into a set of processes which is motivated by the split automata; and an algorithm for translating a sequence diagram to a never claim. We give a simple case study in Section 5. Section 6 concludes and some future research directions are discussed.

2 Sequence Diagrams

In this paper we consider sequence diagrams as a static model. Thus the syntax of the sequence diagram is a simplified version of the ones in [14].

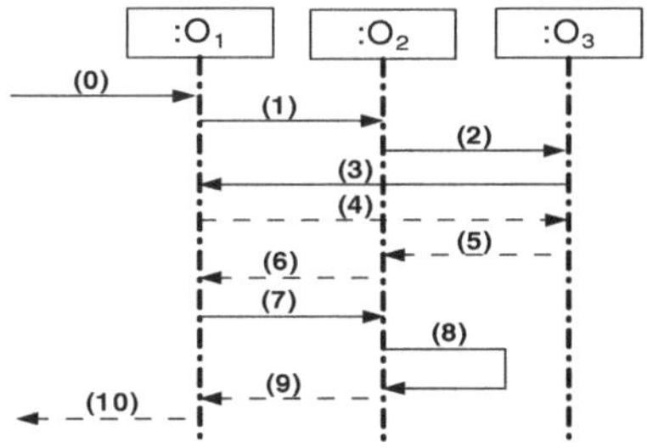

Fig. 1. A sequence diagram

A sequence diagram *SD* consists of three main parts:

1. A sequence of *time-points* $\langle p_1, p_2, \cdots, p_n \rangle$ representing the time points during the lifetime of all objects under consideration. These points represent the order of messages sending and receiving. The set of these points is called $Points$.
2. A sequence of objects: $\langle O_1, O_2, \cdots, O_m \rangle$, which is denoted by *SD.Objects*. Each object O_i has the following structure:
   - O_i is associated with a *type*, denoted by *type*(O), which is a class name. Since we consider only the consistency between sequence and statecharts diagrams, the details of the class declaration are not important here. (Please refer [14] for details of class diagrams)
   - There is a sequence of *time-points* $\langle p_{i_1}, p_{i_2}, \cdots, p_{i_k} \rangle$ which represents the time points during the lifetime of O_i, where $O_i.Points \subseteq Points$. The set of these points, namely $O_i.Points$, is a subset of the global set $Points$. Furthermore, for any i_a and i_b in $O_i.points$, if $a < b$, then $i_a < i_b$, that is, p_{i_a} appears before p_{i_b} in the global sequence.

     We have a function *stamp* at each time-point on an object O. For $p \in O.Points$, *stamp*$(p, O) \in$ {*send*, *ack*, *receive*, *receiveack*}. *stamp*(p, O)=*send* means a message (or equivalently, a method call) is sent from object O at time p, where $p \in O.Points$. Similarly, *receive* means a message reaches O at p. The message between a *send* point and a *receive* point will be drawn as a solid line arrow in the graph, e.g. the message (0) and (1) in Fig. 1. *ack* and *receiveack* points are used to denote the returned messages which are dotted line back to the sending lifeline, e.g. the message (4) and (5) in Fig. 1. Because we have "call back" messages (such as the message (3) in Fig. 1), so we need to draw all the returned messages.
3. A set *MSG* of messages: *msg* $\in$ *MSG* is of the form (*source*, m, *target*, p) where
   - *source*, denoted by *src*(*msg*), represents the source object of the message.
   - *target*, denoted by *tgt*(*msg*), represents the target object of the message.
   - m, denoted by *method*(*msg*), represents a method call[3]. If the source and the target are identical, it represents an internal action (e. g. message (8) in Fig. 1). Finally, a message can be a return signal and in this case m is the empty message ϵ.

[3] To simplify the syntax, we ignore the parameters of methods, which can be easily added.

– p, denoted by *time*(*msg*), represents the time-point when the message occurs. We suppose that the message transfer does not consume time; therefore, when the message occurs in the source object *src*(*msg*), it simultaneously occurs in the target object *tgt*(*msg*).

Moreover, the target or source object may be empty. If the target is empty, then the message is an outgoing message of the whole sequence diagram (message (10) in Fig. 1); or an incoming message (message (0) in Fig. 1) when the source is empty.

2.1 Semantics

We will consider only the *well-formed* sequence diagrams. The well-formedness of a sequence diagram concerns the following items:

- For each message *msg* in the sequence diagram, the *stamp* of the source point of *msg* must be a *send* or *ack* and the *stamp* of target point of *msg* must be a *receive* or *receiveack*, respectively.
- It should be ensured that the sequence diagram indeed represents a scenario of method calls. This means (a) the order of the message sending and receiving must be consistent, and for all messages from the same object, the earlier it is sent, the earlier it is received by the target object; (b) if a message *msg* invokes message msg_1, then msg_1 must return before *msg* does. This can be checked easily by a simple token-traverse algorithm.

The semantics of the sequence diagram is defined as a trace of messages that occurs according to the order of the time-points. Since our main focus is the consistency between the sequence diagram and the statechart diagrams, we ignore the returned messages in the semantics.

Definition 2.1 (Sequence Diagram). For a given sequence diagram SD involving objects $O_1, \cdots, O_m$, its semantics, denoted by $[\![SD]\!]$ is defined as

$$[\![SD]\!] \stackrel{def}{=} \langle msg_1, msg_2, \cdots, msg_n \rangle$$

where each message msg_i is in the set *MSG* of *SD*, and $time(msg_i) < time(msg_{i+1})$ for each $i < n$. □

3 Statechart Diagrams and Split Automata

In this section we will give the syntax and semantics of statecharts. With respect to the model checking strategy in this paper, we will also introduce our special formalism *Split Automata* which is essentially an automata network plus a special controlling mechanism by which an automaton can activate or stop other automata. We will present the syntax and the operational semantics of Split Automata. Based on the semantics, we will prove that the transition system of the corresponding split automata can *simulate* the one of the original statechart.

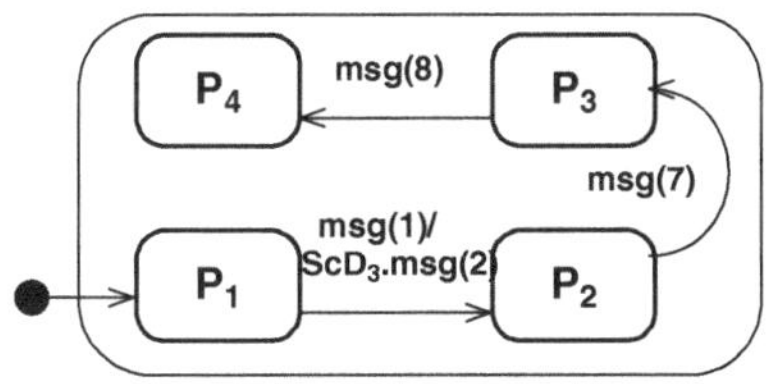

Fig. 2. A statechart ScD_2

3.1 Statechart Diagram

To facilitate our discussion, we use similar textual representation for statecharts in [15]. We only support a small subset of UML statecharts related to consistency checking. In order to keep the formalism concise, we omit guards, entry/exit actions, history states, OCL constraints in the statechart, and only allow one action in each transition. The formal syntax for statecharts is given as follows.

Suppose we have the following sets:

- N: The set of names used to denote statecharts.
- Π: The set of all possible events corresponding to the messages in the sequence diagrams. In this paper, the words "message" and "event" mean the same thing. The empty event ϵ is also included in Π.
- $\mathcal{T}$: The set of all possible transitions, $\mathcal{T} \subseteq N \times \Pi \times (N \times \Pi) \times N$, where
  - The first N denotes the source sub-statechart, while the last N is the target sub-statechart.
  - Π denotes the trigger. Note that we do not allow guards here. Since guards do not appear in sequence diagrams, they are not useful in consistency checking.
  - $(N \times \Pi)$ denotes the action, which stands for new event generated by the transition. For example, if (n, e) is an element of the action of the transition, e stands for what event the transition generates and n stands for which statechart should receive the newly generated event. Potentially, n can be the name of another statechart. We only allow one action in each transition here to simplify the semantics. It is not hard to extend the notation to support multiple actions.

  Thus, (p_i, e, A, p_j) is a transition from sub-statechart p_i to p_j with trigger e and action set A. For example, in Fig. 2, we have three transitions:

$$\tau_1 = (P_1, msg(1), ScD_3.msg(2), P_2)$$
$$\tau_2 = (P_2, msg(7), \epsilon, P_3)$$
$$\tau_3 = (P_3, msg(8), \epsilon, P_4)$$

Definition 3.1 (Statechart diagram). The set *ScD* of statecharts is defined inductively as follows:

1. Basic: $N \rightarrow ScD$:

$$Basic(n) \stackrel{def}{=} [n]$$

2. Or: $N \times \langle ScD \rangle \times 2^{\mathcal{T}} \rightarrow ScD$:

$$Or(n, \langle P_1, \cdots, P_m \rangle, T) \stackrel{def}{=} [n, \langle P_1, \cdots, P_m \rangle, T]$$

3. And: $N \times 2^{ScD} \rightarrow ScD$:

$$And(n, \{P_1, \cdots, P_m\}) \stackrel{def}{=} [n, \{P_1, \cdots, P_m\}]$$ □

Note that we use square brackets to enclose one statechart, and use $\langle \cdots \rangle$ to denote a sequence of statecharts. Here are some explanations.

- $Basic(n)$ denotes a basic statechart named n.
- $Or(n, \langle P_1, \cdots, P_m \rangle, T)$ denotes an Or-statechart named n with a sequence of sub-statecharts $\langle P_1, \cdots, P_m \rangle$, where P_1 is the default sub-state. T is the set composed of all possible transitions among the sub-statecharts of n.
- $And(n, \{P_1, \cdots, P_m\})$ denotes the And-statechart named n, which contains a number of parallel sub-statecharts $P_1, \cdots, P_m$, where $P_1, \cdots, P_m$ are basic statecharts or Or-statecharts (but not And-statecharts).

Fig. 2 shows an Or-statechart with four sub-statecharts.

The behavior of a statechart is composed of a sequence of macro-steps, each of which comprises a sequence of micro-steps. A statechart reacts to any stimuli from the environment at the beginning of each macro-step by performing a sequence of transitions and generating some internal events (by the actions of the transitions it performs), which can in turn fire other state transitions. These lead to a chain of micro-steps. During this chain of micro-steps, the statechart does not respond to any (potentially) further external stimulus. In case that no more transitions are enabled, the macro-step comes to the end. Please notice that the action of a transition can be invocations to other statecharts, which will consider them as external stimulus.

Let us consider the operational semantics of the statecharts. We give the definition of *configurations* by adding the label of the active immediate sub-statechart and the current event e for each Or-statechart. For an And-statechart, all immediate sub-statecharts are active simultaneously.

Definition 3.2 (Configuration). A configuration C of a statechart *ScD* is defined as follows,

- For an Or-statechart $ScD = [n, \langle P_1, \cdots, P_m \rangle, T]$, its configuration has the form $[n, \langle P_1, \cdots, P_m \rangle, \dot{P_l}, T, e]$ where $\dot{P_l}$ is a configuration of P_l; l denotes that the sub-statechart P_l is the current active state $(1 \leq l \leq m)$; and e represents the current incoming event. When there is no event coming from the environment for the statechart, we have $e = e_\epsilon$, where e_ϵ is the dummy event.
- For an And-statechart $ScD = [n, \{P_1, \cdots, P_m\}]$, its configuration has the form $[n, \{\dot{P_1}, \cdots, \dot{P_m}\}]$, where $\dot{P_i}$ is a configuration of P_i.
- The configuration of a basic statechart $[n]$ has the form $[n]$.

We give the following operational transition rules, where we assume that the default configuration has the dummy event e_ϵ at the beginning.

The first transition rule initiates a macro-step for a statechart. It performs only when event e arrives (due to the environment which is composed of the actor of the system or other statecharts) and the statechart is ready to accept it.

Rule 3.3 (***Initiate***)**.** Assume $C_P = [n, \langle P_1, \cdots, P_m\rangle, P_l, T, e_\epsilon]$ is a stable configuration, i.e., a configuration with dummy event, and e is an incoming event form the environment. Then we have

$$\frac{e}{C_P \longrightarrow [n, \langle P_1, \cdots, P_m\rangle, P_l, T, e]} \qquad \square$$

For an Or-statechart, if a transition between two immediate connected sub-statecharts is enabled, the transition can be performed.

Rule 3.4 (***Or***)**.** Suppose P is an Or-statechart $[n, \langle P_1, \cdots, P_m\rangle, T]$ and configuration $C_P = [n, \langle P_1, \cdots, P_m\rangle, P_l, T, e]$. Then we have

$$\frac{\tau \in En(C_P, e)}{(C_P \stackrel{trig(\tau)}{\longrightarrow} [n, \langle P_1, \cdots, P_m\rangle, a2d(tgt(\tau)), T, e_\epsilon])||Update(act(\tau))}$$

where

- $En(C_P, e) \stackrel{def}{=} \{\tau \in T | src(\tau) = P_l \wedge trig(\tau) = e\}$ is the set of transitions enabled in current configuration on the "highest level". Note that there will be a non-deterministic choice when there are multiple transitions in the set.
- $src(\tau)$ and $tgt(\tau)$ are the source and target states of transition τ, respectively.
- $trig(\tau)$ denotes the event triggers the transition τ, and $act(\tau)$ denotes the event generated by transition τ.
- $(C_P \rightarrow [..])||Update(...)$ means to change the configuration and simultaneously execute the *Update* function.
- $Update(act(\tau))$ is equivalent to the following execution: Suppose $act(\tau) = (n, e)$ and n is the name of a (sub)statechart, then the incoming event of n becomes e, i.e. $n.e = e$.
- The function $a2d(C)$ maps the sub-statecharts of C to its default sub-states (recursively). Its definition is:

$$\begin{aligned} &a2d([n]) \stackrel{def}{=} [n] \\ &a2d([n, \langle P_1, \cdots, P_m\rangle, T]) \stackrel{def}{=} [n, \langle P_1, \cdots, P_m\rangle, a2d(P_1), T, e_\epsilon] \\ &a2d([n, \{P_1, \cdots, P_m\}]) \stackrel{def}{=} [n, \{a2d(P_1), \cdots, a2d(P_m)\}] \end{aligned} \qquad \square$$

If no transition among immediate sub-states of an Or-statechart is enabled, then the transitions in its active sub-state can be performed.

Rule 3.5 (***Or-Substate***)**.** Suppose $C_P = [n, \langle P_1, \cdots, P_m\rangle, P_l, T, e]$ is a configuration of an Or-statechart, then

$$\frac{En(C_P, e) = \emptyset, [P_l] \stackrel{trig(\tau)}{\longrightarrow} [P_l']}{C_P \stackrel{trig(\tau)}{\longrightarrow} [n, \langle P_1, \cdots, P_m\rangle, P_l', T, e]} \qquad \square$$

Rule 3.6 (***And***)**.** Suppose $C_P = [n, \{P_1, \cdots, P_m\}]$ is a configuration of an And-statechart. For $i = 1, 2, \cdots, m$, P_i is a basic statechart or a configuration of an Or-statechart,

$$\frac{P_i \stackrel{trig(\tau_i)}{\longrightarrow} P_i', \ i = 1, \ldots, m}{C_P \stackrel{\bigwedge_{i=1}^m trig(\tau_i)}{\longrightarrow} [n, \{P_1', \cdots, P_m'\}]}$$

If no transition can be performed in P_i and its all sub-statecharts, then the sub-configuration is considered as staying the same. That is

$$P_i \rightarrow P_i$$ □

Please note that as the execution goes, the incoming event e may become e_ϵ because of Rule 3.4. If all the incoming events become empty, the execution of the statecharts will end. Thus we do not need a transition rule for the ending of the execution explicitly.

3.2 Split Automata

As stated, the formalism of split automata is motivated by the use of model checking. A split automaton is a network of automata defined as follows.

Definition 3.7 (Split Automata). A Split Automaton is a set of interactive automata $\mathcal{A} = \{A_1, \cdots, A_n\}$ where each A_i has the following structure:

1. A set of states S_i
2. A set $\mathcal{T}_i$ of transitions with the form $\langle s_1, e_1, A', e_2, s_2\rangle$, where $s_1 \in S_i$ and $s_2 \in S_i$ are the source and the target state; e_1 is the name of a trigger event; e_2 is the event name of the action triggered by e_1, and A' is the target automaton of e_2.
3. A mapping $\mathit{switch}_i : \mathcal{T}_i \rightharpoonup 2^{\mathcal{A}} \times \{0, 1\}$ denoting the activation relationship between the events and the corresponding automaton. □

Here are some explanations:

- A split automaton is actually an automata network, where each automaton is an ordinary automaton plus that each transition has an action. The action is a pair of an automaton A' and an event name which stands for the event within the target automaton A'.
- The mapping *switch* denotes the interactions between different automata. If $(A, 1) \in \mathit{switch}(\tau)$, then A will be activated when executing the transition τ; while $(A, 0) \in \mathit{switch}(\tau)$ will stop A.
- Please notice that all the automata are at the same level. The hierarchical data structures of the statechart is encoded in the control structure of the split automata.

The intention of defining split automata is to bridge the statechart to the formalism accepted by model checkers. We want to translate a statechart to a corresponding split automaton, which can correctly simulate the behavior of the statechart. For the statechart shown in Fig. 3, the correspondent split automaton is shown in Fig. 4. We have $\mathit{switch}(\tau_1) = \{(A_2, 1), (A_3, 1)\}$, $\mathit{switch}(\tau_2) = \{(A_2, 0), (A_3, 0), (A_4, 0)\}$, and $\mathit{switch}(\tau_3) = \{(A_4, 1)\}$. The other transitions have empty switches. The formal definition of the translation will be presented soon.

Now we define the semantics of the split automata.

Definition 3.8 (Configuration). Suppose $\mathcal{A}$ is a split automaton. Its *Configuration* $C_{\mathcal{A}}$ has the form $[\mathcal{A}, \{(A_1, s_{i_1}, e_{i_1}), \cdots, (A_m, s_{i_m}, e_{i_m})\}]$, which denotes the fact that $\{A_1, \cdots, A_m\}$ are the active automata with active states $\{s_{i_1}, \cdots, s_{i_m}\}$ and incoming event $\{e_{i_1}, \cdots, e_{i_m}\}$. □

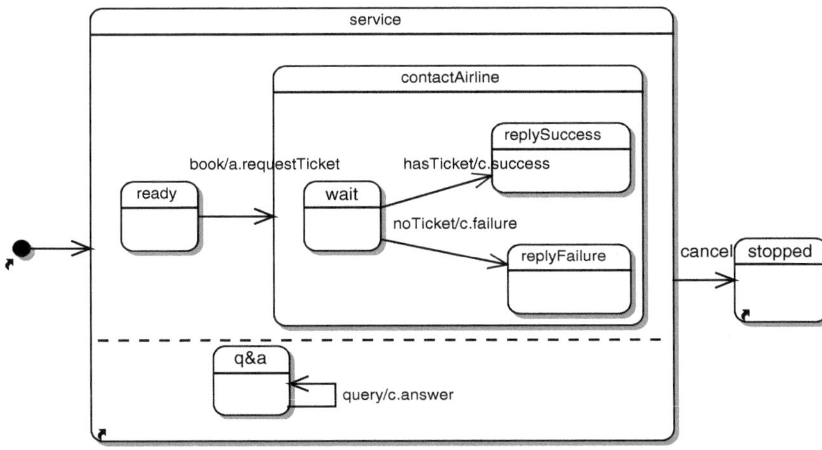

Fig. 3. Travel Agency Statechart

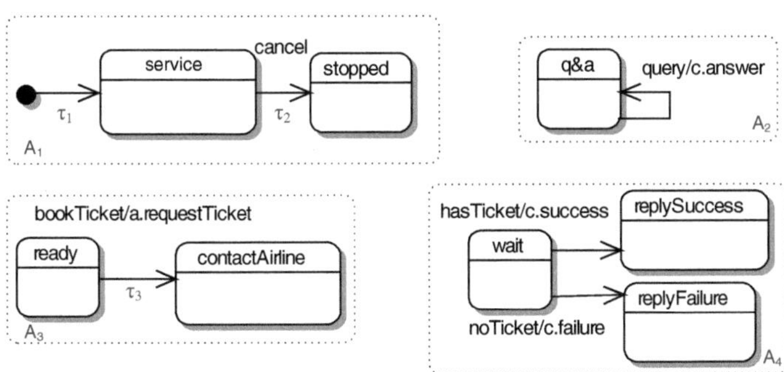

Fig. 4. Split Automaton Example

In contrast to the complicated rules of statecharts, the execution of split automata is quite simple. Its operational semantics has only one rule as follows, which tells us that the automaton will switch its state and active (or stop) some corresponding automata when the related incoming event occurs.

Rule 3.9 (*Split Automata*). Suppose a configuration of split automaton $C_{\mathcal{A}}$ is of the form $[\mathcal{A}, \{(A_1, s_{i_1}, e_{i_1}), \cdots, (A_k, s_{i_k}, e_{i_k}), \cdots, (A_j, s_j, -), \cdots, (A_m, s_{i_m}, e_{i_m})\}]$, and

- $\tau \in \mathcal{T}_k$ is a transition in automaton A_k with the form $\langle s_{i_k}, e_{i_k}, A_j, e_j, s_l \rangle$
- $\mathit{switch}(\tau) = \{(A'_1, 0), \cdots, (A'_p, 0), (A'_{p+1}, 1), \cdots, (A'_q, 1)\}$

Then we have

$$\frac{}{C_{\mathcal{A}} \xrightarrow{\tau} [\mathcal{A}, \{(A_1, s_{i_1}, e_{i_1}), \cdots, (A_k, s_l, e_\epsilon), \cdots, (A_j, s_j, e_j), \cdots, (A_m, s_{i_m}, e_{i_m})\} \\ /\{(A'_1, \text{-}, \text{-}), \cdots, (A'_p, \text{-}, \text{-})\} \oplus \{(A'_{p+1}, s'_{p+1}, e_\epsilon), \cdots, (A'_q, s'_q, e_\epsilon)\}]}$$

where $s'_{p+1}, \cdots, s'_q$ are the initial states of the corresponding automata. We use / to denote set difference without considering the state and incoming event of the automata, and $\oplus$ to denote basically the set union, except overriding the existing automata with the same names[4]. □

In the above we have only considered the configuration for one statechart and one split automaton. For multiple statecharts, we can view them as a big And-statechart, thus the configuration and the operational semantics remain the same. Therefore, there is no need to consider multiple split automata.

3.3 Simulation

In this subsection we give the definition of *Simulation* and prove that our split automata can simulate statecharts. We also define a translation to obtain a split automaton from a given statechart. Suppose $\mathcal{A}$ is a split automaton and S is a statechart. We use $C_S \Rightarrow_S C'_S$ to denote that the configuration C_S can reach another configuration C'_S by the operational rules defined by the statechart S. Similarly, we use $C_\mathcal{A} \Rightarrow_\mathcal{A} C'_\mathcal{A}$ to denote that the configuration $C_\mathcal{A}$ can reach another configuration $C'_\mathcal{A}$ by the operational rules defined by $\mathcal{A}$.

Definition 3.10 (Simulation). Suppose $\mathcal{A}$ is a split automaton and S is a statechart. We say $\mathcal{A}$ can *Simulate* S, if and only if there exists a binary relation $\mathscr{S}$ between the configuration spaces of $\mathcal{A}$ and S such that

- For the initial configuration C^0_S of S and the initial configuration $C^0_\mathcal{A}$ of $\mathcal{A}$, we have $C^0_\mathcal{A} \mathscr{S} C^0_S$
- For any given configuration C_S of S and configuration $C_\mathcal{A}$ of $\mathcal{A}$, if $C_\mathcal{A} \mathscr{S} C_S$ and $C_\mathcal{A} \Rightarrow_\mathcal{A} C'_\mathcal{A}$, then there exists another statechart configuration C'_S, such that $C'_\mathcal{A} \mathscr{S} C'_S$ and $C_S \Rightarrow_S C'_S$ □

As stated, the split automata is an unfolded statechart. We define a translation from a given statechart to a split automaton as follows:

Definition 3.11. Suppose S is a statechart. We recursively define a translation mapping $f : S \rightharpoonup \mathcal{A}$ as follows, where all A represent fresh automata names:

- Basic: If $S = [n]$, then $f([S]) = \{A\}$, where the state set of A is $\{n\}$, and $\mathcal{T}_A = \emptyset$, $switch_A = \emptyset$.
- Or: If $S = [n, \langle P_1, \cdots, P_m \rangle, T]$, then $f([S]) = \{A\} \cup f(P_1) \cup \cdots \cup f(P_m)$, where the state set of A is $\{s_1, \cdots, s_m\}$, and
  - $\mathcal{T}_A = \{\langle s_i, e, f(P_k), a, s_j \rangle \mid \langle P_i, e, P_k, a, P_j \rangle \in T\}$
  - suppose $\tau = \langle s_i, e, A', a, s_j \rangle$, then $switch_A(\tau) = R$, and the construction of set R is defined as follows:
    1. initially, let $R = \{(f(P_i), 0)\} \cup \{(f(P_j), 1)\}$
    2. if $P_i = [n_1, \{P_{i_1}, \cdots, P_{i_p}\}]$, add $\{(f(P_{i_1}), 0), \cdots, (f(P_{i_p}), 0)\}$ to R.
    3. if $P_j = [n_2, \{P_{j_1}, \cdots, P_{j_q}\}]$, add $\{(f(P_{j_1}), 1), \cdots, (f(P_{j_q}), 1)\}$ to R.

[4] In fact, as will be seen later, this overriding will not happen in the split automata generated from statecharts.

- And: If $S = [n, \{P_1, \cdots, P_m\}]$, then $f([S]) = \{A\} \cup f(P_1) \cup \cdots \cup f(P_m)$, where the state set of A is $\{n\}$, and $\mathcal{T}_A = \emptyset$, $switch_A = \emptyset$.

The definition of *switch* ensures that when we leave or enter an And-statechart, all the corresponding automata are activated or stopped. In the translation of the basic And-statechart, we have introduced a redundant automaton A to assist the definition and implementation, which can be eliminated by a post processing (optimizing).

As shown in Fig.4, the statechart diagram depicted in Fig.3 will be translated into a split automaton using the mapping given above. Note that the redundant automata have been omitted.

Following theorem guarantees that our split automata simulates the corresponding statechart.

Theorem 3.12 (Simulation). For a given statechart S, the split automaton $\mathcal{A}$ generated by $f(S)$ simulates S. □

PROOF: The essence of this proof is to give the binary relation between configurations of S and $\mathcal{A}$.

We give it as follows:

1. For the initial configurations, we denote the statechart configuration which has only dummy incoming events as C_S^0, and the split automaton configuration which has only dummy events as $C_{\mathcal{A}}^0$. As expected, it is defined that $C_S^0 \mathscr{S} C_{\mathcal{A}}^0$.
2. For other configurations, we recursively give the as follows:
   - Basic: If $C_S = [n]$ is a configuration, then let $(C_S, f([n])) \in \mathscr{S}$,
   - Or: If $C_S = [n, \langle P_1, \cdots, P_m \rangle, P_l, T, e]$ is a configuration of S, and $P_i \mathscr{S} C_{\mathcal{A}_i}$ $(i = 1, \cdots, m)$. then let $C_S \mathscr{S} [f(S), \langle (A_0, s_l, e), C_{\mathcal{A}_1}, \cdots, C_{\mathcal{A}_m} \rangle]$, where A_0 is the first automaton defined in $f(S)$, s_l is the state corresponding to P_l.
   - And: If $C_S = [n, \{P_1, \cdots, P_m\}]$ is a configuration of S, and $P_i \mathscr{S} C_{\mathcal{A}_i}$ $(i = 1, \cdots, m)$, then let $C_S \mathscr{S} [f(S), \langle (A, n, e_\epsilon), C_{\mathcal{A}_1}, \cdots, C_{\mathcal{A}_m} \rangle]$, where n is the only state of A. □

By structural induction on the combination of configurations of statecharts, it is trivial to prove that the above defined $\mathscr{S}$ is a simulation.

4 Consistency Checking

A well-formed sequence diagram is consistent with a set of statecharts if the trace of the sequence diagram is in the trace set of the statecharts. Supported by the notion of split automata, in this section, we discuss how to verify the consistency between a given sequence diagram and a set of statecharts using the SPIN model checker [8].

The input language of SPIN is called Promela, which is a language for modeling finite-state concurrent processes. SPIN can verify or falsify (by generating counterexamples) linear temporal logic properties of Promela specifications using an exhaustive state space search. It also allows to specify the "never claim", which is a process describing unwanted behaviors.

Given the diagrams, we design an algorithm which automatically generates the corresponding Promela specification. It consists of some communicating concurrent processes in which each process denotes an automaton in the corresponding split automata and a never claim denoting the sequence diagram. Afterwards, if SPIN reports that the system has a trace that agrees with the never claim, then we know the sequence diagram is consistent with the statecharts. Otherwise, if SPIN reports that the system will never act as the never claim, then there must be some inconsistency.

4.1 Translation from Split Automata to Promela

Suppose that we have translated the statecharts into split automata. Now we go ahead to translate each automaton into a Promela process, specified by the `proctype` keyword. In Promela, local variables can be defined in processes; values can be sent or received from channels, using the exclamation mark and the question mark, respectively. A channel is defined (using keyword `chan`) for each automaton, in order to send or receive events, which are stored in an enumeration set `mtype`. An auxiliary variable `msg` is used to record the event that has just been transferred through a channel, which will be used in the never claim later to describe the sequence diagram.

The control flow in an automaton is implemented by a `do` loop with a variable `state` that enumerates on states $S = \{s_1, \cdots, s_n\}$. The loop has the form of

```
do
::state == s1 -> ...
   ...
::state == sn -> ...
od
```

where the guard `state==si` is enabled only when the current active state is s_i. For a transition $\langle s_i, e_1, A', e_2, s_j \rangle$ in automaton A, we implement it as a guarded command: `state==s_i -> if ::A?e_1 -> {A'!e_2; msg=e_2; state = s_j} fi`. The trigger is implemented as channel receiving `A?e_1`, while the action is implemented as channel sending `A'!e_2`. The current state is changed by `state=s_j`, thus the guard for s_j will be enabled in the next round of the loop. If there are more than one transitions leaving s_i, we can add corresponding trigger/action statements in the `if` statement. Finally, we use an auxiliary variable `msg` to record the event that just happens.

The *switch* mechanism in split automata requires us to implement the activation and stop of an automata. The activation is directly implemented by keyword *run* which creates a new instance of a process. To implement stop, we introduce an auxiliary event *stop*. The automaton may stop other automata by sending *stop* event to them. We also add a simple guarded command `A?stop -> break` in each process. That is, when the process receives *stop*, we simply break the loop; then the process terminates. For example, statement `atomic {run A1(); run A2(); A3!stop;}` represents a corresponding *switch* $= \{(A_1, 1), (A_2, 1), (A_3, 0)\}$. Note that we use keyword `atomic` to make sure that these statements are executed as a non-interruptible atomic block.

A complete translation algorithm (from statechart to Promela) is shown in Fig. 5 and Fig. 6. Note that in the algorithm we have also considered the translation from a state in a statechart to an automaton, hence the cases for And-statechart and Or-statechart are distinguished. The algorithms are quite detailed and we do not need more explanations here.

```
void Or-State (State s) {
  output ("proctype p_" + s.name + " () {");
  output ("mtype state = " + s.initState.name + ";"); // init state
  output ("do");
  foreach (State substate in s.states) {
    if (exists t in s.transitions s.t. substate == t.source){ // has transition
      output (":: state == " + substate.name + "->");
      output ("if");
      foreach (t in s.transitions s.t. substate == t.source) { // do transition
        output ("::");
        if (t.trigger != null)
          output ("c_" + s.chartName + "?" + t.trigger); // trigger
        output ("-> atomic { msg = " + t.trigger + ";");
        if (substate.isCompositeState) {
          output ("c_" + substate.name + "! stop"); // stop substate
          output ("c_" + substate.name + "? finish"); // substate stopped
        }
        if (t.target.isCompositeState)
          output ("run p_" + t.target.name + "();" //run next substate
        foreach (Action a in t.actions) { // do actions
          output ("c_" + a.name + "! " + a.event);
        }
        output ("state = "+t.target.name); // goto next substate
        output ("}");
      } // end for
      output (":: c_" + s.name + "?stop -> atomic {"); // receive stop signal
      if (substate.isCompositeState) {
        output ("c_" + substate.name + "! stop;"); // stop substate
        output ("c_" + substate.name + "? finish;");
      }
      output ("break;}"); // exit s
    output ("fi");
    } //end if
  } // end for
  output ("od"); output ("c_" + s.name + "! finish;"); // s is finished
}
```

Fig. 5. Or-state Translation Algorithm

4.2 Translation from Sequence Diagrams to Promela

Compared with the translation of statecharts, the translation of sequence diagrams is trivial. Since we have used the variable `msg` to record every event that takes place, we can simply translate each event as a loop with guard `msg==x`, where x is the name of the event. When the guard is true, we know that event `x` has taken place, then we break the loop and try to match the next event; otherwise we do nothing but wait. If we can match all the events, then we know that the system does have a trace as claimed, which means that the diagrams are consistent. SPIN will report a counter example for the trace, which can run in the simulator to present a visual way for the user to analyze the statecharts. Fig. 7 shows an example of the never claim. Note that we have defined a macro `Event` to simplify the code, which is an adopted technique from [8]. The event sequence is listed in the `never` block.

If the diagrams are not consistent and the trace is not valid, SPIN will simply tell the user "inconsistent" as the result. However, we may want to find out the longest valid sub-trace (LVS) of the given trace, which may be helpful in the analysis of the reason for inconsistency. There is not an automatic way to get the LVS. We can try to find it using a binary search method: given a trace t, we cut the invalid trace into two sub-traces of equal length, namely t_1 and t_2. Then we try to verify the first half, i.e. t_1. When it is still

```
void And-State (State s) {
  output ("proctype p_" + s.name + " () {");
  output ("atomic {"); // run each substate
  foreach (State substate in s.states) {
    output ("run p_" + substate.name + " ();");
  }
  output ("}");
  output ("atomic {");
  output ("c_" + s.name + "? stop;"); // receive stop signal
  foreach (State substate in s.states) { // stop each substate
    output ("c_" + substate.name + "! stop;");
  }
  output ("}");
  foreach (State substate in s.states) { // each substate is finished
    output ("c_" + substate.name + "? finish;");
  }
  output ("c_" + s.name + "! finish;"); // s is finished
}
```

Fig. 6. And-state Translation Algorithm

```
#define Event(x) do :: msg == x -> break :: else od
never{
  Event(book);
  Event(requestTicket);
  Event(hasTicket);
  Event(success);
}
```

Fig. 7. Translated Sequence Diagram Example

invalid, we know that the LVS must be a sub-trace of t_1, hence in the next try we shrink our sub-trace by testing only the first half of t_1, i.e. the first quarter of the full trace. Otherwise when t_1 is a trace of the statecharts, we know that t_1 must be a sub-trace of the LVS, hence we extend the sub-trace as t_1 followed by the first half of t_2, i.e. the first three quarters of the full trace. We need to do $\lg(n)$ rounds of verification when the length of the sequence is n. For example, 6 rounds of verification is needed when the sequence's length is 100. After the LVS is found, the user can simulate it with SPIN and try to get a clue to solve the inconsistency.

5 Example

In this section we present an example of travel agency. Agency t acts as a middle-man between airline company a and client c who wants to book an air ticket. The client may consult the travel agency by querying the flight number and time information, or try to book a ticket from the airline company through the agency. The Fig. 3 and Fig. 8 show the statecharts of the agency, airline company and client respectively.

The airline company statechart is the simplest; it only has one state named *ticket-Service*. When there is a trigger *requestTicket*, the airline company may respond either *t.hasTicket* or *t.noTicket*, depending on whether there is any available ticket left for the flight. We use t here to denote the travel agency statechart. Similarly we use c and a to denote the client and airline company statechart, respectively.

The client statechart begins from *try* state, where he may try to ask the agency by action *t.query*. When the trigger *answer* happens, then the client receives the queried

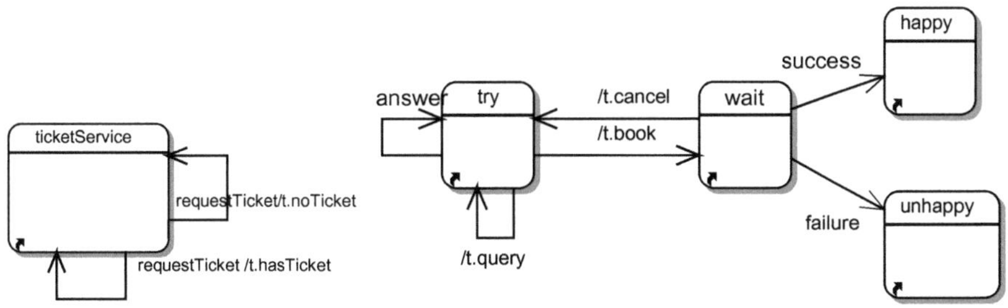

Fig. 8. Airline company and Client Statechart

information. However, the client may be inpatient and do not wait for the answer, or has enough knowledge about the flight so he does not need to ask. In these cases, the client simply book the ticket by proceeding to *wait* state with the action *t.book*. Note that this transition does not has a trigger, so it can happens at any time. After this, the client have to wait for the answer from the agency. If trigger *success* happens, meaning the ticked is successfully booked, then the client moves and stays in *happy* state. The situation is similar when *Failure* happens. But when the client waits for too long without receiving a reply, he can cancel the transaction by action *t.cancel*.

The travel agency statechart (Fig. 3) is the most complex one in the three. The two services run in parallel, thus results in an And-state named *sevice*. The agency will stop working if the client cancels the request. This is ensured by putting the *cancel* trigger on the transition starting from *service*. According to the kind of service requested, the travel agency will answer the client's information query (this service does not require interaction with the airline company) as described in the lower pane of *service*, or try to buy the ticket from the airline company as described in the upper pane. The information query service is represented simply by one state *q&a*, which does action *c.answer* when trigger *query* happens. For the booking service, when trigger *book* happens, the agent will first call the airline company by action *a.requestTicket* and then go to the Or-state *contactAirline*. In the Or-state, the agency waits for the airline company's reply and will forward the reply to the client, as described by the two transitions.

The sequence diagram shown on the left side of Fig. 9 shows a consistent scenario where the booking is successful. The client first sends a *book* message to the agency. Then the agency forwards this message by sending *requestTicket* to the airline com-

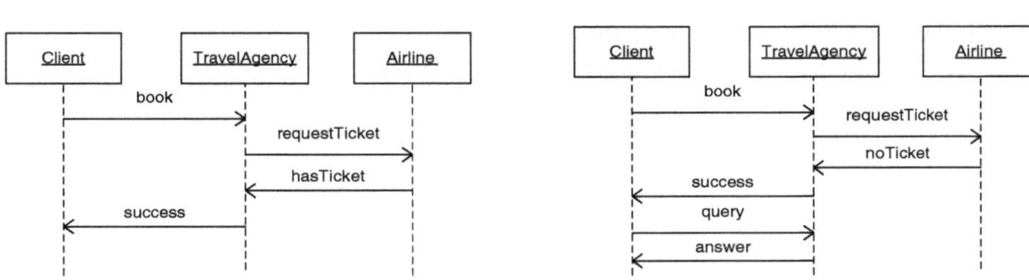

Fig. 9. Two Scenarios

pany. After the airline company replies the *hasTicket* message, the agency will reply the client a *success* message. Although syntactically correct, the diagram on the right side is inconsistent with the statecharts. Firstly, the agency has wrongly replied *success* when the airline company does not have a ticket. Secondly, suppose we correct the first mistake, there is still another problem: the *query* and *answer* happens after the booking is reasonable, but it is not allowed by the client's statechart. This may imply that the client's statechart is not very well designed.

We have translated both the statecharts and the sequence diagrams into Promela codes, as shown in the Appendix. Using SPIN we have successfully verified that the first sequence diagram is consistent while the second one inconsistent, as expected. The verification procedure only costs a few seconds and 3.7MB memory in a Pentium-4 machine, showing that our method is both effective and efficient.

6 Conclusions and Future Work

In this paper, we have syntactically defined sequence diagrams and statechart diagrams and given the semantics as well. What is more, we propose the notion of split automata by advancing the traditional concept of automata. It encodes the hierarchy data structures of statechart diagrams to its control structure hence can be implemented in model checker easily and effectively. Based on these definitions we developed a framework to check the inconsistency between the sequence and statechart diagrams in which the central parts are the algorithms for translating the diagrams to Promela, which is the input language of model checker SPIN.

Compared with the concept of "flattened automata" which unfolds all the hierarchical structure of the original statechart, split automata can prevent the states from explicitly exponential increasing. Also, the split automata can make the specifications in Promela much clearer than those written with flattened automata. What we have to point out is that, in essence, the split automata do NOT solve the problem of state explosion problem because the model checker, say, SPIN itself will generate exponential increasing states when it does verification. However, what we would like to argue is that the model checker can use the *on-the-fly* strategy to reduce the states existing at the same time, hence ease the problem quite a lot.

As for the future work, we can promise the following three aspects. Firstly, we will give fully tool support for the algorithm designed in this paper. Secondly, we will continue investigate semantics for the sequence diagrams which supports all the features of sequence diagrams in UML 2.0, and develop the corresponding algorithm as well. The last, but not the least one, is that we will develop the refinement calculus in UML design models with respect to the consistency in this paper and our earlier work [14]. We hope with this calculus, the modelers who use UML can develop their systems step by step without worrying about inconsistencies between different models.

Acknowledgement. We would like to thank Dr. Zhiming Liu and the anonymous reviewers for many helpful comments on the research of UML consistency checking and much other help.

References

1. E. Astesiano and G. Reggio. An attempt at analysing the consistency problems in the UML from a classical algebraic viewpoint. In *WADT 2002, LNCS 2755*. Springer, 2003.
2. J. R. Burch, E. M. Clarke, K. L. McMillan, and David L. Dill. Sequential circuit verification using symbolic model checking. In *DAC '90: Proceedings of the 27th ACM/IEEE conference on Design automation*, pages 46–51, New York, NY, USA, 1990. ACM Press.
3. E. M. Clarke, O. Grumberg, and D. A. Peled. *Model Checking*. The MIT Press, 2000.
4. M. Fowler. What is the point of UML. In *LNCS 1618*. Springer, 1998.
5. J.M. Kuester G. Engels and L. Groenewegen. Consistent interaction of software components. *Proc. of IDPT 2002*, 2002.
6. M. M. Gallardo, P. Merino, and E. Pimentel. Debugging UML designs with model checking. *Journal of Object Technology*, 1(2):101–117, 2002.
7. J. He, X. Li, and Z. Liu. rCOS : A refinement calculus for object-oriented systems. Accepted for publication in *Theoretical Computer Science*. Also available as Technical Report 322. UNU/IIST, P.O.Box 3058, Macao SAR China (`http://www.iist.unu.edu`).
8. G. J. Holzmann. *The SPIN Model Checker: Primer and Reference Manual*. Addison-Wesley, 2003.
9. P. Inverardi, H. Muccini, and P. Pelliccione. Checking consistency between architectural models using SPIN. In *Proc. of STRAW'01*, 2001.
10. I. Jacobson, J. Rumbaugh, and G. Booch. *The Unified Modelling Language Reference Manual*. Addison-Wesley, 1999.
11. A. Knapp, S. Merz, and C. Rauh. Model checking timed UML state machines and collaborations. In *7th Int. Symp. Formal Techniques in Real-Time and Fault Tolerant Systems*, volume 2469 of *LNCS*, pages 395–416. Springer, 2002.
12. J.M. Küster and J. Stehr. Towards explicit behavioral consistency concepts in the UML. In *Proc. of the 2nd International Workshop on Scenarios and State Machines: Models, Algorithms, and Tools*, Portland, USA, 2003.
13. J. Lilius and I. P. Paltor. Formalising UML state machines for model checking. In Robert France and Bernhard Rumpe, editors, *UML'99 - The Unified Modeling Language. Beyond the Standard. Second International Conference, Fort Collins, CO, USA, October 28-30. 1999, Proceedings*, volume 1723 of *LNCS*, pages 430–445. Springer, 1999.
14. Q. Long, Z. Liu, X. Li, and J. He. Consistent code generation from UML models. In *Proc. of Australian Software Engineering Conference (ASWEC'2005)*, Brisbane, Australia, 2005. IEEE Computer Society.
15. Q. Long, Z. Qiu, and S. Qin. The equivalence of statecharts. In Jin Song Dong and Jim Woodcock, editors, *Formal Methods and Software Engineering, ICFEM'03, LNCS 2885*, Singapore, 2003. Springer.
16. T. Schäfer, A. Knapp, and S. Merz. Model checking UML state machines and collaborations. *Electronic Notes in Theoretical Computer Science*, 55(3), 2001.
17. W. Visser, K. Havelund, G. Brat, and S.J. Park. Model checking programs. In *ASE'00*, Washington, DC, USA, 2000. IEEE Computer Society.

Appendix: Promela Code of the Travel Agency Example

```
mtype {s_init, s_try, s_wait, s_happy, s_unhappy, s_service, s_stop,
s_ready, s_contactAirline, s_replySuccess, s_replyFailure, s_qanda,
s_ticketService, finish, stop, nil, query, answer, book, cancel,
requestTicket, hasTicket, noTicket, success, failure }; chan
c_client = [0] of {mtype}; chan c_travelAgency = [0] of {mtype};
chan c_airline = [0] of {mtype}; chan c_service = [0] of {mtype};
```

```
chan c_service1 = [0] of {mtype}; chan c_service2 = [0] of {mtype};
chan c_contactAirline = [0] of {mtype}; mtype msg = nil;

active proctype client() {
  mtype state = s_try;
  do
  ::state == s_try ->
    if
    :: atomic {c_travelAgency! query; state = s_try;}
    :: atomic {c_travelAgency! book; state = s_wait;}
    :: c_client? answer -> atomic {msg = answer; state = s_try;}
    fi
  ::state == s_wait ->
    if
    :: c_client? success -> atomic {msg = success; state = s_happy;}
    :: c_client? failure -> atomic {msg = failure; state = s_unhappy;}
    :: atomic {c_travelAgency! cancel;  state = s_try;}
    fi
  od;
}

active proctype airline() {
  mtype state = s_ticketService;
  do
  ::state == s_ticketService ->
    if
    ::c_airline? requestTicket ->
      atomic {msg = requestTicket; c_travelAgency! hasTicket; state = s_ticketService;}
    ::c_airline? requestTicket ->
      atomic {msg = requestTicket; c_travelAgency! noTicket; state = s_ticketService;}
    fi
  od;
}

active proctype travelAgency() {
  mtype state = s_init; /* initial state */
  do
  ::state == s_init -> atomic {state = s_service; run p_service();}
  ::state == s_service ->
    if
    :: c_travelAgency? cancel ->
       atomic {msg = cancel; c_service! stop; c_service? finish; state = s_stop;}
    fi
  od;
}

proctype p_service() {
  atomic {run p_service1(); run p_service2();}
  atomic {c_service? stop; c_service1! stop; c_service2! stop;}
  c_service1? finish; c_service2? finish; c_service! finish;
}

proctype p_service1() { /* the upper parallel region */
  mtype state = s_ready;
  do
  ::state == s_ready ->
    if
    ::c_service1? stop -> break;
    ::c_travelAgency? book -> atomic {msg = book; c_airline! requestTicket;
      run p_contactAirline(); state = s_contactAirline;}
    fi
  ::state == s_contactAirline ->
    if
    ::c_service1? stop ->
      atomic {c_contactAirline! stop; c_contactAirline? finish; break;}
    fi
  od;
  c_service1! finish;
```

```
}

proctype p_contactAirline() {
  mtype state = s_wait;
  do
  ::state == s_wait ->
    if
    :: c_contactAirline? stop -> break;
    :: c_travelAgency? hasTicket ->
      atomic {msg = hasTicket; c_client! success; state = s_replySuccess;}
    :: c_travelAgency? noTicket ->
      atomic {msg = noTicket; c_client! failure; state = s_replyFailure;}
    fi
  od;
  c_contactAirline! finish;
}

proctype p_service2() { /* the lower parallel region */
  mtype state = s_qanda;
  do
  ::state == s_qanda ->
    if
    ::c_service2? stop -> break;
    ::c_travelAgency? query ->
      atomic {msg = query; c_client! answer; state = s_qanda;}
    fi
  od;
  c_service2! finish;
}

/* never claim */
#define Event(x) do :: msg == x -> break :: else  od
never {
  Event(book);
  Event(requestTicket);
  Event(hasTicket);
  Event(success);
}
```

Conditions for Avoiding Controllability Problems in Distributed Testing

Jessica Chen and Lihua Duan

School of Computer Science, University of Windsor
Windsor, Ont. Canada N9B 3P4
{xjchen, duan1}@uwindsor.ca

Abstract. Finite-state-machine-based conformance testing has been extensively studied in the literature in the context of centralized test architecture. With a distributed test architecture which involves multiple remote testers, the application of a test sequence may encounter controllability problems. This problem can be overcome by introducing additional external coordination messages exchanged among remote testers. Such an approach requires for extra resources for the communication among remote testers and sometimes suffers from unexpected delay. It is thus desirable to avoid the controllability problem by selecting suitable test sequences. However, this is not always possible. For some finite state machines, we cannot generate a test sequence without using external coordination messages and apply it without encountering controllability problems during testing. In this paper, we present *sufficient and necessary conditions* on a given finite state machine for constructing test sequences so that it does not involve external coordination messages and its application to the *implementation under test* is free from controllability problems.

Keywords: Conformance testing, finite state machine, controllability, test sequence, unique input/output sequence.

1 Introduction

Given an *implementation under test* (IUT) from which we can only observe its input/output behavior, conformance testing can be conducted to improve our confidence that this implementation *conforms* to its specification M. Conformance testing is often carried out by i) constructing a *test sequence*, which is an input/output sequence, from the specification of the system; ii) applying the input portion of this sequence to the IUT, which is considered as a *black box*, according to the given test architecture; and iii) determining whether the actual output sequence is produced as expected. Conformance testing has been extensively studied in the context where M is a Finite State Machine (FSM). This was mainly motivated by the fact that FSMs have been widely used to model the abstract behavior of sequential circuits [11,28], lexical analysis systems [15,17], and communications protocols [1,8,24,36]. Our interest in FSM-based conformance testing is further stimulated by the fact that quite some more expressive

Z. Liu and J. He (Eds.): ICFEM 2006, LNCS 4260, pp. 460–477, 2006.

specification languages such as SDL, Estelle and Statecharts are based on *extensions* of FSMs, and that FSM-based conformance testing techniques can be *applied* to the settings where system specifications are given in such languages [2,12,22,30,33].

In the context where the system is modeled as an FSM, an essential task to carry out conformance testing is to automatically generate an efficient and effective test sequence from the given FSM specification. Various approaches have been explored in this regard according to different test criteria. See [21,19] for comprehensive surveys on this topic.

For *centralized* test architecture, the *same tester* can apply a test sequence derived from the specification of an IUT, observe its external input/output behavior and determine whether the behavior is as expected. When we consider *distributed* systems, the testing may involve *multiple testers*, each residing on a separate *interface* called *port.*

When we apply a test sequence to an IUT in a distributed architecture, the existence of multiple testers may introduce possible coordination problems known as *controllability problem* (or *synchronization problem*) [31] and *observability problem* [23]. Controllability problem occurs if a tester cannot determine *when* to apply a particular input to an IUT. It manifests itself when the tester who is expected to send an input to the IUT does not get involved in the previous transition, i.e., both the input and the output of the previous transition are observed by other testers. Observability problem occurs if a tester cannot determine whether a particular output is a response to a specific input. It manifests itself when the tester is expected to receive an output in response to either a previous input or the current input and because the tester is not the one who sends the current input, it is unable to determine *when* to start and stop waiting.

There are typically two approaches to solving controllability and observability problems: one is to allow testers to communicate with each other by exchanging external coordination messages [4,35]. The other is to try to eliminate the need for explicit coordination by selecting a *suitable* test sequence [7,31]. Using external coordination messages introduces the necessity to set up a separate communication network as well as delays which can be problematic if we have timing issues in our testing. Thus the second approach is often preferred. However, there exist finite state machines with which we cannot generate a test sequence without using external coordination messages and that can be applied without encountering controllability or observability problems. In [5], a *sufficient and necessary condition* is given on a specification FSM for resolving *observability problems* without employing external coordination messages. In this paper, we present *sufficient and necessary conditions* on a given specification FSM for avoiding *controllability problems* without employing external coordination messages. Various conditions are given here according to different criteria on the test sequences well-used in the literature.

The rest of the paper is structured as follows. Section 2 introduces the basic concepts and notations used in this paper. In Section 3, we present our sufficient and necessary conditions for avoiding controllability problems in constructing test sequences. This is followed by discussions (Section 4) on these conditions including the time complexity to check if a given FSM satisfies these conditions. Concluding remarks are given in Section 5.

2 Preliminaries

Figure 1 shows a test architecture proposed by *International Organization for Standardization (ISO)* for testing distributed systems [16]. Here, IUT can be part of the *System Under Test (SUT)* and include a set of protocols, namely, P_1, P_2, ..., P_n. IUT has an explicit boundary to its local tester, i.e., it can provide services to its upper layer. Therefore, we call this local tester an *upper tester (U)*. IUT can also be accessed by a remote tester through underneath service provider platform which has an explicit boundary to the outer environment. We call this remote tester a *lower tester (L)*. Sometimes, a *Test Coordination Procedure* is built to coordinate the cooperation between the upper and the lower testers.

This 2-port test architecture can be generalized into an n-port one [23], which allows n testers to participate in the testing. Formally, we use *n-port FSM* to describe the abstract behavior of the distributed systems with n ports.

An *n-port finite state machine* M (simply called FSM M below) is defined as $M = (S, I, O, \delta, \lambda, s_0)$ where

- S is a finite set of states of M;
- $s_0 \in S$ is the initial state of M;
- $I = \bigcup_{i=1}^{n} I_i$, where I_i is the input alphabet of port i, and $I_i \cap I_j = \emptyset$ for $i, j \in [1, n]$, $i \neq j$;

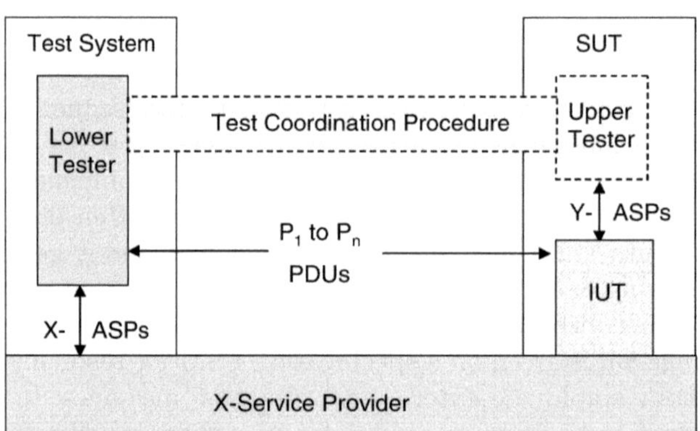

(N) - ASP: abstract N-service primitive, an implementation-independent description of an interaction between a service-user and a service-provider at an (N)-service boundary.
PDU: protocol data unit.

Fig. 1. A test architecture of distributed systems [16]

- $O = \prod_{i=1}^{n}(O_i \cup \{-\})$, where O_i is the output alphabet of port i, and $-$ means null output;
- δ is the transition function that maps $S \times I$ to S, i.e., δ: $S \times I \rightarrow S$;
- λ is the output function that maps $S \times I$ to O, i.e., λ: $S \times I \rightarrow O$.

By definition, an FSM M is: i) *deterministic* in the sense for each input $x \in I$, there is at most one transition defined at each state of M; ii) *completely specified*, i.e., for each input $x \in I$, there is a transition defined at each state of M.

Like in the literature, we assume "slow environment", i.e., whenever an input reaches the system, the system will prompt the output for it before the second input can reach the system.

Note that each $y \in O$ is a vector of outputs, i.e., $y = \langle o_1, o_2, \ldots, o_n \rangle$ where $o_i \in O_i \cup \{-\}$ for $i \in [1, n]$. In the rest of the paper, $p \in [1, n]$ is a port, $x \in I$ is a general input, and $x_p \in I_p$ is an input at the specific port p. We use $y|_p$ to denote the output at port p in y.

We extend *input symbols* and *output symbols* of the transition function δ and output function λ to *strings* as follows: For input $x_1, \ldots, x_k \in I$, output $y_1, \ldots, y_k \in O$, and $s_1, \ldots, s_{k+1} \in S$, if $\lambda(s_i, x_i) = y_i$ and $\delta(s_i, x_i) = s_{i+1}$ for $i \in [1, k]$, then $\lambda(s_1, x_1 \ldots x_k) = y_1 \ldots y_k$, $\delta(s_1, x_1 \ldots x_k) = s_{k+1}$.

We will use 2-port FSMs in all examples in this paper. In a 2-port FSM, U and L stand for the upper port and the lower port of the FSM, respectively. An output vector $y = \langle o_1, o_2 \rangle$ in a transition of a 2-port FSM is a pair of outputs with $o_1 \in O_1$ at U and $o_2 \in O_2$ at L.

A *transition* of an FSM is a triplet $t = (s_1, s_2, x/y)$, where $s_1, s_2 \in S$, $x \in I$, and $y \in O$ such that $\delta(s_1, x) = s_2$, and $\lambda(s_1, x) = y$. s_1 and s_2 are called the *starting state* and the *ending state* of t respectively. The input/output pair x/y is called the *label* of the transition.

A *path* ρ in M is either *null*, denoted by ϵ, or a finite sequence of transitions $t_1 t_2 \ldots t_k$ $(k \geq 1)$ in M such that for $k \geq 2$, the ending state of t_i is the starting state of t_{i+1} for all $i \in [1, k-1]$. A *transition tour*, simply called *tour* below, is a special path ρ such that the starting state of t_1 and the ending state of t_k are the same. Let $t_i = (s_i, s_{i+1}, x_i/y_i)$ for $i \in [1, k]$. The *label* of ρ is the sequence of input/output pairs of the transitions in ρ: $l = x_1/y_1\ x_2/y_2 \ldots x_k/y_k$. $in = x_1 x_2 \ldots x_k$ and $out = y_1 y_2 \ldots y_k$ are called the input sequence and output sequence of ρ respectively. For convenience, we also use the pair of input and output sequence *in/out* for the input/output sequence $x_1/y_1\ x_2/y_2 \ldots x_k/y_k$.

When $\rho \neq \epsilon$, we use *first*(ρ) and *last*(ρ) to denote the first and last transition in ρ respectively. The starting state of ρ, denoted by *start*(ρ), is the starting state of the first transition of ρ, and the ending state of ρ, denoted by *end*(ρ), is the ending state of the last transition of ρ. Sometimes, we also use $(s_1, s_{k+1}, in/out)$ for path ρ with starting state s_1, ending state s_{k+1}, and whose label is *in/out*. Let ρ_1, ρ_2 be two paths in M. When *end*(ρ_1) and *start*(ρ_2) are the same state, we use $\rho_1 \rho_2$ to denote the *concatenation* of ρ_1 and ρ_2. For clarity, sometimes we also use $\rho_1 @ \rho_2$ for $\rho_1 \rho_2$.

Two states s_i and s_j are equivalent if applying any input sequence at s_i and s_j results in the same output sequence. Two FSMs M and M' are equivalent if for every state in M there is a corresponding equivalent state in M', and vice versa. An FSM M is *minimal* if for any two states s_i, $s_j \in S$, $i \neq j$ implies s_i, s_j are not equivalent. In this paper, we assume that the given specification FSM M is minimal.

2.1 Test Sequence

Various test criteria have been used to conduct conformance testing. They were originally defined on single-port FSMs and have been used in general on n-port FSMs as well. We summarize three most commonly-used ones below.

a) The corresponding path of the generated test sequence in the specification FSM M should start from and end at the initial state of M and covers each transition of M at least once.

This is the criterion adopted in T-method [27,35] and below we use *T-sequence* to denote a test sequence satisfying this criterion. As showed in [32], although T-sequence may have a shorter length compared to test sequences satisfying some other criteria, it does not have a good fault detection capability.

Given FSM M that models the required behavior of an IUT, it is normal to assume that the IUT behaves like some (unknown) FSM N with the same input and output alphabets as M. To achieve better fault coverage, the following stronger criterion is required:

b) The corresponding path of the generated test sequence in the specification FSM M should start from and end at the initial state of M and contain each transition in M *followed by a path to verify the corresponding ending state of this transition in* N.

We will use *U-sequence* to denote a test sequence satisfying this criterion as most of the discussions considering this criterion are based on U-method [1,24,29,31].

The generation of U-sequence involves the use of *UIO-sequences*. A UIO-sequence is an input sequence such that the output sequence produced in response to this input sequence by M on a particular state is unique from those on any other states. We use UIO_i to denote the UIO-sequence for state s_i. Formally, given an FSM $M = (S, I, O, \delta, \lambda, s_0)$, UIO_i is a *UIO-sequence for* $s_i \in S$ if for any $s_j \in S, s_j \neq s_i$ implies $\lambda(s_i, UIO_i) \neq \lambda(s_j, UIO_i)$.

When we assume the existence of a UIO-sequence for each state of M, a *test segment* for a transition $t = (s_i, s_j, x/y)$ of M is $x/y@UIO_j/\lambda(s_j, UIO_j)$ which consists of the label of t followed by a test sequence to verify the ending state in N by using UIO-sequence for state s_j.

Criterion b) essentially requires that the test sequence contains at least one test segment for each transition in M. During the testing, for each transition in M, we first use a so-called *transfer sequence* to lead to the starting state of this transition, and then apply *its* test segment. The study of [26,32] shows that U-sequences are quite effective in detecting faults in the IUT.

Neither T-sequence nor U-sequence supports for full fault coverage: having applied a T-sequence or U-sequence successfully to the IUT does not guarantee that if we apply *any* input/output sequence generated from M to test the IUT, the observed output will be consistent to the expected one.

A more rigorous criterion is expressed in *checking sequence* which, under certain assumptions, supports for full fault coverage.

c) The corresponding path of the generated test sequence in the specification FSM M should start from and end at the initial state of M and contain each transition in M such that the corresponding starting state of this transition in N is *recognized* and the ending state of this transition in N is *verified.*

This criterion has been adopted in W-method [8] and D-method [10,11,36] and a test sequence satisfying this criterion is called a *checking sequence.*

As a common assumption used in the literature, N does not have more states than M. Let $\Phi(M)$ denote the set of FSMs that have the same input and output alphabets as M and have no more states than M. A *checking sequence* of M guarantees that when we apply it to the IUT, it can distinguish M from any element of $\Phi(M)$ not equivalent to M. Since M is minimal, the correct output from applying a checking sequence of M to the IUT actually ensures that N is isomorphic to M.

The problem of generating a checking sequence from an FSM M is simplified when M has a set of UIOs or a *distinguishing sequence.* A *distinguishing sequence* of M is an input sequence *DS* with the following characteristics: the output sequences produced by M in response to *DS* on different states of M are all different. Formally, *DS* is a *distinguishing sequence of* M if for any $s_i, s_j \in S, s_j \neq s_i$ implies $\lambda(s_i, DS) \neq \lambda(s_j, DS)$. In the literature, there has been much interest in generating efficient checking sequence from an FSM M when a set of UIOs [14] or a distinguishing sequence is known [10,11,13,36]. We use *UIO-based* and *DS-based* checking sequence to denote the checking sequence generated using a set of UIOs and using a distinguishing sequence respectively.

Example 1. Figure 2 shows a specification of a 2-port FSM. Here $u_1 \in I_1$, $o_1 \in O_1$ at U, $l_1 \in I_2$, $o_2 \in O_2$ at L. Let $\rho = t_1t_2t_3t_2t_5t_4t_5t_6$. As ρ covers each transition in M at least once, its input/output sequence $u_1/\langle o_1, -\rangle$ $l_1/\langle o_1, o_2\rangle$ $l_1/\langle o_1, -\rangle$ $l_1/\langle o_1, o_2\rangle$ $u_1/\langle -, o_2\rangle$ $u_1/\langle o_1, o_2\rangle$ $u_1/\langle -, o_2\rangle$ $l_1/\langle o_1, -\rangle$ is a T-type sequence. The UIOs for each states are $UIO_1 = UIO_2 = UIO_3 = u_1$. In this case, u_1 is also a distinguishing sequence.

2.2 The Controllability Problem

Given an FSM M and an input/output sequence $x_1/y_1\ x_2/y_2 \ldots x_k/y_k$ of M, where $x_i \in I$ and $y_i \in O$, $i \in [1, k]$, a *controllability problem* occurs when, in the labels x_i/y_i and x_{i+1}/y_{i+1} of any two consecutive transitions, $\exists p \in [1, n]$ such that $x_{i+1} \in I_p$, $x_i \notin I_p$, $y_i|_p = -$ $(i \in [1, k-1])$.

Example 2. In Figure 2, suppose we apply the input/output sequence of $\rho = t_1t_2t_3t_2t_5t_4t_5t_6$ to the IUT. For the consecutive transitions t_1t_2, the tester at L

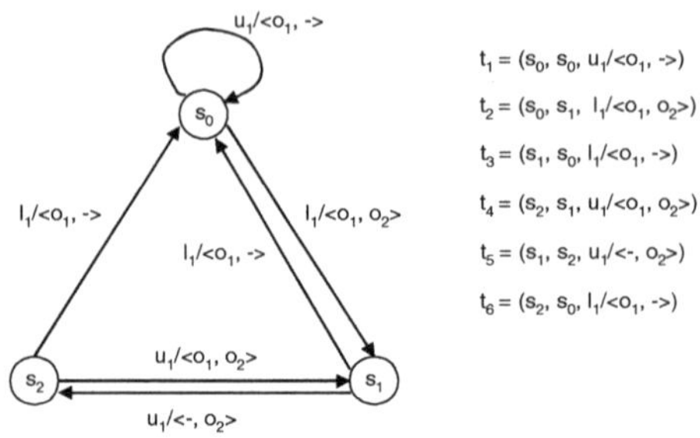

Fig. 2. A given FSM

is not involved in the input or output activity in t_1, so it cannot determine *when* to provide input l_1 of t_2 during the application of this input/output sequence on IUT, and thus a controllability problem occurs.

Two consecutive transitions t_i and t_{i+1}, whose labels are x_i/y_i and x_{i+1}/y_{i+1}, form a *synchronizable pair* of transitions (t_i, t_{i+1}) if t_{i+1} can follow t_i without causing a controllability problem. Any path in which every pair of transitions is synchronizable is called a *synchronizable path.* An input/output sequence is said to be synchronizable if it is the label of a synchronizable path.

Clearly, our ultimate goal is to generate *synchronizable* T-sequence, U-sequence, and checking sequence. Let ρ be a synchronizable input/output sequence of a transition tour $t_1 \ldots t_k$. ρ is called *closed* if (t_k, t_1) is a synchronizable pair of transitions. The conditions we present here are to guarantee the existence of synchronizable T-sequence, U-sequence, and checking sequence that are *closed.* This gives us the flexibility to start the testing from any (known) state in N: we can open tour ρ from any state and obtain its input/output sequence as a *synchronizable* one.

One of the major requirements for an FSM to have a synchronizable test sequence is that the FSM should be *intrinsically synchronizable* [6]. An FSM M is *intrinsically synchronizable* if for any ordered pair of transitions (t_1, t_2), there exists a path ρ such that $t_1@\rho@t_2$ is synchronizable. The FSM M in Figure 2 is not intrinsically synchronizable because there is no path ρ such that $t_1\rho t_2$ is synchronizable.

3 Conditions for Avoiding Controllability Problems

In this section, we present the sufficient and necessary conditions for generating synchronizable T-type sequences, U-type sequences, and checking sequences.

3.1 Conditions for T-Sequences

Theorem 1. *There exists a synchronizable T-sequence in an FSM M if and only if M is intrinsically synchronizable.*

Proof. ($\Rightarrow$) Suppose a synchronizable T-sequence γ exists in M, and its corresponding path is ϱ. According to the definition of T-sequence, ϱ is a path starting from and ending at the initial state. So $\varrho' = \varrho_1 @ \varrho_2$, where $\varrho_1 = \varrho_2 = \varrho$, is also a path in M. Since γ is synchronizable and closed, ϱ' is synchronizable. Now given any ordered pair of transitions (t_1, t_2) in M, since ϱ covers every transition in M at least once, there exists an occurrence of t_1 in ϱ_1 and an occurrence of t_2 in ϱ_2. Let ρ be the path between these two occurrences in ϱ' (including these two transitions). Apparently, ρ is synchronizable, $\mathit{first}(\rho) = t_1$ and $\mathit{last}(\rho) = t_2$. Therefore, M is intrinsically synchronizable.

($\Leftarrow$) Given an intrinsically synchronizable FSM M, we show how to construct a synchronizable path ϱ whose input/output sequence can form a synchronizable T-sequence.

Suppose there are m transitions t_1, ..., t_m in M where the starting state of t_1 is the initial state. Let $\varrho = \rho_1 \rho_2 \dots \rho_m$, where ρ_i ($\rho_i \in [1, m]$) is defined as follows:

(1) for $i \in [1, m-1]$, ρ_i is a synchronizable path such that $\mathit{first}(\rho_i) = t_i$, $(\mathit{last}(\rho_i), t_{i+1})$ is a synchronizable pair. The existence of ρ_i is guaranteed because M is intrinsically synchronizable.
(2) ρ_m is a synchronizable path such that $\mathit{first}(\rho_m) = t_m$ and $(\mathit{last}(\rho_m), t_1)$ is a synchronizable pair. Again, the existence of ρ_m is guaranteed because M is intrinsically synchronizable.

Now, ϱ contains all the transitions in M and is a closed synchronizable path starting from and ending at the initial state, i.e. the starting state of t_1. Thus, the label of ϱ is a synchronizable T-sequence.

3.2 Conditions for U-Sequences

Most of the discussions on generating U-sequences are UIO-based, so we first present our result for UIO-based synchronizable U-sequence with detailed proof. Similar result for DS-based synchronizable U-sequence is given thereafter. Its proof can be analogously given and is omitted.

Theorem 2. *There exists a UIO-based synchronizable U-sequence in an FSM M if and only if*

C_1: *M is intrinsically synchronizable;*
C_2: *for any transition $t = (s_i, s_j, x/y)$ in M, there exists a* UIO_j *such that*

$$t @ (s_j, \delta(s_j, \mathrm{UIO}_j), \mathrm{UIO}_j / \lambda(s_j, \mathrm{UIO}_j))$$

is synchronizable.

Proof. ($\Rightarrow$) Suppose there exists a UIO-based synchronizable U-sequence in M. Let the corresponding path of this U-sequence in M be ϱ.

First, U-sequence is a special T-sequence: it includes one test segment for each transition in M, and thus ϱ apparently covers each transition in M at least once.

So, given a synchronizable U-sequence, similar as in the proof of Theorem 1, we can show that M is intrinsically synchronizable.

For UIO-based test sequence, a test segment for a transition $t = (s_i, s_j, x/y)$ is

$$t@(s_j, \delta(s_j, UIO_j), UIO_j/\lambda(s_j, UIO_j))$$

for some UIO_j. Since a U-sequence includes one test segment for each transition in M, there exists a UIO_j such that

$$t@(s_j, \delta(s_j, UIO_j), UIO_j/\lambda(s_j, UIO_j))$$

appears in ϱ. As ϱ is synchronizable, clearly the above path is also synchronizable.

($\Leftarrow$) Suppose we are given an intrinsically synchronizable FSM M with m transitions $t_1, \ldots, t_m$, and for each transition t_i ($i \in [1, m]$), there exists a UIO_j such that $s_j = end(t_i)$ and $t_i@(s_j, \delta(s_j, UIO_j), UIO_j/\lambda(s_j, UIO_j))$ is synchronizable. We show how to construct a synchronizable path ϱ whose label is a U-sequence.

Let $\rho_i = t_i@(s_j, \delta(s_j, UIO_j), UIO_j/\lambda(s_j, UIO_j))$ ($i \in [1, m]$). Let σ_i ($i \in [1, m-1]$) be a path such that $last(\rho_i)@\sigma_i@t_{(i \bmod m)+1}$ is synchronizable. The existence of σ_i ($i \in [1, m]$) is guaranteed because M is intrinsically synchronizable. Let $\varrho = \rho_1\sigma_1\rho_2\sigma_2 \ldots \rho_m\sigma_m$. Apparently, ϱ is synchronizable. According to the construction of ϱ, its label is a synchronizable U-sequence. Note that σ_i ($i \in [1, m]$) may be ϵ if $(last(\rho_i), first(\rho_{(i \bmod m)+1}))$ forms a synchronizable pair.

Since DS is a special set of UIO-sequences such that the UIO sequence for each state is the same, similar result of Theorem 2 can be induced for DS-based synchronizable U-sequence as stated below.

Theorem 3. *There exists a DS-based synchronizable U-sequence in an FSM M if and only if*

C_1: *M is intrinsically synchronizable;*
C_3: *There exists a distinguishing sequence* DS *of M such that for any transition $t = (s_i, s_j, x/y)$ in M, $t@(s_j, \delta(s_j, \mathrm{DS}), \mathrm{DS}/\lambda(s_j, \mathrm{DS}))$ is synchronizable.*

3.3 Conditions for Checking Sequence

Most discussions in the literature on checking sequence generation are DS-based. Various techniques have been proposed to reduce the length of the checking sequences. Typically, the checking sequence generation is divided into two phases: *state identification* and *transition verification*. In the first phase, the states in N are identified for their correspondence in M. This is accomplished by applying distinguishing sequence to each state: from the output sequence of applying the distinguishing sequence, we can *identify* the state where we have applied the distinguishing sequence. In the second phase, we verify each transition t in M by applying the input of t to the state in N that has been recognized as the corresponding state of the starting state of t, and verify that the output of this transition in N is correct and that the ending state in N after this transition does correspond to the ending state of t by applying the distinguishing sequence. The so-called *transfer sequence* is used wherever necessary to connect these subsequences.

Below we present our condition for the existence of a DS-based synchronizable checking sequence, providing full details of the proof. The proof is based on the following Proposition 1, which claims if an FSM M is intrinsically synchronizable, then for any outgoing transition t of $s_i \in S$, there exists an incoming transition t' of s_i such that (t', t) is a synchronizable pair of transitions.

Proposition 1. *If an FSM M is intrinsically synchronizable, then for any transition t of M, there exists transition t' of M such that (t', t) is a synchronizable pair of transitions.*

Proof. Given any transition t of M, let t'' be any transition of M. Since M is intrinsically synchronizable, there exists a synchronizable path ρ such that $first(\rho) = t''$ and $last(\rho) = t$. If $\rho = t''@t$, then (t'', t) is a synchronizable pair. If $\rho = t''@\rho'@t$ where $\rho' \neq \varepsilon$, then $(last(\rho'), t)$ is a synchronizable pair.

Theorem 4. *There exists a DS-based synchronizable checking sequence in FSM M if and only if*

C_1: *M is intrinsically synchronizable;*
C_3: *There exists a distinguishing sequence* DS *of M such that for any transition $t = (s_i, s_j, x/y)$ in M, $t@(s_j, \delta(s_j, \mathrm{DS}), \mathrm{DS}/\lambda(s_j, \mathrm{DS}))$ is synchronizable.*

Proof. ($\Rightarrow$) Suppose there exists a DS-based synchronizable checking sequence in M. Let the corresponding path of this checking sequence in M be ϱ.

Note that checking sequence is a special T-sequence: for each transition t, it includes a test segment to recognize its starting state, and verify its output and its ending state. Thus ϱ apparently covers each transition in M at least once. So, given a synchronizable checking sequence, similar as in the proof of Theorem 1, we can show that M is intrinsically synchronizable.

Checking sequence ϱ needs to verify the ending state of each transition. For DS-based checking sequence, this means there exists a distinguishing sequence DS such that for each transition $t = (s_i, s_j, x/y)$,

$$t@(s_j, \delta(s_j, DS), DS/\lambda(s_j, DS))$$

appears in ϱ. As ϱ is synchronizable, clearly the above path is also synchronizable.

($\Leftarrow$) Given an FSM M where conditions C_1 and C_3 hold. We show how to construct a synchronizable path ϱ whose label is a checking sequence.

Suppose there are k states s_0, ..., s_{k-1} where s_0 is the initial state, and m transitions t_1, ..., t_m in M. Let $\varrho = \varrho_1@\varrho_2@\varrho_3$, where ϱ_1, ϱ_2, and ϱ_3 are defined as follows.

(1) ϱ_1 is for state identification:
Let $\rho_i = (s_i, \delta(s_i, DS), DS/\lambda(s_i, DS))$, i.e., ρ_i is the path obtained by applying input sequence DS at s_i ($i \in [0, k-1]$).

(i) for any s_i $(i \in [0, k-1])$, we compute the minimal set of transitions MS_i such that for any outgoing transition t from s_i, there exists $t' \in MS_i$ such that (t', t) forms a synchronizable pair of transitions. According to Proposition 1, MS_i is non-empty. Give an arbitrary order to the transitions in MS_i and we use $t'_{i,j}$ to denote the j-th incoming transition to state s_i in MS_i. For any transition $t'_{i,j} \in MS_i$, we construct a path $\rho'_i = t'_{i,1}@\rho_i@\gamma_{i,1}@\ldots t'_{i,|MS_i|-1}@\rho_i@\gamma_{i,|MS_i|-1}@t'_{i,|MS_i|}@\rho_i$, where $\gamma_{i,j}$ (for $j \in [1, |MS_i|-1]$) is a synchronizable transfer sequence starting from $end(t'_{i,j}@\rho_i)$ and ending at $start(t'_{i,j+1})$ such that $last(t'_{i,j}@\rho_i)@\gamma_{i,j}$ $@t'_{i,j+1}$ is synchronizable. $\gamma_{i,j}$ exists because M is intrinsically synchronizable. As $t'_{i,j}@\rho_i$ is also synchronizable according to condition C_3, ρ'_i is synchronizable.

(ii) for $i \in [0, k-2]$, find a transfer sequence σ_i from $end(\rho'_i)$ to $t'_{i+1,1}$ such that $last(\rho'_i)@\sigma_i@first(\rho'_{i+1})$ is a synchronizable path.

(iii) find a transfer sequence σ_{k-1} from $end(\rho'_{k-1})$ to s_0 such that $last(\rho'_{k-1})@\sigma_{k-1}@first(\rho'_0)$ is a synchronizable path.

(iv) let $\varrho_1 = \rho'_0@\sigma_0@\ldots@\rho'_{k-1}@\sigma_{k-1}@\rho_0$.

According to the above definition, ϱ_1 identifies all states in N and it is synchronizable.

(2) ϱ_2 is for transition verification:
For $t_i = (s_u, s_v, x/y)$ $(i \in [1, m])$, let

$$\theta'_i = \theta_i@t_i@(end(t_i), \delta(end(t_i), DS), DS/\lambda(end(t_i), DS)).$$

The label of this path will be used to verify transition t_i. It contains a transfer sequence θ_i leading to t_i, transition t_i, and the path for applying DS on $end(t_i)$. The transfer sequence θ_i is defined as follows:

(i) For t_1, let θ_1 be the transfer sequence from $end(\varrho_1)$ to t_1. According to Proposition 1 and our definition of MS, we know there exists a transition $t'_{u,j}$ in MS_u such that $(t'_{u,j}, t_1)$ is a synchronizable pair of transitions.

If $j = 1$ and $u \neq 0$, find a transfer sequence ς_1 from state $end(\varrho_1)$ to $start(t'_{u-1,|MS_{u-1}|})$, such that $last(\varrho_1)@\varsigma_1@t'_{u-1,|MS_{u-1}|}$ is a synchronizable path. In this case, $\theta_1 = \varsigma_1@t'_{u-1,|MS_{u-1}|}@\rho_{u-1}@\sigma_{u-1}@t'_{u,1}$.

If $j = 1$ and $u = 0$, find a transfer sequence ς_1 from state $end(\varrho_1)$ to $start(t'_{k-1,|MS_{k-1}|})$, such that $last(\varrho_1)@\varsigma_1@t'_{k-1,|MS_{k-1}|}$ is a synchronizable path. In this case, $\theta_1 = \varsigma_1@t'_{k-1,|MS_{k-1}|}@\rho_{k-1}@\sigma_{k-1}@t'_{0,1}$.

If $j > 1$, find a transfer sequence ς_1 from state $end(\varrho_1)$ to $start(t'_{u,j-1})$, such that $last(\varrho_1)@\varsigma_1@t'_{u,j-1}$ is a synchronizable path. In this case, $\theta_1 = \varsigma_1@t'_{u,j-1}@\rho_u@\gamma_{u,j-1}@t'_{u,j}$.

(ii) for t_i $(i \in [2, m])$, let θ_i be the transfer sequence from $last(\theta'_{i-1})$ to t_i. According to Proposition 1 and our definition of MS, we know there exists a transition $t'_{u,j}$ in MS_u such that $(t'_{u,j}, t_i)$ is a synchronizable pair of transitions.

If $j = 1$ and $u \neq 0$, find a transfer sequence ς_i from state $end(\theta'_{i-1})$ to $start(t'_{u-1,|MS_{u-1}|})$, such that $last(\theta'_{i-1})@\varsigma_i@t'_{u-1,|MS_{u-1}|}$ is a synchronizable path. In this case, $\theta_i = \varsigma_i@t'_{u-1,|MS_{u-1}|}@\rho_{u-1}@\sigma_{u-1}@t'_{u,1}$.

If $j = 1$ and $u = 0$, find a transfer sequence ς_i from state $end(\theta'_{i-1})$ to $start(t'_{k-1,|MS_{k-1}|})$, such that $last(\theta'_{i-1})@\varsigma_i@t'_{k-1,|MS_{k-1}|}$ is a synchronizable path. In this case, $\theta_i = \varsigma_i@t'_{k-1,|MS_{k-1}|}@\rho_{k-1}@\sigma_{k-1}@t'_{0,1}$.

If $j > 1$, find a transfer sequence ς_i from state $end(\theta'_{i-1})$ to $start(t'_{u,j-1})$, such that $last(\theta'_{i-1})@\varsigma_i@t'_{u,j-1}$ is a synchronizable path. In this case, $\theta_i = \varsigma_i@t'_{u,j-1}@\rho_u@\gamma_{u,j-1}@t'_{u,j}$.

(iii) Let $\varrho_2 = \theta'_1@\theta'_2@\ldots@\theta'_m$.

Finally, let ϱ_3 be a transfer sequence from $end(\varrho_2)$ to s_0 such that $last(\varrho_2)@\varrho_3@first(\varrho_1)$ is synchronizable. Again, such a ϱ_3 exists since M is intrinsically synchronizable.

Now, let $\varrho = \varrho_1@\varrho_2@\varrho_3$. From the above construction, ϱ is synchronizable. So the label of ϱ is synchronizable. Moreover, $\varrho_1@\varrho_2$ contains both state identification for each state in M and transition verification for each transition in M. So the label of ϱ forms a checking sequence.

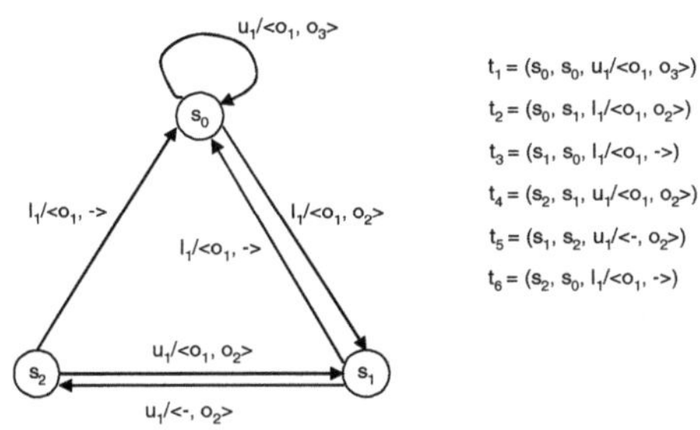

Fig. 3. An example that satisfies both C_1 and C_3

Example 3. To illustrate the proof of Theorem 4, we use the example of Figure 3 to show how a synchronizable checking sequence is constructed. Here $u_1 \in I_1$, $o_1 \in O_1$ at U, $l_1 \in I_2$, $o_2, o_3 \in O_2$ at L. $DS = u_1$.

In this example, $\varrho_1 = t_1t_2t_5t_4t_3t_1$; $\varrho_2 = t_2t_5t_4t_3t_1t_1\ t_2t_5t_4t_3t_2t_5\ t_6t_1t_2t_3t_1\ t_2t_5t_4t_5\ t_6t_1t_2t_5t_4\ t_5t_6t_1$; $\varrho_3 = \epsilon$. The synchronizable checking sequence is the label of the concatenation of ϱ_1, ϱ_2 and ϱ_3:

$$
\begin{array}{l}
u_1/\langle o_1,o_3\rangle\ l_1/\langle o_1,o_2\rangle\ u_1/\langle -,o_2\rangle\ u_1/\langle o_1,o_2\rangle\ l_1/\langle o_1,-\rangle\ u_1/\langle o_1,o_3\rangle\\
l_1/\langle o_1,o_2\rangle\ u_1/\langle -,o_2\rangle\ u_1/\langle o_1,o_2\rangle\ l_1/\langle o_1,-\rangle\ u_1/\langle o_1,o_3\rangle\ u_1/\langle o_1,o_3\rangle\\
l_1/\langle o_1,o_2\rangle\ u_1/\langle -,o_2\rangle\ u_1/\langle o_1,o_2\rangle\ l_1/\langle o_1,-\rangle\ l_1/\langle o_1,o_2\rangle\ u_1/\langle -,o_2\rangle\\
l_1/\langle o_1,-\rangle\ u_1/\langle o_1,o_3\rangle\ l_1/\langle o_1,o_2\rangle\ l_1/\langle o_1,-\rangle\ u_1/\langle o_1,o_3\rangle\ l_1/\langle o_1,o_2\rangle\\
u_1/\langle -,o_2\rangle\ u_1/\langle o_1,o_2\rangle\ u_1/\langle -,o_2\rangle\ l_1/\langle o_1,-\rangle\ u_1/\langle o_1,o_3\rangle\ l_1/\langle o_1,o_2\rangle\\
u_1/\langle -,o_2\rangle\ u_1/\langle o_1,o_2\rangle\ u_1/\langle -,o_2\rangle\ l_1/\langle o_1,-\rangle\ u_1/\langle o_1,o_3\rangle
\end{array}
$$

The generation of *UIO-based* checking sequence is a bit more complicate: in the first phase, we need to apply UIO_i for each state s_i in M to the same state in N in order to identify this state in N. In the second phase, we verify each transition in the same way as in the setting of using distinguishing sequence: to verify the ending state of the transition being verified, the UIO-sequence for the ending state is used instead of the distinguishing sequence.

We use the following example to show that the satisfaction of C_1 and C_2 cannot guarantee the existence of a *UIO-based* synchronizable checking sequence. We leave it open to find the sufficient and necessary conditions for the existence of *UIO-based* synchronizable checking sequence.

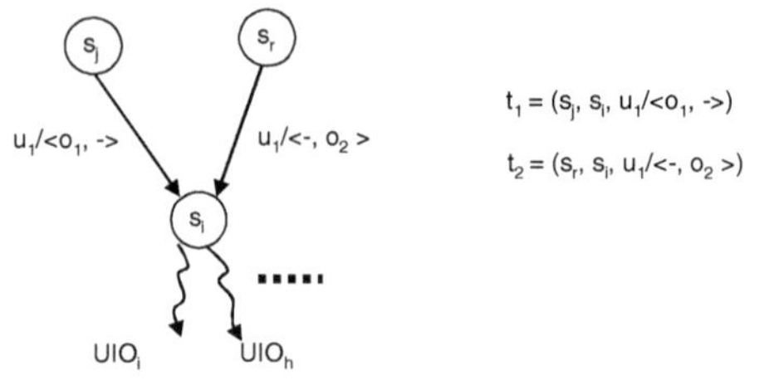

Fig. 4. An example to show C_1 and C_2 are not sufficient for generating a UIO-based synchronizable checking sequence

Example 4. Figure 4 shows part of an FSM M. We assume M is intrinsically synchronizable, and the set of UIO sequences for M is $\{UIO_i | \forall s_i \in S\}$. u_1 is an element of the input alphabet for port U. o_1 and o_2 are elements of the output alphabet for port U and L respectively. For a specific state s_i, there are two incoming transitions t_1 and t_2. We assume $t_1@(s_i, \delta(s_i, UIO_i), UIO_i/\lambda(s_i, UIO_i))$ and $t_2@(s_i, \delta(s_i, UIO_i), UIO_i/\lambda(s_i, UIO_i))$ are synchronizable.

For state identification, every element in $\{UIO_i | \forall s_i \in S\}$ should be applied at state s_i; however, there may exist UIO_h such that neither t_1 nor t_2 followed by the test sequence with UIO_h as the input portion can form a synchronizable path. Therefore, no synchronizable checking sequence can be constructed.

4 Discussions on the Conditions

In this section, we discuss the time complexity to determine if a given FSM holds conditions C_1, C_2 or C_3, and the relationships among these conditions.

4.1 Checking If the Conditions are Satisfied

First, we unveil the relationship between an intrinsically synchronizable FSM and a strongly connected FSM.

A *directed graph (digraph)* G is defined by a pair (V, E) where V is a set of vertices and E is a set of directed edges between vertices. Each edge may have a label. As we know, an FSM can be represented by a digraph where i) each vertex represents a state; ii) each edge represents a transition; iii) the label of an edge is the label of its corresponding transition. A *walk* is a sequence of pair-wise adjacent edges in G. A digraph is *strongly connected* if for any ordered pair of vertices (v_i, v_j) there is a walk from v_i to v_j. An FSM M is *strongly connected* if the digraph that represents M is strongly connected, i.e., for every pair of states s_i and s_j, there exists an input sequence in such that $\delta(s_i, in) = s_j$.

Apparently an FSM M is strongly connected if M is intrinsically synchronizable, while the reverse is not true.

Let $G_M = \langle V, E\rangle$ be the digraph representing FSM M. Define digraph $G'_M = \langle V', E'\rangle$ as follows:

- $V' = \{v_e \mid \forall e \in E\}$
- $E' = \{(v_{e_1}, v_{e_2}) \mid \forall e_1, e_2 \in E,\ (e_1, e_2) \text{ is a synchronizable pair }\}$

Then we have that M is intrinsically synchronizable if and only if G'_M is strongly connected. While most of the discussions in test sequence generation require that G_M be strongly connected, for avoiding controllability problem, it is also important that G'_M is strongly connected.

An algorithm adapted from Depth First Search Algorithm [34] can be implemented to check if a digraph G is strongly connected. This algorithm has time complexity $O(|V| + |E|)$, where $|V|$ and $|E|$ are the number of vertices and the number of edges in G respectively. Given an FSM M with m transitions, it takes time $O(m^2)$ to transform G_M to G'_M. In the worst case, there are m^2 transitions in G'_M. Therefore, it takes time $O(m^2)$ to check whether M is intrinsically synchronizable.

Determining the existence of UIOs or a DS of an FSM is a PSPACE-complete problem [20]. If UIO_i exists for any $s_i \in S$, and the maximum length of UIO_i is l, then determining whether C_2 is satisfied takes time $O(ml)$. Similarly, determining whether C_3 is satisfied takes time $O(m|DS|)$.

4.2 Relationship Among the Conditions

The *intrinsically synchronizable* condition is stronger than the negation of the *intrinsically non-synchronizable* condition [31]. An FSM is intrinsically non-synchronizable if it has non-synchronizable transitions or non-synchronizable states. A *transition* $t = (s_i, s_j, x/y)$ *is non-synchronizable* if t fails to form a synchronizable pair of transitions with any incoming transition to state s_i. A *state* s_i *is non-synchronizable* if it has no outgoing transition t' which forms a synchronizable pair of transitions with any of its incoming transitions. If a given FSM is *intrinsically non-synchronizable*, then there is no synchronizable T-sequence, U-sequence or checking sequence [31].

Clearly, if an FSM M is intrinsically synchronizable, then M is not intrinsically non-synchronizable. However, it is possible that M is not intrinsically non-synchronizable, and it is also not intrinsically synchronizable.

Example 5. The FSM in Figure 2 is not intrinsically non-synchronizable because there is no non-synchronizable transition and there is no non-synchronizable state. However M is not intrinsically synchronizable: there is no synchronizable path to connect t_1 and t_2.

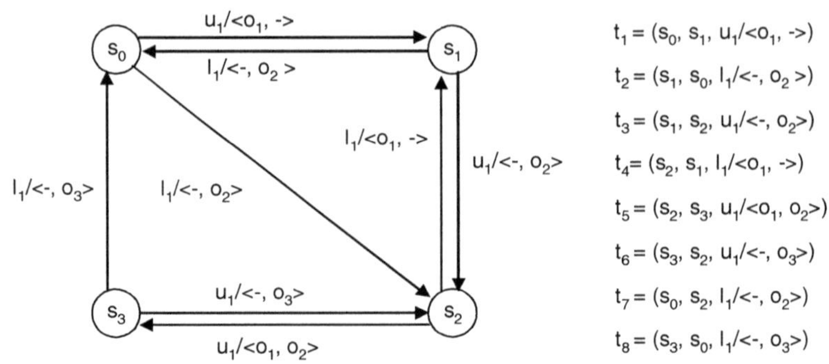

Fig. 5. An example that does not satisfy C_3

Next, we give an example to show that conditions C_1 and C_2 are independent. Analogously, conditions C_1 and C_3 are also independent.

Example 6. Figure 2 gives an example where C_1 is not satisfied while conditions C_2 and C_3 are satisfied. C_1 is not satisfied because there is no synchronizable path to connect t_1 and t_2. It is obvious that no synchronizable checking sequence can be constructed because there is no way to leave state s_1 after executing t_1 without encountering controllability problem.

Figure 5 gives an example where C_1 is satisfied while C_3 is not. This example has the same input and output alphabets as the one in Figure 3, and $DS = u$. C_2 is not satisfied because

$$t_2@(end(t_2), \delta(end(t_2), DS), DS/\lambda(end(t_2), DS))$$
$$t_7@(end(t_7), \delta(end(t_7), DS), DS/\lambda(end(t_7), DS))$$
$$t_8@(end(t_8), \delta(end(t_8), DS), DS/\lambda(end(t_8), DS))$$

are not synchronizable. In this case, the ending state of t_2, t_7, and t_8 cannot be verified without encountering controllability problem, and thus no synchronizable U-sequence or checking sequence can be constructed.

5 Conclusion and Final Remarks

We have presented sufficient and necessary conditions for generating three commonly used test sequences so that applying these sequences to the IUT will not invoke controllability problems. We have considered test sequences whose corresponding paths in the specification FSM are transition tours that start from and end at the initial state. In particular, we require that the last and the first transition of the tour should form a synchronizable pair. This is based on the following facts: i) It is very often desirable that the IUT returns to its initial state after testing. ii) Many systems have the so-called *reliable reset* feature, in the sense that there is a special input that can lead the system from any state back to the initial state. So we can always start the testing from the initial state by applying the generated test sequence. iii) In the absence of *reliable reset* feature, sometimes there exists a *homing sequence* [18,25] or a *synchronizing sequence* [9,18] in the specification FSM. This means after applying the homing sequence or the synchronizable sequence, the IUT will be led to a specific state s. In this case, if we have generated a test sequence whose corresponding path in M is a synchronizable tour such that its last and the first transitions form a synchronizable pair, then we can break the generated test sequence tour so that the test sequence is to be applied at s. Of course, for U-sequence and checking sequence, we cannot break the test sequence (tour) at any place. For example, the test sequence cannot be broken within a subsequence used for transition verification.

Sometimes, it suffices to have a synchronizable test sequence where the last and the first transition of its corresponding path do not form a synchronizable pair. In this setting, the above conditions can be weakened: A weaker condition is given in [3] for generating synchronizable T-sequence. What remain open are the conditions in this setting for generating synchronizable U-sequences and synchronizable checking sequences.

Given a specification FSM satisfying the conditions for the existence of a synchronizable T-sequence, U-sequence or checking sequence, a procedure for constructing the corresponding test sequence is actually given in the proof of the theorems. Of course, such procedures in general do not yield the shortest test sequences. In this regard, various methods have been proposed in the literature on how to minimize the length of T-sequence, U-sequence, or checking sequence [1,13,24,36].

Acknowledgements

This work is supported in part by the Natural Sciences and Engineering Research Council of Canada under grant number RGPIN 209774.

References

1. A.V. Aho, A.T. Dahbura, D. Lee, and M.U. Uyar. An optimization technique for protocol conformance test generation based on UIO sequences and Rural Chinese Postman Tours. *IEEE Trans Comm.*, 39(11):1604–1615, Nov. 1991.
2. G.v. Bochmann, A. Petrenko, O. Bellal, and S. Maguiraga. Automating the process of test derivation from SDL specifications. In *proc. of 8th SDL Forum*, 1997.
3. S. Boyd and H. Ural. The synchronization problem in protocol testing and its complexity. *Information Processing Letters*, 4(3):131–136, Nov. 1991.
4. L. Cacciari and O. Rafiq. Controllability and observability in distributed testing. *Information and Software Technology*, 41:767–780, 1999.
5. J. Chen, R. M. Hierons, and H. Ural. Conditions for resolving observability problems in distributed testing. In *proc. of 24th International Conference on Formal Techinques in Networked and Distributed Systems (FORTE 2004), LNCS 3235*, pages 229–242. Springer-Verlag, 2004.

6. J. Chen, R.M. Hierons, and H. Ural. Overcoming observability problems in distributed test architectures. *Information Processing Letter*, 98(5):177–182, June 2006.
7. J. Chen and H. Ural. Detecting observability problems in distributed testing. In *proc. of 19th IFIP International Conference on Testing of Communicating Systems (TestCom 2006), LNCS*, 2006. To appear.
8. T.S. Chow. Testing software design modeled by finite-state machines. *IEEE Trans. Software Eng.*, SE-4(3):178–187, May 1978.
9. D. Eppstein. Reset sequences for monotonic automata. *SIAM J. Computing*, 19(3):500–510, 1990.
10. G. Gonenc. A method for the design of fault detection experiments. *IEEE Trans. Computers*, 19(6):551–558, June 1970.
11. F.C. Hennie. Fault detecting experiments for sequential circuits. In *proc. of 5th Ann. Symp. Switching Circuit Theory and Logical Design*, pages 95–110, 1964.
12. R. M. Hierons and M. Harman. Testing conformance to a quasi-non-deterministic stream X-machine. *Formal Aspects of Computing*, 12(6):423–442, 2000.
13. R. M. Hierons and H. Ural. Reduced length checking sequences. *IEEE Transactions on Computers*, 51(9):1111–1117, 2002.
14. R. M. Hierons and H. Ural. UIO sequence based checking sequences for distributed test architectures. *Information and Software Technology*, 45(12):793–803, 2003.
15. J.E. Hopcroft, R. Motwani, and J.D. Ullman. *Introduction to automata theory, languages, and computation.* Addison-Wesley, 2001.
16. ISO/IEC 9646. *Information technology – Open Systems Interconnection – Conformance testing methodology and framework – Part 1-7.* ISO, June 1996.
17. W.L. Johnson, J.H. Porter, S.I. Ackley, and D.T. Ross. Automatic generation of efficient lexical processors using finite state techniques. *Communications of the ACM*, 11(12):805–813, 1968.
18. Z. Kohavi. *Switching and finite automata theory.* New York: McGraw-Hill, 2nd edition, 1978.
19. R. Lai. A survey of communication protocol testing. *Journal of Systems and Software*, 62:21–46, 2002.
20. D. Lee and M. Yannakakis. Testing finite state machines: state identification and verification. *IEEE Tran. Computers*, 43:306–320, 1994.
21. D. Lee and M. Yannakakis. Principles and methods of testing finite state machines — a survey. *Proceedings of The IEEE*, 84(8):1090–1123, Aug 1996.
22. G. Luo, A. Das, and G. von Bochmann. Generating tests for control portion of SDL specification. In *proc. of Protocol test systems VI*, pages 51–66, 1994.
23. G. Luo, R. Dssouli, G.V. Bochmann, P. Venkataram, and A. Ghedamsi. Test generation with respect to distributed interfaces. *Computer Standards and Interfaces*, 16:119–132, 1994. Elsevier.
24. R.E. Miller and S. Paul. On the generation of minimal length conformance tests for communications protocols. *IEEE/ACM Transactions on Networking*, 1(1):116–129, 1993.
25. E.F. Moore. Gedanken-experiments on sequenctial machines. *Automata Studies*, 34:129–153, 1956. Princeton Univ. Press.
26. H. Motteler, A. Chung, and D. Sidhu. Fault coverage of UIO-based methods for protocol testing. In *proc. of IFIP TC6/WG6.1 6th International Workshop on Protocol Test Systems*, pages 21–33, 1994.
27. S. Naito and M. Tsunoyama. Fault detection for sequential machines by transition tours. In *proc. of 11th. IEEE Fault Tolerant Computing Symposium*, pages 238–243, 1981.

28. I. Pomeranz and S. M. Reddy. Test generation for multiple state-table faults in finite-state machines. *IEEE Transactions on Computers*, 46:783–794, 1997.
29. K.K. Sabnani and A.T. Dahbura. A protocol test generation procedure. *Computer Networks and ISDN Systems*, 4(15):285–297, 1988.
30. K. Saleh, H. Ural, and A. Williams. Test generation based on control and data dependencies within system specifications in SDL. *Computer Communications*, 23(7):609–627, 2000.
31. B. Sarikaya and G. V. Bochmann. Synchronization and specification issues in protocol testing. *IEEE Transactions on Communications*, 32:389–395, 1984.
32. D. P. Sidhu and T.-K. Leung. Formal methods for protocol testing: A detailed study. *IEEE Transactions on Software Engineering*, 15(4):413–426, 1989.
33. Q. M. Tan, A. Petrenko, and G.v. Bochmann. Modeling basic LOTOS by FSMs for conformance testing. In *proc. of 15th International Symposium on Protocol Specification, Testing and Verification (PSTV 15)*, pages 137–152, 1995.
34. R. Tarjan. Depth-first search and linear graph algorithms. *J. SIAM Comput.*, 1(2):146–160, 1972.
35. H. Ural and D. Whittier. Distributed testing without encountering controlability and observability problems. *Information Processing Letters*, 88:133–141, 2003.
36. H. Ural, X. Wu, and F. Zhang. On minimizing the lengths of checking sequences. *IEEE Transactions on Computers*, 46(1):93–99, 1997.

Generating Test Cases for Constraint Automata by Genetic Symbiosis Algorithm

Samira Tasharofi[1], Sepand Ansari[1], and Marjan Sirjani[1,2]

[1] Department of Electrical and Computer Engineering, University of Tehran, Tehran, Iran
[2] School of Computer Science, Institute for Studies in Theoretical Physics and Mathematics (IPM), Niavaran Square, Tehran, Iran
{s.tasharofi, sepans}@ece.ut.ac.ir
msirjani@ut.ac.ir

Abstract. Constraint automata are a semantic model for Reo modeling language. Testing correctness of mapping black-box components in Reo to constraint automata is an important problem in analyzing the semantic model of Reo. This testing requires a suite of test cases that cover the automaton states and transitions and also examine different paths. In this paper, Genetic Algorithm (GA) is employed to generate such suite of test cases. This test data generation is improved by Genetic Symbiosis Algorithm (GSA). The results show that GSA approach brings us a suite of test cases with full coverage of automata states and transitions and also diversity of examined paths.

Keywords: Constraint automata, finite-state machine testing, automatic test data generation, genetic algorithms, symbiotic evolutionary algorithms.

1 Introduction

Software systems are getting more complex day after day. Therefore, there is a need for techniques to reduce the complexity and consequently development cost and time of these systems. As a result, many new software design and modeling techniques have been introduced. Most of these approaches are shaped by decomposition of software into several smaller subsystems, called components. By acquiring component-based design techniques, new software is designed by using pre-existing and new components in a combination, to achieve the desired functionality. Reo [1] is a coordination language for modeling component-based systems. This language is based on a calculus of channels and consists of components that are connected via connectors which coordinate their activities. Composability and reconfiguration of connectors in Reo make it suitable for modeling systems. This modeling language is used for modeling different application including software architectures, network protocols and multi-agent systems.

Constraint automata [2] are a semantic model for Reo. Each element of Reo such as the black-box components must be mapped to a constraint automaton

Z. Liu and J. He (Eds.): ICFEM 2006, LNCS 4260, pp. 478–493, 2006.

and the behavior of a system is obtained by composing constraint automata of its constituent elements.

Now, the question is how we can make sure that the automaton precisely defines the behavior of our components. One of the approaches is formal verification, but this approach has the problem of state-space explosion and high cost, when the automaton is large. Another approach is testing the automaton; in this approach, we need a suite of tests that gives us the confidence of traversing all the reachable states and transitions from the initial state and also examine a wide range of paths (behaviors).

Genetic Algorithms (GAs) have been used for generating test data for software systems. Pargas [3] examined statement and branch coverage; in [4], GAs are applied to branch testing; boundary conditions are analyzed in [5]; and in [6,7,8] GAs are used for path testing. In [9], functional testing is considered in which program is treated as a black box and the necessary information is extracted from the code to calculate the objective function and in [10] the time it takes for a process is measured.

In order to generate test cases for automated-based languages, classical testing frameworks based on Mealy machines [11,12] or finite labeled transition systems, LTSs are developed [13,14,15,16,17].

A type of problem in FSM (Finite State Machine) testing is conformance testing. In this problem, a specification of finite state machine is given, for which we have its transition diagram, and an implementation, which is a "black box" for which we can only observe its I/O behavior, we want to test whether the implementation conforms to the specification.

Some proposed approaches for conformance testing are the D-method based on distinguishing sequences [18], the U-method based on UIO (Unique Input Output) sequences [19], the T-method based on transition tours [20] and the W-method based on characterization sets [11] which is improved in [21] and the generalized form of it for generating test sequences for NFSM's (Nondeterministic Finite-State Machines) is appeared in [22].

In [23,24] conformance testing methods are proposed for real-time systems based on specifications modeled as timed automata and are based on on-the-fly determinization of the specification automaton during the execution of the test, which in turn relies on reachability computations. These methods focused on generating a suite of tests which covers the specification with respect to a number of criteria: location, edge or state coverage. A conformance testing method for timed I/O automata is presented in [25].

But, constraint automata are different from LTS, FSM, I/O automata and timed automata as multiple inputs/outputs can be activated in each transition. Also, unlike I/O automata which at every state must be receptive towards every possible input action (input enabled) for constraint automata at every state some inputs may be illegal.

These characteristics of constraint automata cause that the presented testing approaches couldn't be applied for constraint automata. So, testing a constraint automaton is an open problem in testing area. In this paper, we are going to use two evolutionary algorithms, ordinary Genetic Algorithm (GA) and Genetic Symbiosis Algorithm (GSA), for generating a suite of tests for constraint automata. Our goal is not only coverage of states and transitions but also examination of different paths (behaviors) by the test cases.

Structure of the paper. The next section is an introduction to the primitive concepts of Reo and constraint automata. Section 3, contains a brief overview of ordinary Genetic Algorithm (GA) and Genetic Symbiosis Algorithm (GSA). The details of our applied algorithms are described in Section 4. The experimental results are presented in Section 5. Finally, Section 6 contains the conclusions derived from these results and the future work.

2 Constraint Automata

Reo is a coordination language for modeling systems based on components. The components in Reo are coordinated through connectors called channels and nodes. So, each Reo circuit is constructed from channels, nodes and components.

Constraint automata [2] are proposed as compositional semantics for Reo based on timed data streams [26]. Each element of a timed data stream is a pair of time and a data item, where the time indicates when the data item is being input or output. A transition fires if it observes data item in a port of the component and according to the observed data, the automaton may change its state. A constraint automaton (over the data domain Data) is a tuple $A = (Q, Names, \longrightarrow, Q0)$ where:

- Q is a finite set of states
- $Names$ is a finite set of names (I/O ports)
- $\longrightarrow$ is a finite subset of $Q \times 2^{Names} \times DC \times Q$, called the transition relation of A
- $Q0 \subseteq Q$ is the set of initial states

In this model, DC is data constraint that plays the role of guard for transition. For example $d(A) = d(B)$ is a data constraint that imposes the observed data on ports A and B must be equal together.

For example, Fig. 1 shows the modeling of the Exclusive-Router component that has one input A and two outputs B and C. This component accepts data by its input if it can simultaneously dispenses data on one of its outputs. The data is copied only on one of its outputs. So, if B and C can accept data, one of them is selected non-deterministically.

In order to obtain the behavior of a Reo circuit (entire system) by constraint automata, first, each element is modeled by a constraint automaton; in the next steps, by composing the automata of Reo elements, the behavior of the entire system is achieved.

Each component in Reo, may be constructed out of a Reo circuit or may be a black box that its I/O behavior is specified. In the case that the component is a Reo circuit, its corresponding constraint automaton can be obtained via a composition process, which is automated in [27]; otherwise, the constraint

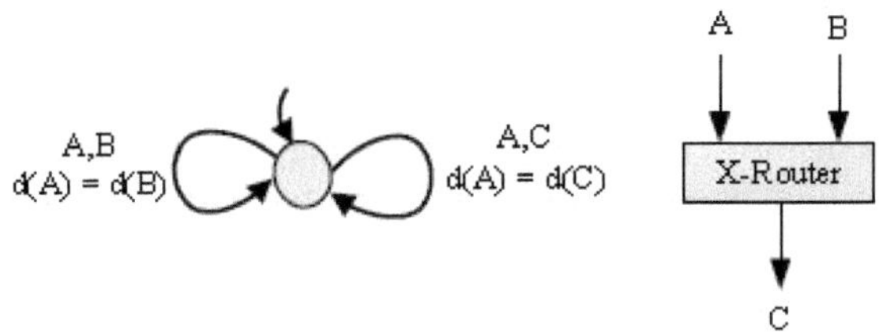

Fig. 1. Exclusive-Router component and its modeling by constraint automata

automaton must be defined with respect to the specification of the component behavior. In the latter case, the correctness of this mapping is a problem.

A constraint automaton is defined in an XML format which is validated by its corresponding schema provided in [28]. As an example, the XML specification of the automaton in Fig. 1 is depicted in Fig. 2. The elements *node* and *edge* are used for defining the states and transitions of an automaton respectively. The *edge* element is a composite element that consists of two elements, *signal* and *constraint*, for defining the *names* and *data constraints* of the transition respectively.

```
<gxl><graph>
    <signals>
        <signal>A</signal>
        <signal>B</signal>
        <signal>C</signal>
    </signals>
    <node id="*st0"> *st0  </node>
    <edge id="edge0" from="*st0" to="*st0">
            <signal>A</signal>
            <signal>B</signal>
            <constraint>d(A)=d(B)</constraint>
    </edge>
    <edge id="edge1" from="*st0" to="*st0">
            <signal>A</signal>
            <signal>C</signal>
            <constraint>d(A)=d(C)</constraint>
    </edge>
</graph></gxl>
```

Fig. 2. XML specification of Exclusive-Router constraint automaton which is shown in Fig. 1

3 Genetic and Genetic Symbiosis Algorithms

Genetic algorithms (GAs) [29] are a particular class of evolutionary algorithms that use techniques inspired by evolutionary biology and natural selection theory. GA is a search technique based to find approximate solutions to optimization and search problems where the problem space is large and complex, and the problem contains difficulties such as high dimensionality, multiple optima, discontinuity and noise. In GA, the parameters and properties of a possible solution to the problem is encoded as a string. Genetic Algorithm maintains a *population* of these encodings as *chromosomes*, each called an *individual*. Each position of the chromosome is called a *gene*, the chromosomal encoding of a solution is called the *genotype*, and the encoded properties of solution are called the *phenotype* of the individual. In every iteration of GA, called a *generation*, an *objective function* quantifies the fitness of each individual or in other words, measures how good a solution coded in the chromosomes solves the problem. According to the fitness of the individuals, certain proportion of the population is selected using the *natural selection* mechanism. Most selection mechanisms are stochastic and designed so that a small proportion of less fit solutions are selected. This helps keep the diversity of the population large, preventing premature convergence on poor solutions. One of the most popular and well-studied selection methods is roulette wheel selection. Using the survived individuals, new offsprings are produced for the next generation. Usually, reproduction is performed using two operations: *crossover* and *mutation*. Crossover is used to create offspring from two parent individuals by randomly exchanging parts of their chromosomes, which can be performed in various ways. An example of one-point crossover is given in the left hand side of Fig. 3. Subsequently, mutation may be applied to individuals by randomly changing pieces of their representations, as shown in the right hand side of Fig. 3. The purpose of mutation in GA is to allow the algorithm to avoid local minima by preventing the population of chromosomes from becoming too similar to each other, thus slowing or even stopping evolution and mutation plays the exploration role in the search. Both crossover and mutation are applied with a certain probability, called crossover rate and mutation rate, respectively. A high-level description of Genetic Algorithm is shown in Fig. 4. For more information on Evolution Strategies, see references [30,31].

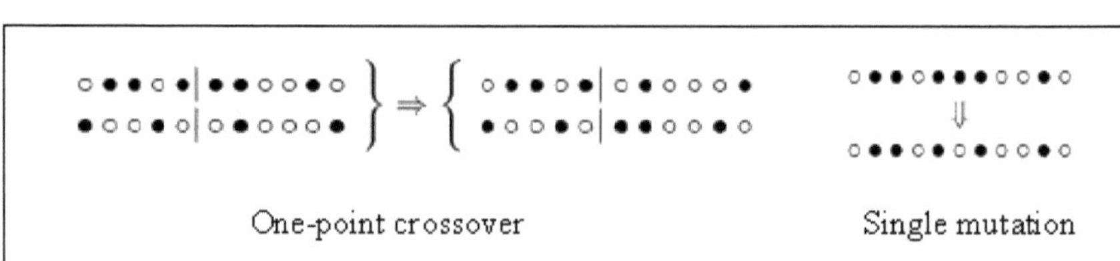

Fig. 3. One-point crossover and single mutation are shown in the left hand side and right hand side respectively

Randomly generate or seed initial population P
Repeat
 Evaluate fitness of each individual in P
 Select parents from P according to selection mechanism
 Recombine parents to form new offspring
 Construct new population P' from parents and offspring
 Mutate P'
 $P \longleftarrow P'$
Until stopping condition reached

Fig. 4. A high level description of Genetic Algorithm

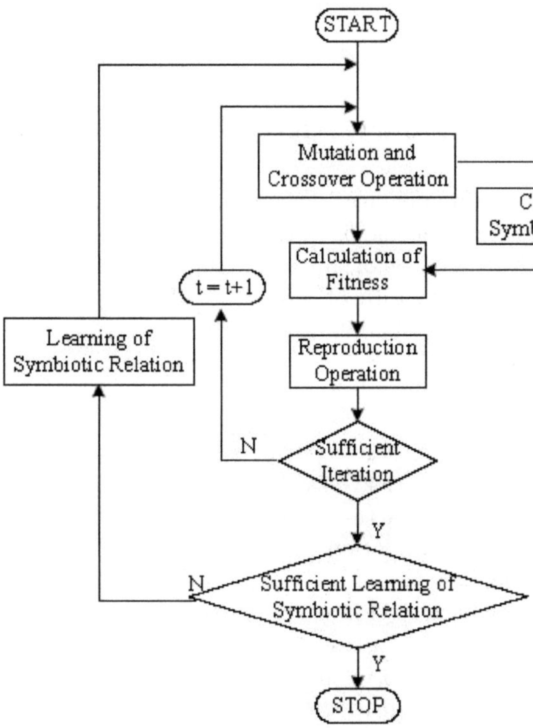

Fig. 5. Structure of GSA

Another variation of Genetic Algorithms is called Genetic Symbiosis Algorithms which is wide spread in complex systems, especially in ecosystems. In the symbiotic systems, the fitness of each individual is dependent to other individuals and interaction between different individuals form the fitness. So two individuals can complement each others and fit into the environment, while none of them would have fit individually. Four different kinds of symbiotic relations exist:

- parasitism: in which the association is disadvantageous or destructive to one of the organisms and beneficial to the other (+ -)
- mutualism: in which the association is advantageous to both (+ +)
- commensalisms: in which one member of the association benefits while the other is not affected (+ 0)
- amensalism: in which the association is disadvantageous to one member while the other is not affected (- 0)

In [32], the Genetic Symbiosis Algorithms has formulized by introducing *symbiotic parameters*. These parameters represent the symbiotic relations such as competition, predation, altruism and mutualism between two individuals. The GSA updates the fitness of individuals according to the symbiotic parameters before applying the selection mechanism. After a certain number of iterations, the symbiotic parameters are recalculated using a fuzzy inference function. The structure of GSA is shown in Fig. 5.

4 The Applied Evolutionary Algorithms

In our algorithms, the problem specification is mapped to GA specification. A test case corresponds to a chromosome or individual which should be evaluated according to its fitness for the decision of survival in natural selection mechanism. Accordingly, the population is a suite of test cases. In the following we will describe the required steps for problem mapping.

4.1 Planning the Chromosomes

The first step is planning the chromosomes (sequence of genes), representing each test case. Each gene is an alphabet that corresponds to each *name* of constraint automata (component I/O ports). A test case consists of a sequence of *names* that represents the sequence of activation of transitions in the automaton and consequently one path (behavior).

As multiple *names* can be activated in each transition, in order to clarify the sequence of traversing transitions by a test case, there must be a signature that specifies the *names* of each transition in the test case. Therefore, each sequence of multiple *names* must be separated to show the synchronization of them and so activation of a transition. So, as well as the *names* of the automaton; we use another alphabet, the comma ",", that plays the role of separator in a test case. Therefore, the set of genes consists of the *names* of the automaton and comma.

Each sequence of alphabet that is separated by a comma represents the *names* of one transition traversed by the test case. An example of a test case (chromosome) and its interpretation for the Exclusive-Router automaton in Fig. 1 is illustrated in Fig. 6. According to this test case, if the data constraints of both transitions are satisfied, first {A,C}-transition is traversed and then {A,B}-transition and finally {A,C}-transition is traversed again.

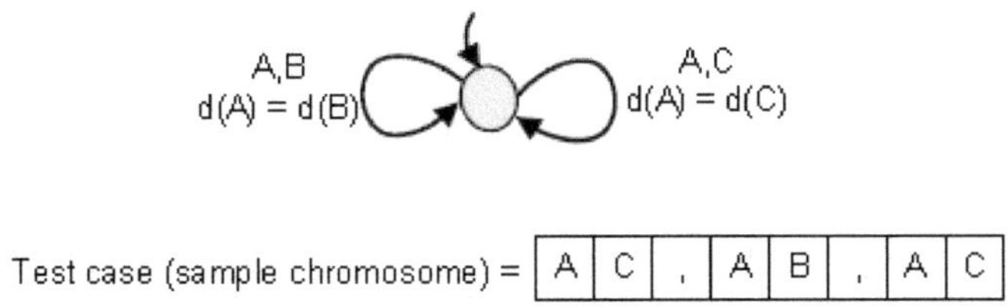

Fig. 6. Example of a test case (chromosome) for the automaton of Exclusive-Router in Fig. 1

4.2 Fitness Function

We need a suite of tests that covers maximum number of reachable states and transitions as well as examination of various paths. In order to achieve these goals, we applied two evolutionary algorithms, ordinary Genetic Algorithm (GA) and Genetic Symbiosis Algorithm (GSA) for defining fitness function of individuals (test cases):

First approach: ordinary GA. In this approach, the fitness value of each test case is determined independent of the other test cases in the test suite. So, the goal is to generate test cases that maximize the number of states visited and transitions taken, while minimizing the length of the test case. In view of the fact that traversing more transitions is much more important than the length of the test case, the fitness function is defined as:

$$f_{GA}(t_i) = \frac{(n_t + n_s)^5}{length_{t_i}} \tag{1}$$

where t_i is a test case, n_t and n_s are the number of distinct transitions and states respectively which are visited by the test case, and $length_{t_i}$ is the length of the test case (length of the string that represents the test case).

Because of the non-deterministic nature of constraint automata, with a certain sequence of names, different paths can be traversed. In our algorithm, the path that traverses maximum number of distinct states and transitions, or has maximum fitness value, is considered.

*Second approach: GSA.*The main problem with the ordinary GA approach is the convergence of test cases to similar sequences of names that traverse the maximum number of states and transitions. This convergence causes to lose the maximum coverage, because paths that face dead end very soon get a low fitness value and is eliminated from the test suite; so many states and transitions have never been visited by the suite of test cases.

In order to address this problem, we use GSA (Genetic Symbiosis Algorithm) approach. Although in [32], a formal framework for Genetic Symbiotic Algorithms has been proposed, in our work, the GSA is formulated in a simpler model.

By this approach, when a test case visits a new state or transition, instead of increasing the fitness value equally for all new states and transitions, the fitness is increased according to how rarely a transition or state is visited by other test cases in the test suite. We have for the less visited states or transitions, more increase in fitness value.

Thus, a test case that passes the small number of transitions and states that have not been passed by the other test cases must have larger fitness than a test case that passes a lot of transitions and states that have also been passed by the other test cases.

Accordingly, before evaluating the fitness values, the number of times a state or transition is visited by all test cases (the chromosome pool) is counted. $freq_{tr}$ and $freq_s$ are the visited frequency of the transitions and states and used for this purpose. Using the visited frequency variables, the fitness function is defined as below:

$$f_{GSA}(t_i) = \left(\sum_{tr \in TR_i} \frac{1}{freq_{tr}} + \sum_{s \in S_i} \frac{1}{freq_s}\right) \times \left(\frac{length_{t_i}}{length_{t_i} - 1}\right) \tag{2}$$

where TR_i and S_i are the set of transitions and states visited by the test case t_i. The second term of multiplication is used to converge test cases to less possible length.

When multiple paths can be traversed by a test case, for each path, the fitness is evaluated and the path that has maximum fitness is selected for that test case.

4.3 Selection Mechanism

We use a common selection method, roulette wheel selection, in which individuals are selected stochastically in proportion to their fitness.

4.4 Crossover Operator

In our implementation, regular one point crossover is used. The crossover rate is set to $population\_size/2$.

4.5 Mutation Operator

The mutation operator randomly mutates a certain proportion of genes to a random value taken from automaton names. The proportion of genes that are stochastically mutated, mutation rate, is set to 0.06.

5 Experimental Results

We have implemented a tool for traversing a constraint automaton which receives the specification of the constraint automata in XML format and also a suite of test cases. This tool traverses the automaton by using the test cases and evaluates the fitness value of each test case according to both methods of ordinary GA and GSA described in Section 4.

These two methods are examined on several constraint automata with different number of transitions and states which are shown in Table 1. The proportion

Table 1. Specification of the automata tested

Automaton	# of States	# of Transitions	Proportion of transitions to states	Connectivity
1	9	20	2.22	high
2	14	21	1.50	low
3	7	25	3.57	high
4	17	28	1.67	low
5	14	33	2.35	high
6	30	44	1.46	low
7	21	45	2.14	high
8	31	53	1.70	low
9	22	70	3.18	high
10	45	60	1.33	low

of the number of transitions to the number of states for each automaton is also shown in Table 1. This information is used to judge about the connectivity of each automaton. If this proportion is larger than or equal to 2, the automaton is considered as high connected automaton otherwise, it is categorized as less connected automaton. So, the automata 1, 3, 5, 7, 9 are considered as high connected and the automata 2, 4, 6, 8, 10 are low connected.

In our experiments, the number of test cases in each test suite (population size) is approximately two times of the number of automaton transitions.

The results of applying GA and GSA on these automata for 500 generations are described in the following with respect to the parameters of a good suite of test cases (state and transition coverage and diversity of paths they pass).

5.1 Transition and State Coverage

According to our results, by using GSA approach, in all of the automata, before the last generation we have reached the transition coverage of 100% and consequently state coverage of 100%. However, in ordinary GA approach, after a certain number of generations the coverage is decreased. By the fitness function of the first approach (ordinary GA), the test cases that pass more different transitions will have the largest fitness value. Therefore, after generating these test cases in a generation, the selection mechanism in the following generations causes other test cases to get similar to these test cases. So, the test cases that pass different shorter paths are not selected and consequently the coverage is reduced.

Another point in our results is that in the case of less connected automaton, the variation of transition coverage between ordinary GA and GSA is higher than in high connected automaton. Because, less connectivity causes the number of unique large paths and as a result, the number of unique test cases that pass large number of transitions (large paths) reduces. So, the selection mechanism causes more similar test cases are generated and the coverage is decreased more.

The transition coverage of the test suite for one of the high connected (automaton 9) and low connected (automaton 8) automata are shown in Fig. 7 and 8 respectively.

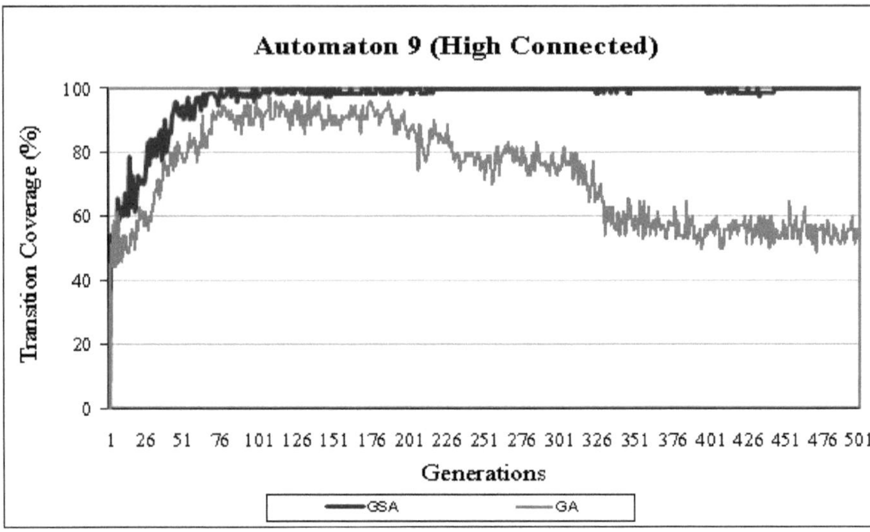

Fig. 7. Transition coverage of the test suite generated by GA and GSA approaches for one of the high connected automaton (automaton 9)

5.2 Diversity of Examined Paths

The results show that in GSA approach, as the algorithm converges, the diversity of paths that test cases traverse is increased and after a threshold, it remains approximately constant. It means that despite of the ordinary GA, the test cases pass divergent transitions and do not get similar to each other.

But, in the ordinary GA approach, as the algorithm converges, the diversity of paths is decreased. It can be concluded that the number of similar test cases is increased. Because ordinary GA is going to select only the test cases that pass more transitions, while there exists test cases that pass less but not yet been visited transitions and these test cases are not selected in the ordinary GA approach.

The variation of unique paths passed by the test suite by using GA and GSA approaches in the case of low connected automata is higher than high connected automata. It is clear that this phenomenon is the direct consequence of generating more similar test cases in ordinary GA approach for low connected automata as explained in Section 5.1. In Fig. 9 and 10 the number of unique paths traversed by the test suite for one of the high connected (automaton 9) and low connected (automaton 8) automata are shown.

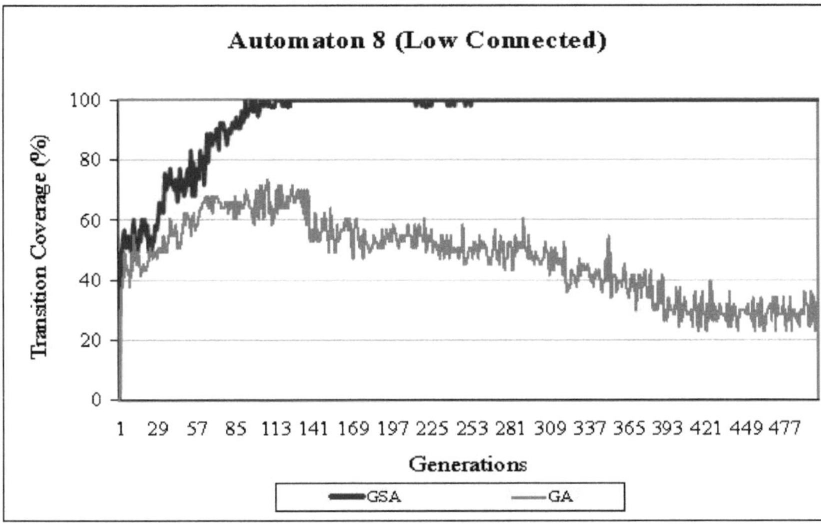

Fig. 8. Transition coverage of the test suite generated by GA and GSA approaches for one of the low connected automaton (automaton 8)

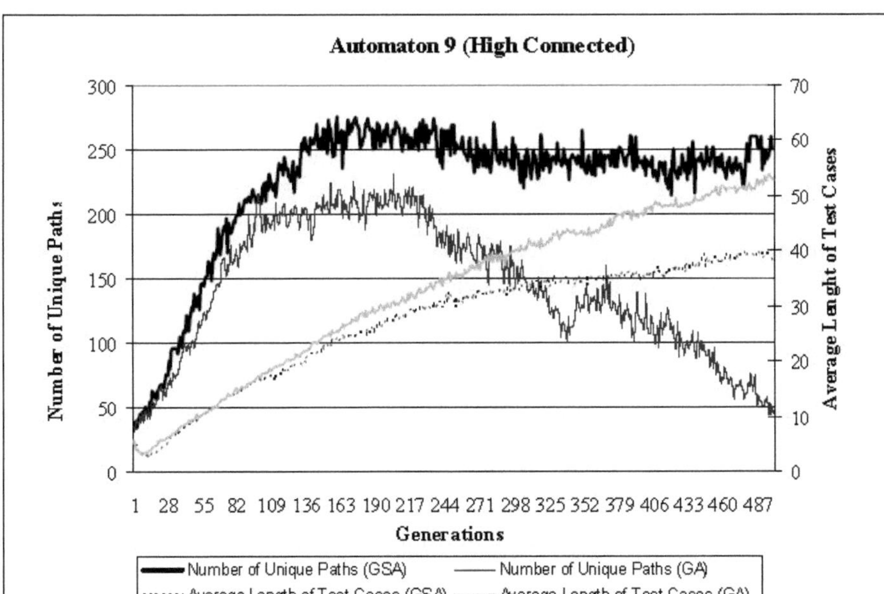

Fig. 9. Number of unique paths traversed by the test suite generated by GA and GSA approaches for one of the high connected automaton (automaton 9)

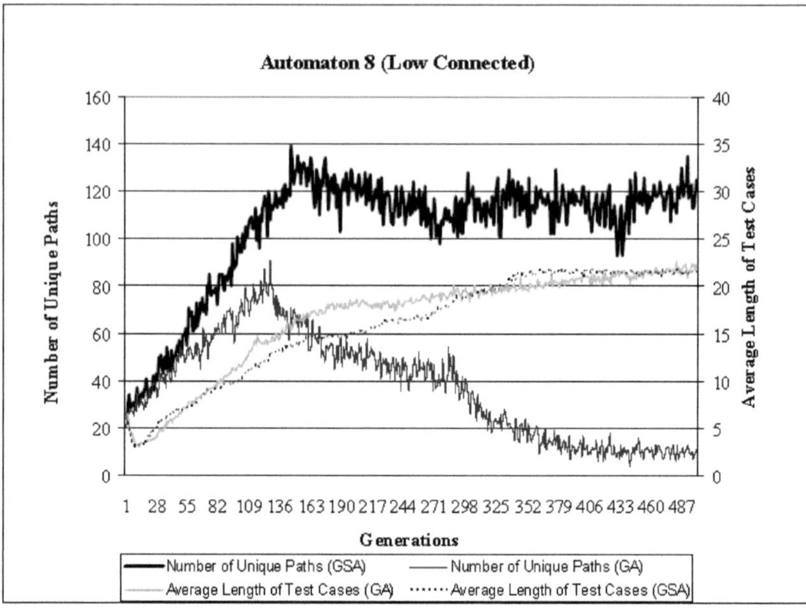

Fig. 10. Number of unique paths traversed by the test suite generated by GA and GSA approaches for one of the low connected automaton (automaton 8)

6 Conclusion and Future Work

Constraint automata are a semantic model for Reo, which is a modeling language for the systems based on the components. The black-box components in Reo language is modeled by constraint automata. In order to check the correctness of this modeling which corresponds to conformance testing in testing area of FSMs (Finite State Machines), two evolutionary algorithms for generating test cases for constraint automata are examined. The purpose is to generate a test suite that cover maximum number of transitions and states and also examine more different paths (behaviors).

In the first approach, we used ordinary GA (Genetic Algorithm) in which we generate test cases that each one of them can traverse more different number of transitions and states. In the second approach, which is based on GSA (Genetic Symbiosis Algorithm), the test cases are generated in which each test case traverses transitions and states that are not or less traversed by the other test cases in the test suite.

The results show that GSA provides a suite of test cases that leads better state/transition coverage and diversity of examined unique paths than ordinary GA approach. By applying GSA, in all of the examined automata we obtain the coverage of 100% before 500 generations. In GSA, as the algorithm converges, the number of examined unique paths is increased and after a threshold, it remains approximately constant. It means that they do not get similar to each other.

Therefore, by using GSA we can generate test cases that satisfy our desired of a test suite which are coverage and diversity of examined paths.

Although ordinary GA is going to improve each test case (individual), the generated test suite is not good. The selection of test cases that pass more different transitions causes the number of similar test cases increases along generations and as a result, after a threshold, coverage and diversity of paths traversed by the test suite are decreased.

In addition, the variation of coverage and number of unique paths traversed by the test suite between two approaches, ordinary GA and GSA, get clearer when the connectivity of the examined automaton is low (the ratio of number of transitions to states is less than 2).

In future developments of this work, it is intended to increase the size of the problem, applying the same approaches for automata with more transitions and states and also on the other types of constraint automata, e.g. parameterized constraint automata and timed constraint automata. Moreover, other kinds of evolutionary algorithms would be explored, in order to verify its influence on the completeness of generated test cases. Investigating the effect of other characteristics of an automaton other than the connectivity, on the results of the proposed approaches is also envisioned.

Acknowledgments. We are grateful to Mehdi Amoui for many inspiring discussions on the issues raised in this paper. Additionally, the third author is partly supported by a grant from IPM, project number CS1385-3-01.

References

1. Arbab, F.: Reo: A channel-based coordination model for component composition. Mathematical Structures in Computer Science **14**(3) (2004) 329–366
2. Baier, C., Sirjani, M., Arbab, F., Rutten, J.J.: Modeling component connectors in Reo by constraint automata. (Science of Computer Programming) accepted 2005, to appear.
3. Pargas, R.P., Harrold, M.J., Peck, R.: Test-data generation using genetic algorithms. Software Testing, Verification & Reliability **9**(4) (1999) 263–282
4. Wegener, J., Baresel, A., Sthamer, H.: Evolutionary test environment for automatic structural testing. Information & Software Technology **43**(14) (2001) 841–854
5. Tracey, N., Clark, J., Mander, K.: Automated program flaw finding using simulated annealing. In: Proceedings of the 1998 ACM SIGSOFT international symposium on Software testing and analysis(ISSTA '98), New York, USA, ACM Press (1998) 73–81
6. Watkins, A.: The automatic generation of software test data using genetic algorithms. In: Proceedings of the Fourth Software Quality Conference. Volume 2., Dundee, Scotland (1995) 300–309
7. Borgelt, K.: Software Test Data Generation from a Genetic Algorithm. Industrial Applications of Genetic Algorithms. CRC Press, Boca Raton, FL (1998)
8. Lin, J.C., Yeh, P.L.: Automatic test data generation for path testing using GAs. Inf. Sci. **131**(1-4) (2001) 47–64
9. Michael, C.C., McGraw, G., Schatz, M.A.: Generating software test data by evolution. IEEE Trans. Softw. Eng. **27**(12) (2001) 1085–1110

10. Alander, J.T., Mantere, T., Turunen, P.: Genetic algorithm based software testing. In: Artificial Neural Nets and Genetic Algorithms, Wien, Austria, Springer-Verlag (1998) 325–328
11. Chow, T.S.: Testing software design modeled by finite-state machines. IEEE Trans. Software Eng. **4**(3) (1978) 178–187
12. Lee, D., Yannakakis, M.: Principles and methods of testing finite state machines - A survey. In: Proceedings of the IEEE. Volume 84. (1996) 1090–1126
13. Belinfante, A., Feenstra, J., de Vries, R.G., Tretmans, J., Goga, N., Feijs, L.M.G., Mauw, S., Heerink, L.: Formal test automation: A simple experiment. In: 12th Int. Workshop on Testing of Communicating Systems (IWTCS), Kluwer (1999) 179–196
14. Brinksma, E., Tretmans, J.: Testing transition systems: An annotated bibliography. In: Proceedings of the 4th Summer School on Modeling and Verification of Parallel Processes(MOVEP). Volume 2067 of Lecture Notes in Computer Science., London, UK, Springer-Verlag (2001) 187–195
15. Clarke, D., Jeron, T., Rusu, V., Zinovieva, E.: STG: A symbolic test generation tool. In: Proceedings of the 8th International Conference on Tools and Algorithms for the Construction and Analysis of Systems(TACAS'02). Volume 2280 of Lecture Notes in Computer Science., Springer-Verlag (2002) 470–475
16. J. C. Fernandez, C. Jard, T. Jeron, G. Viho: Using on-the-fly verification techniques for the generation of test suites. In Rajeev Alur, Thomas A. Henzinger, eds.: Proceedings of the Eighth International Conference on Computer Aided Verification CAV. Volume 1102 of Lecture Notes in Computer Science., New Brunswick, NJ, USA, Springer-Verlag (1996) 348–359
17. Tretmans, J.: Testing techniques. Lecture notes, University of Twente, The Netherlands (2002)
18. Hennie, F.C.: Fault detecting experiments for sequential circuits. In: FOCS. (1964) 95–110
19. Sabnani, K., Dahbura, A.: A protocol test generation procedure. Comput. Netw. ISDN Syst. **15**(4) (1988) 285–297
20. Naito, S., Tsunoyama, M.: Fault detection for sequential machines by transitions tours. In: Proceedings of IEEE Fault Tolerant Computing Symposium, IEEE Computer Society Press (1981) 238–243
21. Fujiwara, S., von Bochmann, G., Khendek, F., Amalou, M., Ghedamsi, A.: Test selection based on finite state models. IEEE Trans. Softw. Eng. **17**(6) (1991) 591–603
22. Luo, G., von Bochmann, G., Petrenko, A.: Test selection based on communicating nondeterministic finite-state machines using a generalized Wp-Method. IEEE Trans. Softw. Eng. **20**(2) (1994) 149–162
23. Krichen, M., Tripakis, S.: Black-box conformance testing for real-time systems. In: 11th International SPIN Workshop on Model Checking of Software (SPIN'04). Volume 2989 of Lecture Notes in Computer Science., Springer-Verlag (2004) 109–126
24. Krichen, M., Tripakis, S.: Real-time testing with timed automata testers and coverage criteria. In: FORMATS/FTRTFT. Volume 3253 of Lecture Notes in Computer Science., Springer-Verlag (2004) 134–151
25. Higashino, T., Nakata, A., Taniguchi, K., Cavalli, A.R.: Generating test cases for a timed I/O automaton model. In: Proceedings of the IFIP TC6 12th International Workshop on Testing Communicating Systems, Deventer, The Netherlands, The Netherlands, Kluwer, B.V. (1999) 197–214

26. Arbab, F., Rutten, J.: A coinductive calculus of component connectors. In Wirsing, M., Pattinson, D., Hennicker, R., eds.: Recent Trends in Algebraic Development Techniques, Proceedings of 16th International Workshop on Algebraic Development Techniques (WADT 2002). Volume 2755 of Lecture Notes in Computer Science., Springer-Verlag (2003) 35–56 http://www.cwi.nl/ftp/CWIreports/SEN/SEN-R0216.pdf.
27. Ghassemi, F., Tasharofi, S., Sirjani, M.: Automated mapping of reo circuits to constraint automata. Electr. Notes Theor. Comput. Sci. **159** (2006) 99–115
28. Ghadiri, A.: A tool for constraint automata join, BS project. Technical report, ECE Department University of Tehran (2004)004)
29. Holland, J.H.: Adaptation in Natural and Artificial Systems. The University of Michigan Press, Ann Arbor, MI (1975)
30. Goldberg, D.E.: Genetic Algorithms in Search, Optimization and Machine Learning. Addison-Wesley Longman Publishing Co., Inc., Boston, MA, USA (1989)
31. Mitchell, M.: An Introduction to Genetic Algorithms. MIT Press, Cambridge, MA, USA (1996)
32. Hirasawa, K., Ishikawa, Y., Hu, J., Murata, J., Mao, J.: Genetic symbiosis algorithm. In: Proc. of the 2000 Congress on Evolutionary Computation, Piscataway, NJ, IEEE Service Center (2000) 1377–1384

Checking the Conformance of Java Classes Against Algebraic Specifications

Isabel Nunes, Antónia Lopes, Vasco Vasconcelos, João Abreu, and Luís S. Reis

Faculty of Sciences, University of Lisbon, Campo Grande, 1749–016 Lisboa, Portugal
{in, mal, vv, joao.abreu, lmsar}@di.fc.ul.pt

Abstract. We present and evaluate an approach for the run-time conformance checking of Java classes against property-driven algebraic specifications. Our proposal consists in determining, at run-time, whether the classes subject to analysis behave as required by the specification. The key idea is to reduce the conformance checking problem to the runtime monitoring of contract-annotated classes, a process supported today by several runtime assertion-checking tools. Our approach comprises a rather conventional specification language, a simple language to map specifications into Java types, and a method to automatically generate monitorable classes from specifications, allowing for a simple, but effective, runtime monitoring of both the specified classes and their clients.

1 Introduction

The importance of formal specification in software development is widely recognized. Formal specifications are useful for developers to reuse existing software. They also help programmers in understanding what they have to provide. Furthermore, they can be used as test oracles, i.e., system behavior can be checked against the specification.

Currently, Design by Contract (DBC) [18] is the most popular approach for formally specifying OO software. In this approach, specifications are class interfaces (Java interfaces, Eiffel abstract classes, etc.) annotated with pre/post conditions pairs expressed in a particular assertion language. At runtime, the implementation can be tested against its specification by means of contract monitorization.

Although the DBC methodology has become very popular, programmers rarely specify contracts—the strong restrictions to the kind of properties that are both expressible and monitorable, contribute to the frustration of being left with very poor specifications. Furthermore, as argued by Barnett and Schulte [3], contract specifications do not allow the level of abstraction to vary and do not support specifying components independently of the implementation language and its data structures.

Algebraic specification [2, 10, 6] is another well-known approach to the specification of software systems that supports a higher-level of abstraction. Algebraic approaches can be divided into two classes: *model-oriented* and *property-driven*.

From the two, *model-oriented* approaches to specification, like the ones promoted by Z [20], Larch [11] and JML [17], definitely prevail within the OO community. In most of these approaches, the behavior of a class is specified through a very abstract implementation, based on primitive elements available in the specification language.

Z. Liu and J. He (Eds.): ICFEM 2006, LNCS 4260, pp. 494–513, 2006.

Implementations can be tested against specifications by means of runtime assertion-checking tools. This requires an *abstraction function* to be explicitly provided. In JML, for instance, a concrete implementation is expected to include JML code defining the relation between concrete and abstract states. Although we recognize the important role played by model-based approaches, we believe that, for a significant part of programmers, understanding or writing this kind of specifications can be rather difficult. Moreover, programmers implementing a specification have to define the appropriate abstraction mapping, which can also be rather difficult to obtain.

In contrast, for a certain class of programs, in particular for *Abstract Data Types* (ADTs), *property-driven* specifications [8, 6] can be very simple and concise: the observable behavior of a program is specified simply in terms of a set of abstract properties. The simplicity and expressive power of property-driven specifications may encourage more programmers to use formal specifications. However, the support for checking OO implementations against property-driven specifications is far from being satisfactory. As far as we know, it is restricted to previously-presented approaches [13,1], whose limitations are discussed in detail in Section 8.

This paper presents a new approach for runtime checking OO implementations against property-driven specifications. The key idea is to reduce the problem to the runtime monitoring of contracts, which is supported by many runtime assertion checking tools (e.g., [5, 15, 16, 17, 21]). The classes under testing become wrapped by automatically generated classes. The wrapper classes are annotated with run-time checkable contracts automatically generated from the corresponding specifications.

A distinguishing feature of the approach is that our module specifications not only specify behavioral properties required from implementations, but they also define the required architecture of the implementations, i.e., how the implementation should be structured in terms of classes. This is important to support reuse: it allows to enforce that the implementation of a module M is achieved in terms of classes that can be reused in the implementation of other modules that have elements in common with M.

The approach is tailored to Java and JML [17] but it could as well be defined towards other OO programming and assertion languages (or other programming languages with integrated assertions [4,18]). It comprises a specification language that allows automatic generation of JML contracts, and a language for defining refinement mappings between specification modules and collections of Java classes. Refinement mappings define how sort names are mapped to class names and operation signatures are mapped to method signatures. Because this activity does not require any knowledge about the concrete representation of data types or component states, refinement mappings are quite simple to define. Our approach offers several benefits. More significantly:

- Specifications are easier to write and understand since they are written in a more abstract, implementation independent, language. The same applies to refinement mappings, whose definition does not require any knowledge about the concrete representation of data types or component states, as happens for instance in JML.
- Several Java classes or packages can be tested against the same specification. This contrasts with, for example, the JML approach in which different implementations may require different JML specifications. For instance, JML contract specifications appropriate for immutable classes are not suitable for mutable classes.

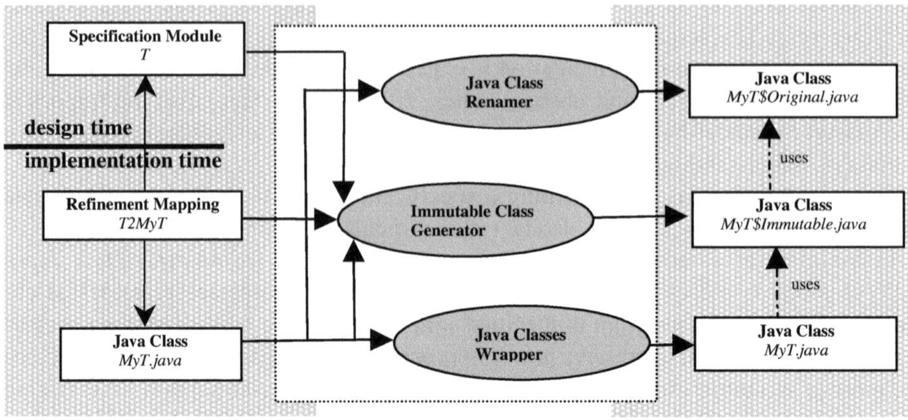

Fig. 1. Approach overview

- The same Java class or package can be tested against several specifications without requiring any additional effort.

In Section 2 we present a quick overview of our approach. Section 3 describes the structure of specification modules and our specification language. In Section 4 the world of specifications and that of implementations are related through the notion of refinement mappings. In Section 5 we describe the wrapper and immutable classes equipped with contracts that are generated, and illustrate their use through an example. In Section 6 we focus on the methodology for generating contracts from specification axioms. Section 7 reports on the results of our experiments. Section 8 presents related work, and Section 9 concludes, describing limitations of our approach, and topics that need further work.

2 Approach Overview

The process of checking the conformance of a collection of Java classes against a specification module consists in inspecting, during execution, the variances between actual and required behavior. This presumes that the implementation is structurally consistent with the specification module which, in our approach, means that there is a *refinement mapping* between the module specification and the collection of Java classes, defining which class implements each sort, and which method implements each operation.

For the purpose of this overview, we start by considering a simplified scenario in which we want to check a single Java class MyT against a single specification *T*. In this case, the user must supply the refinement mapping defining the relationship between the operation and predicate symbols of *T* and the method names of MyT.

Figure 1 illustrates the several entities involved in our approach. The left part includes the entities that the user must supply. The right part shows the classes that are generated—MyT$Original which is just MyT after renaming, MyT$Immutable equipped with the contracts generated from the axioms in specification *T*, and finally MyT which is the generated wrapper class. This last one uses MyT$Original, and MyT$Immutable in order to achieve validation, by contract inspection, of the results of invoking the original methods.

The approach consists in replacing class MyT by an automatically generated *wrapper class*. The wrapper class is client to other classes, automatically generated from specification *T*, one of which annotated with contracts. In this way, during the execution of a system involving classes that are clients of MyT, we have that:

1. The behavior of MyT objects is checked (monitored) against specification T;
2. The correctness of clients' behavior with respect to MyT operations is monitored;

provided that the system is executed under the observation of a contract monitoring tool. In both cases violations are reported. Underlying these conditions are the following notions of correction, applicable whenever consistency between class MyT and specification *T* is ensured by the existence of a refinement mapping.

Behavioral correctness. This condition assumes the following notion of behavioral correctness of class MyT with respect to the specification: class MyT is correct if every axiom of *T* (after the translation induced by the refinement mapping) is a property that holds in every execution of a system in which MyT is used. Consider, for instance, that *Stack* is a specification of stacks including the axiom *pop(push(s, e))* = *e* and that MyStack is an implementation of integer stacks with methods **void** push(**int**) and **int** pop(). Class MyStack is a correct implementation of specification *Stack* only if the property **let** t = s **in** (s.push(i); s.pop(); s.equals(t)) holds for all objects MyStack during their entire life. Axiom translation is addressed in detail in Section 6.

Client's correction. This condition relies on a notion of correctness targeted at the clients' classes. As we shall see in Section 3, specifications may include conditions under which the interpretations of some operations are required to be defined. These are called the *domain* conditions. A client class is a correct user of MyT, if it does not invoke MyT methods in states that do not satisfy the domain conditions of the corresponding operations. For instance, if *Stack* is a specification of stacks including a domain condition saying that operation *pop(s)* is required to be defined if *not isEmpty(s)*, then a class C is a correct client only if it never invokes method pop on objects o of type MyStack, such that o.isEmpty() is true.

As mentioned before, a class is generated that has the same name as the original one—MyT. This class has exactly the same interface as, and their objects behave the same as those of, the original MyT class, as far as any client using MyT objects can tell. The generated MyT class is what is usually called a *wrapper class* because each of its instances hides an instance of the original MyT class, and uses it when calling the methods of an immutable version of MyT—the generated class MyT$Immutable—in response to client calls. MyT clients must become clients of the wrapper instead. To avoid modifying them, the original class MyT is renamed—its name is postfixed with $Original— making the wrapping of the original class transparent to client classes.

MyT$Immutable is the class that gets annotated with contracts automatically generated from specification *T*: pre-conditions are generated from domain conditions, and

```
import IntegerSpec
sort IntStack
operations and predicates
  constructors
    clear: IntStack --> IntStack;
    push: IntStack Integer -->
                              IntStack;
  observers
    top: IntStack -->? Integer;
    pop: IntStack -->? IntStack;
    size: IntStack --> Integer;
  derived
    isEmpty: IntStack;
domains
  s: Stack;
  top(s), pop(s) if not isEmpty(s);
axioms
  s: Stack; i: Integer;
  top(push(_, i) = i;
  pop(push(s, _)) = s;
  size(clear(_)) = zero(_);
  size(push(s, _)) = suc(size(s));
  isEmpty(s) iff size(s) = zero(_);
```

```
sort Integer
operations and predicates
  constructors
    zero: Integer --> Integer;
    suc: Integer --> Integer;
    pred: Integer --> Integer;
  observers
    lt: Integer --> Integer;
axioms
  i, j: Integer
  lt(zero(_), suc(zero(_)));
  lt(suc(i), suc(j)) if lt(i, j);
  lt(pred(zero(_)), zero(_));
  lt(pred(i), j) if lt(i, j);
  lt(pred(suc(i)), i);
  pred(suc(i)) = i;
  suc(pred(i)) = i;
```

Fig. 2. Specification of (a) integer stacks, (b) integers

post-conditions from the axioms that give semantics to the specification operations. Monitoring these contracts correspond to checking (i) whether the properties obtained by translating the specification axioms hold in some particular situations, for some particular objects (these are determined by the contract generation process which is described in Section 6), and (ii) whether client objects do not invoke methods in states that do not satisfy the domain conditions. The fact that MyT$Immutable is, by construction, immutable is essential to ensure that the contracts that are generated are monitorable. Section 5 describes the generated wrapper and immutable classes in more detail.

This approach overcomes the limitations of the direct use of DBC that were mentioned in the introduction. All properties are expressible and monitorable because they are translated into pre- and post-conditions involving only calls to methods that do not change the objects under monitorization.

3 Specifications and Modules

The specification language is, to some extent, similar to many existing languages. In general terms, it supports the description of partial specifications with conditional axioms. It has, however, some specific features, such as the classification of operations in different categories, and strong restrictions on the form of the axioms. It was conceived so that conformance checking with respect to OO implementations can be supported through run-time monitoring of automatically derived contracts. Figure 2 a) presents a typical example in this setting [13, 1, 14]: the ADT integer stack. Figure 2 b) illustrates a specification for integers.

A specification defines exactly *one* sort and the first argument of every operation and predicate in the specification must belong to that sort. Furthermore, operations are classified as ***constructors***, ***observers*** or ***derived***. These categories comprise, respectively, the operations from which all values of the type can be built, the operations that provide fundamental information about the values of the type, and the redundant (but potentially useful) operations. Predicates can only be classified as either ***observers*** or ***derived***.

Specifications are partial because operation symbols declared with $-->?$ can be interpreted by partial functions. In the section ***domains***, we describe the conditions under which interpretations of these operations are required to be defined. For instance, in the specification of integer stacks, both *top* and *pop* are declared as partial operations. They are, however, required to be defined for all non empty stacks.

As usual in property-driven specifications, other properties of operations and predicates can be expressed through axioms, which in our case are closed formulæ of first-order logic restricted to the following specific forms:

- $\forall\vec{y}(\phi \Rightarrow op'_c(op_c(\vec{x}),\vec{t}) = t)$ (relating constructors)
- $\forall\vec{y}(\phi \Rightarrow op_o(op_c(\vec{x}),\vec{t}) = t)$, $\forall\vec{y}(\phi \Rightarrow pred_o(op_c(\vec{x}),\vec{t}))$, $\forall\vec{y}(\phi \Rightarrow \neg pred_o(op_c(x),\vec{t}))$ (defining the result of observers on constructors)
- $\forall\vec{y}(\phi \Rightarrow op_d(\vec{x}) = t)$, $\forall\vec{y}(\phi \Rightarrow pred_d(\vec{x}))$, $\forall\vec{y}(\phi \Rightarrow \neg pred_d(\vec{x}))$ (describing the result of derived operations/predicates on generic instances of the sort).
- $\forall\vec{y}(\phi \Rightarrow x = x')$ (pertaining to sort equality).

where $\vec{y}, \vec{x}$ are lists of variables, x, x' are variables, ϕ is a quantifier free-formula, $\vec{t}$ is a list of terms over $\vec{y}$, t is a term over $\vec{y}$. We use the indexes c, o, d to indicate the kind of operations and predicates that are allowed (constructors, observers, derived).

Notice that, because operations may be interpreted by partial functions, a term may not have a value. The equality symbol used in the axioms represents strong equality, that is to say, either both sides are defined and are equal, or both sides are undefined.

The structure of axioms that is imposed is not only intuitive and easy to understand and to apply, but it is also effective in driving the automatic identification of contracts for classes. In what concerns the expressive power of the language, it is only limited by the fact that we require the sort of the first argument of every operation and predicate in a specification to be the sort introduced in that specification. This rule forces a specific method of organizing specifications which, per se, does not constitute a limitation in the expressive power of the language. The problem is that the rule forbids specifications with constant constructors to be described. Although these constructors are prevalent in algebraic specifications, this limitation has short impact in our approach because it is not possible to provide OO implementations for 0-ary constructors in terms of object methods. Object creation, with a default initialization, is natively supported by OO languages and is not under the control of programmers. These can only define constructors (which are not methods) overriding the default initialization.

Specifications may declare, under ***import***, references to other specifications, and may use external symbols, i.e., sorts, operations and predicates that are not locally declared. For instance, the specification of integer stacks imports *IntegerSpec* and uses sort *Integer* and operation symbols *zero* and *suc*, which are external symbols. Notice that the specification of integers is self-contained since it does not import any specification. We call it a *closed specification*.

```
public class IntArrayStack implements Cloneable {
  private static final int INITIAL_CAPACITY = 10;
  private int [] elems = new int [INITIAL_CAPACITY];
  private int size = 0;
  public void clear() { size = 0; elems = new int [INITIAL_CAPACITY]; }
  public void push(int i) {
   if (elems.length == size) reallocate();
   elems[size++] = i;
  }
  public void pop() { size--; }
  public int top() { return elems[size - 1]; }
  public int size() { return size; }
  public boolean isEmpty() { return size == 0; }
  public boolean equals (Object other) { ... }
  public Object clone() { ... }
  private void reallocate() { ... }
}
```

Fig. 3. Java implementation of an integer stack

The meaning of external symbols is only fixed when the specification is embedded, as a component, in a *module*. A *module* is simply a surjective function from a set N (of names) to a set of specifications, such that, for every specification: *(i)* the referenced specification names belong to N and *(ii)* the external symbols are provided by the corresponding specifications in the module. The set N defines the set of components of the module. For instance, by naming the two specifications presented in Figure 2a) and b) as *IntStackSpec* and *IntegerSpec*, respectively, we obtain a module *IntegerStack*.

4 Refinement Mappings

In order to check Java classes against specification modules, a user of our approach must supply a *refinement mapping* that bridges the gap between the two worlds. These mappings provide the means for explicitly defining which class implements each type and which method implements each operation and predicate.

A *refinement mapping* $\mathcal{R}$ between a module and a collection of Java classes identifies the type (class or primitive) that implements each module component, as well as the binding between the operations and predicates of the corresponding specification in the module and the methods of the class. Only closed specifications can be implemented by primitive types. Furthermore, bindings are subject to some constraints: predicates must be bound to methods of type boolean; every $n+1$-ary operation or predicate *opp*$(s, s_1, \ldots, s_n)$ must be bound to an n-ary method $m(t_1, \ldots, t_n)$ such that t_i is the type of the class that, according to $\mathcal{R}$, implements sort s_i. Furthermore, for components that are implemented by primitive types, the binding defines how operations and predicates are expressed in terms of built-in Java operations. Within the structure imposed by the specification, there are several implementation styles that can be adopted.

For instance, the most common implementation of stacks in Java is through a class such as IntArrayStack, presented in Figure 3, where instance methods provide the predicates and mutable implementations for operations. In this case, the first argument of operations and predicates is implicitly provided—it is the target object of the method invocation—and the application of an operation whose result type is IntegerStack

```
IntegerSpec is primitive int
  zero(x: Integer): Integer is 0;
  suc(x: Integer): Integer is x + 1;
  pred(x: Integer): Integer is x - 1;
  lt(x: Integer, y: Integer) is x < y;
IntStackSpec is class IntArrayStack
  clear(s: IntStack): IntStack is void clear();
  push(s: IntStack, e: Elem): IntStack is void push(int e);
  pop(s: IntStack): IntStack is void pop();
  top(s: IntegerStack): Elem is int top();
  size(s: IntStack): Integer is int size();
  isEmpty(s: IntStack) is boolean isEmpty();
```

Fig. 4. An example of a refinement mapping

induces a state change of the current object. Methods implementing these operations are usually procedures (**void** methods) but in some cases programmers decide that the method should also return some useful information about the object (for example, the pop method in the Sun's JDK java.util.Stack class, returns the top element). Although less common, stacks can also be implemented by immutable classes. The difference in this case is that the methods that implement the operations whose result type is IntegerStack return an object of the class; the state change in the current object, if it exists, is not relevant. Another dimension of variability in the implementation of the *IntegerStack* module is related to the choice of the implementation for integers: there is still the possibility of choosing a (Java) primitive type to implement the type.

An admissible refinement mapping for the module *IntegerStack* is presented in Figure 4. It expresses the fact that specification *IntStackSpec* is implemented by the class IntArrayStack whereas sort *Integer* is implemented by the Java primitive type **int**.

Refinement mappings are quite simple to define because they only involve the interfaces of Java classes, that is to say, no knowledge about the concrete representation of data types or component states is needed. The independence from concrete representation makes it possible to test several Java classes or packages against a same specification module—we just have to create the corresponding refinement mappings. Contracts are automatically generated. The approach also allows a refinement mapping to define a mapping from two different components into the same type (class or primitive). This promotes the writing of generic specifications that can be reused in different situations.

5 The Architecture of Wrapped Implementations

As explained in Section 2, our approach for checking Java implementations against specifications comprises wrapping these classes with other, automatically generated, classes. In this section we describe this process in more detail.

Let again T be a specification, MyT a given class, and *MyRef* describe a refinement mapping between specification T and class MyT. From these, a series of classes are generated that allow a client class ClientC to invoke methods of MyT while checking whether MyT correctly implements T. Remember that the wrapper class gets its name from the original MyT class, while this is renamed to MyT$Original.

The immutable class equipped with contracts. For each MyT method **void** m($\vec{p}$), class MyT$Immutable defines a **static** method:

```
public class IntArrayStack implements Cloneable {
  private IntArrayStack$Original stack = new IntArrayStack$Original();
  public void clear() { stack = IntArrayStack$Immutable.clear(stack); }
  public void push(int i) { stack = IntArrayStack$Immutable.push(stack, i); }
  public void pop() { stack = IntArrayStack$Immutable.pop(stack); }
  public int size() {
    int$Pair pair = IntArrayStack$Immutable.size(stack);
    stack = pair.state;
    return pair.value;
  }
  public int top() {
    int$Pair pair = IntArrayStack$Immutable.top(stack);
    stack = pair.state;
    return pair.value;
  }
  ...
}
```

Fig. 5. Partial view of the wrapper class that results from applying our approach to the specification IntStackSpec and the original IntArrayStack class

```
public class int$Pair {
  public final int value;
  public final IntArrayStack$Original state;
  public int$Pair (int value, IntArrayStack$Original state) {
    this.value = value; this.state = state;
  }
}
```

Fig. 6. The auxiliary class int$Pair composed of an integer and an original IntArrayStack

```
  static MyT$Original m (MyT$Original o, p⃗) {
    MyT$Original aClone = (MyT$Original) clone(o);
    aClone.m(p⃗);
    return aClone;
}
```

and for each MyT method SomeType m($\vec{p}$), class MyT$Immutable defines a method:

```
  static SomeType$Pair m (MyT$Original o, p⃗) {
    MyT$Original aClone = (MyT$Original) clone(o);
    return new SomeType$Pair(aClone.m(p⃗), aClone);
  }
```

where SomeType$Pair is a generated class that declares two public final attributes—MyT$Original state and SomeType value—and a constructor that receives the values to initialize those attributes. Contracts are generated for the methods in MyT$Immutable that are a translation (see Section 6) of the axioms of the corresponding specification.

The wrapper class. MyT defines a single attribute MyT$Original wrappedObject, implements each method **void** m($\vec{p}$) with the following code:

```
  {wrappedObject = MyT$Immutable.m(wrappedObject, p⃗);}
```

and implements each method SomeType m($\vec{p}$) with the following code:

```
  {SomeType$Pair pair = MyT$Immutable.m(wrappedObject, p⃗);
   wrappedObject = pair.state;
   return pair.value;
  }
```

```
public class IntArrayStack$Immutable {
  //@ ensures size(\result).value == 0;
  static public IntArrayStack$Original clear (IntArrayStack$Original s) {
    IntArrayStack$Original aClone = (IntArrayStack$Original) clone(s);
    aClone.clear();
    return aClone;
  }
  //@ ensures size(\result).value == size(s).value + 1;
  //@ ensures top(\result).value == i;
  //@ ensures equal(pop(\result).state, s).value;
  static public IntArrayStack$Original push (IntArrayStack$Original s, int i) {
    IntArrayStack$Original aClone = (IntArrayStack$Original) clone(s);
    aClone.push(i);
    return aClone;
  }
  //@ requires ! isEmpty(s).value;
  static public IntArrayStack$Original pop (IntArrayStack$Original s) {
    IntArrayStack$Original aClone = (IntArrayStack$Original) clone(s);
    aClone.pop();
    return aClone;
  }
  static public int$Pair size (IntArrayStack$Original s) {
    IntArrayStack$Original aClone = (IntArrayStack$Original) clone(s);
    return new int$Pair (aClone.size(), aClone);
  }
 //@ ensures (* See Section 6 *);
    static public boolean equals (IntArrayStack$Original s, Object t) {
    IntArrayStack$Original aClone = (IntArrayStack$Original) clone(s);
    return new boolean$Pair (aClone.equals(t), aClone);
  }
  ...
}
```

Fig. 7. Partial view of the immutable class that results from applying our approach to the *IntegerStack* module and the original IntArrayStack class

The wrapper class uses the value part of the pair to return the value to the client, and retains the state part in its only attribute (in order to account for methods that, in addition to returning a value, also modify the current object).

Whenever a class, client to the original class, is executed within the context of this framework, every call to a method m in the original class is monitored since the wrapper redirects the call through the corresponding method in the immutable class, forcing the evaluation of the pre and post-conditions. These are such that the original methods behavior is monitored without any side effect on the objects created by client classes.

An Example. Figures 5, 6, and 7 illustrate the classes that are generated according to our approach in the context of the Stack example used throughout the paper—the specification in Figure 2, the class in Figure 3, and the refinement mapping in Figure 4. Consider the following code snippet in a client of IntArrayStack class:

```
IntArrayStack s = new IntArrayStack();
s.push(3);
```

Figures 8 and 9 present UML interaction diagrams showing the interaction between the several objects that participate in the realization of the above instructions. The value of aClone (the return value of the push(stack, 3) operation invoked in 2.1, Figure 9) is monitored by checking the contracts associated with method push in class

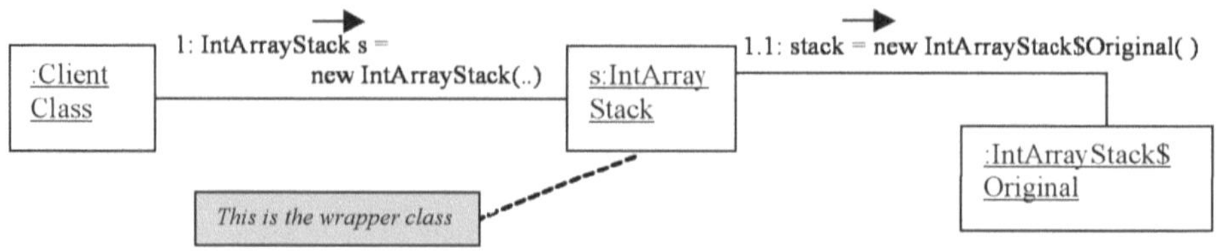

Fig. 8. Creating an IntArrayStack

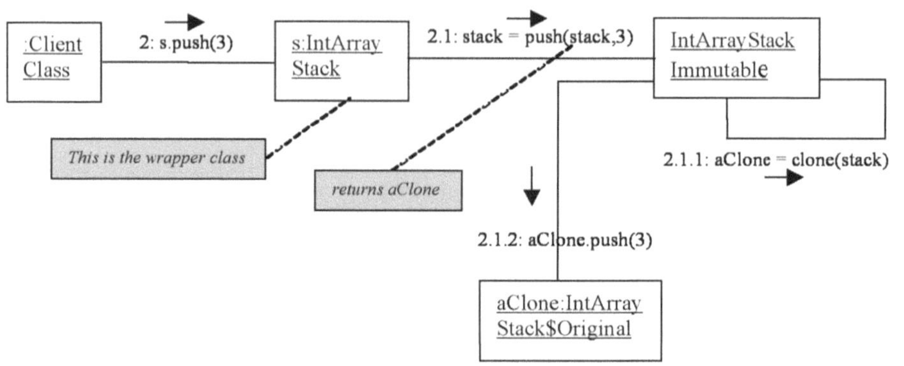

Fig. 9. Invoking a method upon an IntArrayStack

IntArrayStack$Immutable. The post-condition of push invokes methods size, top, and pop of the immutable class on object aClone. These methods do not change object aClone since they invoke the original versions of size, top, and pop on a clone of aClone. The contracts for these methods are not monitored: the contracts of methods invoked from contracts are not monitored—this is a feature of JML, crucial to our approach since it prevents infinite invocation chains.

This example also illustrates what happens in situations where a primitive type is chosen to implement a specification (in the example, integers are implemented by **int**). While monitoring a given implementation for a module, situations may arise where a class MyT is accused of not correctly implementing specification *T* because a closed specification *T'* was mapped to a Java primitive type that does not correctly implement it. This is due to the fact that our approach does not check the conformance of specifications that are mapped into primitive types. However, this problem can only be overcome with client-invasive approaches, i.e., that require the modification of client classes.

We experienced the situation just described in one of the modules we used to evaluate our approach—a Rational module consisting of specifications of integers and rational numbers, available elsewhere [7]. A traditional immutable implementation of rationals was found to be incorrect during the manipulation of fractions with large numerators and denominators, involving cross-products greater than $2^{31} - 1$. This is due to the fact that Java **int** type does not correctly implements the integer specification, namely properties such as $(i < suc(i))$ and $(n \neq 0 \wedge m \neq 0 \Rightarrow n \times m \neq 0)$ do not hold (for example, $2^{31} - 1 + 1$ is a negative number).

6 Contract Generation

In this section we discuss how contracts are generated from specifications. This process can be described in two parts: translation of domain-specific properties described by axioms, and translation of generic properties of equational logic.

6.1 From Axioms to Contracts

Contract generation that captures the properties that are explicitly specified in a given specification *T*, is such that:

- a domain restriction for an operation *op* generates a pre-condition for the method that implements *op*;
- axioms which relate constructors op_c and op'_c, and axioms that specify the result of observers on a given constructor op_c generate post-conditions for the method that implements op_c;
- axioms that describe the result of a given derived operation/predicate opp_d on generic instances of the sort, generate post-conditions for the method that implements opp_d;
- axioms that pertain to sort equality generate post-conditions for the equals method.

A refinement mapping induces a straightforward translation of formulæ and terms into Java expressions. There are a few points of complexity however: (1) the translation of terms $op(t_1, \ldots, t_n)$ into method invocations; (2) the translation of strong equality used in axioms; (3) avoiding calls to methods, within contracts, in cases where their arguments are undefined.

In what concerns point (1), the return type of the method that implements *op* of specification *T* dictates the form of the translation: *(i)* if method m of class MyT that implements *op* is **void**, then $op(t_1, \ldots, t_n)$ is translated into an expression of the form MyT$Immutable.m(...); *(ii)* if method m of class MyT that implements *op* is not **void**, then a pair <value, state> must be returned by the MyT$Immutable version of method m, where value stands for the result of the method, and state stands for the target object state after m's invocation. $op(t_1, \ldots, t_n)$ is translated into an expression of the form MyT$Immutable.m(...).state if the sort of *op* is *T*, and MyT$Immutable.m(...).value in all other cases.

In what concerns point (2), the meaning of an equality $t_1 = t_2$ in the axioms of a specification is that the two terms are either both defined and have the same value, or they are both undefined. To be consistent with this definition, the evaluation of equals(t1, t2) within contracts should only be performed if t_1 and t_2 are both defined. If t_1 and t_2 are both undefined then the equality $t_1 = t_2$ is considered to hold and if just one of them is undefined, then the equality is false.

Finally, point (3) has to do with the fact that contracts of methods invoked within contracts are not monitored by the JML runtime assertion checker. Thus, we have to avoid making, in our contracts, method invocations with undefined arguments. A *def* function is defined and used in the translation process that supplies the definedness conditions for both terms and formulæ of our specification language (see [19] for the definition). As an example, the definedness condition for an operation call $op(t_1, \ldots, t_n)$ is the

```
IntegerSpec is primitive int
  zero(x: Integer): Integer is 0;
  suc(x: Integer): Integer is x + 1;
  pred(x: Integer): Integer is x - 1;
  lt(x: Integer, y: Integer) is x < y;
ElemSpec is class String;
StackSpec is class StringArrayStack
  clear(s: Stack): Stack is void clear();
  push(s: Stack, e: Elem): Stack is void push(String e);
  pop(s: Stack): Stack is String pop();
  top(s: Stack): Elem is String top();
  size(s: Stack): Integer is int size();
  isEmpty(s: Stack) is boolean isEmpty();
```

Fig. 10. A refinement mapping for *GenericStack*

```
public class StringArrayStack implements Cloneable {
  ...
  public void clear() { ... }
  public void push(String i) { ... }
  public String pop() { ... }
  public String top() { ... }
  public int size() { ... }
  public boolean isEmpty() { ... }
  public boolean equals (Object other) { ... }
  public Object clone() { ... }
}
```

Fig. 11. Java implementation of a String array stack

conjunction of the definedness conditions of terms t_1 to t_n with the domain condition of *op*.

We now present in more detail, for each type of axiom, the contract that result from applying the automatic translation process rules. A more complete description of the translation process can be found elsewhere [19]. We use $[\phi]$ to denote the translation of a formula ϕ, and *def*(ϕ) to denote the definedness condition for ϕ.

We illustrate the translation rules with a module *GenericStack*, with three components: the specification of integers presented in Figure 2 under the name *IntegerSpec*, a specification that simply declares the sort *Elem* under the name *ElemSpec* and a specification of stacks, under the name *StackSpec*, that only differs from the one in Figure 2 by the sort of its elements, which is the external sort *Elem* belonging to the imported specification *ElemSpec*. We choose the classes StringArrayStack and java.lang.String to refine module *GenericStack* through the refinement mapping of Figure 10.

Translation of Domain Restrictions. A domain restriction ϕ for an operation *op* generates a pre-condition for the method that implements *op*. In JML, pre-conditions are preceded by keyword **requires** and, thus, the pre-condition that results from translating the domain condition is **requires** $[def(\phi) \Rightarrow \phi]$.
Example: Domain restriction *top(s): **if** not isEmpty(s)* in specification *StackSpec*, Figure 2, produces pre-condition

```
requires true ==> !isEmpty(s).value;
```

in method String$Pair top(StringArrayStack$Original s) of class StringArrayStack$Immutable. The expression **true** is the definedness condition of variable s.

Translation of Axioms about Constructors and Observers. Axioms that specify the result of both constructors and observers on a given constructor op_c generate post-conditions for the method that implements op_c. In JML, post-conditions are preceded by keyword **ensures**. The post-conditions that result from translating axioms of the form $(\phi \Rightarrow op(op_c(\vec{x}), \vec{t}) = t)$ and $(\phi \Rightarrow pred_o(op_c(\vec{x}), \vec{t}))$ are

ensures $[def(\phi) \wedge \phi \Rightarrow op(r, \vec{t}) = t]$
ensures $[def(\phi) \wedge \phi \wedge def(pred_o(r, \vec{t})) \Rightarrow pred_o(r, \vec{t})]$

where op is a constructor or an observer operation, $pred_o$ is an observer predicate, and where r stands for the result of $op_c(\vec{x})$.
Example: Axiom *pop(push(s, i))* $=$ *s* produces post-condition

```
ensures true ==>                                    [φ] implies
  !(true && !isEmpty(\result).value) && !true ||    both undefined or
  (true && !isEmpty(\result).value) && true &&      (both defined and
    equals(pop(\result).state, s).value;             equal)
```

for method StringArrayStack$Original push (StringArrayStack$Original s, String i) in class StringArrayStack$Immutable. The expression **result** in JML represents the result of the method to which the post-condition is attached. The argument of *pop* in the axiom is *push(s, i)* which is precisely the result of method push. This post-condition is the translation of an equality between the terms *pop(push(s, i))* and *s*, thus it must evaluate to true if either both terms are undefined or they are both defined and have the same value. Remember that the definedness condition of an operation invocation is the conjunction of the definedness conditions of its arguments and the domain condition of the operation itself. The translation of the axiom *top(push(s, i))* $=$ *i* would be similar, except in the last part where we would have String$Immutable.equals(top(**result**).value, i).

Translating Axioms about Derived Operations/Predicates. Axioms that describe the result of a given derived operation/predicate opp_d on generic instances of the sort, generate post-conditions for the method that implements opp_d. The post-conditions that result from translating axioms $(\phi \Rightarrow op_d(\vec{x}) = t)$ and $(\phi \Rightarrow pred_d(\vec{x}))$ are

ensures $[def(\phi) \wedge \phi \Rightarrow r = t]$
ensures $[def(\phi) \wedge \phi \Rightarrow r]$

where op_d and $pred_d$ denote derived operations and predicates, and r stands for the result of $op_d(\vec{x})$ or $pred_d(\vec{x})$.
Example: Axiom *isEmpty(s)* ***if*** *size(s)* $=$ *zero(_)* translates into the following post-condition in method boolean$Pair isEmpty (StringArrayStack$Original s).

```
ensures !(true && true) && !true ||         both undefined or
  (true && true) && true &&                 (both defined and
  size(s).value == 0 ==>                     equal) imply
  \result.value                             [r]
```

Translation of Axioms about Equality. Equality between values of a given type are regarded, to some extent, as type-specific predicates. In this way, axioms of the form $(\phi \Rightarrow x = x')$ generate post-conditions **ensures** $[def(\phi) \wedge \phi]$==> **result**.value for method equals. We do not illustrate this case since no specification in module *Generic-Stack* defines axioms of this kind.

Closing Assertions. Whenever the assertions (pre and post-conditions) contain a variable v that does not correspond to any of the parameters of the method to which the assertion belongs, the assertion must be preceded by a JML quantifier \ **forall** that quantifies over that variable within a given domain. Populating these domains is orthogonal to contract generation. In a technical report [19] we present a specific strategy for populating these domains—the one we have used for benchmarking our approach.

6.2 Enforcing Generic Properties

So far we have focused on the generation of contracts capturing user-defined properties, specific for a given type. In addition, there are generic properties concerning equality and cloning that are important to capture through contracts.

Contract for equals. In equational logic, any two terms that are regarded as equal must produce equal values for every operation and predicate. In order to check the consistency of an implementation in what respects these properties, our approach involves the automatic generation of post-conditions for the equals method that test the results given by all methods that implement observer operations and predicates when applied to the two objects being compared. More concretely, for every observer operation and predicate opp_o, the post-condition

```
ensures \result.value ==> (other instanceof C$Original &&
                          [opp_o(one, x⃗) = opp_o((C$Original) other, x⃗))]
```

is generated for the boolean$Pair equals(C$Original one, Object other) method of a class C$Immutable, where C is the class that implements the given specification.

The first part of the above expression is a Java boolean expression, while the second part denotes the translation of an equality between terms of our specification language extended with the (C) x term. The translation of this new term is itself, as expected. The translation of the term equality follows the rules previously explained.

Example: Returning to our StringArrayStack example, the contract generated for method boolean$Pair equals(StringArrayStack$Original one, Object other) in class StringArrayStack$Immutable includes the following pre-condition.

```
ensures \result.value ==> other instanceof StringArrayStack$Original &&
  (!!isEmpty(one).value &&
    (!!isEmpty((StringArrayStack$Original) other).value ||
    (true && !isEmpty(one).value && true) &&
    (true && !isEmpty((StringArrayStack$Original) other).value && true) &&
    String$Immutable.equals(top(one).value,
                            top((StringArrayStack$Original) other).value))
```

This contract does not completely capture congruence—it only tests observers applied to the left and right terms of equality. The process of testing equality between all terms obtained from the application of all combinations of observers is not realistic in this context. Instead, we rely on the not completely exhaustive process of monitoring, which heavily uses the equals method. Although the contracts of methods invoked from contracts are not monitored, we may force the execution of equals from within the immutable class equipped with contracts—this is a subject for further work.

We do not generate post-conditions for properties other than congruence, e.g. reflexivity and symmetry. Although these properties are crucial (as testified by the Java API contract for equals saying that it should implement an equivalence relation), given that they are independent of the target specification we chose not to enforce their checking—it would impose an important overhead.

Contracts for clone. Our approach makes use of cloning so, its soundness can be compromised if given implementations for clone do not meet the following correctness criteria: *(i)* the clone method is required not to have any effect whatsoever on **this**; *(ii)* clone's implementation is required to go deep enough in the structure of the object so that any references shared with the cloned object cannot get modified through the invocation of any of the remaining methods of the class. For example, an array based implementation of a stack, in which one of its methods changes the state of any of its elements, requires the elements of the stack to be cloned together with the array itself.

The post-condition that we want for method clone is one that imposes equality between the cloned object and the original one: **ensures** equals(**result**, o) is generated as a post-condition for the method Object clone(C$Original o) of class C$Immutable.

7 Congu

Congu [7] is a prototype that supports the approach by checking the consistency of specification modules and refinement mappings, and generating the classes required for monitorization. Given the user supplied entities—specification module, refinement mapping and classes—the following situations are identified as errors: the refinement mapping refers to an operation that is not present in the specification module; the refinement mapping refers to a method that is not present in the implementing classes; there are specification operations that are not mapped into any class method; among many others. Once contracts are generated and execution is monitored, the usual pre and post-condition exceptions are launched whenever invocations violate specification domain conditions, and operation implementations violate specification axioms.

We have tested our architecture on four data types: the stack specification described in this paper (both with *Stack* refined into an array-based "standard" class (Figure 3) and into java.util.Stack), a data type representing rational numbers, and a data structure *Vector* whose elements are indexed by integer values. The source code for the test cases can be found elsewhere [7]. For each data type we assessed the time and space used in five different situations.

1. The user's class and the test class only, both compiled with Sun's Java compiler, thus benchmarking the original user's class only;
2. The whole architecture compiled with Sun's Java compiler, thus benchmarking the overhead of our architecture, irrespective of the contracts;
3. The class responsible for checking the contracts, with its contracts removed, compiled with the JML compiler; all other classes in the architecture compiled with Sun's Java compiler.
4. As above but with all contracts in place, except that JML **forall** ranges were not generated;

5. As above but monitoring **forall** assertions with a limit of 20 elements in each range (see below).

All tests were conducted on a PC running Linux, equipped with a 1150 MHz CPU and 512Mb of RAM. We have used J2SE 1.4.2_09-b05 and JML 5.2. The runtime in seconds for 1.000.000 random operations, average of 10 runs, are as follows.

	Case 1	Case 2	Case 3	Case 4	Case 5	Slowdown
StringArrayStack	2.71	3.26	11.58	21.21	21.21	7.8
java.util.Stack	2.27	4.35	10.66	23.07	23.07	10.2
Rational	2.97	4.71	26.74	38.06	58.72	19.8
Vector	3.80	5.24	15.30	26.34	425.18	111.9

Inspecting the numbers for the first and the fifth case one concludes that monitoring introduces a 10 to 100-fold time penalty, depending on how many **forall** assertions are needed (none for the stacks, very little for the rational, a lot for the vector). The numbers for the second case indicate that conveying all calls to the data structure under testing through the Immutable class imposes a negligible overhead, when compiled with Sun's Java compiler. The numbers for the third case allow to conclude that roughly half of the total overhead reported in the fourth column is due to contract monitoring alone, while the other half to the fact that we are using the JML compiler. Comparing the fourth to the fifth case one concludes that monitoring **forall** assertions can impose quite an overhead, if the number of elements inside the **forall** domain is not properly limited. We omit the results on the space used; it suffices to say that the largest increase was reported for the *Vector* test, where we witnessed a negligible 5% increase from case 1 to case 5.

8 Related Work

There is a vast amount of work in the specification and checking of ADTs and software components in general; the interested reader may refer to previous publications [9, 12] for a survey. Here we focus on attempts to check OO implementations for conformance against property-driven algebraic specifications.

Henkel and Diwan developed a tool [13] that allows to check the behavioral equivalence between a Java class and its specification, during a particular run of a client application. This is achieved through the automatic generation of a prototype implementation for the specification which relies on term rewriting. The specification language that is adopted is, as in our approach, algebraic with equational axioms. The main difference is that their language is tailored to the specification of properties of OO implementations whereas our language supports more abstract descriptions that are not specific to a particular programming paradigm. Being more abstract, we believe that our specifications are easier to write and understand.

Figure 12 presents an example. The axioms define that removeLast operation provides the last element that was added to the list and define the semantics of get operation: get(l, i) is the i-th element in the list l. The symbols retval and state are primitive

```
forall l: LinkedList forall o: Object forall i: int
  removeLast(add(l, o).state).retval == o
  if i > 0 get(addFirst(l, o).state, intAdd(i, 1).retval).retval == get(l,i).retval

axioms
  l: LinkedList; o: Elem, i: Integer;
  removeLast(add(_, o)) = o;
  get(AddFirst(l, o), suc(i)) = get (l, i) if gt(i, zero(_));
```

Fig. 12. An example of the specification of two properties of linked lists as they are presented by Henkel and Diwan [13] and as they would be specified in our approach

constructs of the language adopted by Henkel and Diwan [13] to talk about the return value of an operation and the state of the current object after the operation, respectively.

When compared with our approach, another difference is that their language does not support the description of properties of operations that modify other objects, reachable from instance variables, nor does the tool. In contrast, our approach supports the monitoring of this kind of operation.

Another approach whose goal is similar to ours is Antoy and Hamlet's [1]. They propose an approach for checking the execution of an OO implementation against its algebraic specification, whose axioms are provided as executable rewrite rules. The user supplies the specification, an implementation class, and an explicit mapping from concrete data structures of the implementation to abstract values of the specification. A self-checking implementation is built that is the union of the implementation given by the implementer and an automatically generated direct implementation, together with some additional code to check their agreement. The abstraction mapping must be programmed by the user in the same language as the implementation class, and asks user knowledge about internal representation details. Here lies a difference between the two approaches: our refinement mapping needs only the interface information of implementing classes, and it is written in a very abstract language. Moreover, there are some axioms that are not accepted by their approach, due to the fact that they are used as rewrite rules; for example, equations like *insert (X, insert (Y, Z)) = insert (Y, insert (X,Z))* cannot be accepted as rewrite rules because they can be applied infinitely often. We further believe that the rich structure that our specifications present, together with the possibility to, through refinement mappings, map a same module into many different packages all implementing the same specification, is a positive point in our approach that we cannot devise in the above referred approaches.

9 Conclusion and Further Work

We described an approach for testing Java classes against specifications, using an algebraic, property-driven, approach to specifications as opposed to a model-driven one. We believe that the simplicity of property-driven specifications will encourage more software developers to use formal specifications. Therefore, we find it important to equip these approaches with tools similar to the ones currently available for model-driven ones.

Specifications define sorts, eventually referring to other sorts defined by other specifications, which they import. Specifications are nameless, so, the decision of which specification to choose to define a given sort, is made only at module composition time. This promotes reuse at the specification level.

Due to the abstract, implementation independent, nature of the specification language we adopted, it is easy to check different Java packages against the same specification module. This only requires the definition of appropriate refinement mappings. In the case of different classes that implement the same interface, refinement mappings can be reused as well.

Our approach has some limitations, some of these being *structural* in the sense that they are not solvable in any acceptable way while maintaining the overall structure:

- Self calls are not monitored. This limitation has a negligible impact if client classes call all the methods whose behavior needs to be tested.
- The approach is highly dependent on the quality of the clone methods, supplied by the user.
- Conformance checking ignores properties of specifications when implemented by primitive types. However, as described at the end of Section 5, our approach unveiled a problem we were not aware of, in a given module. This problem can only be overcome with client-invasive approaches.

We intend to investigate the best way to solve the problem of side-effects in contract monitoring due to changes in the state of method parameters—our approach does not cover this problem yet. Cloning all parameters in every call to a method in the generated immutable class—as we do for the target object—does not seem a plausible solution. We believe that methods that change the parameters' state do not appear very often in OO programming, except perhaps in implementations of the *Visitor* pattern and other similar situations. In our opinion a better solution would allow the user to explicitly indicate in the refinement mapping whether parameters are modified within methods (the default being that they are not modified).

The relation between domain conditions of specifications and exceptions raised by implementing methods is also a topic to investigate and develop, insofar as it would widen the universe of acceptable implementation classes.

We also plan to investigate possible extensions of both the specification and refinement languages in order to be possible to define 0-ary constructors, and refine them into Java constructors that override the default initialization.

A further topic for future work is the generation, from specifications and refinement mappings, of Java interfaces annotated with human readable contracts. Once one is convinced that given classes correctly implement a given module, it is important to make this information available in the form of human-readable contracts to programmers that want to use these classes and need to know how to use and what they can expect from them.

Acknowledgments. This work was partially supported through the POSI/CHS/48015/2002 Project Contract Guided System Development project. Thanks are due to José Luiz Fiadeiro for many fruitful discussions that have helped putting the project together.

References

1. S. Antoy and R. Hamlet. Automatically checking an implementation against its formal specification. *IEEE TOSE*, 26(1):55–69, 2000.
2. E. Astesiano, H.-J. Kreowski, and B. Krieg-Brckner, editors. *Algebraic Foundations of Systems Specification*. IFIP State-of-the-Art Reports. Springer, 1999.
3. M. Barnett and W. Schulte. Spying on components: A runtime verification technique. In *Proc. WSVCBS — OOPSLA 2001*, 2001.
4. Mike Barnett, K. Rustan M. Leino, and Wolfram Schulte. The spec# programming system: An overview. In *Proc. of CASSIS 2004*, number 3362 in LNCS. Springer, 2004.
5. D. Bartetzko, C. Fisher, M. Moller, and H. Wehrheim. Jass - Java with assertions. *ENTCS*, 55(2), 2001.
6. M. Bidoit and P. Mosses. *CASL User Manual*. Number 2900 in LNCS. Springer, 2004.
7. Contract based system development. http://labmol.di.fc.ul.pt/congu/.
8. H. Ehrig and G. Mahr, editors. *Fundamentals of Algebraic Specification 1: Equations and Initial Semantics*. Springer, 1985.
9. J. Gannon, J. Purtilo, and M. Zelkowitz. Software specification: A comparison of formal methods, 2001.
10. J. Goguen, J. Thatcher, and E. Wagner. An initial algebra approach to the specification, correctness, and implementation of abstract data types. In *Current Trends in Programming Methodology*, volume IV: Data Structuring, pages 80–149. Prentice-Hall, 1978.
11. J. Guttag, J. Horning, S. Garland, K. Jones, A. Modet, and J. Wing. *Larch: Languages and Tools for Formal Specification*. Springer, 1993.
12. J. Henkel and A. Diwan. Discovering algebraic specifications from java classes. In *Proc. ECOOP 2003*, LNCS, 2003.
13. J. Henkel and A. Diwan. A tool for writing and debugging algebraic specifications. In *Proc. ICSE 2004*, 2004.
14. M. Huges and D. Stotts. Daistish: Systematic algebraic testing for OO programs in the presence of side-effects. In *Proc. ISSTV*, pages 53–61. ACM, 1996.
15. M. Karaorman, U. Holzle, and J. Bruno. jContractor: A reflective Java library to support design by contract. In *Proc. of Meta-Level Architectures and Reflection*, number 1616 in LNCS. Springer, 1999.
16. R. Kramer. iContract - The Java Design by Contract Tool. In *Proc. TOOLS USA'98*. IEEE Computer Society Press, 1999.
17. G. Leavens, K. Rustan, M. Leino, E. Poll, C. Ruby, and B. Jacobs. JML: notations and tools supporting detailed design in java. In *OOPSLA'00 Companion*, pages 105–106. ACM Press, 2000.
18. B. Meyer. *Object-Oriented Software Construction*. Prentice-Hall PTR, 2nd edition, 1997.
19. I. Nunes, A. Lopes, V. Vasconcelos, J. Abreu, and L. Reis. Testing implementations of algebraic specifications with design-by-contract tools. DI/FCUL TR 05–22, 2005.
20. J. Spivey. *The Z Notation: A Reference Manual*. ISCS. Prentice-Hall, 1992.
21. Man Machine Systems. Design by contract for java using jmsassert. Published on the internet, 2000.

Incremental Slicing*

Heike Wehrheim

Universität Paderborn, Institut für Informatik
33098 Paderborn, Germany
wehrheim@uni-paderborn.de

Abstract. Slicing is one of a number of techniques for reducing the state space of specifications during verification. Unlike techniques as e.g. data abstraction slicing is *precise*: the slice exactly reflects the property to be verified. This necessitates keeping large parts of the specification.

In this paper we relax this requirement and instead compute slices *overapproximating* the behaviour of the specification. This can lead to substantially smaller slices. We consequently adapt the technique of *abstraction refinement* to slicing as to improve the slice once a false negative is detected. Slicing thus becomes an *incremental* method: it starts with a small, minimal part of the specification and successively adds further parts until either the property under interest holds on the slice or a real counterexample is found. We show correctness and termination of our technique.

1 Introduction

Model checking [3] is a technique for automatically verifying that a certain property (usually written in a temporal logic) holds for a specification / program / hardware design. One of the major hurdles to a widespread use of model checking is the state explosion problem: model checking algorithms need to search the whole state space of specifications and thus often fail due to its complexity. A large number of different techniques for fighting this problem has been developed, e.g. data abstractions [5,11], partial order [14] or symmetry reductions [10] or heuristic search [6]. All of these techniques aim at reducing the number of states to be inspected during model checking.

Slicing is another one of these techniques. Slicing originates from program analysis where it was first applied in debugging [17,18]. In contrast to data abstractions which *change* data domains of variables, predicates and operations, slicing essentially *removes* all parts of a program which cannot influence a certain property under interest (called the slicing criterion). This technique has also successfully been employed for model checking [8,13,16]; in this area the slicing criterion is usually a temporal logic formula. Slicing is a *precise* (or conservative) technique in that the property holds on the reduced specification if and only if

* This work was partly supported by the German Research Council (DFG) as part of the Transregional Collaborative Research Center "Automatic Verification and Analysis of Complex Systems" (SFB/TR 14 AVACS, www.avacs.org).

Z. Liu and J. He (Eds.): ICFEM 2006, LNCS 4260, pp. 514–528, 2006.

it holds on the full specification. This requirement usually necessitates keeping large parts of the specification. Data abstraction techniques on the other hand take a different approach [4]: The abstraction usually makes an *overapproximation* of the behaviour which, however, still guarantees that properties holding on the abstracted specification hold on the original one as well. Counterexamples found in the abstraction thus have to be validated on the original specification. If the counterexample is *spurious* the abstraction has to be *refined* and verification to be repeated. The advantage of this approach is that it allows for much coarser abstractions yielding smaller state spaces, however, at the prize of additional refinement steps.

In this paper, we develop a slicing technique which basically follows the same approach. We determine a small, minimally necessary part of the specification. On this slice the property to be verified is checked. When the property holds on the slice we are done and can conclude validity on the full specification as well. When a counterexample is found it has to be checked against the full specification. If it is found to be spurious the slice has to be refined, i.e., further parts of the specification have to be added to the slice. This is repeated until finally the property holds or a real counterexample is found. Slicing thus gets an incremental technique. On a small example we show that this way smaller slices can indeed be obtained.

We exemplify our approach on a tiny specification formalism containing facilities for defining variables and operations as well as describing the ordering of operations (by means of a finite state automaton). Besides developing an approach for slicing and not abstraction, it is the latter which distinguishes our approach from [4]. The existence of an automaton defining orderings of operations and the fact, that slicing removes operations, necessitates a new refinement technique. The reason for including automata as part of our specification formalism lies in our ultimate goal of applying incremental slicing to CSP-OZ specifications [7] which consist of state-based parts (described in Object-Z) and dynamic behaviour parts (given in the process algebra CSP). This formalism has the two dimensions of static / dynamic behaviour as well and furthermore an ordinary slicing algorithm already exists for CSP-OZ [1]. Here, we refrain from using CSP-OZ directly and instead move to a simpler formalism which allows for a straightforward illustration of the main techniques.

The paper is structured as follows: The next section shortly introduces the specification formalism, its semantics and the logic used for describing properties. It furthermore gives an example which is used throughout the whole paper. Section 3 defines ordinary slicing for this specification formalism. Sections 4 and 5 develop incremental slicing and the refinement technique. The last section concludes.

2 Background and Example

In this section we shortly describe the formalism that we use for specification, give its semantics and explain how slicing in general works.

2.1 Specifications

The specification language is a very simple formalism, used for the purpose of illustration only. The ultimate goal is to use the technique presented here on CSP-OZ specifications [7], for which ordinary slicing has already been developed [1]. CSP-OZ is a combination of the process algebra CSP and the state-based formalism Object-Z, thus allowing for the modelling of static as well as dynamic behaviour. Our tiny formalism will thus have these ingredients as well: variables and operations define the state space and an automaton specifies possible orderings of operations.

A specification *Spec* has the following ingredients:

- A set of variables $V = \{v_1, \ldots, v_n\}$ and operations $OP = \{op_1, \ldots, op_m\}$,
- for every variable v a data domain D_v, letting $D = \bigcup_{v \in V} D_v$,
- a finite state automaton A (without final states) for fixing the ordering of operations: $A = (Q, q_0, \longrightarrow)$ contains a set of states Q, an initial state $q_0 \in Q$ and a transition relation $\longrightarrow \subseteq Q \times OP \times Q$,
- an initialisation of variables given by a (sort-respecting) mapping $Init : V \rightarrow D$,
- a description of the semantics of operations given by a mapping $M : OP \rightarrow (Atom_V \times Ass_V)$ assigning to each operation a *guard* and an *effect*.

Here, $Atom_V$ is the set of predicates over V comparing variables with constants (e.g. $x < 1 \wedge y = 2$). Ass_V are assignments to variables in V of the form $v := expr$, where *expr* is an expression possibly involving other variables of V (e.g. $x := y + 2$, $y := 0$ are assignments). A tupel (or valuation of variables) $(d_1, \ldots, d_n) \in D_{v_1} \times \ldots \times D_{v_n}$ will often be abbreviated as d. A predicate p holds for d, i.e., $p(d)$ is true, if the predicate evaluates to true when replacing variable v_i with d_i. The effect of an operation op on some value d ($effect(op, d)$) with effect of op defined as $v_i := expr$ is some valuation d' which coincides with d except for v_i, for which the value of *expr* (in d) is taken. For an expression or predicate p we refer to $vars(p)$ as the set of variables appearing in p.

Note that in contrast to [4] we also allow for a specification of the dynamic behaviour in terms of an automaton here.

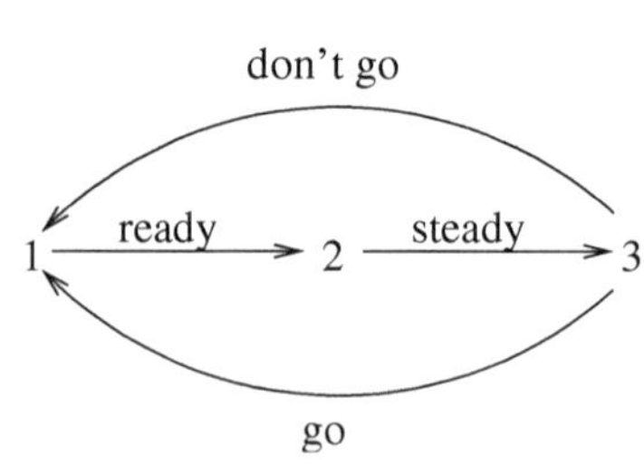

Fig. 1. Automaton of RSG-Specification

As running example, consider the following simple specification of a system continously performing the operations *ready*, *steady* and *go* (thus called RSG-specification). Another operation is *don't go* which can however be shown never to be taken. The system has three variables: $x, y, reset$ with domains $D_x = D_y = \{0, \ldots, 5\}, D_{reset} = \{0, 1\}$ and $Init(x) = Init(y) = Init(reset) = 0$. The automaton is depicted in Figure 1, the meaning of operations is given in the table below.

	guard	effect
ready	$true$	$x := 5$
steady	$x > 0$	$y := 5$
go	$y > 0$	$reset := 0$
don't go	$y = 0$	$reset := 1$

2.2 Kripke Structures and Temporal Logic

The semantics of this simple language can be defined in terms of a Kripke structure, labelled over the operation names OP and predicates $Atom_V$.

Definition 1. *A* Kripke structure $M = (S, R, L, I)$ *over a set of operations OP and a set of atomic propositions $Atom_V$ consists of*

- *a set of states S,*
- *transitions $R \subseteq S \times OP \times S$,*
- *a labelling of states with atomic propositions $L : S \rightarrow 2^{Atom_V}$ and*
- *$I \in S$ an initial state.*

Note that we only consider one initial state here. We often use a mapping like $Init$ as also denoting a tuple or a predicate, i.e. $Init = (d_1, \ldots, d_n)$ if $Init(v_i) = d_i$, and $Init(d_1, \ldots, d_n)$ is true precisely if $Init(v_i) = d_i$. For a subset $V' \subseteq V$ we let $d|_{V'}$ denote the tuple consisting of values for variables in V' only.

Definition 2. *The Kripke structure of a specification Spec with automaton $A = (Q, q_0, \longrightarrow)$ is defined as $S = D_{v_1} \times \ldots \times D_{v_n} \times Q$, $I = (Init, q_0)$ and*

- *$R((d, q), op, (d', q'))$ iff $q \xrightarrow{op}_A q'$, $guard(op, d) \wedge d' = effect(op, d)$,*
- *$L(d, q) = \{p \in Atom_V \mid p(d)\}$.*

The Kripke structure of the RSG specification is depicted in Figure 2. States are denoted as tuples (d_{reset}, d_x, d_y, q).

Our interest is now in verifying such specifications. The temporal logic which we use for describing properties is linear-time temporal logic (LTL) [12].

Definition 3. *The set of LTL formulae over AP is defined as the smallest set of formulae satisfying the following conditions:*

- *$p \in Atom_V$ is a formula,*
- *if φ_1, φ_2 are formulae, so are $\neg\varphi_1$ and $\varphi_1 \vee \varphi_2$,*
- *if φ is a formula, so are $X\varphi$ (Next), $\Box\varphi$ (Always), $\Diamond\varphi$ (Eventually),*
- *if φ_1, φ_2 are formulae, so is $\varphi_1\ U\ \varphi_2$ (Until).*

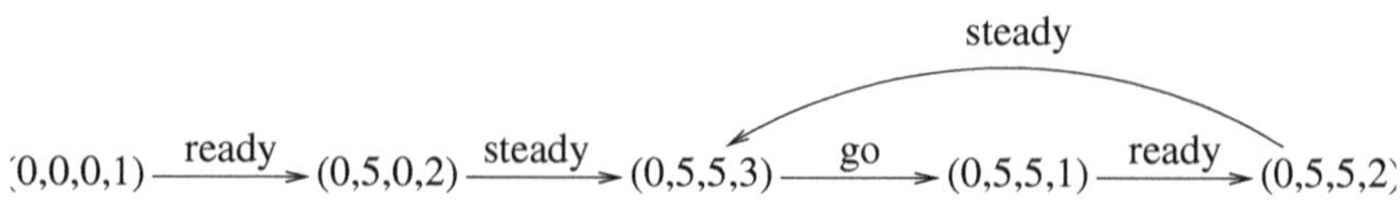

Fig. 2. Kripke structure of RSG specification

As usual, other boolean connectives can be derived from $\neg$ and $\vee$. The next-less part of LTL is referred to as LTL-X. LTL formulae are interpreted on *paths* of the Kripke structure, and a formula holds for the Kripke structure if it holds for all of its paths. In the following we assume that the transition relation of the Kripke structure is total, i.e. $\forall\, s \in S\, \exists\, op, s' : (s, op, s') \in R$.

Definition 4. *Let $K = (S, R, L, I)$ be a Kripke structure. An infinite sequence of states and operations $\pi = s_0\, op_0\, s_1\, op_1\, s_2 \ldots$ is a* path *of K iff $s_0 = I$ and $(s_i, op_i, s_{i+1}) \in R$ for all $0 \leq i$. For a path $\pi = s_0\, op_0\, s_1\, op_1\, s_2 \ldots$ we write $\pi[i]$ to stand for s_i (note that this is the state only) and π^i to stand for $s_i\, op_i\, s_{i+1}\, op_{i+1}\, s_{i+2} \ldots$.*

We furthermore let

$$inf(\pi) = \{op \mid op = op_i \text{ for infinitely many } i\}\ .$$

A path is fair *with respect to a set of operations $F \subseteq OP$ if $inf(\pi) \cap F \neq \varnothing$.*

Fairness is needed later when we move from a full to a reduced specification. Here, it is defined with respect to a set of operations: paths are fair if they infinitely often contain operations from a fairness set. Next, we give the interpretation of LTL formulae.

Definition 5. *Let π be a path, φ an LTL formula.*
$\pi \models \varphi$ is inductively defined as follows:

- $\pi \models p$ *iff* $p \in L(\pi[0])$,
- $\pi \models \neg\varphi$ *iff not* $\pi \models \varphi$,
- $\pi \models \varphi_1 \vee \varphi_2$ *iff* $\pi \models \varphi_1$ *or* $\pi \models \varphi_2$,
- $\pi \models X\ \varphi$ *iff* $\pi^1 \models \varphi$,
- $\pi \models \Box\varphi$ *iff* $\forall\, i \geq 0 : \pi^i \models \varphi$,
- $\pi \models \Diamond\varphi$ *iff* $\exists\, i \geq 0 : \pi^i \models \varphi$,
- $\pi \models \varphi_1\ U\ \varphi_2$ *iff* $\exists\, k \geq 0 : \pi^k \models \varphi_2$ *and* $\forall\, j, 0 \leq j < k : \pi^j \models \varphi_1$.

For the Kripke structure K a formula holds iff it holds for all of K's paths. In addition we will need the notion of fair satisfaction: K *fairly* satifies φ with respect to a fairness constraint $F \subseteq OP$ ($K \models_F \varphi$) iff $\pi \models \varphi$ holds for all F-fair paths π of K.

2.3 Simple Slicing

Usually, Kripke structures may become quite large, due to the possibly large data domains of the specification, and might thus make model checking infeasible.

Slicing allows to remove those parts of the specification which are irrelevant for the property to be verified. Slicing is usually an *exact* reduction technique: given a property φ (specified in LTL-X) and a specification *Spec*, slicing computes a reduced specification $Spec^{red}_{\varphi}$ such that the following holds:

$$Spec \models \varphi \text{ iff } Spec^{red}_{\varphi} \models \varphi$$

The Next operator X has to be left out since the full and the reduced specification differ in the number of steps they make: the full specification has more steps and these are considered as *stuttering* steps with respect to the formula.

Here, we will present a very simple slicing algorithm (ignoring the flow of control) which just serves the purpose of illustrating the concept. A more elaborate slicing algorithm for CSP-OZ is given in [1]; an overview of slicing techniques in general is given in [15].

The slicing algorithm incrementally constructs a set of variables which are relevant for the property to be checked. It starts with the variables appearing in the formula φ itself, $vars(\varphi)$.

$$\begin{aligned} V_0 &= vars(\varphi) \\ V_{i+1} &= V_i \cup \bigcup_{v \in V_i, op \in OP, (v := expr) = effect(op)} vars(effect(op)) \cup vars(guard(op)) \end{aligned}$$

This is repeated until some k is reached with $V_k = V_{k-1}$. The idea is simply to compute the variables which can directly or indirectly influence the valuation of $vars(\varphi)$. First, we need the variables which are in expressions *expr* such that a variable v in φ is set to *expr* in some operation *op*. In addition, since the guard of *op* determines whether this operation is executed at all, we also need the variables in the guard of *op*. The repetition of this computation also gives us indirect influences; the variable sets are closed under influences. Note that in more elaborate algorithms the flow of control is taken into account as well. We let V' denote the variables of this set V_k. These are the variables of the reduced specification. The operations of the reduced specification are

$$\begin{aligned} OP' = \{op \in OP \mid \exists\, v \in V' : (v := expr) = effect(op) \\ \vee\ vars(guard(op)) \subseteq V'\} \end{aligned}$$

We take all operations which either in their guard or in their effect refer to variables in V'. We demonstrate this on our example. Assume that the property to be verified is $\Box(reset = 0)$ (which holds). Thus $V_0 = vars(\varphi) = \{reset\}$.

$$\begin{aligned} V_1 &= \{reset, y\} \\ V_2 &= \{reset, y, x\} \end{aligned}$$

Hence $V' = V$ and $OP' = OP$. We thus do not get any reduction at all. Note that x and y are in V because we have included variables of *guards* in our computation of the set V'. However, looking at the specification we see that operation *ready* and variable x are actually irrelevant. *ready* sets the variable x in such a way that the guard of the following operation is always true. Thus it would not do us any harm to remove both x and *ready* and the guard of *steady*. On the other hand *steady* and y are important since they determine which of the following operations are taken. If we remove them both *go* and *don't go* can be executed in the reduced specification and the formula becomes false. Thus it neither seems to be correct to leave out variables in guards in general, nor does it seem that keeping them in general is necessary.

3 Approximative Slicing

This section proposes a slicing algorithm which overcomes this problem by successively adding variables of guards, however, only when needed. It adopts a technique which has successfully been employed for *abstraction* under the name counterexample-guided abstraction refinement [4]. The approach works as follows: first, a reduced specification which *overapproximates* the behaviour of the original specification is computed. On this reduction the property to be verified is checked. If it holds we are done. If it does not hold, we check feasibility of the counterexample. If the counterexample is possible in the full specification, a real counterexample has been found and we are done. If it is not, the slice has to be "refined", i.e., we have to add some variables and operations as to make the reduced specification more precise.

We start with explaining the modification of the slicing algorithm, which now computes slices overapproximating the behaviour of the original specification. For this, we change the algorithm at one point: we do not consider guards anymore, both in the computation of the set of relevant variables and for the set of relevant operations.

$$V_0 = vars(\varphi)$$

$$V_{i+1} = V_i \cup \bigcup_{v \in V_i, op \in OP, (v := expr) = effect(op)} vars(effect(op))$$

$$OP' = \{op \in OP \mid \exists\, v \in V' : (v := expr) = effect(op)\}$$

Since we will get some reduction for our example now, we also have to explain how the reduced specification is constructed. The guards of the operations $op \in OP'$ in $Spec^{red}$ only contain predicates over variables of V': $guard^{red}(op) = true$ if[1] $vars(guard(op)) \not\subseteq V'$, $guard^{red}(op) = guard(op)$ else. By leaving out some guards although considering the operation we can get new behaviour in $Spec^{red}$.

For the RSG-specification, we now arrive at the following: $V_0 = V_1 = \{reset\}$, thus $V' = \{reset\}$, $OP' = \{go, don't\ go\}$, $Init^{red}(reset) = 0$ and guard and effect are as given in the following table.

	guard	effect
go	*true*	$reset := 0$
don't go	*true*	$reset := 1$

[1] Note that in our current definition of $Atom_V$ there is never more than one variable in $guard(op)$.

The automaton of the specification has to be reduced as well: we collapse all those states into one, which can be reached from one another without performing operations in OP'. For a set $O \subseteq OP$ we define $q \equiv_O q'$ if $q \xrightarrow{O}{}^{*} q'$ or $q' \xrightarrow{O}{}^{*} q$. The automaton A^{red} is $([Q]_{\equiv_{OP \setminus OP'}}, [q_0]_{\equiv_{OP \setminus OP'}}, \longrightarrow_{A^{red}})$ with $[q] \xrightarrow{op}_{A^{red}} [q']$ iff $\exists\, q_1 \in [q], q_2 \in [q'] : q_1 \xrightarrow{op}_A q_2$. If not stated differently $\equiv$ will always stand for $\equiv_{OP \setminus OP'}$. The reduced RSG-automaton is shown in Figure 3.

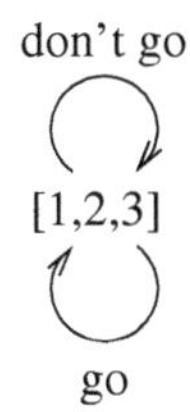

Fig. 3. Automaton of reduced specification

The slice overapproximates the behaviour of the specification, thus the exactness of the reduction technique is lost and instead we only get:

$$Spec_{\varphi}^{red} \models \varphi \Rightarrow Spec \models \varphi$$

This can be proven in two steps: by showing that the reduced specification *simulates* the full specification and proving that the validity of LTL-X formulae is preserved under simulation.

Definition 6. *Let $M = (S, R, L, I)$ and $M' = (S', R, L', I')$ be Kripke structures labelled over OP, OP' and $Atom_V$, $Atom_{V'}$, respectively, $OP \supseteq OP'$, $V \supseteq V'$. M' simulates M ($M \preceq M'$) if there is a relation $H \subseteq S \times S'$ such that the following holds:*

1. *$(I, I') \in H$,*
2. *$\forall (s_1, s_2) \in H$ we have*
   (a) *$L(s_1) \cap Atom_{V'} = L'(s_2)$,*
   (b) *$\forall (s_1, op, s_1') \in R$:*
      - *if $op \in OP'$ then $\exists\, s_2' : (s_2, op, s_2') \in R' \wedge (s_1', s_2') \in H$ or*
      - *if $op \notin OP'$ then $(s_1', s_2) \in H$.*

Theorem 1. *Let $M = (S, R, L, I)$ be the Kripke structure of the full specification Spec, $M' = (S', R', L', I')$ the Kripke structure of $Spec_{\varphi}^{red}$ for some formula φ. Then*

$$M \preceq M' \ .$$

Proof: Let V' and OP' be the set of variables and operations occuring in the reduced specificiation. We use the following simulation relation H

$$H = \{((d, q), (d|_{V'}, [q])) \mid d \in D_{v_1} \times \ldots \times D_{v_n}, q \in Q\}$$

We have to show all simulation conditions.

1. $((Init, q_0), (Init^{Red}, [q_0]))$ is in H by construction of the reduced specification.
2. $L((d,q)) \cap Atom_{V'} = \{p \in Atom_{V'} \mid p(d)\} = \{p \in Atom_{V'} \mid p(d \mid_{V'})\} = L'(d \mid_{V'}, [q])$.
3. Let $(s_1, s_2) \in H$, $(s_1, op, s_1') \in R$. Assume $s_1 = (d,q)$, $s_2 = (d', q')$.
   - $op \in OP'$:
     Hence $guard(op, d)$ holds, $d' = effect(op, d)$ and $q \xrightarrow{op}_A q'$. It follows that $[q] \xrightarrow{op}_{A^{red}} [q']$ in the reduced automaton, and $guard^{red}(op, d \mid_{V'})$ and $d' \mid_{V'} = effect^{red}(op, d \mid V')$. Hence $((d \mid_{V'}, [q]), op, (d' \mid_{V'}, [q'])) \in R'$ and $((d', q'), (d' \mid_{V'}, [q'])) \in H$.
   - $op \notin OP'$:
     We first show that the following holds in M: $\forall (s, op, s') \in R, op \notin OP' : L(s) \cap Atom_{V'} = L(s') \cap Atom_{V'}$ ($op \notin OP'$ are stuttering steps wrt. $Atom_{V'}$). This can be proven by contradiction: assume $L(s) \cap Atom_{V'} \neq L(s') \cap Atom_{V'}$. Hence there is some $v \in V'$ on which s and s' differ, thus $(v := expr) = effect(op)$. But then by definition of OP' op should be in OP'.
     By this we get $d \mid_{V'} = d' \mid_{V'}$. Furthermore $q \equiv q'$. Hence $((d', q'), (d \mid_{V'}, [q])) \in H$.

Theorem 2. *Let $M = (S, R, L, I)$ and $M' = (S', R, L', I')$ be Kripke structures labelled over OP, OP' and $Atom_V, Atom_{V'}$, respectively, $OP \supseteq OP'$, $V \supseteq V'$. Let φ be an LTL-X formula over $Atom_{V'}$ and $M \preceq M'$. Then*

$$M' \models_{OP'} \varphi \Rightarrow M \models_{OP'} \varphi$$

Fairness is needed here since there can in principle be paths in M executing no operations of OP' at all. The validity of a property on such paths cannot be checked in M' since there is no corresponding path in M'.

Proof: The proof proceeds as follows. We assume that $M' \models_{OP'} \varphi$ holds but there is some OP'-fair path π in M such that $M \not\models \varphi$. From such a path we construct a *stuttering equivalent* (wrt. propositions in $Atom_{V'}$) path π' of M'. Stuttering equivalent paths are known to satisfy the same set of LTL-X formulae (over $Atom_{V'}$) [3]. Hence $M' \not\models \varphi$ which gives us the contradiction.

Let H be the relation showing simulation of M by M'. Let π be an OP'-fair path of M, $\pi = s_0\, op_0\, s_1\, op_1 \ldots$. The path π' of M' is inductively constructed.

Induction base: $\pi' = I'$.

Induction hypothesis: $\pi' = s_0'\, op_0'\, s_1' \ldots s_i'$ has already been constructed, having proceeded in path π to state s_j. Then $(s_j, s_i') \in H$. (Note that this is given in the induction base).

Induction step: Assume $op_j \notin OP'$. Then π' is not extended and in π we move to s_{j+1}. By definition of the simulation relation H we get $(s_{j+1}, s_i') \in H$. If $op_j \in OP'$ then we take as s_{i+1}' the state s such that $(s_i', op_j, s) \in R'$ and $(s_{j+1}, s) \in H$.

Due to the fairness assumption π is an infinite path. Due to condition 2(a) of simulation π and π' are stuttering equivalent wrt. the atomic propositions in $Atom_{V'}$. □

Thus, for the reduced RSG specification we can be sure that if a formula holds it will hold for the full specification as well. Unfortunately, the formula $\Box(\mathit{reset} = 0)$ does not hold anymore on the current reduction. The overapproximation we have made has been too coarse. The counterexample trace simply consists of one operation: *don't go*. Hence we next need some means of detecting whether this is an actual counterexample or a spurious one. In case of having found a spurious counterexample we have to construct a new reduced specification which is more precise, i.e., does not exhibit this counterexample anymore.

4 Refining the Slice

For checking counterexamples we use (almost) the same approach as [4]. The difference lies in our explicit treatment (and removal) of operations, which necessitates a different technique for refining the slice. In general, there may be two different kinds of counterexamples: *path* and *loop* counterexamples. Loop counterexamples arise when checking liveness properties. As [4] shows loop counterexamples can be reduced to path counterexamples, thus we only treat the latter here.

4.1 Checking Feasibility of Counterexamples

In the following we always let $M = (S, R, L, I)$ be the Kripke structure of the full specification, A its automaton and V', OP' the set of variables / operations computed during slicing. Assume that we are given a finite path $\tilde{\pi} = \tilde{s}_1\, op_1\, \tilde{s}_2\, op_2 \ldots \tilde{s}_n$ of the reduced system representing a counterexample for the property to be verified. The states in this counterexample are of the form $(\tilde{d}, [q])$ where $\tilde{d}$ is a valuation of variables in V' and $[q]$ an equivalence class of states of the automaton. For a state (d, q) of the full specification we denote by $\mathit{red}(d, q)$ the projection $(d|_{V'}, [q])$ onto the reduced specification. For checking whether $\tilde{\pi}$ is actually possible in the full specification we have to try to find a path π of the full specification whose projection onto variables in V' and operations in OP' gives $\tilde{\pi}$. Thus, contrary to [4], we might need to fill in additional operations. The set of concrete paths corresponding to $\tilde{\pi}$ is the following:

$$\begin{array}{l}\{s_1^1\, op_1^1\, s_1^2 \ldots op_1^{j_1}\, s_1^{j_1+1}\, op_1\, s_2^1\, op_2^1 \ldots op_2^{j_2}\, s_2^{j_2+1}\, op_2\, s_3^1 \ldots op_{n-1}\, s_n^1 \mid \\ \quad \forall\, k : op_k^1, \ldots, op_k^{j_k} \notin OP', R(s_k^l, op_k^l, s_k^{l+1}), R(s_k^{j_k+1}, op_k, s_{k+1}^1), \\ \quad I(s_1^1), \mathit{red}(s_k^1) = \ldots = \mathit{red}(s_k^{j_k}) = \tilde{s_k}\}\end{array}$$

The question is hence whether this set is empty or contains at least one path. To determine this we incrementally construct sets of concrete states corresponding to the states appearing in $\tilde{\pi}$. We start in the initial state and then successively determine the sets of states reachable from this state by first executing operations outside of OP' and then the next operation in $\tilde{\pi}$. This set is then compared with the next state $\tilde{s}_i$ and we remove those states which cannot be projected onto $\tilde{s}_i$.

We use the notation $R_{op}(T)$ to denote $\{s \in S \mid \exists\, s' \in T : (s', op, s) \in R\}$. R^* is the reflexive and transitive closure of this relation, and $R_M, M \subseteq OP$, its extension to sets of operations.

$$S_1 = R^*_{OP\setminus OP'}(I)$$
$$S_{k+1} = \{s \in R^*_{OP\setminus OP'}(R_{op_k}(S_k)) \mid red(s) = \tilde{s}_{k+1}\}$$

Then the following holds.

Proposition 1. *π is a* spurious counterexample *if there is some k such that $S_k = \varnothing$.*

If such an empty set exists then there is no concrete path starting in the initial state and executing the operations in $\tilde{\pi}$, possibly with some operations from $OP \setminus OP'$ in between. Thus we have to compute the sets S_i, $i \geq 1$, until we either reach an empty set or the nonempty set S_n.

We again illustrate this on our sample specification. The counterexample for the formula $\Box(reset = 0)$ is depicted in Figure 4. The state on the left hand side is $\tilde{s_1}$, on the right hand side $\tilde{s_2}$, $\tilde{\pi} = \tilde{s_1}\, don't\ go\, \tilde{s_2}$.

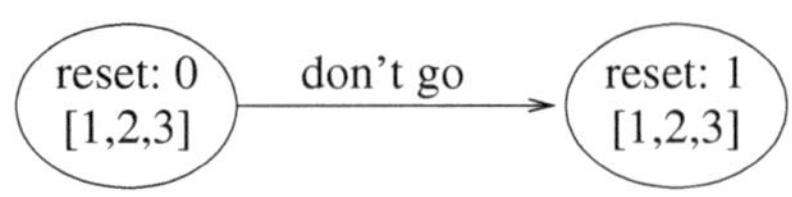

Fig. 4. Counterexample of reduced RSG

For this counterexample we next determine the sets $S_1, S_2 \dots$. We again represent states as tuples (d_{reset}, d_x, d_y, q) (the last element is the state of the automaton).

$$S_1 = \{(0,0,0,1), (0,5,0,2), 0,5,5,3)\}$$
$$S_2 = \varnothing$$

S_2 is empty: starting from S_1 we compute the set of states reached by executing $don'tgo$. Since $don'tgo$ is not enabled in any of these states the resulting set is empty. The counterexample is thus spurious.

4.2 Refinement Step

The basic idea is next to refine the slice (add more variables and/or operations) and redo the verification step on the improved reduced system. This refinement step has to be repeated until either the property holds or the counterexample found turns out to exist in the full specification as well. For avoiding a repetition of this step ad infinitum we have to make sure that each refinement actually adds variables or operations so that we (in the worst case) end when the full specification is reached.

Our primary goal is, however, to avoid getting the same counterexample again in the repetition of the verification step. To this end we more closely examine the sets of states we have computed and those appearing in the counterexample. Assume S_k to be the first set of states being empty. S_{k-1} contains the states reachable from the initial state but operation op_{k-1} was not possible from there.

In the slice this operation can however be executed in $\tilde{s}_{k-1}$. This holds because there are states $s \in S$ from which operation op_{k-1} is possible and which projected onto V' equal $\tilde{s}_{k-1}$. These are called *bad* states (they cause the spurious counterexample):

$$S_B = \{s \in S \mid red(s) = \tilde{s}_{k-1} \wedge \exists\, s' \in S, red(s') = \tilde{s_k} \wedge s' \in R_{op_{k-1}}(s)\}$$

As a first observation note that S_B and S_{k-1} are disjoint.

Proposition 2. $S_B \cap S_{k-1} = \varnothing$.

This is simply due to the fact that S_k is empty and thus op_{k-1} cannot be executed from a state in S_{k-1}. To get rid of the spurious counterexample we have to ensure that states in S_{k-1} and S_B are not collapsed into the same state in the reduced specification. There are two possible ways of doing so:

1. by adding *variables* to V' such that states in S_B and S_{k-1} will disagree on their values,
2. or by adding *operations* to OP' such that the automaton states in S_B and S_{k-1} are not equivalent anymore.

The ideal candidate for 1. are the variables in $guard(op_{k-1})$.

Rule 1: If $vars(guard(op_{k-1})) \nsubseteq V'$ then set V' to $V' \cup vars(guard(op_{k-1}))$.

An addition of these variables might already be sufficient for improving the slice. After adding them to V' we make the closure from slicing again, i.e., we start the computation of relevant variables and operations with this new set V' instead of with $vars(\varphi)$.

We exemplify this on our example: the first set S_k which is empty is S_2, thus $k = 2$. Operation op_{k-1} is *don't go*. The variable in the guard of *don't go* is y which is not yet in V'. Thus V' is extended to $\{reset, y\}$. The closure does not give us additional variables, however, operation *steady* modifying y is included into OP'. The reduced specification this time is thus:

	guard	effect
steady	*true*	$y := 5$
go	$y > 0$	$reset := 0$
don't go	$y = 0$	$reset := 1$

The reduced automaton is depicted in Figure 5. When checking the formula $\Box(reset = 0)$ on this reduced specification we find that it holds this time. By Theorem 2 we thus get validity of the formula for the full specification as well.

However, rule 1 does not always yield an extension of V', namely if the variables in $guard(op_{k-1})$ are already in V'. Even in the case that it does this might not yield a complete separation of S_B from S_{k-1}. Nevertheless, when rule 1 is not applicable anymore we at least know that the reason why op_{k-1} is possible from states in S_B but not in S_{k-1} must lie in the component denoting the state of the automaton. In this case, we in addition have to separate the automaton

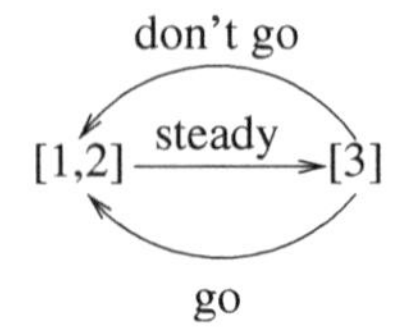

Fig. 5. Reduced automaton after refinement step

states. Let $Q_B = \{q \in Q \mid \exists(d,q) \in S_B\}$ and $Q_{k-1} = \{q \in Q \mid \exists(d,q) \in S_{k-1}\}$ be the automaton states of bad and reachable states. We have to make sure to have $q \not\equiv p$ for all $q \in Q_B, p \in Q_{k-1}$. First note that the following holds.

Proposition 3. *If* $vars(guard(op_{k-1})) \subseteq V'$ *then* $Q_B \cap Q_{k-1} = \varnothing$.

Proof: Assume the contrary, i.e., assume there is some $q \in Q_B \cap Q_{k-1}$. Since operation op_{k-1} is possible from S_B, $guard(op_{k-1})(d)$ and $p \xrightarrow{op_{k-1}}_A$ holds for all $(d,p) \in S_B$, hence in particular $q \xrightarrow{op_{k-1}}_A$. Since the states in S_B and S_{k-1} agree on variables in V' and $vars(guard(op_{k-1})) \subseteq V'$ we also have $guard(op_{k-1})(d')$ holds for all $(d',p') \in S_{k-1}$. But op_{k-1} is not executable in S_{k-1}, hence q cannot be in Q_{k-1}. □

Thus these two sets of states can in fact be separated (wrt. the equivalence $\equiv$). We have to compute a (at the best minimal) set of operations O such that adding O to OP' yields the following property: $\forall\, q \in Q_B, p \in Q_{k-1} : q \not\equiv_{OP \setminus (OP' \cup O)} p$. We only give a brute force approach to computing such a set of operations O here (a more refined technique is the topic of future work). A simple idea is to take every operation which is the first one on a path from a state in Q_B to a state in Q_{k-1} (or vice versa). Thus set O to be the set of operations $op \in OP \setminus OP'$ such that there is some $q_B \in Q_B$, $q_{k-1} \in Q_{k-1}$ with $q_B \xrightarrow{op} \rightarrow^* q_{k-1}$ or $q_{k-1} \xrightarrow{op} \rightarrow^* q_B$. This is certainly not a minimal set (which is to be aimed at), but it separates the two sets.

The second rule uses the result of this procedure.

Rule 2: Let $O \subseteq OP \setminus OP'$ be a set of operations which separate Q_B from Q_{k-1}. Then set OP' to $OP' \cup O$.

This guarantees separation of Q_B and Q_{k-1}. We now (possibly) get operations op in the reduced specification without having the variables they manipulate in V'. For the reduced specification we then simply set $\mathit{effect}^{red}(op) = \mathit{skip}$ (no assignment).

The refinement step thus consists of two smaller steps. First, rule 1 is applied. If this changes the variable set V' verification is repeated. When this results in the same counterexample again rule 2 is applied. The prior application of rule 1 guarantees that rule 2 can separate the automaton states (due to Proposition 3), thus the spurious counterexample is eliminated.

The refinement step on the one hand enlarges the reduced specification and on the other hand makes it more precise (wrt. the full specification). Thus, the refinement and the successive repetition of the verification will eventually end, in the worst case with a slice that ordinary slicing would have computed. Giving up exactness of slicing can however lead to much smaller slices, as has been shown in section 2.

5 Conclusion

In this paper we have developed an incremental slicing technique transferring the idea of abstraction refinement to slicing. The technique introduces additional refinement steps into verification, successively making the slice more precise wrt. to the property to be verified. We have shown that incremental slicing can help in reducing the size of the slices. In fact, the idea of developing such a form of slicing grew out of our experiments with slicing CSP-OZ, where it often turns out that parts of a specification are kept in the slice although they are not strictly necessary (only for exactness). As future work we thus plan to transfer this technique to CSP-OZ. The main challenge for this is the adaption of the refinement step to CSP. Another issue for future work is the improvement of the algorithm for separating Q_B from Q_{k-1} as to compute a minimal set of operations.

Related work. The work closest to ours is that of counterexample guided abstraction refinement (CEGAR), as used for instance in [4,2,9]. The main difference to the work presented here lies in the fact that we employ slicing and not abstraction, and thus also *remove operations* whereas abstraction only collapses the state space. Thus an abstraction will never have less steps than the concrete system, though it represents an overapproximation of it. Operations are explicitly modelled here and are moreover first class entities like variables, which can be kept or removed in a slice. Operations (or events) are also treated in [2] giving a CEGAR approach for state/event-based model checking, however, there the abstraction and the concrete system are built over the same alphabet and thus operations are always kept.

References

1. I. Brückner and H. Wehrheim. Slicing an Integrated Formal Method for Verification. In *ICFEM 2005: Seventh International Conference on Formal Engineering Methods*, volume 3785 of *LNCS*, pages 360–374. Springer, 2005.
2. S. Chaki, E. M. Clarke, J. Ouaknine, N. Sharygina, and N. Sinha. State/event-based software model checking. In Eerke A. Boiten, John Derrick, and Graeme Smith, editors, *IFM*, volume 2999 of *Lecture Notes in Computer Science*, pages 128–147. Springer, 2004.
3. E. Clarke, O. Grumberg, and D. Peled. *Model checking*. MIT Press, 1999.
4. E. M. Clarke, O. Grumberg, S. Jha, Y. Lu, and H. Veith. Counterexample-guided abstraction refinement for symbolic model checking. *JACM*, 50(5):752–794, 2003.
5. E.M. Clarke, O. Grumberg, and D.E. Long. Model checking and abstraction. In *19th ACM POPL*, 1992.

6. S. Edelkamp, A. Lluch-Lafuente, and S. Leue. Directed model-checking in HSF-SPIN. In *8th International SPIN Workshop on Model Checking Software*, number 2057 in Lecture Notes in Computer Science, pages 57–79. Springer, 2001.
7. C. Fischer. CSP-OZ: A combination of Object-Z and CSP. In H. Bowman and J. Derrick, editors, *Formal Methods for Open Object-Based Distributed Systems (FMOODS '97)*, volume 2, pages 423–438. Chapman & Hall, 1997.
8. J. Hatcliff, M. Dwyer, and H. Zheng. Slicing software for model construction. *Higher-order and Symbolic Computation*, 13(4):315–353, 2000.
9. T. A. Henzinger, R. Jhala, R. Majumdar, and G. Sutre. Lazy abstraction. In *POPL*, pages 58–70, 2002.
10. C. Ip and D. Dill. Better verification through symmetry. In *International Conference on Computer Hardware Description Languages*, 1993.
11. C. Loiseaux, S. Graf, J. Sifakis, A. Bouajjani, and S. Bensalem. Property preserving abstractions for the verification of concurrent systems. *Formal methods in system design*, 6:1–35, 1995.
12. Z. Manna and A. Pnueli. *The temporal logic of reactive and concurrent systems (Specification)*. Springer, 1991.
13. L. Millett and T. Teitelbaum. Issues in slicing PROMELA and its applications to model checking, protocol understanding, and simulation. *Software Tools for Technology Transfer*, 2(4):343–349, 2000.
14. D. Peled. All from one, one for all: On model checking using representatives. In *Proc. 5th Workshop on Computer Aided Verification*, number 697, 1993.
15. F. Tip. A survey of program slicing techniques. *Journal of programming languages*, 3(3), 1995.
16. N. Shankar V. Ganesh, H. Saidi. Slicing SAL. Technical report, SRI International, http://theory.stanford.edu/, 1999.
17. M. Weiser. Program slicing. In *Proceedings of the 5th international conference on Software engineering*, pages 439–449. IEEE Press, 1981.
18. M. Weiser. Programmers use slices when debugging. *Communications of the ACM*, 25(7):446–452, 1982.

Assume-Guarantee Software Verification Based on Game Semantics*

Aleksandar Dimovski and Ranko Lazić

Department of Computer Science
University of Warwick
Coventry CV4 7AL, UK
{aleks, lazic}@dcs.warwick.ac.uk

Abstract. We show how game semantics, counterexample-guided abstraction refinement, assume-guarantee reasoning and the L^* algorithm for learning regular languages can be combined to yield a procedure for compositional verification of safety properties of open programs. Game semantics is used to construct accurate models of subprograms compositionally. Overall model construction is avoided using assume-guarantee reasoning and the L^* algorithm, by learning assumptions for arbitrary subprograms. The procedure has been implemented, and initial experimental results show significant space savings.

1 Introduction

One of the most effective methods for automated software verification is model checking [8]. A software system to be verified is modelled as a finite-state transition system and a property to be established is expressed as a temporal logic formula. Given that the state explosion problem is particulary acute in software model checking, the most desirable feature of this approach is *scalability*. *Compositional modelling and verification* achieve scalability by breaking up a larger software system in smaller systems which can be modelled and verified independently. Hence, the properties of a program can be established from the properties of its individually checked components without requiring to check the whole program as an atomic "flat" entity.

Game semantics meets the first requirement for achieving scalability: *compositional modelling*. Game semantics is denotational, i.e. defined recursively on the syntax, therefore the model of a larger program is constructed from the models of its subprograms, using a notion of strategy composition. The other benefits that game semantics brings to software model checking, compared with classical state-based approaches [6,17], are:

Modularity. There is a model for any open program, which enables verification of program fragments which contain free variable and procedure names.

* We acknowledge support by the EPSRC (GR/S52759/01). The second author was also supported by the Intel Corporation, and is also affiliated to the Mathematical Institute, Serbian Academy of Sciences and Arts, Belgrade.

Z. Liu and J. He (Eds.): ICFEM 2006, LNCS 4260, pp. 529–548, 2006.

Correctness. The generated model is fully abstract (sound and complete), i.e., two programs have the same models if and only if they cannot be distinguished with respect to operational tests (such as abnormal termination) in any program context. This means that the model can be used to deduce properties of programs (soundness), and moreover every observable property of programs is captured by the model (completeness).

Efficiency. Programs are modelled by how they interact with their environments. Details of their internal state during computations are not recorded, which results in small models with a maximum level of abstraction.

Assume-guarantee reasoning addresses the second challenge: *compositional verification*. To check that a property P is satisfied by a model M composed of two components M_1 and M_2, it suffices to find an assumption A such that

1. the composition of M_1 and A satisfies P, and
2. M_2 is a refinement of A

If such an assumption A can be found and it is significantly smaller than M_2, then we can verify whether M satisfies P (by checking 1 and 2) without having to build the whole M.

In this paper, we describe an automatic procedure which generates assumptions as above using the L^* algorithm for learning a game strategy. L^* iteratively learns a minimal deterministic finite automaton, which represents the unknown strategy, from membership and equivalence queries. In each iteration, L^* produces a candidate assumption A which is used to check 1 and 2. Depending on results of the checks, we may conclude that the required property is satisfied, violated in which case a witness counterexample is reported, or the current A needs to be revised. This procedure is set within an abstraction refinement loop which automatically extracts a game-semantic model from a data-abstracted program and refines the program if a spurious counterexample is found.

Programs are abstracted through approximating infinite integer data types by partitionings. Any partitioning contains a finite number of partitions, i.e. sets of integers, which are called abstracted integers. Abstracted programs operationally behave like their concrete counterparts, but an abstracted integer argument in any operation is nondeterministically replaced by some concrete integer from its set of integers (partition), and the concrete integer result is replaced by the abstracted integer (partition) to which it belongs. As shown in [11], this is a conservative abstraction. By quotienting over abstracted integers, the models become finite and can be model-checked. Whenever a spurious counterexample is found, it is used to refine the partitionings of the program, by splitting some of their partitions.

We have implemented this approach in the GameChecker tool [12]. We report some initial experimental results, which indicate significant memory savings compared to a non assume-guarantee approach.

The paper is organized as follows. After discussing related work, Section 2 introduces the programming language we are considering. Game semantics of the language is presented in Section 3, followed by a description of the L^* algorithm in Section 4. Details of the verification framework are given in Section 5. Finally, we present the implementation in Section 6, and conclude in Section 7.

1.1 Related Work

Game semantics emerged in the last decade as a potent framework for modelling programming languages [2,3,16,18]. The first applications of game-semantic models to model checking were proposed in [14,1,10]. They were then extended by adapting the counterexample-guided abstraction refinement technique to this setting [11]. A tool (GAMECHECKER) based on these ideas was presented in [12].

The assume-guarantee paradigm is the best studied approach to compositional reasoning [20]. The primary difficulty in applying this approach to realistic systems is that, in general, the appropriate assumptions have to be constructed manually.

The work presented in this paper is motivated by a recently proposed approach [9], which uses learning algorithms to automate assume-guarantee reasoning. In [9], a variant of Angluin's L^* algorithm [5,21] for learning a regular language is used to generate appropriate assumptions. Compared to this approach, which is applied at the design level of a software system, our work makes the following contributions. Firstly, we apply the method at the implementation level, and verify safety properties of open program fragments. Secondly, while in [9] the method is used for verifying multi-threaded programs by building models and checking their constituting threads independently, here we apply compositional verification on sequential programs where individually checked components can be arbitrary subprograms of the given input program. Then, the L^* algorithm is adapted to the specific game semantics setting for learning a game strategy. Finally, the method is integrated with a counterexample-guided abstraction refinement style loop. We thus obtain a procedure which embodies both compositional modelling and compositional verification.

The L^* learning algorithm has found a number applications to automatic verification. For example, adaptive model checking [15] uses learning to compute an accurate finite state model of an unknown system starting from an approximate model; substitutability analysis of evolving software systems [7] verifies an upgraded software system by learning; [4] uses a symbolic implementation of the L^* algorithm for compositional reasoning about symbolic modules, etc.

2 The Programming Language

The language which will be considered, Abstracted Idealized Algol (AIA), is an expressive programming language combining usual imperative features, locally-scoped variables and call-by-name procedures. It also incorporates data abstraction annotations, which enable the writing of abstracted programs in a syntax similar to that of concrete programs.

The data types of AIA are booleans and *abstracted integers* ($D ::= \mathsf{bool} \mid \mathsf{int}_\pi$). The phrase types are expressions, variables and commands ($B ::= \mathsf{exp}D \mid \mathsf{var}D \mid \mathsf{com}$) plus functions ($T ::= B \mid T \to T$).

The *abstractions* π range over computable finite partitionings of the integers $\mathbb{Z}$. Any such partitioning consists of a finite number of partitions (i.e. sets of integers). To say that $m, n \in \mathbb{Z}$ are in the same partition of π, we write $m \approx_\pi n$. In particular, we use the following abstractions:

$$[] = \{\mathbb{Z}\} \qquad [n, m] = \{<n, \{n\}, \{n+1\}, \ldots, \{0\}, \ldots, \{m-1\}, \{m\}, >m\}$$

where $<n = \{n' \mid n' < n\}$, $>n = \{n' \mid n' > n\}$. Instead of $\{n\}$, we may write just n. Abstractions are refined by splitting abstract values: $[]$ to $[0, 0]$ by splitting $\mathbb{Z}$, $[n, m]$ to $[n-1, m]$ by splitting $<n$, or to $[n, m+1]$ by splitting $>m$.

We write $\Gamma \vdash M : T$ to indicate that term M with free identifiers in Γ has type T. The syntax of the language is defined by the standard typing rules for forming and applying functions ($\lambda\, x.M$, MN), augmented with rules for logic and arithmetic ($M \,\mathsf{op}\, N$), branching ($\mathsf{if}\ B\ \mathsf{then}\ M\ \mathsf{else}\ N$), iteration ($\mathsf{while}\ B\ \mathsf{do}\ M$), sequencing (M ; N, expressions with side effects are also allowed), assignment ($M := N$), de-referencing ($!M$), local variable declaration ($\mathsf{new} D\ x := M\ in\ N$), then "do nothing" command (skip), and a command which causes abnormal termination (abort). The typing rules can be found in [11].

The operational semantics is defined as a big-step reduction relation $M, s \Longrightarrow \mathcal{K}$, where M is a term whose free identifiers are assignable variables (i.e. of type var), s is a state which assigns data values to the free variables, and $\mathcal{K}$ is a final configuration. The final configuration can be either a pair V, s' with V a value (i.e. a language constant or an abstraction $\lambda\, x : T.M$) and s' a state, or a special error configuration $\mathcal{E}$.

The reduction rules are similar to those for IA, with two differences. First, whenever an integer value n with data type int_π participates in an operation, any other integer n' can be used nondeterministically so long as $n' \approx_\pi n$.

$$\frac{N_1, s_1 \Longrightarrow n_1, s_2 \qquad N_2, s_2 \Longrightarrow n_2, s}{N_1 \,\mathsf{op}\, N_2, s_1 \Longrightarrow n', s}\; n_i' \approx_{\pi_i} n_i,\ n' \approx_\pi n_1' \,\mathsf{op}\, n_2'$$

Assignment and de-referencing have similar non-deterministic rules.

Second, the abort program with any state reduces to $\mathcal{E}$, and a composite program reduces to $\mathcal{E}$ if a subprogram is reduced to $\mathcal{E}$.

$$\mathsf{abort}, s \Longrightarrow \mathcal{E} \qquad \frac{M, s \Longrightarrow \mathcal{E}}{M \,\mathsf{op}\, N, s \Longrightarrow \mathcal{E}}$$

A term M of type com is said to *terminate* in state s if there exists configuration $\mathcal{K}$ such that $\mathcal{K} = \mathcal{E}$, or $\mathcal{K} = \mathsf{skip}, s'$ for some state s' such that $M, s \Longrightarrow \mathcal{K}$. M is *safe* iff it cannot be reduced (from any state) to $\mathcal{E}$.

Term $\Gamma \vdash M : T$ *approximates* term $\Gamma \vdash N : T$, denoted by $\Gamma \vdash M \precsim N$ if and only if for all contexts $\mathcal{C}[-] : \mathsf{com}$, i.e. terms with a hole such that $\vdash \mathcal{C}[M] : \mathsf{com}$ and $\vdash \mathcal{C}[N] : \mathsf{com}$ are well formed closed terms of type com, if $\mathcal{C}[M]$ may terminate abnormally (resp. successfully) then $\mathcal{C}[N]$ also may terminate abnormally (resp. successfully). If two terms approximate each other they are considered safe-equivalent, denoted by $\Gamma \vdash M \cong N$.

A context is safe if it does not include occurrences of the abort command. A term is *safe* if for any safe context $\mathcal{C}_{\mathsf{safe}}[-]$ program $\mathcal{C}_{\mathsf{safe}}[M]$ is safe; otherwise the term is *unsafe*.

3 Game Semantics of AIA

In this section we review the fundamental concepts of game semantics for call-by-name programming languages [3].

Game semantics is denotational semantics which models types as *games*, computation as *plays* of a game, and programs as *strategies* for a game. In this approach, a kind of game is played by two participants. The first, Player, represents the program under consideration, while the second, Opponent, represents the environment (context) in which the program is used. The two take turns to make moves, each of which is either a question (a demand for information) or an answer (the supply of information).

We now proceed by presenting game semantics formally. A game is played in an *arena* which can be thought of as a playing area setting out basic rules and conventions for the game.

Definition 1. *An* arena *A is a triple $\langle M_A, \lambda_A, \vdash_A \rangle$ where:*

- *M_A is a countable set of* moves
- *$\lambda_A : M_A \to \{\mathsf{O}, \mathsf{P}\} \times \{\mathsf{Q}, \mathsf{A}\}$ is a labelling function which indicates whether a move is by* Opponent(O) *or* Player(P), *and whether it is a* question(Q) *or an* answer(A). *We write λ_A^{OP} for the composite of λ_A with the left projection, so that $\lambda_A^{\mathsf{OP}}(m) = \mathsf{O}$ if $\lambda_A(m) = \mathsf{OQ}$ or $\lambda_A(m) = \mathsf{OA}$. λ_A^{QA} is defined as λ_A followed by the right projection in a similar way. We denote by $\overline{\lambda}_A$ the labelling with O/P part reversed, i.e. $\overline{\lambda}_A^{\mathsf{OP}}(m) = \mathsf{O}$ iff $\lambda_A^{\mathsf{OP}}(m) = \mathsf{P}$.*
- *$\vdash_A$ is a binary relation between $M_A + \{*\}$ ($* \notin M_A$) and M_A, called* enabling *(if $m \vdash_A n$ we say that m enables move n), which satisfies the following conditions:*
  - *Initial moves (a move enabled by $*$ is called* initial*) are Opponent questions, and they are not enabled by any other moves besides $*$;*
  - *Answer moves can only be enabled by question moves;*
  - *Two participants always enable each others moves, never their own (i.e. an Opponent move can only enable a Player move and vice versa).*

A *justified sequence* in arena A is a finite sequence of moves of A together with a pointer from each non-initial move n to an earlier move m such that $m \vdash_A n$. We say that n is (explicitly) justified by m. A *legal play* is a justified sequence with some additional constraints: *alternation* (Opponent and Player moves strictly alternate), *well-bracketed* condition (when an answer is given, it is always to the most recent question which has not been answered), *visibility* condition (a move to be played depends upon a certain subsequence of the play so far, rather than on all of it), and *haltness* (no moves can follow an *abort* move). The set of all legal plays in arena A is denoted by L_A.

We say that n is *hereditarily justified* by a move m in a legal play s if there is a subsequence of s starting with m and ending in n such that every move is justified by the preceding move in it. We write $s\lceil m$ for the subsequence of s containing all moves hereditarily justified by m. We similarly define $s\lceil I$ for a set I of initial moves in s to be the subsequence of s consisting of all moves hereditarily justified by a move of I.

Definition 2. *A game is a structure* $A = \langle M_A, \lambda_A, \vdash_A, P_A\rangle$ *where* $\langle M_A, \lambda_A, \vdash_A\rangle$ *is an arena, and* P_A *is a non-empty, prefix-closed subset of* L_A*, called the* valid plays*, such that for* $s \in P_A$ *and* I *a set of initial moves of* s *we have* $s\lceil I \in P_A$.

Example 1. The simplest game is the empty game $I = \langle \emptyset, \emptyset, \emptyset, \epsilon\rangle$, where ϵ is the empty sequence. The base types are interpreted by the following games:

$$M_{[\![\mathsf{exp}D]\!]} = \{q, abort, n \mid n \in D\} \qquad M_{[\![\mathsf{com}]\!]} = \{run, done, abort\}$$
$$\lambda(q) = \mathsf{OQ},\ \lambda(n, abort) = \mathsf{PA} \qquad \lambda(run) = \mathsf{OQ},\ \lambda(done, abort) = \mathsf{PA}$$
$$* \vdash_{[\![\mathsf{exp}D]\!]} q;\ \ q \vdash_{[\![\mathsf{exp}D]\!]} n, abort \qquad * \vdash_{[\![\mathsf{com}]\!]} run;\ \ run \vdash_{[\![\mathsf{com}]\!]} done, abort$$
$$P_{[\![\mathsf{exp}D]\!]} = \{\epsilon, q, q \cdot abort, q \cdot n \mid n \in D\} \quad P_{[\![\mathsf{com}]\!]} = \{\epsilon, run, run \cdot done, run \cdot abort\}$$

$$M_{[\![\mathsf{var}D]\!]} = \{read, n, write(n), ok, abort \mid n \in D\}$$
$$\lambda_{[\![\mathsf{var}D]\!]}(read, write(n)) = \mathsf{OQ},\ \lambda_{[\![\mathsf{var}D]\!]}(n, ok, abort) = \mathsf{PA}$$
$$* \vdash_{[\![\mathsf{var}D]\!]} read, write(n);\ \ read \vdash_{[\![\mathsf{var}D]\!]} n, abort;\ \ write(n) \vdash_{[\![\mathsf{var}D]\!]} ok, abort$$
$$P_{[\![\mathsf{var}D]\!]} = \big\{\epsilon, read, write(n), read \cdot \{n, abort\}, write(n) \cdot \{ok, abort\} \mid n \in D\big\}$$

Thus in the game $[\![\mathsf{exp}D]\!]$, there is an initial move q (a question: "What is the value of the expression?") and corresponding to it a value from D or *abort* [1] (an answer to the question). In the game $[\![\mathsf{com}]\!]$, there is an initial move *run* to initiate a command, an answer move *done* to signal successful termination of a command, and *abort* to signal abnormal termination. In the game $[\![\mathsf{var}D]\!]$, for each $n \in D$ there is an initial move $write(n)$, representing an assignment. There are two possible responses to this move: *ok*, which signals successful completion of the assignment, and *abort*. For dereferencing, there is an initial move *read*, to which Player may respond with any element of D or *abort*. □

Given games A and B, we define new games $A \times B$ and $A \multimap B$ as follows:

$$M_{A\times B} = M_A + M_B \text{ (disjoint union)}$$
$$\lambda_{A\times B} = [\lambda_A, \lambda_B]$$
$$* \vdash_{A\times B} n \Leftrightarrow * \vdash_A n \vee * \vdash_B n$$
$$m \vdash_{A\times B} n \Leftrightarrow m \vdash_A n \vee m \vdash_B n$$
$$P_{A\times B} = P_A + P_B$$

$$M_{A\multimap B} = M_A + M_B$$
$$\lambda_{A\multimap B} = [\overline{\lambda}_A, \lambda_B]$$
$$* \vdash_{A\multimap B} n \Leftrightarrow * \vdash_B n$$
$$m \vdash_{A\multimap B} n \Leftrightarrow m \vdash_A n \vee m \vdash_B n \vee [* \vdash_B m \wedge * \vdash_A n]$$
$$P_{A\multimap B} = \{s \mid s \upharpoonright A \in P_A, s \upharpoonright B \in P_B\}$$

where $s \upharpoonright A$ is the subsequence of s consisting of moves from M_A. A valid play of $A \times B$ is either a play from A or a play from B. Valid plays of $A \multimap B$ are interleavings of single plays from A and B, and each such play has to begin in B and only Player can switch between the interleaved plays.

[1] Since expressions with side effect are allowed in AIA, evaluating an expression may indeed abort.

Given a game A, we define the game $!A$ as follows: $M_{!A} = M_A$, $\lambda_{!A} = \lambda_A$, $\vdash_{!A} = \vdash_A$ and $P_{!A} = \{s \in L_{!A} \mid \text{for each initial move m, s}\lceil \text{m} \in \text{P}_\text{A}\}$. Hence, legal plays of $!A$ are interleavings of a finite number of plays from P_A. Finally, the arena $A \Rightarrow B$ is defined as $!A \multimap B$. From now on, we work with (*well-opened*) games where initial moves can only happen at the first move.

Definition 3. *A strategy σ for a game A (written as $\sigma : A$) is a prefix-closed non-empty set of even-length plays in P_A.*

A strategy specifies what options Player has at any given point of a play, and it does not restrict the Opponent moves. We say that a play in σ is *complete* if either the opening question is answered, or the special move *abort* has been played.

Example 2. The only strategy for the empty game I is the empty strategy $\perp = \{\epsilon\}$. For the game $[\![\mathsf{expint}]\!]$, there is the empty strategy, and one strategy interpreting each natural number n, namely $\{\epsilon, q \cdot n\}$. A strategy which interprets the successor function $\mathsf{succ} : \mathbb{N} \to \mathbb{N}$ is as follows:

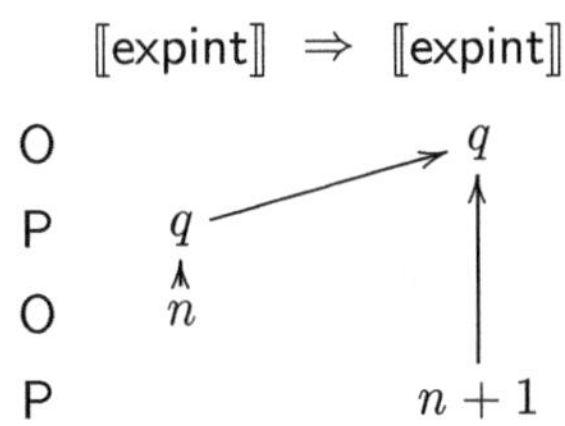

Here Opponent begins a play by asking for output of succ, and Player replies asking for input. When Opponent provides input n (which can be any number since a strategy does not restrict O moves), Player will give output $(n + 1)$. The above strategy can be represented as a regular language (pointers are disregarded) $\sum_{n \in \mathsf{int}} q \cdot q \cdot n \cdot (n + 1)$, where suitable closure operator is applied. □

The notion of composition of strategies is central to game semantics: just as small programs can be put together to form large ones, so strategies can be composed to form new strategies. Strategies compose in a way which is reminiscent of the two stage process of "parallel composition plus hiding" in CSP [22].

Given a strategy $\sigma : A \Rightarrow B$, we define its *promotion* $\sigma^\dagger : !A \multimap !B$, which can play several interleaved copies of σ, by:

$$\sigma^\dagger = \{s \in L_{!A \multimap !B} \mid \text{for all initial m, } s\lceil \text{m} \in \sigma\}$$

Let $\sigma : A \Rightarrow B$ and $\tau : B \Rightarrow C$ are two strategies. Then the composition $\sigma \fatsemi \tau : A \Rightarrow C$ is defined as $\sigma^\dagger; \tau$, where ; is linear composition of strategies.

Given strategies $\sigma : A \multimap B$ and $\tau : B \multimap C$, the linear composition $\sigma; \tau : A \multimap C$ is defined in the following way. For a sequence u of moves from games A, B, C with justification pointers, we define $u \upharpoonright B, C$ to be the subsequence of u consisting of all moves from B and C (if a pointer from one of these points to a move of A, delete that pointer). Similarly define $u \upharpoonright A, B$. We say that u is an *interaction sequence* of A, B, C if $u \upharpoonright A, B \in P_{A \multimap B}$ and $u \upharpoonright B, C \in P_{B \multimap C}$. The set of all such sequences is written as $int(A, B, C)$.

The parallel composition is defined by

$$\sigma \parallel \tau = \{u \in int(A, B, C) \mid u \upharpoonright A, B \in \sigma,\ u \upharpoonright B, C \in \tau\}$$

So $\sigma \parallel \tau$ consists of sequences generated by playing σ and τ in parallel, making them synchronize on moves in B.

Suppose $u \in int(A, B, C)$. Define $u \upharpoonright A, C$ to be the subsequence of u consisting of all moves from A and C, but where there was a pointer from a move $m_A \in M_A$ to an initial move $m \in I_B$ extend the pointer to the initial move in C which was pointed to from m. Thus, we complete the definition of composition by hiding the interaction between σ and τ in B.

$$\sigma;\ \tau = \{u \upharpoonright A, C \mid u \in \sigma \parallel \tau\}$$

The *identity strategy* $id_A : A \Rightarrow A$ for a game A is defined by

$$\{s \in P_{A \Rightarrow A} \mid \forall\, s' \sqsubseteq^{even} s.\ s' \upharpoonright A_l = s' \upharpoonright A_r\}$$

where we use the l and r tags to distinguish between the two occurrences of A and $s' \sqsubseteq^{even} s$ means that s' is an even-length prefix of s. So, in any identity strategy id_A, a move by Opponent in either occurrence of A is immediately copied by Player to the other occurrence.

A term $\Gamma \vdash M : T$, where $\Gamma = x_1 : T_1, \ldots, x_n : T_n$, is interpreted by a strategy $[\![\Gamma \vdash M : T]\!]$ for the game:

$$[\![\Gamma \vdash T]\!] = [\![T_1]\!] \times \ldots \times [\![T_n]\!] \Rightarrow [\![T]\!]$$

Language constants and constructs are interpreted by strategies and compound terms are modelled by composition of the strategies that interpret their constituents. For example, some of the strategies [16] are: $[\![\mathsf{n} : \mathsf{expint}]\!] = \{\epsilon, q \cdot n\}$, $[\![\mathsf{skip} : \mathsf{com}]\!] = \{\epsilon, run \cdot done\}$, $[\![\mathsf{abort} : \mathsf{com}]\!] = \{\epsilon, run \cdot abort\}$, free identifiers are interpreted by identity strategies, etc.

Using standard game-semantic techniques, it has been shown in [11] that this model is fully abstract for AIA.

Theorem 1 (Full abstraction). *For any terms $\Gamma \vdash M, N : T$, we have $\Gamma \vdash M \cong N$ iff $[\![\Gamma \vdash M : T]\!] = [\![\Gamma \vdash N : T]\!]$.*

We say that a play is *safe* if it does not terminate in *abort*, and a strategy if it consists only of safe plays; otherwise, we will call plays and strategies *unsafe*. From the full abstraction result, it follows that:

Corollary 1 (Safety). *$\Gamma \vdash M : T$ is safe iff $[\![\Gamma \vdash M : T]\!]$ is safe.*

This result ensures that, for any term, model-checking its strategy for safety (i.e. for unreachability of the *abort* move) is equivalent to proving the safety of a term.

In the rest of the paper, we work with the 2nd-order recursion-free fragment of AIA (i.e., AIA_2). The 2nd-order restriction means that the function types are restricted to $T ::= B \mid B \to T$. Also, without loss of generality, we only consider terms in β-normal form. For this language fragment, terms define strategies for which justification pointers are uniquely determined by plays, and they can be disregarded. Thus, it has been shown in [11] that:

Proposition 1. *For any finitely abstracted AIA_2 term $\Gamma \vdash M : T$, the strategy $[\![\Gamma \vdash M : T]\!]$ is a regular language.*

Example 3. Consider the term [2]

$$f : \mathsf{com} \to \mathsf{com} \;\vdash\; \mathsf{newint}\, x := 0\, \mathsf{in} \quad f(x := x+1)\,; \quad \mathsf{if}\,(x == 0)\,\mathsf{then\,abort;}$$

in which x is a local block-allocated variable and f is a non-local (safe) procedure. The procedure-call mechanism is by-name, so every call to the first argument of f increments x.

The strategy interpreting this term is shown in Fig 1, where dashed edges indicate moves of the Opponent and solid edges moves of the Player. Accepting states are designated by an interior circle. The states whose interior circles are filled in, correspond to complete plays in the strategy. We use subscripts to indicate the component of the context ($[\![\Gamma]\!]$), i.e. the free identifier, to which a move belongs to. For example, the subscript '$f, 1$' denotes that a move corresponds to the first argument of the procedure f. The model illustrates only the possible behaviors of this term: if the non-local procedure f does not evaluate its argument at all then the term terminates abnormally; otherwise if f calls its argument, one or more times, then the term terminates successfully. Notice that no references to the variable x appear in the model because it is locally defined and so not visible from the outside of the term. □

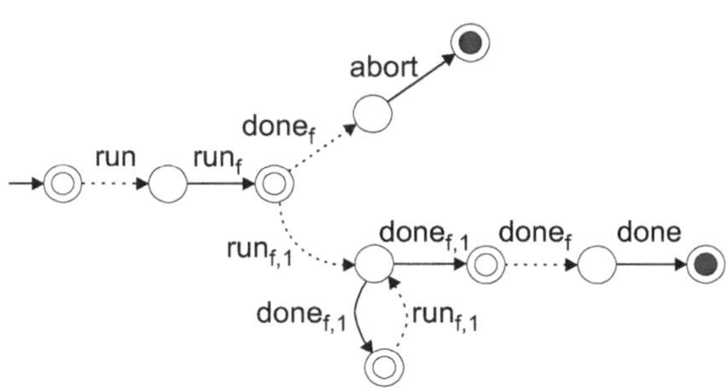

Fig. 1. A strategy as a finite automaton

Definition 4. *If σ and τ are strategies for a game A, we define a binary relation,* refinement, *$\leq$ as: $\sigma \leq \tau \Leftrightarrow \sigma \subseteq \tau$*

[2] This is actually an IA_2 term since no data-abstractions are applied to x.

4 The Learning Algorithm

Central to our compositional verification procedure is an algorithm for learning strategies, which can be represented as regular languages (see Proposition 1). The algorithm is an adaptation of the L^* algorithm introduced by Angluin [5] which learns an unknown regular language. Since L^* needs to learn strategies, the adaptation will consider only non-empty prefix-closed sets of even-length sequences (words) in which Opponent and Player moves alternate, thus achieving greater efficiency.

Let $A = \langle M_A, \lambda_A, \vdash_A, P_A \rangle$ be a game. Let $\mathsf{O}^A = \{m \in M_A \mid \lambda_A^{\mathsf{OP}}(m) = \mathsf{O}\}$ and $\mathsf{P}^A = \{m \in M_A \mid \lambda_A^{\mathsf{OP}}(m) = \mathsf{P}\}$ denote the sets of *Opponent* and *Player* moves in A, respectively. Since λ_A is a total function, $\{\mathsf{O}^A, \mathsf{P}^A\}$ is a partition of M_A. Given that the sequences from a strategy for a game A are valid and satisfy the alternation condition, it follows that they are sequences from $(\mathsf{O}^A\mathsf{P}^A)^*$.

Let σ be an unknown strategy for a game A. L^* iteratively learns the structure of σ using assistance from a *Teacher* who can answer two kinds of questions about σ:

Membership query. Given a sequence s from $(\mathsf{O}^A\mathsf{P}^A)^*$, the Teacher answers *true* if $s \in \sigma$, and *false* otherwise.

Equivalence query. Given a DFA (Deterministic Finite Automaton) D, the Teacher replies that D is either correct, when $\mathcal{L}(D) = \sigma$, or incorrect, and in the latter case gives a counterexample which is a sequence in the symmetric difference of $\mathcal{L}(D)$ and σ.

The basic data structure of the L^* algorithm is a two-dimensional table, called observation table (S, E, T), which keeps information about a finite collection of sequences over $(\mathsf{O}^A\mathsf{P}^A)^*$, classified as members or non-members of σ. S is a *prefix-closed* set of even-length sequences, $E \subseteq (\mathsf{O}^A\mathsf{P}^A)^*$ is a *suffix-closed* set of even-length sequences, and T is a function mapping $(S \cup S \cdot \mathsf{O}^A\mathsf{P}^A) \cdot E \to \{\mathit{true}, \mathit{false}\}$, such that:

$$\forall\, s \in S \cup S \cdot \mathsf{O}^A\mathsf{P}^A . \forall\, e \in E : T(s, e) = \mathit{true} \Leftrightarrow s \cdot e \in \sigma$$

The rows of the table are the elements of $(S \cup S \cdot \mathsf{O}^A\mathsf{P}^A)$, while the columns are the elements of E. Finally T denotes the table entries.

Let us define a function $\mathit{row}(s)$ for any $s \in S \cup S \cdot \mathsf{O}^A\mathsf{P}^A$ as follows:

$$\forall\, e \in E : \mathit{row}(s)(e) = T(s, e)$$

A table is *closed* if for each $s \cdot m_O m_P \in S \cdot \mathsf{O}^A\mathsf{P}^A$ such that $T(s, \epsilon) = \mathit{true}$, there is some $s' \in S$ such that $\mathit{row}(s') = \mathit{row}(s \cdot m_O m_P)$. A table is *consistent* if for each $s, s' \in S$ such that $\mathit{row}(s) = \mathit{row}(s')$, either $T(s, \epsilon) = T(s', \epsilon) = \mathit{false}$, or for each $m_O m_P \in \mathsf{O}^A\mathsf{P}^A$, we have that $\mathit{row}(s \cdot m_O m_P) = \mathit{row}(s' \cdot m_O m_P)$.

We define an equivalence relation $\equiv$ over sequences in $S \cup S \cdot \mathsf{O}^A\mathsf{P}^A$ such that $s \equiv s'$ iff $\mathit{row}(s) = \mathit{row}(s')$. Denote by $[s]$ the equivalence class which includes s. Given a closed and consistent table (S, E, T), L^* constructs a candidate DFA

$D = (Q, q_0, \mathsf{O}^A\mathsf{P}^A, \delta)$ as follows: $Q = \{[s] \mid s \in S, T(s,\epsilon) = true\}, q_0 = [\epsilon]$, and for every $s \in S$ and $m_O m_P \in \mathsf{O}^A\mathsf{P}^A$, the transition from $[s]$ on input $m_O m_P$ is enabled iff $T(s \cdot m_O m_P, \epsilon) = true$ and then $\delta([s], m_O m_P) = [s \cdot m_O m_P]$. The facts that the table is closed and consistent guarantee that the transition relation is well-defined. All states in the automaton are accepting, since the language we learn is prefix closed. Note that every transition in this automaton is labelled by two-letters sequence: an Opponent and a Player move.

let $L^*(S,E)$ **be**
  repeat :
    Update T using queries
    while (S,E,T) is not consistent **or** not closed **do**
      if (S,E,T) is not consistant **then**
        find $s \in S,\ m_O m_P \in \mathsf{O}^A\mathsf{P}^A,\ e \in E$:
          $row(s) = row(s')$ and $T(s \cdot m_O m_P, e) \neq T(s' \cdot m_O m_P, e)$
        $E = E \cup \{m_O m_P \cdot e\}$
        Update T using queries
      if (S,E,T) is not closed **then**
        find $s \in S,\ m_O m_P \in \mathsf{O}^A\mathsf{P}^A$
          $s \cdot m_O m_P \notin [t]$, for all $t \in S$
        $S = S \cup \{s \cdot m_O m_P\}$
        Update T using queries
    $D =$ MakeAutomaton(S,E,T)
    if D is correct **then**
      return D
    else
      let c be reported counterexample
      foreach $(s \in$ even_prefix(c) and $s \notin S)$ $S = S \cup \{s\}$

Fig. 2. L^* algorithm

Fig. 2 contains the L^* algorithm. Each iteration of this algorithm starts with either a table with $S = E = \{\epsilon\}$, or a table which was prepared in the previous step. Then T is updated using membership queries until the table is consistent and closed. Next a candidate automaton D is proposed and an equivalence query with D is made. If the answer for the equivalence query is *true*, L^* terminates and returns the automaton D. Otherwise, L^* analyzes the counterexample c reported by the Teacher and adds all even-length prefixes of c to S. Then, a new iteration is started.

L^* is guaranteed to construct a minimal DFA equivalent to the unknown strategy using at most $n-1$ equivalence queries where n is the number of states in the minimal DFA, and in time polynomial in n and the length of the longest counterexample provided by the Teacher.

Each new call to L^* starts normally with $S = E = \{\epsilon\}$. But in cases where a previously learned candidate exists, we want to start the algorithm by reusing the information proposed in the previous table. Thus with this *dynamic version* of L^*, we try to speed up the learning by reusing the previously inferred sets S and E for strategy σ, to learn a new modified strategy σ' which differs slightly from σ. We apply this optimisation using the fact that if L^* starts with any non-empty valid table (i.e. valid function T) then it will terminate with a correct result [7]. A table is said to be valid if the answers to the membership queries for all sequences in the table are correct with respect to the unknown language which is learned by L^*.

We can apply some further optimizations to the L^* algorithm specific for the languages we learn. Since the sequences from an strategy are valid plays, we test for membership only valid plays. All other sequences are certainly not in the strategy, and they are marked as *false* without any checks. Then, a prefix closed language has the property that extensions of rejected sequences are rejected, i.e., if $s \notin \sigma$, then no extension of s is in σ. Therefore, since the language we learn is prefix closed, before any membership query $s \in \sigma$, we first test whether it is an extension of a sequence already observed to be rejected. If so, we add the result immediately to the table.

5 Compositional Verification

In this section we describe in detail the compositional verification procedure which combines assume-guarantee reasoning and abstraction refinement.

5.1 Overview

We first examine how the game semantics of β-normal AIA_2 terms $\Gamma \vdash M : B$ is obtained. Since terms are interpreted recursively over the typing rules, consider a derivation tree of such a term $\Gamma \vdash M : B$. At the leaves, we have base subterms, which are language constants and free identifiers, and are interpreted by appropriate constant and identity strategies. At each node, there is a subterm obtained by a language construct c from some children subterms $M_1, \ldots, M_n$. Then, $\mathsf{c}(M_1, \ldots, M_n)$ is interpreted by composing the interpretations of the subterms and of the construct σ_{c}:

$$[\![\mathsf{c}(M_1, \ldots, M_n)]\!] = ([\![M_1]\!], \ldots, [\![M_n]\!]) \fatsemi \sigma_{\mathsf{c}} = ([\![M_1]\!]^{\dagger}, \ldots, [\![M_n]\!]^{\dagger})\ ;\ \sigma_{\mathsf{c}}$$

We also note that $\dagger$ is applied only to strategies σ for games of the form $[\![\Gamma]\!] \Rightarrow [\![B']\!]$, where B' are base types. The games $[\![B']\!]$ are flat, i.e. all their questions are initial and Player moves can only be answers. So $\sigma^{\dagger}$ consists of iterated plays of σ, such that a new play of σ can be started only when the previous one is completed. Basically, $\sigma^{\dagger}$ contains plays of the form $s_1 \ldots s_k s_{k+1}$ where each s_i is a play of σ and $s_1, \ldots, s_k$ are complete. That is a regular language operation.

Now, for any strategies $\sigma_1, \ldots, \sigma_n$ and τ, we have $\big((\sigma_1^{\dagger}, \ldots, \sigma_n^{\dagger})\ ;\ \tau\big)^{\dagger} = (\sigma_1^{\dagger}, \ldots, \sigma_n^{\dagger})\ ;\ \tau^{\dagger}$ [3]. By thus distributing $\dagger$ over ; , we conclude that the game semantics of $\Gamma \vdash M : B$ can be obtained by repeatedly applying ; to promoted strategies for base subterms and language constructs. In other words, † does not need to be applied to any composite strategy.

By the same argument, if $\Gamma' \vdash N : B'$ is a subterm of $\Gamma \vdash M : B$, the game semantics of $\Gamma \vdash M : B$ is given by:

$$[\![\Gamma \vdash M[N] : B]\!] = [\![\Gamma \vdash M[-] : B]\!]([\![\Gamma' \vdash N : B']\!]^{\dagger})$$

where $[\![\Gamma \vdash M[-] : B]\!](\sigma)$ is an operator on regular languages, which is obtained from the game semantic definitions for $\Gamma \vdash M : B$ by replacing the promoted interpretation of the subterm $\Gamma' \vdash N : B'$ by σ, and in which only ; is applied to languages obtained from σ.

To check safety of $[\![\Gamma \vdash M[N] : B]\!]$, we use the concept of assume-guarantee (AG) reasoning. We define an *assumption* for a game A as a prefix-closed non-empty set of even-length sequences from $(\mathsf{O}^A\mathsf{P}^A)^*$.

Let σ be an assumption for $[\![\Gamma']\!] \Rightarrow ![\![B']\!]$. We use the following AG rule:

$$\frac{\begin{array}{l}[\![\Gamma \vdash M[-] : B]\!](\sigma) \ \text{ is SAFE} \\ [\![\Gamma' \vdash N : B']\!]^{\dagger} \ \leq \sigma\end{array}}{[\![\Gamma \vdash M[N] : B]\!] \ \text{ is SAFE}}$$

The rule states that if there is an assumption σ for $[\![\Gamma']\!] \Rightarrow ![\![B']\!]$, such that $[\![\Gamma \vdash M[-] : B]\!](\sigma)$ is safe and σ is an abstraction of $[\![\Gamma' \vdash N : B']\!]^{\dagger}$, then $[\![\Gamma \vdash M[N] : B]\!]$ is safe. Our goal is to construct such an assumption σ.

Theorem 2. *The AG rule is sound and complete.*

Proof. By monotonicity of composition of strategies with respect to the $\leq$ ordering, we have that if $\sigma \leq \sigma'$ then $[\![\Gamma \vdash M[-] : B]\!](\sigma) \leq [\![\Gamma \vdash M[-] : B]\!](\sigma')$. To establish soundness, we use the fact that if σ' is safe and $\sigma \leq \sigma'$ then σ is also safe. Completeness follows by taking $\sigma = [\![\Gamma' \vdash N : B']\!]^{\dagger}$. □

For any operator $[\![\Gamma \vdash M[-] : B]\!]$, where the hole $-$ is in the place of a subterm of type $\Gamma' \vdash B'$, we define the *weakest safe strategy* $\sigma_W : [\![\Gamma']\!] \Rightarrow ![\![B']\!]$ as follows. Given an even-length play s of $[\![\Gamma']\!] \Rightarrow ![\![B']\!]$, let τ_s be the strategy consisting of s and all its even-length prefixes. Let σ_W consist of all s such that $[\![\Gamma \vdash M[-] : B]\!](\tau_s)$ is safe.

Proposition 2. *For any AIA_2 term with a hole $\Gamma \vdash M[-] : B$, σ_W is a regular language.*

By the definitions of $[\![\Gamma \vdash M[-] : B]\!]$ and ; , we have that, for any strategy $\sigma : [\![\Gamma']\!] \Rightarrow ![\![B']\!]$,

$$[\![\Gamma \vdash M[-] : B]\!](\sigma) = \bigcup \{[\![\Gamma \vdash M[-] : B]\!](\tau_s) \mid s \in \sigma\}$$

Hence, $[\![\Gamma \vdash M[-] : B]\!](\sigma)$ is safe if and only $\sigma \leq \sigma_W$. For this strategy σ_W, the AG rule is guaranteed to return conclusive results: either the resulting term is safe or unsafe, and in the latter case a counterexample is reported. We use the L^* algorithm to learn σ_W.

The verification procedure **CompVer** which uses the AG rule is presented in Fig. 3. Given two terms $\Gamma \vdash M[-] : B$ and $\Gamma' \vdash N : B'$, it checks safety of $\Gamma \vdash M[N] : B$. The procedure uses an **AGCheck** algorithm, and iteratively performs the following steps:

1. Let $[\![\Gamma_1 \vdash M_1[-] : B_1]\!]$ and $[\![\Gamma_1' \vdash N_1 : B_1']\!]$ be obtained by data abstraction, and $S_1^1 = E_1^1 = \{\epsilon\}$.
2. Apply **AGCheck** on $[\![\Gamma_i \vdash M_i[-] : B_i]\!]$ and $[\![\Gamma_i' \vdash N_i : B_i']\!]$, using S_i^1 and E_i^1. If the result is *true*, then terminate with answer SAFE. Otherwise, a counterexample c is returned as well as updated values of S_i^k and E_i^k.
3. If c is a nondeterministic (i.e. spurious) play, obtain $[\![\Gamma_{i+1} \vdash M_{i+1}[-] : B_{i+1}]\!]$ and $[\![\Gamma_{i+1}' \vdash N_{i+1} : B_{i+1}']\!]$ by refining the abstractions in the current terms which were involved in causing the nondeterminism in c. Set $S_{i+1}^1 = S_i^k$ and $E_{i+1}^1 = E_i^k$ [3], and repeat from 2.
4. Otherwise, c is deterministic (i.e. genuine) and the procedure terminates with answer UNSAFE.

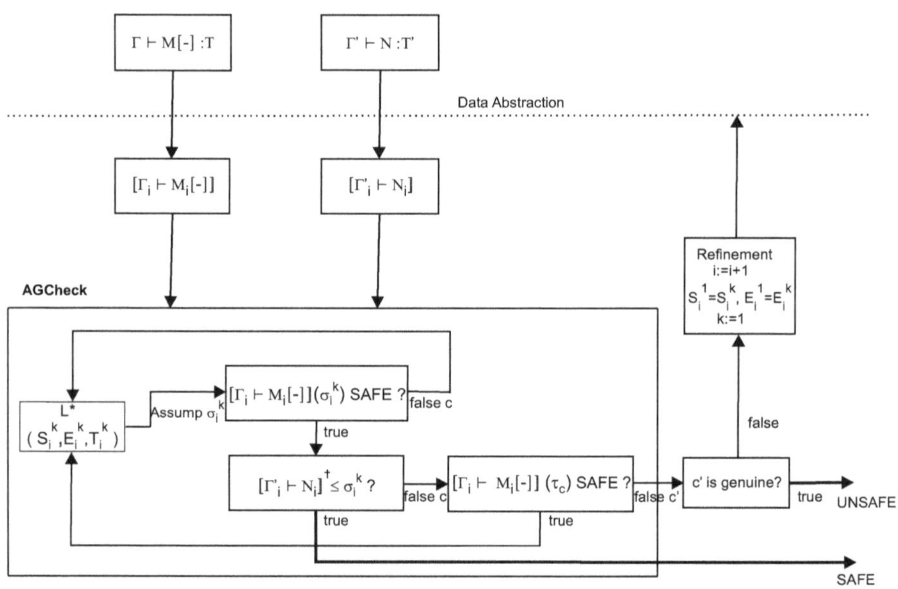

Fig. 3. The compositional verification procedure **CompVer**

We say that a play is *nondeterministic* if it contains a special marker move *nd*, which identifies points in plays at which abstraction gives rise to nondeterminism. This happens when an arithmetic/logic operation produces more than one result.

[3] If some sequences in S_i^k (E_i^k) contain abstract values whose abstractions are refined, we replace them with sequences which are compatible with newly refined abstractions.

We continue by describing the **AGCheck** algorithm. Details of the data abstraction procedure and the abstraction refinement process are beyond the scope of this paper and can be found in [11].

5.2 Assume-Guarantee Algorithm

The **AGCheck** algorithm takes as inputs $[\![\Gamma_i \vdash M_i[-] : B_i]\!]$ and $[\![\Gamma'_i \vdash N_i : B'_i]\!]$ as well as S_i^1 and E_i^1, and returns as answer *true* or a counterexample. **AGCheck** is actually the L^* algorithm given in Fig. 2, where the membership and equivalence queries are answered using model checking. **AGCheck** proceeds as follows:

1. Generate a candidate assumption σ_i^k using L^*.
2. If $[\![\Gamma_i \vdash M_i[-] : B_i]\!](\sigma_i^k)$ is not safe, then return a counterexample to the L^* algorithm, set $k := k + 1$ and repeat from 1.
3. If $[\![\Gamma'_i \vdash N_i : B'_i]\!]^\dagger \leq \sigma_i^k$ is true, terminate with answer *true*.
4. Otherwise, among the even-length counterexamples from $[\![\Gamma'_i \vdash N_i : B'_i]\!]^\dagger$, report a deterministic one, c. If such one does not exist, then report a nondeterministic one, c.
5. Generate a strategy τ_c from the sequence c which contains c and all its even-length prefixes. If $[\![\Gamma_i \vdash M_i[-] : B_i]\!](\tau_c)$ is safe, then report c to L^*, set $k := k + 1$ and repeat from 1.
6 Otherwise, terminate reporting a deterministic counterexample c'. If such one does not exist, report a nondeterministic play c'.

If in Step 2 a counterexample c is returned to L^*, then $c \in \sigma_i^k \backslash \sigma_W$, i.e. the current assumption σ_i^k is too weak and it has to be strengthened by removing some sequences from it. Similarly, if in Step 5 a counterexample c is reported to L^*, then $c \in \sigma_W \backslash \sigma_i^k$, i.e. the current σ_i^k must be weakened by adding some sequences.

In the above procedure, L^* iteratively learns the strategy σ_W, but the procedure terminates as soon as conclusive results are obtained. This is often before the weakest safe strategy σ_W is computed by L^*. The Teacher which interacts with L^* is implemented using model checking. To answer a membership query for a sequence s, the Teacher first builds a strategy $\tau_s = \{s' \mid s' \sqsubseteq^{\text{even}} s\}$. The Teacher then model checks $[\![\Gamma \vdash M[-]]\!](\tau_s)$ for safety. If true is returned, then $s \in \sigma_W$ and the Teacher answers *true*, otherwise it answers *false*. An equivalence query is answered by model-checking two premises of the AG rule in Steps 2 and 3. If both checks succeed, then the answer is *true*, otherwise either a counterexample is reported to L^* or an unsafe counterexample is found.

Theorem 3. *Given* $[\![\Gamma_i \vdash M_i[-] : B_i]\!]$ *and* $[\![\Gamma'_i \vdash N_i : B'_i]\!]$, *the* **AGCheck** *algorithm terminates with either true or an unsafe play from* $[\![\Gamma_i \vdash M_i[N_i] : B_i]\!]$.

Proof. The algorithm returns true when both premises of the AG rule return true, and therefore correctness is guaranteed by the AG rule. An unsafe play is returned when there is a sequence s of $([\![\Gamma'_i \vdash N_i]\!])^\dagger$ which, when applied to $[\![\Gamma_i \vdash M_i[-]]\!]$ produces an unsafe play, which implies that $[\![\Gamma_i \vdash M_i[N_i] : B_i]\!]$ is not safe.

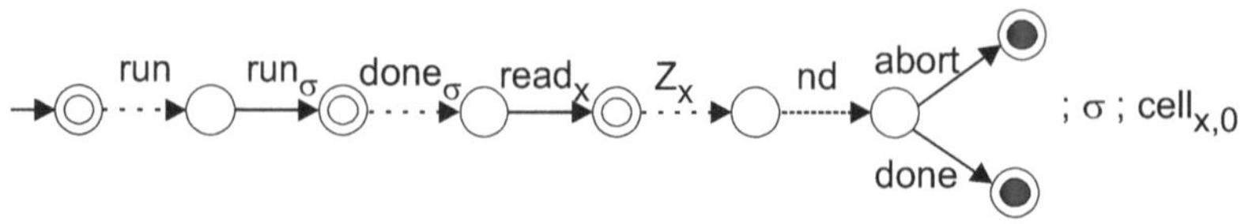

(a)

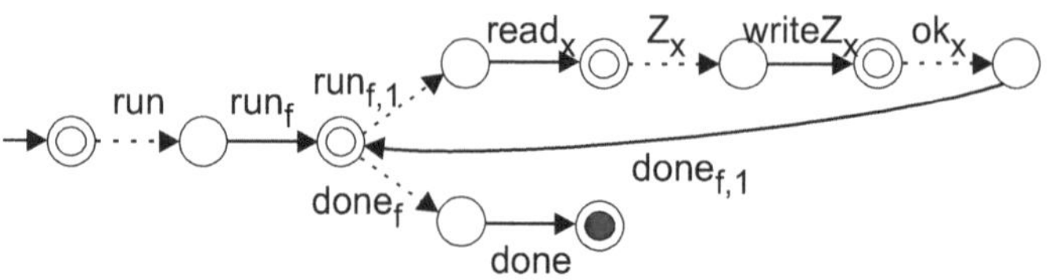

(b)

Fig. 4. Strategies at AR iteration 1: (a) $[\![f \vdash M[-]]\!](\sigma)$ (b) $[\![f, x \vdash f(x := x + 1)]\!]$

Termination of **AGCheck** algorithm is implied by the termination of the L^* algorithm. At any iteration, **AGCheck** either terminates or provides a counterexample to L^*. Thus, L^* will eventually produce σ_W at some iteration and the algorithm will return conclusive results and terminate. □

Theorem 4. *If* **CompVer** *terminates, its answer is correct.*

Proof. This follows from the correctness of the abstraction refinement procedure, which was shown in [11], and Theorem 3. □

5.3 Example

Consider the term

$$f : \mathsf{com} \rightarrow \mathsf{com} \vdash \mathsf{newint}\, x := 0 \,\mathsf{in}\quad f(x := x + 1)\,;\quad \mathsf{if}\ (x == 0)\ \mathsf{then\ abort};$$

in which x is a local variable, and f is a non-local (safe) function. We want to check whether this term is safe from terminating abnormally for all safe instantiations of f. The program is not safe if function f does not use its argument at all.

We start with applying the coarsest abstraction $[\,]$ to x, which means that x can only have the value $\mathbb{Z}$ (i.e. a nondeterministic choice over all integers).

Let the arbitrary subterm N be $f(x := x + 1)$. The model of the whole term is obtained by composing the model for the scope of variable declaration with the strategy $\mathsf{cell}_{x,0}$, which is used for remembering the initial (0) or the most recently written value into the variable x. This strategy ensures "good variable" behavior of x.

In Fig. 4 are shown the models $[\![f \vdash M[-]]\!](\sigma)$ and $[\![f, x \vdash f(x := x + 1)]\!]$ at the first Abstraction Refinement iteration. The *nd* move [4] in the first strategy

[4] It is neither Opponent nor Player, but a special marker move.

	T_1^1	E_1^1
		ϵ
S_1^1	ϵ	*true*
	$run \cdot done$	*false*
$S_1 \cdot \mathsf{O^A P^A}$	$run \cdot done$	*false*
	$run \cdot read_x$	*true*
	$run \cdot writeZ_x$	*true*
	$run \cdot run_f$	*true*

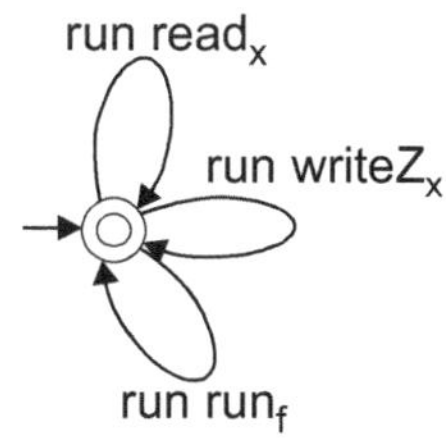

Fig. 5. Observation table and assumption at AR iteration 1

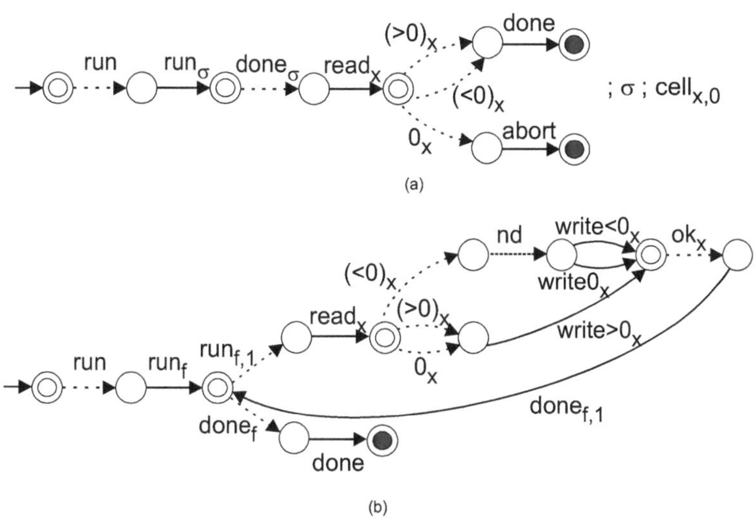

Fig. 6. Strategies at AR iteration 2: (a) $[\![f \vdash M[-]]\!](\sigma)$ (b) $[\![f, x \vdash f(x := x+1)]\!]$

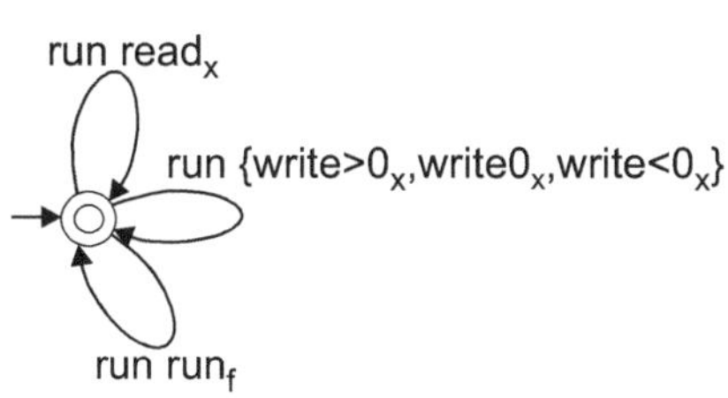

Fig. 7. Assumption at AR iteration 2

marks that nondeterminism has occurred due to abstraction. In this case, the guard of 'if' command has been evaluated nondeterministically to *true* or *false*, since the value of x might be any integer.

At each iteration, L^* updates its observation table and constructs a candidate assumption whenever the table becomes consistent and closed. The first such table produced and its associated assumption are given in Fig. 5. Note that in observation tables we list only sequences from $S \cdot \mathsf{O}^{\mathsf{A}}\mathsf{P}^{\mathsf{A}}$ which are valid plays, and all other sequences are *false* by default. The equivalence query is then asked. The second AG premise fails and the Teacher returns a negative answer with a counterexample $s = \langle run \cdot run_f \cdot done_f \cdot done \rangle$, which is not safe when applied to $[\![f \vdash M[-]]\!]$. Thus, **AGCheck** reports $s' = \langle run \cdot run_f \cdot done_f \cdot nd \cdot abort \rangle$. Since this play is nondeterministic, our procedure decides to refine abstractions that caused the nondeterminism in s' and to continue. In this case, the abstraction of x is refined to $[0, 0]$, which contains three possible values: < 0, 0 and > 0.

At the second abstraction refinement iteration, the strategies $[\![f \vdash M[-]]\!](\sigma)$ and $[\![f, x \vdash f(x := x + 1)]\!]$ are given in Fig. 6.

Since we use a dynamic version of L^*, it starts with an observation table where S_2^1 and E_2^1 are the same as in the previous table T_1^1. The next candidate assumption is shown in Fig. 7. The second AG rule premise fails giving $s = \langle run \cdot run_f \cdot done_f \cdot done \rangle$. Now, **AGCheck** reports a genuine counterexample $s' = \langle run \cdot run_f \cdot done_f \cdot abort \rangle$, and the procedure terminates informing that the input term is not safe.

6 Implementation

We implemented the compositional verification procedure in the GameChecker tool [12]. GameChecker compiles an abstracted open program into a process in the CSP process algebra (e.g. [22]), whose finite traces set represents the game-semantic model of the program. Membership and equivalence queries are answered using the FDR refinement checker [13]. If a counterexample is reported by the procedure, GameChecker is used to analyse the counterexample and do abstraction refinement.

Consider the following implementation of a stack of maximum size n (a meta variable). After implementing the stack by a sequence of local declarations, we export the functions $push(x)$ and pop by calling $ANALYSE$ with arguments $push(p)$ and pop. In effect, the model contains all interleavings of calls to $push(p)$ and pop, corresponding to all possible behaviours of the non-local expression p and non-local function $ANALYSE$.

$\mathsf{empty} : \mathsf{com}, \mathsf{overflow} : \mathsf{com}, p : \mathsf{exp\,int},$
$ANALYSE(\mathsf{com}, \mathsf{exp\,int}) : \mathsf{com} \vdash$
$\mathsf{new\,int}\, buffer[n] := 0 \;\mathsf{in}\; \mathsf{new\,int}\, top := 0 \;\mathsf{in}$
$\mathsf{let\,com}\, push(\mathsf{int}\, x)\, \{$
$\quad \mathsf{if}\ (top == n)\ \mathsf{then\ overflow\ else}\ \{buffer[top] := x;\ \ top := top + 1\}\}\ \mathsf{in}$
$\mathsf{let\,exp\,int}\, pop\, \{$
$\quad \mathsf{if}\ (top == 0)\ \mathsf{then\ empty\ else}\ \{top := top - 1;\ \ \mathsf{return}\ buffer[top + 1]\}\}\ \mathsf{in}$
$ANALYSE(push(p), pop)$

Table 1. Experimental results for checking a stack implementation

	empty		overflow	
n	Direct	AG	Direct	AG
3	271	107	286	147
10	306	135	937	441
15	331	155	1462	651
25	381	195	2662	1071

By replacing the free identifier empty (resp. overflow) with the abort command, we can check the safety property that there are no reads from empty stacks (resp. writes to full stacks). Both errors are present for any n. For the 'empty' error, a genuine counterexample is reported after refining the abstraction of *top* to $[0, 0]$. For the 'overflow' error, the abstraction is $[0, n]$. The counterexamples correspond to a single call of the *pop* method (resp. $n + 1$ consecutive calls of the *push* method) after which abort is executed. We applied the AG procedure by learning an appropriate assumption for the *push* (resp. *pop*) method. In both cases, we obtain conclusive assumptions with 0 states, since counterexamples are reported for all valid plays of the subterms we learn.

Table 1 contains the experimental results for checking the two properties by using the AG procedure and the direct verification procedure without AG reasoning [12]. We list the size of the largest generated transition system in each case for different values of n.

7 Conclusion

This paper presents a fully compositional approach for verifying safety properties of open programs. Game semantics is used for compositional modelling of programs and an automated assume-guarantee procedure with learning is used for compositional verification.

Important topics for future work are extending data abstractions to arbitrary predicates, dealing with concurrent programs, and using assume-guarantee reasoning for verifying liveness properties.

References

1. S. Abramsky, D. R. Ghica, A. S. Murawski, and C.-H. L. Ong. Applying Game Semantics to Compositional Software Modeling and Verification. In Proceedings of *TACAS*, LNCS **2988**, (2004), 421–435.
2. S. Abramsky, R. Jagadeesan, and P. Malacaria. Full Abstraction for PCF. *Information and Computation*, **163(2)**, (2000).
3. S. Abramsky and G. McCusker. Linearity, sharing and state: a fully abstract game semantics for Idealized Algol with active expressions. In P.W.O'Hearn and R.D.Tennent, editors, *Algol-like languages*. (Birkhaüser, 1997).
4. R. Alur, P. Madhusudan, and W. Nam. Symbolic Compositional Verification by Learning Assumptions. In Proceedings of *CAV*, LNCS **3576**, (2005), 548–562.

5. D. Angluin. Learning Regular Sets from Queries and Counterexamples. *Information and Computation*, **75(2)**, (1987), 87–106.
6. T. Ball and S. K. Rajamani. Automatically Validating Temporal Safety Properties of Interfaces. In Proceedings of *SPIN*, LNCS **2057**, (2001), 103–122.
7. S. Chaki, E. Clarke, N. Sharygina, and N. Sinha. Dynamic Component Substiutability Analysis. In Proceedings of *FM*, LNCS **3582**, (2005), 512–528.
8. E.M. Clarke, O. Grumberg and D. Peled, *Model Checking*. (MIT Press, 2000).
9. J. M. Cobleigh, D. Giannakopoulou, and C. S. Pasareanu. Learning Assumptions for Compositional Verification. In Proceedings of *TACAS*, LNCS **2619**, (2003), 331–346.
10. A. Dimovski and R. Lazic. CSP Representation of Game Semantics for Second-Order Idealized Algol. In Proceedings of *ICFEM*, LNCS **3308**, (2004), 146–161.
11. A. Dimovski, D. R. Ghica, and R. Lazic. Data-Abstraction Refinement: A Game Semantic Approach. In Proceedings of *SAS*, LNCS **3672**, (2005), 102–117.
12. A. Dimovski, D. R. Ghica, and R. Lazic. A Counterexample-Guided Refinement Tool for Open Procedural Programs. In Proceedings of *SPIN*, LNCS **3925**, (2006).
13. Formal Systems (Europe) Ltd (http://www.fsel.com), *Failures-Divergence Refinement: FDR2 Manual*, 2000.
14. D. R. Ghica and G. McCusker. The Regular-Language Semantics of Second-order Idealized Algol. Theoretical Computer Science **309** (1–3), (2003), 469–502.
15. A. Groce, D. Peled, and M. Yannakakis. Adaptive Model Checking. In Proceedings of *TACAS*, LNCS **2280**, (2002), 357–370.
16. R. Harmer. Games and Full Abstraction for Nondeterministic Languages. PhD thesis, Imperial College, 1999.
17. T. A. Henzinger, R. Jhala, R. Majumdar, and G. Sutre. Software Verification with BLAST. In Proceedings of *SPIN*, LNCS **2648**, (2003), 235–239.
18. J. M. E. Hyland and C.-H. L. Ong. On Full Abstraction for PCF: I, II, and III. *Information and Computation* **163**, (2000), 285–400.
19. J. Laird. A Fully Abstract Game Semantics of Local Exceptions. In Proceedings of *LICS*, (2001), 105–114.
20. A. Pnueli. In Transition from Global to Modular Temporal Reasoning about Programs. *Logic and Models of Concurrent Systems* **13**, (1984), 123–144.
21. R.L. Rivest and R.E. Schapire. Inference of finite automata using homing sequences. *Information and Computation*, **103(2)**, (1993), 299–347.
22. A. W. Roscoe. *Theory and Practice of Concurrency*. (Prentice-Hall, 1998).

Optimized Execution of Deterministic Blocks in Java PathFinder

Marcelo d'Amorim, Ahmed Sobeih, and Darko Marinov

Department of Computer Science
University of Illinois at Urbana-Champaign
201 N. Goodwin Ave., Urbana IL, 61801 USA
{damorim, sobeih, marinov}@cs.uiuc.edu

Abstract. Java PathFinder (JPF) is an explicit-state model checker for Java programs. It explores all executions that a given program can have due to different thread interleavings and nondeterministic choices. JPF implements a backtracking Java Virtual Machine (JVM) that executes Java bytecodes using a *special representation* of JVM states. This special representation enables JPF to quickly store, restore, and compare states; it is crucial for making the overall state exploration efficient. However, this special representation creates overhead for each execution, even execution of *deterministic blocks* that have no thread interleavings or nondeterministic choices.

We propose *mixed execution*, a technique that reduces execution time of deterministic blocks in JPF. JPF is written in Java as a special JVM that runs on top of a regular, host JVM. Mixed execution works by translating the state between the special JPF representation and the host JVM representation. We also present *lazy translation*, an optimization that speeds up mixed execution by translating only the parts of the state that a specific execution dynamically depends on. We evaluate mixed execution on six programs that use JPF for generating tests for data structures and on one case study for verifying a network protocol. The results show that mixed execution can improve the overall time for state exploration up to 36.98%, while improving the execution time of deterministic blocks up to 69.15%. Although we present mixed execution in the context of JPF and Java, it generalizes to any model checker that uses a special state representation.

1 Introduction

Software model checking [3, 6, 12, 27, 19, 32] is a promising approach for increasing the reliability of programs. The goal of model checking is to explore the program's state space to find property violations or confirm absence of violations. While "state-space explosion" is the key issue in model checking, time efficiency is also an important problem. Several recent model checking tools—including AsmLT [12], BogorVM [27], JPF [19], and SpecExplorer [32]—make the trade-off to speed up the overall state exploration by slowing down a straight-line execution. This work focuses on speeding up the straight-line execution.

We present our approach in the context of the Java PathFinder (JPF) [33, 19], an explicit-state model checker for Java programs. JPF takes as input a Java program and an optional bound on the length of program execution. JPF explores all executions (up

Z. Liu and J. He (Eds.): ICFEM 2006, LNCS 4260, pp. 549–567, 2006.

to the given bound) that the program can have due to different thread interleavings and nondeterministic choices. JPF can generate as output those executions that violate a given (temporal) property, for example violate an assertion or lead to a deadlock. JPF can also generate as output test inputs for the given program [34, 35].

JPF is implemented in Java as a special Java Virtual Machine (JVM) that runs on top of the host JVM. The main difference between JPF and a regular JVM is that JPF can (quickly) backtrack the program execution by restoring any state previously encountered during the execution. Backtracking allows exploration of different executions from the same state. To achieve fast backtracking, JPF uses a *special representation* of states and executes program bytecodes by modifying this representation. The special state representation makes the overall exploration of *all different executions efficient*, although it makes *each single execution inefficient* compared to a regular JVM. An alternative to using special state representation is using the native state representation of the host JVM throughout model checking; however, while native representation makes each single execution efficient, it can slow down the overall exploration.

We propose *mixed execution*, a technique that can reduce execution time in JPF. The main idea of mixed execution is to execute *some* parts of the program not on JPF but directly on the host JVM. With mixed execution, JPF still as usual executes the other parts of the program and stores, restores, and compares the states. Mixed execution executes on the host JVM only *deterministic blocks*, i.e., parts of the execution that have no thread interleavings or nondeterministic choices. To achieve this, mixed execution translates the state from JPF to JVM at the beginning of a block and from JVM to JPF at the end of a block. These two translations introduce an overhead, but the speedup obtained by executing on the host JVM can easily outweigh the slowdown due to the translations. Although we present mixed execution in the context of JPF, our main idea—executing parts of model checking on different state representations—generalizes to all other model checkers—including AsmLT [12], BogorVM [27], and SpecExplorer [32]—that use some special state representation; these checkers do not need to be for Java or even based on virtual machines.

We have implemented mixed execution by modifying the source code of JPF. Our implementation uses, in a novel way, a mechanism that already exists in JPF; to quote from the JPF manual [19]:

> Host VM Execution - JPF is a JVM that is written in Java, i.e. it runs on top of a host VM. For components that are not property-relevant, it makes sense to delegate the execution from the state-tracked JPF into the non-state tracked host VM. The corresponding Model Java Interface (MJI) mechanism is especially suitable to handle IO simulaion [sic] and other standard library functionality.

MJI is an API that allows the host JVM to manipulate JPF state. The novelty of mixed execution is the use of MJI to *delegate the execution* from the state-tracked JPF into the non-state tracked host JVM *even for components that are property-relevant*. Indeed, mixed execution executes on the host JVM some program code that can modify the program state and thus affect a property, for example assertion violation. For example, we use our technique in the execution of property-relevant fragments during the model checking of a network protocol. In contrast, the previous use of MJI in JPF did not execute such program code on JVM and did not translate the state between JPF and JVM representations.

We also present *lazy translation*, an optimization that speeds up mixed execution by translating only the parts of the state that an execution dynamically depends on. The basic, *eager* mixed execution always translates from JPF to JVM the entire state reachable from a set of roots at the beginning of a deterministic block. (Note that even this state can be a tiny part of the entire JVM state.) Effectively, the eager mixed execution translates the entire state that any execution of the deterministic block *may* read or write. In contrast, lazy translation starts the execution without translation and then, during the execution, translates on demand those state parts that the specific execution *does* read or write. As a result, lazy mixed execution performs less translation and can speed up the eager mixed execution. We have implemented lazy translation by providing an instrumentation for the classes executed on the host JVM.

We evaluate mixed execution and lazy translation on six subject programs that use JPF to generate tests for data structures. The experimental results show that mixed execution can improve the overall time for state exploration in JPF up to 36.98%, while improving the time for execution of deterministic blocks up to 69.15%. Additionally, lazy translation can improve the eager mixed execution up to 25.02%. We also evaluate mixed execution on a case study that uses JPF to find a bug in a fairly complex routing protocol, AODV [25]. Note that mixed execution only reduces the execution time for deterministic blocks and thus the overall exploration time; mixed execution does not affect the order of exploration, the number of explored states, or any other aspect of the state exploration. The techniques that improve the latter aspects are orthogonal to mixed execution, which can be used to further improve them.

2 Example

We next present an example that illustrates how mixed execution can speed up JPF's state exploration. Figure 1 shows the example code that was previously used in several studies on JPF [34, 35, 36]. The code explores the state space of the `java.util.TreeMap` class from the standard Java libraries. This class implements the map interface using red-black trees. The basic operations on the map are `put` (which adds a given key-value pair; the example sets all values to `null`), `remove` (which removes the key-value pair for a given key), and `get` (which gets the value for a given key). The code represents a driver that explores all sequences of `put`, `remove`, and `get` operations up to the given bounds `M` (for the sequence length) and `N` (for the range of input values). JPF's library method `Verify.random(int n)` nondeterministically returns a number between zero and the given bound `n`. JPF's library methods `beginAtomic` and `endAtomic` mark an *atomic* block; these (manually added) annotations instruct JPF to ignore thread interleavings within a given block.

Figure 1 shows relevant fields and methods of the class `TreeMap`. Objects of the `Entry` class represent the nodes of red-black trees. Each node has a key-value pair, a color (red or black), and pointers to the parent node and the left and right children. Executions of the `put`, `remove`, and `get` methods manipulate the tree (passed as the implicit `this` argument). The goal of the driver is to explore different trees that can

```
public static void main(String[] args) {
    int M = Integer.parseInt(args[0]); // length of the sequence
    int N = Integer.parseInt(args[1]); // range of inputs
    // initialize N method arguments
    Integer[] elems = new Integer[N];
    for (int i = 0; i < N; i++) elems[i] = new Integer(i);
    // create an empty tree, the root object for exploration
    TreeMap t = new TreeMap();
    // explore method sequences up to length M
    for (int i = 0; i < M; i++) {
        Verify.beginAtomic();
        switch (Verify.random(2)) {
        case 0: t.put(elems[Verify.random(N-1)], null); break;
        case 1: t.remove(elems[Verify.random(N-1)]);  break;
        case 2: t.get(elems[Verify.random(N-1)]); break;
        }
        Verify.endAtomic();
        Verify.ignoreIf(storeIfNotAlreadyStored(t));
    }
}

public class TreeMap {
    Entry root;
    int size;
    static class Entry {
        Object key;
        Object value;
        boolean color;
        Entry left;
        Entry right;
        Entry parent; ...
    }
    public Object put(Object key, Object value) { ... }
    public Object remove(Object key) { ... }
    public Object get(Object key) { ... } ...
}
```

Fig. 1. Driver for bounded-exhaustive exploration and parts of TreeMap code

arise during the executions. JPF in general considers the entire state when comparing different executions, but the driver uses *abstract matching* [35, 36, 37] to compare only the state of the tree, namely the state of all objects reachable from the root `t`. If the state has been already visited, the JPF's library method `Verify.ignoreIf` instructs JPF to backtrack the execution.

As already mentioned, JPF uses a special representation of the JVM state to efficiently store, restore, and compare states. Without mixed execution, JPF executes `put`, `remove`, and `get` methods on the special representation, which slows down every field read and write. Note, however, that JPF needs the state of the tree only at the beginning and at the end of these methods; in other words, each method can execute atomically. Mixed execution therefore executes these three methods on the host JVM:

- At the beginning of each method execution, mixed execution translates the objects reachable from the method parameters (including the tree reachable from `this`) from the JPF representation into the host JVM representation. (Lazy translation does not translate all objects at the beginning but only on demand during the execution.)
- Mixed execution then invokes the method on the translated state in the host JVM. The method execution can then modify this state.

– At the end of each method execution, mixed execution translates the state back from the host JVM representation into the JPF representation. JPF then compares whether it has already explored the resulting state, appropriately backtracks the execution (restores the state), and the process continues.

The speedup (or slowdown) that mixed execution achieves depends on the size of the state and the length of the method execution. The smaller the state is, the less mixed execution has to copy between the JPF and JVM representations. (Lazy translation further reduces this cost such that it does not depend on the size of the state at the beginning of the method but on the size of the state that the execution accesses.) Also, the longer the execution is, the more mixed execution saves by executing on JVM rather than on JPF.

In our running example with `TreeMap`, the results depend on the value for the bounds `M` and `N`. We set `M` = `N` in all experiments, and the value ranges from 6 to 10, as done in the previous studies with abstract matching [35, 36, 37]. For these bounds, JPF with mixed execution (and lazy translation) takes from 9.44% to 36.98% less time for overall state exploration than JPF without mixed execution. Considering only the executions of `put`, `remove`, and `get` methods, mixed execution provides from 43.15% to 54.95% speedup. Besides the executions of these methods, the overall state exploration includes state comparison, backtracking, and other JPF operations. Mixed execution only reduces the method execution time, while the cost of the rest of state exploration remains the same.

3 Background

We briefly review the parts of JPF relevant for mixed execution. More details on JPF can be found elsewhere [19, 33]. We first describe how JPF represents state. More specifically, we focus on how JPF represents the heap. While JPF also represents stack, thread information, class information, and all other parts of a JVM state, mixed execution directly manipulates only the heap. We then describe the Model Java Interface (MJI), an existing mechanism in JPF for accessing the JPF state from the host JVM. Mixed execution uses MJI to translate the heap between the JPF and JVM representations.

3.1 Heap Representation

Each Java heap consists of a set of objects and some values for the fields of these objects. Each object has an identity, and each field has a type that can be either primitive (`int`, `boolean`, `float`, etc.) or a pointer to another object (which can hold the special value `null`).

Recall that JPF is implemented in Java. JPF uses Java integers to represent object identifiers. JPF also uses Java integers to encode all field values, be they primitive or pointers. (JPF determines the meaning of various integers based on the field types kept in the class information.) Conceptually, JPF represents each object as an integer array, and the entire heap is an array of integer arrays. Figure 2 shows an example red-black tree represented in JVM (as an object graph) and in JPF (as an array of integer arrays); this example `TreeMap` object can result from the sequence `TreeMap t = new TreeMap(); t.put(new Integer(2), null); t.put(new Integer(1), null); t.put(new Integer(3), null)`. Figure 2 shows for each object its type,

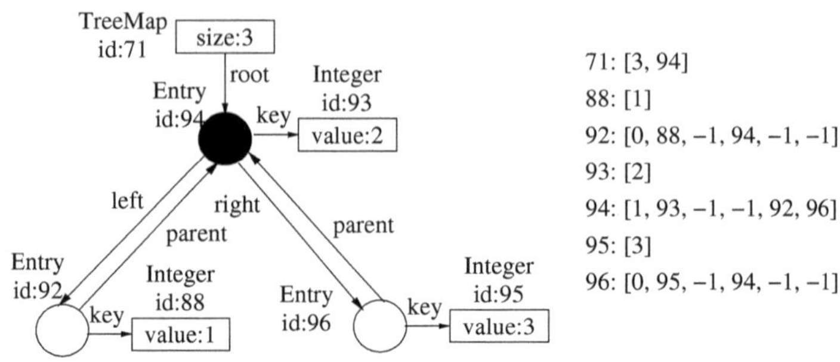

Fig. 2. An example TreeMap as an object graph and in the JPF heap representation

integer identifier, and the values of primitive fields (with the full and empty circles representing the color of the `Entry` objects). The pointer fields not shown in the graph have the value `null`, represented as -1 in JPF.

3.2 Model Java Interface

Model Java Interface (MJI) is a JPF mechanism that allows parts of JPF execution to be delegated from the JPF into the host JVM. MJI is analogous to the Java Native Interface (JNI) [2] that allows parts of JVM execution to be delegated from the JVM into the native code, written in say the C language. MJI, like JNI, splits executions at the method granularity; namely, each method can be marked to be executed either in JPF or in the host JVM. (JPF uses special name mangling to mark methods for the host JVM execution.) MJI also provides API that allows the host JVM execution to manipulate the JPF state representation, for example to read or write field values or to create new objects.

The libraries distributed with JPF use MJI to implement several parts of the standard Java library. MJI, like JNI, is used to implement functionality that either requires higher performance or is not available at the target level (e.g., reflection [11] in Java). Specifically, JPF uses MJI to implement several classes and methods from the `java.io` and `java.lang` packages. These existing methods do not modify the heap; they either only affect the IO or only return primitive values or new objects. In contrast, our mixed execution leverages MJI to execute code that can and does modify the heap. Also, mixed execution does not operate on the JPF representation of state; instead, mixed execution translates the state between the JPF representation and the host JVM representation.

4 Technique

We next present mixed execution in more detail. Like MJI and JNI (Section 3), mixed execution operates at the method granularity: the user can mark each method to be executed either in JPF or in the host JVM. We first present how mixed execution invokes the methods to be executed on the host JVM. We then present the basic version of mixed execution that eagerly translates the state between JPF and JVM at the boundaries of a

```
void jpfInvoke(Method m, int[] args) {
    if (m.shouldBeExecutedOnJVM()) {
        // get the JPF execution environment
        MJIEnv env = JPF.getMJIEnv();
        // translate arguments from JPF to JVM
        Object[] inputs = translateJPF2JVM(env, args);
        try {
            // use reflection to invoke the method on JVM,
            // giving it the translated values as the arguments
            Object result = m.invoke(inputs);
            // translate the heap reachable from the roots from JVM to JPF
            translateJVM2JPF(env, inputs);
            // translate the return value
            int jpfResult = translateObjectJVM2JPF(env, result);
            MJI.pushOnStack(jpfResult);
        } catch (Throwable t) {
            translateJVM2JPF(env, inputs);
            // translate the exception
            int jpfThrowable = translateObjectJVM2JPF(env, t);
            MJI.raiseJPFException(jpfThrowable);
        }
    }
}
```

Fig. 3. Pseudo-code of the method invocation for the host JVM execution

method call. We finally present lazy translation, an optimization that translates only the parts that the execution actually needs.

4.1 Overview

Figure 3 shows how mixed execution invokes methods for host execution. Whenever the program is about to execute a method, mixed execution checks whether the method is marked to be executed in the host JVM. If so, mixed execution translates the state from JPF to JVM, executes the method, and then translates the state back from JVM to JPF. Note that mixed execution handles both cases when the method returns normally and when the method throws an exception; mixed execution catches the (JVM) exceptions and translates them accordingly (into the JPF exceptions), together with the rest of the post-state.

Mixed execution assumes that the methods marked for execution in the host JVM are deterministic, i.e., are not affected by any interleaving of threads and have no nondeterministic choices. (This is always the case when JPF is used to explore method sequences as shown in Section 5.1; the code is single-threaded and there are no `Verify.random` calls in the methods.) Each method takes several arguments (one of which is the implicit `this` argument for instance methods). Some of the arguments may be pointers to objects, and a method execution can access or modify a field of any object reachable from these pointers. The arguments thus represent the roots for the part of the heap that the method can manipulate. The heap may be much larger than the part reachable from the roots, but the method cannot manipulate the part that is not reachable from the roots. (In general, the roots should also include all static fields.)

4.2 Eager Translation

Figure 4 shows the pseudo-code of the method that translates the state from JPF to JVM. The inputs to the method are an `MJIEnv` object, which encodes the entire envi-

```
Map<int, Object> mapJPF2JVM;
Map<Object, int> mapJVM2JPF;
// main method that translates all arguments in the pre-state
Object[] translateJPF2JVM(MJIEnv env, int[] args) {
    mapJPF2JVM = new Map<int, Object>();
    mapJVM2JPF = new Map<Object, int>();
    Object[] result = new Object[args.length];
    for (int i = 0; i < args.length; i++) {
        Type t = env.typeOf(args[i]);
        if (t.isPrimitive()) {
            result[i] = correspondingPrimitiveObject(t, args[i]);
        } else {
            result[i] = translateObjectJPF2JVM(env, args[i]);
        }
    }
    return result;
}
// helper method that translates all fields reachable from a reference
Object translateObjectJPF2JVM(MJIEnv env, int jpfPointer) {
    if (jpfPointer == MJIEnv.NULL) return null;
    if (mapJPF2JVM.contains(jpfPointer)) return mapJPF2JVM.get(jpfPointer);
    // create a new object
    Object o = translateOneReferenceJPF2JVM(env, jpfPointer);
    // set the fields of the object recursively
    foreach (field f in o.getFields()) {
        int value = env.getFieldValue(jpfPointer, f);
        Type t = env.typeOf(f);
        if (t.isPrimitive()) {
            setField(o, f, correspondingPrimitiveObject(t, value));
        } else {
            setField(o, f, translateObjectJPF2JVM(env, value));
        }
    }
    // return the new object with all fields translated
    return o;
}
// helper method that translates only one reference
Object translateOneReferenceJPF2JVM(MJIEnv env, int jpfPointer) {
    if (jpfPointer == MJIEnv.NULL) return null;
    if (mapJPF2JVM.contains(jpfPointer)) return mapJPF2JVM.get(jpfPointer);
    // get the type of JPF object "jpfPointer"
    Class c = env.getClass(jpfPointer);
    // create a new object of class "c" using reflection
    Object o = c.newInstance();
    // update the mappings between JPF and JVM objects
    mapJPF2JVM.put(jpfPointer, o);
    mapJVM2JPF.put(o, jpfPointer);
    return o;
}
```

Fig. 4. Pseudo-code of the algorithm that translates the state from JPF to JVM

ronment/state of the JPF execution, and an array of method arguments, encoded in JPF as integers (Section 3). (For instance methods, the first argument represents `this`.) The output of the method is an array of JVM objects that correspond to the arguments. The method uses a depth-first traversal of the JPF heap reachable from `args` to create an *isomorphic* JVM heap [5]. The method creates two maps that keep the correspondence between the JPF and JVM object identities. These maps initially start empty, but the helper method adds for each JPF object an appropriate JVM object. The method uses the map from JPF to JVM to handle heap aliases. (The use of the map also ensures that the translation terminates when the heap has cycles.) The map from JVM to JPF will be used during the translation at the end of the execution. The method and the helper use

```
Set<Object> visited;
// main method that translates the post-state
void translateJVM2JPF(MJIEnv env, Object[] inputs) {
    visited = new Set<Object>();
    for (int i = 0; i < inputs.length; i++) {
        if (!(env.typeOf(inputs[i]).isPrimitive())) {
            translateObjectJVM2JPF(env, inputs[i]);
        }
    }
}
// helper method that translates one object
int translateObjectJVM2JPF(MJIEnv env, Object o) {
    if (o == null) return MJIEnv.NULL;
    if (!visited.contains(o)) {
        visited.add(o);
        // get type of the object
        Class c = o.getClass();
        // get (or create if necessary) the corresponding JPF object
        int jpfPointer;
        if (!mapJVM2JPF.contains(o)) {
            // create new JPF object of the same type
            jpfPointer = env.createNewObject(c);
            mapJVM2JPF.add(o, jpfPointer);
        } else {
            jpfPointer = mapJVM2JPF.get(o);
        }
        // set the fields of the object recursively
        foreach (field f in c.getFields()) {
            // use reflection to get the field value
            Object value = f.getFieldValue(o);
            Type t = f.getType();
            if (t.isPrimitive()) {
                env.setFieldValue(jpfPointer, f, correspondingPrimitiveJPF(t, value));
            } else {
                env.setFieldValue(jpfPointer, f, translateObjectJVM2JPF(env, value));
            }
        }
    }
    return mapJVM2JPF(o);
}
```

Fig. 5. Pseudo-code of the algorithm that translates the state from JVM to JPF

several MJI calls (on the env objects) to get the values of fields and to get the types of the arguments and fields.

Figure 5 shows the pseudo-code of the method that translates the state from JVM to JPF. The inputs to the method are an MJIEnv object and an array of the inputs, which represent the roots of the heap at the beginning of the execution. The effect of the method is to update the JPF state. The method uses a depth-first traversal of the JVM heap reachable from the inputs roots to appropriately update the JPF heap to be isomorphic to the corresponding JVM heap. The traversals keep the set of visited objects. It is important to distinguish this set and the map from JVM to JPF objects. In the translation from JPF to JVM, a map is used both to keep track of visited (JPF) objects and to provide the mapping of identities. However, in the translation from JVM to JPF, a map is only used to provide the mapping of identities, because an object should be traversed even if it is in the map. Moreover, the translation must preserve the original JPF identity of nodes. The translation method and its helper use several MJI calls (on the env objects) to create new objects and set the values of fields.

```
// Original code, before instrumentation.
public class TreeMap {
    static class Entry {
        Entry left;
        ...
    }
    public Object put(Object key, Object value) {
        ... = e.left; // field read
        e.left = ...; // field write
    } ...
}

// Code after instrumentation.
public class TreeMap {
    static class Entry {
        Entry left;
        boolean _mixed_is_copied_left = false;
        Entry _mixed_get_left() {
            if (!_mixed_is_copied_left) {
                MJIEnv env = JPF.getMJIEnv();
                int jpfPointer = env.getFieldValue(mapJVM2JPF(this), "left");
                left = translateOneReferenceJPF2JVM(env, jpfPointer);
                _mixed_is_copied_left = true;
            }
            return left;
        }
        void _mixed_set_left(Entry e) {
            left = e;
            _mixed_is_copied_left = true;
        }
        ...
    }
    public Object put(Object key, Object value) {
        ... = e._mixed_get_left(); // field read
        e._mixed_set_left(...); // field write
    } ...
}
```

Fig. 6. Example code before and after instrumentation

4.3 Lazy Translation

Lazy translation is an optimization that translates between JPF and JVM only the parts of the heap that a method execution actually needs. While eager translation translates the entire heap at the beginning of the execution, lazy translation translates only the arguments and not all fields reachable from them. During the execution, however, lazy translation performs a check for each field read and write to determine whether the field has been translated from JPF to JVM. If not, lazy translation translates only that one field and continues the execution. By the end of the execution, lazy translation typically translates into JVM only a small part of the heap reachable from the method arguments at the beginning.

Lazy translation requires some changes to the code of the methods executed by mixed execution. Specifically, lazy translation requires the checks for each field read and write. We achieve those checks using *code instrumentation*. Figure 6 shows a part of the code from the `TreeMap` example before and after instrumentation. For each field, the instrumentation adds (i) a boolean flag that tracks whether the field has been translated from JPF to JVM, (ii) a method for reading the field value (translating it from JPF if necessary), and (iii) a method for writing the field value. The instrumentation also replaces all field reads and writes in the original code with the invocations of appropriate methods. Finally, the instrumentation adds a special constructor to create objects without setting the flags. A similar instrumentation has been used previously in testing and model checking [5, 34].

At the end of a method execution on the host JVM, mixed execution with lazy translation traverses the JVM heap similarly as mixed execution with eager translation. In contrast to eager translation, however, only those fields whose flags are set to `true` are translated from JVM to JPF and recursively followed further. A further optimization would be to have "dirty flags" to avoid translation from JVM to JPF for the fields whose value was not changed.

5 Experiments

We next discuss the experiments used to evaluate mixed execution. We have implemented mixed execution by modifying the JPF code [19] to include the algorithms from figures 3, 4, and 5. We have also implemented a prototype tool that automates instrumentation for lazy translation as shown in Figure 6.

We evaluate mixed execution on six subject programs that use JPF for state exploration in data structures. We also evaluate mixed execution on a network protocol for which JPF finds an injected error. The blocks of code delegated to mixed execution are deterministic: they are sequential code without non-deterministic choices (`Verify.random` calls).

We conducted all the experiments on a dual-processor Intel Xeon 2.8 GHz machine running Linux version 2.6.15 with 2 GB memory. We used Sun's 1.4.2_06-b03 JVM, allocating 1.5 GB for the maximum heap size. We compare the time that JPF takes for exploration with and without mixed execution. In both cases, we set JPF to use breadth-first state exploration. We also enable all JPF optimizations, including partial-order reductions [33], the use of MD5 hashing function [19], and the exact state comparison with respect to isomorphism [35, 36].

5.1 Data Structures

We evaluate mixed execution on the six data structures listed in Figure 7. We take the subjects from previous studies on model checking and testing:

- `UBStack` is an implementation of a stack bounded in size, storing integer objects without repetition [30, 37, 8, 23].
- `DisjSet` is an implementation of a union-find data structure implementing disjoint sets [37].
- `Trie` implements a dictionary, i.e., it stores a collection of strings sorted lexicographically [38].
- `Vector`, `LinkedList`, and `TreeMap` are from the Java 1.4 Collection Framework.

Our state exploration considers the methods that add, remove, and search for elements in each data structure, as listed in Figure 7.

Each experiment uses an execution driver similar to that in Figure 1. By default, we use mixed execution with lazy translation. Figure 8 tabulates the results. We set

subject	methods explored
UBStack	push, pop
DisjSet	union, find
Trie	add, is_word, is_proper_prefix
Vector	addElement, removeElement, elementAt
LinkedList	add, removeLast, contains
TreeMap	put, remove, get

Fig. 7. Subjects used in the experiments

			# bytecodes		total time			method exec. only		
subject	bound	# states	JPF	mixed	JPF	mixed	speedup	JPF	mixed	speedup
					[ms]	[ms]	[%]	[ms]	[ms]	[%]
UBStack	5	929	181217	19677	2318	2137	7.81	490	276	43.67
UBStack	6	5776	1561823	132475	5605	4367	22.09	1836	726	60.46
UBStack	7	41094	14940706	1038230	31602	20889	33.90	14301	4412	69.15
DisjSet	5	624	207261	21507	2546	2500	1.81	187	233	-24.60
DisjSet	6	4653	2067901	161408	9602	8902	7.29	1146	789	31.15
DisjSet	7	47480	27152409	1874435	92054	82169	10.74	14133	8194	42.02
Trie	5	129	120869	4839	1686	1636	2.97	262	221	15.65
Trie	6	257	293899	10855	2068	1966	4.93	419	287	31.50
Trie	7	513	690129	24359	2804	2572	8.27	752	460	38.83
Trie	8	1025	1679127	54311	4834	4149	14.17	1440	847	41.18
Trie	9	2049	4018501	120103	9329	7730	17.14	2929	1446	50.63
Trie	10	4097	9190465	263549	18946	15599	17.67	6547	3064	53.20
Vector	5	7057	892349	120244	4513	4074	9.73	1001	522	47.85
Vector	6	91706	13596654	1605126	38360	30534	20.40	11504	4462	61.21
Vector	7	1466919	247371240	26241690	1276992	1124545	11.94	206508	74046	64.14
LinkedList	5	5471	302914	105134	4390	4256	3.05	914	808	11.60
LinkedList	6	74652	4218361	1446823	35109	33453	4.72	10128	9367	7.51
LinkedList	7	1235317	70962644	24157788	578847	553095	4.45	175267	151016	13.84
TreeMap	5	187	92740	7586	1841	1735	5.76	364	201	44.78
TreeMap	6	534	361600	25864	2532	2293	9.44	761	410	46.12
TreeMap	7	1480	1223256	79470	4294	3490	18.72	1738	988	43.15
TreeMap	8	4552	4629574	277476	10489	7556	27.96	5718	2805	50.94
TreeMap	9	13816	16681289	952976	32254	20897	35.21	20096	9424	53.11
TreeMap	10	39344	54581750	3008954	98633	62162	36.98	66336	29887	54.95

Fig. 8. Comparison of JPF without and with mixed execution

the same bounds for the method-sequence length and for the range of values. For each subject and several bounds, we tabulate the number of states that JPF explores (which is the same with or without mixed execution), the total number of bytecodes that JPF executes (with mixed execution, the host JVM executes some bytecodes), the overall time for exploration, and the time for execution of methods marked for mixed execution. All times are in milliseconds. The columns labeled *JPF* and *mixed* represent the runs of JPF without and with mixed execution, respectively. The *speedup* columns show the improvement that mixed execution provides.

The results show that mixed execution can reduce the overall state exploration time up to 36.98%, while reducing the method execution time up to 69.15%. Note that for very short executions (such as `DisjSet` for bound 5), mixed execution may actually slow down JPF as the overhead of translation outweighs the benefit of execution on the host JVM. As a matter of fact, for all subjects and small bounds, mixed execution slows

			total time			method exec. only		
name	bound	# states	eager	lazy	speedup	eager	lazy	speedup
			[ms]	[ms]	[%]	[ms]	[ms]	[%]
Trie	5	129	1785	1748	2.07	234	202	13.68
Trie	6	257	2118	2052	3.12	393	295	24.94
Trie	7	513	2842	2650	6.76	635	465	26.77
Trie	8	1025	4958	4574	7.75	1660	833	49.82
Trie	9	2049	10150	7911	22.06	3595	1446	59.78
Trie	10	4097	20678	15730	23.93	8217	3018	63.27
TreeMap	5	187	1842	1820	1.19	305	218	28.52
TreeMap	6	534	2685	2651	1.27	571	403	29.42
TreeMap	7	1480	3901	3498	10.33	1338	962	28.10
TreeMap	8	4552	9089	7548	16.95	4308	2864	33.52
TreeMap	9	13816	27595	21014	23.85	15235	9425	38.14
TreeMap	10	39344	83744	62789	25.02	49212	29600	39.85

Fig. 9. Comparison of eager and lazy translations

down JPF. However, the more important cases are when the execution is long. As the results show, the longer the execution gets, the more benefit mixed execution provides.

All above experiments with mixed execution use lazy translation. Figure 9 shows the benefit of this optimization. For two subjects and several sizes, we tabulate the overall execution time for state exploration and the time for execution of methods marked for mixed execution. Compared to eager translation, lazy translation reduces the overall time up to 25.02%, while reducing the method execution time up to 63.27%. Note again that the longer the execution gets, the more benefit lazy translation provides.

5.2 The AODV Case Study

We next present the evaluation of mixed execution on Ad-Hoc On-Demand Distance Vector (AODV) routing [26], a widely used network protocol for wireless multihop ad hoc networks. We consider an implementation of AODV based on the AODV Draft (version 11) [25] and implemented in J-Sim [1, 31], a component-based network simulator written entirely in Java. AODV is a fairly complex network protocol whose J-Sim implementation (not including the J-Sim library) has about 1200 lines of code. This case study was used previously to evaluate a model checker specialized for J-Sim [28, 29].

We first give an overview of AODV and its *loop-free* safety property. We then explain the details of the driver for AODV and an error that we injected in the AODV code. We finally present the improvements obtained by using mixed execution to find the error.

An ad hoc network is a wireless network that comes together when and where needed, as a collection of wireless nodes, without relying on any assistance from an existing network infrastructure such as base stations or routers. Due to the lack of complete connectivity and routers, the nodes are designed to serve as routers (i.e., relays) and assist each other in delivering data packets. Hence, the route between two nodes may consist of multiple wireless hops through other nodes; this is called *multihop routing*.

In AODV, each node n in the ad hoc network maintains a routing table. A routing table entry (RTE) at node n to a destination node d contains, among other fields: a next hop address $nexthop_{n,d}$ (the address of the node to which n forwards packets destined for d), a hop count $hops_{n,d}$ (the number of hops needed to reach d from n), and a destination sequence number $seqno_{n,d}$ (a measure of the freshness of the route information). Each RTE is associated with a lifetime. Periodically, a route timeout event is triggered invalidating (but not deleting) all the RTEs that have not been used (e.g., to send or forward packets to the destination) for a time interval that is greater than the lifetime. Invalidating a RTE involves incrementing $seqno_{n,d}$ and setting $hops_{n,d}$ to ∞.

Each node n also maintains two monotonically increasing counters: a node sequence number $seqno_n$ and a broadcast ID bid_n. When node n requires a route to a destination d to which n does not already have a valid RTE, n creates an invalid RTE to d with $hops_{n,d}$ set to ∞. Node n then *broadcasts* a route request (RREQ) packet with the fields $\langle n, seqno_n, bid_n, d, seqno_{n,d}, hopCount_q\rangle$ and increments bid_n. The $hopCount_q$ field is initialized to 1. The pair $\langle n, bid_n\rangle$ uniquely identifies a RREQ packet. Each node m, receiving the RREQ packet from node n, keeps the pair $\langle n, bid_n\rangle$ in a broadcast ID cache so that m can later check if it has already received a RREQ with the same source address and broadcast ID. If so, the incoming RREQ packet is discarded. If not, m either satisfies the RREQ by *unicasting* a route reply (RREP) packet back to n if it has a fresh enough route to d (or it is d itself) or rebroadcasts the RREQ to its own neighbors after incrementing the $hopCount_q$ field if it does not have a fresh enough route to d (nor is it d). An intermediate node m determines whether it has a fresh enough route to d by comparing the destination sequence number $seqno_{m,d}$ in its own RTE with the $seqno_{n,d}$ field in the RREQ packet. Each intermediate node also records a reverse route to the requesting node n; this reverse route can be used to send/forward route replies to n. The requesting node's sequence number $seqno_n$ is used to maintain the freshness of this reverse route. Each entry in the broadcast ID cache has a lifetime. Periodically, a broadcast ID timeout event is triggered causing the deletion of cache entries that have expired.

Overview of AODV. A RREP packet, which is sent by an intermediate node m, contains the following fields $\langle hopCount_p, d, seqno_{m,d}, n\rangle$. The $hopCount_p$ field is initialized to $1 + hops_{m,d}$. If it is the destination d that sends the RREP packet, it first increments $seqno_d$ and then sends a RREP packet containing the following fields $\langle 1, d, seqno_d, n\rangle$. The unicast RREP travels back to the requesting node n via the reverse route. Each intermediate node along the reverse route sets up a forward pointer to the node from which the RREP came, thus establishing a forward route to the destination d, increments the $hopCount_p$ field and forwards the RREP packet to the next hop towards n.

If node m offers node n a new route to d, n compares $seqno_{m,d}$ (the destination sequence number of the offered route) to $seqno_{n,d}$ (the destination sequence number of the current route), and accepts the route with the greater sequence number. If the sequence numbers are equal, the offered route is accepted only if it has a smaller hop count than the hop count in the RTE; i.e., $hops_{n,d} > hops_{m,d}$.

Safety property. An important safety property in a routing protocol such as AODV is the *loop-free* property. Intuitively, a node must not exist at two points on a routing path; therefore, at each hop along a path from a node n to a destination d, either the destination sequence number must increase or the hop count must decrease. Formally,

AODV			# bytecodes		total time			method exec. only		
# nodes	path len.	# states	JPF	mixed	JPF	mixed	speedup	JPF	mixed	speedup
					[ms]	[ms]	[%]	[ms]	[ms]	[%]
8	8	5806	24571290	17425293	61347	54384	11.35	9107	3457	62.04
9	9	7960	37106325	26683825	92266	82231	10.88	13520	4892	63.82
10	10	10585	54077303	39272619	161578	110132	31.84	19495	6578	66.26

Fig. 10. Model checking AODV without and with mixed execution

consider two nodes n and m such that m is the next hop of n to some destination d; i.e., $nexthop_{n,d} = m$. The loop-free property can be expressed as follows [4, 22]:

$$seqno_{n,d} < seqno_{m,d} \lor (seqno_{n,d} = seqno_{m,d} \land hops_{n,d} > hops_{m,d})$$

Test driver. We wrote a test driver for the J-Sim implementation of AODV. The driver produces an environment that executes all sequences of protocol events up to a configurable bound. The driver considers these events [29]:

- Initiation of a route request to a destination d: This event is enabled if the node does not have a valid RTE to the destination d. The event is handled by broadcasting a RREQ.
- Restart of the AODV process at node n: This event may take place because of a node reboot. The event is always enabled and is handled by reinitializing the state of the AODV process at node n.
- Broadcast ID timeout at node n: This event is enabled if there is at least one entry in the broadcast ID cache of node n. The event is handled by deleting this entry.
- Timeout of the route to destination d at node n: This event is enabled if n has a valid RTE to d. The event is handled by invalidating this RTE.
- Delivering an AODV packet to node n: This event is enabled if the network contains at least one AODV packet such that n is the destination (or the next hop towards the destination) of the packet and n is one of the neighbors of the source of the packet. The event is handled by removing this packet from the network and forwarding it to node n in order to be processed according to the AODV implementation.
- Loss of an AODV packet destined for node n: This event is enabled if the network contains at least one AODV packet that is destined for node n. The event is handled by removing this packet from the network.

Since JPF could not execute the code for the entire J-Sim simulator and the AODV protocol, we created a simplified version of the networking layer used by AODV. This version does not have the full generality of the J-Sim simulator but provides the functionality needed to run AODV.

Finding error. We consider an initial state of an ad hoc network consisting of K nodes: n_0, n_1, ..., n_{K-1} (where n_{K-1} is the only destination node) arranged in a chain topology where each node is a neighbor of both the node to its left and the node to its right (if they exist). In the initial state, nodes n_i for all $0 \leq i \leq K-2$ have valid routing table entries to the destination n_{K-1}. We manually injected an error as follows:

a RTE is deleted (instead of invalidated) when a route timeout event occurs. Consider the case of $K = 3$. A routing loop may occur because if $nexthop_{0,2} = 1$ and a route timeout event takes place at n_1, if n_1 is later offered a route to n_2 by n_0, this route will be accepted because $seqno_{0,2} > seqno_{1,2}$. The case of $K > 3$ is similar. The interested reader can find a detailed explanation of this injected error elsewhere [28]. We instruct JPF to stop the exploration as soon as it finds this error.

Mixed execution. To apply mixed execution on AODV, we needed to determine which parts of the AODV code to execute on the host JVM. We first marked for host execution the data structures (such as vectors) that AODV uses to represent protocol data (including routing tables and packet queues). We then used profiling to find that AODV spends a lot of execution time in the methods of the J-Sim library class `Port` that handles sending and receiving of packets between network nodes [31], so we also marked those methods for host execution. Figure 10 shows the improvements obtained with mixed execution on AODV. We tabulate, for a range of number of nodes and length of the event path, the overall state-space exploration time and the method execution time. Mixed execution improves the overall exploration time from 10.88% to 31.84%, and the method execution time from 62.04% to 66.26%.

6 Related Work

Traditional model checkers such as SPIN [15], SMV [18], or Murphi [9] have been extensively used in formal reasoning of both hardware and software systems. These tools analyze the models written in the special modeling languages. To analyze a system, the user thus needs either to manually write a model of the system in a language understood by the tools [4] or to automatically translate an implementation of the system from a programming language (e.g., Java) into the modeling language of the tools [24,14,7,10]. Our work considers model checkers that directly analyze the systems written in a programming language.

Verisoft [13] was the first model checker to directly analyze the implementation code, specifically code written in the C language. Several recent model checkers such as CMC [22], BogorVM [27], or JPF [33] also focus on analyzing the actual code written in a programming language (C or Java). For example, CMC has been used to model check Linux implementations of networking code (e.g., AODV and TCP) and file systems [22, 21, 39]. We have also developed a model checker [29] tailored for the J-Sim network simulator [1] and used it to find errors in the J-Sim implementation of AODV [29]. The model checker extends J-Sim with the capability to explore the state space created by a network protocol, whose simulation code is written in Java. The model checker operates on the concrete memory state and clones/copies large portions of the state for each transition. Our current work targets model checkers that operate on a special representation of state such as AsmLT, BogorVM, JPF, or SpecExplorer.

Handling state is a central issue in explicit-state model checkers [15,17,16,20]. Work in this area focuses on efficient implementation of state operations, including updating, storing, restoring, and comparing states. For example, JPF implements techniques such as efficient encoding of Java program state and symmetry reductions to help reduce the state-space size [17]. As another example, Musuvathi and Dill recently proposed an algorithm for incremental heap canonicalization [20], which speeds up the hashing of states and thus state comparisons. While these techniques focus on *speeding up the operations* on state (or the overall state-space exploration), we propose mixed execution that focuses on *speeding up the executions* that operate on the state that can be translated between the special (JPF) and the host (JVM) representation. Our technique is thus orthogonal to the techniques for state operations and can be combined with them to achieve even higher speed ups.

Our evaluation of mixed execution uses data-structure subjects and the AODV case study. The data-structure subjects have been used in other projects on testing and model checking [30, 37, 8, 38, 23], including in the context of JPF [34, 35, 36]. The most recent work in the context of JPF [35, 36] proposes test-input generation techniques that depend on the *abstract state matching* to avoid the generation of redundant tests. Our experiments rely on that work because our drivers match the state of the data structure (reachable from a root) and not the entire heap. As the results show, however, mixed execution still achieves significant improvements even when used with abstract matching. Finally, the AODV case study presented in this paper is, to the best of our knowledge, one of the largest case studies that have been model checked using JPF.

7 Conclusions

We have presented mixed execution, a technique that reduces the execution time of deterministic blocks in Java PathFinder (JPF). JPF is a special JVM that runs on top of a regular, host JVM; mixed execution translates the state between the special JPF representation and the host JVM representation to enable faster execution of Java bytecodes. We have also presented lazy translation, an optimization that speeds up mixed execution by translating only the parts of the state that an execution dynamically depends on. Our evaluation shows that mixed execution can significantly improve the time for execution of deterministic blocks and thus the overall time for state-space exploration.

Mixed execution points out the importance of studying the trade-offs used in state-space explorations for model checking and testing. We plan to further investigate these trade-offs, focusing on the differences between stateful and stateless search (i.e., between backtracking and re-execution). We also plan to consider the use of memoization and incremental computation in speeding up re-execution. We believe that the straight-line execution in model checkers can be further improved, building on the ideas of mixed execution.

Acknowledgments

We thank Willem Visser for repeatedly and promptly helping us with JPF, Corina Pasareanu and Mahesh Viswanathan for discussing mixed execution with us, and Steven Lauterburg and Nikolai Tillmann for their comments on a previous draft of this paper. This work was partially supported by CAPES fellowship under grant #15021917. We also acknowledge support from Microsoft Research.

References

1. J-Sim. http://www.j-sim.org/.
2. Java Native Interface: Programmer's Guide and Specification. Online book. http://java.sun.com/docs/books/jni/.
3. T. Ball and S. K. Rajamani. Automatically validating temporal safety properties of interfaces. In *SPIN '01: Proc. of the 8th international SPIN workshop on Model checking of software*, pages 103–122, New York, NY, 2001.
4. K. Bhargavan, D. Obradovic, and C. A. Gunter. Formal verification of standards for distance vector routing protocols. *Journal of the ACM*, 49(4):538–576, July 2002.
5. C. Boyapati, S. Khurshid, and D. Marinov. Korat: automated testing based on Java predicates. In *Proc. International Symposium on Software Testing and Analysis*, pages 123–133, 2002.
6. E. Clarke, D. Kroening, and F. Lerda. A tool for checking ANSI-C programs. In *Tools and Algorithms for the Construction and Analysis of Systems (TACAS 2004)*, volume 2988 of *LNCS*, pages 168–176, 2004.
7. J. C. Corbett, M. B. Dwyer, J. Hatcliff, S. Laubach, C. S. Pasareanu, Robby, and H. Zheng. Bandera: extracting finite-state models from Java source code. In *Proc. 22nd International Conference on Software Engineering*, pages 439–448, 2000.
8. C. Csallner and Y. Smaragdakis. JCrasher: an automatic robustness tester for Java. *Software: Practice and Experience*, 34:1025–1050, 2004.
9. D. L. Dill, A. J. Drexler, A. J. Hu, and C. H. Yang. Protocol verification as a hardware design aid. In *IEEE International Conference on Computer Design (IEEE ICCD)*, pages 522–525, 1992.
10. A. Farzan, F. Chen, J. Meseguer, and G. Rosu. Formal analysis of Java programs in JavaFAN. In *Proc. of CAV'04*, July 2004.
11. D. Flanagan. *Java In A Nutshell*. O'Reilly, 1997.
12. Foundations of Software Engineering at Microsoft Research. The AsmL test generator tool. http://research.microsoft.com/fse/asml/doc/AsmLTester.html.
13. P. Godefroid. Model checking for programming languages using Verisoft. In *Proc. 24th ACM SIGPLAN-SIGACT Symposium on Principles of Programming Languages*, pages 174–186, 1997.
14. K. Havelund. Java Pathfinder, a translator from Java to Promela. In *Proc. of SPIN'99*, 1999.
15. G. J. Holzmann. The model checker SPIN. *IEEE Trans. on Software Engineering*, 23(5):279–295, 1997.
16. R. Iosif. Symmetry reduction criteria for software model checking. In *Proc. 9th SPIN Workshop on Software Model Checking*, volume 2318 of *LNCS*, pages 22–41, July 2002.
17. F. Lerda and W. Visser. Addressing dynamic issues of program model checking. In *SPIN '01: Proc. of the 8th international SPIN workshop on Model checking of software*, pages 80–102, Toronto, Canada, 2001.
18. K. L. McMillan. *Symbolic Model Checking*. Kluwer Academic Publishers, 1993.
19. P. C. Mehlitz, W. Visser, and J. Penix. The JPF runtime verification system. Online manual. http://javapathfinder.sourceforge.net/JPF.pdf.
20. M. Musuvathi and D. L. Dill. An incremental heap canonicalization algorithm. In *SPIN*, pages 28–42, 2005.
21. M. Musuvathi and D. Engler. Model checking large network protocol implementations. In *Proc. of The First Symposium on Networked Systems Design and Implementation (NSDI)*, pages 155–168, 2004.
22. M. Musuvathi, D. Park, A. Chou, D. R. Engler, and D. L. Dill. CMC: A pragmatic approach to model checking real code. In *Proc. 5th Symposium on Operating Systems Design and Implementation*, pages 75–88, December 2002.

23. C. Pacheco and M. D. Ernst. Eclat: Automatic generation and classification of test inputs. In *Proc. 19th European Conference on Object-Oriented Programming*, pages 504–527, Glasgow, Scotland, July 2005.
24. D. Y. Park, U. Stern, J. U. Skakkebæk, and D. L. Dill. Java model checking. In *Proc. of IEEE ASE'00*, 2000.
25. C. E. Perkins, E. M. Belding-Royer, and S. Das. Ad hoc on demand distance vector (aodv) routing, January 2002. IETF Draft.
26. C. E. Perkins and E. M. Royer. Ad-hoc on-demand distance vector routing. In *Proc. IEEE Workshop on Mobile Computing Systems and Applications (WMCSA)*, pages 90–100. IEEE Computer Society Press, 1999.
27. Robby, M. B. Dwyer, and J. Hatcliff. Bogor: an extensible and highly-modular software model checking framework. In *Proc. 9th European Software Engineering Conference held jointly with 11th ACM SIGSOFT International Symposium on Foundations of Software Engineering*, pages 267–276, 2003.
28. A. Sobeih, M. Viswanathan, and J. C. Hou. Incorporating bounded model checking in network simulation: Theory, implementation and evaluation. Technical Report UIUCDCS-R-2004-2466, Department of Computer Science, University of Illinois at Urbana-Champaign, Urbana, Illinois, July 2004.
29. A. Sobeih, M. Viswanathan, D. Marinov, and J. C. Hou. Finding bugs in network protocols using simulation code and protocol-specific heuristics. In K.-K. Lau and R. Banach, editors, *ICFEM*, volume 3785 of *LNCS*, pages 235–250, 2005.
30. D. Stotts, M. Lindsey, and A. Antley. An informal formal method for systematic JUnit test case generation. In *Proc. 2002 XP/Agile Universe*, pages 131–143, 2002.
31. H.-Y. Tyan. *Design, Realization and Evaluation of a Component-based Compositional Software Architecture for Network Simulation*. Ph.D., Department of Electrical Engineering, The Ohio State University, 2002.
32. M. Veanes, C. Campbell, W. Schulte, and N. Tillmann. Online testing with model programs. In *ESEC/FSE-13: Proc. of the 10th European Software Engineering Conference and the 13th ACM SIGSOFT International Symposium on Foundations of Software Engineering*, pages 273–282, New York, NY, 2005. ACM Press.
33. W. Visser, K. Havelund, G. Brat, and S. Park. Model checking programs. In *Proc. 15th IEEE International Conference on Automated Software Engineering*, 2000.
34. W. Visser, C. S. Pasareanu, and S. Khurshid. Test input generation with Java PathFinder. In *Proc. 2004 ACM SIGSOFT International Symposium on Software Testing and Analysis*, pages 97–107, 2004.
35. W. Visser, C. S. Pasareanu, and R. Pelanek. Test input generation for red-black trees using abstraction. In *Proc. of IEEE/ACM International Conference on Automated Software Engineering (ASE)*, pages 414–417, 2005.
36. W. Visser, C. S. Pasareanu, and R. Pelanek. Test input generation for Java containers using state matching. In *Proc. 2006 ACM SIGSOFT International Symposium on Software Testing and Analysis*, 2006.
37. T. Xie, D. Marinov, and D. Notkin. Rostra: A framework for detecting redundant object-oriented unit tests. In *Proc. 19th ASE*, pages 196–205, Sept. 2004.
38. T. Xie, D. Marinov, W. Schulte, and D. Notkin. Symstra: A framework for generating object-oriented unit tests using symbolic execution. In *Proc. 11th TACAS*, pages 365–381, Apr. 2005.
39. J. Yang, P. Twohey, D. R. Engler, and M. Musuvathi. Using model checking to find serious file system errors. In *OSDI*, pages 273–288, 2004.

A Tool for a Formal Pattern Modeling Language

Soon-Kyeong Kim and David Carrington

School of Information Technology and Electrical Engineering
The University of Queensland 4072, Australia
soon@itee.uq.edu.au, davec@itee.uq.edu.au

Abstract. This paper presents a formal but practical approach for defining and using design patterns. Initially we formalize the concepts commonly used in defining design patterns using Object-Z. We also formalize consistency constraints that must be satisfied when a pattern is deployed in a design model. Then we implement the pattern modeling language and its consistency constraints using an existing modeling framework, EMF, and incorporate the implementation as plug-ins to the Eclipse modeling environment. While the language is defined formally in terms of Object-Z definitions, the language is implemented in a practical environment. Using the plug-ins, users can develop precise pattern descriptions without knowing the underlying formalism, and can use the tool to check the validity of the pattern descriptions and pattern usage in design models. In this work, formalism brings precision to the pattern language definition and its implementation brings practicability to our pattern-based modeling approach.

Keywords: Design Pattern, Object-Z, Formal Pattern Modeling Language, Model Evolution, Model Transformation, Pattern Tool.

1 Introduction

Design patterns are often proposed as a means to evolve models in a model-driven development approach such as MDA [16]. Since design patterns describe solutions for well-known design problems, evolving models based on design patterns seems an effective approach. While design patterns can provide an effective basis for model evolution, the current approaches to describing patterns fall short of what design patterns can offer for model evolution in the MDA context. Patterns are typically defined imprecisely using natural language descriptions with graphical annotations. It is also common to describe patterns using a concrete design or a specific example of a pattern use, as is done in [13,6]. The problem typically originates from the limitations of using object notations for describing patterns (e.g. OMT and UML [17]). Object notations are basically designed to describe concrete designs and they are not appropriate for describing patterns in an abstract manner [1,5]. Object notations also typically lack precision in their notations. To enhance this situation, the following problems have to be solved:

- There must be a way to define patterns precisely, so a tool applying patterns can interpret the properties of the patterns, and a set of transformation rules can be applied to the patterns for model evolution.

Z. Liu and J. He (Eds.): ICFEM 2006, LNCS 4260, pp. 568–587, 2006.

- Patterns must be described in an abstract manner allowing various deployments of the patterns in different applications.

To address these issues, we define a formal pattern modeling language in terms of a role metamodel using Object-Z [18]. The role metamodel defines role concepts that are commonly used to define design patterns. It also defines consistency constraints that must be preserved when the role concepts are used together to define a pattern. Using Object-Z, each role concept and its associated consistency constraints are formally defined as an Object-Z class. Given the Object-Z classes, we can define patterns precisely by using the instantiation mechanism in Object-Z (see Section 2.3 for an example). Since the pattern modeling language is designed to describe design patterns, patterns developed in this way are abstract allowing various deployments of the patterns. Despite its potential, developing patterns using a formalism may not be practical due to difficulty using the formalism. In addition, pattern descriptions in Object-Z cannot be directly interpreted by most existing modeling tools. These drawbacks potentially limit the practicability of our approach to support pattern-based modeling.

To overcome these drawbacks, we transform the role metamodel in Object-Z to an ecore model (role.ecore[1]) in the Eclipse Modeling Framework (EMF) [7], and implement it using the code generation facility provided in the EMF. The artefacts of this implementation are Java code implementing meta-classes defined in the role metamodel and an editor to create pattern models. We incorporate these artefacts as a plug-in for Eclipse (called the pattern plug-in). Since the detailed constraints of the role metamodel expressed in Object-Z cannot be implemented directly using the EMF, we customize the generated Java code and the editor to implement the constraints (see Figure 1 for the overall architecture of our approach). Given the plug-in, users can define and check patterns using the role concepts without knowing the underlying formalism used to define the concepts. The patterns defined in this way are in an XMI format, so they are understood by MDA tools.

In our approach, patterns are deployed in a design model by developing a role binding model that maps pattern entities to the design model entities. When a pattern is deployed in a design model, certain constraints must be preserved to make the pattern deployment valid. We define these properties using Object-Z, and implement the properties as a plug-in for Eclipse (called the binding plug-in) in the same way that we implement the role metamodel. The binding plug-in maintains a pattern repository, and allows the user to select a pattern and deploy it in their design models. Once a binding model is developed, an automatic model transformation takes place to evolve the design model into a pattern-deployed design model, but we do not discuss this automatic model evolution in this paper, instead focusing on explaining the tool for the formal pattern modeling language. With the two plug-ins, we are able to provide an

[1] Ecore is an object-oriented modeling language used to create models in EMF. It defines simple class constructs in object-orientation such as classes, attributes, operations, and references. These concepts are compatible to the class concepts used in Object-Z, so we map an Object-Z class to an Ecore class in our translation.

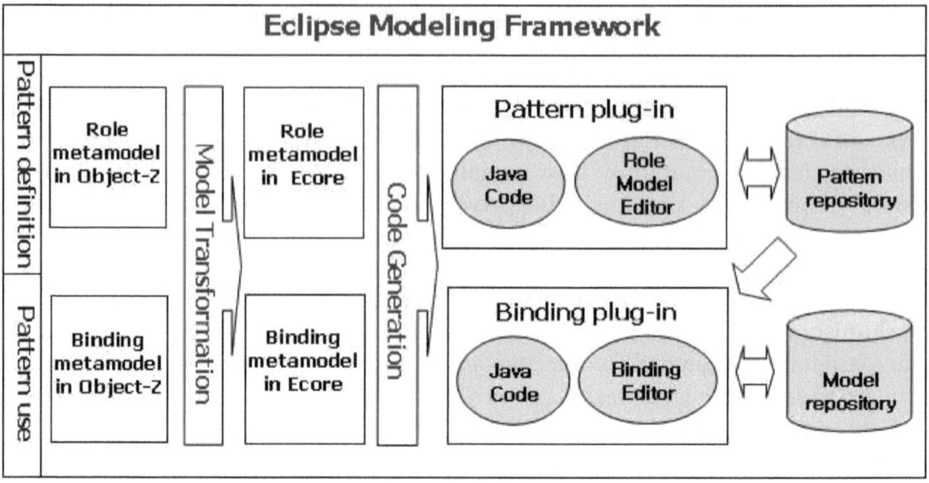

Fig. 1. Architecture of Formal Metamodeling Framework

integrated modeling framework where both developing patterns and deploying them in designs takes place in a single development environment.

In our work, formalism brings precision to the language definition and MDA techniques are used to develop tools for the formal technique. In fact, the approach introduced in this paper proposes a Formal Metamodeling Framework (FMF) where a formal language is used as a rigorous means to define a domain-specific modeling language (in this paper the pattern modeling language). Existing modeling tools are used as a means to implement the language. This approach brings precision and practicability to defining and implementing a domain-specific modeling language.

The rest of this paper is structured as follows. Section 2 provides a review of the role concepts used in our work and their formal definition in Object-Z. Section 3 presents how we implement these role concepts using EMF and how to describe patterns precisely and abstractly using this implementation. Section 4 provides a formal definition of the constraints that must be preserved when a pattern is deployed in a design model and describes the implementation of these constraints using EMF. Section 5 discusses related work. Section 6 draws some conclusions and discusses future work.

2 A Formal Definition of Role Concepts Used in Design Patterns

In the literature, roles are often used for describing design patterns [19,12,5]. However, the notion of role differs in each work (see Section 5 for details). In our approach, we first identify the underlying role concepts that are commonly used to define existing design patterns and then abstract these concepts as metamodeling elements in a role metamodel that constitutes our pattern modeling language. The following sections provide a brief summary of the pattern modeling language. We assume that all metaclasses defined in the role metamodel are formalized as Object-Z classes and refer readers to [11] for a full formal definition of the pattern modeling language.

2.1 Role Concepts in Patterns

A pattern involves a set of roles that are played by participants in the pattern. Figure 2 shows a class diagram visualizing the role concepts we define.

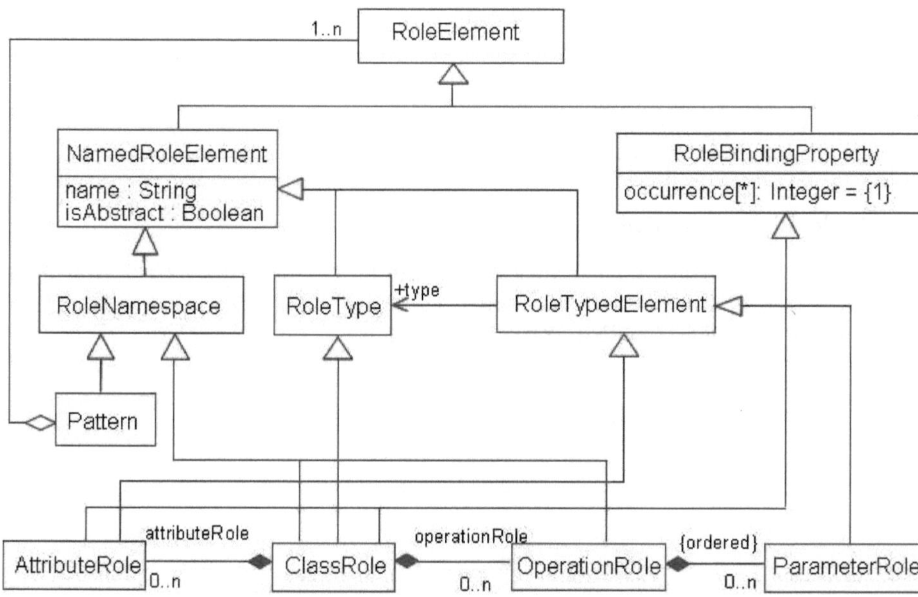

Fig. 2. Role model elements and their structure [11]

The metaclass RoleElement is the top-level model element from which all role concepts in our role modeling language are drawn. Inheriting from this class, we have two metaclasses: *NamedRoleElement* and *RoleBindingProperty*. *NamedRoleElement* is an abstract metaclass from which all role elements with a name are drawn. *RoleBindingProperty* defines the occurrence property of a role in a single pattern realization in a design model (e.g. the *ConcreteFactory* class role in the Abstract Factory pattern [6] can occur multiple times in a single pattern realization). *RoleNamespace* is an element that can own other elements (such as class roles or operation roles).

Using these concepts, we define a class role. A class role owns feature roles such as attribute roles and operation roles, and it can occur multiple times in a single pattern realization, so it inherits from both *RoleNamespace* and *RoleBindingProperty*. A class role is a role type, so it also inherits from *RoleType*. The following Object-Z class is a formal definition of the class role concept. Within a class role, attribute role names and operation role names should be unique (the © symbol stands for object containment in Object-Z). This property is formalized as a constraint in the Object-Z class.

ClassRole

RoleType
RoleNameSpace
RoleBindingProperty

$attributeRoles : \mathbb{P}\ AttributeRole©$
$operationRoles : \mathbb{P}\ OperationRole©$

$\forall\, a1, a2 : attributeRoles \bullet a1.name = a2.name \Rightarrow a1 = a2$
$\forall\, o1, o2 : operationRoles \bullet o1.name = o2.name \Rightarrow o1 = o2$

2.2 Role Relationships in Patterns

Roles in a pattern may have relationships between them. These relationships also play a role in the pattern. We define the relationships as a role element in our modeling language (see Fig. 3).

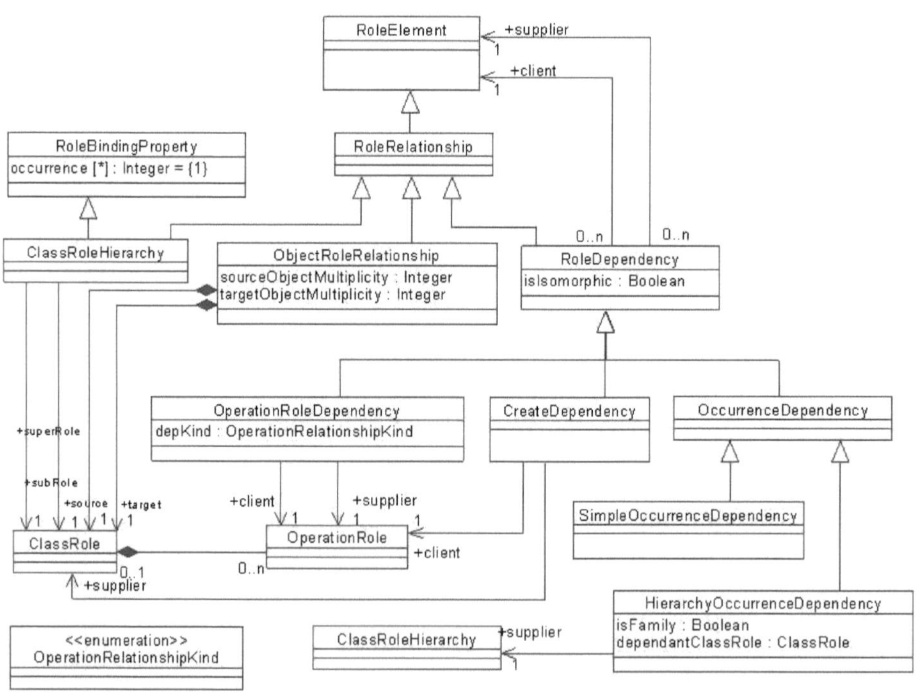

Fig. 3. Various role relationships [11]

In the metamodel, *RoleRelationship* is an abstract metaclass from which all types of relationships between role elements can be drawn. One relationship often found in patterns is a hierarchical relationship between class roles. The metaclass *ClassRoleHierarchy* captures this relationship. Since a hierarchy relationship can appear several times in a single pattern realization (e.g. the hierarchy between AbstractProduct and ConcreteProduct class roles in the Abstract Factory pattern), it inherits from *RoleBindingProperty*. A hierarchy relationship also has a super class role that defines abstract role features (e.g., operation roles) and a subclass role that realizes the abstract role features. The following Object-Z class is a formal definition of the class role hierarchy concept. In each class role hierarchy, the super class role is abstract and may occur only once, but the subclass role is not abstract and may occur multiple times, so its occurrence property remains unconstrained. A subclass role cannot be its own super class role. These properties are formalized as constraints in the Object-Z class.

```
┌─ ClassRoleHierarchy ──────────────────────────────
│ RoleBindingProperty
│ RoleRelationship
│
│ ┌───────────────────────────────────────────────
│ │ superRole : ClassRole
│ │ subRole : ClassRole
│ ├──────────────
│ │ superRole.isAbstract ∧ superRole.occurrence = 1
│ │ ¬ subRole.isAbstract ∧ superRole ≠ subRole
│ │ ...
│ └───────────────────────────────────────────────
└───────────────────────────────────────────────────
```

Another type of relationship often found in patterns is a dependency relationship between various role elements (RoleDependency). Due to page limits, we refer readers to [11] for a full definition of these relationships.

2.3 Developing Patterns Using Role Concepts

Given the Object-Z classes, defining patterns is achieved by instantiating the Object-Z classes and assigning values for the features defined in the classes. Integrity consistency between role elements is ensured by constraints defined in the Object-Z classes. We use the Abstract Factory pattern as an example in this section. The Abstract Factory pattern has two class hierarchies *Factory* and *Product* each of which contains two class roles. For example, the Factory hierarchy has two class roles: *AbstractFactory* and *ConcreteFactory*. Each of these class roles has one operation role, *CreateProduct*. The following Object-Z class is a formal description of the Factory class role hierarchy in the Abstract Factory pattern.

Factory

$$
\begin{array}{l}
factoryHierarchy : ClassRoleHierarchy \\
absFactory : ClassRole \\
absCreateProduct : OperationRole \\
conFactory : ClassRole \\
conCreateProduct : OperationRole \\
absCreateProductConCreateMethod : OperationRoleDependency \\
\hline
factoryHierarchy.superRole = absFactory \\
factoryHierarchy.subRole = conFactory \\
absCreateProduct \in absFactory.operationRoles \\
absCreateProduct.isAbstract \land absCreateProduct.owner = absFactory \\
conFactory.occurrence \geq 1 \\
conCreateProduct \in conFactory.operationRoles \\
\neg\ conCreateProduct.isAbstract \land conCreateProduct.owner = conFactory \\
absCreateProductConCreateMethod.client = absCreateProduct \\
absCreateProductConCreateMethod.supplier = conCreateProduct
\end{array}
$$

Once each class role hierarchy in the pattern is defined, we can define the entire pattern using the inheritance mechanism in Object-Z.

AbstractFactory

Including Factory and Product class role hierarchies

Factory *Product*

$$
\begin{array}{l}
absCreateProductAbsProduct : SimpleOccurrenceDependency \\
conFactoryConProduct : HierarchyOccurrenceDependency \\
conCreateProductConProduct : CreateDependency \\
\hline
absCreateProductAbsProduct.client = absCreateProduct \\
absCreateProductAbsProduct.supplier = absProduct \\
absCreateProductAbsProduct.isIsomorphic \\
conFactoryConProduct.client = conCreateFactory \\
conFactoryConProduct.supplier = productHierarchy \\
conFactoryConProduct.supplier.dependentClassRole = conProduct \\
conFactoryConProduct.supplier.isFamily \\
conCreateProductConProduct.client = conCreateProduct \\
conCreateProductConProduct.supplier = conProduct \\
conCreateProductConProduct.isIsomorphic
\end{array}
$$

Role occurrence properties at the pattern-level

$$
\begin{array}{l}
factoryHierarchy.occurrence = 1 \land productHierarchy.occurrence \geq 1 \\
absCreateProduct.occurrence \geq 1 \land conCreateProduct.occurrence \geq 1
\end{array}
$$

The Object-Z class *AbstractFactory* is a formal definition of the Abstract Factory pattern. It inherits from the Object-Z classes *Factory* and *Product.* Since the product hierarchy can occur multiple times, the occurrence property of the product roles is defined as greater than or equal to 1. In addition, various dependency relationships between the roles are formally defined using their corresponding Object-Z classes. For example, the variable *absCreateProductAbsProduct* formally defines the isomorphic occurrence dependency between the create operation role of the factory class role and an abstract product class role.

3 Implementation of the Formal Role Concepts

We use an existing modeling framework, EMF, to implement the role metamodel in Object-Z. EMF is a Java framework for building applications based on simple class models. EMF plays a very important part in our pattern-based modeling approach as it is used to implement the role metamodel and to develop pattern models. The implementation is achieved by developing an ecore model *(role.ecore)* for the role metamodel. From the ecore model, we can generate Java code using the Java code generation facility provided in EMF. It should be noted that we automatically generate an ecore model from the Object-Z role metamodel using a model transformation tool, Tefkat [23]. That is, given the metamodels of Ecore and Object-Z, we define a set of transformation rules between the two languages, and use these rules to generate an ecore model from the role metamodel in Object-Z. Previously we presented model transformation between Object-Z and UML. Transformation between Object-Z and Ecore is similar, so we refer readers to [10] for details on this topic.

Once we have an ecore model of the role metamodel, using the code generation facility of EMF we can generate Java code implementing the metaclasses in the role metamodel. Given this Java code, EMF also allows the automatic generation of an editor to create instance models of the metamodel. Using this editor, users can develop pattern models based on the role concepts defined in the role metamodel. Figure 4 shows the editor generated by EMF from the role.ecore. The editor shows a list containing all role elements definable at the model level such as class roles and relationship roles. To create a pattern model, we simply choose ClassRole from the list and fill in properties such as role name in the property window. Once an instance of a class role is created, we can define attribute roles and operation roles using the editor. Once a pattern model is created, EMF generates an XMI output file and this file can be understood by MDA tools.

The example pattern model in Fig. 4 defines the AbstractFactory pattern. It contains several class roles: an AbstractFactory class role, a ConcreteFactory class role, an AbstractProduct class role and a ConcreteProduct class role. Since the product hierarchy can occur multiple times when the pattern is realized in a design, the occurrence property of the product roles is defined as greater than or equal to 1. On the other hand, the AbstractFactory has 1 for the value of its occurrence feature because this role can be bound only once when the pattern is realized in a design. Complex occurrence dependencies between the roles are also precisely defined. For example, the isomorphic occurrence dependency between the abstract CreateProduct operation role and the AbstractProduct class role is modelled by defining a SimpleOccurrenceDependency between the roles. The dependency between the ConcreteFactory class role and a family of the ConcreteProduct class roles in the Product hierarchy is also modelled by defining a HierarchyOccurrence Dependency between the role elements. Patterns developed in this way capture the properties defined using Object-Z in Section 2.3.

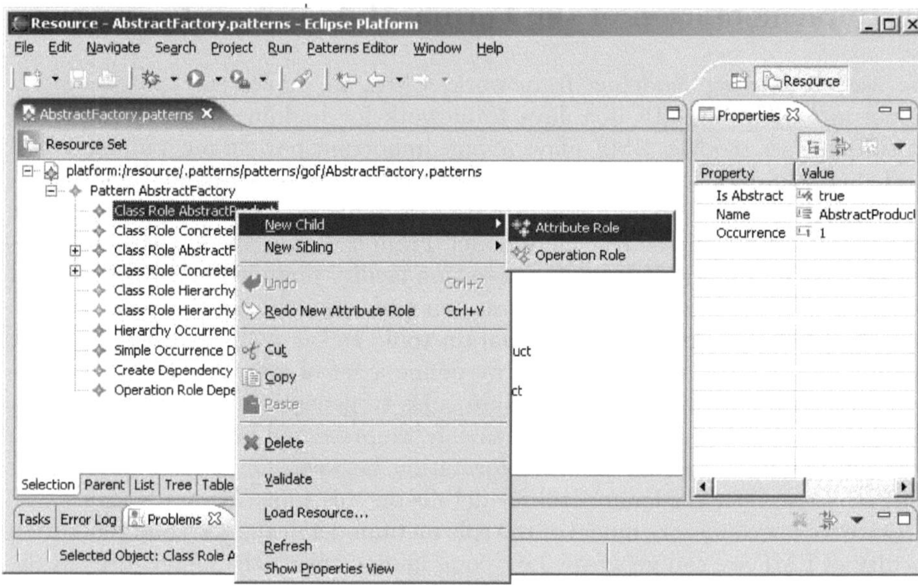

Fig. 4. The pattern model editor generated by EMF

3.1 Validation of Pattern Models

Although we implement the ecore model generated from the formal role metamodel using EMF, constraints expressed in Object-Z in the formal model cannot be implemented directly using the EMF code generation facility. This means that using the editor generated by EMF, users cannot check the conformance of patterns to the constraints defined in the role metamodel in Object-Z. We address this issue by adding several validation features to the generated pattern editor. For example, we use the EMF Validation Framework [7] to implement a validation facility to check pattern descriptions against the role metamodel. When we implement the role metamodel using EMF, EMF generates Java classes implementing the meta-classes defined in the ecore role metamodel (i.e. these Java classes are called model classes). Within these model classes, we implement a method named invariant that checks the constraints of the meta-classes that we defined using Object-Z in the formal role metamodel. When invariant methods are found in the model classes, EMF generates a special Validator class called PatternsValidator. This class is used by the EMF Validation Framework to check user-defined constraints in the model classes. The generated EMF editor includes a user-invoked action for validating instances of the role metamodel.

We also customize the generated editor to provide interactive feedback while a pattern model is being edited by displaying error messages in the Problems tab. This ensures that if the pattern model violates any constraints, the problem is reported immediately. Consider the constraint that says that every class role in a pattern must have a different role name, which is a constraint defined for the metaclass Pattern in Fig. 2. The following is partial Java code implementing this constraint using the EMF Validation framework. The method is added to the generated Java class that implements the Pattern metaclass in the role metamodel.

```
public boolean invariant(DiagnosticChain diagnostics, Map context) {
    // Check for duplicate named role element names

        for(int j = i; j < names.size(); j++) {
        String nextName = (String)names.get(j);
        if(nextName != null && nextName.equals(name)) {
                if (diagnostics != null) {
                        diagnostics.add(new BasicDiagnostic(
                        Diagnostic.ERROR, PatternsValidator.DIAGNOSTIC_SOURCE,
                    PatternsValidator.PATTERN__INVARIANT,
                        "Duplicate named role element: " + name,
                                new Object [] { this }));    }
            ...
        }
```

The example pattern in Fig. 5 violates this constraint since it has two class roles with the same name. An error message is displayed in the problem tab.

3.2 Customization to Prevent Errors

It is always better to prevent errors if possible rather than identify and correct them after they are introduced. To prevent user errors, we constrain the choices that the editor offers to the user in a selection. For example, one of the constraints in the HierarchyOccurrenceDependency class requires that the supplier role must be an instance of ClassRoleHierarchy. However, since the supplier reference is inherited from the RoleDependency class, its type is RoleElement. Although the invariant in the model class requires that the supplier is an instance of ClassRoleHierarchy, the generated editor allows any RoleElement to be selected, since the type of the reference is RoleElement. A better approach is to restrict the possible values that can be selected to just the ClassRoleHierarchy instances. EMF generates two different plugins that deal with user interface code. The edit plugin provides code that is meant to be reused, while the editor plugin provides the specific editor code for Eclipse. The editor plugin uses item providers to

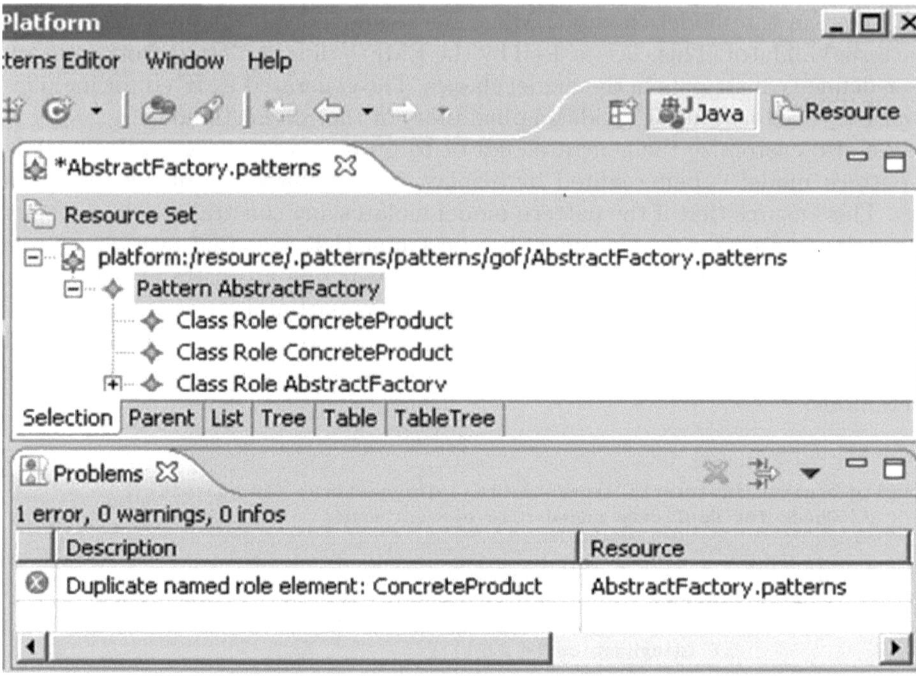

Fig. 5. The problems tab showing errors

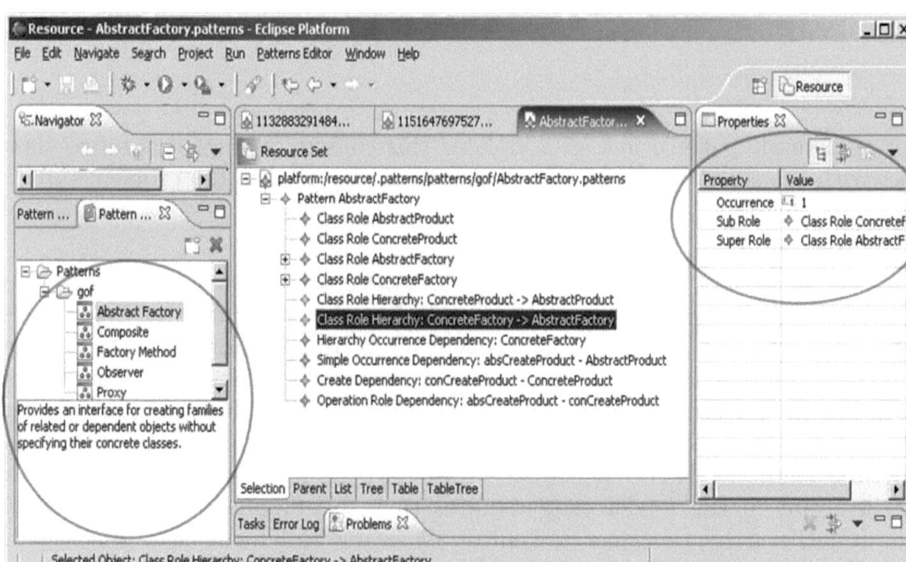

Fig. 6. Customized Pattern Editor and a pattern browser

interact with the model. Item providers adapt model objects so they can provide interfaces to be viewed or edited. We customize the editor plugin to provide constraints at the editor level that involve restricting the possible items (e.g. the dropdown menu in Fig. 6 only shows class roles to define a class role hierarchy). In this way, the pattern editor now only displays role elements that are relevant, thus preventing potential user errors.

Once pattern models are defined, they are placed in a pattern repository. A pattern browser that allows the user to browse and select patterns is added to the pattern modeling framework. A general description of each pattern such as intent and motivation is also displayed in the pattern browser (see the left hand side in Fig. 6).

4 Deploying Patterns in Models

In our approach, a pattern is deployed in a design model by developing a binding model that maps pattern entities to the design entities. This separation of role binding information from the design model has several advantages:

- It does not increase the complexity of the design model, which can occur if pattern deployment information is included in the model.
- After a design model evolves, pattern deployment information remains in the binding model. Any modifications of pattern use in the design model or checking any conflicts with pattern properties after design model evolution can be achieved by tracing the binding models.

4.1 Formal Definition of the Role Binding Model

A role binding metamodel captures all information linking role elements defined in a pattern to model elements defined in a design model. Figure 7 shows the structure of a role binding model. A role binding model is associated with a pattern model and a design model. It has a set of bindings; each binding maps a role element to a design model element in the design model.

Our role binding metamodel is generic and does not restrict pattern realization in a particular way. Instead it defines a small set of integrity constraints that must be preserved in any pattern realization to make the pattern realization

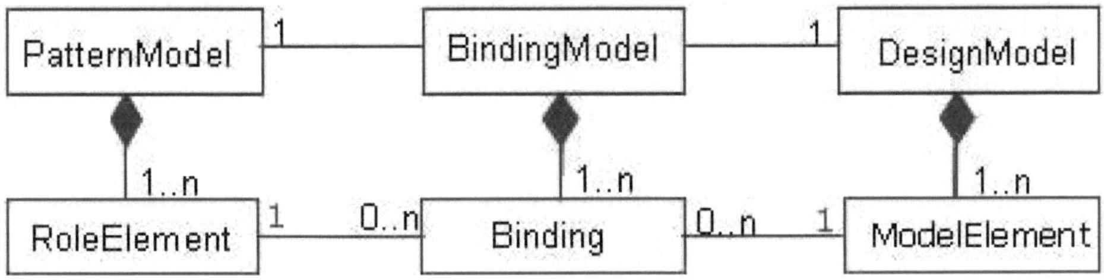

Fig. 7. Role binding model structure

valid. The validity of the pattern realization can be checked using the binding model. Since patterns are realized mainly in class models, we restrict design models to class models.

Prior to providing a formal definition of the role binding model, we give a formal definition of a class model below. A class model has a set of classes and relationships between the classes. A class has attributes and operations and a relationship has associated information such as its source, target and multiplicity.

$$ClassConstruct == Class \bigcup Attribute \bigcup Operation \bigcup Relationship \bigcup Parameter$$

ClassModel

$class : \mathbb{P}\ Class$
$rel : \mathbb{P}\ Relationship$

We then define an Object-Z class Binding to describe mappings from a role element to a design model element. Since roles can be instances of any subclasses of the metaclass RoleElement, the ↓ operator defining polymorphism in Object-Z [18] is attached to the type of the roleElement attribute.

Binding

$roleElement : \downarrow RoleElement$
$designElement : ClassConstruct$

Using the concepts above, we give a formal definition of a role binding model. A role binding model has a role model defining a pattern and a class model realizing the pattern, and a set of role bindings between role elements and design elements. The integrity constraints that must be preserved in any pattern realization are defined as constraints in the Object-Z class. For example, for each role in a pattern except dependencies (which will be realized by the bindings of their associated roles), the occurrence property of each role must be preserved in the binding. This integrity constraint of the binding model is formalized as a constraint in the Object-Z class (see [11] for a full formal description of the role binding model).

RoleBindingModel

$classModel : ClassModel$
$pattern : RoleModel$
$bindings : \mathbb{P}\ Binding$

$\bigcup\{b : bindings \bullet b.roleElement\} \subseteq pattern.roles$
$\bigcup\{b : bindings \bullet b.designElement\} \subseteq classModel.class \cup classModel.rel$
$\forall r : \{rr : pattern.roles \mid rr \notin RoleDependency\} \bullet$
$\quad \#\{b : bindings \mid b.roleElement = r\} \leq r.occurrence$
$\ldots$

4.2 Implementation of the Role Binding Model and Consistency Checking

The role binding model is implemented using EMF in the same way as we implement the role metamodel. The binding editor, like the pattern editor, is based on the generated EMF editor for the binding meta-model. Patterns can be used in software development in various ways[2], so we support pattern use in any class model that is defined as a MOF or Ecore model (see Fig. 8).

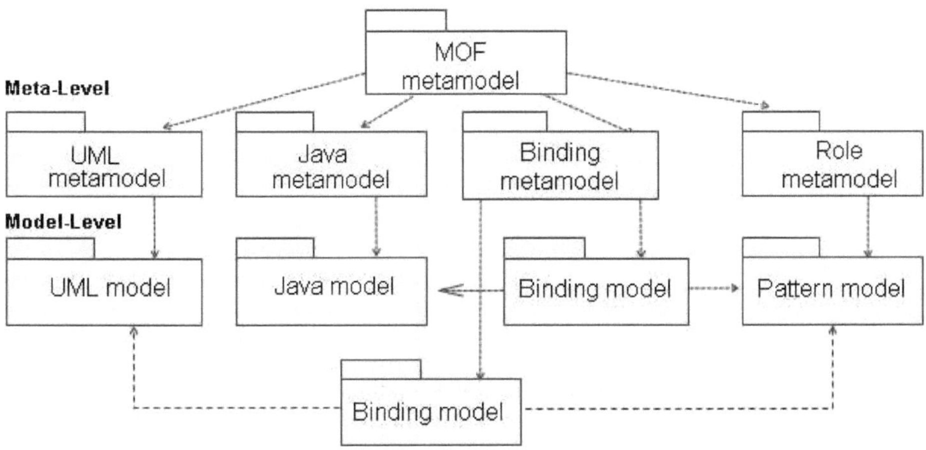

Fig. 8. Generic Pattern Binding Architecture

To provide generic support for any class model, some customizations are required since the generated editor refers to two different models (the target class model and the role model defining a pattern) and the user should be able to select any element in the class model as the target for a binding instance model. We have developed a Pattern Deployment Wizard that allows the user to choose a class model to deploy patterns. Once a model is selected, a role binding editor generated by EMF is displayed (see Fig. 9). Using this editor, a user can define how to deploy a pattern in that design model. The role binding editor lists all the roles defined in the pattern and provides the pattern description. When a role is selected, the property window shows relevant model elements that can be mapped to this role. The validity of binding models can be checked at binding time or when the binding is completed. The validity checks are implemented as class invariants. When a binding model is incomplete (some role elements not mapped to design model elements), the validator displays warnings and checks the integrity of the binding model for the mapped role elements (see the Problems view in Fig.9).

2 [4,21] use patterns to build a design model while others use patterns for refactoring existing models [20] or code refactoring [8].

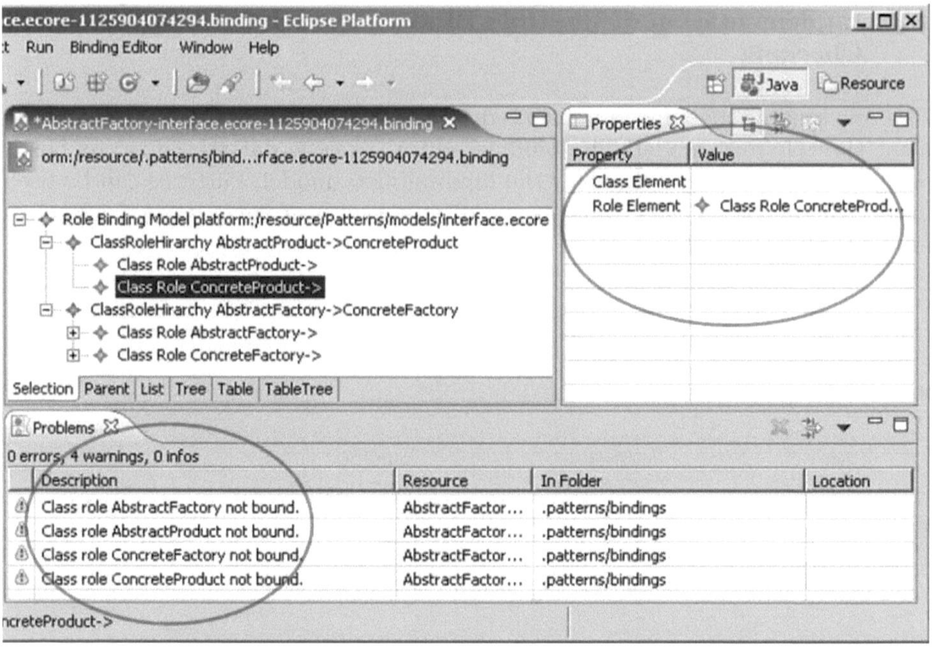

Fig. 9. Role binding editor and binding model validator

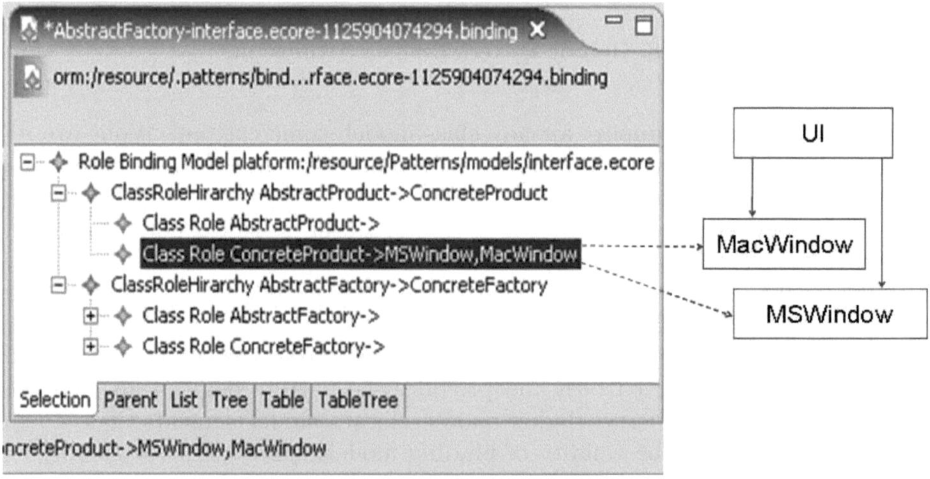

Fig. 10. Role binding model example 1 deploying the AbstractFactory pattern

4.3 Examples of the Role Binding Model

Figures 10 and 11 show two different binding model examples for the Abstract-Factory pattern. The example in Fig. 10 shows a simple application of this

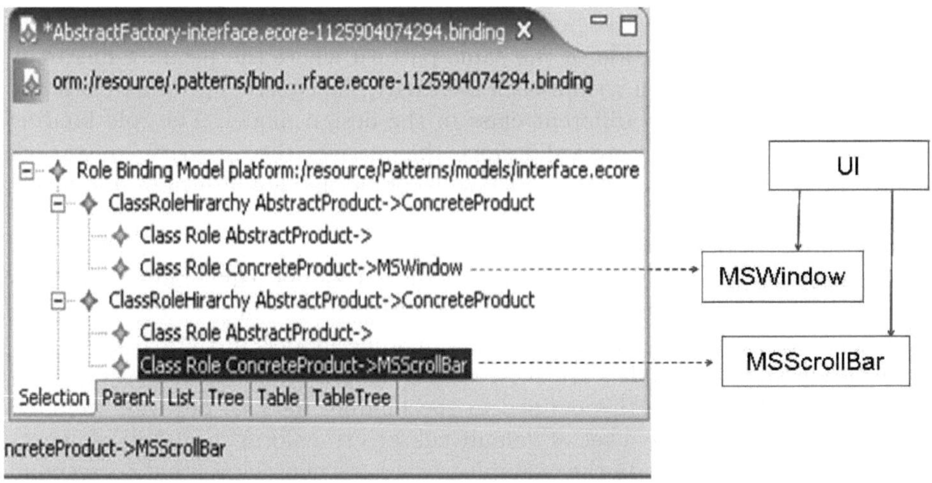

Fig. 11. Role binding model example 2 deploying the AbstractFactory pattern

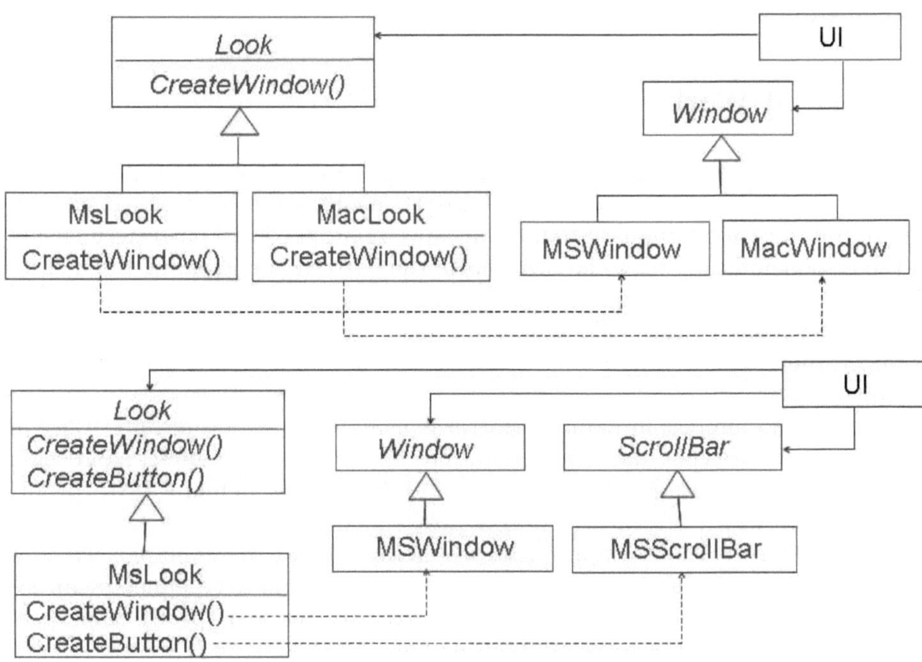

Fig. 12. Evolved design model example deploying the AbstractFactory pattern

pattern where the product class role hierarchy is mapped once to a design model. Within the product hierarchy, the concrete product class role is mapped to two different classes in the design model (see the partial class diagram added to the example purely for descriptive purposes). On the other hand, the example in Fig. 11 shows another application of the same pattern where the product hierarchy is mapped twice, and then within each hierarchy, the concrete product class role is mapped just once to a different class in the design model. The role binding models of both examples are valid since they satisfy the integrity constraints defined in the role binding metamodel, so the binding validator does not report any errors.

As mentioned, once a binding model is created for a design model, the model is automatically evolved into a pattern-deployed model using model transformation techniques. Figure 12 shows the resulting design models deploying the AbstractFactory pattern based on the two binding models in Fig. 10 and 11.

The original design models are evolved by adding new model elements according to the binding properties defined in the binding models. For any unbound role elements, we provide a set of default rules to transform those role elements to design model elements. In the examples, we create new classes that correspond to the factory class role and the abstract product class role in the pattern. Then the relationships between these classes are defined based on the relationships between their corresponding class roles in the pattern. The default rules are readily customized by the user.

5 Related Work

Lano et. al [9] formalize patterns using VDM++ and prove design patterns as refinement transformations using the Object Calculus. Flores et al. [2] use the RAISE Specification Language to formally specify properties of patterns focusing on the responsibilities and collaborations of the pattern participants. Eden et al. [1] present patterns as formulae in LePUS, a language defined as a fragment of higher order monadic logic. These works bring precision to pattern descriptions. However, they focus mainly on pattern creation and do not cover pattern use as we do.

There is also interest in defining patterns using UML. Fontoura and Lucena [13] use new stereotypes and tagged values to improve the presentation of design pattern configurations. Similarly, Sanada and Adams [24] define a UML profile for patterns in which several stereotypes are defined to support the presentation of design patterns. Another approach uses metamodeling to define pattern concepts in the context of the UML metamodel. For example, Guennec et al. [3] use meta-level collaborations to present design patterns and specify some pattern properties as a set of constraints using OCL. Mak et al. [14] present similar work to [3] using meta-level UML collaborations to present design patterns. All these works discuss patterns in the context of UML and limit their application to UML.

Using role modeling techniques, Riehle [5] and Lauder et al. [12] use role concepts to describe patterns, but they limit the role concepts mainly to objects and do not capture other roles played by different entities in a pattern such as classes, features of the classes and relationships between classes. Also object notations used by Riehle and Lauder et al. such as type models in [12] or class templates in [5] do not reflect the full generality of patterns. France et al. [19] reduce these problems by extending the role concepts beyond objects to all features in UML such as classes, attributes, operations, associations, and generalizations. They also use OCL to specify those pattern properties that can be only decided at pattern instantiation time in terms of meta-level pattern constraints. The use of roles facilitates describing patterns in an abstract manner by utilizing roles as placeholders for types or classes. Nevertheless, France et al. discuss role concepts in the context of UML only. Also utilizing role concepts in any UML model construct makes the overall pattern description unnecessarily complex.

Neal et al. [21] define the Pattern Constraints Language (PCL) to describe patterns based on roles and role behaviours. They also developed a tool to check that the behaviour of a system implementing a pattern is consistent with the pattern specification. Soundarajan et al. [15] present an approach to specifying patterns based on roles and their responsibilities. Nevertheless, the main focus of these approaches is on describing patterns using role concepts. They do not consider pattern use as we do in the context of MDA. Also their approaches are not as generic as ours, which is applicable to any modeling language at any level of abstraction.

There is also research that uses patterns for software evolution. For example, Mens et al. [22] present a declarative metamodeling approach to specify design patterns and their evolution in the software. Mapelsden et al. [4] introduce a tool that supports pattern use in UML models. They use a notation called the Design Pattern Modeling Language (DPML) to specify patterns. A design pattern instantiation model is created by copying the structure of the pattern specification. This instantiation model is then used to check correct usage of the pattern in a UML model by linking all design pattern instance elements to the UML design model elements. Unlike our work, this work is not generic just supporting pattern use in UML; they do not separate pattern usage information from the design model; they do not use model transformation techniques to evolve models based on patterns.

France et al. [20] present a metamodeling approach to model refactoring based patterns. This approach shares some ideas with our work, but it is not generic like ours and they do not implement their ideas as a supporting tool. In addition, most of the tools introduced in this area are stand-alone, while we incorporate the pattern development environment into an existing modeling environment providing an integrated modeling framework.

6 Conclusions and Future Work

In this paper we have presented a formal pattern modeling language that is designed specifically to describe design patterns and we have implemented the language using an existing modeling framework. We have provided a plugin tool for the same modeling framework that supports the creation and validation of pattern descriptions and also supports pattern-based model evolution in the

MDA context. When a model is completed based on patterns, we can apply an MDA tool to generate code from the model. Using formalism, we bring precision to the language definition. Using an existing modeling framework, we provide tools for the formal technique. We have defined the design patterns in the GoF's pattern book [6] using the pattern language and built a pattern repository. Currently we are investigating the scalability and feasibility of our approach using enterprise scale applications, and improving the usability of the role binding process.

Acknowledgements

This research is funded by an Australian Research Council Discovery grant, DP0451830: Formalizing Software Design Pattern Concepts and Pattern Specifications using Metamodeling. We wish to thank Alejandro Metke for his assistance in implementing the plugins.

References

1. Eden A., Y. Hirshfeld, and A. Yehudai. Lepus - a declarative pattern specification language. Technical Report 326/98, Department of Computer Science, Tel Aviv Uni., http://www.math.tau.ac.il/ eden/bibliography.html#lepus, 1998.
2. Flores A., L. Reynoso, and R. Moore. A formal model of object-oriented design and GoF patterns. Technical Report 200, UNU/IIST, 2000.
3. Guennec A., G. Sunye, and J. Jezequel. Precise modeling of design patterns. In *UML2000*, volume 1939 of *LNCS*, pages 482–496. Springer, 2000.
4. Mapelsden D, J. Hosking, and J. Grundy. Design pattern modeling and instantiation using DPML. In *TOOLS Pacific*, pages 3–11, 2002.
5. Riehle D. Describing and composing patterns using role diagrams. In *Ubilab Conference*, pages 137–152, 1996.
6. Gamma E., R. Helm, R. Johnson, and J. Vlissidese. *Design Patterns: Elements of Reusable Object-Oriented Software*. Addison Wesley, 1995.
7. EMF. Eclipse modeling framework, http://www.eclipse.org/emf/.
8. Kerievsky J. *Refactoring to Patterns*. Addison Wesley, 2005.
9. Lano K., S. Goldsack, and J. Bicarregui. Formalizing design patterns. In *BCS-FACS, http://www1.bcs.org.uk/DocsRepository/02700/2790/lano.pdf*, 1996.
10. Soon-Kyeong Kim, Damian Burger, and David A. Carrington. An MDA approach towards integrating formal and informal modeling languages. In *Formal Methods*, volume 3582 of *LNCS*, pages 448–464. Springer, 2005.
11. Soon-Kyeong Kim and David A. Carrington. A rigorous foundation for pattern-based design models. In *International Conference of B and Z Users*, volume 3455 of *LNCS*, pages 242–261. Springer, 2005.
12. Anthony Lauder and Stuart Kent. Precise visual specification of design patterns. In *ECOOP*, volume 1445 of *LNCS*, pages 114–134. Springer, 1998.
13. Fontoura M. and C. Lucena. Extending UML to improve the representation of design patterns. *Journal of Object-Oriented Programming*, 13(11):12–19, 2001.
14. Jeffrey Ka-Hing Mak, Clifford Sze-Tsan Choy, and Daniel Pak-Kong Lun. Precise modeling of design patterns in UML. In *International Conference on Software Engineering*.

15. Soundarajan N. and J. Hallstrom. Responsibilities and rewards: Specifying design patterns. In *International Conference on Software Engineering*, pages 666 – 675, 2004.
16. Object Management Group, Framingham, Massachusetts. *MDA Guide Version 1.0.1*, June 2003.
17. Object Management Group, Framingham, Massachusetts. *UML 2.0 Superstructure Specification*, October 2004.
18. Duke R. and G. Rose. *Formal Object-Oriented Specification Using Object-Z*. Macmillan, 2002.
19. France R., D.-K. Kim, G. Sudipto, and E. Song. A UML-based pattern specification technique. *IEEE Transactions on Software Engineering*, 30(3):193–206, 2004.
20. France R., G. Sudipto, E. Song, and D.-K. Kim. A metamodeling approach to pattern-based model refactoring. *IEEE Software*, 20(5):52–58, 2003.
21. Neal S. and P. Linington. Tool support for development using patterns. In *International Enterprise Distributed Object Computing*, pages 237–248, 2001.
22. Mens T. and Tourwe T. A declarative evolution framework for object-oriented design patterns. In *International Conference on Software Maintenance*, pages 570–579, 2001.
23. Tefkat. The EMF transformation engine, https://sourceforge.net/projects/tefkat/.
24. Sanada Y. and R. Adams. Representing design patterns and frameworks in UML - towards a comprehensive approach. *Journal of Object-Oriented Programming*, 2:143–154, 2002.

An Open Extensible Tool Environment for Event-B*

Jean-Raymond Abrial[1], Michael Butler[2], Stefan Hallerstede[1], and Laurent Voisin[1]

[1] ETH Zurich, Switzerland
{jabrial, halstefa, lvoisin}@inf.ethz.ch
[2] University of Southampton, United Kingdom
M.J.Butler@ecs.soton.ac.uk

Abstract. We consider modelling indispensable for the development of complex systems. Modelling must be carried out in a formal notation to reason and make meaningful conjectures about a model. But formal modelling of complex systems is a difficult task. Even when theorem provers improve further and get more powerful, modelling will remain difficult. The reason for this that modelling is an exploratory activity that requires ingenuity in order to arrive at a meaningful model. We are aware that automated theorem provers can discharge most of the onerous trivial proof obligations that appear when modelling systems. In this article we present a modelling tool that seamlessly integrates modelling and proving similar to what is offered today in modern integrated development environments for programming. The tool is extensible and configurable so that it can be adapted more easily to different application domains and development methods.

1 Introduction

We consider modelling of software systems and more generally of complex systems to be an important development phase. This is certainly the case in other engineering disciplines where models are often produced in the form of blueprints. We also believe that more complex models can only be written when the method of stepwise refinement is used. In other words, a model is built by successive enhancement of an original simple "sketch" carefully transforming it into more concrete representations. As an analogy, the first sketchy blueprint of an architect is gradually zoomed in order to eventually represent all the fine details of the intended building. On the way decisions are made concerning the way it can be constructed, thus yielding the final complete set of blueprints. We believe that formal notation is indispensable in such a modelling activity. It provides the foundation on which building models can be carried out, similar to the formal conventions that are used when drawing blueprints. Simply writing a formal text is insufficient, though, to achieve a model of high quality. However, we cannot test or execute a model to verify that the model has the properties that we demand of it. Similarly, we cannot open a window in the blueprint of a building. The only serious way to analyse a model is to reason about it, proving in a mathematically rigorous way that the properties are satisfied.

* This research was carried out as part of the EU research project IST 511599 RODIN (Rigorous Open Development Environment for Complex Systems) http://rodin.cs.ncl.ac.uk

Z. Liu and J. He (Eds.): ICFEM 2006, LNCS 4260, pp. 588–605, 2006.

In order for formal modelling to be used safely and effectively in engineering practice, good tool support is necessary. Present day integrated development environments used for programming do carry out many tasks automatically in the background, e.g. [13], and provide fast feedback when changes are made to a program text. In particular, there is no need for the user to start processes like compilation. A program is written and then run or debugged without compiling it. We present a tool for Event-B [3] that applies these techniques used in programming to formal modelling. Instead of compilation, we are interested in proof obligation generation and automatically discharging trivial proof obligations. Instead of running a program we reason about models or analyse them.

Verification by proof is not restricted to modelling. It has a long tradition in programming methodology, too, e.g. [17]. Software tools that support formal verification methods in programming have been developed, e.g. [7,14]. We mention [7], in particular, because the Boogie architecture presented in the article provides characteristics similar to the Event-B tool. We quote two points from [7] about Boogie and present our view of them:

(1) "Design-Time Feedback". The tool is very responsive and provides almost immediate feedback that easily relates to the program, (resp. model).
(2) "Distinct Proof Obligation Generation and Verification phases". This allows decoupling the development of the programming (resp. modelling) method and prover technologies. It also allows the origin of a proof obligation to be traced easily. This is particularly important when proofs fail.

The third point in the list describing Boogie in [7] is "Abstract Interpretation and Verification Condition Generation". The corresponding problem does not exist in the Event-B notation because it has been designed to be very close to the proof obligations by means of which we reason about Event-B. Technical difficulties encountered in Event-B stem more from the support of refinement and from the requirement that proof obligations appear transparent to the user. By transparency we mean that the user should look at the proof obligation as being part of the model. When a proof obligation cannot be proved, it should be almost obvious what needs to be changed in the model. When modelling, we usually do not simply represent some system in a formal notation. At the same time we learn what the system is and eliminate misunderstandings, inconsistencies, and specification gaps. In particular, in order to eliminate misunderstandings, we first must develop an understanding of the system. The situation is quite different when programming. When we start programming we should already understand what we are implementing. We do not look any longer at the system as a whole but only at the parts that we have to implement, and our main concern is doing this correctly. The task of a tool is to point out programming errors to the user.

In this article we focus on the Event-B tool. This tool is implemented on top of the RODIN open tools kernel [24] which is developed alongside the Event-B tool. The motivation and background of the RODIN open tools kernel is discussed in Section 1.2.

1.1 Existing Tools for Modelling and Proof

We review a selection of formal modelling tools. It is not intended to be complete but to explain the kind of problems that we try to overcome with the Event-B tool described in this article.

The use of general purpose theorem provers with modelling notations like Z [10,29], Action Systems [4,19], or Abstract State Machines [6,9] usually requires a lot of expert knowledge in order to make efficient use of them when reasoning about formal models. This is not a problem of bad design of the theorem prover, but more a problem of bridging the gap between the notation and the logic underlying the theorem prover. General purpose theorem provers are well-suited to proving mathematical theorems in mathematical domains. The main problem solved by the theorem prover is to provide efficient ways to prove theorems. They are not specifically geared for modelling or the typical proof obligations associated with modelling. Theorem provers do assume that the problems to be proved, i.e. the proof obligations, are stated by the user and their proofs as such matter to the user. However, if the main interest of the user is modelling, the user is more concerned with understanding and learning about a model than with the proofs. In particular, generation of the proof obligations should be build into the tool to free the user from tedious work of writing them explicitly. In addition, we expect such a tool to be extensible and adaptable to cope with new and changing applications. This is not an issue with a general purpose theorem prover because proof obligation generation is manual anyway. In the Event-B tool we ensure that proof obligation generation remains extensible and adaptable.

Isabelle [23,30] has been used with Z [10]. Although well-integrated the main problem remains that the user must explicitly specify proof obligations and is responsible for maintaining them. Another problem is that the user must understand the Isabelle logic as well as that of Z. To some degree this is alleviated by the Isar language [22] that extends Isabelle with more legible proofs. Similarly, abstract state machines (ASM) have been used with the KIV theorem prover [6]. The refinement theory used with ASM is stated in KIV and the user has to state the relevant theorems (proof obligations). When dealing with large models the amount of proof obligations is simply to high to load the user with this task [5]. Our tool overcomes these problems by maintaining proof obligations and by providing a prover that is tailored for first-order logic and set theory (which are the basic mathematical theories of Event-B). In the design of the tool great care has been taken to easily relate proof obligations to a model, so that the user can quickly return to the model when a proof fails. The prover interface has also been designed to appear as natural as possible to the user. It gives a graphical representation of a sequent calculus for classical logic that has been further developed from the Click'n'Prove tool [2]. The major shortcoming of Click'n'Prove is that it is built on top of a theorem prover that executes proof scripts. As a consequence, feedback to the user is slow. In addition, the user must explicitly start tools to type-check a model, or generate proof obligations for it. Because the proof obligation generator has been developed for models of sequential programs with the B-Method [1], some proof obligations have variables renamed or are rewritten to a point where they are difficult to relate to the model. This violates our requirement for transparency. Following the experience with Click'n'Prove, we have also simplified Event-B (see Section 2) so that it does not hinder the design of a transparent proof obligation generator. In the Event-B tool, models are stored in a repository and manipulated like spread sheets. Furthermore, all elements of a model (e.g. invariants, axioms) are named. This makes it possible for the tool to analyse models differentially, only generating proof obligations when necessary. The proof obligations are connected to the model by referring to involved repository elements.

The Z/EVES system [26] has a graphical front-end for Z specifications. It has automatic support for type-checking and some related properties. Although its prover is part of the tool, the user is responsible for stating relevant proof obligations. Z/EVES mostly provides a good interface for entering models graphically but less so for reasoning about them.

The approach of embedding a modelling notation into a general purpose theorem prover [10] like Isabelle [23] or Coq [8] provides a strong logical foundation. This is very satisfactory from a logicians point of view. From an industrial point of view, logical soundness is only one design consideration. We also need reactivity, i.e. immediate feedback, speed, and a notation and logic that is familiar to the user of the tool. This is very difficult to achieve in embedded designs. In the area of safety-critical embedded software, the approach of directly implementing provers has been proved fruitful. The Atelier B tool [11] has been used in large scale industrial projects, e.g. [5].

1.2 The Significance of Extensibility and Configurability

We take the view that no one tool can solve all our development problems and that it is important to apply a range of tools in a complementary way in rigorous development. For example, it makes sense to apply model checking as a pre-filter, before applying a theorem prover to a proof obligation. Similarly the use of a diagrammatic views (e.g., UML) of a formal model can aid with construction and validation. Many analysis tools, such as model checkers, theorem provers, translation tools (e.g., UML to B and code generators), have been developed, some of which are commercial products and some research tools. However a major drawback of these tools is that they tend to be closed and difficult to use together in an integrated way. They also tend to be difficult for other interested parties to extend, making it difficult for the work of a larger research community to be combined. Our aim with the RODIN open tools kernel is to greatly extend the state of the art in formal methods tools, allowing multiple parties to integrate their tools as plug-ins to support rigorous development methods. This is likely to have a significant impact on future research in formal methods tools and will encourage greater industrial uptake of these tools.

As well as supporting the combination of different complementary tools, openness and customizability is very important in that it will allow users to customize and adapt the basic tools to their particular needs. For example, a car manufacturer using Event-B to study the overall design of a car information system might be willing to plug some special tools able to help defining the corresponding documentation and maintenance package. Likewise, a rocket manufacturer using Event-B might be willing to plug a special tool for analysing and developing the failure detection part of its design.

2 The Event-B Method

Event-B is defined in terms of a few simple concepts that describe a discrete event system and proof obligations that permit verification of properties of the event system. We present the notation using some syntactical conventions. The keywords **when**, **then**,

end, and so on, are just delimiters to make the textual representation more readable. Introduction of a syntax in the definition of the notation would make it much more difficult to extend the notation, e.g. by introducing probabilities [21].

An Event-B *model* consists of *contexts* and *machines*. In this description we focus on machines. A complete description of Event-B can be found in [3].

Contexts contain the static parts of a model. These are *constants* and *axioms* that describe the properties of these constants.

Machines contain the dynamic parts of a model. A machine is made of a *state*, which is defined by means of *variables*. Variables, like constants, correspond to simple mathematical objects: sets, binary relations, functions, numbers, etc. They are constrained by *invariants* $I(v)$ where v are the variables of the machine. Invariants are supposed to hold whenever variable values change. But this must be proved first (see Section 2.1).

Besides its state, a machine contains a number of *events* which show the way it may evolve. Each event is composed of a *guard* and an *action*. The guard is the necessary condition under which the event may occur. The action, as its name indicates, determines the way in which the state variables are going to evolve when the event occurs.

An event may be executed only when its guard holds. Events are *atomic* and when the guards of several events hold simultaneously, then *at most one of them* may be executed at any one moment. The choice of event to be executed is non-deterministic. Practically speaking, an event, named evt, is presented in one of the three following simple forms:

$$\begin{array}{l}\mathsf{evt} \mathrel{\widehat{=}} \mathbf{begin}\ S(v)\ \mathbf{end}\\ \mathsf{evt} \mathrel{\widehat{=}} \mathbf{when}\ P(v)\ \mathbf{then}\ S(v)\ \mathbf{end}\\ \mathsf{evt} \mathrel{\widehat{=}} \mathbf{any}\ t\ \mathbf{where}\ P(t,v)\ \mathbf{then}\ S(t,v)\ \mathbf{end} \quad ,\end{array}$$

where $P(\ldots)$ is a predicate denoting the guard, t denotes some variables that are local to the event, and $S(\ldots)$ denotes the action that updates some variables. The variables of the machine containing the event are denoted by v.

The action consists of a collection of *assignments* that modify the state simultaneously. An assignments has one of the following three simple forms:

Assignment		Before-After Predicate
$x := E(t,v)$	–	$x' = E(t,v)$
$x :\in E(t,v)$	–	$x' \in E(t,v)$
$x :\mid Q(t,v,x')$	–	$Q(t,v,x')$,

where x are some variables, $E(\ldots)$ denotes an expression, and $Q(\ldots)$ a predicate. Simultaneity of the assignments is expressed by conjoining the before-after predicates of an action. Variables y that do not appear on the left hand side of an assignment of action do not change. Formally this is achieved by conjoining $y' = y$ to the before-after predicate of the action. Note, that Event-B requires actions to be feasible under the guard of the corresponding events. For instance, for the non-deterministic assignment we must prove

$$I(v) \ \wedge\ P(t,v) \Rightarrow (\exists x' \cdot Q(t,v,x')) \quad ,$$

where $I(v)$ is the invariant of the machine and $P(t,v)$ the guard of the event.

In order to be able to provide better tool support invariants, guards, actions are lists of named predicates and assignments. These names can be used to refer to these objects from within the documentation of a machine. But foremost, these names are used to identify all objects and provide helpful information about the origin of proof obligations in the prover interface. The different predicates in the list are implicitly conjoined.

2.1 Consistency of a Machine

Once a machine has been written, one must prove that it is *consistent*. This is done by proving that each event of the machine preserves the invariant. More precisely, it must be proved that the action associated with each event modifies the state variables in such a way that the modified variables satisfy the invariant, under the hypothesis that the invariant holds presently and the guard of the event is true. For a machine with state variable v, invariant $I(v)$, and an event $\mathbf{when}\ P(v)\ \mathbf{then}\ v\ :=\ E(v)\ \mathbf{end}$ the statement to be proved is the following:

$$I(v)\ \wedge\ P(v)\ \Rightarrow\ I(E(v))\quad . \tag{1}$$

Note that, in practice we carry out a decomposition of (1) according to the lists of named invariants, guards, and actions. So statement (1) is not the proof obligation the user gets to see. Instead the user sees a collection of simpler proof obligations.

2.2 Refining a Machine

Refining a machine consists of refining its state and its events. A concrete machine (with regards to the more abstract one) has a state that should be related to that of the abstraction by a so-called *glueing invariant*, which is expressed in terms of a predicate $J(v,w)$ connecting the abstract state represented by the variables v and the concrete state represented by the variables w.

Each event of the abstract machine is refined to one or more corresponding events of the concrete one. Informally speaking, a concrete event is said to refine its abstraction (1) when the guard of the former is stronger than that of the latter (guard strengthening), (2) and when the glueing invariant is preserved by the conjoined action of both events. In the case of an abstract event *abs* and a corresponding concrete event *con* of the form

$$\begin{array}{l}\mathsf{abs} \mathrel{\widehat{=}} \mathbf{when}\ P(v)\ \mathbf{then}\ v\ :=\ E(v)\ \mathbf{end}\\ \mathsf{con} \mathrel{\widehat{=}} \mathbf{when}\ Q(w)\ \mathbf{then}\ w\ :=\ F(w)\ \mathbf{end}\quad ,\end{array}$$

the statement to prove is the following:

$$I(v)\ \wedge\ J(v,w)\ \wedge\ Q(v)\ \Rightarrow\ P(v)\ \wedge\ J(E(v),F(w))\quad , \tag{2}$$

where $I(v)$ is the abstract invariant and $J(v,w)$ is the glueing invariant.

Similarly to (1) the user never gets to see (2) but only the decomposed form.

2.3 Adding New Events in a Refinement

When refining a machine by another one, it is possible to *add new events*. Such events must be proved to refine a dummy event that does nothing (skip) in the abstraction.

Moreover, it may be proved that the new events cannot collectively take control forever. For this, a unique *variant expression* $V(w)$ has to be provided, that is decreased by each new event. In case the new event has the form:

$$\mathsf{evt} \mathrel{\widehat{=}} \textbf{when } R(w) \textbf{ then } w := G(w) \textbf{ end} \quad ,$$

the following statements have to be proved:

$$I(v) \land J(v,w) \Rightarrow J(v,G(w)) \tag{3}$$

$$I(v) \land J(v,w) \Rightarrow V(w) \in \mathbb{N} \land V(G(w)) < V(w) \quad , \tag{4}$$

where we assume that the variant expression is a natural number (but it can be more elaborate).

2.4 More on Event-B

We have kept the presentation of Event-B concise in order to avoid too many definitions. The article [3] provides more detail. The work on Event-B originates in the Action System formalism [4]. So techniques developed for Action Systems can often also be used with Event-B. However, unlike Action Systems the distinguishing characteristic of Event-B is that the notation has been designed with efficient tool support in mind. Action Systems impose less restrictions in modelling but are difficult to support efficiently by means of a software tool.

3 The Event-B Modelling Tool

The software tool support for Event-B should not be just another theorem prover. It should be a modelling tool that constrains modelling activity as little as possible. Powerful theorem provers are available [8,12,16,23] but not enough attention has been paid in formal methods to tool support for the modelling activity per se. Traditionally, it is assumed that one begins a formal development with a specification and develops it into a correct implementation. The flaw in this description is that, initially, there is no specification. Writing a specification involves making errors. The Event-B modelling tool takes this into account by being reactive and efficiently supporting incremental changes to models. Development towards an implementation will profit from this, too. In fact, we consider both, writing a specification and implementing it, to be part of the modelling activity.

Modelling the Modelling Tool. Although, we do not have translators that could generate plug-ins for the RODIN platform, modelling its components is still useful. As a matter of fact, formal models for most kernel components concerned with Event-B have been created before they were implemented. Some models use Event-B itself, but not all. In this section we also describe the different models that have been created and discuss their use and usefulness.

Architecture of the Tool. The tool for Event-B (see Figure 1) is incorporated into the RODIN platform which is an extension of the Eclipse platform. We do not explain Eclipse in this article but only refer to the existing literature [15].

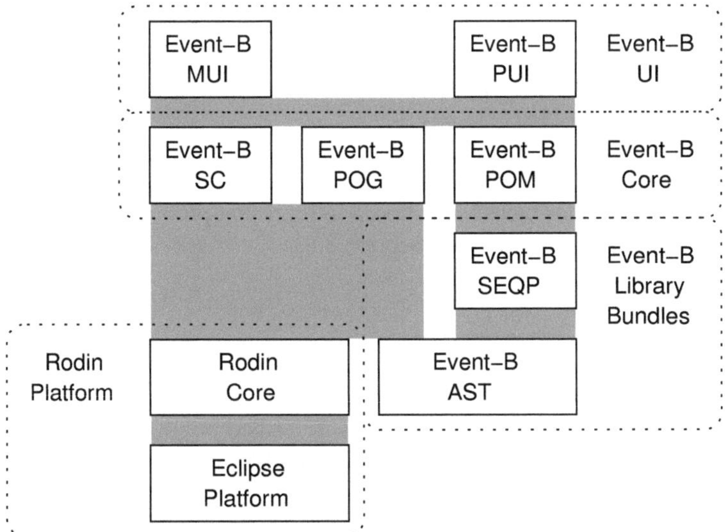

Fig. 1. Architectural Overview of the Event-B Tool

3.1 The RODIN Core

The RODIN Core consists of two components: the RODIN repository and the RODIN builder. These two components are tightly integrated into Eclipse based on designs derived from the Java Development Tools of Eclipse. Informal specifications for the repository and the builder have been developed. Their functionality is simple. They are however very dependent on the resources and concurrency model of Eclipse. Neither the repository nor the builder make any assumptions about elements being stored. In particular, they are independent of Event-B. The use of a repository instead of a fixed syntax for the modelling notations makes extending, e.g. Event-B, much easier. It is not necessary to change the syntax or to make extensions inside comments (in order not to change the syntax).

The RODIN repository manages persistence of data elements. There is a simple correspondence between data elements in form of Java objects and their persistent storage in XML files. The main design characteristic of the RODIN repository is easy extensibility.

The RODIN builder schedules jobs depending on changes made to files contained in the RODIN repository. The builder concept is supplied by the Eclipse platform. It is responsible for automatically launching jobs in the background to achieve higher responsiveness. The builder can be extended by adding new tools to it that keeps derived data elements in the RODIN repository up to date.

3.2 The Event-B Library Packages

Event-B as a whole does not have a syntax that needs to be parsed. Event-B models are kept in a repository. However, the mathematical notation used, e.g., in invariants or guards, has a syntax. It is specified by an attributed grammar that is used to produce the abstract syntax tree (AST) package. The grammar has not been specified in Event-B, although, in principle this should be possible similarly to the technique proposed by Lamport based on TLA+ [18].

The sequent prover (SEQP) library provides the proof engine. It contains the necessary data types, notably the sequent data type, some inference rules and support for tactics. The inference rules have been chosen to represent proof trees that can be easily manipulated in interactive proofs (see Section 3.4).

3.3 The Event-B Core

The Event-B Core consists of three components: the static checker (SC), the proof obligation generator (POG), and the proof obligation manager (POM). Their connection is shown in Figure 2 and their purpose is described below. The scheduling of the three components is taken care of by the RODIN builder (see Section 3.1).

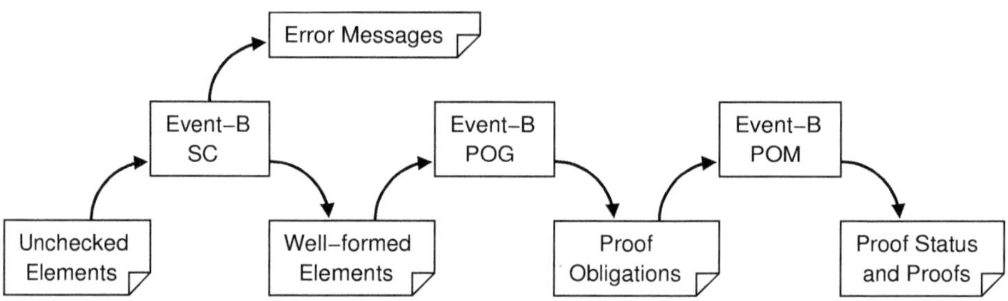

Fig. 2. Tool-Chain in Event-B Core

The static checker for Event-B analyses Event-B contexts and Event-B machines and provides feedback to the user about syntactical and typing errors in them. The mathematical notation of Event-B is specified by a context-free grammar, whereas the rest of Event-B is specified by a graph grammar based on the repository elements. The static checker rejects data elements that do not satisfy the Event-B grammar and produces error messages. It does, however, accept machines and contexts that only partially satisfy the grammar. It filters (and annotates) data elements that are grammatically correct for use by the proof obligation generator that is described in the next paragraph. The static checker can be extended by rejecting more elements and by dealing with new elements that can be added to the repository.

The proof obligation generator for Event-B is specified in a simplified notation used with generalised substitutions described in [1]. Compared to the classic B Method [1], Event-B has been simplified with proof obligation generation in mind. The specification of the proof obligation generator does not just serve for its implementation, it has also inspired some simplifications of the mathematical notation. The proof obligation generator produces proof obligations that have already been simplified. This makes them easier to prove automatically and to read in case automatic proof fails. Information about the origin of a proof obligation in a model is also provided in order to easily relate them to the model. The role of the static checker is to filter all elements from the repository that would cause errors in the proof obligation generator. Separating the two yields a much simplified proof obligation generator. This separation is similar to that of front-end and code generator in a compiler.

The proof obligation manager keeps track of proof obligations and associated proofs. It offers three functionalities:

(1) it matches existing proofs with proof obligations that have changed;
(2) it discharges proof obligations automatically (i.e. without user interaction) if possible;
(3) it provides an interface for interactive proof, in particular, proof tree manipulation.

The functionality referred to in Figure 2 concerns points (1) and (2). Support for interactive proof (3) is used by the graphical user interface (see Section 3.4).

3.4 The Graphical User Interface

The graphical user interface consists of two parts: one user interface for modelling (MUI) and one user interface for proving (PUI). Figure 3 shows how the core components and the user interface are integrated. The proving user interface does not access proof obligations and proofs directly but uses the services of the proof obligation manager. Appendix A contains a screen shot of the modelling perspective and the proving perspective respectively.

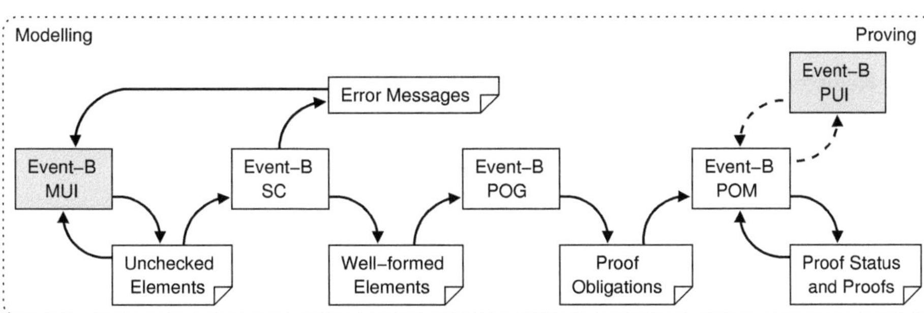

Fig. 3. The User Interface

The two user interfaces are connected by the tool chain of the Event-B core. They are available to the user in form of Eclipse perspectives between which the user can switch easily. The two perspectives are seamlessly integrated so that it is not suggested that modelling and proving are different activities. The user is intended to perceive reasoning about models as being part of modelling. Proof obligations are equipped with hypertext links so that the user can select instantaneously modelling elements related to that proof obligation.

3.5 On Openness

Integrating formal methods requires a lot of foresight. We would like the integrated method to be used for years to come, estimating where the integrated method could be useful and making reasonable restrictions on the development processes in which it would be used. Next we would develop a tool that would support the integrated method to support its use. Can this work? Being pessimistic about our capacity of predicting the future and the ability to dictate changes, radical or not, to industries that could profit from the integrated method, we choose not to integrate in advance. Instead, we propose an approach where the method from which we depart is open with respect to extensions and even changes. We have the same requirement for the accompanying tool to be open for extension and change. By adopting the open source model, we allow users to integrate their own tools into the tool.

4 Incremental Construction of a Small Example

In this section we outline the construction of a small Event-B model using the tool. Our aim is to illustrate the reactive nature of the support provided by the tool as we incrementally construct the model.

The model is of a system for checking registered users in and out of a building. We start the construction of the model by dealing only with registration of users. In the tool we create a new context and introduce a given set $USER$ in the context. We create a new machine and add a variable $register$ to the machine to represent the set of registered users. We create an invariant to type the register:

$$\mathsf{inv1} \quad register \subseteq USER$$

We also create an event to add a new user to the register:

$$\begin{array}{l}\mathsf{Register} \mathrel{\widehat{=}} \textbf{any } u \textbf{ where} \\ \qquad u \in USER \setminus register \\ \quad \textbf{then} \\ \qquad register := register \cup \{u\} \\ \quad \textbf{end}\end{array}$$

Notice that the guard of this event ensures that the new user is not already in $register$.

With the above elements (set $USER$, variable $register$, invariant inv1 and event $Register$) added to the project, the only error message we get is that the $register$ variable has not been initialised. This is remedied by adding the action $register := \varnothing$ to the machine initialisation. The resulting model results in 2 proof obligations, both of which are automatically discharged.

Now we add variables to represent the set of people who are in the building (in) and those that are outside the building (out). These are typed through the following invariants:

$$\begin{array}{ll}\mathsf{inv2} & in \subseteq register \\ \mathsf{inv3} & out \subseteq register\end{array}$$

We ensure that in and out are initialised to be empty. We have an obvious requirement that a user cannot be simultaneously inside and outside the building so we add a further invariant:

$$\mathsf{inv4} \quad in \cap out = \varnothing$$

The resulting model now gives rise to 7 proof obligations all of which are discharged automatically.

We add events to model users entering and leaving the building. Our first attempt at the $Enter$ event is

$$\begin{array}{l} \mathsf{Enter} \mathrel{\widehat{=}} \textbf{any } u \textbf{ where} \\ \qquad u \in out \\ \quad \textbf{then} \\ \qquad in := in \cup \{u\} \\ \quad \textbf{end} \end{array}$$

This event gives rise to 3 new proof obligations, 1 of which is not automatically discharged. Using the proof obligation explorer we can inspect this unproved proof obligation and see that it has hypotheses and a goal as follows:

$$\begin{array}{ll} \mathsf{Hyp1}: & in \cap out = \varnothing \\ \mathsf{Hyp2}: & u \in out \\ & \\ \mathsf{Goal}: & (in \cup \{u\}) \cap out = \varnothing \end{array}$$

Clearly this cannot be proved so either the invariant it is associated with (inv4) is wrong or the $Enter$ event is wrong and one or both need to be changed. The obligation explorer provides hyperlinks to both inv4 and $Enter$ to facilitate any changes to either. In this case we decide that the error is in the $Enter$ operation since we neglected to remove the user from the variable out. We remedy this by clicking on the link to the $Enter$ event and adding the following action to this event:

$$out := out \setminus \{u\}$$

This addition results in all 10 proof obligations being discharged automatically. Note that having a proof obligation that is not automatically discharged does not necessarily mean there is an error in the model. It may be that the proof obligation can be proved using the interactive prover.

A further requirement on the model is that each registered user must either be inside or outside the building. Our existing invariants are not sufficient to express this property so we add a further invariant:

$$\mathsf{inv5} \quad register \subseteq in \cup out$$

This addition gives rise to 3 new proof obligations, 1 of which is not automatically discharged:

$$\begin{array}{ll} \mathsf{Hyp1}: & register \subseteq in \cup out \\ \mathsf{Hyp2}: & u \in USER \setminus register \end{array}$$

$$\mathsf{Goal}: \ (register \cup \{u\}) \subseteq in \cup out$$

Clearly this obligation is not provable: if u is not in $register$, then it is not in $in \cup out$. The obligation explorer tells us that this proof obligation arises from both inv5 and the $Register$ event. Inspection of the $Register$ event shows that it adds a user u to $register$ but not to either in or out. We remedy this by deciding that newly registered users should be recorded as being outside the building and adding the following action to the existing $Register$ event:

$$out := out \cup \{u\}$$

The resulting model gives rise to 14 proof obligations, all of which are automatically discharged.

We have now completed our construction of the small Event-B model. With the old style tools for B, after constructing the model, we would have separately invoked the proof obligation generator and then the automatic prover. With our new Event-B tool, this is taken care of automatically as we construct the model. Our experience is that by making use of the feedback from the tool as we construct the model, e.g., the unproved proof obligations, we are guided towards construction of a model that has less errors and is more easily proved than if we were to delay any proof analysis until after constructing the full model.

5 Extensions

The RODIN open tools platform will allow other parties to integrate their tools, such as model checkers and theorem provers, as plug-ins to support rigorous development. This will allow many researchers to contribute to the provision of a comprehensive integrated toolset and we believe it will encourage greater industrial uptake of these tools. Along with the open tools platform, RODIN is developing a collection of plug-in tools to be integrated in the RODIN platform [25]. Developing these plug-in tools has two major aims:

- To provide extra functionality on top of the core platform to support more fully the application of the RODIN methodology being.
- To validate the open architecture of the platform by populating it with a collection of plug-in tools covering a range of functionalities.

This section outlines our initial effort at providing a collection of plug-in tools.

5.1 Animation and Model-Checking

The PROB animator and model checker has been presented in [20]. Based on Prolog, the PROB tool supports automated consistency checking of B machines via *model checking*.

For exhaustive model checking, the given sets must be restricted to small finite sets, and integer variables must be restricted to small numeric ranges. This allows the checking to traverse all the reachable states of the machine. ProB can also be used to explore the state space non-exhaustively and find potential problems. The user can set an upper bound on the number of states to be traversed or can interrupt the checking at any stage. ProB will generate and graphically display counter-examples when it discovers a violation of the invariant. ProB can also be used as an animator of a B specification. So, the model checking facilities are still useful for infinite state machines, not as a verification tool, but as a sophisticated debugging and testing tool.

The interactive proof process with the B tools can be quite time consuming. We see one of the main uses of ProB as a complement to interactive proof in that errors that result in counterexamples should be eliminated before attempting interactive proof. For finite state B machines it may be possible to use ProB for proving consistency without user intervention. We also believe that ProB can be very useful in teaching B, and making it accessible to new users. Finally, even for experienced B users ProB may unveil problems in a specification that are not easily discovered by existing tools.

5.2 Unified Modelling Language

The UML-B [27] is a profile of UML that defines a formal modelling notation. It has a mapping to the Event B language. UML-B consists of class diagrams with attached statecharts, and an integrated constraint and action language, called μB, based on the Event B notation. UML-B provides a diagrammatic, formal modelling notation based on UML. The popularity of the UML enables UML-B to overcome some of the barriers to the acceptance of formal methods in industry. Its familiar diagrammatic notations make specifications accessible to domain experts who may not be familiar with formal notations. UML-B consists of:

- A subset of the UML - including packages, class diagrams and state charts
- Specialisations of these features via stereotypes and tagged values,
- Structuring mechanisms (systems, components and modules) based on specialisations of UML packages
- UML-B clauses - a set of textual tagged values to define extra modelling features for UML entities,
- μB - an integrated action and constraint language based on Event B,
- Well-formedness rules

The U2B [27] translator converts UML-B models into Event B models. Translation from UML-B into Event B enables the Event B checkers and provers to be utilised. Since the B language is not object-oriented, class instances must be modelled explicitly in the generated B. Attributes and associations are represented as variables whose type is a function from the class instances to the attribute type or associated class. Operation behaviour may be represented textually in μB, as a state chart attached to the class, or as a simultaneous combination of both. Further details of UML-B are given in [27]. Examples of previous case studies using UML-B and U2B are given in [27,28].

5.3 More

Other plug-ins currently under development in RODIN include a petri-net based model checker for an integration of B and the π-calculus, documentation tools for B models, graphical animation tools, code generation tools and test generation tools.

6 Conclusion

We have presented the architecture of a modelling tool that offers the same comfort for writing models as do modern integrated development environments for programming.

We believe that modelling will remain difficult. This does not mean, however, that it is impossible to develop a productive modelling tool. Programming is difficult, too. Still we have very efficient programming tools. But we also have many people who simply got used to the difficulties of programming. Hopefully, they will also get used to the difficulties of modelling when appropriate tools are available.

The Event-B tool presented in this article provides a seamless integration between modelling and proving. This is important for the user to focus on the modelling task and not on switching between different tools. The purpose of modelling is not just to write a specification. It also serves to improve our understanding of the system being modelled. The Event-B tool tries to reflect this view by providing a lot of help for exploring a model and reasoning about it.

The tool is extensible and configurable because we cannot predict future uses of Event-B. The architecture has been designed to make this as easy as possible to invite users who need a (formal) modelling tool tailor it to their needs. We hope this will make it possible to employ the tool in very different development processes.

Acknowledgements

We would like to thank all members of the RODIN project who have contributed to the toolset especially Thai Son Hoang, Cliff Jones, Thierry Lecomte, Michael Leuschel, Farhad Mehta, Christophe Métayer, Colin Snook and Francois Terrier.

References

1. Jean-Raymond Abrial. *The B-Book: Assigning Programs to Meanings*. Cambridge University Press, 1996.
2. Jean-Raymond Abrial and Dominique Cansell. Click'n'Prove: Interactive Proofs within Set Theory. In *Theorem Proving in Higher Order Logics*, volume 2758 of *LNCS*, pages 1–24, 2003.
3. Jean-Raymond Abrial and Stefan Hallerstede. Refinement, decomposition and instantiation of discrete models. *Fundamentae Informatica*, 2006. To appear.
4. R. J. R. Back. Refinement calculus, part II: Parallel and reactive programs. In J. W. de Bakker, W.-P. de Roever, and G. Rozenberg, editors, *Stepwise Refinement of Distributed Systems*, volume 430 of *Lecture Notes in Computer Science*, pages 67–93. Springer-Verlag, 1990.

5. Frédéric Badeau and Arnaud Amelot. Using B as a high level programming language in an industrial project: Roissy VAL. In Helen Treharne, Steve King, Martin Henson, and Steve Schneider, editors, *ZB 2005*, volume 3455 of *LNCS*, pages 334–354, 2005.
6. M. Balser, W. Reif, G. Schellhorn, K. Stenzel, and A. Thums. Formal system development with KIV. In T. Maibaum, editor, *Fundamental Approaches to Software Engineering*, number 1783 in LNCS. Springer, 2000.
7. Mike Barnett, Bor-Yuh Chang, Robert DeLine, Bart Jacobs, and K. Rustan M. Leino. Boogie: A Modular Reusable Verifier for Object-Oriented Programs. In *FMCO 2005*, volume LNCS. Springer-Verlag, 2005. to appear.
8. Yves Bertot and P. (Pierre) Castéran. *Interactive theorem proving and program development: Coq'Art: the calculus of inductive constructions*. Texts in theoretical computer science. Springer-Verlag, 2004.
9. Egon Börger and Robert Stärk. *Abstract State Machines: A Method for High-Level System Design and Analysis*. Springer-Verlag, 2003.
10. Achim D. Brucker, Frank Rittinger, and Burkhart Wolff. HOL-Z 2.0: A proof environment for Z-specifications. *Journal of Universal Computer Science*, 9(2):152–172, February 2003.
11. Clearsy. Atelier B tool homepage. http://www.atelierb.societe.com/.
12. David Detlefs, Greg Nelson, and James B. Saxe. Simplify: a theorem prover for program checking. *J. ACM*, 52(3):365–473, 2005.
13. Eclipse. Eclipse platform homepage. http://www.eclipse.org/.
14. J.-C. Filliâtre. Verification of Non-Functional Programs using Interpretations in Type Theory. *Journal of Functional Programming*, 13(4):709–745, July 2003.
15. Erich Gamma and Kent Beck. *Contributing to Eclipse*. Addison Wesley, 2003.
16. Matt Kaufmann and J. Strother Moore. An industrial strength theorem prover for a logic based on common lisp. *IEEE Transactions on Software Engineering*, 23(4):203–213, 1997.
17. James C. King. A new approach to program testing. In *Proceedings of the international conference on Reliable software*, pages 228–233, New York, NY, USA, 1975. ACM Press.
18. Leslie Lamport. *Specifying Systems, The TLA+ Language and Tools for Hardware and Software Engineers*. Addison-Wesley, 2002.
19. Thomas Långbacka and Joakim von Wright. Refining reactive systems in HOL using action systems. In Elsa L. Gunter and Amy P. Felty, editors, *Theorem Proving in Higher Order Logics, 10th International Conference, TPHOLs'97*, volume 1275 of *Lecture Notes in Computer Science*, pages 183–197. Springer, 1997.
20. M. Leuschel and M. Butler. ProB: A Model Checker for B. In Keijiro Araki, Stefania Gnesi, and Dino Mandrioli, editors, *Proceedings FME 2003, Pisa, Italy*, LNCS 2805, pages 855–874. Springer, 2003.
21. Carroll Morgan, Thai Son Hoang, and Jean-Raymond Abrial. The challenge of probabilistic event B - extended abstract. In Helen Treharne, Steve King, Martin C. Henson, and Steve A. Schneider, editors, *ZB 2005: Formal Specification and Development in Z and B, 4th International Conference of B and Z Users*, volume 3455 of *Lecture Notes in Computer Science*, pages 162–171. Springer, 2005.
22. Tobias Nipkow. Structured Proofs in Isar/HOL. In H. Geuvers and F. Wiedijk, editors, *Types for Proofs and Programs (TYPES 2002)*, volume 2646 of *LNCS*, pages 259–278. Springer, 2003.
23. Lawrence C. Paulson. *Isabelle: A Generic Theorem Prover*, volume 828 of *Lecture Notes in Computer Science*. Springer Verlag, 1994.
24. RODIN. RODIN project homepage. http://rodin.cs.ncl.ac.uk/.
25. RODIN. Deliverable D16: Prototype Plug-in Tools. `http://rodin.cs.ncl.ac.uk/deliverables.htm`, 2006.

26. Mark Saaltink. The Z/EVES system. In Jonathan P. Bowen, Michael G. Hinchey, and David Till, editors, *ZUM '97: The Z Formal Specification Notation, 10th International Conference of Z Users*, volume 1212 of *Lecture Notes in Computer Science*, pages 72–85. Springer, 1997.
27. C. Snook and M. Butler. UML-B: Formal modelling and design aided by UML. *ACM Transactions on Software Engineering and Methodology*, 2006. To appear. eprints.ecs.soton.ac.uk/10169/.
28. C. Snook and K. Sandstrom. Using UML-B and U2B for formal refinement of digital components. In *Proceedings of Forum on specification and design languages (FDL03)*, 2003.
29. J. Michael Spivey. *The Z Notation: A Reference Manual.* International Series in Computer Science. Prentice-Hall, New York, NY, second edition, 1992.
30. Daniel Winterstein, David Aspinall, and Christoph Lüth. Proof general / eclipse: A generic interface for interactive proof. In *IJCAI*, pages 1587–1588, 2005.

A The User Interface

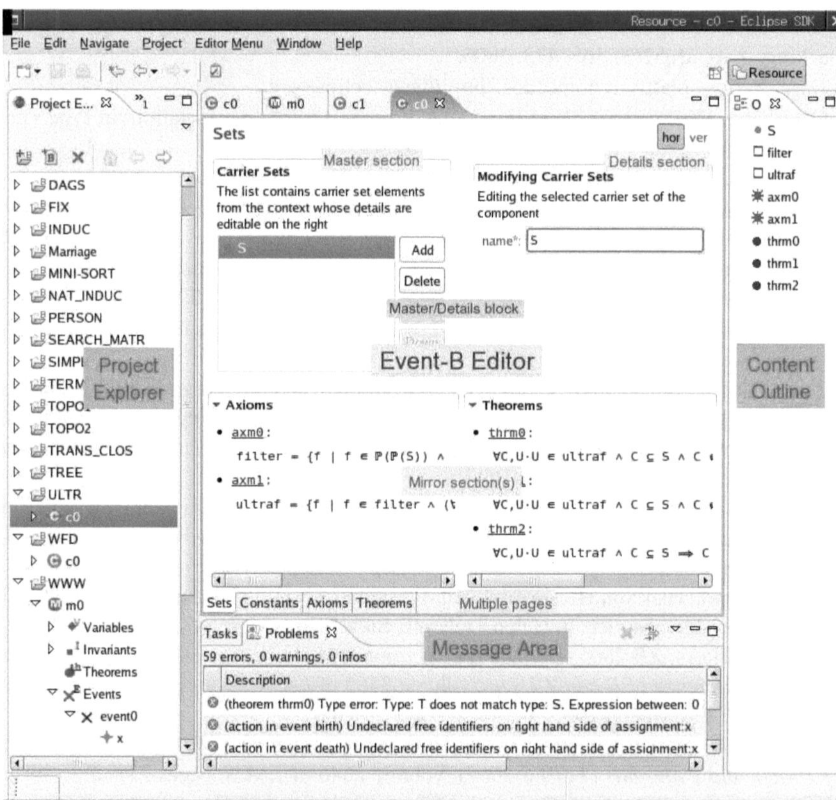

Fig. 4. The Modelling Perspective

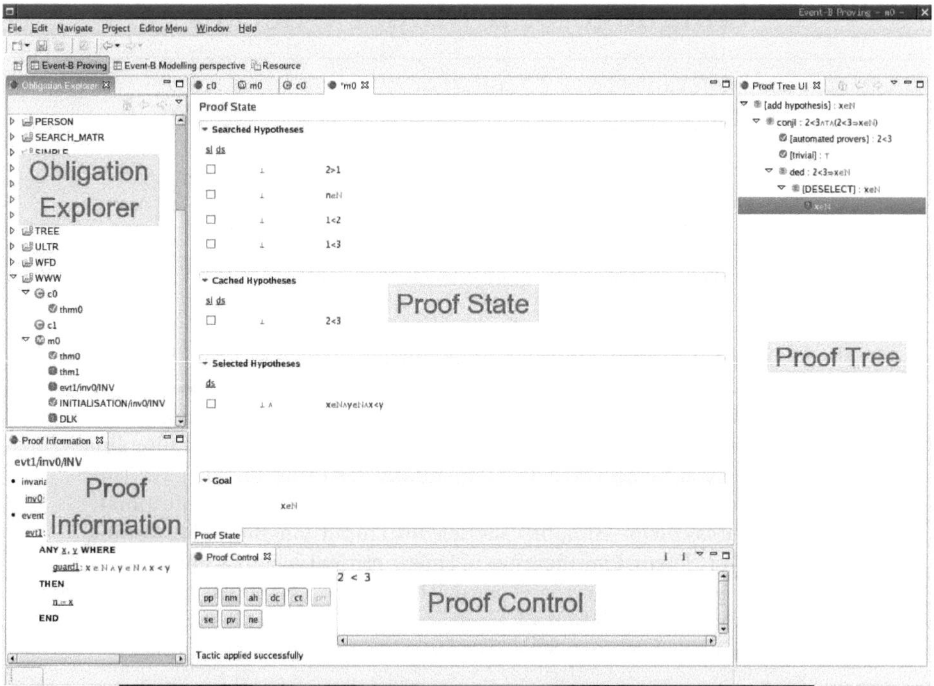

Fig. 5. The Proving Perspective

Tool for Translating Simulink Models into Input Language of a Model Checker

Meenakshi B., Abhishek Bhatnagar, and Sudeepa Roy*

Honeywell Technology Solutions Lab
Bangalore 560076, India
Meenakshi.Balasubramanian@honeywell.com

Abstract. Model Based Development (MBD) using Mathworks tools like Simulink, Stateflow etc. is being pursued in Honeywell for the development of safety critical avionics software. Formal verification techniques are well-known to identify design errors of safety critical systems reducing development cost and time. As of now, formal verification of Simulink design models is being carried out manually resulting in excessive time consumption during the design phase. We present a tool that automatically translates certain Simulink models into input language of a suitable model checker. Formal verification of safety critical avionics components becomes faster and less error prone with this tool. Support is also provided for reverse translation of traces violating requirements (as given by the model checker) into Simulink notation for playback.

1 Introduction

Model Based Development (MBD) is a concept of software development in which *models* are developed as work products at every stage of the development life-cycle. Models are concise and understandable abstractions that capture critical decisions pertaining to a development task and have semantics derived from the concepts and theories of a particular domain. Models supersede text and code as the primary work products in MBD and most development activities are carried out by processing models with as much automation as possible.

MBD is known to improve the quality of the product being developed. Formal models of design are used for proving the design correct with respect to functional requirements, identifying errors early in the life-cycle. Automatic methods for generating code and test cases helps to reduce coding errors and save total development time spent in coding and testing phases.

Formal verification techniques like *theorem proving* and *model checking* are well-known to reduce defects in the design stage by checking if a design meets its functional requirements [9]. Presence of formal models in MBD gives room for analysis using formal verification. Both MBD and formal verification are practices that put emphasis on detecting design errors (that have high leakage rate) rather than implementation errors (that have low leakage rate).

* Presently at Google, Bangalore, India.

Z. Liu and J. He (Eds.): ICFEM 2006, LNCS 4260, pp. 606–620, 2006.

DO-178B [1] standard produced by Radio Technical Commission for Aeronautics Inc. defines guidelines for development of avionics software and is the accepted means of certifying all new avionics software. DO-178B is obsolete with respect to MBD process but recognizes formal methods as a way to prevent and eliminate requirements, design and code errors throughout the development lifecycle. The benefit of formally verifying models at design stage is also validated by its successful use in various industrial examples [9].

In spite of all the above advantages, formal verification has not been successfully integrated into many development processes. The main issues are related to making it easy to use by the system engineers. Formal verification tools typically do not support standard design modeling notations but have their own notations related to the theories of the tool. The extra effort to learn the notations to use these tools is usually not welcome due to the delays it causes in development time. Consequently, there is a need to automate the formal verification process as much as possible for use by system engineers.

One possible step towards automation is to make formal verification tools available in notations that system engineers typically use. Mathworks tools like Simulink [2], Stateflow [3] etc. are extensively used in Honeywell for avionics software development. For system engineers to formally verify their design, it would be ideal if these modeling tools can automatically link to suitable model checking tools. We meet such a need in this paper by developing a *translator* from Simulink to the model checker NuSMV [4]. NuSMV is an open source symbolic model checker jointly developed by ITC-IRST, CMU, University of Genova and University of Trento. The translator takes a Simulink model as input and generates an equivalent NuSMV model.

The translator supports all the basic blocks that constitute a *finite state* subset of Simulink, i.e., any Simulink model obtained by putting together these blocks constitutes a finite state machine. The model generated by the translator can be formally verified against temporal logic requirements using the NuSMV model checker. We are working on providing support for specifying requirements by using a template based tool along the lines of the specification pattern system developed in [11]. These two tools put together would constitute a full-fledged verification tool for Simulink models.

Some other tools have been developed for formally verifying Simulink models. Commercial tools like SCADE design verifier [8], Embedded Validator [5] support formal verification of Simulink models against safety properties and work with their customized library of Simulink blocks, again mainly blocks from the discrete library. These tools were not expressive enough to translate some of models used in Honeywell, one such model involving an avionics triplex sensor voter is presented in the paper.

Checkmate [6] is a research tool developed to translate Simulink models into hybrid automata notation and verification is done using abstraction and certain semi-decision procedures involving reachability analysis of hybrid automata which are not guaranteed to terminate. Since Checkmate can translate Simulink models into hybrid automata, the translation also supports certain continuous basic blocks of Simulink. Thus, even though a larger set of Simulink models can be translated, fully automated verification of models is not possible as the reachability analysis procedures of the considered class of hybrid automata are not guaranteed to terminate.

Our algorithm works with standard Simulink notation and semantics and the models are translated into NuSMV which is an open source verification tool supporting the fully automatic technique of model checking. This achieves the main goal of providing a fully automated formal verification support to system engineers using MBD based on Simulink models.

2 Preliminaries

We briefly describe Simulink and NuSMV tools in this section.

2.1 Simulink

Simulink is a computer aided design tool widely used in the aerospace industry to design, simulate and auto code software for avionics equipment [2]. A Simulink model of a system is a hierarchical representation of the design of the system using a set of blocks that are interconnected by lines. Each block represents an elementary dynamic system that produces an output either continuously (continuous block) or at specific points in time (discrete block). The lines represent connections of block inputs to block outputs. Simulink provides various libraries of such blocks and in addition, some additional blocks can also be user-defined. Interconnected blocks are used to build sub-systems which in turn are put together to form a system model.

Simulink, considered as a de-facto standard in control design, is proven to be expressive enough to model many avionics systems and offers extensive simulation capabilities for de-bugging the design model.

2.2 NuSMV Model Checker

NuSMV [4] is a symbolic model checker based on Binary Decision Diagrams (BDDs) [7]. It allows for the description of systems as finite state machines, both synchronous and asynchronous. Specifications regarding the system can be given as Computation Tree Logic (CTL) and Linear Temporal Logic (LTL) formulas. Model checking algorithms in NuSMV check if the system meets the specifications using BDD-based and SAT-based model checking techniques and are ideally suited for verifying hardware designs.

The data flow block diagram of a Simulink model resembles control flow like that of hardware design even though Simulink models are finally implemented in software. This is the main reason behind choosing NuSMV as the target model checking tool for formally verifying Simulink diagrams apart from the fact that NuSMV is an open source tool. Also, NuSMV being a symbolic model checker is capable of handling systems with huge state space size. We illustrate this fact by applying the translator algorithm on the Simulink model of an avionics triplex sensor voter. The details are described in a subsequent section.

NuSMV input language. The input language of NuSMV is designed to allow for specification of system models as finite state machines. The data types provided by the language are Booleans, bounded integer sub-ranges, symbolic enumerated types and bounded arrays of these basic data types.

Complex system models can be described by decomposing it into *modules*. Each module defines a finite state machine and can be instantiated many times. Modules can be composed either synchronously or asynchronously to get the full system description. In synchronous computation, a single step in the composed model corresponds to a single step in each of the modules. In asynchronous computation, a single step in the composed model corresponds to a single step performed by exactly one module.

3 The Translator Algorithm

We describe the translator algorithm from Simulink models into NuSMV model checker in this section along with details about the execution semantics and the reverse translation. Working of the algorithm along with its use in formal verification of Simulink models will be illustrated in the next section with an example from the avionics domain.

3.1 Description of the Algorithm

The translator algorithm takes the MDL file format (textual representation) of the Simulink model as input and outputs its equivalent model in the input notation of NuSMV as described in Section 2.2.

Each basic block in Simulink (in the libraries supported by the translator algorithm) is translated into its equivalent module in NuSMV. For a given Simulink model, the NuSMV model that is output by the translator varies with the type of input ports of the Simulink model. Basic blocks of Simulink are generic, for example, the basic block corresponding to addition can add two scalars or two vector inputs, type matching and conversion are taken care of automatically. However, this is not the case with NuSMV, the module that adds two scalar inputs is different from the one that adds two vector inputs. Consequently, there is one NuSMV module corresponding to a given basic block and input type in Simulink.

A *library of routines* to generate NuSMV modules equivalent to basic blocks in Simulink are written to be re-used while generating NuSMV models from given Simulink models. The routines in this library respect the correspondence between basic blocks and modules mentioned above. For example, consider the standard relational operator block in Simulink given in Figure 1. Assume that the first input (`in1`) to the block is a vector of length 2, the second input (`in2`) is a scalar and the operation being checked for is $\leq$. The NuSMV module equivalent to the relational operator basic block is given below:

```
MODULE _relational_operator_2(in1, in2)

VAR
    out : array 0..1 of boolean;

ASSIGN
    out[0] := in1[0] <= in2;
    out[1] := in1[1] <= in2;
```

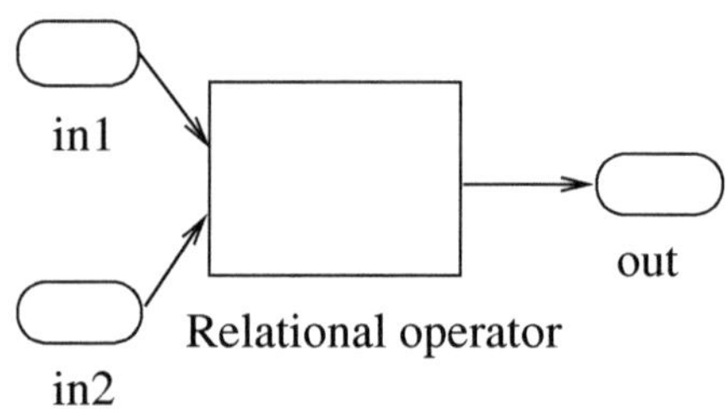

Fig. 1. Relational operator block in Simulink

The above module will be generated by a routine in the library to be re-used whenever the relational operator block with two inputs (of types as above) is being used in a model.

The translator algorithm is divided into the following steps:

1. **Parsing the model:** The model is read from its textual representation, irrelevant information involving the graphics of the model (like color, font size etc.) are discarded and information regarding blocks and subsystems, input and output ports, variables, inter-connection of blocks etc. is extracted.
2. **Computing input type of blocks and sub-systems:** In this step, a walk through the output of the graph structure extracted from step (1) is done wherein the type of input of each block is computed depending upon the output of preceding blocks.
   (a) For each block of source library of Simulink, input types of all the connected blocks is populated. Output type information for source block can be calculated directly from Simulink model.
   (b) If depending upon the input type, any decision regarding block output type can be taken (For example, in the case of Add block, if one of the inputs is a vector of n-dimension then output will be of n-dimension, where $n > 1$, or when all input port types are of 1-dimension then output will also be of type 1-dimension), then all the blocks further connected to this block are populated with input port type.

(c) The above step is continued for all the blocks in the graph until a block for which output type cannot be computed is reached. At this stage, control is transferred to the parent of this block in the model and the previous step and this one are repeated for the other connected blocks from the output port of the parent. This is done iteratively till all the blocks connected to one of the source blocks (in the first step above) are exhausted.
Note that this step is guaranteed to terminate as the input model has a fixed number of blocks.
If block is of type subsystem, then, blocks inside this sub-system are populated as per step 2 above. Once output port is reached, all the blocks connected to this output port of the subsystem are populated as done in step 2(c).

3. **Writing the final file:** In the final step, routines from the library described above are used to write the NuSMV model wherein each basic block is replaced by its equivalent modules(s). Here again, sub-systems are translated first respecting the hierarchy in the model.

Notice that the translation preserves the structure (hierarchy of the blocks, their names and interconnections) of the input Simulink model. The NuSMV model output by the translator follows the same hierarchical structure as the input Simulink model and variable names are also retained to be the same. Also, there is one module in NuSMV model corresponding to each basic block in the Simulink model. These features are important in MBD for answering traceability related questions and also for the verification of requirements as some of them might be specified by fully exploiting the structure in the model.

The above algorithm has been implemented and has been tested on some examples to check for the translation preserving the model. We present a detailed example involving the translation of Simulink model corresponding to an avionics triplex sensor voter in the next section.

3.2 Simple Abstraction Feature

The size of the translated NuSMV model is an important factor to make it amenable for verification. Many abstraction techniques are used to avoid the famous *state space explosion problem*. The fact that NuSMV is a symbolic model checker comes in useful here as such model checkers are well-known to handle systems with large state space size.

We have provided a simple state abstraction feature to be able to model check Simulink models that are too huge even for symbolic model checkers like NuSMV. While running the above translation algorithm, the system engineer has the option of bounding the ranges of certain/all variables that occur in the model. If no ranges are specified, the translator assumes maximum range. Otherwise, ranges of certain variables can be bounded by the system engineer and are incorporated into the translated model. This will help in reducing the state space size whenever required, while retaining the features required for verification of requirements.

3.3 Execution Semantics

Some points are worth noting regarding the translator algorithm preserving the behavior of the Simulink model. Semantics of systems modeled using Simulink is presented through simulations, which are done by sampling the data in the model. As mentioned above, Simulink models have both discrete and continuous blocks. *Sample time* parameter talks about the rate at which the states of the Simulink model are updated. The sample time is by definition, continuous for continuous blocks and is explicitly specified by the user for discrete blocks.

The scope of the translator algorithm presented in this paper is restricted to the discrete blocks of Simulink as the model checker NuSMV is capable of modeling discrete finite state systems only. We assume that one sample time in the Simulink model is equivalent to one *execution step* (modeled by a transition from one state to another) in the NuSMV model. The NuSMV model is equivalent to the given Simulink model as generated by the translator with respect to this assumption. Also, as noted in the previous section, for a given Simulink model, the NuSMV model generated by the translator varies with the type of input ports. Given the above, the translator algorithm preserves the given Simulink model as follows: at any point of execution, for every *state* of the Simulink model (given by the values which all the variables in the model take), there is a corresponding state in the NuSMV model wherein the variables take the same values. Also, transitions between states that arise because of change of values of certain variables in the Simulink model also result in corresponding transitions between corresponding states in the NuSMV model.

3.4 Finite State Simulink Models

As mentioned in the previous section, the scope of the translator is restricted to discrete Simulink models only, mainly due to the fact that the model checker NuSMV is capable of modeling discrete systems only. Here again, the model checker NuSMV is a finite state verification tool, that is, the class of models that can be formally verified using NuSMV are finite state machines. Consequently, the translator can support all the basic blocks of Simulink that, when put together, form a finite state model of a system.

Basic blocks of Simulink are organised into libraries of those with similar properties. In the translator algorithm, all the blocks of the signal routing, logic and bit operations, math operations (discrete), sources, discontinuities and discrete libraries are supported as of now with integer and Boolean data types for variables. As we illustrate in a subsequent section, the translator algorithm is expressive enough to translate non-trivial avionics Simulink models that are built using basic blocks from these libraries. Detailed list of the various blocks (listed within the libraries they belong to) are given below.

- Signal routing library
  - Demux and mux blocks
  - Switch block

    - Selector block
    - Multi-port switch, index vector blocks
    - Merge block
  - Logic and bit operations library
    - Relational block
    - Logical block
    - Interval test block
    - Interval test dynamic block
    - Compare to zero, compare to constant blocks
  - Math operations library
    - Sum, add, subtract and sum of elements blocks
    - Product, divide and product of elements blocks
    - Abs block
    - Unary minus block
    - Sign block
    - Bias block
    - Min-max block
    - Gain block
  - Sources library
    - Ground block
    - Constant block
    - In port block
    - Uniform Random Number
    - Step
    - Counter Free Running
    - Counter Limited
    - Read From File
  - Discontinuities library
    - Saturation block
    - Saturation dynamic block
    - Dead zone block
    - Dead zone dynamic block
    - Wrap to zero block
    - Coulomb and vicious function block
  - Discrete blocks library
    - Unit delay and integer delay blocks
  - Sinks blocks Library
    - Out port Block

3.5 Reverse Translation

NuSMV (and many other model checking tools) take a system model and a requirement as input and provide a yes/no answer depending on whether the system satisfies the requirement or not respectively. In the latter case, a system run violating the requirement is also output by the model checking tool as evidence to the fact the system does not meet the requirement. This feature is very useful in de-bugging the system design to meet the requirement.

In order to facilitate the Simulink system engineer to de-bug the model, we provide a *reverse translation routine* that takes a system run produced by NuSMV (as counter example) as input and translates it back into a textual notation that a Simulink designer can understand.

Since the translation algorithm preserves the structure of the input model, the counter example output by NuSMV reveals the structure fully in its description. Consequently, the reverse translation routine is a simple scripting program that re-writes the example in a notation that a Simulink designer can understand and simulate. Simulation of a violating run helps in de-bugging the design.

4 Sensor Voter Example

We describe an example involving a Simulink model used in digital flight control, namely that of an *avionics triples sensor voter*. This model was automatically translated into NuSMV by the algorithm and various computational and fault-handling requirements of the model were verified using NuSMV.

4.1 Triplex Sensor Voter

Almost all digital flight control systems utilize redundant hardware to meet high reliability requirements. Use of redundant hardware poses two problems: distinguishing between operational and failed units and computing the "mean" value of the various units for use by other components. A key part of redundant systems are redundant sensors and algorithms that focus on managing redundant sensors to provide a high integrity measurement for use by down-stream control calculations. We consider a *voter algorithm* that manages three redundant sensors in this paper. This class of algorithms is applicable to a variety of sensors used in modern avionics, including air data sensors, surface position sensors etc. The voter model has been translated by hand into the model checking tool SMV and many requirements were verified [10]. We now describe the sensor voter model and our work related to its formal verification using the translation algorithm.

Sensor voter operation. Simulink model corresponding to the sensor voter is described in Figure 2. The voter takes input from three sensors and produces a single reliable sensor output. Each sensor produces a measured data value and a self-check bit indicating whether or not the sensor considers itself to be operational.

The operation of the voter algorithm is described in the steps below:

- All valid sensor data are combined to produce output.
- If three sensors are available, a weighted average is used in which an outlying sensor value is given less weight than those that are in closer agreement.
- If only two sensors are available, a simple average is used.
- If only one sensor is available, it becomes the output.

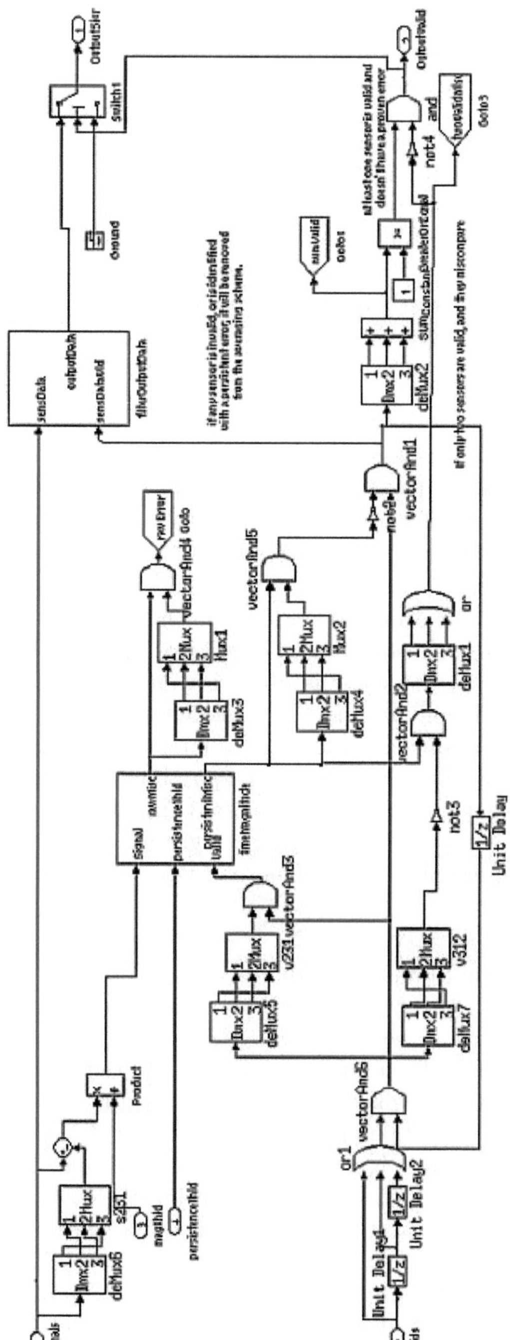

Fig. 2. Simulink model of avionics triplex sensor voter

A faulty sensor value is not used in failure comparisons or in the production of the output signal. The following are the mechanisms by which a faulty sensor can be detected and eliminated:

- Any sensor input whose own self-check bit is false is not used.
- Next, all the sensor values are compared two at a time. If difference exceeds threshold, magnitude error is set. If magnitude error persists longer than magnitude threshold, persistent miscompare is set. (threshold, magnitude error and persistent miscompare are variables in the model).
- If sensors 1 and 2 have persistent miscompare and so do sensors 2 and 3, sensor 2 is flagged as persistent sensor error and is not used.
- If only two sensors are valid and then miscompare, output depends on the self-check bit.

Requirements of the sensor voter were either relating to the value of the output signal computed by the voter or they were fault handling requirements that talk about mechanisms to detect and isolate faulty sensors. We translated the requirements manually into CTL formulas for verification using NuSMV.

Sensor voter modeling. In order to perform formal verification, it is just not sufficient to translate the sensor voter model into NuSMV. We need to model the *environment* in which the voter is used so that faults can be injected into the model externally. The environment was modeled by using a *world block* that acts as an abstraction of all the components that provide inputs for the sensors to measure. There are also three blocks corresponding to the sensors that model the physical sensors that generate the measured signal. The sensor blocks were used to inject faults to test the ability of the voter to identify them. These blocks were added to the original Simulink model to create a model amenable to formal verification.

Formal verification. The Simulink model of sensor voter (as given in Figure 2) was modified by adding the world and sensor blocks as described above. The new model constitutes what we call a *fault model* where different values can be injected to perform "what if" analysis to check if the requirements are met.

The translator tool was invoked to translate the fault model of sensor voter into NuSMV. Since the sensor voter model is big, the NuSMV code of the model as generated by the translator is not fully presented. Figure 3 gives a snapshot of part of the NuSMV model containing the declarations of the modules corresponding to the sub-systems and the blocks in the outermost level of the sensor voter model.

We now present the results of verifying two requirements related to the sensor voter. The requirements were given as CTL formulas to NuSMV.

1. The first property relates to the requirement that detection and elimination of a faulty sensor is final, i.e. once a sensor is detected and eliminated as being faulty, it is never available as an active sensor again. This requirement

```
VAR
      Constant : __constant_18();
      GreaterOrEqual : __relational_operator_4(sum._1000, Constant
      Ground : __ground_1();
      Mux1 : __subsystem_6(deMux3._3, deMux3._1, deMux3._2);
      Mux2 : __subsystem_7(deMux4._3, deMux4._1, deMux4._2);
      Product : __product_1(Sum.out1, magThld);
      Sum : __add_1(InSignals, s231.Mux);
      Switch1 : __switch_1(filterOutputData.outputData, and._1000,
      Unit_Delay : __unit_delay_4(vectorAnd1._1000);
      Unit_Delay1 : __unit_delay_5(Valids);
      Unit_Delay2 : __unit_delay_6(Unit_Delay1.out1);
      and : __subsystem_8(GreaterOrEqual.out1, not4._2);
      deMux1 : __subsystem_9(vectorAnd2._1000);
      deMux2 : __subsystem_10(vectorAnd1._1000);
      deMux3 : __subsystem_11(timeMagnitude.rawMisc);
      deMux4 : __subsystem_12(timeMagnitude.persistentMisc);
      deMux5 : __subsystem_13(vectorAnd6._1000);
      deMux6 : __subsystem_14(InSignals);
      deMux7 : __subsystem_15(vectorAnd6._1000);
      filterOutputData : __subsystem_16(InSignals, vectorAnd1._10C
      not2 : __subsystem_29(vectorAnd5._1000);
      not3 : __subsystem_30(v312.Mux);
      not4 : __subsystem_31(or._1000);
      or : __subsystem_32(deMux1._1, deMux1._2, deMux1._3);
      or1 : __subsystem_33(Valids, Unit_Delay1.out1, Unit_Delay2.c
      s231 : __subsystem_34(deMux6._2, deMux6._3, deMux6._1);
      sum : __subsystem_35(deMux2._1, deMux2._2, deMux2._3);
      timeMagnitude : __subsystem_36(Product.out1, persistenceThlc
      v231 : __subsystem_40(deMux5._2, deMux5._3, deMux5._1);
      v312 : __subsystem_41(deMux7._3, deMux7._1, deMux7._2);
      vectorAnd1 : __subsystem_42(not2._2, vectorAnd6._1000);
      vectorAnd2 : __subsystem_43(timeMagnitude.persistentMisc, nc
      vectorAnd3 : __subsystem_44(v231.Mux, vectorAnd6._1000);
      vectorAnd4 : __subsystem_45(timeMagnitude.rawMisc, Mux1.Mux)
      vectorAnd5 : __subsystem_46(timeMagnitude.persistentMisc, Mu
      vectorAnd6 : __subsystem_47(or1._1000, Unit_Delay.out1);
DEFINE
      OutputSignal := Switch1.out1;
      OutputValid := and._1000;
      __Goto__1[0] := vectorAnd4._1000[0];
      __Goto__1[1] := vectorAnd4._1000[1];
      __Goto__1[2] := vectorAnd4._1000[2];
      __Goto1__1 := sum._1000;
      __Goto3__1 := or._1000;
      __Goto5__2[0] := timeMagnitude.__Goto5__1[0];
      __Goto5__2[1] := timeMagnitude.__Goto5__1[1];
      __Goto5__2[2] := timeMagnitude.__Goto5__1[2];
```

Fig. 3. Main module of the NuSMV code of triplex sensor voter

is specified by using the following CTL formula which specifies that there is no execution path where the number of valid sensors increases.

```
 AG (
(voting3signals.OutputValid = 0 ->
!EF voting3signals.OutputValid = 1)
& (voting3signals.OutputValid = 1 ->
!EF voting3signals.OutputValid = 2)
& (voting3signals.OutputValid = 2 ->
!EF voting3signals.OutputValid = 3))
```

NuSMV reported this specification to be true. We first ran verification with unbounded ranges and since NuSMV model checker took about a week to produce the results, we tried verification algorithm by bounding the range of one variable, namely, unit delay, to vary from -30 to 30. With this option, the state space size reduced drastically and verification of the model with respect to the above property completed with the same result within a few seconds. This acts as a good illustration of the static abstraction feature explained earlier.

2. The second requirement relates to fault handling requirements of the sensor voter. If the number of valid sensors is 2 and the voter output is valid and the second sensor becomes faulty then in the future, the number of valid sensors is 1 and the voter output is still valid.

```
 AG (
((voting3signals._Goto1_1 = 2
& voting3signals.OutputValid) & fault2) ->
AF (voting3signals._Goto1_1 = 1
& voting3signals.OutputValid))
```

NuSMV reported this property to be false and gave a violating run. The property turned out to be false due to a problem with our fault model (and not the voter model). We had modeled the sensors in such a way that a faulty sensor will never exhibit any faulty behavior in terms of the way in which the values are measured.

5 Model Based Formal Analysis

Engineers traditionally perform well-established but, informal analysis techniques like Fault Tree Analysis (FTA) and Failure Modes and Effects Analysis (FMEA) for checking for safety requirements of their system. These techniques are well established and are used extensively during the design of safety critical systems. Despite this, most of the techniques are highly subjective and dependent on the skill of the practitioner as they are based on informal system models that are derived in an ad hoc fashion. This results is excessive consumption of resources and time.

Due to these reasons, there is an increasing shift towards using MBD techniques for analysis of the design of safety-critical systems. In this approach, various development activities including design and simulation, verification, testing and code generation are based on a formal model of the system. The presence of formal models makes the development process amenable to using formal verification techniques like model checking. However, there are certain gaps to be filled for model checking techniques to be directly used by system engineers.

We already discussed one of the gaps in the introduction, namely that of the model checking notations not being easy-to-use by system engineers. The translator algorithm presented in this paper fills this gap. Few more questions need to be answered to fully integrate techniques like model checking with MBD. The first among them is to be able to formalize a *fault model* of the system under test. Fault model captures the various ways in which the components of the system can malfunction. This information is provided by modeling the entities that the system interacts with so that faults can be externally introduced into the system without altering the system model. For example, in the verification of sensor voter presented in the previous section, fault model comprises of abstract models of the sensors and the world block gives data to the sensors. This step has to be done by the system engineers themselves, manually.

The second gap comes from the requirements side. Functional requirements which ensure safe behavior of the system are usually specified in text document along with other requirements. The safety properties must be expressed in some formal notation to support automated analysis. There are several formal specification languages like CTL, LTL, finite state machines etc. that are supported by many model checkers. We are working on automating this step by exploiting the work done in [11] where the authors provide a repository of commonly occurring specification patterns in the specification of concurrent, reactive systems. There is a mapping from these specification patterns to a number of formalisms that are supported by tools for formal analysis. LTL and CTL languages that are supported by NuSMV are also provided amongst the formalisms.

A template-based description of these specification patterns is being developed with facilities to include model specific values to the specification templates. These will be translated into equivalent CTL/LTL formulas so that they can be fed into the model checker NuSMV for verification automatically. This step would fill all the gaps that exist for fully automated use of model checking techniques by Simulink system engineers.

6 Conclusions

We have presented a translator algorithm that translates a subset of Simulink into input language of the model checker NuSMV. The subset of Simulink blocks supported by the translator is expressive enough to translate many interesting classes of avionics models like the avionics triplex sensor voter presented in this paper. The tool aids in automating formal verification of Simulink models and will be of valuable use in model based formal safety analysis of systems.

References

1. DO-178B guidelines. Available from: http://www.rtca.org/.
2. Simulink web page: http://www.mathworks.com/products/simulink/.
3. Stateflow web page: http://www.mathworks.com/products/stateflow/.
4. NuSMV web page: http://nusmv.irst.itc.it/.
5. Embedded Validator web page: http://www.dspaceinc.com/ww/en/inc/home/products/sw/pcgs/automatic_model_validation.cfm.
6. Checkmate web page: http://www.ece.cmu.edu/~webk/checkmate/.
7. Randal E. Bryant. Graph-based algorithms for boolean function manipulation. *IEEE Transactions on Computers*, 35(8):677–691, 1986.
8. Jean-Louis Camus and Bernard Dion. Efficient development of airborne software with scade-suite. Technical report, Esterel Technologies, 2003.
9. Edmund M. Clarke and Jeannette M. Wing. Formal methods: state of the art and future directions. *ACM Computing Surveys*, 28(4):626–643, 1996.
10. Samar Dajani-Brown, Darren Cofer, Gary Hartman, and Steve Pratt. Formal modeling and analysis of an avionics triplex sensor voter. In *Proc.SPIN*, pages 34–48. Springer, 2003.
11. Matthew B. Dwyer, George S. Avrunin, and James C. Corbett. Property specification patterns for finite-state verification. In Mark Ardis, editor, *Proc. 2nd Workshop on Formal Methods in Software Practice (FMSP-98)*, pages 7–15, New York, 1998. ACM Press.

Verifying Abstract Information Flow Properties in Fault Tolerant Security Devices

Tim McComb and Luke Wildman

School of Information Technology and Electrical Engineering
The University of Queensland, 4072, Australia
{tjm, luke}@itee.uq.edu.au

Abstract. The verification of information flow properties of security devices is difficult because it involves the analysis of schematic diagrams, artwork, embedded software, etc. In addition, a typical security device has many modes, partial information flow, and needs to be fault tolerant. We propose a new approach to the verification of such devices based upon checking abstract information flow properties expressed as graphs. This approach has been implemented in software, and successfully used to find possible paths of information flow through security devices.

1 Introduction

High-grade security devices, like data-diodes, encryption hardware, and context filters, are used to electronically separate high-security domains from low-security domains, and thus provide a degree of protection against unwanted information flow. These devices are commonly used by intelligence agencies and corporations to safeguard confidential information – a *domain* in this sense normally referring to a computer or a network of computers. The devices need to be carefully designed and evaluated to ensure that the requirement of *domain separation* is always satisfied, that is, to ensure that information cannot flow from a high-security domain to a low-security one where it is impermissible to do so, even in the presence of component failures.

A previous approach [12] has considered the problem from a graph theoretic standpoint, analysing transitive connectivity between vertices to establish whether there exists the possibility of information flow, both when the device is operating normally and when subcomponents have failed. A significant limitation of this theory is its inability reason about partial connectivity. Partial connectivity arises when certain types of information flow are permissible and these types need to be distinguished from impermissible information flow. The previous approach considered any connectivity to be disallowed, and this lack of expressiveness inhibits the analytical power of the framework.

In this paper, we present an alternative framework for analysing the information flow properties of systems. Our approach is based upon checking consistency relations between abstract and concrete models, where the information flow characteristic to be checked is expressed in the abstract model, and the

Z. Liu and J. He (Eds.): ICFEM 2006, LNCS 4260, pp. 621–638, 2006.

concrete model contains the relevant implementation detail. Since the abstract models are in themselves arbitrary, this allows an evaluator to express and verify information flow properties (with respect to points-of-failure), including those that pertain to partial connectivity.

Our approach only considers static connectivity, that is, we do not consider the dynamic properties (control flow etc.) of the system in the analysis. However, we do allow for modes to be expressed at the system (rather than component) level, which can capture such properties. This approach is safe in that all possible information flows are explored, however, because some combinations of modes may not be possible in reality, it can report false-positives. The benefit of this approach is that it can scale to systems of a reasonable size (thousands of components), with components each having several normal modes and fault modes. (In fact we treat all modes, normal or faulty, equally, except that fault modes may be shared amongst components.).

In this paper we use the Z specification language [1] to specify the modelling and analytical framework, and also briefly discuss an implementation of the specification. This implementation has allowed us to utilise the technique to automatically verify existing devices, and also to detect possible single points-of-failure.

Frameworks for analysing information flow properties over networks (particularly hardware devices) have been previously presented by Rae and Fidge [12] and McComb and Wildman [6]. Our approach improves upon that work in the sense that we can effectively reason about partial connectivity without having to identify and eliminate false positives. Our abstraction based modelling approach also lends itself to the validation of designs at a high level, which provides a scalable alternative to the previous work (for which no abstraction mechanism was considered).

In the following section we discuss our technique for analysing information security in relation to existing methods. In Section 3 we describe a graph-based model of information flow and introduce our example: a simple cryptographic device. Here, we give a description of a connectivity model without modes and define a simple consistency relation between such models. In Section 4 we extend this model with alternative information flows corresponding to different modes; either normal or faulty. Section 5 details the consistency analysis for the combined model (connectivity and modes) and applies it to the example cryptographic device. We conclude in Sections 6 and 7 with related work, and a summary of our approach (with some directions for future work) respectively.

2 Motivation

Non-interference based approaches to the verification of information flow properties such as theorem proving [13] or static analysis techniques such as those applied to programs [14] are difficult to apply to the problem of information flow analysis of hardware devices in the presence of faults. Firstly, these approaches do not scale well to the size of the circuits that need to be evaluated in practice.

The devices that we consider typically have thousands of components. Secondly, interference based approaches infer information flow from the logical functions of the components. In order to extend this approach to include fault modes of hardware components one would have to create a logical characterisation of the faults: this introduces an additional step in the evaluation process which it turns out can be avoided. Thirdly, logical approaches to the characterisation of information flow do not apply to all aspects of the devices under consideration. For instance, we need to consider the potential for information flow to be introduced by failure modes which occur due to the placement of multiple logical components on a single chip. We must also consider information flow introduced by both the normal and faulty behaviour of the circuitry intended to supply power to the components, and additionally the potential for information flow to introduced by EMF (electromagnetic field) interference across the circuit.

For these reasons we have abstracted the notion of information flow to reachability across a graph. This allows us to combine multiple sources of information together and allows very large circuits to be analysed. However, we consequently rely on information flow details to be supplied from a number of different sources. The information flow across components in both normal and failure modes is supplied by a pre-fabricated (but extensible) component library. Information flow across the circuit (and from global fault modes) is supplied by the logical connectivity of the circuit and from the failure analysis technique described in [10]. Information flow introduced by the physical layout of the circuit and the grouping of logical components into common packages/chips is supplied by an analysis of the PCB (printed circuit board) artwork.

A final criticism of non-interference based approaches is that it is difficult to deal with partial information flow. That is, domain separation devices are typically used to enforce a security policy that allows some information to be transmitted (e.g. encrypted streams or trusted words) but not all (e.g. unencrypted streams or untrusted words). In our approach we are able to specify the information flow that we allow through the device, and then check that no other flow is present. The same technique can also be applied to partial information flow introduced by faults. That is, we are able to specify that certain information flow introduced by some faults is acceptable. This is often the case if the (non-silent) failure is mitigated against in some way.

A consequence of our approach is that it can produce false positives (report undesired information flow that does not exist). For example, information flow may be reported that is produced by combinations of modes that cannot occur in practice. More seriously, it can also suffer false negatives (fail to report undesired information flow where some exists). This may be due to an inadequacy of the model, where there is incompleteness in the information flows supplied. The problem of false positives is partially addressed by the ability to specify the desired information flow in the manner described above. However, to completely eliminate false positives and negatives, one would need to augment our approach with a more sophisticated technique such as those based on non-interference or traditional model-checking. Note that this is easily achieved because of our abstraction of information flow. However, it is likely that such techniques will only need to be applied to specific subcomponents, such as programmable chips, or to particularly complicated configurations of logic.

3 Connectivity Model

Abstractly, we consider information flow as a graph of possibilities, where a directed edge between two vertices in the graph represents the possibility of information flow from one vertex to another. Vertices may in reality be any entity, but we are interested in electronic devices so they typically correspond to ports or pins on a circuit board. We also assume that information flow is *transitive*, that is, if two components each communicate information in certain modes then if those components are connected, information will also flow through the combination of those components when they are in those modes. Thus, we calculate the potential for information flow by reasoning about connectivity.

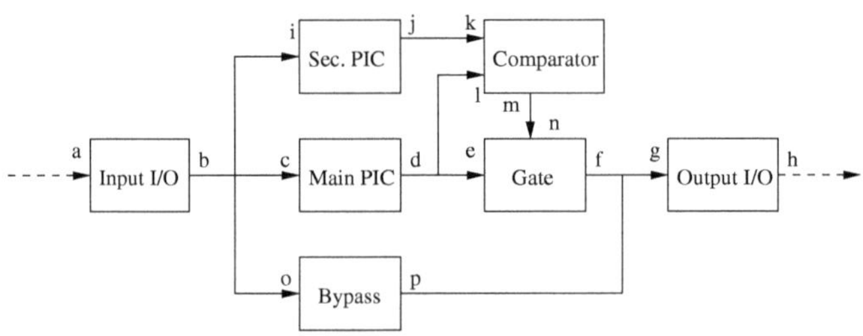

Fig. 1. Block diagram for cryptographic device

Consider the cryptographic device represented by Figure 1. This device has two PIC processors that perform an encryption function over the data streaming through the input I/O, where each processor performs precisely the same encryption operation. The comparator unit compares the output of the two processors and releases data from the main processor to the output I/O through the gate only when the output from the two processors match. In the event that the output from the processors does not match, no data is released to the output I/O, and the circuit is disabled. Additionally, the device has a bypass channel, through which plain-text may be sent if the unit is in the appropriate mode.

We consider this device design as a *GRAPH*, which is illustrated in Figure 2. A *GRAPH* is a relation between *PORT* types,

$$[PORT]$$
$$GRAPH == PORT \leftrightarrow PORT$$

where the ports correspond to the vertices labelled a through p.

Paths from a high-security input to a low-security output are referred to as *leaks*. If we trace all of the leaky paths, we find that there are four:

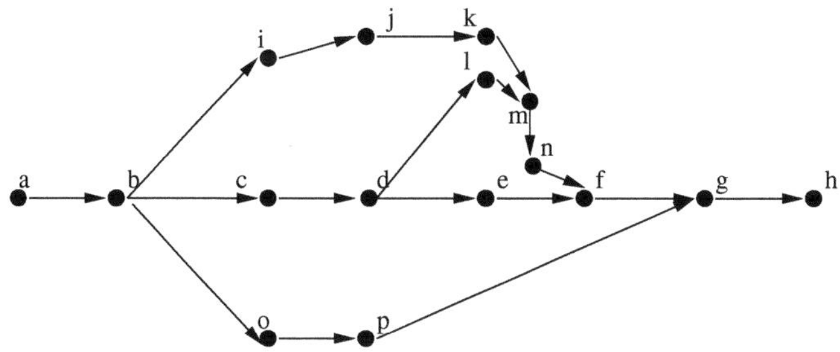

Fig. 2. Information flow graph for cryptographic device

1. $a \to b \to c \to d \to e \to f \to g \to h$
2. $a \to b \to c \to d \to l \to m \to n \to f \to g \to h$
3. $a \to b \to i \to j \to k \to m \to n \to f \to g \to h$
4. $a \to b \to o \to p \to g \to h$

Of these paths, we must ensure that each achieves the function of domain separation. In this example, the four paths do so because the connections from c to d (paths 1 and 2) and from i to j (path 3) both encrypt the data, and removing these connections disconnect all of the paths except for the bypass channel (path 4), which we must assume is not active.

While this is a rather straight-forward way to reason about information security, it becomes unwieldy for large systems . There are three reasons for this: first, we are required to demonstrate the security property with rigour, and to do so requires that the graph of the device is constructed directly from the schematic diagrams. These devices may have thousands of components, and thus the accompanying graphs become too large, with thousands of ports and edges. Secondly, we need to reason about partial connectivity. Some paths of information flow are perfectly acceptable (and expected), like the bypass channel, while others may indicate a potential problem — through our formalisation we need to express these properties in order to carefully direct and focus the analysis. Thirdly, we need to consider the possibility of component and multiple-component faults, and the resulting effects upon information flow.

3.1 Abstraction of Information Flow

We address these issues through abstraction, where an abstract model of the device is created which captures the intended security function, and this model is then checked for consistency against the much larger concrete representation. For example, the model in Figure 3 abstractly captures the fact that the encryption device has one part that is responsible for separating the domains through encryption, and a bypass channel; the details of the secondary processor, the comparator, and the gate have been elided.

There are fewer paths through this abstract model than in the concrete one, but our primary concern is that the abstraction is not deceptive with respect to the cut-sets of the concrete information flow graph. That is, the edges of

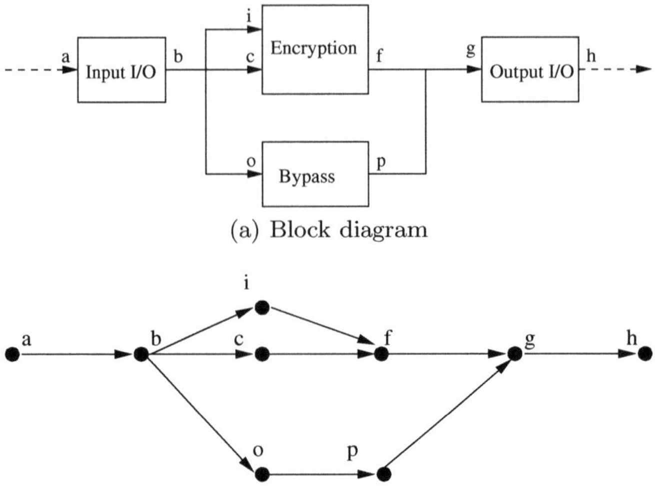

(a) Block diagram

(b) Information flow graph

Fig. 3. Abstract cryptographic device

the abstract graph that are critical for obtaining domain separation over all of the paths (the cut-sets) should accurately represent the reality of the concrete model.

3.2 Analysis

Port labels must be shared between the models to indicate that they refer to common parts of the system; the abstract model must be similar to the concrete model in this respect. By comparing the possible paths through the abstract model with those in the concrete model, we can observe whether any discrepancies exist. To do this, we consider only the ports on the paths through the concrete graph that also appear in the abstract graph, so that we can rewrite the concrete paths with respect to the abstract model. In our example,

1. $\mathbf{a} \rightarrow \mathbf{b} \rightarrow \mathbf{c} \rightarrow d \rightarrow e \rightarrow \mathbf{f} \rightarrow \mathbf{g} \rightarrow \mathbf{h}$
   becomes $a \rightarrow b \rightarrow c \rightarrow f \rightarrow g \rightarrow h$
2. $\mathbf{a} \rightarrow \mathbf{b} \rightarrow \mathbf{c} \rightarrow d \rightarrow l \rightarrow m \rightarrow n \rightarrow \mathbf{f} \rightarrow \mathbf{g} \rightarrow \mathbf{h}$
   becomes $a \rightarrow b \rightarrow c \rightarrow f \rightarrow g \rightarrow h$
3. $\mathbf{a} \rightarrow \mathbf{b} \rightarrow \mathbf{i} \rightarrow j \rightarrow k \rightarrow m \rightarrow n \rightarrow \mathbf{f} \rightarrow \mathbf{g} \rightarrow \mathbf{h}$
   becomes $a \rightarrow b \rightarrow i \rightarrow f \rightarrow g \rightarrow h$
4. $\mathbf{a} \rightarrow \mathbf{b} \rightarrow \mathbf{o} \rightarrow \mathbf{p} \rightarrow \mathbf{g} \rightarrow \mathbf{h}$
   becomes $a \rightarrow b \rightarrow o \rightarrow p \rightarrow g \rightarrow h$

Each of these (filtered) concrete paths corresponds to a path through the abstract graph, so we consider the two models to be consistent. If the abstract model were such that the encryption function did not connect i to f, then the third path enumerated above would not appear in the abstract model and the models would be inconsistent. Thus, our abstraction needs to contain all of the connectivity of the concrete model, but need not use all of the ports from the concrete model to do so.

Formally, we consider a path to be an injective sequence of ports (an injective sequence contains no repetitions).

$$PATH[X] == \mathrm{iseq}\, X$$

The paths over a graph then correspond to all such sequences where each adjacent pair of ports in each path are contained in the graph.

$$\begin{array}{l} [R] \\ \hline pathsOver : (R \leftrightarrow R) \rightarrow \mathbb{P}\, PATH[R] \\ \hline (\forall\, g : R \leftrightarrow R \bullet pathsOver(g) = \\ \quad \{p : PATH[R] \mid (\forall\, i1, i2 : (\mathrm{dom}\, p) \mid i2 = i1 + 1 \bullet (p\ i1, p\ i2) \in g)\}) \end{array}$$

Given an *abstract* and a *concrete* graph, with ports connected to the *high* and *low* domains, we ensure that all paths over the concrete graph can be matched by a path in the abstract graph when we only consider the ports from the concrete paths that appear in the abstract graph. Furthermore, we only consider paths that result in a leak (paths from *high* to *low*) — this is advantageous for forming succinct security arguments: parts of the system that are irrelevant for information security may be ignored.

$$high, low : \mathbb{P}\, PORT$$

$$\begin{array}{l} ConnectivityConsistency \\ \hline abstract, concrete : GRAPH \\ \hline \forall\, p : pathsOver(concrete) \mid head(p) \in high \wedge last(p) \in low \bullet \\ \quad p \upharpoonright (\mathrm{dom}\, abstract \cup \mathrm{ran}\, abstract) \in pathsOver(abstract) \end{array}$$

The filter operator ($\upharpoonright$) above is used to restrict the sequence p to the ports appearing in the abstract graph, and 'squash' them into a sequence.

4 Mode Model

The analysis of information flow consistency over different levels of abstraction presented in Section 3 does not distinguish the multiple operating modes of components, nor does it allow us to express the way in which component faults may contribute to information flow. To address this, we abandon the single *GRAPH* as a model of information flow properties through a system. Instead, we model a system as an interconnected set of *COMPONENT*s, where each component is associated with a set of possible *MODE*s (*ComponentModes*), and each mode is (possibly) related to a set of edges (*ModeEdges*).

$$[COMPONENT, MODE]$$
$$ComponentModes == COMPONENT \leftrightarrow MODE$$
$$ModeEdges == MODE \leftrightarrow (PORT \times PORT)$$

The contents of both the abstract model and the concrete model are expressed formally by populating these data structures.

Some of the modes are considered to be fault modes, so we distinguish between normal operating modes and fault modes for the purpose of counting points of failure later. The schema *Model* consolidates the data required to form a complete model, and, as a convenience, in the *Model* schema we also derive the set of all ports used. Note that we ensure every component has at least one mode that is not a fault.

Model

$$componentModes : ComponentModes$$
$$faultModes : \mathbb{P}\, MODE$$
$$modeEdges : ModeEdges$$
$$allPorts : \mathbb{P}\, PORT$$

$$allPorts = \mathrm{dom}(\mathrm{ran}\, modeEdges) \cup \mathrm{ran}(\mathrm{ran}\, modeEdges)$$
$$\mathrm{dom}(componentModes \rhd faultModes) = \mathrm{dom}\, componentModes$$

The edges that connect components, as opposed to those that are internal to components, are modelled by a special component called the "parent". The parent component has only one mode for which all such edges are associated.

For example, the concrete model in Figure 1 is represented by *ExampleConcreteModel* in Figure 4. Here, each component has associated with it a set of modes, some of which are categorised as fault modes. The parent component's mode, "parent_mode", holds all of the interconnecting edges.

4.1 Fault Modes

It is unusual to consider a component fault to be an operating mode of the component. Normally, behaviour under fault conditions is reasoned about independently using analysis techniques like Fault Trees [8] or Failure Modes and Effects Analysis [7]. Our application, however, is rather unusual. Failures are considered as connections across the circuit; faults which contribute to failures introduce connectivity into the circuit. Consequently, there is a symmetry between the architecture of the device under analysis and the corresponding fault tree which would model that device for domain separation failure. For example, consider the simple design presented in Figure 3(a). Figure 5 shows a fault tree for this device, modelling the circumstances under which the device fails to ensure domain separation.

Components that lay serially along the path translate to conjuncts in the tree, while components that are in parallel become disjuncts. This semantics is identical to our connectivity analysis (the paths from cause to effect trace along the same lines), so there is no need to perform this translation explicitly.

$$
\begin{array}{|l}
\hline
\textit{ExampleConcreteModel} \\
\textit{Model} \\
\hline
\textit{componentModes} = \\
\quad \{inputIO \mapsto inputIO\_normal, inputIO \mapsto inputIO\_fault, \\
\quad mainPIC \mapsto mainPIC\_normal, mainPIC \mapsto mainPIC\_fault, \\
\quad secPIC \mapsto secPIC\_normal, secPIC \mapsto secPIC\_fault, \\
\quad comparator \mapsto comparator\_normal, comparator \mapsto comparator\_fault, \\
\quad comparator \mapsto comparator\_signal\_fault, gate \mapsto gate\_open, \\
\quad gate \mapsto gate\_closed, gate \mapsto gate\_fault, \\
\quad gate \mapsto comparator\_signal\_fault, bypass \mapsto bypass\_on, \\
\quad bypass \mapsto bypass\_off, outputIO \mapsto outputIO\_normal, \\
\quad outputIO \mapsto outputIO\_fault, parent \mapsto parent\_mode\} \\
\textit{faultModes} = \\
\quad \{inputIO\_fault, mainPIC\_fault, secPIC\_fault, comparator\_fault, \\
\quad gate\_fault, comparator\_signal\_fault, outputIO\_fault\} \\
\textit{modeEdges} = \\
\quad \{inputIO\_normal \mapsto (a \mapsto b), mainPIC\_fault \mapsto (c \mapsto d), \\
\quad secPIC\_fault \mapsto (i \mapsto j), comparator\_fault \mapsto (l \mapsto m), \\
\quad comparator\_fault \mapsto (k \mapsto m), gate\_open \mapsto (e \mapsto f), \\
\quad gate\_fault \mapsto (n \mapsto f), comparator\_signal\_fault \mapsto (e \mapsto f), \\
\quad bypass\_on \mapsto (o \mapsto p), outputIO\_normal \mapsto (g \mapsto h), \\
\quad parent\_mode \mapsto (b \mapsto i), parent\_mode \mapsto (b \mapsto c), \\
\quad parent\_mode \mapsto (b \mapsto o), parent\_mode \mapsto (j \mapsto k), \\
\quad parent\_mode \mapsto (d \mapsto l), parent\_mode \mapsto (d \mapsto e), \\
\quad parent\_mode \mapsto (m \mapsto n), parent\_mode \mapsto (p \mapsto g), \\
\quad parent\_mode \mapsto (f \mapsto g)\} \\
\hline
\end{array}
$$

Fig. 4. Example concrete model

However, this method assumes that all possible faults are component-level faults. Unfortunately, we know this to not always be the case. For example, Figure 6 represents a simple system where a common controller C opens and closes a data channel at two distinct points A and B. Assume that both A and B are normally closed. If we consider only component-level faults then to send information over the channel it would require both A and B to be open. If this was a fault mode for these components, then it counts as two faults for the entire channel to be open. Otherwise, if this is not a fault mode, then it requires no faults. For an accurate model, it should only require one fault—that of component C—to cause the failure.

To provide for such scenarios, we allow fault modes to be shared amongst components. In this case, components A, B, and C could all share a fault mode *controller_signal_fault* that modelled the situation described above. Thus, the connectivity over the channel is correctly modelled as requiring a single fault.

The example concrete model shown in Figure 4 illustrates one fault mode that is shared between two components. Here, the fault mode is *comparator_signal_fault*

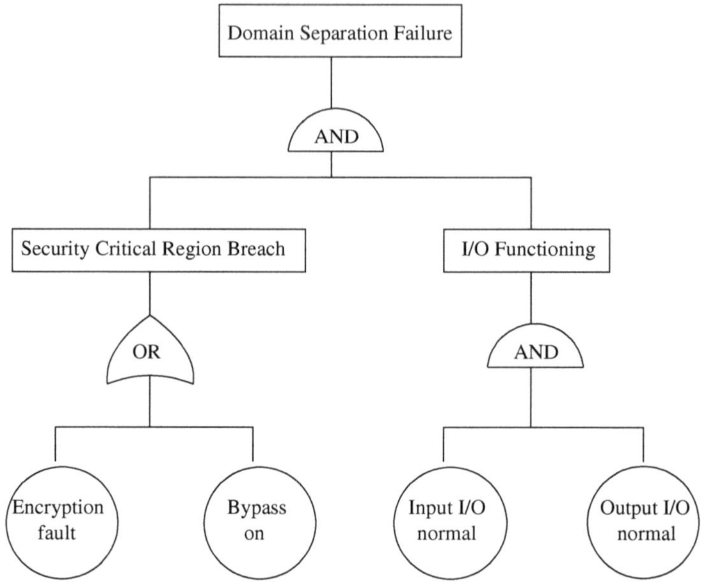

Fig. 5. Fault tree for abstract cryptographic device

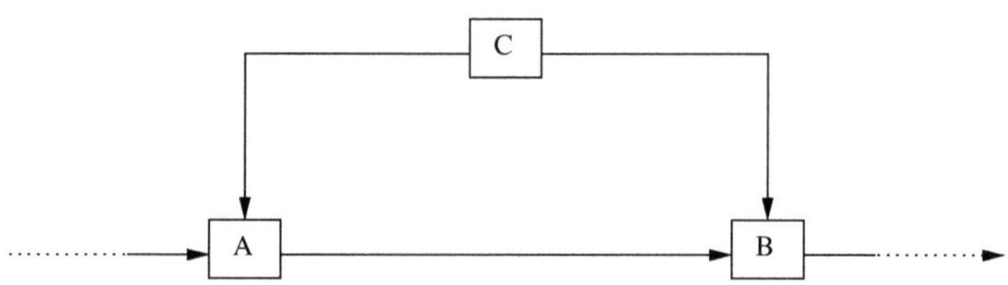

Fig. 6. Faults in controlling circuitry

and it is shared between the *comparator* and the *gate*. It models the scenario when the comparator fails to close the gate, allowing a signal to propagate from e to f.

4.2 Modes and Consistency

In Section 3 we described connectivity consistency by matching paths from the concrete model to paths in the abstract model. Consistency was achieved if every concrete path could be matched by an abstract path. When considering fault modes, if a path exists in the concrete model that requires the presence of a fault, then the matching abstract path should also require a fault. Intuitively, the abstract paths should exactly match the number of faults in the concrete model to form an accurate representation. However, this constraint is too strong; it is difficult to achieve because the abstract model will most likely have fewer components than the concrete model. Therefore, the abstract model will have fewer faults along those paths involving extra concrete components. Consequently, we require that the concrete model be 'at least as safe' as the abstract model under failure. Every path in the concrete model must be matched by a path in the abstract model in terms of connectivity, and additionally the concrete path must always require at least as many faults to form a complete connection across the graph than the corresponding abstract path requires. As the concrete path requires at least as many faults, it is at least as safe.

While this technique ensures that the abstract model accurately portrays the concrete model in terms of the number of faults required to compromise the domain separation functionality, it is possible that the abstraction has the faults in different places to the concrete model. This might occur if the number of points-of-failure required to cross one part of the circuit were decreased (making that part more fault prone) but a corresponding increase in points-of-failure were to occur somewhere else. For the purpose of showing the consistency between models of information flow with respect to points of failure, it is not clear whether we should allow this much flexibility. For the sake of being able to report when such differences occur we have chosen the stronger consistency relationship, that is, we check that between *any* two matching abstract ports along a pair of matching paths, the number of faults in the abstract model between those ports is fewer than, or equal to, the number of faults in the concrete model.

In the next section, we present the method we use to translate the model such that we are able to consider faults and connectivity simultaneously, and then revise our notion of model consistency accordingly.

4.3 Combining Connectivity and Modes

To simultaneously reason about connectivity and faults, we must derive a graph that describes the connectivity by assigning to each component a specific mode, some of which may be fault modes. We then consider all possible combinations of such assignments, ensuring that the abstract and concrete graphs are consistent regardless of the combination of modes (i.e., the abstraction is always a genuine representation of the system, regardless of the system state).

We specify the set of possible mode assignments for a graph by taking the set of all total functions that can be formed from the *componentModes* relation. Components may share fault modes, so we also stipulate that whenever a fault is selected it applies to all components that are capable of expressing that fault.

$$assignments : ComponentModes \rightarrow \mathbb{P}\, ComponentModes$$

$$\begin{array}{l} \forall\, rel : ComponentModes \bullet assignments(rel) = \\ \quad \{fs : ((\mathrm{dom}\, rel) \rightarrow MODE) \cap \mathbb{P}\, rel \mid \\ \qquad \forall\, f : fs \bullet \forall\, fault : (\mathrm{ran}\, f) \cap faultModes \bullet \\ \qquad\quad f \rhd \{fault\} = componentModes \rhd \{fault\}\} \end{array}$$

For a particular assignment, we construct a *CombinedGraph* where each vertex is a schema binding that contains both a port label and the set of faults required to reach that port.

$$\begin{array}{|l}
\hline
\textit{Reachable} \\
port : PORT \\
modes : \mathbb{P}\, MODE \\
\hline
\end{array}$$

$$CombinedGraph == Reachable \leftrightarrow Reachable$$

To construct a *CombinedGraph* we first start with an initial graph containing just a reflexive map of the *high* ports with no faults (it requires no faults to "reach" a port designated as *high*).

$$\begin{array}{|l}
initialGraph : CombinedGraph \\
\hline
initialGraph = \mathrm{id}\ \{r : Reachable \mid r.port \in high \wedge r.modes = \varnothing\}
\end{array}$$

We then extend it by progressively adding edges and vertices that correspond to the connectivity graph, and the modal assignment over that graph. This effectively mimics a breadth-first search, such that when a fixed point is reached (when further extending the search is futile) the combined graph is fully constructed.

The higher-order function *extend*, when given the set of fault modes, and a *ModeEdges* relation, returns a function that extends a combined graph with respect to the *ModeEdges* and the fault modes.

$$\begin{array}{l}
extend == (\lambda\, faults : \mathbb{P}\, MODE;\ connectivity : ModeEdges \bullet \\
\quad (\lambda\, g : CombinedGraph \bullet g \cup \bigcup\{s : \mathrm{ran}\, g \bullet \\
\qquad \{t : connectivity \mid (t.2).1 = s.port \bullet \\
\qquad\quad s \mapsto ((t.2).2, s.modes \cup \{t.1\} \cap faults)\}\}))
\end{array}$$

We also introduce the function *fix* which, given a function and an argument, finds and returns the fixed-point of that function with respect to the argument (if there exists a fixed-point, otherwise *fix* is undefined).

$$\begin{array}{|l}
\hline
[X] \\
fix : (X \rightarrow X) \times X \rightarrowtail\!\!\!\!\!\!+ \ X \\
\hline
\forall f : X \rightarrow X;\ x : X \bullet \\
\quad (f(x) = x \Rightarrow fix(f, x) = x) \wedge \\
\quad (f(x) \neq x \Rightarrow fix(f, x) = fix(f, f(x))) \\
\hline
\end{array}$$

We can now generate a combined graph *searchGraph* by finding the fixed-point of the *extend* function as applied to the *initialGraph*:

$$\begin{array}{l}
searchGraph == \\
\quad (\lambda\, faults : \mathbb{P}\, MODE;\ connectivity : ModeEdges \bullet \\
\qquad fix(extend(faults, connectivity), initialGraph))
\end{array}$$

For example, the following *assignment* models the case where the bypass mode is off, the gate is open, and the main processor has a fault, in the *ExampleConcreteModel* (Figure 4):

$$
\begin{aligned}
&assignment == \\
&\quad \{(bypass, bypass\_off), (comparator, comparator\_normal), \\
&\quad\ (gate, gate\_open), (inputIO, inputIO\_normal), \\
&\quad\ (mainPIC, mainPIC\_fault), (outputIO, outputIO\_normal), \\
&\quad\ (parent, parent\_mode), (secPIC, secPIC\_normal)\}
\end{aligned}
$$

Given *conc* as an instance of *ExampleConcreteModel*, Figure 7[1] illustrates the *searchGraph* resulting from restricting the *modeEdges* relation in *conc* to the modes in *assignment*.

$$searchGraph(conc.faultModes, (\operatorname{ran} assignment) \lhd conc.modeEdges)$$

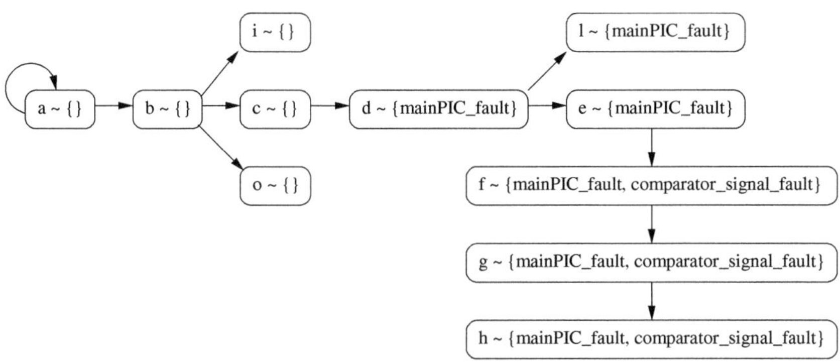

Fig. 7. An example search graph (for the concrete model)

Although the search graph may contain paths to sinks that are not in *low*, (i, o, and l exemplify this), when determining consistency we are only interested in the set of paths that connect *high* and *low*, so such dead-ends are eventually disregarded.

5 Analysis of Combined Model

It is possible to construct a *searchGraph* for every assignment of modes to components in both the concrete and the abstract models. The abstract model must be consistent with the concrete model regardless of the concrete model's state. Therefore, the consistency property ensures that for every path through every *searchGraph* in the concrete model, an assignment can be found for the abstract model that produces a *searchGraph* matching that path — in terms of connectivity, number of points of failure, and the location of failures.

We begin by finding the set of all paths *allLeaks*, over every possible *searchGraph* (mode assignment), that exist in a model where the path constitutes a leak.

[1] For brevity, we use the following abbreviation to denote a schema binding of *Reachable*: $a \leadsto b == \langle\!|\ port == a;\ modes == b\ |\!\rangle$.

$$
\begin{array}{|l}
allLeaks : Model \rightarrow \mathbb{P}\, PATH[Reachable] \\
\hline
\forall\, m : Model \bullet allSearchPaths(m) = \\
\quad \bigcup\{assignment : assignments(m.componentModes) \bullet \\
\quad\quad \{path : pathsOver(searchGraph(m.faultModes, \\
\quad\quad\quad\quad (\mathrm{ran}\ assignment) \lhd m.modeEdges)) \wedge \\
\quad\quad\quad first(path).port \in high \wedge last(path).port \in low\}\}
\end{array}
$$

We only consider paths that breach domain separation (leaks), so our concept of consistency only extends that far. Like the model of connectivity presented in Section 3, one need not capture in the abstraction parts of the concrete model that cannot possibly contribute to a leak.

Our consistency constraint ensures not only that a matching path can be found in the abstract model for every path through the concrete model, but also that the matching abstract path is consistent with respect to points of failure. *Consistency*, defined below, relates an abstract and a concrete model under these conditions.

$$
\begin{array}{|l}
\text{\_\_ } Consistency \text{ \_\_\_\_} \\
abs, conc : Model \\
\hline
\forall\, c\_path : allLeaks(conc) \bullet \\
\quad (\mathbf{let}\ c\_filtered == c\_path \upharpoonright \{r : Reachable \mid r.port \in abs.allPorts \wedge \\
\quad\quad\quad r.modes \in \mathbb{P}\, conc.faultModes\} \bullet \\
\quad\quad (\exists\, a\_path : allLeaks(abs) \bullet \\
\quad\quad\quad (\forall\, i_1, i_2 : \mathrm{dom}\ a\_path \mid i_2 > i_1 \bullet \\
\quad\quad\quad\quad (a\_path\ i_1).port = (c\_filtered\ i_1).port \wedge \\
\quad\quad\quad\quad (a\_path\ i_2).port = (c\_filtered\ i_2).port \wedge \\
\quad\quad\quad\quad \#(a\_path\ i_2).modes - \#(a\_path\ i_1).modes \leq \\
\quad\quad\quad\quad\quad \#(c\_filtered\ i_2).modes - \#(c\_filtered\ i_1).modes))) \\
\hline
\end{array}
$$

In Section 3.2 we filtered concrete paths by removing ports that did not appear in the abstract model, and in *Consistency* we filter the concrete paths on the same premise. The variable *c_filtered* represents the concrete path *c_path*, after the *Reachable* vertices that contain port labels not appearing in the abstract model are filtered out. This filtering occurs irrespective of the fault modes in the concrete path, such that the only vertices retained are those where the port is in *abs.allPorts* and the fault mode set is any subset of *conc.faultModes*.

For a particular filtered concrete path, we find an abstract path and examine all possible sub-paths. Since *a_path* is a sequence, its domain contains natural numbers that index the values in the sequence: the variables i_1 and i_2 thus denote a sub-path from index i_1 to index i_2. The predicate stipulates that at both indices, the port labels in the tuples match. Furthermore, *between* both indices the number of faults accrued in *a_path* is less than, or equal to, the number of faults accrued in *c_filtered*.

$$
\begin{array}{l}
\textit{ExampleAbstractModel} \\
\hline
\textit{Model} \\
\hline
\textit{componentModes} = \\
\quad \{\textit{inputIO} \mapsto \textit{inputIO\_normal}, \textit{inputIO} \mapsto \textit{inputIO\_fault}, \\
\quad \textit{encryption} \mapsto \textit{encryption\_normal}, \\
\quad \textit{encryption} \mapsto \textit{encryption\_fault}, \textit{encryption} \mapsto \textit{encryption\_leak} \\
\quad \textit{bypass} \mapsto \textit{bypass\_on}, \textit{bypass} \mapsto \textit{bypass\_off}, \\
\quad \textit{outputIO} \mapsto \textit{outputIO\_normal}, \textit{outputIO} \mapsto \textit{outputIO\_fault}, \\
\quad \textit{parent} \mapsto \textit{parent\_mode}\} \\
\textit{faultModes} = \\
\quad \{\textit{inputIO\_fault}, \textit{encryption\_fault}, \textit{encryption\_leak}, \textit{outputIO\_fault}\} \\
\textit{modeEdges} = \\
\quad \{\textit{inputIO\_normal} \mapsto (a \mapsto b), \textit{encryption\_fault} \mapsto (c \mapsto f), \\
\quad \textit{encryption\_leak} \mapsto (i \mapsto f), \textit{bypass\_on} \mapsto (o \mapsto p), \\
\quad \textit{outputIO\_normal} \mapsto (g \mapsto h), \textit{parent\_mode} \mapsto (b \mapsto i), \\
\quad \textit{parent\_mode} \mapsto (b \mapsto c), \textit{parent\_mode} \mapsto (b \mapsto o), \\
\quad \textit{parent\_mode} \mapsto (f \mapsto g), \textit{parent\_mode} \mapsto (p \mapsto g)\}
\end{array}
$$

Fig. 8. Example abstract model

5.1 Example

Revisiting the example in Section 4, we presented a concrete model and we also illustrated a possible abstraction of this model as a block diagram (refer to Figure 3). We now compliment that block diagram with the model in Figure 8, which includes information pertaining to the modes of the abstract components.

We wish to verify *ExampleAbstractModel* to ensure that it can match all leaky paths through *ExampleConcreteModel* according to *Consistency*. If we enumerate *allLeaks* for our *ExampleConcreteModel*, then *c_filtered* can take the following values:

1. $\langle a \backsim \varnothing,\ b \backsim \varnothing,\ c \backsim \varnothing,\ f \backsim \{\textit{mainPIC\_fault}, \textit{comparator\_signal\_fault}\},$
   $g \backsim \{\textit{mainPIC\_fault}, \textit{comparator\_signal\_fault}\},$
   $h \backsim \{\textit{mainPIC\_fault}, \textit{comparator\_signal\_fault}\}\rangle$
2. $\langle a \backsim \varnothing,\ b \backsim \varnothing,\ c \backsim \varnothing,\ f \backsim \{\textit{mainPIC\_fault}, \textit{comparator\_fault}, \textit{gate\_fault}\},$
   $g \backsim \{\textit{mainPIC\_fault}, \textit{comparator\_fault}, \textit{gate\_fault}\},$
   $h \backsim \{\textit{mainPIC\_fault}, \textit{comparator\_fault}, \textit{gate\_fault}\}\rangle$
3. $\langle a \backsim \varnothing,\ b \backsim \varnothing,\ i \backsim \varnothing,\ f \backsim \{\textit{secPIC\_fault}, \textit{comparator\_fault}, \textit{gate\_fault}\},$
   $g \backsim \{\textit{secPIC\_fault}, \textit{comparator\_fault}, \textit{gate\_fault}\},$
   $h \backsim \{\textit{secPIC\_fault}, \textit{comparator\_fault}, \textit{gate\_fault}\}\rangle$
4. $\langle a \backsim \varnothing,\ b \backsim \varnothing,\ o \backsim \varnothing,\ p \backsim \varnothing,\ g \backsim \varnothing,\ h \backsim \varnothing\rangle$

Likewise, *a_path* can take on the following values if we consider *allLeaks* over the *ExampleAbstractModel*:

1. $\langle a \backsim \varnothing,\ b \backsim \varnothing,\ i \backsim \varnothing,\ f \backsim \{encryption\_leak\},\ g \backsim \{encryption\_leak\},$ $h \backsim \{encryption\_leak\}\rangle$
2. $\langle a \backsim \varnothing,\ b \backsim \varnothing,\ c \backsim \varnothing,\ f \backsim \{encryption\_fault\},\ g \backsim \{encryption\_fault\},$ $h \backsim \{encryption\_fault\}\rangle$
3. $\langle a \backsim \varnothing,\ b \backsim \varnothing,\ o \backsim \varnothing,\ p \backsim \varnothing,\ g \backsim \varnothing,\ h \backsim \varnothing\rangle$

Consistency requires that for every *c_filtered* path we can find an *a_path* to match it in terms of connectivity. In Section 3.2 we have already shown that this is indeed the case. Further to this constraint, the matching *a_path* must not require a greater number of faults to traverse any particular sub-path than the *c_filtered* path for the same sub-path.

For example, *c_filtered* path numbers (1) and (2) above both match with *a_path* number (2). The only point on any of the paths where faults are added to the fault sets is between c and f. In the abstract path, one fault is added, and in the filtered concrete paths *at least* one fault is added on this step. Since no faults are added anywhere else, the *a_path* is a match for both filtered concrete paths. Similarly, *c_filtered* path number (3) above matches with *a_path* number (1), and *c_filtered* path number (4) matches *a_path* number (3).

6 Related Work

The relational algebra system RelView [2] makes possible the specification and exploration of relational problems likes ours. They employ model checking techniques in order to automatically calculate the solutions to problems expressed in a general relational programming language. They do not address problems in security, fault tolerance, or graph consistency specifically.

The ability to restate our problem as a model checking problem was discovered early in the project: one may consider an edge in the information flow model as a transition in a finite state machine (FSM) and check that there are no leaks from high to low by way of a state reachability analysis. If our abstract model were also expressed as an FSM then the consistency problem may also be expressed as a variant of Kripke-structure abstraction refinement [3].

This paper has avoided the discussion of particular implementation issues in order to focus on the specification of the problem domain.

7 Conclusion and Future Work

In this paper we have presented an abstraction mechanism that is suitable for the large scale analysis of information flow properties over systems in the presence of faults. Although we have concentrated on hardware devices, the theory can be applied to arbitrary networks of objects. We are implementing the approach into the SIFA[2] (Secure Information Flow Analyser) software [6], which has resulted in the identification of previously unknown possible information flow pathways

[2] `http://www.itee.uq.edu.au/~infosec/SIFA`

through two prototype security devices. The concrete models for these devices are directly imported into the tool from VHDL (a hardware description language) and checked for consistency against an abstract model created by hand from the design documentation. A primary advantage of using SIFA is the tool's ability to compose together multiple views to form a single model: normally this involves overlaying the electronic schematics (logical connectivity) with the artwork design (physical connectivity).

Our technique for checking consistency is analogous to symbolic model checking [4] in many respects, but we only deal with abstract states, i.e. states that have no associated semantic model (guards, transitions, etc.) Additionally, we do not require a deep semantic model for representing failure modes as these just correspond to connectivity. In further work we hope to automatically incorporate control flow into the dynamic properties of states (giving a richer semantic model), so the dependencies between states that give rise to shared fault modes may be automatically derived [9,11].

Our analysis technique overlooks the potential for information flow *between* component operating modes, i.e., via components that store information in one mode and release it in another [5]. Thus, the possibility for information flow paths to be present over sequences of modes is not detected. In future work we will extend the consistency checking technique presented in this paper to incorporate information flow over sequences of mode changes.

Additionally, we plan to increase the expressiveness of our methodology with a probabilistic model of failure. Of particular interest is the likelihood, impact, and observability of failures. For instance, unlikely failures with a low impact may be ignored, and we need to be able to distinguish failures that occur silently from those that do not, as silent failures can lead to a catastrophic (and unmitigated) leak of information.

Acknowledgements. This research is funded by an Australian Research Council Linkage grant, LP0347620: *Formally-Based Security Evaluation Procedures* conducted in conjunction with the Defence Signals Directorate.

References

1. ISO/IEC 13568, Information Technology—Z Formal Specification Notation—Syntax, Type System and Semantics, 2002. First edition 2002-07-01.
2. R. Behnke, R. Berghammer, E. Meyer, and P. Schneider. RELVIEW – a system for calculating with relations and relational programming. In *FASE*, pages 318–321, 1998.
3. E. Clarke, O. Grumberg, S. Jha, Y. Lu, and H. Veith. Counterexample-guided abstraction refinement for symbolic model checking. *J. ACM*, 50(5):752–794, 2003.
4. E. M. Clarke, O. Grumberg, and D. A. Peled. *Model checking.* MIT Press, Cambridge, MA, USA, 1999.
5. C. Fidge and T. McComb. Tracing information flow through mode changes. In Vladimir Estivill-Castro and Gillian Dobbie, editors, *Twenty-Ninth Australasian Computer Science Conference (ACSC 2006)*, volume 48 of *CRPIT*, pages 303–310, Hobart, Australia, 2006. ACS.

6. T. McComb and L. Wildman. SIFA: A tool for evaluation of high-grade security devices. In *ACISP*, pages 230–241, 2005.
7. MIL-STD. *Procedures for performing a failure mode, effects and criticality analysis.* Department of Defense (USA), 1629A.
8. U. S. Nuclear Regulatory Commission NRC. *Fault Tree Handbook.* NUREG-0492, Springfield, 1981.
9. A. Rae and C. Fidge. Identifying critical components during information security evaluations. *Journal of Research and Practice in Information Technology*, 37(4), November 2005.
10. A. Rae, C. Fidge, and L. Wildman. Fault evaluation for security-critical communications devices. *Computer*, 39(5):61–68, 2006.
11. A. Rae, C. Fidge, and L. Wildman. Information security fault mode evaluation for communications devices. *IEEE Computer*, 39(3), March 2006.
12. A. J. Rae and C. J. Fidge. Information flow analysis for fail-secure devices. *The Computer Journal*, 48(1):17–26, January 2005.
13. J. Rushby. Noninterference, transitivity, and channel-control security policies. Technical Report CSL-92-02, Computer Science Laboratory, SRI International, December 1992.
14. A. Sabelfeld and A. C. Myers. Language-based information-flow security. *IEEE Journal on Selected Areas in Communications*, 21(1):5–19, 2003.

A Language for Modeling Network Availability

Luigia Petre, Kaisa Sere, and Marina Waldén

IT Department, Åbo Akademi University, FIN-20520 Turku, Finland
{luigia.petre, kaisa.sere, marina.walden}@abo.fi

Abstract. Computer networks have become ubiquitous in our society and thus, the various types of resources hosted by them are becoming increasingly important. In this paper we study the resource availability in networks by defining a dedicated middleware language. This language is a conservative extension of the action system formalism, a general state-based approach to modeling and analyzing distributed systems. Our language formally treats aspects such as resource accessibility, replicated and homonym resources, their mobility, as well as node failure and maintenance in networks. The middleware approach motivates the separation of the views and formalisms used by the various roles such as the network user, the application developer, and the network manager.

1 Introduction

The networks have become an ubiquitous component of our society. Network applications range from e-commerce and Internet banking to digital TV, video-on-demand, and network games. Envisioned applications link the existing networks with more mundane appliances already containing embedded software, such as microwave ovens, refrigerators, VCRs, or the house clocks. With these applications it would be possible to check online the contents of the fridge, schedule the recording of a TV programme from work, or have the clocks automatically switched to the daylight saving time [25]. As users of such a network-oriented world, we would like to access all the applications we need at any time, without having to know about the network functioning mechanisms.

Meeting such a goal requests a high degree of reliance on the correct functioning and availability of the networks. Numerous formal frameworks have been developed to address the former issue, namely to specify a network-oriented application and then analyze its properties. Examples of such frameworks are CSP [11] and CCS [17], UNITY [7], Object-Z [24], and action systems [1]. To partially address the latter issue of network availability, some formalisms define concepts such as *locations* and *mobility*: π-calculus [18], Ambient Calculus [5], Mobile UNITY [22], and topological action systems [21]. These formalisms are mostly targeted to application developers who need the concepts of location and mobility in their specifications. The proper network availability is to be treated at a more specialized lower level. Hence, we need to separately analyze the *network user* requirements using any formal framework dedicated to network-aware applications. These requirements may need to be expressed more precisely in terms of locations and mobility by the *application developer*, using a properly equipped

Z. Liu and J. He (Eds.): ICFEM 2006, LNCS 4260, pp. 639–659, 2006.

formal framework. Then, the capabilities of the network in handling the functioning of various applications can be expressed by the *network manager* at an even lower layer. This layer is commonly referred to as the *middleware* layer.

In this paper we present a middleware language called MIDAS (MIDdleware based on Action Systems) for supporting resource-centric computing. Our proposed language is based on topological action systems introduced in [21] as a framework extending the action system formalism conservatively towards location-aware computing. Here we build on this work by providing an approach dedicated to the network resources and nodes. A resource can be a *data-oriented repository*, a *piece of code*, or a combination of data and code, the latter referred to as a *computation unit*. Our language handles resource accessibility, replicated and homonym resources, their mobility, as well as node failure and maintenance.

To make a clear distinction between the contribution of the application developer and that of the network manager, we employ action system *refinement* [1,2]. This technique ensures that a high-level system specification can be transformed by a sequence of *correctness-preserving steps* into an executable and more efficient system that satisfies the original specification. In this paper we assume to have two specification levels: one expressed with topological action systems and written by the application developer, say *Level1Spec* and another written in MIDAS by the network manager, say *Level2Spec*. The latter includes the former together with additions handling the network availability for the application, so that *Level1Spec* is refined by *Level2Spec*. The two specifications are thus intermediate steps between requirements and implementation, preserving the refinement relation that needs to exist between them. Namely, $\mathit{Requirements} \sqsubseteq \mathit{Level1Spec} \sqsubseteq \mathit{Level2Spec} \sqsubseteq \mathit{Implementation}$, where '$\sqsubseteq$' is the refinement relation notation. The table below summarizes this.

Role	Specification	Represents
User	Requirements	
Application Developer	Level1Spec	Application
Network Manager	Level2Spec	Middleware
Programmer	Implementation	Code

We proceed as follows. In Section 2 we present the language of topological action systems used throughout the paper. Based on some properties of this language, we define in Section 3 the network resource and its location. We also explain the difference between the specifications written by the application developer and the network manager. The following sections treat various aspects of MIDAS: Section 4 introduces the replicated resources, Section 5 the homonym resources, Section 6 the resource mobility, and in Section 7 we discuss the failure and maintenance of network nodes. Conclusions and related work are presented in Section 8.

2 Topological Action Systems

A topological action system is defined based on a connected graph. The nodes of this graph model the nodes of a network where computation can take place or where data can reside, i.e., the set of possible *locations* for resources. Let therefore $G = (V, E)$ be a *connected* graph, where V is the finite, non-empty set of nodes in the graph and E the set of edges.

A topological action system consists of a finite set of *actions* that can evaluate and modify a finite set of *variables*. The values of the variables form the *state* of the system. In the following, we first concentrate on the variables and actions and then define formally the topological action system.

Variables. Let Var be a finite set of *variable names*. We define a *variable* of a topological action system to be a quadruple (v, loc, Val, val) where $v \in Var$, $loc \subseteq V$, Val is a nonempty set of *values*, and $val \in Val$. The first field v denotes the name of the variable, the second (loc) its location in the network (V, E), the third (Val) the variable type, and the fourth (val) the current value of the variable. To avoid working with this quadruple in specifications, a few shorthand notations are introduced. We express the location of a variable called v by the expression $v.loc$ and the names of the variables located at a location α by the expression $\alpha.var$. The value of a variable called v is given by the expression $v.val$ and the type of a variable called v by the expression $v.type$. When we are interested only in the location of a variable, we can express this by $v@\alpha$, where $\alpha \in v.loc$ ($\alpha \in V$) or $v@\Gamma$, where $\Gamma \subseteq v.loc$ ($\Gamma \subseteq V$). When $|v.loc| > 1$ we say that the variable is *replicated*. We assume that the type of a variable is unchangeable.

Actions. Let Act be a finite set of *action names*, distinct from Var. We define an *action* of a topological action system to be a triple (a, loc, A) where $a \in Act$ is an informal, optional name for the action, $loc \subseteq V$ is its location in the network (V, E), and A is its body, i.e., a statement that can model evaluation and updates of the variables. A set of shorthand notations is introduced to avoid working with such triples in specifications. We express the location of an action (a, loc, A) by the expression $a.loc$ or $A.loc$ and the bodies of the actions located at a location α by the expression $\alpha.action$. When we are interested only in the location of an action, this is given by $A@\alpha$, where $\alpha \in A.loc$ ($\alpha \in V$) or $A@\Gamma$, where $\Gamma \subseteq A.loc$ ($\Gamma \subseteq V$); a similar notation is used with the name a of the action instead of its body A. When $|A.loc| > 1$ (or $|a.loc| > 1$) we say that the action is *replicated*. The name of an action is unchangeable. The body A of an action named a is described by the following grammar:

$$A ::= abort \mid skip \mid v.val := e \mid b \rightarrow A \mid A \,;\, A \mid [\!]_{i \in I} A \mid \textsf{if } b \textsf{ then } A \textsf{ else } A \textsf{ fi} \qquad (1)$$

Here (v, loc, Val, val) is a variable so that $v \in Var$, $e \in Val$, b is a predicate, and I an index set. Intuitively, $abort$ is the action that always deadlocks, $skip$ is the stuttering action, $v.val := e$ is an assignment, $b \rightarrow A$ is a guarded action, that can be executed only when b evaluates to true, $A_1 \,;\, A_2$ is the sequential composition of two actions A_1 and A_2, $[\!]_{i \in I} A_i$ is the non-deterministic choice among actions A_i, $i \in I$, and $\textsf{if } b \textsf{ then } A_1 \textsf{ else } A_2 \textsf{ fi}$ is the conditional composition of two actions A_1 and A_2. The nondeterministic assignment $[\!]_{v' \in Val} v.val := v'$ is denoted by $v.val :\in Val$.

Action semantics. The semantics of the action bodies in a topological action system is expressed with the *weakest precondition predicate transformer* (wp) [2].

Assume an action body A and a postcondition q for A, i.e., a predicate describing the state after the execution of A. A and q are then mapped into the weakest predicate $wp(A, q)$ describing the state before A was executed, so that A establishes q. For the action bodies described by the grammar (1) we give below their corresponding wp expressions:

$$\begin{array}{ll}
wp(abort, q) & \hat{=}\ false \\
wp(skip, q) & \hat{=}\ q \\
wp(v.val := e, q) & \hat{=}\ q[e/v.val] \\
wp(b \rightarrow A, q) & \hat{=}\ (b \Rightarrow wp(A, q)) \\
wp(A_1 \ ; A_2, q) & \hat{=}\ wp(A_1, wp(A_2, q)) \\
wp([\!]_{i\in I} A_i, q) & \hat{=}\ \forall i \in I \cdot wp(A_i, q) \\
wp(\mathsf{if}\ b\ \mathsf{then}\ A_1\ \mathsf{else}\ A_2\ \mathsf{fi}, q) & \hat{=}\ (b \Rightarrow wp(A_1, q) \wedge \neg b \Rightarrow wp(A_2, q)).
\end{array}$$

We say that an action behaves miraculously when it establishes any postcondition, including *false* which models an aborting state. The *guard condition* $g(A)$ defined as $g(A) \hat{=} \neg wp(A, false)$ gives those states in which the action behaves non-miraculously.

Topological action systems. The computation unit in the network (V, E) is modeled by a *topological action system*, defined in the following form:

$$\begin{array}{l}
\mathcal{A} \hat{=} |[\ \mathbf{exp}\ y; \\
\quad\quad \mathbf{var}\ x; \\
\quad\quad \mathbf{imp}\ z; \\
\quad\quad \mathbf{do}\ [\!]_{i\in I}\ A_i\ \mathbf{od} \\
\quad\ ]|
\end{array} \quad (2)$$

The first three sections are for variable declaration and usage, while the last describes the computation involved in $\mathcal{A}$, when I is finite. We assume that x, y and z are lists of variables whose names are pairwise disjoint, i.e., the name of a variable is unique in a topological action system.

The **exp** section describes the *exported* variables y of $\mathcal{A}$, $y = \{(y_l,\ y_l.loc,\ y_l.type,\ y_l^0)\}_{l\in L}$, where L is a finite index set. These variables can be used within $\mathcal{A}$, as well as within other topological action systems that import them. Initially, they are assigned the values y_l^0 and are located at $y_l.loc$. If the initialization is missing, arbitrary values from the type sets $y_l.type$ are assigned as initial values, while a default location $\{\lambda\}$, $\lambda \notin V$ is assigned as initial location. As the exported variables can be imported by other systems, their names are unchangeable.

The **var** section describes the *local* variables x of $\mathcal{A}$, $x = \{(x_j, x_j.loc, x_j.type, x_j^0)\}_{j\in J}$, where J is a finite index set. These variables can be used only within $\mathcal{A}$. Initially they are assigned the values x_j^0 and locations $x_j.loc$, or, if the initialization is missing, some arbitrary values from their type sets and $\{\lambda\}$ for location. As the variables are local to $\mathcal{A}$, their names can be changed. This change has to respect the requirement of unique names for variables in a topological action system and has to be propagated in all the action bodies that use the respective local variables.

The **imp** section describes the *imported* variables z, $z = \{(z_k, \Gamma_k, T_k)\}_{k\in K}$, where K is a finite index set. These variables are specified by name (z_k), desired locations of import (Γ_k), and desired import type (T_k). They are used in $\mathcal{A}$ and are declared as exported in other topological action systems. The imported and the exported variables form the *global* variables of $\mathcal{A}$, used for communication between topological action systems. The desired locations of import Γ_k can also be denoted by $z_k.iloc$ and the desired type of import T_k by $z_k.itype$. The locations Γ_k can also be left unspecified ($z = \{(z_k, T_k)\}_{k \in K}$), denoting the need of $\mathcal{A}$ to use variables with predefined names and types, independently of their location. In this case we write $z_k.iloc = \emptyset$. As the imported variables refer to exported variables of other topological action systems, their names are unchangeable.

The **do**...**od** section describes the computation involved in $\mathcal{A}$, modeled by a non-deterministic choice between actions with bodies A_i described by the grammar (1). If some of these actions are replicated, $|A_i.loc| > 1$, then A_i in the **do**...**od** section stands for $A_i@\rho_{i_1} \parallel A_i@\rho_{i_2} \parallel ... \parallel A_i@\rho_{i_{h_i}}$, where $|A_i.loc| = h_i$ and $A_i.loc = \{\rho_{i_1}, \rho_{i_2}, ..., \rho_{i_{h_i}}\}$. We refer in the following to actions of the form[1] $(a, \rho, A), \rho \in V$.

Assume that the names of all the variables used by an action (a, ρ, A) are in the set vA and the names of the used imported variables are in the set iA, $iA \subseteq vA$. It can often be the case that the variables vA and the action a are located at different nodes of the network and, hence, the accessibility of the variables from the action is not necessarily guaranteed. To model the network accessibility of an action $(a, \rho, A), \rho \in V$, we define a function depending on the action and its location, called *cell*: $cell(A, \rho) \subseteq V$. The cell comprises the set of accessible locations for each action A at a certain location $\rho \in V$.

To model that the variables vA are accessible to the action $(a, \rho, A), \rho \in V$, we define a predicate called *location guard*, denoted $lg(A@\rho)$:

$$lg(A@\rho) \mathrel{\hat{=}} \forall v \in vA \cdot (\exists \alpha \in cell(A, \rho) \cdot (v \in \alpha.var) \wedge \\ (v \in iA \wedge v.iloc \neq \emptyset \Rightarrow \alpha \in v.iloc)) \tag{3}$$

Before executing the action, the location guard verifies that, for each variable named $v, v \in vA$, there is a location α in the cell of the action that contains a variable with this name. Furthermore, if an imported variable $v \in iA$ is specified together with its desired locations of import ($v.iloc \neq \emptyset$), then the location α is one of the desired locations of import $v.iloc$.

Enabledness. The *guard* of the action (a, ρ, A) is defined as

$$gd(A@\rho) \mathrel{\hat{=}} lg(A@\rho) \wedge g(A), \tag{4}$$

where $g(A)$ is the guard condition. An action (a, ρ, A) of a topological action system is said to be *enabled*, if its guard $gd(A@\rho)$ evaluates to true. An action can be chosen for execution only if it is enabled.

The topological action system $\mathcal{A}$ in formula (2) thus models computation via the action $\parallel_{i \in I}(A_i@\rho_{i_1} \parallel A_i@\rho_{i_2} \parallel ... \parallel A_i@\rho_{i_{h_i}})$. Hence, $\mathcal{A}$ is a set of actions with bodies A_i at locations ρ_{i_j}, $i \in I, j \in \{1, 2, ..., h_i\}$, operating on local and global variables. First, the local and exported variables whose values form the state of $\mathcal{A}$ are initialized. Then, repeatedly, enabled actions at various locations in $\{A_i.loc\}_{i \in I}$ are non-deterministically chosen and executed, typically updating the state of $\mathcal{A}$. Actions that do not access each other's variables and are enabled at the same time can be executed in parallel. This is possible because their

[1] The correct form of an action located at a single location $\rho \in V$ is $(a, \{\rho\}, A), \rho \in V$. Here we use $(a, \rho, A), \rho \in V$ instead, for simplicity.

sequential execution in any order has the same result and the actions are taken to be atomic. Atomicity means that, if an enabled action is chosen for execution, then it is executed to completion without any interference from the other actions of the system. The computation terminates if no action is enabled, otherwise it continues infinitely.

Example 1. Consider an electronic library that provides books and other reading material as PDF-files on a server. A topological action system modeling such a library has the form below:

$$\begin{array}{ll} \mathcal{L}ibrary \mathrel{\widehat{=}} |[& \mathbf{exp}\ (books, \{\alpha\}, set\ of\ PDF); \\ & \mathbf{var}\ \ (x, \{\alpha\}, PDF); \\ & \mathbf{do}\ add :: x.val :\in PDF; books.val := books.val \cup \{x.val\} \\ & \ \ \| \, delete :: x.val :\in books.val; books.val := books.val \setminus \{x.val\} \\ & \ \ \| \, skip \\ & \mathbf{od} \\ ]| & \end{array} \quad (5)$$

An action (a, ρ, A) is denoted as $a :: A$ in the body of the topological action system. The variable *books* stores a finite set, $books.val = \{book_l | l \in L\}$, where L is a finite index set. The actions *add* and *delete* model the updating of the book collection. The execution of $\mathcal{L}ibrary$ is a nondeterministic choice between doing nothing (*skip*), adding books (*add*), or deleting books from the library collection (*delete*). We assume that all the resources of $\mathcal{L}ibrary$ are located at the server's location, $\alpha \in V$: $books.loc = x.loc = add.loc = delete.loc = skip.loc = \{\alpha\}$. The location guard of the action *add* is $\exists \beta \in cell(add, \alpha) \cdot \{x, books\} \subseteq \beta.var$. Since $x.loc = books.loc = \{\alpha\}$, then $\{x, books\} \subseteq \alpha.var$ and, hence, the location guard reduces to $\alpha \in cell(add, \alpha)$. Similarly, $lg(delete@\alpha) = \alpha \in cell(delete, \alpha)$.

3 Modularity Techniques, Resources, and Role Views

In this section we employ two modularity techniques that topological action systems inherit from the action system formalism. First, via *parallel composition*, we define our concept of resource and its location. Second, via *refinement*, we show the distinction between the specifications written by the application developer and the network manager.

Parallel composition. The topological action system is defined as the basic computation unit. Yet, in order to model complex systems we need to compose such units. This operation is described using the *parallel composition* operator.

Consider the topological action systems $\mathcal{A}$ and $\mathcal{B}$ below:

$$\begin{array}{ll} \mathcal{A} = |[& \mathbf{exp}\ \ y; \\ & \mathbf{var}\ \ x; \\ & \mathbf{imp}\ \ z; \\ & \mathbf{do}\ \ \|_{i_1 \in I_1} A_{i_1}\ \ \mathbf{od} \\ ]| & \end{array} \qquad \begin{array}{ll} \mathcal{B} = |[& \mathbf{exp}\ \ v; \\ & \mathbf{var}\ \ w; \\ & \mathbf{imp}\ \ t; \\ & \mathbf{do}\ \ \|_{i_2 \in I_2} B_{i_2}\ \ \mathbf{od} \\ ]| & \end{array}$$

We *assume* that the local variables of $\mathcal{A}$ and $\mathcal{B}$ have distinct names: $\{x_{j_1}\}_{j_1 \in J_1} \cap \{w_{j_2}\}_{j_2 \in J_2} = \emptyset$. If this is not the case, we can always rename a local variable to meet this requirement. The exported variables declared in $\mathcal{A}$ and $\mathcal{B}$ are *required* to have distinct names: $\{y_{l_1}\}_{l_1 \in L_1} \cap \{v_{l_2}\}_{l_2 \in L_2} = \emptyset$. The *parallel composition* $\mathcal{A} || \mathcal{B}$ of $\mathcal{A}$ and $\mathcal{B}$ has the following form:

$$\begin{array}{rl} \mathcal{A} \,||\, \mathcal{B} \mathrel{\widehat{=}} |[& \textbf{exp } u; \\ & \textbf{var } s; \\ & \textbf{imp } r; \\ & \textbf{do } A \parallel B \textbf{ od} \\ ]| & \end{array} \tag{6}$$

where $u = y \cup v$, $s = x \cup w$ and $r = (z \cup t) \setminus u$. Also, $A = \|_{i_1 \in I_1} A_{i_1}$ and $B = \|_{i_2 \in I_2} B_{i_2}$. The initial values and locations of the variables, as well as the actions in $\mathcal{A} \,||\, \mathcal{B}$ consist of the initial values, locations, and the actions of the original systems, respectively. The well-definedness of $\mathcal{A}||\mathcal{B}$ is ensured by the fact that all its variables have unique names. Thus, the exported and local variables of $\mathcal{A}$ and of $\mathcal{B}$ have distinct names and, moreover, the local variables of $\mathcal{A}$ can always be renamed in order not to be homonym with the exported variables of $\mathcal{B}$ (and vice versa). The binary parallel composition operator '$||$' is associative and commutative and thus extends naturally to the parallel composition of a finite set of systems.

Scalability and network resources. Based on the parallel composition operator, our approach is enabled to *scale up*, i.e., to model larger systems. We can thus specify the computation of entire networks, including the location of their various resources. Based on this operator, more flexibility of the approach has been demonstrated in [21]. Thus, we can decompose a topological action system into parallel 'smaller' units, so small that they encompass only a variable or an action. For instance, if the topological action system $\mathcal{A}$ in (2) has only two exported variables, two local variables, one imported variable and two actions ($I = \{1, 2\}$), then we can rewrite it as follows:

$$\begin{aligned} \mathcal{A} &= |[\textbf{exp } y_1]| \,||\, |[\textbf{exp } y_2]| \,||\, |[\textbf{var } x_1]| \,||\, |[\textbf{var } x_2]| \,||\, \mathcal{C}_1 \,||\, \mathcal{C}_2 \\ \mathcal{C}_1 &= |[\textbf{imp } z, y_1, x_1 \;;\, \textbf{do } A_1 \textbf{ od}]| \\ \mathcal{C}_2 &= |[\textbf{imp } z, y_2, x_2 \;;\, \textbf{do } A_2 \textbf{ od}]| \end{aligned} \tag{7}$$

where z, y_i, x_i are the names of the variables imported by $\mathcal{C}_i$, $i \in I$. Hence, we have a collection of topological action systems, each describing only one variable or action and running in parallel with each other.

We define a *network resource* to be a topological action system. The flexibility provided by the topological action systems approach allows the computation unit to *scale down* to fine grains of data and code resources. This is important because it provides a unique notation for modeling different kinds of resources in a network. Thus, a topological action system denotes not only an entire computation unit that acts via actions over a set of variables, but also a data repository (a variable or a set of variables) or mere code resources (an action or a set of actions).

Location of resources. Topological action systems of the form $\mathcal{A}_1 = |[\textbf{exp } y@\Gamma_1]|$, $\mathcal{A}_2 = |[\textbf{var } y@\Gamma_2]|$, and $\mathcal{A}_3 = |[\textbf{imp } z\,; \textbf{do } A@\Gamma_3 \textbf{ od}]|$ can be seen as taking the location of their declared entities: $\mathcal{A}_1@\Gamma_1, \mathcal{A}_2@\Gamma_2, \mathcal{A}_3@\Gamma_3$. This rises the question of defining locations also for the entire computation unit, i.e., the topological action system, not only for base resources such as variables and actions. If all the components of a topological action system have the same location, then this location is propagated to the topological action system. In case the locations differ, the topological action system gets the default location $\{\lambda\}$. Thus, we define the location of a topological action system $\mathcal{A}$,

$$
\begin{aligned}
\mathcal{A} = |[\ & \mathbf{exp}\ \{(y_1, \Phi_1, \cdots),\ \cdots, (y_n, \Phi_n, \cdots)\};\\
& \mathbf{var}\ \{(x_1, \Psi_1, \cdots),\ \cdots, (x_m, \Psi_m, \cdots)\};\\
& \mathbf{imp}\ z;\\
& \mathbf{do}\ \|_{i \in I}\ A_i\ \mathbf{od}\\
]|\ &
\end{aligned}
$$

with $A_i.loc = \Delta_i, \forall i \in I$ as:

$$
\mathcal{A}.loc \mathrel{\widehat{=}} \begin{cases} \Phi_i, & \Phi_i = \Psi_j = \Delta_k,\ \forall i, j, k \\ \{\lambda\}, & otherwise. \end{cases} \tag{8}
$$

We also use the notation $\mathcal{A}@\alpha$ or $\mathcal{A}@\Gamma$ for expressing that $\alpha \in \mathcal{A}.loc$ or $\Gamma \subseteq \mathcal{A}.loc$, respectively. The reverse relation, of a topological action system propagating its location to its components holds in the following form. If $\mathcal{A}.loc \subseteq V$, then all the components of $\mathcal{A}$ have the same location $\mathcal{A}.loc$. Yet, if $\mathcal{A}.loc = \{\lambda\}$ then we cannot say anything about the locations of the topological action system components.

Refinement. In the Introduction we defined informally the concept of refinement. When discussing refinement techniques for a system $\mathcal{A}$ we refer to the *behavior* of $\mathcal{A}$ as the set of state sequences that correspond to all the possible executions of $\mathcal{A}$. In this context, we say that the system $\mathcal{A}_1$ is *superposition* refined [2] by the system $\mathcal{A}_2$ when the behavior of $\mathcal{A}_1$ is still modeled by $\mathcal{A}_2$ and the new behavior introduced by $\mathcal{A}_2$ does not influence or take over the behavior of $\mathcal{A}_1$. This means that new variables and actions can be added by $\mathcal{A}_2$, in addition to those of $\mathcal{A}_1$, but in such a manner that they do not modify or take over the state evolution of $\mathcal{A}_1$. Superposition (only one of the refinement types) is the technique we employ in this paper to show the distinction between the specifications written by the application developer and the network manager.

More precisely, a specification written by the application developer (say *Level1Spec*) contains the resources and their locations as introduced so far. These resources can be composed in parallel and may contain finer grained resources: a topological action system typically contains variables and actions with their own location. Some other features, introduced in the following sections, can also be a part of the application developer domain and thus, of *Level1Spec*.

A MIDAS specification written by the network manager (say *Level2Spec*) contains *Level1Spec* and the necessary additions for handling the network availability. In particular, the guards of the actions are strengthened and some new actions that do not influence or take over the state evolution of *Level1Spec* are added. Thus, we can informally[2] say that $Level1Spec \sqsubseteq Level2Spec$.

Strengthening the guards here means considering a guard as a conjunction between the guard condition and the location guard, as defined in (4). The

[2] The formal rules for strengthening the guards and introducing new action are given in [2].

application developer is only concerned with specifying the guard condition, while the network manager is interested in the location guard. The location guards together with the definitions of the *cell* functions model the *resource accessibility* in MIDAS. The example below extends (5) in Section 2 and emphasizes the parts of the specifications that belong to the application developer and the network manager.

Example 2. The library system defined in (5) has the location $\{\alpha\}$: $\mathcal{L}ibrary.loc = \{\alpha\}$ (8). For using the collection of books, we define below a set of topological action systems, called $\mathcal{R}eader_k$, $k \in K$, where K is a finite index set:

$$
\begin{array}{rl}
\mathcal{R}eader_k \mathrel{\widehat{=}} |[& \textbf{var}\ \{(x, \{\beta_k\}, PDF), (books\_to\_read, \{\beta_k\}, set\ of\ PDF, \emptyset)\}; \\
& \textbf{imp}\ (books, set\ of\ PDF); \\
& \textbf{do}\ borrow :: x.val :\in books.val; \\
& \quad books\_to\_read.val := books\_to\_read.val \cup \{x.val\} \\
& \| return :: \exists z \in books\_to\_read.val \cdot duedate(z) \rightarrow \\
& \quad x.val :\in \{z | z \in books\_to\_read.val \wedge duedate(z)\}; \\
& \quad books\_to\_read.val := books\_to\_read.val \setminus \{x.val\} \\
& \| skip \\
& \textbf{od} \\
]| &
\end{array}
\qquad (9)
$$

We assume that the actions of $\mathcal{R}eader_k$, $k \in K$ are located at $\{\beta_k\}$ as are its variables: $borrow.loc = return.loc = skip.loc = \{\beta_k\}$. Hence, we have $\mathcal{R}eader_k.loc = \{\beta_k\}$ (8). A reader keeps track of all its borrowed books using the variable *books_to_read*, initially set to $\emptyset$. Borrowing a book implies choosing it from the list of books exported by the library system ($x.val :\in books.val$) and adding it to the set *books_to_read*. We assume that the files storing the reading material come with an embedded application, that removes them from the reader's location when the returning date comes. The latter condition is modeled by the predicate $duedate(x), x \in PDF$. The book returning is then expressed by the guarded action *return* that chooses among the books with expired due dates and removes their copies from the collection of borrowed books.

In order for the library example to function properly, the topological action systems $\mathcal{L}ibrary$ and $\mathcal{R}eader_k, k \in K$ are composed in parallel: $\mathcal{L}ibrary \parallel (\parallel_{k \in K} \mathcal{R}eader_k)$. The local variables of $\mathcal{R}eader_k$ can be renamed from x to x_k and from *books_to_read* to $books\_to\_read_k$. The application developer has thus produced a working specification of an electronic library: $Level1Spec = \mathcal{L}ibrary \parallel (\parallel_{k \in K} \mathcal{R}eader_k)$.

What does the network manager add in *Level2Spec*? First, a list of the *cell* functions for the actions *add*, *delete*, *borrow*, and *return* is specified. Second, the location guards are defined for each of these actions. The *skip* actions do not access any variable and, hence, their location guards evaluate to *true*.

We have already specified the location guards of *add* and *delete* in Section 2. For the actions *borrow* and *return*, we need to ensure that the local variables x and *books_to_read* as well as the imported variable *books* are located in the cell of each action. For the local variables, the location guard reduces to $\beta_k \in cell(borrow, \beta_k)$ and $\beta_k \in cell(return, \beta_k)$, following a similar reasoning as in

Example 1. For the imported variable of action *borrow* we need to ensure the less obvious condition $\exists \gamma \in cell(borrow, \beta_k) \cdot books \in \gamma.var$ and similarly for the *return* action.

Compatibility. The default location $\{\lambda\}$ models the location of a server for which the entire network is accessible and vice versa, any resource located at $\{\lambda\}$ is accessible to every action located in V. More precisely, an action with body A so that $A.loc = \{\lambda\}$ has $cell(A, \lambda) = V$, hence $lg(A@\lambda) = true$. This action is therefore enabled whenever the guard condition $g(A)$ holds. We also assume that $\lambda \in cell(A, \rho)$, for every action (a, ρ, A), $\rho \in V$. Thus, if an action requires some variable located at $\{\lambda\}$, then the variable is accessible. This mechanism of default location is intended as a compatibility means with the more traditional local area networks where there is no replication and no significant mobility, and hence no location information is necessary. Such a local area network can be seen as located at $\{\lambda\}$, and so, is location-transparent.

4 Replicated Resources

Besides resource accessibility, another aspect of MIDAS is the definition and maintenance of replicated resources. The replication mechanism is intended for optimal availability of resources and, thus, we do not replicate resources located at $\{\lambda\}$. Such resources are anyway accessible to the whole network as explained above. In the following, we study the replication of each resource type in turn: first we consider variables, then actions, and then topological action systems. All the actions defined in this section as well as their necessary location guards are the job of the network manager, hence, they belong to *Level2Spec*.

4.1 Variables

In the previous sections we have seen the impact of variable names, in the definition of action enabledness as well as in the well-definedness of parallel composition. We now study variables having the same name.

A *replicated variable* is by definition a variable whose location has more than one element. More precisely, the replicas of a variable named v and located at $\Gamma = \{\alpha_1, \alpha_2, ..., \alpha_n\}$, $\Gamma \subseteq V$ have the same name, type, and value, but different locations excluding $\{\lambda\}$: $v@\alpha_1, v@\alpha_2, ..., v@\alpha_n$. Moreover, it makes no sense to have more than one replica of the same resource at the same location.

Accessing replicated variables depends on whether the access is (only) for reading or for (reading and) updating the variable value. If a variable is only accessed for reading, then no special rule is needed, hence the location guard in (3) is used. We can reinterpret this rule as follows: For any variable named $v, v \in vA$, we choose a location of one of its replicas so that this location is in the cell of the action. If a variable is accessed also for updating its value, then all its replicas have to be updated simultaneously to the same value. We model this case in two steps. First, we enforce a more restrictive form of the location guard than the one in (3):

$$lg(A@\rho) \mathrel{\widehat{=}} \forall v \in vA \cdot (\exists \alpha \in cell(A,\rho) \cdot (v \in \alpha.var) \wedge \\ (|\mathbf{v.loc}| > \mathbf{1} \Rightarrow \mathbf{v.loc} \subseteq \mathbf{cell}(\mathbf{A},\rho)) \wedge \\ (v \in iA \wedge v.iloc \neq \emptyset \Rightarrow \alpha \in v.iloc)) \tag{10}$$

This restricted form ensures that we can access all the replicas of a variable named v that needs to be updated. Second, if the above action with body A is enabled and chosen for execution, then every assignment to the replicated variable named v is replaced by the sequential composition of assignments to all its replicas. As an example, the action in the topological action system

$$|[\mathbf{exp}\ (y, \{\alpha, \beta\}, \cdots)\ ;\ \mathbf{do}\ (y.val \neq 5 \rightarrow y.val : = 5)@\rho\ \mathbf{od}]|$$

first checks the guard condition $y.val \neq 5$, then the location guard $(\exists \delta \in cell(y.val \neq 5 \rightarrow y.val : = 5, \rho) \cdot y \in \delta.var) \wedge \{\alpha, \beta\} \subseteq cell(y.val \neq 5 \rightarrow y.val : = 5, \rho)$. If both conditions evaluate to *true*, then both $y@\alpha$ and $y@\beta$ are updated to the value 5. The atomicity property for actions ensures that other computations will not access the variable named y until all its copies are updated.

Creating replicas. There are two ways to create replicas for a variable. We can either declare the variable as replicated or we can update its location via actions during the execution of the topological action system. In the latter case, consider that we have a variable named v. We create another replica of this variable at the location Γ, $\Gamma \subseteq V$ using a special *copy* action:

$$\begin{array}{lcl} A & ::= & \ldots \mid copy(v,\Gamma), \\ copy(v,\Gamma) & \mathrel{\widehat{=}} & v.loc \neq \{\lambda\} \rightarrow v.loc : = v.loc \cup \Gamma \end{array} \tag{11}$$

This action is semantically sound, its *wp* expression having the following form:

$$wp(copy(v,\Gamma), q) = (v.loc \neq \{\lambda\} \Rightarrow q[(v.loc \cup \Gamma)/v.loc])$$

Its guard condition is $v.loc \neq \{\lambda\}$. To create replicas at Γ, the action *copy* needs to have Γ accessible to its cell. Hence, the location guard is

$$lg(copy(v,\Gamma)@\rho) = \exists \alpha \in cell(copy(v,\Gamma),\rho) \cdot v \in \alpha.var \\ \wedge\ \mathbf{\Gamma} \subseteq \mathbf{cell}(\mathbf{copy}(\mathbf{v},\mathbf{\Gamma}),\rho)$$

Since $copy(v,\Gamma)$ does not modify $v.val$, the fact that this variable may already be replicated or may be imported makes no difference. We only need to access one of its copies and the set Γ, as expressed above. Hence, the last two conjunctions of (10) are not needed in the location guard of the $copy(v,\Gamma)$ action.

Removing replicas. The reverse of the *copy* operation is that of removing replicas of a variable named v:

$$\begin{array}{lcl} A & ::= & \ldots \mid remove(v,\Gamma), \\ remove(v,\Gamma) & \mathrel{\widehat{=}} & \textsf{if}\ v.loc \setminus \Gamma \neq \emptyset\ \textsf{then}\ v.loc : = v.loc \setminus \Gamma \\ & & \textsf{else}\ v.loc : = \{\lambda\}\ \textsf{fi} \end{array} \tag{12}$$

This action is semantically sound having the following *wp* expression:

$$wp(remove(v,\Gamma), q) = (v.loc \setminus \Gamma \neq \emptyset \Rightarrow q[(v.loc \setminus \Gamma)/v.loc]) \wedge \\ (v.loc \setminus \Gamma = \emptyset \Rightarrow q[\{\lambda\}/v.loc]),$$

while its guard condition is *true* and its location guard is similar to the location guard of $copy(v,\Gamma)$. If $v.loc = \Gamma$ and we want to remove all its replicas, then the copies at Γ are indeed removed, but the variable is saved at the default location $\{\lambda\}$.

4.2 Actions

Actions have a different replication pattern compared to variables. They model *active* code resources, i.e., code which executes itself following its own semantic rules. Executing $A \parallel A$ is equivalent to executing A, except that some of the nodes containing A may be unavailable (see Section 7). Hence, by having replicas of an action executed in parallel at different locations, we increase the enabledness of the code modeled by this action, i.e., we ensure a better code availability.

A replicated action is by definition an action whose location has more than one element. More precisely, the replicas of an action (a, loc, A) so that $A.loc = \{\rho_1, \rho_2, ..., \rho_n\}$ have the same name and body, but different locations excluding $\{\lambda\}$: $A@\rho_1$, $A@\rho_2$,..., $A@\rho_n$. It makes no sense to have more than one replica of an action at the same location.

Creating replicas. There are two ways to create replicas for an action. We can either declare the action as replicated or we can update its location via actions during the execution of the topological action system. In the latter case, consider that we have an action with body A. We create another replica of this action at the location Γ, $\Gamma \subseteq V$ using a special *copy* action:

$$\begin{array}{lcl} A & ::= & ... \mid copy(A, \Gamma), \\ copy(A, \Gamma) & \hat{=} & A.loc \neq \{\lambda\} \rightarrow A.loc := A.loc \cup \Gamma \end{array} \tag{13}$$

This action is semantically sound, its *wp* expression having the following form:

$$wp(copy(A, \Gamma), q) = (A.loc \neq \{\lambda\} \Rightarrow q[(A.loc \cup \Gamma)/A.loc])$$

Its guard condition is $A.loc \neq \{\lambda\}$ and its location guard is

$$\begin{array}{rl} lg(copy(A, \Gamma)@\rho) = & \exists \alpha \in cell(copy(A, \Gamma), \rho) \cdot A \in \alpha.action \\ & \wedge\, \boldsymbol{\Gamma} \subseteq \mathbf{cell}(\mathbf{copy}(\mathbf{A}, \boldsymbol{\Gamma}), \rho) \end{array}$$

We note that the action body needs to be appropriately located in order for the *copy* operation to succeed. In this case, the action (code resource) to be copied behaves more like a data resource.

Removing replicas. The reverse of the *copy* operation is that of removing replicas of an action with body A:

$$\begin{array}{lcl} A & ::= & ... \mid remove(A, \Gamma), \\ remove(A, \Gamma) & \hat{=} & \mathsf{if}\ A.loc \setminus \Gamma \neq \emptyset\ \mathsf{then}\ A.loc := A.loc \setminus \Gamma \\ & & \mathsf{else}\ A.loc := \{\lambda\}\ \mathsf{fi} \end{array} \tag{14}$$

This action is semantically sound having the following *wp* expression:

$$\begin{array}{rl} wp(remove(A, \Gamma), q) = & (A.loc \setminus \Gamma \neq \emptyset \Rightarrow q[(A.loc \setminus \Gamma)/A.loc]) \wedge \\ & (A.loc \setminus \Gamma = \emptyset \Rightarrow q[\{\lambda\}/A.loc]), \end{array}$$

while its guard condition is *true* and its location guard is similar to the location guard of $copy(A, \Gamma)$. If $A.loc = \Gamma$ and we want to remove all its replicas, then the copies from Γ are indeed removed, but the action is saved at the default location $\{\lambda\}$.

4.3 Topological Action Systems

Consider a topological action system $\mathcal{A}$ as in (2) so that $\mathcal{A}.loc \neq \{\lambda\}$. $\mathcal{A}$ is called *replicated* if $|\mathcal{A}.loc| > 1$. This means that all the variables and actions of $\mathcal{A}$ are replicated at $\mathcal{A}.loc$. Creating and removing replicas of $\mathcal{A}$ is based on creating and removing replicas for all the variables and actions of $\mathcal{A}$. We formally extend the action grammar (14) with two more actions:

$$\begin{array}{lll} A & ::= & ... \mid copy(\Gamma) \mid remove(\Gamma), \\ copy(\Gamma) & \hat{=} & \mathcal{A}.loc \neq \{\lambda\} \rightarrow \\ & & \quad \forall l \in L \cdot copy(y_l, \Gamma); \\ & & \quad \forall j \in J \cdot copy(x_j, \Gamma); \\ & & \quad \forall i \in I \cdot copy(A_i, \Gamma) \\ remove(\Gamma) & \hat{=} & \textsf{if } \mathcal{A}.loc \setminus \Gamma \neq \emptyset \textsf{ then} \\ & & \quad \forall l \in L \cdot remove(y_l, \Gamma); \\ & & \quad \forall j \in J \cdot remove(x_j, \Gamma); \\ & & \quad \forall i \in I \cdot remove(A_i, \Gamma) \\ & & \textsf{else } \mathcal{A}.loc := \{\lambda\} \textsf{ fi} \end{array} \tag{15}$$

These actions are semantically sound, having tedious but obvious *wp* expressions. The actions $copy(\Gamma)$ and $remove(\Gamma)$ refer to the topological action system they are specified in, hence, we cannot manipulate other systems based on these actions. Namely, computation units can only duplicate themselves and similarly for reducing their number of replicas.

Example 3. The library system introduced in (5) provides data to be used by readers (9). If the reading data is only stored on one server, then it is lost in case this server fails. Hence, the $\mathcal{L}ibrary$ system should have some replicas in the network (V, E). For this, the network manager adds an action in $\mathcal{L}ibrary$: $\cdots \,\|\, skip \,\|\, \mathbf{copy}(\alpha')$, at the middleware layer. This action creates a replica of $\mathcal{L}ibrary$ at the α' node, $\alpha' \in V$, so that $\mathcal{L}ibrary.loc = \{\alpha, \alpha'\}$. The *copy* action executes every time it is chosen for execution; however, the library system's location is changed from $\{\alpha\}$ to $\{\alpha, \alpha'\}$ only following its first execution, due to the form of the action *copy* (see (11), (13), (15)).

Adding the action $copy(\alpha')$ in *Level2Spec* preserves the refinement relation between *Level1Spec* and *Level2Spec*. However, it implies some other modifications in *Level2Spec*. The location guards of actions *borrow* and *return* do not change, even though we now have $|books.loc| > 1$; this is because these actions only read the variable *books*. On the contrary, the actions *add* and *delete* modify the value of the variable *books*. Due to the condition $|books.loc| > 1$, we need to ensure that $books.loc \subseteq cell(add, \alpha) \wedge books.loc \subseteq cell(add, \alpha')$ and similarly for the action *delete*. This means strengthening the guards of actions *add* and *delete* and, thus, $Level1Spec \sqsubseteq Level2Spec$ holds. Moreover, we need to update both copies of the variable *books*, $books@\alpha$ and $books@\alpha'$ in the body of the actions *add* and *delete*, as explained in Section 4.1. Since these changes do not influence the behavior of *Level1Spec*, the refinement relation is preserved. Similar guard strengthening and updates need to be made for the local and replicated variable x in the actions *add* and *delete*. All these changes preserve $Level1Spec \sqsubseteq Level2Spec$.

5 Homonym Variables

Another capability of MIDAS is the treatment of homonym variables. The general case of such variables having the same name, but possibly different types and values, is different with respect to replication. These resources can be declared in different topological action systems: $\mathcal{T}_1 = |[\mathbf{exp}\ (z_k, \{\alpha\}, T_1, a)]|$ and $\mathcal{T}_2 = |[\mathbf{exp}\ (z_k, \{\beta\}, T_2, b)]|$, where z_k is their common name, $\{\alpha\}$ and $\{\beta\}$ their distinct locations, T_1 and T_2 their types, and a and b their values. The types T_1 and T_2 can be identical. The difference with respect to a replicated variable located at $\{\alpha, \beta\}$ is that each homonym variable has its own update history, i.e., their updates are independent of each other.

Clearly, the systems where homonym variables are declared cannot compose in parallel with each other. However, another topological action system importing the variable $(z_k, \Gamma_k, z_k.type)$ can compose with either of $\mathcal{T}_1$ or $\mathcal{T}_2$. In this case, for importing a variable both its name and its type have to match with its specification $(z_k, \Gamma_k, z_k.type)$. Hence, the last conjunction in the location guard formula (3) $(v \in iA \wedge v.iloc \neq \emptyset \Rightarrow \alpha \in v.iloc)$ becomes $(v \in iA \Rightarrow v.type = v.itype \wedge (v.iloc \neq \emptyset \Rightarrow \alpha \in v.iloc))$, where $v.iloc = \Gamma_k$. In this way, the rightly typed variable is imported.

Besides the above modification, we need to ensure that at a certain location there is only one variable with a certain name v, $\forall v \in Var$. This integrity condition is modeled by a function that records, for every location in V and every variable name in Var, the number of variables having that name and located there: $\forall v \in Var, \forall \alpha \in V \cdot \alpha.no(v) \in \{0, 1\}$. Thus, $\alpha.no(v) = 1$ means that a variable called v is located or has a replica at α and $\alpha.no(v) = 0$ means that there is no variable called v located or with a replica at α. The network manager has to ensure the well-definedness of this function: a replicated variable named v has only one copy at every $\alpha \in v.loc$ and there are no homonym variables named v with common locations, $\forall v \in Var$. Hence, the guards of the actions that could modify the values of the function during execution have to prohibit this. The action $copy(v, \Gamma)$ thus becomes: $copy(v, \Gamma) \mathrel{\hat{=}} (v.loc \neq \{\lambda\}) \wedge (\forall \alpha \in \mathbf{\Gamma} \cdot \alpha.\mathbf{no}(\mathbf{v}) = \mathbf{0}) \rightarrow v.loc :\!= v.loc \cup \Gamma$.

The declaration of homonym variables z_k is typically done by the application developer. Hence, they belong to *Level*1*Spec* together with the possible modifications for importing the variables z_k. The well-definedness of the function $\alpha.no(v), \forall v \in Var, \forall \alpha \in V$ and the location guards above are the job of the network manager, and, hence, belong to *Level*2*Spec*. As before, the relationship *Level*1*Spec* $\sqsubseteq$ *Level*2*Spec* is preserved.

Example 4. The example (5),(9) can also include the specification of a homonym variable *books*, exported by a bookshop system like the one sketched below:

$$\begin{array}{l} \mathcal{B}ookshop \mathrel{\hat{=}} |[\ \mathbf{exp}\ (books, \{\alpha''\}, set\ of\ Book) \\ \qquad\qquad\qquad \mathbf{do} \cdots \mathbf{od} \\ \qquad\qquad\quad]| \end{array} \tag{16}$$

In this case, the two homonym variables called *books* (the one declared in $\mathcal{L}ibrary$ and the one in $\mathcal{B}ookshop$) have different types and locations. Hence, the $\mathcal{R}eader_k$

system specifies the importing of the variable *books* together with its desired import type: **imp** (*books*, *set of PDF*). The location guards of the actions *borrow* and *return* need to check the extra conjunction $books.type = books.itype$, which ensures that the variable *books* from $\mathcal{L}ibrary$ is the one used.

If $\mathcal{B}ookshop$ declares **exp** $(books, \{\alpha''\}, set\ of\ PDF)$, then the location is the only way to differentiate between the variables to be used in $\mathcal{R}eader_k$ (we assume that $\alpha'' \notin \{\alpha, \alpha'\}$). Hence, when importing the variable *books* in this system, the desired import location has to also be specified: **imp** $(books, \{\alpha, \alpha'\}, set\ of\ PDF)$. This ensures that the actions *borrow* and *return* will choose one of the library locations for the imported variable *books*.

6 Mobility of Resources

Mobility is a central feature in network computations as well as in the middleware language handled by the network manager. We can model data, code, as well as computation unit mobility using the topological action system framework. Hence, we obtain a model for *resource mobility*.

We start by extending the grammar (15) with the following actions:

$$\begin{array}{lll} A & ::= & \ldots \mid move(v, \alpha_0, \alpha) \mid move(A, \alpha_0, \alpha) \mid move(\alpha_0, \alpha), \\ & & \alpha_0, \alpha \in V \\ move(v, \alpha_0, \alpha) & \widehat{=} & \alpha_0 \in v.loc \rightarrow v.loc := v.loc \setminus \{\alpha_0\} \cup \{\alpha\} \\ move(A, \alpha_0, \alpha) & \widehat{=} & \alpha_0 \in A.loc \rightarrow A.loc := A.loc \setminus \{\alpha_0\} \cup \{\alpha\} \\ move(\alpha_0, \alpha) & \widehat{=} & \alpha_0 \in \mathcal{A}.loc \rightarrow \\ & & \quad \forall l \in L \cdot move(y_l, \alpha_0, \alpha); \\ & & \quad \forall j \in J \cdot move(x_j, \alpha_0, \alpha); \\ & & \quad \forall i \in I \cdot move(A_i, \alpha_0, \alpha) \end{array} \quad (17)$$

Here v is the name of a variable, A is the body of an action, and $\mathcal{A}$ is a topological action system. The *move* actions model the movement of resources (variable, action, topological action system) from the initial location α_0 to a location α in the network. These actions are guarded by the condition that the initial location of the resource contains the location α_0. The *move* actions are semantically sound; the first two have the following *wp* expressions and guard conditions:

$$\begin{array}{ll} wp(move(v, \alpha_0, \alpha), q) & = (\alpha_0 \in v.loc \Rightarrow q[(v.loc \setminus \{\alpha_0\} \cup \{\alpha\})/v.loc]) \\ wp(move(A, \alpha_0, \alpha), q) & = (\alpha_0 \in A.loc \Rightarrow q[(A.loc \setminus \{\alpha_0\} \cup \{\alpha\})/A.loc]) \\ g(move(v, \alpha_0, \alpha)) & = \alpha_0 \in v.loc \\ g(move(A, \alpha_0, \alpha)) & = \alpha_0 \in A.loc \end{array}$$

Moving $\mathcal{A}$ from α_0 to α is based on moving all the variables and actions of $\mathcal{A}$. The corresponding action is also semantically sound, its *wp*-expression being based on the above given expressions. The action $move(\alpha_0, \alpha)$ refers to the topological action system it is specified in. Hence, computation units can only move themselves; we cannot manipulate other systems based on this action.

We note the role of the guard condition $\alpha_0 \in r.loc$ (see (17)) of a *move* action for the replicated resource r, $|r.loc| > 1$. This condition ensures that only the copy located at α_0 is moved to α while the rest of the copies of r do not change their location.

Similarly as for the *copy* action, the guard condition of the *move* action is strengthened so that $\forall v \in Var, \forall \alpha \in V$ the function $\alpha.no(v)$ remains well-defined. The action $move(v, \alpha_0, \alpha)$ thus becomes:

$$move(v, \alpha_0, \alpha) \mathrel{\widehat{=}} \alpha_0 \in v.loc \wedge \alpha.\mathbf{no(v)} = \mathbf{0} \rightarrow v.loc := v.loc \setminus \{\alpha_0\} \cup \{\alpha\}$$

The actions specified in (17) are usable by both the application developer and the network manager. However, the network manager has to handle the necessary location guards.

Location guards. In order for the *move* actions to be executable, the target location α needs to be accessible. Furthermore, the variable called v and the action with body A have to be available in the cell of their *move* actions. Hence, since these resources are located at α_0 (as ensured by the guard condition), the location α_0 also needs to be available to the *move* actions. We have the following location guards:

$$\begin{aligned} lg(move(v,\alpha_0,\alpha),\rho) &= \{\alpha_0,\alpha\} \subseteq cell(move(v,\alpha_0,\alpha),\rho)\\ lg(move(A,\alpha_0,\alpha),\rho) &= \{\alpha_0,\alpha\} \subseteq cell(move(A,\alpha_0,\alpha),\rho)\\ lg(move(\alpha_0,\alpha),\rho) &= \{\alpha_0,\alpha\} \subseteq cell(move(\alpha_0,\alpha),\rho) \wedge\\ &\quad \textstyle\bigwedge_{l\in L} lg(move(y_l,\alpha_0,\alpha),\rho_l) \wedge\\ &\quad \textstyle\bigwedge_{j\in J} lg(move(x_j,\alpha_0,\alpha),\rho_j) \wedge\\ &\quad \textstyle\bigwedge_{i\in I} lg(move(A_i,\alpha_0,\alpha),\rho_i) \end{aligned} \tag{18}$$

The location guard of the action $move(\alpha_0, \alpha)$ also contains the location guards of the *move* actions for the variables and actions of $\mathcal{A}$.

Example 5. For the $\mathcal{R}eader_k$ system we can assume that it will not be replicated: $|\mathcal{R}eader_k.loc| = 1$. This ensures the natural requirement that no clones are created for such systems (the condition can be handled by either the network manager or the application developer). However, the initial β_k location can be modified via movement through the network. The following additions are made to the form specified in (9):

$$\begin{aligned} \mathcal{R}eader_k \mathrel{\widehat{=}} |[\ & \mathbf{var}\ \{\cdots, (x', \{\beta_k\}, V), (x'', \{\beta_k\}, V)\}\ ;\ \cdots\\ & \mathbf{do}\ \cdots\\ & \ []\ goto :: x'.val :\in \mathcal{R}eader_k.loc; x''.val :\in V; move(x'.val, x''.val)\\ & \mathbf{od}\\ ]|& \end{aligned} \tag{19}$$

The action *goto* can change the location of $\mathcal{R}eader_k$ (and thus, the location of all its resources). The new location $x''.val$ is chosen nondeterministically from the network nodes V, hence, it can also be the location $\mathcal{R}eader_k.loc$. In such a case *goto* is equivalent to *skip*.

Having the $\mathcal{L}ibrary$ system replicated on two network nodes provides even more useful when we take into account the movement of $\mathcal{R}eader_k$. The exported variable *books* of $\mathcal{L}ibrary$ is then imported from α or α', depending on the current position of $\mathcal{R}eader_k$. If both α and α' are accessible to the cells of actions *borrow* or *return* from $\mathcal{R}eader_k$, then one is chosen by the middleware location guard. If neither location is accessible, then these actions of $\mathcal{R}eader_k$ cannot execute until $\mathcal{R}eader_k$ has moved to a more suitable location in the network.

7 Node Failure and Maintenance

The status of the network nodes greatly influences the availability of the network resources. We model the node status in MIDAS as described below. Consider a partition of the network nodes V into active nodes, nodes under maintenance, and failed nodes: $V = V_{act} \cup V_{maint} \cup V_{fail}$, so that $V_{act} \cap V_{maint} = \emptyset$, $V_{act} \cap V_{fail} = \emptyset$, $V_{maint} \cap V_{fail} = \emptyset$. We extend the grammar (17) with the following actions:

$$\begin{array}{lcl} A & ::= & ... \mid \mathit{fail}(\alpha) \mid \mathit{begin\_maint}(\alpha) \mid \mathit{end\_maint}(\alpha), \\ \mathit{fail}(\alpha) & \widehat{=} & \alpha \in V_{act} \rightarrow V_{act} := V_{act} \setminus \{\alpha\};\ V_{fail} := V_{fail} \cup \{\alpha\} \\ \mathit{begin\_maint}(\alpha) & \widehat{=} & \alpha \in V_{act} \rightarrow V_{act} := V_{act} \setminus \{\alpha\};\ V_{maint} := V_{maint} \cup \{\alpha\} \\ \mathit{end\_maint}(\alpha) & \widehat{=} & \alpha \in V_{maint} \rightarrow V_{act} := V_{act} \cup \{\alpha\};\ V_{maint} := V_{maint} \setminus \{\alpha\} \end{array} \tag{20}$$

We assume here that $\alpha \in V, \alpha \neq \lambda$, i.e., the server does not fail and does not need to be maintained. Intuitively, we want to interpret the above actions as follows. The action $\mathit{fail}(\alpha)$ models the failure of node α, hence the node changes its status from active to failed. The action $\mathit{begin\_maint}(\alpha)$ models that the node α will have some maintenance procedures performed for it and the action $\mathit{end\_maint}(\alpha)$ models that the node α has returned to normal operation after certain maintenance procedures have been performed for it.

Besides modeling the node status, it is important to model in MIDAS what happens to the resources located at these nodes. For instance, if the node α fails, then we want to model that all its resources disappear or become unavailable. We do this by refining $\mathit{fail}(\alpha)$ to the following form:

$$\begin{array}{l} \mathit{fail}(\alpha) \widehat{=} \alpha \in V_{act} \rightarrow V_{act} := V_{act} \setminus \{\alpha\};\ V_{fail} := V_{fail} \cup \{\alpha\}; \\ \qquad \forall v \in \alpha.var \cdot \mathit{remove}(v, \alpha); \\ \qquad \forall A \in \alpha.action \cdot \mathit{remove}(A, \alpha) \end{array}$$

We observe that such a fail operation is relatively safe: in the worst case – when a resource is only located at the failing node α – it saves a copy of each such resource at the default location $\{\lambda\}$. This is ensured by the remove actions defined in (12) and (14).

When a node α is not in V_{act} due to maintenance procedures, then we would like to 'save' the resource information so that we can restore it when the node functions normally again. This is modeled by keeping the form of the actions $\mathit{begin\_maint}(\alpha)$ and $\mathit{end\_maint}(\alpha)$ as in (20), but ensuring that all the resources having $\alpha \in V_{maint}$ as location are not used or executed. We do this by enforcing slightly stronger location guards. First, actions will execute only when their accessed variables are located at active locations. Thus, instead of $(\forall v \in vA \cdot (\exists \alpha \in \mathit{cell}(A, \rho) \cdot (v \in \alpha.var) \wedge ...))$ in the location guard, we require $(\forall v \in vA \cdot (\exists \alpha \in \mathit{cell}(A, \rho) \cap \mathbf{V_{act}} \cdot (v \in \alpha.var) \wedge ...))$. Second, the location guard $lg(A@\rho)$ of an action (a, ρ, A) also needs to verify the extra condition $\rho \in \mathbf{V_{act}}$, and so $lg(A@\rho) = \rho \in \mathbf{V_{act}} \wedge (\forall v \in vA \cdot ...)$.

Moreover, the actions that handle locations need to ensure their active status. It is meaningless to create replicas or move resources to locations that are inactive or to remove replicas from inactive locations, since the resources there might already have been removed by the safe failure operation. Hence, the condition

$\alpha \in V_{act}$ has to be conjuncted with the location guards of the actions *copy*, *move*, and *remove*.

Specifying node failure and maintenance together with the strengthened location guards for the actions of the system is the job of the network manager. The application developer should not have to deal with such issues. Since treating failure and maintenance implies only adding actions and strengthening guards according to [2], this middleware aspect also keeps the relationship $Level1Spec \sqsubseteq Level2Spec$ preserved. Thus, the node failure and maintenance in MIDAS offers a simple model for describing the status of the network nodes, building on the resource model presented in the previous sections.

Example 6. The network manager can use the system below to model unexpected node failure:

$$\mathcal{A} \mathrel{\widehat{=}} |[\ \mathbf{var}(x, \{\gamma\}, V);\ \mathbf{do}\ x.val :\in V \ \| \ fail(x.val) \ \| \ skip\ \mathbf{od}]| \qquad (21)$$

Any system $\mathcal{S}$ that can have unexpected node failures can be modeled as $\mathcal{S} \,||\, \mathcal{A}$.

8 Conclusions and Related Work

In this paper we have focused on the network availability to applications. We have addressed issues such as resource accessibility, replicated and homonym resources, their mobility, as well as failure and maintenance of network nodes. These network aspects are expressed in a dedicated language named MIDAS. This is rigorously defined by a grammar of actions (20) and supplemented with various location guards and functions as explained throughout the paper. Thus, MIDAS is a language that treats network resources in a general and thorough manner. Compared with our earlier work in [21], the focus shifted from a general view of networks expressed by action systems with locations to a clearly scoped language, addressing the network availability to applications. Therefore, we have provided here a careful systematization and extension of the material introduced in [21].

Expressing issues of network availability for applications belongs to the *middleware* level of specification. Numerous middleware approaches have been developed in the last decade or so [15] to address the network availability to application developers. *Location-aware middleware* systems [20,9] have been built to integrate different positioning technologies such as outdoor GPS and indoor infrared via a common interface. Location is only one aspect of the more general *context* information that an application can use. *Context-aware middleware* systems have also been developed [23], allowing the application to influence the middleware by inspecting and modifying the context. Various middleware systems are oriented towards *data sharing* as a communication paradigm that maximizes data availability via replicas. These replicas are not necessarily kept consistent with each other. For instance, Bayou [8] employs a weak consistency that ensures that only eventually all the copies will be synchronized; the application developer is aware of the fact and can provide specific procedures to resolve intermediate conflicts. XMIDDLE [16] focuses on representing the data as XML trees that can be shared when their declaring devices are connected; if these devices are disconnected, then offline operations can be performed on the trees. Reconciliation takes place when the devices are reconnected later on. Each device has access points for each of its trees, defining the branches that can be read or modified by other connected devices that previously linked to that tree. Thus, the unit of replication is very adaptable. Another class of middleware systems use *tuple spaces* (as introduced by the coordination language Linda [10]) for computation and communication. For instance, Lime [19] adapts Linda to mobility by breaking the centralized tuple space into multiple tuple spaces, each owned by a mobile entity. These exclusive spaces are dynamically recomputed to illustrate the tuple spaces of all the devices that are connected.

Following the middleware classification introduced in [15], MIDAS is supporting systems with mobile entities, intermittent connection, and a dynamic execution context. The computational load is not intended as heavy-weight, except that our replicas are kept consistent with each other at all times. However, since the propagation of changes is done only when all the copies are in the action's cell, this does not seem a restriction. The communication paradigm is asynchronous, via data sharing, and the context of the application is available to the developer. For instance, the application is aware that a resource is replicated or not and can use locations in its specification. More context-awareness in the action system framework was analyzed earlier [26]. A missing feature of MIDAS is the discovery of resources and the dynamic adaptation to them. We did not discuss how to define new resources nor how can a system use any resources that are not declared in its specification. However, we can employ refinement techniques towards this goal, as shown in [3].

An advantage of our approach is in its formal semantics that enables the verification of various properties. A similar foundation based on Mobile UNITY [22] has been used for Lime and EgoSpaces [12], the latter being a middleware approach to the development of context-aware applications. A special framework based on co-algebras has been introduced in [4], for defining orchestrators – a form of middleware agents. Another interesting approach called MTLA [13] has been devised (based on Lamport's TLA [14]) for the specification, verification, and formal development of mobile code systems. MTLA is a spatio-temporal logic resembling the modal logic for mobility developed for the Ambient Calculus in [6]. MTLA semantics is used to identify refinement strategies for the mobile code systems. We use refinement in this paper in a special manner – for distinguishing the specifications written by the application developer and the network manager. Still, we can also employ the refinement technique in the traditional way: the application developer specification can be refined by either making the algorithms more deterministic or by making the data structures more precise and implementable.

References

1. R. J. Back and R. Kurki-Suonio. Decentralization of process nets with centralized control. In *Proceedings of the 2nd ACM SIGACT-SIGOPS Symposium on Principles of Distributed Computing*, pp. 131-142, 1983.
2. R. J. Back and K. Sere. Superposition Refinement of Reactive Systems. In *Formal Aspects of Computing*, Vol. 8, No. 3, pp. 324-346, Springer-Verlag, 1996.

3. M. Bonsangue, J. N. Kok, and K. Sere. An Approach to Object-Orientation in Action Systems. In *J. Jeuring (ed), Proceedings of MPC'98 – Fourth International Conference on Mathematics of Program Construction.* Lecture Notes in Computer Science, Vol. 1422, pp. 68-95, Springer-Verlag, 1998.
4. M. A. Barbosa and L. S. Barbosa. An Orchestrator for Dynamic Interconnection of Software Components. In *Proceedings of the 2nd International Workshop on Methods and Tools for Coordinating Concurrent, Distributed and Mobile Systems (MTCoord06)*, Elsevier, 2006 (to appear).
5. L. Cardelli. Abstractions for Mobile Computation. In *J. Vitek and C. Jensen (eds). Secure Internet Programming: Security Issues for Mobile and Distributed Objects.* Lecture Notes in Computer Science, Vol. 1603, pp. 51-94, Springer-Verlag, 1999.
6. L. Cardelli and A. D. Gordon. Anytime, Anywhere: Modal Logics for Mobile Ambients. In *Proceedings of the 27th ACM Symposium on Principles of Programming Languages*, pp. 365-377, 2000.
7. K. M. Chandy and J. Misra. *Parallel Program Design: A Foundation.* Addison-Wesley, 1988.
8. A. Demers, K. Petersen, M. Spreitzer, D. Terry, M. Theimer, and B. Welch. The Bayou Architecture: Support for Data Sharing among Mobile Users. In *Proceedings of the IEEE Workshop on Mobile Computing Systems and Applications*, pp. 2-7, 1994.
9. D. Fritsch, D. Klinec, and S. Volz. NEXUS - Positioning and Data Management Concepts for Location Aware Applications. In *Proceedings of the 2nd International Symposium on Telegeoprocessing*, pp. 171-184, 2000.
10. D. Gelernter. Generative Communication in Linda. In *ACM Transactions on Programming Languages and Systems (TOPLAS)*, Vol. 7, No. 1, pp. 80-112, 1985.
11. C.A.R. Hoare. Communicating Sequential Processes. In *Communications of the ACM*, Vol. 21, No. 8, pp. 666-677, 1978.
12. C. Julien and G.-C. Roman. EgoSpaces: Facilitating Rapid Development of Context-Aware Mobile Applications. In *IEEE Transactions on Software Engineering*, 2006 (to appear).
13. A. Knapp, S. Merz, M. Wirsing, and J. Zappe. Specification and Refinement of Mobile Systems in MTLA and Mobile UML. In *Theoretical Computer Science*, Vol. 351, No. 2, pp. 184-202, Elsevier, 2006.
14. L. Lamport. The Temporal Logic of Actions. In *ACM Transactions on Programming Languages and Systems (TOPLAS)*, Vol. 16, No. 3, pp. 872-923, 1994.
15. C. Mascolo, L. Capra, and W. Emmerich. Mobile Computing Middleware. In *E. Gregori et al. (eds), Networking 2002 Tutorials*, Lecture Notes in Computer Science, Vol. 2497, pp. 20-58, Springer-Verlag, 2002.
16. C. Mascolo, L. Capra, S. Zachariadis and W. Emmerich. XMIDDLE: A Data-Sharing Middleware for for Mobile Computing. In *Wireless Personal Communications Journal*, Vol. 21, No. 1, pp. 77-103, Springer, 2002.
17. R. Milner. *A Calculus of Communicating Systems.* Lecture Notes in Computer Science, Vol. 92, Springer-Verlag, 1980.
18. R. Milner, J. Parrow, and D. Walker. A Calculus of Mobile Processes I and II. In *Information and Computation*, Vol. 100, No. 1, pp. 1-77, 1992.
19. A. L. Murphy, G. P. Picco, and G.-C. Roman. LIME: A Middleware for Physical and Logical Mobility. In *Proceedings of the 21st International Conference on Distributed Computing Systems*, pp. 524-533, 2001.
20. Oracle Technology Network. Oracle Application Server Wireless, 10g. http://www.oracle.com/technology//products/iaswe/index.html, 2005.

21. L. Petre, K. Sere, and M. Waldén. A Topological Approach to Distributed Computing. In *Proceedings of WDS 99 – Workshop on Distributed Systems*, Electronic Notes in Theoretical Computer Science, Vol. 28, pp. 97-118, Elsevier Science, 1999.
22. G.-C. Roman and P. J. McCann. A Notation and Logic for Mobile Computing. In *Formal Methods in System Design*, Vol. 20, No. 1, pp. 47-68, 2002.
23. M. Roman, C. Hess, R. Cerqueira, A. Ranganat, R. Campbell, and K. Nahrstedt. A middleware infrastructure for active spaces. In *IEEE Pervasive Computing*, Vol. 1, No. 4, pp. 74-83, 2002.
24. G. Smith. *The Object-Z Specification Language.* Kluwer Academic Publishers, 2000.
25. A. S. Tanenbaum. *Computer Networks*, fourth edition. Pearson Education, Inc., Prentice Hall PTR, 2003.
26. L. Yan and K. Sere. A Formalism for Context-Aware Mobile Computing. In *Proceedings of ISPDC/HeteroPar'04*, pp. 14-21, IEEE Computer Society Press, 2004.

Multi-process Systems Analysis Using Event B: Application to Group Communication Systems

J. Christian Attiogbé

LINA - FRE CNRS 2729 - University of Nantes, France
Christian.Attiogbe@univ-nantes.fr

Abstract. We introduce a method to elicit and to structure using Event B, processes interacting with ad hoc dynamic architecture. A Group Communication System is used as the investigation support. The method takes account of the evolving structure of the interacting processes; it guides the user to structure the abstract system that models his/her requirements. The method also integrates property verification using both theorem proving and model checking. A B specification of a GCS is built using the proposed approach and its stated properties are verified using a B theorem prover and a B model checker.

Keywords: Event B, Group Communication Systems, Dynamic Architecture, Property verification.

1 Introduction

The rigorous description of dependable systems starts from the formal specifications of their requirements. It is crucial for the subsequent development steps to use an adequate specification. But according to the features of the system to be studied the elicitation and structuring of formal specifications is still a challenging concern. Moreover asynchronous systems with evolving structure are especially difficult. Structuring not only deals with the readability of the produced specifications but it is also important for the requirement capture and for the specification analysis.

The B method [2,4] is one of the well-mechanized formal methods that cover the development process from specification to code generation. However there is no specific guidance at the specification level. This is a shortcoming shared by general purpose formal methods such as PVS or Isabelle.

The general motivation of this work is the search for practical methods, techniques and tools to help the developers in specifying and analysing their systems; the emphasis is put on methods appropriate for the class of systems to be treated.

Distributed systems design, analysis and implementation are difficult engineering tasks. They still pose challenging specification and analysis problems. To master this difficulty several layers of concerns are distinguished. The lower one is the network and operating system layer; a group communication layer is built on the top of the former. Finally the application layer is the one close to the user. The reliability of distributed applications requires the proof of correctness at various layers: a layered property verification approach. We consider

Z. Liu and J. He (Eds.): ICFEM 2006, LNCS 4260, pp. 660–677, 2006.

Group Communication Systems [14,11] as our investigation support as it concentrates non-trivial modelling and analysis concerns, and also will contribute to the layered property verification of distributed applications.

In this article we focus on the systematic specification and analysis of multi-process systems, especially those with evolving structure. The contribution of this work is threefold: *i)* a method to guide the development of systems with multi-processes and dynamic architecture; *ii)* a proof of concept of group communication modelling and analysis using B; *iii)* a combined use of theorem proving and model checking to hasten correctness analysis of non-trivial system.

The remainder of the article is organized as follows: in the Section 2 we provide an overview of the used Event B framework. Section 3 introduces the features of group communication systems. Section 4 deals with the proposed specification method. In Section 5 we consider the properties that are verified. Finally Section 6 concludes the article.

2 Event B Method

2.1 An Overview of Event B

Within the Event B framework, asynchronous systems may be developed and structured using *abstract systems* [2,4]. *Abstract systems* are the basic structures of the so-called *event-driven* B, and they replace the *abstract machines* which are the basic structures of the earlier *operation-driven* approach of the B method[1]. An *abstract system* [2,4] describes a mathematical model of a system behaviour[1]. It is made mainly of a state description (constants, properties, variables and invariant) and several *event* descriptions. Abstract systems are comparable to Action Systems [6]; they describe a nondeterministic evolution of a system through guarded actions. Dynamic constraints can be expressed within abstract systems to specify various liveness properties [4,10]. The state of an abstract system is described by variables and constants linked by an invariant. Variables and constants represent the data space of the system being formalized. Abstract systems may be refined like abstract machines [10,3].

Data of an Abstract System. At a higher level an abstract system models and contains the data of an entire model, be it distributed or not. Abstract systems have been used to formalize the behaviour of various (including distributed) systems [2,9,10,3]. Considering a global vision, the data that are formalized within the abstract system may correspond to all the elements of the distributed system.

Events of an Abstract System. Within B, an event is considered as the observation of a system transition. Events are spontaneous and show the way a system evolves. An event e is modelled as a *guarded sustitution*: $e \mathrel{\widehat{=}} eG \Longrightarrow eB$ where eG is the event *guard* and eB the event *body* or *action*.

[1] A system behaviour is the set of its possible transitions from state to state beginning from an initial state.

(SELECT Form)	(ANY Form)
`eventName` $\widehat{=}$ SELECT $P_{(gcv)}$ THEN $GS_{(gcv)}$ END	`eventName` $\widehat{=}$ ANY bv WHERE $P_{(bv,gcv)}$ THEN $GS_{(bv,gcv)}$ END

Fig. 1. General Forms of Events

An event may occur or may be observed only when its guard holds. The action of an event describes with generalized substitutions how the system state evolves when this event occurs. Several events may have their guards hold simultaneously; in this case, only one of them occurs. The system makes internally a nondeterministic choice. If no guard is true the abstract system is blocking (deadlock). An event has one of the general forms (Fig. 1) where gcv denotes the global constants and variables of the abstract system containing the event; bv denotes the bound variables (variables bound to ANY). $P_{(bv,gcv)}$ denotes a predicate P expressed with the variables bv and gcv; in the same way $GS_{(bv,gcv)}$ is a generalized substitution S which models the event action using the variables bv and gcv. The SELECT form is a particular case of the ANY form. The guard of an event with the SELECT form is $P_{(gcv)}$. The guard of an event with the ANY form is $\exists(bv).P_{(bv,gcv)}$.

Semantics and Consistency. The semantics of an abstract system relies on its invariant and is guaranteed by proof obligations(POs). The *consistency* of the model is established by such proof obligations: *i) the initialisation U should establish the invariant I*: $[U]I$;

ii) each event of the given abstract system should preserve the invariant of the model. The proof obligation of an event with the ANY form (Fig. 1) is:

$$I_{(gcv)} \wedge P_{(bv,gcv)} \Rightarrow [GS_{(bv,gcv)}]I_{(gcv)}$$

where $I_{(gcv)}$ stands for the invariant of the abstract system. Moreover the events should terminate: $I_{(gcv)} \wedge P_{(bv,gcv)} \Rightarrow \mathsf{fis}(GS_{(bv,gcv)})$. The predicate $\mathsf{fis}(S)$ expresses that the substitution S does not establish *False*: $\mathsf{fis}(S) \Leftrightarrow \neg\, [S]False$.

The deadlock-freeness should be established for an abstract system: the disjunction of the event guards should be true. The B method is supported by theorem provers which are industrial tools (Atelier-B [12] and B-Toolkit [5]).

The event-based semantics of an abstract system A is the event traces of A ($traces(A)$); the set of finite event sequences generated by the evolution of A.

2.2 Overview of the ProB Tool

The ProB tool [18,19] is an animator and a model checker for B specifications. It provides functionalities to display graphical view of automata. It supports automated consistency checking of B specifications (an abstract machine or a refinement with its state space, its initialization and its operations). The consistency checking is performed on all the reachable states of the machine. ProB also provides a constraint-based checking; with this approach ProB does not explore the state space from the initialization, it checks whether applying one of the operation can result in an invariant violation independently from the initialization.

ProB offers many functionalities. The main ones are organized within three categories: *Animation*, *Verification* and *Analysis*. Several functionalities are provided for each category but here, we just list a few of them which are used in this article.

The *Animation* category gathers the following functionalities:

Random Animation: it starts from an initial state of the abstract machine and then, it selects in a random fashion one of the enabled operations, it computes the next state accordingly and proceeds the animation from this state with one of the enabled operations;
View/Reduced Visited States: it displays a minimized graph of the visited states after an animation;
View/Current State: it displays the current state which is obtained after the animation.

In the *Verification* category, the following functionalities are available:

Temporal Model Checking: starting from a set of initialization states (initial nodes), it systematically explores the state space of the current B specification. From a given state (a node), a transition is built for each enabled operation and it ends at a computed state which is a new node or an already existing one. Each state is treated in the same way.
Constraint Based Checking: it checks for invariant violation when applying operation independently of initialization states.

In the *Analysis* category we have the following functionalities:

Compute Coverage: the state space (the nodes) and the transitions of the current specification are checked, some statistics are given on deadlocked states, live states[2], covered and uncovered operations.
Analyse Invariant: it checks if some parts of the current invariant are true or false;
Analyse Properties: the property clause of the current specification is checked.

The ProB tool is used to check liveness properties. Besides, note that if a B prover has been used to perform consistency proof, the invariant should not be violated; the B consistency proof consists in checking that the initialization of an abstract machine establishes the invariant and that all the operations preserve the invariant. In the case where the consistency is not completely achieved ProB can help to discover the faults.

3 Group Communication System: Experiment Support

GCSs have motivated several works [14,11] and there are several well-know GCSs such as Isis[8], Horus[25], Ensemble[16,17]. In this experiment we do not

[2] Those already computed.

consider a specific GCS but the main features that are common to most of the GCSs.

3.1 Overview of Group Communication System

A process group is a set of processes interacting to achieve a common goal defined by their designer. A group communication system (GCS) [14] is the support of multicast communication among a process group. This communication support should have a *reliability* property which is the main property of GCS: a message sent by a process to a process group is delivered once to each current member of the group. Therefore the main task of a GCS (with regard to a given user application) is to simulate an environment in which message delivery is reliable between the involved processes. There are various kind of groups: *open group* where processes outside the group may send a message to the group taken as an entity; *closed group* where a process outside the group can send a message to a given process of the group but not to all the members.

The processes which are members of a group exchange messages between themselves. Message exchange between one process of a group and other processes outside the group is permitted in the case of open group.

Sending a message to a group (*multicast*) is the basic communication action. Unlike *unicast* message which is sent by one process to one other process, a multicast message is a message sent to all the members of a group. The structure of a GCS is changing as well as the structure of a group. At a given moment the processes and groups that pertain to the GCS form its *view*. View changing is notified to the environment. A group is created at any time by one process. The process that creates a group is the owner of it and also the first member of the created group (*Self Inclusion* property). A group can be removed by its owner if there is no other member in the group. A process may join (becoming member) or leave a group. A process may be member of several groups. A process may own several groups. A group owner cannot leave its group.

Membership changes are reported through messages to the environment (application layer).

The interaction between an application and a GCS is structured as follows: the application sends/receives messages to/from the GCS. The GCS notifies memberships changes to the application. The interaction at the GCS layer involves group installation, group deletion, memberships action (joining or leaving a group).

3.2 Analysis and Modelling Assumptions

To model a GCS we need to describe several sets of interacting processes; each set identifies a group. A group has some members which are processes. The number of processes in a set is varying. A group is identified and thus it is distinguished from the others; it has a view which is its current members. The union of the views of groups forms the GCS view. A GCS is a multi-process system whose architecture is dynamic.

The main events (observed from an abstract point of view) that describe the evolution of a GCS are:

- *newPrc*: a (new) process appears;
- *byeProc*: a process leaves the system;
- *newGrp*: a process creates a group;
- *rmvGrp*: a process removes a group;
- *joinGrp*: a process joins a group;
- *leaveGrp*: a process leaves a group;
- *snd2grp*: a process sends a message to a group;
- *rcvFgrp*: a process receives a message from the group.

The behaviour of a GCS is the combined behaviours of the processes that constitute the groups. A process behaviour is characterized by several events: an alphabet. At this stage we may describe a process with an abstract system equipped with the event alphabet: *newPrc*, *leaveSys*, *newGrp*,*rmvGrp*, *joinGrp*, *leaveGrp*, *snd2grp*, *rcvFgrp*. A precise investigation of the process behaviour within the GCS reveals that the events should be more specific than the listed ones. This is detailed in the sequel (see Section 4.4).

The processes of a GCS exchange messages which are unique: two different sent messages cannot be confused. The messages convey data. Therefore a good abstraction is to consider a *set* of messages exchanged within the GCS; each one is made with an (unique) identifier and a data part. A message is viewed as a pair: $\langle identifier, data \rangle$.

We then consider a set of identifiers (*MId*) to catch the unicity of exchanged messages. The set of messages to be considered is the union of the messages exchanged by all the processes that participate in the GCS.

A process that joins the system should be able to interact with the existing processes. A process also has a data storage where the received messages are stored. Acknowledgement may be sent for received data. We study in the following a method to specify such an interacting system that has an ad hoc evolving structure. The logical behaviour of the system is handled as event orderings or event traces.

4 Specifying Interacting Group Processes in B

The interaction between several processes which cooperate to achieve a given common goal is often handled using communication between the processes. Two main paradigms support communication: message passing and variable sharing. The former is adapted to distributed systems and therefore used for GCS. The architecture of a group communication system is dynamic. The processes involved in a group interact using the current ad hoc structure of the processes. This structure is changing as the processes evolve. We focus here on the systematic specification of the interacting processes.

4.1 Dynamic Process Architecture

Process algebras (such as CCS [22], CSP[24], LOTOS[20]) generalize state transition approaches and are widely used to model interacting processes; herein the behaviours of elementary processes are described and then the parallel composition operators are used to combine the processes. Therefore the architecture of a system is a static composition of a finite number of processes. The $\pi-$calculus [23] permits the description of evolving structures of processes but it is not well supported by tools.

In many specification circumstances, one has to deal with dynamic configuration of the system architecture: an example is the growing number of client processes in a resource allocation problem. Such circumstances are often dealt with by considering the reasoning on an arbitrary high number of processes. However, it is a biased solution of the problem.

The approach proposed here combines a process-oriented approach and B system; it copes with the specification of dynamic interacting processes and deals with the limitations of both cited approaches.

State Transitions Approach. Capturing a process behaviour is intuitive but state transition systems lack high level structures for complex processes. Handling an undefined, variable number of processes is not tractable. Dealing with several instances of the same processes is not possible. Synchronization of processes should be made explicit.

B System Approach. A difficult concern is that of the completeness with respect to event ordering (liveness concerns): did the specification covers all the possible evolution (event sequences) expressed in the requirement? Indeed one can have a consistent system (with respect to the stated invariant) which does not meet the desired logical behavioural requirements.

Rigorous guidelines may help to discover and express the desired behaviours; liveness properties help to cover the related completeness aspect. That is the basis of the proposed approach.

4.2 Event Orderings: Causality and Liveness

In this section we explain our policy to constrain event occurrences according to the user requirements. We make it clear the event orderings. This enable us to express event causality. But liveness property (*something good eventually happens*) may also be expressed considering the event orderings.

Because we do not want to change the B method and its semantics in our approach to obtain B models for multi-process systems, we avoid using temporal logics to state liveness properties and checking the obtained models again these properties (that is the more classical way). Therefore instead of pure liveness properties, we consider causalities which are more intuitive at modelling level. It is easier for the developper to express the ordering of his/her system events as causality relation; for example a requirement such as "the event e_1 always precede the event e_2" is simply captured by a causality: e_2 follow e_1. Implicitely, each event of the ongoing system alphabet should possibly occurs (liveness).

Using a LTL formula, the same example requirement is expressed as follows:

$$\Box(e_1 \rightarrow \Diamond e_2)$$

Therefore the user's requirements related to event orderings can be easily expressed with a collection of event causalities as above. That is the principle we use in our approach: the user makes it explicit the ordering of the system events. Technically, considering a process behaviour, the analysis of liveness properties can only be performed on infinite traces (from the exploration of the process behaviour graph); that means using a Büchi automata.

From a methodological point of view, we use a (directed) graph to describe the process behaviours. The graph described with a relation on events. This relation is called *follow* in the sequel and it describes a transition relation labelled with events. The *follow* relation is given by the user to capture the needed event orderings.

The *follow* relation is sufficient to describe even complicated situation; for example a causality such as: "an event e_3 is caused by a disjunction of e_1 and e_2" is captured by the relation $\{(e_1, \{e_2, e_3\}), (e_2, \{e_1, e_3\})\}$. That is graphically

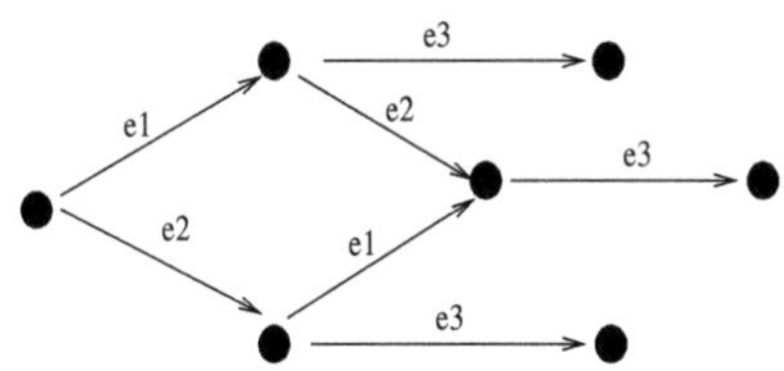

According to a B system to be constructed, the constraints that are captured with event orderings (through the *follow* relation) should appear in event guards, hence the B abstract system is correctly built.

4.3 The Proposed Specification Method: Illustration with a GCS

According to a given requirement statement (here a GCS), one has to build an abstract system $\mathcal{A}$ that models the behaviour of a set $\mathcal{P}_r$ of interacting processes. This behaviour is described with a set of events that are observed when the system evolves. The interacting processes may be of different types; they may use resources or data which are shared or not.

The proposed method is a methodological approach to build the behaviour of the given system in such a way that it corresponds to the stated informal requirements. Accordingly the built system should ensure safety and the event orderings should be the expected ones. Several steps are distinguished for the method.

Step 1. General frame of the abstract system

• Begin the construction of an abstract system $\mathcal{A}$ that is the B formal model of the studied system. The semantics of $\mathcal{A}$ (see Section 2.1) is not modified. $\mathcal{A}$ is made of S, E, *follow*, *Evts* where S is the state space that will be described with variables and predicates, E is an event alphabet, *follow* is a transition relation on E and *Evts* is a set of event specifications. The relation *follow* is neither reflexive nor symmetric nor transitive. Moreover when $(e_1, e_2) \in \mathit{follow}$, each occurrence of e_2 should be preceded (immediately or not; depending on the other elements of *follow*) by an occurrence of e_1. This evolution constraint is introduced latter (**Step 5.**) through the guard of events.

As $\mathcal{A}$ is a multi-process system, several process types will contribute to define its behaviour. These process types are described in the following.

• Identify the set $\mathcal{P}_r$ of (types of) processes that interact within $\mathcal{A}$: $\mathcal{P}_r = \{P_1, P_2, \cdots\}$. Put into the SET clause of $\mathcal{A}$ an abstract set P_i for each process type.

For the GCS a process type *PROCESS* is considered. It does not matter the number of the process of each type.

• For each process type $P \in \mathcal{P}_r$

- consider a new variable to model the set of processes of this type. According to the GCS we have $\mathit{processes} \subseteq \mathit{PROCESS}$.
- Identify the system resources or data and distinguish the shared ones. The data manipulated in the GCS are a set of process groups (GROUP), a set of messages; each message is made with an identifier (*MId*) and a data part (*DATA*).
- Fill in the SET clause of $\mathcal{A}$ with the identified abstract sets: GROUP, DATA, MId, ...

• The shared resources need a specific access policy. For each kind of shared resources,

- define a B *event* to access/get/free the resource. Typically an event that reads a common data is to be distinguished from the one that write the data.

The resources of the GCS are not shared.

• Identify the set of events that make the system evolves: E. These events may be split into two classes of events: the *general events* (GE) that affect the whole system and the *process-specific events* (SE) which correspond to the evolution of the identified (type of) processes.

As far as the GCS is concerned, we have the following events:

$GE = \{\mathit{newPrc},\ \mathit{newGrp},\ \cdots\}$;

$SE = \{\mathit{joinGrp},\ \mathit{mleaveGrp},\ \mathit{ojoinGrp},\ \mathit{oleaveGrp},\ \mathit{snd2grp},\ \mathit{rcvFgrp},\ \cdots\}$.

This distribution of the events into classes favours the decomposition of the abstract system since the events may be shared between subsystems.

Step 2. Modelling the state space: S

• Identify the global resources and properties with an invariant predicate that characterizes S. For the GCS we have a set of groups, a set of processes, etc.

• Fill in the VARIABLES clause and the INVARIANT clause of $\mathcal{A}$ with the resource declarations and the identified properties. The result for the GCS is as follows:

$$processes \subseteq PROCESS$$
$$groups \subseteq GROUP$$
$$data \subseteq DATA$$
$$mesgs \subseteq MId \times data$$

The set of exchanged messages is: $mesg \subseteq MId \times DATA$. The sent messages with their senders are handle with a function:

$$sender : mesgs \rightarrow process$$

The messages received by the processes are modelled with a relation:

$$store : mesgs \leftrightarrow processes$$

The set of messages sent to the groups are also recorded with a relation:

$$sent2gr : mesgs \leftrightarrow groups$$

A function $msgId$ gives the identifier of each message.

$$msgId : mesgs \rightarrow MId$$

The members of a process group are handled with a relation:

$$members : groups \leftrightarrow processes$$

These relations and other identified properties are gathered in the INVARIANT clause of $\mathcal{A}$.

Step 3. Describing event ordering: the *follow* relation
• Identify the properties of the behaviour of the whole system; that is a specific ordering of the event occurrences according to the *liveness* requirements. The relation $follow : E \leftrightarrow E$ (see **Step 1**) captures the required ordering of the events.

According to the GCS an example is: a process cannot leave a group that it had not joined; that means an event *joinGrp* is observed before the occurrence of the *leaveGrp* one; therefore *leaveGrp* follows *joinGrp*. It remains to complete *follow* according to the classes (GE, SE) of events in E.

Step 4. Defining the general events: $Evts_{GE}$
• Increase $\mathcal{A}$ with the B specifications of the general events. For illustration the events *newPrc* and *newGrp* are considered for the GCS. The first one is specified as follows:

```
newPrc ≙                /* a new process enters the system */
  ANY pr WHERE
    pr ∈ PROCESS − processes
  THEN
    processes := processes ∪ {pr}
  END
```

Step 5. Defining specific process behaviour: $Evts_{SE}$

• For each process type $P \in \mathcal{P}_r$ we supplement $\mathcal{A}$ with $\mathcal{A}_P$ which is made of S_P, E_P, $follow_P$, $Evts_P$. Consider *PROCESS* as an illustration of P.

1. E_P: identify the event subset of *SE* that make the evolution of P;
2. $follow_P$: define an ordering relation on these events by considering the specific requirements on P; this results in describing a subset of *follow* related to P: $follow_P$. A rather small state transition system (a behaviour graph where the transitions are labelled with the event names) may help here. The following table illustrates a part of the ordering relation for the *PROCESS* type.

$follow_{PROCESS}$	
newPrc	{*snd2grp*, *snd2prc*, *rcvFgrp*, *newGrp*, *joinGrp*, *byePrc*}
snd2grp	{*snd2grp*, *snd2prc*, *rcvFgrp*, *joinGrp*, *newGrp*, *byePrc*}
snd2prc	{*snd2grp*, *snd2prc*, *rcvFgrp*, *joinGrp*, *newGrp*, *byePrc*}
...	...

The process event alphabet should be more precise than it was described previously (Section 3.2); a thorough analysis of the process behaviour is needed (see Section 4.4) to discover the event alphabet of process types. All the processes that reach a given evolution stage (corresponding to a state of the behaviour graph)) may nondeterministically evolve in the same way. This is captured with variables denoting sets of processes that reach given evolution stages; the guard of events are then written with these variables. For instance a variable *siprocesses* denotes the set of processes in a given state s_i;

```
joinGrp ≙
  ANY pr WHERE
    pr ∈ siprocesses ∧ ···
  THEN
    siprocesses := siprocesses − {pr}
    sjprocesses := sjprocesses ∪ {pr}
    ...
  END
```

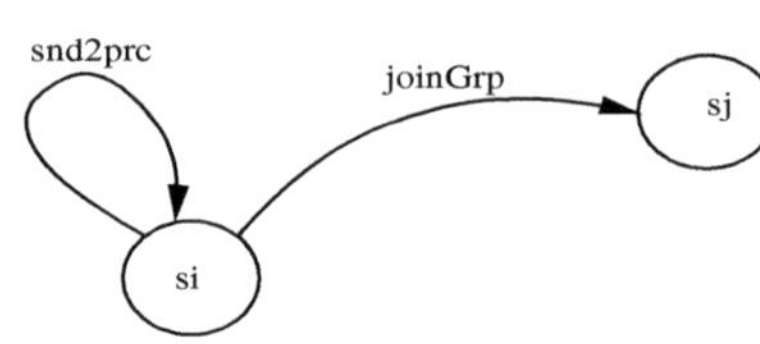

Thereafter only the processes in the state s_i may perform the events associated to this state. The event guards handle this constraint.

3. $Evts_P$:
   – Describe each event of the current process P as a B event (guard and substitution).
   – Increase the EVENTS clause of $\mathcal{A}$ with the new described event.

The following example gives the specification of the *mleaveGrp* event.

```
mleaveGrp ≙                /* a process leaves a group */
  ANY pr, gr, ngm WHERE
     pr : grpMembers ∧ gr : groups
  ∧ (gr, pr) ∈ members ∧ ngm ⊆ processes
  ∧ ngm = ran(members − {gr ↦ pr})
  THEN
     members := members − {gr ↦ pr}
  || grpMembers := ngm
  END
```

In the same way the B specifications are described for all the events of the alphabet E_P.

After the current step, the abstract system $\mathcal{A}$ under construction is equipped with the B specifications of all the events.

Step 6. Consistency

• Complete the abstract system $\mathcal{A}$ with the desired properties; fill in the INVARIANT clause with the related predicates and
• prove its consistency using B provers such as Atelier B (theorem proving aspect). All the proof obligations should be discharged. However we have not yet the means to guarantee the liveness requirements captured within *follow*; we shall prove that *traces*($\mathcal{A}$) coincides with the *follow* relation. That is the role of the following step.

Step 7. Completeness and Liveness

• Analyze and improve the $\mathcal{A}$ abstract system; this is achieved with the help of model checking and animation with ProB. First, model-check (see 2.2) the $\mathcal{A}$ abstract system to detect deadlocks. Correct the specification accordingly.
• When $\mathcal{A}$ is deadlock-free, check that it fulfills the requirements in *follow*. Using ProB (see 2.2), check that all the events are enabled (this corresponds to no uncovered operations).
Moreover, we have to check that each event (*evt*) enables the events in *follow*(*evt*). This is checked by visualizing the reduced visited states (see 2.2). Another way to check this is by stepwise animations; ProB displays the operations enabled by each activated operation; they should be in correspondence with the given *follow* relation. The $\mathcal{A}$ abstract system is updated accordingly, by tuning the B specification of the events.

As the *follow* relation expresses the set of all possible orderings of the events that could happen in the system, after the **Step 7.**, the logical behaviour analysis is complete and we get a *correct* specification of $\mathcal{A}$ with respect to the requirements.

Proof: The occurrences of event orderings of $\mathcal{A}$ are checked with respect to *follow*. Formally, the occurrence of an event $e_1 \mathrel{\widehat{=}} eG_1 \Longrightarrow eB_1$ is:

$$\exists\, v_i, v_{i+1}.[v := v_i]eG_1 \wedge [v, v' := v_i, v_{i+1}]\mathsf{prd}_v(eB_1)$$

The occurrence of a sequence of two events $e_1.e_2$ is:

$$\exists\, v_i, v_{i+1}, v_{i+2}.[v := v_i]eG_1 \wedge [v, v' := v_i, v_{i+1}]\mathsf{prd}_v(eB_1) \wedge$$
$$[v := v_{i+1}]eG_2 \wedge [v, v' := v_{i+1}, v_{i+2}]\mathsf{prd}_v(eB_2)$$

This generalizes easily to the sequences of n events and it corresponds to $traces(\mathcal{A})$. $\mathsf{prd}_v(S)$ is the before-after predicate of the substitution S; it relates the values of the state variable just before (v) and just after (v') the substitution S. The closure of *follow* (noted *follow**) is the event occurrences that correspond to the requirements captured by *follow*. Therefore we have

$$\boxed{follow^* = traces(\mathcal{A})}$$

4.4 Enhancement of Process Behaviour

The B specification of a process strongly depends on the set of events that are considered. Remenber that an event is guarded and simulates an evolution step of the system. Specific care should be taken to identify the appropriate event granularity. We give here some rules that govern the improvement of the process specification.

Rule *BasicEvent.* A process event alphabet and a transition relation sholud be considered to get the basic behaviour of each process type (**Step 3.** above). This basic behaviour constitutes a starting point to discover and improve the process behaviour. A state transition system (a behaviour graph) is helpful but insufficient; it may be too complex and even practically indescribable for complex behaviour.

Rule *EvtSplit.* An event with a disjunctive guard and related effects on the substitution should be split into different events with each disjunct as a guard.

Indeed there are multiple conditions where a given event is observed. Consider for instance the behaviour of a process $p1$ that joins a group, sends multicast messages and leaves the group versus the behaviour of a process $p2$ that creates a group, joins another group, sends multicast messages and then leaves the recently joined group. The remainder of the process behaviour depends on its history. When the event *joinGrp* is observed, it may be the case where $p1$ (not yet member of any group) joins a group. It also may be the case where the process $p2$ which is a group owner joins another group. The specification of the event depends on the considered case: in this circumstance two specific events should be considered to distinguish between the cases and to prepare the remainder of the behaviours. The event *mjoinGrp* is used in the first case; its substitution updates a variable (*nonMembers*) that represents the process which are not members of a group. The event *ojoinGrp* is used in the second case; its substitution updates a variable *groupOwners* but does not modifies the variable *nonMembers*.

Rule *StepEvent.* The evolution of a process, described by a set of events, depends on the current evolution phase and also on the history of this evolution. For example the following four evolution phases distinguish a process of the GCS: it is not a member of a group, it is a member of a group, it is a group owner, it is both a group owner and member of other groups. At each phase, the process can perform or not some actions that correspond to the observed events. During the specification these phases are then distinguished and constrain the events.

When we put these rules into practice on the GCS, we have the following ordering of events:

$follow_{PROCESS}$	
newPrc	$\{snd2grp, snd2prc, rcvFgrp, newGrp, joinGrp, byePrc\}$
snd2grp	$\{snd2grp, snd2prc, rcvFgrp, joinGrp, newGrp, byePrc\}$
snd2prc	$\{snd2grp, snd2prc, rcvFgrp, joinGrp, newGrp, byePrc\}$
joinGrp	$\{msnd2grp, msnd2prc, mrcvFprc, mleaveGrp, mjoinGrp, mnewGrp\}$
mrcvFgrp	$\{msnd2grp, msnd2prc, mrcvFprc, mleaveGrp\}$
mrcvFprc	$\{snd2grp, snd2prc, rcvFgrp, newGrp, joinGrp, byePrc\}$
msnd2prc	$\{snd2grp, snd2prc, rcvFgrp, newGrp, joinGrp, byePrc\}$
msnd2grp	$\{snd2grp, snd2prc, rcvFgrp, newGrp, joinGrp, byePrc\}$
mleaveGrp	$\{snd2grp, snd2prc, rcvFgrp, newGrp, joinGrp, byePrc\}$
newGrp	$\{ormvGrp, osnd2grp, osnd2prc, orcvFprc, ojoinGrp, omrmvGrp, onewGrp\}$
rmvGrp	$\{snd2grp, snd2prc, rcvFgrp, newGrp, joinGrp, byePrc\}$
...	...

This ordering is partially summarized in the Figure 2. We indicate with the [g] anotation the events that are specifically strengthened according to their history.

Using the presented method we have specified the described group communication system: a GCS formal model that incorporates goals and assumptions that drive the GCS. The specification obtained is improved by performing stepwise formal analysis.

5 Analysis Issues

The obtained B specification enables us to explore in detail the formal model of the GCS and to overcome problems. The analysis of the specification is performed during **Step 6** and **Step 7** in the method. It is worth noting that the combined use of theorem proving (via Atelier B) and model checking (via ProB) enhances the study of the system. Consistency checking alone is definitely not satisfactory for a complex study; it is well supplemented by model checking. The approach to combine both is as follows. First of all theorem proving is performed by considering the properties expressed within the invariant and the assertion clauses of the abstract system. Either the POs are all discharged or not. In any case, model checking is applied; deadlock states are revealed and corrected by

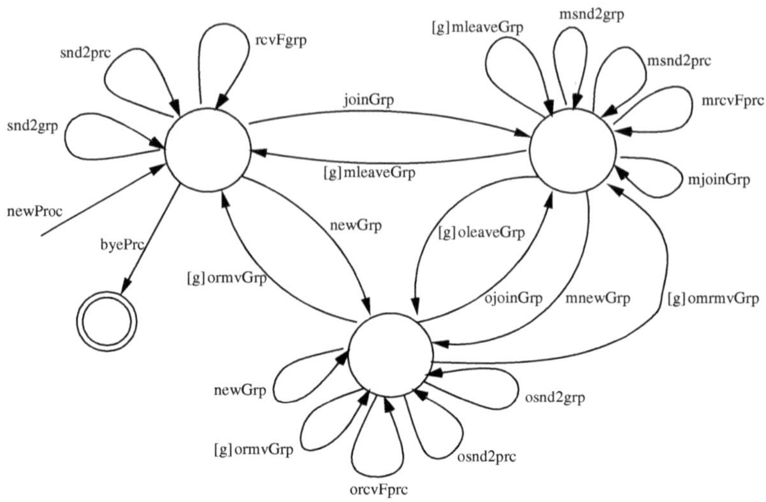

Fig. 2. A Partial State Model of a GCS Behaviour

examining the involved states and variables. When the system is deadlock-free we perform a random traversal of the whole specification (with a high number of generated states) to be sure that all the events are enabled at least once. Something is wrong in the specification if there is at least one uncovered event. We discovered many uncovered events after discharging all the proof obligations of the abstract system. This is due to imprecise guards (that cannot be detected by the AtelierB). The specification is then gradually corrected. The main properties of the GCS are formalised and proved correct.

Reliability. The main property of a GCS is that an event sent to a group is received by all the member of the group. This property is expressed as follows:

$$(m, g) \in sent2gr \Rightarrow store(m) = members(g)$$

It is also simply expressed using relation composition $sent2gr \mathbin{;} members = store$.

Message uniqueness. This property is guaranteed through the use of sets to model the exchanged messages ($mesgs$ and $store$ relation).

Causality. Every delivered message must have been sent before. Two partial functions are used to manage logical time;

$$sendDate : Mid \rightarrowtail \mathbb{N}$$
$$rcvDate : MId \rightarrowtail \mathbb{N}$$

Thereafter the messages received by processes (in $store$) are such that:

$$(m, p) \in store \Rightarrow sendDate(msgId(m)) < rcvDate(msgId(m))$$

Integrity. The messages that are delivered have been sent by a trusted processes. This property is captured with the *sender* function whose range is the (trusted) processes;

$$ran(sender) = processes$$

Virtual Synchrony. If two processes $p1$ and $p2$ move to a new view W from a previous view V, then any message received by $p1$ in the view V is also received by $p2$.

In order to ensure this property, the constructed GCS model was increased with a function $previousGr : groups \rightarrow groups$ that is updated each time the GCS view is changed.

The virtually synchrony is expressed as

$$\begin{aligned}&\forall\, gr.((gr \in groups \cap \mathrm{dom}(previousGr)) \Rightarrow\\ &\qquad store[sent2gr^{-1}(previousGr(gr))]) =\\ &\qquad\quad members(gr) \cap members(previousGr(gr)))\end{aligned}$$

where $store[sent2gr^{-1}(previousGr(gr))]$ gives the processes that received the messages sent to the previous group of gr.

6 Concluding Remarks

We have presented a specification method dedicated to the specification and the analysis of multi-process systems in Event B. The specification and analysis of a group communication system are achieved in light of the proposed method. A GCS is asynchronous, distributed and it has an ad hoc interaction structure; processes may join, leave or interact within the system at any time. These features make it non-trivial to specify and analyse. We show how such a system can be systematically treated using Event B increased with the proposed method. For the analysis our formal model of the GCS integrates the desired GCS properties (consistency, reliability, integrity, causality, virtual synchrony) and we have combined theorem proving and model checking to formally analyse the model. The Atelier B and the ProB tools are used for this purpose. This work is a step towards a global policy for the layered verification of software systems in distributed environment where reliability of a software system is not a local concern. Each involved layer should guarantee correctness.

Related works. As far as the GCS case is concerned the experimental support of the current work follows the stream of a series of works. In [7] the authors describe a formal model of the Ensemble GCS to support a switching mechanism for a set of protocols. The NUPRL development system [15] is used to model and to prove both meta-properties and specific properties on the described model. A trace semantics is used. A similar work is presented in [17] where the authors focus on specific properties of the Ensemble GCS. The I/O automaton model [21] is used for their modelling and NUPRL is use to support proofs. Compared to these works the current one provides a formal model that supports the dynamic aspects of the GCSs and the model makes it easy proof of some of the GCS properties.

Perspectives. Providing Event B oriented specification methods adapted to other classes of systems is the general perspective of this work. But as a short term perspective we intend to cover liveness properties which are not fully considered in the current experiment. We also plan to extend the proposed method and experiment in other layers of distributed interacting systems which are not considered here. The other topic planned in our agenda is the refinement into existing GCS systems such as Ensemble or Transis [13] which have practical supports for distributed-application programming.

Acknowledgments. Many thanks to my colleagues and to the anonymous referees for their valuable comments on the current work.

References

1. J-R. Abrial. *The B Book.* Cambridge University Press, 1996.
2. J-R. Abrial. Extending B without Changing it (for developping distributed systems). *Proc. of the 1st Conf. on the B method, H. Habrias (editor), France*, pages 169–190, 1996.
3. J-R. Abrial, D. Cansell, and D. Mery. Formal Derivation of Spanning Trees Algorithms. In D. Bert et al., editor, *ZB'2003 – Formal Specification and Development in Z and B*, volume 2651 of *LNCS*, pages 457–476. Springer-Verlag, 2003.
4. J-R. Abrial and L. Mussat. Introducing Dynamic Constraints in B. In *Proc. of the 2nd Conference on the B method, D. Bert (editor)*, volume 1393 of *Lecture Notes in Computer Science*, pages 83–128. Springer-Verlag, 1998.
5. B-Core. *B-Toolkit, www.b-core.com.* UK, consulted in 2006.
6. R.J. Back and R. Kurki-Suonio. Decentralisation of Process Nets with Centralised Control. In *Proc. of the 2nd ACM SIGACT-SIGOPS Symp. on Principles of Distributed Computing*, pages 131–142, 1983.
7. M. Bickford, C. Kreitz, R. Van Renesse, and R. Constable. An Experiment in Formal Design Using Meta-Properties. In *DISCEX*, volume 02, pages 100–107, Los Alamitos, CA, USA, 2001. IEEE Computer Society.
8. K. Birman and R. van Renesse. Reliable Distributed Computing with the Isis Toolkit. IEEE Computer Society Press, 1994.
9. M. Butler and M. Walden. Distributed System Development in B. *Proc. of the 1st Conference on the B method, H. Habrias (editor), France*, pages 155–168, 1996.
10. D. Cansell, G. Gopalakrishnan, M. Jones, and D. Mery. Incremental Proof of the Producer/Consumer Property for the PCI Protocol. In D. Bert, J. P. Bowen, M. C. Henson, and K. Robinson, editors, *ZB'2002 – Formal Specification and Development in Z and B*, volume 2272 of *LNCS*, pages 22–41. Springer-Verlag, 2002.
11. Gregory V. Chockler, Idid Keidar, and Roman Vitenberg. Group Communication Specifications: a Comprehensive Study. *ACM Comput. Surv.*, 33(4):427–469, 2001.
12. ClearSy. *Atelier B V3.6, www.clearsy.com.* Steria, Aix-en-Provence, France, consulted in 2006.

13. D. Dolev and D. Malki. The Design of the Transis System . In *Theory and Practice in Distributed Systems*, volume 938 of *LNCS*, pages 83–98. Springer-Verlag, 1995.
14. D. Powel (Guest Editor). Special Issue on Group Communications Systems. *Communications of the ACM*, 39(4), 1996.
15. R. L. Constable et al. *Implementing Mathematics with the Nuprl Proof Developemnt System.* Prentice Hall, 1986.
16. Mark Hayden and Robbert Van Renesse. Optimizing Layered Communication Protocols. In *HPDC '97: Proceedings of the 6th International Symposium on High Performance Distributed Computing (HPDC '97)*, page 169, Washington, DC, USA, 1997. IEEE Computer Society.
17. J. Hickey, N. Lynch, and R. van Renesse. Specifications and Proofs for Ensemble Layers. In R. Cleaveland, editor, *5th International Conference on Tools and Algorithms for the Construction and Analysis of Systems*, number 1579 in Lecture Notes in Computer Science, pages 119–133. Springer-Verlag, 1999.
18. M. Leuschel and M. Butler. ProB: A Model Checker for B. In Keijiro A., Stefania G., and Dino M., editors, *FME 2003: Formal Methods*, LNCS 2805, pages 855–874. Springer-Verlag, 2003.
19. M. Leuschel and E. Turner. Visualizing Larger State Spaces in ProB. In *Proc. of ZB'05*, volume 3455 of *LNCS*, pages 6–23. Springer-Verlag, April 2005.
20. ISO LOTOS. *A Formal Description Technique Based on The Temporal Ordering of Observational Behaviour.* International Organisation for Standardization - Information Processing Systems - Open Systems Interconnection, Geneva, 1988. International Standard 8807.
21. N. Lynch and M. Tuttle. Hierarchical Correctness Proofs for Distributed Algorithms, 1987.
22. Robin Milner. *Communication and Concurrency.* Prentice-Hall, NJ, 1989. Englewood Cliffs.
23. Milner R., Parrow J., and Walker D. A Calculus of Mobile Processes. *Journal of Information and Computation*, 100, 1992.
24. A.W. Roscoe. *The Theory and Practice of concurrency.* Prentice-Hall, 1998.
25. Robbert van Renesse, Kenneth P. Birman, and Silvano Maffeis. Horus: a Flexible Group Communication System. *Commun. ACM*, 39(4):76–83, 1996.

Issues in Implementing a Model Checker for Z

John Derrick, Siobhán North, and Tony Simons

Department of Computing, University of Sheffield, Sheffield, S1 4DP, UK
J.Derrick@dcs.shef.ac.uk

Abstract. In this paper we discuss some issues in implementing a model checker for the Z specification language. In particular, the language design of Z and its semantics, raises some challenges for efficient model checking, and we discuss some of these issues here. Our approach to model checking Z specifications involves implementing a translation from Z into the SAL input language, upon which the SAL toolset can be applied. In this paper we discuss issues in the implementation of this translation algorithm and illustrate them by looking at how the mathematical toolkit is encoded in SAL and the resultant efficiency of the model checking tools.

Keywords: Z, model-checking, SAL.

1 Introduction

Computing is a tool-based activity, and this applies to design and specification as much as to programming. Furthermore, all design and development methods which have ultimately gained acceptance have been supported, if not based on, toolsets for integral parts of their activity, and this is true for both formal as well as informal methods.

For example, it is inconceivable to imagine UML without tool support, and similarly the use of, say, B or SDL depend on their associated toolsets. Indeed, many notations have been designed with tool support in mind, resulting in efficient type-checkers, simulators, proof assistants etc. for these languages.

However, this is not the case for the specification language Z [14,1], where the notation and needs of abstraction have been the driver behind the language and its development rather than tool support. The language itself has been very successful and the challenge now is to develop usable tool support for it. The CZT (Community Z Tools) project (see http://czt.sourceforge.net/ or [10]) aims to tackle some of these issues, and is building a range of tools around a common exchange format. In this paper we discuss some issues in implementing a model checker for Z which is being developed by the Universities of Queensland, Australia, and Sheffield, England. In particular, the language design of Z and its semantics raises some challenges for efficient model checking and we illustrate some of these issues here.

Model checking [4], which aims to determine whether a specified system satisfies a given property, works by exhaustively checking the state space of a specification to determine whether or not the property holds. Model checkers will also provide a counter-example when the property does not hold, thus giving some insight into

Z. Liu and J. He (Eds.): ICFEM 2006, LNCS 4260, pp. 678–696, 2006.

the failure of the property on the current specification. There has been a considerable amount of success in applying model checking to real large-scale systems, and the technique is now applied routinely in some industrial sectors.

Originally model checking technology was only feasible for small, finite state spaces, and this meant that their application was restricted to notations suited to modelling systems where the complexity lay in the control structure, rather than the data, e.g., hardware systems and communication protocols. However, these factors have become less of an issue due to the maturity of the technology. For example, it is now feasible to model check systems involving very large state-spaces (e.g., systems with 10^{20} states), and the restriction to specification notations with control rather than data has now gone. In addition, automatic techniques for property-preserving abstraction [7,12,3] and bounded model checking allow systems with infinite state spaces to be checked. Furthermore, powerful automatic decision procedures allow model-checker languages to support high-level specification constructs such as lambda expressions, set comprehensions and universal and existential quantifiers [5].

Instead of implementing a model-checker from scratch we have been investigating using an intermediate format into which we translate a Z specification. In particular, we have been using the SAL input format as our intermediate format. SAL [5] is a tool-suite for the analysis and verification of systems specified as state-transition systems. Its aim is to allow different verification tools to be combined, all working on an input language designed as a format into which programming and specification languages can be translated. The input language provides a range of features to support this aim, such as guarded commands, modules, definitions etc., and can, in fact, be used as a specification language in its own right. The tool-suite currently comprises a simulator and four model checkers including those for LTL and CTL.

The basis of the translation algorithm of Z into SAL was defined by Smith and Wildman in [13], and in this paper we discuss the implementation of these ideas. The advantage of using SAL is that many aspects of Z, such as structuring via schemas, use of primes for after-state etc., can have a similar representation in SAL. The focus of the translation thus comes down to how the mathematical toolkit (i.e., sets, relations, sequences etc.) is encoded. We illustrate this point by discussing the approach, and problems, of representing sets in SAL.

The structure of the paper is as follows. In Section 2 we introduce our running example. The basic approach to translation is discussed in Section 3 which briefly explains how a Z specification is translated into a SAL module. Subsequent sections discuss the implementation of types (Section 4) and axiomatic definitions (Section 5) before we focus on the issues surrounding the implementations of sets in Section 6. Section 7 discusses the use of the tool, and Sections 8 and 9 provide a discussion and some conclusions respectively.

2 Example

A Z specification defines a number of components, including types, constants, abbreviations and schemas. The schemas define the state space of the system under consideration, its initial configuration and the operations which define the transitions of the system.

For example, the following defines the process of joining an organisation which has a set of *members* and a set of people *waiting* to join.

$$[NAME]$$

$$Report ::= yes \mid no$$

$$total : \mathbb{N}_1$$
$$total = 4096$$

$$capacity : \mathbb{N}_1$$
$$1 < capacity \leq 4096$$

$$\# NAME > capacity$$

State

$$member, waiting : \mathbb{P}\, NAME$$

$$member \cap waiting = \varnothing$$
$$\# member \leq 4096$$
$$\# waiting \leq total$$

Init

$$State'$$

$$member' = \varnothing$$
$$waiting' = \varnothing$$

Join

$$\Delta State$$
$$n? : NAME$$

$$n? \in waiting \land \# waiting < capacity$$
$$member' = member \cup \{n?\}$$
$$waiting' = waiting \setminus \{n?\}$$

$$\begin{array}{|l}
\multicolumn{1}{l}{\textit{JoinQ}} \\
\Delta State \\
n? : NAME \\
\hline
n? \notin (waiting \cup member) \\
\# waiting < total \\
waiting' = waiting \cup \{n?\} \\
member' = member \\
\hline
\end{array}$$

$$\begin{array}{|l}
\multicolumn{1}{l}{\textit{Remove}} \\
\Delta State \\
n? : NAME \\
\hline
n? \in member \\
waiting' = waiting \\
member' = member \setminus \{n?\} \\
\hline
\end{array}$$

$$\begin{array}{|l}
\multicolumn{1}{l}{\textit{Query}} \\
\Xi State \\
n? : NAME \\
ans! : Report \\
\hline
n? \in member \Rightarrow ans! = yes \\
n? \notin member \Rightarrow ans! = no \\
\hline
\end{array}$$

3 Basic Translation

Our approach to model checking Z involves implementing a translation from Z into the SAL input language upon which the SAL toolset can be applied.

The translation scheme is based upon that presented in [13], whose aim was to preserve the Z-style of specification including predicates where primed and unprimed variables are mixed, and the approach of the Z mathematical toolkit to the modelling of relations, functions etc., as sets of tuples. No claim is made about how optimised the translation is; the aim of [13] was simply to show how much of the Z style could be preserved within SAL. Here we consider some of the implementation issues.

A Z specification is translated to a SAL module, which groups together a number of definitions which include types, constants and modules for describing the state transition system. In general a SAL module will have the following form (where elided parts are written ...):

```
State : MODULE =
  BEGIN
   INPUT ...
```

```
    LOCAL ...
    OUTPUT ...
    INITIALIZATION [ ... ]
    TRANSITION [
                  ....
               ]
  END
```

3.1 State and Initialisation Schemas

As seen in the example above, in a states plus operations style, schemas form one of the basic building blocks of a Z specification. Different schemas take on different roles, and the translation into SAL needs to take account of the intended role of each schema in the specification. In our current implementation, we assume that there is a single state and initialisation schema, and that the first schema in the Z input is the state schema, and that the second is the initialisation schema. All other schemas are taken as operation schemas.

In general, schema references are allowed within a schema, and are used in initialisation and operation schemas, e.g., $\Xi State$ in the operation *Query* above. However, the schema references can be expanded, and then there is no need for a predicate in the state schema, since it will be included in the initial and operation schemas, and for the latter in both primed and unprimed form. Our tool does this expansion of schema references in the declaration part of any schema automatically. Once this has been done, the (single) state schema contains only a list of declarations. These declarations will be translated to local variables of the SAL module.

In translating the initialisation schema we note that all schema references to the state will have been expanded out, and the translation of the state schema will have produced local variables. Currently we do not allow new declarations (e.g., of inputs) in the initialisation schema, it thus remains to translate the predicate of the initialisation which becomes a guard of the initialisation section of the module. The guard is followed by a list of assignments, one for each declaration in the state schema. We allow both styles of specification where the initialisation can contain either primed or unprimed components in the Z specification, but all are unprimed in the resultant SAL output. In the translation these assignments allow any value of the appropriate type to be assigned.

Thus the state and initialisation schemas in our example above produce the following SAL fragment.

```
State : MODULE =
  BEGIN
    INPUT ...
    LOCAL member : set{NAME;}!Set
    LOCAL waiting : set{NAME;}!Set
    OUTPUT ...
    INITIALIZATION [
```

```
      member = set{NAME;}!empty_set  AND
      waiting = set{NAME;}!empty_set
    -->
  ]
```

3.2 Operation Schemas

For the operation schemas, all schema references to the state will have been expanded out. The translation of the state schema will have produced local variables as above. It thus remains to translate the predicate (which will include the predicate of the expanded state schema reference) and the input and output of the schema.

Variables of the state schema (e.g., *member*, *waiting* but not the primed versions) have become local variables of the module. Inputs and outputs of the operations are translated to input and output variables of the module, respectively. Output variables need to be renamed since ! is not allowed as part of the variable name in SAL. We choose to translate an output variable *output*! in Z to `output_` in SAL prefixed by the schema name and two underscores to avoid ambiguity. This is possible because the translator ensures unique names are used by restricting the acceptable Z input to having names involving a single consecutive _ character so we can safely use double underlining for system generated names.

Each operation is translated into one branch of a guarded choice in the transitions of the SAL module. We choose to label each choice by the name of the operation in the Z specification, although, strictly speaking this is optional for SAL.

In addition, it is necessary to ensure that the transition relation is total (for soundness of the model checking). This is achieved in the translation by a final guarded command which is an `else` branch to provide a catch-all, and will evaluate to true only when all other guards evaluate to false.

Each choice in the transition (e.g., `Join : ...`) consists of a guarded assignment as in the initialisation. The predicate in the operation schema becomes a guard of the particular choice. The guard is followed by a list of assignments, one for each output and primed declaration in the operation schema. In the translation these assignments allow any compatible value to be assigned.

For example, the translation of our example will result in input and output declarations and a transition as follows:

```
INPUT Join__n? : NAME
INPUT JoinQ__n? : NAME
INPUT Remove__n? : NAME
INPUT Query__n? : NAME
OUTPUT Query__ans_ : Report

TRANSITION [
  Join : ...
```

```
        ...
          -->
             member' IN { x : set{NAME;}!Set | TRUE};
             waiting' IN { x : set{NAME;}!Set | TRUE}
   []
     JoinQ : ...
        ...
          member' = member
          -->
             member' IN { x : set{NAME;}!Set | TRUE};
             waiting' IN { x : set{NAME;}!Set | TRUE}
   []
               ...
   []
     Query : ...
       ...
          member' = member AND
          waiting = waiting'
          -->
             member' IN { x : set{NAME;}!Set | TRUE};
             waiting' IN { x : set{NAME;}!Set | TRUE};
             Query__ans_' IN { x : Report | TRUE}
   []
     ELSE -->
     ]
```

where we have elided parts of the translation we have not yet defined. In particular, the assignment of after-state values occurs before the `-->` in the transitions in this style of encoding.

Any local declarations, i.e., those not arising from a state schema but declared locally in the operation are translated with the `Op__` prefix as in the inputs and outputs (where *Op* is the name of the schema).

4 Implementing Types

The above fragment already includes translations of some types defined in the specification, and Z includes a limited number of built in types. In particular, arithmos is defined which provides 'a supply of values to be used in specifying number systems'. In practice it is assumed that $\mathbb{N}$ and $\mathbb{Z}$ are available.

In contrast SAL supports the basic types NATURAL of natural numbers, and INTEGER of integers. These types can only be used with some of the SAL model-checkers, thus we will translate them into finite subranges. We translate the Z types $\mathbb{Z}$ and $\mathbb{N}$ into bounded SAL types `INT` and `NAT` respectively. We also translate the nonzero Z type $\mathbb{N}_1$ into the SAL type `NZNAT`. SAL definitions for these bounded types are included if the Z specification requires them.

The default finite subrange for `NAT` contains 4 elements in our implementation. Thus if $\mathbb{N}$ occurs in the LaTeX input, then `NAT: TYPE = [0..3]` will be generated at the start of the SAL specification. Likewise, the `NZNAT` type has a default subrange of 3 elements starting at 1 and the `INT` type has a default subrange of 5 elements starting at -1. This is to ensure that every type has at least three elements, while preserving the Z inclusion relationships: $\mathbb{N}_1 \subset \mathbb{N} \subset \mathbb{Z}$. However, the user can supply different bounds as parameters to the translator if desired, and a larger subrange will automatically be used if the specification contains a constant which is out of range. Our example uses the type $\mathbb{N}_1$ and a constant value 4096 occurs of this type. The translator therefore defines `NZNAT: TYPE = [1..4097]` automatically.

A given type, as in $[NAME]$ above, represents a user defined unstructured type. Although SAL supports a range of types, in general, the model checkers work with finite types. Thus we need to provide a finite enumeration of the given set *NAME*, and we translate it to:

```
NAME: TYPE = {NAME__1,NAME__2,NAME__3};
```

The number of elements in a given set enumeration is whatever the user has supplied as a parameter as the upper bound - or 3 by default.

Free types in Z define types whose values are either constants or constructors. The latter construct values of the free type from other values (see [13] for how these free types are dealt with). In the example above, we translate *Report* directly as

```
Report: TYPE = DATATYPE
  yes,
  no
END;
```

5 Axiomatic Descriptions

After the type declarations, a Z specification continues with the declaration of uninterpreted constants, which may or may not be constrained. A basic constant declaration has the form $capacity : \mathbb{N}_1$ and a constrained constant is declared using an axiomatic definition, given in standard schema format:

$$
\begin{array}{|l}
capacity : \mathbb{N}_1 \\
\hline
1 < capacity \leq 4096
\end{array}
$$

In the SAL language definition [5] it is clear that the intention is to support uninterpreted constants, eventually. The obvious translation of an uninterpreted constant would be `capacity : NZNAT;`, and the translation of a constrained constant would rely on SAL's definition by set comprehension:

```
capacity : { x : NZNAT | 1 < x <= 4096 };
```

However, the current SAL toolset does not support uninterpreted constants, which are rejected by the semantic analyser. This means that the translation from Z into SAL has the choice of initialising all such uninterpreted constants with suitable sentinel values, or treating them like SAL local variables. The tradeoff is that the precise sentinel values to choose may be difficult to find; whereas SAL variables range over many values, causing a state explosion in the checking tools.

The SAL variable translation treats all uninterpreted constants as LOCAL variables. If they are constrained, this translation is identical to the translation of state schemas (see Section 3). Because of the state explosion this approach may cause, the preferred translation is to choose suitable precise values for constants. The heuristic chosen is to initialise constants by default to some value within the range of the type concerned. For example, where `NZNAT: TYPE = [1..2]` it would make sense to define:

```
capacity : NZNAT = 2;
```

for both of the above cases (constrained and unconstrained). The main concern is to find a suitable value which satisfies all the predicates in which the constants appear, otherwise the specification would, as a whole, be false. The assignment of values to constants is relatively simple for predicates which consist of an identifier compared to a literal. These straightforward predicates are used to determine the set of possible values each constant could be given and an initial value is chosen from these at random. If the predicates are unsatisfiable, our translation tool displays an error message and halts.

Predicates which compare constants with each other, such as $x < y$, or, worse still, $(u + v) \leq (y - z)$ are dealt with when the limits on each constant have been determined from the simple predicates. Currently, our tool uses a naive algorithm which cycles through the remaining possible initial values until a combination is found that satisfies all of the predicates. After 20 iterations the translator gives up with a message that the initial constraints cannot be resolved. Clearly, a more sophisticated constraint solving approach might be used; however the need to solve large systems of constraints rarely arises in typical Z specifications.

In our particular example we have the following pair of constraints:

$$\begin{array}{|l} \mathit{capacity} : \mathbb{N}_1 \\ \hline 1 < \mathit{capacity} \leq 4096 \end{array}$$

$$\begin{array}{|l} \#\mathit{NAME} > \mathit{capacity} \end{array}$$

In the SAL translation, a value for *capacity* is chosen (at random) which satisfies all the constraints, e.g., one possible value it will be instantiated to is:

```
capacity : NZNAT = 2;
```

This simplification is possible because the tool knows the size of the given type NAME and so $\#\mathit{NAME}$ is replaced by a constant 3. The largest *capacity* that is smaller than 3 is 2. The predicate $\mathit{capacity} \leq 4096$ is redundant and is eliminated by the tool.

6 Implementing Sets

A basic translation scheme for sets is given in the *set.sal* context, provided with the SAL distribution, and this represents a set as a function from elements to Booleans. All of the set operations can be expressed in a logically succinct way, for example the set membership function *contains?* simply applies the set to the element. In [13] the *set.sal* context was extended to include a means of determining the cardinality of nonempty sets. We have adapted this encoding to work with all sets as follows:

```
set{T : TYPE; } : CONTEXT =
BEGIN

  Set : TYPE = [T -> BOOLEAN];

  empty_set : Set = LAMBDA (e : T) : FALSE;

  full_set : Set = LAMBDA (e : T) : TRUE;

  insert (aset : Set, e : T) : Set =
    LAMBDA (e1 : T) : e = e1 OR aset(e1);

  remove (aset : Set, e : T) : Set =
    LAMBDA (e1 : T) : e /= e1 AND aset(e1);

  contains? (aset : Set, e : T) : BOOLEAN =
    aset(e);

  empty? (aset : Set) : BOOLEAN =
    (FORALL (e : T) : aset(e) = FALSE);

  union(aset1 : Set, aset2 : Set) : Set =
    LAMBDA (e : T) : aset1(e) OR aset2(e);

  intersection(aset1 : Set, aset2 : Set) : Set =
    LAMBDA (e : T) : aset1(e) AND aset2(e);

  difference(aset1 : Set, aset2 : Set) : Set =
    LAMBDA (e : T) : aset1(e) AND NOT aset2(e);

  size?(aset:Set, n:NATURAL) : BOOLEAN =
    (n = 0 AND empty? (aset)) OR
    (n > 0 AND
    (EXISTS (f:[[1..n] -> T]) :
      (FORALL (x1,x2:[1..n]) : f(x1)=f(x2) => x1=x2) AND
      (FORALL (y:T) : aset(y) <=> (EXISTS (x:[1..n]) : f(x) =y))));
END
```

This allows a succinct translation of declarations and predicates involving sets. A declaration $member : \mathbb{P}\,NAME$ is translated to `member : set{NAME;}!Set`. Predicates involving set operators are also translated in the obvious way. For example, $member = \varnothing$ becomes

```
member = set{NAME;}!empty_set
```

Similarly, $n? \in waiting$ in the operation *Join* becomes

```
set{NAME;}!contains?(waiting, Join__n?)
```

and $member' = member \cup \{n?\}$ becomes

```
member' = set{NAME;}!insert(member, Join__n?)
```

Set cardinality (the most troublesome operator) cannot be expressed directly as a function returning the element count in SAL, since nowhere does SAL store a representation of the set as a whole, but only as a distributed collection of function-valued variables. Instead, the *size* function computes the relation between sets and natural numbers, returning true when a set is of a given size. Z predicates involving the cardinality of sets, such as $\#waiting < total$, can be translated to the following existentially quantified SAL predicate:

```
EXISTS(n: NAT) : set{NAME;}!size?(waiting,n) AND n < total.
```

Although this implementation of the translation algorithm is correct, a number of issues arose, some of which were to do with representation, others with efficiency, and we deal with each in turn.

6.1 Literals

The translation of literal sets causes particular problems as they can only occur in type declarations in SAL, but can be used in variable declarations or predicates in Z. The translation process addresses the problem of set literals in declarations by introducing a named type. Thus a state variable

$$s : \mathbb{P}\{1, 2, 3\}$$

becomes

```
LOCAL s : set{Set__1__2__3;}!Set
```

and `Set__1__2__3: TYPE = { x : NZNAT | x < 4 };` appears before the state module. Any other use of the same or an equivalent (e.g., $\{3, 2, 1\}$) set literal in a declaration will be translated to the type name. Literal sets in predicates can be dealt with more simply: $x \in \{1, 2\}$ becomes `(x=1 OR x=2)`.

6.2 Re-implementing Set Cardinality

It was soon discovered that Z specifications that made reference to the cardinality of sets generated SAL translations which did not execute in any sensible amount of time. Simulations did not terminate in half a day, whilst some model checks terminated, depending on how the checked LTL theorem further constrained the state space search. We therefore experimented with alternative set encodings that might have a more efficient implementation of `size?`.

Attempt I - A recursive definition of sets. According to the SAL language manual it should be possible to define inductive data types, similar to the illustrated definition of lists, which have recursive operations. In this case, `size?` could be provided as an efficient recursive function on sets. Thus one would define:

```
cset{T : TYPE; } : CONTEXT =
BEGIN
  Set : TYPE = DATATYPE
        add(elem : T, rest : Set),
        empty
        END;

  insert (set : Set, e : T) : Set =
    IF empty?(set)
      THEN add(e, set)
    ELSIF e = elem(set)
      THEN set
    ELSE
      add (elem(set), insert(rest(set), e))
    ENDIF;
...

  size?(set : Set) : NATURAL =
    IF empty?(set)
          THEN 0
    ELSE
          1 + size?(rest(set))
    ENDIF;
END
```

In this, `empty` and `add` are the primitive type constructors and `elem` and `rest` are the implicitly defined deconstructors that break apart a set. Set operations like `insert` are defined recursively by always `add`ing a new element to an empty set, otherwise deconstructing the head `elem` to see if this is equal to the new element, returning the set unchanged if so, otherwise inserting the new element into the `rest` of the set and `add`ing the deconstructed head back onto this. The `size?` function recursively counts the number of `add`s wrapping the `empty?` set.

Unfortunately, it was discovered afterwards that the current release of the SAL toolset does not yet support simulation or model checking with inductively defined datatypes. Even a simple recursive definition of `size?` fails to load into the simulator, because SAL attempts to expand all possible recursive trees and runs out of memory. A future release of the toolset is planned to handle recursively defined functions and inductive types.

Attempt II - countable finite sets. After experimenting with other encodings, a workable SAL translation was found for encoding counted finite sets. This is a brute-force encoding that is specific to the maximum expected set cardinality. Various set contexts `setN` were designed for different `N`, corresponding to the maximum expected cardinality. This is reasonable in SAL, since every scalar type must have a known lower and upper bound. Our translation fixes the range of scalar types for small `N`. The following excerpt is from the `set5` context, which holds a maximum of five elements.

```
set5{T : TYPE; e1, e2, e3, e4, e5 : T} : CONTEXT =
BEGIN

%% A countable set over a domain of 5 elements.  The context
%% parameters are: the element type T, and an exhaustive
%% enumeration of all the elements e1..e5 of the domain.

  Set : TYPE = [T -> BOOLEAN];

  empty_set : Set =
    LAMBDA (e : T) : FALSE;

  full_set : Set =
    LAMBDA (e : T) : TRUE;

  size? (set : Set) : NATURAL =
    IF set(e1) THEN 1 ELSE 0 ENDIF +
    IF set(e2) THEN 1 ELSE 0 ENDIF +
    IF set(e3) THEN 1 ELSE 0 ENDIF +
    IF set(e4) THEN 1 ELSE 0 ENDIF +
    IF set(e5) THEN 1 ELSE 0 ENDIF;

  ... %% the rest as per the set.sal context
END
```

The main difference between this and the standard `set.sal` context is that the context accepts value-parameters for all possible elements of the set, as well as the usual element type-parameter. This allows a brute-force encoding of the `size?` function, which tests for the presence of each element in turn. This encoding executes very efficiently, since it builds a shallow symbolic execution tree, in contrast with a recursively-defined function. The rest of the context is defined exactly as per the original `set.sal` context, using the encoding of sets as Boolean-valued functions over its elements, since this is the optimal encoding for translation to BDDs in the SAL tools.

A number of contexts may be pre-generated, for different `N`. We have also successfully generated different `setN.sal` on demand, to cater for unknown ranges. The only changes are the number of value parameters required and the number of subexpressions in the `size?` function. To use these bounded contexts, it is preferred to instantiate all parameters once in a new named context, in the following style:

```
PersonSet : CONTEXT =
  set3{PERSON; PERSON__1, PERSON__1, PERSON__3};
...
LOCAL set : PersonSet!Set
INITIALIZE set = PersonSet!empty_set
```

Then, all types and operations are accessed from the new named context. This makes the rest of the generated code easier to read than if the contexts were instantiated at every point of use.

Attempt III - Direct enumeration. Our current approach to problems in SAL with cardinality are to limit the state space explosion possibilities in SAL during the translation process. In general the structure of a predicate in Z is much the same as its translation in SAL, but not where `size?` is involved. When the cardinality of a set is tested for equality (or inequality) the test can be transformed fairly simply because the SAL `size?` function is designed to test for a particular cardinality. Thus $\#waiting = capacity$ becomes

`set{NAME;}!size?(waiting, capacity).`

Our initial approach to translating comparisons like $\#waiting < 3$ was to use an existential quantifier in the translated expression. However, since the standard translation of `size?` already used nested quantification, this merely exacerbated the state space explosion. Our current solution is to exploit the translator's knowledge of the maximum cardinality of the sets we are using to produce an expression which does not involve an existential quantifier. So if the maximum cardinality of *waiting* was 3 the translation of $\#waiting < 3$ is `NOT set{NAME;}!size?(waiting, 3)`, whereas if the the set *waiting* could have up to 5 elements the translation is

```
(set{NAME;}!size?(waiting, 0) OR set{NAME;}!size?(waiting, 1) OR
              set{NAME;}!size?(waiting, 2))
```

Where the comparison is with a variable the expression is slightly more complex. So $\#waiting < capacity$, where the maximum cardinality of the sets is 3 and the variable's upper bound is 3, becomes

```
(((0<capacity) AND set{NAME;}!size?(waiting,0) ) OR ((1<capacity)
          AND set{NAME;}!size?(waiting, 1) ) OR ( (2<capacity) AND
          set{NAME;}!size?(waiting, 2) ) OR ( (3<capacity) AND
          set{NAME;}!size?(waiting, 3) ))
```

This assumes that SAL does a lazy evaluation of the expression but experimental results seem to confirm this. Evaluating $\#member > \#waiting$ is possible by this technique too although the resulting expression does get rather long:

```
((set{NAME;}!size?(member,0) AND NOT set{NAME;}!size?(waiting,0))
    OR
 (set{NAME;}!size?(member, 1) AND (set{NAME;}!size?(waiting, 2)
          OR set{NAME;}!size?(waiting, 3)) )
    OR
 (set{NAME;}!size?(member, 2) AND (set{NAME;}!size?(waiting, 3))))
```

7 Using the Translation Tool

Currently we use a command line interface. As input format we use the LaTeX markup as given in the Z standard, and the output a plain SAL file. Since XML markups exist for both Z and SAL, these might eventually be the ultimate exchange format.

The components of the SAL toolset can now be applied to the output. For example, we can simulate the specification or use one of the model checkers on it. As we alluded to above, experiments revealed substantial efficiency problems with the naive version of `size?`.

Labelling the three implementations as Original (the first in Section 6), Canonical (Attempt III) and Alternate (Attempt II) we can compare the efficiency of the different size implementations.

For example, if we run the SAL simulator on the above example using the Canonical set representation, we find that it takes 2 seconds to create the initial state(s) of the system. Then invoking

```
(display-curr-states)
```

reports that 162 possible initial states were generated.

```
(display-curr-trace)
```

gives a single trace (one of the sets of initialisations leading to one of the initial states):

```
sal > (display-curr-trace)
Step 0:
--- Input Variables (assignments) ---
(= Join__n? NAME__3);
(= JoinQ__n? NAME__3);
(= Remove__n? NAME__3);
(= Query__n? NAME__3);
--- System Variables (assignments) ---
(= (member NAME__1) false);
(= (member NAME__2) false);
(= (member NAME__3) false);
(= (waiting NAME__1) false);
(= (waiting NAME__2) false);
(= (waiting NAME__3) false);
(= Query__ans_ yes);
```

The next stage is to try to step through the simulation.

```
(step!)
```

advances by a single step.

```
(display-curr-states)
```

reports that 648 states were created in this first step. This is consistent with attempting 4 transitions for each of the 162 states in the initialisation (4 * 162 = 648). The simulation can then be continued by exploring subsequent traces, working our way through the specification.

The performance of the Alternate representation was similar, however, the Original representation failed to create an initial state of the system in the simulator in over 12 hours. Experiments with the model checker produced similar results. We formalised the following three theorems:

th1 : the size of the *member* set can never reach 3 (expected false)
th2 : the size of the *waiting* set can never reach 3 (expected false)
th3 : the combined sizes of both sets is always ≤ 3 (expected true)

For the Canonical example, the theorems are expressed:

```
th1 : THEOREM State |- NOT F(set{NAME;}!size?(member', 3));
th2 : THEOREM State |- NOT F(set{NAME;}!size?(waiting', 3));
th3 : THEOREM State |- G( (FORALL(x,y:NZNAT) :
                  (set{NAME;}!size?(member', x) AND
                   set{NAME;}!size?(waiting', y)) => x+y <= 3));
```

For the Alternate example, the same theorems were supplied slightly differently, reflecting the simpler `size?` function:

```
th1 : THEOREM State |- NOT F(FSet!size?(member') = 3);
th2 : THEOREM State |- NOT F(FSet!size?(waiting') = 3);
th3 : THEOREM State |- G( (FSet!size?(member) +
                                   FSet!size?(waiting)) <= 3);
```

The following table gives the approximate timings for the simulation and proof or refutation of the theorems. The entries marked "> 12 hours" mean that, for example, the Canonical representation took over 12 hours for the third theorem without terminating.

	Original	Canonical	Alternate
Simulation	> 12 hours	2 sec	1.5 sec
th1	> 12 hours	4 sec	3 sec
th2	> 12 hours	4 sec	3 sec
th3	> 12 hours	> 12 hours	3 sec

Where the model checking was feasible, for theorems *th*1 and *th*2, both examples discovered the path of $3 * JoinQ$ to fill the waiting set, and the path of $3 * JoinQ + 3 * Join$ to fill the member set.

As can be seen, the original encoding does not model check in a feasible time. The Canonical encoding is feasible for some properties (and some specifications), and we have yet to find an example where the Alternate encoding is infeasible.

8 Discussion

Although, it is feasible in general to model check specifications with very large state spaces, model checking Z specifications poses some serious challenges. The inclusion of non-trivial data types is well known to cause state-space explosions, and even the use of small sets in the above example pushed the model checker to its limits in its memory and time capabilities in some of the encodings. The restriction to small set sizes and the fact that generic parameters (e.g., *capacity* in the example above) have to be instantiated mean that we are really using model checking to explore the specification rather than to perform the complete verification of a property. The use of data abstraction to alleviate this problem is a topic for further investigation.

However, in addition to the inclusion of data, the approach to the semantics in Z adds to the overhead. Specifically, everything in Z is modelled in the semantics as a set, thus relations are sets of pairs, functions are relations with a constraint, sequences are partial functions with a constraint, and so on. If this approach is preserved in the translation to SAL, as we have done so far, then this results in a computational overhead for the model checker which is likely to become prohibitive for any non-trivial specification.

The alternative would be to code the data structures in the mathematical toolkit directly. For example, SAL has total relations as one of the built in data-types, but does not have partial relations, however, the latter could be encoded as total functions with an undefined element to represent elements outside the precondition (i.e., one would model a partial relation as its *totalisation*). This is likely to give a better efficiency than the existing approach but there are complications in the translation. For example, in Z it is acceptable to write (for a function $f : \mathbb{N} \rightarrow\!\!\!\!\!+ \mathbb{N}$):

$$f' = f \cup \{(1, 3)\}$$

This is translated easily at present, but if functions are coded directly then a version of set union needs to be defined on the function space, which also has to be able to mix total and partial functions freely.

9 Conclusions

In this paper, we have discussed our current approach to building a model checker for Z specifications. This is work in progress, and there is much to be done. For example, we need to explore the use of constraint solvers in resolving the instantiation of constants introduced by axiomatic definitions. Similarly we need to investigate alternative representations for the mathematical toolkit which are not just their set-based expansion, and to compare the efficiency of such an approach. Finally, the current prototype is stand-alone, and a re-engineered version would involve integration with the CZT platform of tools.

Of course, this is not the first attempt to provide model checking facilities for Z. For example, there have been a number of encoding of subsets of Z-based languages in FDR [6,11,8]. However, FDR is not a temporal logic model checker, but rather is designed to check whether a refinement relation holds between two specifications. Additionally, FDR was developed for a process algebra, rather than a state-based notation, thus encoding a language such as Z is non-trivial, and to date there is no full encoding of Z in FDR.

Other relevant work directly concerned with state-based languages includes that on the ProB model checker [9] which provides model checking capabilities for B. Bolton has recently experimented with using Alloy to verify data refinements in Z [2]. The Alloy Analyzer is a SAT-based verification tool that automatically determines whether a model exists for a specification within given set bounds for the basic types. Bolton translates a Z specification into Alloy by encoding its relational semantics in Alloy and using the latter to see if a simulation can be found. However, the encoding of the relational semantics is not automatic in contrast to the implemented Z to SAL translation discussed above.

Acknowledgements. This work was done as part of collaborative work with the University of Queensland, and in particular, Graeme Smith and Luke Wildman. Tim Miller also gave valuable advice on the current CZT tools. Thanks is also due to the financial support of the EPSRC via the *RefineNet* grant.

References

1. ISO/IEC 13568:2002. Information technology—Z formal specification notation—syntax, type system and semantics. International Standard.
2. C. Bolton. Using the Alloy Analyzer to Verify Data Refinement in Z. *Electronic Notes in Theoretical Computer Science*, 137(2):23–44, 2005.
3. E. Clarke, O. Grumberg, S. Jha, Y. Lu, and H. Veith. Counterexample-guided abstraction refinement. In E.A. Emerson and A.P. Sistla, editors, *International Conference on Computer Aided Verification (CAV'00)*, volume 1855 of *LNCS*, pages 154–169. Springer-Verlag, 2000.
4. E. Clarke, O. Grumberg, and D. Peled. *Model Checking.* MIT Press, 2000.
5. L. de Moura, S. Owre, and N. Shankar. The SAL language manual. Technical Report SRI-CSL-01-02 (Rev.2), SRI International, 2003.
6. C. Fischer and H. Wehrheim. Model-checking CSP-OZ specifications with FDR. In K. Araki, A. Galloway, and K. Taguchi, editors, *International Conference on Integrated Formal Methods (IFM'99)*, pages 315–334. Springer-Verlag, 1999.
7. S. Graf and H. Saïdi. Construction of abstract state graphs with PVS. In *International Conference on Computer Aided Verification (CAV'97)*, volume 1254 of *LNCS*, pages 72–83. Springer-Verlag, 1997.
8. G. Kassel and G. Smith. Model checking Object-Z classes: Some experiments with FDR. In *Asia-Pacific Software Engineering Conference (APSEC 2001)*. IEEE Computer Society Press, 2001.
9. M. Leuschel and M. Butler. Automatic refinement checking for B. In K. Lau and R. Banach, editors, *International Conference on Formal Engineering Methods, ICFEM 2005*, volume 3785 of *LNCS*, pages 345–359. Springer-Verlag, 2005.
10. Tim Miller, Leo Freitas, Petra Malik, and Mark Utting. CZT Support for Z Extensions. In Judi Romijn, Graeme Smith, and Jaco Pol, editors, *Integrated Formal Methods, IFM 2005*, volume 3771 of *LNCS*, pages 227–245. Springer-Verlag, 2005.

11. A. Mota and A. Sampaio. Model-checking CSP-Z: strategy, tool support and industrial application. *Science of Computer Programming*, 40:59–96, 2001.
12. H. Saïdi and N. Shankar. Abstract and model check while you prove. In N. Halbwachs and D. Peled, editors, *International Conference on Computer Aided Verification (CAV'99)*, volume 1633 of *LNCS*, pages 443–453. Springer-Verlag, 1999.
13. G. Smith and L. Wildman. Model checking Z specifications using SAL. In H. Treharne, S. King, M. Henson, and S. Schneider, editors, *International Conference of Z and B Users (ZB 2005)*, volume 3455 of *LNCS*, pages 87–105. Springer-Verlag, 2005.
14. J.M. Spivey. *The Z Notation: A Reference Manual.* Prentice Hall, 2nd edition, 1992.

Taking Our Own Medicine: Applying the Refinement Calculus to State-Rich Refinement Model Checking

Leo Freitas, Ana Cavalcanti, and Jim Woodcock

Department of Computer Science
University of York, UK
{leo, alcc, jim}@cs.york.ac.uk

Abstract. In this paper, we advocate the use of formal specification and verification in software development for high-integrity and safety-critical systems, where mechanical proof plays a central role. In particular, we emphasise the crucial importance of applying verification in the development of formal verification tools themselves. We believe this approach is very useful to increase the levels of confidence and integrity of tools that are built to find bugs based on formally specified models. This follows the trend set out by a UK grand challenge in computer research for verified software repository.

In this direction, we present our experiences on a case study on the development process of a refinement model checking tool for *Circus*, a concurrent refinement language that combines Z, CSP, guarded commands, and the refinement calculus, with the Unifying Theories of Programming of Hoare and He as the theoretical background.

Keywords: model checking, theorem proving, formal verification.

1 Introduction

Increased complexity in hardware and software systems has created a demand for precision and reliability, particularly in the high-integrity and safety-critical domains [2]. One effective way of achieving this goal is through the use of formal specification and verification. When it comes to the development of formal tools, which ultimately will perform such verification, we see the use of formalism as essential. The same principles apply for critical systems.

A well-known programming technique is stepwise development through refinement, where correctness is guaranteed by construction. That is, starting from an abstract specification, the system is formally developed by the application of refinement laws that transform its representation to an artifact closer to a computer implementation (or program), where the properties of the specification are preserved, provided that generated proof obligations are discharged.

Specifications, intermediate designs, and concrete implementations are usually represented as mathematical models, where we are mostly interested in their data and behavioural aspects. The refinement laws enabling correct transformations are part of a refinement calculus of sequential programs [1, 15].

Z. Liu and J. He (Eds.): ICFEM 2006, LNCS 4260, pp. 697–716, 2006.

The problem with applying a refinement calculus is that it is a laborious task, and rigorous proof is needed. When the complexity and number of operations involved is high, the proofs become error prone, painstakingly long, and some sort of tool support would be very helpful, if not an imperative factor.

In this paper, we present our experience in using a refinement calculus in the development process of a model checking tool, where we have used the Z/Eves theorem prover [21] to mechanise the proof obligations. With the mechanised application of the refinement calculus, we strengthened the claims for correctness of the model checker.

The most important results obtained by this work are: (i) mechanical discharge of proof obligations; (ii) hints or counterexamples for failed proofs, hence invaluable suggestions for possible amendments in pre or postconditions, or loop invariants; (iii) hints about efficient use of Z/Eves that enables great reuse between different proof obligations, hence gained performance and productivity; and (iv) an informal strategy to translate Z and specification statements into JML [4], a modelling language that enables formal verification of Java code. This was developed while applying an extended version of the *Z Refinement Calculus* (ZRC) [5], the *Circus* refinement calculus [17], to an algorithm for refinement model checking of *Circus* [11, Chapter 4], which integrates model checking and theorem proving, in systems where data and behavioural aspects are combined.

The result of applying formal methods in the development of a model checker, was rewarding: since the encoding of the calculated algorithm, the code has not changed. Furthermore, as it is possible to (informally) translate these findings with some level of confidence to JML, we believe we have narrowed the gap between the concrete model of guarded commands and a Java implementation.

This sort of bootstrapping, where we have used *Circus* to specify and refine its own model checker, allows us to find early design flaws, as well as to ensure the algorithm is correct by construction. Thus, important properties, such as loop invariants, are precisely documented. That is, we took our own medicine to formally specify key aspects of the architecture, in order to enhance the consistency of the whole tool throughout the development process.

Whilst the model checker is still a prototype, various examples have been analysed and no bugs in the refinement algorithm have been found. We believe that for a formal verification tool, such an approach is essential for the assurance and credibility of any flaws they might find. This decision follows the trend set by a grand challenge in computer science research in verified software [2].

In the literature, there are few examples of such an approach, to the extent of our knowledge. The *Mural* theorem prover is one tool we know stepwise refinement was used throughout its development process [12] was used. Nevertheless, other tools, such as *Perfect Developer* [7], have applied verification of its own code after being developed.

In the next section, we present *Circus* and its refinement calculus by illustrating the application of some laws on simple examples. After that, Section 3 presents how we use Z/Eves to encode the proof obligations from the refinement calculus.

In Section 4, we present our case study. Finally, Section 5 presents conclusions and future work.

2 *Circus*

Circus is a concurrent language built for refinement, which allows the combination of different language paradigms [23]. It combines Z [22], CSP [9, 20], and specification statements found in refinement calculi. Other executable commands are also available, such as assignments, conditionals, and loops. This enables one to use *Circus* for both abstract specifications, intermediate designs, and actual code. Because its semantic model is based on the UTP [10], it is amenable for extension, and considerable work has already been done in this direction. The result is a unified programming language that can be used for developing concurrent programs through refinement.

Circus provides a refinement calculus that extends ZRC, hence we can formally specify and derive code not only for abstract data types, but also for concurrent programs. There is considerable effort in building a set of tools supporting the language. At the time of writing, there is a parser, a typechecker, a prototype refinement model checker, and the basis of a theorem prover. In fact the model checker combines both fully automatic verification with interactive theorem proving due to the presence of state-rich features of *Circus*.

One of the greatest challenges in combining different programming paradigms and notions of refinement is the provision of a suitable semantic model. The UTP model of *Circus* embeds all the features of Z and CSP. In this framework, we can guarantee that we can safely use both ZRC and CSP refinement laws, as well as new *Circus* laws.

In terms of data or behaviour dealt separately, one can apply either Z or CSP refinement laws. In situations where both paradigms cannot (or should not) be separated, new *Circus* refinement laws can be applied, and they are given in [17, App C]. This includes ZRC laws, CSP laws, and new *Circus* laws. For instance, using the *Circus* law (*C.141*) of interchange between alternation and guarded external choice, we could transform an alternation into an external choice.

For the implementation of a model checker for *Circus*, we face many challenges: (i) how to represent Z schemas without loosing their characteristic abstraction; (ii) how to represent predicate calculus finitely in order to allow model checking; (iii) how to model check behavioural and data aspects of systems; (iv) how to maximise the levels of automation, while combining model checking with theorem proving, whenever theorem proving is required; *etc.*

3 Refinement Calculus Automation Strategy in Z/Eves

Firstly, from a *Circus* specification we apply the refinement strategy proposed in [6]. As *Circus* specifications involve specification statements, guarded commands, and Z and CSP operators, we need to find a way to represent these structures in a theorem prover in order to enable mechanisation. Luckily, proof obligations can be described as specification statements mentioning a frame of variables that can be updated, as well as pre and postconditions with predicate calculus, hence we can use theorem provers for discharging proof obligations that would otherwise require to be done by hand. That is, we have used Z/Eves not to apply refinement laws, but to discharge the proof obligations these laws generate. Also, as we do not have a suitable refinement calculus tool, the translation of proof obligations to Z/Eves is done manually. A further step, would be the construction of a refinement calculation tool for *Circus*, such as Refine [16] for ZRC, where the application of laws and the transformations they represent could also be done by formal tools.

From the *Circus* specification of the model checker, we decided to apply the refinement calculus to the refinement model checking algorithm in order to get to code. This choice was made because we believe this to be the crucial part of the whole architecture. By using the refinement calculus to reach the code from the abstract specification, we ensure that the algorithm is correct by construction, and important properties such as loop invariants are precisely documented. Furthermore, other parts of the architecture have also been formalised in Z/Eves, but no refinement calculation was performed.

Firstly, from the Z aspect of the *Circus* specification, we needed to prove simulation between the abstract and concrete models, which include the state and related operations. These simulation proofs have been done mechanically in Z/Eves. This was achieved through simulation laws and corresponding applicability and correctness proof obligations. After that, with the concrete model at hand, we started applying ZRC laws to transform the Z part of the specification into guarded commands. Moreover, proof obligations coming from the application of CSP and *Circus* laws can be discharged similarly to the simulation proofs by using Z/Eves. In this process, various properties of interest were discovered and altered, such as state and loop invariants. As postconditions of concrete specifications tend to be quite complex, with predicates often involving schema inclusions, predicate simplifications were also often important. Thus, whenever stepwise refinement or formal verification was applied and proof obligations were generated, we see mechanisation via theorem proving as an essential requirement for correctness.

For different problems, one can follow a similar strategy. With an abstract specification either in *Circus*, if concurrent aspects are relevant, or pure Z, if only data is under concern, the same ideas for of applying the refinement calculus hold. In this way, the strategy can be reused to refine specifications down JML annotations in the actual code.

Mechanisation with Z/Eves means encoding the proof obligations using the Z schema calculus. For that, we apply the ZRC law of basic conversion (bC) backwards from specification statements to schemas, and then syntactically rearrange the corresponding schema so that it is amenable for mechanical proof in Z/Eves. Obviously, during the first iterations of stepwise refinement, where one starts from schemas and usually goes to specification statements, this is not very helpful. Nonetheless, later on when specification statements are to be refined to the most common guarded commands, such as alternations and assignments, this strategy pays off as it allows proof obligations to be mechanically discharged, like the ones in our case study in the next section.

For instance, assuming square root is well-defined in Z/Eves with signature as $sqrt \in \mathbb{N} \rightarrow \mathbb{N}$, where domain checks were discharged. Let us illustrate how we encode the proof obligation generated by the application of strengthening the postcondition (in the example from [15, p. 5])

$$y : [0 \leq x \leq 9,\ sqrt\ y = x] \overset{sP}{\sqsubseteq} y : [0 \leq x \leq 9,\ sqrt\ y = x \land y \geq 0]$$

$$\textbf{provided that} \quad \forall x, y, y' : \mathbb{Z} \bullet (0 \leq x \leq 9) \land (sqrt\ y' = x \land y' \geq 0) \bullet (sqrt\ y' = x)$$

which is true based on properties of *sqrt* defined in Z/Eves as one expected *sqrt* to behave, bearing in mind specification/mechanisations issues. Firstly, we encode the state variables carefully according in the *Frame* schema. Next, we encode the pre and post conditions as schemas *Pre*, *Post*, and *NewPost* coming directly from the specification statement predicates (via *bC* backwards).

$$\begin{array}{lcl} Frame & \widehat{=} & [x, y, y' : \mathbb{Z}] \\ Pre & \widehat{=} & [Frame \mid 0 \leq x \leq 9] \\ Post & \widehat{=} & [Frame \mid sqrt\ y' = x] \\ NewPost & \widehat{=} & Post \land [Frame \mid y' \geq 0] \end{array}$$

As the precondition does not mention the after state, we include a read-only (Ξ) version of *Frame* in *Pre*. Finally, we can discharge the proof obligation by proving the conjecture *posP*1 as a theorem

theorem posP1
$\forall Frame \mid Pre \land Post \Rightarrow NewPost$

The complete set of translation strategies for the various ZRC laws used throughout the formal derivation of the refinement algorithm code can be found in Section 6 of [11, App. A]. In this reference, we also include extensive information on how to drive Z/Eves, so that one can achieve efficient and acceptable (or higher) levels of automation.

The use of the schema calculus to represent the ZRC proof obligations makes the proofs concise, elegant, and easier to follow. For example, in our case study, due to the sheer number and complexity of predicates involved, it soon became impossible to handle the proofs reliably, as they would easily spread across two or more A4 pages of mathematical formulae. In spite of some auxiliary lemmas needed to improve automation in Z/Eves, the mechanised result was much more tidy, organised, elegant, and reliable than the alternative by hand.

Some Conventions for Z/Eves

For every declaration that might include undefinedness, such as type inconsistencies or partial functions called outside their domain, Z/Eves introduces proof obligations as *Domain Checks*. These are sufficient conditions for definedness one needs to prove, even if the definitions involved are not being used.

For most declared functions that might become involved in future domain checks or proof obligations, some housekeeping theorems should be included. Although these housekeeping theorems are usually obvious, quite repetitive, and straightforward to prove, they do increase the levels of automation to a great extent. For instance, we can axiomatically define a total function f that nondeterministically creates sequences of size n as

$$f : \mathbb{N} \rightarrow \operatorname{seq} \mathbb{N}$$
$$\forall n : \mathbb{N} \bullet \#(f\ n) = n$$

In this case, Z/Eves introduces a trivial domain check as the proof obligation

$$f \in \operatorname{seq} \mathbb{N} \land n \in \mathbb{N} \land s \in \operatorname{seq} \mathbb{N} \Rightarrow n \in \operatorname{dom} f \land f\ n \in \operatorname{dom} \#$$

Discharging this proof obligation is important in order to ensure we have not given a definition that might introduce inconsistencies in the model whenever f is used. If f is not used, one ends up proving more than what is necessary.

We also introduce additional facts about the function's domain, and result maximal types, to increase automation of other definitions that depend on f. In Z/Eves syntax, these facts are introduced as named conjectures to be proved as theorems, where the names are preceded by modifiers used for controlling automation granularity.

theorem grule gFMaxType
$f \in \mathbb{P}(\mathbb{Z} \times \mathbb{P}(\mathbb{Z} \times \mathbb{Z}))$
theorem grule gFRelMaxType
$f \in \mathbb{Z} \leftrightarrow \mathbb{P}(\mathbb{Z} \times \mathbb{Z}))$
theorem rule rFResultMaxType
$\forall n : \mathbb{N} \bullet f\ n \in \mathbb{P}(\mathbb{Z} \times \mathbb{Z})$
theorem rule rFIsTotal
$\forall n : \mathbb{N} \bullet n \in \operatorname{dom} f$

In Z/Eves, assumptions (*grule*) rules are used by every tactic that rewrites the goal, hence it enables coarse-grained automation for commonly needed type consistency checks that often appear in later proofs where f is used. On the other hand, rewriting (*rule*) rules are used by only a few specialised tactics, hence they enable fine-grained automation for more specialised scenarios.

As we use the schema calculus throughout our case study, and in the proof obligations from the refinement calculus, it is sometimes necessary to inform Z/Eves about obvious facts regarding the (maximal) types of the schema components, depending on which components are used later on. For instance, in a schema such as

$$S \mathrel{\widehat{=}} [n : \mathbb{N};\ s : \operatorname{seq} \mathbb{N} \mid \forall i : \operatorname{dom} s \bullet s\ i < n]$$

Z/Eves includes a domain check about the application of s to i that is easily discharged, since $i \in \operatorname{dom} s$. Depending on how S might appear, perhaps with

s being created using f, one needs to include additional information about the type of s with theorems, such as

theorem frule fSsMaxType
$\forall S \bullet s \in \mathbb{P}(\mathbb{Z} \times \mathbb{Z})$

This kind of theorem, among other reasons, is useful to avoid the need to always expand the schema definitions in order to discharge goals where s is involved. This "use without expansion" is the most useful tool for higher degrees of automation and modularity of proofs when complex schema inclusions occur. That is, because we can surgically guide specific aspects of the goal without the need to expand (possibly a great amount of) unrelated assumptions from included schemas. This kind of usage is defined as a forward rule (*frule*).

More details about Z/Eves are beyond the scope of this paper, and are omitted here for space constraints. An extensive tutorial including detailed information on how to precisely drive Z/Eves, with higher levels of automation for a variety of scenarios, can be found in Section 1.1.1 of [11, App. A].

4 Case Study: Witness Search Model Checking Algorithm

In this section we briefly present the *Circus* model checker architecture, detailing its refinement checking module. From this module, we include parts of the abstract model, parts of the sequential algorithm derivation via forward simulation, and the complete refined code of a sequential algorithm from the concrete model. Moreover, we discuss our findings and present some benchmarks of the whole project of the model checker tool.

Model Checker Architecture Overview
The architecture of the *Circus* model checker is inspired by FDR, the refinement model checker for CSP [8, 18], and it has four components: (i) a parser, (ii) a typechecker, (iii) a compiler, and (iv) a refinement checker, as shown in Figure 1. The arrows in the Figure represent the date flow from a *Circus* specification in LaTeXto the actual set of witnesses the model checker could find. In this flow, firstly the parser creates an *Abstract Syntax Tree* (AST) that the typechecker annotates with type information (AST_+). The compiler then transforms the annotated AST_+ using the operational semantics of *Circus* into a labelled transition system with predicates embedded on the arcs (PTS) [11, Chapter 3]. Finally, these automata are analysed by the witness search algorithm we present here in order to find possible flaws.

From this architecture, an automaton theory (for PTS), the operational semantics of *Circus*, and the refinement checker module have been formally defined as *Circus* specifications, and mechanical proof of properties and proof obligations have been carried out using Z/Eves.

The refinement checker module takes two compiled automata representing the *Circus* specification and implementation sides of the refinement order, together

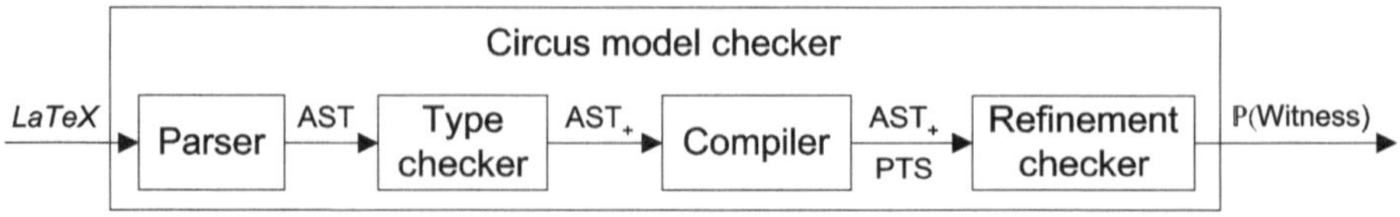

Fig. 1. *Circus* model checker architecture

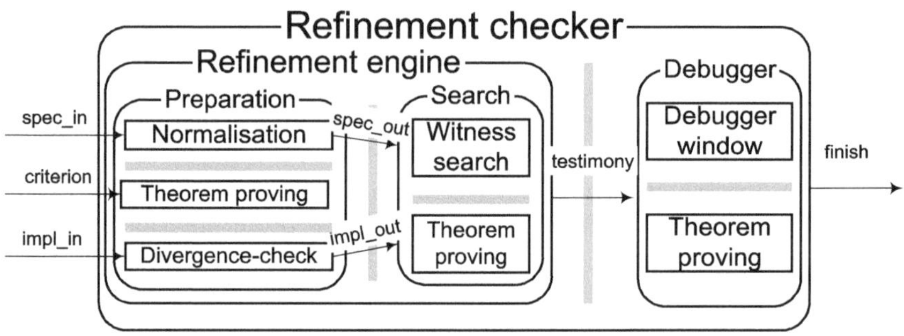

Fig. 2. *Circus* refinement checker

with a criterion (or level of detail) to perform the search. The refinement checker is defined in *Circus* by the parallel composition of various processes, as shown in Figure 2. The gray bars represent parallel composition of *Circus* processes, whereas the arrows represent (visible and internal) CSP events. For our case study, we detail the witness search process only. A full account of each of these processes, as well as the other components of the whole architecture is given in [11].

Witness Search

Witness search establishes whether a specification S is refined by a design or implementation I, denoted by $S \sqsubseteq I$. If it does, a successful report is generated. If it does not, we provide sufficient debugging information that can be used to produce a suitable human-readable account of the failures as a set of witnesses. It works over PTS automata representing the state-rich aspects of *Circus*.

Witnesses are characterised as a nonempty joint path of node pairs coming from both automata, since a witness is the result of a search that found at least one incompatible node pair.

$$\begin{array}{lll} JointPath & == & \{ SNP : \text{iseq } NodePair;\ SCL : \text{seq } \mathbb{N} \mid \# SCL = \# SNP \} \\ Witness & == & JointPath \setminus \{ (\langle\rangle, \langle\rangle) \} \end{array}$$

A joint path is formed by a pair of sequences, where the first element is an injective sequence of node pairs, and the second element is a sequence of layers of the *Breadth First Search* performed. It enforces that both sequences must have the same size, hence both node pairs, and their corresponding search levels, are accessed at the same index. Injectivity of node pairs is important because it ensures no pairs are searched twice. Nevertheless, different pairs can searched at the same level. Search levels are important for memory efficient extraction of debugging information from witnesses.

Next, we define the conditions for a valid witness: (i) the last element of the node pair sequence of a witness (sN, iN) must be valid (*NodePairInv*), but no information about their compatibility is known, since it is the current pair being checked; (ii) on the other hand, every node pair in the *front* of a witness must be valid ($NodePairInv[dn/sN, n/iN]$) and compatible ($\neg GenVl[dn/sN, n/iN]$); (iii) there must exist a trace (*wtsTrace*) from both automata of S (normalised *nf*) and I (*ip*) corresponding to each node pair sequence that is part of a witness; and (iv) the search level of each node pair recorded strictly increases.

WitnessInv

$m : Criterion;\ nf : NFPTS;\ ip : IPTS;\ w : Witness;\ NodePairInv$

$$
\begin{array}{l}
(sN, iN) = last\,(w.1) \\
\forall\, dn : DNode;\ n : Node \mid (dn, n) \in \operatorname{ran}(front\ w.1) \bullet \\
\qquad NodePairInv[dn/sN, n/iN] \land \neg GenVl[dn/sN, n/iN] \\
\exists\, T : \operatorname{seq} \Sigma \bullet T = wtsTrace\,(nf, ip, w) \\
\forall\, i : 1 \mathinner{..} (\#\, w.2 - 1) \bullet w.2\,(i) \leq w.2\,(i+1)
\end{array}
$$

The existence of a trace in S (*nf*) and I (*ip*) from the node pairs in the current witness (w) establishes the nodes that are mutually reachable, while searching for new successor pairs. That means, if one can create a valid non-empty sequence of node pairs from the two automata, then it must be possible to retrieve the unique trace related to such witness. The trace of events is unique because of the deterministic property of the normalised automaton of S. Finally, it ensures that lower level nodes must appear before higher level ones. As we do not store the whole trace a witness represents, these levels allow memory efficient representation of flaws. This consistency on the levels information is important for the debugger to provide accurate information while rebuilding the transition system from the failed pair up to the root of the search. Many of these properties were found due to failed proofs while mechanising.

The abstract model. Witness search is responsible for finding whether all the behaviours of I are allowable by at least one behaviour of S, such that they have a trace in common. The behaviours of interest depend on the selected criterion to establish refinement, which in turn has specific violation criterion. Due to space restrictions, we present only the relevant parts.

The general violation criterion is defined next. Regardless of the criterion being traces, nondeterminism, or divergences, every node pair from S and I must be valid (*NodePairInv*), and checked for traces violation (*TrVl*). For the traces criterion (*tr*), this is enough. Other different criteria, such as nondeterminism (*sfl*), can also be checked for stable-failures violation (*SFlVl*). Finally, the divergence violations (*DvVl*) are checked only for the failures-divergences criterion (*fldv*). The violation of each criterion is defined as a Z schema that establishes the relationship between node pairs from the automata of S and I.

$$
\begin{array}{|l}
\textit{GenVl} \\
\hline
m : \textit{Criterion};\ \textit{NodePairInv} \\
\hline
\textit{TrVl} \lor (\lnot m = tr \land (\textit{SFlVl} \lor (m = \textit{fldv} \land \textit{DvVl})))
\end{array}
$$

In this way, we separate concerns at the specification level.

The abstract state includes the refinement search parameters (*RSParams*), and the set of witnesses found (*wts*). The invariant of the abstract state (*RSState*) guarantees that: (i) the number of witnesses searched ($\#wts$) does not exceed the amount requested (*wr*); (ii) the automata involved after the transformations occurred during normalisation and divergence checking are valid with respect to the operational semantics (*enabled*) (see arrows in Figure 2); and (iii) witnesses that have been found, must satisfy the witness invariant (*WitnessInv*), and have the last node pair violating some compatibility criteria (*GenVl*). The *enabled* function receives a transition system and a node and return the set of arcs available from this point.

$$
\begin{array}{|l}
\textit{RSState} \\
\hline
\textit{RSParams};\ wts : \mathbb{P}\ \textit{Witness} \\
\hline
wts \in \mathbb{F}\ \textit{Witness} \land \#wts \leq wr \\
\forall sN : \textit{DNode};\ iN : \textit{Node};\ a : \mathbb{P}_1\ \Sigma \mid \textit{NodePairInv} \land \lnot\ \textit{GenVl} \land \\
\qquad a \in \textit{enabled}\,(ip.ts, iN) \bullet \lnot \bigcup(\textit{enabled}\,(nf.ts, sN)) \cap a = \{\,\} \\
\forall w : \textit{Witness} \mid w \in wts \bullet \exists sN : \textit{DNode};\ iN : \textit{Node} \bullet \\
\qquad \textit{WitnessInv} \land \textit{GenVl}
\end{array}
$$

That is, for consistency, if a node pair $((sN, iN))$ is valid (*NodePairInv*), compatible ($\lnot$*GenVl*), and has visible events ($a \neq \varnothing$) immediately available (*enabled*) in the implementation I (*ip*), then there must be some event in common with the normalised specification S (*nf*). Otherwise, either the operational semantics, or the model checking compatibility criteria, would have been wrongly specified. These consistency elucidations are due to mechanical proof.

Next is the signature of refinement search operations. It establishes that the search parameters that are part of the state do not change (Ξ), and that the set of witnesses (*wts*) may increase (to wts'), but previously found witnesses are not lost ($wts \subseteq wts'$).

$$
\begin{array}{|l}
\textit{RSOps} \\
\hline
\Xi\ \textit{RSParams};\ \Delta\ \textit{RSState} \\
\hline
wts \subseteq wts'
\end{array}
$$

In the general violation criterion (*GenVl*), we factor the searching for witnesses with respect to each violation criterion. This allows a modular combination of criteria within the different aspects of the compatibility check. Thus, for each criterion, we define an operation to search for witnesses. The set of witnesses found (wts') must be a subset of the set containing all valid witnesses (w) according to the witness invariant ($WitnessInv$), and related violation criteria for traces ($TrVl$) for a pair of nodes coming from the specification (sN) and the implementation (iN) automata.

$$\begin{array}{l} \underline{\quad TrWtsSearch \quad} \\ RSOps \\ \hline m = tr \land wts' \subseteq \{\, w : Witness;\ sN : DNode;\ iN : Node \mid \\ \qquad\qquad\qquad\qquad WitnessInv \land TrVl \bullet w \,\} \end{array}$$

As we do not need to necessarily find all witnesses, but a specific number requested (wr), the value of wts' is a subset of, rather than equal to, the entire space of witnesses. Similarly, for the other criteria, each violation schema is disjoined to form the other sets of witnesses

$$\begin{array}{ll} WitnessInv \land (TrVl \lor SFlVl) & \text{for stable-failures} \\ WitnessInv \land (TrVl \lor SFlVl \lor DvVl) & \text{for failures-divergences} \end{array}$$

Finally, we define a total operation for finding witnesses, regardless of the criteria, as the disjunction of the witness search operations.

$$FindWitnesses \mathrel{\widehat=} (TrWtsSearch \lor SFlWtsSearch \lor FlDvWtsSearch)$$

This modular approach gives room for future extensions in a precise fashion. For instance, one could encode one of the extended failures models for CSP defined in [3] as an additional violation schema, with the corresponding criterion flag and schema characterising the space of witnesses to search for. Moreover, for all available operations in the abstract model, we have proved applicability theorems about the operation preconditions.

The concrete model. We applied (a trivial) data refinement over the state of the abstract model ($RSState$), so that the concrete model has additional components: (i) two injective sequences for pending (pd), and already checked node pairs (ck); (ii) the node pair (wnp) currently being searched; (iii) a sequence of working levels used to register at which level of the search each (working) node pair appeared; and (iv) the abstract refinement search parameters. The sequential state invariant gathers properties about the variables (pd, ck, lvl, wnp, $swts$) used in the algorithm's code, instead of scattered in postconditions of later specification statements. This decision was taken in order to minimise and modularise the complexity of proof obligations generated, as the first s (harder) attempt to discharge the proof obligations when predicates were scattered showed. The first predicates are about finiteness of witnesses, and an equivalence for wnp used for better automation. Next we have the number witness we can search ($\#swts \leq wr$). The consistency between progress of node pairs from the implementation (ip) and the normal form (nf) as defined by the operational semantics (*enabled*) comes next, and it is similar to the abstract state (*RSState*), but mentioning the working node pair (*wnp*). A series of predicates establishing that the working node pair, and the pending and checking sequences elements are valid in the product automata (*PA*), are also included. The product automata is just the cross product of the available nodes from both the specification and implementation automata.

SeqRSState

$$\begin{array}{l}
RSParams;\ swts : \mathbb{P}\ Witness;\ ck, pd : \mathrm{iseq}\ NodePair;\ lvl : \mathrm{seq}\ \mathbb{N} \\
wnp : NodePair;\ wsN : DNode;\ wiN : Node;\ wl : \mathbb{N} \\
\hline
swts \in \mathbb{F}\ Witness \land wnp = (wsN, wiN) \land \#swts \leq wr \\
\forall a : Arc \mid \neg GenVl[wsN/sN, wiN/iN] \land \neg a = \{\} \land \\
\quad a \in enabled\,(ip.ts, wiN) \bullet \neg \bigcup (enabled\,(nf.ts, wsN)) \cap a = \{\} \\
\#ck = \#lvl \land wnp \in PA\,(nf, ip) \land NodePairInv[wsN/sN, wiN/iN] \\
ck \in \mathrm{iseq}\,(PA\,(nf, ip)) \land pd \in \mathrm{iseq}\,(PA\,(nf, ip)) \\
\forall sNck : DNode;\ iNck : Node \mid (sNck, iNck) \in \mathrm{ran}\ ck \bullet \\
\quad NodePairInv[sNck/sN, iNck/iN] \land \neg GenVl[sNck/sN, iNck/iN] \\
\forall sNpd : DNode;\ iNpd : Node \mid (sNpd, iNpd) \in \mathrm{ran}\ pd \bullet \\
\qquad NodePairInv[sNpd/sN, iNpd/iN] \\
\mathrm{ran}\ pd \cap \mathrm{ran}\ ck = \{\} \\
\forall i : 1 \mathrel{..} (\#lvl - 1) \bullet lvl\,(i) \leq lvl\,(i+1) \\
\forall j : 1 \mathrel{..} \#lvl \bullet lvl\,(j) \leq wl \\
\forall w : Witness \mid w \in swts \bullet \mathrm{ran}\ pd \cap \mathrm{ran}\ w.1 = \{\} \\
\forall w : Witness \mid w \in swts \bullet WitnessInv[wsN/sN, wiN/iN] \land \\
\qquad GenVl[wsN/sN, wiN/iN]
\end{array}$$

Next, comes the property that pending and checked pairs are disjoint, hence the search is closed under the elements of these sequences. This is important to establish the main loop variant, and hence guarantee that the whole search terminates. Finally, we include a series of properties regarding search levels useful for debugging, together with information about how witnesses relate to pending and checked pairs, which are further detailed latter. Many of these were discovered through formal proof.

This is possible by the application of forward simulation rules with a quite trivial retrieve relation: the set of witness from the abstract world equals the set of witnesses used in the concrete world. Thus, we have an operational refinement, rather than data refinement. At first we have used an injective sequence to represent *swts*, and the retrieve schema as $wts = \mathrm{ran}\ swts$, but it increased the complexity of the proofs in a great extent, because the Z toolkit does not have great automation for this data type. Fortunately, this was not a problem for the proof obligations related to the injective sequence of pending and checked node pairs. Finally, as Java and JML support sets, this choice did not become an implementation issue.

At this stage, in order to establish refinement, we needed to prove that, for every available operations of the abstract model, the corresponding concrete version satisfies the two proof obligations of applicability and correctness generated [17, Law C.4]. In particular, we have done this for the entire *Circus* specification. In here we want to emphasise that the refinement algorithm simulates the abstract specification.

$$FindWitnesses \preceq SeqWitnesses$$

Finally, Like in the abstract model, we calculate the preconditions of all concrete operations to ensure their applicability as well.

The algorithm. It defines how node pairs are checked for compatibility, as well as how new pairs are found. To give an overview of the algorithm we provide the entire derived code in Figure 3, which is written in *Circus*. This code has been derived using ZRC, and action refinement laws for *Circus* [17, Appendix C]. Although our algorithm is similar to the algorithm of FDR presented in [19, 14], the mechanised proof effort precisely exposed loop invariants, and a great amount of hidden information that is interesting for the understanding of the witness search problem for refinement model checking in general.

The algorithm is divided into two stages: (i) compatibility check; and (ii) successor node pairs search. In the compatibility check, we first assign to the working node pair (wnp), update the pending pairs (pd), and increment the working level of the search accordingly. If wnp is incompatible ($GenVl$), then it must be included as a new witness in $swts$. It is formed by the previous checked pairs, together with the offending working node pair at the working level. Otherwise, if wnp is compatible, then the sequence of checked pairs and search level are updated likewise, and the next stage of finding successor pairs starts. The search is performed while there are pending pairs ($pd \neq \langle\rangle$) to be searched, and witness to be found ($\#swts < wr$).

While searching for successors, the arcs immediately available for communication in the implementation are retrieved through the *enabled* function representing all events immediately available from a given node. For each of those arcs, one needs to progress appropriately in the automata of S and I, according to the loop invariant. In order to exhaust all enabled implementation arcs ($arcS$), we choose the specification node successor (sN), and select all available implementation successor nodes ($iN \in iNS$) on the same arc. If it is a silent or internal transition, here specified as an empty arc, it represents nondeterminism (from an internal choice, for instance) being resolved in I. Since after normalisation the automaton of S is deterministic and has no silent transitions left, there is no successor node for S in this case. Otherwise, in the case of visible communication, the selection of successors follows from the *arcStep* function. It determines the set of nodes we can reach through a given arc at a particular node. These two functions represent the formally specified operational semantics of *Circus* [11, Chapter 3].

Interesting Properties We Have Discovered

Although this way of building up the witness from the sequence of checked pairs comes from FDR's algorithm, some properties to enable us to derive thecode are

```
SeqWitnesses ≙
  do_L0 (#swts < wr ∧ pd ≠ ⟨⟩) →
    wnp, pd, wl := head pd, tail pd, (wl + 1) ;
    if (GenVl[wsN/sN, wiN/iN]) →
        swts := swts ∪ { ((ck ⁀ ⟨wnp⟩), (lvl ⁀ ⟨wl⟩)) }
      ▯ (¬ GenVl[wsN/sN, wiN/iN]) →
        ck, lvl := (ck ⁀ ⟨wnp⟩), (lvl ⁀ ⟨wl⟩) ;
        |[ var arcS : 𝔽 Arc •
          arcS := enabled (ip.ts, wiN) ;
          do_L1 (arcS ≠ ∅) →
            |[ var arc : Arc; sN : DNode •
              arc := elem (arcS) ;
              arcS := arcS \ { arc } ;
              ( if (arc ≠ ∅) →
                      sN := arcStep (nf.ts, wsN, arc)
                  ▯ (arc = ∅) →
                      sN := wsN
                fi ) ;
              |[ var iNS : 𝔽 Node •
                iNS := arcStep (ip.ts, wiN, arc) ;
                do_L2 (iNS ≠ ∅) →
                  |[ var iN : Node •
                    iN := elem (iNS) ;
                    iNS := iNS \ { iN } ;
                    ( if ((sN, iN) ∈ ran pd ∪ ran ck) →
                            Skip
                        ▯ ((sN, iN) ∉ ran pd ∪ ran ck) →
                            pd := pd ⁀ ⟨(sN, iN)⟩
                      fi )
                  ]|
                od
              ]|
            ]|
          od
        ]|
    fi
  od
```

Fig. 3. Sequential witness search algorithm

not documented, to the extent of our knowledge. In FDR's algorithm description [19], it is mentioned that the elements of *pd* and *ck* are disjoint. Because of the mechanisation of proof obligations, these well-known and some other facts must be formally specified. For instance, we need to precisely include obvious facts not mentioned in [19], such as: (i) all node pairs in *ck* and *pd* are valid (or are part of) the automaton of S and I; (ii) all node pairs in *ck* are compatible in the chosen model (*GenVl*); (iii) node pairs from *ck* and *pd* can only come from the product automata of S and I, and not any valid node pair from other automata; and so on.

There are, however, some not entirely obvious facts as well. They must be clearly stated, otherwise the proof obligations cannot be mechanically discharged. We see this as a very interesting contribution to the field of refinement model checking. These facts are mostly related to the normalisation of S that occurs at the preparation process (see Figure 2), the various relationships between the witnesses found and the data structures used in the sequential search, and about loop invariants.

Normalisation properties. During normalisation, the automaton of S is transformed to become deterministic and free of silent transitions. Among other reasons, this is useful because it makes the sequence of node pairs unique, and hence it enables memory-efficient representation of the search space without compromising its results. Nonetheless, as witness search and normalisation are independent *Circus* processes, we must record that the automata received were built by the operational semantics. Another example is that, since the normal form of S is a deterministic automaton, and elements of pd and ck are disjoint, when the search finishes, the union of elements from pd and ck must be the size of the product automata of S and I. In this way, we ensure that all node pairs are checked, hence a precise characterisation of search exhaustiveness is given.

Witness properties related to the sequential state. As pd and ck belong to the product automata of S and I, and the normalisation guarantees the search paths to be unique, node pairs from witnesses already found can never appear as pending. Furthermore, valid node pairs in the product automata that have not yet being searched (*i.e.,* they are neither pending nor checked), can never be part of any witnesses that have already been found. These facts are included in the last predicates of $SeqRSState$.

Properties of the main loop. Let us explain the invariant, guard, and variant of each labelled loop from Figure 3. With application of appropriate laws and further simplifications, the main loop (L_0) invariant is reduced to the sequential state invariant already presented in schema $SeqRSState$. That is not surprising as we moved the algorithm main variables to the state on purpose at the beginning, in order to have the main loop invariant clear from the state invariant itself. This is crucial for concentrating the proof effort at one hard/difficult point, whereas the remaining proofs become simpler. The main loop guard defines the termination condition for the algorithm as

$$\#swts < wr \land \neg pd = \langle\rangle$$

which means that either enough witnesses have been found, or there are no more pending pairs to be checked. It has been previously introduced by strengthening the postcondition right after initialisation of the corresponding variables via assignment. The main loop variant is defined as

$$(PS\,(nf, ip) - \#ck) + (wr - \#swts)$$

because only ck or $swts$ will increase at each iteration but not both, as every valid node pair being searched is either compatible or not. As a loop variant is an integer expression whose value is strictly decreased by the loop body, we need to find the boundaries for both ck and $swts$. The checking sequence is bound by the product size of both automata ($PS\,(nf, ip) \in \mathbb{N}_1$), as we can never check more than what is available, whereas the set of witnesses is bound by the number requested on wr. Moreover, pd cannot be used in the variant because it may not vary at every iteration.

Properties of loop L_1. The next loop encodes the search for successor pairs from a compatible node pair. As each arc from the set of enabled arcs (*enabled*) is being explored, we need to establish via the assignment that the following properties about arcs hold

$$arcS \subseteq enabled\,(ip.ts, wiN) \land$$
$$(\forall\, a : Arc \mid a \in arcS \bullet \neg arcStep\,(ip.ts, wiN, a) = \varnothing\,)$$

That is, subset containment with respect to the operational semantics (*enabled*) guarantees that exploring new arcs ($arcS$) preserves the amount remaining to be searched, and valid normal form nodes have no silent transitions. This forms part of the loop invariant. Moreover, after the assignment on $arcS$, we also establish the new properties about a compatible working node pair (wnp)

$$\neg wnp \in \operatorname{ran} pd \land wnp \in \operatorname{ran} ck \land$$
$$(\forall\, w : Witness \mid w \in swts \bullet \neg\, wnp \in \operatorname{ran} w.1)$$

That is, wnp is not pending, has already been checked, and cannot be part of any witnesses previously found. This is also important for re-establishing the main loop invariant, as well as make both loops L_0 and L_1 work. They are dischargeable because the normal form is unique, the injective sequences (pd and ck) are disjoint, and because of the witness properties related to the sequential state and witness invariant mentioned above. Finally, the invariant of L_1 is given in four parts: (i) the guard from the alternation ensuring the working node pair is compatible ($\neg\, GenVl[wsN/sN, wiN/iN]$); (ii) a simplified version of the state invariant (*SeqRSState*) with information about well-formed witnesses removed, as to search for successors it is irrelevant; (iii) the new properties of the working node pair after the update of ck; and (iv) the properties of $arcS$ just mentioned. Also, since we use the cardinality of $arcS$ as the variant, $arcS$ must be finite. The loop guard is given as ($arcS \neq \varnothing$), and the variant is $\#\, arcS$.

Properties of loop L_2. The final part of the algorithm is the possible inclusion of new successor pairs as pending, whenever they have not been already checked. We need to iterate over the set of reachable implementation nodes (iNS) to form new node pairs (sN, iN), where the normal form node (sN) has already been fixed. Loop L_2 has the invariant of L_1 conjoined with the property about iNS

$$iNS \subseteq arcStep\,(ip.ts, wiN, arc)$$

which is dischargeable as the nodes in *iNS* are reaches from *arcS enabled* by the operational semantics. Finally, the guard of L_2 is $(iNS \neq \varnothing)$, whereas the variant is $\# iNS$.

These, and other properties that were found throughout the mechanical formalisation process, have proved the whole idea of applying formal methods in the development of formal tools worthwhile for this case study. Although mechanisation can incur some burden and time constraints, in the longer run, we believe it to be indispensable in discovering information that is crucial for correctness, and a better understanding of the problem at hand.

Translation into JML

At last, we translate the various predicates representing different properties of the algorithm into JML notation. They appear as comments in the Java code that implements the algorithm in Figure 3.

As the proof obligations normally come from specification statements, it is usually straightforward to translate, because JML allows pre and postconditions on methods as special predicates directly, as the *requires* and *ensures* clauses of JML annotations, respectively. Similarly, the JML *assignable* clause is a direct representation of the specification statement frame.

It is more challenging to translate the loop invariants. At the time when this case study was performed, the JML documentation and language support for encoding loop invariants was not as thorough as it is today, where the available annotations are better documented and supported by the JML tools. Because of that, we needed to provide an intermediate solution: the predicate's annotation and the algorithm's code were scattered into various methods of Java inner classes, so that the frame, pre and postconditions could be precisely specified at each different stage. Nonetheless, although this specifies/documents the problem precisely, it unfortunately complicates the code. Furthermore, the lack of Z toolkit definitions within the available JML data structures, such as injective sequences, also limited this translation effort altogether.

Some Benchmarks

In total, the whole formalisation effort in the development of the *Circus* model checker is summarised in Table 1. It includes: (i) an extended Z toolkit to handle finiteness and injections better; (ii) the automata theory for *PTS*; (iii) the normalisation, divergence checking, refinement search, and debugger *Circus* specifications; and (iv) the refinement proofs for the derivation of the sequential witness search algorithm.

The complete process took one person working full-time for around one whole year. For the algorithm derivation alone, we applied around 101 refinement laws, which generated 42 proof obligations, including: (i) 14 trivial proofs discharged directly by Z/Eves; (ii) 12 easy proofs with (possibly lengthy) straightforward manipulations; (iii) 10 hard proofs usually depending on case analysis and Z/Eves rules; and (iv) 6 difficult proofs that exposed most of the inconsistencies in the automata theory, and in the formal definitions.

Although the number of Z/Eves automation theorems is high, they are repetitive and straightforward to prove. Also, many of the given theorems are in fact

Table 1. Summary of formal declarations for *Circus* model checker

Formal item	Ext. Z toolkit	PTS theory	Normal form	Div. check	Ref. search	Debugger	Total
Abbrev.	2	15	0	0	3	2	**22**
Given sets	0	2	0	0	0	1	**3**
Free types	0	2	0	0	4	0	**6**
Ax. defs.	0	16	6	0	6	1	**29**
Gen. defs.	10	7	0	0	0	0	**17**
Schemas	0	8	4	6	108	8	**134**
Z/Eves rules	81	191	18	5	90	12	**397**
Lemmas	14	24	0	0	73	0	**111**
Theorems	11	44	5	1	25	1	**87**
Proof scripts	103	259	23	6	214	1	**606**
Domain checks	3	25	7	0	43	0	**78**
Channels	—	—	3	3	6	2	**14**
Actions	—	—	3	7	25	9	**44**
Variables	—	—	0	0	14	1	**15**
Total	**224**	**593**	**69**	**28**	**611**	**38**	**1563**

specification statements and proof obligations encoded as schemas by our automation strategy. To the extent of our knowledge, this code derivation is the biggest case study in the application of ZRC, and one of the few related to the development of a formal tool.

5 Conclusion

We expect the experiences shown in this case study to motivate the application of formal specification and verification, both in theory and practice, for tools aimed at formal verification, as well as computer systems in general. We advocate the use of mechanical proof throughout formal specification and verification.

We believe that formalisation plays a crucial role in increasing the integrity levels of the model checker through a combination of techniques. Together with the refinement algorithm and the architecture, the operational semantics and the underlying automata theory are also formally defined. Throughout the development process, Z/Eves was used to discharge proof obligations from the algorithm derivation, animate the operational semantics, prove properties of the theory of automata, and so on. In this process we presented a recipe showing how to use a theorem prover to discharge proof obligations generated by the application of the *Circus* refinement calculus.

This sort of bootstrapping, where we have used *Circus* to specify and refine its own model checker, allows us to find early design flaws, as well as to ensure the algorithm is correct by construction. For instance, the various properties about witnesses, pending, and checking sequences, enabled us to properly understand why some witnesses could not be properly interpreted by the debugger process due to lack of information. Moreover, to bridge the gap between formal specification and actual code, we use JML annotations to document our findings at the level of the Java code. Thus, important properties, such as loop invariants, are precisely documented and amenable to further verification. This exercise of taking our own medicine shows how one can go from an abstract formal specification to code mechanically, hence gathering the knowledge to step forward on the roadmap for building formal verification tools formally. In this process, we found not only bugs, but also unkonwn/undocumented important properties.

Foreseeable extensions to the work are a formal derivation from the abstract specification of witness search to a parallel refinement model checking algorithm. Apart from concurrency complexity, there is a further burden while integrating theorem proving and model checking in a parallel setting, such as dependencies between their results. Another interesting work is to extend the JML type system to include most of the Z toolkit, hence enabling more Z specifications to be translated and analysed by JML tools. At this point, an automated translation tool could be created, in the spirit of another interesting tool that already partially converts B to JML [13].

References

[1] Ralph-Johan Back and Joakim von Wright. *Refinement Calculus: A Systematic Introduction.* Graduate Text in Computer Science. Springer-Verlag, 1998.

[2] J. C. Bicarregui, C. A. R. Hoare, and J. C. P. Woodcock. The Verified Software Repository: a Step Towards the Verifying Compiler. UK Grand Challenge for Computer Research, Steering Committee, 2004.

[3] Christie Bolton and Gavin Lowe. A Hierachy of Failures-Based Models: Theory and Application. *Theoretical Computer Science Journal*, June 2004.

[4] Lilian Burdy, Yoonsik Cheon, David R. Cok, Michael D. Ernst, Joseph R. Kiniry, Gary T. Leavens, K. Rustan M. Leino, and Erik Poll. An Overview of JML Tools and Applications. In *Eighth International Workshop on Formal Methods for Industrial Critical Systems (FMICS)*, Electronic Notes in Theoretical Computer Science, pages 73–89. University of Nijmegen, Elsevier, March 2003.

[5] A. L. C. Cavalcanti and J. C. P. Woodcock. *ZRC—A Refinement Calculus for Z.* Formal Aspects of Computing Journal, 10(3):267–289, 1999.

[6] A. L. C. Cavalcanti and A. C. A. Sampaio and J. C. P. Woodcock. *A Refinement Strategy for Circus.* Formal Aspects of Computing Journal, 15(2-3):146–181, 2003.

[7] Escher Technologies. *Perferct Developer User's Guide, v.3.0, 2004.* Available on-line at `www.eschertech.com/product_documentation/UserGuide.htm`

[8] M. Goldsmith. *FDR2 Manual (v2.82).* Formal Systems (Europe) Ltd., June 2005.

[9] C. A. R. Hoare. *Communicating Sequential Process.* International Series in Computer Science. Prentice-Hall, 1985.

[10] C. A. R. Hoare and He Jifeng. *Unifying Theories of Programming.* International Series in Computer Science. Prentice-Hall, 1998.

[11] Leo Freitas. *Model Checking Circus.* PhD thesis, Univeristy of York, October 2005.

[12] C.B. Jones, K.D. Jones, P.A. Lindsay, and R. Moore. **Mural**: *a Formal Development Support System.* Springer-Verlang, 1991. ISBN: 3-540-19651-X.

[13] Petra Malik and Mark Utting. CZT: A Framework for Z Tools. In Helen Treharne, Steve King, Martin Henson, and Steve Schneider, editors, *ZB 2005: Formal Specification and Development in Z and B: 4th International Conference of B and Z Users, Guildford, UK*, pages 13–15. Springer-Verlag, April 2005.

[14] J. M. R. Martin and Y. Huddart. Parallel Algorithms for Deadlock and Livelock Analysis of Concurrent Systems. *Communicating Process Architectures*, 2000.

[15] Carroll Morgan. *Programming from Specifications.* Prentice-Hall, 1994.

[16] M. V.M. Oliveira and M. A. Xavier and A. L. C. Cavalcanti. *Refine and Gabriel: Support for Refinement and Tactics.* In J. R. Cuellar and Z. Liu editors, *2nd IEEE International Conference on Software Engineering and Formal Methods*, pages 310–319. IEEE Computer Society Press, 2004.

[17] Marcel Oliveira. *Formal Derivation of State-Rich Reactive Programs using* Circus. PhD thesis, University of York, 2006.

[18] Peter Ryan, Steve Schneider, Bill Roscoe, Michael Goldsmith, and Gave Lowe. *Modelling and Analysis of Security Protocols.* Addison Wesley, 2001.

[19] A. W. Roscoe. *Model Checking CSP* in *A Classical Mind: Essays in Honour of C. A. R. Hoare.* International Series in Computer Science. Prentice-Hall, 1994. Chapter 21, pages 353–378.

[20] A. W. Roscoe. *The Theory and Practice of Concurrency.* Prentice-Hall, 1997.

[21] Mark Saaltink. *Z/Eves 2.0 User's Guide.* ORA Canada, 1999.

[22] Jim Woodcock and Jim Davies. *Using Z: Specification, Refinement, and Proof.* International Series in Computer Science. Prentice-Hall, 1996.

[23] J. C. P. Woodcock and A. L. C. Cavalcanti. *The Semantics of* Circus. In D. Bert and J. P. Bowen and M. C. Henson and K. Robinson, editors, *ZB 2002: Formal Specification and Development in Z and B*, number 2272 in Lecture Notes in Computer Science, pages 184–203, Springer-Verlag, 2002.

Discovering Likely Method Specifications

Nikolai Tillmann[1], Feng Chen[2], and Wolfram Schulte[1]

[1] Microsoft Research, One Microsoft Way, Redmond, Washington, USA
{nikolait, schulte}@microsoft.com
[2] University of Illinois at Urbana-Champaign, Urbana, Illinois, USA
fengchen@cs.uiuc.edu

Abstract. Software specifications are of great use for more rigorous software development. They are useful for formal verification and automated testing, and they improve program understanding. In practice, specifications often do not exist and developers write software in an ad-hoc fashion. We describe a new way to automatically infer specifications from code. Our approach infers a likely specification for any method such that the method's behavior, i.e., its effect on the state and possible result values, is summarized and expressed in terms of some other methods. We use symbolic execution to analyze and relate the behaviors of the considered methods. In our experiences, the resulting likely specifications are compact and human-understandable. They can be examined by the user, used as input to program verification systems, or as input for test generation tools for validation. We implemented the technique for .NET programs in a tool called Axiom Meister. It inferred concise specifications for base classes of the .NET platform and found flaws in the design of a new library.

1 Introduction

Specifications play an important role in software verification. In formal verification the correctness of an implementation is proved or disproved with respect to a specification. In automated testing a specification can be used for guiding test generation and checking the correctness of test executions. Most importantly specifications summarize important properties of a particular implementation on a higher abstraction level. They are necessary for program understanding, and facilitate code reviews. However, specifications often do not exist in practice, whereas code is abundant. Therefore, finding ways to obtain likely specifications from code is highly desired if we ever want to make specifications a first class artifact of software development.

Mechanical specification inference from code can only be as good as the code. A user can only expect good inferred specifications if the code serves its purpose most of the time and does not crash too often. Of course, faithfully inferred specifications would reflect flaws in the implementation. Thus, human-friendly inferred specifications can even facilitate debugging on an abstract level.

Several studies on specification inference have been carried out. The main efforts can be classified into two categories, static analysis, e.g., [16,15,14], and dynamic analysis, e.g., [13,19]. The former tries to understand the semantics of the program by analyzing its structure, i.e., treating the program as a white-box; the latter considers the implementation as a black box and infers abstract properties by observations of program runs. In

Z. Liu and J. He (Eds.): ICFEM 2006, LNCS 4260, pp. 717–736, 2006.

this article we present a new technique to infer specifications which tries to combine the strengths of both worlds. We use symbolic execution, a white box technique, to explore the behaviors of the implementation as thoroughly as possible; then we apply observational abstraction to summarize explored behaviors into compact axioms that treat the implementation as a black box.

We applied the technique to infer specifications for implementations of abstract data types (ADTs) whose operations are given as a set of *methods*, for example, the public methods of a class in C#. The technique infers a likely specification of one method, called the *modifier method*, by summarizing its behavior, e.g. its effect on the state and its result value, using other available methods, called *observer methods*. Interestingly, our technique does neither require that the modifier methods changes the state nor that observer methods do not change it.

The inferred specifications are highly abstract and human beings can review them. In many cases, they describe all behaviors of the summarized method. For example, our tool, called Axiom Meister, infers the following specification for the `Add` method of the BCL `Hashtable` class using the observer methods `ContainsKey`, the property `Count` and the indexer property `[]`.

```
void Add(object key, object value)
  requires key != null otherwise ArgumentNullException;
  requires !ContainsKey(key) otherwise ArgumentException;
  ensures ContainsKey(key);
  ensures value == this[key];
  ensures Count == old(Count) + 1;
```

Our technique obtains such a specification in three steps, illustrated in Figure 1.

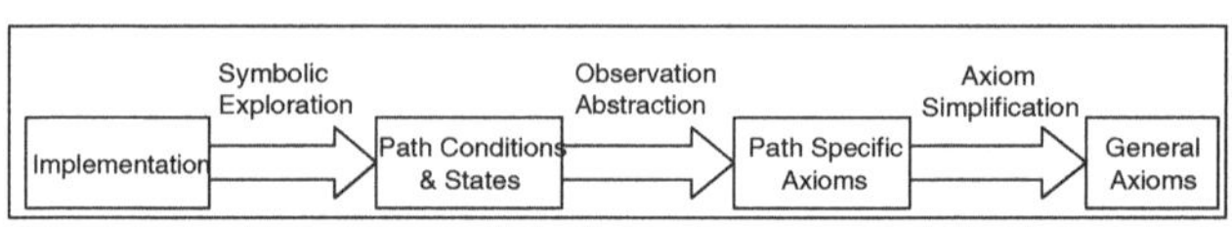

Fig. 1. Overview of the Specification Inference Process

Firstly, we symbolically execute the modifier method from an arbitrary symbolic state with arbitrary arguments. We assume single-threaded, sequential execution. Symbolic execution attempts to explore all possible execution paths. Each path is characterized by a set of constraints on the inputs called the *path condition*. The inputs include the arguments of the method as well as the initial state of the heap. The number of paths may be infinite if the method contains loops or employs recursion. Our approach selects a finite set of execution paths by unrolling loops and unfolding recursion only a limited number of times. A path may terminate normally or have an exceptional result.

Secondly, we evaluate observer methods to find an observational abstraction of the path conditions which may contain constraints referring to the private state of the implementation. Specifications must abstract from such implementation details. Observer methods are used to obtain a representation of the path conditions on a higher abstraction level. This step yields many path-specific axioms, each describing the behavior of the method under certain conditions, in terms of the observer methods.

Thirdly, we merge the collected path-specific axioms (to build comprehensive descriptions of behaviors from different cases), simplify them (to make the specification more concise), and generalize them (to eliminate concrete values inserted by loop unfolding).

The contributions of our paper are:

- We introduce a new technique for inferring formal specifications automatically. It uses symbolic execution for the exploration of a modifier method and it summarizes the results of the exploration using observer methods.
- In certain cases it can detect defective interface designs, i.e., insufficient observer methods. We show an example in Section 5 that we found when we applied our technique on code currently being developed at Microsoft.
- We can represent the inferred specifications as traditional Spec# [7] pre- and postconditions or as parameterized unit tests [26].
- We present a prototype implementation of our technique, Axiom Meister, which infers specifications for .NET and finds flaws in class designs.

The rest of this paper is organized as follows. Section 2 presents an illustrative example describing our algorithm to infer axioms, and gives an overview of symbolic execution. Section 3 describes the main steps of our technique. Section 4 discusses the heuristics we have found useful in more detail. Section 5 discusses features and limitations. Section 6 contains a brief introduction to Axiom Meister. Section 7 presents our initial experience of applying the technique on various classes. Section 8 discusses related work, and Section 9 future work.

2 Overview

We will illustrate our inference technique for an implementation of a bounded set of nonzero integers (Figure 2). Its public interface contains the methods `Add`, `IsFull`, and `Contains`. The nonzero elements of the `repr` are the elements of the set.

Here is a reasonable specification of the `Add` method in the syntax of Spec#'s pre- and postconditions [7], using `IsFull` and Contains as observer methods.

```
void Add(int x)
  requires x != 0                       otherwise ArgumentException;
  requires !Contains(x) && !IsFull()    otherwise InvalidOperationException;
  ensures Contains(x);
```

Each `requires` clause specifies a precondition. Violations of preconditions cause exceptions of certain types. `requires` and `ensures` clauses are checked sequentially, e.g., `!IsFull() && !Contains(x)` will only be checked if `x!=0`. Only if all preconditions hold we can be sure that the method will not throw an exception and that the `ensures` clause's condition will hold after the method has returned.

We can also write an equivalent specification in the form of independent implications, which we call *axioms*:

$$\texttt{x==0} \Rightarrow \textit{future}(\texttt{ArgumentException})$$
$$\texttt{x!=0} \wedge (\texttt{Contains(x)} \vee \texttt{IsFull()}) \Rightarrow \textit{future}(\texttt{InvalidOperationException})$$
$$\texttt{x!=0} \wedge \neg\texttt{Contains(x)} \wedge \neg\texttt{IsFull()} \Rightarrow \textit{future}(\texttt{Contains(x)})$$

```
public class Set {
  int[] repr;
  public Set(int maxSize) { repr = new int[maxSize]; }

  public void Add(int x) {
    if (x == 0) throw new ArgumentException();
    int free = -1;
    for (int i = 0; i < repr.Length; i++)
      if (repr[i] == 0) free = i;                              // remember index
      else if (repr[i] == x) throw new InvalidOperationException(); // duplicate
    if (free != -1) repr[free] = x;                              // success
    else throw new InvalidOperationException(); // no free slot means we are full
  }

  public bool IsFull() {
    for (int i = 0; i < repr.Length; i++) if (repr[i] == 0) return false;
    return true;
  }

  public bool Contains(int x) {
    if (x == 0) throw new ArgumentException();
    for (int i = 0; i < repr.Length; i++) if (repr[i] == x) return true;
    return false;
  }
}
```

Fig. 2. Implementation of a set

Here we used the expression *future*(_) to wrap conditions that will hold and exceptions that will be thrown when the method returns. We will later formalize such axioms.

It is easy to see that the program and the specification agree:

The `Add` method first checks if `x` is not zero, and throws an exception otherwise. Next, the method iterates through a loop, guaranteeing that the `repr` array does not contain `x` yet. The expression `!Contains(x)` checks the same condition. If the set already contains the element, `Add` throws an exception.

As part of the iteration, `Add` stores the index of a free slot in the `repr` array. After the loop, it checks if a free slot has indeed been found. `!IsFull()` checks the same condition. If the set contains no free slot, `Add` throws an exception.

Finally, `Add` stores the element in the `repr` array's free slot, so that `Contains(x)` will return `true` afterwards.

2.1 Symbolic Exploration

Our automated technique uses symbolic execution [20] to obtain an abstract representation of the behavior of the program. A detailed description of symbolic execution of object oriented programs is out of the scope of this paper, and we refer the interested reader to [17] for more discussion. Here we only briefly illustrate the process by comparing it to normal execution.

Consider symbolic execution of a method with parameters. Instead of supplying normal inputs, e.g., concrete numeric values, symbolic execution supplies symbols that represent arbitrary values. Symbolic execution proceeds like normal execution except that the computed values may be terms over the input symbols, employing interpreted functions that correspond to the machine's operations. For example, Figure 3 contains terms arising from during the execution of the `Add` method in elliptic nodes. The terms are built over the input symbols `me`, representing the implicit receiver argument, and `x`.

The terms employ the interpreted functions, including `!=`, `==`, `<`, selection of a field, and array access.

Symbolic execution records the conditions that determine the execution path. The conditions are Boolean terms over the input symbols. The path condition is the conjunction of all individual conditions along a path. For example, when symbolic execution reaches the first *if*-statement of the `Add` method, it will continue by exploring two execution paths separately. It conjoins the *if*-condition to the path condition of the *then*-path and the negated condition to the path condition of the *else*-path. Note that some branches are implicit, for example, accessing an object member might raise an exception if the object reference is `null`, and accessing an array element might fail if the index is out-of-bounds.

Not all potential execution paths are feasible. For example, after successfully accessing an object member, any subsequent member access on the same object will never fail. We use an automatic theorem prover to prune infeasible path conditions. Figure 3 shows a tree representing all feasible execution paths of `Add` up to a certain length. A path condition has a conjunct $c = v$ iff the path includes an arc labeled v from a node labeled with condition c. The figure omits arcs belonging to infeasible paths. It also omits nodes with only one outgoing arc.

The diamond nodes S2, S8, S15, S16, S23, and S24 are ends of paths that throw exceptions, and S4 and S6 represent paths terminating with errors caused by the accesses of an object member using a `null` reference. The rectangular node S14 represents a path with normal termination of the `Add` method.

2.2 Discovering Specifications from Paths

For each path, symbolic execution derives the path condition and a final program state. We could declare this knowledge as the method's specification. However, it would not be a good specification: While some of the conditions shown in Figure 3 are simple expression, e.g., `x!=0`, most expressions involve details that should be hidden from the user, like the `repr` array. And even though there are many different cases with detailed information, it is not even a complete description of the `Add` method's behavior, because symbolic exploration stopped unfolding the loop at some point. While the partial execution tree might be useful for the developer of the `Set` class, the information is simply at the wrong level of abstraction for a user of the class, who is only interested in the public interface of the ADT.

We use observational abstraction to transform the information obtained by symbolic execution into a specification, i.e., we will try to express the implementation-level conditions of the explored paths with equivalent observations that we can make on the level of the class interface. Before we discuss the general process, we will go through the steps of our technique for our example.

Consider the paths to S4 and S6 in Figure 3. They terminate with a `null` dereference error, because either `me` or `me.repr` was `null`. Symbolic execution found these paths because it started with no assumptions about the `me` argument or the values of fields. However, C# semantics preclude a call to an instance-method using a `null`-receiver, and the constructor of the `Set` class will initialize the `repr` field with a proper array. Thus, we can safely ignore the paths S4 and S6.

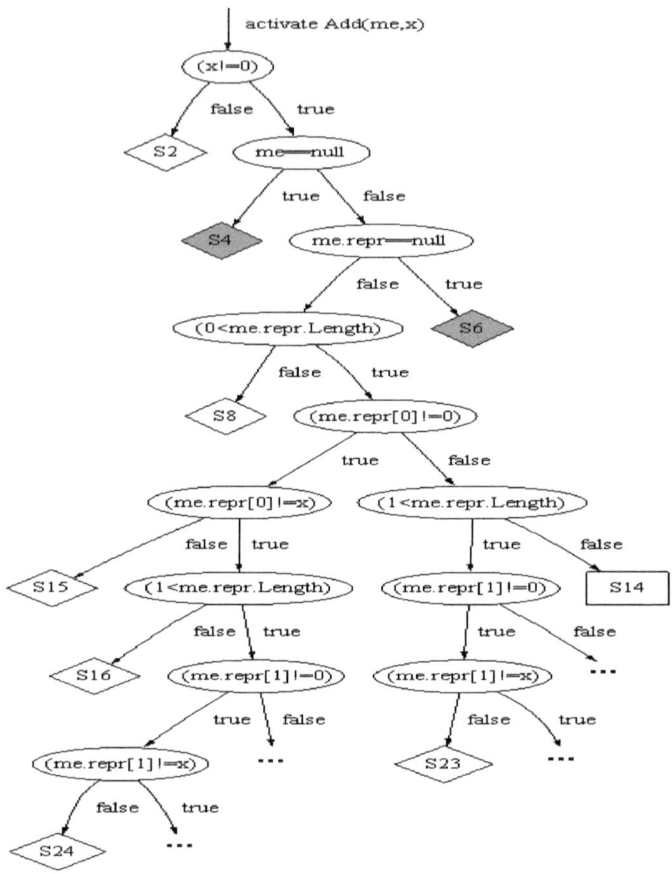

Fig. 3. Tree representation of feasible execution paths of `Set.Add` up to a certain length. See Subsection 2.1 for a detailed description.

Consider the path to S2. If `x` is zero, `Add` throws an exception. Since `x` is not private to the class, no further abstraction is necessary. We get the following precondition.

```
requires x != 0        otherwise ArgumentException;
```

Consider the paths to S15, S23 and S24. They all terminate with the same exception. In each path, the last condition establishes that `x` is equal to some element of the `repr` array. For all such `x`, `Contains(x)` clearly returns `true`. Using this characteristic behavior of `Contains`, we can summarize the paths as follows

```
requires !Contains(x) otherwise InvalidOperationException;
```

Consider the path to S8. Along the way we have `me!=null`, `me.repr!=null` and `0>=me.repr.Length`. It is easy to see that under these conditions the `IsFull` method returns `true`. Later, we will obtain this result automatically by symbolically executing `IsFull` under the constraint of path S8. The conditions along the path to S16 are more involved; they describe the case where the `repr` array has length one and its element is nonzero. Again, `IsFull` also returns `true` under these conditions. Using this characteristic behavior of `IsFull`, we deduce:

```
requires !IsFull() otherwise InvalidOperationException;
```

We can combine the last two findings into a single `requires` clause since they have the same exception types:

```
requires !Contains(x) && !IsFull() otherwise InvalidOperationException;
```

Finally consider S14, the only normally terminating path. Its path condition implies that the `repr` array has size one and contains the value zero. Under these conditions, `IsFull` and `Contains` return `false`. (Note that when inferring preconditions, we only impose the path conditions, but do not take into account any state updates that the `Add` might perform.)

We can also deduce postconditions. Consider `Contains` under the path condition of S14 with the same arguments as `Add`, but starting with the heap that is the result of the updates performed along the path to S14. In this path the loop of `Add` finds an empty slot in the array in the first loop iteration, and then the method updates `me.repr[0]` to `x`, which will be reflected in the resulting heap. Operating on this resulting heap, `Contains(x)` returns `true`: the set now contains the added element. Consider `IsFull` under the path condition of S14 with the resulting heap. It will also return `true`, because the path condition implies that the array has length one, and in the resulting heap we have `me.repr[0]==x` where `x` is not zero according to the path condition.

After the paths we have seen so far, we are tempted to deduce that the postcondition for the normal termination of `me.Add(x)` is `Contains(x) && IsFull()`. However, when symbolic execution explores longer paths, which are not shown in Figure 3, we will quickly find another normal termination path whose path condition implies `x!=0`, with the `repr` array of size two and containing only zeros. Under these conditions, `IsFull` and `Contains` return `false` initially, the same as for S14. But for this new path, `IsFull` will remain `false` after `Add` returns since `Add` only fills up the first element of the array. Thus, the deduced postcondition will be `Contains(x) && (IsFull() || !IsFull())`, which simplifies to `Contains(x)`, in Spec#:

```
ensures Contains(x);
```

Combined, we obtain exactly the entire specification of `Add` given at the beginning. In our experiments on the .NET base class library the inferred specifications are often as concise and complete as carefully hand-written ones.

3 Technique

We fix a modifier method and a set of observer methods for this section.

3.1 Exploration of Modifier Method

As discussed in Section 2.1, we first symbolically explore a finite set of execution paths of the modifier method. Since the number of execution paths might be infinite in the presence of loops or recursion, we unroll loops und unfold recursion only a limited number of times.

3.2 Observational Abstraction

The building stones of our specifications are observations at the level of the class interface. The observations we have constructed for our example in Section 2 consisted of calls to observer methods, e.g., `Contains`, with certain arguments, e.g., `me` and `x`. In this subsection, we introduce the concepts of observer terms and observer equations which represent such observations, and we describe how we build path-specific axioms using observations.

We described in Section 2.1 how symbolic execution derives terms to represent state values and branch conditions. Consider Figure 3. While it mentions `me` explicitly, it omits another essential implicit argument: the heap. The (updated) heap is also an implicit result of each method. We view the heap as a mapping of object references to the values of their fields or array elements. Every access and update of a field or array element implicitly involves the heap. We denote the initial heap by h, and the updated heap after the method call by h'.

We extend the universe of function symbols by functions for observer methods. We write the function symbol of a method in italics. For example, the term representing the invocation `me.Contains(x)` in the initial heap h is $\mathit{Contains}(h, \mathit{me}, x)$. We write all input symbols in cursive.

The arguments are not necessarily plain input symbols, but can be terms themselves. Consider for example a method `int f(int x)`, then we can construct arbitrarily nested terms of the form $f(h, \mathit{me}, f(h, \mathit{me}, \ldots))$. We call terms over the extended universe of function symbols *observer terms*, as opposed to *ordinary terms*.

Observer equations are equations over observer terms. A *proper observer equation* does not contain heap-access subterms, e.g., field selection terms or array update terms. An example of a proper observer equation is $\mathit{Contains}(h, \mathit{me}, x) = \mathbf{true}$. In the following, we use shorthand notations for simple equations, e.g. x for $x = \mathbf{true}$, $\neg x$ for $x = \mathbf{false}$, and $x \neq y$ for $(x == y) = \mathbf{false}$.

For each explored path of the modifier method, we select a finite set of proper observer equations that is likely equivalent to the path condition. We will discuss our selection strategies in Section 4. We call those equations that do not mention the updated heap h' *(likely) preconditions*, and all other remaining equations *(likely) postconditions*. The implication from a path's preconditions to its postconditions is a *(likely) path-specific axiom*. For example, here is the axiom for path S14 in Figure 3:

$$x \neq 0 \wedge \neg \mathit{IsFull}(h, \mathit{me}) \wedge \neg \mathit{Contains}(h, \mathit{me}, x) \Rightarrow \\ \mathit{Contains}(h', \mathit{me}, x) \wedge \mathit{IsFull}(h', \mathit{me})$$

3.3 Summarizing Axioms

For each explored path of the modifier method we compute a likely path-specific axiom. However, in most cases, the number of explored paths and thus the number of axioms is large. Obviously a human reader prefers a compact description to hundreds of such axioms. So the final step of our specification inference technique is to merge and simplify the path-specific axioms as follows:

1. Disjoin preconditions with the same postconditions
2. Simplify merged preconditions
3. Conjoin postconditions with the same preconditions
4. Simplify merged postconditions

This algorithm computes and simplifies the conjunctions of implications. The order of step 1 and 3 is not strict; changing it might result in equivalent axioms in different representations.

If a path terminates with an exception, we add a symbol representing the type of the exception to the postcondition. Section 5 discusses some exceptions to this rule.

$$\begin{array}{llll}
x = 0 & & & \Rightarrow \textit{ArgumentException} \\
x \neq 0 \wedge & \textit{IsFull}(h, me) \wedge & \neg \textit{Contains}(h, me, x) & \Rightarrow \textit{InvalidOperationException} \\
x \neq 0 \wedge & \neg \textit{IsFull}(h, me) \wedge & \neg \textit{Contains}(h, me, x) & \Rightarrow \textit{IsFull}(h', me) \wedge \textit{Contains}(h', me, x) \\
x \neq 0 \wedge & & \textit{Contains}(h, me, x) & \Rightarrow \textit{InvalidOperationException} \\
x \neq 0 \wedge & \textit{IsFull}(h, me) \wedge & \neg \textit{Contains}(h, me, x) & \Rightarrow \textit{InvalidOperationException} \\
x \neq 0 \wedge & \neg \textit{IsFull}(h, me) \wedge & \textit{Contains}(h, me, x) & \Rightarrow \textit{InvalidOperationException} \\
x \neq 0 \wedge & & \textit{Contains}(h, me, x) & \Rightarrow \textit{InvalidOperationException}
\end{array}$$

Fig. 4. All Path-Specific Axioms for `Set.Add`

$$\begin{array}{ll}
x = 0 & \Rightarrow \textit{ArgumentException} \\
x \neq 0 \wedge (\textit{IsFull}(h, me) \vee \textit{Contains}(h, me, x)) & \Rightarrow \textit{InvalidOperationException} \\
x \neq 0 \wedge \neg \textit{IsFull}(h, me) \wedge \neg \textit{Contains}(h, me, x) & \Rightarrow \textit{IsFull}(h', me) \wedge \textit{Contains}(h', me, x)
\end{array}$$

Fig. 5. Merged and Simplified Axioms for `Set.Add`

Figure 4 shows all path-specific axioms of Figure 3. Figure 5 shows the equivalent merged and simplified axioms. As we discussed in Section 2.2, only when exploring longer execution paths the spurious consequence $\textit{IsFull}(h', me)$ will disappear from the summarized implications in Figure 5.

```
public class Set {
  ...
  public int Count() {
    int count=0;
    for (int i = 0; i < repr.Length; i++) if (repr[i] != 0) count++;
    return count;
  }
}
```

Fig. 6. Implementation of `Set.Count`

Unrolling loops and unfolding recursion sometimes causes a series of concrete values in our axioms. Consider the extension of the bounded set class by a new observer method `Count`, given in Figure 6. The number of execution paths of the `Add` method depends on the number of loop unrollings that also determines the return value of `Count`. As a consequence, our technique infers many path-specific axioms of the following form, where α appears as a concrete number.

$$\ldots \wedge \textit{Count}(h, me) = \alpha \quad \Rightarrow \quad \ldots \wedge \textit{Count}(h', me) = \alpha + 1$$

Before we can merge and simplify these concrete conditions we need to generalize them into more abstract results. In this example, we are able to generalize this series of path-specific axioms by substitution:

$$\ldots \quad \Rightarrow \quad \ldots \wedge Count(h', me) = Count(h, me) + 1$$

We have also implemented the generalization of linear relations over integers.

4 Observational Abstraction Strategies

This section discusses our strategies to select proper observer equations which are likely equivalent to a given path condition. Developing these strategies is a nontrivial task and critical to the quality of inferred specifications. What we describe in this section is the product of our experience.

Since observer equations are built from observer terms, we choose the latter first.

4.1 Choosing Proper Observer Terms

A term representing an observer method call, `m(h, me, x`$_1$`, ..., x`$_n$`)`, involves a function symbol for the observer method, a heap, and arguments including the receiver. In the following we describe our strategies to select such proper observer term.

Choosing observer methods. Intuitively, observer methods should be *observationally pure* [8], i.e., its state changes (if any) must not be visible to a client. Interestingly, this is not a requirement for our technique since we ignore state changes performed by observer methods. However, if the given observer methods are not observationally pure, the resulting specifications might not be intuitive to users, and they might violate requirements of other tools that want to consume our inferred specifications. For example, pre- and postconditions in Spec# may not perform state updates. Automatic observational purity analysis is a non-trivial data flow problem, and it is a problem orthogonal to our specification inference. Our tool allows the user to designate any set of methods as observer methods (Figure 7). By default, it selects all property getters and query methods with suggestive names (e.g. `Get...`), which is sufficient in many cases. Since it is well known that the problem of determining a minimal basis for an axiomatic specification [12] is undecidable, we do not address this problem in our current work. In our experience, the effort of manually selecting a meaningful subset from the suggested observer methods is reasonable with the help of the GUI provided in our interactive tool which requires only a few clicks to remove or add observer methods and re-generate the specification. Our tool also allows the user to include general observer methods that test properties like $\_ =$ **null** which have been found useful [13,19].

Choosing heaps. We are not interested to observe intermediate states during the execution of the modifier method since the client can only make observations before calling the modifier method and after the modifier method has returned. Therefore, we choose only the initial heap h or the final heap h'. The final heap represents all updates that the modifier method performs along a path.

Choosing arguments. Recall that we use symbols representing arbitrary argument values to explore the behaviors of the modifier method. A naive argument selection strategy for an observer method is to also simply choose fresh symbols for all arguments. The following example shows when this strategy fails to detect relationships. Let `x` and `y` be two unrelated symbols, then `Contains(x)` does not provide any useful information about the behavior of `Add(y)`. As a consequence, the only symbols we use to build observer terms are the input symbols of the modifier method. And the constructed terms should be type correct.

However, for some classes this strategy is still too liberal. For example, legacy code written before generic types were available often employs parameters and results whose formal type is `object`, obscuring the assumptions and guarantees on passed values. Similarly, the presented `Set` class uses values of type `int` for two purposes: As elements of the set, e.g. in `void Add(int x)` and `bool Contains(int x)`, and to indicate cardinality, e.g. in `int Count()`.

To reduce the set of considered observer terms, we introduce the concept of *observer term groups*, or short *groups*. We associate each formal parameter and method result with a group. By default, there is one group for each type, and each parameter and result belongs to its type group. Intuitively, groups refine the type system in a way such that the program does not store a value of one group in a location of another group, even if allowed by the type system.

Lackwit [23] is a tool which infers such groups, called *extended types*, automatically for C programs. We want to implement such an analysis for .NET programs in future work. Currently, our tool allows the user to manually annotate parameters and results of methods with grouping information.

We only build group-correct observer terms: The application of an observer-method function belongs to the group of the result of the observer method, all other terms belong to the groups that are compatible with the type of the term, and the argument terms of an observer-method function must belong to the respective formal parameter group.

For example, we can assign the `int` parameters of `Add` and `Contains` to a group called `ELEM`, and the result of `Count` to a group `CARD`. When we instantiate the parameter of `Add` with x, then we will build $Contains(h, me, x)$ as an observer term. However, we will not consider $Contains(h, me, Count(h, me))$.

Also, our tool only builds single-nested observer terms, i.e., $f(g(x))$, and negations and equations over such terms. This has been sufficient in our experience.

4.2 Choosing Proper Observer Equations

It is easy to see how symbolic execution can reduce observer terms to ordinary terms: Just unfold the observer method functions from a given state. For example, the observer term $Contains(x)$ reduces to **true** when symbolically executing `Contains(x)` after `Add(x)`. The reduction is not unique if there is more than one execution path. For example, before calling `Add(x)`, we can reduce $Contains(x)$ to both **true** and **false**.

We fix a path p of the modifier method for the remainder of this subsection. We reduce each chosen proper observer term t relative to p as follows. We symbolically execute the observer method under the path condition of p, i.e. we only consider those paths of the observer method which are consistent with the path condition of p. Again, we only explore a limited number of execution paths. We ignore execution paths of observer methods which terminate with an exception, and thus the reduction may also result in the empty set, in which case we omit the observer term.

For each execution path of the observer method, we further simplify the resulting term using the constraints of the path condition. For example, if the resulting term is $x = 0$ and the path condition contains $x > 0$, we reduce the result to **false**.

If all considered execution paths of the observer method yield the same reduced term, we call the resulting term the *reduced observer term of* t, written as t_R.

Given a finite set T of observer terms, we define the *basic observer equations* as $\{t = t_R : t \in T \text{ where } t_R \text{ exists}\}$. This set characterizes the path p of the modifier method by unambiguous observations. For example, the basic observer equations of S14 in Figure 3 are:

$$\{\ x = 0, \mathit{IsFull}(h, me) = \mathbf{false}, \mathit{Contains}(h, me, x) = \mathbf{false},$$
$$\mathit{Contains}(h', me, x) = \mathbf{true}, \mathit{IsFull}(h', me) = \mathbf{true}\ \}$$

However, the reductions of the observations may refer to fields or arrays in the heap, and a specification should not contain such implementation details. Consider for example a different implementation of the `Set` class where the number of added elements is tracked explicitly in a private field `count`, and the `Count` method simply returns `count`. Then the observer term $\mathit{Count}(h, me)$ reduces to the field access term $me.count$.

We substitute internal details by observer terms wherever possible, and construct the *completed observer equations* as follows. Initially, our completed observer equations are the basic observer equations. Then we repeat the following until the set is saturated: For two completed observer equations $t = t'$ and $u = u'$, we add $t = t'[u'/u]$ to the set of completed observer equations if the term $t'[u'/u]$ contains less heap-access subterms than t.

For example, let h' be equal to the heap for a path where `Add` returns successfully and increments the private field `count` by one, then $\mathit{Count}(h, me)$ reduces to $me.count$ and $\mathit{Count}(h', me)$ to $me.count + 1$ in the initial heap h. Then the completed observer equations will include the equation $\mathit{Count}(h', me) = \mathit{Count}(h, me) + 1$ which no longer refers to the field `count`.

We select the set of observer equations likely equivalent to p's path condition as follows: the completed observer equations less all tautologies and all equations which still refer to fields or arrays in a heap. (This way, all the remaining equations are proper observer equations.)

5 Further Discussion

Detecting insufficient observer methods. When we applied our tool to a code base that is currently under development (a refined DOM implementation [3]), our tool inferred a specification for the method `XElement.RemoveAttribute` that we did not expect.

```
void RemoveAttribute(XAttribute a)
  requires HasAttributes() && a!=null;
  ensures false;
```

This axiom is contradictory. The reason is the set of available observer methods: For some paths, `RemoveAttribute` assumes that the element contains only one attribute, then after removal, `HasAttributes` will be false. For other paths, it assumes that the element contains more than one attribute, which makes `HasAttributes` true after removal. The existing observer methods of the class `XElement` cannot distinguish these two cases. Therefore, for the same preconditions, we may reach two contradictory postconditions. This actually indicates that the class should have more observer methods. We call a set of observer methods *insufficient* if they cause our analysis to derive contradictory postconditions.

Indeed, after adding a new observer method called `AttributesCount` to the class `XElement`, we obtain the following consistent specification where `old(`e`)` denotes the value of e at the entry of the method.

```
void RemoveAttribute(XAttribute a)
  requires HasAttributes() && a!=null;
  ensures old(AttributesCount() > 1) => HasAttributes();
  ensures old(AttributesCount() < 2) => !HasAttributes();
```

This way, our tool examines if a class interface provides sufficiently many observer methods for the user to properly use the class.

Pruning unreachable states. Since we explore the modifier method from an arbitrary state, we might produce some path-specific axioms that have preconditions which are not enabled in any reachable state.

For example, for the .NET `ArrayList` implementation the number of elements in the array list is at most its capacity; a state where the capacity is negative or smaller than the number of contained elements is unreachable. Symbolic execution of a modifier like `Add` will consider all possible initial states, including unreachable states. As a consequence, we may produce specifications which describe cases that can never happen in concrete sequences of method calls. These axioms are likely correct but useless.

Ideally, the class would provide an observer method which describes when a state is reachable. Fortunately, our experiments show that this is usually not necessary. Exploration from unreachable states often results in violations of contracts with the execution environment, e.g., `null` dereferences. Since our approach assumes that the implementation is "correct," our tool prunes such error cases.

Computing the set of reachable states precisely is a hard problem. A good approximation of reachable states are states in which the class-invariant holds. If the class provides a Boolean-valued method that detects invalid program states, our tool will use it to prune invalid states.

Redundancy. Two observations might be equivalent, e.g., `IsEmpty()` is usually equivalent to `Size()==0`. While this may cause some redundancy in the generated specifications, it does not affect the soundness of the specifications. We do not provide an automatic analysis to find an expressive and minimal yet sufficient set of observer methods but leave it to the user to select an appropriate set. As we discussed in Section 4, the required effort of manually selecting observer methods has been reasonable in our experiences.

Limitations. There is an intrinsic limitation in any automatic verification technique of nontrivial programs: there cannot be an automatic theorem prover for all domains. Currently, our exploration is conservative for the symbolic exploration: if the theorem prover cannot decide a path condition's satisfiability, exploration proceeds speculatively. Therefore, it might explore infeasible paths. The consequences for the generated axioms are similar to the ones for unreachable, unpruned states.

Moreover, as mentioned, our technique considers only an exemplary subset of execution paths and observer terms. In particular, we unroll loops and recursion only a certain number of times, but the axioms in terms of the observer methods often abstract from that number, pretending that the number of unrollings is irrelevant. Without precise summaries of loops and recursion, e.g., in the form of annotated loop invariants, we cannot do better. The generalization step introduces another source of errors, since it postulates general relations from exemplary observations using a set of patterns.

While our implementation has the limitations discussed above, in our experience the generated axioms for well-designed ADTs are comprehensive, concise, sound and actually describe the implementation.

6 Implementation

We have implemented our technique in a tool called Axiom Meister. It operates on the methods given in a .NET assembly.

We built Axiom Meister on top of XRT [17], a framework for symbolic execution of .NET programs. XRT represents symbolic states as mappings of locations to terms plus a path condition over symbolic inputs. XRT can handle not only symbols for primitive values like integers, but also for objects. It interprets the instructions of a .NET method to compute a set of successor states for a given state. It uses Simplify [11] or Zap [6] as automatic theorem provers to decide if a path condition is infeasible.

Corresponding to the three steps of the inference process, Axiom Meister consists of three components: the observer generator, the summarization engine, and the simplification engine. The observer generator manages the exploration process. It creates exploration tasks for the modifier and observer methods which it hands down to the XRT framework. From the explored paths it constructs the observation equations, as discussed in Section 4.1. The simplification engine uses Maude [4].

Axiom Meister is configurable to control the execution path explosion problem: The user can control the number of loop unrollings and recursion unfoldings, and the user can control the maximum number of terminating paths that the tool considers. By default, Axiom Meister will terminate the exploration when every loop has been unrolled three times, which often achieves full branch coverage of the modifier method. So far, we had to explore at most 600 terminating paths of any modifier method to create comprehensive axioms.

Axiom Meister can output the inferred specifications as formulas, parameterized unit tests [26], or as Spec# specifications.

The user can control Axiom Meister from the command line and it has a graphical user interface (Figure 7). The user can choose the modifier method to explore, *Hashtable.Add* in this example, and a set of observer methods on the left panel. The

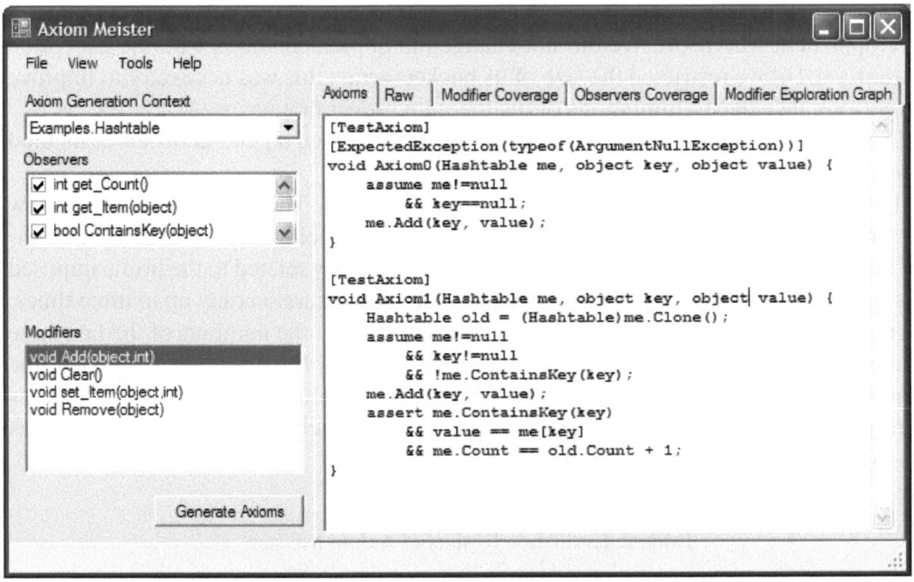

Fig. 7. Screenshot of Axiom Meister

right window shows the generated axioms, here as parameterized unit tests. It also provides views of the modifier exploration tree (Figure 3), and the code coverage of the modifier and observer methods.

7 Evaluation

We have applied Axiom Meister on a number of nontrivial implementations, including several classes of the .NET base class library (BCL), classes from the public domain, as well as classes currently under development by a Microsoft product group.

Table 1. Example Classes for Evaluating Axiom Meister

Class	Modifiers	Observers	LOC	Source
`Stack`	3	3	200	.NET BCL
`BoundedStack`	2	4	160	Other
`ArrayList`	7	6	350	.NET BCL
`LinkedList`	6	4	400	Other
`Hashtable`	5	4	600	.NET BCL
`XElement`	2	3	800	MS internal

Table 1 shows some of the investigated classes along with the numbers of the chosen modifier and observer methods. The LOC column gives the number of lines of non-whitespace, non-comment code. We took `Stack`, `ArrayList` and `Hashtable` from the BCL; `BoundedStack` is a modified version of `Stack` with a bounded size; `LinkedList` from [1] implements a double linked list with an interface similar to

ArrayList; XElement is a class of a refined DOM model [3], which is currently under development at Microsoft. We did not change the implementations with the exception of Hashtable: we restricted the size of its buckets array; this was necessary to improve the performance due to limitations of the theorem prover that we used.

In addition to the regular observer methods, we included a general observer method which checks if a value is null.

Table 2 gives the evaluation results of these examples. The first two columns show the number of explored paths and the time cost to infer specifications for multiple modifier methods of the class. Both measurements are obviously related to the limits imposed on symbolic exploration: exploration unrolls loops and recursion only up to three times. We inspected the inferred specifications by hand to collect the numbers of the last three columns. They illustrate the number of merged and simplified axioms generated, the number of sound axioms, the number of methods for which complete specifications were generated, and the percentage of methods for which full branch coverage was achieved during symbolic execution.

Table 2. Evaluation Results of Axiom Meister

Class	Paths	Time(s)	Axioms	Sound	Complete	Coverage
Stack	7	1.78	6	6	3	100%
BoundedStack	17	0.84	12	12	2	100%
ArrayList	142	28.78	26	26	7	100%
LinkedList	59	9.28	16	13	6	100%
Hashtable	835	276.48	14	14	5	100%
XElement	42	2.76	14	13	2	100%

Most BCL classes are relatively self-contained. They provide sufficient observer methods whereas new classes under development, like XElement, as discussed in Section 5, often do not. In these examples branch coverage was always achieved, and the generated specifications are complete, i.e., they describe all possible behaviors of the modifier method. However, some of the generated specifications are unsound. A missing class invariant causes the unsound axioms for LinkedList, and we discussed the unsound axioms for XElement in Section 5. After adding additional observer methods, we infer sound axioms only.

8 Related Work

Due to the importance of formal specifications for software development, many approaches have been proposed to automatically infer specifications. They can be roughly divided into static analysis and dynamic detection.

8.1 Static Analysis

For reverse engineering Gannod and Cheng [16] proposed to infer detailed specifications by computing the strongest postconditions. But as mentioned, pre/postconditions obtained from analyzing the implementation are usually too detailed to understand and too specific to support program evolution. Gannod and Cheng [15] addressed this deficiency by generalizing the inferred specification, for instance by deleting conjuncts, or adding disjuncts or implications. This is similar to the merging stage of our technique. Their approach requires loop bounds and invariants, both of which must be added manually. There has been some recent progress in inferring invariants using abstract interpretation. Logozzo [22] infers loop invariants while inferring class invariants. The limitation of his approach are the available abstract domains; numerical domains are best studied. The resulting specifications are expressed in terms of the fields of classes. Our technique provides a fully automatic process. Although loops can be handled only partially, in many cases, our loop unrolling has explored enough behavior to deduce reasonable specifications.

Flanagan and Leino [14] present another lightweight verification based tool, named Houdini, to infer ESC/Java annotations from unannotated Java programs. Based on specific property patterns, Houdini conjectures a large number of possible annotations and then uses ESC/Java to verify or refuse each of them. This way it reduces the false alarms produced by ESC/Java and becomes quite scalable. But the ability of this approach is limited by the patterns used. In fact, only simple patterns are feasible, otherwise Houdini generates too many candidate annotations, and consequently it will take a long time for ESC/Java to verify complicated properties. Our technique does not depend on patterns and is able to produce complicated relationship among values.

Taghdiri [25] uses a counterexample-guided refinement process to infer over-approximate specifications for procedures called in the function being verified. In contrast to our approach, Taghdiri aims to approximate the behaviors for the procedures within the caller's context instead of inferring specifications of the procedure.

There are many other static approaches that infer some properties of programs, e.g., shape analysis [24] specifies which object graph the program computes, termination analysis decides which functions provide bounds to prove that a program terminates [10]. All these analyses are too abstract for us; we really wanted to have axioms that describe the precise input/output behavior.

8.2 Dynamic Analysis

Dynamic detection systems discover general properties of a program by learning from its execution traces.

Daikon [13] discovers Hoare-style assertions and loop invariants. It uses a set of invariant patterns and instruments a program to check them at various program points. Numerous applications use Daikon, including test generation [30] and program verification [9]. Its ability is limited by patterns which can be user-defined. We use observer methods instead: they are already part of the class may carry out complicated computations that are hard to encode as patterns, e.g., membership checking. Also, Daikon is not well-suited for automatically inferring conditional invariants. The Java front end of Daikon, Chicory [2], can make observations using pure methods. However, it only supports pure methods without arguments, which are essentially derived variables of the class state. Daikon and our technique have different goals. We focus on inferring pre- and postconditions for methods, whereas Daikon infers invariants.

Groce and Visser [18] recently integrated Daikon [13] into JavaPathFinder [27]. Their main goal is to find the cause of a counterexample produced by the model checker. Their approach compares invariants of executions that lead to errors and those of similar but correct executions. They use Daikon to infer the invariants.

Henkel and Diwan [19] have built a tool to discover algebraic specifications for interfaces of Java classes. Their specifications relate sequences of method invocations. The tool generates many terms as test cases from the class signature. It generalizes the resulting test cases to algebraic specifications. Henkel and Diwan do not support conditional specifications, which are essential for most examples we tried.

Dynamic invariant detection is often restricted by a fixed set of predefined patterns used to express constraints and the code coverage achieved by test runs. Without using patterns, our technique can often detect relationships between the modifier and observer methods from the terms over the input symbols that symbolic execution computes. We also do not need a test suite.

Xie and Notkin [29] recently avoid the problem of inferring preconditions by inferring statistical axioms. Using probabilities they infer which axiom holds how often. But of course, the probabilities are only good with reference to the test set; nevertheless, the results look promising. They use the statistical axioms to guide test generation for common and special cases.

Most of the work on specification mining involves inferring API protocols dynamically. Whaley et al. [28] describe a system to extract component interfaces as finite state machines from execution traces. Other approaches use data mining techniques. For instance Ammons et al. [5] use a learner to infer nondeterministic state machines from traces; similarly, Evans and Yang [31] built Terracotta, a tool to generate regular patterns of method invocations from observed program runs. Li et al. [21] mine the source code to infer programming rules, i.e., usage of related methods and variables, and then detect potential bugs by locating violations of these rules. All these approaches work for different kinds of specifications and our technique complements them.

9 Future Work

Although this paper focuses on examples of classes implementing ADTs, we believe that our technique can be adopted to work for cooperating classes, like collections and their iterators, or subjects and their observers. We intend to address these challenges next. Other future work includes inferring specifications for sequences of modifier methods, inferring grouping information automatically, and inferring class invariants.

Acknowledgements

We thank Wolfgang Grieskamp for many valuable discussions and for his contributions to the Exploring Runtime, XRT, which is the foundation on which we built Axiom Meister. We also thank Tao Xie, who participated in the initial discussions that shaped this work, and Michael D. Ernst for his comments on an early version of this paper. We thank Colin Campbell and Mike Barnett for proof-reading. The work of Feng Chen was conducted while being an intern at Microsoft Research.

References

1. Codeproject. http://www.codeproject.com.
2. Daikon online manual. http://pag.csail.mit.edu/daikon/download/doc/daikon.html.
3. Document object model(DOM). http://www.w3.org/DOM/.
4. Maude. http://maude.cs.uiuc.edu.
5. G. Ammons, R. Bodik, and J. R. Larus. Mining specifications. In *Proc. 29th ACM SIGPLAN-SIGACT Symposium on Principles of Programming Languages*, pages 4–16, 2002.
6. T. Ball, S. Lahiri, and M. Musuvathi. Zap: Automated theorem proving for software analysis. Technical Report MSR-TR-2005-137, Microsoft Research, Redmond, WA, USA, 2005.
7. M. Barnett, R. Leino, and W. Schulte. The Spec# programming system: An overview. In M. Huisman, editor, *Construction and Analysis of Safe, Secure, and Interoperable Smart Devices: International Workshop, CASSIS 2004*, volume 3362 of *LNCS*, pages 49–69, 2005.
8. M. Barnett, D. A. Naumann, W. Schulte, and Q. Sun. 99.44% pure: Useful abstractions in specifications. In *Proc. 6th Workshop on Formal Techniques for Java-like Programs*, June 2004.
9. L. Burdy, Y. Cheon, D. Cok, M. D. Ernst, J. Kiniry, G. T. Leavens, K. R. M. Leino, and E. Poll. An overview of JML tools and applications. *International Journal on Software Tools for Technology Transfer*, 7(3):212–232, June 2005.
10. A. R. Byron Cook, Andreas Podelski. Abstraction-refinement for termination. In *12th International Static Analysis Symposium(SAS'05)*, Sept 2005.
11. D. Detlefs, G. Nelson, and J. Saxe. Simplify: A theorem prover for program checking. Technical Report HPL-2003-148, HP Labs, Palo Alto, CA, USA, 2003.
12. H. Ehrig and B. Mahr. *Fundamentals of Algebraic Specification I.* Springer-Verlag New York, Inc., Secaucus, NJ, USA, 1985.
13. M. D. Ernst, J. Cockrell, W. G. Griswold, and D. Notkin. Dynamically discovering likely program invariants to support program evolution. *IEEE Transactions on Software Engineering*, 27(2):99–123, 2001.
14. C. Flanagan and K. R. M. Leino. Houdini, an annotation assistant for esc/java. In *FME '01: Proceedings of the International Symposium of Formal Methods Europe on Formal Methods for Increasing Software Productivity*, pages 500–517, London, UK, 2001.
15. G. C. Gannod and B. H. C. Cheng. A specification matching based approach to reverse engineering. In *ICSE '99: Proceedings of the 21st international conference on Software engineering*, pages 389–398, Los Alamitos, CA, USA, 1999.
16. G. C. Gannod and B. H. C. Cheng. Strongest postcondition semantics as the formal basis for reverse engineering. In *WCRE '95: Proceedings of the Second Working Conference on Reverse Engineering*, pages 188–197, July 1995.
17. W. Grieskamp, N. Tillmann, and W. Schulte. XRT - Exploring Runtime for .NET - Architecture and Applications. In *SoftMC 2005: Workshop on Software Model Checking*, Electronic Notes in Theoretical Computer Science, July 2005.
18. A. Groce and W. Visser. What went wrong: Explaining counterexamples. In *10th International SPIN Workshop on Model Checking of Software*, pages 121–135, Portland, Oregon, May 9–10, 2003.
19. J. Henkel and A. Diwan. Discovering algebraic specifications from Java classes. In *Proc. 17th European Conference on Object-Oriented Programming*, pages 431–456, 2003.
20. J. C. King. Symbolic execution and program testing. *Commun. ACM*, 19(7):385–394, 1976.
21. Z. Li and Y. Zhou. PR-Miner: Automatically extracting implicit programming rules and detecting violations in large software code. In *13th ACM SIGSOFT Symposium on the Foundations of Software Engineering (FSE'05)*, Sept 2005.

22. F. Logozzo. Automatic inference of class invariants. In *Proceedings of the 5th International Conference on Verification, Model Checking and Abstract Interpretation (VMCAI '04)*, volume 2937 of *Lectures Notes in Computer Science*, Jan. 2004.
23. R. O'Callahan and D. Jackson. Lackwit: a program understanding tool based on type inference. In *ICSE '97: Proceedings of the 19th international conference on Software engineering*, pages 338–348, New York, NY, USA, 1997.
24. M. Sagiv, T. Reps, and R. Wilhelm. Parametric shape analysis via 3-valued logic. *ACM Trans. Program. Lang. Syst.*, 24(3):217–298, 2002.
25. M. Taghdiri. Inferring specifications to detect errors in code. In *19th IEEE International Conference on Automated Software Engineering (ASE'04)*, Sept 2004.
26. N. Tillmann and W. Schulte. Parameterized unit tests. In *Proceedings of the 10th European Software Engineering Conference held jointly with 13th ACM SIGSOFT International Symposium on Foundations of Software Engineering,*, pages 253–262, 2005.
27. W. Visser, K. Havelund, G. Brat, and S. Park. Model checking programs. In *Proc. 15th IEEE International Conference on Automated Software Engineering*, pages 3–12, 2000.
28. J. Whaley, M. C. Martin, and M. S. Lam. Automatic extraction of object-oriented component interfaces. In *Proc. the International Symposium on Software Testing and Analysis*, pages 218–228, 2002.
29. T. Xie and D. Notkin. Automatically identifying special and common unit tests for object-oriented programs. In *Proceedings of the 16th IEEE International Symposium on Software Reliability Engineering (ISSRE 2005)*, November 2005.
30. T. Xie and D. Notkin. Tool-assisted unit test generation and selection based on operational abstractions. *Automated Software Engineering Journal*, 2006.
31. J. Yang and D. Evans. Dynamically inferring temporal properties. In *Proc. the ACM-SIGPLAN-SIGSOFT Workshop on Program Analysis for Software Tools and Engineering*, pages 23–28, 2004.

Time Aware Modelling and Analysis of Multiclocked VLSI Systems

Tomi Westerlund[1,2] and Juha Plosila[2]

[1] Turku Centre for Computer Science
Lemminkäisenkatu 14 A, FI-20520 Turku, Finland
[2] Department of Information Technology, University of Turku
University of Turku, Department of Information Technology, FI-20014 Turku, Finland
{tomi.westerlund, juha.plosila}@utu.fi

Abstract. We introduce a formal, time aware framework for modelling and analysis multiclocked VLSI systems. We define a delay calculus framework for our timed formalism, and, furthermore, constraints with which to confine the correctness of the system under development, not only logically but also with respect to timing characteristics. We give an elaborate definition of the timed formalism, Timed Action Systems, and its delay models. With the timing aware formal development framework it is possible to obtain information of multiclocked VLSI systems already at high abstraction levels as our application, a GALS (globally asynchronous, locally synchronous) system, shows.

Keywords: Timed Action Systems, GALS, formal methods, time.

1 Introduction

The traditional communication schemes are facing the reality of being unable to answer the challenges given by the continuously increasing system complexities and the level of integration. Furthermore, large Systems-on-Chip (SoC) designs need large and power hungry clock distribution network that has been recognised one of the major challenges in modern deep-submicron VLSI designs.

A commonly used method to alleviate the problems indicated above is to use globally asynchronous, locally synchronous (GALS) design method introduced in [7]. Furthermore, by adopting formal methods we gain the capability to specify, design and validate these systems with the benefits of a rigorous mathematical basis. Therefore, in industry and academia the interest towards formal methods and GALS architecture is continuously increasing. The formal basis for our study is provided by the timing information spiced Action Systems, called Timed Action System [24]. The base formalism, Action Systems [3], henceforward called conventional Action Systems, is based on an extended version of Dijkstra's guarded command language [8]. The timing information allows us to model both logical and temporal aspects of multiclocked VLSI systems. One of the benefits on using Timed Action Systems is the ability to use it throughout the design project. However, in this paper we do not cover the synthesis problem of transforming an abstract system specification down to an implementable specification.

The main contribution of this study is the introduction of the delay calculus as well as the definition of constraints that are used to ensure the correct operation of the VLSI

Z. Liu and J. He (Eds.): ICFEM 2006, LNCS 4260, pp. 737–756, 2006.

systems, not only logically but also with respect to temporal properties. We define a constraint that behaves as a *skip* action, an empty statement, if the condition holds, but otherwise as *abort*, an abnormal termination. Furthermore, we give an elaborate introduction of the revised time enhanced Action Systems.

To model VLSI systems several synchronous formalisms exists such as *Lustre* [11], *Signal* [10] and ESTEREL [4]. From these languages ESTEREL is extended to multiple clock domains in two studies [20, 5]. However, for our knowledge these synchronous formalisms do not support rigorous stepwise development of an abstract specification down to an implementation level as our formalism does [27]. In addition to mentioned synchronous languages, there exists several powerful formalisms that are applied to the time aware modelling of VLSI designs, see for example [23, 12, 2].

Outline. The rest of the paper is organised as follows: In Sect. 2 we start by introducing Timed Action Systems after which we introduce how the temporal properties of timed actions are modelled and constrained in Sect. 3. Then, in Sect. 4 we show how multi-clocked VLSI systems are modelled in our framework. Finally, in Sect. 5 we end with concluding remarks.

2 Timed Action Systems

Let us start this section by giving a short overview of conventional actions that form the formal basis for our timed formalism after which we continue to a quite elaborate introduction to our timed notation.

2.1 Conventional Actions

An *action* A is defined (for example) by:

$A ::= abort$	(*abortion, non-termination*)
$\mid skip$	(*empty statement*)
$\mid \{p\}$	(*assert statement*)
$\mid [p]$	(*assumption statement*)
$\mid x := x'.R$	(*non-deterministic assignment*)
$\mid x := e$	(*(multiple) assignment*)
$\mid p \rightarrow A$	(*guarded action*)
$\mid A_1 \; [] \; A_2$	(*non-deterministic choice*)
$\mid A_1; A_2$	(*sequential composition*)
$\mid \lvert[\mathbf{var}\ x := x_0;\ A]\rvert$	(*block with local variables*)
$\mid \mathbf{do}\ A\ \mathbf{od}$	(*iterative composition*)

where A and A_i, $i = 1, 2$, are actions; x is a variable or a list of variables; x_o some value(s) of variable(s) x; e is an expression or a list of expressions; and p and R are predicates (boolean conditions). The variables which are assigned within the action A are called the *write variables* of A, denoted by wA. The other variables present in the action A are called the *read variables* of A, denoted by rA. The write and read variables form together the *access set* vA of A: $vA \widehat{=} wA \cup rA$.

Semantics of actions. The *total correctness* of an action A with respect to a precondition p and a postcondition q is denoted pAq and defined by: $pAq \widehat{=} p \Rightarrow \mathbf{wp}(A, q)$, where $\mathbf{wp}(A, q)$ stands for the *weakest precondition* for the action A to establish the postcondition q. We define, for example: $\mathbf{wp}(skip, q) = q$, $\mathbf{wp}((A_0 \;[\!]\; A_1), q) = \mathbf{wp}(A_0, q) \wedge \mathbf{wp}(A_1, q)$, $\mathbf{wp}(\{p\}, q) = p \wedge q$, $\mathbf{wp}([p], q) = p \Rightarrow q$, $\mathbf{wp}((A_0; A_1), q) = \mathbf{wp}(A_0, \mathbf{wp}(A_1, q))$, $\mathbf{wp}(x := e, q) = q[e/x]$, $\mathbf{wp}(p \rightarrow A, q) = p \Rightarrow \mathbf{wp}(A, q)$ and $\mathbf{wp}(\mathbf{do}\; A\; \mathbf{od}, q) = (\exists k . k \geq 0 \wedge H(k))$, where $H(0) = Q \wedge \neg gA, k = 0$ and $H(k) = (gA \wedge \mathbf{wp}(A, H(k-1))) \vee H(0), k > 0$, where gA is the guard of A. That is, the weakest precondition of the iterative composition requires that after k repetitions of A the loop terminates, that is, A becomes disabled in a state where the post-condition Q holds. If $k = 0$, A is disabled and the iteration behaves as the *skip* action.

Quantified composition. A *quantified composition* of actions is defined by: $[\bullet\; 1 \leq i \leq n : A_i]$, and it is defined by: $A_1 \bullet \ldots \bullet A_n$, where the bullet $\bullet$ denotes any of the composition operators, and n is the number of actions.

Substitution. A *substitution* operation within an action A_i, denoted by $A[e'/e]$, where e refers to an element such as variables and predicates of the original action A_i and e' denotes the new element, which replaces e in A_i. The same notation is applied to action systems as well.

Prioritised composition. A prioritised (' // ') composition [21] is a composition in which the execution order of enabled actions is prioritised. We have: $A \;/\!/\; B \widehat{=} A \;[\!]\; \neg gA \rightarrow B$, where the highest priority belongs to the leftmost action in the composition; thus, the leftmost enabled action is always chosen for execution.

Synchronous composition. For modelling locally synchronous components in a GALS system, we use a synchronous composition of actions that is defined by:

$$
\begin{aligned}
A_1 \vee A_2 \widehat{=} |[\mathbf{var}\; & uA_1, uA_2; gA_1 \vee gA_2 \rightarrow uA_1, uA_2 := wA_1, wA_2 \\
& ; [; 1 \leq i \leq 2 : A_i[uA_i/wA_i] \;/\!/\; skip] \qquad (\textit{synchronous composition}) \\
& ; wA_1, wA_2 := uA_1, uA_2 \,]|
\end{aligned}
$$

where only enabled actions are executed. The enabledness of an action A_i is evaluated based on its guard gA_i. Those actions that are disabled at the time of execution perform the *skip* action. The variable substitution resolves possible read-write conflicts by storing the write variables ($wA_1 \cap wA_2 = \emptyset$) onto local, internal variables uA_1 and uA_2. The actions write on the local variables and after all the actions are executed the write variables are updated. Thus, there is no possibility for read-write conflicts during operation.

Procedures. Body P of a *procedure* p: $p(\mathbf{val}\; x; \mathbf{res}\; y) : P$, is in general any atomic action A, possibly with some auxiliary local variables w initialised to $w0$ every time the procedure is called. The action A accesses the global and local variables g and l of the host/enclosing system and the formal parameters x and y. Hence, the body P can be generally defined by: $P \widehat{=} |[\mathbf{var}\;\; w; \mathbf{init}\; w := w0; A(g, l, w, x, y)]|$. If there are no local variables, the begin-end brackets $|[\;]|$ can be removed all together: $|[A(g, l, x, y)]| =$

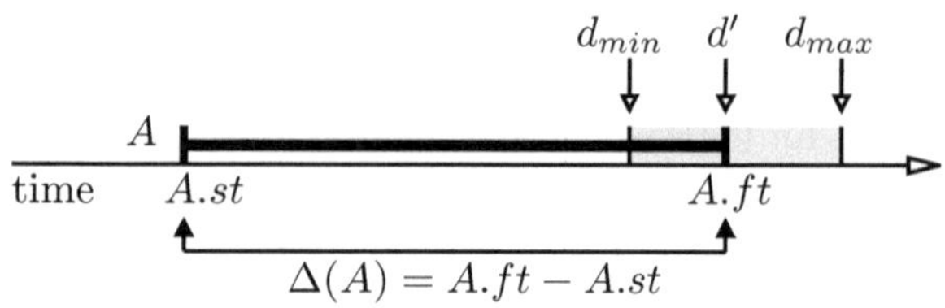

Fig. 1. Illustration of a non-deterministic delay predicate dA_{nd}

$A(g, l, x, y)$. If there are neither local variables nor parameters, the action A only accesses the global and local variables of the host system, then the procedure p can be written as: **proc** $p : A(g, l)$.

2.2 Timed Action

The computation of conventional Action Systems does not take time, a reaction is instantaneous – and therefore atomic in any possible sense. Atomicity means that only pre- and post-states of actions are observable, and when they are chosen for execution they cannot be interrupted by external counterparts. This is due to its software tailored background. In modelling digital VLSI systems it is important to know the time consumed by actions, because the operation speed is determined by the delay of those actions. Therefore, in Timed Action Systems we take the view that every computation takes time. This approach is also justified by the atomicity of actions and the fact that a state of the system can be observed after each execution of actions. It should be observed that the complexity of a timed action is not restricted, and thus the operation time is not bounded either.

The time domain $\mathbb{T} = \mathbb{R}_{\geq 0}$ is dense and continuous, and the lapse of time is modelled by postponing the update of the write variables. The time when the computation is commenced is set in the initialisation of the system, but it is of no importance as only the relative ordering of timed actions is important.

Delay models. A delay of a timed action, say A, is determined by a predicate dA. In this section we introduce the two most commonly used delay predicates: a deterministic dA_n and non-deterministic dA_{nd} delay predicates for which we have the following abbreviations $A[\![d]\!]$ and $A[\![d_{min}, d_{max}]\!]$, respectively. They are defined by:

$dA_d \mathrel{\widehat{=}} d' = d$	*(delay (deterministic))*
$dA_{nd} \mathrel{\widehat{=}} d_{min} \leq d' \leq d_{max}$	*(delay (bounded, non-deterministic))*

where d' is a variable of type $\mathbb{T}$ and d, d_{min} and d_{max} are numerical values of type $\mathbb{T}$.

Timed action. *A timed action* A is defined by:

$A[\![dA]\!] \mathrel{\widehat{=}} (A_f \;[\!]\; A_k) \;/\!\!/\; A_s \;/\!\!/\; Pt$	*(timed action)*

where we can identify three operational segments: *commence*, *end* and *time*. The commence segment contains *the start action* A_s whose execution initiates the operation of timed action, and the operation is terminated in the end segment which consists of *the finish action* A_f and *the kill action* A_k. The one which will be executed depends on the enabledness of the timed action. The time is advanced in the time segment after the execution of the start action by executing *the time propagation action* Pt. This execution sequence ensures that all the enabled timed actions will be executed before time is advanced. A timed action whose operation is performed, but its write variables are not yet updated, is considered *a scheduled timed action*.

The use of *the kill action* A_k is twofold: (1) It prevents a timed action being *deadlocked*, when it is disabled during the delay. This kind of situation may arise when several timed actions are enabled and executed at the same time, and, moreover, they are modelled to disable each other. The result of the described behaviour is that only the winning action (chosen non-deterministically) may proceed, whereupon other timed actions are disabled forever; (2) It models an inertial delay. The inertial delay model absorbs all incoming pulses that are shorter than a circuit component's delay is. Real circuit components have always some inertia in their operation due to presence of capacitance, resistance and inductance.

Let us next introduce the timed action components in detail. Thereafter, the composition of timed actions and the time propagation action will be introduced. Timed action components are defined by:

$$A_s \mathrel{\hat{=}} \neg bA \wedge gA \rightarrow stateA := (wA, gt, gt + d'.dA)$$
$$;\, A[stateA.wA/wA]; bA := T; \qquad \textit{(timed action (start))} \quad (1)$$

$$A_f \mathrel{\hat{=}} bA \wedge gA \wedge (gt = stateA.ft) \rightarrow bA := F$$
$$;\, wA := stateA.wA; \qquad \textit{(timed action (finish))} \quad (2)$$

$$A_k \mathrel{\hat{=}} bA \wedge \neg gA \rightarrow bA := F; \qquad \textit{(timed action (kill))} \quad (3)$$

---

where boolean variable bA sequences the operation into operation and write parts; gA is the guard of the timed action; $stateA$ stores *the new state* of the action. It is of type: **type** $state$: **record**(wA; st, ft: $\mathbb{T}$), where wA is the write variables of A, st a start time and ft a finish time. The start time is set to the global time gt and the finish time is obtained by adding the value of a delay to the global time. Observe that $stateA.ft$ actually stores the time when the write variable is scheduled to be updated by A_w assuming that it remains enabled during the delay, that is, the kill action A_k is disabled the mentioned time period.

The composition of timed actions A_i is:

`composition of timed actions` $A_i \mathrel{\hat{=}}$ *(timed action composition)*

$[\,[\!]\, 1 \le i \le n\colon (A_{f,i} \;[\!]\; A_{k,i})]$ *(finish the operation of scheduled timed action(s))*

$/\!/\; [\,[\!]\, 1 \le i \le n\colon A_{s,i}]$ *(commence the operation of enabled timed action(s))*

$/\!/\; Pt$ *(progress time)*

---

where n is the number of actions. Observe that time propagation action Pt is shared amongst the timed actions. It sets the global time to the nearest scheduled finish time. It is defined by:

$$Pt \widehat{=} [\,[]\ 1 \leq i \leq n : min[i] \rightarrow gt := stateA_i.ft] \qquad \text{(time propagation action)}$$

where the guard $min[i]$ is given as:

$$min[i] \widehat{=} (stateA_i.ft > gt) \wedge (\forall j : 1 \leq j \leq n : j \neq i : stateA_j.ft > gt \Rightarrow stateA_i.ft \leq stateA_j.ft) \qquad \text{(guard min)}$$

It explores the values of finish times $stateA_i.ft$ of scheduled timed actions. It evaluates to $true$ if a finish time $stateA_i.ft$ of a timed action A_i is greater than gt (a requirement for a timed action being a scheduled timed action) and no other scheduled timed actions' finish time $stateA_j.ft$ is smaller than it is. In other words, it chooses the smallest scheduled finish time greater that the global time gt, which then becomes a new global time in Pt.

Weakest precondition of a timed action. The weakest precondition defines the total correctness of an action with respect to its pre- and postcondition. The weakest precondition of a timed action divides into two parts depending on its enabledness during execution: (a) a timed action is enabled throughout its operation allowing write variables to be updated after the specified delay and (b) a timed action becomes disabled during execution preventing the update of the write variables and enabling the timed action for further executions. That is, it behaves as the *skip* action. The weakest precondition of a timed action is:

$$\mathbf{wp}((A[\![dA]\!]), Q) = \mathbf{wp}(A, Q[stateA.st, stateA.ft, stateA.ft / A.st, A.ft, gt]) \wedge (\neg gA \Rightarrow \mathbf{wp}(skip, Q)) \qquad (\textbf{wp} \textit{ of a timed action})$$

2.3 Timed Action System

Let us commence the introduction of Timed Action System by first showing its form, and then introducing its elements and computation model.

A timed action system $\mathcal{A}$ has a form:

sys $\mathcal{A}$ (**imp** p_I; **exp** p_E;)(g;) ::
|[**delays** dA_i, dp, dp_E;
  proc $p[\![dp]\!](x) : (P); p_E[\![dp_E]\!](e) : (P_E)$;
  var l;
  actions $A_i[\![dA_i]\!] : (aA_i)$;
  init $g, l := g0, l0$;
  exec do `composition of timed actions` A_i **od**]|

where aA_i is any kind of the defined atomic actions generated by the syntax given previously, A_i its symbolic name and dA_i its delay. In the above system we can identify three main sections: *interface*, *declarative* and *iteration*. The interface part declares those variables, g, that are visible outside the action system boundaries, and thus accessible by other action systems. It also introduces interface procedures that are either imported (hence, introduced by some other timed action system) (p_I) or introduced and

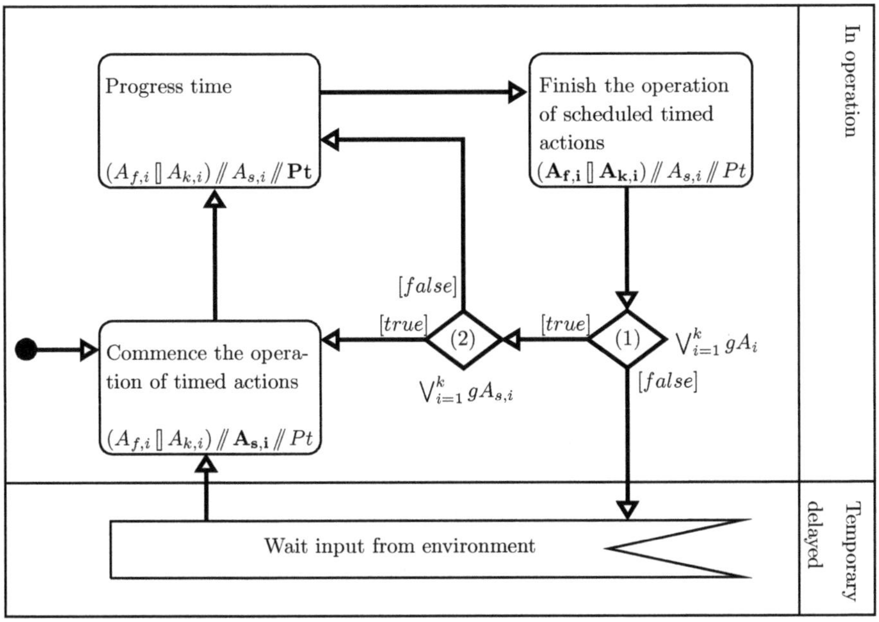

Fig. 2. A computation model of a timed action system

exported (p_E) by the system. If an action system does not have any interface variables or procedures, it is *a closed action system*, otherwise it is *an open action system*. The declarative part introduces delay definitions, the local variables l, local p and exported p_E procedures, and, furthermore, actions that perform operations on local and global variables. Finally, the iteration section, the **do-od** loop of the system, contains the composition of the actions defined in the declarative part.

2.4 Modelling the Behaviour of a Digital VLSI Circuit

Let us have two timed action systems $\mathcal{A}$ and $\mathcal{E}nv$ whose local variables and actions are distinct and the latter is the environment of the former. Consider the parallel composition of these systems, denoted by $\mathcal{A} \parallel \mathcal{E}nv$. The parallel composition is defined to be another action system whose global and local identifiers (variables and actions) consist of the identifiers of component systems and whose **exec** clause has the form: **do** $[\,[\!]\, 1 \leq i \leq n\colon A_i] \;[\!]\; E$ **od**, where A_i and E are actions of the systems $\mathcal{A}$ and $\mathcal{E}nv$, respectively. The constituent systems communicate via their shared interface variables. The definition of the parallel composition is used inversely in system derivation to decompose a system description into a composition of smaller separate systems or internal subsystems. In modelling the behaviour of a digital VLSI circuit $\mathcal{A}$ and its environment $\mathcal{E}nv$, it is assumed that there is always one enabled timed action. In other words, the system must satisfy the following invariant: $\vee_{i=1}^{n} gA_i \vee gE$.

Computation model. (Fig. 2) The computation of a timed action system is commenced in an initialisation in which the variables (both local and global) are set to predefined values. In the iteration part, the **exec** section, actions are sequentially selected for execution based on the composition and enabledness of the start actions $A_{s,i}$. After all the enabled start actions are executed, the global time gt is set to nearest scheduled finish time in the time propagation action Pt. Then, either finish $A_{f,i}$ or kill $A_{k,i}$ action of those scheduled timed actions whose delay is consumed are executed. This is repeated as long as there are either enabled (1) or scheduled (2) timed actions. However, if there are no such timed actions, the timed action system is considered *temporary delayed*. The computation resumes execution when some other timed action systems enables an action via the interface variables or calls an exported procedure.

Weak fairness. The conventional Action Systems formalism does not contain any fairness assumptions. However, to describe the behaviour of a digital VLSI circuits accurately, enabled actions are executed in a *weakly fair* manner in [18]. In other words, it is not possible to infinitely select some timed action A_i for execution, if there are some other action A_j, which remains enabled simultaneously with A_i. In Timed Action Systems, however, the weak fairness assumption is unnecessary due to the timed action model that ensures the execution of all the enabled timed actions.

3 Temporality

In this section we introduce delay calculation rules for the Timed Action Systems formalism, and, furthermore, we define constraints with which the operation of timed action can be restricted, not only logically but also temporally.

3.1 Delay Calculus

Let us start by defining a semantics to calculate delays of timed actions and their compositions. Given a timed action A we write $\Delta(A)$ to calculate the set of possible delays for the system. Rules of the delay calculation are defined recursively as follows:

$$
\begin{aligned}
\Delta(A) ::= {} & d'.dA = A.ft - A.st && \textit{(action delay)} \quad (4)\\
| {} & \Delta(A_1; A_2) = \Delta(A_1) + \Delta(A_2) && \textit{(sequential delay)} \quad (5)\\
| {} & \Delta(p \to A) = \Delta([p]; A) = \Delta(p) + \Delta(A) && \textit{(guarded action delay)} \quad (6)\\
| {} & \Delta(A_1 \; [] \; A_2) = \{\Delta(A_1), \Delta(A_2)\} && \textit{(alternative delay)} \quad (7)\\
| {} & \Delta(A_1 \; /\!/ \; A_2) = \{\Delta(A_1), \Delta(A_2)\} && \textit{(alternative delay)} \quad (8)\\
| {} & \Delta(A_1 \vee A_2) = \mathbf{Max}(\Delta(A_1), \Delta(A_2)) && \textit{(synchronous delay)} \quad (9)\\
| {} & \Delta(|[\mathbf{var}\ x := x_0;\ A]|) = \Delta(A) && \textit{(block delay)} \quad (10)\\
| {} & \Delta(\mathbf{do}\ A\ \mathbf{od}) = \textstyle\sum_{i=k}^{0} \Delta(A) && \textit{(iterative delay)} \quad (11)
\end{aligned}
$$

where (4) defines a timed action delay. The delay is also defined using the start and finish times of a timed action; (5) sums the delays of sequentially executed timed actions; (6) defines a delay for a guarded timed action. It consists of the *predicate delay* and the *action delay* based on the definition of a guarded action; (7) and (8) gives a set of delays each of which reflect an alternative delay path. To extract either the best or worst case propagation delay, one may use the **Min** or **Max** functions, respectively. For example, in critical timing path analysis one utilise the **Max** function to observe the slowest path from input to output; In (9) a delay is the maximum delay of the synchronous timed actions because the slowest action (the largest delay) of the composition defines the overall performance of a synchronous VLSI component; (10) defines a delay for a block of timed actions; Finally, in (11) is defined the delay for the iterative composition. It equals the sum of the delays of those timed actions which are executed in k iterations. The definition is justified by the weakest precondition of the iterative composition given earlier. It states that after k selections of an action the **do-od** loop will terminate properly.

Using the above delay calculation rules we are able to define *a static delay* for a system. In the static delay analysis the expected timing information of the system is computed without requiring simulations. The static delay analysis returns a set of delays each of which corresponds a possible computation path. From the obtained set, it is possible to calculate, for example, the worst case delay for the circuit under analysis using the **Max** function or the best case delay using the **Min** function.

Delay definitions. The basis for delay definitions is that one must be able to calculate a delay information for every timed action used in a timed action system's iteration section. In other words, in the declarative section a timed action may or may not have a specific delay information.

System delay. As stated earlier we assume that there is always at least one enabled action in a system. Therefore, when one is computing a delay for a system (and its environment), only computation paths are considered. This approach facilitates the timing analysis, and, furthermore, it provides sufficient information of the system. In determining computation paths for a circuit it is required to have information of the logical behaviour of the circuit. That is, it is required to know how timed actions interact with each other. A computation path from action A to action B, denoted by $A \mapsto B$, is a sequence of immediate successors which leads from A to B. An immediate successor is an action that is enabled by its predecessor in the path where no loops are allowed. A computation path delay between timed actions A and B is defined by:

$$\Delta({}^*A \mapsto B^*) ::= B.ft - A.st \qquad \textit{(computation path delay)}$$

where, the symbol * indicates, by its position, whether the delay of an action is included into the computation path delay or not. In the above rule both delays are included. For excluding either or both of the delays we have: $\Delta({}^*A \mapsto {}^*B) \widehat{=} \Delta({}^*A \mapsto B^*) - \Delta(B) = B.st - A.st$, $\Delta(A^* \mapsto B^*) \widehat{=} \Delta({}^*A \mapsto B^*) - \Delta(A) = B.ft - A.ft$, $\Delta(A^* \mapsto {}^*B) \widehat{=} \Delta({}^*A \mapsto B^*) - \Delta(B) - \Delta(A) = B.st - A.ft$. Without specifying actions or interface signals for a timed action system, $\Delta(\mathcal{A})$, we obtain a set of delays each of which corresponds one computation path. Let us next have an exemplification of the delay definitions as well as the above defined delay calculus for timed action and timed action systems.

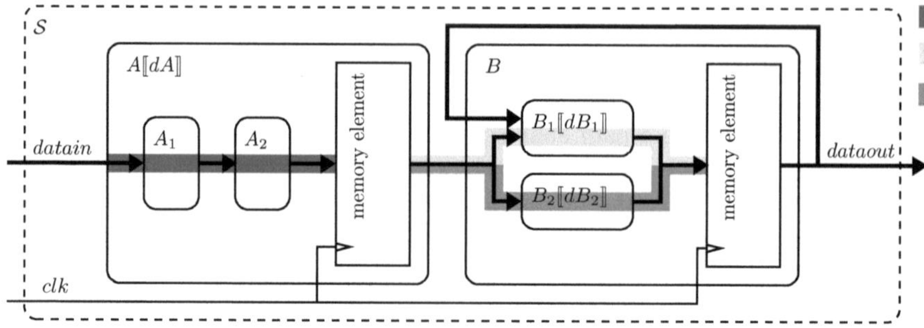

Fig. 3. Delay paths of the timed action systems $\mathcal{S}$

Example 1. Consider the following timed action system $\mathcal{S}$:

sys $\mathcal{S}$ ($datain, dataout$: $data$;) ::
|[**delays** dA, dB_1, dB_2;
var l;
actions A_1: (aA_1); A_2: (aA_2);
$A[\![dA]\!]$: $(A_1; A_2)$;
$B_1[\![dB_1]\!]$: (aB_1); $B_2[\![dB_2]\!]$: (aB_2);
B: $(B_1 \;[\!]\; B_2)$;
init $l := l0$;
exec do $A \vee B$ **od**]|

where we have six timed actions, two of which are utilised in the iteration loop. The timed actions A_1 and A_2, of which the timed action A is composed of, do not have a delay information. However, as stated earlier we need or must be able to calculate delay information only for those actions that are used in the iteration loop, and therefore it is adequate to have $A[\![dA]\!]$ (path 1 in Fig. 3). The timed action B, on the other hand, does not have a specific delay, although, it is used in the iteration loop. Its delay is obtained using (7): $dB = \{dB_1, dB_2\}$ (paths 2 and 3 in Fig. 3, respectively). Because of the synchronous composition it is not required to model the clock signal clk (depicted in Fig. 3)in the above system.

Using the delay calculus we are able to calculate the clock cycle time for the above system by observing the composition in the execution loop of the system. We have: $\Delta(A \vee B) = \Delta(A \vee (B_1 \;[\!]\; B_2)) = \mathbf{Max}(\Delta(A), \Delta(B_1 \;[\!]\; B_2)) = \mathbf{Max}(dA, \{dB_1, dB_2\}) = \mathbf{Max}(dA, dB_1, dB_2)$. That is, the delay of the synchronous composition is the maximum of the three delays, which, based on the definition of the synchronous composition, is the delay information used by timed action model.

The calculation of a system delay, as defined earlier, requires information of the logical behaviour of the system. In other words, one needs to know the operation sequence of the actions, the computation path. In Fig. 3 is represented one possible circuit construct for the given system $\mathcal{S}$ as the model itself does not provide detailed information of how timed actions A and B interact with each other. Thus, based on Fig. 3 we have the following computation path: $A \mapsto B$, and a computation path delay $\Delta(*A \mapsto B*) = 2 * \mathbf{Max}(dA, dB_1, dB_2)$.
End of example.

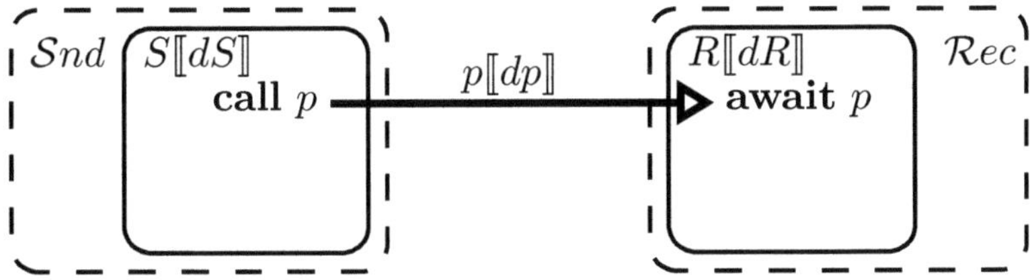

Fig. 4. $\mathcal{S}nd$ and $\mathcal{R}ec$ communicate directly with each other

Procedure delay. Let us next define a delay for a procedure p. We have:

$$\Delta(p) ::= \Delta(P) = \Delta(A) \qquad \textit{(procedure delay)}$$

That is, the delay of a procedure p is a delay of its body P, which, on the other hand, is in general any atomic action A as stated in the procedure definition. We call this delay also a *static delay*. The name comes from the use of procedures in communication modelling. The static part of the communication delay is known *a priori* and it is not affected by external counterparts.

Procedure based communication delay. The procedure based communication [19] uses remote procedures to model communication channels between action systems, see Fig. 4. Consider the timed action systems $\mathcal{S}nd$ and $\mathcal{R}ec$ whose internal activities are denoted with actions $S[\![dS]\!] \mathrel{\widehat{=}} (S_1; \textbf{call}\ p(l_S); S_2)$ and $R[\![dR]\!] \mathrel{\widehat{=}} (R_1; \textbf{await}\ p; R_2)$, where p is an interface procedure defined in and exported by the receiver ($\mathcal{R}ec$), and imported and called by the sender ($\mathcal{S}nd$), with the variables l_S (sender's local variables) as actual value parameters. The body P of $p[\![dp]\!]$ can be any atomic action writing onto the variables l_R (receiver's local variables). In Action Systems (untimed and timed ones) systems are combined using *parallel composition*. In parallel composition of action systems, the **exec** clause of the composed system $\mathcal{S}nd \parallel \mathcal{R}ec$ has the form: **do** $S \;[\!]\; R$ **od**. The construct $S \;[\!]\; R$, where S calls p (**call** command) and R awaits such a call (**await** command), is regarded as a single atomic action SR, defined by: $SR \mathrel{\widehat{=}} (S_1; R_1; P[l_S/x]; R_2; S_2)$. Hence, communication is based on sharing an action in which data is atomically passed from $\mathcal{S}nd$ to $\mathcal{R}ec$ by executing the body P of the procedure p hiding the details of the communication into the procedure call. A static delay for the above presented procedure based communication is therefore:

$$\Delta_{comm} ::= \Delta(SR) = \Delta(S) + \Delta(p) + \Delta(R) \qquad \textit{(communication delay)}$$

That is, the communication delay is a sum of its components' delays: the delay of the calling timed action $\Delta(S)$, the delay of the communication procedure $\Delta(p)$ and the delay of the called timed action $\Delta(R)$.

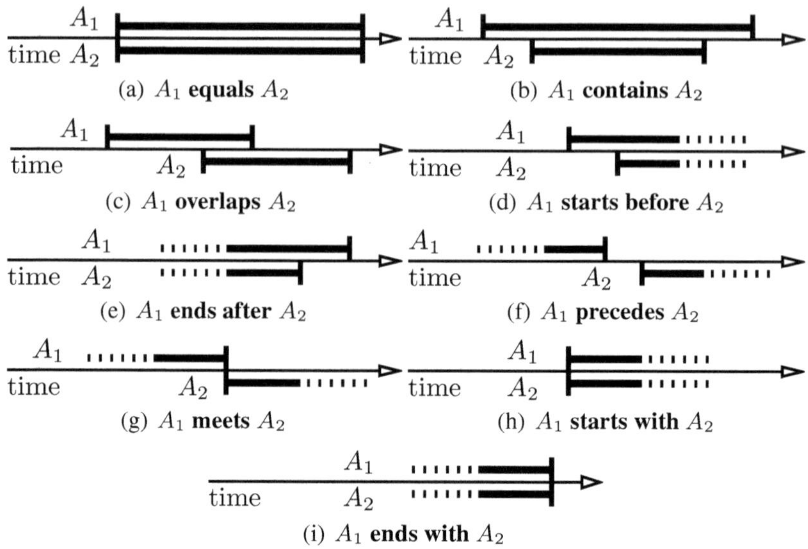

Fig. 5. Temporal relations in a graphical form

3.2 Constraints

In this section we give a new, revised form of the constraint [26] with which we are able to restrict the temporal and functional operation of a timed action system. A constraint is an expression according to which involved timed actions are obliged to operate. That is, a constraint defines a condition whose strict adherence is mandatory; violation of such a condition results an unpredictable computation. In other words, the violation of a constraint denotes a useless computation. In text we use a symbol $\Box$ to denote a constraint. Formally it behaves as an assert statement. We have:

$$\Box\{B\} = \begin{cases} abort, \text{ when } B = false \\ skip, \text{ when } B = true \end{cases} \qquad (constraint)$$

where B is a predicate (boolean condition). An assert statement behaves as a $skip$ statement if B holds but otherwise it behaves like $abort$. In other words, if constraints are satisfied they operate as empty statements that do not change the state at all. On the other hand, if a constraint is *not* satisfied, it is a never terminating statement, which hence does not establish any postconditions causing an abnormal termination of the system.

Relative ordering. Being able to define relative ordering of actions is useful in designing VLSI systems. Relative timing defines the ordering of operations in the time domain. Relative timing is not a novel idea, and it is widely used in databooks and applied in several studies, see for example [22, 13, 17]. We define the relative timing constraints (see Fig. 5) applying the temporal interval notation introduced in [1]. We define:

A_1 **starts before** $A_2 \mathrel{\widehat{=}} A_1.st < A_2.st$	(*starts before*)	(12)
A_1 **ends after** $A_2 \mathrel{\widehat{=}} A_2.ft < A_1.ft$	(*ends after*)	(13)
A_1 **precedes** $A_2 \mathrel{\widehat{=}} A_1.ft < A_2.st$	(*precedes*)	(14)
A_1 **meets** $A_2 \mathrel{\widehat{=}} A_1.ft = A_2.st$	(*meets*)	(15)
A_1 **starts with** $A_2 \mathrel{\widehat{=}} A_1.st = A_2.st$	(*starts with*)	(16)
A_1 **ends with** $A_2 \mathrel{\widehat{=}} A_1.ft = A_2.ft$	(*ends with*)	(17)

where $A_i.st$ and $A_i.ft$ are the start and finish times of a timed action, respectively. In (15), for example, the time constraint defines that the execution of A_2 must be started at the same time point in which A_1 finished its execution. Observe, that those relative orderings that define overlapping operations denotes parallel operation of timed actions, too.

The above relative orderings are called *elementary relative orderings*. Relative orderings composed of these orderings are called *composite relative orderings*. We have, for example, **equals, contains** and **overlaps**, which are defined by:

A_1 **equals** $A_2 \mathrel{\widehat{=}} (A_1$ **starts with** $A_2) \wedge (A_1$ **ends with** $A_2)$	(*equals*)
A_1 **contains** $A_2 \mathrel{\widehat{=}} (A_1$ **starts before** $A_2) \wedge (A_1$ **ends after** $A_2)$	(*contains*)
A_1 **overlaps** $A_2 \mathrel{\widehat{=}} (A_2.st < A_1.ft) \wedge (A_1$ **starts before** $A_2)$ $\wedge (A_2$ **ends after** $A_1)$	(*overlaps*)

where the **overlaps** is defined with two elementary relative orderings in addition to time points because defining the **overlaps** only with the elementary relative orderings does not guarantee the intended temporal behaviour of the composite relative ordering as depicted in Fig. 5(c).

The abstraction level in which the above temporal relations are used is of no importance. Let us next give a low-level circuit example of the use of relative orderings after which an example at a higher abstraction level.

Example 2. Assume that we have two signals a and b and that the rising transition ($\uparrow$) of a must always happen before than that of b. The timed actions that determines the transition are: $A[\![dA]\!] : a \wedge v \rightarrow v := F$; and $B[\![dB]\!] : b \wedge w \rightarrow w := F$;, where the boolean variables v and w disables the actions after the rising transition as otherwise the actions are enabled, and therefore executed, whenever a and b were $true$. To guarantee that the circuit always fulfils this requirement we specify the following time constraint using a relative ordering **precedes**: $\Box\{A$ **precedes** $B\} \mathrel{\widehat{=}} \{A.st < B.st\}$.
End of example.

Example 3. Let us consider the timed actions $A[\![dA]\!]$, $B_1[\![dB_1]\!]$ and $B_2[\![dB_2]\!]$ given in Fig. 3 composed with synchronous operator $\vee$ as earlier: P: $\big(A \vee (B_1 \;[\!]\; B_2)\big)$, where P is a processing action. To confirm that the operation of the timed actions A, B_1 and B_2 is performed within the clock cycle time, we define: $\Box\{P$ **ends after** $A\}$,

Fig. 6. A timed action A satisfying $\{T\}$ and dissatisfying $\{F\}$ a deadline

$\Box\{P$ **ends after** $B\}$ and $\Box\{P$ **ends after** $B_2\}$. That is, the operation of the timed actions must finish their operation before memory elements are updated. The defined constraints also reflect the requirements of register-transfer level design where the sampled signal must be stable prior to rising clock signal. Observe, however, that from the logical point of view, the synchronous composition ensures the correct operation, these constraint are essential in back-annotation to formally validate the real timing values that are obtained from a synthesised design [25].
End of example.

Deadlines. Let us then revise the deadline [25] that defines *the maximum time* a timed action is allowed to consume in its operation. A deadline (⊟) defines a time point upon which the operation of involved timed actions are obliged to finish their operation. Applying the time constraint definitions we define:

$\boxminus\{E, d\} \widehat{=} \Box\{TE \leq d\}$ *(deadline)*

---

where TE is a time expression that evaluates to a time value ($\mathbb{T}$). Time expressions are composed of mathematical operations, e.g. $+$ and $-$.

Example 4. A deadline for a timed action is defined by: $\boxminus\{A, d\} \widehat{=} \Box\{\Delta(A) \leq d\}$, shown in Fig. 6, where the correct execution is marked with $\{T\}$. The dashed line denotes a false computation, marked with $\{F\}$, as the computation of the timed action ends after the deadline constraint. The shaded area denotes the false computation area.
End of example.

4 Modelling Multiclocked VLSI Systems

Thus far we have mainly concentrated on our formal, time aware modelling language. In this section we utilise the formalism in modelling a multiclocked VLSI system, to be exact, a globally asynchronous, locally synchronous (GALS) system. We chose GALS based systems due to their non-trivial structure as well as both asynchronous and synchronous systems can be seen a special cases of a GALS architecture. In GALS design we have locally synchronous islands whose clocks are independent of each other. The communication between these independent synchronous modules is commonly implemented using asynchronous wrappers, see for example [16, 28, 9, 6]. The wrapper based design supports highly modular design structure making it attractive to be used with IP (intellectual property) blocks that are provided with several industrial vendors. Hence, we adopted the wrapper based design paradigm to our GALS model.

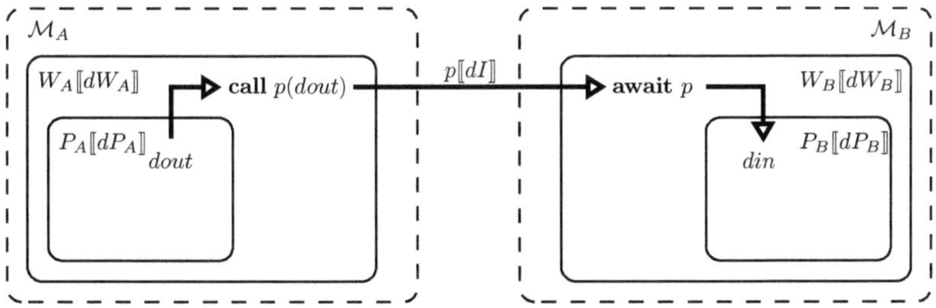

Fig. 7. Wrapped sender and receiver communicating directly with each other

4.1 GALS Concept

Consider two closed synchronous modules, say $\mathcal{M}_A$ and $\mathcal{M}_B$, both of which have a clock of their own independent of each other. The action systems have the form:

sys $\mathcal{M}_A$ ( ) ::
|[**delays** dP_A;
  var l_A;
  actions A_i: (aA_i);
    $P_A[\![dP_A]\!]$: $(A_1 \vee \ldots \vee A_n)$;
  init $l_A := l0_A$;
  exec do P_A **od**]|

sys $\mathcal{M}_B$ ( ) ::
|[**delays** dP_B;
  var l_B;
  actions B_j: (aB_j);
    $P_B[\![dP_B]\!]$: $(B_1 \vee \ldots \vee B_m)$;
  init $l_B := l0_B$;
  exec do P_B **od**]|

where the operation of the above systems is performed synchronously in the processing actions P_A and P_B. The delay of these synchronous actions are dP_A and dP_B, respectively. The given delay defines also the clock cycle time of the processing actions. Observe that as we only define the delay information for the synchronous composition, we have: $P_A[\![dP_A]\!]: (A_1 \vee \ldots \vee A_n) \equiv P_A: (A_1[\![dP_A]\!] \vee \ldots \vee A_n[\![dP_A]\!])$ and $P_B[\![dP_B]\!]: (B_1 \vee \ldots \vee B_m) \equiv P_B: (B_1[\![dP_B]\!] \vee \ldots \vee B_m[\![dP_B]\!])$ giving us $dP_A \equiv dA_i$ and $dP_B \equiv dB_j$. That is, we have equal delays for all the synchronously composed timed actions.

Placing the modules into the same SoC design requires that special attention is paid on their communication due to the different clock periods. Based on the assumption that the clock periods are not allowed to be changed, the communication scheme between the modules have to be defined with care. Possible difficulties that may be created by the different clock periods in communication are, for example, synchronisation problems such as lost and duplication of data. Therefore, we utilise the earlier introduced procedure based communication that ensures the data integrity during communication. The action systems becomes (see Fig. 7):

sys $\mathcal{M}_A$ (**imp** p_C;) ::
|[**delays** dW_A, dP_A;
  var l_A;
  actions A_i: (aA_i);
    $P_A[\![dP_A]\!]$: $(A_1 \vee \ldots \vee A_n)$;
    $W_A[\![dW_A]\!]$: $(S_1;$ **call** $p_C(l_A); S_2)$;
  init $l_A := l0_A$;
  exec do W_A // P_A **od**]|

sys $\mathcal{M}_B$ (**exp** p_C;) ::
|[**delays** dW_B, dP_B, dI;
  var l_B;
  proc $p_C[\![dI]\!]$(**val** x): (P);
  actions B_j: (aB_j);
    $P_B[\![dP_B]\!]$: $(B_1 \vee \ldots \vee B_m)$;
    $W_B[\![dW_B]\!]$: $(R_1;$ **await** $p_C; R_2)$;
  init $l_B := l0_B$;
  exec do W_B // P_B **od**]|

where the system $\mathcal{M}_B$ introduces and exports the communication procedure p_C, and the system $\mathcal{M}_A$ imports the procedure. The communication procedure is called and awaited in special actions, called wrapper actions (W_A and W_B). These actions hide the communication details from the processing actions allowing one to design the communication apart from the functionality; thus, enabling the use of existing IP components.

Observe that the direction of data is not identified in the procedure based communication: to or from the callee. The type of the communication channel is identified in the definition of a procedure. In our abstract GALS model we have used *push* channel between the components: $p_C(\textbf{val}\ x) : P$, where the direction of data is identified by the **val** specifier. A *pull* channel is defined using **res** specifier; we have: $p(\textbf{res}\ x) : P$.

The parallel composition of these two systems, denoted by $\mathcal{M}_A \parallel \mathcal{M}_B$, is:

$$
\begin{array}{l}
\textbf{sys}\ \mathcal{M}_A \parallel \mathcal{M}_B\ (\quad) :: \\
|[\ \textbf{delays}\ dW_A, dW_B, dI, dA_i, dB_j; \\
\quad \textbf{var}\ l_A \cup l_B; \\
\quad \textbf{proc}\ p_C[\![dI]\!](\textbf{val}\ x) : (P); \\
\quad \textbf{actions}\ A_i : (aA_i);\ B_j : (aB_j); \\
\qquad\qquad P_A[\![dP_A]\!] : (A_1 \vee \ldots \vee A_n); \\
\qquad\qquad W_A[\![dW_A]\!] : (S_1; \textbf{call}\ p_C(l_A); S_2); \\
\qquad\qquad P_B[\![dP_B]\!] : (B_1 \vee \ldots \vee B_m); \\
\qquad\qquad W_B[\![dW_B]\!] : (R_1; \textbf{await}\ p_C; R_2); \\
\quad \textbf{init}\ l_A \cup l_B := l0_A \cup l0_B; \\
\quad \textbf{exec do}\ (W_A\ /\!/\ P_A)\ [\!]\ (W_B\ /\!/\ P_B)\ \textbf{od}\ \ ]|
\end{array}
$$

where it is required that the local variables are distinct: $l_A \cap l_B = \emptyset$. The local identifiers (procedures, variables, actions) are the identifiers of the component action systems.

4.2 Communication

Let us consider the iteration loop in more detail by writing the operators based on their definitions and using the definition of the procedure based communication. The iteration loop of the above system is regarded as the following composition:

$$
\begin{aligned}
\textbf{do}\ (W_A\ /\!/\ P_A)\ [\!]\ (W_B\ /\!/\ P_B)\ \textbf{od} &= \textbf{do}\ W_{AB}\ /\!/\ (P_A\ [\!]\ P_B)\ \textbf{od} \\
&= \textbf{do}\ W_{AB}\ [\!]\ \neg g W_{AB} \rightarrow (P_A\ [\!]\ P_B)\ \textbf{od}
\end{aligned}
$$

By opening the prioritised composition it is clearly seen that when the communication between the processing units is initiated, the calling action disables itself and the other processing action due to use of prioritised composition: $\neg g W_{AB}$ becomes *false*. This naturally prevents all activities in the processing actions until the data is safely transferred by successful operation of the composed wrapper action W_{AB} ensuring the data integrity during communication activities.

4.3 Delay Calculations

Let us next analyse the delay characteristics of the above presented GALS system and its synthetic, but possible, operation sequences. Let us first determine the clock cycle time for the synchronous modules $\mathcal{M}_A$ and $\mathcal{M}_B$. We have:

$$\Delta(P_A) = dP_A \qquad \textit{(clock cycle time of } \mathcal{M}_A)$$
$$\Delta(P_B) = dP_B \qquad \textit{(clock cycle time of } \mathcal{M}_B)$$

where the clock cycle time equals the delay of the processing actions.

Then we consider the delay of the systems. We have, assuming the pipelined operation (similar the one shown in Fig. 3) for the systems $\mathcal{M}_A$ and $\mathcal{M}_B$ with three ($n = 3$) and two ($m = 2$) pipeline stages in the system, respectively. The computation path without the wrapper actions and the communication delay between the systems are:

$$\Delta(*A_1 \mapsto A_3*) = \Delta(A_1) + \Delta(A_2) + \Delta(A_3) \qquad \textit{(computation path delay of } P_A)$$
$$\Delta(*B_1 \mapsto B_2*) = \Delta(B_1) + \Delta(B_2) \qquad \textit{(computation path delay of } P_B)$$
$$\Delta_{comm} = \Delta(W_{AB}) = \Delta(W_A) + \Delta(p_C) + \Delta(W_B) \qquad \textit{(communication delay)}$$

Datapath delay. Let us compute a datapath delay, for example, a dataflow application in which the two presented synchronous modules are sequentially connected. Examples of such applications are FIR filter (3 sequentially connected modules in [29]), digital down conversion (DDC)(5 modules in [15]) and WLAN baseband processor (transmitter side composed of 3 modules in [14]). For our datapath we obtain the following delay:

$$\Delta(*A_1 \mapsto B_2*) = \Delta(A_1) + \Delta(A_2) + \Delta(A_3) \qquad \textit{(computation path delay of } P_A)$$
$$+ \Delta(W_A) + \Delta(p_C) + \Delta(W_B) \qquad \textit{(communication delay)}$$
$$+ \Delta(B_1) + \Delta(B_2) \qquad \textit{(computation path delay of } P_B)$$

Equal clock cycle times. Let us first assume that the synchronous modules have equal clock cycle times, that is, we have: $dP_A = dP_B$. We obtain an execution sequence shown in Fig. 8(a): $E : (P_A, P_B); W_{AB}; (P_A, P_B); (P_A, P_B); \ldots$, where the timed actions in parentheses are started at the same time instant ($P_A.st = P_B.st$). Observe that the order in which the processing units appear in the parenthesis is of no importance due to their parallel operation. The action W_{AB}, on the other hand, is executed individually due to prioritised composition allowing safe transformation of data items. For the sequence with equal clock cycle times (Fig. 8(a)) we obtain the following delays for the systems $\mathcal{M}_A$ and $\mathcal{M}_B$, denoted by $\Delta(Seq_{\mathcal{M}_A})$ and $\Delta(Seq_{\mathcal{M}_B})$:

$$\Delta(Seq_{\mathcal{M}_A}) \ldots + dP_A + dW_{AB} + dP_A + dP_A + \ldots + dW_{AB} + \ldots \qquad \textit{(iteration delay of } \mathcal{M}_A)$$
$$\Delta(Seq_{\mathcal{M}_B}) \ldots + dP_B + dW_{AB} + dP_B + dP_B + \ldots + dW_{AB} + \ldots \qquad \textit{(iteration delay of } \mathcal{M}_B)$$

where $dP = dP_A = dP_B$; thus, we have: $\Delta(Seq_{\mathcal{M}_A}) = \Delta(Seq_{\mathcal{M}_B})$.

Unequal clock cycle times. With unequal clock cycle times, for example $dP_A < dP_B$, we obtain the action sequence: $E : (P_A, P_B); W_{AB}; (P_A, P_B); P_A; P_B; \ldots$, as shown in Fig. 8(b). The number of execution rounds of the processing unit P_A with respect to P_B depends on their operation speed. We have:

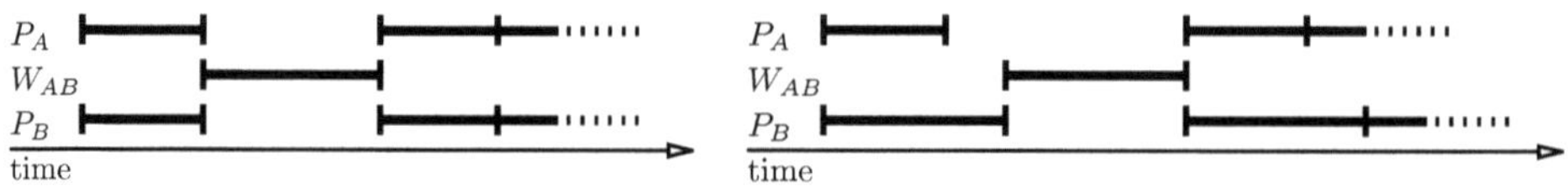

(a) $dP_A = dP_B$ (b) $dP_A < dP_B$

Fig. 8. Communication activity with equal (a) and unequal (b) clock cycle times

$$\Delta(Seq_{\mathcal{M}_A}) = \ldots + dP_A + d(idle) + dW_{AB} + dP_A + dP_A + \ldots \quad \textit{(iteration delay of } \mathcal{M}_A)$$
$$\Delta(Seq_{\mathcal{M}_B}) = \ldots + dP_B + dW_{AB} + dP_B + dP_B + \ldots \quad \textit{(iteration delay of } \mathcal{M}_B)$$

where $d(idle)$ denotes the time that P_A must wait for the commence of communication.

4.4 Constraints

Above we analysed the temporal operation of the described GALS system. We showed how to calculate delays for the processing units as well as for the communication with equal and unequal clock cycle times. Let use next consider both the logical and temporal constraints of the GALS model.

Logical constraints. From the logical point of view the synchronous composition itself guarantees that all the timed actions perform their operation within the given limits. In addition, the prioritised composition used in the wrapper based computation ensures that sent data items are transferred safely and correctly.

Temporal constraints. From the time point of view the operation of the synchronously coupled timed actions can be ensured by defining the following deadlines: $\boxminus_i\{A_i, dP_A\}$ and $\boxminus_j\{B_j, dP_B\}$. That is, the time elapsed by the timed actions A_i and B_i are not allowed to exceed the clock cycle time. Moreover, to define relation between the synchronously coupled timed actions A_i, B_j and the synchronous timed actions P_A and P_B, respectively, we confine that all the timed actions finish their operation before the active clock edge: $\Box_i\{P_A$ **ends after** $A_i\}$ and $\Box_j\{P_B$ **ends after** $B_j\}$. The defined constraints can be used in the validation process as well as in the back-annotation of timing information to ensure the correct temporal operation of the system under development.

5 Conclusions

We presented a formal, time aware modelling environment for multiclocked VLSI systems. We gave an elaborate definition of the timed formalism, Timed Action Systems, for which we defined different delay types. We presented a delay calculus framework for our timed formalism, and, furthermore, we presented constraints with which to confine temporal as well as logical behaviour of VLSI systems. These constraints terminate the operation of the system if violated due to unpredictable result of computation in such a case. The future studies will include the utilisation of the constraints in modelling robust fault-tolerant designs and also the possibility to model constraint whose violation is not critical for the system's operation; although, the result of computation might not be predictable. This includes the investigation of decreasing usefulness of computation as time elapses after its violation. The decline of the value of usefulness as used in *soft* constraints in real-time system modelling is of no use in VLSI system design, and therefore not considered in this paper. However, in the future studies concerning embedded system modelling where both software and hardware point of view are equally important, soft constraints shall be addressed. In addition, the revised deadlines bound the maximum allowable operation time of timed actions. The introduced constraints are essential in the validation of the multiclocked VLSI systems, not only logically but also with respect to given temporal constraints.

We illustrated the defined time aware formalism and its delay calculus by modelling a GALS systems. In our GALS model the integrity of data during communication activities is ensured using the procedure based communication and the prioritisation of actions. The prioritisation disables the processing units while the communication activities are in operation; thus, new data cannot be written until the old one is transferred. The application showed the usability of our formalism in designing such systems, and, furthermore, as both self-timed and synchronous systems can be seen as special cases of GALS systems our approach is also applicable to model those systems as well. The scope of this paper was the introduction of the formal, time aware modelling and analysis framework, and therefore the synthesis problem from an abstract specification down to implementable model is not discussed.

Acknowledgements. Tomi Westerlund gratefully acknowledges financial support for this work from the Nokia foundation.

References

[1] J. F. Allen. Maintaining knowledge about temporal intervals. *Commun. ACM*, 26(11):832–843, 1983.
[2] R. Alur and D. L. Dill. A theory of timed automata. *Theoretical Computer Science*, 126(2):183–235, 1994.
[3] R.-J. Back and K. Sere. From modular systems to action systems. In *Proc. of Formal Methods Europe '94*, Spain, October 1994. Lecture notes in comp. sci., Springer-Verlag.
[4] G. Berry and G. Gonthier. The Esterel synchronous programming language: Design, semantics, implementation. *Science of Computer Programming*, 19(2):87–152, 1992.
[5] G. Berry and E. Sentovich. Multiclock Esterel. In *Correct Hardware Design and Verification Methods*, volume 2144/2000, pages 110–125. LNCS, 2001.
[6] D. S. Bormann and P. Y. Cheung. Asynchronous wrapper for heterogeneous systems. In *Computer Design: VLSI in Computers and Processors*, pages 307–314, 1997.
[7] D. M. Chapiro. *Globally-Asynchronous Locally-Synchronous Systems*. PhD thesis, Standford University, 1984.
[8] E. W. Dijkstra. *A Discipline of Programming*. Prentice-Hall International, 1976.
[9] R. Dobkin, R. Ginosar, and C. Sotiriou. Data synchronisation issues in gals socs. In *International Conference on Asynchronous Circuits and Systems*, pages 170–179, 2004.
[10] P. L. Guernic, T. Gautier, M. L. Borgne, and C. L. Maire. Programming real-time applications with SIGNAL. *Proceedings of the IEEE*, 79(9):1321–1335, September 1991.

[11] N. Halbwachs, P. Caspi, P. Raymond, and D. Pilaud. The synchronous data-flow programming language LUSTRE. *Proceedings of the IEEE*, 79(9):1305–1320, September 1991.
[12] J. He and K. J. Turner. Specifying hardware timing with ET-LOTOS. In *Correct Hardware Design and Verification Methods*, volume 2144/2000, pages 161–166. LNCS, 2001.
[13] H. Kim, P. A. Beerel, and K. Stevens. Relative timing based verification of timed circuits and systems. In *Proceedings of the Eighth International Symposium on Asynchronous Circuits and Systems*, pages 115 – 124, April 2002.
[14] M. Krstic, E. Grass, and C. Stahl. Request-driven gals technique for wireless communication system. In *Proceedings of the 11th IEEE International Symposium on Asynchronous Circuits and Systems*, pages 76–85. IEEE, March 2005.
[15] J. Mekie, S. Chakraborty, G. Venkatarami, P. Thiagarajan, and D. Sharma. Interface design for rationally clocked gals systems. In *Proceedings of the 12th IEEE International Symposium on Asynchronous Circuits and Systems*, pages 160–171. IEEE, March 2006.
[16] J. Muttersbach, T. Villiger, and W. Fichtner. Practical design of globally-asynchronous locally-synchronous systems. In *Advanced Research in Asynchronous Circuits and Systems*, pages 52 – 59, 2000.
[17] R. Negulescu and A. Peeters. Verification of speed-dependences in single-rail handshake circuits. In *Advanced Research in Asynchronous Circuits and Systems*, pages 159–170, 1998.
[18] J. Plosila. *Self-Timed Circuit Design - The Action System Approach.* PhD thesis, University of Turku, 1999.
[19] J. Plosila, P. Liljeberg, and J. Isoaho. Modelling and refinement of an on-chip communication architecture. In *Formal Methods and Software Engineering: 7th International Conference on Formal Engineering Methods*, volume 3785/2005, pages 219–234. LNCS, 2005.
[20] B. Rajan and R. Shyamasundar. Multiclock Esterel: a reactive framework for asynchronous design. In *Parallel and Distributed Processing Symposium*, pages 201–209, 2000.
[21] E. Sekerinski and K. Sere. A theory of prioritizing composition. *The Computer Journal*, 39(8):701–712, 1996. The British Computer Society. Oxford University Press.
[22] K. Stevens, R. Ginosar, and S. Rotem. Relative timing. In *IEEE Transactions on Very Large Scale Integration (VLSI) Systems*, pages 129 – 140, Feb 2003.
[23] K. J. Turner and R. O. Sinnott. DILL: Specifying digital logic in LOTOS. In *Proc. Formal Description Techniques VI*, pages 71–86. North-Holland, 1994.
[24] T. Westerlund and J. Plosila. Formal timing model for hardware components. In *Proceedings of the 22nd NORCHIP Conference*, pages 293–296, Norway, Nov 2004.
[25] T. Westerlund and J. Plosila. Back-annotation of timing information into a formal hardware model: A case study. In *International Symposium on Signals, Circuits, and Systems - ISSCS 2005*, pages 625–628, Romania, July 2005.
[26] T. Westerlund and J. Plosila. Formal modelling of synchronous hardware components for system-on-chip. In *International Symposium on System-On-Chip*, pages 116–119, Finland, Nov 2005.
[27] T. Westerlund and J. Plosila. Time aware system refinement. In *REFINE 2006 Workshop*, page To appear, Septemper 2006.
[28] S. Zhuang, J. Carlsson, and L. Wanhammar. A design approach for gals based systems-on-chip. In *Solid-State and Integrated Circuits Technology*, pages 1368 – 1371, 2004.
[29] S. Zhuang, J. Carlsson, and L. Wanhammar. A design approach for gals based systems-on-chip. In *7th Internation Conference on Solid-State and Integrated Circuits Technology*, volume 2, pages 1368–1371, October 2004.

SALT—Structured Assertion Language for Temporal Logic

Andreas Bauer, Martin Leucker*, and Jonathan Streit

Institut für Informatik, Technische Universität München
{baueran, leucker, streit}@informatik.tu-muenchen.de

Abstract. This paper presents SALT. SALT is a general purpose specification and assertion language developed for creating concise temporal specifications to be used in industrial verification environments. It incorporates ideas of existing approaches, such as specification patterns, but also provides nested scopes, exceptions, support for regular expressions and real-time. The latter is needed in particular for verification tasks to do with reactive systems imposing strict execution times and deadlines. However, unlike other formalisms used for temporal specification of properties, SALT does not target a specific domain. The paper details on the design rationale, syntax and semantics of SALT in terms of a translation to temporal (real-time) logic, as well as on the realisation in form of a compiler. Our results will show that the higher level of abstraction introduced with SALT does not deprave the efficiency of the subsequent verification tools—rather, on the contrary.

1 Introduction

Temporal logics, such as linear time temporal logic (LTL)[Pnu77], are specification formalisms suited to express desired properties of a set of traces and come with a rigorous semantics. Yet more importantly, automatic verification techniques, such as model checking[CGP99], are successfully used to verify such specifications over finite-state system models.

However, despite obvious advantages over semi-formal or even informal notations, temporal logic is often completely disregarded in (industrial) practice. Instead, a considerable amount of verification related questions are answered only partially by means of testing and simulation—with well-known drawbacks, namely that testing alone can never show the absence of bugs, but merely their presence if at all (cf.[DDH72]). Temporal logic, on the other hand, is still widely considered to be a vehicle for specially skilled verification engineers, if not even an academic toy.

We argue that this point-of-view is misleading. We do, however, admit that, for example, LTL's syntax—together with the typical reduction to a minimal set of operators which is done in most research papers—makes it additionally hard for formulating concise and correct specifications, even for specialists.

* Part of this work was done during the author's stay in Stanford, USA, and supported by ARO DAAD 19-03-1-0197.

Z. Liu and J. He (Eds.): ICFEM 2006, LNCS 4260, pp. 757–775, 2006.

For example, consider the simple requirement "s precedes p after q", which is formulated in LTL by Dwyer et al.[DAC99] as $(\Box\neg q) \vee \Diamond(q \wedge (\neg p \text{ W } s))$. At first sight, this looks correct: "either q never holds or, when q becomes true, there is no p before an s". Nevertheless, the formula contains a very subtle error: it states that *eventually* $q \wedge (\neg p \text{ W } s)$ holds, but does not require it to be the first occurrence of q. The sequence `qpqs` satisfies the formula, although it is clear that it should not. Consequently, the correct formula would be $(\Box\neg q) \vee \neg q \text{ U } (q \wedge (\neg p \text{ W } s))$. Avoiding this kind of mistake in specifications altogether is practically impossible. LTL's minimalistic set of operators, however, forces its users to build complex, error-prone formulas for even very simple requirements as can be seen above.

Despite this, it is very unlikely that a completely different specification formalism—of whatever kind—would stand a chance to compete with LTL for at least two different reasons: 1. LTL has a well-accepted precise semantics, 2. powerful model checking tools and runtime verification approaches based on LTL exist already.

Contribution. In this paper, we remedy LTL's and timed LTL's (short: TLTL [RS97, D'S03]) weaknesses for industrial specifications by introducing the specification and assertion language SALT, which is an acronym for *Structured Assertion Language for Temporal Logic* (see also `http://salt.in.tum.de/`).

To programmers, SALT looks a lot like a programming language, while still being translatable to LTL, or—in case real-time operators are used—to TLTL. As such, SALT is also suitable as a front end to already existing model checking and runtime verification tools. Furthermore, a precise semantics of SALT is given in terms of translation rules, which are realised in an accompanying SALT compiler prototype.

More importantly, being closer to a general purpose (programming) language, SALT is—as the examples throughout the paper will show—more intuitive to use and understand than standard LTL. For example, besides LTL's temporal operators, SALT provides sophisticated scoping rules, support for (limited) regular expressions, exceptions, iterators, counting quantifiers, and user-defined macros.

In other words, using SALT, users are able to specify properties on a higher level of abstraction than with many other formalisms, such as standard LTL.

While compiling a high level programming language to a low level representation often has a negative impact in terms of efficiency, we will show that LTL (resp. TLTL) formulas resulting from SALT specifications tend to be rather compact when compared to their manually-written counterparts in LTL; one reason lies in that humans tend to choose the most readable formula among equivalent ones, while our compiler can optimise purely for the size of a formula.

However, plain LTL's limited flexibility in real-world scenarios has also been noted by other users (see Section 2). For instance, for the hardware domain, Sugar/PSL [BBDE$^+$01] has been designed as a high level specification language aimed as a "syntactic sugaring" for temporal logic.

Dwyer et al. [DAC99] have analysed real-world specifications to identify typical *patterns* for property specifications, similar to *design patterns* encountered in software engineering [GHJV94]. Using patterns allows even inexperienced users to reuse expert knowledge.

SALT takes over some of the ideas present in PSL and is heavily inspired by the pattern approach. However, SALT is a language and patterns are turned into operators of the language. Furthermore, the additional concepts listed above, like macro definitions, counting quantifiers etc., round off the specification language and push SALT ahead of existing approaches.

SALT's language reference, a compiler, an interactive web interface, as well as further example specifications written in SALT are available from the web site (`http://salt.in.tum.de/`).

Outline. Section 2 describes the context of SALT by means of already existing and mostly domain-specific approaches, as well as a classification of SALT with respect to its underlying semantics and expressiveness. Then, in Section 3, we take a detailed look at the language itself and highlight its main features. We discuss SALT's formal semantics in Section In Section 5, we will show that SALT specifications can be efficiently compiled to standard temporal (real-time) logics, often resulting in even more compact representations. Section 6 concludes the paper.

2 Classification

In the following, we detail on the context of SALT in terms of related work as well as in terms of its underlying semantics and expressiveness.

2.1 Existing Approaches

Sugar/PSL. Sugar/PSL (Property Specification Language) [BBDE+01] is a high level specification language tailored for hardware design, originally aimed as a "syntactic sugaring" of the branching time logic CTL. Sugar 2.0 is based on a linear view of time while keeping branching time as an optional extension and is currently undergoing standardisation by the IEEE under the name PSL [FMW05].

The PSL specification language is structured into boolean, temporal, verification, and modelling *layers*. The boolean layer provides operators for propositional logic, while the operators of the temporal layer are used to combine propositional formulas to temporal ones. The verification layer allows to define what the verification tool is expected to do with the specified properties (e. g., check that a property holds, assume that a property holds, etc.). The modelling layer, in turn, is used to model the input to the design or external hardware.

PSL provides a rich set of operators for reasoning over boolean conditions (e. g., bit-vector operations) and for regular expressions. A so-called clocking operator allows to state that an expression is evaluated only in cycles where its clocking condition holds. PSL comes with an abort operator that can be used to model resets: it evaluates a pending expression to false on the occurrence of an exceptional (abort) condition. Furthermore, PSL allows the use of macro directives similar to those of the C preprocessor. Parameterised properties can be instantiated for a set of concrete values. However, PSL does not contain temporal past operators which can be rather intuitive to use as well as make specifications more succinct (cf. [Mar03]), and no real-time constraints used frequently for modelling and verifying properties of reactive systems imposing strict execution times and deadlines, such as embedded systems.

PSL is often directly used as input to a verification tool, both for formal verification and for generating checks that are executed by a simulation tool. The latter corresponds to a runtime analysis of a simulated hardware design. However, PSL is specific to the hardware domain and a translation into LTL is possible only for a subset of PSL [TS05]. Therefore it cannot be easily used with existing LTL-based verification tools.

PSL's goals are orthogonal to the SALT approach. With SALT, we wanted to go further in terms of abstracting from LTL's syntax and thus providing a more convenient-to-use language. On the other hand, SALT is not dedicated to either model checking, runtime verification, or strictly to the hardware domain. As such, SALT does not impose its own verification and modelling layer.

SpecPatterns. The SALT approach was also influenced by work of Dwyer et al., in which various real-world specifications have been analysed [DAC99]. Frequently used patterns have been identified and a *pattern system* for property specifications, similar to the design patterns in software engineering [GHJV94] has been elaborated. A pattern provides a solution to a reoccurring problem, often including notes about its advantages, drawbacks, and alternatives. As such it enables inexperienced users to reuse expert knowledge.

Basically, the patterns of Dwyer et al. consist of *requirements*, such as "absence" (i. e., a condition is false) or "response" (i. e., an event triggers another one), that can be expressed under different *scopes*, like "globally", "before an event r", "after an event q", or "between two events r and q". The specification pattern approach has been adopted by the Bandera Specification Language [CDHR01] and a compiler that translates such specifications into LTL is part of the Bandera system.

Dwyer et al. convincingly argue that scopes are needed in many real-world specifications. However, specification patterns as defined by Dwyer et al. suffer from the fact that they cannot be nested: only propositional formulas may be used as their parameters. In other words, adding a new requirement to the pattern system means having to manually write an LTL formula for each scope.

Others. The previous two approaches are not the only specification languages tailored for domain specific tasks. For instance, the ForSpec Temporal Logic (FTL) [AFF$^+$02] is a specification language developed at INTEL, and is based on a linear view of time, aimed for the formal verification of hardware circuits. Much like Sugar/PSL, ForSpec provides regular and clocked expressions as well as accept and reject operators for modelling resets. However, ForSpec does not contain real-time operators, only limited support for references to the past, and cannot be completely translated to LTL.

EAGLE [BGHS04] is a temporal logic with a small but flexible set of primitives. The logic is based on recursive parameterised equations with fix-point semantics and merely three temporal operators: next-time, previous-time, and concatenation. Using these primitives, one can construct the operators known from various other formalisms, such as LTL or regular expressions. While EAGLE allows the specification of real-time constraints, it lacks most high level constructs such as nested scopes, exceptions, counting quantifiers currently present in SALT.

Duration calculus [CHR91] and similar interval temporal logics overcome some of the limitations of LTL that we mentioned. These logics can naturally encode past operators, scoping, regular expressions, and counting. However, it is unclear how to translate specifications in these frameworks to LTL such that standard model checking and runtime verification tools based on LTL can be employed.

2.2 Expressiveness

Clearly, existing approaches have shaped various practical considerations in the design rationale of the language SALT. However, from a purely theoretical point-of-view, SALT's features are more oriented towards the varying expressiveness of the supported logics.

SALT currently supports translation into propositional logics, LTL, as well as TLTL, a natural extension of LTL for the formulation of real-time constraints [RS97]. D'Souza has shown [D'S03] that TLTL corresponds exactly to the first-order fragment of monadic second order logic interpreted over timed words. This resembles the correspondence of LTL and first-order logic over words, shown by Kamp [Kam68]. However, LTL is strictly less expressive than second-order logic over words, which is expressively equivalent to ω-regular expressions. This implies that full support of regular expressions is not possible when LTL properties are in question (see Figure 1).

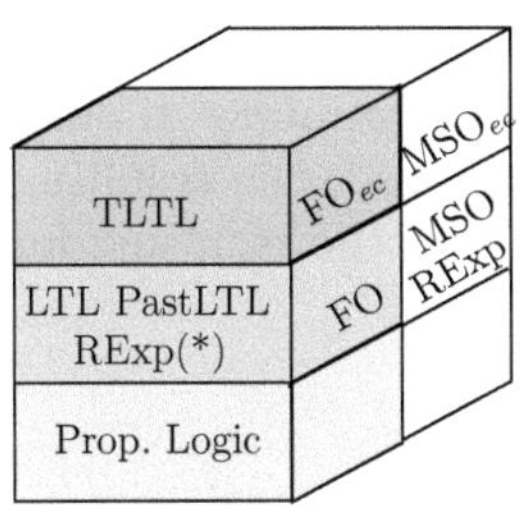

Fig. 1. Relationships between propositional, first-order, and temporal logics

For practitioners, regular expressions are an established formalism, often used to specify custom search-patterns. Therefore, SALT provides support for simplified regular expressions that do not go beyond star-free languages (where "star" refers to the Kleene operator) and that can be efficiently translated into LTL.

The design of the language SALT also follows a strictly layered approach (see Section 3), in that the language supports specifications that can be translated into either formalism depicted in Figure 1. More so, by reflecting and differentiating between the different levels of expressiveness in the language, SALT is extensible to support other logics in the future as well.

3 Features of the SALT Language

A SALT specification contains one or many assertions that together formulate the requirements associated with a system under scrutiny. Each assertion is translated into a separate LTL /TLTL formula, which can then be used in, say, a model checker or a runtime verification framework. SALT uses mainly textual operators, so that the frequently used LTL formula $\Box(p \rightarrow \Diamond q)$ would be written as

```
assert always (p implies eventually q).
```

Basically, the SALT language consists of the following three layers, each covering different aspects of the specification:

- *The propositional layer* provides the atomic, boolean propositions as well as the well-known boolean operators.
- *The temporal layer* encapsulates the main features of the SALT language for specifying temporal system properties. The layer is divided into a future fragment and a symmetrical past fragment.
- *The timed layer* adds real-time constraints to the language. It is equally divided into a future and a past fragment, similar to the temporal layer.

Within each layer, macros and parameterised expressions can be defined and instantiated by iteration operators, enlarging the expressiveness of each layer into the orthogonal dimension of functions.

Depending on which layers are used for specification, the SALT compiler generates either LTL or TLTL formulas (resp. with or without past operators). For instance, if only operators from the propositional layer are used, the resulting formulas are purely propositional formulas. If only operators from the temporal and the propositional layer are used, the resulting formulas are LTL formulas, whereas if the timed layer is used, the resulting formulas are TLTL formulas.

3.1 Propositional Layer

Atomic propositions. Boolean propositions are the atomic elements from which SALT expressions are built. They usually resemble variables, signals, or complete expressions of the system under scrutiny. SALT is parameterised with respect to the propositional layer: any term that evaluates to either *true* or *false* can be used as atomic proposition. This allows, for example, propositions to be Java expressions when used for runtime verification of Java programs, or, simple bit-vectors when SALT is used as front end to verification tools like SMV [McM92].

Usually, every identifier that is used in the specification and that was not defined as a macro or a formal parameter is treated as an atomic proposition, which means that it appears in the output as it has been written in the specification. Additionally, arbitrary strings can be used as atomic propositions. For example,

```
assert always "state!=ERROR"
```

is a valid SALT specification and results in the output (here, in SMV syntax)

```
LTLSPEC G state!=ERROR.
```

However, the SALT compiler can also be called with a customized parser provided as a command line parameter, which is then used to perform additional checks on the syntactic structure of the propositions thus, making the use of structured propositions more reliable.

Boolean operators. The well-known set of boolean operators $\neg$, $\wedge$, $\vee$, $\rightarrow$ and $\leftrightarrow$ can be used in SALT both as symbols (`!`, `&`, `|`, `->`, `<->`), or as textual operators (`not`, `and`, `or`, `implies`, `equals`).

Additionally, the conditional operators `if-then` and `if-then-else` can be used, which appear similarly also in the ForSpec language. Conditional operators tend to make specifications easier to read, because `if-then-else` constructs are familiar to programmers of almost every language. Using this operator, the introductory example could be reformulated as

```
assert always (if p then eventually q).
```

More so, any such formula can be arbitrarily combined using the boolean connectives.

3.2 Temporal Layer

The temporal layer consists of a future and a past fragment. Although past operators do not add expressiveness [GPSS80], they can help to write formulas that are easier to understand and more efficient for processing [Mar03].

In the following, we concentrate on the future fragment of SALT. The past fragment is, however, completely symmetrical. SALT's future operators are translated using only LTL future operators, and past operators are translated using only LTL past operators. This leaves users the complete freedom as to whether they do or do not want to have past operators in the result.

Standard LTL operators. SALT provides the common LTL operators U, W, R, $\Box$, $\Diamond$ and $\circ$, written as `until`, `until weak`, `releases`, `always`, `eventually`, and `next`. Thus, untimed SALT has the same expressiveness as LTL (see Section 2.2).

Extended operators. Similar to Sugar/PSL, SALT also provides a number of extended operators that help express frequently used requirements.

- `never`. The `never` operator is dual to `always` and requires that a formula never holds. While this could of course be easily expressed with the standard LTL operators, using `never` can help to make specifications easier to understand.
- Extended `until`. SALT provides an extended version of the LTL U operator. The user can specify whether they want it to be *exclusive* (i. e., in φ U ψ, φ has to hold until the moment ψ occurs) or *inclusive* (i. e., φ has to hold until and during the moment ψ occurs) [1]
  They can also choose whether the end condition is *required* (i. e., must eventually occur), *weak* (i. e., may or may not occur), or *optional* (i. e., the expression is only considered if the end condition eventually occurs).
  The `until` operator family of Sugar/PSL provides a similar choice between inclusive/exclusive and weak/strong end conditions.
- Extended `next`. Instead of writing long chains of `next` operators, SALT users can specify directly that they want a formula to hold at a certain step in the future. It is also possible to use the extended `next` operator with an interval, e. g., specifying that a formula has to hold at some time between 3 and 6 steps in the future. Note that this operator refers only to states at certain positions in the sequence, not to real-time constraints.

Counting quantifiers. SALT provides two operators, `occurring` and `holding`, that allow to specify that an event has to occur a certain number of times. `occurring` deals with events that may last more than one step and are separated by one or more steps in which the condition does not hold. `holding` considers single steps in which a condition holds. Both operators can also be used with an interval, e. g., expressing the fact that an event has to occur *at most* 2 times in the future. To express this requirement manually in LTL, one would have to write

$$\neg p \text{ W } (p \text{ W } (\neg p \text{ W } (p \text{ W } \Box\neg p))).$$

The corresponding SALT specification is written as

```
assert occurring[<=2] p.
```

Exceptions. SALT includes the exception operators `rejecton` and `accepton` that interrupt the evaluation of a formula upon occurrence of an abort condition. `rejecton` evaluates a formula to false if the abort condition occurs and the formula has not been accepted before. For example, monitoring a formula $\Diamond\varphi$ when there has been no occurrence of φ yet would evaluate to false. The dual operator, `accepton`, evaluates a formula to true if it has not been rejected before.

[1] This has nothing to do with strict or non-strict U: strictness refers to whether the present state (i. e., the left end of the interval where φ is required to hold) is included or not in the evaluation, while inclusive/exclusive defines whether φ has to hold in the state where ψ occurs (i. e., the right end of the interval). Strict SALT operators can be created by adding a preceding `next`-operator.

Exceptions can be useful, for example, when specifying a communication protocol that requires certain messages to be sent, but allows to abort the communication at any time by sending a reset message. This would be expressed in SALT as

```
assert (con_open and next (data until con_close))
    accepton
reset.
```

Similar `rejecton` and `accepton` operators can be found in ForSpec and in PSL. The formal semantics of LTL enriched with those two operators (called Reset-LTL) is explored in detail elsewhere [ABKV03].

Scope operators. Many temporal specifications use requirements restricted to a certain *scope*, i. e., they state that the requirement has to hold only before, after, or between some events, and not on the whole sequence [DAC99]. This can be expressed in SALT using the operators `upto` (or `before`), `from` (or `after`) and `between`.

Figure 2 illustrates scopes. It should be clear from the figure that it is mandatory in SALT to specify whether the delimiting events are part of the interval (i. e., *inclusive*) or not (i. e., *exclusive*).

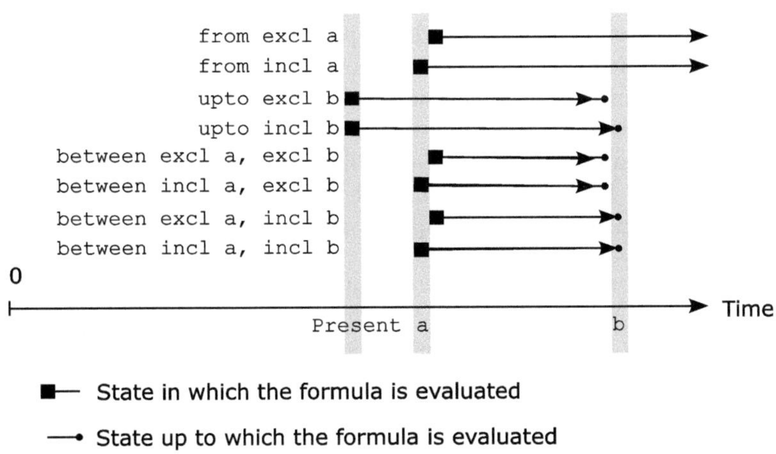

Fig. 2. Scopes of `upto`, `from` and `between`

Furthermore, for scope operators, it has to be stated whether the occurrence of the delimiting events is strictly required. For example, the following specification

```
assert p
  between inclusive optional call,
          inclusive optional answer
```

means that p has to hold within the interval delimited by *call* and *answer*, provided such an interval exists. Without the keyword *optional*, such an interval would be required and within this interval, p must occur.

Scopes have been identified by Dwyer et al. as an important issue in the specification pattern system, and the Bandera language. However, their pattern system is restricted to predefined requirements. It does not allow nested scopes, and by default only certain combinations of inclusive/exclusive and required/optional delimiters. Some—but by far not all—scopes can also be expressed in Sugar/PSL using the `next_event` and `before` operators. SALT's distinguishing feature here is that scope operators can be used with arbitrary formulas, even with nested scope operators.

While it is possible to implement a translation of the `from` operator into LTL relatively straightforward (see Section 4), the `upto` operator proves to be more difficult, as can be seen in the following example.

A specification `always` φ `upto` b expresses that φ must always hold until the occurrence of the end condition b. A naïve translation into LTL would be φ W b. This is in order for a purely propositional φ, but might be wrong when temporal operators are used: Consider for example $\varphi :=$ `p-> (eventuallys)` yielding the formula $(p \rightarrow \Diamond s) \mathrm{W} b$, intending to say "`p` should be followed by `s` before `b`". The sequence pbs is a model for the latter formula, although `s` occurs after the end condition `b`, which clearly violates our intuitions. To meet our intuition, the negated end condition b has to be inserted into the U and ○ statements of φ in various places, e. g., like this: $(p \rightarrow (\neg b \; \mathrm{U} \; (\neg b \wedge s))) \; \mathrm{W} \; b$. Dwyer et al. describe this procedure in the notes of their specification pattern system [DAC99]. It is however a tedious and highly error-prone task if undertaken manually.

SALT supports automatic translation by internally defining a stop operator. Using stop , the above example can be formulated as $((p \rightarrow \Diamond s)$ stop $b)\mathrm{W}b$ with stop b expressing that $(p \rightarrow \Diamond s)$ shall not take into account states after the occurrence of b. It is then transformed into an LTL expression in a similar way as the `rejecton` and `accepton` operators. Details can be found in Section 4.

Regular expressions. Regular expressions are well-known to many programmers. They provide a convenient way to express complex patterns of events, and appear also in many specification languages, e. g., such as Sugar/PSL. However, arbitrary regular languages can be defined using regular expressions, while LTL only allows to define so-called *star-free* languages. Thus, regular expressions have to be restricted in SALT.

SALT regular expressions provide concatenation (`;`), union (`|`) and Kleene-star operators (`*`), but no complement. The argument of the Kleene-star is required to be a propositional formula. The advantage of this operator set—in contrast to the usual operator set for star-free regular expressions, which contains concatenation, union and complement—is that it can be translated efficiently into LTL. We agree with Sugar/PSL, which also provides regular expressions without a complement operator, that many relevant properties can be expressed conveniently without it.

Additionally, SALT provides operators that do not increase the expressiveness of its regular expressions, but makes dealing with them more convenient for users. The overlapping sequence operator `:` is inspired by Sugar/PSL and states that one expression follows another one, overlapping in one step. The `?` and `+` operators (optional expression and repetition at least once) are common extensions of regular expressions. The `*` operator extended with a range of natural numbers allows to specify that an expression has to hold at least, at most, exactly, or in between n and m times.

Traditional regular expressions match finite sequences. A SALT regular expression holds on an (infinite) sequence if it matches a finite prefix of the sequence.

With the help of regular expressions, we can rewrite the example using exception operators as

```
assert /con_open; data*; con_close/ accepton reset.
```

3.3 Timed Layer

SALT contains a timed extension that allows the specification of real-time constraints. Timed operators are translated into TLTL [RS97, D'S03], a timed variant of LTL.

Timing constraints in SALT are expressed using the modifier `timed[`$\sim$`]`, which can be used together with several untimed SALT operators in order to turn them into timed operators. $\sim$ is one of `<`, `<=`, `=`, `>=`, `>` for `next timed` and either `<` or `<=` for all other timed operators.

- `next timed[`$\sim c$`]` φ
  states that the next occurrence of φ is within the time bounds $\sim c$. This corresponds to the operator $\rhd_{\sim c}\varphi$ in TLTL.
- φ `until timed[`$\sim c$`]` ψ
  states that φ is true until the next occurrence of ψ, and that this occurrence of ψ is within the time bounds $\sim c$. The extended variants of `until` can be used as timed operators as well.
- `always timed[`$\sim c$`]` φ
  states that φ must always be true within the time bounds $\sim c$.
- `never timed[`$\sim c$`]` φ
  states that φ must never be true within the time bounds $\sim c$.
- `eventually timed[`$\sim c$`]` φ
  states that φ must be true at some point within the time bounds $\sim c$.

3.4 Macros and Parameterised Expressions

SALT allows user-defined sub-expressions as *macros* and to parameterise macros and sub-expressions. Macros can be called in the same way as built-in SALT operators. Within certain limits, this allows the user to extend the SALT language using their own operators. For example, the following macro is called in infix notation:

```
define respondsto(x, y) := y implies eventually x
   assert always
(reply respondsto request)
```

Iteration operators allow to instantiate a parameterised sub-expression or macro with a list of values provided by the user. For example, the following specification states that either `a` or `!b` or `c` must hold forever.

```
assert someof list [a, !b, c] as i in always i
```

Parameters defined in a macro or an iteration expression can also be used to parameterise boolean variables, as in the following example, which states that exactly one of the four variables, `state_1`, `state_2`, `state_3` and `state_4`, must be true.

```
assert exactlyoneof enumerate[1..4] as i in state_$i$
```

Macros can help to make a specification easier to understand, because complicated sub-expressions can be transparently hidden from the user, and accessed via an intuitive name that explains what the expression actually stands for. Sub-expressions that are used several times have to be written down only once.

Up to an extent, support for user-defined macros and iteration over parameterised expressions is a part of many high-level specification languages, e. g., such as Sugar/PSL.

3.5 Example

Let us conclude this section by looking at a slightly longer example showing most of SALT's features. The following specification describes an elevator and is partially based on an example presented by Dwyer et al. [DAC99]: On all three floors in a building, calling the elevator at floor i implies that it may pass at most two times at that floor without opening its doors, and that it must finally open its doors at that floor within 60 seconds.

```
define max_twice_at_floor_before_open(i) :=
 always (occurring[<=2] atfloor_$i$
            between inclusive optional call_$i$,
                    exclusive optional open_$i$)

define max_60s_before_open(i) :=
 always (call_$i$ implies
        eventually timed[<=60.0] open_$i$)

assert allof enumerate[1..3] as floor in
            max_twice_at_floor_before_open(floor)
        and max_60s_before_open(floor)
```

Note that the modifiers `optional` in the `between`-statement make sure that `atfloor_`i is only checked provided `call_`i occurs.

4 Semantics

SALT comes with a precisely defined semantics. As outlined in Section 2.2, SALT can be translated into either LTL or TLTL; the latter only when timed operators are used in a specification. Therefore, we define the semantics of SALT's operators by means of their corresponding LTL or respectively TLTL formulas.

More precisely, we define a translation function $\mathcal{T}$ to translate a valid SALT specification ψ into a temporal logic formula $\mathcal{T}(\psi)$, and define that an infinite word w over a finite alphabet of actions satisfies ψ iff $w \models \mathcal{T}(\psi)$ (using the standard satisfaction relation $\models$ defined for LTL /TLTL [MP95]).

For brevity, we exemplify the translation on a few selected operators only and refer to the extensive language reference and manual available from SALT's homepage at `http://salt.in.tum.de/` for the remaining cases.

In what follows, let ψ, φ, and φ' denote SALT specifications. Many of SALT's operators can be considered as simple syntactic sugaring and are easily translated to LTL. For example, $\mathcal{T}(\varphi\ \texttt{or}\ \varphi'))$ is translated inductively to $\mathcal{T}(\varphi) \vee \mathcal{T}(\varphi')$. The operator `never` is then translated as $\mathcal{T}(\texttt{never}\ \varphi) = \neg\Diamond\mathcal{T}(\varphi)$, whereas a weak inclusive until as in φ_1 `untilinclweak` φ_2 is then defined, for instance, as

$$\mathcal{T}(\varphi_1\ \texttt{untilinclweak}\ \varphi_2) = \mathcal{T}(\varphi_1)\ \mathrm{W}\ (\mathcal{T}(\varphi_1) \wedge \mathcal{T}(\varphi_2)).$$

However, not all SALT operators translate in such a straightforward inductive manner, since their translation depends on what is defined by the according sub-formulas occurring in a given expression. To guide the translation process for such operators, we have introduced an artificial or helper operator, `stop`, which is inductively defined as follows:

$$\begin{aligned}
\mathcal{T}(b\ \mathrm{stop}_{\mathrm{excl}}\ s) &= b\\
\mathcal{T}((\neg\varphi)\ \mathrm{stop}_{\mathrm{excl}}\ s) &= \neg\mathcal{T}(\varphi\ \mathrm{stop}_{\mathrm{excl}}\ s)\\
\mathcal{T}((\varphi \wedge \psi)\ \mathrm{stop}_{\mathrm{excl}}\ s) &= \mathcal{T}(\varphi\ \mathrm{stop}_{\mathrm{excl}}\ s) \wedge \mathcal{T}(\psi\ \mathrm{stop}_{\mathrm{excl}}\ s)\\
\mathcal{T}((\varphi \vee \psi)\ \mathrm{stop}_{\mathrm{excl}}\ s) &= \mathcal{T}(\varphi\ \mathrm{stop}_{\mathrm{excl}}\ s) \vee \mathcal{T}(\psi\ \mathrm{stop}_{\mathrm{excl}}\ s)\\
\mathcal{T}((\varphi\ \mathrm{U}\ \psi)\ \mathrm{stop}_{\mathrm{excl}}\ s) &= (\neg s \wedge \mathcal{T}(\varphi\ \mathrm{stop}_{\mathrm{excl}}\ s))\ \mathrm{U}\ (\neg s \wedge \mathcal{T}(\psi\ \mathrm{stop}_{\mathrm{excl}}\ s))\\
\mathcal{T}((\varphi\ \mathrm{W}\ \psi)\ \mathrm{stop}_{\mathrm{excl}}\ s) &= \mathcal{T}(\varphi\ \mathrm{stop}_{\mathrm{excl}}\ s)\ \mathrm{W}\ (s \vee \mathcal{T}(\psi\ \mathrm{stop}_{\mathrm{excl}}\ s))\\
\mathcal{T}((\circ\varphi)\ \mathrm{stop}_{\mathrm{excl}}\ s) &= \circ(\neg s \wedge \mathcal{T}(\varphi\ \mathrm{stop}_{\mathrm{excl}}\ s))\\
\mathcal{T}((\circ_W\varphi)\ \mathrm{stop}_{\mathrm{excl}}\ s) &= \circ(s \vee \mathcal{T}(\varphi\ \mathrm{stop}_{\mathrm{excl}}\ s))
\end{aligned}$$

$$\begin{aligned}
\mathcal{T}((\Box\varphi)\ \mathrm{stop}_{\mathrm{excl}}\ s) &= \mathcal{T}(\varphi\ \mathrm{stop}_{\mathrm{excl}}\ s)\ \mathrm{W}\ s\\
\mathcal{T}((\Diamond\varphi)\ \mathrm{stop}_{\mathrm{excl}}\ s) &= (\neg s)\ \mathrm{U}\ (\neg s \wedge \mathcal{T}(\varphi\ \mathrm{stop}_{\mathrm{excl}}\ s))
\end{aligned}$$

where b denotes an atomic proposition from the action alphabet and s an arbitrary formula, possibly atomic also.

Thus, `stop` selects certain aspects of a formula, and in $\psi \equiv \varphi_1$ `stop` φ_2, intuitively asserts that the validity of ψ does not depend on events occurring after φ_2 has occurred. Again, for brevity, we consider only the exclusive variant of `stop` and only for the future fragment of SALT. The past fragment and inclusive semantics, however, are each symmetrical.

The more complicated scope operator `upto`, which was discussed earlier in Section 3.2, and whose translation depends on `stop`, is then defined as:

$$
\begin{array}{lll}
\mathcal{T}(\varphi\ \texttt{upto excl req}\ b) & & = \\
& \text{if } \mathcal{T}(\varphi) = \Box\psi: & (\psi\ \text{stop}_{\text{excl}}\ b)\ \mathrm{U}\ b \\
& \text{if } \mathcal{T}(\varphi) = \neg\Diamond\psi: & (\neg\psi\ \text{stop}_{\text{excl}}\ b)\ \mathrm{U}\ b \\
& \text{else:} & (\Diamond b) \wedge (\mathcal{T}(\varphi)\ \text{stop}_{\text{excl}}\ b) \\
\mathcal{T}(\varphi\ \texttt{upto excl opt}\ b) & & = \\
& \text{if } \mathcal{T}(\varphi) = \Diamond\psi: & \neg((\neg\psi\ \text{stop}_{\text{excl}}\ b)\ \mathrm{U}\ b) \\
& \text{else:} & (\Diamond b) \rightarrow (\mathcal{T}(\varphi)\ \text{stop}_{\text{excl}}\ b) \\
\mathcal{T}(\varphi\ \texttt{upto excl weak}\ b) & & = (\mathcal{T}(\varphi)\ \text{stop}_{\text{excl}}\ b) \\
\mathcal{T}(\texttt{req}\ \varphi\ \texttt{upto excl req}\ b) & & = \\
& \text{if } \mathcal{T}(\varphi) = \Box\psi: & \neg b \wedge ((\psi\ \text{stop}_{\text{excl}}\ b)\ \mathrm{U}\ b) \\
& \text{if } \mathcal{T}(\varphi) = \neg\Diamond\psi: & \neg b \wedge ((\neg\psi\ \text{stop}_{\text{excl}}\ b)\ \mathrm{U}\ b) \\
& \text{else:} & (\Diamond b) \wedge \neg b \wedge (\mathcal{T}(\varphi)\ \text{stop}_{\text{excl}}\ b) \\
\mathcal{T}(\texttt{req}\ \varphi\ \texttt{upto excl opt}\ b) & & = \\
& \text{if } \mathcal{T}(\varphi) = \Diamond\psi: & \neg((\neg\psi\ \text{stop}_{\text{excl}}\ b)\ \mathrm{U}\ b) \\
& \text{else:} & (\Diamond b) \rightarrow (\neg b \wedge (\mathcal{T}(\varphi)\ \text{stop}_{\text{excl}}\ b)) \\
\mathcal{T}(\texttt{req}\ \varphi\ \texttt{upto excl weak}\ b) & & = \neg b \wedge (\mathcal{T}(\varphi)\ \text{stop}_{\text{excl}}\ b) \\
\mathcal{T}(\texttt{weak}\ \varphi\ \texttt{upto excl req}\ b) & & = \\
& \text{if } \mathcal{T}(\varphi) = \Box\psi: & (\psi\ \text{stop}_{\text{excl}}\ b)\ \mathrm{U}\ b \\
& \text{if } \mathcal{T}(\varphi) = \neg\Diamond\psi: & (\neg\psi\ \text{stop}_{\text{excl}}\ b)\ \mathrm{U}\ b \\
& \text{else:} & (\Diamond b) \wedge (b \vee (\mathcal{T}(\varphi)\ \text{stop}_{\text{excl}}\ b)) \\
\mathcal{T}(\texttt{weak}\ \varphi\ \texttt{upto excl opt}\ b) & & = \\
& \text{if } \mathcal{T}(\varphi) = \Diamond\psi: & b \vee \neg((\neg\psi\ \text{stop}_{\text{excl}}\ b)\ \mathrm{U}\ b) \\
& \text{else:} & (\Diamond b) \rightarrow (b \vee (\mathcal{T}(\varphi)\ \text{stop}_{\text{excl}}\ b)) \\
\mathcal{T}(\texttt{weak}\ \varphi\ \texttt{upto excl weak}\ b) & & = b \vee (\mathcal{T}(\varphi)\ \text{stop}_{\text{excl}}\ b) \\
\mathcal{T}(\varphi\ \texttt{upto incl req}\ b) & & = (\Diamond b) \wedge (\mathcal{T}(\varphi)\ \text{stop}_{\text{incl}}\ b) \\
\mathcal{T}(\varphi\ \texttt{upto incl opt}\ b) & & = (\Diamond b) \rightarrow (\mathcal{T}(\varphi)\ \text{stop}_{\text{incl}}\ b) \\
\mathcal{T}(\varphi\ \texttt{upto incl weak}\ b) & & = \\
& \text{if } \mathcal{T}(\varphi) = \Box\psi: & \neg(\neg b\ \mathrm{U}\ \neg(\psi\ \text{stop}_{\text{incl}}\ b)) \\
& \text{if } \mathcal{T}(\varphi) = \neg\Diamond\psi: & \neg(\neg b\ \mathrm{U}\ (\psi\ \text{stop}_{\text{incl}}\ b)) \\
& \text{else:} & (\mathcal{T}(\varphi)\ \text{stop}_{\text{incl}}\ b)
\end{array}
$$

where, of course, $\text{stop}_{\text{excl}}$ and $\text{stop}_{\text{incl}}$ are references to the exclusive and inclusive variants of `stop`, respectively.

Similar translation schemes are defined for SALT's exception operators, i. e., `accepton` and `rejecton`. Those and the remaining operators' semantics are detailed in the SALT language reference and manual.

5 Realisation and Results

We have implemented our concepts in terms of a compiler for the SALT language. The compiler front end is currently implemented in Java, while its back end, which also optimises specifications for size, is realised via the functional programming language Haskell.

5.1 The SALT Compiler

Basically, the compiler's input is a SALT specification and its output a temporal logic formula. Like with programming languages, compilation of SALT is done in several stages. First, user-defined macros, counting quantifiers and iteration operators are expanded to expressions using only a core set of SALT operators. Then, the SALT operators are replaced by expressions in the subset SALT--, which contains the full expressiveness of LTL /TLTL as well as exception handling and stop operators. The translation from SALT-- into LTL /TLTL is treated as a separate step since it requires weaving the abort conditions into the whole subexpression. The result is an LTL /TLTL formula in form of an abstract syntax tree that is transformed easily into concrete syntax via a so-called *printing function*. Currently, we provide printing functions for SMV [McM92] and SPIN [Hol97] syntax, but the users can easily provide additional printing functions to support their tool of choice.

The use of optimised, context-dependent translation patterns as well as a final optimisation step performing local changes also help reducing the size of the generated formulas.

5.2 Experimental Results

As the time required for model checking depends exponentially on the size of the formula to check, efficiency was an important issue for the development of SALT and its compiler. One might suspect that generated formulas are bigger and less efficient to check than handwritten ones. But our experiments show that this is not the case.

In order to quantify the efficiency of the SALT compiler, existing LTL formulas were compared to the formulas generated by the compiler from a corresponding SALT specification. This was done for two data sets: the specification pattern system [DAC99] (50 specifications) and a collection of real-world example specifications, mostly from the Dwyer's et al.'s survey data [DAC99] (26 specifications). The increase or decrease of the formula was measured using the following parameters:

BA [Fri]: Number of states of the Büchi automaton (BA) generated using the algorithm proposed by Fritz [Fri03], which is one of the best currently known. This is probably the most significant parameter, as a BA is usually used for model checking, and the duration of the verification process depends highly on the size of this automaton.

BA [Odd]: Number of states of the BA generated using the algorithm proposed by Oddoux [GO01].
U: Number of U, R, $\Box$ and $\Diamond$ in the formula.
X: Number of $\circ$ in the formula.
Boolean: Number of boolean leafs, i. e., variable references and constants. This is a good parameter for estimating the length of the formula.

The results can be seen in Figure 3. The formulas generated by the SALT compiler contain a greater number of boolean leafs, but use *less temporal operators* and, therefore, also yield a smaller BA. The error markers in the figure indicate the simple standard error of the mean.

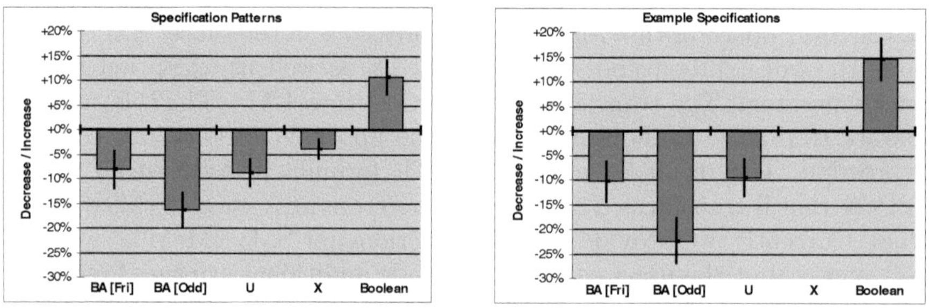

Fig. 3. Size of generated formulas

Discussion. Using SALT for writing specifications does not deprave model checking efficiency. On the contrary, one can observe that it often leads to more succinct formulas.

The reason for this result is that SALT performs a number of optimisations. For instance, when translating a formula of the form $\varphi W \psi$, the compiler can choose between the two equivalent expressions

$$\neg(\neg\psi \text{ U } (\neg\varphi \wedge \neg\psi)) \quad \text{and} \quad (\varphi \text{ U } \psi) \vee \Box\varphi.$$

While the first expression duplicates ψ in the resulting formula, the second expression duplicates φ, and introduces a new temporal operator. In most cases, the first expression, which is less intuitive for humans, yields better technical results.

Another equivalence utilised by the compiler is: $\Box(\varphi \text{ W } \psi) \iff \Box(\varphi \vee \psi)$. With $\varphi \text{ W } \psi$ being equivalent to $(\varphi \text{ U } \psi) \vee \Box\varphi$, the left hand side reads as $\Box((\varphi \text{ U } \psi) \vee \Box\varphi)$. When φ and ψ are propositions, this expression results in a BA with four states (using the algorithm proposed by Fritz [Fri03]). $\Box(\varphi \vee \psi)$, however, is translated into a BA with only a single state.

Of course, the benefit obtained from using the SALT approach is of no principle nature: The rewriting of LTL formulas could be done without having SALT as a high-level language. What is more, given an LTL-to-BA translator that produces a minimal BA for the language defined by a given formula, no optimisations on the formula level would be required, and such a translation function exists—at least theoretically.[2] Nevertheless, the high abstraction level realised by SALT makes the mentioned optimisations *easily* possible, and produces BAs that are smaller than without such optimisations—despite the fact that today's LTL-to-BA translators already perform many optimisations.

6 Conclusions

In this paper we presented SALT, a high-level extensible specification and assertion language for temporal logic. It is designed for intuitive usage for both verification experts as well as more practically oriented system engineers.

The development of SALT originates mainly from difficulties we faced in our industrial cooperations, when trying to apply and transfer certain state-of-the-art verification methods into industrial practice. But also within our academic cooperations (see, e. g., [BKKS05]), we have learned that LTL is often difficult to use for a typical software engineer.

SALT aims to ease some of these problems by introducing on the one hand side a higher level of abstraction for the specification of temporal assertions. This makes specifications easier to understand and more convenient to express for its users. At the same time, SALT is designed to look and feel like a programming language to be easily accessible to software engineers.

Our experimental results have shown that the higher level of abstraction does not result in an efficiency penalty, as compiled specifications are often considerably smaller than manually-written ones.

We have integrated SALT into AUTOFOCUS [HSSS96], a modelling and verification tool used within several industrial cooperations, and first reactions of AutoFocus users are very promising.

SALT as presented in this paper is ready to use and we invite the reader to explore it in-depth via its interactive web interface at `http://salt.in.tum.de/`.

References

[ABKV03] R. Armoni, D. Bustan, O. Kupferman, and M. Y. Vardi. Resets vs. aborts in linear temporal logic. In *International Conference on Tools and Algorithms for Construction and Analysis of Systems*, pages 65–80. Springer, 2003.

[AFF$^+$02] Roy Armoni, Limor Fix, Alon Flaisher, Rob Gerth, Boris Ginsburg, Tomer Kanza, Avner Landver, Sela Mador-Haim, Eli Singerman, Andreas Tiemeyer, Moshe Y. Vardi, and Yael Zbar. The ForSpec temporal logic: A new temporal property-specification language. In *Tools and Algorithms for Construction and Analysis of Systems*, pages 296–211, 2002.

[2] As the class of BAs is enumerable and language equivalence of two BAs decidable, it is possible to enumerate the class of BAs ordered by size and take the first one that is equivalent to the one to be minimised. Clearly, such an approach is not feasible in practice—and feasible minimisation procedures are hard to achieve.

[BBDE+01] Ilan Beer, Shoham Ben-David, Cindy Eisner, Dana Fisman, Anna Gringauze, and Yoav Rodeh. The temporal logic Sugar. In *Proceedings of the 13th International Conference on Computer Aided Verification (CAV)*, pages 363–367, London, UK, 2001. Springer.

[BGHS04] H. Barringer, A. Goldberg, K. Havelund, and K. Sen. Rule-based runtime verification. In *Fifth International Conference on Verification, Model Checking and Abstract Interpretation*, 2004.

[BKKS05] J. Botaschanjan, L. Kof, C. Kühnel, and M. Spichkova. Towards Verified Automotive Software. In ACM Press, editor, *Proceedings of the 2nd International ICSE Workshop on Automotive Software*. ACM, New York, May 2005.

[CDHR01] James Corbett, Matthew Dwyer, John Hatcliff, and Robby. Expressing checkable properties of dynamic systems: The Bandera specification language. Technical Report 04, Kansas State University, Department of Computing and Information Sciences, 2001.

[CGP99] Edmund M. Clarke, Orna Grumberg, and Doron A. Peled. *Model Checking*. The MIT Press, Cambridge, Massachusetts, 1999.

[CHR91] Zhou ChaoChen, Tony Hoare, and Anders P. Ravn. A calculus of durations. *Information Processing Letters*, 40(5):269–276, 1991.

[DAC99] Matthew B. Dwyer, George S. Avrunin, and James C. Corbett. Patterns in property specifications for finite-state verification. In *Proceedings of the 21st International Conference on Software Engineering*, 1999.

[DDH72] O.J. Dahl, E.W. Dijkstra, and C.A.R. Hoare. *Structured Programming*. Academic Press, London, 1972.

[D'S03] Deepak D'Souza. A logical characterisation of event clock automata. *International Journal of Foundations of Computer Science (IJFCS)*, 14(4):625–639, August 2003.

[FMW05] Harry Foster, Erisch Marschner, and Yaron Wolfsthal. IEEE 1850 PSL: The next generation. In *DVCon*, 2005.

[Fri03] Carsten Fritz. Constructing Büchi automata from linear temporal logic using simulation relations for alternating Büchi automata. In Oscar H. Ibarra and Zhe Dang, editors, *Implementation and Application of Automata. Eighth International Conference (CIAA)*, volume 2759 of *Lecture Notes in Computer Science*, pages 35–48, Santa Barbara, CA, USA, 2003.

[GHJV94] E. Gamma, R. Helm, R. Johnson, and J. Vlissides. *Design Patterns: Elements of Reusable Object-Oriented Software*. Addison-Wesley, 1994.

[GO01] Paul Gastin and Denis Oddoux. Fast LTL to Büchi automata translation. In *Proceedings of the 13th International Conference on Computer Aided Verification (CAV)*, pages 53–65, London, UK, 2001. Springer.

[GPSS80] Dov Gabbay, Amir Pnueli, Saharon Shelah, and Jonathan Stavi. On the temporal analysis of fairness. In *Proceedings of the 7th ACM SIGPLAN-SIGACT symposium on Principles of programming languages (POPL)*, pages 163–173, New York, NY, USA, 1980. ACM Press.

[Hol97] Gerard J. Holzmann. The model checker Spin. *IEEE Trans. on Software Engineering*, 23:279–295, May 1997.

[HSSS96] Franz Huber, Bernhard Schatz, Alexander Schmidt, and Katharina Spies. AutoFocus: A tool for distributed systems specification. In *Proceedings of Formal Techniques in Real-Time and Fault Tolerant Systems*, pages 467–470. Springer, 1996.

[Kam68] Johan Anthony Willem Kamp. *Tense Logic and the Theory of Linear Order*. PhD thesis, University of California, Los Angeles, 1968.

[Mar03] Nicolas Markey. Temporal logic with past is exponentially more succinct, concurrency column. *Bulletin of the EATCS*, 79:122–128, 2003.

[McM92] K. L. McMillan. The SMV system, symbolic model checking - an approach. Technical Report CMU-CS-92-131, Carnegie Mellon University, 1992.

[MP95] Zohar Manna and Amir Pnueli. *Temporal Verification of Reactive Systems*. Springer, New York, 1995.

[Pnu77] Amir Pnueli. The temporal logic of programs. In *Proceedings of the 18th IEEE Symposium on the Foundations of Computer Science (FOCS-77)*, pages 46–57, Providence, Rhode Island, October 31–November 2 1977. IEEE Computer Society Press.

[RS97] Jean-François Raskin and Pierre-Yves Schobbens. State clock logic: A decidable real-time logic. In Oded Maler, editor, *HART*, volume 1201 of *Lecture Notes in Computer Science*, pages 33–47. Springer, 1997.

[TS05] T. Tuerk and K. Schneider. From PSL to LTL: A formal validation in HOL. In *Theorem Proving in Higher Order Logic (TPHOL)*, Lecture Notes in Computer Science, Oxford, UK, 2005. Springer.

Author Index

Lecture Notes in Computer Science

For information about Vols. 1–4177

please contact your bookseller or Springer

Vol. 4272: P. Havinga, M. Lijding, N. Meratnia, M. Wegdam (Eds.), Smart Sensing and Context. XI, 267 pages. 2006.

Vol. 4270: H. Zha, Z. Pan, H. Thwaites, A.C. Addison, M. Forte (Eds.), Interactive Technologies and Sociotechnical Systems. XVI, 547 pages. 2006.

Vol. 4269: R. State, S. van der Meer, D. O'Sullivan, T. Pfeifer (Eds.), Large Scale Management of Distributed Systems. XIII, 282 pages. 2006.

Vol. 4267: A. Helmy, B. Jennings, L. Murphy, T. Pfeifer (Eds.), Autonomic Management of Mobile Multimedia Services. XIII, 257 pages. 2006.

Vol. 4265: N. Lavrač, L. Todorovski, K.P. Jantke (Eds.), Discovery Science. XIV, 384 pages. 2006. (Sublibrary LNAI).

Vol. 4264: J.L. Balcázar, P.M. Long, F. Stephan (Eds.), Algorithmic Learning Theory. XIII, 393 pages. 2006. (Sublibrary LNAI).

Vol. 4260: Z. Liu, J. He (Eds.), Formal Methods and Software Engineering. XII, 778 pages. 2006.

Vol. 4257: I. Richardson, P. Runeson, R. Messnarz (Eds.), Software Process Improvement. XI, 219 pages. 2006.

Vol. 4254: T. Grust, H. Höpfner, A. Illarramendi, S. Jablonski, M. Mesiti, S. Müller, P.-L. Patranjan, K.-U. Sattler, M. Spiliopoulou (Eds.), Current Trends in Database Technology – EDBT 2006. XXXI, 932 pages. 2006.

Vol. 4253: B. Gabrys, R.J. Howlett, L.C. Jain (Eds.), Knowledge-Based Intelligent Information and Engineering Systems, Part III. XXXII, 1301 pages. 2006. (Sublibrary LNAI).

Vol. 4252: B. Gabrys, R.J. Howlett, L.C. Jain (Eds.), Knowledge-Based Intelligent Information and Engineering Systems, Part II. XXXIII, 1335 pages. 2006. (Sublibrary LNAI).

Vol. 4251: B. Gabrys, R.J. Howlett, L.C. Jain (Eds.), Knowledge-Based Intelligent Information and Engineering Systems, Part I. LXVI, 1297 pages. 2006. (Sublibrary LNAI).

Vol. 4249: L. Goubin, M. Matsui (Eds.), Cryptographic Hardware and Embedded Systems - CHES 2006. XII, 462 pages. 2006.

Vol. 4248: S. Staab, V. Svátek (Eds.), Engineering Knowledge in the Age of the Semantic Web. XIV, 400 pages. 2006. (Sublibrary LNAI).

Vol. 4247: T.-D. Wang, X. Li, S.-H. Chen, X. Wang, H. Abbass, H. Iba, G. Chen, X. Yao (Eds.), Simulated Evolution and Learning. XXI, 940 pages. 2006.

Vol. 4245: A. Kuba, L.G. Nyúl, K. Palágyi (Eds.), Discrete Geometry for Computer Imagery. XIII, 688 pages. 2006.

Vol. 4243: T. Yakhno, E.J. Neuhold (Eds.), Advances in Information Systems. XIII, 420 pages. 2006.

Vol. 4241: R.R. Beichel, M. Sonka (Eds.), Computer Vision Approaches to Medical Image Analysis. XI, 262 pages. 2006.

Vol. 4239: H.Y. Youn, M. Kim, H. Morikawa (Eds.), Ubiquitous Computing Systems. XVI, 548 pages. 2006.

Vol. 4238: Y.-T. Kim, M. Takano (Eds.), Management of Convergence Networks and Services. XVIII, 605 pages. 2006.

Vol. 4236: L. Breveglieri, I. Koren, D. Naccache, J.-P. Seifert (Eds.), Fault Diagnosis and Tolerance in Cryptography. XIII, 253 pages. 2006.

Vol. 4234: I. King, J. Wang, L. Chan, D. Wang (Eds.), Neural Information Processing, Part III. XXII, 1227 pages. 2006.

Vol. 4233: I. King, J. Wang, L. Chan, D. Wang (Eds.), Neural Information Processing, Part II. XXII, 1203 pages. 2006.

Vol. 4232: I. King, J. Wang, L. Chan, D. Wang (Eds.), Neural Information Processing, Part I. XLVI, 1153 pages. 2006.

Vol. 4229: E. Najm, J.F. Pradat-Peyre, V.V. Donzeau-Gouge (Eds.), Formal Techniques for Networked and Distributed Systems - FORTE 2006. X, 486 pages. 2006.

Vol. 4228: D.E. Lightfoot, C.A. Szyperski (Eds.), Modular Programming Languages. X, 415 pages. 2006.

Vol. 4227: W. Nejdl, K. Tochtermann (Eds.), Innovative Approaches for Learning and Knowledge Sharing. XVII, 721 pages. 2006.

Vol. 4225: J.F. Martínez-Trinidad, J.A. Carrasco Ochoa, J. Kittler (Eds.), Progress in Pattern Recognition, Image Analysis and Applications. XIX, 995 pages. 2006.

Vol. 4224: E. Corchado, H. Yin, V. Botti, C. Fyfe (Eds.), Intelligent Data Engineering and Automated Learning – IDEAL 2006. XXVII, 1447 pages. 2006.

Vol. 4223: L. Wang, L. Jiao, G. Shi, X. Li, J. Liu (Eds.), Fuzzy Systems and Knowledge Discovery. XXVIII, 1335 pages. 2006. (Sublibrary LNAI).

Vol. 4222: L. Jiao, L. Wang, X. Gao, J. Liu, F. Wu (Eds.), Advances in Natural Computation, Part II. XLII, 998 pages. 2006.

Vol. 4221: L. Jiao, L. Wang, X. Gao, J. Liu, F. Wu (Eds.), Advances in Natural Computation, Part I. XLI, 992 pages. 2006.

Vol. 4219: D. Zamboni, C. Kruegel (Eds.), Recent Advances in Intrusion Detection. XII, 331 pages. 2006.

Vol. 4218: S. Graf, W. Zhang (Eds.), Automated Technology for Verification and Analysis. XIV, 540 pages. 2006.

Vol. 4217: P. Cuenca, L. Orozco-Barbosa (Eds.), Personal Wireless Communications. XV, 532 pages. 2006.

Vol. 4216: M.R. Berthold, R. Glen, I. Fischer (Eds.), Computational Life Sciences II. XIII, 269 pages. 2006. (Sublibrary LNBI).

Vol. 4215: D.W. Embley, A. Olivé, S. Ram (Eds.), Conceptual Modeling - ER 2006. XVI, 590 pages. 2006.

Vol. 4213: J. Fürnkranz, T. Scheffer, M. Spiliopoulou (Eds.), Knowledge Discovery in Databases: PKDD 2006. XXII, 660 pages. 2006. (Sublibrary LNAI).

Vol. 4212: J. Fürnkranz, T. Scheffer, M. Spiliopoulou (Eds.), Machine Learning: ECML 2006. XXIII, 851 pages. 2006. (Sublibrary LNAI).

Vol. 4211: P. Vogt, Y. Sugita, E. Tuci, C. Nehaniv (Eds.), Symbol Grounding and Beyond. VIII, 237 pages. 2006. (Sublibrary LNAI).

Vol. 4210: C. Priami (Ed.), Computational Methods in Systems Biology. X, 323 pages. 2006. (Sublibrary LNBI).

Vol. 4209: F. Crestani, P. Ferragina, M. Sanderson (Eds.), String Processing and Information Retrieval. XIV, 367 pages. 2006.

Vol. 4208: M. Gerndt, D. Kranzlmüller (Eds.), High Performance Computing and Communications. XXII, 938 pages. 2006.

Vol. 4207: Z. Ésik (Ed.), Computer Science Logic. XII, 627 pages. 2006.

Vol. 4206: P. Dourish, A. Friday (Eds.), UbiComp 2006: Ubiquitous Computing. XIX, 526 pages. 2006.

Vol. 4205: G. Bourque, N. El-Mabrouk (Eds.), Comparative Genomics. X, 231 pages. 2006. (Sublibrary LNBI).

Vol. 4204: F. Benhamou (Ed.), Principles and Practice of Constraint Programming - CP 2006. XVIII, 774 pages. 2006.

Vol. 4203: F. Esposito, Z.W. Raś, D. Malerba, G. Semeraro (Eds.), Foundations of Intelligent Systems. XVIII, 767 pages. 2006. (Sublibrary LNAI).

Vol. 4202: E. Asarin, P. Bouyer (Eds.), Formal Modeling and Analysis of Timed Systems. XI, 369 pages. 2006.

Vol. 4201: Y. Sakakibara, S. Kobayashi, K. Sato, T. Nishino, E. Tomita (Eds.), Grammatical Inference: Algorithms and Applications. XII, 359 pages. 2006. (Sublibrary LNAI).

Vol. 4200: I.F.C. Smith (Ed.), Intelligent Computing in Engineering and Architecture. XIII, 692 pages. 2006. (Sublibrary LNAI).

Vol. 4199: O. Nierstrasz, J. Whittle, D. Harel, G. Reggio (Eds.), Model Driven Engineering Languages and Systems. XVI, 798 pages. 2006.

Vol. 4198: O. Nasraoui, O. Zaiane, M. Spiliopoulou, B. Mobasher, B. Masand, P. Yu (Eds.), Advances in Web Minding and Web Usage Analysis. IX, 177 pages. 2006. (Sublibrary LNAI).

Vol. 4197: M. Raubal, H.J. Miller, A.U. Frank, M.F. Goodchild (Eds.), Geographic, Information Science. XIII, 419 pages. 2006.

Vol. 4196: K. Fischer, I.J. Timm, E. André, N. Zhong (Eds.), Multiagent System Technologies. X, 185 pages. 2006. (Sublibrary LNAI).

Vol. 4195: D. Gaiti, G. Pujolle, E. Al-Shaer, K. Calvert, S. Dobson, G. Leduc, O. Martikainen (Eds.), Autonomic Networking. IX, 316 pages. 2006.

Vol. 4194: V.G. Ganzha, E.W. Mayr, E.V. Vorozhtsov (Eds.), Computer Algebra in Scientific Computing. XI, 313 pages. 2006.

Vol. 4193: T.P. Runarsson, H.-G. Beyer, E. Burke, J.J. Merelo-Guervós, L.D. Whitley, X. Yao (Eds.), Parallel Problem Solving from Nature - PPSN IX. XIX, 1061 pages. 2006.

Vol. 4192: B. Mohr, J.L. Träff, J. Worringen, J. Dongarra (Eds.), Recent Advances in Parallel Virtual Machine and Message Passing Interface. XVI, 414 pages. 2006.

Vol. 4191: R. Larsen, M. Nielsen, J. Sporring (Eds.), Medical Image Computing and Computer-Assisted Intervention – MICCAI 2006, Part II. XXXVIII, 981 pages. 2006.

Vol. 4190: R. Larsen, M. Nielsen, J. Sporring (Eds.), Medical Image Computing and Computer-Assisted Intervention – MICCAI 2006, Part I. XXXVVIII, 949 pages. 2006.

Vol. 4189: D. Gollmann, J. Meier, A. Sabelfeld (Eds.), Computer Security – ESORICS 2006. XI, 548 pages. 2006.

Vol. 4188: P. Sojka, I. Kopeček, K. Pala (Eds.), Text, Speech and Dialogue. XV, 721 pages. 2006. (Sublibrary LNAI).

Vol. 4187: J.J. Alferes, J. Bailey, W. May, U. Schwertel (Eds.), Principles and Practice of Semantic Web Reasoning. XI, 277 pages. 2006.

Vol. 4186: C. Jesshope, C. Egan (Eds.), Advances in Computer Systems Architecture. XIV, 605 pages. 2006.

Vol. 4185: R. Mizoguchi, Z. Shi, F. Giunchiglia (Eds.), The Semantic Web – ASWC 2006. XX, 778 pages. 2006.

Vol. 4184: M. Bravetti, M. Núñez, G. Zavattaro (Eds.), Web Services and Formal Methods. X, 289 pages. 2006.

Vol. 4183: J. Euzenat, J. Domingue (Eds.), Artificial Intelligence: Methodology, Systems, and Applications. XIII, 291 pages. 2006. (Sublibrary LNAI).

Vol. 4182: H.T. Ng, M.-K. Leong, M.-Y. Kan, D. Ji (Eds.), Information Retrieval Technology. XVI, 684 pages. 2006.

Vol. 4180: M. Kohlhase, OMDoc – An Open Markup Format for Mathematical Documents [version 1.2]. XIX, 428 pages. 2006. (Sublibrary LNAI).

Vol. 4179: J. Blanc-Talon, W. Philips, D. Popescu, P. Scheunders (Eds.), Advanced Concepts for Intelligent Vision Systems. XXIV, 1224 pages. 2006.

Vol. 4178: A. Corradini, H. Ehrig, U. Montanari, L. Ribeiro, G. Rozenberg (Eds.), Graph Transformations. XII, 473 pages. 2006.

MIX
Papier aus verantwortungsvollen Quellen
Paper from responsible sources
FSC® C105338

If you have any concerns about our products,
you can contact us on
ProductSafety@springernature.com

In case Publisher is established outside the EU,
the EU authorized representative is:
Springer Nature Customer Service Center GmbH
Europaplatz 3, 69115 Heidelberg, Germany

Printed by Libri Plureos GmbH
in Hamburg, Germany